Syngress know̶ ; to
you and to yc ̶
are often financing your own training and
certification; therefore, you need a system that is
comprehensive, affordable, and effective.

Boasting one-of-a-kind integration of text, DVD-quality
instructor-led training, and Web-based exam simulation, the
Syngress Study Guide & DVD Training System guarantees 100% coverage of exam
objectives.

The Syngress Study Guide & DVD Training System includes:

- **Study Guide with 100% coverage of exam objectives** By reading
  this study guide and following the corresponding objective list, you
  can be sure that you have studied 100% of the exam objectives.

- **Instructor-led DVD** This DVD provides almost two hours of virtual
  classroom instruction.

- **Web-based practice exams** Just visit us at **www.syngress.com/
  certification** to access a complete exam simulation.

Thank you for giving us the opportunity to serve your certification needs. And
be sure to let us know if there's anything else we can do to help you get the
maximum value from your investment. We're listening.

www.syngress.com/certification

SYNGRESS®

COVERS ALL
100% CERTIFIED
EXAM OBJECTIVES

MCSA/MCSE

Exam 70-291: Implementing, Managing, and Maintaining a Windows Server 2003 Network Infrastructure

STUDY GUIDE & DVD TRAINING SYSTEM

Deborah Littlejohn Shinder

Dr. Thomas W. Shinder

Chad Todd   Technical Reviewer

Laura Hunter   DVD Presenter

KEY	SERIAL NUMBER
001	PV43SLUGGY
002	Q2TQRGN7VA
003	8C38A9R7FF
004	Z6TDAVAN9Y
005	P33JEET8MS
006	3SHX6SN$RK
007	CH3W7E42AK
008	9EU6V4DER7
009	SUPACM4NFH
010	5BVF3MEV2Z

PUBLISHED BY
Syngress Publishing, Inc.
800 Hingham Street
Rockland, MA 02370

Implementing, Managing, and Maintaining a Windows Server 2003 Network Infrastructure Guide & DVD Training System

Printed in the United States of America

1 2 3 4 5 6 7 8 9 0

ISBN: 1-931836-92-2

Technical Editor: Deborah Littlejohn Shinder
and Thomas W. Shinder M.D
Technical Reviewer: Chad Todd
Acquisitions Editor: Jonathan Babcock
DVD Production: Michael Donovan

Cover Designer: Patricia Lupien
Page Layout and Art by: Patricia Lupien
Copy Editors: Adrienne Rebello
Indexer: Nara Wood
DVD Presenter: Laura Hunter

Acknowledgments

We would like to acknowledge the following people for their kindness and support in making this book possible.

Karen Cross, Meaghan Cunningham, Kim Wylie, Harry Kirchner, Kevin Votel, Kent Anderson, Frida Yara, Jon Mayes, John Mesjak, Peg O'Donnell, Sandra Patterson, Betty Redmond, Roy Remer, Ron Shapiro, Patricia Kelly, Andrea Tetrick, Jennifer Pascal, Doug Reil, David Dahl, Janis Carpenter, and Susan Fryer of Publishers Group West for sharing their incredible marketing experience and expertise.

Duncan Enright, AnnHelen Lindeholm, David Burton, Febea Marinetti, and Rosie Moss of Elsevier Science for making certain that our vision remains worldwide in scope.

David Buckland, Wendi Wong, Daniel Loh, Marie Chieng, Lucy Chong, Leslie Lim, Audrey Gan, and Joseph Chan of Transquest Publishers for the enthusiasm with which they receive our books.

Kwon Sung June at Acorn Publishing for his support.

Jackie Gross, Gayle Voycey, Alexia Penny, Anik Robitaille, Craig Siddall, Darlene Morrow, Iolanda Miller, Jane Mackay, and Marie Skelly at Jackie Gross & Associates for all their help and enthusiasm representing our product in Canada.

Lois Fraser, Connie McMenemy, Shannon Russell, and the rest of the great folks at Jaguar Book Group for their help with distribution of Syngress books in Canada.

David Scott, Annette Scott, Delta Sams, Geoff Ebbs, Hedley Partis, and Tricia Herbert of Woodslane for distributing our books throughout Australia, New Zealand, Papua New Guinea, Fiji Tonga, Solomon Islands, and the Cook Islands.

A special thanks to Deb and Tom Shinder for going the extra mile on our core four MCSE 2003 guides. Thank you both for all your work.

And to Laura Hunter, thank you for the exceptional work on the DVD for this book.

Technical Editors

Debra Littlejohn Shinder (MCSE) is a technology consultant, trainer, and writer who has authored a number of books on networking, including *Scene of the Cybercrime: Computer Forensics Handbook,* published by Syngress Publishing (ISBN: 1-931836-65-5), and *Computer Networking Essentials,* published by Cisco Press. She is co-author, with her husband, Dr. Thomas Shinder, of *Troubleshooting Windows 2000 TCP/IP* (ISBN: 1-928994-11-3), the best-selling *Configuring ISA Server 2000* (ISBN: 1-928994-29-6), and *ISA Server and Beyond* (ISBN: 1-931836-66-3). Deb is also a technical editor and contributor to books on subjects such as the Windows 2000 MCSE exams, the CompTIA Security+ exam, and TruSecure's ICSA certification. She edits the Brainbuzz A+ Hardware News and Sunbelt Software's WinXP News and is regularly published in TechRepublic's TechProGuild and Windowsecurity.com. Deb currently specializes in security issues and Microsoft products. She lives and works in the Dallas-Fort Worth area and can be contacted at deb@shinder.net or via the website at www.shinder.net.

Thomas W. Shinder M.D. (MVP, MCSE) is a computing industry veteran who has worked as a trainer, writer, and a consultant for Fortune 500 companies including FINA Oil, Lucent Technologies, and Sealand Container Corporation. Tom was a Series Editor of the Syngress/Osborne Series of Windows 2000 Certification Study Guides and is author of the best selling books *Configuring ISA Server 2000: Building Firewalls with Windows 2000* (Syngress Publishing, ISBN: 1-928994-29-6) and *Dr. Tom Shinder's ISA Server and Beyond* (ISBN: 1-931836-66-3). Tom is the editor of the Brainbuzz.com *Win2k News* newsletter and is a regular contributor to TechProGuild. He is also content editor, contributor and moderator for the World's leading site on ISA Server 2000, www.isaserver.org. Microsoft recognized Tom's leadership in the ISA Server community and awarded him their Most Valued Professional (MVP) award in December of 2001.

Technical Reviewer

Chad Todd (MCSE: Security, MCSE, MCSA: Security, MCSA, MCP+I, MCT, CNE, A+, Network+, i-Net+) author of the best-selling *Hack Proofing Windows 2000 Server* co-owns a training and integration company (Training Concepts, LLC) in Columbia, SC. Chad first certified on Windows NT 4.0 and has been training on Windows operating systems ever since. His specialties include Exchange messaging and Windows security. Chad was awarded MCSE 2000 Charter Member for being one of the first two thousand Windows 2000 MCSEs and MCSA 2002 Charter Member for being one of the first five thousand MCSAs. Chad is a regular contributing author for *Microsoft Certified Professional Magazine*. Chad has worked for companies such as Fleet Mortgage Group, Ikon Office Solutions, and Netbank.

Chad would like to first thank his wife Sarah. Without her love and support all of the late nights required to write this book would not be possible. He would also like to thank Kirk Vigil and Jim Jones for their support and encouragement. Lastly, Chad would like to thank Olean Rabon and Theresa Johnson for being his greatest fans.

Contributors

Susan Snedaker (MCP, MCT, MCSE+I, MBA) is a strategic business consultant specializing in business planning, development, and operations. She has served as author, editor, curriculum designer, and instructor during her career in the computer industry. Susan holds a Master of Business Administration and a Bachelor of Arts in Management from the University of Phoenix. She has held key executive and technical positions at Microsoft, Honeywell, Keane, and Apta Software. Susan has contributed chapters to five books on Microsoft Windows 2000 and 2003. Susan currently provides strategic business, management and technology consulting services (www.virtualteam.com).

Hal Kurz (MCSE, CCDP, CCNP, CCDA, CCNA) is CIO of Innovative Technology Consultants and Company, Inc. (www.itccinc.com), a computer consulting and training company located in Miami, FL as well as chief technologist for ITC-Hosting (www.itc-hosting.com) a web hosting and web-based application development company. He holds Microsoft MCSE certifications for Windows 2000 and Windows NT 4.0. He is currently gearing up for his CCIE lab exam. Hal is a University of Florida engineering graduate with experience in VMS, Unix, Linux, OS/400, and Microsoft Windows. He lives in Miami with his wife Tricia and four children Alexa, Andrew, Alivia, and Adam. *Thank you again Tricia and kids for all of your support!*

Kirk Vigil (MCSE, MCSA) is a senior network consultant for Netbank, Inc. in Columbia, SC. He has worked in the IT integration industry for over 11 years, specializing in Microsoft messaging and network operating system infrastructures. He has worked with Microsoft Exchange since its inception and continues to focus on its advancements with the recent release of Exchange 2003 as well as its integration with Windows Server 2003. Kirk holds a bachelor's degree from the University of South Carolina. He also works as an independent consultant for a privately owned integration company, lending technical direction to local business practices. He is a contributing author for the monthly technical subscription Microsoft Certified Professional Magazine. Beginning his career in Information Technology for a small startup company, The Computer Group, he helped integrate that company into the technology division of the worldwide IKON Office Solutions.

Kirk would first like to thank his family for their continuous love and support. Thanks also go to Chad Todd for his introduction to Syngress Publishing as well as his counsel. Special appreciation goes to Jim Jones for his encouragement and understanding, making the writing of this book possible. Lastly, Kirk is grateful to editors Jon Babcock, Deborah Littlejohn Shinder, and Thomas Shinder for their technical guidance and leadership throughout the editorial process.

Dan Douglass (MCSE+I, MCDBA, MCSD, MCT) is a software developer and trainer with a cutting edge medical software company in Dallas, Texas. He currently provides software development skills, internal training and integration solutions, as well as peer guidance for technical skills development. His specialties include enterprise application integration and design, HL7, XML, XSL, Visual Basic, database design and administration, Back Office and .NET Server platforms, Network design, including LAN and WAN solutions, Microsoft operating systems and FreeBSD. Dan is a former US Navy Submariner and lives in Plano, TX with his very supportive and understanding wife, Tavish.

DVD Presenter

Laura E. Hunter (CISSP, MCSE, MCT, MCDBA, MCP, MCP+I, CCNA, A+, Network+, iNet+, CNE-4, CNE-5) is a Senior IT Specialist with the University of Pennsylvania, where she provides network planning, implementation and troubleshooting services for various business units and schools within the University. Her specialties include Microsoft Windows NT and 2000 design and implementation, troubleshooting and security topics. As an "MCSE Early Achiever" on Windows 2000, Laura, was one of the first in the country to renew her Microsoft credentials under the Windows 2000 certification structure. Laura's previous experience includes a position as the Director of Computer Services for the Salvation Army and as the LAN administrator for a medical supply firm. She also operates as an independent consultant for small businesses in the Philadelphia metropolitan area and is a regular contributor to the TechTarget family of websites.

Laura has previously contributed to the Syngress Publishing *Configuring Symantec Antivirus, Corporate Edition* (ISBN 1-931836-81-7). She has also contributed to several other exam guides in the Syngress Windows Server 2003 MCSE/MCSA DVD Guide and Training System series as a DVD presenter, contributing author and technical reviewer.

Laura holds a bachelor's degree from the University of Pennsylvania and is a member of the Network of Women in Computer Technology, the Information Systems Security Association, and InfraGard, a cooperative undertaking between the U.S. Government other participants dedicated to increasing the security of United States critical infrastructures.

MCSA/MCSE 70-291 Exam Objectives Map and Table of Contents

All of Microsoft's published objectives for the MCSA/MCSE 70-291 Exam are covered in this book. To help you easily find the sections that directly support particular objectives, we've listed all of the exam objectives below, and mapped them to the Chapter number in which they are covered. We've also assigned numbers to each objective, which we use in the subsequent Table of Contents and again throughout the book to identify objective coverage. In some chapters, we've made the judgment that it is probably easier for the student to cover objectives in a slightly different sequence than the order of the published Microsoft objectives. By reading this study guide and following the corresponding objective list, you can be sure that you have studied 100% of Microsoft's MCSA/MCSE 70-291 Exam objectives.

Exam Objective Map

Objective Number	Objective	Chapter Number
1	**Implementing, Managing, and MaintainingIP Addressing**	1, 3
1.1	Configure TCP/IP addressing on a server computer.	1
1.2	Manage DHCP.	3
1.2.1	Manage DHCP clients and leases.	3
1.2.2	Manage DHCP Relay Agent.	3
1.2.3	Manage DHCP databases.	3
1.2.4	Manage DHCP scope options.	3
1.2.5	Manage reservations and reserved clients.	3
1.3	Troubleshoot TCP/IP addressing.	1
1.3.1	Diagnose and resolve issues related to Automatic Private IP Addressing (APIPA).	3
1.3.2	Diagnose and resolve issues related to incorrect TCP/IP configuration.	3
1.4	Troubleshoot DHCP.	3

Objective Number	Objective	Chapter Number
1.4.1	Diagnose and resolve issues related to DHCP authorization.	3
1.4.2	Verify DHCP reservation configuration.	3
1.4.3	Examine the system event log and DHCP server audit log files to find related events.	3
1.4.4	Diagnose and resolve issues related to configuration of DHCP server and scope options.	3
1.4.5	Verify that the DHCP Relay Agent is working correctly.	3
1.4.6	Verify database integrity.	3
2	**Implementing, Managing, and Maintaining Name Resolution**	**5, 6**
2.1	Install and configure the DNS Server service.	6
2.1.1	Configure DNS server options.	6
2.1.2	Configure DNS zone options.	6
2.1.3	Configure DNS forwarding.	6
2.2	Manage DNS.	6
2.2.1	Manage DNS zone settings.	6
2.2.2	Manage DNS record settings.	6
2.2.3	Manage DNS server options.	5
2.3	Monitor DNS. Tools might include System Monitor, Event Viewer, Replication Monitor, and DNS debug logs.	6
3	**Implementing, Managing, and Maintaining Network Security**	**9, 10**
3.1	Implement secure network administration procedures.	9
3.1.1	Implement security baseline settings and audit security settings by using security templates.	9
3.1.2	Implement the principle of least privilege.	9
3.2	Monitor network protocol security. Tools might include the IP Security Monitor Microsoft Management Console (MMC) snap-in and Kerberos support tools.	10

Objective Number	Objective	Chapter Number
3.3	Troubleshoot network protocol security. Tools might include the IP Security Monitor MMC snap-in, Event Viewer, and Network Monitor.	10
4	**Implementing, Managing, and Maintaining Routing and Remote Access**	**7, 8**
4.1	Configure Routing and Remote Access user authentication.	7
4.1.1	Configure remote access authentication protocols.	7,8
4.1.2	Configure Internet Authentication Service (IAS) to provide authentication for Routing and Remote Access clients.	8
4.1.3	Configure Routing and Remote Access policies to permit or deny access.	8
4.2	Manage remote access.	8
4.2.1	Manage packet filters.	8
4.2.2	Manage Routing and Remote Access routing interfaces.	8
4.2.3	Manage devices and ports.	8
4.2.4	Manage routing protocols.	8
4.2.5	Manage Routing and Remote Access clients.	8
4.3	Manage TCP/IP routing.	8
4.3.1	Manage routing protocols.	8
4.3.2	Manage routing tables.	2
4.3.3	Manage routing ports.	8
4.4	Implement secure access between private networks.	7
4.5	Troubleshoot user access to remote access services.	8
4.5.1	Diagnose and resolve issues related to remote access VPNs.	7
4.5.2	Diagnose and resolve issues related to establishing a remote access connection.	8

Objective Number	Objective	Chapter Number
4.5.3	Diagnose and resolve user access to resources beyond the remote access server.	8
4.6	Troubleshoot Routing and Remote Access routing.	8
4.6.1	Troubleshoot demand-dial routing.	8
4.6.2	Troubleshoot router-to-router VPNs.	7
5	**Maintaining a Network Infrastructure**	**3, 4, 6, 8, 10**
5.1	Monitor network traffic. Tools might include Network Monitor and System Monitor.	10
5.2	Troubleshoot connectivity to the Internet.	10
5.3	Troubleshoot server services.	3, 4, 6,8
5.3.1	Diagnose and resolve issues related to service dependency.	3, 4, 6, 8
5.3.2	Use service recovery options to diagnose and resolve service-related issues.	3, 4, 6, 8

Contents

Foreword   **xxix**

Chapter 1 Reviewing TCP/IP Basics   **1**

Introduction 2

Understanding the Purpose and Function of Networking Models ...2

    Understanding the Department

      of Defense (DoD) Networking Model 3

        Layer One: Network Interface 4

        Media Access Control 6

        Network Interface Hardware/Software 6

        Layer Two: Internet (or Internetworking) 7

        Layer Three: Host to Host (or Transport) 7

        Layer Four: Application 8

    Understanding the OSI Model 8

        Layer 1: Physical 9

        Layer 2: Data Link 11

        Layer 3: Network 13

        Layer 4: Transport 14

        Layer 5: Session 16

        Layer 6: Presentation 17

        Layer 7 Application 17

    The Microsoft Model 18

        Understanding the Function of Boundary Layers 19

        Understanding Component Layers 21

1.1/1.3   Understanding the TCP/IP Protocol Suite 22

        Layer 1: Network Interface 24

        CSMA/CD 24

        CSMA/CA 25

        Token Passing 25

        Other Access Control Methods 26

        Layer 2: Internet 27

Internet Protocol 27

Internet Control Message Protocol 28

Internet Group Management Protocol 28

Address Resolution Protocol 29

Layer 3: Host-to-Host Transport 30

Transmission Control Protocol 30

User Datagram Protocol 34

Layer 4: Application 35

NetBIOS over TCP 35

Windows Internet Name Service 36

Server Message Block/Common Internet File System 37

Internet Printing Protocol 37

Windows Sockets 38

Telnet 38

Dynamic Host Configuration Protocol 39

Simple Mail Transport Protocol 40

Post Office Protocol 40

Internet Message Access Protocol 40

Hypertext Transport Protocol 41

Network News Transfer Protocol 41

File Transfer Protocol 41

Domain Naming System 42

Routing Information Protocol 43

SNMP 43

1.1/1.3   Understanding IP Addressing 45

Converting from Decimal to Binary 45

Network ID and Host ID 50

Rules for Network IDs 52

Rules for Host IDs 52

Class A 52

Class B 53

Class C 53

Class D and Class E 54

Address Class Summary 54

Understanding Subnetting 55

Understanding Subnet Masking 57

How Bitwise ANDing Works 57

Default Subnet Mask 59

Custom Subnet Mask 60
  Determine the Number of Host Bits to Be Used 61
  Determine the New Subnetted Network IDs 62
  Determine the IP Addresses for Each New Subnet 64
  Creating the Subnet Mask 64
Public and Private IP Addresses 67
Understanding Basic IP Routing 68
  Name and Address Resolution 68
    Host Name Resolution 68
    NetBIOS Name Resolution 70
  How Packets Travel from Network to Network 72
    IP Routing Tables 73
    Route Processing 75
    Physical Address Resolution 76
    Inverse ARP 77
    Proxy ARP 77
    Static and Dynamic IP Routers 77
    Routing Utilities 82
    Conclusion 83
  Example of a Simple Classful Network 83
Summary of Exam Objectives 85
Exam Objectives Fast Track 86
Exam Objectives Frequently Asked Questions 89
Self Test 91
Self Test Quick Answer Key 96

**Chapter 2 Variable Length Subnet Masking
and Client Configuration   97**
Introduction 98
Review of Classful Subnet Masking 98
Variable Length or Nonclassful (Classless) Subnet Masking 104
  Example of Subnetting a Class A Network 107
  Requirement #1:
    Reserve Half the Addresses for Future Use 107
  Requirement #2:
    Twelve Networks with 8,190 Hosts per Subnet 107
  Requirement #3:
    Ten Networks with 2,046 Hosts per Subnet 108

Requirement #4:
Five Networks with 250 Hosts per Subnet 109
Example of Subnetting a Class B Network 110
Requirement #1: One Subnet of Up to 30,000 Hosts 110
Requirement #2: Twelve Subnets with Ip to 1,500 Hosts ...110
Requirement #3: Six Subnets with Up to 250 Hosts 112
Requirement #4: Reserve at
Least Five Subnets with 250 Hosts for Future Use 112
Example of Subnetting a Class C Network 113
Requirement #1:
Create One Subnet with at Least 60 Host Addresses 113
Requirement #2: Create at
Least Five Subnets with Up to Six Host Addresses 114
Requirement #3: Save at
Least Two Subnets for Future Use 114
Variable Length Subnetting Summary 119
Supernetting Class C Networks 120
Example of Supernetting a Class C Network 121

4.3.2   The Windows XP/Windows 2000 Routing Table 124
Adding Routing Table Entries 127
Removing Routing Table Entries 128

4.3.2   The Windows Server 2003 Routing Table 128
Creating Routing Table Entries 134
Removing Routing Table Entries 136
Assigning IP Addressing Information to Network Clients 138
Static IP Addressing 138
Dynamic IP Addressing 141
APIPA 143
Configuring Alternate
IP Addressing Configurations 145
Summary of Exam Objectives 147
Exam Objectives Fast Track 148
Exam Objectives Frequently Asked Questions 152
Self Test 153
Self Test Quick Answer Key 159

Chapter 3 The Dynamic Host Configuration Protocol   161

Introduction 162

1.2   Review of DHCP 162

1.2.1   DHCP Leases 164

    General Lease Duration Rules 165

    The DHCP Lease Process 166

        IP Lease Request (Discover) 168

        IP Offer Response 170

        IP Selection Request 171

        IP Lease Acknowledgement 172

    Lease Renewal 173

        Automatic Renewal 174

        Manual Renewal 175

1.2.1/1.2.4 Configuring the Windows

1.2.5/1.4.4 Server 2003 DHCP Server 176

    Installing the DHCP Service 176

1.2.4   Configuring DHCP Scopes 179

    Configuring DHCP Options 186

        Server Options 189

        Scope Options 189

    User and Vendor Class Options 189

1.2.5   Configuring DHCP Reservations 197

    Configuring BOOTP Tables 199

    Configuring Superscopes 201

        When to Use Superscopes 202

        How to Create a Superscope 202

    Configuring Multicast Scopes 203

    Configuring Scope Allocation of IP Addresses 206

        Conflict Detection 207

1.2.2/1.4.5 Configuring the DHCP Relay Agent 209

    BOOTP versus DHCP Relay 210

    Configuring the DHCP Relay Agent 211

    Integrating the DHCP Server with Dynamic DNS 214

    Dealing with Windows NT 4.0 and Win9x Clients 216

        DNS Updating Options 217

        DNSUpdateProxy Group 218

        Security Concerning the DNSUpdateProxy Group 220

1.4/1.4.1 Integrating the DHCP Server with Routing and Remote Access ...222

    DHCP and RRAS Scenarios 223

Scenario 1: RRAS Acts as DHCP Server 223
Scenario 2: RRAS Passes Requests to Another
DHCP Server 224
Scenario 3: Static IP Assigned to User 224
Integrating DHCP with Active Directory 226
Authorizing DHCP Servers in the Active Directory 229
Rogue DHCP Server Detection 230
1.3.1/1.3.2 Understanding Automatic Private IP Addressing (APIPA) 231
How APIPA Works 232
Disabling APIPA 232
1.2/1.4.6 Managing the Windows Server 2003 DHCP Server 235
1.2.3 Managing the DHCP Server Database 235
Viewing and Recording DHCP Server Statistics 239
Delegating DHCP Administration 241
Enterprise Admins Group 242
1.4.3/1.4 DHCP Administrators Group 242
DHCP Users Group 242
1.4/1.4.3 Monitoring and Troubleshooting
1.4.4/5.3/ the Windows Server 2003 DHCP Server 243
5.3.1/5.3.2
Using the Event Viewer 243
Using System Monitor 245
1.4.3 Real World Data Sniffing 248
1.4.3 Using the DHCP Server Audit Log 250
Using DHCP Log Files 251
Client-Side Troubleshooting 254
Summary of Exam Objectives 256
Exam Objectives Fast Track 258
Exam Objectives Frequently Asked Questions 262
Self Test 266
Self Test Quick Answer Key 277

Chapter 4 NetBIOS Name Resolution and WINS   279
Introduction 280
Review of NetBIOS Name Resolution 281
Network Browsing 283
NetBIOS Name Registration 283
NetBIOS Name Registration 284

NetBIOS Name Discovery 284
NetBIOS Name Release 284
Standard NetBIOS Name Resolution 285
Local Broadcast 285
NetBIOS Name Cache 287
NetBIOS Name Server 288
NetBIOS Over TCP/IP 289
Resolving NetBIOS Names to IP Addresses 289
The NetBIOS Node Types 290
b-node (Broadcasts) 291
p-node (Peer-to-peer) 291
m-node (Mixed) 291
h-node (Hybrid) 292
Enhanced h-node 292
The LMHOSTS file 294
The Windows Server 2003 Windows Internet Name Server 300
Overview of WINS 300
Client Name Registration 302
Client Name Renewal 303
Client Name Release 304
Client Name Resolution Query 305
Installing the WINS Server 307
Configuring and Managing the WINS Server 309
Configuring WINS Replication 310
Managing WINS Records and Its Database 321
Back Up and Restore the WINS Database 344
Configuring the WINS Client 354
Possible WINS Clients 356
WINS Proxy Agent 357
Non-WINS NetBIOS Registration 357
Non-WINS NetBIOS Resolution 357
Network Service Interoperability 359
WINS and DHCP 359
WINS and DNS 361
WINS and RRAS 365
WINS and Active Directory 366
WINS and the Browser Service 367
WINS and Win9x/NT Clients 368

5.3

5.3/5.3.1/ Monitoring and Troubleshooting
5.3.2   the Windows Server 2003 WINS Server 368
    WINS System Monitor Objects 369
    Troubleshooting WINS Clients 373
    Troubleshooting WINS Servers 378
        WINS Monitoring and Statistics 379
    Summary of Exam Objectives 383
    Exam Objectives Fast Track 385
    Exam Objectives Frequently Asked Questions 388
    Self Test 392
    Self Test Quick Answer Key 407

Chapter 5 Domain Naming System Concepts   409
    Introduction 410
    Review of DNS 411
        Comparing NetBIOS and DNS Naming Conventions 412
            Flat versus Hierarchical 413
            Naming Conventions 413
            NetBIOS Name Resolution Review 415
            NetBIOS and Winsock Interface Name Resolution 417
        The DNS Namespace 417
            Domain and Host Names 420
            Naming Subdomains 421
        Basic DNS Concepts 421
            DNS Servers 422
            DNS Resolvers 422
            Resource Records 422
            Zones 422
            Zone Files 422
        DNS Zones 423
            Commonly Used Resource Records 427
        Delegation and Glue Records 431
        DNS Zone Transfer 434
    Host Name Resolution 435
        Order of Host Name Resolution 436
        Recursive Queries 436
        Iterative Queries 438
        Forward Lookups 439
        Reverse Lookups 440

Root Hints File 440

2.2.3   Windows Server 2003 DNS Server Roles 440
Standard Primary DNS Server 441
Standard Secondary DNS Server 441
Caching-only DNS Server 442
DNS Forwarder and DNS Slave Servers 442
Testing the DNS Server 444
Dynamic DNS Servers 447
Aging and Scavenging of Stale Records 452
DNS Extensions 453
Windows Server 2003 Active Directory Integrated DNS Servers ...454
Secure Dynamic Updates 455
Active Directory Integrated Zones 455
Active Directory Related DNS Entries 456
Summary of Exam Objectives 457
Exam Objectives Fast Track 459
Exam Objectives Frequently Asked Questions 462
Self Test 464
Self Test Quick Answer Key 470

Chapter 6 The Windows Server 2003 DNS Server   471
Introduction 472
2.1/2.1.1/   Installing and Configuring the Windows Server
2.1.2/2.1.3/   2003 DNS Server 472
2.2/2.2.1/2.2.2
2.1.1   Configuring Your DNS Server 480
Configuring Forward Lookup Zones 483
Adding DNS Database Records 487
Configuring Reverse Lookup Zones 490
2.1.1   Configuring Your DNS Server 492
2.1.2   Configuring Your DNS Zones 502
2.2   Configuring DNS Clients 508
Using DHCP to Configure DNS Clients 510
Integrating the Windows
Server 2003 DNS Server with DHCP 517

DNS Updating Options 518
 Enabling DNS Dynamic Updates 519
DNSUpdateProxy Group 520
 Security Concerning the DNSUpdateProxy Group 522
Integrating the Windows Server 2003 DNS Server with WINS ...524
 WINS and DNS 524
Integrating the Windows Server 2003 DNS Server with BIND ...528

2.3 Monitoring the Windows Server 2003 DNS Server 533
 DNS Console 533
 System Monitor 536
 Network Monitor 542

5.3/5.3.1/ Troubleshooting the Windows Server 2003 DNS Server 544
5.3.2

 Logging 544
 Diagnostic Tools 546
Summary of Exam Objectives 550
Exam Objectives Fast Track 551
Exam Objectives Frequently Asked Questions 554
Self Test 557
Self Test Quick Answer Key 568

**Chapter 7 Configuring the Windows Server 2003
Routing and Remote Access Service VPN Services 569**
Introduction 570
Review of Windows Server 2003 Remote Access Concepts 570
Enabling the Windows Server 2003 Remote Access Service 575

4.1/4.1.1/ Configuring the Windows Server 2003 VPN Server 584
4.5.1

 Supporting Network Infrastructure 584
  Underlying Network Connection 585
  VPN Server Placement 585
  Certificate Infrastructure 586
  Centralized Accounting 587
 PPP Authentication Process and Protocols 588
  The PPP Authentication Process 588
 VPN Tunneling Protocols 597
  Understanding Tunneling 597
  Tunneling Protocols Supported by Windows Server 2003 ...598

Configuring the VPN Server 602

Planning Your VPN Server Deployment 603

IP Addressing for VPN Clients 605

Adding Ports on the VPN Server 606

4.5/4.5.1/ Configuring the Windows Server 2003 VPN Gateway 613
4.6.2

Supporting Network Infrastructure 615

Creating the Demand-Dial Connection 616

IP Addressing Support for VPN Gateways 619

Creating the Local and Remote Gateways 620

Creating the Static Packet Filter 621

Troubleshooting Windows Server 2003 VPN Services 629

Summary of Exam Objectives 632

Exam Objectives Fast Track 634

Exam Objectives Frequently Asked Questions 637

Self Test 639

Self Test Quick Answer Key 647

Chapter 8 Configuring the Windows 2003 Routing and Remote Access Service LAN Routing, Dial-up Services, and Routing Protocols   649

Introduction 650

4.3.3/4.6/ Configuring LAN Routing 650
4.6.1

4.2/4.2.1/ Configuring RRAS Packet Filters 659
4.2.2/4.2.3

4.5.3/4.6.1 Configuring the Windows 2003 Dial-up RAS Server 665

Configuring the Windows
2003 Dial-up RAS Gateway 672

PPP Multilink and Bandwidth Allocation Protocol (BAP) 680

PPP Multilink Protocol 680

BAP Protocols 681

4.1.1 Configuring Wireless Connections 685

Categorizing Wireless Networks 685

Wireless Security 686

4.1.3/4.2.5 Configuring Remote Access Policies 699

4.2.4/4.3 Understanding Router Protocols 706
4.3.1/4.3.3

RIP 711

OSPF 720

IGMP 731

Configuring Basic Firewall Support 731

4.2.5/5.3/   RRAS NAT Services 736
5.3.1/5.3.2

ICMP Router Discovery 742

4.2.5/4.5/   Troubleshooting Remote Access Client Connections 743
4.5.2/4.5.3

5.3/5.3.1/   Troubleshooting Remote Access Server Connections 748
5.3.2

Configuring Internet Authentication Services 751

Summary of Exam Objectives 758

Exam Objectives Fast Track 760

Exam Objectives Frequently Asked Questions 765

Self Test 771

Self Test Quick Answer Key 778

Chapter 9 Security Templates and Software Updates   779

Introduction 780

3.1/3.1.1/   Security Templates 780
3.1.2

Types of Security Templates 782

Network Security Settings 783

Analyzing Baseline Security 788

Applying Security Templates 795

secedit.exe 795

Group Policy 796

Security Configuration and Analysis 797

Software Updates 798

Install and Configure Software Update Infrastructure 799

Install and Configure Automatic Client Update Settings 807

Supporting Legacy Clients 816

Testing Software Updates 819

Summary of Exam Objectives 821

Exam Objectives Fast Track 821

Exam Objectives Frequently Asked Questions 823

Self Test 824

Self Test Quick Answer Key 830

Chapter 10 Monitoring and Troubleshooting Network Activity   831

Introduction 832

3.3/5.1   Using Network Monitor 832

Installing Network Monitor 833

Basic Configuration 840

Network Monitor Default Settings 840

Configuring Monitoring Filters 841

Configuring Display Filters 843

Interpreting a Trace 843

5.2   Monitoring and Troubleshooting Internet Connectivity 848

NAT Logging 848

Name Resolution 857

Host Name Resolution 857

NetBIOS Name Resolution 858

Using IPConfig to Troubleshoot Name Resolution 860

IP Addressing 862

Client Configuration Issues 862

Network Access Quarantine Control 864

DHCP Issues 865

3.2/3.3   Monitoring IPSec Connections 867

IPSec Monitor Console 867

Network Monitor 869

netsh 869

ipseccmd 870

netdiag 871

Event Viewer 871

Summary of Exam Objectives 872

Exam Objectives Fast Track 873

Exam Objectives Frequently Asked Questions 875

Self Test 877

Self Test Quick Answer Key 882

Self Test Appendix   883

Index   1003

Foreword

This book's primary goal is to help you prepare to take and pass Microsoft's exam number 70-291: *Implementing, Managing, and Maintaining a Microsoft Windows Server 2003 Network Infrastructure.* Our secondary purpose in writing this book is to provide exam candidates with knowledge and skills that go beyond the minimum requirements for passing the exam, and help to prepare them to work in the real world of Microsoft computer networking.

What is Exam 70-291?

Exam 70-291 is one of the two core networking systems requirements (along with exam 70-290) for the Microsoft Certified Systems Administrator (MCSA) and one of the four core requirements for the Microsoft Certified Systems Engineer (MCSE) certifications. Microsoft's stated target audience consists of IT professionals with at least six months to one year of work experience on a medium or large company network. This means a multi-site network with at least three domain controllers, running typical network services such as file and print services, database, firewall services, proxy services, remote access services and Internet connectivity, as well as messaging, intranet and client computer management.

However, not everyone who takes Exam 70-291 will have this ideal background. Many people will take this exam after classroom instruction or self-study as an entry into the networking field. Many of those who do have job experience in IT will not have had the opportunity to work with all of the technologies covered by the exam. In this book, our goal is to provide background information that will help you to understand the concepts and procedures described even if you don't have the requisite experience, while keeping our focus on the exam objectives.

Exam 70-291 covers the basics of managing and maintaining a network environment that is built around Microsoft's Windows Server 2003. Objectives are task-oriented, and include the following:

- **Implementing, Managing and Maintaining IP Addressing**: This includes configuring TCP/IP on a server, managing DHCP (clients and server, including the relay agent, DHCP database, scope options and reservations), troubleshooting

TCP/IP addressing (manual addressing, DHCP addressing and APIPA), and troubleshooting DHCP (including authorization issues, server configuration, and use of log files).

- **Implementing, Managing and Maintaining Name Resolution:** This focuses on DNS and includes the installation and configuration of the DNS server (including server options, zone options and DNS forwarding), DNS management (zone settings, record settings and server options) and monitoring of DNS with System Monitor, Event Viewer, Replication Monitor and DNS debug logs.

- **Implementing, Managing and Maintaining Network Security:** This includes the implementation of security templates and applying the principle of least privilege, monitoring protocol security using the IPSec Monitor and Kerberos tools, and troubleshoot IPSec, using Event Viewer and Network Monitor.

- **Implementing, Managing and Maintaining Routing and Remote Access:** This includes configuration of RRAS user authentication (including authentication protocols, IAS, and remote access policies), management of remote access (including packet filters, RRAS routing, devices, ports, routing protocols, and RRAS clients), management of TCP/IP routing, implementation of secure access between networks, troubleshooting user access to remote access services, and troubleshooting RRAS routing.

- **Maintaining a Network Infrastructure:** This includes monitoring network traffic with Network Monitor and System Monitor, troubleshooting Internet connectivity, and troubleshooting server services, including issues related to service dependency and use of service recovery options.

Path to MCP/MCSA/MCSE

Microsoft certification is recognized throughout the IT industry as a way to demonstrate mastery of basic concepts and skills required to perform the tasks involved in implementing and maintaining Windows-based networks. The certification program is constantly evaluated and improved; the nature of information technology is changing rapidly and this means requirements and specifications for certification can also change rapidly. This book is based on the exam objectives as stated by Microsoft at the time of writing; however, Microsoft reserves the right to make changes to the objectives and to the exam itself at any time. Exam candidates should regularly visit the Certification and Training web site at www.microsoft.com/traincert/ for the most updated information on each Microsoft exam.

Microsoft presently offers three basic levels of certification:

- **Microsoft Certified Professional (MCP):** to obtain the MCP certification, you must pass one current Microsoft certification exam. For more information on exams that qualify, see http://www.microsoft.com/traincert/mcp/mcp/requirements.asp.

- **Microsoft Certified Systems Administrator (MCSA):** to obtain the MCSA certification, you must pass three core exams and one elective exam, for a total of four exams. For more information, see http://www.microsoft.com/TrainCert/mcp/mcsa/requirements.asp.

- **Microsoft Certified Systems Engineer (MCSE):** to obtain the MCSE certification on Windows Server 2003, you must pass six core exams (including four network operating system exams, one client operating system exam and one design exam) and one elective. For more information, see http://www.microsoft.com/traincert/mcp/mcse/windows2003/.

Exam 70-291 applies toward all of the above certifications.

NOTE

Those who already hold the MCSA in Windows 2000 can upgrade their certifications to MCSA 2003 by passing one upgrade exam (70-292). Those who already hold the MCSE in Windows 2000 can upgrade their certifications to MCSE 2003 by passing two upgrade exams (70-292 and 70-296).

Microsoft also offers a number of specialty certifications for networking professionals and certifications for software developers, including the following:

- **Microsoft Certified Database Administrator (MCDBA)**

- **Microsoft Certified Solution Developer (MCSD)**

- **Microsoft Certified Application Developer (MCAD)**

Exam 70-291 does not apply to any of these specialty and developer certifications.

Prerequisites and Preparation

There are no mandatory prerequisites for taking Exam 70-291, although Microsoft recommends that you meet the target audience profile described earlier. Most candidates will take Exam 70-291 as their second MCSA or MCSE certification exam, following Exam 70-290, which is the logical choice for the first step in completing the requirements for MCSA 2003 or MCSE 2003.

Preparation for this exam should include the following:

- Visit the web site at http://www.microsoft.com/traincert/exams/70-291.asp to review the updated exam objectives.

- Work your way through this book, studying the material thoroughly and marking any items you don't understand.

- Answer all practice exam questions at the end of each chapter.

- Complete all hands-on exercises in each chapter.

- Review any topics that you don't thoroughly understand.

- Watch the companion DVD.

- Consult Microsoft online resources such as TechNet (http://www.microsoft.com/technet/), white papers on the Microsoft web site, and so forth, for better understanding of difficult topics.

- Participate in Microsoft's product-specific and training and certification newsgroups if you have specific questions that you still need answered.

- Take one or more practice exams, such as the one available at www.syngress.com/certification.

Exam Overview

In this book, we have tried to follow Microsoft's exam objectives as closely as possible. However, we have rearranged the order of some topics for a better flow, and included background material to help you understand the concepts and procedures that are included in the objectives. Following is a brief synopsis of the exam topics covered in each chapter:

- **Chapter 1 Review of TCP/IP:** You will start by learning about the two most popular networking models: the Department of Defense (DoD) model and the Open Systems Interconnection (OSI) model, both of which provide a layered structure for vendors of networking hardware and software. We'll then take a look at the various protocols of the TCP/IP protocol suite, and where each fits into the networking models. We'll review the basics of IP addressing, from binary/decimal conversion to the function of the host and network IDs. You'll learn about subnet masking, including how bitwise ANDing works, and we'll introduce the basics of IP routing, focusing on classful networks.

- **Chapter 2 Variable Length Subnet Masking and Client Configuration:** We start with a review of classful subnet masking and then introduce the concept of variable length (non-classful) subnet masking. We'll provide examples of how to subnet class A, B, and C networks, and as well as how to supernet a class C network. You'll learn about the Windows XP/2000 routing table and how it differs from the Windows Server 2003 routing table, and we'll show you how to create and remove routing table entries. Next, we discuss the methods of assigning IP addressing information to network clients, including static addressing, dynamic (DHCP) addressing and automatic private addressing (APIPA), as well as how to use the new alternate configuration feature.

- **Chapter 3 The Dynamic Host Configuration Protocol:** First, we provide an overview of DHCP: how it works, leases and the lease process, and lease renewal. Then we move on to DHCP Server configuration and you learn about DHCP scopes, options and reservations, as well as superscopes and BOOTP tables. We discuss the function of the DHCP relay agent and show you how to configure it, then we cover how DHCP is integrated with Dynamic DNS in Windows Server 2003 and discuss how to deal with Windows NT 4.0 and 9x clients. We also discuss integration of DHCP with RRAS and go over a number of common scenarios. Finally, we deal with how DHCP is integrated with Active Directory, and show you how to authorize DCHP servers in the Active Directory. You'll learn about how rogue DHCP server detection works, and we'll discuss the management of the DHCP server, including how to manage the DHCP database and viewing and recording of DHCP server statistics. We'll go into some detail about monitoring and troubleshooting DHCP using the Event Viewer, System Monitor, DHCP server audit log and DHCP log files.

- **Chapter 4 NetBIOS Name Resolution and WINS:** We start with an overview and review of the history and function of NetBIOS naming and discuss NetBIOS over TCP/IP (NetBT) and how NetBIOS names are resolved to IP addresses. We discuss the NetBIOS node types (b, p, m, h and enhanced h) and also discuss how NetBIOS names can be resolved using an LMHOSTS file. Then we get into the use of NetBIOS name servers and specifically the Windows Internet Name Server (WINS). You'll find out how WINS works, how to install and configure a WINS server, how to manage WINS records, how to configure replication and how to back up and restore the WINS database. We'll also cover how to configure the WINS client, and you'll learn about WINS interoperability with DHCP, DNS, RRAS, Active Directory, the browser service, and Windows 9x and NT 4.0 clients. Finally, we'll discuss troubleshooting WINS, including both WINS clients and WINS servers.

- **Chapter 5 Domain Naming System Concepts:** We begin with an overview and review of DNS and compare the NetBIOS and DNS naming conventions. You'll learn about the hierarchical DNS namespace, the functions of domain and host names, and how subdomains are named. Next, we discuss DNS zones and zone transfer, then we get into the nitty-gritty of host name resolution. You'll learn the order of host name resolution methods and we'll discuss the differences between recursive and iterative queries and forward and reverse lookups. We take a look at Windows Server 2003 DNS server roles, including standard primary DNS server, standard secondary DNS server, caching only DNS server, DNS forwarder and slave servers and dynamic DNS (DDNS) servers. We'll show you how DNS is integrated with Active Directory in Windows Server 2003, and you'll learn about the benefits of dynamic updates, AD integrated zones and AD related DNS entries.

- **Chapter 6 The Windows Server 2003 DNS Server:** Moving from concepts to practical matters, we get into the "how to" of installing and configuring a Windows Server 2003 DNS server. You'll learn to configure the DNS server properties, how to create reverse and forward lookup zones (including configuration of zone properties and creation and management of resource records), how to configure zone transfers, create zone delegations and create stub zones. Next, we deal with how to configure the DNS clients, using primary and alternate DNS server settings and configuring the client Advanced DNS settings. We'll discuss how to integrate DNS with DHCP, BIND, and Internet publishing, then you'll learn how to monitor the DNS server using the Performance console and the DNS server logs, and how to test simple and recursive queries. Finally, we cover troubleshooting issues, and you'll learn how to use nslookup, DNSCMD and DNSLint utilities to troubleshoot common DNS problems.

- **Chapter 7 Configuring the Windows Server 2003 Routing and Remote Access Service VPN:** After an overview of Windows Server 2003 Remote Access concepts, we discuss how to enable the Remote Access Service (RAS). Then we show you how to configure a virtual private networking (VPN) server. You'll learn about the authentication protocols that are supported as well as the VPN tunneling protocols (PPTP and L2TP). You'll learn about the VPN Server Configuration Wizard and how to use it and we'll discuss IP addressing for VPN clients. Next, we show you how to configure a VPN gateway, including how to create a demand dial connection, how to create the local and remote gateways and how to create static packet filters.

- **Chapter 8 Configuring the Windows Server 2003 RRAS LAN Routing, Dialup Services and Routing Protocols:** We show you how to configure local area network (LAN) routing, how to configure RRAS packet filters, and how to configure dialup remote access servers and dialup RAS gateways. We discuss how to configure connections using multilink and Bandwidth Allocation Protocol (BAP), and we also discuss the configuration of wireless connections. Next, we address the configuration of RRAS policies and you'll learn about the supported dynamic routing protocols: RIP, OSPF and IGMP. We also cover basic firewall support and Network Address Translation (NAT) services, and you'll learn about ICMP router discovery, as well as how to configure and use the Internet Authentication Services (IAS). Finally, we turn to troubleshooting both Remote Access client and server connections.

- **Chapter 9 Security Templates and Software Updates:** We'll introduce you to the concept of security templates and explain their function in your Windows Server 2003 network. You'll learn about different types of templates, network security settings, how to analyze baseline security and how to apply security templates, as well as how to use the default templates and how to create your own custom templates. Next, we discuss software updates and how to install and configure the software update infrastructure. You'll learn to install and configure automatic client update settings and we'll discuss support of legacy clients. Finally, we show you how to test software updates.

- **Chapter 10 Monitoring and Troubleshooting Network Activity:** We start with an overview of the Network Monitor protocol analysis tool. You'll learn how to install Network Monitor (which is not installed in Windows Server 2003 by default) and we'll discuss basic configuration. You'll learn about the default settings and we'll show you how to configure both capture and display filters. We show you how to interpret a trace. Next, we cover how to monitor and troubleshooting Internet connectivity; this includes the use of NAT logging, name resolution problems, and IP addressing problems. We'll also show you how to monitor secure connections (those using IPSec) with the IPSec Monitor console, as well as how to use other tools such as netsh, ipseccmc, netdiag and the Event Viewer.

Exam Day Experience

Taking the exam is a relatively straightforward process. Both Vue and Prometric testing centers administer the Microsoft 70-291 exam. You can register for, reschedule or cancel an exam through the Vue web site at http://www.vue.com/ or the Prometric web site at http://www.2test.com/index.jsp. You'll find listings of testing center locations on these sites. Accommodations are made for those with disabilities; contact the individual testing center for more information.

Exam price varies depending on the country in which you take the exam.

Exam Format

Exams are timed. At the end of the exam, you will find out your score and whether you passed or failed. You will not be allowed to take any notes or other written materials with you into the exam room. You will be provided with a pencil and paper, however, for making notes during the exam or doing calculations.

In addition to the traditional multiple choice questions and the select and drag, simulation and case study questions introduced in the Windows 2000 exams, Microsoft has developed a number of innovative question types for the Windows Server 2003 exams. You might see some or all of the following types of questions:

- *Hot area* questions, in which you are asked to select an element or elements in a graphic to indicate the correct answer. You click an element to select or deselect it.

- *Active screen* questions, in which you change elements in a dialog box (for example, by dragging the appropriate text element into a text box or selecting an option button or checkbox in a dialog box).

- *Drag and drop* questions, in which you arrange various elements in a target area.

You can download a demo sampler of test question types from the Microsoft web site at http://www.microsoft.com/traincert/mcpexams/faq/innovations.asp#H.

Test Taking Tips

Different people work best using different methods. However, there are some common methods of preparation and approach to the exam that are helpful to many test-takers. In this section, we provide some tips that other exam candidates have found useful in preparing for and actually taking the exam.

- Exam preparation begins before exam day. Ensure that you know the concepts and terms well and feel confident about each of the exam objectives. Many test-takers find it helpful to make flash cards or review notes to study on the way to the testing center. A sheet listing acronyms and abbreviations can be helpful, as the number of acronyms (and the similarity of different acronyms) when studying IT topics can be overwhelming. The process of writing the material down, rather than just reading it, will help to reinforce your knowledge.

- Many test-takers find it especially helpful to take practice exams that are available on the Internet and with books such as this one. Taking the practice exams not only gets you used to the computerized exam-taking experience, but also can be used as a learning tool. The best practice tests include detailed explanations of why the correct answer is correct and why the incorrect answers are wrong.

- When preparing and studying, you should try to identify the main points of each objective section. Set aside enough time to focus on the material and lodge it into your memory. On the day of the exam, you be at the point where you don't have to learn any new facts or concepts, but need simply to review the information already learned.

- The value of hands-on experience cannot be stressed enough. Exam questions are based on test-writers' experiences in the field. Working with the products on a regular basis, whether in your job environment or in a test network that you've set up at home, will make you much more comfortable with these questions.

- Know your own learning style and use study methods that take advantage of it. If you're primarily a visual learner, reading, making diagrams, watching video files on CD, etc. may be your best study methods. If you're primarily auditory, classroom lectures, audiotapes you can play in the car as you drive, and repeating key concepts to yourself aloud may be more effective. If you're a kinesthetic learner, you'll need to actually *do* the exercises, implement the security measures on your own systems, and otherwise perform hands-on tasks to best absorb the information. Most of us can learn from all of these methods, but have a primary style that works best for us.

- Although it might seem obvious, many exam-takers ignore the physical aspects of exam preparation. You are likely to score better if you've had sufficient sleep the night before the exam, and if you are not hungry, thirsty, hot/cold or otherwise distracted by physical discomfort. Eat prior to going to the testing center (but don't indulge in a huge meal that will leave you uncomfortable), stay away from alcohol for 24 hours prior to the test, and dress appropriately for the temperature in the testing center (if you don't know how hot/cold the testing environment tends to be, you may want to wear light clothes with a sweater or jacket that can be taken off).

- Before you go to the testing center to take the exam, be sure to allow time to arrive on time, take care of any physical needs, and step back to take a deep breath and relax. Try to arrive slightly early, but not so far in advance that you spend a lot of time worrying and getting nervous about the testing process. You may want to do a quick last minute review of notes, but don't try to "cram" everything the morning of the exam. Many test-takers find it helpful to take a short walk or do a few calisthenics shortly before the exam, as this gets oxygen flowing to the brain.

- Before beginning to answer questions, use the pencil and paper provided to you to write down terms, concepts and other items that you think you may have difficulty remembering as the exam goes on. Then you can refer back to these notes as you progress through the test. You won't have to worry about forgetting the concepts and terms you have trouble with later in the exam.

- Sometimes the information in a question will remind you of another concept or term that you might need in a later question. Use your pen and paper to make note of this in case it comes up later on the exam.

- It is often easier to discern the answer to scenario questions if you can visualize the situation. Use your pen and paper to draw a diagram of the network that is described to help you see the relationships between devices, IP addressing schemes, and so forth.

- When appropriate, review the answers you weren't sure of. However, you should only change your answer if you're sure that your original answer was incorrect. Experience has shown that more often than not, when test-takers start second-guessing their answers, they end up changing correct answers to the incorrect. Don't "read into" the question (that is, don't fill in or assume information that isn't there); this is a frequent cause of incorrect responses.

- As you go through this book, pay special attention to the Exam Warnings, as these highlight concepts that are likely to be tested. You may find it useful to go through and copy these into a notebook (remembering that writing something down reinforces your ability to remember it) and/or go through and review the Exam Warnings in each chapter just prior to taking the exam.

- Use as many little mnemonic tricks as possible to help you remember facts and concepts. For example, to remember which of the two IPSec protocols (AH and ESP) encrypts data for confidentiality, you can associate the "E" in encryption with the "E" in ESP.

Pedagogical Elements

In this book, you'll find a number of different types of sidebars and other elements designed to supplement the main text. These include the following:

- **Exam Warning** These focus on specific elements on which the reader needs to focus in order to pass the exam (for example, "Be sure you know the difference between symmetric and asymmetric encryption").

- **Test Day Tip** These are short tips that will help you in organizing and remembering information for the exam (for example, "When preparing for the exam on test day, it may be helpful to have a sheet with definitions of these abbreviations and acronyms handy for a quick last-minute review").

- **Configuring & Implementing** These are sidebars that contain background information that goes beyond what you need to know from the exam, but provide a "deep" foundation for understanding the concepts discussed in the text.

- **New & Noteworthy** These are sidebars that point out changes in W2003 Server from the old Windows 2000/NT family, as they will apply to readers taking the exam. These may be elements that users of W2K/NT would be very familiar with that have changed significantly in W2003 Server, or totally new features that they would not be familiar with at all.

- **Head of the Class** These are discussions of concepts and facts as they might be presented in the classroom, regarding issues and questions that most commonly are raised by students during study of a particular topic.

The book also includes, in each chapter, hands-on exercises in planning and configuring the features discussed. It is essential that you read through and, if possible, perform the steps of these exercises to familiarize yourself with the processes they cover.

You will find a number of helpful elements at the end of each chapter. For example, each chapter contains a *Summary of Exam Objectives* that ties the topics discussed in that chapter to the published objectives. Each chapter also contains an *Exam Objectives Fast Track,* which boils all exam objectives down to manageable summaries that are perfect for last minute review. *The Exam Objectives Frequently Asked Questions* answers those questions that most often arise from readers and students regarding the topics covered in the chapter. Finally, in the *Self Test* section, you will find a set of practice questions written in a multiple-choice form that will assist you in your exam preparation These questions are designed to assess your mastery of the exam objectives and provide thorough remediation, as opposed to simulating the variety of question formats you may encounter in the actual exam. You can use the *Self Test Quick Answer Key* that follows the *Self Test* questions to quickly determine what information you need to review again. The *Self Test Appendix* at the end of the book provides detailed explanations of both the correct and incorrect answers.

Additional Resources

There are two other important exam preparation tools included with this Study Guide. One is the DVD included in the back of this book. The other is the practice exam available from our Web site.

- **Instructor-led training DVD provides you with almost two hours of virtual classroom instruction.** Sit back and watch as an author and trainer reviews all the key exam concepts from the perspective of someone taking the exam for the first time. Here, you'll cut through all of the noise to prepare you for exactly what to expect when you take the exam for the first time. You will want to watch this DVD just before you head out to the testing center!

- **Web based practice exams.** Just visit us at **www.syngress.com/certification** to access a complete Exam 70-291 practice test. These remediation tools are written to test you on all of the published certification objectives. The exam runs in both "live" and "practice" mode. Use "live" mode first to get an accurate gauge of your knowledge and skills, and then use practice mode to launch an extensive review of the questions that gave you trouble.

Chapter 1

MCSA/MCSE 70-291

Reviewing TCP/IP Basics

Exam Objectives in this Chapter:

1.1   Configure TCP/IP addressing on a server computer.

1.3   Troubleshoot TCP/IP addressing.

☑   Summary of Exam Objectives

☑   Exam Objectives Fast Track

☑   Exam Objectives Frequently Asked Questions

☑   Self Test

☑   Self Test Quick Answer Key

Introduction

To prepare for the Microsoft Windows Server 2003 Network Infrastructure exam (Exam 70-291), you should begin by reviewing the foundations of networking: the models on which networks are built, the protocols they use to communicate, the addressing schemes by which they identify individual devices on the network, and the technologies they use to ensure that data reaches its destination. The vast majority of networks today (including the Internet) use Transmission Control Protocol/Internet Protocol (TCP/IP) to transmit information among computers and networks in a wide area network (WAN). Together, TCP and IP are referred to as a *protocol stack* or as *network/transport* protocols because they work together at two different levels (called the Network and Transport layers) to enable computers to communicate with each other.

A thorough understanding of TCP/IP is essential to successfully maintain servers and networks efficiently and securely, and to understand the Windows Server 2003 network services (such as DNS, WINS, and Routing and Remote Access) that will be discussed throughout this book.

In this chapter, we'll examine the history and evolution of TCP/IP from its humble beginnings in the 1960s to its current implementation in Windows Server 2003 networks. We'll look at the networking models that provide guidelines for vendors of networking products, including the early Department of Defense (DoD) model as well as the International Organization of Standardization's Open Systems Interconnection (OSI) model.

Next, we'll move into the specifics of TCP/IP. You'll learn about the individual components of TCP/IP, a suite of protocols that are used throughout the network communication process to ensure that data sent from a computer reaches its intended destination.

Due to the explosive growth of networking as a means of communication and sharing of resources and information, a method was needed to subdivide assigned public network addresses. This is called *subnetting*, and is widely used by organizations to reduce the number of computers on a network segment, improving the speed of the network for the users. Subnetting requires unique addressing schemes that utilize IP addresses, subnet masks, and gateways. The foundation of IP addressing as well as IP routing is the binary numbering system. In this chapter, you'll learn how to convert from binary to decimal and back again, how to decipher IP addresses in the dotted decimal format, and how to use Boolean logic to determine network and host addresses from IP addresses.

Finally, we'll discuss how data is routed through a network to reach its intended destination quickly and accurately. All of this will be covered in our in-depth look at TCP/IP.

Understanding the Purpose and Function of Networking Models

This chapter discusses several specific networking models, so it's important to begin our discussion with an overview of the purpose and function of networking models. Just about everywhere we look in the world today, we can see examples of agreed-upon rules that help people work together more effectively to achieve a specific aim. This is especially true in the world of technology where standards, specifications, and protocols are used to accomplish a particular task. Why is it you can pop a DVD in your player and watch it, regardless of who made the DVD, the DVD player, or the television? It's because everyone involved agreed to certain parameters such as the circumference of the DVD disk, the method of recording and reading the DVD, and the interface between the DVD player and the television.

The same is true in computer technology. A wide variety of methods can be used to transmit and receive data across a network. Models are used to broadly define the required elements. This helps break down complex tasks into more manageable segments. It also provides frameworks from which standards can be developed. Organizing networking tasks in this way provides standardization, which is critical for any technology to be widely adopted. It also reduces development time and cost because common tasks are defined and can be implemented without "reinventing the wheel."

The Department of Defense networking model was originally created to solve the problem of people needing to share information across large computer systems. That model was used as the basis for an expanded model known as the OSI model. Microsoft networks also rely upon a networking model, which incorporates the required elements from the OSI model and defines additional elements specific to Microsoft technologies. Software and hardware vendors that want to develop products that will work seamlessly with Microsoft products use the Microsoft networking model as the basis for designing their products. For example, it's very helpful for software developers to know how Microsoft technologies interface with a Network Interface Card (NIC). They can create products (software, hardware, or both) that follow the requirements of the model, knowing that their products will interoperate with other hardware and software that adhere to the same model.

Understanding the Department of Defense (DoD) Networking Model

In the mid-1960s, computer systems were huge mainframes that were all owned and maintained by large companies, universities, and governmental agencies. Users, especially in the academic, scientific, and governmental arenas, often needed to share data with other users. The problem was that mainframe computers all ran different proprietary software, and operating systems could not easily communicate with one another. In order to share data, programmers had to write code that would allow one mainframe to communicate with another specific mainframe.

This cumbersome one-to-one process was prohibitive, both in terms of the time and cost required to develop unique, proprietary solutions, and in terms of the limitations those solutions often imposed. After an interface was written, that mainframe still could communicate only with its specified counterpart. If either mainframe's operating system changed, the interface might be broken and programmers would have to be called back in to reestablish the communication system between the two mainframes.

The U.S. Department of Defense's *Advanced Research Projects Agency* (DARPA) tackled this problem with an experiment designed to demonstrate a way to share computer data across a wide area network. This experiment was called ARPANET (Advanced Research Projects Agency Network), and it became the foundation for what we know today as the Internet. It also resulted in the development of the TCP/IP protocols in the late 1960s. TCP/IP is one of the few computer technologies from the 1960s that is still in use today—a testament to the superb design of the TCP/IP suite. There have been efforts to replace it with other, more elegant protocol suites (most notably, the OSI protocol suite) but these efforts have, for the most part, met with failure. Although it has undergone some modifications over time, TCP/IP is still the "protocol suite of choice" for almost all large networks and for the global Internet, and it is only recently that the limitations of its networking layer protocol (IP) have been reached. A new version of the IP protocol, IPv6, addresses those limitations, as we'll discuss later in this book.

The DARPA architecture, known as the *DARPA model* or the DoD model, defines four layers starting at the network cable (or interface) and working its way up:

- Network Interface
- Internet (or Internetworking)
- Host to Host (or Transport)
- Application

Each layer is designed with a specific function and together they provide the foundation for internetworking. Different protocols within the TCP/IP suite work at different layers, as you'll discover when we examine the individual components of the TCP/IP suite.

Layer One: Network Interface

The *Network Interface* layer of the DoD model corresponds to the lowest level of the TCP/IP protocol architecture and correlates to Layers 1 and 2 in the OSI model. The Network Interface layer provides most of the capabilities provided for in the Physical and Data Link layers of the OSI model.

Let's begin with a brief overview of the hardware involved in the network at this level. We have the network medium, typically coaxial or twisted pair cabling (although wireless networking is increasing in popularity); and we have the network interface card (NIC) that has both a physical MAC address and a logical IP address (we'll discuss the IP address a bit later). The NIC has logic (a circuit board and chips) built into it that gives it basic functionality. It uses a driver, which is a small software program that interfaces between the hardware and the operating system, to provide additional functionality. The NIC typically is involved at Layers 1 and 2 of the OSI model, thus it operates at Layer 1 in the TCP/IP model.

The specifications related to how the network technology is implemented are defined by an international association of engineers called the *Institute of Electrical and Electronics*

Engineers (IEEE, called the "Eye-triple E" by industry members). The IEEE helps define common standards for use in a variety of technical fields, including computing. One such standard is the 802 standard, so named because the initial committee meeting was in 1980, in February (the second month). This standard defines specifications for the lower level networking technologies; that is, those at the physical level (NIC, connectors, and cables) and at the data link level (access methods).

As you'll see, the standards vary, depending on the network technology (Ethernet, Token Ring, ATM, Frame Relay, and so forth). Because TCP/IP works independently of network technology, it can be used with each of these types of networks, and can be used to send information between two dissimilar networks as well. For more information on the IEEE, you can visit their Web site at www.ieee.org.

The standards set by the 802 committee pertaining to networking are as follows:

- **802.1** Internetworking standards that deal with the management of local area networks (LANs) and metropolitan area networks (MANs), including bridges and the spanning tree algorithm used by bridges to prevent looping

- **802.2** Logical link control, and the division of OSI Layer 2 into two sublayers, LLC and MAC

- **802.3** CSMA/C, the media access control method used on Ethernet networks, and frame formats for Ethernet

- **802.4** Token Bus networks that use 75ohm coaxial or fiber optic cabling and the token passing access method

- **802.5** Token Ring, the technology developed by IBM that uses a physical star and logical ring topology with twisted pair cabling (shielded or unshielded) and the token passing access method

- **802.6** MANs, networks of a size and scope that falls between that of the LAN and the WAN

- **802.7** Broadband transmissions that use Frequency Division Multiplexing (FDM), including CATV

- **802.8** Fiber optics networks, including Fiber Distributed Data Interface (FDDI) using the token passing access method

- **802.9** Integrated services (voice and data) over ISDN

- **802.10** Virtual private networking to create a secure connection to a private network over the public Internet

- **802.11** Wireless networking technologies, including the most common 802.11b, faster 802.11a, and newest 802.11g wireless communications methods

- **802.12** The 100VG AnyLAN technology developed by Hewlett Packard, which uses the demand priority access method

Media Access Control

Media access control (MAC) refers to the method used to allocate use of the medium among the computers and devices on the network. The media access control method performs a function similar to the chairperson of a meeting, whose responsibility it is to recognize each speaker in turn and keep everyone from talking at once.

In networking, access control is important only when many devices share a common medium, such as a coaxial cable or twisted pair cable—and then it is *very* important. Various schemes have been devised to control access to the media by the connected devices. If no methods were in place, all devices would send data whenever it suited them. On a small network, this might not be a problem, but if there are more than a few devices, it quickly causes congestion, collisions, and errors because everybody's talking at once. Therefore, as the size of the typical network grew, it was important to develop standard methods to control access to the shared media so that communication would proceed in an orderly and predictable manner. The access control method lays out rules defining how access is allocated, just as Robert's Rules of Order govern how meetings proceed.

MAC is performed by MAC layer protocols. Although there are many different MAC protocols for a wide variety of media used by many different communications technologies (cellular, cable TV, satellite, etc.), we're going to concentrate on those that are most common in computing today. These include:

- CSMA/CD
- CSMA/CA
- Token passing

We will discuss each of these in detail later in this chapter.

Network Interface Hardware/Software

The network interface is established through the Network Interface Card. Each type of NIC uses a different type of connector to connect to the physical medium. The connector types are delineated in the IEEE 802 specifications. Each network technology is delineated in its own section of the 802 specification, as described previously. Most significantly, Ethernet is defined in 802.3, Token Ring in 802.5, and Wireless Networking in 802.11.

The NIC employs both hardware and software in connecting the device to the network media. The TCP/IP Network Interface layer defines protocols used by the NIC to receive, assemble, address, and transmit. For example, most Ethernet networks in use today employ an Ethernet NIC, which, among other things, uses CSMA/CD to control media access. The most common type of Ethernet NIC uses a Category 5 or greater unshielded twisted pair cable (typically referred to as UTP CAT5, CAT5e, or CAT6) with specified pin connections. In some cases, Ethernet is still deployed over thin (1/4 inch diameter) or thick (1/2 inch diameter) coaxial cable. Ethernet can also be deployed over fiber optic cable. Regardless of the cable type, Ethernet networks use the same contention-based access control method.

UTP cabling connects to the NIC via an RJ-45 modular plug and jack (similar to a large phone jack), and thin coax (thinnet) connects via a BNC connector (Bayonet Neill Concelman, after its twist-on style and the two men who invented it) shaped like a T. Thick coaxial (thicknet) is connected via a vampire tap (a metal pin that penetrates the cable) to an external transceiver, which in turn connects to the NIC. Other types of Ethernet NICs have the transceiver built onto the NIC itself. Some NICs, called *combo cards*, have connectors for more than one type of cable.

The Ethernet NIC is also responsible for receiving/sending and assembling/disassembling data to and from the network connection. The Network Interface layer in the DoD model encompasses the functions of the OSI model's Physical and Data Link Control layers and controls media access and the assembly/disassembly of data at the lowest level of the hierarchy.

Layer Two: Internet (or Internetworking)

The next layer in the DoD model is the *Internet* layer, which maps to the Network layer of the OSI model. The Internet layer, so called because of the addressing scheme that makes communications possible across a network of networks, or internetwork, is responsible for packaging, addressing, and routing the data. When this layer was originally conceived, the Internet as we know it today did not exist. The concept behind this layer was to define a framework for two computers to connect to one another to share data. This laid the foundation for widespread internetworking, which led to what we now know as the Internet.

Before data can be sent out over the Network Interface, it must have a standard format, size, and addressing scheme. The Network Interface layer is responsible only for taking the data it is given and translating that to signals on a physical medium. The Internet layer defines packet structure (what each bit of a data segment means), addressing, and routing. Later in this chapter, we'll discuss the four primary protocols used by TCP/IP that work at the Internet layer: the Internet Protocol (IP), Internet Control Message Protocol (ICMP), Internet Group Management Protocol (IGMP), and Address Resolution Protocol (ARP).

Layer Three: Host to Host (or Transport)

Layer 3 in the DoD model is the *Host-to-Host Transport* layer, sometimes called the *Transport* layer since this layer maps to the Transport layer (Layer 4) in the OSI model. As the name implies, this layer is responsible for transporting the data. It sets up communications between the Application layer and the lower layers. The Internet layer is responsible for formatting, addressing, and routing the data, and the Host-to-Host Transport layer is responsible for setting up the connection between hosts so that formatted data can be sent.

Because this layer establishes a connection, it can also take on some of the responsibilities of the Session layer of the OSI model. In TCP/IP, the two core protocols used at the Host-to-Host Transport layer are the *Transmission Control Protocol* (TCP) and the *User Datagram Protocol* (UDP). TCP is a more complex protocol that provides reliable data transport—the application sending the data receives acknowledgement that the data was received. UDP is a much simpler protocol that does not provide acknowledgement messages. Although this makes UDP data transport less reliable, it is a very useful protocol in certain applications where fast, simple communication is required. Both of these protocols are discussed in detail later in this chapter.

Layer Four: Application

The *Application* layer of the DoD model operates at the Session, Presentation, and Application layers of the OSI model. This layer enables applications to communicate with one another and it provides access to the services of the other underlying layers (Network Interface [1], Internet [2], and Host-to-Host Transport [3]). There are a wide variety of Application layer protocols, and more are continually being developed because they can rely on all the services beneath them. If you think of how your computer's software is configured, you use many different applications that rely upon the services of the underlying operating system. Each application does not have to provide duplicate services such as a routine for accessing your disk drive. That is provided by the operating system and the application utilizes that functionality. This is how the Application layer of the networking model works as well: It relies upon the underlying services. In this way, developers do not have to write code continually to provide the underlying functionality, but can simply access that functionality by adhering to agreed-upon standards and specifications. We'll look at a number of Application layer protocols when we look at TCP/IP in detail.

We've discussed the four layers of the DARPA or DoD model of internetworking. Throughout, we've mentioned the OSI model. Now, let's take an in-depth look at the OSI model to understand how the OSI model expands upon the functionality defined in the DoD model.

Understanding the OSI Model

The *Open Systems Interconnection* (OSI) model was originally developed at Honeywell in the mid-1970s, and expanded upon the DoD model. In 1977, the *International Organization for Standardization,* commonly known as ISO, recognized the need to develop a communication standard for computing. They formed a subcommittee called the OSI committee, and asked for proposals for a communication standard. Honeywell's solution, called a *distributed systems architecture* (DSA), included seven layers for communications. This framework was adopted by the OSI, and is still used as the model for distributed communications.

The seven layers of the OSI model are:

- Physical
- Data Link
- Network
- Transport
- Session
- Presentation
- Application

We'll explore each of the seven layers of the OSI model in the following subsections. The first two layers of the OSI model involve both hardware and software. In the five upper layers (Layers 3 through 7), the OSI model typically is implemented via software only.

TEST DAY TIP

Some exams may ask you to identify the seven layers of the OSI model, as well as to identify the definitions of one or more of the layers. An acronym used to remember the seven layers of the OSI model is **All People Seem To Need Data Processing**. This equates to **Application, Presentation, Session, Transport, Network, Data Link,** and **Physical.** By remembering this acronym, you'll easily remember the seven layers (in reverse order). Remember that numbering starts at the "bottom" of the model.

More commonly, the Microsoft exams require you to know and understand what happens at each layer, and which protocols operate there (rather than just rote memorization of the layers themselves) in order to be able to troubleshoot common networking problems.

Figure 1.1 shows the OSI model. It is represented as a *stack* because data that is sent across the network has to move through each layer at both the sending and receiving ends. The sending computer generally initiates the process at the Application layer. The data is then sent down the stack to the Physical layer and across the network to the receiving computer. On the receiving end, the data is received at the Physical layer and the data packet is sent up the stack to the Application layer.

Layer 1: Physical

The first, most basic layer of the OSI model is the *Physical* layer. This layer specifies the electrical and mechanical requirements for transmitting data bits across the transmission medium (cable or airwaves). It involves sending and receiving the data stream on the carrier—whether that carrier uses electrical (cable), light (fiber optic) or radio, infrared or laser (wireless) signals. The Physical layer specifications include:

- Voltage changes
- Timing of voltage changes
- Data rates
- Maximum transmission distances
- Physical connectors to the transmission medium
- Topology or physical layout of the network

Figure 1.1 The OSI Model

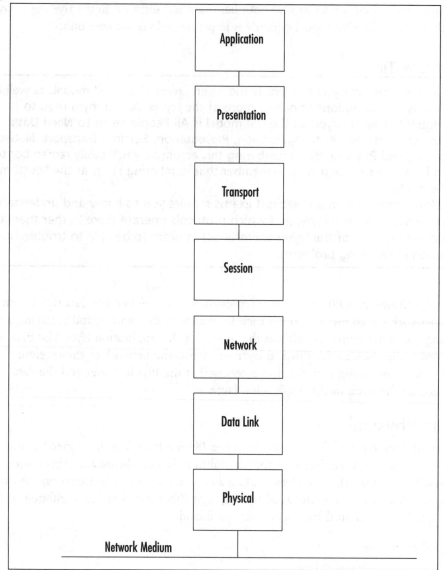

Many complex issues are addressed at the Physical layer, including digital versus analog signaling, baseband versus broadband signaling, whether data is transmitted synchronously or asynchronously, and how signals are divided into channels (multiplexing).

Devices that operate at the Physical layer deal with signaling, such as the transceivers on the NIC, repeaters, basic hubs, and simple connectors that join segments of cable.

The data handled by the Physical layer is in bits—literally 1s and 0s. These 1s and 0s are represented by pulses of light or electricity, and by the state of those pulses (on generally representing a 1 and off generally representing a 0).

How these bits are arranged and managed is a function of the next layer in the OSI model.

Layer 2: Data Link

Layer 2 is the *Data Link* layer. This layer is responsible for maintaining the data link between two computers, typically called *hosts* or *nodes*. It also defines and manages the ordering of bits to/from data segments, called packets. *Frames* contain data arranged in an organized manner, which provides for an orderly and consistent method of sending data bits across the medium. Without such control, the data would be sent in random sizes or configurations and the data that was sent on one end could not be decoded on the other end. The Data Link layer manages the physical addressing and synchronization of the data packets (as opposed to the logical addressing that is handled at the Network layer). The Data Link layer is also responsible for flow control and error notification on the Physical layer. Flow control is the process of managing the timing of sending and receiving data so that it doesn't exceed the capacity (speed, memory, etc.) of the physical connection. Since the Physical layer is responsible only for physically moving the data onto and off of the network medium, the Data Link layer also receives and manages error messaging related to physical delivery of packets.

Network devices that operate at this layer include Layer 2 switches (switching hubs) and bridges. A Layer 2 switch decreases network congestion by sending data out only on the port to which the destination computer is attached, instead of sending it out on all ports, as a physical layer hub does. Bridges provide a way to segment a network into two parts and filter traffic by building tables that define which computers are located on which side of the bridge, based on their MAC addresses.

The Data Link layer is divided into two sublayers: the *Logical Link Control* (LLC) sublayer and the *Media Access Control* (MAC) sublayer.

The LLC Sublayer

The LLC sublayer provides the logic for the data link, thus it controls the synchronization, flow control, and error checking functions of the Data Link layer. This layer can handle connection-oriented transmissions (unlike the MAC sublayer below it), although connectionless service can also be provided by this layer. Connectionless operations are known as Class I LLC, whereas Class II can handle either connectionless or connection-oriented operations. With connection-oriented communication, each LLC frame that is sent is acknowledged. The LLC sublayer at the receiving end keeps up with the LLC frames it receives (these are also called Protocol Data Units or PDUs), and if it detects that a frame has been lost during the transmission, it can send back a request to the sending computer to start the transmission over again, beginning with the PDU that never arrived.

The LLC sublayer sits above the MAC sublayer, and acts as a liaison between the upper layers and the protocols that operate at the MAC sublayer such as Ethernet, Token Ring, and so on (IEEE standards). The LLC sublayer itself is defined by IEEE 802.2. Link addressing, sequencing, and definition of Service Access Points (SAPs) also take place at this layer.

The MAC Sublayer

The MAC sublayer provides control for accessing the transmission medium. It is responsible for moving data packets from one NIC to another, across a shared transmission medium such as an Ethernet or fiber optic cable.

Physical addressing is addressed at the MAC sublayer. Every NIC has a unique MAC address, also called the physical address, which identifies that specific NIC on the network. The MAC address of a NIC usually is burned into a read-only memory (ROM) chip on the NIC card. Each manufacturer of network cards is provided a unique set of MAC addresses so that (theoretically, at least) every NIC that is manufactured has a unique MAC address. Obviously, it would be confusing if there were two or more NICs with the same MAC address. A packet intended for NIC #35 (a simplification of the MAC address) would not know to *which* NIC #35 it was destined. To avoid this confusion, MAC addresses, in most cases, are permanently burned into the NIC's memory. This is sometimes referred to as the Burned-In Address or BIA.

NOTE

On Ethernet NICs, the physical or MAC address (also called the hardware address) is expressed as 12 hexadecimal digits, arranged in pairs with colons between each pair: 12:3A:4D:66:3A:1C. In binary notation, this translates to a 48-bit (or 6-byte) number, with the initial three bytes representing the manufacturer and the last three bits representing a unique network interface card made by that manufacturer. On Token Ring NICs, the MAC address is six bytes long, too, but the bits of each byte are reversed. That is, Ethernet transmits in *canonical or LSB mode,* with the least significant bit first, whereas Token Ring transmits with the most significant bit first (*MSB or non-canonical* mode). Although duplicate MAC addresses are rare, they do show up because some manufacturers have started to use their numbers over again. This usually is not a problem because the duplicates almost never show up on the same network. Some cards allow you to change the MAC address by using special software to "flash" the card's chip.

Another important issue that's handled at the MAC sublayer is media access control. This refers to the method used to allocate network access to computers and prevent them from transmitting at the same time, causing data collisions. Common media access control methods include Carrier Sense Multiple Access/Collision Detection (CSMA/CD), used by Ethernet networks, Carrier Sense Multiple Access/Collision Avoidance (CSMA/CA), used by AppleTalk networks, and token passing, used by Token Ring and FDDI networks.

Layer 3: Network

As we travel up the OSI model, the next layer we encounter is the *Network* layer. At the Network layer, packets are sequenced and logical addressing is handled. Logical addresses are nonpermanent, software-assigned addresses that can be changed by administrators. The IP addresses used by the TCP/IP protocols on the Internet and the IPX addresses used by the IPX/SPX protocols on NetWare networks are examples of logical addresses. These protocol stacks are referred to as *routable* because they include addressing schemes that identify both the network or subnet and the particular client on that network or subnet. Other network/transport protocols, such as NetBEUI, do not have a sophisticated addressing scheme and thus cannot be routed across different networks.

NOTE

To understand the difference between physical and logical addresses, consider this analogy: If you buy a house, it has a physical address that identifies exactly where it is located on the earth, at a specific latitude and longitude. This never changes (unless you have a mobile home that can be moved from one plot of land to another). This is like the MAC address on a NIC. Your house also has a logical address assigned to it by the Post Office, consisting of a street number and street name. The city can (and occasionally does) change the names of streets, or renumber the houses located on them. This is like the IP address assigned to a network interface.

The Network layer is also responsible for creating a virtual circuit (a logical connection, not a physical connection) between points or nodes. A node is a device that has a MAC address, which typically includes computers, printers, and routers. This layer is also responsible for routing, Layer 3 switching, and forwarding of packets. *Routing* refers to forwarding packets from one network or subnet to another. Without routing, computers can communicate only with other computers that are on the same network. Routing makes it possible for computers to send data through many networks to other computers that are on the other side of the world. Routing is the key to the global Internet, and is one of the most important duties of the Network layer.

Finally, the Network layer provides additional levels of flow control and error control. As mentioned earlier, from this point on, the primary methods of implementing the OSI model architecture involve software rather than hardware.

Devices that operate at this layer include, most prominently, routers and Layer 3 switches.

Head of the Class...

Different Switches for Different Layers

Troubleshooting network problems requires that you understand which protocols and devices operate at which layers of the networking model. It's important to understand that all switches are not created equal. There are actually several different types of devices that are called switches, and they operate at different layers.

Layer 2 switches are sometimes called *standard switches*. They operate at the Data Link layer, and function like sophisticated hubs. When a computer sends data to a hub, the hub sends it back out on all ports, to all the connected computers. A switch sends the data only out the port to which the destination computer (based on the addressing information in the headers) is attached. This decreases the amount of unnecessary traffic on the network and also increases security.

Layer 3 switches also operate at the Network layer, and are really a specialized type of router. They're sometimes called switched routers. Layer 3 switches use the information in the packet headers to apply policies, in addition to performing normal routing functions.

Layer 4 switches operate at the Transport layer (in addition to the lower layers) and can use the port number information from TCP or UDP headers. They can provide Access Control Lists (ACLs) to filter traffic for better security, and are able to control bandwidth allocation for load balancing purposes. Many routers also function as Layer 4 switches.

Layer 4: Transport

Layer 4 is the *Transport* layer. As the name implies, it is responsible for transporting the data from one node to another. It provides transparent data transfer between nodes and manages the end-to-end flow control, error detection, and error recovery.

The Transport layer protocols initiate contact between host computers and set up a virtual circuit. The transport protocols on each host computer verify that the application sending the data is authorized to access the network and that both ends are ready to initiate the data transfer. When this synchronization is complete, the data can be sent. As the data is being transmitted, the transport protocol on each host monitors the data flow and watches for transport errors. If transport errors are detected, the transport protocol can provide error recovery.

The functions performed by the Transport layer are very important to network communication. Just as the data link layer provides lower level reliability and connection-oriented or connectionless communications, the Transport layer does the same thing at a higher level. In fact, the two protocols most commonly associated with the Transport layer are defined by their connection state: The Transmission Control Protocol (TCP) is connection-oriented, whereas the User Datagram Protocol (UDP) is connectionless.

Connection-Oriented versus Connectionless Protocols

What's the difference between a connection-oriented and a connectionless protocol? A connection-oriented protocol such as TCP creates a connection between the two computers before actually sending the data, and then verifies that the data has reached its destination by using acknowledgements (messages sent back to the sending computer from the receiving computer that acknowledge receipt). Connectionless protocols send the data and trust that it will reach the proper destination.

Consider an analogy: You need to send a very important letter to a business associate, containing valuable papers that must not get lost along the way. You call him before mailing the letter, to let him know he should expect it (establishing the connection). You might even insure it or send it via certified mail. After a few days have passed, your friend calls you back to let you know that he did receive the letter, or you get back the return receipt that you requested (acknowledgement). This is the way a connection-oriented communication works. It's different from mailing a relatively unimportant item, such as a postcard to a friend when you're on vacation. In that case, you just drop it in the mailbox and hope it gets to the addressee. You don't expect or require any acknowledgement. This is like a connectionless communication.

What else does the Transport layer do? It handles another aspect of logical addressing: ports. If you think of a computer's IP address as analogous to the street address of a building, you can think of a port as a suite number or apartment number within that building. It further defines exactly where the data should go.

A computer might have several network applications running at the same time: a Web browser sending a request to a Web server for a Web page, an e-mail client sending and receiving mail, and a file transfer program uploading or downloading information to and from an FTP server. There must be some mechanism to determine which incoming data packets belong to which application, and that's the function of port numbers. The FTP protocol used by that program is assigned a particular port, whereas the Web browser and e-mail clients use different protocols (HTTP and POP3 or IMAP) that have their own assigned ports. Thus the information that is intended for the Web browser doesn't go to the e-mail program by mistake. Port numbers are used by the Transport layer protocols (TCP and UDP).

Finally, the Transport layer deals with name resolution. Because human beings prefer to identify computers by names instead of IP addresses (after all, it's easier to remember "www.microsoft.com" for Microsoft's Web server than 207.46.249.222), but computers know only how to interpret numbers (and binary numbers, at that), there must be a way for names to be matched with numerical addresses so that people and computers don't drive one another crazy. Name resolution methods such as the Domain Name System (DNS) solve this problem, and they generally operate at the Transport layer.

Layer 5: Session

After the Transport layer has established the virtual connection, a communication session can be established. A communication session occurs between two processes on two different computers. The *Session* layer is responsible for establishing, monitoring, and terminating sessions, using the virtual circuits established by the Transport layer.

The Session layer is also responsible for putting header information into data packets to indicate where the message begins and ends. Once header information is attached to the data packets, the Session layer performs synchronization between the sender's Session layer and the receiver's Session layer. The use of acknowledgement messages (ACKs) helps coordinate transfer of data at the Session layer level.

A very important function of the Session layer is controlling whether the communications within a session are sent as full duplex or half duplex messages. Half duplex communication goes in both directions between the communicating computers, but information can travel in only one direction at a time (as with walkie-talkie radio communications, in which you have to hold down the microphone button to transmit and cannot hear the person on the other end when you do). With full duplex communication, information can be sent in both directions at the same time (as in a regular telephone conversation, in which both parties can talk and hear one another at the same time).

Whereas the Transport layer establishes a connection between two machines, the Session layer establishes a connection between two processes. A *process* is a defined task related to an application. An application may run many processes simultaneously to accomplish the work of the application. These processes are small executable files that together do the work required by the application. You can view the processes running on your Windows 9*x* computers by pressing **CTL+ALT+DEL** and clicking the **Processes** tab. You'll notice you have far more processes running than applications since each application typically runs more than one process at a time.

The Session layer, then, is responsible for setting up the connection between an application process on one computer and an application process on another computer, after the Transport layer has established the connection between the two machines.

NOTE

Computer communications can be in half duplex or full duplex mode. *Simplex,* or unidirectional (one-way) communication generally is not used in computer networking. It is the type of communication used for radio and over-the-air TV broadcasts (many CATV transmissions now use two-way signaling to allow for interactive TV).

There are a number of important protocols that operate at the Session layer, including Windows Sockets (the WinSock interface) and NetBIOS (the Network Basic Input/Output interface).

Layer 6: Presentation

Data translation is the primary activity of Layer 6, the *Presentation* layer. When data is sent from sender to receiver, the data is translated at the Presentation layer. The sender's application passes data down to the Presentation layer, where it is put into a common format. When the data is received on the other end, the Presentation layer changes the data from the common format back into a format that is useable by the application. Protocol translation, the conversion of data from one protocol to another so that it can be exchanged between computers that use different platforms or operating systems, takes place here.

This is the layer at which many gateway services operate. Gateways are connection points between networks that use different platforms or applications. Examples include e-mail gateways (that allow for communications between two different e-mail programs using a common protocol such as SMTP), Systems Network Architecture (SNA) gateways (that allow PCs to communicate with mainframe computers), and gateways that cross platforms or file systems (for example, allowing Microsoft clients that use the Server Message Block protocol for file sharing to access files on NetWare servers that use NetWare Core Protocol). Gateways are usually implemented via software, such as the Gateway Services for NetWare (GSNW). Software redirectors also operate at this layer.

This layer is also where data compression can take place, to minimize the actual number of bits that must be transmitted on the network media to the receiver. Data encryption and decryption take place in the Presentation layer as well.

Layer 7 Application

The *Application* layer is the point at which the user application program interacts with the network. This layer of the networking model should not be confused with the application itself. Application processes, such as file transfers or e-mail, are initiated within a user application (for example, an e-mail program). Then the data created by that process are handed to the Application layer of the networking software. Everything that occurs at this level is application-specific. File sharing, remote printer access, network monitoring and management, remote procedure calls, and all forms of electronic messaging occur at this level.

Both *File Transfer Protocol* (FTP, a common way of transferring files across WANs or the Internet) and *Telnet* function within the Application layer, as do the *Simple Mail Transfer Protocol* (SMTP), *Post Office Protocol* (POP), and *Internet Message Access Protocol* (IMAP), all of which are used for sending or receiving e-mail. There are many other Application layer protocols, including the Hypertext Transfer Protocol (HTTP), Network News Transfer Protocol (NNTP), and Simple Network Management Protocol (SNMP).

Be sure to distinguish between the protocols mentioned and applications that may bear the same names. There are many different FTP programs made by different software vendors, but all of them use the FTP protocol to transfer files.

TEST DAY TIP

Although it's important to *understand* the details of the OSI model for the exam, you're likely to run into a limited number of questions related to the specific layers of the model. Understanding the basic functions of each layer will help you easily identify correct answers to the questions you may see on the exam. It is especially important to remember that, when troubleshooting, you should start with Layer 1 (Physical) and work your way up. A common error among technicians and network administrators is starting to troubleshoot at Layer 7.

It is important to understand how data flows through the OSI model. This can be helpful not only on the exam, but also in maintaining and troubleshooting your network. Figure 1.2 provides a visual representation of how data moves through the OSI layers. Notice that each layer adds a header to the data packet so that by the time it reaches the Physical layer, it is much longer than when it started at the Application layer. When data are received by the receiving host, the headers are stripped off as the data moves back up the stack, one layer at a time, by the layer that corresponds to the one that added it. This means that each layer on the sending computer communicates only with the layer of the same name on the receiving machine.

The Microsoft Model

Prior to the release of Windows NT 3.1, users that wanted to connect to a network had to obtain the TCP/IP protocol suite from a third party and install it. TCP/IP did not come bundled with the software. At times, the TCP/IP software that was purchased didn't work well with the operating system (OS) because it handled various tasks of network communication in a slightly different way than did the operating system. This sometimes led to intermittent network problems or time spent troubleshooting TCP/IP and operating system interoperability.

With the release of Windows NT 3.1, TCP/IP was built into the operating system, providing a seamless integration of networking functionality in the OS. Since that time, it has become standard to provide TCP/IP with the operating system since so many computers today connect to a network in one form or another.

The *Microsoft model* (see Figure 1.3) provides a standard platform for application developers. This modular design enables the developer to rely upon the underlying services of the OS through the use of standard interfaces. These interfaces provide specific functionality developers can use as building blocks to develop an application. This makes development time shorter and provides common interfaces for users, making learning and using new applications easier.

Though the Microsoft model is used primarily by programmers, it's important to understand the framework of how TCP/IP works on a Microsoft Windows-based computer.

Figure 1.2 Data Moving through the OSI Layers

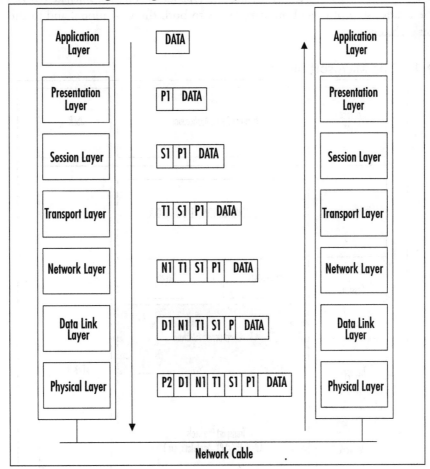

Understanding the Function of Boundary Layers

The Microsoft model describes software and hardware components and the connections between them that facilitate computer networking. This modular approach both allows and encourages hardware and software vendors to develop products that work together through the Microsoft operating system. Boundary layers are interfaces that reside at the boundaries of functionality. They interact with the layer below and the layer above, providing an interface from one layer to the next.

Within each layer, various components perform the tasks defined at the layer. A variety of components can provide similar functionality at any given layer. This modular approach provides flexibility for developers while providing common interfaces that reduce development time and cost. A vendor can provide new functionality at any of these layers, knowing their products will integrate with the other layers to provide seamless network communications. The interfaces defined by Microsoft are the *Network Device Interface Specification* (NDIS), *Transport Driver Interface* (TDI), and the *Application Program Interface* (API). Figure 1.3 shows the relationship of these boundary layers to both the OSI model and to the Microsoft architecture.

Figure 1.3 The Microsoft Model

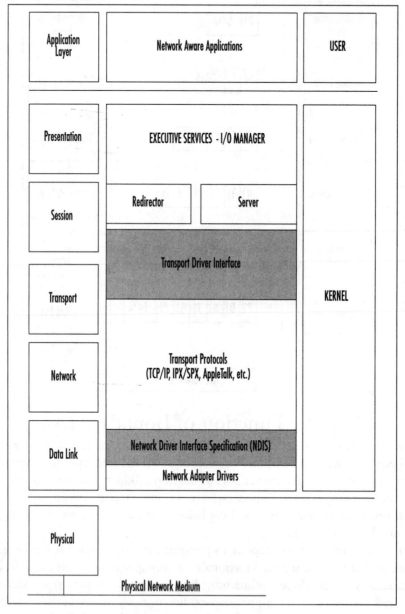

The Windows OS is divided into three primary areas: the User, the Executive, and the Kernel. The Kernel is the core of the Microsoft operating system architecture and it manages the most basic operations including interacting with the hardware abstraction layer that interacts with the hardware (CPU, memory, etc.). The Kernel also synchronizes activities with the Executive level, which includes the Input/Output (I/O) Manager and the Process Manager. The User level interacts with the Executive level; this is the level at which most applications and user interfaces reside.

The Network Driver Interface Specification Boundary Layer

The *Network Driver Interface Specification* (NDIS) works at the bottom of the networking architecture and maps to the Data Link layer of the OSI model and the Network Interface layer of the DARPA model. The NDIS layer is the boundary between the physical network (Physical layer of the OSI model) and the higher level transport protocols. This layer provides the standardized functions that allow various transport protocols to use any network device driver that is compatible with the specifications of this layer, providing both flexibility and reliability to developers. The earliest versions of NDIS were developed by a Microsoft and 3Com joint effort. Current NDIS versions are proprietary to Microsoft operating systems.

The Transport Driver Interface Boundary Layer

The *Transport Driver Interface* (TDI) provides a portal into the transport protocols for kernel mode components such as servers and redirectors. In essence, it is the gateway between the Transport layer and the Session layer in the OSI model, providing a common interface developers can use to access both Transport and Session layer functionality.

The Application Program Interface Boundary Layer

The *Application Program Interface* (API) is the interface through which developers can access network infrastructure services such as various Application layer protocols. *Dynamic Host Configuration Protocol* (DHCP), *Domain Name Service* (DNS), and *Windows Internet Name Service* (WINS) all work at this level and connect to the lower layers through APIs. There are also *Windows Sockets* (WinSock), *NetBIOS,* telephony, and messaging APIs used to assist in carrying out lower level network functions.

Understanding Component Layers

Within each layer are component layers that provide very specific functionality.

The NDIS Wrapper

The NDIS wrapper is a library of common NDIS functions that can be used both by the MAC protocols beneath it and by TCP/IP above it. The NDIS wrapper is implemented by a file called *ndis.sys*, which is software code that surrounds all NDIS device drivers. It provides a common interface for device drivers and protocol drivers. The NDIS wrapper is used to reduce platform dependencies during development of network interface devices.

Network Transport Protocols

Network transport protocols allow applications or clients to send and receive data over the network. Although we're discussing TCP/IP specifically in this chapter, other network transport protocols include Internet Packet Exchange/Sequenced Packet Exchange (IPX/SPX), ATM, NetBEUI, Infrared Data Association (IrDA), AppleTalk, and SNA. These protocols are used on a variety of non-Microsoft operating systems including Novell, Apple, and IBM.

File System Drivers

The file system drivers are the *Redirector* and the *Server service.* When there is a request to open a shared file, the I/O Manager sends a request to the Redirector, which selects the appropriate Transport layer protocol via the TDI layer. When there is a request to access a local file, the Server service responds to requests from the remote Redirector and provides access to the requested file. Named pipes, mailslots, server service, and redirector are file system drivers that work at both the Presentation and Session layers of the OSI model.

Applications and User Mode Services

Applications must interface with the lower layer protocols and must interact in some manner with the user. These services are implemented in a number of ways, but there are four commonly used APIs implemented at this point that provide access to lower transport protocols.

The WinSock API allows Windows-based applications to communicate with the lower layers. Winsock is a protocol-independent networking API that provides standardized access to datagram and session services over TCP/IP, IPX/SPX, AppleTalk, and others.

Telephony integrates computers with telephone technology and utilizes the *Telephony API* (TAPI) to provide a standardized interface to networking protocols for various telephony applications. The *NetBIOS API* has been used for developing client/server applications and is supported in Windows Server 2003 for backward compatibility. The *Messaging API* (MAPI) is an industry standard that assists applications in interfacing with messaging services via a single interface. Microsoft Exchange uses MAPI.

Understanding the TCP/IP Protocol Suite

In the first section of this chapter, we discussed the DoD model, which has four layers: *Network Interface, Internet, Transport,* and *Application.* Since TCP/IP is an outgrowth of the DoD's DARPA model, the TCP/IP protocol architecture uses those same four layers. However, there is a direct correlation between the OSI model's seven layers and TCP/IP's four layers, as shown in Figure 1.4.

Figure 1.4 The TCP/IP Protocol Suite and OSI Model

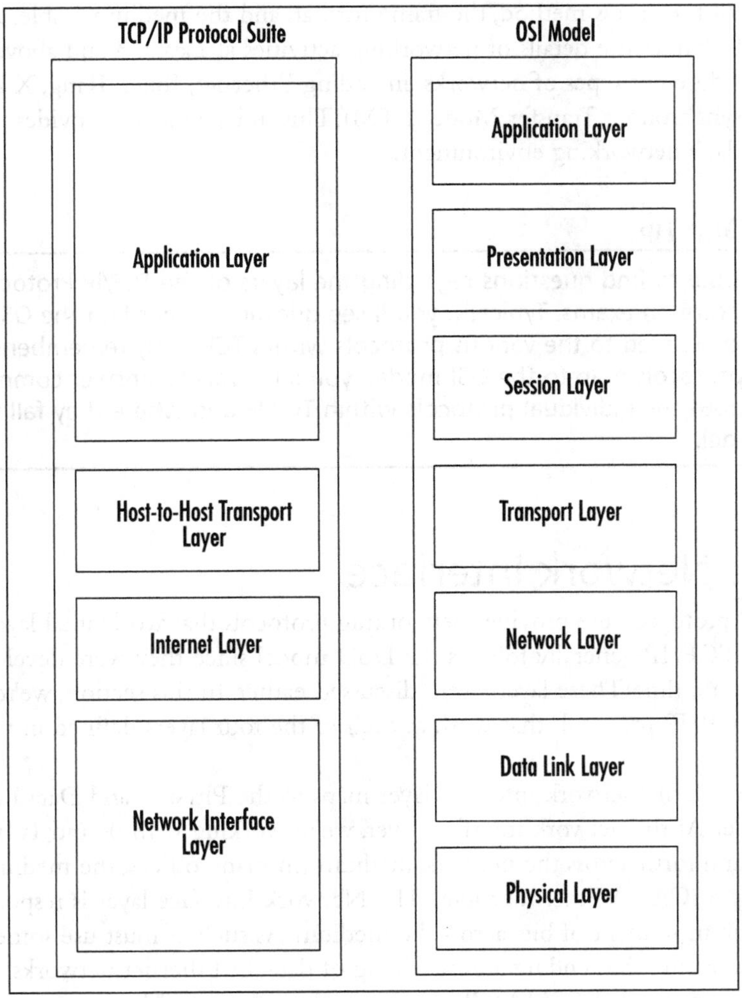

TCP/IP Protocol Suite	OSI Model
Application Layer	Application Layer
	Presentation Layer
	Session Layer
Host-to-Host Transport Layer	Transport Layer
Internet Layer	Network Layer
Network Interface Layer	Data Link Layer
	Physical Layer

TCP/IP's *Network Interface* layer translates into Layers 1 and 2 of the OSI model, performing the same functions as the latter's Physical and Data Link layers. The TCP/IP *Internet* layer maps to the Network layer in the OSI model. In both models, the *Transport* layer is the next layer up, though in the DoD model, it originally was referred to as the Host-to-Host layer. The *Application* layer in the DoD model maps to the top three layers of the OSI model: Session, Presentation, and Application.

As you can see, the TCP/IP protocol suite, based on the DoD model, provides all the functionality delineated by the OSI model, but with a slightly different schema. As we discuss the protocols that comprise the TCP/IP suite, we'll continue to correlate the TCP/IP schema to the OSI model.

TCP/IP was designed to work independently of network design or architecture. It is independent of the access method, the frame format, and the medium (cable, airwaves, etc.) itself. TCP/IP defines the details of networking activities at Layers 3 and above. Thus, it is used in many different types of networks, including Ethernet, Token Ring, X.25, Frame Relay, and Asynchronous Transfer Mode (ATM). This independence provides the flexibility needed in today's networking environment.

Test Day Tip

It's unusual to find questions regarding the layers of the TCP/IP Protocol Architecture on exams. Typically, you'll see questions regarding the OSI model and questions related to the various protocols within TCP/IP. By remembering how the TCP/IP protocols map to the OSI model, you'll be able to answer common questions about the individual protocols within TCP/IP and where they fall within the OSI model.

Layer 1: Network Interface

The TCP/IP protocol suite provides networking protocols that work at all layers of the DoD model. TCP/IP generally follows the DoD model since they were developed at roughly the same time. These layers were discussed earlier. In this section, we're going to look at the TCP/IP protocols that work at each of the four layers defined in the DoD model.

As you recall, the network interface layer maps to the Physical and Data Link layer in the OSI model. At the network interface layer, we're working with 0s and 1s being transmitted back and forth across the network medium (in many offices, the medium is twisted-pair Category 5 (CAT5) Ethernet cable). The Network Interface layer is responsible for controlling the movement of bits across the medium. As such, it must use some organized method of managing the sending and receiving of data. In Ethernet networks, the most common method is called CSMA/CD. However there are other, less common methods of managing data on the network including Carrier Sense Multiple Access/Collision Avoidance (CSMA/CA) and Token Passing. Each is discussed in turn.

CSMA/CD

Ethernet, a common network architecture used in PC networking, uses CSMA/CD to manage media access. CSMA/CD is used on multiple access networks as defined in the IEEE 802.3 specification. Using this method, devices that have data to transmit listen for an opening on the line before transmitting (Carrier Sense). That is, they wait for a time when there are no signals traveling on the cable. When a device detects an opening, it transmits its data. The problem is that several devices may sense simultaneously that the line is clear and they may all transmit at the same time. When this happens, the data packets collide and the data is lost (this is called a collision).

Using the CSMA/CD protocol, the devices will detect that a collision has occurred (collision detection) and each of the devices that transmitted at the same time will wait a random amount of time and then retransmit. The likelihood of one or more devices *randomly* selecting the same delay is almost zero, so the retransmission is likely to be successful. Higher network traffic, larger numbers of computers on a network segment, and longer cables all contribute to an increased number of collisions, which in turn lowers the efficiency of the network because even more traffic is generated by larger number of retransmissions. A *collision domain* is a segment of cable on which two stations can't transmit at the same time without causing a collision. For example, all computers attached to the same hub in a star topology network, or all the computers on the same bus (linear segment) in a bus topology network, comprise a single collision domain. By using a switch, you can create separate collision domains and reduce network traffic.

With CSMA/CD, unlike with some access control protocols (such as demand priority) all stations or nodes are equal in their ability to send data when there is an opening; no station gets higher priority than any other.

A number of IEEE working groups continue to develop new standards for CSMA/CD, such as those pertaining to gigabit Ethernet and Ethernet over fiber (100BaseFX).

CSMA/CA

A media access protocol that is related to CSMA/CD is *Carrier Sense Multiple Access/Collision Avoidance* (CSMA/CA), which is also used on multiple access networks. With CSMA/CA, a device listens for an opportunity to transmit its data just as devices do on CSMA/CD networks. However, when the device senses an opening, it does not immediately transmit the data; instead it transmits a signal notifying other devices that it is transmitting (a sort of warning message) before actually sending the data. This means data packets will never collide (although warning packets may).

CSMA/CA was most commonly used by AppleTalk networks. However, today most Apple computers can use Ethernet hardware, and this access method has fallen out of favor because it creates significant overhead—it adds unnecessary traffic to the network, slowing everything down. The preferred method of dealing with collisions is the collision detection method, which is the method now employed in Ethernet networking technologies.

Token Passing

In the 1980s and 1990s, IBM's Token Ring was a popular network technology. Its method of media access control involved the use of a token, a signal that was passed around the network (which was laid out in a logical ring configuration). A device that wanted to transmit data had to wait until it received the token. Once it had the token, it was free to transmit. This is referred to as a *noncontention* access method, because the devices don't contend or compete for access to the media. This certainly prevents packet collisions on the line, but it is also a slower process because of the time it takes for the token to pass from device to device. Token ring networks typically operate at 4Mbps or 16Mbps, so they have generally fallen out of favor as Ethernet has gained speed (going from 10Mps to 100Mps to 1000Mps). Vendors such as IBM, Cisco, and 3Com have developed implementations of High Speed Token Ring (HSTR), including 100Mbps over copper and gigabit Token Ring over fiber, but high speed Ethernet had a big head start, and organizations such as the 10 Gigabit Ethernet Alliance (www.10gea.org) are devoted to taking it to even greater speeds.

However, FDDI networks are in use as high-speed backbones for mission-critical traffic. FDDI was designed to transfer data at 100Mbps, comparable to the most common implementation of Ethernet. FDDI uses a dual ring topology: traffic flows in opposite directions on the two rings. Stations on the network can be attached to both rings or to a single ring. Computers connected to both rings are called Class A stations, and those attached to only one are called Class B stations. The second ring usually is used for failover in case of problems with the primary ring. Unlike a Token Ring network, a FDDI network can have more than one frame traveling on the ring at the same time. Because it is faster than Token Ring, highly reliable, and fault tolerant, FDDI is great for networks that need both high bandwidth and high reliability. However, it is also relatively expensive.

Other network architectures have used the token passing method of access control. Attached Resource Computer Network (ARCnet), popular in the 1970s, used a special type of token passing in which the token moved from computer to computer in order of the node address on the NIC, rather than around a ring as with Token Ring and FDDI. ARCnet is slow (2.5Mbps in its original configuration, 20Mbps in a later version), so even though it is stable and reliable, it is slowly disappearing from the networking world.

Other Access Control Methods

There are other ways that computer networks can control access to the media, but they are limited in use. For example, Hewlett Packard designed an architecture it called 100VG-AnyLAN, based on the *demand-priority* access control method. These networks were designed in a tree configuration, with child hubs cascading off a root hub, and computers connected to each child hub. This creates multiple small collision domains, preventing problems associated with broadcasts that are sent to the entire network. The hubs (also called multiport repeaters because they boost the signals they receive before sending them back out) monitor the nodes that are attached to them, in a round-robin fashion, detecting requests to transmit on the network. An advantage of this access method is the fact that you can set priorities according to data type, to ensure that the most important data is processed first. The equipment, however, is proprietary, and despite its reliability, performance, and security advantages, demand-priority-based networks are not common.

EXAM WARNING

When taking the exam, you should read each question carefully before reading the answers. Access control methods are needed only on networks where there are multiple connection points, not on point-to-point connections such as a one-to-one dial-up connection. This is an important distinction. You may see questions regarding how data is managed on the physical medium. Make sure you understand what the question is asking. The most frequently asked media access questions have to do with CSMA/CD, because it is the most widely used in networking today. However, you might find a tricky question that asks you to identify CSMA/CA instead. It is rare to encounter a question about token passing on a Microsoft exam, but you should be prepared for anything covered in this material.

Layer 2: Internet

The TCP/IP suite has four core protocols that work at the *Internet* layer, which maps to the Network layer of the OSI model. The Internet layer is responsible for packaging, addressing, and routing the data. The four core protocols used in the TCP/IP suite are:

- The Internet Protocol (IP)
- The Internet Control Message Protocol (ICMP)
- The Internet Group Management Protocol (IGMP)
- The Address Resolution Protocol (ARP)

Internet Protocol

The *Internet Protocol* (IP) is probably the best known of the TCP/IP protocols. Many people, especially those who have even a passing familiarity with computer technology, have heard or used the term *IP address*. Later in this chapter, we'll take an in-depth look at how the IP protocol works and you'll learn the intricacies of IP addressing.

With regard to the TCP/IP architecture, IP is a routable protocol (meaning it can be sent across networks) that handles addressing, routing, and the process of putting data into or taking data out of packets. IP is considered to be *connectionless* because it does not establish a session with a remote computer before sending data. Data sent via connectionless methods are called *datagrams*. An IP packet can be lost, delayed, duplicated, or delivered out of sequence and there is no attempt to recover from these errors. Recovery is the responsibility of higher layer protocols including Transport layer protocols such as TCP.

IP packets contain data that include:

- **Source IP address** The IP address of the source of the datagram.
- **Destination IP address** The IP address of the destination for the datagram.

- **Identification** Identifies a specific IP datagram as well as all fragments of a specific IP datagram if the datagram becomes fragmented.

- **Protocol** Indicates to which protocols the receiving IP should pass the packets.

- **Checksum** A simple method of error control that performs a mathematical calculation to verify the integrity of the IP header.

- **Time-to-Live (TTL)** Designates the number of networks the datagram can travel before it is discarded. This prevents datagrams from circling endlessly on the network.

Internet Control Message Protocol

The *Internet Control Message Protocol* (ICMP) is not as well known as its famous cousin, IP. It is responsible for handling errors related to IP packets that cannot be delivered. For instance, if a packet cannot be delivered, a message called *Destination Unreachable* is sent back to the sending device so it will know that there was an undelivered message. The Destination Unreachable message has several subtypes of messages that can be sent back to the host to help pinpoint the problem. For instance, *Network Unreachable* and *Port Unreachable* are two examples of *Destination Unreachable* messages that may be returned to help the host determine the nature of the problem.

If you have ever used the Ping utility (discussed at the end of this chapter) and received an error, it was ICMP that was responsible for returning the error. In addition to announcing errors, ICMP also announces network congestion (*source quench* messages) and timeouts (which occur when the TTL field on a packet reaches zero).

NOTE

For more information about ICMP, see RFC 792 at www.freesoft.org/CIE/RFC/792/index.htm, which defines the specifications for this protocol.

Internet Group Management Protocol

The *Internet Group Management Protocol* (IGMP) manages host membership in multicast groups. IP multicast groups are groups of devices (typically called *hosts*) that listen for and receive traffic addressed to a specific, shared multicast IP address. Essentially, IP multicast traffic is sent to a specific MAC address but processed by multiple IP hosts. (As you'll recall from our earlier discussion, each NIC has a unique MAC address, but multicast MAC addresses use a special 24-bit prefix to identify them as such.) IGMP runs on the router, which handles the distribution of multicast packets (often, multicast routing is not enabled on the router by default and must be configured).

Multicasting makes it easy for a server to send the same content to multiple computers simultaneously. IP addresses in a specific range (called Class D addresses) are reserved for multicast assignment. The IGMP protocol allows for different types of messages, used to join multicast groups and to send multicast messages.

A unicast message is sent directly to a single host, whereas a multicast is sent to all members of a particular group. Both utilize connectionless datagrams and are transported via the *User Datagram Protocol* (UDP) that we'll discuss in the Host-to-Host Transport Layer section. A multicast is sent to a group of hosts known as an *IP multicast group* or *host group*. The hosts in this group listen for IP traffic sent to a specific IP multicast address. IP multicasts are more efficient than broadcasts because the data is received only by computers listening to a specific address. A range of IP addresses, Class D addresses, is reserved for multicast addresses. Windows Server 2003 supports multicast addresses and, by default, is configured to support both the sending and receiving of IP multicast traffic.

NOTE

For more information about IGMP, see RFC 1112 at www.cis.ohio-state.edu/cgi-bin/rfc/rfc1112.html, which defines the specifications for IP multicasting.

EXAM WARNING

Although their acronyms are very similar and they function at the same layer of the networking models, ICMP and IGMP perform very different functions, so be sure you don't get them confused on the test.

Address Resolution Protocol

The *Address Resolution Protocol* (ARP) is the last of the four core TCP/IP protocols that work at the Internet layer. As we've discussed, each NIC has a unique MAC address. Each NIC also is assigned an IP address that is unique to the network on which it resides. When a packet is sent on a TCP/IP network, the packet headers include a destination IP address (along with other information). The IP address must be translated into a specific MAC address in order for the data to reach its intended recipient. Without ARP, computers must send broadcast messages each time an IP address needs to be matched to a MAC address.

ARP is responsible for maintaining the mappings of IP addresses to MAC addresses. These mappings are stored in the *arp cache* so if the same IP address needs to be matched to a MAC address again, the mapping can be found in the cache; it's not necessary to repeat the discovery process.

The protocol includes four different types of messages: ARP request, ARP reply, RARP request, and RARP reply. RARP refers to Reverse Address Resolution protocol, which resolves addresses in the opposite direction (MAC address to IP address). These messages are used to discover the MAC addresses that correspond to specific IP addresses (and vice versa). When the MAC address is correlated to the specific IP address, the data can be sent to the proper host.

ARP was originally designed for DEC/Intel/Xerox 10Mbps Ethernet networks, but is now used with other types of IP-based networks as well.

These are the four primary protocols involved in TCP/IP at the Internet layer, which is responsible for addressing, packaging, and routing packets of data. As we move up the protocol stack, we will examine the Transport layer.

NOTE

For more information about ARP and RARP, see RFCs 826 and 903 at www.networksorcery.com/enp/rfc/rfc826.txt and www.networksorcery.com/enp/rfc/rfc903.txt.

Layer 3: Host-to-Host Transport

Layer 3 in TCP/IP is the *Host-to-Host Transport* layer, sometimes called the *Transport* layer. It maps to the Transport layer (Layer 4) in the OSI model. As the name implies, this layer is responsible for transporting the data. It sets up communications between the Application layer and the lower layers.

Because this layer establishes a connection, it can also take on some of the responsibilities of the Session layer of the OSI model. In TCP/IP, the two core protocols used at the Host-to-Host layer are the *Transmission Control Protocol* (TCP) and the *User Datagram Protocol* (UDP). As we discussed earlier, one of the key distinguishing features of these two protocols is that TCP is considered connection-oriented and UDP is connectionless.

Transmission Control Protocol

The *TCP* provides reliable one-to-one communications because it establishes a connection with the receiving host prior to transmitting and because it provides a number of control features to ensure reliable communications. TCP is connection-oriented because it establishes a TCP connection prior to sending data. This is similar to the way a modem works when the modem dials another computer and establishes a connection before data is transmitted. This ensures that someone is on the other end before data is sent. TCP sequences the packets, acknowledges sent packets, and helps recover lost packets. Data is transmitted in segments and each segment is numbered sequentially. When the receiving host receives data, it sends an ACK message to the sender. If the sender does not receive this ACK within a specified amount of time, the data segment is re-sent, based on the assumption the data was not received.

Data from the Transport layer's TCP is organized into segments. These are sent down through the protocol stack and headers are added. Each network technology (Ethernet, Token Ring, etc.) has a particular way it encapsulates data. This particular encapsulation is called the *frame format*. Each technology uses its own frame format. In Ethernet technologies, the frame of data is a fixed-length and is generally referred to as a *packet*. The Ethernet IP packet contains a preamble, destination and source address, data, and an error-checking sequence, among other things. The frame format describes the required data and the order in which is appears inside the data packet, which is the unit of data sent across the network medium.

Each TCP segment has a header that contains, among other things, the following important fields:

- TCP port to send the data
- TCP port to receive the data
- Sequence number for the segment
- Acknowledgement number
- Window size (not to be confused with the Microsoft *Windows* operating system), which indicates the current size of the TCP buffer on the sending host's end. The TCP buffer is used to hold incoming segments and must have room to accept additional segments when received.

Head of the Class…

TCP Window Size

The TCP Window is used to help control the sending and receiving of data between two hosts. The sender can send only as much data as the receiver's buffer can hold. New data is sent only when the receiver indicates its buffer is ready to receive more data. The sender can send only data that fits within the window and the window slides along the outbound and inbound data stream.

In Windows XP and Windows Server 2003, the TCP/IP maximum receive window is set to 16,384 bytes by default. The default maximum receive window is negotiated during the establishment of the TCP connection. The maximum receive window size can be set through the registry. There are two settings that are related to the TCP window size: GlobalMaxTcpWindowSize and TcpWindowSize.

The GlobalMaxTcpWindowSize is found in the following location:
HKEY_LOCAL_MACHINE\SYSTEM\CurrentControlSet\Services\Tcpip\Parameters

It sets the default maximum receive window for all interfaces unless that is overridden by the TcpWindowSize setting.

The TcpWindowSize setting is found in the following locations:
HKEY_LOCAL_MACHINE\SYSTEM\CurrentControlSet\Services\Tcpip\Parameters and HKEY_LOCAL_MACHINE\SYSTEM\CurrentControlSet\Services\Tcpip\Parameters\Interfaces\InterfaceGUID

Continued

In the case of both the GlobalMaxTcpWindowSize and the TcpWindowSize, values greater than 65,535 can be used only if window scaling is enabled and other computers support window scaling.

On older networks, the default window size is defined by RFC 793 and allows for a 16-bit field of data, which translates into 65,535 bytes of data. This means that the sender can send only 65K bytes of data before receiving an acknowledgement. Newer network technologies have much higher throughput and sending only 65K of data before awaiting a response is inefficient. RFC 1323 defines a larger window size called the TCP Window Scale. It provides a scaling factor that can be combined with the 16-bit TCP window to increase the maximum size of the window to 1,073,725,440 bytes (approximately 1 gigabyte). When supported, windows scaling occurs when TCP establishes the connection and both hosts indicate their respective receive window sizes. This allows for a more flexible and efficient use of network bandwidth.

TCP also avoids sending and receiving small segments through a method called the *Nagle Algorithm.* The Nagle Algorithm, named for its creator John Nagle and described in RFC 896, works on the principle that only one small segment can be sent and not acknowledged. For interactive sessions such as Telnet, each individual keystroke entered is a single segment of data, which must make a round trip in order to be shown on the user's screen. Obviously, these small segments must be sent in order for the user to see on the screen what's been typed on the keyboard. Using the Nagle Algorithm, the many small segments (such as a user typing on a keyboard) are stored in a buffer. Once the first segment is acknowledged, the next segment is sent. That second segment may contain many smaller segments (for instance, several individual keystrokes).

Finally, there is a syndrome that occurs called *Silly Window Syndrome* (SWS). Whenever data is sent to the receiver's Application layer protocol, the receive window opens and a new window size is advertised. Depending on a number of factors, this can cause one of several behaviors. Each time the Application layer protocol retrieves data, it may accept only one byte of data at a time. Thus, the sender's window advances by only one byte at a time. These are small segments that do not make optimal use of the network's total capabilities.

To avoid SWS, the receiver does not advertise a new window size unless it is half of the maximum receive window size or at least the maximum segment size (MSS).

In order to establish a connection, TCP uses a three-part handshake, which works as follows:

1. The client computer sends a SYN (synchronization request) message with a sequence number that is generated by the client.

2. The server computer responds with an ACK (acknowledgement) message. This consists of the original sequence number plus 1. The server also sends a SYN number that it generates.

3. The client adds a 1 to the SYN number that was sent by the server, and returns it as an ACK.

This process, with each computer acknowledging the other, results in the establishment of a connection. A similar process is used to terminate the connection. TCP establishes this one-to-one (host-to-host) connection and also adds header information to ensure reliable communications. The downside to this reliability is that it adds both time and data in the transmission, which slows down communication somewhat.

Figure 1.5 shows the process TCP uses to establish a connection. There are three distinct steps used to establish a reliable connection. These same steps are used to end a connection. This handshake process is what creates a reliable connection because both hosts must indicate that they are ready to send/receive and that they are finished sending/receiving. As you can see in Figure 1.5, the first step is to establish the connection. The sending host (we'll call it Host A for clarity) sends a TCP segment to the receiving host (Host B) with an initial Sequence Number for the connection and the TCP window size, which indicates the sender's receiving buffer size. The receiving computer, Host B, replies with a TCP segment that contains its chosen Sequence Number and its initial TCP window size. Host A sends a segment back to Host B acknowledging Host B's chosen Sequence Number.

Figure 1.5 TCP Handshake

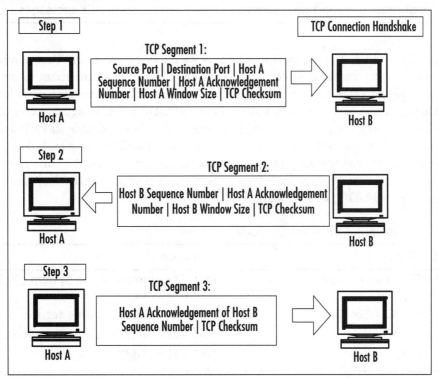

User Datagram Protocol

In some cases, it's appropriate to send a quick message without needing to sequence the data or to get an acknowledgement that it's been received. In these cases, an application developer might choose to use the UDP instead of TCP. Remember that protocols are agreed-upon rules that developers use to ensure their applications work within the TCP/IP framework. UDP is often described as connectionless or "best-effort delivery" because it does not establish a connection before sending, it does not sequence packets before sending, and it does not provide error control through retransmission. In short, it's a one-shot deal that is fast but not always reliable.

The UDP header contains three important fields:

- The source port
- The destination port
- The UDP Checksum

NOTE

The UDP Checksum is the only error control mechanism within UDP. It is used to verify the integrity of the UDP header and data. UDP is used, for instance, in NetBIOS name service and Simple Network Management Protocol (SNMP) because both of these use short data segments and do not require ACK messages.

Both TCP and UDP utilize port numbers, as we discussed previously. Port numbers are assigned by the Internet Assigned Numbers Authority (IANA). It is important to have a centralized body to assign these numbers so that everyone will use the same ports for the same functions. There are many well-known TCP and UDP ports, as well as many obscure ports. When you secure a network server, it is usually advisable to disable all TCP and UDP ports that are not in use so they cannot be used by hackers looking for a back door.

TCP and UDP may use the same port numbers, but they are not the same ports. Each uses its own distinct set of ports. TCP Port 20 is different than UDP Port 20. A few of the common TCP and UDP ports are shown in Table 1.1.

Table 1.1 Common TCP and UDP Ports

Common TCP Ports	Common UDP Ports
Port 20 – FTP (Data Channel)	Port 53 – Domain Name System (DNS) Name Queries
Port 21 – FTP (Control Channel)	Port 137 – NetBIOS name service
Port 23 – Telnet	Port 138 – NetBIOS datagram service
Port 80 – HTTP	Port 161 – SNMP

For a listed of commonly hacked (or probed) ports, see www.linux-firewall-tools.com/linux/ports.html. Although the site is a Linux site, the TCP and UDP ports used by TCP/IP services (and by hackers) are the same regardless of the operating system.

TEST DAY TIP

You are very likely to run into one or more questions on the exam that are related to TCP and UDP. It's critical to understand the difference between these two transport protocols. UDP is an unreliable, connectionless, fast transport protocol used for sending short messages or messages that do not require acknowledgement of receipt. An easy way to remember the difference is: **TCP** is *Trustworthy*; **UDP** is *Unreliable*.

What's important to remember about TCP and UDP is that although one is considered reliable and the other unreliable, it does not mean that one is inherently better than the other. TCP establishes a connection before information is sent to the receiver; UDP does not. Many applications do not require acknowledgement that sent data was received because it sends the data in small amounts. In these scenarios, using a connectionless UDP datagram is far more efficient. Therefore, UDP datagrams are used in a variety of applications including NetBIOS name service, NetBIOS datagram service, SNMP, and DNS.

Layer 4: Application

The *Application* layer protocols of the TCP/IP protocol suite operate at the Session, Presentation, and Application layers of the OSI model. In the DoD model, this layer enables applications to communicate with one another and it provides access to the services of the other underlying layers (DoD Layers 1 through 3). There is a wide variety of Application layer protocols, and more are being developed, because they can rely on all the TCP/IP services beneath them in the protocol stack.

We briefly mentioned some of the Application layer protocols in our discussion of the OSI Application layer. In the following sections, we will describe some of these in more detail. We won't cover every single Application layer protocol in use today (we couldn't, without turning this book into a multivolume tome), but we will cover some of the protocols and services that you're not only likely to work with on the job, but that you're also likely to encounter on the certification exam.

NetBIOS over TCP

In Windows Server 2003, *NetBIOS over TCP* as a naming service is largely supplanted by the use of DNS, discussed later. However, in organizations running operating systems or applications that cannot use DNS for name services, NetBIOS over TCP must still be enabled.

NetBIOS over TCP (NetBT) is an Application layer set of protocols that provides *name*, *session*, and *datagram* services for NetBIOS applications. NetBIOS was originally developed for IBM by Systek Corporation, to extend the capabilities of the BIOS (Basic Input Output System) to include the ability to work across a network. It is a software interface and a naming convention, not a protocol (although you will see it referred to in some documentation as the *NetBIOS protocol*). NetBIOS over TCP supplies the programming interface provided for by NetBIOS, along with communication protocols provided for by TCP.

- NetBT's *name* service allows host computers to attain and retain (or defend) a NetBIOS name. It also assists other hosts in locating a computer with a specific NetBIOS name. Additionally, the name service resolves a specific NetBIOS name to an IP address. This process utilizes *broadcast* messages that are sent to all hosts on the network. The name service uses UDP Port 137.

- The *session* service of NetBT provides for the reliable exchange of messages between two NetBIOS applications, typically on two different computers. The session service uses TCP Port 139.

- The *datagram* service within NetBT provides connectionless, unreliable message delivery between NetBIOS applications via UDP Port 138. As mentioned earlier, when data length is short or reliability is not critical, the datagram service is a faster method than session-based communication.

Together, the session and datagram services provide the NetBIOS applications with the ability to exchange information with one another. NetBIOS is discussed in detail in Chapter 4 and will cover the NetBIOS name, name service, session service, as well as the differences between a NetBIOS application and a Winsock application.

Windows Internet Name Service

Windows Internet Name Service, or WINS, is a NetBIOS name server that NetBIOS clients can use to attain, register, and resolve NetBIOS names. WINS is specific to Microsoft networks and is not used (or available for use) on non-Microsoft operating system-based computers. Computers running UNIX, Linux, and other non-Microsoft operating systems typically use DNS for name resolution, although there are other, non-WINS NetBIOS name services available. Generally other operating systems will be concerned with NetBIOS names only when they're on a network with Microsoft machines; for example, when using SAMBA.

WINS provides NetBIOS functionality but expands it by replicating this information for faster name resolution services across a large network. WINS generates a database that contains each NetBIOS name and its associated IP address. A WINS Server resolves NetBIOS names and provides the associated IP addresses when it receives requests.

WINS is implemented in two parts: the Server service and the Client service. The Server service maintains the database containing both NetBIOS names and associated IP addresses. It also replicates the database to other WINS Servers for faster name resolution across a large network. This reduces network broadcast traffic because names can be acquired and defended using direct requests to the WINS Server, rather than by using network broadcasts. The Client service runs on the individual computers and it uses WINS to register the computer name, as well as to provide name resolution services to the local applications and services.

All Windows Server 2003 versions (Standard Edition, Enterprise Edition, Web Edition, and Datacenter Edition) include a WINS service, but it is *not* installed by default. All Windows clients include a WINS client that is installed automatically.

For backward compatibility, Windows Server 2003 also provides support for using the LMHOST file. This plain text file is unique to Windows-based computers and provides a map of the computer's NetBIOS name with an IP address. This static file was used prior to the implementation of dynamic Windows name resolution found in WINS. NetBIOS name resolution and WINS are discussed in detail in Chapter 4.

Server Message Block/Common Internet File System

The *Server Message Block* (SMB) protocol was originally developed by IBM in the 1980s and later expanded upon by IBM, Microsoft, Intel, and 3Com. SMB was primarily used for file and print sharing, but is also used for sharing serial ports and abstract communications technologies such as named pipes and mail slots. SMB is also now known as *Common Internet File System* (CIFS); both names are used interchangeably.

CIFS is a protocol that, like many Application layer protocols, is operating system-independent. It evolved from SMB and NetBIOS file and print sharing methods in earlier versions of the Windows operating system. It can be used by different platforms and operating systems and across different network/transport protocols; it is not TCP/IP dependent. The connection from client to server can be made via NetBEUI or IPX/SPX. After the network connection from client to server is established, then SMB commands can be sent to the server so that the client can open, read and write files, and so on.

CIFS is being jointly developed by Microsoft and other vendors, but no published specification currently exists. UNIX and Linux clients can connect to SMB shares using *smbclient* from SAMBA or *smbfs* for Linux. Server implementations of SMB for non-Microsoft operating systems include SAMBA and LAN Manager for OS/2 and SCO.

NOTE

For more detailed information about SMB, see http://samba.anu.edu.au/cifs/docs/what-is-smb.html.

Internet Printing Protocol

The *Internet Printing Protocol* (IPP) is related to SMB and CIFS. It provides the ability to perform various printing operations across the network (including an internetwork) using HTTP version 1.1.

In Windows Server 2003, IPP requires that the IPP Server be running Microsoft Internet Information Services 6 (IIS 6.0), which is *not* installed by default.

NOTE

There are a large number of RFCs that define different specifications for IPP. For more information, see the IEEE's PWG (Printer Working Group) Web site at www.pwg.org/ipp/.

Windows Sockets

WinSock is a Microsoft Windows *Application Programming Interface* (API) that provides a standard programming interface for accessing TCP/IP in Windows. Sockets were originally developed at the University of California in Berkeley, and Microsoft developed WinSock to work specifically in the Windows operating system environment.

Vendors who develop software that runs on Windows can use this API to access standard TCP/IP functionality. A number of built-in Windows tools rely on Windows Sockets, including *Packet InterNet Groper* (ping) and *Trace Route* (tracert). In addition, the FTP and DHCP servers and clients use Windows Sockets, as does the Telnet client.

Telnet

Telnet is a terminal emulation protocol that allows you to log onto a remote computer. The remote computer must be using TCP/IP and have the Telnet Server service running. To connect to a remote host, you must start the Telnet client and must possess a username and password for the remote host computer. In Windows Server 2003, the Telnet Server service is present but must be started in order to service Telnet clients.

If you have never used the command prompt in Windows, here's how: click **Start | Run** and type **cmd** in the dialog box. (In Windows operating systems prior to Windows 98, the 16-bit command was **command**. In Windows 98 and beyond, the 32-bit command, **cmd**, is supported.) This will open a command window. Type **telnet** at the prompt. Use **help** for a list of commands and **quit** to close Telnet. Use **exit** to close the command prompt window. Figures 1.4 and 1.5 show how to initiate a Telnet session. This is also the method used to initiate other Application layer communication utilities such as *ping* and *tracert*. Figures 1.6 and 1.7 show opening the command prompt and starting a Telnet session using the command line.

Figure 1.6 Opening a Command Prompt Window

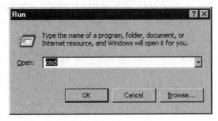

Figure 1.7 Starting a Telnet Session

Dynamic Host Configuration Protocol

The *Dynamic Host Configuration Protocol* (DHCP) is used to automatically (or dynamically) assign IP addresses to host computers on a network running TCP/IP. Prior to DHCP, network administrators had to assign IP addresses to host computers manually. This was not only a time-consuming endeavor, but also made it easy for errors (either in IP assignment or in entering in the IP address) to creep in and cause network problems.

Why is DHCP so important? Because each host must have a unique IP address, a problem occurs when two hosts have the same IP address. DHCP was devised as an efficient method to alleviate both the problems caused by errors and the time it took to assign and resolve errors, by maintaining a database of the addresses it assigns, ensuring that there will never be duplicate addresses among the DHCP clients.

DHCP is implemented as both a Server service and a Client service. The DHCP Server service is responsible for assigning the IP address to individual hosts and for maintaining the database of IP address information, including IP addresses that are assigned, IP addresses that are available, and other configuration information that can be conveyed to the client along with the IP address assignment. The DHCP Client service interacts with the Server service in requesting an IP address and in configuring other related information including the *subnet mask* and *default gateway* (both are discussed in detail later in this chapter).

We will discuss the DHCP Service in much greater detail in Chapter 3.

Simple Mail Transport Protocol

SMTP is a protocol used to transfer e-mail messages and attachments. SMTP is used to transmit e-mail between e-mail servers and from e-mail clients (such as Microsoft Outlook) *to* e-mail servers (such as Microsoft Exchange). However, most e-mail clients use other protocols, POP3 or IMAP, to *retrieve* e-mail from the server. These two server applications (SMTP and POP or IMAP) may exist on the same physical server machine.

As with the other protocols and services discussed in this section, SMTP operates at the Application layer and relies on the services of the underlying layers of the TCP/IP suite to provide the actual data transfer services.

Post Office Protocol

POP is a widely used e-mail application protocol that can be used to retrieve e-mail from an e-mail server for the client application, such as Microsoft Outlook. The current version of POP is POP3.

POP servers set up mailboxes (actually directories or folders) for each e-mail account name. The server receives the mail for a domain, and sorts it into these individual folders. Then a user uses a POP client program (such as Microsoft Outlook or Eudora) to connect to the POP server and download all the mail in that user's folder to the user's computer. Usually, when the mail messages are transferred to the client machine, they are deleted from the server.

Internet Message Access Protocol

IMAP, like POP, is used to retrieve mail from a server, and creates a mailbox for each user account. It differs from POP in that the client program can access the mail and allow the user to read, reply to, and delete it while it is still on the server. Microsoft Exchange functions as an IMAP server. This is convenient for users because they never have to download the mail to their client computers (saving space on their hard disks), but especially because they can connect to the server and have all their mail available to them from any computer, anywhere. When you use POP to retrieve your mail, old mail that you've already downloaded is on the computer you were using when you retrieved it, so if you're using a different computer, you won't be able to see it. IMAP is preferred for users who use different computers (for example, a home computer, an office computer, and a laptop) to access their e-mail at different times.

Hypertext Transport Protocol

HTTP is the protocol used to transfer files used on the Internet to display Web pages. When you type an Internet address (called a *Uniform Resource Locator* or URL) into your browser's Address window, it uses the HTTP protocol to retrieve and display the files located at that address.

A URL typically contains a server name, a second level domain name, and a top-level domain name, with the parts of the address separated by dots. Individual folder and file names may follow, separated by slashes. For example, www.shinder.net/documents/essay.html indicates an HTML document (Web page) in a folder called documents on a Web server named www in the shinder.net domain. The first part of the URL may also be entered as an IP address.

HTTP was defined and used as early as 1990. However, there were no published specifications for HTTP in the beginning, and different vendors modified HTTP as they saw fit. As the World Wide Web continued to evolve and grow to be the enormous resource that it is today, additional functionality was needed in HTTP. The first formal definition was labeled HTTP/1 and it was later replaced by HTTP/1.1. Windows Server 2003 and Microsoft Internet Information Server (IIS) both use HTTP/1.1.

HTTP is implemented as a Server and a Client. IIS provides the HTTP Server functionality, and a Web browser, such as Netscape Navigator or Microsoft Internet Explorer, provides the client functionality.

Network News Transfer Protocol

NNTP is similar to the SMTP, in that it allows servers and clients to exchange information. In this case, however, the information is exchanged in the form of news articles. This feature originally was implemented in the Internet's predecessor network, ARPANET. Network bulletins were exchanged using this protocol. Today there are thousands of news-groups devoted to discussion of every topic imaginable. Usenet has grown into a huge network of news servers hosting news groups. Newsgroups differ from other forums such as Internet mailing lists (in which all messages posted come into your inbox if you're a member) and Web discussion boards (which are accessed through the browser).

NNTP is now implemented as an Application layer client/server protocol. The news server (for example, msnews.microsoft.com) manages news articles and news clients. IIS contains the NNTP server service and can be used to host news groups. A news client is an application that runs on a client computer and is used to both read and compose news articles. Outlook Express contains a news reader component.

For more information about Usenet newsgroups, see the Usenet FAQ and references at www.faqs.org/usenet.

File Transfer Protocol

The *File Transfer Protocol* (FTP) is used to transfer files from one host to another, regardless of the hosts' physical locations. It is one of the oldest Application layer protocols and was

www.syngress.com

used on ARPANET to transfer files from one mainframe to another. Still in use today, FTP is widely used on the Internet to transfer files. One of the problems with FTP is that it transmits users' passwords in clear text, so it is not a secure protocol.

In contrast to the single connections used by NNTP, HTTP, and SMTP, two separate connections are established for an FTP session. One transmits commands and replies and the other transmits the actual data. The command and control information is sent, by default, via TCP Port 21. The data, by default, is sent via TCP Port 20.

Configuring & Implementing…

FTP Ports

Understanding the configuration and implementation of FTP is important for a number of reasons. FTP Ports 20 and 21 are used for FTP Data and FTP Control, respectively. It is possible to modify the ports used for data and control transmissions when developing or implementing an application. However, by default, a program interface that uses FTP listens at TCP Port 21 for FTP traffic. Thus, if your application is sending TCP control information on a different port, the other application interface may not hear the FTP traffic.

TCP Ports 20 and 21 are well-known port numbers and hackers often try to exploit these ports. As a security measure, all servers that are not running the FTP Server service should have TCP Ports 20 and 21 disabled. This prevents attackers from exploiting these ports to gain unauthorized access to the server, and perhaps to the entire network.

A common method of attack is via port scanning where the attacker scans for open ports to gain access to a network. There are a number of ways to secure FTP servers to thwart these kinds of attacks, but that is beyond the scope of this chapter. Beware of vulnerabilities and security methods when implementing FTP Servers on your network.

Domain Naming System

DNS is used to resolve a host name to an IP address in order to facilitate the delivery of network data packets. As mentioned previously, DNS is now the primary method used in Microsoft Windows Server 2003 to resolve host names to IP addresses. DNS is also the protocol used on the Internet to resolve host names (such as those in URLs) to IP addresses.

Prior to DNS, host name-to-IP resolution was accomplished via a text file called *hosts*. In the days of ARPANET, this file was compiled and managed by the Network Information Center at the Stanford Research Institute. This plaintext file contained the name and address of every single computer, but there were only a handful of computers on the network at the time. When a new computer was added, or a computer changed its IP address, the file had to be edited manually and distributed to all the other computers. As computers and networks proliferated, another, more automated solution had to be devised and the specifications for a distributed naming system, called the DNS, were developed. Windows Server 2003 still supports the use of the hosts file for backward compatibility.

DNS Servers on the Internet store copies of the DNS database. Due to the explosive growth of the Internet in the past decade, DNS databases are specialized. For instance, a set of databases is responsible for top-level domain information only. Examples of top-level domains are .com, .gov, .edu, .net, .org, and so on. All requests for an address ending with .com will be forwarded to a particular set of DNS servers. These servers will query their databases to find the specific .com domain requested (for example, microsoft.com). DNS databases are replicated periodically to refresh the data. DNS is discussed at length in Chapter 5.

Routing Information Protocol

As the name implies, the RIP is used to exchange routing information among IP routers. RIP is a basic routing protocol designed for small- to medium-sized networks. It does not scale well to large IP-based networks (including the Internet). Windows Server 2003 computers can function as routers, and as such, they support RIP.

RIP and other routing protocols will be discussed in more detail in Chapter 8.

SNMP

SNMP is used for communications between a network management console and the network's devices, such as bridges, routers, and hubs. This protocol facilitates the sharing of network control information with the management console. SNMP employs a management system/agent framework to share relevant network management information. This information is stored in a *Management Information Base* (MIB) and contains a set of objects, each of which represents a particular type of network information such as an event, an error, or an active session. SNMP employs UDP datagrams to send messages between the management console and the agents.

Configuring & Implementing...

Name Resolution Services

Naming and name resolution services in TCP/IP have evolved in each subsequent release of the Microsoft Windows operating network systems. Prior to Windows 2000, naming services were typically provided for by both WINS (providing the functions of NetBT) and DNS. WINS was primarily used to assign, defend, and locate NetBIOS names in a Windows network. DNS was used primarily to do the same for host names across networks or across dissimilar networks (Windows NT to UNIX, for example).

Windows Server 2003 provides name resolution through direct hosting (as did Windows 2000), thus eliminating the need for WINS in networks that don't have *downlevel* clients and servers on the network (those running operating systems older than Windows 2000 or based on the 9x line). Direct hosting uses DNS for name resolution and the network communication is sent directly over TCP (instead of NetBIOS over TCP) using TCP Port 445 (rather than TCP Port 139 as used by NetBT). However, most networks are still running a mix of prior operating systems, including Windows 95 or 98, Windows Millennium, and Windows NT. These operating systems, as well as many of the applications and services running on them, require the use of WINS. Disabling WINS in a mixed environment can cause needed services and applications to cease functioning.

Clearly, the Application layer is complex, primarily because applications and services can be developed that rely upon the services of the lower layers. This modular approach to network communications makes development less time consuming and more consistent across vendors, networks, and systems. As a result, new Application layer protocols are constantly being developed. This section is not meant to serve as an exhaustive look at the wide array of application protocols available today, but to give you a better idea of the more common protocols and services that operate at this layer and provide an understanding of how the layered approach works.

We've reviewed the seven layers of the OSI model (physical, data link, network, transport, session, presentation, application) and the four layers of the DoD (TCP/IP) model (network interface, Internet, host-to-host, application) and we've learned how these layers map to one another. We've also taken a look at the very different Microsoft networking model. We've examined many of the common protocols of the TCP/IP protocol suite that work at each layer and looked at the services and functions that each provides. In the next section, you'll learn about the IP protocol and how it is used to send data to the correct location, no matter where the destination host resides.

Understanding IP Addressing

IP is widely used today as the foundation of network addressing in both private networks and across the Internet. In order to effectively manage a network in today's complex environment, it's critical to understand IP addressing in depth.

We previously discussed the importance of a unique host (computer or device) address on each network. IP addressing is used to assign a unique address. Assigning the IP address to a host is a relatively simple process, especially if the host uses DHCP to automatically acquire that address. However, most networks are divided into more efficient segments called subnets. Understanding addressing related to subnets is a bit more complex, so we'll begin by understanding some of the mathematics underlying this process.

IP addresses are expressed in four sets of three numbers, such as 136.14.117.5. Each of the numbers between the dots is called an octet because, when converted to binary notation, it represents eight binary digits (bits). Every IP address has 32 bits and can be notated as *www.xxx.yyy.zzz or w.x.y.z*. This is called *dotted decimal notation*. When the value of any one of the octets is less than three digits, it is written without leading zeroes. Therefore, you'll see IP addresses with one, two, or three digits in each section, such as 254.4.27.112. However, when the value of the octet is zero, it is still written as zero because each octet must be represented (for example, 129.48.0.95). The notation is often shortened to *w.x.y.z* to represent the four octets. The longer notation, *www.xxx.yyy.zzz* is used to indicate that each position can be a maximum of three digits. In this chapter, we'll use both notations.

Each IP address contains two elements, the network address space and the host address space. Throughout this text, we'll use "address" and "ID" interchangeably, thus we may also refer to the "network ID" or the "host ID." Understanding how to work with IP addressing is a fundamental skill that will be used throughout your career in Information Technology and throughout the various Microsoft Windows Server exams. Take time to understand this information thoroughly if you want to ensure your success on the exam and on the job.

Converting from Decimal to Binary

In everyday life, we use the decimal numbering system for counting. The decimal system relies on the digits 0 through 9. This is the system we use for the standard math that we do in our heads. However, this is not the only way to denote numbers. The binary system relies on only two digits: 0 and 1. It's the language of the computer because electrical components are either on or off, and thus electrical signals (or RF signals or light impulses) can easily represent 0 by an off status and 1 by an on status. Although there are some exceptions, for the purpose of this discussion, we will use this convention. Each binary digit is called a *bit* and in IP addressing, eight bits form an *octet*. An IP address has four octets, or a total of 32 bits.

Any whole number from our decimal system can be represented in binary. Each location, or bit position, in a binary number has a certain weight, just as in our decimal system. For example, we know that in the decimal system, a digit in the first position from the right represents ones, a digit in the second position represents tens, a digit in the third position represents hundreds, and so forth. When we see the number 384, we don't even have to stop and think to know that it means 3 hundreds, 8 tens (eighty) and 4 ones.

As with decimal, the weighting in a binary number moves from low-order on the right to high-order on the left. Although our eyes are accustomed to understanding decimal numbers when we read them left to right, many people find it easier to work with binary numbers from right to left. Choose whichever way works best for you, because on the certification exam, you'll probably be required to translate binary to decimal in answering one or more questions.

 EXAM WARNING

It is unlikely that the exam will contain any straightforward conversion questions such as "what does the binary number 1001 0001 1111 1011 represent in decimal?" If only it were that easy! Instead, you'll need to know how to do the conversion as part of a more complex process, usually in calculating subnet masks.

Binary numbers typically are counted beginning with Bit 0, the right-most bit. This has a value of 2^0, or 1. Each bit to the left is raised (exponentially) to the next power, which effectively doubles the number. Thus, Bit 1 is 2^1 or 2, and so forth, as shown in Table 1.2. This formula is typically expressed as 2^n where n is the bit number.

Table 1.2 Binary and Decimal Values

Bit Number	Bit 7	Bit 6	Bit 5	Bit 4	Bit 3	Bit 2	Bit 1	Bit 0
Notation	2^7	2^6	2^5	2^4	2^3	2^2	2^1	2^0
Decimal Value	128	64	32	16	8	4	2	1

If you're not familiar with binary numbers, you may be wondering why this numbering system is set up this way. If you take the right-most position, the Bit 0 position, and set it to 0, the number is 0. If you set Bit 0 to 1, the number is 1. How do we get to 2? We set the next bit, Bit 1, to 1 and reset Bit 0 to 0. This is just like in the decimal numbering system in which you count, in the right-most position, from 0 to 9. After nine, you move to the next position, set it to 1 and reset the first position to 0, resulting in the decimal number 10. Binary works the same way, except that each bit position can be only 0 or 1, thus you need more positions in order to represent decimal numbers.

To create a binary number, we set the desired bit to 1. For instance, to represent the number 128, we would set the eighth position, or Bit 7 (remember, we're counting from 0 to 7, not 1 to 8), to 1. What if we wanted to create the number 132? We'd set Bit 7 and Bit 2 to 1. The rest of the bits would remain 0, as shown in Table 1.3. Any number can be expressed this way.

Table 1.3 Setting Bits to Create Dotted Decimal Values

Bit Number	Bit 7	Bit 6	Bit 5	Bit 4	Bit 3	Bit 2	Bit 1	Bit 0
Notation	2^7	2^6	2^5	2^4	2^3	2^2	2^1	2^0
Decimal Value	128	64	32	16	8	4	2	1
Bit Values for 132	1	0	0	0	0	1	0	0

To convert a binary number to decimal, add the value of each bit position set to 1. Thus, the binary number 10000100 converts to decimal 132.

To convert a decimal number to a binary number, look at the decimal number and find the largest binary bit represented. If we want to convert 184 to binary, we do the math shown in Table 1.4. For each number we subtract, we set the corresponding bit to 1.

Table 1.4 Calculating Binary Bits from Dotted Decimal

Converting Decimal to Binary	Subtraction
Decimal number	184
Largest binary number (in octet) that can be subtracted from this number	−128
Remainder	56
Largest binary number that can be subtracted	−32
Remainder	24
Largest binary number that can be subtracted	−16
Remainder	8
Largest binary number that can be subtracted	−8
Remainder	0

Using this example, 184 can be notated as 10111000 with the 128, 32, 16, and 8 bits set to 1, and the rest set to 0. As you become accustomed to working with both binary and decimal conversions, you may not need to do this lengthy math; eventually you might simply be able to do this in your head.

EXERCISE 1.01

CONVERTING DECIMAL AND BINARY NUMBERS

These exercises are designed to reinforce what we've learned about binary and decimal conversions. Each activity is followed by a step-by-step explanation.

1. Convert the following number to binary: 24. Using the technique just described, we first write out the bit values of an octet: 128 64 32 16 8 4 2 1. Next, we look for the highest value that is less than the number given. In this case, the highest number is 16. We set the Bit 4, which is equivalent to decimal 16, to 1. Next we subtract 16 from our number: 24 – 16 = 8. We set Bit 3, equivalent to decimal 8, to 1. We subtract 8 – 8 = 0 and we have no remainder. Thus, we have the 16 and 8 bits set to 1, and all other bits are zero: 00011000.

2. Convert the following number to decimal: 00001011. In this case, we have to do just the opposite of what we did in the first conversion. Now, we write the bit values of the octet and add up any bit values set to 1. The octet numbers are 128 64 32 16 8 4 2 1. The following bits are set to 1: 8, 2, 1. We add 8 + 2 + 1 to yield 11, the decimal equivalent of this binary notation.

3. Convert the following number to binary: 255.0.132.2. Let's work on each octet, one at a time. Let's begin with the left-most octet, 255. By now, you might recognize that the 255 is all 1s. If not, this is a handy fact to remember. To calculate its value, we begin by subtracting the highest bit value less than 255. (The bit value being subtracted is in **bold** to make it easier to read). In this case, that's 128. 255 – **128** = 127. Again, we subtract the largest bit value: 127 – **64** = 63. Repeating this process we get: 63 – **32** = 31. 31 – **16** = 15. 15 – **8** = 7. 7 – **4** = 3. 3 – **2** = 1. 1 – **1** = 0. For each bit value we subtract (128, 64, etc.) we set the corresponding bit position to 1. Thus, the binary equivalent is 11111111. The next octet (x) is easy, it's all 0s. The octet is written as 00000000. The third octet (y) is equal to 132. Using our subtraction technique, we know that the 128 bit will be set to 1. 132 – 128 = 4. Thus, we set the 4 bit to 1, yielding this octet: 10000100. The final (z) octet is 2. This is easy to figure out—the second bit is set to 1, the rest of the bits are 0. The octet is 00000010. Putting this all together, we have 11111111.00000000.10000100.00000010

4. Convert the following number to dotted decimal notation: 00001000.00001111.00101101.10101010. In this case, we need to convert this number to dotted decimal by adding the values of each bit position set to 1. Again, we'll start on the left. In the first octet, the only position set to 1 is the 8 position. In the second octet, the right-most four bits are set to 1. If you're becoming familiar with the different bit patterns, you'll immediately recognize 15. Otherwise, add the bit values of 1, 2, 4, and 8 together to yield 15. The next octet (y) has the following bit positions set to 1: 32, 8, 4, 1. If you have difficulty with this, write out the bit values 128 64 32 16 8 4 2 1, and then write

out the octet underneath. You'll see which bit positions are set to 1 and you can add those values. In this case, it equals 45. The final octet, *z*, has the following bit positions set to 1: 128, 32, 8, 2. Adding these results in 170. The resulting dotted decimal notation for this is 8.15.45.170.

5. Convert the following number to binary: 112.64.117.3 Again, we'll use our subtraction method to find the largest bit value that is lower than the number and subtract it from the number. We'll repeat the process until the remainder is 0. For each number we subtract (shown in bold), we set the corresponding bit to 1. Our answer looks like this:

First octet (*w*): 112 − **64** = 48. 48 − **32** = 16. 16 − **16** = 0 = 01110000

Second octet (*x*): 64 − **64** = 0 = 01000000

Third octet (*y*): 117 − **64** = 53. 53 − **32** = 21. 21 − **16** = 5. 5 − **4** = 1. 1 − **1** = 0 = 01110101.

Fourth octet (*z*): 3 − **2** = 1. 1 − **1** = 0 = 00000011
    Putting the four octets together yields this dotted decimal notation: 01110000.01000000.01110101.00000011

Although the adding and subtracting may seem simplistic, it's important to practice this over and over, so you can actually look at an octet and add up the values in your head or at least recognize the values and add them with a calculator. It's simple math that simply requires close attention to detail. It's easy to inadvertently miss a bit position. Writing down the sequence can help you avoid these kinds of errors.

It's a good idea to practice converting binary to decimal, as you'll need to know how to do this when working on your network and for the exam. The key is to break each octet down individually and check your work by adding up the value of the bits you've set. This will help ensure that your math and your logic are both correct and will reduce common errors when you set up subnets, subnet masks, and other IP addresses.

 TEST DAY TIP

Binary to Decimal Conversion. After you're situated in the exam room at the testing computer, use a minute or two before starting the test to write down all your tips and tricks for the exam on the blank paper provided (and make sure you get this before you start the exam because your allocated time doesn't begin until you actually start). It's a good idea to write down **128 64 32 16 8 4 2 1**. Then, when you're asked a question about binary or decimal conversions, you won't make an error simply because you forgot that 32 is in between 16 and 64. If you practice these conversions enough, you'll actually begin to recognize patterns immediately—you'll know that 00001111 is 15 and 00001010 is 10, and so on. It's not difficult math, but you have to pay very careful attention to the details. One missed bit changes everything!

Network ID and Host ID

Now that you've learned how to convert binary to decimal and back again, let's look at the principals underlying networking with IP addresses. An IP address has two elements, the *network address* or ID and the *host address* or ID. As we've discussed, the IP address is a unique address assigned to a computer or device (printer, router, etc.) connected to the network. The network address is a fixed address used to identify a common network—sometimes a separate *physical* network and sometimes a separate *logical* network. Within each IP address is a network address (shared by all computers on that network) and a unique host address. When combined, the result is a single unique IP address on the network.

NOTE

We often refer to IP addresses as being assigned to devices, but actually each network interface on a device generally has a separate IP address. Thus, when we speak of a computer's IP address, the terminology holds true only if that computer has a single NIC. If the computer is multihomed (has two or more NICs), it will generally have multiple IP addresses, one for each NIC. The same is true of a router, which has an IP address on each network to which it is connected (and a multihomed computer often *is* a router).

All hosts (also called *nodes* when talking about connected network devices) on the same network segment must have the same network ID. A good analogy is the U.S. zip code system. There are many houses on a street, each with a unique street address (host ID) but all of them have the same zip code within a certain area (network ID). The street address combined with the zip code is a unique combination that identifies a particular house or building just as an IP address identifies a particular host. Figure 1.8 illustrates this concept.

Figure 1.8 Network and Host IDs

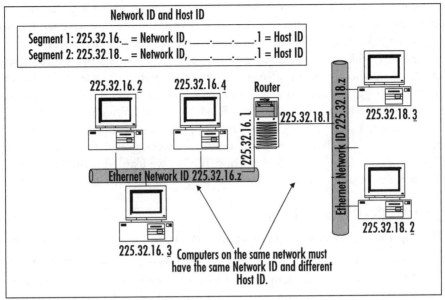

Large networks usually are divided by routers. Routers separate one segment from another and only pass along data destined for external networks (those on the other side of the router). If the data is intended for a host within the segment, the router does not forward it to the external segment(s). This reduces network traffic and increases response times. In order for this to work, however, each segment of the network must have a unique identifier, which is the network address or network ID. Primary network IDs are managed by the *Internet Network Information Center* (InterNIC), an organization that manages top-level network addresses to prevent two organizations from using the same network ID. Two networks connected to the Internet cannot use the same network ID (Networks that are completely standalone and have no connection to the Internet can use any network ID you wish).

Originally, network IDs were divided into classes: Class A, B, C, and D. Each class had a specific purpose and a defined range of allowable addresses. The goal was to provide for three common scenarios in networking:

- Small number of very large networks (large number of nodes per network)

- Moderate number of medium-sized networks

- Large number of very small networks (small number of nodes per network)

This class-based system worked well for quite some time. However, in the 1990s, when the Internet boom period began, it became clear that the addressing scheme would not support the many hundreds of thousands of networks that were popping up (and getting connected to the global network) around the world. A new *classless* system was devised. It still uses

IP addressing fundamentals, but it extends the original concept. The class-based system now often is referred to as *classful*, to differentiate it from the *classless* addressing system. We'll discuss the classless system (also called *variable length subnet masking*) in the next chapter. For now, let's look at the class-based system to understand network addressing fundamentals.

The 32-bit IP address is subdivided into two portions: the network address space and the host address space. The use of 32-bits does not change, but the use of the bits *within* the 32-bit address changes in order to define four classes of addresses. There are currently five defined address classes: Class A, B, C, D, and E. Microsoft Windows Server 2003 supports four address classes: A, B, C, and D. It does not support Class E addresses, which are considered experimental at this time. In addition, there are several guidelines regarding allowable or legal addresses for network IDs and for host IDs. As we learned earlier, the notation used is called *dotted decimal* and is also represented as *w.x.y.z* to denote the four octets used.

Rules for Network IDs

The following rules apply to creating or using network IDs in a class-based system.

1. Network IDs cannot begin with 127 as the first octet, such as 127.14.102.6. 127.x.y.z is reserved for loopback addresses. A loopback address is used to test IP software on the host computer and is not associated with the computer's hardware.

2. All bits of a Network ID cannot be set to 1. This configuration is reserved for broadcast addresses.

3. All bits of a Network ID cannot be set to 0. This configuration is reserved for indicating a host on the local network.

4. A Network ID must be unique to the IP network. If you have three network segments in your corporate network, each segment must have a unique network ID.

Rules for Host IDs

The following rules apply to creating and assigning host IDs.

1. All bits in a Host ID cannot be set to 1. This configuration is reserved for broadcast addresses.

2. All bits in a Host ID cannot be set to 0. This configuration is reserved for the expression of IP network IDs.

3. A Host ID must be unique to the network on which it resides.

Class A

Class A addresses are designed for very large networks with few logical network segments and many hosts. Class A addresses always have the high-order bit (or left-most bit) set to zero. The first octet (the left-most eight bits) is used to define the network ID. The host addresses use the second, third, and fourth octets. This can also be represented as w = network ID, $x.y.z$ = host ID (using the convention that all IP addresses are composed of four octets and represented as $w.x.y.z$). Let's look at an example: **01110000 00000000 00001100 00001111** is a Class A address. The network ID (in **bold**) is 112. The host ID is 0.12.15. Thus, this IP address is 112.0.12.15. Other hosts on the same network would all have IP addresses that begin with 112.

With the high-order bit set to 0, by definition, then a Class A address cannot be greater than 127 since a value of 128 would require the left-most bit be set to 1. To calculate the number of possible networks, use the formula $2^{\wedge}n$ or 2^n, where n is the number of bits in the octet than can be used. In this case, we cannot use the left-most bit, so n in this case is 7. $2^{\wedge}7$ or 2^7 equals 128. However, we know that we cannot have a network set to 127 (loopback) and we cannot have a network of all 0s or all 1s. Therefore, we have 126 useable network addresses. We can also calculate how many possible host addresses we have in a Class A network by using the same formula. In this case, we're using three octets for host IDs. Therefore, we have 2^{24} or 16,777,216. Again, we cannot use addresses of all 0s or all 1s, so we have 16,777,214 useable host addresses available.

Class B

Class B addresses are used for medium-sized networks that have a moderate number of hosts connected to them. Class B addresses always have the first two high-order bits (left-most) set to **10**. The Class B network ID uses the first *two* octets for the network ID. This allows for more network IDs and fewer hosts than a Class A network. Since it uses an additional octet for the network, there is one less octet available for host IDs, reducing the number of hosts that can be addressed on this network by approximately a factor of two.

Here's a Class B IP address: **10010001 00001100** 00001010 00001001. This translates into 160.12.10.9. The first two octets (160.12) represent the network ID and the last two octets (10.9) represent the host ID portion of this IP address. Thus, the schema is $w.x$ = network ID, $y.z$ = host ID. Notice that the two high-order bits are set to 10.

Class B networks use the first two octets for the network ID. However, we cannot set the second bit to 1 (Class B left-most two bits must be 10). Therefore, we can calculate that there are a total of 2^{14} or 16,384 Class B network addresses (16 bits for network ID but we cannot use the first two bits because they must be set to 10). Since we are required to set the first two bits to 10, we will not end up with a network address that is all 0s or all 1s; therefore we do not need to subtract from our total network IDs to find available network IDs. To calculate the number of hosts on a Class B network, we know that we use 16 bits (two octets) for the host ID. Thus, we have 65,536 total host IDs and we cannot use all 0s or all 1s, resulting in 65,534 available host IDs on a Class B network.

Class C

Class C addresses are for small networks with few hosts. These addresses have the first three high-order bits set to **110**. Class C addresses use the first *three* octets for the network ID and the last octet for the host ID. Using your understanding of IP addressing at this point, how many host addresses will be available in each Class C network? If you answered 256 (0 through 255), you'd be close. If you add each bit ($128 + 64 + 32 + 16 + 8 + 4 + 2 + 1$), it totals 256, but remember we cannot use an address of all 0s or all 1s. We're left with 254 possible addresses. The schema for the Class C IP address is $w.x.y$ = network ID, z = host ID.

Class C networks use the left-most three bits set to 110. To calculate the number of networks available, we calculate the total bits available, in this case 24 (three octets) − 3 (first three bits must be 110) = 21. Using the formula 2^{21} we see that the number of Class C networks is 2,097,152. Again, because the left-most three bits must be set to 110, we do not need to subtract for network IDs of all 0s or all 1s. As we saw, the number of host IDs is 254 based on $2^8 − 2 = 256 − 2$ or 254.

Class D and Class E

Recall our earlier discussion of IP multicasting. Class D is reserved for IP multicast addresses. The first four high-order bits are set to 1110. The remaining 28 bits are used for individual IP multicast addresses. *Multicast Backbone on the Internet* (MBONE) is an extension to the Internet that supports IP multicasts and uses Class D addresses. MBONE allows a single packet to have multiple destinations and is most often used in real-time audio and video applications.

Class E addresses are not supported in Microsoft Windows Server 2003. This class is considered experimental and the addresses are defined as "reserved for future use." The first five high-order bits are set to 11110.

Address Class Summary

IP addresses are 32-bit addresses divided into four octets. Each octet has eight bits and a maximum value of 255, which is when all eight bits are set to 1. Each address class defines the maximum number of networks (or subnets, actually) and hosts. These are summarized in Tables 1.5 and 1.6.

Table 1.5 Network Address Classes

Address Class	Octets Used	First Network ID	Last Network ID	Number of Networks
Class A	1	1.x.y.z	126.x.y.z	126
Class B	2	128.0.y.z *	191.255.y.z	16,384
Class C	3	192.0.0.z	223.255.255.z	2,097152

Remember that a valid network address cannot begin with 127.0.0.0, which is reserved for loopback addresses.

Table 1.6 Host Address Classes

Address Class	Octets Used	First Host ID	Last Host ID	Number of Host
Class A	3	w.0.0.1	w.255.255.254	16,777,214
Class B	2	w.x.0.1	w.x.255.254	65,534
Class C	1	w.x.y.1	w.x.y.254	254

Understanding Subnetting

A Class A network could theoretically have 16,777,214 hosts. However, in a real world application, this would be impractical. As you recall, there are some instances when information is broadcast on a network. Imagine broadcasts to and from 16 millions hosts. The network would come to a grinding halt from all that traffic. Therefore, although a company may have a Class A network ID, it will segment (divide) that network to avoid having 16 million hosts per network. This process of segmenting is called *subnetting*. Each segment or subnet must have a unique identifier so that traffic can be sent to the correct location. Since the network ID is a fixed number assigned by the InterNIC, a method was devised to subdivide the assigned network ID by borrowing bits from the host address space. An assigned Class A network assigns the network ID using only the first octet. A subnetted Class A network might use bits from the second and third octets to create new subnetworks.

Although it's theoretically possible to use any host octet bits, in practice they are always used starting from the left-most host address space bit moving to the right. In other words, we take the high-order host address bits first. Table 1.7 shows the resulting number of subnets and number of host bits used when subnetting a Class A network.

Table 1.7 Subnets Using Host ID Bits

Number of Subnets	Number of Host Bits Used in Network ID	Binary (network ID in bold)
0	0	**01000010** . 00000000 . 00000000 . 00000000
1–2	1	**01000010** . 00000000 . 00000000 . 00000000
3–4	2	**01000010** . 00000000 . 00000000 . 00000000
5–8	3	**01000010** . 00000000 . 00000000 . 00000000
9–16	4	**01000010** . 00000000 . 00000000 . 00000000
17–32	5	**01000010** . 00000000 . 00000000 . 00000000
33–64	6	**01000010** . 00000000 . 00000000 . 00000000
65–128	7	**01000010** . 00000000 . 00000000 . 00000000
129–256	8	**01000010** . 00000000 . 00000000 . 00000000

The process is identical to extend the number of subnets on a Class A network beyond 256 by taking additional host address bits from the next octet (where *w.x* and *y* are used for network and only *z* is left for host addresses). This process is similar for Class B and Class C networks as well, although the number of subnets and hosts will vary.

We can identify the number of bits used for the network by notating how many total bits (counting left to right) are used in the network address. From there, we can calculate how many bits remain for host addresses. Using the information from Table 1.7, a Class A network subdivided to allow up to 16 subnets uses 12 bits for the network ID, leaving 20 bits for host addresses. This is commonly denoted with a /12 to show that 12 bits are used for the network ID. An example of this notation is 66.192.15.4/12.

Head of the Class…

Calculating the Number of Hosts

When you begin subnetting, each bit you take from the host address space reduces the number of hosts by a factor of 2. If you can have a maximum of 65,534 hosts and you take 1 bit from the host address space, you reduce the number of hosts you can have by approximately half, or 32,767 (65,534 / 2). If you keep this in mind, you'll have an easier time assessing correct scenarios on the exam and in configuring subnets on the job.

There are two ways to calculate the total number of possible hosts on any given network. First, you can determine the number of host address bits and total the bit values for each bit position that is a host bit. Although we've discussed only the weighted binary values up to 128, they extend far beyond that. To extend these values further to the left, (writing this in reverse order to make it easier to read) we would have 1 2 4 8 16 32 64 128 256 512 1024 2048 4096 8192 16384, and so on. To place this sequence in the proper order, we simply write it from right to left: 16384, 8192, 4096, 2048, and so on. If we want to calculate the number of hosts, we just keep adding, from right to left, the number of host bits. Since a traditional Class A network uses the first octet (w) as the network address, that generally leaves 24 bits for host addresses. You would have to extend the previous example out to 24 bits (the previous example goes out to only 15 bits), doubling the previous number. Remember, though, that you must subtract 2 from any result since legal addresses cannot be all 0s or all 1s in the classful addressing scheme.

Another way to calculate this, which is much faster and easier if you have a scientific calculator function available to you, is to use the formula $[(2^n)-2]$. Most people can't do this kind of math in their heads but you can use the **x^y** function on the Windows Calculator. Start the Calculator by selecting **Start | Run** and typing **calc** in the **Run** dialog box, and then pressing **Enter**. Choose **View | Scientific** from the menu. Enter the number **2**, click the button labeled **x^y**, then enter the number of bits used for the problem and press **Enter** or click **=**. For instance, 2^{21} equals 2,097,152. If you're using 21 bits for the host address space, you will have (2,097,152 – 2) bits available to you, or 2,097,150. The same holds true for network

Continued

addresses. So, rather than memorizing the many different configurations, use this formula to check your logic, your math, and your answers.

To become familiar with the conversions, we recommend creating conversion tables for yourself by writing a conversion on an index card and running through these flash cards until you're doing conversion in your sleep. On exam day, you'll be glad you did.

Understanding Subnet Masking

Large networks are subdivided to create smaller subnetworks to reduce overall network traffic by keeping local traffic on the local subnet and sending all nonlocal traffic to the router. In order to create a subnetwork, we need to have a system for addressing that allows us to use the network ID and host ID within the class-based system. This is accomplished through the use of a *subnet mask*. In essence, a subnet mask is a 32-bit number that is combined with the IP address (network address and host address) to shield or mask certain bits, thus creating a new, unique number.

The 32-bit IP address is composed of the network ID and the host ID. The number of host IDs on a network is variable, but the network ID must be the same for all hosts on a segment. For example, in a Class C network, you can have from 1 to 254 hosts. Suppose you wanted to divide your Class C network into two networks with 100 hosts each? You could use your Class C network ID with a subnet mask and virtually divide your network into two parts. This is done by borrowing bits from the host ID portion of the IP address. When you take bits from the host address space, you reduce the number of potential host addresses roughly by a factor of two. If this sounds a bit confusing, don't worry. We're going to walk through this step-by-step. The underlying concept of subnets and subnet masking involves a binary process called *bitwise ANDing*.

How Bitwise ANDing Works

The term *ANDing* comes from a form of mathematics called Boolean algebra. Computers use *Boolean operators* in their circuitry. Integrated circuits contain components known as gates and inverters. A gate (or inverter) has one or more inputs. Their output is based on the *state* of those inputs. The state can only be off (0) or on (1). In Boolean terms, it can only be true (1) or false (0). AND gates will return (or output) 1 if *all* inputs are 1 and will return 0 if *any* input is not 1. An OR gate will return 1 if *any* input is 1 and will return 0 only if no input signals are 1.

You may be familiar with Boolean operators in using search engines. You can refine your search by using Boolean operators, including AND and OR. There are other, less commonly used operators such as *NAND* (not AND) and *XOR* (exclusive OR), but these are outside the scope of this discussion.

Bitwise ANDing simply means that we are performing the logical AND function on each bit. The simple AND statements can be expressed as shown here. Rather than a mathematical *plus* function, this is a comparison between two (or more) values.

- $0 + 0 = 0$
- $0 + 1 = 0$
- $1 + 0 = 0$
- $1 + 1 = 1$

Notice that the logical AND function results in a 1 only when *both* inputs are 1; otherwise, the result is 0. Next, let's take a slightly more complicated example, still using bitwise ANDing.

First input	1010	1010	1010
Second input	0001	1000	1100
Result of ANDing	**0000**	**1000**	**1000**

Again, the result is 1 only when both inputs are 1; otherwise the result is 0. Now let's explore how bitwise ANDing is used in subnetting.

EXERCISE 1.02

BITWISE ANDING

This exercise is designed to give you practice with bitwise ANDing. Each question is followed by a step-by-step answer.

1. What is the result of the following bitwise ANDing? Convert your answer from binary to dotted decimal. Compare 146.64.160.9 and 255.255.224.0.

    Answer: The result is 146.64.160.0

Inputs	Dotted Decimal Notation	Binary Notation
IP address	146.64.160.9	10010001.01000000.10100000.00001001
Subnet mask	255.255.224.0	11111111.11111111.11100000.00000000
Result	146.64.160.0	10010001.01000000.10100000.00000000

As you can see, the result from our bitwise ANDing of an IP address and our subnet mask is the underlying network ID, in this case 146.64.160.0. Once you have delineated your subnet IDs and determined your subnet mask, you can check your work by performing the ANDing process to verify the result is the underlying subnet network ID.

2. What is the result of the following bitwise ANDing? Convert your answer from binary to dotted decimal. Compare 146.64.195.36 and 255.255.224.0.
Answer: The result is 146.64.192.0

Inputs	Dotted Decimal Notation	Binary Notation
IP address	146.64.195.36	10010001.01000000.11000011.00100100
Subnet mask	255.255.224.0	11111111.11111111.11100000.00000000
Result	146.64.192.0	10010001.01000000.11000000.00000000

In this example, the underlying network ID was not readily apparent. By using bitwise ANDing, we were able to extract the network ID.

3. What is the network ID of this IP address: 146.64.187.112/20? As you recall, the notation /20 indicates we're using 20 bits from the network address space. Thus, we know that our subnet mask must use 1 in the left-most 20 locations. Our bitwise ANDing results in a network ID of:

Inputs	Dotted Decimal Notation	Binary Notation
IP address	146.64.187.112	10010001.01000000.10111011.01110000
Subnet mask	255.255.240.0	11111111.11111111.11110000.00000000
Result	146.64.176.0	10010001.01000000.10110000.00000000

Default Subnet Mask

A subnet mask is a four-octet number used to identify the network ID portion of a 32-bit IP address. A subnet mask is required on all class-based networks, even on networks that are not subnetted. A *default subnet mask* is based on the IP address classes we discussed earlier and is used on networks that are not subdivided. If your network is not subnetted, you must use the subnet mask associated with your IP address class. The default subnet masks are shown in dotted decimal format in Table 1.8.

Table 1.8 Default Subnet Masks

IP Address Class	Default Subnet Mask
Class A	255.0.0.0
Class B	255.255.0.0
Class C	255.255.255.0

We've already discussed the fact that a Class A network uses the first octet as the network address. You can see from the default subnet mask shown in the preceding table that the first octet is set to all 1s (dotted decimal 255). Recall that a network ID cannot be set to all 1s. Thus, when you use logical ANDing with any Class A network and the default subnet mask, it will always yield the Class A network ID. For example, if the Class A network ID is 66.x.y.z, it would be represented as 01000010.x.y.z. The default subnet mask is represented as 11111111.x.y.z. The logical AND function, shown in Table 1.9, yields 01000010.x.y.z.

Table 1.9 ANDing Network ID and Default Subnet Mask

Class A Network ID = 66	01000010
Default Subnet Mask = 255	11111111
Bitwise AND result = 66	01000010

Custom Subnet Mask

Most networks are subnetted because the number of hosts allowed in both Class A and Class B networks is well beyond what could be used in practical application. Subnetting is accomplished by using bits from the host address space for the network address space.

The custom subnet mask (also called a variable length subnet mask) is used *to identify the bits used for a network address versus the bits used for a host address.* Custom subnet masks are used when *subnetting* or *supernetting*. As we've discussed, subnetting is the process of dividing one network into many. Supernetting uses a single IP address to represent many unique IP addresses. *Supernetting* is the process of allocating a range or block of network IDs (typically Class C) instead of a single Class A or B network ID to preserve Class A and B networks for uses that require a large number of host addresses.

To determine the appropriate custom subnet mask (typically referred to simply as *subnet mask*) for a network, you must first:

1. Determine the *number of host bits to be used* for subnetting.
2. Determine the *new subnetted network IDs.*
3. Determine the *IP addresses for each new subnet.*
4. Determine the appropriate *subnet mask.*

Determine the Number of Host Bits to Be Used

We can create a subnet mask by using bits that would normally be used for host addresses. *The number of subnets needed will determine the number of host bits to be used.* An important element of this process is determining the maximum number of subnets you may need in the future, to avoid having to reassign addresses when your network grows. Allow for more subnets than you plan to use, within reason. Also keep in mind that the more host bits you use for subnets, the fewer host IDs you'll have left for assigning to your connected devices. There is a trade-off between allowing for adequate subnet growth and retaining adequate host IDs for all connected devices.

Let's look at an example using a Class B network, which uses the two left-most octets for the network ID and the two right-most octets for the host ID. If you had no subnets, you would have 65,534 host addresses available to use. Suppose you wanted to have two subnets? How would you determine your subnet mask and how many host IDs would you have available to you?

If you take one bit from the host address space, you would be able to create two networks, each with 32,768 host addresses. If you take two bits from the host address space, you can create three to four subnets of 16,384 host addresses per subnet. Remember, we can't use host addresses with all 0s or all 1s, so the number of *available* host addresses is reduced by two each time.

> **NOTE**
>
> The rule that network IDs could not consist of all 0s or all 1s came about because at one point in time, router software wasn't capable of handling such network IDs. The routers being made today are perfectly capable of handling network IDs of all 0s or all 1s, so this rule—while still imposed by Microsoft on their networks—no longer is a technical limitation but merely one of convention. However, although network IDs of all 0s and all 1s are permissible now, you still cannot use host IDs that consist of all 0s or all 1s.

For this section, we're going to use the following data. We're going to use a Class B network with the IP address of 145.64.0.0. We'll assume we need up to eight subnets to handle our future expansion. We'll also assume that having up to 8,190 host addresses per subnet will be acceptable for our configuration. We've determined our maximum number of subnets and the resulting number of host addresses per subnet.

Now that we've decided we need a maximum of eight subnets, we must next determine how many host bits we'll need to use to accomplish this. Thus, we use bits from the third octet (*y*) and determine how many we'll need to create eight (remember, counting starts with 0). We can see that we need three bits from the third octet to give us up to eight subnets. We know that 00000111 = 7. Since we're including 0, using three bits would allow a total of eight subnets. It's important not to get confused between bit values and number of bits. At this point, we simply need to figure out how *many* bits are needed, so we start on the right. If we needed 64 networks, we'd need six bits (00111111 = 63) and so on. Table 1.10 shows the bit configuration for up to eight subnets using our sample network 145.64.0.0.

Table 1.10 Dotted Decimal and Binary Configuration for Subnetted Networks

Network Dotted Decimal	Binary (network address in bold)	Subnet Range
145.64.0.0	**10010001.01000000.**00000000.00000000	Undivided Class B network
145.64.0.0	**10010001.01000000.000**00000.00000000	First subnet address
145.64.224.0	**10010001.01000000.111**00000.00000000	Last subnet address

Notice that we used three bits—the three bits contiguous to our original network ID. Essentially these bits extend the network address space by three bits. An important thing to remember is that these bits retain their original bit value and that they stay in their original octet—we don't move the decimal place. For example, the left-most bit of the third octet, while incorporated into the network ID, still retains its value of 128. When we add together the values of the four left-most bits from the third octet, it results in 224 (128 + 64 + 32), yielding our highest network ID.

Determine the New Subnetted Network IDs

Once we've taken the number of host address bits we need to create our requisite number of subnets, we must determine the resulting addresses of our new subnets. There are two steps in this process.

1. List all the possible binary combinations of the bits taken from the host address space.
2. Calculate the incremental value to each subnet and add to the network address.

The possible combinations of the four bits taken from the host address space are shown in Table 1.11. The number of combinations can be denoted as 2^n, where *n* is the number of bits. In this case, we could represent all possible combinations as 2^3 or 8.

Table 1.11 Binary Combinations

Combination Number	Binary Representation
1	000
2	001
3	010
4	011
5	100
6	101
7	110
8	111

Next, we need to calculate the incremental values. Again, we begin with the bit that is contiguous with the original network ID. Table 1.12 shows the results.

Table 1.12 Incremental Binary Values

Network Dotted Decimal	Binary (network address in bold)
145.64.0.0	**10010001.01000000.000**00000.00000000
	10010001.01000000.00100000.00000000
	10010001.01000000.00100000.00000000
	10010001.01000000.01000000.00000000
	10010001.01000000.01100000.00000000
	10010001.01000000.10000000.00000000
	10010001.01000000.10100000.00000000
	10010001.01000000.11000000.00000000
	10010001.01000000.11100000.00000000

Determine the IP Addresses for Each New Subnet

Earlier we learned that we could denote the number of network ID bits by using the convention w.x.y.z/## where ## is the total number of network ID bits. In this case, we have a Class B network, so we know we're starting with 16 bits for the network. We've taken three bits from the host address space, so our total network bits are now 19. Thus, we can denote our new subnetted network in this way: 146.64.0.0/19. Each of the subsequent subnet IDs can be denoted in a similar fashion as shown in Table 1.13.

Table 1.13 Incremental Dotted Decimal and Binary Values

Network Dotted Decimal	Binary (network address in bold)
145.64.0.0 /19	**10010001.01000000.000**00000.00000000
145.64.0.0 /19	**10010001.01000000.000**00000.00000000
145.64.32.0 /19	**10010001.01000000.001**00000.00000000
146.64.64.0 /19	**10010001.01000000.010**00000.00000000
146.64.96.0 /19	**10010001.01000000.011**00000.00000000
146.64.128.0 /19	**10010001.01000000.100**00000.00000000
146.64.160.0 /19	**10010001.01000000.101**00000.00000000
146.64.192.0 /19	**10010001.01000000.110**00000.00000000
146.64.224.0 /19	**10010001.01000000.111**00000.00000000

Creating the Subnet Mask

We've determined our subnets, and now we need to create a subnet mask that will work with each subnet ID we created. Recall that we use bitwise ANDing to compare the bits of the IP address and the subnet mask. The result of the comparison is the network ID. Using Table 1.13, we know that we need to set to 1 any bits used for the network ID portion of the IP address. In this case, the subnet mask would be set to:

11111111.11111111.11100000.00000000

Notice that we have set the left-most 19 bits to 1. Thus, our subnet masks can be written in dotted decimal notation as 255.255.224.0. Let's compare this subnet mask to a sample IP address from within our subnetted addresses to see how this works.

146.64.193.14 IP address	= 10010001.01000000.11000001.00001110
255.255.224.0 subnet mask	= 11111111.11111111.11100000.00000000
Result of bitwise ANDing	= 10010001.01000000.11000000.00000000
Underlying network ID	= 146.64.192.0

EXERCISE 1.03

DEFINING SUBNET MASKS

In this exercise, we'll practice defining subnets and subnet masks. Use the following scenario: Your start up company has been assigned a Class C address. You have only six computers, one router, and three printers attached to your network. You'd like to subnet your network before your company's planned expansion and you'll need a maximum of six to seven networks in the future.

1. How many host address bits will you need to take from the host address space to create seven subnets? To solve this problem, we need to think in terms of the bit value of the binary bits in an octet. What bit values, added together, equal 7? The answer is the right-most three bits, or 00000111. This tells us we need three bits from the host address space to add to the network address space. However, it's important to remember that we don't *use* the right-most bits. This may be confusing, but we used the bit values simply to determine how many bits we'll need. We use the bits closest to the octet used for the network ID.

2. What is the binary representation of the subnet mask used for this configuration? Class C uses the *w.x.y* octets for network ID. Therefore, we know that the default subnet mask is 255.255.255.0. We've determined that we need to take three bits from the host ID space. We take the three left-most bits from the fourth octet so they remain contiguous with the network address space. The result is a subnet mask with the 1s in 27 of the 32 bits, moving left to right, as shown. 11111111.11111111.11111111.11100000

3. What is the dotted decimal value of the binary configuration shown in Problem 2? 10.255.255.255.224

4. What is one way of representing this network configuration, given that we are using three bits from the host address space for network IDs? As you may recall, a common notation for showing how many bits represent the network ID (and therefore the subnet mask) is *w.x.y.z* /27 where *w.x.y.z* are the dotted decimal values of the four octets that comprise an IP address and the /27 denotes the number of bits used for the network address.

5. If we use three bits from the host space for network IDs, what is the maximum number of hosts we can have per subnet? We know that an IP address has 32 bits and that we're using 27 of those bits for network addresses. 32 − 27 leaves 5 bits for host addresses. If we use the formula 2^n, we have 2^5, or 32 addresses. However, this includes an address of all 0s and all 1s, both of which cannot be used, resulting in 30 possible host addresses per subnet.

This exercise should help you find out if you have any areas of confusion. If so, go back and work on the specific area that is giving you trouble. The Microsoft exam is likely to have questions that rely upon this knowledge. You'll have scenarios that require you to perform these calculations in order to discern the correct answer.

Head of the Class...

Creating Subnet Masks

This topic always causes some confusion in the classroom because it requires us to work left to right *and* right to left. As we work through examples, some people get it immediately and some people don't. Usually the area of most confusion deals with taking bits from the host address space. This is because we use the bits with the lowest bit values first. However, when we're using those bits, they shift over to the left because we always want to use the bits contiguous with the network address space.

We emphasize that the bits retain their weighted binary values within the octets, regardless of their use. In the preceding exercise, we saw that there were both *network* and *host* bits in the fourth octet (the *z* octet). Although the bits are used for two different purposes, they must be calculated into a single dotted decimal number. The first thing we always calculate is how many subnets we're going to need. We convert that number to weighted binary, to determine how many bits we need. This essentially tells us how many possible bit combinations there are and therefore how many subnets we can delineate.

One example we use to make this point clear is a simple one. If we need one network ID, we don't need any bits from the host address space. There is only one combination. If we need two networks, we need one bit. Why? Because that one bit can be either 0 or 1, and that's two different combinations.

If we need one bit, we take that bit and use it on the left side of the octet. That's where some people get confused. After we figure out how many bits we need, we extend the network address space by that number of bits, which is the reason they shift to the left while retaining their weighted value based on their placement within the octet.

You should work through lots of examples so that you can fully understand both the concepts and the practical applications of subnetting. Work through the examples in this chapter and make up some of your own. If you have a study buddy, you can help each other by testing your knowledge of this crucial topic.

EXAM WARNING

You will likely run into several questions that test your ability to apply your understanding of network IDs, subnetting, and subnet masks. This is a critical part of the TCP/IP section and will likely be tested extensively. Make sure you are very comfortable with these concepts and practice binary-to-decimal conversion, subnetting, and custom subnet masks. Review these areas frequently during your studies and particularly a day or two before the exam. You will be asked questions about how to define subnet ranges, number of host address available, and so on, and you will see some tricky answers designed to make sure you really know what you're doing.

Public and Private IP Addresses

Class A, B, and C network addresses are assigned by the InterNIC. This is important to avoid duplication of network IDs that communicate via the public network, better known as the Internet. However, if your network will never connect in any manner to the Internet, you can have any address class or any specific network ID you choose. If you do connect to the Internet, you can have direct (routed) or indirect (proxy or translator) connectivity using *public* or *private* addresses. You will always need at least one public address to connect your network to the Internet.

Public addresses are assigned by the InterNIC and can be *classful* (Class A, B, C) or *classless* (CIDR blocks, discussed in Chapter 2). They are guaranteed to be unique across the entire worldwide Internet network. When these addresses are assigned, Internet routers are programmed so that traffic for these addresses reaches the intended destination.

A network address can be any address you choose, as long as you do not connect to the Internet. You can, in fact, choose addresses that are already in use on the Internet because all traffic on your network remains private and does not reach the Internet. If your company later decides to connect its network to the Internet, it will have to contact the InterNIC to obtain a useable public address. This will entail changing network addressing to the new, public addressing scheme. If the company does not change its addressing scheme and attempts to use addresses already assigned to someone else by the InterNIC (and that have assigned routes in public routing tables), the company's network will not be able to connect to the Internet. These are considered *illegal addresses.*

With the explosive growth of the Internet, the InterNIC realized that some devices may never connect directly to the Internet. A good example of this is that many computers in a company connect to the Internet via an intermediate device such as a firewall, proxy server, or router. Consequently, those devices behind the firewall or other intermediate device don't need globally unique IP addresses. Three address blocks are defined as private address blocks, for situations in which the host does not connect directly to the Internet.

- **10.0.0.0/8** This is a private Class A network address with the host ID range of 10.0.0.1 through 10.255.255.254. This private network has 24 bits that can be used for any subnetting configuration desired by the company.

- **172.16.0.0/12** This scheme uses Class B addresses and allows for up to 16 Class B networks or 20 bits can be used for host IDs. The range of valid addresses on this private network is from 172.16.0.1 through 172.31.255.254.

- **192.168.0.0/16** This configuration can provide up to 256 Class C networks or 16 bits can be used for host addresses. The value range of IP addresses in this private network is 192.168.0.1 through 192.168.255.254.

These private addresses are not assigned publicly and therefore will never exist in Internet routing tables. This makes these private addresses unreachable via the Internet. If a host using a private network IP address requires access to the Internet, it must use the services of an Application layer gateway such as a proxy server or it must have its address translated into a legal, public address. A process called *Network Address Translator* (NAT) performs this translation before sending data out to the Internet from a private address host ID.

Another use of private addressing is called Automatic Private IP Addressing (APIPA). If a computer (Windows 98 or later) is configured to obtain its address automatically from a DHCP Server and it cannot locate a DHCP Server, it will configure itself using APIPA. The computer randomly selects an address from the 169.254.0.0/16 address range and then checks the network for uniqueness. If the address is unique, it will use that address until it can reach a DHCP Server. If the address is not unique, it will randomly select another address from that range. APIPA is discussed in greater detail in Chapter 2.

Understanding Basic IP Routing

In this section, we're going to learn about how data is routed on a network using the IP protocol. We'll begin by learning how names and addresses are resolved. Then, we'll look at how packets of data are sent from one network to another to understand the process of basic IP routing.

Name and Address Resolution

Names are often used for computers and devices because it's much easier for humans to remember names than numbers. You're more likely to remember that your computer name is HTaylor than to remember that your IP address is 196.55.141.6. There are two types of names—*NetBIOS names*, which are used by NetBIOS applications and *host names*, used by Windows Sockets applications and TCP/IP applications. Since names are often used, there must be a method for translating or resolving names—both NetBIOS and host names—to unique IP addresses.

Host Name Resolution

A host name is a name, or alias, assigned to a device (also called *host* or *node*) to identify it as a TCP/IP host device. This host name can be up to 255 characters long, can contain both alpha and numeric characters, and can contain the "-" (hyphen) and "." (dot, or period) characters. A computer or device can actually have multiple host names assigned to it. Beginning with Windows 2000, the host name and computer name do not have to be the same.

WinSock-based applications can use either the host name or the IP address. Both Internet Explorer and FTP are examples of WinSock-based applications that use either the host name or IP address. If a host name is used for the destination, it must be resolved to the IP address associated with the host name.

Host names take a variety of forms, but the two most common are nicknames (aliases) and domain names. A nickname might be Galileo or JohnS. Domain names are host names that follow the commonly known Internet naming conventions.

The InterNIC created a hierarchical namespace called DNS, which allows organizations to create custom names based on an agreed-upon hierarchy. This system is similar to a directory structure on a disk drive. A unique name for the host within this type of hierarchy is referred to as a *Fully Qualified Domain Name* (FQDN). An example of a FQDN is *server01.example.somecompany.com*. The root is indicated with a null "". The top-level domain is "com," familiar to most people in today's environment. "Somecompany" represents the second-level domain, "example" represents the third-level domain, and "server01" is the host (computer name). The unique host name is the entire string. It is possible, for example, to have a host named server01 on another domain such as example2, in which case the FQDN would be *server01.example2.somecompany.com*. Each name is still unique because the entire string serves as the name. Domain names are not case sensitive. FQDNs need to be resolved to IP addresses in order for data to be sent and received properly. Host names (whether alias or FQDN) can be resolved through the use of a static hosts file, through the use of a DSN Server for lookup, or through a combination of the two.

Hosts File

UNIX has long used the *hosts* file to store host name-to-IP address mappings. This file can also be used on Windows-based computers. On UNIX systems, the hosts file typically is located in /etc/hosts. On a Windows Server 2003 machine (or Windows 2000), it is located in the \%SystemRoot%\system32\drivers\etc directory. The file is a simple text file (but saved *without* the .TXT extension) that lists the IP address and the host name of each defined device. Below is an example of a hosts file.

```
#
# Table of IP addresses and host names
#
127.0.0.1      localhost
132.14.29.1    router
191.87.221.2   server2.example.somecompany.com
191.87.221.3   server3.example.somecompany.com  galileo
```

Notice that the IP address is given first, then the host name. On the last line of this sample hosts file, notice that there are two names: *server3.example.somecompany.com* and *galileo*. In a hosts file, you can map both a FQDN and an alias (nickname) to the same associated IP address. Thus, there are three ways someone could reach that device: using *galileo*, *server3.example.somecompany.com*, or *191.87.221.3*. Hosts files in Windows NT, 2000, and 2003 are not case sensitive and are named *hosts*. In other operating systems, such as in UNIX, the hosts file is case sensitive.

There are two big problems with using a hosts file. First, it is a static file. If any names or addresses change, they must be changed manually in the hosts file. If you have a hosts file on 1,500 computers that defines the location and name of a router and information changes, you may have a big job ahead of you when you need to change that hosts file on all 1,500 computers and other devices that use that router. Also, if the number of defined hosts in a hosts file gets long, it can take a long time to parse the file. This results in a delay as your computer reads through a long file in an attempt to locate a host name and associated IP address.

Domain Name System Name Resolution

An alternative to the hosts file is to use a DNS Server. DNS Servers store FQDN-to-IP address translations. A computer runs the DNS client called the *DNS resolver*, which is configured with the IP address of the DNS Server. When an IP address is needed, the DNS resolver requests the information from the DNS Server by first translating the FQDN provided into a *DNS name query*. When the IP address is returned from the DNS Server, the DNS resolver provides that information to the requesting application. DNS is a distributed system, so not all mappings reside on all DNS Servers. Each DNS Server is responsible for a particular segment of the names and it either returns the requested information or forwards it to the appropriate DNS Server. We'll learn more about DNS later in this book.

In the Windows implementation of TCP/IP, both a hosts file and DNS are used to resolve host names. The hosts file is checked first and if the desired mapping is not present, DNS will be queried.

NetBIOS Name Resolution

There are essentially four ways a NetBIOS name can be resolved:

- The client's NetBIOS name cache is checked to see if the NetBIOS name-to-IP address has already been resolved and is sitting in memory.

- A WINS Server can be queried to see if the information is in a WINS database.

- The client can use a file called LMHOSTS (that works similarly to the hosts file for host names).

- The NetBIOS name is converted to a host name and host name resolution methods are employed.

The method by which NetBIOS names are resolved depends on the node's configuration. There are four types of configurations, described in Table 1.14, that are referred to as NetBIOS Node Types.

Table 1.14 NetBIOS Node Types

Node Type	Description of Node
B-node (Broadcast) Benefit: Broadcast sends message to network for response. Potential Problem: Increased network traffic.	B-node clients broadcast a message to the local network. If the queried name exists on the local network, a positive *name query response* is generated, which contains the IP address of the associated NetBIOS name. Once resolved, this information resides in the NetBIOS cache until it times out.
P-node (Peer-to-peer) Benefit: Message is sent only to WINS Server, reducing network traffic. Potential Problem: Names may be resolved over WAN, which is both slower and less efficient.	P-node clients send a unicast (a directed message) to the defined WINS Server. If the WINS Server database contains the needed information, it responds with a positive name query response along with the requested IP address. If the WINS Server does not respond, the client will try additional WINS Servers.
M-node (Mixed) Benefit: Useful when the client is on the other side of a WAN link from the desired resource. Potential Problem: Broadcasts may cause increased traffic on the local network.	M-node clients use B-node to resolve the name-to-address first. If this is unsuccessful, it will then use P-node for resolution.
H-node (Hybrid) Benefit: Works well if names are located on a WINS Server and are resolved via WINS. Potential Problem: Can still generate excess local network traffic through the use of broadcasts.	H-node clients use a process just the opposite of M-node clients. Resolution is first attempted using P-node and if unsuccessful, B-node is used.

You may be thinking that a single broadcast to resolve a name on a network may not be significant in increasing network traffic. However, depending on the number of hosts on a subnet, the attempts at name resolution could cause substantial network traffic. It's also important to remember that these broadcasts use UDP datagrams. If you recall our earlier discussions, UDP datagrams are connectionless and therefore not reliable. If a client does not receive a positive response from a name query, the client doesn't really know whether the request ever reached its destination. In order to make sure the request is received, these UDP datagram broadcasts are sent out three times with a 750ms delay in between. Thus, each attempt at name resolution generates three packets, not just one. The number of attempts and the delay can be changed in the registry, though these default settings are typically adequate.

In Windows Server 2003 (and going as far back as Windows 98), a client can be configured with up to 12 WINS Servers, significantly increasing the chances of receiving a positive name query response from a configured WINS Server. However, if the name is still not resolved using these methods, the client will continue to try to resolve the name.

How Packets Travel from Network to Network

Now that we understand how names are translated into IP addresses, let's look at how a data packet from one host travels to another across the span of networks. After a sending host receives the needed IP address, the packet is sent from the host through the TCP/IP suite to the physical medium for delivery at the target IP address. *Routing* is the process of sending the packet to its destination. A *router* is a device that forwards packets from one network to another and is also referred to as a *gateway*. (The term gateway is used in several different contexts; in all cases, a gateway connects one thing with another.)

When the sending host has a packet ready, it already has determined the destination's IP address by using one of the many name-to-IP resolution methods discussed. However, it may not know where that IP address is located if it is not located on the same subnet as the sending host.

When TCP/IP on a host is initialized, it automatically creates a routing table, which consists of default entries, manual entries, and entries made automatically through communication with network routers. In order to route the packet properly, the IP layer of a host will consult with the routing table that is stored in memory. Depending on whether the destination is on the same network or across the network boundaries (which is determined by examining the network ID of the destination address), the packet will be sent by *direct delivery* or *indirect delivery*.

Direct delivery is when the router is not used to forward the packet because the destination is on the same network (subnet or network segment) as the sending host. In this case, the packet is sent directly to its destination. When the packet leaves the sending host, the data is encapsulated in a frame format for the Network Interface layer with the destination's physical address included (as you'll recall, the physical or MAC address that matches the IP address in the destination header is determined by ARP).

If the packet is destined for another network, it is sent to an intermediate point for forwarding. This is called indirect delivery. The IP data is encapsulated in a frame format that is actually addressed to the physical address of the network interface of the IP *router* that is on the sending computer's subnet. Thus, the packet is sent from the sending host directly to the router. The router takes a look at the packet and determines where it should be sent in order to reach its final destination. The router passes the packet from its *internal interface* (the one with an address on the same subnet as the sender) to its *external interface* (the interface that's on a different subnet). From there, the packet may make its way across many routers before reaching the subnet or network on which the destination computer resides.

IP Routing Tables

Any IP node that initializes the TCP/IP stack will generate a default routing table based on the configuration of that node. For instance, when your network-connected desktop boots up and initializes the TCP/IP stack, it will create a default routing table based on your computer's unique IP address, which includes the network ID as well as the default gateway (default router) and subnet mask. The table also contains the logical or physical interface, typically the network interface card, to be used to forward the packet.

IP Routing Table Entries

Routing table entries can be default, manual, or dynamic.

- The default values are created when the TCP/IP stack is initialized, as shown in Figure 1.6.

- Manual entries can be placed in the table for specific routes that may be desired. Some organizations, for instance, want specific traffic to go through specific routers. In that case, those routes can be entered into the routing table manually.

- Routes can be added dynamically if the router supports dynamic routing tables.

We'll discuss the differences between manual and dynamic routing in a moment. For now, let's look at the specific entries in a routing table.

Figure 1.9 Default Routing Table Entries

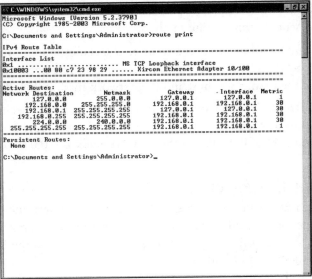

Routing table entries contain a number of elements in a specified order. Each of those elements is required and each is described briefly here. Figure 1.9 shows a typical routing table.

- **Network Destination** The network ID can be class-based, subnetted, or supernetted.

- **Netmask** The mask used to match the destination network with the IP address in the data.

- **Next Hop or Gateway** The IP address of the next router. (A hop is one segment between routers. If a packet needs to go through two routers, that would be two hops.)

- **Interface** Identifies which network interface is used to forward the packet. Remember that every router has at least two interfaces.

- **Metric** The metric is a number used to help determine the best route for the packet. This typically is used to identify the route with the fewest hops. The metric is often expressed as the "cost of the route."

Routing tables can also store four specific types of routes:

- **Directly Attached Network IDs** For packets destined for the local or attached network. If the sending and receiving hosts are both on the same subnet, for instance, the packet would be sent via this method.

- **Remote Network IDs** Any packets destined for networks reachable via routers would be sent via this routing method.

- **Host Routes** A host route is a route to a specific IP address. This type of route allows a packet to be sent to a specific IP address. The network ID is the IP address of the destination host and the network mask is 255.255.255.255.

- **Default Route** The default route is used when a more specific network ID or route cannot be found. When all else fails, the default route is used. This is defined as a network ID of 0.0.0.0, and the network mask is 0.0.0.0.

Route Determination Process

Each IP packet has a destination IP address, which is used to determine how the packet will be routed. Using the logical ANDing process, the destination IP address and the subnet mask (or netmask) are compared. If they match, the packet stays on the local network and is sent directly to the destination IP address.

If the destination IP address and the subnet mask do not match, the entries in the routing table are compared to the destination IP address. If a match is found (i.e., the destination IP address and the subnet mask AND to a value found in the routing table), the packet is sent to the gateway listed in the routing table. If no matching entries can be found, the packet is sent to the defined default gateway. If more than one match is found in the routing table entries, the *metric* is used and the route with the fewest hops typically is selected. Table 1.15 shows a sample routing table list. To view the route table on your Windows Server 2003 computer, open the command prompt and type **route print**.

Table 1.15 Sample Static Routing Table

Destination IP	Subnet Mask	Gateway	Interface	Metric	Purpose
0.0.0.0	0.0.0.0	166.42.8.1	166.42.14.62	20	Default route
127.0.0.0	255.0.0.0	127.0.0.1	127.0.0.1	1	Loopback network
166.42.8.0	255.255.224.0	166.42.14.62	166.42.14.62	20	Directly attached network
166.42.14.62	255.255.255.255	127.0.0.1	127.0.0.1	20	Local host
166.42.255.255	255.255.255.255	166.42.14.62	166.42.14.62	1	Network broadcast
224.0.0.0	224.0.0.0	166.42.14.62	166.42.14.62	1	Multicast address
255.255.255.255	255.255.255.255	166.42.14.62	166.42.14.62	1	Limited broadcast

Route Processing

On a Windows Server 2003 family computer, the IP routing process is as follows.

1. Perform the route determination process as described previously, choosing the route that is either the best match or the fewest hops (lowest metric).

2. Examine the gateway (router) and interface IP address of the selected route.

3. If the gateway IP address is the same as the interface IP, the next-hop IP address is set to the destination IP address.

4. If the gateway IP address is different than the interface IP address, the next-hop IP address is to the gateway IP address.

For example a host with the IP address 166.42.14.62/22 sends a packet to 166.42.16.5/22. The network ID of the source is compared to the network ID of the destination. If they are the same, the packet is delivered directly to 166.42.16.5/22. Since the network portions are not the same (166.42.14._/22 is different from 166.42.16._/22), the destination will be compared with entries in the routing table. If there is a matching entry in the routing table, the packet is forwarded to that entry. For instance, if the routing table included the entry 166.42.16.5/22, the packet would be forwarded to that gateway. If there is no matching entry in the routing table, the packet will be sent to the default gateway for forwarding. When this process is complete, the resulting IP address (either destination IP address or gateway IP address) is then resolved to a physical address. This process uses the *Address Resolution Protocol* or ARP.

Physical Address Resolution

ARP, as discussed earlier, resolves IP addresses to physical addresses. ARP is used to resolve the next-hop IP address to a physical media access control (MAC) address. This is done using network broadcasts. The resolved MAC address is placed in the header of the packet as the destination MAC address.

ARP Cache

Just as a routing table is stored on the local host, so too is a list of the resolved IP to MAC addresses. This information is held in the ARP cache. Each time a request and resolution occur, both the sender and receiver store the other's IP to MAC address mapping. When a packet is received, the ARP cache is checked to see if the resolution has already been added to the cache. If so, the packet is immediately forwarded to the resolved address. If the ARP cache does not contain the listing, a process must be initiated to resolve the IP address to the MAC address. Resolved entries are stored for a specified period of time and then discarded. If the same IP address is used within the specified time frame, the MAC address is already known and the packet is simply forwarded. If the ARP cache entry has expired, it no longer exists and the discovery process must be used, even if the MAC address was previously discovered.

ARP Process

There are two steps involved in resolving the IP to MAC address: the *ARP Request* and *ARP Reply*. The node responsible for forwarding the packet (either the sender or a gateway) will use the ARP Request message to request the MAC address for the next-hop IP address. The format of the ARP Request is a MAC-level broadcast that is sent to all nodes on the same physical segment as the sender. Whichever node sends the ARP Request message is called the *ARP requester*.

The ARP Reply is the return process. The node whose address matches the MAC address in the ARP Request will respond by sending an ARP Reply. This is a unicast (directly back to the sender only) MAC frame sent by the node called the *ARP responder*. The ARP responder's unicast message contains both its IP address and its MAC address.

Once this process is complete, both nodes now have new information about an IP address and the associated MAC address. This information is stored in the ARP cache for a specified amount of time. When it expires, if this address is needed again, the same Request and Reply process is used.

EXAM WARNING

The process of resolving an address to its physical (MAC) address is a very important one and is likely to be the subject of at least one exam question. Typically, questions have to do with how ARP actually resolves the address. Remember that the *ARP Request* is a broadcast datagram and the *ARP Reply* is a unicast datagram. Datagrams, unlike other messages, do not require the ACK message to acknowledge receipt. The broadcast datagram is sent out to all hosts, which process the ARP Request. If a host's IP address matches the ARP Request, it sends an ARP Reply. The ARP Reply is a unicast because it is sent from the matching host directly back to the requesting host. No other hosts receive this datagram. If it does not match the request, the ARP Request is simply discarded. You may see a question on the exam that incorporates these facts.

Inverse ARP

On nonbroadcast-based multiple access (NBMA) networks, such as wide area technologies including ATM, frame relay, and X.25, the network interface address is not the MAC address. Instead, it is a virtual circuit. In these cases, the IP address is mapped to the virtual circuit over which the packet is traveling. In resolving addresses in NBMA networks, the virtual circuit identifier is known but the receiving node's IP address is not. Inverse ARP (InARP) is used to resolve the IP address on the other end of the virtual circuit. InARP was specifically designed for frame relay circuits. InARP uses a query on each virtual circuit to determine the IP address of the interface on the other end. A table is built using the results of these queries for use in resolving addresses in NBMA networks.

NOTE

Don't confuse inverse ARP with reverse ARP (RARP).

Proxy ARP

Proxy ARP occurs when one node answers ARP Requests on behalf of another node. This is typically the case in subnets where no router is present. An ARP Proxy device is placed between nodes on the network. This device is aware of all nodes on its physical segment and can respond to ARP Requests and facilitate the forwarding of packets on the network. An ARP Proxy device is often a routing device but it does not act as an IP router.

Static and Dynamic IP Routers

Routing tables can be updated manually or dynamically. If the table must be updated manually, it is considered to be *static*. If the table can be updated automatically, it is considered to be *dynamic.* Static routing works well in small environments but does not scale well to larger networks. Another useful application of static routing is in subnets that are separated from the rest of the network. Rather than using routing protocols across WAN connections, static routes can be entered manually at both the main office and remote office routers to make each network segment reachable. A third common use of static routes is to connect a network to the Internet. A Windows Server 2003 computer can be used as a static router when it is configured as a multihomed computer. This entails installing two or more network interface cards, each with a separate IP address and subnet mask. Static routes can then be configured for the two (or more) networks directly attached to the multihomed computer.

Configuring & Implementing…

Static Routes in Multihomed Windows Server 2003-based Computers

If you use default routing, you may be tempted to configure a default gateway on *each* of the network interface cards in your multihomed computer. However, you should only configure a default route for the NIC attached to the network that contains the router you want to use on the default route. Configuring multiple default routes on multiple NICs can cause undesirable behavior. The result of setting multiple default routes in this manner is that there will be several routes with exactly the same metric. Thus, TCP/IP will select the route associated with the first NIC binding. When this occurs, the route selected actually may not be the best route to use.

If you choose to set up a multihomed computer as a static IP router, you'll also need to enable the Routing and Remote Access service. To do this, you must set the IpEnableRouter key in the registry to 1. Use the following path to set this registry value:

```
HKEY_LOCAL_MACHINE\System\CurrentControlSet\Services\Tcpip\

    Parameters\IpEnableRouter
```

When you've enabled static routing via the registry key value, add the appropriate routes to your routing table through Routing and Remote Access administrative tool or via the **route add** command at the command prompt. For parameters used in the **route add** command, type **route ?** (there is a space between the word **route** and the question mark) at the command prompt (**cmd**) for a list of the available commands.

Exercise 1.04

Enabling Static Routing on a Multihomed Windows Server 2003 Computer

Even if the computer you are working on does not have two NICs cards installed, you can walk through the process of setting up a multihomed computer as a static router. This exercise also helps you become more familiar with working in the registry. Remember, you should work in the registry *with extreme care*. Inadvertently changing values in the registry can make your computer unstable or even unusable. Therefore, it is highly recommended to back up your registry before making changes. We'll walk through the steps in this exercise to help you become familiar with this process.

1. Click **Start | Run** and type **regedt32** in the **Run** dialog box. The 16-bit equivalent (for older Windows operating systems that use the registry) is the command is **regedit**.

2. The Registry Editor opens with the registry HKEYs displayed on the left and related values on the right.

3. To export the registry, which can be used to restore the registry if you inadvertently make changes that impact your system, click **File | Export**. An *Export Registry File* dialog box opens, allowing you to select the location to which you want to save the registry file. The registry file can be a large file, so you most likely do not want to save this file repeatedly without removing old, unneeded files. Note that there are backup and emergency restore routines that save the registry that can be used to restore it as well. The method described here is simply one quick method of creating a registry backup.

4. Select the location to which you'd like to save the registry file and provide a desired registry name in the **Save as type** box. The .REG extension will automatically be appended to the name you select. Then click **Save**.

5. If you (or someone else) have worked in the registry previously, the HKEYs may already be expanded. Collapse the listing by clicking on any – (minus) signs shown in the left side of the registry. The default setting shows the five HKEYs, each with a + (plus sign) to the left of the key.

6. Click the + to the left of HKEY_LOCAL_MACHINE. You'll see five listings beneath this key: HARDWARE, SAM, SECURITY, SOFTWARE, SYSTEM.

7. Click the + to the left of SYSTEM. A list beneath SYSTEM is displayed.

8. Click the + to the left of CurrentControlSet.

9.   Click the + to the left of Services. When you expand services, it's likely the list is so long that it will not be completely contained in the left pane of the window. Use the scroll bar between the left and right panes of the window to navigate.

10. Scroll down to locate **Tcpip** and click the + to the left of **Tcpip** to expand the list.

11. Click the word **Parameters** under **Tcpip**. When you click on that registry key, a list of values is displayed in the right pane of the window, as seen in Figure 1.10.

12. Locate IPEnableRouter in the list on the right. When you locate it, double-click the word **IpEnableRouter**. Alternately, once you have selected the desired value, you can click **Edit | Modify** or you can right-click the value and select **Modify** from the shortcut menu.

13. When you choose Modify, the Edit DWORD Value dialog box opens and shows both the value name that you selected and the value data. The default value data for IpEnableRouter is 0. To enable static routing in a multihomed computer, type the number **1** (one) in the Value data box and click **OK**. If you do not want to change this value, click **Cancel** to exit without saving any changes.

14. You will notice that the data shown to the right of the IpEnableRouter now appears as 0 x 00000001 (1) instead of the default setting 0x00000000(0).

15. If desired, collapse the listing on the left side by clicking any minus (–) signs present.

16. Click **File | Exit**. If you've made changes, you will not be prompted or reminded and there is no **File | Save As** command available. For this reason, it is important to back up your registry file before making changes if there is any doubt at all about working in the registry.

Dynamic routing occurs when routing tables are automatically and periodically updated. Dynamic routers rely upon routing protocols. The two most commonly used routing protocols, both supported by Windows Server 2003's RRAS, are:

- Routing Information Protocol (RIP)
- Open Shortest Path First (OSPF)

Figure 1.10 Using the Registry Editor

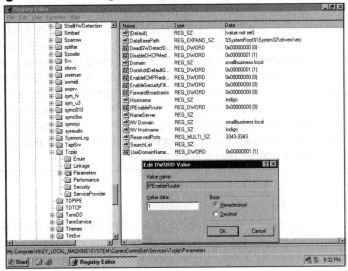

RIP was originally designed for use on classful networks. RIP is a distance vector routing protocol and determines routes based on number of hops (how many routers it must pass through). Any route more than 15 hops away is considered unreachable. For this reason, RIP does not scale well to large networks. RIP routing tables are dynamically updated using a route-advertising mechanism.

In contrast to RIP, OSPF is a link state routing protocol. The method of dynamically updating routing information is through link state advertisements (LSAs) that have information containing both the connected networks and their costs. The *cost* of each router interface is determined by the administrator in order to use best connections first. The combined cost of a connection using this classless routing protocol must be less than 65,535.

A Windows Server 2003 computer can be configured as a dynamic router, using either of these protocols. As with static configurations, multiple NICs must be installed and the RRAS must be enabled. In dynamic routing, default routes are seldom used. Thus, it is not necessary to configure a default gateway on any NIC. When the RRAS is enabled, static routing is enabled. To enable dynamic routing, add the RIP and OSPF protocols and enable them on your NICs by adding your NICs to the appropriate routing protocol. RIP is more appropriate for small-to-medium networks and OSPF is appropriate for large networks. Therefore, you are most likely to enable one or the other protocol, depending on your network configuration.

EXAM WARNING

One or more questions about routing protocols may come up on the exam. Remember that RIP and OSPF both support dynamic routing but RIP is not a good choice for a larger network. Look for questions that may include more than 16 hops—you'll immediately know that RIP can't be used in this case. Since OSPF was specifically designed for frame relay circuits, questions about OSPF will likely revolve around frame relay as opposed to other NBMA types of networks. Also keep in mind that a multihomed computer must have the Routing and Remote Access service enabled to function as a router, and that it sets up static routing by default. The only way dynamic routing occurs is if you install the RIP or OSPF protocols and bind your NIC to them.

Routing Utilities

There are four commonly used routing utilities. Each typically is run from the command line (**Start | Run | cmd**). The specific command line options available are displayed when the command is typed in at the prompt. See Figure 1.11 for an example of the command line options available for the **tracert** and **ping** commands.

- **route** Used to view and modify the entries in the routing table.
- **ping** Used to verify reachability of intended destinations using ICMP Echo messages.
- **tracert** Used to send ICMP Echo messages to discover the path between a node and a destination.
- **pathping** Used to discover the path between a host and destination or to identify high-loss links.

Figure 1.11 *Route* and *Ping* Command Line Options

```
C:\WINDOWS\system32\cmd.exe

Microsoft Windows [Version 5.2.3790]
(C) Copyright 1985-2003 Microsoft Corp.

C:\Documents and Settings\Administrator>tracert

Usage: tracert [-d] [-h maximum_hops] [-j host-list] [-w timeout]
               [-R] [-S srcaddr] [-4] [-6] target_name

Options:
    -d                 Do not resolve addresses to hostnames.
    -h maximum_hops    Maximum number of hops to search for target.
    -j host-list       Loose source route along host-list (IPv4-only).
    -w timeout         Wait timeout milliseconds for each reply.
    -R                 Trace round-trip path (IPv6-only).
    -S srcaddr         Source address to use (IPv6-only).
    -4                 Force using IPv4.
    -6                 Force using IPv6.

C:\Documents and Settings\Administrator>ping

Usage: ping [-t] [-a] [-n count] [-l size] [-f] [-i TTL] [-v TOS]
            [-r count] [-s count] [[-j host-list] | [-k host-list]]
            [-w timeout] [-R] [-S srcaddr] [-4] [-6] target_name

Options:
    -t                 Ping the specified host until stopped.
                       To see statistics and continue - type Control-Break;
                       To stop - type Control-C.
    -a                 Resolve addresses to hostnames.
    -n count           Number of echo requests to send.
    -l size            Send buffer size.
    -f                 Set Don't Fragment flag in packet (IPv4-only).
    -i TTL             Time To Live.
    -v TOS             Type Of Service (IPv4-only).
    -r count           Record route for count hops (IPv4-only).
    -s count           Timestamp for count hops (IPv4-only).
    -j host-list       Loose source route along host-list (IPv4-only).
    -k host-list       Strict source route along host-list (IPv4-only).
    -w timeout         Timeout in milliseconds to wait for each reply.
    -R                 Trace round-trip path (IPv6-only).
    -S srcaddr         Source address to use (IPv6-only).
    -4                 Force using IPv4.
    -6                 Force using IPv6.

C:\Documents and Settings\Administrator>
```

A very common use of the ping utility is to check connectivity from one computer to another. From your computer, you can run the ping utility from the command window. You can ping using an IP address or host name. If your computer cannot connect to the network, you can try to ping a known server or another computer (by IP address or name) on your network. If that does not work, the next step is to ping the local computer, which tests the internal network communication functions of your computer (NIC and TCP/IP stack) by using the following command: **ping localhost** or **ping 127.0.0.1** (the loopback address). If this fails, the problem is with the configuration of the TCP/IP stack on your computer. If pinging the loopback address is successful, the problem is probably external to the NIC.

Exam Warning

Before exam day, try each of these utilities on a networked computer. Once you see how the utility works and what the return values are, you'll have a much clearer idea of how each is used. Scenarios based on using these utilities may trip you up if you're not certain which utility has which function. Memorize the functions of these four utilities. You'll probably see one or more of them used in a network scenario.

Conclusion

IP routing involves using both direct and indirect routes to deliver packets to their intended destinations. Static and dynamic routing tables are used to determine how to best send the packet. With the use of the IP protocol and other associated protocols (Application layer protocols, UDP datagrams, ICMP messages, routing protocols), messages are reliably and quickly encoded, sent, and decoded. Many of the topics covered in this section will be discussed in even greater detail in subsequent chapters of this book.

Example of a Simple Classful Network

Class A, B, and C networks are often subnetted to increase efficiency of the network. Broadcasts are kept on local subnets, preventing wider distribution of broadcast traffic, and IP data that is intended for a host on the local subnet is kept local and not passed across a router. Routing tables are used to determine how an IP packet will be sent. If its destination IP address matches the local network, the data is sent to the destination host. If the address does not match the local network ID, the packet is sent to the router, or gateway for forwarding. Figure 1.12 shows two segments of a Class B network and a sample routing table for a host on Subnet A.

Figure 1.12 Example of Classful Network and Routing Table

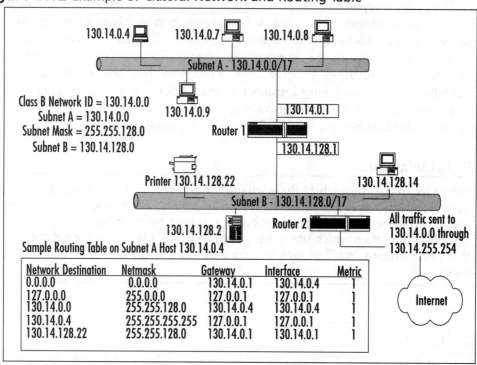

The routing table contains several entries that should look familiar. The first entry is the default route, which is used if no other entries in the routing table match the destination IP's network ID. Notice that the gateway is Router 1 and the interface is the IP address for the host. The second entry in the routing table is the loopback address, which is the same for each host. The third entry is for the directly attached network. The Class B network ID is 130.14.0.0 with a subnet mask of 255.255.128.0. Data intended for the directly attached network is not forwarded to a router but is delivered directly to the destination IP address from the source address. The gateway and interface IP addresses are set to the host IP address to indicate the data originated at the host. The next entry, 130.14.0.4 is the host address. Data sent from the host to the host is looped back, as reflected by the gateway and interface addresses of 127.0.0.1. Finally, a route exists to the printer on Subnet B. The destination IP address is on the other subnet and the gateway and interface addresses are those belonging to Router 1.

As you can see, classful subnetting and routing is relatively easy to understand conceptually but can be quite complex in its implementation. Understanding these foundation concepts will help you as we move into more detail throughout this book.

Summary of Exam Objectives

Understanding TCP/IP from the ground up is required to effectively manage a Windows Server 2003-based computer. TCP/IP is a suite of protocols originally developed by the Department of Defense in a project called the Advanced Research Projects Agency (DARPA). The first wide area network implemented using these protocols was called the Advanced Research Projects Agency Network (ARPANET). It was during this time that TCP/IP was designed and developed as a standardized way for computers to communicate across a network.

From the DARPA experiment came the understanding that networking would become increasingly common—and increasingly complex. The OSI model was developed, based on the DARPA model, and approved by Open Systems Interconnection (OSI) subcommittee of the International Organization for Standardization (ISO). The OSI model defined seven layers for standard, reliable network communications: Physical, Data Link, Network, Transport, Session, Presentation, and Application. The acronym commonly used to remember this is (in reverse order): **A**ll **P**eople **S**eem **T**o **N**eed **D**ata **P**rocessing.

The TCP/IP protocol suite provides the functionality specified in the OSI model using the four related layers of the DoD model: Network Interface, Internet, Host-to-Host, and Application. The Network Interface maps to the Physical and Data Link layers; the Internet layer maps to the OSI's Network layer. The Host-to-Host layer maps to the Transport layer and DoD's Application layer maps to the Session, Presentation, and Application layers of the OSI model. Some of the more commonly known Application layer protocols are FTP, HTTP, POP3, WINS, DNS, and DHCP.

At the Internet layer is the Internet protocol used for addressing data for delivery across a network. Understanding IP addressing is a fundamental skill needed both on the job and for this exam. IP addresses are 32-bit addresses represented in dotted decimal format ($w.x.y.z$). The 32 bits contain both a network and host ID. To understand IP addressing, you must first understand how to convert the dotted decimal numbers into binary and back to decimal. In order to send data to the correct location, the IP address in the packet is compared, using bit-wise ANDing, to the subnet mask. If the result is the local network address, the packet stays on the local network. If ANDing indicates that the network address is external to the local network, the packet is forwarded to the defined default gateway for forwarding.

Network addresses were originally designed in a class-based system. Class A networks use the first octet (w) and have an address range of $1.x.y.z$ to $126.x.y.z$. Class B networks use the first two octets for the network ID and have an address range of $128.0.y.z$ to $191.255.y.z$. Class C networks use the first three octets for the network ID and have an address range of $192.0.0.z$ to $223.255.255.z$. Each class of network, when undivided, uses a default subnet mask, which identifies which bits of the IP address represent the network ID. The default subnet masks are: Class A: 255.0.0.0; Class B: 255.255.0.0; Class C: 255.255.255.0.

Classful networks can be subdivided for greater efficiency by reducing the number of hosts per segment and thus reducing network traffic. Subnetting requires the subdividing of the class-based network IDs using custom subnet masks. These are developed by using bits from the host address space. The number of subnets that can be created from the network ID depends on the number of bits taken from the host address space. There is an inverse relationship between the number of subnets and the number of hosts per subnet. Typically, organizations choose to have a maximum of 256 devices per subnet for the most efficient use of network bandwidth.

Packets destined for networks that are not local are forwarded using gateways or routers. IP routing involves resolving the hostname or NetBIOS name to an IP address and resolving the IP address to a MAC address. NetBIOS name resolution uses four different node types to resolve names to IP addresses: Broadcast (B-node), Peer-to-Peer (P-node), Mixed (M-node), and Hybrid (H-node). Names can also be resolved by using a hosts file or through the Domain Naming Service (DNS). Names must be resolved to IP addresses. The Address Resolution Protocol (ARP) is used to resolve the IP address to the Media Access Control (MAC) address that is unique to each Network Interface Card (NIC) manufactured.

Routing on a Windows Server 2003-based computer can be static or dynamic, depending on whether or not dynamic routing protocols are installed. Many computers designed as routers include this function but a Windows Server 2003 computer can be set up as a router by installing two NICs, enabling the Routing and Remote Access Service via the Registry and installing and configuring both the Routing Information Protocol (RIP) and Open Shortest Path First (OSPF) dynamic routing protocols. Four commonly used routing utilities are route, ping, tracert, and pathping. Each can be run from the command line in Windows. To get a list of parameters for each utility, type the command followed by the word **help**.

Understanding the details of the TCP/IP protocol suite is fundamental to managing computers in today's networked environment. Being able to subnet, assign IP addresses, create subnet masks, and set up routing are essential skills you'll need on the job and to successfully master the material on this exam.

Exam Objectives Fast Track

Understanding the Purpose and Function of Networking Models

- ☑ The Department of Defense (DoD) model was originally designed to share computer data across a wide area between several large, mainframe computers.

- ☑ The DoD's Advanced Research Projects Agency (DARPA) formed an internetworking experiment called ARPANET.

- ☑ The DoD model used four layers: Network Interface, Internet, Host-to-Host, and Application.

- ☑ The OSI model is based on the DoD model and has seven defined layers.

☑ The seven layers of the OSI model are Physical, Data Link, Network, Transport, Session, Presentation, Application.

☑ An acronym commonly used to remember the seven layers is All People Seem To Need Data Processing.

☑ Each layer of the OSI model is responsible for a specific set of network communication functions.

☑ FTP and Telnet are both implemented at the Application layer.

Understanding the TCP/IP Protocol Suite

☑ The TCP/IP Protocol Suite is modeled after the DARPA (DoD) model and is implemented at four layers.

☑ The four layers of TCP/IP are Network Interface, Internet, Host-to-Host, and Application.

☑ The Internet layer uses the Internet Protocol (IP) for network communication functions.

☑ The Host-to-Host layer uses the connection-based Transmission Control Protocol (TCP) and the connectionless User Datagram Protocol (UDP).

☑ NetBIOS over TCP and Windows Sockets are examples of Application layer interfaces.

Understanding IP Addressing

☑ IP addresses are 32-bit addresses expressed in dotted decimal notation of four octets, *w.x.y.z.*

☑ IP addresses contain the network address space followed by the host address space.

☑ Originally, IP addresses were assigned four classes: A, B, C, and D. Class E is considered experimental and is not supported in Windows Server 2003.

☑ The growth of networking required a new solution. CIDR was implemented as a classless addressing schema.

☑ Dotted decimal notation can be converted to its binary equivalent by using weighted binary bits notated with 2^n where *n* is the number of bits.

Understanding Subnet Masking

☑ Default subnet masks are defined for undivided Class A,B, C, and D networks.

☑ The default subnet masks for Class A, B, C, and D are, respectively, 255.0.0.0, 255.255.0.0, 255.255.255.0, and 255.255.255.255.

☑ Custom subnet masks (also called variable length subnet masks) are used when a network is divided, by using bits from the host address space that are added to the network address space.

☑ A logical bitwise AND comparison is used to compare the bits of the IP address to the subnet mask. The result of the comparison is the network ID.

Understanding Basic IP Routing

☑ Packets are sent with a destination name or IP address included in the packet headers.

☑ Name resolution occurs using WINS or an LMHOSTS file (for NetBIOS names) or DNS or a HOSTS file (for host names).

☑ NetBIOS name resolution occurs using one of four types of broadcasts: Broadcast node (B-node), Peer-to-Peer node (P-node), Mixed node (M-node), and Hybrid node (H-node).

☑ IP address resolution of host names occurs using Hosts files or DNS.

☑ IP address to MAC address resolution occurs through ARP Request and Reply messages. The reverse, MAC to IP resolution, uses Reverse ARP (RARP) Requests and Replies.

☑ Routers can use static or dynamic routing. Static routing requires new entries to be entered manually. Dynamic routing updates route information automatically.

☑ Dynamic routing in Windows Server 2003 uses Route Information Protocol (RIP) or Open Shortest Path First (OSPF) Protocol.

Exam Objectives
Frequently Asked Questions

The following Frequently Asked Questions, answered by the authors of this book, are designed to both measure your understanding of the Exam Objectives presented in this chapter, and to assist you with real-life implementation of these concepts. You will also gain access to thousands of other FAQs at ITFAQnet.com.

Q: How likely am I to see a question related to the DoD/DARPA model or ARPANET on the exam?

A: It's unusual to see a question directly related to these topics but you will see questions that rely upon your understanding of both the OSI model and the TCP/IP suite. Understanding the origins of these models will help you answer questions related to the networking models.

Q: Isn't ARPANET the same thing as the Internet? Why do I need to know this anyway?

A: ARPANET was the first working implementation of internetworking. The structures devised in the experiment as well as the knowledge gained during that project form the foundation of the Internet. The ARPANET was a network of a few mainframe computers and was not universally available, as the Internet is today, nor was it a commercial network (all nodes were located at universities or government agencies). It is possible that you'll see an exam question that uses ARPANET as an answer. Understanding the origins of the Internet can help you answer other questions on the exam, sometimes by simply helping you eliminate wrong answers.

Q: How exactly does the Network Interface layer of the DoD model map to the Physical and Data Link layers of the OSI model?

A: The DoD's Network Interface layer maps directly to the Physical and Data Link layers of the OSI model, with one notable exception. There are two parts to the Data Link layer—the Logical Link Control and the Media Access Control sublayers. TCP/IP does not implement the Logical Link Control element at the Network Interface layer. This function is handled further up the protocol stack at the Host-to-Host (Transport) layer.

Q: How likely am I to see questions on the exam related to media access control?

A: Remember that the exam typically includes a specific number of questions per topic. Also, Microsoft exams typically include more questions on technologies and features that are new to the exam topic being tested. In this case, it is expected to include many questions on new features of Windows Server 2003. That said, TCP/IP is a fundamental technology that must be well understood in order to effectively manage any Microsoft network. You will see questions on TCP/IP, especially on subnetting. If you see a specific question on media access control, the information in this chapter should be sufficient for you to select the correct answer.

Q: There are a lot of Application layer protocols in the TCP/IP suite. Am I expected to memorize them all?

A: There is an ever-expanding set of Application layer protocols in use today. It's important to get a firm understanding of the most common protocols and to have at least a familiarity with the less common protocols. At the very least, you should be very familiar with NetBIOS over TCP, Windows Sockets, DNS, DHCP, WINS, Telnet, SMTP, HTTP, FTP, RIP, and SNMP.

Q: I'm still a bit rusty with binary, dotted decimal, conversions, and so forth. Can't I use a program to do all this for me when I'm working on my corporate network?

A: Yes, there are programs available that will do all the conversions and subnet calculations you need. However, those won't be available on the exam and they may not always be available to you on the job. Keep working through the conversions and examples in this chapter until you feel confident of your understanding and application of the material. You may see only one or two questions or you may see five or ten questions on this topic. Remember, Microsoft exams are adaptive. This means that the content of each question is based on your answer to the previous question. If you're having trouble with subnetting, you're likely to see even more questions about it than will someone who has it down cold.

Q: Will I be given a table of Class A, B, and C networks, subnets and subnet masks for the exam?

A: No, you will not. You'll need to memorize the definitions of Class A, B, and C networks, along with their associated default subnet masks. You'll also be required to calculate subnets and resulting numbers and address ranges for subnets and hosts.

Q: Will I have access to a calculator with scientific notation to calculate a number such as 2^{12}?

A: You should have access to the default calculator provided in the Windows operating system. To switch to scientific notation to gain access to the $x^\wedge y$ function, click **View | Scientific.** If for some reason this is not available, you can use the standard calculator function and multiply the results. For instance, Bit 0 is 2^0 or 1, 2^1 is 2, 2^2 is 4, 2^3 is 8. Looking at the pattern, you could probably guess that 2^4 is 16 and 2^5 is 32. Continue doubling the previous value and incrementing the exponent to derive the number you need.

Q: Is bitwise ANDing really tested on the exam?

A: Yes, it is. You're not likely to see a question that says, "Use bitwise ANDing to compare…." Instead, you'll need to use bitwise ANDing to compare an IP address to a subnet mask to figure out the underlying network ID. There's a very good chance you'll see one or more of these questions on your exam.

Self Test

A Quick Answer Key follows the Self Test questions. For complete questions, answers, and explanations to the Self Test questions in this chapter as well as the other chapters in this book, see the Self Test Appendix.

Understanding the Purpose and Function of Networking Models

1. A beta version of an application you're testing to send and receive data on your network does not seem to be sending compressed data before sending packets across the network. You're looking at the architecture of the application to see if you can determine where the problem likely originates. Using the OSI model, from where is the problem probably originating?

   A. Transport layer

   B. Application layer

   C. Presentation layer

   D. Physical layer

2. Your firm is designing a new software driver that will employ a proprietary method of flow control for data being sent across a network medium. On which layer of the OSI model would be this flow control likely be implemented?

   A. Application

   B. Data Link

   C. Transport

   D. Media Access Control

Understanding the TCP/IP Protocol Suite

3. You disabled TCP Port 80 on your Windows Server 2003, which is also running Web services via IIS, in hopes of increasing security on your network. However, users are now complaining that they can't reach your Web site. What is the most likely result of your actions?

   A. Disabling TCP Port 80 has no effect on your Web site, there must be another problem.

   B. FTP uses Port 80 and therefore the FTP function for your Web site was disabled.

   C. HTTP uses TCP Port 80 and therefore the HTTP protocol was disabled.

   D. The users need to enable HTTP on their local machines in order for them to browse to the Web site.

4. A user notifies you that her computer is having trouble receiving e-mail via the corporate network. She has no trouble sending e-mail or connecting to files on public shares. She can also connect to the Internet. What would you check to begin troubleshooting this problem?

   A. Check to see if her computer is configured to use SMTP.

   B. Check to see if TCP/IP is installed on her computer.

   C. Check to see if she can ping localhost.

   D. Check to see if her computer is configured to use POP3.

Understanding IP Addressing

5. Your computer seems to have a problem with name resolution and you decide the problem may be in your hosts file. Your computer's IP address is 66.212.14.8. You open the hosts file and spot the likely problem. Which line from the hosts file is the most likely the cause of your name resolution problem?

   A. 66.214.41.1 router1

   B. 127.0.0.1 localhost

   C. 191.87.221.2 server.company.com pisces

   D. 66.212.14.8 localhost

6. You've just accepted a job at a small company as the IT Manager. The company network is not yet connected to the Internet and you've been asked to make this your top priority. You examine the IP addresses on several computers and find these addresses in use: 192.168.0.4, 192.168.0.19, 192.168.0.11. What is the next step you would have to take to connect your network to the Internet?

A. Purchase, configure, and install a server to act as a firewall for Internet connectivity.

B. Apply to the InterNIC for the appropriate IP address assignment.

C. Install and configure the common Internet protocols including SMTP, FTP, and HTTP.

D. Subnet the current network configuration using a custom Class C subnet mask.

7. A user contacts you to let you know his computer won't connect to the corporate network. You ask the user to go into his Network Connections properties and tell you both his IP address and subnet mask. He tells you his IP address is 180.10.254.36 and his subnet mask is 255.255.240.0. Based on this information, what is the correct binary representation of the network ID to which this user is connected?

A. 10110100.00001001.11110000.00000000

B. 10110100.00001010.11100000.00000000

C. 10110110.00001010.11110000.00000000

D. 10110100.00001010.11110000.00000000

8. Another IT staff person, Mike, tells you about a problem he's troubleshooting. He says that Jake's computer doesn't connect to the corporate network. The network uses DHCP to automatically assign IP addresses to computers, so he believes the IP address is correct and unique. He's tried pinging the localhost and that works fine but when he pings a server that is on the same subnet as Jake's computer, he gets an error message. What is the most likely cause of this problem?

A. Mike's NIC card has a duplicate IP address.

B. Mike's NIC card has a duplicate MAC address.

C. Mike's NIC card has no IP address.

D. Mike's Ethernet cable is loose.

9. You're designing a network scheme from a Class A network address. You want to be able to have about 16,000 hosts on each subnet. Based on this, what is the maximum number of host address bits you can take to still allow up to 16,000 hosts per subnet?

A. 8

B. 16

C. 24

D. 17

Understanding Subnet Masking

10. As you review your firm's subnetting scheme, you notice that it was originally set up with a Class C network ID of 198.255.8.0 and was subdivided to yield four subnets, three of which are in use. Based on this information, what are the starting addresses of the available subnets?

    A. 198.255.8.0; 198.255.8.64;198.255.8.128

    B. 198.255.8.64; 198.255.8.128; 198.255.8.192; 198.255.8.224

    C. 198.255.8.0; 198.255.8.64; 198.255.8.128; 198.255.8.192

    D. 198.255.8.0; 198.255.8.1; 198.255.8.2; 198.255.8.3

11. You're working on a subnetting problem and you notice a host with the IP address of 146.64.195.36 and a subnet mask of 255.0.0.0. You compare this to another computer whose IP address is 146.64.195.38 and subnet mask is 255.0.0.0. Although you're not sure what's wrong, you do know that the maximum number of hosts your subnet supports is 65,534. What is the most likely cause of your subnetting problem?

    A. The IP address is an illegal address.

    B. The network portion of the IP address is incorrect.

    C. The subnet mask is incorrect.

    D. The host portion of the IP address is incorrect.

12. The Class B network your firm was assigned needs to be subnetted. You have four divisions that are located in six cities around the U.S. You have approximately 5,000 employees, most of whom have computers on their desktops. In addition, you have approximately 47 servers and routers on your network. You want to create the most efficient network possible while providing for future growth, which is not yet quantified. Based on this information, what is the optimal number of bits to use for your subnetting task?

    A. 20

    B. 8

    C. 24

    D. 16

Understanding Basic IP Routing

13. A remote user reports that her computer doesn't seem to be able to connect to the corporate network. From your computer, you use the ping utilities to try to contact her computer, using its IP address. This returns the following message: "Packets: sent = 4, Received = 0, Lost = 4 (100% loss)." You also try pinging her computer by its name, *cooperjones*. Ping returns the following message: "Ping request could not find host cooperjones. Please check the name and try again." Based on these results, what would be your next logical step?

   A. Verify her IP address.

   B. Ask her to use the following command: **ping 127.0.0.1.**

   C. Ask her to use the following command: **ping 127.0.0.1 localhost.**

   D. Ask her to check her connection to the network cable.

14. You work for a very small company that has computers in two physical locations, which are not currently connected. You're tasked with connecting the two locations. You purchase a server to act as both a server for the organization and as a dynamic router. You add a second NIC, and install Windows Server 2003. After you've enabled Routing and Remote Access on the server, what is the next step you must take to configure this computer as a dynamic router?

   A. No additional steps. Once Routing and Remote Access is enabled, dynamic routing is enabled by default.

   B. Bind your NIC to RIP and OSPF.

   C. Add RIP and OSPF.

   D. Set a default gateway for each NIC.

15. You notice that there are two servers on your network with the same name: salero215. You use the route utility to view your routing table and see the following entries:

   196.6.14.5   salero215.building1.phoenix.somecompany.com salero215

   196.6.17.5   salero215.building1.tubac.somecompany.com salero215

   To solve this problem, you recommend the following change:

   A. Change the first listing to salero215a.building1.phoenix.somecompany.com salero215.

   B. Change the second listing to salero215.building2.tubac.somecompany.com.

   C. Change the first listing to salero215.building1.phoenix.somecompany.com.

   D. No change is needed. The FQDN for each server is unique.

Self Test Quick Answer Key

For complete questions, answers, and explanations to the Self Test questions in this chapter as well as the other chapters in this book, see the Self Test Appendix.

1.	**C**	9.	**B**
2.	**B**	10.	**C**
3.	**C**	11.	**C**
4.	**D**	12.	**C**
5.	**D**	13.	**B**
6.	**B**	14.	**C**
7.	**D**	15.	**C**
8.	**D**		

Chapter 2

MCSA/MCSE 70-291

Variable Length Subnet Masking and Client Configuration

Exam Objectives in this Chapter:

4.3.2   Manage Routing Tables.

- ☑   Summary of Exam Objectives
- ☑   Exam Objectives Fast Track
- ☑   Exam Objectives Frequently Asked Questions
- ☑   Self Test
- ☑   Self Test Quick Answer Key

Introduction

The explosive growth of networking and the Internet over the past decade has brought to light one of the few limitations of class-based, or classful, IP addressing. Under the current addressing scheme based on IPv4, Class A and B networks allow for a large number of hosts per network but fewer networks with unique network IDs, thus limiting the number of Class A and B networks in the world. Class C networks are more plentiful, but they are limited in the number of hosts allowed per network. As we learned in Chapter 1, there is always a trade off between the number of networks and the number of hosts you can have in the classful system.

In an effort to mitigate the looming shortage of unique public network addresses, two additional addressing schemes were devised:

- The first method subnets a network to yield more network segments with fewer hosts per segment. The subnets are not equal divisions of the subnet, but can be of various sizes. This is known as *variable length subnetting*, which uses a *Variable Length Subnet Mask* (VLSM) to define subnets of different sizes based on the original network ID.

- The second method combines unique network IDs into larger segments, essentially the reverse of subnetting, and is called *supernetting*.

In this chapter, we'll begin by reviewing how classful subnetting works and then we'll examine both variable length subnetting and supernetting. We'll also look at routing in Windows XP/Windows 2000 and routing in Windows Server 2003. We'll finish by discussing how to assign these IP addresses to clients on the network.

Review of Classful Subnet Masking

As you learned in Chapter 1, IP addresses use dotted decimal notation to represent four binary octets (groups of eight bits each), which can be expressed as *w.x.y.z*. Classful addressing works like this:

- Class A networks use the first (*w*) octet for the network address or ID and the remaining octets for host IDs.

- Class B networks use the first and second octets (*w.x*) to express the network address and the third and fourth octets for host addresses.

- Class C networks use the first three octets (*w.x.y*) to denote the network address and the last octet for host addresses.

To subnet a network, first you have to determine how many subnets you need for future use and how many hosts per subnet is optimal for your specific needs. Once you've determined this, you can devise a subnetting scheme that provides for a set number of fixed subnets with a set number of hosts. Let's look at one example, just as a refresher.

As you recall, the default subnet mask is the same for all undivided subnets in each class. The default Class A subnet mask is 255.0.0.0 and the default subnet mask for a Class C network is 255.255.255.0. Using a Class B network ID of 142.18.0.0, the default subnet mask is 255.255.0.0. If you want to divide this network into eight segments, you will need three bits from the host address space. First, determine how many subnets you need and determine how many bits you need to extend the network address space. You know that 2^3 = 8, so you can take the three highest order bits from the next octet (y) to extend the network address space. This yields up to eight subnets because there are eight possible combinations of the three bits, as shown in Table 2.1.

Table 2.1 Binary Combinations Using Three Bits

Combination	Binary Representation
1	000
2	001
3	010
4	011
5	100
6	101
7	110
8	111

This configuration can be represented as 142.18.0.0/19. Each subnet can have the same maximum number of hosts. This can be calculated by using the formula $2^n - 2$, where n is the number of bits available for host addresses. In this case, you have an assigned Class B network ID, which, by definition uses 16 bits. You should have taken three bits from the host address space, leaving 13 bits ($32 - 19 = 13$) for host addresses. Thus, you have a maximum of ($2^{13} - 2$), or 8190 host addresses per subnet.

You must also define the eight subnet address ranges. To do this, use the bit combinations devised previously and convert those into dotted decimal format, as shown in Table 2.2. The three bits taken from the host address space are shown in bold.

Table 2.2 Dotted Decimal Values for Third Octet

Combinations for Third Octet	Binary Representation	Third Octet Dotted Decimal
1	**000**00000	0
2	**001**00000	32
3	**010**00000	64
4	**011**00000	96
5	**100**00000	128

Continued

Table 2.2 Dotted Decimal Values for Third Octet

Combinations for Third Octet	Binary Representation	Third Octet Dotted Decimal
6	10100000	160
7	11000000	192
8	11100000	224

You now have the starting address for each of eight subnets. Each subnet begins with the first address (derived from the third octet values in Table 2.2) and ends one address before the next beginning address. The beginning and ending address ranges are shown in Table 2.3. As you can see, the third octet value is the beginning address range and the ending address range is one less than the next beginning address.

Table 2.3 Subnet Address Ranges

Combinations for Third Octet	Binary Representation	Third Octet Dotted Decimal	Beginning Address	Ending Address
1	00000000	0	142.18.0.0	142.18.31.254
2	00100000	32	142.18.32.0	142.18.63.254
3	01000000	64	142.18.64.0	142.18.95.254
4	01100000	96	142.18.96.0	142.18.127.254
5	10000000	128	142.18.128.0	142.18.159.254
6	10100000	160	142.18.160.0	142.18.191.254
7	11000000	192	142.18.192.0	142.18.223.254
8	11100000	224	142.18.224.0	142.18.239.254

Based on this configuration, you can also determine the subnet mask needed to differentiate the network address from the host address on the subnets. Since you are using a total of 19 bits for your network ID, you must use a subnet mask that sets the left-most 19 bits to 1. This is represented as 11111111.11111111.11100000.00000000 and can be shown in dotted decimal format as 255.255.224.0.

Bitwise ANDing is used to compare a specific IP address with the subnet mask to find the network ID. Using the same example, you can randomly select an IP address from within the ranges specified in Table 2.3 and use bitwise ANDing to find the underlying network ID.

IP address	142.18.33.66	10001110.00010010.0010001.01000010
Subnet mask	255.255.224.0	11111111.11111111.1110000.00000000
Result	142.18.32.0	10001110.00010010.0010000.00000000

You can see by comparing the result to Table 2.3 that the IP address 142.18.33.66 falls within the range 142.18.32.0 to 142.18.63.254 and the network ID corresponds to the beginning address of that range.

Subnetting takes assigned network addresses and subdivides them for more efficient networking configurations. Each subnet is of equal size. In the previous example, you saw that taking three bits from the host address space resulted in eight subnets each, with up to 8190 host IP addresses per subnet. You could instead have subdivided it to yield up to 16 subnets with a possible 4,094 host addresses per subnet.

EXERCISE 2.01

SUBNETTING REVIEW

In this exercise, we're going to walk through a subnetting scenario to reinforce what you've learned about classful subnetting. Using the network address 134.40.0.0 and the default subnet mask, you will create subnets that will allow for no more than 2,150 hosts per subnet. You'll determine the number of subnets, address ranges, the subnet mask, and the number of network bits used.

1. 134.40.0.0 is a Class B network using 16 network bits by default. This can support up to 65,534 hosts before subnetting. You know that 134.40.0.0 is a Class B subnet because the first octet falls between 128 and 191. As you recall, Class B networks must have the two left-most bits of the first (w) octet set to 10. This means that it must be higher than 128. In addition, you know that Class C networks have the first octet with the three left-most bits set to 110. This means that the Class B range ends at (128 + 64) − 1, or 191. Therefore, you know that you are working with a Class B network.

2. Now that you've determined that you have a Class B network, you can determine the default subnet mask. For a Class B network, the default subnet mask is 255.255.0.0.

3. The total number of hosts is determined by the default configuration. By definition, a Class B network uses 16 bits for the network address space, therefore it has 16 bits left for host addressing. Using our formula, you can calculate $2 \wedge 16$ (or 2^{16}), which equals 65,536. Host IDs of all 0s or all 1s are prohibited, so you have 65,534 possible addresses for use on this network.

4. Next, you need to determine how to subnet this Class B network so that you end up with no more than 2,150 hosts per subnet. You can determine that in one of two ways. The longhand method starts with the right-most bit of the fourth octet (z) and proceeds to the left. Each bit position is double the previous one. Therefore, you can continue

counting bits to the left until the value approaches 2,150. For instance, the values (beginning on the right and moving to the left) are 1, 2, 4, 8, 16, 32, 64, 128, 256, 1024, 2048, 4096, 8192, and so forth. If you count the number of bits, you will see that you need 11 host address bits. Using 12 bits would give you 4,096 addresses, exceeding the maximum stipulated. Remember, too, that 2,048 (2^11) results in 2,046 useable host IP addresses since host addresses cannot be all 0s or all 1s.

5.   A second method you can use to calculate this is by looking at the total number of host addresses (65,536) and using logic to help you estimate the number of bits you'll need. You already know that each bit you borrow from the host addresses reduces the number of hosts per subnet by half. If you start with 16 bits for host addresses and take 1 bit, the number of host addresses available goes down to 32,768. Take a second bit and it drops to 16,384. Take a third bit and the number of host addresses are reduced to 8,192. The fourth bit taken results in 4,096 addresses and the fifth bit taken yields 2,048 addresses. This meets the requirement of no more than 2,150 hosts per subnet. Thus, you have taken five bits away from the host space, resulting in (16 − 5) = 11 host address bits.

6.   If you use 11 bits for the host address space, you know you have 21 bits (32 − 11) for the network address space. To determine how many networks you will have, each with a maximum of 2,048 host addresses, you need to calculate the value of the *additional* network bits. *This is an important distinction*. Remember, by default you're already using 16 bits (octets *w* and *x*) for the network ID. Although there are 21 bits available for network addresses, you are *extending* the network address space by *five bits*, which you've borrowed from the host address space. Thus, the calculation is 2^5 (or 2^5) rather than 2^21. Calculating 2^5 results in 32, so you can create 32 subnets that each have no more than 2,150 host addresses. This meets the requirements. To be more precise, however, you can create 32 total subnets each with a maximum of 2,046 host addresses available on each subnet.

7.   You can check your math by multiplying 32 (number of subnets) x 2,048 (remember that you have 2,048 addresses, of which 2,046 can be used), which equals 65,536. If you came out with more addresses than you started with, you would know that you'd made an error in your calculations or logic.

8.   The default subnet mask of 255.255.0.0 will no longer work, because you have extended the network address space. You'll recall that the subnet mask is used to identify which bits of the 32-bit IP address represent the network ID. You've extended the network address by five

bits, so you need to create a new subnet mask that reflects this change. To do this, you can calculate the value of the bits or, if necessary, write it out in binary notation and then calculate the dotted decimal value. Let's look at both methods.

9. Taking the left-most bits of the third octet (y) from the host address space results in the following bits being set to 1: 128, 64, 32, 16, 8. Adding those together equals 248. Thus, the third octet of the subnet mask is 248, resulting in a new subnet mask for your subnetted Class B network of 255.255.248.0.

10. You can also figure this out by setting the appropriate bits and then converting to decimal. The original network bits are shown in **bold** and the extended bits (borrowed from the host address space) are <u>underlined</u>.

    11111111.11111111.<u>11111</u>000.00000000 = 255.255.248.0

11. Now you have determined the correct number of subnets, maximum host addresses per subnet, and the new subnet mask. The last required task is to determine the address ranges for your new subnets. The network can be notated as 134.40.0.0/21 and the addresses will increment based on the lowest value of the borrowed bits. As you saw, the bit values are 128, 64, 32, 16, and 8. Therefore, each subnet will increment by eight. You can write this out in binary notation to help visualize the process. The right-most *network* bit is shown <u>underlined</u>. Begin by incrementing this bit from 0 to 1.

    134.40.0.0 =   10000110.00100010.00000<u>0</u>00.00000000

    134.40.8.0 =   10000110.00100010.00001<u>0</u>00.00000000

    134.40.16.0 =   10000110.00100010.0001<u>0</u>000.00000000

    134.40.32.0 =   10000110.00100010.0001<u>1</u>000.00000000

    ...

    134.40.240.0 =   10000110.00100010.1111<u>0</u>000.00000000

    134.40.248.0 =   10000110.00100010.1111<u>1</u>000.00000000

The use of three dots (ellipses, shown as ...) indicates information that is omitted. It's clear that the sequence continues but each individual value is not delineated. This saves space and can be used when the pattern is clearly established.

Variable Length or Nonclassful (Classless) Subnet Masking

In classful subnetting, each subnet has the same number of host addresses. In many cases, this is not an optimal solution because we often need some segments that have only a few IP addresses and other segments that have hundreds. For example, administrators commonly group resources that are in physical proximity to one another on the same segment. However, you might want routers and gateways on small segments that are isolated from the rest of the network through subnetting. With classful subnetting, you have only one option: subdividing the network into equal sized segments. This results in one of two situations:

- You can create subnets with thousands of host addresses to meet the largest host addressing requirement.

- You can create subnets with few host addresses to meet the smallest host addressing requirement.

In either case, the network configuration is not optimized.

The ability to create variable length subnets provides you with the flexibility you need to configure network subnets to your organization's specifications without wasting IP addresses. If you have three segments in your network that need only four IP addresses, subnets that allow 8,190 host addresses waste 8,186 IP addresses on each of those segments. Subdividing a network into subnets of various sizes with varying numbers of hosts is called *variable length subnetting* or *nonclassful subnetting*.

Variable length subnetting is a process by which subnets are further divided into smaller segments, as shown in Figure 2.1. You can see that the network is divided into subnets of various sizes. This process is also called *recursive* subnetting because you can continue to subdivide subnets repeatedly. This allows you to take any number of classful subnets and divide them into smaller subnets of varying sizes. For instance, if you divide a network into 8 subnets, you can create 16 smaller subnets that allow only 4 host addresses, 32 smaller subnets that allow 254 host addresses, and 2 subnets that are not further divided that allow 8,190 host addresses. Even after you've done all that, you can still have additional subnets reserved for future use. This type of scheme is far more useful in real world implementations than fixed, or classful, subnetting.

Figure 2.1 Variable Length Subnetting Concept

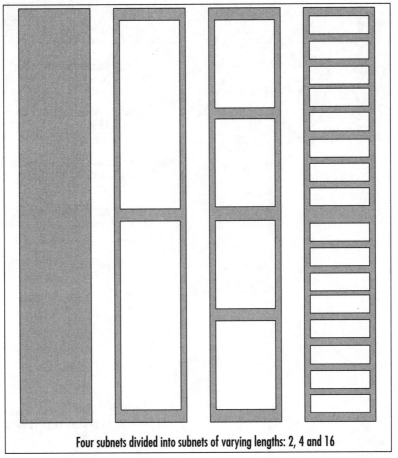

Four subnets divided into subnets of varying lengths: 2, 4 and 16

Variable length subnetting relies upon the subnet mask to differentiate the network address space from the host address space, just as with classful subnetting. This is accomplished in the same way that you configured a classful subnet mask. However, you start with the subnet mask used on the original subnet, not with the default subnet mask. As you subdivide a subnet, you add bits to the network address space, and therefore also to the subnet mask, to indicate the new subnetting scheme. Figure 2.2 shows how several subnets can be subdivided into several smaller (and varying) subnets. In the following sections, we'll look at examples for Class A, B, and C type networks so that you can better understand how variable length subnets can be formed.

Figure 2.2 Network Divided into Variable Length Subnets

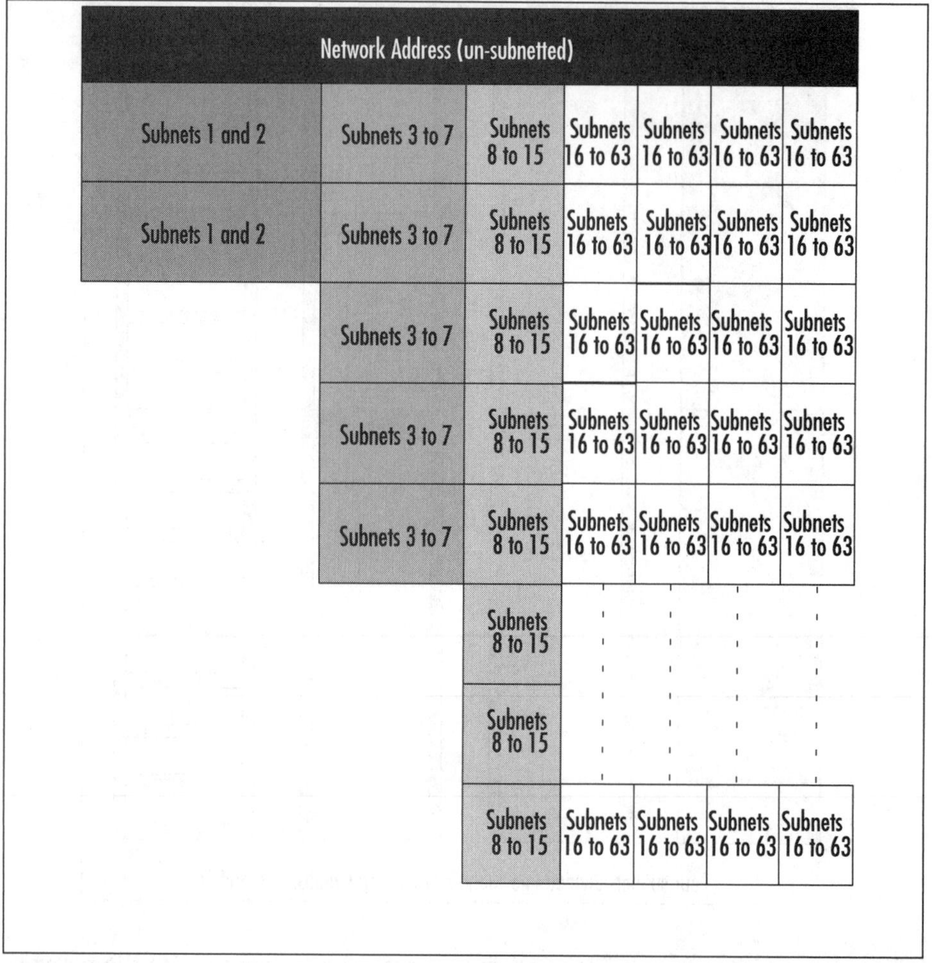

Network Address (un-subnetted)						
Subnets 1 and 2	Subnets 3 to 7	Subnets 8 to 15	Subnets 16 to 63	Subnets 16 to 63	Subnets 16 to 63	Subnets 16 to 63
Subnets 1 and 2	Subnets 3 to 7	Subnets 8 to 15	Subnets 16 to 63	Subnets 16 to 63	Subnets 16 to 63	Subnets 16 to 63
	Subnets 3 to 7	Subnets 8 to 15	Subnets 16 to 63	Subnets 16 to 63	Subnets 16 to 63	Subnets 16 to 63
	Subnets 3 to 7	Subnets 8 to 15	Subnets 16 to 63	Subnets 16 to 63	Subnets 16 to 63	Subnets 16 to 63
	Subnets 3 to 7	Subnets 8 to 15	Subnets 16 to 63	Subnets 16 to 63	Subnets 16 to 63	Subnets 16 to 63
		Subnets 8 to 15				
		Subnets 8 to 15				
		Subnets 8 to 15	Subnets 16 to 63	Subnets 16 to 63	Subnets 16 to 63	Subnets 16 to 63

All 0s and All 1s Addressing

In earlier versions of Windows, subnets using all 0s or all 1s were not allowed because early routers were not able to handle these addresses. Modern routers do not have a problem with this, so in Windows Server 2003, these special subnets are allowed in a classless environment. This change is in accordance with an Internet standard published through a technical specification called Request For Comment (RFC) 1812. RFCs are managed by the Internet Engineering Task Force (IETF).

RFC 1812 allows the use of all 0s and all 1s subnets in classless environments because routing protocols advertise the subnet mask with the network ID, which makes 129.17.0.0/19 distinguishable from 129.17.0.0/21.

New & Noteworthy...

Example of Subnetting a Class A Network

You know that Class A networks use the first octet as the network address and the remaining three octets for host address spaces. In a Class A network that is not subnetted, you can have one network and up to 16,777,214 host addresses. Even if you subdivide the network into 8,000 subnets, you would still have up to 2,046 host addresses per subnet. This is not an optimal solution if 1400 of your subnets need only four host addresses. Instead, you can recursively subdivide subnets to sizes more appropriate for your needs. Let's examine a sample scenario to see exactly how this works.

A company is assigned a Class A network address of 66.0.0.0/8. The default subnet mask is 255.0.0.0. The company has the following minimum requirements:

- Half the addresses must be reserved for future use.

- Twelve networks are required with 8,190 hosts per subnet.

- Ten networks are required with 2,046 hosts per subnet.

- Five networks are required with 254 hosts per subnet.

In the following sections, we break these requirements down and address each of them individually.

Requirement #1:
Reserve Half the Addresses for Future Use

To save half the addresses for future use, you can divide the network into two subnets, use one subnet for your current addressing needs and leave the other one for future use. Your current addresses run from 66.0.0.0/8 to 66.255.255.254/8. An approximate midpoint in this range is 66.128.0.0/9. By dividing the network in half, you save half of all possible addresses for future use. Keep in mind that any addressing scheme that goes past 66.129.0.0 will violate this requirement. This means you have the addresses from 66.0.0.0 through 66.128.255.254 to work with to meet your additional requirements.

Requirement #2:
Twelve Networks with 8,190 Hosts per Subnet

The current configuration gives you one network address (which is a subnet of your original network ID) with a range of 66.0.0.0/9. How do you now create 12 subnets with 8,190 hosts each? You need 13 bits for the host addresses ($2^{13} - 2 = 8190$). That leaves a maximum of 19 bits for the network address space. However, you need to determine how many bits to use. If you create too many of these networks, it might hinder your flexibility later on. You know that there is a trade off between network addresses and host addresses. You can assume, given the requirements, that the largest number of hosts you'll want on any given subnet is 8,190. Using the current configuration, 66.0.0.0/9, and the upper limitation of 66.129.0.0/9, you can subdivide this subnet by using a total of 19 network bits. Each of these subnets can be further divided, if desired, to better utilize this address space. The proper subnet delineation is shown in Table 2.4. As discussed earlier, the ellipses (…) are used to indicate that the entire sequence is not shown but continues in the established pattern.

Table 2.4 Class A Subnet with 8,190 Host Addresses

Class A Subnet Address	Binary Representation
66.0.0.0/19	01000010.00000000.00000000.00000000
66.0.32.0/19	01000010.00000000.00100000.00000000
66.0.64.0/19	01000010.00000000.01000000.00000000
66.0.96.0/19	01000010.00000000.01100000.00000000
66.0.128.0/19	01000010.00000000.10000000.00000000
66.0.160.0/19	01000010.00000000.10100000.00000000
66.0.192.0/19	01000010.00000000.11000000.00000000
…	…
66.127.224.0/19	01000010.01111111.11100000.00000000

The host address ranges available in the first subnet are 66.0.0.1/15 through 66.0.31.254/19. This subnet yields 8,190 host addresses. Therefore, to meet the requirement of 12 subnets, you should use the starting subnet addresses shown in Table 2.5.

Table 2.5 Starting Addresses for 12 Subnets

No.	Starting Address	No.	Starting Address
1	66.0.0.0/19	7	66.0.192.0/19
2	66.0.32.0/19	8	66.0.224.0/19
3	66.0.64.0/19	9	66.1.0.0/19
4	66.0.96.0/19	10	66.1.32.0/19
5	66.0.128.0/19	11	66.1.64.0/19
6	66.0.160.0/19	12	66.1.96.0/19

This configuration uses only a handful of the available networks. The unused subnets, beginning with 66.1.128.0/19, can be reserved for future use or to meet subsequent requirements.

Requirement #3:
Ten Networks with 2,046 Hosts per Subnet

Next, you need to create 10 networks with 2,046 hosts per subnet. Each of the preceding subnets yields 8,190. When subnetted, each can yield three subnets with 2,046 host addresses. To meet this requirement, you would need to create 10 subnets, which would require taking four of the networks developed earlier and subnetting them. In other words, you must start where you left off, since you cannot have overlapping network addresses. The starting network address in this case is 66.1.128.0/19. You need 11 host bits to create 2,046 addresses. This means that you can use 21 network bits (32 − 11) to create these subnets. Table 2.6 defines several of the starting network addresses, as well as the ending network address. The bits that represent the network ID are shown in bold.

Table 2.6 Class A Subnetted Subnet with 2,046 Hosts

Class A Subnet Address	Binary Representation
66.1.128.0/21	**01000010.00000001.10000**000.00000000
66.1.136.0/21	**01000010.00000001.10001**000.00000000
66.1.144.0/21	**01000010.00000001.10010**000.00000000
66.1.152.0/21	**01000010.00000001.10011**000.00000000
66.1.160.0/21	**01000010.00000001.10100**000.00000000
…	…
66.127.248.0/21	**01000010.01111111.11111**000.00000000

As before, you can select the first 10 subnets from this range to meet Requirement #3. The last subnet used in this configuration, then, is 66.2.32.0/21. The subnet mask is 255.255.248.0.

Requirement #4: Five Networks with 250 Hosts per Subnet

The final requirement in subnetting your Class A network is to create five networks that have up to 250 hosts each. In this case, you can use 24 bits for the network ID, leaving eight for host addresses, which will yield 254 host addresses. This meets the final requirement. Though you could take a subnet from an unused space, in this example we will work with the last available address range from earlier, 66.127.248.0/21, and use three additional network bits: 66.127.248.0/24. Table 2.7 shows the network configurations that result.

Table 2.7 Subnets with 250 Hosts

Class A Subnet Address	Binary Representation
66.127.248.0/24	**01000010.01111111.11111000**.00000000
66.127.249.0/24	**01000010.01111111.11111001**.00000000
66.127.250.0/24	**01000010.01111111.11111010**.00000000
66.127.251.0/24	**01000010.01111111.11111011**.00000000
66.127.252.0/24	**01000010.01111111.11111100**.00000000

Continued

Table 2.7 Subnets with 250 Hosts

Class A Subnet Address	Binary Representation
...	...
66.127.255.0/24	01000010.01111111.11111111.00000000

Based on Table 2.7, you can see that the first and last addresses of the five subnets with 250 hosts are 66.127.248.0/24 and 66.127.252.0/24.

You have met all the requirements set out for the Class A network addressing scheme, with many addresses left for future use. Next, let's look at variable length subnetting of a smaller Class B network.

TEST DAY TIP

Reviewing address ranges of Class A, B, and C networks before taking the test will refresh your memory and help you answer questions more quickly. Memorizing the number of host addresses that is available in each network class will help you with subnetting questions and a variety of scenario-based questions.

Example of Subnetting a Class B Network

Now let's look at an example using a Class B network with a network ID of 129.69.0.0/16. You know that the subnet mask is 255.255.0.0. The requirements for subnetting this network are that you need at least one subnet with about 30,000 hosts, 12 subnets with up to 1,500 hosts, and 6 subnets with up to 250 hosts.

Requirement #1: One Subnet of Up to 30,000 Hosts

In order to have up to 30,000 hosts on one subnet, you need 15 bits for host addresses (2^{15} = 32,768). That leaves 17 bits for the network address. Your Class B network, by definition, uses 16 bits for the network ID, so you add one host address bit to the network address space to create a subnet that allows up to 30,000 hosts. This would be defined as 129.69.0.0/17. The subnet mask is 255.255.128.0.

Requirement #2: Twelve Subnets with Ip to 1,500 Hosts

You know that 1111 = 15, so you'll need four bits to create these 12 subnets. When you add these bits to the ones already in use, you end up with /21. The first network subnet, 129.69.0.0/17, is for 30,000 hosts, but you have a second large subnet that can be divided. This network begins at 129.69.128.0. You're using 21 bits for the network ID, so the subnet mask is 11111111.11111111.11111000.00000000, or 255.255.248.0. The first 12 subnets are selected with the last subnet of 129.69.216.0/21. You have 11 bits for use in the host address space, which yield (2^{11} − 2) or (2,048 − 2) host addresses, meeting the minimum requirement for 1,500 hosts. In Table 2.8, we've highlighted (in bold) the additional network bits used to create your networks.

TEST DAY TIP

After you determine how many bits from the host address space you need to take to extend the network address space, you can easily determine by what value the network address ranges will increment. This is helpful not only in delineating each subnet address range but in checking both your math and your logic. If you take five bits from a host address space octet, you know the incremental value is 8. If you take four bits, each subnet range will increment by 16, and so on.

Table 2.8 Class B Variable Length Subnet with 21 Bits

Network Addresses	Binary Equivalent
129.69.128.0/21	10000001.01000101.1**0000**000.00000000
129.69.136.0/21	10000001.01000101.1**0001**000.00000000
129.69.144.0/21	10000001.01000101.1**0010**000.00000000
129.69.152.0/21	10000001.01000101.1**0011**000.00000000
129.69.160.0/21	10000001.01000101.1**0100**000.00000000
129.69.168.0/21	10000001.01000101.1**0101**000.00000000
129.69.176.0/21	10000001.01000101.1**0110**000.00000000
129.69.184.0/21	10000001.01000101.1**0111**000.00000000
129.69.192.0/21	10000001.01000101.1**1000**000.00000000
129.69.200.0/21	10000001.01000101.1**1001**000.00000000
129.69.208.0/21	10000001.01000101.1**1010**000.00000000
129.69.216.0/21	10000001.01000101.1**1011**000.00000000
129.69.224.0/21	10000001.01000101.1**1100**000.00000000
129.69.232.0/21	10000001.01000101.1**1101**000.00000000
129.69.240.0/21	10000001.01000101.1**1111**000.00000000

Let's look at one example to see how you came up with these networks. You started with 129.69.0.0/17. In binary notation, that is **10000001.010000101.00**000000.00000000 (the network address space is in bold). You add to this configuration, using four more bits (underlined). The lowest bit that you use in this octet has the weighted value of 8. You can see that the network addresses incremented by eight each time. The first address after 129.69.0.0/17 for this configuration is 129.69.128.0/21. This is because you created two subnets to meet Requirement #1, 129.69.0.0/17 and 129.69.128.0/17. You further subnet the 129.69.128.0 network by taking an additional four bits, so you begin with 129.69.128.0/21 and increment by eight each time as you increment the selected four bits. This is shown in Table 2.8.

Requirement #3: Six Subnets with Up to 250 Hosts

To meet this requirement, you could use one of the subnets created for Requirement #2 and subnet that. However, you might want to leave the remaining subnets in that configuration for future use. Let's assume that is the case; then you can take the next available network address and subnet it. The next available address is 129.69.248.0/21. To subnet this to meet the requirements, you will need three more bits. Binary 111 = 7, which meets the requirement of six subnets. Adding three more bits to the subnet mask makes the first address 129.69.248.0/24. Notice that you are using 24 bits for the network ID, which leaves eight bits for the host address space. You know that an octet set to all 1s yields 255 decimal, less 2 for all 0s and all 1s, which are not legal host addresses. In Table 2.9, you can see how these addresses are arranged. The subnet mask for this configuration is 255.255.255.0 because you're using 24 bits for the network address. You might notice that this is the same as the default subnet mask for a Class C network, which uses three octets for the network address space by default.

Exam Warning

Although as mentioned earlier, *network* IDs of all 1s or all 0s are now acceptable in Microsoft networking configurations, you still cannot have *host* addresses of all 1s or all 0s. Don't confuse the two.

Table 2.9 Variable Length Subnet with 24 Bits

Network Address	Binary Representation
129.69.248.0/24	10000001.01000101.11111**000**.00000000
129.69.249.0/24	10000001.01000101.11111**001**.00000000
129.69.250.0/24	10000001.01000101.11111**010**.00000000
129.69.251.0/24	10000001.01000101.11111**011**.00000000
129.69.252.0/24	10000001.01000101.11111**100**.00000000
129.69.253.0/24	10000001.01000101.11111**101**.00000000
129.69.254.0/24	10000001.01000101.11111**110**.00000000
129.69.255.0/24	10000001.01000101.11111**111**.00000000

Requirement #4: Reserve at Least Five Subnets with 250 Hosts for Future Use

For Requirement #2, you created 15 subnets but needed only 12. That left three subnets that can have up to 2,046 hosts each. You could further subdivide one or more of these subnets to meet the fourth requirement. You also have one unused subnet left over from Requirement #3. Therefore, you have exceeded this requirement with the current configuration.

As you can see, to create variable length subnets, you simply add to the network bits by borrowing from the host bits. Rather than always starting from a standard classful network address, you start with a subnetted address, but the process is exactly the same.

TEST DAY TIP

Many of the scenarios on the exam center on Class B networks because there are enough host addresses to make many different plausible scenarios, but not so many that the math becomes overly complex. Although you may see questions on subnetting Class A and C networks, expect the bulk to be based on Class B networks.

Example of Subnetting a Class C Network

In real world scenarios, you might need to create subnets that contain only a few IP addresses. This is done to logically isolate devices on separate networks. Examples of networks with a few devices include routers on a network backbone or a point-to-point WAN connection that needs only two addresses. In these cases, you want to create small subnets to avoid wasting IP addresses. This is done with Class C network addresses, which already use 24 bits to denote the network space.

As you subnet a Class C, the number of hosts per subnet will go down by about a factor of 2, quickly reducing the number of host addresses per subnet. The maximum number of hosts in a Class C network is 254. Each subdivision results in roughly half the number of host addresses: 128, 64, 32, 16, 8, 4, 2, 1, following weighted binary values. Let's look at an example so you can better understand the mechanics of this process.

Rather than working on a random Class C network, we will continue the previous example, using one of the Class C-type network addresses you created to meet Requirement #3. Let's take the very last unused network address, 129.69.255.0/24, and assume you will put your routers and WAN connections on these smaller subnets.

Requirement #1: Create One Subnet with at Least 60 Host Addresses

The current configuration uses 24 bits for the network ID. You need at least 60 host addresses on this subnet. You need six bits for host address spaces. This means you can take two bits from the fourth octet for additional network subnetting. The beginning address is 129.69.255.0/24. You take two more bits and create 129.69.255.0/26. The subnet mask is 255.255.255.192.

Using this configuration, the possible network addresses are:

- 129.69.255.0/26
- 129.69.255.64/26
- 129.69.255.128/26
- 129.69.255.192/26

You have four subnets that can be used to meet this requirement and you will use the first one to meet this requirement.

Requirement #2: Create at Least Five Subnets with Up to Six Host Addresses

You can take one of the four subnets created for Requirement #1 and use it to create subnets with up to six host addresses. Begin with 129.69.255.128/26, because you might want to use 129.69.64/26 for future expansion of your 60-host subnets.

Subnetting 129.69.255.128/26 to create up to six host addresses requires that you keep three bits for host addresses ($2^3 = 8$), so you can take up to three more bits for network addresses. The results are shown in Table 2.10.

Table 2.10 Subnet for Six Host Addresses

Network Address	Binary Representation
129.69.255.128/29	10000001.01000101.11111111.10000000
129.69.255.136/29	10000001.01000101.11111111.10001000
129.69.255.144/29	10000001.01000101.11111111.10010000
129.69.255.152/29	10000001.01000101.11111111.10011000
129.69.255.160/29	10000001.01000101.11111111.10100000
129.69.255.168/29	10000001.01000101.11111111.10101000
129.69.255.176/29	10000001.01000101.11111111.10110000
129.69.255.184/29	10000001.01000101.11111111.10111000
...	...
129.69.255.248/29	10000001.01000101.11111111.11111000

By subnetting the previous subnet, you can create 16 subnets that can have up to six host addresses per subnet. You've met the requirement and have subnets left for future expansion. The subnet mask for this configuration is 255.255.255.248.

Requirement #3: Save at Least Two Subnets for Future Use

You have 10 additional subnets for future use, so you already have met this requirement.

EXAM WARNING

Watch for questions related to Class C networks, because they can be tricky. You have relatively few host addresses available, so check first to determine whether the question is really about *subnetting* or *supernetting*.

EXERCISE 2.02

VARIABLE LENGTH SUBNETTING

Although we used examples in the text to help understand variable length subnetting concepts, this exercise will help you to walk through another example to solidify your understanding of this important concept. The requirements are as follows:

- Create three subnets with no more than 8,200 hosts per subnet.
- Create 30 subnets with up to 254 hosts addresses per subnet.
- Create 60 subnets with no more than two host addresses each.
- Reserve half the total addresses for future use.
- The assigned network ID is 133.98.0.0/16.

1. To solve this problem, you have to look at several factors at once. You have a Class B network using 16 bits for the network address and you must reserve half the addresses for future use. You can begin by determining that you have a total of 65,534 host addresses available in an undivided Class B network ($2 \wedge 16 = 65,536$). You need to reserve half of those, or 32,768.

2. Before you begin subnetting, however, it's important to determine the maximum number of hosts required on any given subnet. In this case, you have a requirement of a maximum of 8,200 hosts per subnet on three subnets. The requirement doesn't specifically limit you to three subnets with 8,200 hosts, but it requires no less than three. You must calculate the number of host bits needed. There are a number of methods you can use to figure this out. However, you know that with 16 bits, you have 65,536 hosts. Removing one bit at a time reduces this number by half. Removing 1 bit = 32,768; 2 bits = 16,384; 3 bits = 8,192. Therefore, 16 bits – 3 bits = 13 bits—the number needed for host addresses that will not exceed 8,200.

3. Using 13 bits for the host address space allows you to use 19 bits for the network address space. The network can now be identified as 133.98.0.0/19.

4. Next, you need to define the network address ranges. If you take three bits from the host address space, you can create 2^3 (can also be notated as 2^3) subnets, or 8. These eight subnets will increment by 32 because you're taking the three left-most bits of the third (y) octet, which have the weighted binary value of 128, 64, and 32.

5. The following are the resultant starting address ranges:

    133.98.0.0/19

    133.98.32.0/19

    133.98.64.0/19

    133.98.96.0/19

    133.98.128.0/19

    133.98.160.0/19

    133.98.192.0/19

    133.98.224.0/19

6. You must reserve half the addresses for future use, so reserve the last four address ranges: 133.98.128.0/19 through 133.98.224.0/19.

7. The next requirement is to create three subnets with no more than 8,200 host addresses. Remember that the current subnetting scheme is based on the maximum host address requirement, so each of these subnets currently supports a maximum of 8,190 hosts per subnet. Use the first three starting addresses for this requirement: 133.98.0.0/19, 133.98.32.0/19, and 133.98.64.0/19.

8. The next requirement is to create 30 subnets with 254 host addresses per subnet. Begin with the next available subnet address, 133.98.96.0/19. From there, you need to subnet this segment to allow only 254 hosts per subnet. When you set all the bits of one octet to 1, it equals 255 in decimal, so the fourth octet (z) is used for host addressing, not to exceed 254 hosts per subnet. This means that you use the third octet (y) for network addressing. You have already borrowed three bits from this octet in the earlier subnetting scheme. Now you need to take the remaining bits, resulting in a total of 24 network bits. Your new notation for this subnet is 133.98.96.0/24.

9. You need to define three subnets with a maximum of 254 host addresses. Begin with the first address, 133.98.96.0/24. The last net-

work bit is the right-most bit of the third octet, with the value of 1. Therefore, your network addresses will increment by 1. Since you extended the network address space by five total bits (from /19 to /24), you will be able to create 2^5, or 32 subnets with a maximum of 254 host addresses. These addresses are listed here:

133.98.96.0/24

133.98.97.0/24

133.98.98.0/24

133.98.99.0/24

...

133.98.127.0/24

10. The required three subnets with a maximum of 254 hosts are: 133.98.96.0/24, 133.98.96.97.0/24, and 133.98.98.0/24.

11. The next requirement is to create 60 subnets with no more than two host addresses per subnet. Begin by using the last subnet created in step 9, which is 133.98.127.0/24, as the base address. Two addresses per subnet means you need two host address bits. This might seem odd since you know the 1 bit can be 0 or 1, which equals two values. Remember, though, that the host address cannot be all 0s or all 1s. Thus, you need two bits in order to accommodate this restriction. If you are using only two host bits, you must use 30 network bits. This is an extension of six bits from the previous configuration, which then results in 2^6 or 64 subnets with no more than two host addresses. The requirement calls for 60 subnets of this configuration, so this will work.

12. The subnets for this configuration begin with 133.98.127.0/30. You have extended the network address space into the fourth octet (*z*) and the last bit value is 4. (The 2 and 1 bits are used for host addressing). Thus, the starting subnet addresses will increment by four. The beginning and ending address ranges are shown here:

133.98.127.0/30

133.98.127.4/30

133.98.127.8/30

133.98.127.12/30

133.98.127.16/30

...

133.98.127.248/30

You can verify the ending address by dividing the ending number (248) by the incremental value (4) to yield 62 (the number of subnets you have determined will result from this configuration). You can also multiply the incremental value (4) by the number of subnets created (62) to yield 248 as the last starting number.

13. To meet Requirement #4, choose the first 60 subnets and reserve the last two for future use. These two unused subnets in this configuration are 133.98.127.244/30 and 133.98.127.248/30.

14. You have already met the final requirement, which is to reserve half of all addresses for future use, so you are finished with the exercise. Notice that the last address you defined, 133.98.127.248/30, is still below the first reserved address of 133.98.128.0/19. If these addresses had overlapped, you would have a clear indication that you made an error in your calculations.

TEST DAY TIP

The various methods shown for checking your math and logic can be very useful—both on the job and on the exam. By using these simple methods for checking your work, you can be sure your calculations are accurate.

Head of the Class...

Subnets Using All 0s or All 1s

Although RFC 1812 allows the use of subnets that are all 0s or all 1s, use caution before implementing such a plan. There are a few notable limitations. In the examples we've used, we've continued to disallow all 0s and all 1s because even today, not all routers and hosts support RFC 1812.

To use subnets with all 0s or all 1s, you must use a routing protocol that supports RFC 1812. These protocols include *Routing Information Protocol version 2* (RIPv2), *Open Shortest Path First* (OSPF), and *Border Gateway Protocol version 4* (BGPv4). Some routers and hosts can support all 0s or all 1s subnets, but must be configured to do so. Routers and hosts running Windows Server 2003 support the use of all 0s and all 1s without additional configuration.

If you decide to use subnets with all 0s and all 1s, verify that all the routers and hosts on your network support this configuration before implementing it.

Variable Length Subnetting Summary

Variable length subnetting is the process of subdividing subnets. The process is the same as when subnetting classful network addresses, as we have illustrated using a Class A, B, and C network. Variable length subnetting or nonclassful subnetting allows us to create subnets of unequal size to avoid wasting IP addresses within the network range. By creating subnets with a varying number of available host addresses, you can better utilize your allocated addressing space. This recursive method of subdividing uses the subnetting principle of taking bits from the host address space to add to the network address space. Thus, the number of network ID bits increases, based on the previous subnet's network bits.

Configuring & Implementing...

Variable Length Subnetting

In Chapter 1, we emphasized learning the fundamentals of subnetting, starting with converting decimal to binary and binary to weighted binary. You also learned how to work with dotted decimal notation. You can probably see now why this was so important. Not only is it important for basic networking, it is required for variable length subnetting. With the growing shortage of IP addresses worldwide, new schemes have been devised to help make better use of networks. The flexibility provided by variable length subnetting is needed in today's real world networking environment. If you work in an IT department in a medium-to-large business, you'll likely come across variable length subnetting. We can no longer afford simply to leave thousands of IP addresses unused, so creating subnets from subnets makes efficient use of these IP addresses.

The process of creating variable length subnets is not complex, but it requires full attention to detail. In the world of computer communications, one bit changes everything, so it's important that you not only fully understand the theory but also master the mechanics of performing these routines.

A few tips can make this process easier, both in real world scenarios and on the exam.

- First, identify your starting point. Is your network already subnetted or are you starting with a "fresh" Class A, B, or C network? What is your current subnet mask? This is an instant clue as to what your network

Continued

status is—if you're not using a default subnet mask for the appropriate network type, your network is already subnetted. If you find that's the case, your first step should be to delineate the current configuration. How many subnets do you currently have and how many host addresses are available on each subnet?

- Next, determine your new configuration needs. It's possible that you'll have to backtrack a bit and change your subnets. Remember, this is not a task to be taken lightly, as it often involves changing cabling, routers, and other network configurations. If at all possible, work with your current network configuration as your starting point.

- Finally, determine your subnetting scheme. You should have a list of the new configuration requirements, much like the scenarios we've gone through in this chapter. These requirements help you define your needs and develop solutions to match those needs.

This planning and attention to detail will pay off—by reducing errors and networking configuration problems in a real network and by helping you discern the correct answers to exam questions. Variable length subnetting is not difficult when you understand the foundations of subnetting, but it still requires strict attention to detail.

Supernetting Class C Networks

Useable network addresses have grown scarce as companies have expanded their networks and connected to other networks via the Internet. To prevent the problem of running out of Class A and Class B network addresses that are needed by very large companies, the Internet addressing authorities decided to try to preserve some of these network addresses. For example, if a small company needs about 2,000 addresses for all of its anticipated expansion, assigning it a Class B network would waste thousands of addresses. The total default number of host addresses in a Class B network is 65,534. A small company might never be able to utilize all of those addresses. The problem, however, is that a Class C network allows only 254 hosts per network and that's not enough for this hypothetical company. To address this situation, a method was devised to group two or more Class C networks together to yield a higher number of host address spaces, while preserving Class B networks for larger companies that require more of the 65,534 host addresses.

The concept of grouping Class C networks together is called *supernetting*. If a company needs 2,000 host addresses, the Internet authority, Internet Assigned Numbers Authority (IANA), can assign it a group of eight contiguous Class C network addresses. With 254 hosts per Class C network, the company ends up with 2,032 host addresses across the eight networks.

This concept has one major drawback. If eight network IDs are assigned to the company, routers across the Internet have to store eight separate addresses to identify a single entity. If this is done on a large scale, it potentially could bog down the Internet as routers sort through multiple entries for a particular company. To solve this, a technique called *Classless Interdomain Routing* (CIDR) was developed. CIDR collapses the Class C network IDs into a single entry that points to all the corresponding Class C networks at one organization.

This is done by creating a routing table entry that includes two elements:

- The *Starting Network ID*, which identifies the beginning of the group of Class C addresses

- The *Count*, which indicates how many Class C networks are assigned to the organization

This solution reduces the number of addresses stored in routers but requires that Class C network assignments be contiguous. It also creates another problem with routers, because it requires that the subnet mask be advertised along with the IP address so that the block of addresses can be discerned. Without the subnet mask, the Class C address would be seen as a single address and the remainder of the block of addresses would not be seen. A block of addresses using CIDR is called a *CIDR block*. A CIDR block must contain a sequential group of Class C networks, and the number of allocated Class C networks must be expressed as a power of 2. Let's look at an example of supernetting so you can better understand how this works.

Exam Warning

CIDR uses a notation to indicate the number of network bits used in an IP address, which is denoted using **/xx** at the end of an IP address (for example, 174.42.95.6/22).

Note

For more information on the Internet Assigned Numbers Authority (IANA), visit their Web site at www.iana.org.

Example of Supernetting a Class C Network

Let's consider the following scenario: Your small company is assigned the network address of 242.12.130.0. It is assigned a range of four Class C networks because it anticipates needing no more than a total of 1,000 host addresses. These are the four network addresses:

242.12.136.0   **11110010.00001100.100010**<u>00</u>.00000000

242.12.137.0   **11110010.00001100.100010**<u>01</u>.00000000

242.12.138.0   **11110010.00001100.100010**<u>10</u>.00000000

242.12.139.0   **11110010.00001100.100010**<u>11</u>.00000000

The binary bits in bold are the base network IDs. The underlined bits are the additional Class C network assignments. This gives you four Class C networks with a starting address of 242.12.136.0 and an ending address of 242.12.139.0. Next, you need to determine the appropriate subnet mask to use that will allow your routers to understand that this is a block of addresses. You are using six of the eight bits in the third octet for the starting network address, so a subnet mask of 255.255.252.0 should work. Let's check it against another address, using bitwise ANDing, just to make sure you've calculated correctly.

242.12.138.0   11110010.00001100.10001010.00000000

255.255.252.0   11111111.11111111.11111100.00000000

Result   11110010.00001100.10001000.00000000

Result =   242.12.136.0 [Starting Network ID]

As you can see, by testing the subnet mask against another Class C network in the assigned range, you end up with the Starting Network ID. This means that when any address within this range is used with the subnet mask 255.255.252.0, the routing table will forward the data to your organization.

Routers must be able to store and exchange network information relating to both the network ID and the subnet mask in order to effectively use CIDR blocks. Dynamic routing protocols, discussed in Chapter 1, are designed to support CIDR blocks. The RIP and OSPF protocols both support CIDR blocks. In addition, BGPv4 also supports CIDR.

NOTE

RIP version 1 does *not* support CIDR blocks.

The CIDR block of addresses in our example can be seen in two ways. It can be seen as a block of four Class C network addresses. It can also be seen as a single network that uses 22 bits for network IDs and 10 bits for host IDs. When viewed in the second way, it loses its classfulness and becomes classless.

Essentially, addresses are composed of 32 bits with a set number of bits assigned to network IDs and a set of variable bits used for host addresses. The boundaries of Class A, B, and C networks lose distinction as we move into variable length subnetting and supernetting. One notable guideline is that when you subnet, you use more network bits than in a standard classful network, whereas when you supernet, you use fewer network bits than in a standard classful network. This makes sense because with supernetting, you are combining network IDs to *reduce* the number of networks (many represented by one), thus you have to reduce the number of network bits to accomplish this. When you subnet, on the other hand, you are *increasing* the number of networks (subnetworks) and thus you must increase the number of bits that represent the network ID.

EXERCISE 2.03

SUPERNETTING AND CIDR BLOCKS

In this exercise, you will work through an example of supernetting and creating CIDR blocks. The scenario focuses on a start-up company that anticipates needing about 4000 total host addresses over the next five years. The beginning Class C network ID you'll work with is 226.130.48.0/24. You must determine how to use Class C networks in a supernetted fashion to meet these requirements.

1. You need about 4,000 host addresses. A Class C network can have a maximum of 254 host addresses. Thus, to determine the total number of Class C subnets needed (or the address range, using classless terminology), divide 4,000 by 254, which yields 15.75. The number of Class C networks must be expressed as a power of 2, and you can't have 15.75 networks. Keeping this in mind, select 16, the next largest integer, and a number that can be expressed as a power of 2 ($2 \char`^4$). This means you need 16 Class C networks to meet our requirement for about 4,000 hosts.

2. You can calculate the total number of host addresses you will have available by multiplying 16 (number of networks) x 254 (number of hosts per network), yielding 4,064 total host addresses.

3. To calculate the subnet mask for this configuration, begin with the maximum bits for the network space and work backwards. A Class C default subnet mask is 255.255.255.0/24. If you have two Class C networks, yielding 512 addresses, take one network bit away. The first bit, with a weighted value of 1, can be either 0 or 1, yielding two choices or two addresses. If you have four Class C networks, you require two bits (00, 01, 10, 11). Remember that you must allot Class C networks in numbers expressed as a power of 2 (1, 2, 4, 8, 16, etc.), so you skipped three Class C networks. Next in the sequence is a requirement of eight Class C networks using three bits (000, 001, 010, 011, 100, 101, 110, 111). Following that, you have 16 Class C networks using four bits. The subnet mask must use four fewer bits than the default, resulting in a subnet mask using 20 network bits.

4. To calculate the subnet mask, calculate the value of the third (*y*) octet using four bits. Remember that you began by using 24 bits for the network ID, which would use the entire third octet. You have subtracted four bits, leaving four bits in the octet to be used for the supernetting. You next calculate the third octet as (128 + 64 + 32 + 16), or 240. The resulting supernetted subnet mask is 255.255.240.0/20.

5. Next, calculate the beginning and ending host addresses for this block of addresses. The beginning Class C network ID is 226.130.48.0/24. The supernetted configuration is represented as 226.130.48.0/20. Thus, the range of addresses is as follows, with the bits representing the network ID <u>underlined</u>.

    226.130.48.0/20   =   <u>11100010.10000010.0011</u>0000.00000000

    226.130.49.0/20   =   <u>11100010.10000010.0011</u>0001.00000000

    226.130.50.0/20   =   <u>11100010.10000010.0011</u>0010.00000000

    226.130.51.0/20   =   <u>11100010.10000010.0011</u>0011.00000000

    ...

    226.130.63.0/20   =   <u>11100010.10000010.0011</u>1111.00000000

    Notice that this differs from the process used for subnetting. In this case, you have removed four bits from the network ID and set that as a fixed number (represented by the left-most four bits of the third octet set permanently to 0011, with a value of 48). Next, you incremented the bits remaining in the octet normally used for the Class C network to define the network IDs that are combined in this configuration. The process is the opposite of subnetting but uses the same principles.

6. Your aggregate, the CIDR block, can be expressed as 226.130.48.0/20 with a subnet mask of 255.255.240.0.

EXAM
70-291
OBJECTIVE
4.3.2

The Windows XP/ Windows 2000 Routing Table

Routing is one of the primary functions of the IP. Data packets, or datagrams, contain both the source and destination IP addresses in their headers, and this information is used in making routing decisions. IP compares the destination address with the local address to determine whether the packet should be sent up the stack on the local host, sent to another destination, or ignored.

In Windows XP and Windows 2000 Professional, the only way to access the routing table is through the command line. The routing table includes entries that provide information used to properly route datagrams. Each field in the routing table is explained next.

- **Network Destination** The network ID corresponding to the route. This can be a class-based address, a subnet or supernet address, or an IP address for a host.

- **Netmask** The netmask is the mask used to match the destination address to the network destination.

- **Gateway** The gateway that takes you out of the local network/subnet; the router used to forward data. This is called the *forwarding* or *next-hop* IP address for the network destination.

- **Interface** The IP address of the network interface card (NIC) used to forward the IP data.

- **Metric** This number represents a relative cost of the route. It is used to determine the best route among many choices. Typically the route with the fewest hops (number of routers that must be crossed) has the lowest metric. However, the network administrator can adjust this to prevent certain types of traffic from using specific routes. If two routes have the same network destination and netmask, the route with the lowest metric will be used.

In addition to these required elements, routing tables can contain additional information. If present, the following fields provide the following information:

- **Directly Attached Network ID Routes** These listings are used for routes that are directly attached. The Gateway IP address is the IP address of the interface on that network for networks that are attached.

- **Remote Network ID Routes** These listings are used for routes that are available indirectly, through other routers. In this case, the Gateway IP address is the IP address of a local router that is in between the forwarding node and the remote network.

- **Host Routes** This listing allows you to enter a route to a specific host. The network destination is the IP address of the intended host and the subnet mask is 255.255.255.255.

- **Default Route** If a more specific route cannot be found, a default route can be defined to assist in routing IP data. If the network ID or host route is not found, the default route is used. The default route network destination is 0.0.0.0 and the subnet mask is 0.0.0.0.

EXERCISE 2.04

VIEWING ROUTING TABLES

In this exercise, you will view the entries in the routing table on a computer that is running Windows XP, Windows 2000, or Windows Server 2003.

1. Open a 32-bit command prompt by clicking **Start | Run** and typing **cmd** in the **Run** dialog box. (Note that on older systems such as Windows 9x, the 16-bit equivalent is **command**.)

2. The command prompt window opens, showing the pathname of the current location followed by a > symbol.

3. At the > symbol, type the command **route help,** then press **Enter.** The various commands and parameters that can be used with the **route** command are displayed.

4. At the > symbol, type the command **route print** to display the routing table on the local computer.

5. Notice there are several entries present; these are the default routing table entries that are created every time the TCP/IP protocol is initiated on the computer.

6. The default headings are Network Destination, Netmask, Gateway, Interface, and Metric.

7. The default route is 0.0.0.0 with a subnet mask of 0.0.0.0. This is where packets are sent if no other route can be found.

8. The loopback route is 127.0.0.0. Its subnet mask is 255.0.0.0 and it is sent to the gateway 127.0.0.1 through the interface 127.0.0.1, both of which are internal to the computer.

9. You should also see an entry under **Network Destination** that is the IP address of the local computer. In this case, you will see the subnet mask and default gateway, which are configured in the computer's TCP/IP properties.

10. To end the session, type **exit** at the > symbol. This closes the command prompt window.

Adding Routing Table Entries

The Routing tool is accessed via the command prompt by clicking **Start | Run**, typing **cmd** and pressing **Enter**. This opens a command prompt window in which you can run a variety of command-line utilities including *ping*, *tracert*, and *route*. To add routing table entries, open the command prompt window. Figure 2.3 shows how to access the route command help, which shows you how the commands are formatted and what parameters can be (or must be) included. At the prompt, type **route help** and press **Enter**. This will show you a list of all the route command parameters available to you. Notice the command **add** in the list. Figure 2.4 shows the parameters associated with several commands, including the **add** command. The command line format and a sample entry are shown next. To enter the command, press the **Enter** key.

```
route add [destination] [mask] [gateway] [metric] IF [interface]
route add 157.0.0.0  mask 255.0.0.0  157.55.80.1 metric 3
```

Figure 2.3 Accessing Route Command Help

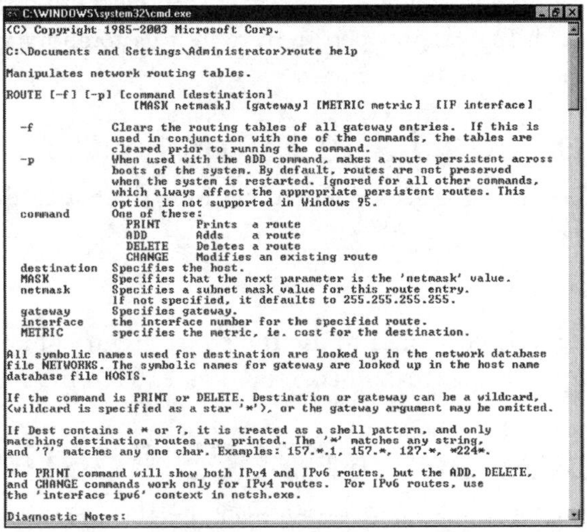

```
C:\WINDOWS\system32\cmd.exe
(C) Copyright 1985-2003 Microsoft Corp.

C:\Documents and Settings\Administrator>route help

Manipulates network routing tables.

ROUTE [-f] [-p] [command [destination]
                  [MASK netmask]  [gateway] [METRIC metric]  [IF interface]

  -f           Clears the routing tables of all gateway entries.  If this is
               used in conjunction with one of the commands, the tables are
               cleared prior to running the command.
  -p           When used with the ADD command, makes a route persistent across
               boots of the system. By default, routes are not preserved
               when the system is restarted. Ignored for all other commands,
               which always affect the appropriate persistent routes. This
               option is not supported in Windows 95.
  command      One of these:
                 PRINT     Prints  a route
                 ADD       Adds    a route
                 DELETE    Deletes a route
                 CHANGE    Modifies an existing route
  destination  Specifies the host.
  MASK         Specifies that the next parameter is the 'netmask' value.
  netmask      Specifies a subnet mask value for this route entry.
               If not specified, it defaults to 255.255.255.255.
  gateway      Specifies gateway.
  interface    the interface number for the specified route.
  METRIC       specifies the metric, ie. cost for the destination.

All symbolic names used for destination are looked up in the network database
file NETWORKS. The symbolic names for gateway are looked up in the host name
database file HOSTS.

If the command is PRINT or DELETE. Destination or gateway can be a wildcard,
(wildcard is specified as a star '*'), or the gateway argument may be omitted.

If Dest contains a * or ?, it is treated as a shell pattern, and only
matching destination routes are printed. The '*' matches any string,
and '?' matches any one char. Examples: 157.*.1, 157.*, 127.*, *224*.

The PRINT command will show both IPv4 and IPv6 routes, but the ADD, DELETE,
and CHANGE commands work only for IPv4 routes.  For IPv6 routes, use
the 'interface ipv6' context in netsh.exe.

Diagnostic Notes:
```

To view the changes you made and to verify that you entered them correctly, you can use the command **route print** to show the current routing table. If you made an error, you can use the **route change** command, but only to modify the gateway or metric. If you made any other errors in the routing table entry, you must use the **route delete** command and then the **route add** command again to enter the correct information.

When adding routes, it's important to remember that these are *temporary* additions to the routing table. When the computer is rebooted, these additions are erased. To make a permanent or persistent entry in the routing table, use the *–p* parameter. The following is an example of how to add a persistent routing table entry:

```
route -p add 157.0.0.0 mask 255.0.0.0 157.55.80.1 metric 3 [enter]
```

Figure 2.4 Accessing *Route Add* Command Line Parameters

This will ensure that the entry you made remains in the routing table even after the system has been rebooted. To change a persistent route to a temporary route, you must remove and re-enter the routing table entry.

Removing Routing Table Entries

Removing routing table entries is accomplished by using the **route delete** command. The format of the command is:

route delete [destination]

For added accuracy, it's a good idea to use the **route print** command to view the routing table after you make changes to make sure you entered the information correctly.

The Windows Server 2003 Routing Table

The Window Server 2003 routing table can be maintained through the command line utility, **route**, as with Windows XP/Windows 2000 Professional. It can also be viewed and maintained with the graphical **Routing and Remote Access** administrative tool (as with Windows 2000 Server) if the RRAS service is enabled. The **route** commands in Windows Server 2003 are the same as in Windows XP/Windows 2000. To view the routing table from the Routing and Remote Access administrative interface, click **Start | Administrative Tools | Routing and Remote Access**.

The IP routing table for a Windows Server 2003 computer consists of the default routes shown in Table 2.11. As you can see, the table shows that six are required:

- Network Destination
- Netmask
- Gateway
- Interface
- Metric
- Protocol

Customizing the Routing Table View

The graphical view of the routing table is accessed by clicking **Start | Programs | Administrative Tools | Routing and Remote Access** to open the RRAS console. In the left console pane, expand the node for the RRAS server, then expand the **IP Routing** node. Right-click **Static Routes** and select **Show IP Routing Table**.

You can customize the information that is shown in the graphical view of the routing table by selecting which columns to show or hide. To do so, right-click on any of the column headers in the routing table (for example, **Destination**) and select **Select columns** from the right context menu. By default, the five parameters listed in the text are all displayed.

To remove a parameter so that it will not be displayed in the table, select it in the right **Displayed parameters** text box and click the **Remove** button. This will move it to the left **Hidden parameters** textbox.

To change the order in which the columns are displayed, select a column and click the **Move Up** or **Move Down** button to change its position in the display.

To return to the default display, click the **Restore Defaults** button.

There are two ways to view the routing table in Window Server 2003—via the command line utility **route** and via the **Routing and Remote Access** interface. Table 2.11 shows a routing table as it would appear using the command-line utility. When viewed via the RRAS interface, persistent static routes are viewed via the **Static Routes** node on the tree in the left pane. To view the routing table, select **Static Routes** from the tree and then click **Action | Show IP Routing Table**. There are two primary differences between the command line **route print** and the RRAS interface **Show IP Routing Table**. First, the RRAS routing table does not list the default gateway separately as does the command line utility. Second, the RRAS routing table shows the *Protocol* field. This field shows how the route was learned. If the entry on the line is anything other than Local, then the router is receiving routes via a routing protocol such as RIP or OSPF.

EXAM WARNING

Open Shortest Path First (OSPF) is neither available on the 64-bit version of Windows Server 2003 nor is it available in the Windows XP 64-bit version.

To understand the routing table entries, first assume that the routing table shown is from IP address 147.98.140.29 with a subnet mask of 255.255.240.0.

Table 2.11 Windows Server 2003 Routing Table Entries

Active Routes:

Line #	Network Destination	Netmask	Gateway	Interface	Metric
1	0.0.0.0	0.0.0.0	147.98.128.1	147.98.140.29	20
2	127.0.0.0	255.0.0.0	127.0.0.1	127.0.0.1	1
3	147.98.128.0	255.255.240.0	147.98.140.29	147.98.140.29	20
4	147.98.140.29	255.255.255.255	127.0.0.1	127.0.0.1	20
5	147.98.255.255	255.255.255.255	147.98.140.29	147.98.140.29	20
6	224.0.0.0	240.0.0.0	147.98.140.29	147.98.140.29	20
7	255.255.255.255	255.255.255.255	147.98.140.29	147.98.140.29	1

8	**Default gateway:** 147.98.128.1
9	**Persistent routes:** None

The line numbers in Table 2.11 are not part of the routing table displayed on a Windows Server 2003 computer but are included here for clarity. The routing table begins with a list of active routes, followed by a list of persistent, or static, routes. Let's examine the information on each line and what it all means:

- **Line 1** In this list, Line 1 begins with the default route of 0.0.0.0 and a netmask (subnet mask) of 0.0.0.0. When there are no other matches for a route for a specified IP address, this route is used. You'll notice that the gateway is the address of the default gateway defined on the computer's TCP/IP properties sheet and the interface is the IP address of the local computer. When the computer sends a packet with an IP address that has no better matching route, this is used as the default to ensure all packets sent from this computer can find their ways to the proper destinations.

- **Line 2** This line shows the loopback address. As we've discussed, the loopback address is internal to the computer and is used to verify that the TCP/IP stack (software) is working properly on the machine. 127.0.0.0 is the loopback network destination address and 127.0.0.1 is both the gateway and interface for this loop-back address. These packets never leave the local computer.

- **Line 3**   The next line shows the directly attached subnet address. This indicates the specific subnet address to which this particular computer is attached. Any packets sent from this computer to any IP address that is also attached to this subnet will be sent directly to the host instead of going through a router. When this route is selected, the packet is sent via this computer, which in a sense acts as the gateway, and through this computer's interface. Since the packet must be routed, the use of this computer's IP address as the gateway and interface makes sense because the packet is being delivered directly from this computer to another host on the same subnet.

- **Line 4**   The network destination IP address of Line 4 is the IP address for the computer on which this routing table resides. Thus, any packets *from* this computer *to* this computer are sent via the loopback IP address of 127.0.0.1 because there is no need for this type of packet to be sent out onto the network medium, only to return back to the same computer.

- **Line 5**   This line contains a route for all-subnets-directed broadcasts. This entry exists only if the network on which the local host computer resides is subnetted. Information on all-subnets-directed broadcasts is covered in greater detail when we discuss the Internet Protocol later in this book. This address shows the under-lying network ID of 147.98.0.0 for the Class B address and the second two octets are set to all 1s, 147.98.255.255. Packets sent to this directed broadcast IP address are sent as MAC-level broadcasts, using the computer's interface IP address of 147.98.140.29. Remember, this is the routing entry on the local computer for traffic originating on the computer. The routing entry on another computer on the same subnet would have the same network destination and subnet mask but the interface would be different; it would be *that* computer's IP address.

- **Line 6**   The network destination IP address in Line 6 is the route for multicast addresses and is used to match all Class D addresses. As you'll recall, Class D is reserved for multicasts, which are messages sent to a single address but received by multiple computers with different IP addresses, which are members of a multicast group. As with all-subnets-directed broadcasts, these messages are sent as MAC-level broadcasts using the computer's assigned IP address and the interface.

- **Line 7**   In Chapter 1, we discussed the reasons why an IP address cannot be all 0s or all 1s, and how those addresses are reserved for broadcasts. This is the case, as well, for the network destination of 255.255.255.255 shown on Line 7. When this computer sends a message for broadcast to 255.255.255.255, the host route for limited broadcasts shown on Line 7 is used. Notice that the netmask is also set to all 1s (255.255.255.255) and that both the gateway and interface are the IP address of the sending computer, 147.98.140.29.

- **Line 8**   On Line 8, you see the address of the default gateway configured for the local computer. This means that any packet intended for a network other than the network to which this computer is attached will be forwarded to the default gateway for delivery.

- **Line 9**   Finally, you can see that this computer has no persistent routes defined. Recall that a persistent route is one that persists through a reboot, meaning that it has been added to the table as a static route. When you add a route to a routing table, you must flag it as persistent in order for it to remain in the routing table permanently (or until you manually remove it). Otherwise, the route will remain in the routing table until the next time the TCP/IP stack is initialized, which typically occurs during a reboot or reinitialization of the computer. Persistent routes are added with the −*p* parameter when using the **route add** command. The persistent routes are stored in the Registry in the following key:

```
HKEY_LOCAL_MACHINE\SYSTEM\CurrentControlSet\Services\Tcpip\

      Parameters\PersistentRoutes
```

NOTE

When you use the **route print** command in Windows Server 2003, the IPv6 routes will be displayed along with the IPv4 routes. However, you cannot use the **route** utilities to add, change, and delete IPv6 routes. Instead, you must use the **netsh.exe** tool. At the **netsh>** prompt, you'll need to change the context by typing **interface ipv6**. Then you can use the **add** and **delete** commands to add and delete table entries.

New & Noteworthy...

Windows Server 2003 Routing Tables

There are two notable differences between routing tables in Windows Server 2003 and Windows operating systems prior to Windows 2000. First, in Windows Server 2003, the netmask for the Class D multicast is set to 240.0.0.0. In earlier versions of Windows (prior to Windows XP/2000, which includes Windows 98 and Windows Millennium), it was set to 224.0.0.0. Though the network destination is 224.0.0.0, the netmask is 240.0.0.0, which is a better match for the Class D range of addresses.

The second notable difference is that the routing metric is determined automatically by TCP/IP based on the speed of the interface. A metric of 20, shown in Table 2.11 indicates a 100 Mps Ethernet interface. This automatic creation of the routing metric can be disabled through TCP/IP properties but is enabled by default. Exercise 2.05 explains how to disable automatic calculation of the metric.

EXAM WARNING

It is very common to see questions on Microsoft exams related to new features of the product. Therefore, you may see questions about the changes to the routing table. One area to pay special attention to is the automatic calculation of the metric, which can be disabled to allow manual entry of the metric in the Advanced TCP/IP settings.

EXERCISE 2.05

DISABLE AUTOMATIC METRIC CALCULATION

In this exercise, we'll walk through the steps required to disable the automatic configuration of the routing metric based on the speed of the interface.

1. On your Windows Server 2003-based computer, click **Start | Control Panel | Network Connections**.

2. Select **Local Area Connection**.

3. **The Local Area Connection Properties** dialog is displayed. In the box entitled **This connection uses the following items**, click **Internet Protocol (TCP/IP)**. *Important note:* Select by clicking on the text, not in the check box to the left of the text. If you remove the checkmark in the box by clicking on it, you will disable TCP/IP on your computer. Ensure the checkmark is present in the box to the left of the Internet Protocol (TCP/IP) text.

4. Once you have selected TCP/IP, click the **Properties** button.

5. The **Internet Protocol (TCP/IP) Properties** dialog is displayed, showing the IP configuration for the computer. On the lower right side of the dialog box, locate and click the **Advanced** button.

6. The **Advanced TCP/IP Settings** dialog is displayed.

7. There are four tabs: **IP Settings**, **DNS**, **WINS**, and **Options**. The **IP Settings** tab is selected by default. On this tab, there are three sections: **IP addresses**, **Default gateways**, and **Automatic metric**. **Automatic metric** is selected by default, indicated by the checkmark in the box to the left of the text.

8. To disable automatic metric calculation, click the box to remove the checkmark. When the checkmark is cleared, the automatic metric calculation is disabled.

9. The Interface metric can be entered manually only after automatic metric calculation is disabled. You'll notice that when the checkmark is present in the **Automatic metric** box, the **Interface metric** field is grayed out, indicating it is disabled.

10. Enter the desired interface metric in the field, then click **OK** to close the **Advanced TCP/IP Settings** dialog box. If you do not desire to make a change, click **Cancel** to exit without saving changes.

11. Click **OK** (or **Cancel** if you do not wish to save changes) to exit the **Internet Protocol (TCP/IP) Properties** dialog box.

12. Click **OK** (or **Cancel** if you do not wish to save changes) to exit the **Local Area Connection Properties** dialog box.

Figure 2.5 shows the **Advanced TCP/IP Settings | IP Settings** dialog box with the entry of a manual Interface metric of 5.

Figure 2.5 Advanced TCP/IP Settings

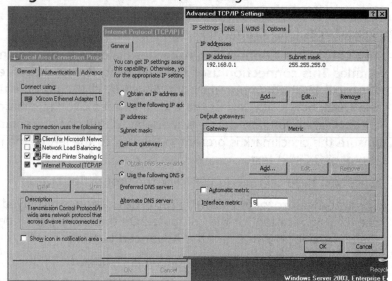

Creating Routing Table Entries

The routing table is created at start up and is stored in temporary memory. Any change made to the routing table is lost when the computer is restarted unless the change is marked as *persistent.* This means it will become a permanent entry in the routing table that will be present every time the computer's routing table is created. To create a persistent routing table entry, the *–p* parameter, described earlier must be used.

The routing table can also be modified via the Routing and Remote Access administrative interface. To access this, click **Start | Administrative Tools | Routing and Remote Access**. This will display the Routing and Remote Access interface. To display the routing table, select an Interface from the list and right-click to display the context menu. Select **Show IP routing Table** from the list, as shown in Figure 2.6. Routes added to via the RRAS interface are static routes. The *–p* parameter is not available in RRAS. Routes added via the RRAS interface can be modified or removed via the RRAS interface or via the command line utility. When you add a static route in RRAS, it will remain in the routing table until you remove it. This means that static routes added via RRAS are persistent by default.

Figure 2.6 Routing and Remote Access Dialog

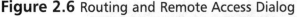
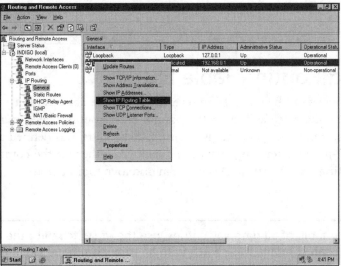

To add static entries to the routing table, select **IP Routing | Static Routes** and right-click to access the context menu. Select **Add Static Route** to display the dialog box shown in Figure 2.7. Select the desired interface from the list in the drop-down box, and then enter the Destination, Network mask, Gateway, and Metric. If you want to use this route to initiate demand-dial connections, leave the checkmark in the box that is so labeled. Otherwise, click the box to remove the checkmark, then click **OK** to complete the addition of the static route.

Figure 2.7 Adding a Static Route via Routing and Remote
Access Administrative Tool

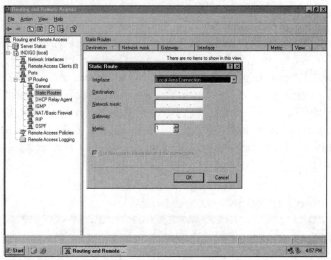

Removing Routing Table Entries

A routing table entry can be removed in several ways. If the command line utility, **route**, was used to create the entry and the entry was not entered using the *–p* parameter, the entry will be lost when the computer is restarted. If the entry was defined as a persistent route using the *–p* parameter, the entry can be removed either via the command line utility or via the **Routing and Remote Access** administrative tool interface.

NOTE

To clear the table of all gateway entries, use the **–f** switch with the **route** command. You can combine this switch with another command (such as **add**), in which case the tables will be cleared before the other command is run.

To remove an entry via the command line, open the command prompt by clicking **Start | Run** and typing **cmd** in the dialog box. Then click **OK** or press **Enter**. The command prompt window will open. To locate the route you want to delete, use the **route print [Enter]** command to see a complete listing of routes in the table. When you identify the route you want to delete, use the **route delete** command in the following format:

```
route delete [destination] [Enter]
```

Although a routing table entry may have several fields (destination, mask, etc.), it is necessary to type only the destination, which by default is the first IP address listed on any routing table entry. This will delete the route and the associated options.

NOTE

When you use the **route delete** command, you can use a wildcard (*) for the destination. For example, if you want to delete all routes with destination addresses that begin with 157 as the first octet, you can enter **157.*** as the destination.

A static route can be removed via the **Routing and Remote Access** tool. After opening the tool by choosing **Start | Administrative Tools | Routing and Remote Access**, expand the node for the RRAS server in the left pane, expand the **IP Routing** node under it, then select **Static Routes**. A list of static routes will be displayed in the right pane. Select the static route you want to remove and right-click to display the context menu. Select **Delete** from the menu. You will not get a dialog box confirming that you want to delete the route and there is no **Edit | Undo** function, so use caution when deleting static routes.

EXAM WARNING

If a route is not marked with a –p when being entered, it will not be in the routing table the next time the computer is rebooted or the TCP/IP stack is reinitialized. Routes entered manually without the –p parameter will remain in the routing table until the next time the TCP/IP stack initializes.

In addition to adding and deleting routes, route information can be changed. A route may need to be modified to reflect a change to the gateway or to modify the metric manually. The route utility accessed via the command line uses the following syntax:

```
route change [destination IP] mask [mask address] [gateway IP]
    metric [xx]
```

As an example, suppose you want to change a route to reflect a new gateway. The current route, when you use the **route print** command, will be displayed as shown:

```
Destination ID    Netmask      Gateway      Interface      Metric
78.114.24.10      255.0.0.0    78.114.0.1   78.114.24.10   30
```

To change this route, the syntax is:

```
route change 78.114.24.10 mask 255.0.0.0 78.114.24.1 20
```

The **route change** command can be used to change only the gateway IP address or the metric. If other changes are needed, such as a different subnet mask, the route must be deleted and the correct route information should be added via the **route add** command.

To modify a route via the RRAS interface, access the RRAS interface (as described earlier) and identify the route to be changed. Double-click the route to open the **Static**

Route dialog box to modify the properties of the route including the *Interface*, *Destination*, *Network mask*, *Gateway*, and *Metric*. You can also access the **Static Route** properties dialog box by clicking on the desired route then selecting **Action | Properties** from the menu.

Assigning IP Addressing Information to Network Clients

In this chapter, we've discussed how to devise IP addresses from classful networks, classless networks, and CIDR blocks. Once you've devised your networking schema, you need to assign IP addresses to the network clients, or hosts. Assigning addresses once required you to physically go to each computer and access the TCP/IP stack to manually enter a *static* IP address and related information (subnet mask, default gateway). This process was time-consuming, but perhaps even more importantly, it was error-prone. One mistyped IP address could bring network communications to a grinding halt. To save the time of manually entering addresses at each client and to reduce the possibility of errors, *dynamic* addressing was developed. In this section, we'll look at both static and dynamic addressing and learn why it is still sometimes necessary or preferable to use static IP addressing for some computers.

Static IP Addressing

Static IP addressing manually assigns a specific IP address to a client or host. The IP address of the client does not change unless someone manually changes it. Although this was the original way IP addresses were assigned, it was largely supplanted by dynamic IP addressing to avoid errors and ease the burden of administration. However, there are still cases in which it is best to assign a static IP address to a device. For example, you might want to configure an IP address on a router manually so that it does not change IP addresses. You can then add static routes to your routing tables and that router would always be found. For instance, you might want to use static addressing in a branch office rather than use a routing protocol (RIPv2, OSPF) across the WAN. Using static addressing on the branch office and main office routers can enable each to find the other across the WAN. In this case, you need to also set up static routing entries in your routing tables on those two routers.

In the following exercise, you'll learn the procedure for configuring a static IP address in Windows Server 2003.

EXERCISE 2.06

CONFIGURING A STATIX IP ADDRESS

To configure a static IP address on a Windows Server 2003 computer:

1. Select **Start | Control Panel | Network Connections**.

2. In Network Connections, double-click **Local Area Connection** (or right-click and select **Properties**). The **Local Area Connection Properties** dialog box will open.

3. On the **General** tab, select **Internet Protocol (TCP/IP)** from the list.

4. If TCP/IP is not shown in the list, click the **Install** button, select **Protocol** from the list provided, click **Add**, and select **TCP/IP** from the network protocol list. Click **OK** to install.

5. Select **Internet Protocol (TCP/IP)** from the list. *Important note:* Do not click the box with the checkmark or you will de-select TCP/IP. If you inadvertently do this, click the box again to place a checkmark in the box.

6. With **Internet Protocol (TCP/IP)** selected, click the **Properties** button, shown in Figure 2.8. The **Internet Protocol (TCP/IP) Properties** dialog box will be displayed, showing two sections for IP address input. The first section is for IP address configuration. The second section is for DNS server addresses.

7. Click the option button next to **Use the following IP address**. If the **Obtain an IP address automatically** is selected, the IP address configuration information is disabled.

8. Enter the static IP address that you want to assign to this network interface in the **IP address** section.

9. Enter the subnet mask for this device in the **Subnet mask** section.

10. Enter the default gateway for this device in the **Default Gateway** section. At this point, you should have three entries in the first section, as shown in Figure 2.8.

11. Click **OK** to accept these changes or click **Cancel** to cancel the changes.

12. In the **Local Area Connection Properties** dialog box, click **OK** to accept changes or **Cancel** to exit without accepting the changes you made.

Figure 2.8 Local Area Connection Properties and TCP/IP Dialog

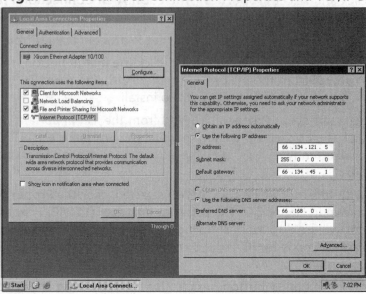

Configuring a Static IP Address

Configuring a static IP address can be useful in a number of situations. For example, there are a number of computer roles that require a static IP address or for which it is preferable to assign a static address:

- A DHCP server must have a static IP address. The DHCP server service will not run on a computer that is configured to obtain its IP address automatically.

- DNS servers need static IP addresses so clients can find them, and their IP addresses can be configured in DHCP options to be handed out to DHCP clients.

- WINS servers need static IP addresses for the same reason.

However, make sure that there is a sound reason for configuring a device with a static IP address. You can run into trouble with static IP addresses in a number of situations. If you're using DHCP to configure IP addresses automatically, you will need to exclude the static IP address(es) from the address pool on your DHCP Server. Otherwise, the static IP address that you manually assigned might be assigned to another device by DHCP, and this can cause connectivity problems for

Continued

either or both devices because they are trying to use identical IP addresses. Also, if you reconfigure your network, you may run into trouble changing static IP addresses or static routes added to routing tables. Keep a list of the static IP addresses you've assigned and any static routing tables that may point to those devices to avoid problems on the network.

Also note that in many cases, using DHCP reservations is a better alternative than assigning static addresses. This ensures that the computer will always have the same IP address, as with static addressing, but also allows for DHCP options to be updated and distributed without having to make the changes on each computer manually.

EXAM WARNING

If you assign a computer a static IP address that is already taken on the subnet, the computer with the duplicate IP address will have a subnet mask of 0.0.0.0. This is a good clue that the IP address is a duplicate.

Dynamic IP Addressing

In most cases, it's desirable to use dynamic IP addressing because you can manage IP addressing from a central location and the addresses are assigned by the system rather than being typed manually. This reduces errors and provides timely, accurate IP addressing to clients. Unlike static IP addressing, dynamic addressing easily scales from small to large networking environments. For very small environments, a special form of dynamic addressing called Automatic Private IP Addressing (APIPA) might be the best solution. We'll discuss APIPA in the next section, but in this section, we'll take a brief look at DHCP.

NOTE

Both DHCP and APIPA are discussed in great detail in Chapter 3.

Dynamic IP addressing is accomplished in Windows Server 2003 via the DHCP. If you recall from our discussion in Chapter 1, DHCP is an Application layer protocol that provides dynamic IP addressing via a server/client model. A DHCP server must be installed and clients must be configured to obtain their IP address configuration data automatically (along with other optional TCP/IP configuration information such as DNS server address, WINS server address, and default gateway) from the DHCP server. All Microsoft Windows Server 2003-

based computers include a DHCP server service that is an installation option (not default). All Microsoft Windows computers running TCP/IP, including servers and workstations running Windows 98, ME, NT, XP, 2000, and Server 2003, install the DHCP client service automatically, as part of TCP/IP.

NOTE

Installing the DHCP server service is done a little differently depending on the edition of Windows Server 2003 you're using. With the Standard, Enterprise, and Datacenter editions, you can install the DHCP server service via the **Configure your Server** wizard, invoked via the **Administrative Tools** menu. In Web edition, you must add the DHCP server service via **Add/Remove Programs** in Control Panel, as a Windows Component (Networking Services).

DHCP is configured by an administrator to provide IP address configuration information to DHCP clients. The information distributed to clients is based on segments called scopes. A *scope* is a set of IP addresses that can be allocated to DHCP clients. Each scope is associated with specific configuration information to be supplied to clients whose IP addresses fall within that scope. The administrator can create one or more scopes on a Windows Server 2003 computer running the DHCP server service. Scope information is specific to the DHCP Server and if you have multiple DHCP servers, they must be configured to use mutually exclusive scopes. Scope information is not shared across DHCP servers and any duplication in the scope range will cause serious network addressing problems. In addition to carefully defining scopes for DHCP servers, administrators must also take care to avoid including static IP addresses that have been manually assigned, in any DHCP server scope.

Scopes are sets of defined IP addresses identified by a subnet mask. When a DHCP client requests an IP address from the DHCP server, an address is used from a specific scope, as shown in Figure 2.9. Since some IP addresses may be assigned manually, such as those for routers or specific servers, those IP addresses can specifically be excluded from a scope. This ensures that duplicate IP addresses are not assigned and allows for static configuration of IP addresses on the network.

In a subnetted environment, routers and remote computers can be configured to be DHCP Relay Agents, which forward DHCP information between subnets. The router forwards requests for IP address configuration assignments to the remote DHCP Server. The entire process of configuring and managing DHCP servers and clients is discussed in detail in Chapter 3.

Figure 2.9 DHCP Server, Scopes, and Clients

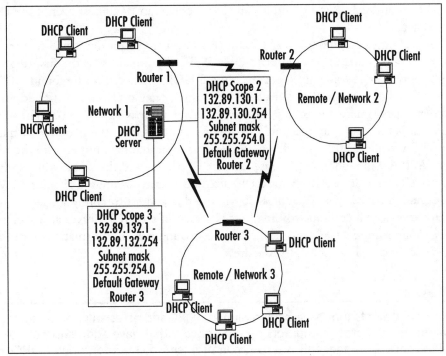

APIPA

For small network environments where scalability is not an issue, APIPA can be used to assign addresses automatically without requiring a DHCP server or the purchase of a server operating system. Beginning with Windows 98, the APIPA service has been included in Microsoft operating systems for the purpose of assigning unique IP addresses automatically to computers in a small networked environment, such as the small office/home office (SOHO). This provides similar capabilities to DHCP but does not require that DHCP be implemented or managed, as in a large scale networking environment. In fact, APIPA is targeted at networks with 25 or fewer clients.

APIPA uses a reserved range of IP addresses and a mathematical calculation, or algorithm, to ensure each assigned IP address is unique on the private network. There are two major benefits of using APIPA versus static IP addressing: The automation reduces IP addressing errors and it will yield to DHCP servers, if one is found on the network. APIPA works seamlessly with DHCP by regularly checking for the presence of a DHCP server on the network. If a DHCP server is detected, APIPA will request an address from the DHCP server to replace the private address it has assigned. This integration with DHCP makes APIPA a viable solution for small, growing companies.

APIPA is also used in cases where a DHCP server is present but unavailable. Though a DHCP server might be unavailable because one has not been placed in service on a network (as described earlier), APIPA can also be used for fault-tolerance to ensure that a DHCP client computer coming online can always obtain an IP address even if the DHCP server is down.

When a client is configured to obtain an IP address automatically, it will first try to find a DHCP server by initiating the standard DHCP discover broadcast as the first step in the DORA negotiation described in Chapter 3. If a DHCP server cannot be found, APIPA automatically will configure the client computer using a randomly chosen IP address from the reserved Class B network 169.254.0.0 with the subnet mask 255.255.0.0. The client computer takes the randomly generated IP address and tests it on the network by transmitting an ARP broadcast. If the IP address is in use (as indicated by a response to the ARP message), APIPA will randomly generate another IP address and the client will test that address via ARP broadcast. APIPA makes 10 attempts to find an unused IP address. When the client finds an acceptable IP address, it will use that address to communicate on the network. However, it will continue to broadcast in search of a DHCP Server at five-minute intervals. If one is found, it obtains new IP address configuration information from the DHCP server and replaces the APIPA address.

NOTE

Note that clients that have been assigned APIPA addresses will not be able to communicate with other computers on the network that have addresses outside the APIPA network range. This is a common problem to check for when a DHCP client is unable to communicate on the network. Use **ipconfig** to determine its IP address; if it is in the 169.254.0.0 range, you know there is a DHCP problem.

New & Noteworthy...

Alternate IP Configuration

A computer can be configured with its IP address information via static address assignment, DHCP, the DHCP allocator, APIPA, or via *alternate configuration information*. In Windows Server 2003 (and Windows XP), an alternate IP configuration can be assigned to a computer in one of two ways. An alternate configuration can be configured manually for a specific network setting or it can obtain a private IP address automatically when the DHCP server is not available. This is helpful when a computer is used on more than one network, as is often the case with laptops. When a laptop is used at the office, the DHCP server is found and the IP configuration is obtained automatically through the DHCP client request. When the laptop is used on a home network, no DHCP server is found and, if configured, the laptop will use an automatically assigned private IP address or it will use the alternate configuration information provided. Without alternate configuration data, APIPA will be used if no DHCP server is found.

Continued

The ability to configure alternate, static IP configuration information is new to Windows XP/Windows Server 2003, and provides additional flexibility for today's mobile devices.

Configuring Alternate IP Addressing Configurations

Windows XP and Windows Server 2003 clients can also be configured with alternate IP address configurations. This is especially helpful for laptop computers that may connect to a variety of networks such as branch office, home office, and vendor sites. The alternate IP addressing configuration also is used if the DHCP server cannot be contacted, as an alternative to APIPA. The alternate configuration includes IP address, subnet mask, default gateway, and DNS and WINS server IP addresses.

Configuring & Implementing...

Alternate IP Addressing

Alternate IP addressing is configured in the **Local Area Connection** settings. Figure 2.10 shows the **Alternate Configuration** options in the Internet Protocol (TCP/IP) Properties dialog.

Follow these steps to configure alternate IP addresses for a Windows XP/Windows Server 2003 device:

1. Select **Start | Control Panel | Network Connections**.

2. Select **Local Area Connection**.

3. In the Local Area Connection Properties dialog box, select **Internet Protocol (TCP/IP)**. *Important note:* Do not click the box or the checkmark will be removed, which will disable TCP/IP.

4. In the Internet Protocol (TCP/IP) Properties dialog box, click the **option** button next to **Obtain IP Address Automatically**, if it is not already selected.

5. Click the **Alternate Configuration** tab. If the **Alternate Configuration** tab is *not* displayed, this means you have **Use the following IP address** selected on the **General** tab. You can set up an alternate configuration only if the computer is configured as a DHCP client. Click **Obtain an IP address automatically** to display the **Alternate Configuration** tab in the Internet Protocol (TCP/IP) Properties dialog.

Continued

6. On the **Alternate Configuration tab, Automatic Private IP address** is selected by default. To configure an alternate IP address, click the **option** button next to **User configured**.

7. The fields below **User configured** are now available. Enter the *IP address, subnet mask, default gateway, Preferred and Alternate DNS servers, and Preferred and Alternate WINS servers.*

8. Click **OK** to accept the changes or **Cancel** to exit without saving the changes.

Figure 2.10 Alternate IP Configuration

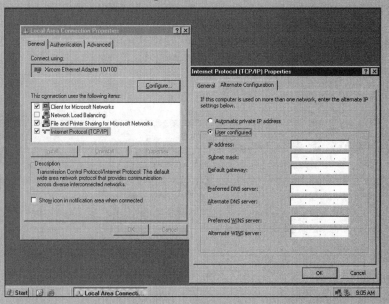

The DHCP Allocator

Another way in which IP addresses can be assigned automatically is via the DHCP *allocator* that is part of the Internet Connection Sharing (ICS) service. An ICS host computer acts as a limited-functionality DHCP server and hands out IP addresses to ICS clients. These addresses are from the private address range 192.168.0.2 to 192.168.0.254. The ICS host itself is configured with an IP address of 192.168.0.1 on its LAN adapter.

Windows Server 2003's Network Address Translation (NAT) service can also use the allocator, or clients can use a full-fledged DHCP server to obtain their addresses. NAT should be used instead of ICS if there are DHCP servers, DNS servers, gateways, or computers with static IPs on the network.

Head of the Class…

Summary of Exam Objectives

To successfully manage a network in today's environment, you must have a firm understanding of IP addressing and how to work with classful and classless subnetting issues. Classful addressing uses standard publicly assigned Class A, B, or C network IDs with the default subnet masks 255.0.0.0, 255.255.0.0, and 255.255.255.0, respectively. In addition, classful networks can be subdivided into smaller, equal-sized segments or subnets. These subnets are created by borrowing bits from the host address space, which then are appended to the network address space. The number of bits taken from the host will increase the number of network IDs available and will also decrease the number of host addresses available per subnet by approximately a factor of 2. This inverse relationship is the foundation of subnetting, whether within the classful boundaries or not.

Classful subnetting requires a strong understanding of binary to decimal conversion, an understanding of weighted binary values, and knowledge of how to create and dissect dotted decimal notations from binary values. In addition, it's critical to know how to determine the number of bits needed to create a desired number of subnets or, conversely, the number of bits that must remain to generate a minimum (or maximum) number of host addresses per subnet. Using a varying number of bits to extend the network space, subnets of equal sizes can be created. Classful subnetting requires that each subnet be equal in size. Thus, you can create 4 or 64 or 16,384 subnets, but each will have the same number of available host addresses per subnet.

Variable length subnetting expands upon classful subnetting and allows you to create subnets of various sizes. This is not only extremely useful in practical application but it is a more efficient use of available IP addresses as well. Most corporate networks today have some subnets that administrators want to limit to one, two, or perhaps three devices. Other subnets might have hundreds or thousands of host devices. Variable length subnetting is accomplished through the use of a variable length subnet mask, which defines which portion of the IP address is the network ID and which portion is the host ID. Thus, one subnet can be limited to two IP addresses, and another subnet can have 65,536 host addresses per subnet. Variable length subnetting has two notable characteristics:

- Variable length subnets are created by subdividing subnets. This is an important concept to understand.

- Although you can subdivide subnets, those subdivisions initially will have an equal number of hosts per subnet (equal-sized). Therefore, variable length subnetting is a recursive process where subnets are divided and divided again, creating a tree-like structure where groups of subnets have different numbers of host addresses per subnet.

IP addresses are routed using routing tables. Default routing tables are created on a Windows-based computer each time the TCP/IP stack is initialized (typically this occurs when you boot the computer). Default routing tables on Windows XP/Windows Server 2003 computers contain several routes, including the default route, 0.0.0.0, which is used if no other suitable route can be found. A routing table entry in Windows XP/2003 must contain at least the destination IP address, the netmask (subnet mask), and gateway or router to which traffic will be sent, the IP address of the physical interface, and a metric to determine best routes. In cases where more than one route is suitable for use, the route with the lowest metric will be chosen. The default routing table can be viewed by clicking **Start | Run | cmd** to open a command window, and typing **route** with various parameters.

Routing tables in Windows Server 2003 differ from routing tables in earlier versions of Windows in two important ways. The Class D netmask is defined as 240.0.0.0 instead of 224.0.0.0. This new subnet mask is better suited to Class D multicast routing. The second difference is that the metric is calculated automatically by TCP/IP. This feature can be disabled in the Advanced properties of TCP/IP.

The most common method of assigning IP addresses to host devices is by using the Dynamic Host Configuration Protocol. A DHCP server manages the automatic process by replying to requests for IP addresses. A unique address from a pool of available IP addresses is assigned to the requesting host. The other related IP configuration data is also assigned, including the subnet mask and default gateway. Optional information, such as DNS and WINS server addresses, can be assigned as well. The configuration and management of a DHCP server is critical to problem-free IP addressing and is covered in greater detail later in this book. If a host is not configured to receive an IP automatically using DHCP, it must be configured manually. The danger in manual configuration is that if a duplicate address is accidentally assigned, one or both devices (the two with duplicate addresses) may be unable to communicate on the network. In addition, the manual assignment of addresses can be time consuming and error prone, so assigned static IP addresses should be limited to devices such as routers and servers for which a static IP address makes sense. It is possible to accomplish basically the same thing (the ability of a device to always have the same address) by using address reservations in DHCP. However, some computers—notably, the DHCP server itself—must have static addresses assigned.

APIPA and the DHCP allocator also assign IP addresses automatically. In addition, Windows Server 2003, like Windows XP, provides the ability to set an alternate configuration as an alternative to APIPA to be used when a DHCP server is not found.

Exam Objectives Fast Track

Review of Classful Subnet Masking

- ☑ Class A networks use the first octet for the network ID and have a default subnet mask of 255.0.0.0.

- ☑ Class B networks use the first two octets (w, x) for the network ID and have a default subnet mask of 255.255.0.0.

☑ Class C networks use the first three octets (*w*, *x*, *y*) for the network ID and have a default subnet mask of 255.255.255.0.

☑ Class D networks are used for multicasts.

☑ Class E networks are not supported in Windows Server 2003 and are currently considered experimental.

☑ Networks can be subdivided to both increase the number of networks and to decrease the number of host addresses available per subnet.

☑ Subnetting is accomplished by taking bits from the host address space and adding them to the network ID space.

☑ The number of bits borrowed for the network ID determines both the number of new subnets that can be created and the number of hosts you can have on each new subnet.

☑ Each bit taken from the host address space for the network ID reduces the number of host addresses available on each subnet by a power of 2.

Variable Length or Nonclassful (Classless) Subnet Masking

☑ The process of creating variable length subnets is a recursive function; this means that subnets are further subdivided (one or more times) to yield subnets with varying numbers of host addresses.

☑ Variable length subnetting forms a tree-like structure of subnets, similar to a directory tree on a disk drive.

☑ Variable length subnetting is accomplished by creating a variable length subnet mask (VLSM). This determines the number of resulting subnets.

☑ The VLSM for a subnet is created from the subnet above it, with bits being added to the network ID space for each subsequent subnetting.

☑ When subnets of varying sizes are created using VLSMs, the distinctions between network ID classes loses distinction. Therefore, this method is known as nonclassful subnet masking.

The Windows XP/Windows 2000 Routing Table

☑ A Windows XP/Windows 2000 routing table has the following fields included, by default: network destination, netmask, gateway, interface, and metric.

☑ A Windows XP/Windows 2000 routing table may also have the following optional fields: Directly Attached Network ID Routes, Remote Network ID Routes, Host Routes, and Default Route.

☑ The network destination is the IP address of the destination for the packet.

☑ The netmask is the subnet mask, used to identify the network ID portion of the IP address.

☑ The gateway is the router that will forward nonlocal packets.

☑ The interface is the IP address of the physical interface.

☑ The metric is a number calculated to assist in automatically determining the best route. If two routes are suitable for forwarding a packet, the route with the lowest metric is selected.

☑ The Directly Attached Network ID Routes entry is used for routes that are connected to the local network.

☑ The Remote Network ID Routes entry is used for routes that can be accessed only via routers, or remotely.

☑ Host Routes allows you to enter a specific route to a specific host. The network destination is the host's IP address and the subnet mask is set to 255.255.255.255.

☑ The Default Route is the route used if no other matching route can be found. It uses all 0s, which sends a MAC-level broadcast.

The Windows Server 2003 Routing Table

☑ The Windows Server 2003 routing table uses the same fields as the Windows XP/2000 routing tables.

☑ The Windows Server 2003 routing table differs from earlier versions of Windows routing tables in two ways: automatic metric calculation and the Class D subnet mask.

☑ If automatically calculated by TCP/IP, the metric indicates the speed of the interface. Administrators can also disable automatic calculation and set their own metrics.

☑ The Class D subnet mask used in earlier versions of Windows was 224.0.0.0 with a network destination of 224.0.0.0. The new subnet mask for the network destination of 224.0.0.0 is 240.0.0.0.

☑ Routing table entries can be temporary or persistent. A route that is added to the routing table with the –*p* parameter is persistent; otherwise, the route is temporary.

☑ A temporary route exists in the routing table only until the TCP/IP stack is reinitialized, which typically happens during a system start up or reinitialization.

☑ A persistent route will remain in the routing table until manually removed.

☑ Static routes can be added via the command line utility **route**, or via the Routing and Remote Access Administration interface.

Assigning Addressing Information to Network Clients

☑ IP configuration information can be provided to host computers either manually or automatically.

☑ Manual IP configuration or static IP configuration can be used for hosts that need a static (or constant) IP address. This might include WINS servers, routers, or other types of servers. The DHCP server itself must have a static address.

☑ Manual IP configuration can be error-prone and is best avoided except for the small number of hosts that require static configuration.

☑ Automatic configuration is accomplished by using the Application layer Dynamic Host Configuration Protocol (DHCP).

☑ Address ranges, called DHCP scopes, contain a set of available IP addresses that can be assigned to hosts requesting an IP address.

☑ The automatic IP configuration information also distributes other parameters to clients, including (at minimum) the IP address, subnet mask, and default gateway. It also can include optional information such as the IP addresses for preferred DNS and WINS servers.

☑ Static addresses assigned to routers, servers, and so forth should be excluded from the DHCP server's scope to avoid duplication of IP addresses, which can disable your network.

Exam Objectives
Frequently Asked Questions

The following Frequently Asked Questions, answered by the authors of this book, are designed to both measure your understanding of the Exam Objectives presented in this chapter, and to assist you with real-life implementation of these concepts. You will also gain access to thousands of other FAQs at ITFAQnet.com.

Q: There's a lot of material on subnetting in this chapter. Do we really need to focus so much on this topic?

A: Yes, for two reasons. First, if you need to do this on the job, you need to have a strong level of comfort and competence to do the job. Disabling your network due to calculation or logic errors would be unacceptable. Also, this foundational knowledge applies not only to specific subnetting questions you'll get on the exam but it will help you understand subsequent material as well. Having a strong foundation in subnetting will pay off in many areas of the exam and on the job.

Q: Isn't variable length subnetting the same as subnetting a subnet?

A: Yes, it is. Variable length subnetting is a recursive process. We take a network and subnet it into some number of segments, each with the same number of host addresses per subnet. We take one of those subnets and further divide it, creating a different number of host addresses per subnet for that one subnet. We can create a different configuration on another subnet.

Q: What's the difference between a regular subnet mask and a variable length subnet mask?

A: On first glance, they can look exactly the same. It's the application that changes. With a standard (not default) subnet mask, the same subnet mask is used for all subnets. With a variable length subnet mask, a different subnet mask is used on each variant. As you subdivide a subnet, you create a new subnet mask that reflects that particular configuration. Overall, on a network on which you've used variable length subnetting, you might have two, three, four, or more different subnet masks in use.

Q: What's the difference between a routing table on a router and a routing table on my computer?

A: The routing tables are used in the same way, to help determine the best route for any IP packet it encounters. However, the primary difference is that your computer will create a default routing table every time it boots and TCP/IP is initialized. Most computers are not configured as routers and do not use routing protocols like RIP or OSPF. However, Windows Server 2003 can function as a router (as can Windows 2000 Server) and run these dynamic routing protocols.

Q: Am I more likely to see command line questions or RRAS console questions on the exam?

A: Microsoft exam questions typically test knowledge and familiarity with new features. However, the command line utilities are fast and easy to use, so they are still in common use in the field. Your chances are about the same in terms of seeing command line or RRAS interface questions regarding routing, so be familiar with both methods. More importantly, understand what the various route parameters accomplish. There are some functions that can be performed only via the command line.

Q: What's the difference between a static IP address and an alternate IP address?

A: A static IP address is any address that is manually entered in the computer's TCP/IP properties (as opposed to configuring the computer to obtain an address automatically). An alternate IP address is an example of a static IP address. A Windows Server 2003 computer that is used in more than one location (on more than one network) can be configured with an alternate, static IP address even if its primary IP address is assigned dynamically via DHCP.

Self Test

A Quick Answer Key follows the Self Test questions. For complete questions, answers, and explanations to the Self Test questions in this chapter as well as the other chapters in this book, see the Self Test Appendix.

Classful Subnet Masking

1. What is the correct subnet mask for the IP address 120.66.10.5/10?

    A. 255.192.0.0

    B. 255.66.0.0

    C. 255.255.10.0

    D. 255.10.0.0

2. Identify the underlying network ID for this IP address: 199.214.36.132/25.

    A. 199.214.36.0/24

    B. 199.214.36.0/25

    C. 199.214.36.128/25

    D. 199.214.36.128/24

Variable Length or Nonclassful Subnet Masking

3. Your corporate network uses variable length subnetting to make more efficient use of IP addresses. One of the IP addresses for a host is 131.39.161.17 with a subnet mask of 255.255.248.0. What is the proper notation for the network to which this host is connected?

   A. 131.39.160.0/21

   B. 131.36.161.0/20

   C. 131.39.161.17/21

   D. 131.36.160.0/20

4. You need to create several subnets for your corporate network. Each subnet should have no more than two host addresses available per subnet. You have a subnet with the address of 136.42.255.0/24. What are the first two subnet addresses that would be created in this configuration?

   A. 136.42.255.0/31, 136.42.255.4/31

   B. 136.42.255.2/30, 136.42.255.4/30

   C. 136.42.255.4/29, 136.42.255.8/29

   D. 136.42.255.0/30, 136.42.255.4/30

5. You've just accepted a position in the IT department at a small, growing company. You've been asked to devise a subnetting scheme for their network that will allow for a maximum of 30 hosts per subnet. The company's assigned network ID is 197.228.69.0. What is the subnet mask for the configuration you must develop?

   A. 255.255.255.248

   B. 255.255.255.240

   C. 255.255.255.224

   D. 255.225.248.0

6. A Class A network is subnetted using the subnet mask 255.254.0.0. You are asked to further subnet this network to create a subnetting scheme that allows up to 65,534 hosts per subnet. The network address you've been given to work with is 65.254.0.0. What is the last network address in the new scheme you're to devise?

   A. 65.254.0.0/16

   B. 65.254.0.0/15

   C. 65.255.0.0/16

   D. 65.255.0.0/15

7. You're working on a subnet with this network address: 155.18.128.0/19. To make the most efficient use of your IP addresses and to improve the efficiency of the network, you are tasked with dividing this segment into subnets that have a maximum of 254 hosts per subnet. What are the last two network addresses you'll create and what is the correct subnet mask?

A. 155.18.128.0/24, 155.18.129.0/24, 255.255.255.0

B. 155.18.188.0/24, 155.18.190.0/24, 255.255.254.0

C. 155.18.254.0/24, 155.18.255.0/24, 255.255.255.0

D. 155.18.158.0/24, 155.18.159.0/24, 255.255.255.0

The Windows XP/Windows 2000 Routing Table

8. Based on the partial routing table provided, what will happen to a packet with the IP address 133.94.228.52 and a default gateway of 133.94.128.1?

Network Destination	Netmask	Gateway	Interface	Metric
0.0.0.0	0.0.0.0	133.94.128.1	133.94.140.26	30
127.0.0.0	255.0.0.0	127.0.0.1	127.0.0.1	1
133.94.128.0	255.255.240.0	133.94.140.26	133.94.140.26	30
133.94.140.26	255.255.255.255	127.0.0.1	127.0.0.1	30

A. The packet will be sent directly to 133.94.228.52 for delivery.

B. The packet will be sent to 133.94.128.1 for delivery.

C. The packet will be sent to 133.94.140.26 for delivery.

D. The packet will be sent to 133.94.128.0 for delivery.

9 . Using the routing table provided, identify the destination of a packet with the IP address of 66.22.221.19 and a default gateway of 66.22.192.1.

Network Destination	Netmask	Gateway	Interface	Metric
0.0.0.0	0.0.0.0	66.22.192.1	66.22.200.13	30
127.0.0.0	255.0.0.0	127.0.0.1	127.0.0.1	1
66.22.192.0	255.255.224.0	66.22.200.13	66.22.200.13	30
66.22.200.13	255.255.255.255	127.0.0.1	127.0.0.1	30

A. 66.22.200.13

B. 66.22.192.0

C. 66.22.192.1

D. 66.22.221.19

The Windows Server 2003 Routing Table

10. You've added several routes to a routing table on a heavily utilized server in the finance department, using the Routing and Remote Administration interface. However, you notice that this seems to be making things worse. You want to remove the routes you added, so you reboot the computer, knowing that the routing table will be recreated when TCP/IP is reinitialized, but the problem persists. What is the most likely cause of the problem?

A. When you add routes using the RRAS interface, they are not added to the routing table until you click Refresh. Therefore, the routes were never added.

B. The routes you added were not flagged with the −p to mark them as persistent. They should have been removed when you rebooted.

C. The routes you added will not be removed through rebooting because you added them through RRAS.

D. The routes you added can be removed only by using the command line interface.

11. You're examining the routing table on a Windows Server 2003. You see the following entries (partial routing table). What can you conclude about this computer?

Network Destination	Netmask	Gateway	Interface	Metric
0.0.0.0	0.0.0.0	66.22.192.1	66.22.200.13	30
10.84.112.0	255.255.255.0	10.84.112.8	10.84.112.8	30
10.84.112.8	255.255.255.255	127.0.0.1	127.0.0.1	1
66.22.192.0	255.255.224.0	66.22.200.13	66.22.200.13	30
66.22.200.13	255.255.255.255	127.0.0.1	127.0.0.1	30
127.0.0.0	255.0.0.0	127.0.0.1	127.0.0.1	1

A. There is a problem with the subnet mask associated with 10.84.112.0.

B. There is a problem with the TCP/IP protocol stack because two addresses are associated with the loopback address.

C. The computer is configured to use an alternate IP address.

D. The computer has two NICs installed.

Assigning Addressing Information to Network Clients

12. Your corporate network uses DHCP to dynamically assign IP addresses to clients. You're installing a new router and have been given the router's assigned static IP address. You configure the router and add it to the network. Immediately, you begin getting calls from users who cannot connect to the network. When you **ping** the router, you get errors. What is the most likely cause of this problem?

    A. The router is using an address within the scope of the DHCP addresses.

    B. The router is using a static IP address assigned to another router.

    C. The router is not configured to use a dynamic routing protocol.

    D. The router is on a different subnet from the DHCP server.

13. Jack was away on vacation for three weeks and decided to come in Sunday afternoon to begin sorting through some of the work he knew would be waiting. Known to be a bit of a "button pusher," Jack started looking through some of his computer settings. He noticed that his IP address had changed to a completely new number. Before his vacation, his IP address was 62.128.47.55 but now it was 169.254.64.15. He wondered if something was wrong with his computer, but he noticed that he could still surf the Internet. When he mentions it to you over coffee Monday morning, what do you tell Jack about this?

    A. Jack's computer is configured to automatically obtain IP configuration information from a backup DHCP server if the primary one is down.

    B. The DHCP server was moved to a new subnet, causing client IP assignments to change.

    C. The DHCP servers were offline for service on Sunday afternoon.

    D. Someone must have changed the TCP/IP settings to a static IP address while Jack was on vacation.

14. A user has a laptop that she uses at home, at work to access both the corporate network and the Internet, and when she travels to client sites. She contacted you Monday morning to say that her laptop wouldn't connect to the network. She did mention something about having trouble on her home network over the weekend and working Sunday at home to fix the problem. You check the laptop's TCP/IP properties, and notice it is configured to "Use the following IP address." The address is 192.168.0.1 and the subnet mask is 255.255.255.0. What is the most likely cause of the user's connectivity problem at work?

A. The subnet mask does not match the network ID portion of the IP address.

B. Her laptop is configured to use a static IP address from the private address range.

C. Her laptop is configured to use an alternate IP address for her home connection.

D. Her laptop is configured to dynamically obtain an IP address, which caused a problem on her home network and is now causing a problem on the corporate network as well.

15. You've configured a DHCP server to use the following range of IP addresses when assigning addresses to clients: 131.107.0.0/19 through 131.107.224.0/19. You set the subnet mask for this range of addresses to 255.255.240.0. Users are complaining that they cannot connect to the network. What is the most likely cause of this problem?

A. The range of addresses is illegal. It should end at 131.107.192.0/19.

B. The subnet mask is wrong. It should be 255.224.0.0.

C. The range of addresses is illegal. The first address cannot be 131.107.0.0/19.

D. The subnet mask is wrong. It should be 255.255.224.0.

Self Test Quick Answer Key

For complete questions, answers, and explanations to the Self Test questions in this chapter as well as the other chapters in this book, see the Self Test Appendix.

1.	**A**		9.	**D**
2.	**C**		10.	**C**
3.	**A**		11.	**D**
4.	**D**		12.	**A**
5.	**C**		13.	**C**
6.	**C**		14.	**B**
7.	**D**		15.	**D**
8.	**B**			

Chapter 3

MCSA/MCSE 70-291

The Dynamic Host Configuration Protocol

Exam Objectives in this Chapter:

1.2 Manage DHCP.

1.2.1 Manage DHCP clients and leases.

1.2.4 Manage DHCP scope options.

1.2.5 Manage reservations and reserved clients.

1.4.4 Diagnose and resolve issues related to configuration of DHCP server and scope options.

1.4.5 Verify that DHCP Relay Agent is working correctly.

1.4 Troubleshoot DHCP.

1.4.1 Diagnose and resolve issues related to DHCP authorization.

1.3.1 Diagnose and resolve issues related to APIPA.

1.3.2 Diagnose and resolve issues related to incorrect TCP/IP configuration.

1.4.6 Verify database integrity.

1.2.3 Manage DHCP databases.

1.4.3 Examine the system event log and DHCP server audit log files to find related events.

5.3 Troubleshoot server services.

5.3.1 Diagnose and resolve issues related to service dependency.

5.3.2 Use service recovery options to diagnose and resolve service-related issues.

Introduction

Prior to the release of Windows NT 4.0, company networks relied heavily on IPX/SPX and even NetBEUI as their primary network/transport protocols, due to their simplicity and ease of configuration. At that time, TCP/IP was still widely referred to as the "protocol of the Internet," and was seldom used for internal networks. It was considered too complex, too clunky and slow, and too difficult to configure and manage. Novell Netware had the greater share of the Network Operating System (NOS) market, although it did not support native IP; UNIX had the majority share of the Internet market and was primarily run with only IP.

One of the deterrents to using TCP/IP for the company network was its complex addressing scheme. In order to be routable across multiple networks—a necessity for an Internet protocol—TCP/IP relies on IP addresses that define both network and host addresses. Each address must be unique, and keeping track of all the addresses assigned to devices in a large network environment could be an administrative nightmare.

However, the Dynamic Host Configuration Protocol (DHCP) provides a mechanism for assigning IP addresses automatically, ensuring that there will be no duplicates on the network and relieving much of the administrative burden. With the introduction of DHCP into the networking world, more and more companies started relying on TCP/IP for their client centric communication protocol.

In the previous two chapters, we discussed the TCP/IP protocol, IP addressing, and how assigned IP address blocks can be divided to fit your network design topology (subnetting). In this chapter, we discuss how the assignment of those IP addresses can be distributed across your client base automatically. We focus on the inner workings of DHCP in your network environment and discuss how it can be integrated with your domain name system (DNS) implementation for complete client manageability. First, we look at how DHCP actually works when clients request IP addresses on your local area network (LAN). Next, we discuss the steps for installing, configuring, and setting up your Windows Server 2003 server as a DHCP server and defining its scopes and specialized classes for a multitude of different situations. Finally, we cover some basic troubleshooting guidelines, disaster recovery preparation methods, and DHCP system monitoring techniques.

Review of DHCP

DHCP is a standardized protocol that is used to dynamically distribute IP address assignments and configuration information to DHCP enabled clients. Whether those clients run Windows, UNIX/Linux, or Macintosh operating systems, they need only be DHCP-aware to be able to receive IP addresses from a Windows Server 2003 DHCP server.

Head of the Class…

History of DHCP

DHCP grew out of BOOTP (Bootstrap protocol), which was defined by RFC 951 as a means for diskless workstations to obtain an IP address (along with information for booting the machine). Sun had started building these diskless workstations in the 1980s, and they used BOOTP to allow the machines to boot up with information from a BOOTP server.

DHCP was developed as an extension to BOOTP; it uses a "lease" method to allow addresses to be reassigned to different clients, and it also allows for the DHCP server to provide additional TCP/IP configuration information (such as DNS server address and default gateway) along with the IP address. The specifications for DHCP were written by Ralph Droms in 1989, and the first implementation was coded by Ted Lemon.

Request for Comment (RFC) 2131 defines the framework for the DHCP protocol and lays the groundwork for changes that may occur in regard to this protocol in the future. In fact, work on improving the protocol is a task of the Dynamic Host Configuration (DHC) working group of the Internet Engineers Task Force (IETF).

Before DHCP, TCP/IP configuration was a manual process. Administrators had to configure each workstation by hand and keep a running list of which machine owned which IP address. As we pointed out in Chapter 2, each IP address on any given connected network has to be unique. If addresses are not unique and multiple workstations are configured to use the same IP address, users on those workstations will receive an IP address conflict message, and will be unable to connect to other resources via the TCP/IP protocol stack.

In most situations, the reasons for using DHCP far outweigh those in favor of statically assigning addresses to all your workstations. TCP/IP is the native network/transport protocol for Windows Server 2003 (as it was for Windows 2000). If you plan to implement a Windows Server 2003 Active Directory (AD), be prepared to implement TCP/IP also, because it is a requirement. If your user community spans more than about 100 users, DHCP is a must, for the following reasons (among others):

- It allows for central management of workstation IP addresses.

- It provides for easy deployment of networking configuration options such as a DNS suffix, default gateway, or NetBIOS name resolution node type.

- It provides the ability to assist downlevel clients in auto-registering their fully qualified domain names (FQDN) in your AD DNS.

With the addition of a Windows Server 2003 DHCP server to your network environment, the problem of difficult-to-trace misconfigured clients will soon fade away.

EXAM
70-291

OBJECTIVE
1.2.1

DHCP Leases

The process a DHCP client goes through in order to obtain an IP address and any network specific configuration options is called the *DHCP lease process*. A DHCP lease is a configurable amount of time that defines for how long a client has permission to use a particular IP address. This time limit is referred to as a *lease duration*. By default, Windows Server 2003 sets this value to eight days (the same default value was assigned to DHCP leases configured using Windows 2000 DHCP server). It is a best practice not to set your lease duration too high, because other DHCP clients on your network may be unable to obtain an IP address lease if all addresses are used up before current leases expire. As discussed in Chapter 2, your IP address class, whether it is classful or classless addressing, determines how many physical nodes or hosts you can have on a physical network segment. Based on this number, you should determine IP address availability for distribution. See Figure 3.1 for the lease duration configuration page (later in the chapter, we will go into the details of how to configure the lease duration).

You can assign a lease duration of *Unlimited*; however, doing this has some drawbacks and should be used with caution. Assigning an unlimited lease duration means that client IP addresses will never expire. Thus, your IP address pool will never be replenished after all of your IP addresses are handed out. There are some situations in which an unlimited lease duration is appropriate. For example, in a smaller network using a Class A address block, where you may have an exorbitant number of extra addresses, you can use this technique to limit the amount of DHCP lease process traffic traversing the wire.

Figure 3.1 Configuring the DHCP Lease Duration

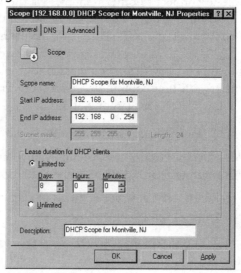

General Lease Duration Rules

DHCP scopes can be defined as a set of configurable IP address options along with hard-coded IP address ranges that ultimately service DHCP clients during their DHCP lease process. Lease duration times are scope independent and thus can be set differently for each scope on your DHCP server. Here are four general rules of thumb you can use when deciding what your lease duration time should be for each network segment's scope:

- If the number of IP addresses available per subnet greatly exceeds your number of physical DHCP aware devices, you can set your lease duration for a longer time interval than the default value of eight days.

- If your DHCP clients tend not to move around (no portable/mobile computers), and your network configuration options do not change often, you can set your lease duration time to a higher interval.

- If your IP address scheme limits the number of IP addresses per subnet in such a way that you are likely to come close to reaching your IP host limit, you might need to set shorter lease duration times to ensure that all clients get an equal share of the allocated IP address space.

- If you are in an environment where configuration changes happen often, or if there are many mobile users, it is best to use a shorter lease duration time. This ensures that mobile users do not "hog" IP addresses for elongated periods of time when those addresses may need to be reused in the production environment.

The DHCP Lease Process

The DHCP lease process has not changed since DHCP was first included in Windows NT 4.0. Before a device can begin transmitting via TCP/IP on your network, it must have a unique IP address assigned to it, either manually or automatically. By design, DHCP is a broadcast-based protocol. For a client to communicate with a DHCP server in order to obtain an IP address, first there must be a process in place by which a non-IP configured client can send a message to an IP configured server. This is done by using a client broadcast along with a limited version of the TCP/IP protocol.

The lease process consists of a four-phase client-server negotiation in which, ultimately, DHCP clients receive a unique address and any other DHCP server configured options. The following list indicates the order in which DHCP messages are exchanged in each of the four phases, and indicates from which computer (client or server) each message type is generated. (See Table 3.1 for a complete listing of all DHCP messages.)

The message types that define the four phases of the DHCP lease process are:

- **DHCPDISCOVER** Initiated by the *DHCP Client* when it comes onto the network
- **DHCPOFFER** Response sent by one or more *DHCP Servers*
- **DHCPREQUEST** Sent by the *DHCP Client* to only one of the responding servers
- **DHCPACK** Sent by the *DHCP Server* to "seal the deal"

TEST DAY TIP

To help remember the four steps of the lease process, it is often referred to as DORA (Discover, Offer, Request, Acknowledgement).

Table 3.1 DHCP Messages

DHCP Messages	Description
DHCPDISCOVER	A *request message* broadcast from *the client* to all devices on the local subnet, asking for an IP address.
DHCPOFFER	An *offer message* sent from any or all *DHCP servers* listening on the local network segment, offering an IP address.
DHCPREQUEST	A *selection message* sent from *the client*, back to the DHCP server that responded first, requesting the selected IP address.
DHCPACK	An *acknowledgement message* sent from the *DHCP server* back to the client, confirming that the IP address is assigned to that client.
DHCPNAK	A *negative acknowledgement message* sent from the DHCP sever back to the client indicating that the requested IP address is no longer valid.
DHCPRELEASE	A *release message* sent from the client to the DHCP server asking for the IP address to be released and the lease expired before its preset expiration time.
DHCPDECLINE	A *decline message* sent from the DHCP client to the offering DHCP server, refusing the acceptance of the offered lease. This is due to an IP address conflict detection on the client side.
DHCPINFORM (Client) DHCPINFORM (Server)	A two-part message used by both the client and server. On the client side, this is a message used to obtain only DHCP options when the client already had a valid IP address. On the server side, this message is used when the DHCP service starts to query Active Directory to determine if it is authorized to lease IP addresses.

TEST DAY TIP

You need to be very familiar with the four message types in the DHCP lease process. Make sure you completely understand the order in which they occur and which device, the client or server, is responsible for sending each type of message. You may also see these message types referred to as *IP request*, *IP offer*, *IP selection*, and *IP acknowledgement*.

IP Lease Request (Discover)

The IP lease request process begins anytime a DHCP client boots up and initializes the TCP/IP stack. A DHCP client is one with its TCP/IP addressing configuration set to **Obtain an IP address automatically**. A Windows Server 2003 computer can be configured as a DHCP client, unless it is functioning as a DHCP server, DNS server, default gateway (router), and so forth. The same lease process occurs when a DHCP client tries to renew its lease agreement with the DHCP server. We will discuss more about lease renewals later.

NOTE

When TCP/IP is configured to use DHCP on a client, only a limited version of the IP stack is actually initialized. Not until the client receives an IP address will the stack become fully functional.

Here's how it works: The client first broadcasts a DHCPDISCOVER message, asking for a valid IP address on its network segment. The limited IP stack in this broadcast uses a source address of 0.0.0.0 and a destination address of 255.255.255.255, a standard broadcast packet address. This message goes to every computer on the network segment. Included in these packets are the Media Access Control (MAC) address of the requesting NIC and the unique NetBIOS name of the client computer. Using both of these pieces of information, any listening DHCP server can return a valid DHCP offer message.

If the client does not receive a response, it will try up to four times before automatically assigning itself a private IP address in the range from 169.254.0.1 to 169.254.255.254 (called an APIPA address). The four attempts at retry occur in intervals of 2, 4, 6, and finally 16 seconds. A random length of time ranging from 0 to 1,000 milliseconds is also added to these retry attempt times. After the fourth attempt, the client will then try to obtain an address every five minutes. The client will continue to keep its auto-generated address until an authorized DHCP server responds. However, with this private address, the client will be able to communicate only with other clients on the same subnet sharing this private range. You will read more about this in the section "Automatic Private IP Addressing (APIPA)."

Head of the Class...

Multiple NICS and DHCP

Have you ever purchased a new server for your company that came with a dual interface network card? These can be used for network load balancing or network card redundancy. In addition to these two NICs, suppose you want to add another Gigabit Ethernet card to take advantage of that new switch your network guys just installed. You now have three NICS in your server, and only the gigabit NIC is configured with a static IP address. In addition, the gigabit NIC is the only physically connected network card, since you don't have any use for the dual card at the moment. There are cables plugged into the dual card, but they're not attached to any device at the other end.

Everything seems to be running fine at first. However, when you boot up the system, you notice a bit of a network lag before the **Ctrl + Alt + Del** logon screen appears. You wonder if you have a network problem, but this is not the case at all. The reason you are experiencing a lag is because each network card in your machine that is configured for DHCP has to go through the lease process separately.

What about Media Sense? Isn't it supposed to disable a NIC that's not connected? Media Sense is a process by which the TCP/IP protocol stack dynamically senses connected or disconnected media types on your network interface cards. The problem arises when there is media (network cables) connected to your NIC, but no live connection at the other end. DHCP is running through its configured retry intervals while you wait for it to eventually time out.

There are a few ways around this if you must keep the unused NICs in your server and physically plugged into your network for possible future use. You can simply disable the NIC in the properties of **My Network Places** by right-clicking the card you do not want to use and choosing **Disable**. Alternatively, you can open the Windows Registry and disable DHCP Media Sense. To do this, open the Registry Editor (run **regedt32.exe**), navigate to the following key and add a new DWORD value key, **DisableDHCPMediaSense**, with a value of **1**.

```
HKLM\SYSTEM\CurrentControlSet\Services\tcpip\Parameters
```

NOTE

Microsoft recommends that you create the Registry key and value when installing Windows Clustering Services, due to an issue with how the local interconnect NICs function when there is a cable disconnect.

See Figure 3.2 for an illustration of the DHCPDISCOVER phase of the lease process.

Figure 3.2 DHCP Client Initiates an IP Address Request (DHCPDISCOVER)

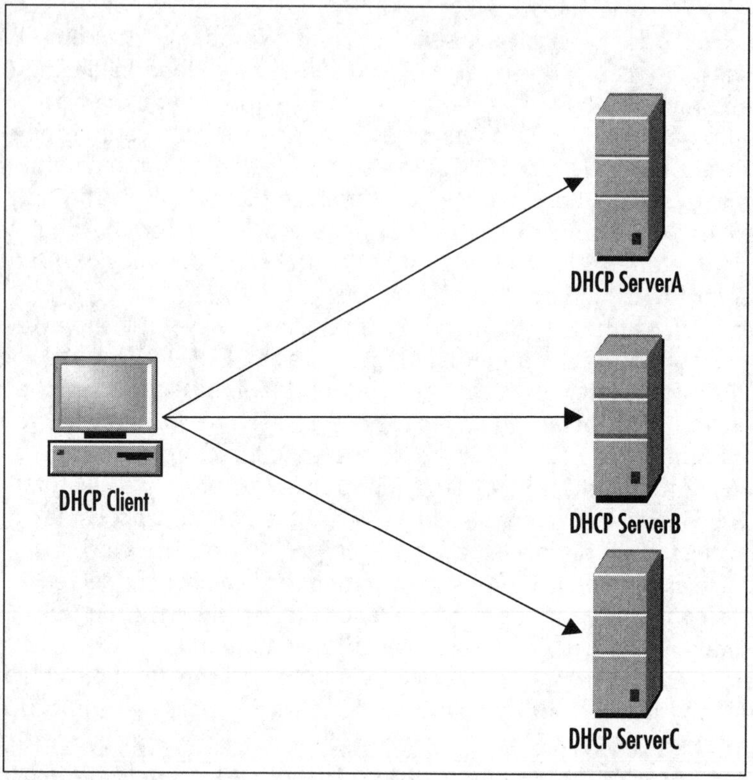

DHCP ServerA

DHCP ServerB

DHCP Client

DHCP ServerC

EXAM WARNING

Although the first stage of the DORA process is referred to as an *IP Lease Request*, it uses a DHCPDISCOVER message. It is physically looking for or trying to discover a DHCP server that can assist it in obtaining an IP address lease. Don't get that confused with the third stage of the DORA process, which actually uses a message called a DHCPREQUEST message. In this stage, called *IP Lease Selection*, the DHCP client is actually selecting the DHCP server it want to use, and requests that that DHCP server issue it an IP address.

IP Offer Response

All DHCP servers running on the same segment that hear a DHCPDISCOVER broadcast message respond to the calling client with a DHCPOFFER message if they have available addresses. These OFFER messages are processed by the client in a first-come, first-served fashion. That is, the client will respond to the first DHCP server response that it receives, by broadcasting a DHCPREQUEST message. The following information is included in each IP offer message:

- The DHCP server's MAC address
- The DHCP server's IP address
- The offered client IP address
- The subnet mask that goes with the offered IP address
- The offered IP address lease duration time
- The client's MAC address

NOTE

Note that when a client is obtaining an address for the first time, all of the messages in the DORA process are broadcast messages. However, after the client has an address and sends a request to renew that address, that message is sent directly to the DHCP server instead of being broadcast to the entire network segment.

As mentioned earlier, all DHCP servers that have available addresses respond with the described offer request information. Regardless of which server wins the offer, they need a way to keep from offering the same address to two computers at the same time. To prevent this, each server must place a reservation for the offer in its own database. This insures that a given address is not offered in response to more than one DHCPDISCOVER message until that address has been refused by the first client, releasing it for use in a subsequent offer. See Figure 3.3 for an illustration of the DHCPOFFER phase.

IP Selection Request

When the client receives the first DHCP server's offer, it uses the information in the OFFER message to reply to the server that made the offer by sending back a DHCPRE-QUEST message. Since the client has not yet accepted the IP address, this is sent as another broadcast message, so that all other DHCP servers will also receive it.

EXAM WARNING

DHCP broadcasts are sent using User Datagram Protocol (UDP) port numbers 67 and 68. This is important to know because, by default, most routers do not forward these types of broadcast messages. If you want to use a DHCP server that sits on the other side of a router interface, you must ensure that the router supports DHCP relaying. This is defined in RFC 2131. Most Cisco routers will support DHCP relay; to enable it, type the **iphelper** protocol command at the router console.

Figure 3.3 DHCP Server Offering an IP Lease (DHCPOFFER)

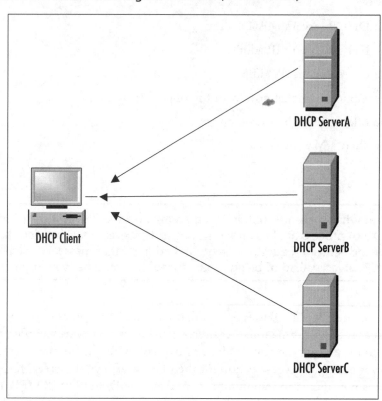

Any other DHCP servers that initially sent a DHCPOFFER will hear this broadcast, determine that the destination IP address in the packet is not for them, and release their IP offer reservations. The IP addresses they had offered are now free to be offered to another client. See Figure 3.4 for an illustration of the DHCPREQUEST message.

IP Lease Acknowledgement

In the fourth and final stage of the DHCP lease process, the original DHCP offering server will respond to the client with a DHCPACK message. This is yet another broadcast message, which includes the IP address to be assigned to the client, along with any additional DHCP configured options, such as a default gateway or DNS server. See Figure 3.5 for an illustration of the DHCPACK message.

In rare instances, the DHCP server will respond with a DHCPNAK message. This is a negative acknowledgement (in other words, the server is saying no to the client's request to lease the offered IP address). This can occur if the IP address is not valid anymore, because it has been assigned to another computer or possibly because the scope has been deactivated.

Figure 3.4 DHCP Client Selecting a DHCP Server's Lease (DHCPREQUEST)

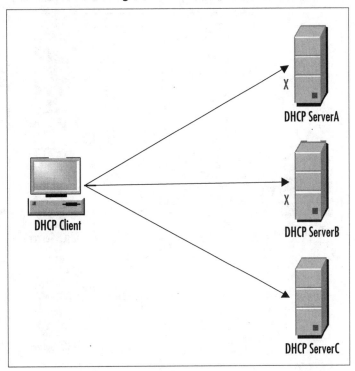

Such messages can be greatly reduced by using the conflict detection options discussed in the section "Conflict Detection." If a client receives a DHCPNAK message, it must start the lease process all over from the beginning by generating a new DHCPDISCOVER broadcast.

Lease Renewal

IP addresses given out by a DHCP server usually are not permanently assigned. Unless you have more than enough IP addresses to hand out and have set your lease duration to *unlimited*, DHCP servers are configured to lease their addresses for a specified duration (on a per-scope basis). Periodically, each client needs to check back in with the DHCP server from which it received its IP address and ask to be allowed to continue using it. At the same time, the client will receive any configuration option changes that need to be applied. This process is called *lease renewal*. Although it is usually an automatic process, it can be manually forced by the DHCP client.

Figure 3.5 DHCP Server Acknowledging Client Selection (DHCPACK)

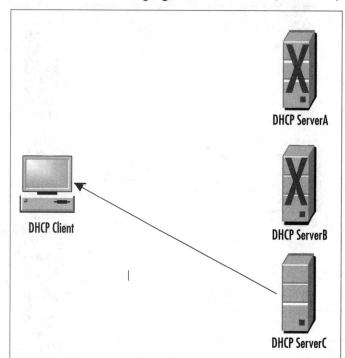

Automatic Renewal

Lease renewal is something that is continually happening on all DHCP clients for which the lease duration has not been set to *unlimited*. By definition, lease renewal is the process by which a configured DHCP client tries to renegotiate its current IP information and options with its leasing DHCP server. Lease renewal is an automatic process and is determined by the *lease duration* settings in the properties of the DHCP scope to which the client's address belongs.

The beginning of the lease renewal process happens when 50 percent of the client's lease duration interval has elapsed. For example, if a computer named CLIENTX has a lease duration of eight days, it will try to renew its lease after four days. The renewal begins at the third stage of the DHCP lease process; issuing a DHCPREQUEST message to the same server that originally leased the IP address to the client (remember, this is not a broadcast message as were all the messages in the original DORA process). If the DHCP server is available, the client receives a DHCPACK from the server, renewing the client lease in accordance with the lease duration interval, and updates any DHCP options that were changed.

If the originating DHCP server is unavailable at the 50 percent mark, the client waits until 87.5 percent of the lease is up and tries again with another DHCPREQUEST message.

If at this time the DHCP server is still unavailable, the client will keep its current IP address only until the lease expires, at which time it will begin at stage one of the DHCP lease process, broadcasting a DHCPDISCOVER message in an effort to find a new DHCP server.

NOTE

If the client issues a request for an address that does not reside on its network segment, possibly because the client was moved from one network to another, the DHCP server will issue a DHCPNAK message. This will force the client to release its address and start at stage one of the DHCP lease process with a DHCPDISCOVER broadcast. A common cause of this scenario is a laptop user who unplugs the computer from one network and into another when moving from one location to another.

Manual Renewal

Manual lease renewal is initiated on the client side and is accomplished by issuing a command line sequence. You might want to renew a client's lease manually when you have made an urgent scope options change, such as adding a new DNS server, and you want to push the change out immediately. The **ipconfig** command is used to manually release and renew your IP address and scope options.

To release a client's IP configuration, use the **ipconfig** command with the **/release** switch. To renew that same client's IP configuration instead, issue the **ipconfig** command with the **/renew** switch.

The basic syntax of the each of these commands is:

```
ipconfig.exe    ipconfig [/release [adapter]
ipconfig.exe    ipconfig [/renew [adapter]
```

EXAM WARNING

Running the **ipconfig** command with the **/release** switch (not specifying an adapter) will release all adapters configured for DHCP of their IP information. On the same note, running it with the **/renew** switch and no adapter specification will renew all DHCP enabled adapters. If you want to configure only one adapter at a time, you will need to use the **[adapter]** identifier as shown:

```
Ipconfig /release "Local Area Connection"

Ipconfig /renew "Local Area Connection"
```

Note that this is based on the assumption you have the default network card name of *Local Area Connection*. Also note that the quotation marks are needed only if there are spaces in the adapter name.

Of course, if there is only one network adapter installed in the computer, there is no need to use the adapter specification.

Configuring the
Windows Server 2003 DHCP Server

To configure your DHCP server, you must first install DHCP as a service, using the source files on your Windows Server 2003 source CD-ROM, or the i386 folder on a network share. Then there are a number of different elements that can be configured. In the following sections, we will discuss:

- Installing the DHCP service
- Configuring scopes
- Configuring DHCP reservations
- Configuring BOOTP tables
- Configuring superscopes
- Configuring multicast scopes
- Configuring scope allocation of IP addresses

Let's begin at the beginning, with installation.

Installing the DHCP Service

There are two methods by which you can install the DHCP service.

1. The first (and probably quickest) way is through the **Advanced** Toolbar on the menu bar of your **Network Connections** folder window. Click **Start | Control Panel | Network Connections** to open the folder. Click **Advanced**, and then click **Optional Network Components** to invoke the wizard, as shown in Figure 3.6.

Figure 3.6 Installing the DHCP Server Service through Network

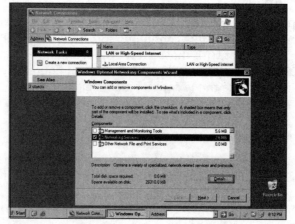

NOTE

If clicking **Network Connections** in the Control Panel opens a menu instead of a folder, you will not see the **Advanced** menu. This occurs if you have set both Control Panel and Network connections to be expanded in your taskbar properties. To remedy it, right-click the task bar in an empty place, and click **Properties.** Select the **Start Menu** tab, choose **Classic Start menu**, and click the **Customize** button. In the **Advanced Start menu options** box, scroll down and uncheck the **Expand Control Panel** and **Expand Network Connections** check boxes. Now the Control Panel and Network Connections will open as folder windows instead of menus.

2. You will see three Components on the **Windows Components** page of the wizard. Highlight **Network Services** and click **Details**.

3. Click **Dynamic Host Configuration Protocol (DHCP)** and click **OK** as shown in Figure 3.7. Click **OK** once more and then click **Next** to begin the installation. Make sure your licensed copy of Windows Server 2003 is inserted in your CD tray or point Setup to the location of the network share that holds the i386 folder. Windows will begin copying the installation files. No reboot is necessary.

4. Alternatively, you can install the DHCP service using the Control Panel's **Add or Remove Programs** applet. After you launch this applet, click **Add/Remove Windows Components**. This will start the Windows Components Wizard. Scroll down until you see **Network Services**, highlight it, and click **Details**. Click on **Dynamic Host Configuration Protocol (DHCP)** and click **OK**. Click **OK** once more and finally **Next** to begin the installation as shown in Figure 3.7.

NOTE

We have found that the Windows Components Wizard invoked through Add/Remove Programs takes longer to initiate than the first installation method invoked through the Network Connections folder.

After the DHCP service is installed, you can start creating your DHCP server scopes, options, reservations, and client-specific vendor classes.

Figure 3.7 Installing the DHCP Server Service Using the Control Panel

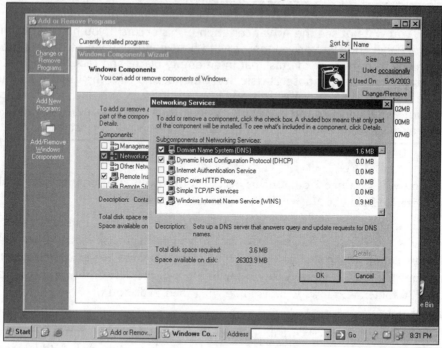

 EXAM WARNING

To successfully use the Windows Server 2003 DHCP service, you must first configure your server's TCP/IP stack with a static IP address, default gateway, and subnet mask. This is a requirement of the DHCP service and avoids potential problems that clients might encounter if the DHCP server's IP address changed because it was using DHCP itself. Although having the server set up as a DHCP client will not prevent you from installing the DHCP service, the installation process will prompt you with two error messages that state the recommended way to configure TCP/IP. See Figures 3.8 and 3.9 for illustrations of these messages.

Figure 3.8 Installation Error 1 when DHCP Server Is Also a DHCP Client

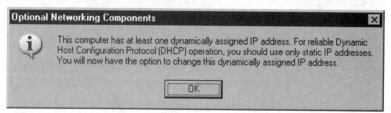

Figure 3.9 Installation Error 2 When DHCP Server Is Also a DHCP Client

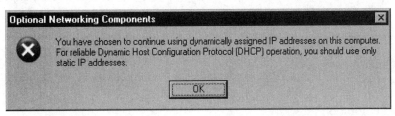

Configuring DHCP Scopes

DHCP scopes are the basic building blocks for developing a framework for network segments on which you want to deploy DHCP clients. By definition, a *scope* is a range of IP addresses. This range has a beginning and an ending IP address that define the inclusive IP addresses that are available for clients to obtain.

Configuring a DHCP scope is done via the DHCP management console snap-in. If you have installed the Administration Pak for Windows Server 2003, you will notice some new Microsoft Management Console (MMC) snap-ins. Particular to DHCP setup and management is the tool labeled *IP Address Management*. Click **Start | Programs | Administrative Tools | IP Address Management** (or click **DHCP** if you have not installed the tools). You will not need to add your new DHCP server as it should already appear in the MMC Console. This is what we call a feature enhancement to the previous Windows 2000 DHCP MMC console, in which you had to add your DHCP server to the console each time you accessed it.

NOTE

The Windows Server 2003 Administration Pak is located in %systemroot%\system32 of your installed server. It is called *adminpak.msi* and can be installed on any machine to locally or remotely manage almost all aspects of the server. Just double-click the .MSI file to start the setup wizard. Note that all instances of the MMC must be closed or setup will fail.

One DHCP sever can hold scopes for many different network segments. Each scope is accessible by DHCP clients across router boundaries, but only if the router that separates those network segments is configured to forward DHCP broadcasts or if each segment has a DHCP Relay Agent configured to forward these broadcasts to the DHCP server holding its scope. See the section "DHCP Relay Agent" to learn more about how to handle the forwarding of DHCP broadcasts.

Each scope is configured with the following options during the New Scope Wizard setup:

- IP Address Range
- Subnet mask
- IP address exclusions
- Lease duration interval

The IP address range and subnet mask are mandatory entries you must make when setting up your DHCP server. The address range is the range of IP addresses that you want to hand out as leases to your DHCP clients. The subnet mask defines the network and host portion of the IP addresses you are assigning. The DHCP scope wizard is configured to understand Classless Interdomain Routing (CIDR), so you can simply enter the length of the subnet mask. As previously discussed, the lease duration is the amount of time a DHCP server allows a client to hold an IP address. In Exercise 3.01, we will walk you through the setup of a new DHCP scope and configure it with a few of the more standard options.

EXERCISE 3.01

SETTING UP A DHCP SCOPE

1. Open the DHCP MMC Management Console. If your server does not appear under DHCP, add it as described in the previous section, "DHCP Scope."

2. Highlight the name of your **DHCP server** so that it expands and you see the **Server options** container. You can either right-click the server name or click the **Action** menu and select **New Scope**.

3. Click **Next** on the **Welcome to the New Scope Wizard** page.

4. Enter a **Name** for your new scope and a **Description** explaining what the new scope represents, as shown in Figure 3.10. We have found that the more descriptive you are, the better it is for other administrators who have to manage and troubleshoot these scopes later. Click **Next**.

5. This brings you to the **IP Address Range** configuration window shown in Figure 3.11. Type a valid IP address range and subnet mask for your network (either as a length in bits or as an address mask) and click **Next**.

Figure 3.10 Configuring Your IP Address Range

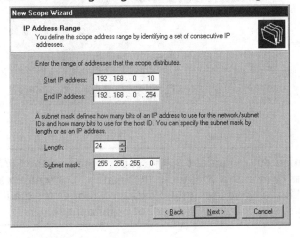

Figure 3.11 Configuring Your IP Address Range

TEST DAY TIP

When entering your Start IP and End IP addresses, be very familiar with IP addresses that are assigned already or that will be assigned statically on your network. You do not want to offer an IP address in your DHCP scope that is already configured statically. If you do so, you may cause an IP address conflict, leaving one of the devices unresponsive. If so desired, you can enter the full range of IP addresses available on your network subnet and then use the Add Exclusions portion of the wizard to specify the addresses that are already in use, such as that of your default router. However, we have found it is usually more effective to begin your start range at an IP address above those already in use on your network. This assumes you have divided your addresses into device- or user-specific ranges, such as 192.168.0.1 to 172.16.0.5 for infrastructure hardware, 192.168.0.6 to 192.168.0.9 for network printers, and 192.168.0.10 to 192.168.0.254 for DHCP.

6. The next page displays the **Add Exclusions** window. Enter either a range of IP addresses or a specific IP address that is included in your original IP address scope range, but that you do not want to be offered to DHCP clients (because it is or will be statically assigned to some device). To enter a single IP address, enter the address in only the Start IP address box shown in Figure 3.12 and click **Add**. Click **Next**.

Figure 3.12 Configuring Any IP Address Exclusions

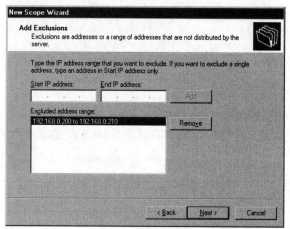

NOTE

If you are configuring redundant DHCP scopes based on the 80/20 configuration that we discuss later in this chapter in the section "Configuring Scope Allocation of IP Addresses," it is a good idea to use exclusion ranges for the IP address ranges that sit opposite each other in the pool of redundant servers.

7. The DHCP **Lease Duration** window appears next, as shown in Figure 3.13. Configure the lease duration by using the **Days, Hours**, and **Minutes** scroll boxes. The default lease duration is set for eight days.

Figure 3.13 Configuring the Lease Duration

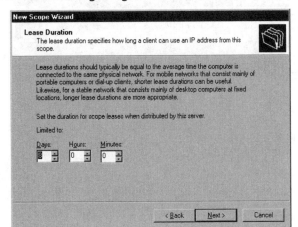

8. On the next page, when prompted with the **Configure DHCP Options** windows, select **Yes, I want to configure these options now** as shown in Figure 3.14. For this exercise, we will configure the most common DHCP options. Click **Next**.

Figure 3.14 Configuring Your DHCP Scope Options

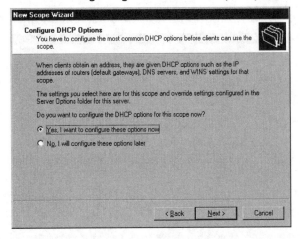

9. The first option presented is the *default gateway.* This is the router that connects your subnet to the rest of your network. Enter the IP address of your default gateway, as shown in Figure 3.15. Click **Add** and then **Next**.

Figure 3.15 Configuring Your Default Gateway

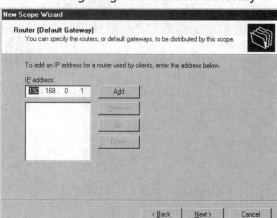

10. The next window will prompt you to enter the default *Parent domain* name you want your clients to use when searching for network hosts, as shown in Figure 3.16. This name will be appended to any host name searches. In the lower section of the dialog box, type any *DNS Server* IP addresses you want your clients to use for name to IP resolution. Click **Add** for each DNS server entry, and **Next** when you are finished.

Figure 3.16 Configuring Your DNS Servers and Parent Domain Name

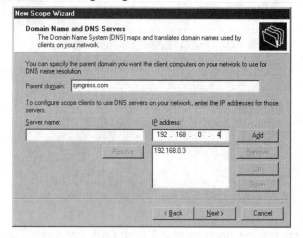

EXAM WARNING

The order in which you place these DNS servers directly relates to the order in which your clients use them to resolve domain names. If the first one in the list is unavailable, the DHCP client will search the second one, and so on. Be on the lookout for questions that deal with DNS resolution timeouts. If you cannot resolve the DNS server error, you may need to change the order of your DNS servers and force a manual renew on each client in order to avoid lengthy DNS queries.

11. If you are still using NetBIOS names on your network, you will need to enter the IP address of your Windows Internet Naming Service (WINS) server as shown in Figure 3.17. Enter each *WINS server IP address* and click **Add**. The same ordering rule holds true for WINS servers as it does for DNS servers. Click **Next** when you are finished.

Figure 3.17 Configuring Your WINS Servers

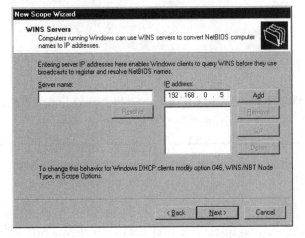

NOTE

If you want to configure only some of these options and not all (for example, you have no WINS servers and are not using NetBIOS), you can skip any of the pages by leaving the fields blank and clicking **Next**.

TEST DAY TIP

If you are going to use WINS servers and are pushing their IP addresses out via DHCP, it is highly recommended that you also configure option 046, which is the node type the client uses for NetBIOS name resolution. Node types define the order in which clients look at resources to resolve a NetBIOS name. You will learn more about NetBIOS node types in Chapter 4.

12. On the last page, the New Scope Wizard will ask you if you would like to activate your scope. Click the **Yes, I want to activate this scope now** radio button and click **Next** when you are finished, as shown in Figure 3.18.

Figure 3.18 Activating Your Scope

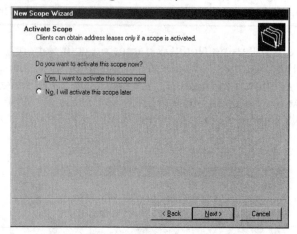

13. Click **Finished** on the Completing the New Scope Wizard window to complete the configuration of your new scope.

EXAM WARNING

Be careful when reading questions that deal with clients not able to receive IP addresses after an administrator has fully configured the DHCP scope. The scope needs to be *Activated* before it is able to hand out its IP addresses in its configured range. If you choose not to *Activate* the scope during the Wizard setup procedure, you can activate it later by right-clicking on the scope and choosing **Activate** from the menu.

Configuring DHCP Options

DHCP Options are configurable settings that an administrator can set on a DHCP server to push out (distribute), along with IP addresses, to DHCP clients. These options are client specific, meaning that if the DHCP client does not support an option you configure, it simply ignores that option. There are over 60 different configurable DHCP options in the

Windows Server 2003 DHCP server. See Table 3.2 for a few of the more common DHCP configurable options.

Table 3.2 Configurable DHCP Options

Option Number	Option Name	Description
003	Router	Specifies the default gateway router
006	DNS Servers	Lists any DNS servers on the network
015	DNS Domain Name	Specifies the parent DNS domain name for the DNS locater service
035	ARP Cache Timeout	Specifies the timeouts in seconds for ARP cache entries
044	WINS Servers	Lists and WINS servers on the network
046	WINS Node Type	Specifies the NetBIOS
249	Classless Static Routes	Specifies destination, mask, and router for static routes

New & Noteworthy...

Distribute Static Routes through DHCP

Windows Server 2003 has introduced a new predefined DHCP option to enable the distribution of network specific static routes. Option number 249—classless static routes—enables the administrator to define any number of static routes desired, to the clients' local routing tables. This option can encompass all of your DHCP scopes if you use it as a server option, or a specific subnet if you configure it as a scope option. Figure 3.19 shows you the graphical interface for adding static routes as a scope option.

Figure 3.19 Adding Static Routes as a Scope Option

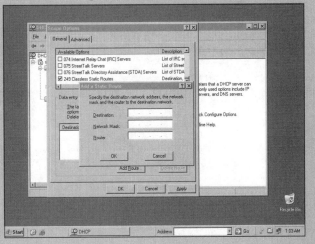

There are four types of DHCP options. These options are applied in a specific order when received by a DHCP client, with the first option being overwritten if followed by a conflicting second option. The list of options in order of precedence are:

1. Server

2. Scope

3. User and Vendor Class

4. Reserved

 EXAM WARNING

Any static client-specific DNS configurations will override any of the four DHCP option settings described in the text. Be prepared to address clients that use DHCP as well as manual settings when troubleshooting exam questions.

You can manipulate these different options to target groups of machines, specific networks, or even individual clients. If used correctly, they are very powerful for managing the distribution of configuration information across your LANs, WANs, and remote clients. However, they can also cripple your network if configured incorrectly, so plan carefully before deploying DHCP options in your network environment.

In the next sections, we discuss each of the option types in detail.

Server Options

Server-level options apply to all scopes configured on a particular server. So, if you are serving up 10 different subnets with ten different DHCP scopes on the same server, and want all clients on all subnets to have the same WINS server and parent DNS domain name, you should configure these as server options. Server options apply to all clients that lease an IP address from the DHCP server. Server options are considered to be at the highest configuration level and are always applied first.

NOTE

If you are familiar with Windows NT 4.0 DHCP scopes, the *global* reference is different in Windows Server 2003. For the exam, just remember that Server options are *global* to all scopes on that DHCP server.

Scope Options

Scope-level options are next in line and are specific only to the scope to which they belong. Using the previous example, if you wanted each of your clients to have a different default gateway, you would configure these as Scope options. Scope options override Server options. For example, if you had configured a global Server option for the distribution of a common DNS server, but had one scope that needed a different DNS server, you would configure this as a separate Scope option. Scope options apply only to clients obtaining IP information from that scope.

EXAM WARNING

Static client-specific DNS configurations will override any of the previous four DHCP option settings. Be prepared to deal with questions about clients that use DHCP as well as manual settings when troubleshooting exam questions.

User and Vendor Class Options

EXAM 70-291 OBJECTIVE 1.2.5

User and *Vendor* classes are optional methods of classifying or grouping machines or users into unique units for individual configuration. Options configured at these levels overwrite any options at the scope or server level. Both of these options were first introduced with Windows Server 2000 and are becoming more widely used to granularly manage and define the client base. They can be defined in the following manner:

Server versus Scope Options

Do any of your DHCP servers host multiple DHCP scopes? Do any of these scopes contain similar DHCP options? It is common practice to have one DHCP server host many of your network segment's DHCP scopes. It is also common to find that many of these scopes contain the same configured options. Multiple scopes configured on the same DHCP server, using the same Scope options, should use Server options instead, making sure they are configured only once per server. Server options should be used whenever possible to cut back on administrative overhead at the scope level. A good rule of thumb is this: If more than half of the scopes on your DHCP server need the same Scope option, configure it as a Server option.

For example, if you have ten scopes and each of those scopes uses the same DNS and WINS servers, configure this at the Server level. Then it will filter down to the Scope level for all scopes on the server and you have to configure it only one time. Let's say out of those ten different scopes, three of them need their own DNS and WINS servers. You should still configure the DNS and WINS servers for the other seven scopes at the server level and then configure individual Scope options for the remaining three unique scopes. This will result in four configuration changes rather than the ten you would make if you were to make them all Scope options.

Always try to look at the similarities when creating your DHCP Scope options first, and then focus on the differences to make your Scope options. Remember that options are processed in order, with the last option being the one that is applied. DHCP options are processed as follows:

- Server Options
- Scope Options
- User/Vendor Options
- Reserved Options

- *User* classes are used for assigning options to clients identified as sharing a common need for similar DHCP options configuration.

- *Vendor* classes are used for assigning vendor-specific options to a group of clients identified as sharing a commonly defined vendor type.

An example of each would be the following:

- *Users* classes can define groups such as laptop users, desktop users, or servers.

- *Vendor* classes can define groups such as Windows 98 machines, Windows 2000 machines, or Machines with CD-ROMS. See Figure 3.20 for an illustration.

When you have defined classes, you can then assign options to these classes. For example, you might want to assign short lease durations to the members of the laptop users class.

Figure 3.20 Defining a Vendor Class

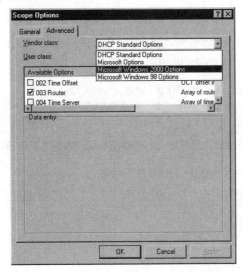

TEST DAY TIP

In order for a client to receive any type of User or Vendor class options that have been set on your DHCP server, you must first set the user's classid from the physical workstation. You can accomplish this by using the **ipconfig** command with the **/setclassid** switch.

For example: Where *Local Area Connection* is the name of your network adapter and *Laptop Users* is the name of the User Class Definition you set up, you would type:

```
Ipconfig /setclassid "Local Area Connection" "Laptop Users"
```

In Exercise 3.02, we will walk you through the steps of creating a specific *user* class for a group of laptop users, creating a specific lease duration interval for that *user* class, and setting the specific *classid* on the individual laptop workstations.

EXERCISE 3.02

SETTING UP A SPECIFIC DHCP UUSER CLASS

The three steps involved in performing this exercise are:

1. Defining a new User Class.

2. Setting a Scope option for a new class.

3. Setting the clients *classid* to receive options from a new class.

To define a User Class:

1. Open the **DHCP MMC** in the Administrative Tools menu bar.

2. Right-click the name of your DHCP server and select **Define User Classes**, as shown in Figure 3.21.

Figure 3.21 Defining a New User Class

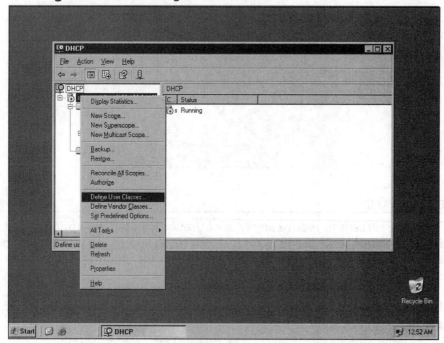

3. The **DHCP User Classes** window appears as shown in Figure 3.22. By default, the **Default Routing and Remote Access Class** and the **Default BOOTP class** are available. Click **Add** to create a new class. The **New Class** window appears.

4. In the **Display name** field, type the name you want to use to define your user class (for example, **Laptop Users**).

5. In the **Description** field, type a detailed description used to identify this user class.

6. In the **ID** data window, type a random data bit to identify this user class. For example, type **1234**. This ASCII or binary string will be set at member clients when you configure them to use this class ID.

7. Click **OK** to create your new class. Click **Close** on the DHCP User Classes window.

Figure 3.22 Creating the User Class

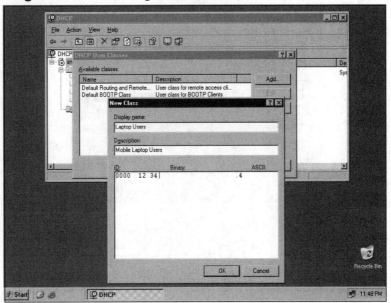

NOTE

Don't make the name of the class too complicated, as it will be used to create all your client-side *classid*s and should be descriptive, yet easy to remember and to type.

To set up a Scope option for your User Class follow these steps:

1. Now that your custom User Class has been created, you can assign some options to that class. In the left pane of the DHCP MMC, expand the scope in which these users will pull DHCP information and right-click **Scope Options**, and select **Configure Options**. This will bring up the *Scope Options* window as shown in Figure 3.23.

NOTE

The **Configure Options** option will be grayed out in the Scope options context menu if you have not yet created a new class.

Figure 3.23 Selecting Your New User Class

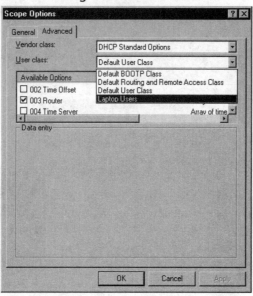

2. In the **User class** drop-down box, you will see the new class you created, called *Laptop Users*. Go ahead and select this class.

3. In the **Available Options** window, scroll down until you find option
   051 Lease, and check its check box. This is illustrated in Figure 3.24.

Figure 3.24 Defining a User Class Option

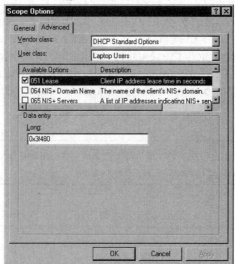

4. Next, configure the *Data Entry* value for the *Long* field. Type **259200** in the field, and then click **OK**.

NOTE

Option **051 Lease** is defined as the lease duration time and is configured in seconds. The value for this option is presented in hexadecimal format. However, you can type the number of seconds, and the software will convert it to hex. For this exercise, we choose 25900 seconds, which is equal to three days.

To set up a ClassID for your clients follow these steps:

1. After both **User Class** and **Scope options** have been set, it is time to configure your local clients to receive these new settings. Go to one of your laptop clients, open a command window by typing **cmd** at the **Run** box, and type the following at the command prompt:

```
ipconfig /setclassid "Local Area Connection" "Laptop Users"
```

NOTE

In this example, *"Local Area Connection"* is the name of your network adapter and *"Laptop Users"* is the name of the User Class Definition you set up. The quotation marks are necessary because there are spaces in the names.

2. Notice the output shown in Figure 3.25, telling you that the *classid* was successfully set.

3. To show the client *Classid* configuration of a client, simply type **ipconfig** at the command prompt. See Figure 3.26.

Note that a client computer can be identified by only one user class at the DHCP server.

Figure 3.25 Setting Your Client ClassID

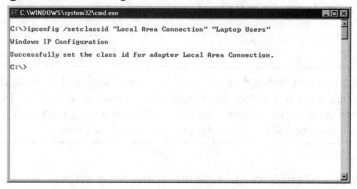

Figure 3.26 Displaying Your Client ClassID

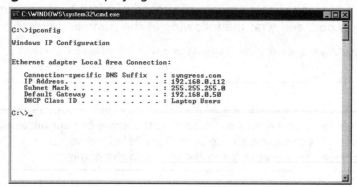

EXAM WARNING

Though NetBIOS is going away in the Microsoft world, be certain to memorize the different WINS node types for the exam. This information is still heavily tested. The four node types are:

- **b-node (Value of 1)** Client initiates a broadcast only.
- **p-node (Value of 2)** Client uses a NetBIOS name server only.
- **m-node (Value of 4)** Client combines both b-node and p-node by first using a broadcast and then a name server.
- **h-node (Value of 8)** Client combines both b-node and p-node but first uses a name server and then a broadcast. This is the most commonly used node type.

- **Microsoft Enhanced b-node (or Modified b-node)** Client checks the NetBIOS name cache, then initiates a broadcast, and lastly checks for a local LMHOSTS file.
- **Microsoft Enhanced h-node** Client checks the NetBIOS name cache, then uses a NetBIOS name server, initiates a broadcast, checks for a local LMHOSTS file, tries DNS named cache, a local HOSTS file, and lastly DNS.

See Chapter 4 for more detailed coverage on the WINS protocol and NetBIOS name resolution service.

Configuring DHCP Reservations

EXAM
70-291
OBJECTIVE
1.2.5

DHCP Reservations provide a way to reserve a particular IP address for a specific client, which is useful for clients that always need to have the same address. Why not just assign a static IP instead? You could, but then the client would not be able to get other configuration options (DNS server, default gateway, etc.) from the DHCP server if/when those options change—you would have to change them manually on every statically assigned computer.

Reservations are treated a bit differently than the other types of DHCP options, because an administrator must manually set up each reservation separately with predefined information from the client machine's network interface card. Aside from *User* and *Vendor* classes, client reservations are the most specific type of setting for assigning IP addresses to clients. To set up a reservation, follow these steps:

1. Expand the nodes for the DHCP Server and Scope in the DHCP MMC console.

2. Right-click **Reservations**.

3. Select **New Reservation** to display the New Reservation configuration box shown in Figure 3.27.

Figure 3.27 Configuring a Client Reservation

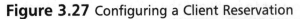
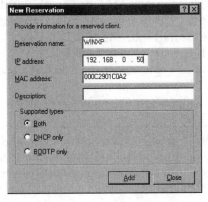

The options that need to be entered into a DHCP reservation are as follows (only the ones followed by asterisks are required):

- **Reservation Name★** Uniquely identifies the client you are reserving
- **IP Address★** A reserved IP address from the range of IPs in the scope
- **MAC Address★** The Media Access Control number of the client's NIC
- **Description** An administrative description to better identify this client

The Supported types configuration boxes refer to the method in which each client obtains DHCP information. Although most Microsoft clients will use *DHCP only*, Windows 2000 Remote Installation Services (RIS) clients use the BOOTP protocol to initialize. Older non–Microsoft clients may use the BOOTP protocol, so unless you are sure, it is probably safe to leave the default of *Both* selected.

Exam Warning

The MAC address is the piece of the reservation that actually identifies the client as it first initiates its DHCPDISCOVER broadcast. The MAC address is a 48-bit binary number, but it is notated as 12 hexadecimal digits arranged in pairs. It is imperative that you type this address correctly. You can find out the MAC address from the client computer by running **ipconfig /all**. If you cannot physically visit the client computer, you can use the **ping** and **arp** commands to identify this number and then use the copy and paste feature to enter it into the reservation.

For example:

1. Ping the client and take notice to the IP address that is returned.
2. Use the **arp** command with the –**a** switch to show the local *arp* cache.
3. Match up the IP address in step one to the MAC address in step 2.
4. Use the copy and paste functionality built into the command interface of Windows Server 2003 to insert the MAC address into the reservation: right-click the title bar of the command window, and select **Edit | Mark**. Then use your cursor to highlight the information you want to copy (in this case, the MAC address). Right-click the title bar again and select **Edit | Copy**. This copies the marked text to the clipboard and it can be pasted into the MAC address field in the *New Reservation* box.

Note

If you have multiple DHCP servers, Microsoft recommends that you create reservations on all of the servers that can be reached by the DHCP client's startup broadcast. This is true even though only one of the DHCP servers has an address pool that contains the client's address.

Configuring BOOTP Tables

The BOOTP protocol was pre-DHCP and was designed primarily to support clients that did not have local bootable disks. To support these types of clients, you must have a Trivial File Transfer Protocol (TFTP) file server and a bootable image file. The Windows Server 2003 DHCP service supports BOOTP clients with its BOOTP Table configuration option. In Figure 3.28, we provide an example of a UNIX BOOTP host configuration entry.

Figure 3.28 Configuring a BOOTP Table

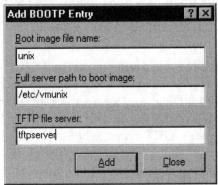

To configure a BOOTP table entry, you must first enable viewing of the BOOTP table folder. To do this, right-click the node for your DHCP server and select **Properties** from within the DHCP MMC. Select the **General** tab, click the check box labeled **Show the BOOTP table folder**.

When this folder appears in your DHCP console, right-click on it and select **New Boot Image**. You will see the **Add BOOTP Entry** dialog box shown in Figure 3.27. Enter the name of your boot file image, the full server path to that boot file image, and the name or IP address of your TFTP server. Click **Add** to finish the creation of your new BOOTP table.

The original BOOTP protocol was different from DHCP in that it did not use a lease period. The only way to receive the BOOTP table was to reboot your workstation and re-initiate the boot strap protocol to go out in search of a downloadable boot image. With the release of Windows 2000, Microsoft introduced dynamic BOOTP. With Dynamic BOOTP, clients now have a default 30-day lease duration.

To add dynamic BOOTP client support for a scope:

1. In the left pane of the DHCP console, right-click the scope to which you want to add dynamic BOOTP client and select **Properties**.

2. Click the **Advanced** tab.

3. Under **Assign IP addresses dynamically to clients of**, click **BOOTP only** or **Both**.

4. Change the default lease duration (30 days) under the **Lease duration for BOOTP clients** section, if desired.

NOTE

Remember that you cannot manually force a release or renewal for a BOOTP client as you can with a DHCP client; you must reboot the machine to initiate an IP address negotiation.

Although BOOTP clients have the ability to receive DHCP options from a Windows Server 2003 server, the more robust and feature-rich options distribution for DHCP clients make DHCP the best choice for client management in most situations; however, you must be familiar with the BOOTP protocol for the exam. Know that BOOTP is used primarily to download a boot image from a TFTP server, whereas DHCP is used just to download client-specific options and an IP address because they already have a bootable operating system. BOOTP clients must also all be configured with a *client reservation* prior to being able to download a boot image (previously discussed in the section "Configuring DHCP Reservations"). These reservations should be configured to use *Both* or *BOOTP only* as their supported types. Both protocols use the same UDP port number 67 for communication to and fro the DHCP/BOOTP server.

NOTE

BOOTP clients have the ability to receive a limited number of configurable parameters compared to DHCP clients using a Windows Server 2003 DHCP/BOOTP server. Although BOOTP parameters are called *vendor extensions*, DHCP parameters are simply called *options*. Table 3.3 shows the available vendor extensions a Windows Server 2003 can offer a BOOTP client. If a BOOTP client is capable of specifying option/parameter 55 in their BOOTP request, other vendor extensions will become available to that client. Windows Server 2003 will provide BOOTP clients with as many options as it can fit into a single datagram response packet.

Table 3.3 BOOTP Client Vendor Extension Parameters

BOOTP Code	Description
1	Subnet Mask
3	Router
4	Time Server

Continued

Table 3.3 BOOTP Client Vendor Extension Parameters

BOOTP Code	Description
5	Name Server
9	LPR Server
12	Computer Name
15	Domain Name
17	Root Path
42	NTP Servers
44	WINS Server
45	NetBIOS over TCP/IP Datagram Distribution Server
46	NetBIOS over TCP/IP Node Type
47	NetBIOS over TCP/IP Scope
48	X Window System Font Server
49	X Window System Display Manager
69	SMTP Server
70	POP3 Server

Exam Warning

Be aware when you are creating your BOOTP/DHCP reservations that both can share configurable BOOTP/DHCP options; thus it is imperative you configure your scopes appropriately.

Configuring Superscopes

Superscopes are used to manage a group of individual scopes on one physical DHCP server in a *multinet* environment. A *multinet* is a configuration in which you have one physical network segment broken up into many logical IP subnets. Superscopes can be further defined as an administrative grouping of preconfigured scopes; they are used as a way to inform the DHCP service that more than one logical IP network exists on the same physical network, so that addresses from any of the scopes in the superscope will work on the network. Although the grouped scopes can be managed as a single entity, configuration options still must be addressed at each individual scope level and cannot be accomplished as a whole at the superscope level.

Superscopes are required for any network or bordering networks that are configured as *multinets* or are *multinets* themselves, forwarding broadcasts via a BOOTP router or DHCP Relay Agent.

When to Use Superscopes

Superscopes allow for the activation and distribution of multiple DHCP scopes and IP leases to clients on the same physical network segment. Examples of when to use a super-scope include:

- You have used up 99 percent of the available address pool on your existing DHCP server scope and now you have 50 more computers that need IP addresses. You originally used the entire address class to create your scope, but now you need to extend that address space by subnetting it for the same physical network segment.

- You have two separate IP networks located on the same physical network segment and you want to use two DHCP servers on the segment.

- You have to change your IP address range for your network, and want to gradually migrate your clients from the old scope of addresses to the new one.

The superscope should be configured on each of the DHCP servers on the network segment.

How to Create a Superscope

First, you need to have at least two scopes created. To create a new scope, in the left pane of the DHCP MMC, right-click the node for the DHCP server and select **New Scope** as described previously.

NOTE

Note that if you try to create a new scope whose addresses overlap with an existing scope, Windows will display a warning message to that effect, and will not allow you to make the scope.

To create the superscope:

1. Right-click the node for the DHCP server and select **New superscope** from the right context menu. This will invoke the New Superscope Wizard. Click **Next** on the welcome page.

2. On the **Superscope Name** page, type a name for the superscope and click **Next.**

3. On the **Select Scopes** page, select one or more of the available scopes that are displayed, and click **Next** (hold down the CTRL key to select multiple scopes).

4. On the **Completing the New Superscope Wizard** page, ensure that the desired scopes are listed, and click **Finish.**

NOTE

The Superscope Wizard will allow you to create a superscope with only one scope. Additionally, a scope does not have to be activated in order to be added to a superscope.

Configuring Multicast Scopes

Multicast scopes provide DHCP functionality to clients via a *multicast* IP address. Multicast addresses are secondary addresses that can be assigned to computers to make them members of a multicast group. This allows messages to be sent to multiple computers by using a single address, as opposed to *unicast* addressing in which messages are addressed to one individual computer.

Multicast addresses fall within the Class D address range of 224.0.0.0 to 239.255.255.255. Multicasting provides a one-to-many relationship and is often used for applications such as live media streaming or video conferencing. A proposed standard protocol called the Multicast Address Dynamic Allocation Protocol (MADCAP) determines how each multicast address is assigned to each MADCAP client. See Figure 3.29 for the Multicast Scope Configuration Wizard dialog box.

Figure 3.29 Configuring a Multicast Scope

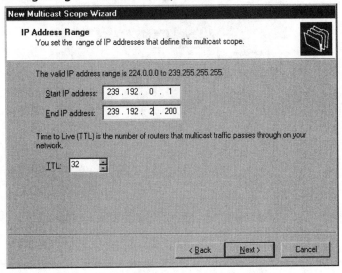

To create a multicast scope, follow these steps:

1.   In the left pane of the DHCP MMC, right-click the node for the **DHCP server**.

2.   Click **New Multicast scope**. This will invoke the New Multicast Scope Wizard.

3. On the welcome page, click **Next**.

4. On the **Multicast Scope Name** page, type a name for the multicast scope and a description if desired. Click **Next**.

5. On the **IP Address Range** page (shown in Figure 3.30), type a starting and ending IP address within the 224.0.0.0 to 239.255.255.255 range. You can also configure the Time to Live (TTL), which represents the number of "hops" (routers) the multicast traffic will go through. Click **Next**.

6. On the **Add Exclusions** page, you can enter any addresses within the scope range that you want to exclude. Click **Next**.

7. On the **Lease Duration** page, you can change the default of 30 days if desired, as shown in Figure 3.30. Click **Next**.

8. On the **Activate Multicast Scope** page, select **Yes** (the default) if you want to activate the scope, and click **Next**.

9. On the last page, click **Finish** to complete the wizard.

Figure 3.30 Configuring a Multicast Scope Lease

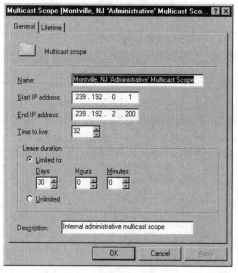

 NOTE

If you use the administratively scoped multicast space (239.0.0.0 to 239.255.255.255), the scope must have at least 256 addresses. Outside this range, you can make smaller scopes.

Unlike the typical DHCP scope, multicast scopes are limited in what they provide—they do not provide any configurable options. Multicast scopes provide only an IP address to multicast clients. Along with the IP address, a default 30-day lease is configured, which you can alter later if desired. Another configurable parameter in the setup of a multicast scope is the scope's lifetime. By default, this is set to *infinite* and the scope will exist until it is removed manually. However, you can change this setting in the DHCP MMC by right-clicking on the *Multicast Scope* and clicking **Properties**. Next, click on the **Lifetime** tab and you will see that you can *expire* the scope on a specific date and time, as shown in Figure 3.31.

Figure 3.31 Configuring a Multicast Scope Lifetime

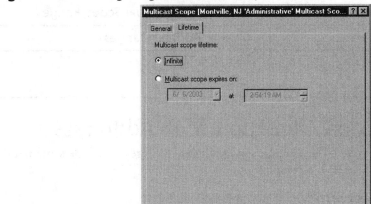

EXAM WARNING

Although you can use any IP address combination in the Class D range to configure your internal multicast scope, Microsoft recommends you use only the IP network 239.192.0.0/14 for your internal *administrative* scoping range. This is to prevent any multicast traffic from traveling out to the Internet or *global* ranges. See Table 3.4 for more detail.

There are two types of multicast scoping IP ranges. One is specific to your internal network, and the other targets your external or Internet interface network. Respectively, they are referred to as administrative and global scoping.

Administrative scoping is used primarily for your internal network. With this type of scope, Microsoft recommends using a special range known as the IPv4 Organization Local Scope range, shown in Table 3.4. Using this table as a beginning administrative scope address range, you can configure up to 262,144 group addresses for use on your internal subnetted network.

Global scoping is used primarily for your external or Internet network. To properly distribute global multicast scope IP addresses, a subnetting scheme has been proposed for MADCAP clients. This address scheme or range can be referenced in Table 3.4. Using this range of addressing, your publicly configured multicast network can use up to 255 multicast group addresses on the Internet.

As a best practice, you do not want to inverse these address ranges when setting up your multicast scopes. Follow Table 3.4 as a guideline and reference RFC2365 when setting up your internal administrative scopes.

Table 3.4 Microsoft Recommended Administrative and Global Scope Ranges

Scope Range Type	CIDR IP Address Ranges
Administrative (internal)	239.192.0.0/14
Global (external)	233.0.0.0/24

Configuring Scope Allocation of IP Addresses

It is common to have more than one DHCP server allocating addresses for the same network segments. The reason for this is twofold:

- DHCP server redundancy
- DHCP load balancing

DHCP server redundancy or fault tolerance provides protection against server outages. If one DHCP server goes down, the other DHCP server can serve DHCP client requests. DHCP load balancing is the dynamic assignment of DHCP addresses across multiple servers, spreading the traffic load across the servers so that one doesn't get too overloaded.

To use multiple DHCP servers effectively, it is important to take advantage of the Address Exclusion option when configuring each scope for redundancy. This is to ensure that you do not have two servers trying to hand out identical IP addresses. The standard guideline for this situation is called the *80/20 rule*. It is so named because it stipulates that you allow one DHCP server to allocate 80 percent of the address class while the other allocates the remaining 20 percent of the addresses. This has been shown to provide the greatest client uptime in case of a server failure.

To get a better look at allocating a particular address scope, study the IP address exclusion ranges in each of the DHCP servers' scopes in Table 3.5.

Table 3.5 DHCP Server 80/20 Rule

DHCP Server	IP Address Range	IP Exclusion Range
DHCP Server A (20%)	192.168.20.10 to 192.168.20.254	192.168.20.1 to 192.168.20.205
DHCP Server B (80%)	192.168.20.10 to 192.168.20.254	192.168.20.206 to 192.168.0.254

Determining How Many DHCP Servers You Need

One DHCP server is usually sufficient for a small network, but on a large network, a single DHCP server will get overloaded.

Additionally, you need to take into consideration how the network is subnetted, and whether to place DHCP servers on each separate subnet. Remember that if you don't, you'll need to use DHCP Relay Agents and you might need to configure superscopes. Bandwidth is another consideration; you won't want to have clients that have to go across a slow link to reach a DHCP server.

The number of clients a DHCP server can service depends on the server's hardware resources. Particularly important is hard disk speed (access time). Microsoft recommends a limit of 10,000 clients for a DHCP server, with no more than 1,000 scopes. You can have more, but performance will deteriorate.

Another idea is to create a backup DHCP server that is not in use, but can be deployed quickly if needed (this is called *hot standby*). You configure the backup server exactly like your primary server, but do not activate its scopes. This does require more administrative effort, however, than implementing multiple active DHCP servers to load balance one another.

Conflict Detection

Have you ever booted up your workstation only to see a big gray warning box, alerting you that you have the same IP address as another node on your network and that you will be unable to connect to any resources using the TCP/IP protocol? This is called an IP address conflict. Each network interface card, along with its unique MAC address, must be configured with a unique IP address for the network on which it is located. If two devices on the same network are configured manually with the same IP address, or if the DHCP servers that service that network segment hand out the same IP address to two different clients, both devices will receive an IP address conflict, and only one of the devices will be allowed to continue using the address. *Conflict Detection* is a process designed to address this problem.

There are two methods of conflict detection:

- Server-side conflict detection
- Client-side conflict detection

Server-Side Conflict Detection

Server-side conflict detection is the ability of your Windows Server 2003 DHCP server to test an IP address and determine if it is in use prior to leasing it to a DHCP client. This process uses the Packet Internet Groper (PING) TCP/IP application program to see if it receives a successful reply from an IP address. If a successful reply is returned, the server assumes that IP address is in use and does not offer it as an available lease. On the other hand, if a negative reply is received, that IP address is flagged for an available client lease.

Server-side conflict detection can be set by following these steps:

1. In the left pane of the DHCP MMC, right-click the node for your DHCP server and select **Properties** from the context menu.

2. Click the **Advanced** tab.

3. Specify the number of times the server should attempt conflict detection for each IP address before leasing that address, as shown in Figure 3.32 (the maximum is 5; the default is 0).

Figure 3.32 Configuring Conflict Detection Attempts

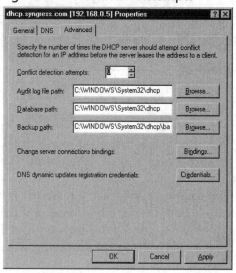

As noted, the number you can assign for conflict detection attempts can be from 0 to 5. Selecting 0 (the default) disables conflict detection completely. If any other number is selected that is the number of ping attempts that will be tried for each address before it is leased.

EXAM WARNING

Although you can set conflict detection attempts up to 5, we recommend that you set this value to not more than 2. This is due to the latency involved in ping attempts. The higher the conflict detection value is set, the longer the lease process will be for every client that uses the DHCP server.

Client-Side Conflict Detection

With the evolution of smarter client operating systems such as Windows 2000 and Windows XP, conflict detection has been integrated into the client side of the DHCP leasing process. A process called *gratuitous arp* defines the steps by which a client attempts to determine if its offered IP lease is already in use on its network segment. The DHCP client sends a gratuitous arp request on the local subnet for the offered IP address. If it receives a positive reply, it knows the address is already in use and sends a DHCPDECLINE message back to the DHCP server. Then the client requests another address. (See Table 3.1 for more information about the DHCPDECLINE message.)

NOTE

With the inclusion of conflict detection in Windows 2000 Professional and Windows XP, Microsoft recommends that you use server-side conflict detection only if down-level DHCP clients (pre-Windows 2000) are used on your network. These include Windows NT, Windows 95/98, or Windows 3.11. Otherwise, client-side detection is preferred. This is the reason server-side detection is disabled by default.

EXAM
70-291

OBJECTIVE
1.2.2
1.4.5

Configuring the DHCP Relay Agent

If you have a routed network, or you are using the Routing and Remote Access Service (RRAS) and DHCP, you will probably need to configure the DHCP Relay Agent. The DHCP Relay Agent is a service that aids in passing of DHCP and BOOTP broadcast messages across interfaces (such as routers) that do not support the forwarding of such messages or that are not RFC 2131 compliant. It *relays* the messages across subnets from clients to servers and vice versa.

Two methods are used to provide remote or dial-up clients access to a DHCP server by means of a DHCP/BOOTP broadcast:

- Through an RFC2131 compliant router with the use of an *iphelper* protocol
- Through the use of the Windows Server 2003 DHCP Relay Agent

www.syngress.com

EXAM WARNING

RFC2131, superceding RFC1542, states that a router supports the passing of DHCP/BOOTP broadcast messages. These RFC numbers may appear on the exam, so be aware of what they mean.

Both of these methods are processes for *forwarding* DHCP/BOOTP messages to a listening DHCP/BOOTP server on a remote subnet, either to download an available image or to begin the DHCP leasing process.

NOTE

You cannot install the DHCP Relay Agent on a computer that is a DHCP server, or on one that is running Internet Connection Sharing (ICS) or Network Address Translation (NAT).

BOOTP versus DHCP Relay

BOOTP is an older protocol used to boot diskless workstations with the use of a network-downloadable operating system image. Like DHCP, it is broadcast-based and runs over UDP port 67 and 68. Most routers are not set up by default to forward this type of broadcast, and need some type of assistance to be able to do so. Hence, the DHCP Relay Agent was born.

A DHCP Relay Agent is set up to listen for DHCP broadcast messages on a network segment on which there is no DHCP server. Its job is to intercept these messages and forward them via a one-to-one (*unicast*) message to a valid DHCP server across a router. The DHCP Relay Agent acts as an intermediary DHCP client, working to provide the real DHCP client with a valid DHCP lease. See Figure 3.33 for an illustration of how the DHCP Relay Agent works.

NOTE

In contrast to a *broadcast,* which is a one-to-all type of message using 255.255.255.255 as its destination subnet, a *unicast* is a one-to-one relationship in which the initiating computer already knows the destination IP address of the destination computer.

Figure 3.33 Placing Your DHCP Relay Agent

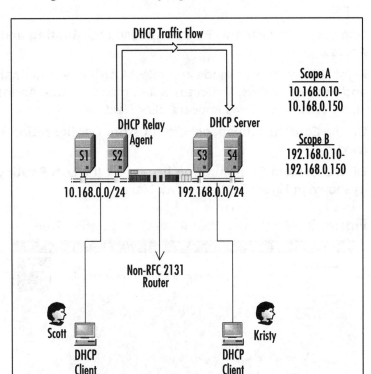

Configuring the DHCP Relay Agent

The procedure for configuring the DHCP Relay Agent has not changed since Windows 2000. It is still configured via the RRAS MMC snap in the Administrative Tools menu tree. Go through Exercise 3.03 to become more familiar with how to configure and set up the DHCP Relay Agent.

EXERCISE 3.03

CONFIGURING YOUR DHCP RELAY AGENT

The three parts of this exercise are:

- Configuring and enabling RRAS
- Adding the DHCP Relay Agent as a new routing protocol
- Configuring the DHCP Relay Agent to forward requests

To configure and enable Routing and Remote Access, perform the following steps:

1. Open the Administrative Tools menu and click **Routing and Remote Access**.

2. Right-click your server node and select **Configure and Enable Routing and Remote Access**. When the Routing and Remote Access Server Setup Wizard windows appears, click **Next**.

3. On the **Configuration** page, click **Custom Configuration** and select **Next**.

4. On the **Custom Configuration** page, click the **LAN Routing** check box, as shown in Figure 3.34, and click **Next**.

Figure 3.34 Selecting Your RRAS Configuration Type

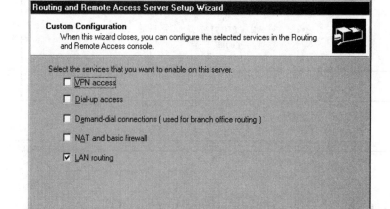

5. On the Summary page, click **Finish** to complete the installation of RRAS.

6. When prompted, select **Yes** to start the RRAS service.

To install the Relay Agent, perform the following steps:

1. Expand the **IP Routing** node and right-click **General**. Select **New Routing Protocol** from the right context menu.

2. In the **New Routing Protocol** dialog box, shown in Figure 3.35, select **DHCP Relay Agent** and click **OK**.

Figure 3.35 Selecting New Routing Protocol

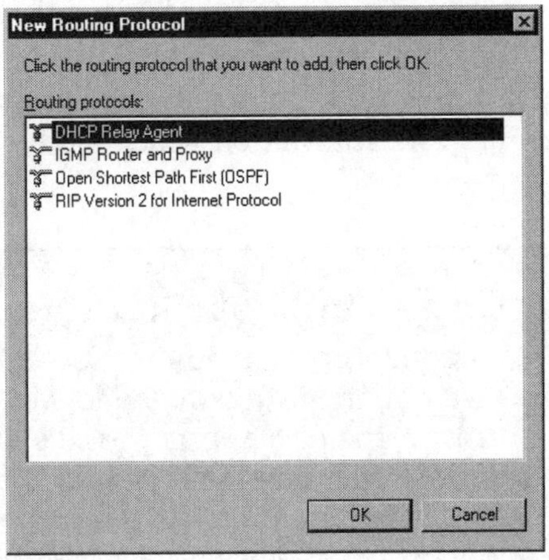

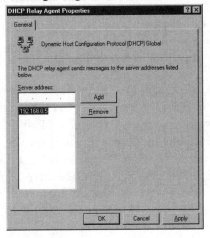

To configure the Relay Agent:

1. Right-click the **DHCP Relay Agent** node and select **New Interface**.

2. If there are multiple interfaces on your server, choose the one that is on the same subnet as your DHCP clients and click **OK**.

3. In the **DHCP Relay Properties** dialog box, click **OK** to keep the default settings.

4. Right-click on the **DHCP Relay Agent** node again and click **Properties**.

5. Enter the **IP Address** of your DHCP server in the dialog box shown in Figure 3.36, and click **Add**. Click **OK**.

Figure 3.36 Configuring the DHCP Server Address

You might need to configure a DHCP Relay Agent for every subnet that does not physically have a DHCP server, if your routers can't forward the needed broadcasts. This does not necessarily mean that you need a different DHCP server for each Relay Agent. All DHCP Relay Agents can point back to the same DHCP server, as long as that DHCP server hosts a scope for each network segment on which the Relay Agents reside.

Configuring & Implementing...

Saving Money by Upgrading Your Routers

In today's world of system administration, automation is the key element. Along with automation comes ease of administration and lower total cost of ownership. Systems administrators want to spend the least possible amount of money, time, and continued effort to implement something new in their already hectic, technology-filled lives.

For this reason, we suggest that you upgrade all of your routers to be RFC 2131 compliant, to support the forwarding of BOOTP and DHCP traffic. Although we discussed the use of the Windows Server 2003 DHCP Relay Agent to aid in environments where RFC2131 routers were not present, this might not be the most cost effective solution if you have many network segments. That's because you need to purchase a physical server and Windows Server 2003 license for each of your different subnets in order to install and configure the DHCP Relay Agent, which can become quite expensive.

In addition, the added administrative overhead of each of these servers could double or even triple the costs of upgrading or purchasing new compliant routers. This is true because most subnets are created within the realm of a single router that contains multiple interfaces. Thus only one new router would need to be purchased to support, for example, the 10 segments it hosts, whereas if you use the DHCP Relay Agent, you must purchase 10 server machines and 10 server licenses.

Integrating the DHCP Server with Dynamic DNS

The primary name resolution mechanism used in Windows Server 2003 Active Directory is the Domain Name System (DNS). DNS provides clients with name-to-IP-address resolution so they can locate network resources. Dynamic DNS is a feature, introduced in Windows 2000, giving your clients the ability to automatically update their own DNS records in your DNS server database. Both Windows 2000 and Windows XP workstations support dynamic updates in a Windows Server 2003 Active Directory environment. However, Windows XP clients are set to update DNS by default, whereas Windows 2000 Professional and Server clients are not. The Windows Server 2003 DHCP service has the ability to dynamically update DNS records on behalf of its clients, solving the problems that arise because of the Windows 2000 default setting.

Figure 3.37 shows the DNS configuration tab on the DHCP server's properties page. This allows you to select your preferred DHCP update method.

Figure 3.37 Configuration of DNS Integration with DHCP

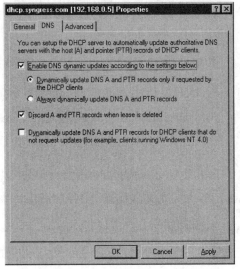

NOTE

The Windows Server 2003 descriptions of each of these options have been revised since Windows 2000. Microsoft documentation is now much clearer and more understandable for administrators trying to decide which options to use in their environments.

Head of the Class...

Multihomed DHCP Servers

DHCP Relay Agents and BOOTP enabled routers are just two of the ways you can service multiple network segments using a single DHCP server. If you find yourself in an environment where router upgrades or additional server licenses to house your DHCP Relay Agents are not feasible, why not throw a few extra network cards in your current DHCP server and multihome it? With the purchase of a few network interface cards, your current DHCP server can physically sit on and service several of your network segments.

A multihomed DHCP server is a server that houses multiple network interface cards that are each physically attached to your network segments servicing DHCP clients. In order to accomplish this successfully, there are a few configuration details that are essential for a successful deployment:

- Each network card must be configured to use a static IP address that is on the same network of the address pool it is to lease its clients.

- Each network interface card's IP address must be configured as an exclusion in the address pool it is to lease its clients.

If you find yourself in a financial bind, network cards are a lot cheaper than routers, servers, and software licensing, so a mutihomed DHCP server may be a good solution for you.

Dealing with Windows NT 4.0 and Win9x Clients

Downlevel DHCP clients do not have the same abilities as Windows 2000 and XP clients to automatically update DNS records in the server's database. Windows NT 4.0, Windows 9x, and Windows for Workgroup clients must use the delegation powers of their issuing DHCP servers to register DNS entries on their behalf. This feature has greatly improved the ability to use DNS for client resolution, because you no longer have to enter IP addresses manually in DNS, and manually update them if they change.

Based on the differences between these clients and the newer Windows 2000 and XP clients, a multitude of updating options arise. These options are discussed in more detail later, in the section, "DNS Updating Options."

TEST DAY TIP

Be very familiar with each of these options, their default settings, and what happens when each is configured independently and separately. This is expected to be the focal point of one or more exam questions, and you might gain some easy points if you study and know this topic inside and out.

DNS Updating Options

The **DHCP updating DNS** configuration options, shown in Figure 3.35, determine exactly how various DHCP client leases are integrated into the DNS database. It is a huge benefit to your network if you take advantage of these options for the most effective integration of DNS and DHCP. The Windows Server 2003 Active Directory is based on DNS and Windows 2000/XP clients using DNS first to resolve name requests. If you can maintain a list of your entire client and server base in your DNS database, whether or not it consists of older downlevel clients, you can guarantee that name resolution for Windows 2000/XP machines will be performed more quickly. This is because each name resolution request will not have to be referred to a WINS server to resolve names for Windows NT 4.0 clients. In the following section, we will define each of the available options in detail and discuss how they can best be used in your environment.

Enable DNS Dynamic Updates

Checking this option turns **off** and **on** the function of allowing your DHCP server to dynamically update *any* of its clients. By default this is turned **on**. This option has two additional settings:

- **Dynamically update DNS A and PTR records only if requested by DHCP clients** If this check box is selected, and the client is a Windows 2000/XP/Server 2003 machine, the DHCP server updates only the PTR record. These clients automatically will update their own A records (if configured to do so on the client side). This option is turned on by default. However, if the clients are downlevel clients, the **Dynamically update DNS A and PTR records for DHCP clients that do not request updates** (for example, clients running Windows NT 4.0) check box must also be selected before DHCP will update the A and PTR records for these clients automatically. The check box is *not* checked by default.

- **Always dynamically update A and PTR records** If this check box is selected, and the client is a Windows 2000/XP/Server 2003 machine, the DHCP server will always update both the A and PTR records in DNS, regardless of what the client requests or how the client is configured. This option is tuned off by default.

NOTE

For more information about the function of A and PTR records in DNS, reference Chapter 6.

Discard A and PTR Records When Lease is Deleted

If the **Discard A and PTR records when lease is deleted** check box is selected, the server will automatically delete the A record associated with a client's PTR record when the client sends a *release message* to the DHCP server. By default, if the **Enable DNS Dynamic updates according to the settings below** check box is also enabled, the DHCP server will already automatically delete the client's PTR record in DNS. This option allows the DHCP server to automatically delete the A record as well. This option is turned **on** by default.

Dynamically Update DNS A and PTR Records for DHCP Clients that Do Not Request Updates

When the Dynamically update DNS A and PTR records for DHCP clients that do not request updates (for example clients running Windows NT 4.0) check box is selected, it enables downlevel clients to participate in DHCP dynamic updates in a way that is similar to Windows 2000/XP and Server 2003 clients. One difference is that *all* DNS updates are funneled through the issuing DHCP server. See the differences illustrated in Figures 3.38 and 3.39.

TEST DAY TIP

The ability for Windows 2000/XP/Server 2003 clients to use dynamic updates relies on the addition of a new client-side DHCP option (option 81). This option allows these types of clients to send their FQDNs to the DHCP server, along with informational data on how they should be updated in DNS. To emulate this ability for downlevel windows clients, you must enable the **Dynamically update DNS A and PTR records for DHCP clients that do not request updates (for example clients running Windows NT 4.0)** option.

DNSUpdateProxy Group

Dynamic DNS provides a way to make sure all your clients, including downlevel clients, get updated in your DNS database. However, when your DHCP server updates its clients in DNS, the ownership of all the A and PTR records points directly back to the DHCP server itself (depending on the configuration discussed in the *DNS Updating Options* section of this chapter). This causes a problem when one of the following situations occur:

- You have to switch to using another DHCP server.
- You change the configuration on your DHCP server to allow clients to update their own records.

If the original DHCP server that registered a client's record becomes unavailable and another DHCP server has to be brought online, the new DHCP server will not have any

Figure 3.38 Displaying Dynamic DNS Requests for Windows 2000/XP/
Server 2003 Clients

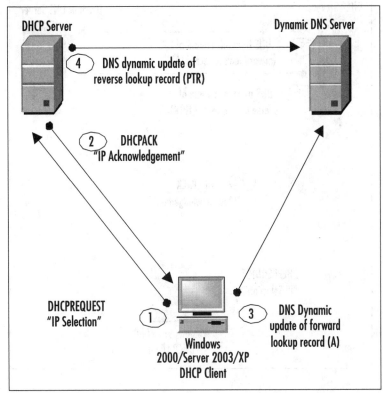

rights to update any of the older, already registered client records. Additionally, if you
change the configuration on your DNS server from **Always dynamically update A and
PTR records** to **Dynamically update DNA A and PTR records only if requested
by DHCP clients** (or if you completely disable dynamic updating), clients will not have
the rights to update their own records in DNS. Both of these situations arise because the
registering DHCP server is the only one that has the proper security permissions to update
these records. To prevent this from happening, Microsoft created the DNSUpdateProxy
Active Directory Group.

The DNSUpdateProxy Group consists of computers that can update records on behalf
of other DHCP clients. By putting all of your DHCP servers into this group, you can allow
them to update records for your clients, but not take ownership of and stamp its security
credentials on these records. This means that the original clients can update records later if
necessary. Ownership of the records is established when the first security principal accesses
these entries. This does not include any member of the DNSUpdateProxy Group itself. It
also means that DHCP servers can update records on behalf of other servers that fail.

Figure 3.39 Displaying Dynamic DNS Requests for Downlevel DHCP Clients

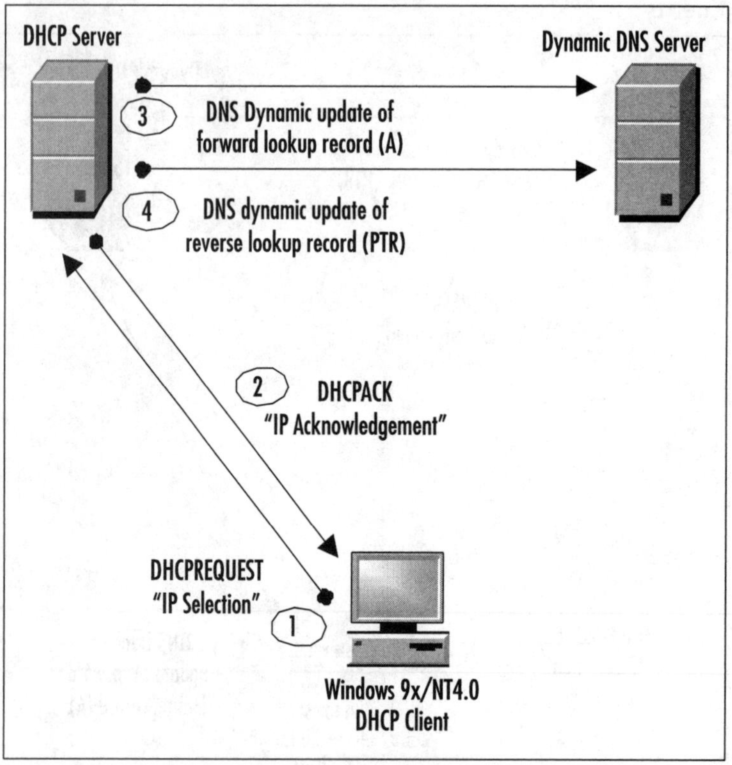

Security Concerning the DNSUpdateProxy Group

There are some security concerns to be aware of when putting the DNSUpdateProxy Group into action. If you put your DHCP servers in this group, all records updated by those servers are not secure in your DNS database. If your DHCP server is a domain controller (as those in many branch office configurations are), all the service location (SRV), and forward lookup (A) records registered when starting the Netlogon service will not be secure. What can you do to address these concerns?

1. Do not put any of your domain controllers in the DNSUpdateProxy Group.

2. If you choose to use the DNSUpdateProxy Group, don't install DHCP on a domain controller.

New & Noteworthy...

Securing the Use of the DNSUpdateProxy Group

Previous versions of Windows posed some serious concerns when dealing with DHCP's dynamic updating of DNS records. For example, if you were using an Active Directory integrated DNS zone configured for **secure updates only**, you were unable to use the DNSUpdateProxy Group, because DHCP servers that are members of the DNSUpdateProxy Group register all client records without ownership.

To address some of these issues, a new **DNS dynamic update credentials** manager was created. The interface is shown in Figure 3.40.

Figure 3.40 Configuring Credentials for Use with Dynamic Updating

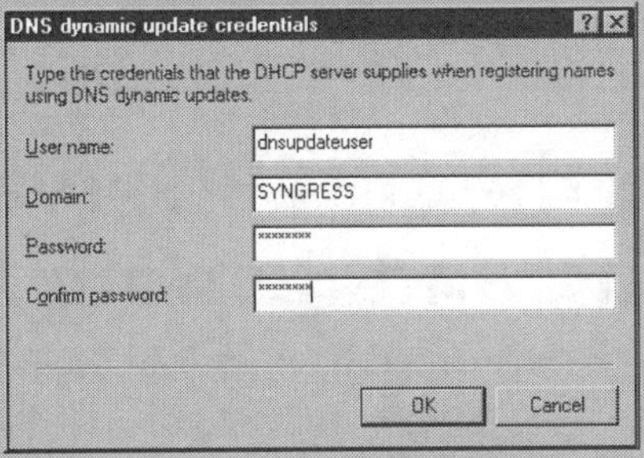

You first need to create a dedicated user account in Active Directory whose credentials will be used by DHCP servers to perform dynamic updates. Then, to configure each DHCP server to use the account, perform the following steps:

1. In the left console pane of the DHCP MMC, right-click the server node and select **Properties**.

2. Click the **Advanced** tab.

3. Under **DNS dynamic updates registration credentials**, click the **Credentials** button.

4. Enter the user name, domain, and password for the account you created for this purpose, and click **OK**.

Do this for all DHCP servers that will use these credentials. The credentials supplied in the **DNS dynamic update credentials** dialog box are used by DHCP servers that are members of the DNSUpdateProxy group to register client records in DNS. This prevents the registration of nonsecure records in DNS. The same account can be used on all your DHCP servers, thus eliminating one of the earlier issues described in the section "Security Concerning the DNSUpdateProxy Group," in reference to switching to a new DHCP server after the original one has already registered client records under its ownership. By using the new credentials option, you create a configuration that allows the use of both the DNSUpdateProxy group and Active Directory integrated DNS with *secure updates only*.

Continued

To configure the dynamic DNS update credentials, you can use the graphical user interface (GUI) shown in Figure 3.40 or you can use the `netsh` command line utility within the *servers context* using the *set dnscredentials* parameter.

NOTE

The user account whose credentials will be used by the DHCP servers for dynamic updates should be dedicated to this one task and should not be used for any other purpose.

EXAM 70-291

OBJECTIVE 1.4 1.4.1

Integrating the DHCP Server with Routing and Remote Access

RRAS support is being implemented by more and more companies as their employees are beginning to work from their homes over fast DSL/Cable Internet services and VPN connections, in addition to traditional dial-up accounts. Most internal networks today use the TCP/IP protocol as the primary (or only) network/transport protocol for internal communication and resource sharing. In order to facilitate the internal use of TCP/IP for remote access, your RRAS server has to be able to allocate TCP/IP addresses to your dial-in clients, thus acting as DHCP servers.

You can configure your RRAS server to do this in one of two ways:

- You can configure your RRAS server with a static pool of addresses that it will itself assign to dial-in clients.

- You can configure the RRAS server to relay clients to your internal DHCP server. For the purpose of this section on DHCP server integration, we will discuss the latter method.

To configure your RRAS server to use DHCP, you first will need to set up a **DHCP Relay Agent** as described in Exercise 3.3. Next, you must configure your server to use the **Dynamic Host Configuration Protocol (DHCP)** option rather that the **Static address pool** option, as shown in Figure 3.41. To do so, perform these steps:

1. Open the **Routing and Remote Access console** from within the Administrative Tools menu.

2. Right-click on the node for the RRAS server and select **Properties**.

3. Click the **IP** tab to display the DHCP configuration dialog window shown in Figure 3.41.

4. Under IP Address assignment, select the **Dynamic Host Configuration Protocol (DHCP)** option button.

5. Click **OK**.

Figure 3.41 Configuring DHCP for Remote Access Users

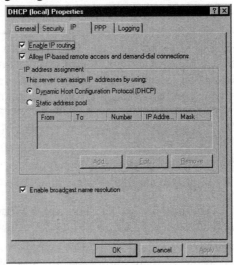

DHCP and RRAS Scenarios

Based on different configuration options, there are a few different scenarios your dial-in clients may go through in order to obtain DHCP information. Which scenario applies to a given client depends on which of the following three IP configurations is set up for the client's dial-in environment.

1. IP address is assigned from static pool on RRAS server.

2. IP address is assigned from DHCP server through use of the DHCP Relay Agent.

3. IP address is assigned statically to the user's security object.

Scenario 1: RRAS Acts as DHCP Server

Scenario 1 assumes that you have chosen the **Static address pool** radio button in Figure 3.41. When choosing this option, you must click **Add** and configure a **Start IP address** and an **End IP address**. The **New Address Range** dialog window automatically will display the number of addresses in the range you have chosen to configure.

In this particular scenario, the RRAS server acts as a DHCP server to the client, issuing IP addresses as clients request them. However, IP addresses are the only configuration information the RRAS server can hand out. In order for the dial-in client to receive any DHCP

IP options, it must contact an authorized DHCP server by means of the DHCP Relay Agent. This means that although the RRAS server is set up to act as a DHCP server, it still must be configured with a DHCP Relay Agent in order to give the client any needed IP option information. Such options might include the IP addresses of a DNS server, WINS server, or DNS domain name suffix.

NOTE

When entering the **Start IP address** and **End IP address** in the RRAS **New Address Range** box shown in Figure 3.41, you might notice that there is no place to enter a subnet mask. This is because the RRAS server automatically configures its own subnet mask for all dial-in clients, based on the configuration of the RRAS server itself.

Scenario 2: RRAS Passes Requests to Another DHCP Server

Scenario 2 assumes that you have chosen the **Dynamic Host Configuration Protocol (DHCP)** radio button in Figure 3.41. When you choose this option, all DHCP lease traffic is sent through the RRAS server by means of the DHCP Relay Agent. The DHCP server configured in the DHCP Relay Agent's properties is responsible for carrying out the entire DHCP lease process with the client, again by means of the DHCP Relay Agent. Both the client IP address and all IP configured options are distributed by the configured DHCP server.

This is the most common setup and the one that is configured by default when you install the DHCP Relay Agent. This option helps to alleviate some management overhead, in that you need to manage only one DHCP distribution point.

Scenario 3: Static IP Assigned to User

Scenario 3 assumes that you have statically configured an IP address for the dial-in client in the properties sheet for that user's security object, as shown in Exercise 3.04. If this is the case, when the user dials into your RRAS server, the settings specified in the Remote Access Policy will be ignored, and it doesn't matter whether or not you have chosen to use DHCP or RRAS DHCP. Instead, the computer will use the IP address set on the user's properties page. This allows the administrator to exert very granular control over dial-in users, possibly using static IP address in specific access or deny lists across network resources.

EXERCISE 3.04

ASSIGNING INDIVIDUAL USER OBJECT IP ADDRESSES

This exercise will show you how to configure the properties of a user account object manually with a static IP address for remote dial-in purposes.

1. Open the **Active Directory Users and Computers** MMC from within the **Administrative Tools** menu.

2. Right click your *domain name* and click **Find**. Type the username to which you wish to statically assign an IP address and click **Find Now**.

3. In the search results window, double-click the **username**.

4. Click the **Dial-In** menu tab of the *<username>* **Properties** dialog box, as shown in Figure 3.42.

5. Click the checkbox next to **Assign a Static IP** Address field and type a valid IP address for one of your dial-in network subnets. Click **OK**.

Figure 3.42 Configuring a User Object with a Static IP Address

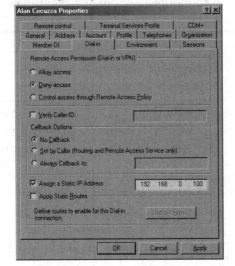

NOTE

The functional level of your Windows Server 2003 Active Directory domain must be at least *Windows 2000 native*, meaning it contains only Windows 2000, and Windows 2000 and Windows Server 2003 domain controllers, in order to support this feature. Otherwise, the **Assign a Static IP Address** field will be grayed out. The default domain functional level is *Windows 2000 mixed,* which allows NT 4.0 domain controllers along with Windows 2000 and Server 2003 domain controllers. You will not have this option if your domain is running at the default level. Domain functional levels are like the domain *modes* in Windows 2000. To raise the functional level of your domain, click **Start | Programs | Administrative Tools | Active Directory Domains and Trusts**. In the left pane of the MMC, right-click the name of the domain and select **Raise domain functional level**. Be aware that the process is not reversible.

EXAM WARNING

Remember, though each of these scenarios is set up a bit differently, all of them have and require the installation and setup of the DHCP Relay Agent. This is because, without the Relay Agent in place, each one of these scenarios lacks the ability to obtain any IP configured options the client may need to further communicate on your network.

TEST DAY TIP

When a client uses the DHCP Relay Agent to obtain an IP option from your DHCP server, the client issues a DHCPINFORM message. This message is solely for the purpose of asking your DHCP server if there are any IP options available for the network subnet on which the client is located. See Table 3.1 for more about the DHCPINFORM message.

Integrating DHCP with Active Directory

With the introduction of DHCP into any network environment, you introduce a substantial amount of risk. Before Active Directory, there was no effective way to secure the implementation of a DHCP server installed on a Microsoft network. All a person needed was the ability to install the DHCP service, configure a scope, and activate it to be able to hand out IP addresses. "Rogue" DHCP servers, operating without the knowledge of the administrator, were not uncommon. In today's Active Directory environments, DHCP has become tightly integrated with the directory services in order to add another layer of security to your IP deployment and management tactics.

A Good Reason to Assign IP Addresses via User Object Properties

Do you work for a company that has a lot of remote or mobile laptop users? Do you often wonder who they are, what they do, and more importantly, what they are doing on your network when they dial in? You might have even been the one who set up these users with VPN access to the network, without knowing why they needed it or when they would be dialing in. Well, if so, you're no different from many other administrators. We just fulfill new user requests as they come in.

However, this is not the best practice. Instead, you should ask question after question about each remote user who needs access to your network. Create a template question form that details why, when, and to what the user needs access via a remote dial-in connection. If this is not enough, and you suspect that a particular user or users are dialing in and doing things they shouldn't, you can use the **Dial-In** tab on each user's **Properties** sheet to assign each user a single static IP address. To do this, follow the steps outlined in Exercise 3.04.

After a user has been set up with a static IP address, you are armed not only with his or her specific Active Directory user account information, but also the IP address with which each user roams around your network. This means you can monitor network traffic to determine exactly where each user goes and what each user does. To directly limit a user from roaming your network, once inside your dial-in server, you can begin setting up boundaries and access lists, using the static IP address as a definitive identifier. Thus, static IP address assignment can enhance security.

A second reason to use static IP address assignment on user objects is purely for administrative purposes. There are many products sold today that heavily rely on security and build into their source code access control lists (ACLs) based on source IP address. Some of these products include:

- Firewall Software
- Antivirus Management Software
- Anti-Spam Content Software
- Intrusion Detection System Software

Because access to manage these software products relies on a source IP address, it is difficult and not a good security practice to use DHCP ranges to allow admittance. However, if administrators who are also dial-in users are configured to use static IP addresses when they dial in, it is easy to add single static IP addresses to each of the management consoles' ACLs.

Here's how it works: Before an Active Directory DHCP server is allowed to distribute IP address leases, it must be authorized to do so in Active Directory. To authorize a Windows Server 2003 DHCP server, you must be a member of the root domain's Enterprise Admins group. This level of security ensures that only the highest level administrators can implement Windows Server 2003 DHCP severs on the network.

One way to authorize a single DHCP server is by right-clicking the DHCP server's name in the left pane of the DHCP MMC Console and clicking **Authorize** (or choosing **Authorize** from the **Action** menu). See Figure 3.43 for an illustration. You may need to press **F5** to refresh the console and show the updated status.

To authorize multiple DHCP servers, work through Exercise 3.05.

TEST DAY TIP

Though DHCP authorization offers a great deal of security, be aware that only Windows 2000 and Server 2003 DHCP servers have to be authorized. Any other OS-dependant DHCP server can be brought online and operate without error. Windows NT 4.0 is a good example.

Figure 3.43 Authorizing a Single DHCP Server

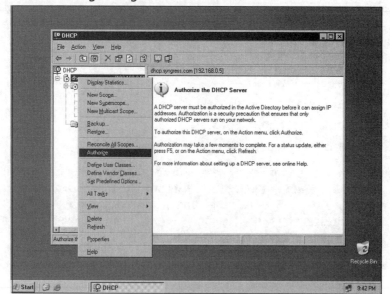

Authorizing DHCP Servers in the Active Directory

Authorizing DHCP server in Active Directory is an important task and should not be taken lightly. It provides the ultimate authority over which servers are deemed secure to serve IP address leases. As noted, you can authorize a single DHCP Server easily from the **Action** or right context menu.

When Active Directory is deployed on your network, DHCP servers should be domain controllers or member servers that belong to the domain, in order to be authorized. In order for a standalone server to function as a DHCP server, there cannot be any other authorized DHCP servers on the subnet. Microsoft recommends that you not use standalone DHCP servers in this way.

The first DHCP server installed on your network should always be a domain controller or member server. If you choose to install standalone servers, they must be installed afterward. Authorization will not work correctly if a standalone is installed as the first DHCP server on the network.

NOTE

If the FQDN of the DHCP server has more than 64 characters, there will be an error returned when you attempt to authorize the server in Active Directory. You can work around this by authorizing the DHCP server by IP address instead of FQDN.

To fully authorize multiple DHCP servers in Active Directory, follow the steps in Exercise 3.05.

EXERCISE 3.05

AUTHORIZING DHCP SERVERS

1. Open the **Administrative Tools** menu and click **DHCP**.

2. In the left pane of the console, right-click **DHCP** and click **Manage authorized servers** in the drop-down menu. You will see a list of authorized DHCP servers.

3. To authorize additional servers, click the **Authorize** button within the **Manage Authorized Servers** dialog window.

4. Type the **Name or IP address** of the DHCP server you want to authorize as shown in Figure 3.44. Click **OK**. A dialog box will show the corresponding name and IP address of the server that is about to be authorized. Click **OK** again.

5. Repeat steps three and four for all the DHCP servers you wish to authorize.

Figure 3.44 Authorizing DHCP Servers

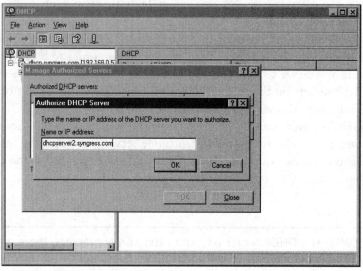

 TEST DAY TIP

At the same time a DHCPINFORM message helps a DHCP server find out whether it is authorized to start, it also determines if an already authorized DHCP server is no longer authorized to continue leasing IP addresses.

Rogue DHCP Server Detection

Rogue DHCP server detection is built into the way that Windows 2000 and Server 2003 DHCP servers announce themselves when starting up the DHCP service. Exactly how this works depends on whether the DHCP server is a member of the domain or a standalone.

If the DHCP server is a domain member, it will query the Active Directory when it starts up, and the Active Directory will return a list of authorized DHCP servers. The querying server checks the list, and if its own IP address is there, it proceeds to initialize the DHCP service and starts providing IP addresses to client computers. If not, it does not initialize the DHCP service. If the member server cannot contact the Active Directory (it is not available for some reason) it will operate in its last known state. That is, if it was authorized when it shut down, it will assume that it is still authorized.

When a standalone DHCP starts up, it broadcasts a DHCPINFORM message on its local network segment. All authorized listening DHCP servers reply to this message with a DHCPACK message (see Table 3.1 for more on these message types). Included in the DHCPACK message is information pertaining to where any domain controllers for the Active Directory root domain reside. The initializing DHCP server then attempts to contact those domain controllers, asking for a valid list of authorized DHCP servers on the network. If the querying DHCP server finds itself on the list, the DHCP service starts. If the DHCP server does not find itself on this list, it will fail to start the service, and log an event in the System Event log. The DHCP server service will broadcast DHCPINFORM messages every five minutes in an effort to find itself on the authorized DHCP list. Until this time, it is considered unauthorized and will refuse client DHCPDISCOVERY messages.

This functionality helps to provide a layer of security by enabling only users of the built-in Enterprise Admins Active Directory group to initially authorize DHCP servers before they are available on your network.

EXAM WARNING

Remember again that DHCP authorization refers only to Windows 2000 and Server 2003 DHCP servers. Other operating systems' rogue DHCP servers may operate freely on your network and cause havoc. There is good reason for mentioning this twice in this chapter!

EXAM
70-291

OBJECTIVE
1.3.1
1.3.2

Understanding Automatic Private IP Addressing (APIPA)

Automatic Private IP Addressing has been supported in all of Microsoft's Windows products since Windows 98SE. This includes the following operating systems:

- Windows 98SE
- Windows ME
- Windows 2000 Professional and Server
- Windows XP
- Windows Server 2003

How APIPA Works

Before APIPA was introduced, DHCP clients would go through the DHCP lease process to obtain an IP address, and if no DHCP server was available, an error message was displayed, telling the client that DHCP was not able to configure an IP address. With APIPA, even if no DHCP server responds, the client will still be configured with an IP address. This IP address is generated form the APIPA IP address range of 169.254.0.0 to 169.254.255.255 with a class B subnet mask of 255.255.0.0. The Internet Assigned Numbers Authority (IANA) reserved this range of addresses for Microsoft as a block of private addresses. Like the other private address ranges, APIPA addresses are not valid on the Internet.

In smaller networks where there are no routers, and where DHCP is not an option because there are no computers running a server operating system that can be configured as DHCP servers, APIPA can be used as a solution for IP address distribution. As long as all the clients on the network support the APIPA technology, all clients will receive valid IP addresses on the same subnet and will be able to talk to each other using their TCP/IP stack. You simply configure them to obtain IP addresses automatically, just as you do for DHCP clients. If there are routers configured on the network, and you want to be able to communicate with resources across router boundaries, APIPA is not the answer. APIPA configures the client only with an IP address and subnet mask. It does not provide default gateway or DNS/WINS information and is not meant to route across network segments.

APIPA uses its own form of conflict detection to make sure that the auto configuration of each client does not conflict with another client on the same network. It does this by broadcasting an *arp* request for the IP address that it is planning to assign to the client and listening for a response. If there is no response, the IP address is assigned to the client. If there is a positive response to the *arp* request, than the IP is assumed to be in use and discarded by APIPA; the same process is repeated with another address in the range.

A computer that has been assigned an APIPA address will continue to check every five minutes for a DHCP server, and if it finds one, will stop the APIPA service and initiate the DHCP lease process.

Disabling APIPA

It is possible to disable the generation of APIPA addresses on your Windows Server 2003 DHCP clients if you want to use only valid DHCP server scope addresses, even in the event that a DHCP server is not available. To do so, you need to edit the windows registry and make the following changes:

1. Open the Registry Editor by running **Reged32.exe** and traverse to the following keys, depending on whether you want to disable APIPA for one network card or all network cards. Use this key, where *InterfaceAdapterKey* is the globally unique identifier (GUID) of your single DHCP NIC, if you want to disable APIPA on one NIC:

```
HKLM\System\CurrentControlSet\Services\Tcpip\Parameters\

    InterfaceAdapterKey
```

Use this key to disable APIPA on a global level for all network cards in the machine:

```
HKLM\SYSTEM\CurrentControlSet\Services\Tcpip\Parameters
```

2. Add the *IPAutoconfigurationEnabled* DWORD registry entry with a value of *0x0*.

NOTE

This is not needed for the test, but something we thought might interest our readers. The APIPA IP address range used to be a viable Internet routable Class B network that was owned by Bill Gates, chairman of Microsoft. He decided to donate the address range to the Windows 98SE project team, and they came up with what Microsoft now calls Automatic Private IP Addressing. This address range is supported and reserved by the Internet Assigned Numbers Authority (IANA).

TEST DAY TIP

APIPA is a great solution for getting around the problem of unavailable DHCP servers, but be aware that it can also make your troubleshooting problems a bit more complicated because errors are not popped up automatically in the client's graphical interface when APIPA is enabled. APIPA does not generate an IP address error and instead just configures itself with an APIPA address. This means you may be unaware that the DHCP server is unavailable, and unable to figure out why the APIPA-assigned computer can't communicate with others on the network. One of your first troubleshooting steps in an APIPA client environment is to run the *ipconfig /all* command to determine if the IP is in the APIPA range, as shown in Figure 3.45.

Figure 3.45 Displaying APIPA Address Configuration

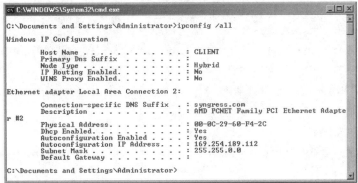

New & Noteworthy...

Alternate IP Configuration

With Windows Server 2003, APIPA is now not the only way to configure an IP address in the absence of a DHCP server. Windows Server 2003 servers can be configured to use an alternate static IP configuration. If you choose to use an alternate IP address configuration, when your DHCP client realizes that no DHCP server is available, it will automatically switch over and configure your TCP/IP stack with the static address information you entered in the alternate configuration tab, as shown in Figure 3.46.

Figure 3.46 Configuring an Alternate IP Address

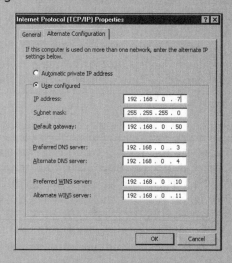

This is an ideal situation for users who travel between two networks with a laptop and need to be statically configured on one of those networks due to the lack of a DHCP server. The Alternate Configuration tab can be configured by performing these steps:

1. Click **Start | Control Panel | Network Connections**.

2. Right-click the network connection for which you want to set an alternate configuration and select **Properties**.

3. On the General tab, highlight **Internet Protocol (TCP/IP)** in the list of items used by the connection.

4. Click the **Properties** button.

5. Click the **Alternate Configuration** tab.

6. Click **User configured**.

7. Enter the TCP/IP configuration information for the second network.

Continued

> The alternate IP address supports a limited manual configuration of the following:
>
> - IP address
> - Subnet mask
> - Default gateway
> - Preferred and alternate DNS servers
> - Preferred and alternate WINS servers

NOTE

To view the Alternate Configuration tab in the TCP/IP properties dialog box, your main TCP/IP configuration must be configured to use DHCP. When your TCP/IP stack is already configured for a static address, the availability of the Alternate Configuration tab disappears.

Managing the Windows Server 2003 DHCP Server

Once your DHCP servers are installed, authorized, and physically handing out IP addresses on your network, you need to ensure that they can continue doing so as efficiently as possible. You should ensure that you have enough DHCP addresses available, ensure that the DHCP lease process is running smoothly, and ensure that your DHCP database is backed up in case of a failure.

You also want to securely manage your DHCP server without compromising productivity. In the following sections, we will discuss several issues important to the management of your DHCP server:

- How to back up and restore your DHCP database in case of complete failure
- How to repair your DHCP database in case of corruption
- How to view and analyze statistical information about your DHCP server
- How to effectively distribute management tasks to your employees

Managing the DHCP Server Database

Managing your DHCP server database includes making sure that it is always backed up in case of a disaster. It also includes regularly checking server event logs to determine if the database is in an inconsistent state and needs to be repaired.

A new feature in Windows Server 2003 will allow you to back up your DHCP database manually via the DHCP MMC console. In earlier versions of Windows DHCP, you had to rely on the command line utility called *netsh* to back up your databases manually. It is important to have a backup copy of your database at all times. Manually backing it up or scheduling it for backup is a critical step in ensuring limited downtime to clients if a DHCP server should fail.

Another new feature in Windows Server 2003 is the ability of the built-in **ntbackup** utility to back up the DHCP database while it is still open and the service is still running. This is due to a new feature called Volume Shadow Copy (VSC). VSC is a configurable service that allows you to periodically take snapshots of files on your server. VSC allows **ntbackup** to take advantage of its imaging abilities and institute its own Open File Transaction Manager. Although this is useful when running nightly backups, it is still a good idea to have a separate backup copy of the database somewhere else. Exercise 3.06 will guide you through the process of manually backing up and restoring your DHCP database.

EXERCISE 3.06

BACKING UP AND RESTORING YOUR DHCP DATABASE

This exercise will show you how to manually back up your DHCP database to an alternate location.

To back up the DHCP database:

1. Open the **DHCP** MMC console from within the **Administrative Tools** menu.

2. Right-click the node for the **DHCP server** and select **Backup** from the context menu, as shown in Figure 3.47.

3. Choose a folder to which you want to back up the database and select **OK**.

To restore the DHCP Database:

1. Open the **DHCP** MMC console from within the **Administrative Tools** menu.

2. Right-click the node for the DHCP server and select **Restore**.

3. Choose the folder that contains the backup copy of your DHCP database and select **OK**.

4. You are prompted with a message stating that your DHCP service must be stopped and restarted. Click **Yes** if you want to do this now, as shown in Figure 3.48.

Figure 3.47 Backing Up Your DHCP Database from within the DHCP MMC Console

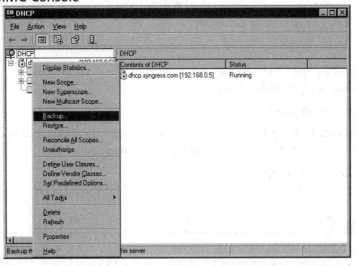

Figure 3.48 Restoring DHCP Database Warning Message

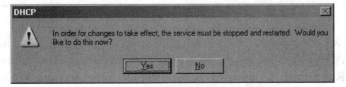

TEST DAY TIP

Although the ability to back up and restore your DHCP database manually from within the DHCP MMC console is a great new feature of Windows Server 2003, you can still use the *netsh* command line utility to schedule a backup your DHCP databases automatically, as you did in Windows 2000. However, by default the DHCP service runs a synchronous backup of the database every 60 minutes. This interval can be changed by editing the following Registry key: HKLM\SYSTEM\CurrentControlSet\DHCPServer\Parameters\BackupInterval

In certain instances, your DHCP databases may become inconsistent or corrupt. Periodically, the DHCP service performs a consistency check against your database to determine whether it is still consistent. If it is not, the DHCP service will attempt to correct these problems. If it cannot, an event will be logged in the System Event log, stating that your DHCP database may be inconsistent or corrupt. This means you will have to use the **jetpack** command line utility to repair the database manually. To use the **jetpack** utility:

1. Open a command prompt window by typing **cmd** in your **Start | Run** box.

2. Navigate to your DHCP database directory (which by default is **%windir%\system32\dhcp**).

3. Type **net stop dhcp**.

4. Type **jetpack dhcp.mdb** <*temp*> (where *temp* is the name and location of a temporary file that will be used to repair the database).

5. Type **net start dhcp**.

TEST DAY TIP

The jetpack program not only repairs consistency errors, but compacts the database size. If you manage very large DHCP client bases and your DHCP databases are consistently growing, it is a good idea to schedule monthly downtime to run the jetpack utility program for this purpose.

To keep track of inconsistencies in your DHCP database scopes, you can manually run the **Reconcile All Scopes** menu selection from the DHCP console, as shown in Figure 3.49. From the **Reconcile All Scopes** dialog window shown in Figure 3.50, you can then click the **Verify** button to check your scopes for inconsistencies against the Registry data.

Figure 3.49 Reconciling Your DHCP Scopes

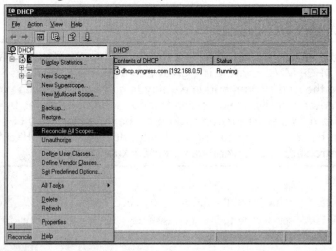

Figure 3.50 Comparing Scope Information with Registry Data

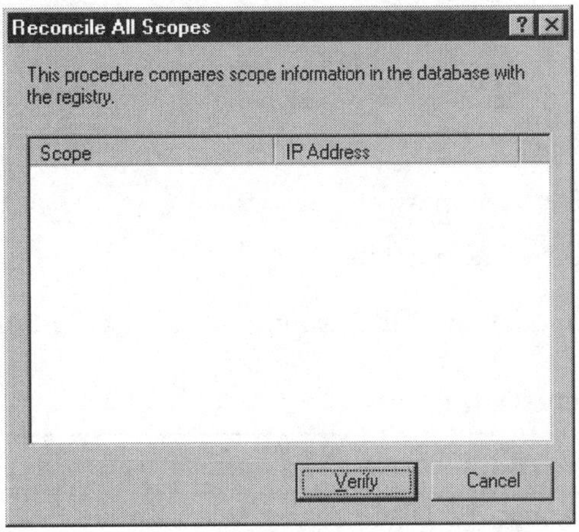

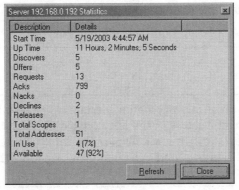

Viewing and Recording DHCP Server Statistics

Periodically, DHCP administrators need to monitor statistical information about how their DHCP servers are serving clients. You can do this from within the DHCP MMC by following these steps:

1. Open the **DHCP MMC** from within the **Administrative Tools** menu.

2. Right-click on the node for your DHCP server and select **Display Statistics**. This will display the Statistics window shown in Figure 3.51.

Figure 3.51 Viewing Your DHCP Server Statistics

The Server Statistics view shown in Figure 3.51 gives you information about the following:

- The DHCP server service
- Your DHCP scopes
- Individual DHCP lease message statistics
- Available IP address information

More detail can be found about the meaning of each of these statistics in Table 3.6.

Table 3.6 Server Statistic Definitions

Statistic Header	Description
Start Time	Time that the DHCP service was started
Up Time	Time since the DHCP service was started
Discovers	Shows many DHCPDISCOVER messages have been received
Offers	Shows many DHCPOFFER messages have been given out
Requests	Shows many DHCPREQUEST messages have been received
Acks	Shows many DHCPACK messages have been given out
Nacks	Shows many DHCPNACK messages have been given out
Declines	Shows many DHCPDECLINE messages have been received
Releases	Shows many DHCPDISCOVER messages have been received
Total Scopes	How many DHCP scopes are configured on this server
Total Addresses	How many IP addresses are available in all scopes
In Use	How many IP addresses are in use
Available	How many IP addresses are left available for lease

NOTE

You can also view statistical information pertaining to a single scope, by right-clicking the name of the scope in the left console pane of the DHCP MMC and selecting **Scope Statistics**. This will display the total number of addresses in the scope, how many are in use, and how many are available (both actual numbers and as percentages of the total).

EXAM WARNING

Statistical data refresh times can be configured at the server level. This is accomplished by selecting the **Properties** option from the context menu when you right-click the node for your DHCP server. The resulting configuration dialog box is shown in Figure 3.52.

Figure 3.52 Changing the Statistical Refresh Rate

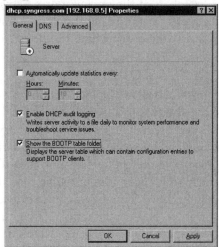

This statistical data can also be found in the DHCP server logs. These are text files that can be opened in NotePad. The information recorded in these logs can be found in the %windir%\system32\dhcp folder on your DHCP server. We will discuss DHCP logging in more detail in the *Monitoring and Troubleshooting DHCP* section of this chapter. Specific information for analyzing these logs can also be found in Tables 3.9 and 3.10 in the section "Using DHCP Log Files."

Delegating DHCP Administration

DHCP administration and control over your DHCP server is now easier than ever with the predelegated built-in local groups of Windows Server 2003 DHCP servers. There are three groups that deal with the administration of Windows Server 2003 DHCP servers:

- Enterprise Admins group
- DHCP Administrators group
- DHCP Users group

In the following sections, we will discuss the purposes of these groups and what rights each group gives to users that are members.

Enterprise Admins Group

The Enterprise Admins group is often called the "all powerful" group in the Active Directory environment. There is good reason for this, because members of this group have the ability to do whatever they want on an enterprise or forest-wide level. This includes full rights over the DHCP servers. One special feature of this group is that it is the only Active Directory group that has the right to authorize a DHCP server. Because the Enterprise Admins group does have so much power over the network, it is a good idea to restrict membership in this group to members of the organization's Active Directory enterprise design team. Even then, in most cases membership should be limited to only a few members of that team, with the actual number depending on the size of the organization.

DHCP Administrators Group

The DHCP Administrators group is created as a local group on every DHCP server. Members of this group have the ability to manage all aspects of the DHCP server. This includes the creation, deletion, and activation of server scopes, the ability to create client reservations and specific user and vendor scope options, and the right to back up and restore the DHCP database. However, this group does not have all the rights of local Administrators; they can perform only those administrative tasks that directly pertain to DHCP. Members of this group might be Systems Administrators or others who are responsible for day-to-day server operations and configuration activities, as well as persons to whom you want to delegate the authority to take care of DHCP servers only.

DHCP Users Group

The DHCP Users group is also created as a local group on all DHCP servers. Members of this group have view-only rights to the DHCP server's configuration and statistical information. Other tasks that can be performed by members of this group include:

- The ability to see whether there is a depletion of IP addresses in any of your servers' scopes.

- The ability to see the options that are being handed out to DHCP clients, as well as which scopes have or have not been activated.

- The ability to determine if there are issues with client connectivity due to DHCP server configuration problems or a lack of IP addresses to lease.

Members of this group might include personnel on your Client Services teams, or those in charge of day-to-day client workstation operations.

Monitoring and Troubleshooting the Windows Server 2003 DHCP Server

An understanding of the tools discussed in this section is essential to the tasks of monitoring your DHCP server's performance and troubleshooting problems that arise. Mastering these tools will not only help you pass the exam, but will prove to be a necessity in the production environment. Windows Server 2003 does a good job of routinely logging data that can be used for troubleshooting, but there are also a number of special tools that can be used to capture and create data after the fact. Many of these tools can be used from the DHCP server itself or from a remote client (as long as you have the proper permissions on the server).

EXAM WARNING

When monitoring your DHCP server, you may encounter the appearance of triangular icons next to one or more of your scopes. It is important to know the meanings of these icons:

- **Yellow triangle icon** This indicates that 90 percent of your DHCP leases are being used.
- **Red triangle icon** This indicates that the DHCP lease pool is depleted.

Using the Event Viewer

The Windows Server 2003 Event Viewer can be found in the **Administrative Tools** menu. All DHCP related events are logged in the *System* log of the event viewer. All DHCP events logged by the event viewer are coded with the same *Source* field of **DhcpServer**, so you can easily sort through DHCP specific events by clicking the *Source* field heading.

The Event Log is used to log events that are specific to the DHCP service itself and to the DHCP server as a whole. For instance, the event viewer will log an event when the DHCP service starts and stops, during periodic authorization checks, indicating whether it is authorized to lease IP addresses in Active Directory and whether or not the DHCP database is inconsistent. Events are also logged if the DHCP service is running but not able to hand out leases. For example, Event ID 1041 is logged when there are no active static IP addresses assigned to any available network adapters. This might be the result of an administrator changing the IP configuration of the DHCP server from static to dynamic. Security events related to DHCP are also logged here. The service will also alert you of an event, stating that your DHCP server service is running under the credentials of the system and not under those specified by the administrator, as shown in Figure 3.53. The server prompts you with this security event and gives you an explanation and recommendation for reconciling it in the description field of the event.

Figure 3.53 Viewing DHCP Event Log Error

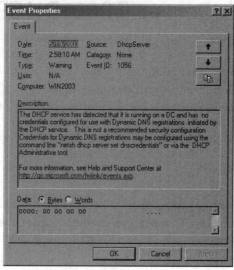

Table 3.7 displays some more common event IDs that you may find in your DHCP server's system event log.

Table 3.7 Common DHCP System Event IDs

Event Type	Event ID	Description
Information	1037	The DHCP service has started to clean up the database.
Information	1038	The DHCP service has cleaned up the database for unicast IP addresses: 0 leases have been recovered and 0 records have been removed from the database.
Information	1039	The DHCP service has cleaned up the database for multicast IP addresses: 0 leases have expired (been marked for deletion) and 0 records have been removed from the database.
Warning	1042	The DHCP/BINL service running on this machine has detected the following servers on the network. Their domains are listed below as well as the authorization status of the local machine as verified against the directory service enterprises of each of these domains. If the servers do not belong to any domain, the domain is listed as empty. The IP address of each of these servers is listed in parentheses. The DHCP/BINL service has not determined if it is authorized in directory domain *syngress.com* (Server IP Address 192.168.0.192).

Continued

Table 3.7 Common DHCP System Event IDs

Event Type	Event ID	Description
Information	1044	The DHCP/BINL service on the local machine, belonging to the Windows Administrative domain *syngress.com*, has determined that it is authorized to start. It is servicing clients now.
Error	1046	The DHCP/BINL service on the local machine, belonging to the Windows Administrative domain *syngress.com*, has determined that it is not authorized to start. It has stopped servicing clients. The following are some possible reasons for this: This machine is part of a directory service enterprise and is not authorized in the same domain. (See **Help** on the DHCP Service Management Tool for additional information.) This machine cannot reach its directory service enterprise and it has encountered another DHCP service on the network belonging to a directory service enterprise on which the local machine is not authorized. Some unexpected network error occurred.
Warning	1056	The DHCP service has detected that it is running on a DC and has no credentials configured for use with Dynamic DNS registrations initiated by the DHCP service. This is not a recommended security configuration. Credentials for Dynamic DNS registrations may be configured using the command line **netsh dhcp server set dnscredentials** or via the DHCP Administrative Tool.

Using System Monitor

The Windows System Monitor is a real-time diagnostics tool for troubleshooting DHCP data traffic flowing between your DHCP server and your DHCP clients. System Monitor allows you to target specific object related counters found on your system and track the data associated with those counters. Found in the **Administrative Tools** menu under the heading **Performance**, System Monitor can be set up to log real time DHCP leasing events and to alert you regarding any number of configurable thresholds. Some of the items System Monitor can track are:

- DHCP lease process
- DHCP server conflict attempts
- Duplicate IP addresses drops

When DHCP is installed on a server, it also installs specific DHCP related object counters to the System Monitor. These can be used to monitor DHCP data. Exercise 3.07 will walk you through the process of configuring the System Monitor to use some of these object counters to track the DHCP leasing process on your network.

EXERCISE 3.07

USING SYSYTEM MONITOR TO SEE DHCP TRAFFIC

This exercise is designed to teach you how to use the Windows Server 2003 System Monitor to pinpoint and track DHCP specific data.

1. Open the **Performance** MMC console (System Monitor) from your **Administrative Tools** menu (or type **perfmon** at the **Run** command).

2. At the bottom of the screen, click on each of the predefined counters (for example *Pages/sec*) and press the **Delete** key. (This will clear all counters except the ones we are interested in seeing.)

3. Click the **Add** button (the *plus* icon) on the middle of the graphical menu bar, or select **Ctrl + I** on your keyboard.

4. Drop down the toggle box under **Performance objects** and select **DHCP Server**.

5. From the **Select counters from list** window, select both **Acks/sec** and **Offers/sec** and click **Add**. Click **Close** to finish.

Your System Monitor will now display all of the DHCPACK and DHCPOFFER messages it is producing in real time, as shown in Figure 3.54.

Figure 3.54 Viewing Live System Monitor Activity

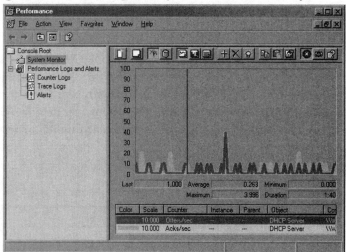

NOTE

In addition to monitoring the local machine, you can also monitor another DHCP server on the network remotely by typing the UNC path for the remote server in the **Select counters from computer** box. If you have previously monitored other machines, their names will be in the drop-down box.

There are a number of other DHCP-related counters that can be monitored. These are included with their description in Table 3.8.

Table 3.8 DHCP Performance Counters

DHCP Counter	Description
Acks/sec	The rate of DHCP Acknowledgements sent by the DHCP server per second
Active Queue Length	The number of packets in the processing queue of the DHCP server
Conflict Check Queue Length	The number of packets in the DHCP server queue waiting on conflict detection (ping attempts)
Declines/sec	The rate of DHCP Declines received by the DHCP server
Discovers/sec	The rate of DHCP Discovers received by the DHCP server
Duplicated Dropped/sec	The rate at which the DHCP server received duplicate packets
Informs/sec	The rate of DHCP Informs received by the DHCP server
Milliseconds per packet (Avg.)	The average time per packet taken by the DHCP server to send a response
Nacks/sec	The rate of DHCP Nacks sent by the DHCP server
Offers/sec	The rate of DHCP Offers sent out by the DHCP server
Packets Expired/sec	The rate at which packets get expired in the DHCP server message queue
Packets Received/sec	The rate at which packets are received by the DHCP server
Releases/sec	The rate of DHCP Releases received by the DHCP server
Requests/sec	The rate of DHCP Requests received by the DHCP server

If you forget the function of any particular counter, you can highlight it and click the **Explain** button for details about what the counter represents.

NOTE

System Monitor defaults to the *View Current Activity* mode, although there is also a *View Log Data* mode. On choosing the *View Log Data* mode, you are prompted to choose a previously recorded data log from a specific **Performance object** and all its counters.

NOTE

To simulate DHCP offer and acknowledgement traffic, we used a batch file that released and renewed two machines' IP addresses every second. We than changed the default scale for each of the object counters to 10, to show it easily in the monitor window. We also increased the size of the display lines to enhance visibility.

Real World Data Sniffing

Although its use might be a bit more complex for the average administrator, there is another tool that can be used for troubleshooting DHCP lease traffic or any other network traffic. This tool requires some practice to become comfortable with it, but when you've mastered it, you have a powerful addition to your troubleshooting arsenal. We're referring to Network Monitor, Windows Server 2003's built-in network "sniffer" or protocol analyzer. Sometimes called *Netmon*, Network Monitor allows you to take a close look at the actual data packets that traverse your network media. Network Monitor has been around since Windows NT, and although it is not as full featured as some of the popular third-party sniffing programs such as Network Associates' Sniffer Pro or Network Instruments' Observer, it gets the job done for most routine needs.

There are two versions of Network Monitor: one that ships with Windows Server 2003 and one that ships with Microsoft's deployment and distribution product, Systems Management Server (SMS). The difference between the two versions is the scope of the data that can be captured by each. The version that ships with Windows Server 2003 captures only data packets going to and coming from the machine on which it is installed. The version that ships with SMS can capture all data that passes on the network segment to which the machine on which it's running is attached. For this discussion, we will focus on the Windows Server 2003 version.

If you want to examine all the DHCP lease traffic that your DHCP server is receiving at the moment, follow these steps:

1. Install the tool from the **Add or Remove Programs** applet in **Control Panel**, as the Network Monitor is not installed by default. Choose **Add/Remove Windows Component | Management and Monitoring Tools | Network Monitor Tools**.

2. Click **OK** and point to your Windows Server 2003 source files.

3. After the installation completes, access the **Network Monitor** utility from the **Administrative Tools** menu.

4. In the Network Monitor interface, click **Capture | Start** from the tools menu to begin capturing data, as shown in Figure 3.55.

NOTE

If there are multiple network interfaces on the server, you will be asked to select a network on which you want to capture data. Select the appropriate interface (for example, the LAN interface).

Figure 3.55 Capturing Data with Network Monitor

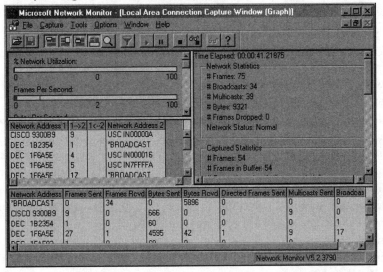

When you believe that enough data traffic has been captured, simply click the **Capture | Stop and View** menu item and you will see all of your DHCP traffic that was captured, as shown in Figure 3.56. Sorting through the data to find the packets you actually need is the time consuming part of using Network Monitor. In cases where there is just too much data to manage, you can use Network Monitor's filtering ability to capture only specific network traffic, or to display only specified traffic out of that which was previously captured.

Network Monitor is a very useful tool and is included with Windows Server 2003. You must understand how to configure and use this tool to effectively troubleshoot networking problems of all types, including those related to DHCP.

Figure 3.56 Viewing Captured DHCP Data with Network Monitor

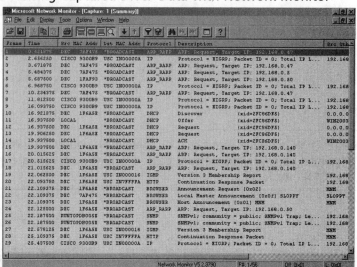

 ## Using the DHCP Server Audit Log

The Windows Server 2003 DHCP Server has the ability to track and log all DHCP server activity. Although this feature has changed only slightly since Windows 2000 DHCP auditing, it is still an invaluable tool for troubleshooting a large DHCP client base.

By default, the DHCP database audit logs are stored in the %windir%\system32\dhcp folder and are named according to the day they were recorded in a .log file format. DHCP Audit logging can be enabled via the **General** tab of the DHCP server properties window. The log file location can be changed if you want to move the files off of the system disk and onto a larger disk with less overhead. To do so, click the **Advanced** tab of the DHCP server properties sheet, and enter or browse to a new **Audit log file path**.

Additional parameters, such as disk space allowed for audit files and frequency of disk space checking, can also be configured; however, configuring these parameters requires that you edit the Windows Registry.

 ### EXAM WARNING

DHCP auditing is a very resource intensive process and can cause excessive server overhead. For this reason, we recommend that it be enabled for troubleshooting purposes only. Nonetheless, DHCP auditing is turned **on** by default.

Using DHCP Log Files

DHCP logging detects and logs many types of events including the following:

- DHCP server events
- DHCP client events
- Leasing operations
- Active Directory authorization
- Rogue server detection events

To use the logs effectively, you need to know how they are formatted and what each of the Event IDs means. See Table 3.9 for a listing of some of the more common DHCP logging Event IDs and the their meaning. These Event IDs should be used for client/server DHCP troubleshooting, as well as for DHCP server installation and service problems.

These log files are text files in standard comma delimited format (which makes it easy to import them into a program such as Excel), and include all the necessary information needed to determine when, where, by whom, and why each event entry was generated. Each entry in the file is shown as a single line of text. The log format includes each of the following items:

- Event ID
- Date
- Time
- Description of Event ID
- IP address of the DHCP client
- Host name of the DHCP client
- MAC address of the DHCP client

Each of these items is important when you are tracking down a DHCP issue and have only one piece of information. The log files use event codes to describe information about the activities being logged. For example, Event ID 00 indicates that the log was started. A listing of the more common event codes is shown in Table 3.9. To see the complete listing of codes above 50, showing the events used in the Windows 2000 and Server 2003 rogue server detection process, see Table 3.10.

Table 3.9 Common DHCP Log Event IDs

Event ID	Event ID Description
00	The log was started.
01	The log was stopped.
02	The log was temporarily paused due to low disk space.
10	A new IP address was leased to a client.
11	A lease was renewed by a client.
12	A lease was released by a client.
13	An IP address was found to be in use on the network.
14	A lease request could not be satisfied because the scope's address pool was exhausted.
15	A lease was denied.
16	A lease was deleted.
17	A lease was expired.
20	A BOOTP address was leased to a client.
21	A dynamic BOOTP address was leased to a client.
22	A BOOTP request could not be satisfied because the scope's address pool for BOOTP was exhausted.
23	A BOOTP IP address was deleted after checking to see it was not is use.
24	IP address cleanup operation has begun.
25	IP address cleanup statistics.
30	DNS update request to the named DNS server.
31	DNS update failed.
32	DNS update successful.
50+	Codes above 50 are used for Rogue Server Detection information.

Table 3.10 Rogue Server Detection DHCP Log Event IDs

Event ID	Event ID Description
50	**Unreachable domain** The DHCP server could not locate the applicable domain for its configured Active Directory installation.
51	**Authorization succeeded** The DHCP server was authorized to start on the network.
52	**Upgraded to a Windows Server 2003 operating system** The DHCP server was recently upgraded to a Windows Server 2003 operating system; therefore, the unauthorized DHCP server detection feature (used to determine whether the server has been authorized in Active Directory) was disabled.

Continued

Table 3.10 Rogue Server Detection DHCP Log Event IDs

Event ID	Event ID Description
53	**Cached Authorization** The DHCP server was authorized to start using previously cached information. Active Directory was not currently visible at the time the server was started on the network.
54	**Authorization failed** The DHCP server was not authorized to start on the network. When this event occurs, it is likely followed by the server being stopped.
55	**Authorization (servicing)** The DHCP server was successfully authorized to start on the network.
56	**Authorization failure, stopped servicing** The DHCP server was not authorized to start on the network and was shut down by the operating system. You must first authorize the server in the directory before starting it again. For more information, see "To authorize a DHCP server in Active Directory."
57	**Server found in domain** Another DHCP server exists and is authorized for service in the same domain.
58	**Server could not find domain** The DHCP server could not locate the specified domain.
59	**Network failure** A network-related failure prevented the server from determining if it is authorized.
60	**No DC is DS Enabled** No Windows Server 2003 domain controller was located. For detecting whether the server is authorized, a domain controller that is enabled for Active Directory is needed.
61	**Server found that belongs to DS domain** Another DHCP server was found on the network that belongs to the Active Directory domain.
62	**Another server found** Another DHCP server was found on the network.
63	**Restarting rogue detection** The DHCP server is trying once more to determine whether it is authorized to start and provide service on the network.
64	**No DHCP enabled interfaces** The DHCP server has its service bindings or network connections configured so that it is not enabled to provide service.

The detailed information found in each log file usually provides an ample amount of data to track down the source of the problem. However, it is important to note that the log files are kept only for a one-week period, and the file for each day of the week is overwritten on that day of the next week.

NOTE

NOTE

The file format for Windows Server 2003 DHCP logs has been improved since Windows 2000. In Windows 2000, each log was named **DHCPSrvLog.Fri** or **DHCPSrvLog.Sat** with the file extension being shortened to indicate the day of the log. Windows Server 2003 uses the **DHCPSrvLog-Fri.log** or **DHCPSrvLog-Sat.log** file format. This relieves administrators of the trouble of having to associate the *.Fri* through *.Sun* file extension formats with NotePad or your favorite text editing program.

NOTE

Event IDs 30 through 32 are new in Windows Server 2003 DHCP logging. They are related to Dynamic DNS updating.

Client-Side Troubleshooting

Now that we have discussed the tools you can use to monitor and troubleshoot DHCP from the server side, we will examine the most commonly used client-side troubleshooting tool: the **ipconfig** command line utility.

ipconfig is used to configure, unconfigure, reconfigure or simply display DHCP client IP information. The basic syntax of the **ipconfig** tool for these functions is:

```
ipconfig.exe    ipconfig [/? | /all | /renew [adapter] | /release
    [adapter] |
```

When attempting to troubleshoot DHCP problems at the client end, we are concerned primarily with the */all* switch. Figure 3.57 shows the output of running **ipconfig** with the */all* switch (by typing **ipconfig /all**).

Figure 3.57 Displaying Client DHCP Output Using the Ipconfig Utility

```
Select C:\WINNT\System32\cmd.exe                                      _ □ x
Windows 2000 IP Configuration

        Host Name . . . . . . . . . . . . : client2000-VM
        Primary DNS Suffix  . . . . . . . : syngress.com
        Node Type . . . . . . . . . . . . : Hybrid
        IP Routing Enabled. . . . . . . . : No
        WINS Proxy Enabled. . . . . . . . : No

Ethernet adapter Local Area Connection 2:

        Connection-specific DNS Suffix  . : syngress.com
        Description . . . . . . . . . . . : AMD PCNET Family PCI Ethernet Adapte
r #2
        Physical Address. . . . . . . . . : 00-0C-29-84-01-A9
        DHCP Enabled. . . . . . . . . . . : Yes
        Autoconfiguration Enabled . . . . : Yes
        IP Address. . . . . . . . . . . . : 0.0.0.0
        Subnet Mask . . . . . . . . . . . : 0.0.0.0
        Default Gateway . . . . . . . . . :
        DHCP Server . . . . . . . . . . . : 255.255.255.255
        DNS Servers . . . . . . . . . . . : 192.168.0.192
        Primary WINS Server . . . . . . . : 192.168.0.3
        Secondary WINS Server . . . . . . : 192.168.0.4

C:\>_
```

The output displayed in Figure 3.57 provides the following information, which is useful in troubleshooting DHCP client problems:

- Whether DHCP is enabled

- The IP address the client has obtained from the DHCP server

- The IP address of the DHCP server from which the client is leasing an IP address

- Whether Autoconfiguration Enabled (APIPA) is turned on and being used

- Some of the more important IP options obtained from your DHCP server (default gateway, subnet mask, DNS servers, WINS servers)

With these pieces of information in hand, you can determine such things as whether the client is using an APIPA address and thus is able to talk only to other APIPA clients, whether there is a misconfigured DNS or WINS server address being handed out that is disabling the client's ability to resolve names to IP addresses, or whether the DHCP server that the client is using is a rogue DHCP server that needs to be tracked down and turned off.

Summary of Exam Objectives

The Dynamic Host Configuration Protocol is a standard protocol, and is described completely in Request For Comment (RFC) 2131. Its main function is to dynamically distribute TCP/IP addresses to client machines or DHCP configured devices on your network. At the same time, it can distribute TCP/IP protocol options that clients can use to find their way around the network. Before DHCP was developed and standardized, administrators had to configure each and every TCP/IP device manually. This was one of the factors that kept TCP/IP out of mainstream network environments, and which made more easily configurable protocols such as IPX/SPX and NetBEUI a more common choice for LANs. All of today's modern operating systems, including Windows Server 2003 and Windows XP, support DHCP.

DHCP works in a sort of ask-and-receive exchange between client and server. This is referred to as the DHCP lease process and contains four vital steps (denoted by the DORA acronym), as follows:

- DHCP request from the client (Discover)
- DHCP offer from the server (Offer)
- DHCP selection from the client (Request)
- DHCP acknowledgement from the server (ACK/NAK)

Due to the nature of what happens during the DHCP lease process, DHCP is a broadcast protocol. Without an IP address, clients and servers cannot locate one another without issuing a broadcast message to every computer that is listening on the wire.

Configuration of a Windows Server 2003 DHCP server should include all of the following steps to ensure that a properly working server will be available for DHCP clients:

- Authorization of the DHCP server in Active Directory
- Creation of DHCP scopes that are appropriate for your networks
- Configuration of scope-specific DHCP options
- Activation of each scope

Customizable steps can make your DHCP environment easier to manage. Inclusion of DHCP reservations and DHCP User and Vendor Options are only a few of the ways that you can customize the distribution of IP addresses and information to your client base. Windows Server 2003 DHCP server also includes support for multinet environments with the use of superscopes, as well as multicast environments with the use of multicast scopes.

Windows Server 2003 gives you the option to configure a DHCP Relay Agent through the Routing and Remote Access Service, if you have an environment that does not support RFC2131 to allow BOOTP/DHCP broadcasts across your routers. A DHCP Relay Agent can be placed statically on each subnet that does not have a DHCP server, and can effectively support all DHCP broadcasts on that subnet, forwarding them to a DHCP server on another subnet. BOOTP clients are also supported by the Windows Server 2003 DHCP server, with the addition of a configurable BOOTP table for locating a downloadable copy of a boot image.

DNS plays a vital role in your Windows Server 2003 Active Directory infrastructure. Because of this, Microsoft has given the DHCP service the ability to tightly integrate and work alongside with your DNS servers. DHCP can be set up in such a manner as to register DHCP clients automatically in the DNS database. It also supports the registration of downlevel Windows 9x and Windows NT 4.0 clients in the DNS database, using a feature Microsoft calls Dynamic DNS.

Routing and Remote Access Server (RRAS) plays an important role for DHCP-configured dial-up clients. Dial-up clients that are not configured with static IP addresses need access to a DHCP server in order to obtain an IP address and IP configurable options so they can communicate on your network. There are three ways to deal with address allocation for remote users:

- Use the DHCP Relay Agent to forward RRAS client requests to an internal DHCP server for address assignment.

- Configure a static pool of IP addresses on the RRAS server itself, for it to hand out to remote clients.

- Configure a static IP address on each individual RRAS user account object via the Active Directory Users and Computers administrative tool.

The DHCP Relay Agent will play a vital role in making sure things work correctly and thus must always be configured when clients are set to use DHCP to connect to your RRAS server.

To use DHCP in an Active Directory environment, Windows 2000 and Server 2003 DHCP servers must be authorized. Only members of the root domain's Enterprise Admins group have the right to authorize DHCP servers. However, Active Directory has the ability to authorize only Windows 2000 and Windows Server 2003 DHCP servers. This means that it is still possible to encounter rogue DHCP servers on your network, for example, a DHCP server running Windows NT 4.0.

Rather than generate error after error when DHCP servers aren't available, most modern Windows clients use the Automatic Private IP Addressing (APIPA) technology first introduced in Windows 98SE. APIPA can also be used in smaller nonrouted network environments of less than 25 machines to configure IP addresses automatically without any need for a DHCP server. However, in large environments that use a DHCP server, you may find it desirable to disable APIPA on the clients.

Managing your DHCP servers and clients can include a variety of sensitive tasks. For that reason, Windows Server 2003 includes two built-in delegated DHCP administration groups:

- **DHCP Administrators Group** Members are granted rights to fully administer the DHCP servers but do not have local administrative rights on the server.

- **DHCP Users Group** Members have rights to view only information kept within the DHCP databases.

Managing a DHCP server includes the task of backing up the DHCP database, either with Windows Server 2003's **ntbackup** utility or manually through the DHCP console. Another important management task is compacting the DHCP database when it gets too large for your client base with the **jetpack** utility. You also need to know how to reconcile DHCP scopes. DHCP database statistics are recorded by the Windows DHCP server and can be accessed through an easy to view graphical window, or through the daily DHCP logs that are stored as text files.

There are many tools and resources available that can be used to monitor and troubleshoot your DHCP client/server activity. The following resources are included in the Windows Server 2003 operating system:

- System Monitor

- Network Monitor

- System Event Logs

- Local DHCP Server Logs

- **ipconfig** command-line utility

All but the last one generally are used on the DHCP server itself. The last can be used as a client utility to view IP configuration information on the client machine, or to initiate DHCP lease communications with your server.

Exam Objectives Fast Track

Review of DHCP

☑ The DHCP protocol provides the ability to dynamically and automatically assign clients an IP address from a prebuilt pool of addresses.

☑ DHCP is a broadcast protocol that uses four steps in the leasing of an IP address: DHCPDISCOVER, DHCPOFFER, DHCPREQUEST, and DHCPACK.

☑ DHCP and BOOTP are different protocols with different purposes, although they share the same broadcast UDP ports of 67 and 68. DHCP is based on BOOTP but provides TCP/IP configuration options in addition to an IP address; BOOTP is used for diskless workstations that need to obtain an address and download an operating system image from the network.

Configuring the Windows Server 2003 DHCP Server

☑ After installing and configuring your DHCP scopes, you must activate them before they will start issuing IP addresses.

☑ DHCP reservations are used when you want to configure a DHCP client with the same IP address every time. To do this, you need to know the client NIC's MAC (physical) address.

☑ User and Vendor classes can be used when you want to differentiate the DHCP options that are leased with IP addresses, based on workstation characteristics such as hardware configuration or operating system type.

Configuring the DHCP Relay Agent

☑ The DHCP Relay Agent is configured on network segments that do not have a DHCP server and are on the other side of a non-2131 compliant router (that does not support BOOTP/DHCP relaying) from a DHCP server.

☑ The DHCP Relay Agent is installed through the Routing and Remote Access wizard and must be installed when using RRAS for dial-in access if remote clients are configured to use DHCP and you want to provide TCP/IP options to them.

☑ When configuring the DHCP Relay Agent with a static pool of IP addresses, you should exclude those addresses from your internal DHCP servers to avoid overlapping scopes.

Integrating the DHCP Server with Dynamic DNS

☑ By default, Dynamic DNS is set up to allow Windows 2000/Server 2003/XP machines to register their own A records while the DHCP server registers their PTR records.

☑ In Windows Server 2003, you can use the Secure only updates along with the DNSUpdateProxy group in your Active Directory Integrated DNS because of the new Dynamic DNS credentials feature.

☑ Downlevel Windows clients cannot use DHCP and Dynamic DNS Updates by default; they must have the option turned on after installation.

Integrating the DHCP Server with Routing and Remote Access

- ☑ The DHCP Relay Agent has to be set up in order to allow RRAS to use DHCP to provide options to clients.

- ☑ The RRAS server can be configured to act as a DHCP server to remote clients, configured with a static pool of IP addresses.

- ☑ If the RRAS server is set up with a static pool of IP addresses, the client will issue only a DHCPINFORM message to the internal DHCP server to obtain a list of its DHCP IP options (if it is configured to obtain options from a DHCP server).

Integrating the DHCP Server with Active Directory

- ☑ Windows 2000 and Server 2003 DHCP servers must be authorized in Active Directory before the DHCP service will be allowed to start.

- ☑ Members of the Enterprise Admins group are the only users with the authority to authorize DHCP servers.

- ☑ DHCP servers other than Windows 2000 and Windows Server 2003 cannot be authorized in Active Directory, and thus can end up on your network as rogue servers.

Understanding Automatic Private IP Addressing (APIPA)

- ☑ APIPA provides a DHCP-configured client with the ability to assign itself its own IP address if a DHCP server is not available.

- ☑ The APIPA range of IP addresses extends from 169.254.255.255 to 169.254.0.0, with a class B subnet mask of 255.255.0.0.

- ☑ As an alternative to APIPA, Windows Server 2003 clients now have the option to configure an alternate static TCP/IP address on the Alternate Configuration tab of their TCP/IP properties, which will be used if a DHCP server doesn't assign an address.

- ☑ APIPA does not assign a default gateway; thus APIPA clients can communicate only with computers whose addresses fall within the same address range (typically, other APIPA clients on the same network segment).

Managing the Windows Server 2003 DHCP Server

☑ The DHCP MMC in Windows Server 2003 allows you to back up and restore the DHCP database without relying on command line utilities.

☑ When a DHCP server is installed, the installation program adds two local administrative groups to the server, called DHCP Administrators and DHCP Users. DHCP Administrators have full administrative control over DHCP (but not over other aspects of the server), whereas DHCP Users have read-only rights to the DHCP configuration and scopes.

☑ DHCP server statistics will alert you with different colored triangular icons when your scopes are getting close to and/or have been depleted of IP addresses.

Monitoring and Troubleshooting the Windows Server 2003 DHCP Server

☑ DHCP Server system event logs are used to log DHCP server based information, warnings, and alerts. DHCP Audit logs can be used for both server information and client information.

☑ The installation of DHCP adds DHCP server object counters (such as Acks/sec and Offers/sec) for use with the System Monitor.

☑ The **ipconfig /all** command can be used to determine whether a client is receiving information from a DHCP server or is using automatic configuration (APIPA).

Exam Objectives
Frequently Asked Questions

The following Frequently Asked Questions, answered by the authors of this book, are designed to both measure your understanding of the Exam Objectives presented in this chapter, and to assist you with real-life implementation of these concepts. You will also gain access to thousands of other FAQs at ITFAQnet.com.

Q: Is it possible to set my lease durations too long?

A: Yes. If you have a limited number of IP addresses, and you have many mobile users who take their laptops out of the office, you potentially could run into problems with long lease periods because all of the IP addresses could be used up.

Q: Will existing DHCP clients automatically start using a second DHCP server that I bring up on their subnet?

A: No. Clients will continue to use their current DHCP server as long as it is up and has already configured them with an IP address. If you want existing clients use a new DHCP server, you must set the current lease to expire and deactivate the current DHCP scope.

Q: Can I set up one DHCP reservation for a user who switches between a laptop machine and desktop workstation?

A: No. DHCP reservations are allocated to computers (actually to NICs), not to users. Configuration of a reservation is dependant on the specific MAC address of a machine's network interface card.

Q: I am trying to install the DHCP server service on one of my Window Server 2003 file servers that is configured for DHCP, but it keeps giving me an error stating that it needs a static IP address. However, it let me finish the installation and the DHCP service is started. Will it work this way?

A: No. A DHCP server cannot be a DHCP client. That's the reason you get an error stating that DHCP must use a static IP to work. Failing to configure it with a static IP does not stop you from finishing the installation and starting the service, but the DHCP server will not be able to lease IP addresses in this state.

Q: I want to configure my DHCP-configured workstation to always receive the same IP address when I am at work. Is this possible?

A: Yes. This is possible through the use of DHCP reservations. All you need is the MAC address of the network card in your workstation and the IP address you want to lease to configure the reservation on the DHCP server.

Q: I am a systems administrator and my network administrator peers have informed me we use multinets to break out our different network segments. I am having trouble getting my DHCP scopes to work correctly. What am I doing wrong?

A: In a multinet environment, you need to configure a DHCP superscope to allow DHCP to function properly.

Q: What is the difference between BOOTP and DHCP?

A: Although both are broadcast-based and use UDP ports 67 and 68, BOOTP is used to provide an IP address so that a client can communicate on the network to download a bootable image. Usually BOOTP clients are diskless workstations. DHCP is used to distribute IP addresses, as well as configurable options, to workstations and servers on the network. BOOTP does not allow the distribution of configurable options.

Q: If I am using RFC 2131 compatible routers for my internal network segments, do I need to install a DHCP Relay Agent for my dial-in RRAS server if I want to distribute options to them?

A: Yes. Although your internal routers support the forwarding of BOOTP/DHCP traffic, RRAS requires the installation and configuration of the DHCP Relay Agent in order for DHCP-configured remote clients to obtain TCP/IP options from a DHCP server.

Q: When I go to the **Add/Remove Programs** applet, I cannot seem to find an option to install the DHCP Relay Agent. Why?

A: The DHCP Relay Agent was installed from the **Add/Remove Programs** applet in Windows NT 4.0. In Windows 2000 and Server 2003, it is installed through the Routing and Remote Access (RRAS) MMC.

Q: I have a single network segment and manage a mixed environment of DHCP-enabled Windows XP and Windows NT machines. I am not using WINS. Is there a way I can limit the broadcast traffic that is created to communicate with my Windows NT machines?

A: Yes. You can enable the use of Dynamic DNS updates for your downlevel NT 4.0 machines on the DHCP server. This will enable your Windows XP machines to locate the Windows NT 4.0 machines via DNS and reduce the broadcast traffic.

Q: I want to allow my DHCP servers to use Dynamic updates to register DNS records without taking ownership of each record in my Windows Server 2003 network. Can I do this and still continue to use secure-only updates in DNS?

A: Yes. Windows Server 2003 introduced the option to supply credentials other than those of the DHCP server to register A and PTR records with your DNS server when your DHCP server is made a member of the DNSUpdateProxy group. This is acceptable to a secure-only Active Directory Integrated DNS server.

Q: Is there a way I can make my DHCP server register both A and PTR records for Windows 2000 and Windows XP clients?

A: Yes. You can enable the **Always dynamically update DNS and PTR records** option on your DHCP server.

Q: Does my RRAS server need to have DHCP installed on it for my VPN clients?

A: No. It needs to have only the DHCP Relay Agent installed and configured to forward DHCP messages to a DHCP server.

Q: Do clients have to use IP addresses from DHCP when I configure my RRAS server for VPN access?

A: No. You can get a bit more granular and configure the individual user account objects with static IP addresses that will override any DHCP configured address when using the VPN.

Q: My VPN users that are DHCP clients are complaining that they are able to connect and access resources on the RRAS server itself, but cannot access anything beyond that server on the network. What is wrong?

A: You have not configured your DHCP Relay Agent to point to an internal DHCP server so that your dial-in clients can receive DHCP options that are needed for name resolution.

Q: I have verified that I am in the DHCP Administrators group, but I still cannot seem to authorize my Windows Server 2003 DHCP server. Why is this?

A: The DHCP Administrators group does not have this right. You must be a member of the Enterprise Admins group to authorize a DHCP server in Active Directory.

Q: I have installed the Windows Server 2003 Active Directory environment and am the only member of the Enterprise Admins Group. Do I finally have complete control to prevent anyone from bringing up a rogue DHCP server?

A: No. Windows 2003 Active Directory authorization protects you only from rogue Windows 2000 or Windows Server 2003 DHCP servers. Other DHCP servers (such as Windows NT) will not be detected and can operate in a rogue state on the network.

Q: How does my Windows Server 2003 Active Directory keep rogue DHCP servers off the network?

A: When the Windows 2000 or Server 2003 DHCP service starts on a standalone DHCP server, it broadcasts a DHCPINFORM message on its local network. An authorized DHCP server responds to this request with the location of a Domain Controller that contains a list of authorized servers that are allowed to lease IP addresses on the network. If the DHCP server is not on this list, its service will fail to start. In addition, if the DHCP server does not receive a response from its DHCPINFORM message it will assume it is unauthorized. If the DHCP server is a member server, it will contact Active Directory Domain Controllers directly when looking for an authorization list.

Q: I have set up all my clients to use APIPA and do not use a DHCP server. I have a routed network and am having problems getting clients to talk across the router. What can I do?

A: Use DHCP. APIPA does not allow cross network communication because it does not assign a default gateway, which is a necessary TCP/IP configuration for computers to send routed messages.

Q: If I have a DHCP server problem and all my clients receive APIPA addresses, how can I make them check for the DHCP server when I get it back online?

A: You don't have to do anything. The local DHCP service on each client will check every five minutes by default for the presence of a DHCP server until it finds one and receives an IP address.

Q: Can I disable APIPA?

A: Yes. You can disable APIPA by editing the local Registry of the machine on which you want to disable the service, or you can configure a static IP address on the **Alternate Configuration** tab of your TCP/IP properties, which also prevents the computer from using APIPA in the absence of a DHCP server.

Q: My boss gave me the job of installing the DHCP service on all of our branch office servers and making sure that clients were able to obtain leases. He informed me I would have all the needed rights to complete my job because my user account was put into the DHCP Administrators group. Is he correct?

A: No. You will not be able to authorize the DHCP servers in Active Directory so that your clients can obtain leases from them. To do that, your account must be added to the Enterprise Admins group.

Q: I want to back up the DHCP database but am uncomfortable with the command line tool I read about called **netsh**. Is there anything else I can use?

A: Yes. You can back up the DHCP database from within the graphical DHCP MMC. You can also use the **ntbackup** program to back up your DHCP database if you enable **Volume Shadow Copy** on the DHCP server.

Q: How can I find out how many IP addresses are remaining to be leased from my DHCP server?

A: Open the DHCP MMC, right-click the node for your DHCP server, and select **Display Statistics**.

Q: The DHCP service on the server will not start. I looked in the event viewer and found a message that states that the database is corrupt. Do I have to start over by uninstalling and reinstalling DHCP?

A: No. Windows Server 2003 comes with a database utility called **jetpack.exe** that you can run on your database to attempt to repair any inconsistencies that might be causing the corruption.

Self Test

A Quick Answer Key follows the Self Test questions. For complete questions, answers, and explanations to the Self Test questions in this chapter as well as the other chapters in this book, see the Self Test Appendix.

Review of DHCP

1. About a week and a half ago, you hired Jamie, a new Systems Engineer, to help you fix some DHCP scope problems you had been having that resulted in a shortage of IP addresses. You configured a scope with a 24-bit mask and a network number of 192.168.0.0. You thought you had plenty of IP addresses because there are only 240 users in the company and this gives you 254 addresses. Your company employs a 50 percent sales force that is in and out of the office; sometimes sales personnel are gone for weeks at a time. With the recent addition of 10 new employees, your scope ran out of IP addresses and has been doing so intermittently for a few days. You put Jamie on the problem and she said she fixed it in a matter of minutes. She was right; you've had no more IP shortages. However, ever since the fix, your employees have been complaining to you about slow network performance. You asked one of your network engineers to

run Network Monitor and he reported that hundreds and hundreds of DHCPRE-QUEST messages are traversing the wire. What did Jamie do to fix the problem?

A. Added more existing IP addresses to the scope range.

B. Turned off Dynamic DNS updating of downlevel Windows clients.

C. Reduced the default lease time.

D. Increased the default lease time.

2. Chris and Keith are two contractors you hired to help with your new data warehouse project for your Web site, the primary function of which is the online purchasing of ski apparel, equipment, and lift tickets for various ski resorts around the Untied States. Chris and Keith are very familiar with your entire product line and have been hired to customize an inventory database that is easily searchable from the Web site. To do this, they need the ability to gather information on site, sync it with the data on their portable Windows 2000 laptops, and bring this data into a prebuilt lab environment in their own office. Due to recent security policies, your company has mandated that consultant laptop machines using DHCP cannot leave the premises with any DHCP lease information from your network. Your manager asks you if this is possible. You reply yes. Was your reply correct?

A. Yes. There is no way to make sure leased IP addresses don't leave the building.

B. No. To do this, you need to make sure the lease duration is set to unlimited.

C. No. To do this, you need to set up a special User and Vendor class.

D. No. To do this, you need to make sure the lease duration is set to only a couple of days.

Configuring the Windows Server 2003 DHCP Server

3. You are a contractor for a brand new mobile advertising company opening up in downtown Boston, MA, called Adstogo, Inc. You have been hired to configure DHCP for their new office of 200 employees. Fifty percent of their employees are mobile and usually out on the road, selling or driving advertising trucks. Every employee at Adstogo was offered a laptop with dial-in capabilities in order to stay in touch with corporate management because most of these road trips last one to two weeks at a time. You arrive onsite and begin configuring the Windows Server 2003 DHCP server as you have done many times before. You configure a scope with a 192.168.0.0/24 network address and exclude a range of 192.168.0.0 to 192.168.0.20 for network hardware and servers' static IP assignments. You configure the lease duration to three weeks and configure all the standard DHCP options. You authorize the server, activate the scope, and alert the 20 or so users in the office to hook up their already config-ured DHCP laptops. Presto! Everything works. You are congratulated, paid in full, and sent on your way. About two weeks later, you get a call from Mark, the owner of Adstogo. He says that he just hired 50 more employees to work in the office and only half of them can connect to network resources or get on the Internet. He rebooted the server and it appears to be working fine, other than the inability of some clients to obtain addresses. What is the problem?

A. All users need to reboot to be assigned a new DHCP address.

B. The DHCP server has crashed and is unable to hand out leases.

C. Address conflicts are preventing clients from obtaining a lease.

D. Your DHCP scope is out of addresses and able to renew only those that are already in use.

4. For the past two years, you have been working as a systems engineer at a local bank in your hometown of Philadelphia. The bank has 17 branch offices that are participating in a Wide Area Network (WAN). Windows Server 2003 Active Directory has already been set up by the infrastructure team and they authorized all the DHCP servers cur-rently in use today. Some of your responsibilities include the management of client and server IP addresses. This encompasses the setup and maintenance of all company DHCP servers. For this reason, your user account has been made a member of the DHCP Administrators group. Your manager, Mike, alerts you that a new branch is opening and asks you to prepare the DHCP scope on the server that the infrastruc-ture team installed. You gather the needed IP network information from your network team and start creating the new scope. About the same time, your manager calls you over with an urgent problem he needs fixed immediately. You select the option to configure the scope options at a later time and click **Finish** to build the new scope. After things have calmed down and the problems have subsided, you go back and

finish configuring all the scope options as detailed in your IP information. You inform your manager that the server is ready to be deployed. However, clients at the new branch complain that they are unable to log on to the domain. You successfully ping the server from the Philadelphia branch to verify that it is up and responding. You also verify with the infrastructure team that they successfully authorized the DHCP server. Why are users unable to log onto the domain?

A. The local Domain Controller has not been activated.

B. The DHCP scope needs to be activated.

C. The users do not have any cached credentials on their local workstations.

D. The WAN link is down.

5. Jennifer, the network administrator at a chain of bakery stores called The Cheesecake Factory, recently upgraded the corporate office of a single segmented network to one that supports four separate virtual networks, or Virtual Local Area Network segments (VLANS). Jennifer is very conscious of production change and thus contacted the systems group in order to make sure all the technical aspects of the project were met. Jennifer wanted to make sure that when all the client workstations were on the new network segments, they were still able to gain IP connectivity to the rest of the network as they had before. The Cheesecake Factory has been running a Windows Server 2003 Active Directory domain at the Windows 2000 mixed functional level for over two months. Jennifer created four network segments and labeled them VLAN1, VLAN2, VLAN3, and VLAN4. VLAN1 was the original network and hosts the original DHCP server, called SERVER1. Its network address did not change. The systems team decided to put DHCP Relay Agents on VLAN2 and VLAN3, configured to relay DHCP messages to the original DHCP server on VLAN1. Due to a reluctance to permit more DHCP broadcast traffic than the router could handle, Jennifer suggested to her systems team that VLAN4 should host its own DHCP server. The systems group installed another DHCP server on VLAN4, set up the appropriate DHCP scopes on that server and set up the additional DHCP scopes for VLAN2 and VLAN3 on SERVER1. After the work was completed, all clients on all VLANs seemed to be working fine for about two weeks, until Jennifer got a call from the Help Desk stating that the users in the warehouse cannot boot up from their diskless workstations, where they run monthly accounting statistics, but can connect from all other workstations. Jennifer looks at her network diagram and determines that the warehouse is located on VLAN4. She also checks with users in the accounting department on VLAN1 to see if they can connect using their diskless workstations. They tell Jennifer that they can and have had no problems. What did the systems team most likely forget to do?

A. Install a DHCP Relay Agent on VLAN4.

B. Configure a BOOTP table on the new DHCP server on VLAN4.

C. Replace the router with an RFC 2131 compliant router.

D. Cold boot all the diskless workstations.

Configuring the DHCP Relay Agent

6. Ceste has been working for the client services department at a local bank in Richmond, Virginia for over a year. He is responsible for client connectivity to the corporate network backbone. Ceste is a member of the DHCP Users group and uses his privileges as a member of this group to gauge the status of DHCP leases and available IP addresses. Jamie is a systems engineer for the same bank, and is responsible for the back-end configuration of all DHCP servers and scope configuration. He is a member of both the Domain Users and DHCP Administrators groups. On Monday morning, SERVER2, the DHCP server servicing the first and second floor of the bank, crashes. SERVER2 sits on the same network segment as the first floor users' client machines. The second floor network segment has a Windows Server 2003 server with RRAS and a DHCP Relay Agent configured. Ceste is the first to be alerted that clients are unable to obtain an IP address, and further notices that he cannot connect to the DHCP Console on SERVER2. He notifies Jamie, telling him that he thinks SERVER2 has crashed. Jamie is already in the process of activating all the pre-existing backup scopes for all the DHCP network segments at the bank. He tells Ceste to have all users on the first and second floor reboot their machines and everything should work. About 10 minutes later, Jamie receives a call from Ceste with the news that all first floor users' computers are now working, but nobody on the second floor can connect to any of their daily resources. What did Jamie forget to do in order to be fully prepared for this type of disaster?

    A. Add the IP address of the backup DHCP server to the DHCP Relay Agents.

    B. Configure a DHCP Relay Agent for the backup DHCP server.

    C. Authorize the backup DHCP server.

    D. Activate the DHCP scopes.

Integrating the DHCP Server with Dynamic DNS

7. You have been using Windows Server 2003 DHCP services to distribute IP addresses successfully to your mixed Windows XP/Windows NT DHCP enabled clients for over two months on your single segment LAN. Your Windows XP clients are configured with only the IP address of your DNS server for name resolution. NetBIOS broadcasts have been disabled on your network. Windows XP machines are able to successfully resolve all Windows NT 4.0 workstations by means of DNS. Recently, you had a disaster with one of your domain controllers and had to promote your only DHCP server to a DC, due to corporate cutbacks and limited budgeting. You are concerned with security due to this situation and decide to update your password policy so that when an account is locked out, it stays locked out until an administrator

unlocks it. You double-check and make sure that you are the only Enterprise and Domain Admin in your single domain forest. You have not made any changes to your network infrastructure since the crash. The problem: Your new DHCP Server/Domain Controller can no longer update any IP addresses for Windows NT clients in the Active Directory integrated DNS database. What is the most likely cause of this problem?

A. The original DHCP server was in the DNSUpdateProxy Group.

B. Coincidentally, someone recently turned on Secure only dynamic updates.

C. DNS and DHCP cannot coexist on the same Windows Server 2003 server.

D. The account credentials specified for Dynamic DNS updates has been locked out.

8. Kim works for a consulting firm that services local Fortune 500 companies in the New York City tri-borough area, using Windows technology. She recently received a priority one call from a brokerage firm, stating that none of their Windows XP users who work collaboratively with each other's workstations can contact each other. Kim begins the troubleshooting process by gathering background data and recording recent changes. The systems administrator at the brokerage firm, Alan, said that the network team subnetted the network over the weekend and added five new virtual networks. He also told Kim that he installed and configured a new DHCP server to service these new networks. He said that the network team told him everything would be fine as long as he set up the correct DHCP server scopes ahead of time on the new DHCP server and had the clients reboot first thing Monday morning. The network team also noted that they were using DHCP forwarding on the routers and that there was no need to set up any DHCP Relay Agents. The DHCP forwarding address pointed to the new DHCP server. Kim asked how Dynamic updates were set up on the old and new DHCP servers and found that Alan always used the option *Always dynamically update DNS A and PTR records*. She asked what happens when a ping is attempted on one of the workstation names. Alan replied that he could ping the workstations by their new IP addresses, but not by name. When he pings the workstations by name, he receives the old DHCP IP addresses of the client machine. What should Kim suggest to fix the problem and make sure it does not happen again?

A. Enable secure dynamic updates on the DNS server.

B. Activate the new DHCP server scopes.

C. Add the new DHCP server to the DNSUpdateProxy Group and delete all the client records from DNS.

D. Add the new DHCP server to the DNSUpdateProxy Group.

Integrating the DHCP Server
with Routing and Remote Access

9. You have been asked by upper management to implement a VPN solution in your newly built Windows Server 2003 Active Directory forest. All your users use Windows 2000 on portable laptops and their machines are successfully configured as DHCP clients. Management has asked that you not invest any more money in hardware or software but use the features that are packaged in the Windows Server 2003 product itself. You decide that this is feasible and begin by installing Routing and Remote Access Service(RRAS) on one of your dual-homed servers that is connected to both your internal network and your Internet Service Provider, and configuring it as a VPN server. You run the installation wizard and provide all the necessary answers. You have decided to use your RRAS server to assign client IP addresses by configuring it with a static pool of addresses that are routable on your internal network. Encouraged by the ease with which RRAS was set up, you send your CIO home for the day with the information needed to connect to your VPN server. You get a call from your CIO after he gets home. He says he is unable to connect to any resources on the internal network via the VPN. Which of the following is the most likely cause of the problem?

A. You forgot to exclude the static pool of IP addresses in your internal DHCP server's scope.

B. You forgot to configure your DHCP Relay Agent with the IP address of your internal DHCP server.

C. You gave your CIO the wrong IP address for the external network interface connected to your ISP.

D. You do not have a DNS server configured as an option on your RRAS server.

10. You are the systems administrator in charge of remote access at the corporate office for a multisite manufacturing company called BodyMetal, based in Chicago, Illinois. You have recently been tasked with the project of setting up a Routing and Remote Access Services (RRAS) server that will allow all of the company managers to work at home one day per week by dialing into the network, regardless of where they physically reside. Remote site managers live all over the United States and usually work from within their respective remote branch offices, using the high speed corporate WAN. You decide to install two RRAS servers to balance the user load, since you know all of your IT staff potentially will benefit from this project. All of your corporate DHCP servers reside on a single server, called SERVER1. You install the RRAS servers and configure them both with a locally hosted range of IP addresses. The two ranges you use do not overlap and have been excluded from the corporate DHCP server's scope. You also set up a DHCP Relay Agent on both RRAS servers and configure them with the internal IP address of your corporate DHCP server. You set up

your external DNS to resolve to the names of your two RRAS servers, REMOTE1 and REMOTE2. You provide directions on setting up the VPN client software to all the users in the remote managers group and members of your IT staff, each randomly defined with a different RRAS server name. A week goes by and you start receiving a handful of calls from your remote VPN users, saying that they are unable to connect to any resources beyond the RRAS server itself. You ask some of your IT staff if they are also having problems. You receive mixed results, as some can connect to the rest of the network and some cannot. As you analyze the data about which users cannot connect, you come up with a common variable: they are all using the REMOTE1 RRAS server. What is the most likely cause of this problem?

A. The DHCP Relay Agent service on REMOTE1 is stopped and needs to be started via the Services MMC.

B. The RRAS server, REMOTE1, does not support BOOTP/DHCP forwarding.

C. The corporate DHCP server is down.

D. The DHCP Relay Agent on REMOTE1 is configured with the wrong IP address for the corporate DHCP server.

Integrating the DHCP Server with Active Directory

11. You are the manager of the security division for an online banking startup company called BankNet.com. Security is of the utmost importance at your company, so you decided to implement Windows Server 2003 in an Active Directory infrastructure to take advantage of all the security features built into the new operating system and the AD environment. One of the features that most impresses you is the ability to control who can bring up DHCP servers on the network. At some of your other security jobs, you have seen a lot of client productivity lost due to the installation of a rogue DHCP server by one of the eager young IT guys. You decide that with Windows Server 2003's rogue detection feature, this will finally be a thing of the past. To assure yourself of this, you make sure that you are the only one who is a member of the Domain Admins, Enterprise Admins, and DHCP Administrators groups. One Tuesday afternoon, you get a call from the head of the Human Resources department, stating that he just rebooted his computer and now cannot connect to any network resources. You walk him through the process of running **ipconfig** with the /**all** switch at the command line, only to determine that this user has an IP address configuration that is not in the range of any scope configured on your DHCP servers. What has most likely happened?

A. One of the IT staff members has authorized a Windows Server 2003 server with the wrong scope information.

B. One of the IT staff members has reconfigured one of your existing scopes with the wrong IP range.

C. One of the IT staff members has installed a Windows NT 4.0 server running the DHCP service.

D. One of the IT staff members has changed the default gateway scope option for the segment on which the HR user's workstations sit.

Understanding Automatic Private IP Addressing (APIPA)

12. You are the systems administrator for a small network of fewer than 10 users on a single network segment, which is configured for peer-to-peer network resource sharing. You are using Windows XP and Windows 2000 on all of your client desktops and you decide to avoid the hassle of installing DHCP or manually configuring static IP addresses by using APIPA. You are using two file servers, both running Windows Server 2003, which also have the ability to use APIPA. Everything is running smoothly and you applaud yourself for implementing such an easy alternative for IP distribution. As your small network grows, however, you start to see your single segment network begin to outgrow itself. You decide to add another segment to your network, and you do so, setting up a network router. You add five new employees and plug their computers into the switch that is attached to the new subnet. All these employees' computers are configured to use APIPA and are able to communicate with each other immediately. However, when the new users try to access anything on the network servers, they are unable to connect. They are also unable to connect to any existing shares on the original network. What have you overlooked in your use of APIPA as an IP alternative?

A. APIPA works only if you have fewer than 10 workstations.

B. APIPA has not been configured properly on the new workstations.

C. The router is not able to forward BOOTP/DHCP broadcasts.

D. APIPA cannot be routed.

Managing the Windows Server 2003 DHCP Server

13. You are working as a desktop engineer for a pharmaceutical company in Washington D.C., called SMB Inc. SMB Inc. has a fully functional Windows Server 2003 Active Directory domain in which they have implemented DHCP. You have been in the IT industry for nine years, working primarily with Windows NT 4.0, and consider yourself quite seasoned. When you hear your manager, Julie, asking one of the systems engineers why she is not able to obtain an IP address from the server, you go to your PC, open your DHCP MMC, and determine that the network scope for her subnet is not activated. You quickly activate it and tell her to try again. It now works. When the same thing happens two months later, you open the DHCP MMC and are pleased to find that is the same problem; you will be the first to fix it again. However, when you try to activate the scope this time, you find that you cannot. You report to Julie that there is a problem with the DHCP server, because it will not let you activate the scope, but it will let you open up the DHCP MMC and view everyone on the DHCP server. Most likely, what really has happened?

    A. You have been removed from the Forest Admins Group.

    B. You have been removed from the DHCP Administrators Group.

    C. You have been placed in the DHCP Users Group.

    D. You are correct that there is a DHCP server problem.

Monitoring and Troubleshooting the Windows Server 2003 DHCP Server

14. Mike is the senior network analyst at a financial firm in downtown Manhattan. On a typical day, Mike monitors network traffic, compiles the traffic into a report, and submits any abnormalities to the appropriate technology team. The network is composed of a Windows Server 2003 Active Directory back end and a combination of Windows 2000 and Windows XP clients on the front end. On one particular Monday morning, Mike notices a large increase in the number of DHCPDECLINE messages coming from a majority of DHCP clients on subnet A. He checks the daily change control logs for any weekend work that might have caused this and comes across one entry of particular interest. The previous weekend, the systems team installed an additional DHCP server on subnet A to help balance the DHCP lease load on the existing DHCP server. With the data that Mike has already gathered, what conclusion can you come to as to the source of so many new DHCPDECLINE messages on Monday morning?

A. Conflict detection was not enabled on the new DHCP server.

B. The new DHCP server was configured with an overlapping scope of IP addresses.

C. The new DHCP server was not authorized, causing clients to decline its IP addresses.

D. The new DHCP server was not running Windows Server 2003.

15. Gary has been the DHCP administrator for T&G Sporting Company for the past five years. When Gary retired last month, he gave the keys to the kingdom to Jeff, a newbie in the field of engineering but very eager to learn. Although new to a lot of Windows technology, Jeff was the only administrator at T&G and thus had full rights to manage anything and everything. Jeff immediately began poking around into all the systems and services to learn as much as he could, as quickly as he could, before something broke and he had to learn it on the fly. Jeff was not quick enough. Jeff's manager, Jim, came up to him a few days after he took over, reporting that nobody on the second floor could access the Internet or anything else on the network. Jeff took a cursory look at the DHCP server service on the second floor and noticed that it was started. He then used the **netsh** utility to view the configuration of the DHCP scope, and noted that it appeared to be unchanged. He then looked at the System logs in the event viewer and noticed many specific errors with the source of DHCP server and Event ID of 1046. What did Jeff accidentally do to cause this problem while poking around in DHCP?

A. He deleted the DHCP database.

B. He unauthorized the DHCP server.

C. He turned off dynamic updates.

D. He created a multicast scope.

Self Test Quick Answer Key

For complete questions, answers, and explanations to the Self Test questions in this chapter as well as the other chapters in this book, see the Self Test Appendix.

1.	**C**	9.	**B**
2.	**C**	10.	**D**
3.	**D**	11.	**C**
4.	**B**	12.	**D**
5.	**B**	13.	**B**
6.	**A**	14.	**B**
7.	**D**	15.	**B**
8.	**C**		

Chapter 4

MCSA/MCSE 70-291

NetBIOS Name Resolution and WINS

Exam Objectives in this Chapter:

5.3   Troubleshoot server services.

5.3.1   Diagnose and resolve issues related to server dependency.

5.3.2   Use service recovery options to diagnose and resolve service-related issues.

   ☑   Summary of Exam Objectives

   ☑   Exam Objectives Fast Track

   ☑   Exam Objectives Frequently Asked Questions

   ☑   Self Test

   ☑   Self Test Quick Answer Key

Introduction

With the release of Microsoft Windows 2000, the primary IP to name resolution method for all service-related queries is the Domain Name System (DNS). Microsoft has committed to using DNS as the backbone for all computer communications for Windows 2000, Windows Server 2003, and for all of its future operating systems (OS). This does not mean they have forgotten their roots with LAN Manager, Windows NT 3.51, and NT 4.0. All of these OSs used Network Basic Input/Output System (NetBIOS) as their primary name to IP resolution method because it worked quite well and got the job done. Though a good protocol for its time, Microsoft is urging its customers to slowly phase out the aging, less-scaleable and chatty protocol, promoting the use of host to IP name resolution for all application developers, and the reliability of a sturdy DNS. Microsoft sends a clear message, but they are dedicated to customers that continue to run and support legacy Windows operating systems, and will continue to support NetBIOS in their core OS. NetBIOS, although a broadcast protocol, can be centralized into a searchable service database, called the Windows Internet Naming Service (WINS). WINS is a database that is intended to receive client name registrations with their identifying IP addresses, cache those credentials, and reply with those cached names and IPs when queried against. WINS works in the same manner as do DNS servers when they resolve hosts names to IP addresses, except that WINS substitutes NetBIOS names. During this chapter's discussion of NetBIOS and the use of the WINS, you will learn about the origin of NetBIOS, its use in today's environments, and how to install, configure, and integrate its WINS database into your existing DHCP and DNS infrastructures.

Head of the Class...

A Brief History of NetBIOS

NetBIOS was developed in 1983, by a systems company called Sytec, Inc., for specific use on International Business Machines Corporation's (IBM) in-house local broadband PC Network. It was used as a means to provide the computers with a Basic Input/Output System (BIOS) as a means of extending itself and communicating on a network. It was first hard-coded into the Network Interface Card (NIC) with a memory resident driver being loaded at boot time, and later developed to ride on top of more prominent protocols like Transmission Core Protocol/Internet Protocol (TCP/IP), Digital Equipment Corporation Network (DECnet), or Novell NetWare's Internet Packet Exchange/Sequenced Packet Exchange (IPX/SPX). It was originally developed as an Application Program Interface (API), so programmers could develop Local Area Network (LAN) aware applications. It was later further extended to be used with IBM's Token Ring in 1985, and given the name NetBIOS Extended User Interface (NetBEUI).

IBM introduced its first NetBIOS Operating System driver in its 1987 Personal Systems /2 (PS/2) computer release. Microsoft later released its first Network Operating System with the use of NetBIOS when it launched its LAN Manager

Continued

product. As mentioned, NetBIOS was originally an API, and was not a protocol. Though not a true protocol by itself, it is often mentioned in that manner because it is used alongside or on top of many other protocols. Due to the many applications that were born out of the NetBIOS API, it is and will continue to be around for quite some time. Though the industry will hold onto NetBIOS due to its heavy infiltration in corporate operating systems for a while longer, Microsoft has introduced Windows 2000 and Server 2003 with the ability to disable NetBIOS over TCP/IP (NetBT) if you are not dependant on them for any downlevel clients or applications. Microsoft recommends disabling NetBT if you have the ability to do so, because it just adds to protocol overhead.

Review of NetBIOS Name Resolution

NetBIOS sat at the heart of Microsoft's earlier operating systems like Windows for Workgroups, Windows 95, and Windows NT, and represented the core means for network communication. Computers use NetBIOS at the session layer of the Open Systems Interface (OSI) model to communicate with each other over the network. The OSI model is standardized by the International Standards Organization (ISO), and represents the fundamental path a bit of data must go through to get from one computer to another computer. NetBIOS is used in this model to establish a name resolution session with another NetBIOS machine in an effort to pass data.

NOTE

In March of 1987, RFC 1001 was published describing the use of NetBIOS as a transport protocol to be used on top of TCP/IP, in "Protocol Standard for a NetBIOS Service on a TCP/UDP Transport."

NetBIOS is considered a broadcast protocol, and works by announcing its name on its local network using a User Datagram Protocol (UDP) query to every listening node. On a NetBIOS LAN, the NetBIOS name is also considered the network address. For this reason it must be unique, and only one device can hold the same NetBIOS network name address in order to communicate without conflict. It is not until used on top of other protocols that it picks up other identifying network address types, like an IP address when used over TCP/IP.

NOTE

It is important to know the standard characters recognized in the NetBIOS name convention. Valid NetBIOS characters supported are: A–Z, a–z, 0–9, – (hyphen), !, @, #, $, %, ^, &, ( ), -, _, ', { }, ., ~.

DNS names are a bit different. DNS Names are broken up by periods. Each section cannot exceed 63 characters and the entire name cannot exceed 255 characters. Acceptable DNS characters are: A–Z, a–z, 0–9, – (hyphen).

Standard DNS does not support the use of underscores (_), which were commonly used with NetBIOS names to separate words. However since the inception of Windows 2000 DNS, Microsoft has supported this functionality.

Unlike DNS, NetBIOS naming is defined as a *flat* namespace, meaning that it does not branch out in a hierarchal manner like DNS. NetBIOS names can be composed of only 16 bytes, thus limiting their size compared to the Fully Qualified Domain Name (FQDN) of DNS names. Fifteen of those bytes make up the physical NetBIOS name, and the sixteenth byte is reserved for identifying a particular service that NetBIOS name may represent or host. This byte is sometimes referred to as a *type* byte as referenced in RFC 1001 and 1002. Because a computer may have several services that it may want to announce, a NetBIOS name registration may appear multiple times for a single computer or group name. NetBIOS registrants can be based on either a unique name or a group name. Mapping a unique name ties that name to a single computer's IP address, whereas mapping a group name maps that name to a group of separate computer IP addresses. An example of a group name would be a Windows Server 2003 NetBIOS workgroup or domain name registration. NetBIOS names can also contain extra characters that make up what is called a NetBIOS scope. A NetBIOS scope is a way to organize chat communities of NetBIOS machines into specific groups. Only computers that contain the exact same NetBIOS scope name can communicate with one another. Although in previous versions of Windows this was a graphical configuration setting, you cannot configure the NetBIOS scopes in the Graphical User Interface (GUI) of Windows 2000 or Server 2003. You also cannot use DHCP to distribute NetBIOS scopes in Windows 2000 and Server 2003. You must add a registry value using **regedt32.exe** as shown:

1. Click **Start | Run** and type **regedt32.exe**.

2. Locate the following key: HKLM\System\CurrentControlSet\Services\NetBT\Parameters.

3. Highlight the **Parameters** subkey and click **Add Value** on the **Edit** menu.

4. Type **ScopeID** (case sensitive) in the Value Name field.

5. Use **REG_SZ** in the Data Type box and click **OK**.

6. Restart the computer.

TEST DAY TIP

NetBIOS scopes are used to group computers into a common NetBIOS boundary, using extra hexadecimal characters at the end of the NetBIOS name. Computers set to use a NetBIOS scope can talk over NetBIOS only to other computers sharing the exact same scope.

NOTE

NetBIOS scopes are not recommended by Microsoft unless there are no other means of creating computer communication boundaries, such as using Virtual Local Area Networks (VLANS) or IPSec. Microsoft even states that they may schedule NetBIOS scopes for omission in upcoming versions of Windows and that you should not count on them for support.

Network Browsing

In order to assist with NetBIOS name resolutions, Windows Server 2003 and all previous versions of Windows create what are known as *Browse Lists*. These are lists of NetBIOS computer names grouped by physical network and replicated across network router interfaces by Master Browsers. These master browse lists contain lists of all the NetBIOS machine names per domain. In an attempt to locate and use these NetBIOS lists to find computers on both the local and remote network segments, computers are said to be *browsing*. Browsing is the act of looking for a NetBIOS computer name for communications purposes. We will focus more on browsing and how WINS is used to aid in the browsing process in the WINS and the Browser Service section of this chapter.

NetBIOS Name Registration

To begin the NetBIOS name resolution process, NetBIOS machines must register their names on the network. NetBIOS name registrations are dynamic in nature, in that they register and unregister themselves as they successfully come onto and off of the network wire, or when they successfully start or stop NetBIOS related services. Registration is important because it defines that name as unique on your network. After the time of registration, no other computer can claim that NetBIOS name as its own. In fact as computers begin registering their names, if a duplicate is found a NetBIOS name conflict occurs, and the second computer that tries to register that name is denied NetBIOS access on that network segment.

The NetBIOS name registration and query process for already registered names happens in the following three steps:

1. NetBIOS Name Registration
2. NetBIOS Name Discovery
3. NetBIOS Name Release

NetBIOS Name Registration

NetBIOS name registration happens when a NetBIOS client's network interface card initializes itself on its local segment. To assure itself of a unique name for NetBIOS communication, it broadcasts a name registration request to all machines on the network, or to a configured name server that hosts all NetBIOS names on the network. In either method, if another name is found matching the name request, a *Negative Name Registration Response* is sent back to the client, prohibiting that client from initializing and using its NetBIOS name. If no objections to the name are received by the NetBIOS client, it will issue a *Name Overwrite Demand*, and register the name.

NetBIOS Name Discovery

Once a NetBIOS name is registered, other computers on the network may want to locate application or file level resources on that workstation or server. To accomplish this, a similar method is performed on the local segment called a NetBIOS name query. A NetBIOS name query takes the destination name it is looking to locate and either broadcasts it or sends it to a configured name server for resolution. Depending on the method, if a positive match is found for the name, either the owner of the NetBIOS name or the corresponding name server replies with a positive query response. The result is a one-to-one NetBIOS communication commencing between the source and destination NetBIOS computers.

NetBIOS Name Release

NetBIOS names are not meant to stay resident on the network if the corresponding NetBIOS computer or service is not alive. This is accomplished by a NetBIOS name release. When NetBIOS computers shutdown or NetBIOS applications and services stop, a name release is sent out, and that name is then considered available to any NetBIOS name registrant. Computers and services requesting that name will receive a positive response during the registration phase.

Exam Warning

NetBIOS registration happens when machine services startup on the network. NetBIOS unregistration or release happens when services are stopped on the network. The releasing of NetBIOS names is apparent only if those services or machines are gracefully shutdown. If they are abruptly taken off of the network, or are taken down by a sudden crash, the previously registered NetBIOS names may remain resident and cause headaches down the road.

A Windows Server 2003 client can be manually released and reregistered if it is configured to use a name server such as WINS. To do this manually, use the nbtstat.exe command and type **nbtstat –RR** (ReleaseRefresh) as shown in Figure 4.1. After this is executed, you must wait at least two minutes for your name server to do its job, or you will receive an error message stating that it failed to release and renew your NetBIOS name with your WINS server.

Figure 4.1 Releasing and Renewing Your NetBIOS Name

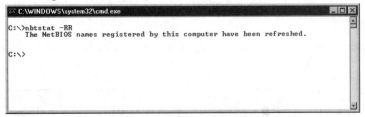

Standard NetBIOS Name Resolution

NetBIOS name resolution refers to the mapping of a NetBIOS name to an IP address. The IP address is yet one step closer to locating the physical network interface card of the destination computer. If you are running applications that require NetBIOS or using Microsoft operating systems prior to Windows 2000 Server, you will need to implement some sort of NetBIOS name resolution method. There are three NetBIOS name resolution methods that are considered standard, and are outlined in RFC 1001 and 1002. They are:

- Local broadcast
- NetBIOS name cache
- NetBIOS name server

Local Broadcast

A local broadcast is a UDP packet that is sent out from a NetBIOS machine to every computer on its network segment, announcing its name. Because it must ask every computer on the network if it is using its name, NetBIOS broadcasts can consume a lot of your network bandwidth, especially if this is the only resolution method in use. NetBIOS was not really developed to scale to thousands of machines on a single segment without the use of a name to IP database like WINS or even a flat name file like LMHOSTS, both of which we will discuss a bit later. You can use the nbtstat.exe utility to view how many names have been resolved via a broadcast by typing **nbtstat –r** as shown in Figure 4.2.

Figure 4.2 Showing Broadcast vs. Name Server Resolve

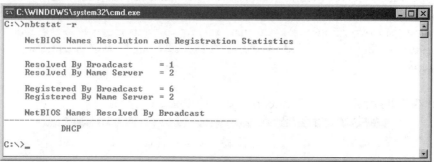

Head of the Class...

Reducing NetBIOS Broadcast Timeouts

Have you ever tried to connect to a computer resource and realized you typed the old computer name, or in fact just typed the wrong name altogether? Doesn't it take forever to time out so you can retype in the correct name? Well, for those of us who seem to be working on a hundred things at a time, this mistake is all too common.

You can configure your system to reduce the amount of time and retries it takes for NetBIOS broadcast resolution. When you accidentally type the wrong NetBIOS name and try to get resolution, your system is eventually going to resort to a broadcast to try and resolve that name. This is because that name does not exist in any NetBIOS name table or server service. If your organization is relying on a name server and all your NetBIOS clients are configured to use that name server, it may be a good idea to look into reducing the broadcast query timeouts as well as the broadcast query count. The broadcast query count is the amount of times a client will try to broadcast a query before it results in a failure to resolve a name. The default setting for this is three times. The broadcast query timeout is the timeout interval for each broadcast attempt. The default value for this is 750ms. To manipulate these values, you can edit the following registry key for each of these settings using regedt32.exe.

Registry Key: **HKLM\SYSTEM\CurrentControlSet\ Services\NetBT\Parameters**

Broadcast Query Count Entry: **BcastNameQueryCount**

Broadcast Query Timeout Entry: **BcastQueryTimeout**

NetBIOS Name Cache

Every NetBIOS machine maintains a local copy of resolved NetBIOS name resolutions it has successfully opened a communications session with. Oddly enough, this cache is called the *remote cache table*, but is commonly referred to as local cache. It is called a remote cache table because it identifies all NetBIOS machine names that have been resolved remotely and cached locally. We use terms *NetBIOS name cache*, *local cache*, and *remote name cache* intermittently to refer to the same thing. This cache remains alive for a configurable time period of 10 minutes and is limited to only 16 entries by default. The NetBIOS cache is the first place a machine will look when trying to resolve a NetBIOS name to an IP address. This means that recently accessed NetBIOS machine names will not go through the broadcast procedure to resolve those names. To view your current NetBIOS name cache, use the nbtstat.exe command line utility and type **nbtstat –c**. Note that if a recently accessed NetBIOS name is cached, and that NetBIOS name reregisters with a different IP address, your client will not be able to communicate until after the 10 minute timeout. To get around this, you can simply use the nbtstat.exe command line utility to flush your cache by typing **nbtstat –R** as shown in Figure 4.3. The syntax casing is important to note because a lowercase **–r** shows which machine resolutions have been resolved via a broadcast and which have used a name server.

Figure 4.3 Purging and Reloading Your NetBIOS Name Cache

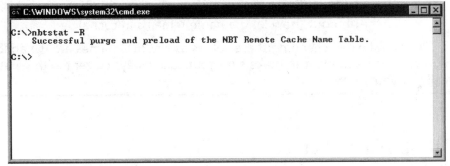

EXAM WARNING

The nbtstat.exe utility has a command syntax that allows the listing of all local NetBIOS names. This is not cache, just a listing of what NetBIOS names are physically present, their name type and their registration status on the network. To issue this command, type **nbtstat –n** at your command prompt window. See Figure 4.4 for an example.

Figure 4.4 Using Nbtstat to View Your Machines NetBIOS Name Registration Status

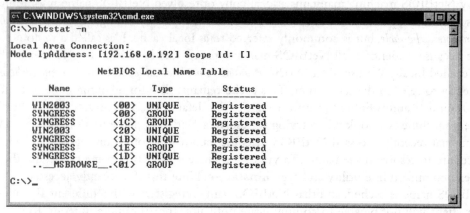

```
C:\WINDOWS\system32\cmd.exe                                          _ □ X
C:\>nbtstat -n

Local Area Connection:
Node IpAddress: [192.168.0.192] Scope Id: []

                   NetBIOS Local Name Table

        Name              Type         Status
    ---------------------------------------------------
        WIN2003      <00>  UNIQUE      Registered
        SYNGRESS     <00>  GROUP       Registered
        SYNGRESS     <1C>  GROUP       Registered
        WIN2003      <20>  UNIQUE      Registered
        SYNGRESS     <1B>  UNIQUE      Registered
        SYNGRESS     <1E>  GROUP       Registered
        SYNGRESS     <1D>  UNIQUE      Registered
        ..__MSBROWSE__.<01>  GROUP     Registered

C:\>_
```

TEST DAY TIP

You can alter the number of cached names as well as the default time to live (TTL) for your NetBIOS name cache by editing the following two registry values using regedt32.exe.

`HKLM\SYSTEM\CurrentControlSet\Services\NetBT\Parameters`

- **Size/Small/Medium/Large** (number of names cached)
- **CacheTimeout** (how long a name remains in cache)

Be careful when changing these values as NetBIOS names are dynamically registered and you want to make sure your cache stays current with what is really on your network.

NetBIOS Name Server

A NetBIOS name server (NBNS) is a server that accepts NetBIOS name registrations and caches them into a centralized database that can later be queried by NetBIOS clients. It is used for name registration, discovery queries, and NetBIOS name release requests. It maps NetBIOS names to IP addresses as NetBIOS clients dynamically roll through the NetBIOS name registration and resolution processes. Name servers can be replicated for redundancy and can be used to help clients cross network router boundaries.

The most commonly used NetBIOS name server is Microsoft's implementation, WINS.

EXAM WARNING

NetBIOS broadcast to do pass through router boundaries by default and are kept within their local domains. These are typically called broadcast domains. In order for NetBIOS discoveries to traverse network boundaries, a name server like WINS or a static mapping of all NetBIOS names in a name file, like an LMHOSTS file, must be used.

NetBIOS Over TCP/IP

NetBIOS over TCP/IP is commonly referred to as NetBT or NBT for short. It refers to the fact that NetBIOS is riding on top of the TCP/IP protocol as its transport. When TCP/IP computers on your network try to resolve a NetBIOS name, they are really looking for an IP address. NetBIOS is used to identify the computer name and TCP/IP is the transport mechanism for NetBIOS communication traffic. In conjunction, they are in need of a way to tie the computer name to its IP address. NetBIOS to IP name resolution is the means to this end and is discussed in the next section.

NOTE

Though name resolution typically is looking for an IP address in order to reach its destination, it is ultimately looking for the Media Access Control (MAC) address of the Network Interface Card (NIC) that is bound to that IP address. It does this with the help of another protocol called the Address Resolution Protocol (ARP).

Resolving NetBIOS Names to IP Addresses

The standard resolution methods for resolving NetBIOS names to IP addresses were mentioned previously in the review of NetBIOS name resolution. Those methods can be used together along with other name resolutions protocols like DNS in order to provide a client with a positive name resolution request. What we will detail here are the different scenarios or name resolution methods that Windows clients can be configured to go through in order to map NetBIOS names to IP addresses. Though NetBIOS can work with IPX/SPX name resolution as well, we will focus just on TCP/IP; it is the key element in this chapter's explanation of WINS and how it brings these two protocols together.

The different methods NetBIOS computers use to resolve names to IP addresses are referred to as nodes. Nodes are a series of name resolution steps that a NetBIOS computer goes through in order to resolve a NetBIOS name. With Windows Server 2003 there are five key NetBIOS node types, discussed next.

The NetBIOS Node Types

NetBIOS client node types can be configured locally on each machine by editing the registry or more commonly can be distributed by means of a Dynamic Host Configuration Protocol (DHCP) server. By default, a Windows 2000/XP/Server 2003 machine that is not configured to use a name server like WINS is said to be using Microsoft Enhanced b-node for name resolution. This means that the client first checks the NetBIOS name cache and if no match is found, initiates a local segment broadcast. Regardless of which node type is in use, all Windows node types check the NetBIOS name cache first. This is important to remember, because you can preload this name cache with static entries on systems you want to configure for fast NetBIOS access to other systems. You can do this with the use of an LMHOSTS file, discussed a bit later in the chapter. Depending on node type, nodes can be configured to use any of the following resolution methods:

- NetBIOS remote name cache
- Local broadcast
- NetBIOS name server (WINS)
- LMHOSTS file
- DNS named cache
- A HOSTS file or a DNS

Because Windows Server 2003 now focuses on DNS as its primary name resolution method, Windows 2000/XP/Server 2003 NetBIOS clients first try to determine if a NetBIOS name request is longer than the standard 15 character limit or if it contains any periods (.). If so, the request is sent to DNS. For example, take a look at the following command using a NetBIOS command line utility.

```
net use s: \\fileserver.syngress.com\docs
```

Though this is considered a NetBIOS command line utility, a DNS server would be queried due to the FQDN naming convention used in its syntax. After clients go through this initial step, the specific configured node type takes over and its resolution path is followed.

TEST DAY TIP

In versions of Windows prior to Windows 2000, if you configured DNS, you had to manually specify that DNS was to be used as an alternative for NetBIOS name resolution. With Windows 2000, Windows XP, and Windows Server 2003, if DNS is configured and the client uses a WINS server (DNS) it is automatically set to be used as a last means to resolve a NetBIOS name. This is Microsoft's Enhanced h-node mode.

b-node (Broadcasts)

b-node type clients use only broadcast to resolve NetBIOS names as well as to register their own NetBIOS names. B-node client types will resolve NetBIOS names in the following order:

- NetBIOS remote name cache
- Broadcast

NOTE

Microsoft has created its own version of the b-node broadcast method and has been named both *Enhanced b-node* and *Modified b-node*, respectively, depending on what you read. These Microsoft specific modes include the addition of an LMHOSTS file in the resolution process if a broadcast is unsuccessful. The name resolution order for these clients is shown in the following order:

- NetBIOS remote name cache
- Broadcast
- LMHOSTS file

This is the default node type for Windows 2000/XP/Server 2003 clients that are not configured as WINS clients.

p-node (Peer-to-peer)

p-node type clients use a configured NetBIOS name server to resolve NetBIOS names as well as to register their own. p-node client types will resolve NetBIOS names in the following order:

- NetBIOS remote name cache
- NetBIOS name server (WINS)

m-node (Mixed)

m-node type clients use a combination of b-node and p-node types to resolve NetBIOS names as well as to register their own. A b-node broadcast is used first, and if it does not result in a resolve, a p-node name server is queried. m-node client types will resolve NetBIOS names in the following order:

- NetBIOS remote name cache
- Broadcast
- NetBIOS name server (WINS)

h-node (Hybrid)

h-node type clients also use a combination of b-node and p-node types to resolve NetBIOS names as well as to register their own. However, the order of resolution changes in that a name server (WINS) is used prior to issuing a broadcast. h-node client types will resolve NetBIOS names in the following order:

- NetBIOS remote name cache
- NetBIOS name server (WINS)
- Broadcast

TEST DAY TIP

h-node is the preferred NetBIOS name resolution method if you want to cut down on broadcast traffic but still allow broadcasts to resolve those names not yet entered into your WINS server. It is recommended by Microsoft and may show up on your exam. It uses a hexadecimal value of 0x8 as shown in Figure 4.5.

Enhanced h-node

Enhanced h-node type clients use the same resolution methodology as regular h-node clients with the addition of DNS in the resolution path. If DNS is also configured on your WINS clients, it will be used to try and resolve NetBIOS names. By default, Microsoft Windows 2000/XP/Server 2003 NetBIOS clients that are configured to use a WINS server use *enhanced h-node* NetBIOS name resolution. Enhanced h-node client types will resolve NetBIOS names in the following order:

- NetBIOS remote name cache
- NetBIOS name server (WINS)
- Broadcast
- LMHOSTS file
- DNS named cache
- HOSTS file
- DNS

TEST DAY TIP

Enhanced h-node is the most commonly found name resolution method found on Windows machines today. To help you remember the name resolution order, use the first letter in each word of the following sentence: *Can we bark like happy dogs?*

- **Can** (*cache*)
- **We** (*WINS*)
- **Bark** (*Broadcast*)
- **Like** (*LMHOSTS*)
- **Happy** (*HOSTS*)
- **Dogs** (*DNS*)

TEST DAY TIP

Enable LMHOSTS lookup is a configurable option located within the advanced properties of your network interface's TCP/IP properties on the WINS configuration tab. This option is what enables these modes to search the LMHOSTS file for NetBIOS name resolution.

EXAM WARNING

Computers running Windows 2000, Windows XP, or Windows Server 2003 are configured to use enhanced/modified b-node resolution by default, unless they are configured to use a WINS server, in which they use enhanced h-node by default.

If you choose to configure a client node type manually, you can do so in your Windows registry by editing the flowing key value: HKLM\SYSTEM\CurrentControlSet\Services\NetBT\Parameters\NodeType

All the available node type values can be found in Table 4.1. These same values are used to configure the node type as a DHCP scope option shown in Figure 4.5.

Table 4.1 NetBIOS Node Type Values

NetBIOS Node Type	Hex Value	Decimal Value
b-node	0x1	1
p-node	0x2	2
m-node	0x4	3
h-node	0x8	4

Figure 4.5 Configuring Your NetBIOS Node Type via DHCP

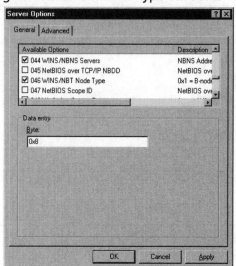

The LMHOSTS file

The LMHOSTS file is a static file, used by Microsoft operating systems to help resolve NetBIOS names to IP addresses. It is used as an alternate method of remote name resolution in the NetBIOS naming resolution order if all of the previous resolution methods fail. It was originally created as a simple method to map NetBIOS names to IP addresses and was limited in functionality. It was created early on in Microsoft's core Windows operating systems and later enhanced in the Windows NT 3.1 version of the OS. Early versions of the LMHOSTS files limitations included:

- Inability to validate logons across subnets
- Inability to be used in a domain design spanning subnets

These limitations were removed in Windows NT 3.1 with the addition of several *tag* lines you could precede in your LMHOSTS file entries. The tag line entries listed here are further explained in Table 4.2. As you can see in the table, even more enhancements have been made with the addition of new tag lines for additional functionality.

- #PRE
- #DOM:<*domain*>
- #INCLUDE <*path to file*>
- #BEGIN_ALTERNATE
- #END_ALTERNATE

The LMHOSTS file is located in the %systemroot%\system32\drivers\etc directory and is the standard location across Microsoft OS platforms. It is a standard text file that is loaded into the NetBIOS name cache upon each boot up of the OS. You can populate your LMHOSTS file with a variety of different tag options to accomplish many NetBIOS resolution queries. Table 4.2 displays all of the available tag options you can use in your LMHOSTS file. The # symbol is preceded by each of these tag entries and lets your system know that it needs to pay special attention to what follows. If it is a valid tag option, the system will do what is outlined in Table 4.2. If it is not valid, it treats the verbiage as plain *comment* text. With the addition of the # symbol, comments can be added to help explain each of your LMHOSTS file entries, though be limited in what you write. LMHOST files are parsed by your system, meaning they are read from top to bottom and not all at once like interpretive programs. This is one reason why you should not use the sample LMHOSTS file that come with Windows Server 2003 as it is filled with unnecessary comments.

You should structure your LMHOSTS file in such a manner that the most frequently queried NetBIOS machine names are at the top and the least queried machine names are below that, and so on. However, there is one exception, and that is with the use of the #PRE tag. The #PRE tag is used to preload entries into your NetBIOS name cache at boot time. These entries remain in the cache as long as the machine is turned on. Normal NetBIOS cache entries remove themselves from the NetBIOS name cache at the default interval of 10 minutes. This is how entries that do not use the #PRE prefix tag are treated. They are loaded into cache at boot time, but expire after 10 minutes if no NetBIOS query is performed against them. Since preloaded NetBIOS names remain in cache for the lifetime of the machine cycle, it is wise to put these entries last in your LMHOSTS file. A sample LMHOSTS file using some of the different tags in Table 4.2 can be found in Figure 4.6.

EXAM WARNING

Though similar to the HOSTS file and located in the same directory, the LMHOSTS file maps NetBIOS names to IP addresses whereas the HOSTS file maps hierarchal FQDN to IP addresses. Though both can be used to help each other out in the name resolution process, be sure you know the difference.

Table 4.2 LMHOSTS File Keywords

Keyword Tag	Function/Description
#PRE	Used to preload name entries into a machine's remote name cache. It will remain in cache until removed from the LMHOSTS file and reloaded.
#DOM:*<domain>*	Used to identify a domain controller for a particular domain.

Continued

Table 4.2 LMHOSTS File Keywords

Keyword Tag	Function/Description
#INCLUDE <path to file>	Used to point a client to use another centrally located LMHOSTS file using a UNC file path. In order to use this tag, statically set the server and IP address in your original LMHOSTS file that is used in the <path to file> location.
#BEGIN_ALTERNATE	Used along with the #INCLUDE statement to list alternative servers hosting centralized LMHOSTS files. Alternative LMHOSTS file locations are attempted only if the previous locations were unaccessible.
#END_ALTERNATE	Used to end the #BEGIN_ALTERNATIVE tag and is used after the last #INCLUDE tag.
#MH	Used to identify multihomed computer systems.
#NOFNR	Used to avoid NetBIOS-directed name queries for LAN Manager UNIX systems.
#SG <name>	Used to define a special (Internet) group specified by a name. These tags along with special groups in general are limited to 25 members.
\0xnn	Used to identify machines with a specific service or application. Use the hexadecimal number of the service or application as the sixteenth character in the NetBIOS name and enclose the entire name in quotation marks.

Figure 4.6 Sample LMHOSTS File

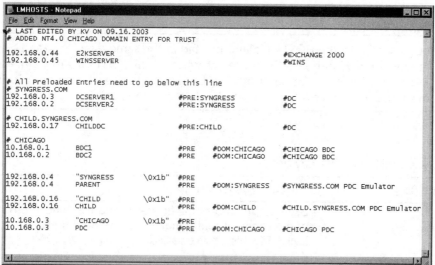

If using an LMHOSTS file, it is a good idea to add a comment to the top of the file that states who last edited the file, the date, and what was changed. This helps clear some of the confusion when problems arise due to LMHOSTS file changes.

Notice that in Figure 4.6 we used one of the hexadecimal tag options described in Table 4.2. These tags are used to clearly identify a particular NetBIOS service registered on your network. Specifically we used the */0x1b* tag, which identifies a Domain Master Browser, or more specifically, a Primary Domain Controller/PDC Emulator. This is useful for down-level domain trusts or down-level domain authentication. Table 4.3 shows you more of the common hexadecimal switches you can take advantage of in your LMHOSTS file.

Table 4.3 Service Specific HEX Locators

HEX Suffix Number (LMHOSTS Tag) Network Service	
1Bh (\0x1b)	Domain Master Browser (PDC or PDC Emulator)
20h (\0x20)	File Server (Server Service)
00h (\0x00)	Workstation (Workstation Service)
01h (\0x01)	Other (—__MSBROWSE__-)
1Ch (\0x1c)	Domain Controller
03h (\0x03)	Messenger Service (username)
00h (\0x00)	Workgroup
1Eh (\0x1e)	Normal Group Name (Browser Service Election)

EXAM WARNING

A default LMHOSTS.SAM file comes with every Microsoft client, including Windows Server 2003. A common mistake is for users to edit this default file and think that it will start helping them resolve NetBIOS names. The default install of Windows Server 2003 is to display file name extensions: This has changed since NT 4.0 and Windows 2000 where at first glance, the LMHOSTS.SAM file appears to be called only LMHOSTS. Though the .SAM file extension is again visible by default, the trick is renaming the file, or better yet, creating a new filename **LMHOSTS** with no file extension. Be careful when using Notepad to create this file as it may append a .TXT extension that may not be visible. This extension, as well as any other LMHOSTS file extension, will cause Windows Server 2003 to disregard it as a valid LMHOSTS file. Alternatively, you can import another text file in the GUI and Windows Server 2003 will auto generate an LMHOSTS file with no extension, as explained in Exercise 4.01. If enabled, all Microsoft operating systems look for a standard flat filename LMHOSTS, and will disregard the default one with a .SAM extension. Don't be fooled on the exam if the question states that the default LMHOSTS file is being used as it is there only as a sample to provide direction.

EXERCISE 4.01

USING AN IMPORT TO CREATE YOUR LMHOSTS FILE

In this exercise, we will show you how to import a standard text file into your Windows Server 2003 system in order to generate an LMHOSTS file. Make sure the file is formatted correctly before importing it, as discussed previously; there is no need to name it or remove the file extension however, because this process will do that automatically.

1. Click **Start | Control Panel | Network Connections | Local Area Connection | Properties**.

2. Scroll down and highlight **Internet Protocol (TCP/IP)** and then click **Properties**.

3. Click the **Advanced** button; in the **Advanced TCP/IP Settings** window, click the **WINS** tab.

4. You will see a window like that in Figure 4.7. Verify that the default setting of **Enable LMHOSTS lookup** is checked. Click the **Import LMHOSTS** button.

Figure 4.7 Importing LMHOSTS File Window

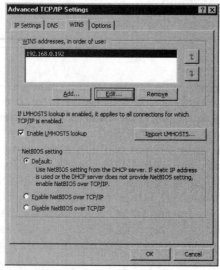

5. An explorer window will appear, allowing you to locate your file. Browse to the location of your saved text file, highlight it, and select **Open** as shown in Figure 4.8.

Figure 4.8 Choosing Import File for LMHOSTS Creation

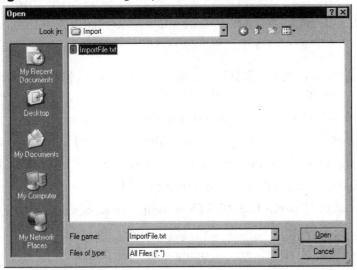

6. Click **OK** in the **Advanced TCP/IP Settings** dialog window.

7. Click **OK** in the **Internet Protocol (TCP/IP) Properties** dialog window.

8. Click **Close** in the **Local Area Connections** dialog window and you have successfully imported a text file and created your LMHOSTS file.

NOTE

To verify your LMHOSTS file creation, navigate to your %systemroot%\system32\ drivers\etc directory and see if there is a file called LMHOSTS. Open your LMHOSTS file with notepad.exe and verify that the data within are the same as that in your original text file.

Though LMHOSTS files are not used much anymore and are not recommended for mass distribution on servers or workstations for resolution, they can become quite handy when troubleshooting NetBIOS name resolution problems. If you are trying to connect to a NetBIOS application or workstation and are having problems, possibly due to a downed name server, create a simple LMHOSTS file, place it in your %systemroot%\system32\ drivers\etc directory, run **nbtstat –R** to reload your name cache, and see if that resolves the problem. If so, look into a possible name server replication problem, or physical name server or service problem.

Another reason to use an LMHOSTS file is if your Windows Server 2003 Active Directory needs to establish a down level trust with an NT 4.0 domain that sits across a firewall boundary. Windows NT 4.0 domains still rely on NetBIOS name resolution and require it for successful trust implementations, even with a Windows 2000 or Server 2003 Active Directory domain.

By default, Windows Server 2003 is configured to use the LMHOSTS file in the NetBIOS name resolution process. To disable this:

1. Open your **Network Connection** applet in the **Control Panel**.
2. Right-click your active **Local Area Connection** and select **Properties**.
3. Highlight your **Internet Protocol (TCP/IP)** protocol and click **Properties**.
4. Click the **Advanced** button and then the **WINS** tab.
5. Deselect the **Enable LMHOSTS lookup** option box.

If at all possible, try to implement and count on a Windows Internet Name Server or WINS server for your NetBIOS name resolution, but don't forget about this handy little file!

The Windows Server 2003 Windows Internet Name Server

In the following sections we will discuss the Windows Internet Naming Server that comes as a configurable service option in Windows Server 2003. Although Windows 2000, Windows XP, and Windows Server 2003 machines rely on DNS for name resolution, you may need to install and configure a Windows Internet Naming Server in your environment to support all of your down level clients and applications. We will look at how to install, configure, and replicate this service with other Windows Internet Naming Servers.

Overview of WINS

Windows Internet Naming Service (WINS) is Microsoft's answer to unicast NetBIOS name resolution. WINS is Microsoft's version of a NetBIOS name server, whose function it is to resolve client requests for NetBIOS name to IP resolution. As DNS is to hosts files, WINS is the database version of the LMHOSTS flat file. In its database, WINS accepts and stores client name registrations. These stored names include the registering clients IP address and any available searchable service that client may want another host to know about. These registrations are then provided to other querying clients looking for those names or services. Clients configured to use this type of service are referred to as *WINS enabled clients*. Clients that are not set up to use this name service are referred to as *broadcast clients*.

Take, for example, the initial boot sequence of a Windows 2000 WINS enabled client. When a Windows 2000 WINS client initializes its TCP/IP stack it registers its NetBIOS name with its configured WINS server. It may also register its workstation and server service and possibly others, like its messenger service. When an alternate WINS client, say a

Windows NT 4.0 client, goes looking for that Windows 2000 client, it queries its configured WINS server for name resolution instead of initiating a local broadcast. The WINS server will search its database for the queried name and return a positive or negative response depending on what it finds. If it finds the NetBIOS name that is in an *active* state, it will return the IP address of that client along with any queried service lookups. The client will then initiate a direct unicast communications session with that IP address. If it does not find the NetBIOS name, it will return a negative response, forcing the client to initiate a broadcast. If it finds the NetBIOS name, and it is in any other state than *active*, it will also return a negative response; but this one does not force the client to initiate a broadcast, it just tells the client the requested name is not available.

WINS client registrations are temporary, and kept only for the configured time to live interval of your WINS servers. In order to keep registration information current within the WINS database, WINS clients go through three separate phases. They are referred to as:

- Client Name Registration
- Client Name Renewal
- Client Name Release

Clients that are configured to use WINS will go through these phases in order to qualify their name against all other names on the network, in order to allow other WINS clients to successfully query and resolve their name. Though WINS servers receive registration, renewal, and release traffic, client queries are usually the most common type of traffic a WINS server will process. See Figure 4.9 for a graphical view of these four steps.

Figure 4.9 Displaying Client and Server WINS Traffic Flow

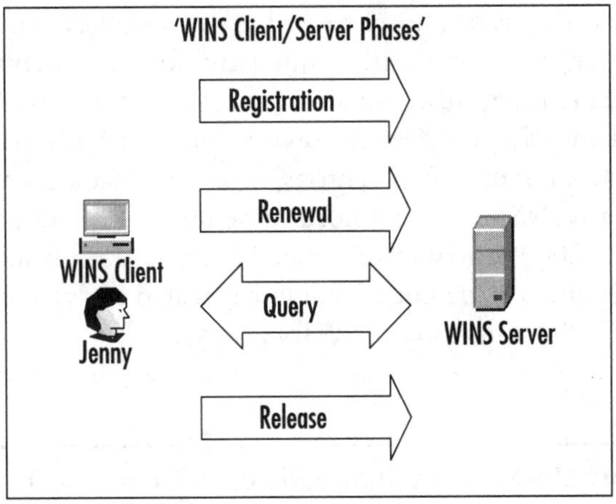

Client Name Registration

WINS enabled clients are configured with the IP address of either one or two WINS servers. The first IP address is referred to as the *primary WINS server* and the second one is called the *secondary WINS server*. When a WINS client starts, it directly registers its name and IP address with the IP address of its primary WINS server. If the first attempt at registering with the primary WINS server fails because the server is unavailable, the client will attempt only two more registration requests with the primary WINS IP address, at which time it will try the secondary WINS server, if configured. If no secondary WINS server is configured, or if the client recognizes it is also unavailable, the client initiates a NetBIOS broadcast.

When a WINS server receives a registration request, it checks its database for the existence of the requested name. If no matching name is found, it sends the client a successful registration message. Within that message is a time to live (TTL) stamp, telling the client how long the WINS server will keep its record alive, and ultimately, when the client needs to refresh its record to keep it alive. If the WINS server receives this request, it finds a NetBIOS name match in its database, and it will send a name query request to the owner of that record in an attempt to see if that name is in fact an active name. If it receives a positive answer, it will send a negative acknowledgement back to the initiating name registration request, denying that client its name registration. The client will display a NetBIOS name conflict error message.

NOTE

When the WINS server tries to determine if a client name is still alive on the network, it will query each TCP/IP bound interface of a multihomed computer.

Static entries in a WINS database are treated as defined; they don't change. Thus if a WINS server goes to register a new name request and finds a matching static entry, regardless of whether that name is responsive or not, the request is denied. An update request is also denied when a client tries to update its own record and finds that record to be static. Microsoft recommends using only static entries for clients that are unable to physically register themselves with a WINS server and need to be queried by other NetBIOS hosts. With the release of Windows 2000, a new feature called Migrate on was introduced, allowing an administrator to determine if static entries could be treated as dynamic. More on this feature will be discussed in "Configuring the WINS Server."

TEST DAY TIP

Using the **Import LMHOSTS** feature outlined in Exercise 4.01 on your WINS server will create static entries. This is a not a good idea, unless all the entries in the file you are importing are clients that cannot register themselves with a WINS server.

Each time a WINS client's IP address changes, it will automatically update its record with its WINS server. This could be due to an administrator manually changing the IP address of a statically assigned WINS client, or because a WINS client receives a new IP address from its DHCP server.

Client Name Renewal

At the TTL extinction period, the WINS client will go through the process of name renewal with its configured WINS server, in an attempt to refresh its existing NetBIOS name registration. Because WINS is a dynamic database, WINS clients can register and unregister their names themselves. They do this at configured time intervals depending on the TTL of their registered name. The default TTL interval configured for Windows Server 2003 WINS server is six days, and is shown in the *Renew interval* setting in Figure 4.10.

Figure 4.10 Configuring WINS Client Intervals

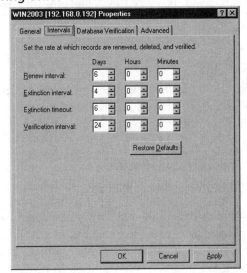

WINS clients will attempt to renew or refresh their NetBIOS names with their WINS servers at 50 percent of the configured *Renew interval* times, received from the WINS server when their name was registered. By default this would be every three days. If for some reason the primary WINS server is not available, the client will try again in 10 minutes. If the client still receives no response, it will continue trying the primary WINS server every 10 minutes for up to one hour. At this time, if configured to use a secondary WINS server, it will try that server. If no response is heard from it, it will also try every 10 minutes for one hour. The WINS client will continue this rotation until its name is refreshed with a WINS server or until its TTL expires.

If you want to manually reregister or refresh your WINS client's NetBIOS record with its WINS server, you can do so in the command interface using the nbtstat.exe utility and typing **nbtstat –RR** as shown in Figure 4.11.

Figure 4.11 Refreshing Your NetBIOS Name with Your WINS Server

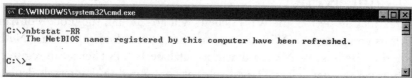

```
C:\>nbtstat -RR
      The NetBIOS names registered by this computer have been refreshed.

C:\>_
```

TEST DAY TIP

When a WINS server successfully receives a client's name renewal or refresh request, it sends the client a new TTL value, starting the cycle over.

Client Name Release

When computers or services are shutdown and essentially taken off the network, they need a way to alert their WINS server to properly update its database, so that other querying clients are not faced with invalid information when looking to communicate with those computers or services. WINS clients do this is one of two ways:

- Properly shutting down the computer
- Stopping a NetBIOS service or application

Both of the methods send what is called a *Name Release* request to their configured WINS server, asking that server to expire their name in the database. Within this name release request sits the computer or applications NetBIOS name along with its IP address. Upon receipt of the request, the WINS server will look in its database for a correlation to that name or service. If it finds a positive match for both name and IP address, it replies to the requesting client with a positive name release response, including a TTL value of zero. At the same time, it marks the entry found as *extinct*. This record is now mapped for extinction and will be removed from the database based on the *extinction interval* discussed further in the section "Configuring the WINS Server." If, however, the WINS server does not find the NetBIOS name or service in its database, or if it finds a different IP address mapped to the requested name release, it will issue a negative name release response back to the client.

TEST DAY TIP

If for some reason a WINS client loses contact with its WINS server, and thus is not able to send a successful name release request before its TTL time expires, the WINS server will also mark that record for extinction.

EXAM WARNING

Have you ever been told that is very important to shut your computer down properly, and not just power it off using the power button or unplugging it from the wall? Well, NetBIOS name release is one of the reasons. When a WINS client computer is improperly shut down on a network, that name is never released from the WINS database. The WINS server continues to think it is alive on the network and will send positive name queries to all requesting clients. This causes the querying clients to wait extra periods of time as the invalid requests timeout. This has been somewhat helped with today's new technology in power management—Windows 2000, Windows XP, and Windows Server 2003 will recognize that a power button has been pressed and will initiate a proper shutdown on APM- and ACPI-compliant BIOS machines.

Client name release request packets contain the source and destination addresses along with the name they wish to release. WINS server name release response requests packets also contain the source and destination address as well as the released name and a TTL value of zero.

Client Name Resolution Query

Clients configured to use a WINS server are said to be using a *hybrid* node type for name query resolution. This type of resolution refers to a specific order in which NetBIOS name resolution methods are queried. Hybrid queries use the following name resolution order when resolving NetBIOS names to IP addresses:

- Local NetBIOS name cache
- Primary WINS server
- Secondary WINS server (if configured)
- Local network broadcast
- Local LMHOSTS file (if configured)

WINS clients first check their local NetBIOS name cache. If no match is found, they send a name query to their configured primary WINS server. If it does not contain a match, the client will issue the same query two more times to the same WINS server. If after three attempts it does not resolve the name, it will attempt the same query with any configured secondary WINS servers. If the secondary WINS server fails to resolve the name after another three attempts, the client will initiate a local broadcast. Lastly, after a broadcast fails name resolution, a WINS client will look to its local LMHOSTS file if it is configured to do so. By default, Windows Server 2003 clients are configured to look for LMHOSTS files.

WINS clients will go through this name resolution process every time they initiate a process that is in need of a NetBIOS name IP address lookup. The following is a list of common NetBIOS name actions requiring a name resolution query:

- Use of the **net use** command, such as **net use x: \\server\share**
- Right-click **My Computer | Map Network Drive | \\server\sharename**
- **Start | Run | \\server\sharename**
- Using NetBIOS client applications that access programs like Exchange Server 5.5 or SQL Server 6.5

Once a client resolves a NetBIOS name the first time, it will cache that name in its local NetBIOS name cache for future use. It keeps that name for a default period of 10 minutes. If within that 10 minute period the client requests that same NetBIOS name, the discussed process ends at the first step and name resolution is very quick. This default name cache time period is configurable by editing the local registry as discussed earlier in this chapter.

TEST DAY TIP

To see if a computer is configured to use a WINS server, use the **ipconfig** command by typing **Ipconfig /all**.

If the output's *Node Type* displays *Hybrid* or *Peer-to-Peer*, the client is using WINS. The output will also display what IP address the client is configured to use for its primary and secondary WINS servers as shown in Figure 4.12.

Figure 4.12 Showing Your WINS Client Configuration

```
C:\WINDOWS\system32\cmd.exe

C:\>ipconfig /all

Windows IP Configuration

        Host Name . . . . . . . . . . . . : Win2003
        Primary Dns Suffix  . . . . . . . : syngress.com
        Node Type . . . . . . . . . . . . : Hybrid
        IP Routing Enabled. . . . . . . . : Yes
        WINS Proxy Enabled. . . . . . . . : No
        DNS Suffix Search List. . . . . . : syngress.com
                                            vigil.ws
                                            columbia.vigil.ws
                                            domain.com

Ethernet adapter Local Area Connection:

        Connection-specific DNS Suffix  . : syngress.com
        Description . . . . . . . . . . . : AMD PCNET Family PCI Ethernet Adapter
        Physical Address. . . . . . . . . : 00-0C-29-F3-7C-80
        DHCP Enabled. . . . . . . . . . . : No
        IP Address. . . . . . . . . . . . : 192.168.0.192
        Subnet Mask . . . . . . . . . . . : 255.255.255.0
        Default Gateway . . . . . . . . . : 192.168.0.50
        DNS Servers . . . . . . . . . . . : 192.168.0.192
        Primary WINS Server . . . . . . . : 192.168.0.192

C:\>_
```

Installing the WINS Server

Like any other network service in Windows Server 2003, you can use the **Add/Remove Programs** Control Panel applet to add WINS as a service to your server. You will need to be a local administrator on the server in order to successfully install the WINS service. Exercise 4.02 will walk you through adding WINS as a network service after the initial install of Windows Server 2003 has been completed.

EXERCISE 4.02

INSTALLING THE WINS SERVICE

In this exercise, we will show you how to install the Windows Internet Naming Service on your Windows Server 2003 server.

1. Click **Start | Control Panel | Add or Remove Programs**.

2. Click **Add/Remove Windows Components** in the Windows Components Wizard dialog window.

3. As shown in Figure 4.13, scroll down and highlight **Network Services** and click **Details**.

Figure 4.13 Adding Windows Network Services

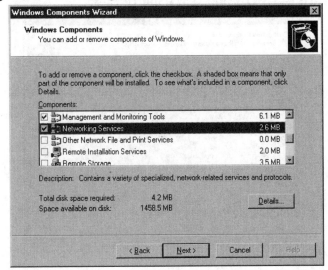

4. Select the **Windows Internet Name Service (WINS)** option checkbox and click **OK** as shown in Figure 4.14.

Figure 4.14 Adding the WINS Service

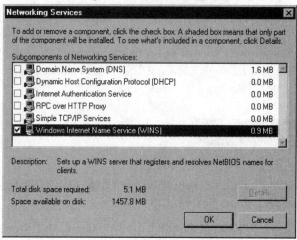

5. Make sure you have your Windows Server 2003 source CD in your CD-ROM drive and click **Next**. Windows Server 2003 will start copying the needed source files and installing the WINS service as shown in Figure 4.15.

Figure 4.15 Copying WINS Source Files

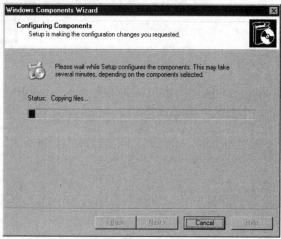

6. Click **Finish**. The WINS service is installed and ready to be accessed.

7. Click **Start | Administrative Tools | WINS** to open your WINS MMC Console and configure your WINS server.

NOTE

You can also install the WINS service via the **Network Connections** window.

1. Click **Start | Control Panel | Network Connections**.
2. Right-click **Network Connections** and select **Open**.
3. Click the **Advanced** toolbar menu and then select **Optional Networking Components**.
4. This will put you at window somewhat similar to Figure 4.13, but with less available options, called **Windows Optional Networking Components Wizard**.

EXAM WARNING

Use common sense and configure your Windows Internet Naming Servers with a static IP address. If clients are to be hard-coded with the IP address of your WINS server, then it is not wise to configure your WINS server with an IP address that uses DHCP and could possibly change over time. If you try to install WINS on a server that is configured to use DHCP, you will receive the errors displayed in Figures 4.16 and 4.17.

Figure 4.16 Installation Error Shown If Your Server Is Using DHCP

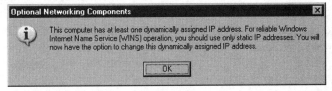

Figure 4.17 Installation Error Shown If You Continue Using DHCP

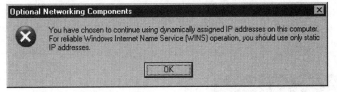

Configuring and Managing the WINS Server

Configuring and managing your WINS server correctly ensures seamless NetBIOS name resolution throughout your network environment. It is important to detail your configuration before it is approved and put into your production environment. To correctly configure your WINS server topology and manage its records, there are several key factors you must consider. These include:

- Configuring WINS replication
    - Manual versus automatic
- Managing WINS records and its database
- Backup and restore of the WINS database

Configuring WINS Replication

For NetBIOS clients on your network, a WINS server is a vital component in the name resolution process. If clients are separated by physical network segments, and your WINS server were to go down, these NetBIOS clients would be able to communicate only via local broadcast to local machines on their own subnet. This is typically going to be only employee workstations and not the production server that they need to do their jobs.

For this reason, it is imperative that you configure redundancy into your WINS topology. You can do this with the use of Windows Server 2003 WINS replication. WINS replication is a method used by WINS servers to *push* or *pull* database information between each other, keeping similar dynamic databases across all WINS servers. With replicated WINS data, you can configure your NetBIOS client community with the IP addresses of multiple WINS servers, thus reducing the risk of losing NetBIOS resolution if one of the servers goes down.

WINS servers need to be set up as replication partners in order to successfully replicate with each other. Replication partners can be set up *manually* by a WINS administrator, or they can be set to *automatically* generate replication relationships with other WINS servers using multicast packets to search out these other servers.

Manually Creating Replication Partners

Manual configuration requires that you know the name or IP address of the WINS server with which you want to replicate. If you want to use the name, you must make sure that you have other methods of name resolution in place in order to recognize the server you are setting up replication. Exercise 4.03 walks you through setting up a replication partner with an NT 4.0 Backup Domain Controller.

EXERCISE 4.03

SEETTING UP MANUAL REPLICATION PARTNERS

In this exercise we will show you how to manually set up a replication partner with another WINS server. In this particular case, it is a Windows NT 4.0 Backup domain controller and thus we use the IP address and not the name in the initial setup.

1. Click **Start | Administrative Tools | WINS** to open your WINS MMC snap-in console.

2. Right-click your **WINS server name** and select **New Replication Partner** as shown in Figure 4.18.

    Figure 4.18 Creating a New Replication Partner

    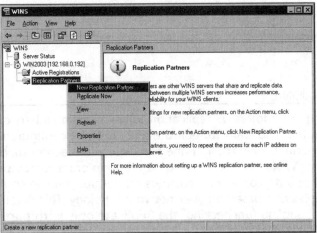

3. Enter the IP address of the WINS server you wish to replicate with as shown in Figure 4.19 and click **OK**.

    Figure 4.19 Adding the Replication Partner's IP Address

    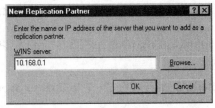

4. You have successfully set up a new replication partner and are ready to do the same on the alternate WINS server. Follow the exact same steps, reversing the replication partner IP address.

NOTE

It is easier to use the IP address of the WINS server with which you are attempting to set up replication because you may not have NetBIOS name resolution with that server until replication is in place. This may be the case if you are configuring replication with a down level NT 4.0 WINS server that may not have an entry in DNS. If you are setting up WINS replication with another Windows 2000 or Windows Server 2003 server, you would be able to use the name because these operating systems use DNS for name resolution first.

EXAM WARNING

By default, in order for WINS replication to work, the members of any WINS server combination that you want to replicate must both be configured with a replication connection partner. Even though one replication connection specifies *push* and *pull*, the other WINS server must also be set up in order to accept the replication requests. Once both connection partners are set up, you can configure the *push/pull* replication based on your network topology. This default behavior can be changed by disabling (unchecking) the **Replicate only with partners** option checkbox. This is located by right-clicking on the **Replication Partners** object in your WINS MMC console and selecting **Properties**.

Automatically Creating Replication Partners

Automatically creating replication partners is done using a Windows 2000 and Windows Server 2003 configuration feature called Automatic Partner Configuration. It is configured by selecting the checkbox option on the **Advanced** tab of the **Properties** of your Replication Partners object.

1. Click **Start | Administrative Tools | WINS** to open your WINS MMC snap-in console.

2. Right-click on **Replication Partners** and select **Properties**.

3. Click the **Advanced** tab and select the checkbox option labeled **Enable automatic partner configuration** as shown in Figure 4.20.

Automatic partner configuration will use multicast packets to find and configure WINS server replication partners. To reduce this multicast traffic, you can change the default values for both the *multicast interval* and *multicast TTL*. The multicast interval defaults to every 40 minutes and is defined as the amount of time between multicast packets sent to the WINS server group address. The multicast TTL defaults to two seconds and is the amount of time a multicast packet waits to hear a response from the WINS server group before timing out.

Figure 4.20 Enabling Automatic Partner Configuration

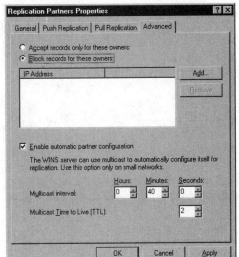

TEST DAY TIP

In order for the automatic partner configuration option to work in Windows Server 2003 WINS, your network router must support multicasting. If your routers do not support multicasting, your WINS replication partners will be set up only with WINS servers that reside on the same physical subnet. Windows Server 2003 WINS servers will use the multicast address 224.0.1.24 to discover and establish WINS replication partners.

Configuring Your Push/Pull Partner Relationships

After you have chosen a replication partner method, you need to establish the way replication takes place between your newly replicating WINS servers. There are two ways in which WINS data is replicated. It is either *pulled* by SERVER1 from SERVER2, or *pushed* from SERVER1 to SERVER2. By default, when replication partners are set up, either manually or automatically, they are set up as both push and pull replication partners. The default settings are displayed in Figure 4.21. You can configure connection-specific replication of push/pull relationships on the **Properties** page of each replication partner.

1. Click **Start | Administrative Tools | WINS** to open your WINS MMC snap-in console.

2. Highlight **Replication Partners** and select the *replication partner* you want in the right-side pane.

3. Right-click on the *replication partner* and select **Properties**.

Figure 4.21 Configuring Push/Pull Partnerships

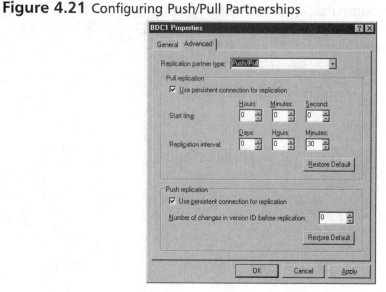

You can also configure general push/pull relationships on the **Properties tab** of the **Replication Partners** main object container as discussed later.

Pull Replication

Pull replication uses a configurable time interval in determining when the WINS server will pull data from a replication partner. By default this time is set to every 30 minutes.

Pull replication should be used if you have slower network connectivity between your WINS servers. Because you can configure the time between replication intervals, you can better determine when you may need more bandwidth and time it accordingly.

There are five configurable parameters you can set up on a Pull partner's configuration page. To open this page:

1. Click **Start | Administrative Tools | WINS** to open your WINS MMC snap-in console.

2. Right-click **Replication Partners** and select **Properties**.

3. Click the **Pull Replication** tab as shown in Figure 4.22.

The parameters that you can set up include the following:

- **Start time** This time interval tells your WINS service what time to start automatic Pull replication. By default this is set to 0:0:0. This states that pull replication will not happen automatically.

- **Replication interval** This time interval tells your WINS service how long it should wait before initiating a pull replication with its partners. It is configured for 30 minutes by default.

- **Number of retries** This is the number of times the WINS service will attempt to connect to one of its replication partners in the event of a failed connection. By default it is set to 3.

- **Start pull replication at service startup** This specifies whether the WINS service will pull replicas from its partners at the initialization of the WINS service.

- **Use persistent connections for pull replication partners** This specifies that after a connection is made to a replication partner, that connection remains open for use in future replication attempts. It is turned on by default.

Test Day Tip

Though pull partners allow you to configure replication based on a set amount of time, be careful when setting this time too high. As dynamic as WINS is, changes happen frequently and if databases are not synchronized that frequently, name resolution requests may fail.

Figure 4.22 Configuring Pull Partnership Parameters

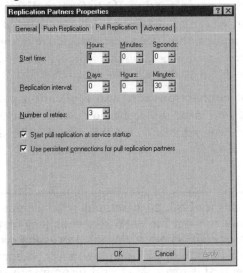

Push Replication

Push replication uses a configurable number, representing the number of changes in its database, before it will send a message to its replication partner informing them that there is data to replicate. Its replication partner must respond with a positive replication request before a push partner will *push* its database changes to its partner.

A push partner should be used if there are high-speed fast links between your WINS servers. This assures that you can keep your WINS databases synchronized more frequently with an up-to-date synchronous copy on each server, at the cost of a little more bandwidth.

There are four configurable parameters you can set up on a push partner's configuration page. To open this page:

1. Click **Start | Administrative Tools | WINS** to open your WINS MMC snap-in console.

2. Right-click **Replication Partners** and select **Properties**.

3. Click the **Push Replication** tab as shown in Figure 4.23.

The four configurable parameters include:

- **At service startup** This instructs the WINS server to notify its partner of its database status upon initialization of the WINS service. It is off by default.

- **When address changes** This specifies whether pull partners are informed when address *changes* are made. This is also off by default.

- **Number of changes in version ID before replication** This specifies the number of database record updates that have to be made before a push partner will inform its replication partners that changes are ready to be pushed. This is set to 0 by default, essentially meaning that although enabled, push replication itself is turned off.

- **Use persistent connections for push replication partners** This specifies that after a connection is made to a replication partner, that connection remains open for use in future replication attempts. It is turned on by default.

TEST DAY TIP

Persistent connections for both push and pull relationships should be used only if high speed data lines connect the WINS servers as they may congest lower bandwidth lines. Persistent connections lower the processing cycles of WINS servers because they do not have to open multiple connection agreements each time a WINS replication request is made. Microsoft recommends using these connections if bandwidth is available.

Figure 4.23 Configuring Push Partnership Parameters

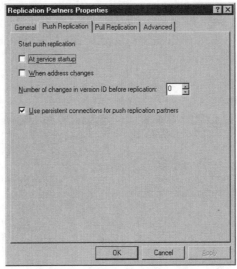

Figure 4.24 displays a graphical visualization of what happens after the configuration of Push/Pull partnerships are in effect.

Figure 4.24 Displaying Push/Pull Replication Traffic

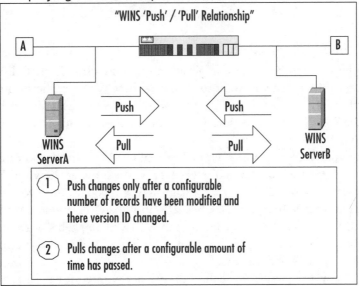

By default, replication is allowed only if the WINS server you wish to replicate SERVER1 with is also set up as a replication partner with *SERVER1*. This is configurable in the **Properties** window of the Replication Partners container's **General** tab, as shown in Figure 4.25. Also configurable on this page is the **Overwrite unique static mappings at this server (migrate on)**. With this option checkbox checked, you are telling WINS to treat static records like dynamic ones, and use the version ID of the record to determine the most recent version is when replicating records. By default, static records are never overwritten and thus remain static.

Figure 4.25 Configuring General Replication Rules

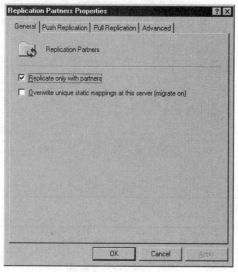

Manually Forcing Replication

Even after you have established a good replication topology using Push/Pull relationships, there may come a time when you want to manually force WINS replication between all replication partners on a server, or just between two WINS servers. This can be accomplished using the WINS MMC Console. Click **Start | Administrative Tools | WINS** to open your WINS MMC snap-in console.

To replicate your WINS database with all its replication partners, you can right-click on your **Replication Partners** object and select **Replicate Now** as shown in Figure 4.26. Selecting **Replicate Now** will display a message asking if you are sure you want to force replication with all your WINS servers. Click **OK** to initiate this request. You will be alerted that your request has been queued on the WINS servers. This warning appears due to the fact that this request may be more bandwidth intensive than the alternative of replicating with just a single WINS server.

To replicate only a single WINS replication partner with your database, you have two options:

- Start Push Replication
- Start Pull Replication

To Start Push Replication, right-click on that replication partner under the **Replication Partners** object, and select **Start Pull Replication** as shown in Figure 4.27. You will be prompted with a warning message stating that this may increase network traffic. Click **Yes** to continue with your request and a message appears stating that your request has been queued on the WINS server. Click **OK** to clear the message.

If you select the **Start Push Replication** option, you will be prompted with the alternate window shown in Figure 4.28, asking you if you want to **start with this partner only**, or to **propagate to all partners**. Select **Start with this partner only** and click **OK**. A message appears stating that your request has been queued on the WINS server. Click **OK** to clear the message.

Figure 4.26 Forcing WINS Replication with All Replication Partners

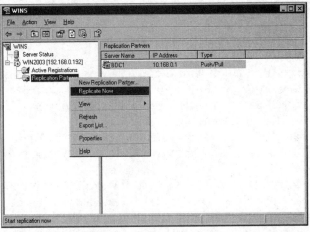

Figure 4.27 Forcing Only Push or Pull Replication with One WINS Server

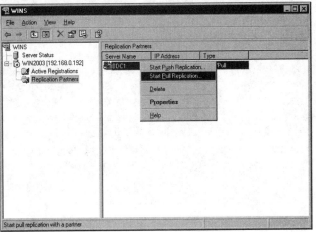

Figure 4.28 Forcing Only Push or Pull Replication with One WINS Server

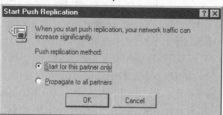

Automatically Configure Replication Partners to Only a Subset of WINS Servers

Windows 2000 first introduced the concept of Automatic Partner Configuration. Automatic Partner Configuration could be set up in order to allow your WINS server to scan the network, picking up other WINS servers and automatically creating replication partner information with them. This was great because administrators no longer had to worry about setting up WINS replication partners, especially on each physical WINS server, as was the case with Windows NT 4.0. However, Automatic Partner Configuration had its drawbacks. What if you did not want to replicate with every WINS server on your network? Well, Windows 2000 allowed you to specify a block list in which server IP addresses on this list were not included in your replication topology.

Windows Server 2003 WINS enhanced this configuration method because it lacked the granularity of securing your WINS servers against other WINS servers that you did not know about—in essence, *rogue* WINS servers. With the use of Automatic Partner Configuration and a block list technique, you (as the administrator) had to be aware of the WINS servers you wanted to physically add to your block list. Windows Server 2003 WINS allows you to specify an acceptance list, allowing only servers entered on this list as valid replication partners. You can do this by selecting the **Accept records only for these owners** option button shown in Figure 4.29.

Windows Server 2003 WINS still has the ability to choose the **Block records for these owners** method of configuration if so desired. However, when using Automatic Partner Configuration, it is a much better idea to stick with entering WINS servers you know about to avoid the possibility of running into a rogue WINS server. Depending on your configuration, replication of static WINS records may overwrite valid dynamic records in your database. If so, a rogue WINS server can render your NetBIOS resolution solution useless in a matter of minutes.

Continued

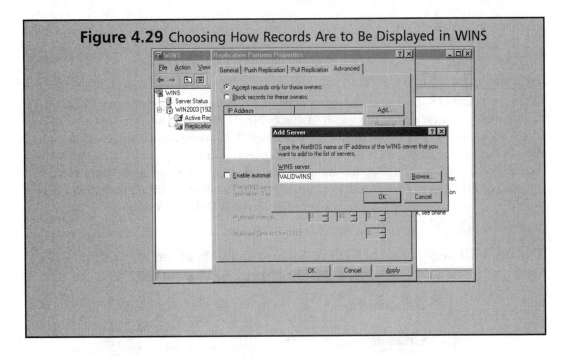

Figure 4.29 Choosing How Records Are to Be Displayed in WINS

TEST DAY TIP

Building a *block* or *accept* list for WINS replication is in no way tied to Automatic Partner Configuration and can be used regardless. However, if you are not using automatic configuration, you should already know the servers you intend to replicate with, because you will have to set them up manually. Thus, choosing the **Block records** option over the **Accept records** option is not a wise decision because it limits you to blocking only servers you know about, but not ones you don't. Using the **Accept records** option allows you to guarantee that only servers you know about will be involved in your WINS replication topology.

Managing WINS Records and Its Database

There are a few identifying tasks we will be discussing next, which define and identify the ways you can successfully manage and maintain your WINS database.

- Searching for WINS records
- Adding and Removing WINS records
- Maintaining your WINS database
  1. Record Reconciliation and Integrity
  2. Database Consistency

3.   Database Size

4.   Advanced Performance Options

Searching for WINS Records

WINS is a database, and like all databases must be maintained to meet the performance requirements of hundreds to thousands of chatty NetBIOS clients on your network. Every WINS client on your network must register its NetBIOS name and IP address with your WINS server. Along with their name, NetBIOS clients register any available NetBIOS service they have running on their machine. Some of these services and applications require special NetBIOS identifiers in order for other NetBIOS clients to locate them. They register themselves as hexadecimal address numbers in the WINS server database as shown under the *Type* field in Figure 4.30.

Figure 4.30 Registration of NetBIOS Services Show Up as Hex Numbers in WINS

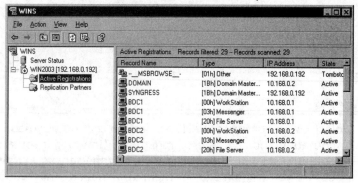

These are the same hexadecimal service locator record identifiers that we discussed earlier for use in your LMHOSTS file. These hex numbers are actually appended as the sixteenth byte in the NetBIOS 15 byte name.

Based on these facts, you may find that some machines register three, four, maybe five times with the same WINS server. This can lead to rather large and complex databases. For this reason, the WINS MMC console allows for you to search for records and filter them by name or IP address. The searchable feature in WINS leads to easier troubleshooting when you are trying to track down a NetBIOS naming conflict or resolution problem. To search the WINS database, follow these two steps:

1.   Click **Start | Administrative Tools | WINS** to open your WINS MMC snap-in console.

2.   Right-click your **WINS** *server name* and select **Display Records**.

New & Noteworthy...

New Ways to Search the WINS Database

Windows Server 2003 has introduced a new way to search for WINS records within the WINS MMC snap-in console interface. Though the WINS database has not been significantly changed, the way you can search for records within the database has a new look and feel as well as some new functionality. The ability to cache searched records is now available, enabling administrators to speed up future searches on similar records. Before the Windows Server 2003 and Windows XP Administrative Tools MMC snap-ins, WINS records had to be searched on by *record name* (Find by Name) or *record owner* (Find by Owner) exclusively. This was apparent in the interface and limited the ability to group these two together for a more detailed centric search. In Windows 2000, you could search for WINS records only by one of two methods:

- By Record Name exclusively
- By Record Owner and record type exclusively

In Windows Server 2003 you can search for WINS records in any of the following combinations:

- By Record Name
- By Owner
- By Type
- Any combination of the three

Following these numbered steps will teach you how to pinpoint specific records in your WINS database:

1. You can search your WINS database using the preceding combinations by right-clicking **Active Registrations** in your WINS MMC console and selecting **Display Records** as shown in Figure 4.31.

Figure 4.31 Displaying Records in Your WINS Database

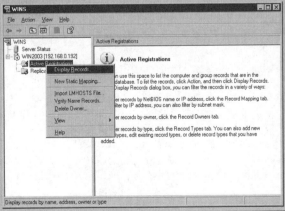

Continued

2. You will be presented with a **Display Records dialogue window** and three configurable tabs (shown in Figure 4.32):

- Record Mapping
- Record Owners
- Record Types

Figure 4.32 Choosing How Records Are to Be Displayed in WINS

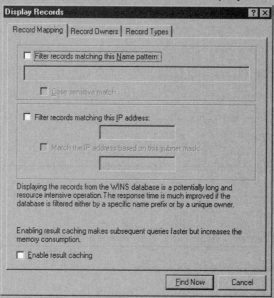

3. Each one of the tabs can contain its own data, and the search will be issued as a combination of all of them.

The new searching console has two other nice features, shown in Figure 4.32:

- The ability to *filter* your record search by a specific IP address or IP subnet

- The ability to *cache* your results

The filter option just gives you one more way to zero in and fine tune your records search. The caching option, on the other hand, helps when you have a very large database and are doing many searches against the same data sorts. By checking the **Enable result caching** option checkbox, all searches that are run against that WINS database, regardless of query type, are cached locally. Thus, if you were going to be running the same query five times in one day, the last four

Continued

times would be significantly faster as they would be read from cache. These results are cached locally on the machine running the query, not the WINS server itself. If one query is cached locally, and a different query is run that may contain a subset of the previous query, data in that subset is obtained locally, whereas the newer data must be obtained from the live WINS server database.

EXAM WARNING

Be careful when using Enable result caching option as there are two potential caveats:

1. Cached queries are stored in local memory and depending on the query size can degrade local system performance.
2. Cached queries are static and thus do not change with the dynamic changes of your WINS database. Don't rely on cached queries over a period of time as by design, WINS records change frequently.

Adding and Removing WINS Records

The WINS database is dynamic in nature, leaving the administrator with little to do as far as record management is concerned. This is a far cry from the static LMHOSTS file, and the main reason why WINS has almost completely eliminated the need to use an LMHOSTS file. However, there may come a time when you need to enter manual records into your WINS database. These records are considered *static*, and by default remain constant in your WINS database tables.

Creating Static Records

Though WINS registers everything dynamically for WINS clients, it does not for non-WINS clients. We discuss more about how non-WINS clients use WINS by means of a proxy later on in the chapter, but for now we will discuss how you can enter entries manually in your WINS database for non-WINS clients. This enables your WINS clients to query all of your non-WINS NetBIOS clients by way of WINS and not a broadcast. Static entries can be entered once and are by default replicated to all configured replication partners. There are five different types of static NetBIOS names you can enter into your WINS database. They are the same NetBIOS names that WINS registers automatically and are outlined in Table 4.4. Exercise 4.04 will walk you through creating a static WINS database record.

Table 4.4 Static NetBIOS Name Types

Type	Description
Unique	Used to identify a single NetBIOS name to IP address. When this type is selected, three entries are created: [00h] WorkStation, [03h] Messenger, and [20h] File Server.
Group (*Normal Group*)	Used to add the static entry of a computer into a workgroup used on your network. If this type is used, the IP address of the computer is resolved via broadcast and not stored in WINS.
Domain Name	Used to identify a domain name mapping of NT domain controllers with a [1ch] entry.
Internet Group	Used to define special groups used for administration. Each Internet group is represented by a shared group name with an entry of [20h].
Multihomed	Used to identify a computer with more than one interface card with different IP addresses or more than one IP address bound to the same interface card.

EXERCISE 4.04

ADDING STATIC WINS RECORDS

In this exercise, we will show you how to manually add static WINS records of type *unique* to your database.

1. Click **Start | Administrative Tools | WINS** to open your WINS MMC snap-in console.

2. Highlight your **Active Registrations** container. Right-click and choose **New Static Mapping** as shown in Figure 4.33.

Figure 4.33 Creating New Static Mapping

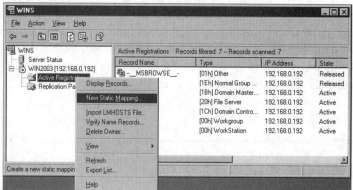

3. In the **New Static Mapping** dialog window, type the **NetBIOS computer name** of the non-WINS client as shown in Figure 4.34. Leave the default type of *unique* and leave the *NetBIOS scope* field blank.

4. In the **IP address** field, type the **IP address** of the non-WINS NetBIOS name.

5. Click **OK**. The three *unique* NetBIOS entries are added immediately in the WINS database as discussed in Table 4.4 and shown in Figure 4.35.

Figure 4.34 Creating New Static Mapping

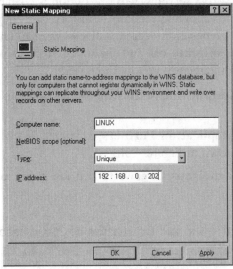

6. Notice the small x under the static column field. Click the Static field to sort the database and view all static entries in order.

Figure 4.35 Showing Static Entry in WINS Database

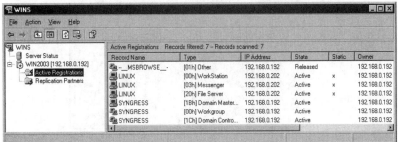

Be forewarned about static WINS entries. By default, they override any dynamic entry with which they conflict. This is particularly evident in the case where an administrator uses the WINS console to import an LMHOSTS file into the WINS database. The importation of an LMHOSTS file into WINS creates static entries by default. If those entries happen to be current entries of Windows type machines in your database, they will soon be changed from dynamic records to static records. This is not a good idea. The LMHOSTS import feature should be used with caution and used only to import non-WINS client records.

This default behavior can be overwritten with an option called **Overwrite unique static mappings at this server (migrate on)**. This is a server by server option and can be set differently on each WINS server. When this option is enabled, it treats static entries as if they were dynamic entries, allowing version ID history to take precedence as to what the most recent record wins in replication decisions. If you want to change the default feature, which is also referred to as **migrate off**, and allow static records on a single WINS server to be overwritten by dynamic records, follow these steps:

1. Click **Start | Administrative Tools | WINS** to open your WINS MMC snap-in console.

2. Highlight your **Replication Partners** container. Right-click and choose **Properties** as shown in Figure 4.36.

3. Click the option checkbox **Overwrite unique static mappings at this server (migrate on)**.

Figure 4.36 Enabling the Migrate On Feature of Static Records

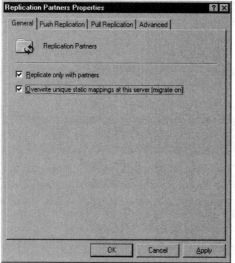

Exam Warning

Using the option **Overwrite unique static mappings at this server (migrate on)** affects only the following two types of static entries:

- Unique entries
- Multihomed entries

Configuring & Implementing...

Manually Stop Static WINS Records from Replicating

By default, static entries are replicated like all other WINS database entries. However, static entries are treated a bit differently by default—if they are in conflict with a valid dynamic record, they will overwrite that dynamic record. A way around this behavior is to specifically configure static entries to not replicate all or just a handful of its configured replication partners. You can do this by editing the Windows registry and adding a **REG_DWORD** value of **OnlyDynRecs** with a data value of 1 to the following registry key:HKLM\SYSTEM\CurrentControlSet\Services\Wins\Partners\Push\IPAddress

Note that the registry key mentioned in the text is present only on machines that are configured to be WINS servers.

In this case IPAddress is the IP address of the replication partner you do not want to replicate static entries.

In additional to adding the preceding registry key entry for each partner you do not want to replicate static entries to, you must have the option **Replicate Only with Partners** enabled. This is enabled by default with these steps:

1. Click **Start | Administrative Tools | WINS** to open your WINS MMC snap-in console.
2. Highlight your **Replication Partners** container. Right-click and choose **Properties.**
3. Verify that **Replicate Only with Partners** is checked.

As records are added to your WINS database, either dynamically or manually, they are organized in a format that is descriptive in determining what the records are, who owns them, whether they are expiring soon, and so on. The WINS database table contains field headers that allow you to sort your WINS data based on the field name. Field names you can sort on and their descriptions are detailed in Table 4.5.

Table 4.5 WINS Record Entry Descriptions

Field Name	Description
Record Name	The registered NetBIOS name, representing a *unique name*, a *group*, an *internet group*, or *multihomed* computer.
Type	The service identifier along with its hexadecimal value.
IP Address	The IP address of the NetBIOS name.
State	The state of the record in the database. This can be *active*, *released*, or *tombstoned*.
Static	Displays a static entry as opposed to a dynamic one.
Owner	Displays the owner of a record or that to which a record was originally registered.
Version	A unique hexadecimal number assigned to each registered record, used to determine the most recent record version during replication.
Expiration	Displays the date and time the record's lease will expire.

Each one of these fields tells something a little bit different about each of the records in WINS. Particularly we will focus on just two, as the rest are covered elsewhere throughout the chapter.

- State
- Expiration

State

A record's *state* tells you as an administrator whether or not it is alive on the network, removed from the network, or whether it is scheduled to be deleted from the database. The three possible states a record can be labeled are defined in Table 4.6.

Table 4.6 WINS Database Record States

Record State	Description
Active	Describes a record that is alive on the network as a NetBIOS name.
Released	Describes a record that has asked to remove its name from the database and is no longer alive on the network, freeing up that NetBIOS name for another.
Tombstoned	Describes a record that is marked for deletion upon the next extinction interval cleanup.

When WINS clients register with their configured WINS server, they are given what is termed a lease. A lease is defined as an amount of time that a NetBIOS name will remain in use and registered to a client before it is marked as expired and eventually removed from the database. Upon time of initial client registration and before the *renewal interval* is reached, a client's record is considered to be *active*.

If a client's NetBIOS machine is shut down properly, a release request is sent to its WINS servers requesting that WINS remove its NetBIOS name from the database so queries against that machine will show that it is not active but offline. Until that client boots up and re-registers or refreshes its name with WINS, another client boots up with the same name and registers itself with WINS or before the *extinction interval* is met, that record will be in a state of being *released*.

Expiration

The expiration field shows the date and time a client's lease is expected to run out. If the client has not contacted the WINS server to renew or refresh its lease at that time, the record will be marked as expired and will eventually be deleted from the database.

The *renewal interval*, *extinction interval*, *extinction timeout*, and *verification timeout* are all configurable times, located on the Intervals tab on the Properties of your WINS *server name* shown in Figure 4.37.

Figure 4.37 Configuring WINS Record Cleanup Intervals

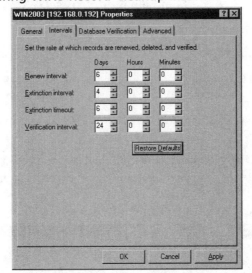

Figure 4.37 shows all of the default timing intervals you can configure on your WINS server. We explain in more detail what each of these different time intervals do for you and your server:

- **Renewal interval** Defined as the frequency a WINS client will renew its name with the WINS server. By default this is six days.

- **Extinction interval** Defined as the interval between when an entry is marked as released from the database and when it is marked as extinct (*scavenged* or removed from the database). The default interval is four days.

- **Extinction timeout** Defined as the interval between when an entry is marked for *extinction* and when the entry is actually *scavenged* or removed from the database. The default is six days and cannot be less than 24 hours.

- **Verification interval** Defined as the interval a WINS server needs to verify that the records in its database that it does not own and has acquired via replication from its partners, are still in fact *active*.

Along with these automatic configuration intervals, it may be necessary for you to manually go in and delete or schedule for deletion (*tombstone*) certain records for yourself. As records go into a *released state*, they stay there for the configured *extinction interval* in order to make sure their state is fully replicated around your WINS replication topology. At that time they are marked as **extinct** and WINS will scavenge or remove them permanently from the database at the scheduled extinction timeout interval.

There are two ways you can manually remove WINS records from your database:

1. Manually initiate scavenging.

2. Manually delete a record from within the WINS database:

   - Manually delete a record from a single WINS server

   - Manually tombstone a record so that it replicates throughout the topology

By manually initiating scavenging, you are telling WINS to skip the extinction interval time and mark everything for removal now. To initiate manual scavenging, do the following:

1. Click **Start | Administrative Tools | WINS** to open your WINS MMC snap-in console.

2. Highlight your **WINS** *server name*. Right-click and select **Scavenge Database**. You will receive the informational message shown in Figure 4.38.

Figure 4.38 Manually Queuing a Request to Scavenge Your WINS Records

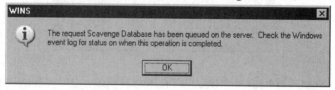

The second two options are completed from within your WINS database, by physically pressing the Delete key on a record you want to remove. Two options exist when trying to remove a record this way (as shown in Figure 4.39):

- **Delete the record only from this server** Deletes the WINS record only from that WINS server and does not replicate the fact that it was deleted. The record is immediately deleted upon clicking **OK** in Figure 4.39.

- **Replicate deletion of this record to other servers (tombstoned)**
  Schedules the record for deletion by expiring the record and replicating the fact
  that it is to be expired on all WINS servers at the configured extinction interval.
  In order to manually tombstone a record, WINS must first take ownership of that
  record, and prompts you with a warning message as shown in Figure 4.40.

Figure 4.39 Choosing a Way to Manually Delete Your WINS Records

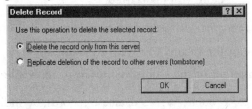

Figure 4.40 Warning Message before Manually Tombstoning a WINS Record

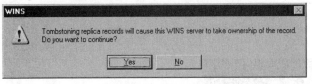

After you confirm that you want to take ownership of the record and manually tombstone it by clicking **Yes** in Figure 4.40, WINS marks the record state as Tombstoned, as
shown in Figure 4.41.

Figure 4.41 Displaying the State of Tombstoned Records in Your WINS Database

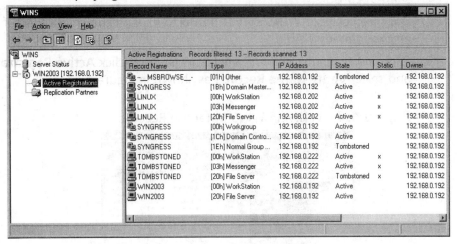

Record Reconciliation and Integrity

Like DHCP, discussed in Chapter 3, WINS is a dynamic database. This means that all these hundreds and thousands of records are constantly being registered, unregistered and reregistered. This causes tremendous activity within your WINS database. It is important to maintain your WINS database and periodically check its data for validity. Data validity is accomplished though *reconciliation*. Reconciling your database records ensures a level of data integrity that is essential in any database. To reconcile your WINS database records, you need to know a few things before you get started:

- IP address of the server you want to reconcile
- NetBIOS name of the record you want to reconcile
- Hexadecimal number of the record you want to reconcile

There are two ways to reconcile WINS database records: by individually typing all the records by hand or by importing multiple records from a text file called *names.txt*. Similarly, you can select each WINS server's IP address you want to reconcile the data against, or you can import a list of WINS servers. In Exercise 4.05 we focus on using the manual method by verifying just a single WINS server record.

EXERCISE 4.05

RECONCILING WINS RECORDS

In this exercise, we will show you how to manually reconcile one of your WINS file server records.

1. Click **Start | Administrative Tools | WINS** to open your WINS MMC snap-in console.

2. Double-click your **WINS server name** to expand the child object if they are not already visible.

3. Click and highlight **Active Registrations**. Right-click **Active Registrations** and select **Verify Name Records** as shown in Figure 4.42.

Figure 4.42 Verifying WINS Database Records

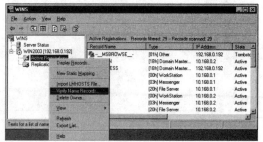

4. On the **Verify Name Records** dialog window click the **List (case sensitive)** option button under the *Name records* box and type the exact name of the WINS record or records you want to reconcile, including in it the hexadecimal service locator as shown in Figure 4.43. Click **Add** when you are done.

Figure 4.43 Specifying WINS Records to Reconcile

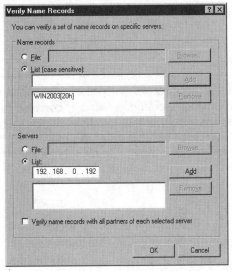

5. Looking at the same dialog window (Figure 4.43), click **List** under the *Servers* box. Type the **IP address** of the WINS server or servers you want to reconcile the preceding record against. Click **Add** when you are done.

6. Click **OK** to verify the records.

7. Figure 4.44 shows the results of a successfully verified record.

Figure 4.44 Verifying WINS Database Records

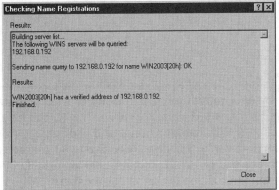

TEST DAY TIP

When typing in WINS database record names, you must use all capital letters because this field is case sensitive and requires that reconciled names match the exact WINS database format. For the same reason, you must append the hexadecimal service locator value in the form of (*hex*), for example, ***20** for a file server or ***03** for the messenger service. You can refer back to Table 4.3 for a reference to these identifiers.

NOTE

If you want to verify the same record with all of your WINS server's replication partners, click the option box labeled **Verify name records** with all partners of each selected servers. Note that this will take considerably longer, as each partner from each server you choose has to be physically communicated to over the network.

Database Consistency

Along with issues of your data validity comes the important matter of database consistency. Verifying database consistency determines if your database has any incorrect entries. Database consistency compares all the records that it pulls from remote WINS databases with those in its local database. Based on what it finds in the comparison, it does one of the following two actions:

- If the record in the local WINS database is an exact match of the record that was pulled from the remote owner database, the local record is time stamped with that of the record owner's database.

- If the record that is pulled from the remote owner database has a higher version ID (meaning that it is the most recent record) than the local copy of that record, it is marked for deletion and the remote record copy is added to the local database.

TEST DAY TIP

All WINS servers have a default version ID number that they stamp on their records when they are initially created via registration. This ID can be altered by going to the **Properties** of your **WINS server name** and clicking the **Advanced** tab. By changing the **Starting Version ID (hexadecimal)** you can essentially force the replication of this server's records using a higher version ID than normal, and effectively making those records appear to be the most current.

Two consistency checks you can run against your WINS database, either manually or automatically via scheduling, are

- Database consistency
- Version consistency

Database consistency checks your WINS database against other replicated WINS server databases to see if its data is consistent. You can manually check your database consistency with these steps:

1. Click **Start | Administrative Tools | WINS** to open your WINS MMC snap-in console.

2. Right-click your **WINS** *server name* and select **Verify Database Consistency** as shown in Figure 4.45.

NOTE

A warning message will pop up, alerting you of the network bandwidth intensive operation you are about to perform. Microsoft is recommending that you run this check during off hours so you do not affect production. The details of this message are displayed in Figure 4.46.

3. Click **Yes** on the pop-up warning message to schedule the consistency check. You will see a second pop-up message in Figure 4.47, telling you that the database consistency check has been queued on the server and will log an event in the event log with details of its operation.

Figure 4.45 Verifying Database Consistency

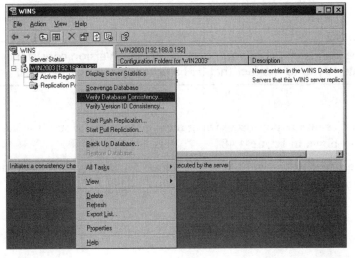

Figure 4.46 Verifying Database Consistency Warning Message

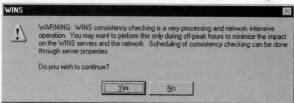

Figure 4.47 Scheduling Database Consistency Success Message

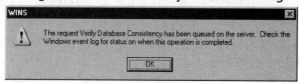

Version consistency is a process that is run against all your WINS servers to verify that each WINS server has the highest version number on all of the records it has as being owned. WINS servers will obtain ownership of any record that is either manually (statically) created on them, or physically registered with them. They do not own records that are replicated to them. Version IDs are kept on each record for replication purposes. They are used in the event replication is set up with multiple WINS servers, and used to ensure that they have the most recent copy of each client data record. *Version consistency* can be verified with these steps:

1. Click **Start | Administrative Tools | WINS** to open your WINS MMC snap-in console.

2. Right-click your **WINS** *server name* and select **Verify Version ID Consistency** as shown in Figure 4.45.

NOTE

A warning message will pop up, explaining what Version consistency checking will do and alerts you to the fact that it is a potentially long operation.

3. Click **Yes** on the pop-up warning message to agree to start the verification process as shown in Figure 4.48.

4. Version consistency will pop up a progress window with the outputted data as shown in Figure 4.49.

Figure 4.48 Verifying Version ID Consistency

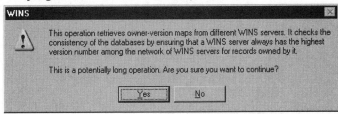

Figure 4.49 Verifying Version ID Output

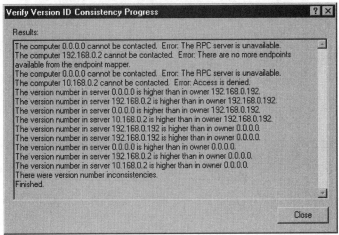

Automatic database verification can also be set up on your WINS servers. This should be set up to run at off-peak hours when your NetBIOS resolution needs are at their lowest. This process is both network and server intensive. To configure your WINS server for automatic database verification, do the following:

1. Click **Start | Administrative Tools | WINS** to open your WINS MMC snap-in console.

2. Right-click your **WINS** *server name* and select **Properties**.

3. Click the **Database Verification** tab and select the checkbox option **Verify database consistency every** as shown in Figure 4.50.

4. Enter the desired frequency in *hour,* as well as the *beginning hour,* and the **Maximum number of records verified each period**.

NOTE

Be careful with this setting because as it increases, so does the load on your WINS server.

5.   You also have the ability to choose whether you want to verify the database against only **Owner servers**, or against **Randomly selected partners**.

Figure 4.50 Automatically Scheduling Database Verification

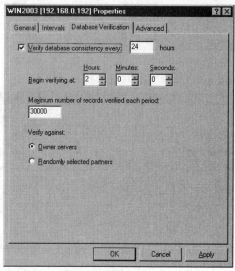

Database Size

As you add more and more WINS clients to your Windows domain, the WINS database will continue to grow larger. By default, the WINS service is intelligent enough to automatically schedule the database to be compacted online at off intervals. However there may be times when you find it necessary to manually compact the database. The WINS database is located in the %systemroot%\system32\wins directory by default and is named wins.mdb. Its database is made up of the long-time Microsoft standard JET database engine. Thus, we use the same jetpack.exe tool we have for years to compact the database. To manually compact your WINS database, follow these steps:

1.   Click **Start | Run** and type **cmd.exe** to enter a command prompt window.

2.   Stop the WINS database by typing **net stop wins**.

3.   Traverse to the directory structure %systemroot%\system32\wins or to where you have placed your database. If using the default location, type cd\ and then type cd %systemroot%\system32\wins.

4.   Run the jetpack compacting utility by typing **jetpack wins.mdb temp_dbname.mdb** where *temp_dbname* is any name you want to assign that **jetpack** will use to compress the database to before copying it back to the name **wins.mdb**.

5.   Type **net start wins**.

The way jetpack compacts your WINS database is by way of a temporary database. Jetpack will compact the database to the temporary file, copy the temporary file back over the original file naming it wins.mdb, and than deleting the temporary file.

NOTE

There are plenty of WINS knowledge base articles on Microsoft's Web site that require the use of this tool in order to troubleshoot or resolve some sort of relevant issue.

Advanced Options

The Advanced tab on the **Properties** page of your WINS server contains a few more settings that we feel are important to identify. You can get to this configuration dialog window as shown in Figure 4.51 by clicking **Start | Administrative Tools | WINS** to open your WINS MMC snap-in console. Right-click your **WINS** *server name* and select **Properties**. Click the **Advanced** tab.

Figure 4.51 Configuring Advanced WINS Options

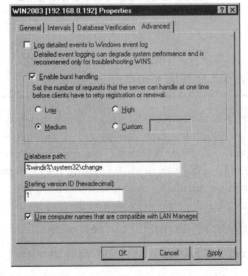

Configuration settings on this tab include:

- **Log detailed events to Windows event log** By checking this option checkbox, you will enable the WINS service to log WINS related events into the System log of your WINS server. By default this option is not enabled as it can be very taxing on your system. Logging should be enabled only when troubleshooting WINS-related problems. When you decide to enable WINS logging, be sure to increase the size of the System logs in the event viewer console because it will easily reach the default size limit quickly.

- **Enable burst handling** Burst handling is enabled by default and should not be disabled if at all possible. Burst handling is a feature introduced in Windows 2000 that allows your WINS server to take on excessive loads of WINS requests at one time. It does this by issuing short lease times to client requests when under a heavy load and cannot add those requests into its database. This may be caused by a sudden power outage that requires your entire company to reboot and log on all at once, trying to register their names with WINS. WINS will not register the names of these short-leased clients, but essentially will delay their registration for a little while until it can catch up with its database entries. When the short lease times expire, clients will again try to register their names with WINS. There are three preset *mode* settings that define the number of requests that can be queued before burst handling kicks in. There is also a custom field where you can enter in your own number. See Table 4.7 for a list of these settings and numbers.

Table 4.7 WINS Burst Handling Modes

Mode Setting	Number of Requests before Bursting Starts
Low	300
Medium	500
High	1000
Custom	Empty field to type a custom number

- **Database path** Microsoft does not recommend changing the path to where your WINS database and log files reside, but gives you the opportunity to do so. Changing this path will cause WINS to be stopped and restarted, so use caution and plan ahead when changing this field. A warning message stating this can be seen in Figure 4.52. If you do decide to change this location, you may need to do some post work cleanup, listed in the following bullets:
  - Copy files from the old path to the new path
  - Initiate immediate manual replication with partners
  - Change any custom scripts that may have been set to back up WINS
- **Starting Version ID** The number entered into this field determines the beginning version ID number of the WINS database. It is used to stamp new WINS records, which are later used to determine which version of a particular record is more recent during WINS replication. This is not usually a field you want to change, although it may be helpful in situations where you want to manually force the replication of a particular WINS database as having the highest record values for all its records. The default value for this field is 1.

Figure 4.52 Configuring the Default Database Path

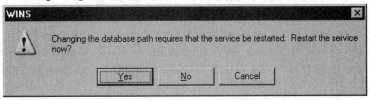

- **Use computer names that are compatible with LAN Manager** Use this setting only if you have non–Microsoft NetBIOS clients in your environment that will be registering with your WINS server. By default it is enabled and allows the registration of only 15 character NetBIOS names. Some non–Microsoft NetBIOS clients may need to register names that are 16 characters long and thus require this setting to be disabled.

EXAM WARNING

Before you change the **Database path** field, be sure the location you specify already exists. If not, WINS will fail to start and may cause you to have to restore WINS from backup.

EXAM WARNING

Prior to the introduction of burst handling support, Microsoft recommended setting up your server's WINS clients with only one address of one WINS server. This was because of the way WINS servers handled busy registration times: They wouldn't. This meant that registering clients would try to register services with their secondary WINS servers. Thus a single client may have its registered services split between two WINS servers. Whether these were set up to replicate or not may cause issues. Workstation clients do not typically register production-specific application services. Servers, on the other hand, do register application-specific services that need to be accessed by everybody. So, if a client goes to access a server service by looking at its primary WINS server, finds the server but not the service because it was registered on another server, that client may fail to connect to the service. This was prevented with the introduction of burst handling, because the WINS server was now able to handle a bigger load of client registrations at one time.

Back Up and Restore the WINS Database

The WINS database, like any other network critical database, must be backed up on a regular basis in case of corruption, disaster, or misconfiguration causing undesirable results. With the introduction of Windows Server 2003's new *Volume Shadow Copy* feature, there is an additional way to back up your WINS database. The most common backup methods are:

1. WINS MMC Console backup

    ■   Automatic Backup

    ■   Manual Backup

2. ntbackup.exe graphical utility

WINS MMC Console Backup

There are two ways to back up your WINS database via the MMC console. You either can back up the database manually, or set the database to be backed up manually upon server shutdown. To set the server to be automatically backed up, you must first provide a backup location.

Automatic Backup

To perform an automatic backup of your WINS database, follow these steps:

1. Click **Start | Administrative Tools | WINS** to open your WINS MMC snap-in console.

2. Right-click your **WINS** *server name* and select **Properties**.

3. In the WINS servers properties window, type the path you want to use to automatically back up the WINS database in the **default backup path** window. For example, *%systemroot%\system32\wins\backup*, as shown in Figure 4.53.

4. Check the **Back up database during server shutdown** option checkbox.

Figure 4.53 Configuring Your WINS Default Database Backup Path

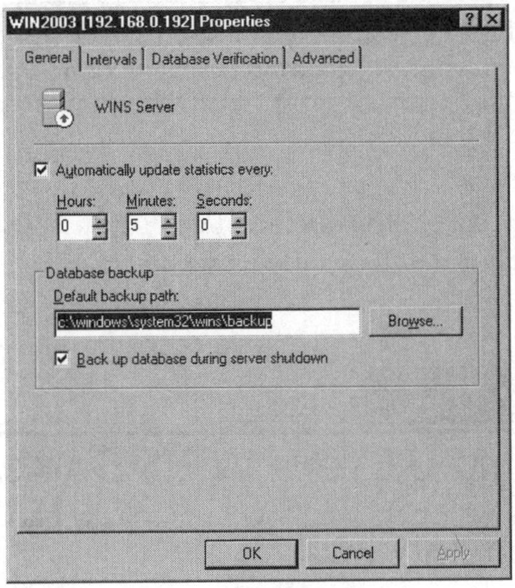

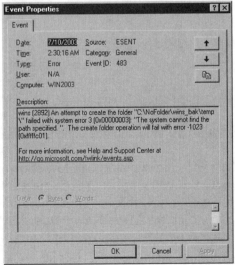

EXAM WARNING

In order for you to be able to select the **Back up database during server shut-down** option checkbox, the **default backup path** must be filled in. The **default backup path** location requires a valid existing folder directory. Although this field will allow you to type an invalid path, upon server shutdown you will receive Application Event errors stating that the path was invalid, as shown in Figure 4.54.

Figure 4.54 Configuring Default Database Backup Path Incorrectly

EXAM WARNING

If you set WINS to back up automatically upon server shutdown, WINS also will automatically back up your WINS database every 24 hours by default.

Manual Backup

You can manually back up your WINS database by using the WINS MMC snap-in found in your administrative tools menu. To manually back up your WINS database, follow the steps in Exercise 4.06.

EXERCISE 4.06

MANUALLY BACKING UP YOUR WINS DATABASE

In this exercise, we will show you how to manually back up your WINS database using the WINS MMC.

1. Click **Start | Administrative Tools | WINS** to open your WINS MMC snap-in console.

2. Right-click your **WINS server name** and select **Back Up Database** as shown in Figure 4.55.

Figure 4.55 Backing Up Your WINS Database

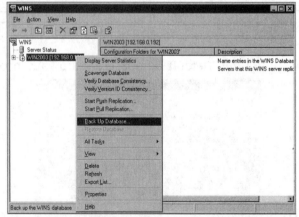

3. In the **Browse For Folder** dialog window shown in Figure 4.56, browse to a folder in which you want to place your WINS database backup. If you need to create a new folder, for example under your original WINS database folder, click the **Make New Folder** button and type the name of your new backup folder, as shown in the same figure.

4. Click **OK** and WINS will come back and alert you that your database has been backed up successfully, as shown in Figure 4.57.

Figure 4.56 Backing Up Your WINS Database

Figure 4.57 Successfully Backing Up Your WINS Database

NOTE

Each time you want to back up your WINS database manually you must select a folder location. You can use the same folder location each time, or select to create a new one in order to have multiple backup copies. If you select the same location each time, the existing backup database will be overwritten.

TEST DAY TIP

When you select to back up your database manually or if you configure it to be backed up automatically upon server shutdown, WINS automatically will create a folder structure beneath the one you provided. The additional folder structure path WINS uses is **\wins_bak\new**. Thus, the actual backup of the WINS database isn't truly in the path you choose. In reference to the example we used previously, the database backup path files would exist in a path resembling the following: **%systemroot%\system32\wins\backup\wins_bak\new**

---

ntbackup Graphical Utility

In prior versions of Windows, in order to use the built in ntbackup.exe utility to back up your WINS database, you had to stop the WINS service prior to starting your backup. This was true because the WINS database was constantly open, and thus could not be backed up. This led to the extra overhead of creating special batch file jobs that would automatically stop the WINS service, start an ntbackup job, and then restart the WINS service. If anyone needed to use WINS for NetBIOS resolution at the time of backup, they were out of luck.

With the introduction of Windows Server 2003 and its new Volume Shadow Copy feature, you can back up your WINS database online. Volume Shadow Copy enables the backup of open files by first caching them to its own database. To enable Volume Shadow Copy on your WINS server, follow the steps in Exercise 4.07.

EXERCISE 4.07

ENABLING VOLUME SHADOW COPY

In this exercise, we will show you how to enable Volume Shadow Copy to allow online backups on your WINS database.

1. Click **Start | My Computer | Open**.

2. Right-click the **system volume** and select **Properties**.

3. In the **systems volume Properties** dialog window, click the **Shadow Copies** tab as shown in Figure 4.58.

   Figure 4.58 Setting Shadow Copies on System Volume for Open WINS Database Backup

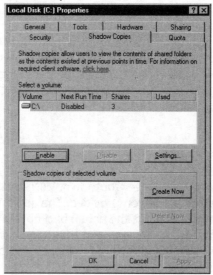

4. Highlight the **system volume** and click **Enable**. You will be presented with a warning message as shown in Figure 4.59. Click **Yes** to enable it.

Figure 4.59 Enabling Volume Shadow Copies Warning Message

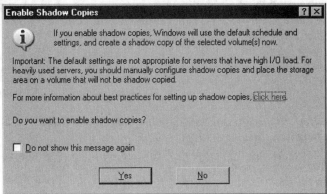

5. It may take a minute to enable, but once completed, you will see the first successful shadow of your system volume as shown in Figure 4.60.

6. You are now ready to run **ntbackup** against your WINS databases, and they will be backed up while they continue to run.

Figure 4.60 Successfully Creating Your First Volume Shadow Copy of the System Drive

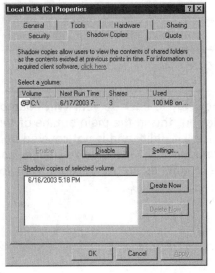

Configuring & Implementing...

Using the Command Line to Back Up WINS

You can back up your WINS database using the command line utility **netsh.exe**. netsh allows you to run interactively for manual backups or as a command script so that you can schedule it for automatic backups. Figure 4.61 shows this command as it would appear in a command shell. The command syntax to run the netsh command utility used in an automatic shell script is:

```
netsh wins \\winsserver init Backup Dir=c:\backupdir Type=0
```

where:

- **\\winsserver** is the name of your WINS server
- **C:\backupdir** is the name of the location you want to back up your database
- **Type=0** is for Full backups and **Type=1** is for Incremental backups

Figure 4.61 Backing Up Your WINS Database Using netsh

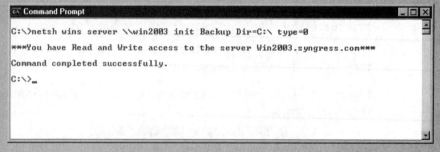

NOTE

There is another handy way to back up your WINS database, a tool called winscl.exe. We did not put this in the main outline of this section because it is a Windows 2000 resource kit utility and is not covered on the test. winsel.exe is included with the Windows 2000 resource kit utilities and not with the Windows Server 2003 resource kit utilities. To use it, run it from your command line, following these steps:

```
C:\>winscl.exe

C:>winscl.exe

TCP/IP or named pipe. Enter 1 for TCP/IP or 0 for named pipe

    -1

Address of Name Server to Contact— WIN2003

Command—BK
```

```
Full (1) or Incremental (any other) - 1

Backup File Path - C:\Backup
```

winscl.exe will automatically create a **/wins_bak** folder under the folder you specify. Make sure the folder you specify is already created because winscl.exe will not create it for you.

Manual Database Restore

To restore a previously backed up WINS database, you must first stop the WINS service, or the option to restore will be unavailable. To restore your WINS database, we will use the WINS MMC snap-in, found in your administrative tools menu. Follow the steps in Exercise 4.08 to become more familiar with WINS database recovery.

EXERCISE 4.08

MANUALLY RESTORING YOUR WINS DATABASE

In this exercise, we will show you how to restore a previously backed up WINS database. In order to restore a WINS database, you must first stop the WINS service.

1. Click **Start | Administrative Tools | WINS** to open your WINS MMC snap-in console.

2. Right-click your **WINS server name** and select **All Tasks | Stop** as shown in Figure 4.62.

Figure 4.62 Stopping Your WINS Service for Database Restore

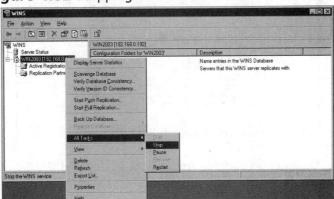

3. Once your WINS service is stopped, a red *X* will appear over your WINS server name. Right-click your **WINS server name** and select **Restore Database** as shown in Figure 4.63.

Figure 4.63 Selecting the Option to Restore Your WINS Database

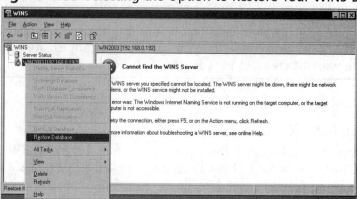

4. In the **Browse For Folder** dialog window shown in Figure 4.64, browse to the same folder location you originally backed up your WINS database in Exercise 4.07. You will want to select the exact folder *you* created, and not the one that was created automatically by the WINS backup procedure earlier (/wins_bak/new). If you select this automatically created folder, WINS will be unable to locate the backup, as it again appends that folder data for you.

Figure 4.64 Browsing to Restore Your WINS Database

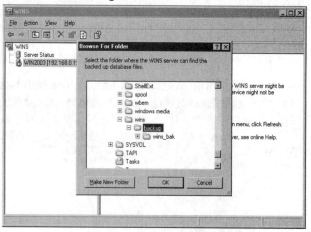

5. Click **OK** once you locate the correct folder and WINS will restore your database and automatically restart your WINS service as shown in Figure 4.65.

6. Figure 4.66 shows the message that appears if the database was restored successfully.

Figure 4.65 Restoring Your WINS Database Automatically Restarts Your WINS Service

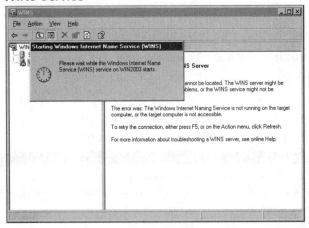

Figure 4.66 Successfully Restoring Your WINS Database

NOTE

You may notice when you try and run a WINS restore that the option is grayed out. This is by design because you cannot restore your WINS database until it knows that you have backed it up. As soon as you run through a backup, this option will become available.

Command-Line Restore

You can restore your WINS database using the command-line utility netsh.exe. netsh allows you to run interactively for manual restores or as a command script so that you can schedule it for automatic restores. Figure 4.67 shows this command as it would appear in a command shell. The command syntax to run the netsh command utility used in an automatic shell script is:

```
netsh wins \\winsserver init Restore Dir=c:\backupdir Type=0
```

where:

- **\\winserver** is the name of you WINS server
- **C:\backupdir** is the name of the location you want to restore your database from

Figure 4.67 Restoring Your WINS Database Using netsh

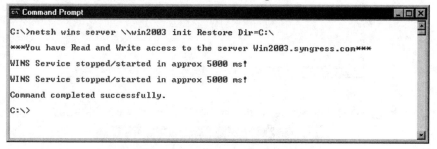

Configuring the WINS Client

WINS clients are clients that are in need of NetBIOS to IP name resolution, when broadcasting is not available or not the preferred method of resolution. Until you set up your clients as WINS clients, you really can't take advantage of the WINS service. Successful registration and reregistration with WINS is what enables clients to query other hosts without using broadcasts. WINS client configuration is accomplished by editing the TCP/IP stack on each client and pointing them to the correct WINS server or servers. Exercise 4.09 will walk you through configuring a Windows Server 2003 server as a WINS client.

TEST DAY TIP

Although you may have read that Microsoft Windows 2000 and Windows Server 2003 Active Directory does not require NetBIOS or WINS to function anymore, that does not negate the fact that applications outside of active directory may require these protocols to work. The following are three instances where you may not need to install WINS and use WINS clients:

- All your client and server operating systems are running Windows 2000, Windows XP, or Windows Server 2003.
- None of your network applications require the use of NetBIOS.
- Active Directory is in place and provides name resolution by means of DNS.

EXERCISE 4.09

CONFIGURING YOUR WINDOWS SERVER 2003 CLIENT TO USE WINS

In this exercise, we will show you how to enable your Windows Server 2003 as a WINS client.

1. Click **Start | Control Panel | Network Connections** and select **Local Area Connection**. Click the **Properties** button.

2. In the **Local Area Connections** dialog window, scroll down until you see **Internet Protocol (TCP/IP)** and highlight it. Click the **Properties** button.

3. In the **Internet Protocol (TCP/IP)** dialog window, click the **Advanced** button.

4. In the **Advanced TCP/IP Settings** dialog window, click the **WINS** tab as shown in Figure 4.68.

5. Click the **Add** button and type the **IP address** of your WINS servers as shown in Figure 4.69. Click **Add**.

6. You can use the two **arrow** buttons to prioritize your WINS servers if entering more than one. Those at the top of the list will be used before those underneath.

Figure 4.68 Configuring Your Client For WINS

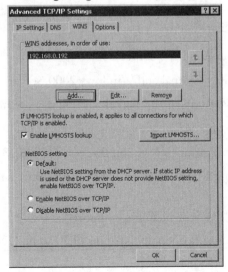

Figure 4.69 Adding Your WINS Server IP Address

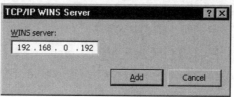

NOTE

In general, when configuring WINS clients, the difference in operating systems means that the configuration will be somewhat different as well, although the concept is the same. WINS is configured within each client's TCP/IP stack because its main goal is registering that stack's IP address with a central WINS database.

Exercise 4.09 showed you how to manually set up your client to use a WINS server. This typically is performed on servers because they are usually configured statically. The recommended and more common configuration is to distribute WINS server information to clients via the use of a DHCP server. For more about configuring the integration of WINS and DHCP, see the section "WINS and DHCP" later in this chapter.

Possible WINS Clients

There are a host of operating systems that can be configured as WINS clients. They include:

- Windows XP and Windows Server 2003

- Windows 2000 Professional and Windows 2000 Server

- Windows NT Workstation and Server version 3.5 or later

- Windows 95/98 and ME

- Windows for Workgroups V3.11 running the TCP/IP-32 stack

- MS-DOS running Microsoft's Network Client V3.0 using real-mode TCP/IP driver

- LAN Manager V2.2c not including support for OS/2

- Various non-Microsoft operating systems like Linux, UNIX, or Macintosh

WINS Proxy Agent

Though it is called Windows Internet Naming Service, WINS is not limited to Microsoft Windows clients using its services. Microsoft supports other clients using its database to register and query its database *if* those clients support using a WINS server as their name server. There are, however, certain circumstances where clients do not support the use of WINS yet understand NetBIOS naming and can use NetBIOS over TCP/IP. Microsoft supports these clients by means of a proxy.

A WINS proxy is a Windows computer, configured to listen for, capture, and forward broadcasts to a WINS server. Without a name server, non-Microsoft NetBIOS computers' only option for name resolution and registration is via broadcasts. A WINS proxy removes these previous limitations and extends the resolution methods used by non-Microsoft NetBIOS clients, enabling them to take advantage of Microsoft's WINS server services.

Non-WINS NetBIOS Registration

When a non-WINS client tries to register its name via a broadcast, the proxy agent hears the registration request and passes it to the WINS server for name verification. If the name is not in use, it replies with a successful name registration message but *does not* register the name in the WINS database. If you want to have WINS manage the NetBIOS name of non-WINS clients, you will need to enter a static entry in the WINS database as discussed earlier in "Managing WINS Records."

Non-WINS NetBIOS Resolution

When a non-WINS client broadcasts a name resolution request, the proxy agent hears the request and first checks its name cache for name resolution. If the name is not present in cache, the proxy agent forwards the request over the WINS server for resolution. The WINS servers resolves the name if it is in the database and passes it back to the WINS proxy. The WINS proxy then caches the name and IP address and sends the answered request back to the non-WINS client. See Figure 4.70 for a graphical interpretation of this process.

To enable a Windows XP computer to be used as a Proxy Agent, you will need to edit the registry. Open your registry editor by typing **regedt32** or **regedit** in your **Run** window. Navigate to the following key: HMLM\SYSTEM\CurrentControlSet\Services\NetBT\Parameters

Add a **REG_DWORD** value named **EnableProxy** with a value of **1** and restart the computer.

Figure 4.70 Resolving a Non-WINS Name Request

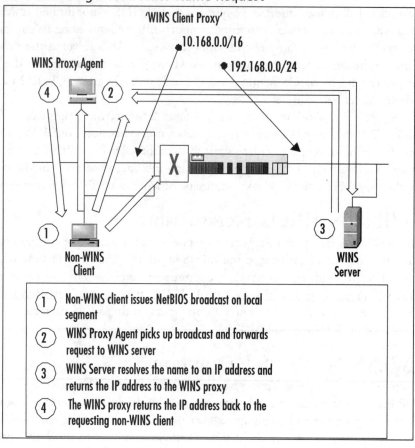

 TEST DAY TIP

When configuring proxy agents for your non-WINS clients, configure at least one, but no more than two agents per network segment. Configuring more than two proxy agents per subnet may cause excessive network traffic or overload your WINS server.

Although set in different registry locations, all versions of Windows later than Windows for Workgroups v3.11, including this version, can be enabled as WINS Proxy Agents.

 EXAM WARNING

If you are using non-Microsoft NetBIOS computers that have the ability to register with a WINS server, be certain to disable the **Use computer names that are com-**

patible with LAN Manager option checkbox on the **Advanced** tab on the **Properties** of your **WINS server name.** Microsoft NetBIOS names allow the registration of only 15 character names, whereas non-Microsoft NetBIOS clients potentially can have 16 character NetBIOS names.

Network Service Interoperability

Windows Internet Naming Service is only one of a handful of back-end network services that assist clients in communicating on your network. All of the services combined enable your clients to successfully send and receive data byte information to and from your application hosts in the most efficient manner. In this section, we discuss these services and how they can be configured to interoperate with each other.

WINS and DHCP

If you are running an environment that requires the use of NetBIOS, WINS is a must-install service for your back-end infrastructure. Previously, we discussed the server side installation of the WINS service as well as the manual client configuration to use the WINS service. In this section, we will discuss how you can integrate the deployment of WINS to your client base via the Dynamic Host Configuration Protocol (DHCP).

DHCP has two configurable options when it comes to pushing out WINS server information (for more details on DHCP options, see Chapter 3):

- 044 WINS/NBSN Servers
- 046 WINS/NBT Node Type

Option 044 allows you to enter all your WINS server IP addresses in the order you want clients to register as well as query when searching for a NetBIOS name. See Figure 4.71 and

Figure 4.71 Adding Your WINS Server IP Address Via DHCP

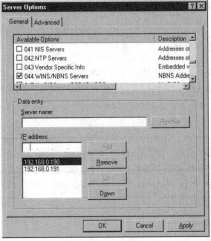

use the **Up** and **Down** buttons to alter the WINS server priority. Those at the top of the list will be used as primary WINS server and those underneath will be secondary. You can enter as many WINS servers as you want in the IP address field.

Option 046 allows you to enter the specific node type you want your client to use. Node types determine the order in which your client tries to resolve NetBIOS names. For more on node types refer to the section "NetBIOS Node Types" earlier in this chapter. See Figure 4.72 for an illustration of the DHCP node type option.

Figure 4.72 Adding Your Client Node Type Via DHCP

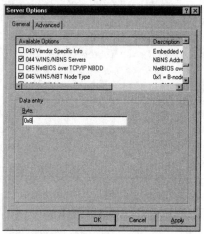

NOTE

Microsoft recommends always configuring a node type if you are also using WINS. They also recommend that you use a node type of *0x8* or *h-node*. This ensures that WINS clients will try to use a WINS server first before initiating a broadcast.

There are a few more settings to consider when configuring your WINS clients. The first is only configurable at the client, but the second is configured using the client or a combination of client and DHCP.

- **Enable LMHOSTS Lookup** Checked by default, this setting tells the client to look for a configured LMHOSTS file under %systemroot%\system32\drivers\etc.

NOTE

If an LMHOSTS file uses any #PRE tag options, those settings are loaded automatically into the clients NetBIOS name cache and used as a means of resolution regardless of whether this option is checked or unchecked.

- **NetBIOS settings** Used to determine if a client is enabled or disabled for NetBIOS use and whether or not it lets a DHCP server decide. Options include the following:

  - **Default** Based on a vendor-specific setting in DHCP, determines if a client is enabled or disabled for the use of NetBIOS. If the DHCP option **Disable NetBIOS over TCP/IP (NetBT)** is used, the client is disabled. If this DHCP option is not set and you are statically configured with an IP address, NetBIOS is enabled.

  - **Enable NetBIOS over TCP/IP** Enables the use of NetBIOS.

  - **Disable NetBIOS over TCP/IP** Disables the use of NetBIOS, in effect making WINS settings useless.

You can use these DHCP options when setting up your DHCP scopes to ensure that your clients are configured to use the correct WINS server IP addresses in the order you specify, as well as make sure they are using the right broadcast ordering method, again defined by the node type you specify.

WINS and DNS

Another network infrastructure service that is heavily relied upon in a Windows Server 2003 Active Directory environment is the Domain Name System Service (DNS). DNS is the backbone of all Windows 2000 and Windows Server 2003 network authentication, name resolution, and service level locator requests. By default, downlevel Windows clients do not use DNS for any of these functions and thus must rely on your WINS server. For similar reasons, your Windows 2000, Windows XP, and Windows Server 2003 clients must use WINS to communicate with your downlevel clients due to their reliance on NetBIOS naming and its IP transport protocol. By default, DNS handles only host to IP name resolution and leaves NetBIOS to IP naming resolution to its partner, WINS. However, these two partners can be tied together to assist your Windows 2000, Windows XP, and Windows Server 2003 DNS dependant clients in creating a more efficient and effective naming resolution solution, since it may make more sense to not configure your non-WINS DNS clients with a WINS server, but to leave that work up to your DNS server.

To integrate your WINS installation with your Active Directory DNS zones, follow the steps outlined in Exercise 4.10.

EXERCISE 4.10

SETTING UP WINS TO INTEROPERATE WITH DNS

In this exercise, we will show you how you can set up your DNS zones to query your WINS database on behalf of your DNS clients for requests not found in DNS. This is useful if the majority of your server names are NetBIOS names stored in WINS, but you wish to use DNS to resolve these names.

1. Click **Start | Administrative Tools | DNS** to open your DNS MMC snap in.

2. Click the "...." to expand your **Forward Lookup Zones** container.

3. Highlight the zone you want to configure, then right-click it and select **Properties**.

4. In your zone names Properties dialog window, select the **WINS** tab as shown in Figure 4.73.

   Figure 4.73 Configuring WINS as a Forward Lookup for Your DNS Zones

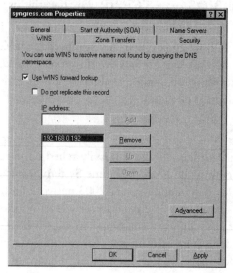

5. Click on the option checkbox **Use WINS forward lookup**.

6. Type the IP address of your WINS server and click the **Add** button as displayed in Figure 4.73. Repeat this step for each server to which you want to forward lookups for name resolution.

NOTE

Check the option checkbox, **Do not replicate this record,** if you do not want WINS related entries replicated, or *transferred*, to your other DNS servers during normal zone transfer operations. This option is useful when you want to avoid zone update failures and loading errors when you have a mixed DNS environment consisting of Microsoft and non-Microsoft DNS servers that may not understand your WINS data records. By default this is not checked when enabling WINS lookup and thus all WINS-related records are slated to be replicated via zone transfers.

7. Click the **Advanced** button to configure both Cache Time-outs and Lookup Time-outs as shown in Figure 4.74. The two advanced configuration options include the following:

- **Cache time-out** TTL value that determines how long other DNS servers are allowed to cache WINS related entries returned through the use of WINS lookup integration. The default value is 15 minutes.

- **Lookup time-out** An interval that determines the amount of time a DNS server will wait to get a successful response from its configured WINS forward lookup server before returning a *name not found* error. The default value is 2 seconds.

Figure 4.74 Configuring Cache and Lookup Time-out Intervals

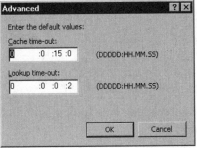

Configuring WINS forward lookup for your DNS implementation is *zone independent*. This means that if you have multiple zones, you will need to run through Exercise 4.10 for each zone you host. This is also true for any reverse lookup zones you may also host. However, reverse lookup zones ask you to specify a *domain name* that you wish to append to the NetBIOS name record. Reverse WINS lookup also gives you the opportunity to return the DNS domain name as the *NetBIOS scope*. The latter should be used only if NetBIOS scopes are used in production already. Reverse WINS lookup is configured on the **WINS-R** tab of your zones property. See Figure 4.75 for an illustration.

To better understand the way non-WINS or DNS-only clients would use the WINS lookup feature of Windows Server 2003's DNS, look at these steps while viewing the diagram depicted in Figure 4.76:

1. The DNS client queries its preferred DNS server.

2. The preferred DNS sever contacts the DNS server that is authoritative for that zone.

Figure 4.75 Configuring Reverse DNS to WINS Lookup

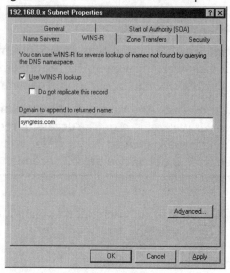

3. The authoritative server for that zone forwards that request to its configured WINS lookup server for resolution.

4. The WINS server resolves the name lookup and forwards the IP address back to the authoritative zone server.

5. The authoritative zone server returns the IP address back to the preferred DNS server.

6. The preferred DNS server returns the IP address back to the DNS client.

Figure 4.76 Tracing the Flow of the DNS to WINS Forward Lookup Process

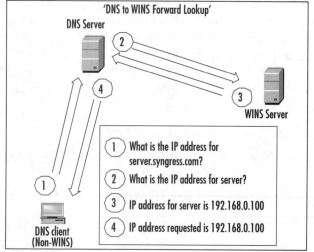

If you want your downlevel Windows clients to use DNS for name resolution, you will need to make sure they are set up as *Enhanced h-node* clients; if set up to use WINS, Windows 2000, Windows XP, and Windows Server 2003 clients are enabled for *enhanced h-node* resolution by default. For more on this, refer to the section "NetBIOS Node Types" earlier in the chapter. It depicts the different name resolution methods you can set up in order for DNS to be used as a means to resolving NetBIOS names.

WINS and RRAS

If you want to extend the functionality of NetBIOS name resolution to remote clients using a Routing and Remote Access Service (RRAS), you must take into account that your RRAS server is not able to resolve the NetBIOS names of your dial-in users without the help of WINS. Because your RRAS server is considered a network router, it does not automatically forward broadcasts to your internal network. Although your internal network may be configured on one physical segment, and all your clients may be able to broadcast and resolve NetBIOS names, they will not be able to do so through your RRAS server. This puts you at a cross roads in that you need to use WINS in order to implement RRAS. However, in order to have a populated WINS database that dial-in clients can resolve names from, you need to implement WINS in your internal network before installing an RRAS server. Once this is done, you can successfully use a DHCP server with the IP addresses of these WINS servers, to hand to your dial-in RRAS users.

To successfully implement an RRAS server, you must configure a DHCP relay agent; that relay agent must point itself back to an internal DHCP server hosting a valid scope of IP addresses for the dial-in segment of the RRAS server. This scope is typically a different scope than that used on your internal network, and thus is configured with different server options. To ensure correct name to IP NetBIOS resolution for your dial-in users, you must configure your dial-in DHCP scope with the IP addresses of a WINS server. Once this is in place, users can dial into your RRAS server, receive an IP address and the configured addresses of your WINS servers, and successfully resolve NetBIOS names. For more on the DHCP relay agent and RRAS refer to Chapter 4. For more on setting up WINS via DHCP, refer to the section "WINS and DHCP" earlier in this chapter.

NOTE

If you did not want to implement WINS in your environment just to install and use an RRAS server and successfully resolve NetBIOS names, you could use LMHOSTS files. Although this would be very tedious and hard to keep up with, it is a way to make sure your dial-in users could resolve names that will work. Just remember that every time you add, remove, or change a server IP address, you have to update your dial-in clients' local LMHOSTS file. We highly recommend that instead, you install a WINS server if you plan on using RRAS.

WINS and Active Directory

Windows 2000 and Windows Server 2003 are designed to allow downlevel clients to authenticate with them via the use of WINS. For this reason, you must set up your Windows 2000 or Windows Server 2003 Active Directory domain controllers as WINS clients, especially if you are operating in a subnetted network environment that does not allow the use of broadcasts to traverse its routers. When you do so, your Active Directory domain controllers will publish downlevel domain and domain controller service locator information into your WINS database. By default, the first Windows Server 2003 domain controller installed or upgraded in your domain holds a special role categorized as one of the Flexible Single Master Operational (FSMO) roles. This role is the *PDC Emulator Role*, and appears to downlevel clients as an NT 4.0 Primary Domain Controller (PDC) server. This is an essential piece of the NT 4.0 domain and its NetBIOS-type downlevel clients, and without it certain domain type functions would not exist. Your Windows Server 2003 PDC Emulator publishes special locator records in the WINS database that trick clients into thinking it is a PDC. These record types, as discussed earlier in the section on LMHOSTS, are a [1bh] Domain Master Browser or PDC Emulator Role record and a [1ch] Domain Controller record. The [1ch] domain controller record allows downlevel clients to authenticate and locate backup domain controller type of actions as they did in NT 4.0 domains. Since NT 4.0 domains had only a single writable copy of the directory SAM database located on the PDC, the [1bh] PDC Emulator record handles the location of this service for functions like:

- Password changes
- Account changes, additions, or deletions
- Workstation changes, additions, or deletions

TEST DAY TIP

To facilitate your downlevel clients it is essential to tie your Active Directory domain controllers together with your WINS database.

WINS is a network-specific service that can be installed only on Microsoft server version products. For this reason, it is installable and configurable only by an Administrator of the server on which WINS is installed. By default this is anyone that is a member of the Enterprise Admins or Domain Admins group. Because it is not highly likely that a lot of administrators will be members of these groups, it used to be difficult to delegate viewable rights to the WINS database in Active Directory. With the release of Windows 2000, Microsoft came up with a predelegated group that allows just the viewing of WINS database information. This group, called the *WINS Users Group*, is created automatically when you promote your first server to a domain controller using the dcpromo.exe utility.

By default, this group is a Domain Local Security group and is located in the default Users container. As you install WINS onto servers that are members of your Active Directory domain, they are added automatically to this group, and thus members of the WINS Users group will have the ability to view their databases.

The WINS Users group is installed with the WINS service, not when the first DC is installed if it isn't a WINS server.

WINS and the Browser Service

Browsing is the ability of any Windows client to actively search its network for other NetBIOS type computer names. You are said to be browsing any time you access the *My Network Places* icon on your desktop with the following steps:

1. Double-click **My Network Places** on your desktop (or on Windows XP and Windows Server 2003's standard shell **Start | My Network Places**).

2. Double-click the **Entire Network** icon.

3. Double-click the **Microsoft Windows Network** icon.

NOTE

In older versions of Windows, or those referred to as downlevel Windows clients, browsing was accomplished by accessing the Network Neighborhood icon on the desktop.

There are automatically elected Windows-based servers or workstations on your network that are configured to gather all of the NetBIOS names on a particular network segment and construct what is called a *browse list*. These lists are gathered by way of each client's browser service broadcasting its name on the network. When you follow the previous steps and begin browsing your network, you are looking at the browse list.

The problem arises when networks are segmented into what are known as broadcast domains (not to be confused with Windows domains, which are security boundaries). These broadcast domains prohibit the use of broadcasts from traversing their routers' border interfaces, thus preventing you from browsing any computers other than those on your network segment. Enter WINS. When you use WINS, all servers, workstations, and browser services configured with the address of your WINS servers register their services with that WINS server. One of these services is the browser service. If you have separate broadcast domains, locating a WINS server on each of these domains and configuring each to replicate with one another allows *all* WINS clients on *all* network segments to browse one another.

EXAM WARNING

The ability to browse across broadcast domains can also be accomplished with the use of an LMHOSTS file. Doing so, however, would require that you create, install, and manually manage and keep up to date this same LMHOSTS file on all of your machines. Microsoft recommends using WINS as a solution for browsing instead of an LMHOSTS file solution.

WINS and Win9x/NT Clients

Windows 9x (Windows 95, 95b, 98, 98SE, and Me) and Windows NT clients are referred to as downlevel Windows clients in the world of Windows 2000 and Windows Server 2003 Active Directory. This is because they still require the use of NetBIOS to communicate and resolve names as well as to authenticate to any domain service. NetBIOS is the heart of the NT domain infrastructure and as such is also used by all its pre-Windows 2000 clients.

Back in the day of single network segments, these older "chatty" clients were able to broadcast name resolution requests throughout the local network and receive valid responses from other NetBIOS listeners. As network designers realized that this was not such a good thing because it seemed to hog bandwidth and slow down network connectivity, they started to design segmented networks. As networks are segmented, they are divided into what are called broadcast domains; each segment created can broadcast packets only on its segment. This is based on the fact that most of the routers that separate these segments do not forward these broadcast messages by default. This makes it a necessity to install WINS servers into your domain infrastructure if you plan on using any of these downlevel clients and want them to be able to log on to your Windows domain and access resources.

As mentioned in the previous section, "WINS and Active Directory," these downlevel clients require the use of WINS in order to find the PDC and its backup domain controllers for authentication. They also use WINS to locate NetBIOS type resources, such as file and print servers, network drive mappings, and distributed file shares (DFS).

Monitoring and Troubleshooting the Windows Server 2003 WINS Server

EXAM 70-291 OBJECTIVE 5.3 5.3.1 5.3.2

Monitoring your WINS server and its clients prior to and after a problem is good practice to aid you in your troubleshooting skills. In this section, we will discuss the different ways by which you can enable logging techniques and initiate monitoring methods for your WINS server as well as ways to identify and troubleshoot issues resulting from a WINS server problem to a WINS client problem.

WINS System Monitor Objects

The Windows System Monitor is a real-time diagnostics tool for troubleshooting WINS data traffic flowing between your WINS server and each of your WINS clients. System Monitor allows you to target specific object-related counters found on your system and track the data associated with those counters. Found in the **Administrative Tools** menu under the heading **Performance**, System Monitor can be set up to log real-time WINS registration, renewal, and query events, and to alert you regarding any number of configurable thresholds. Some of the items System Monitor can track are:

- Number of queries WINS receives

- Number of registrations WINS receives

- Number of releases WINS receives

When WINS is installed on a server, it also installs specific WINS-related object counters to the System Monitor. These can be used to monitor WINS data. Exercise 4.11 will walk you through the process of configuring the System Monitor to use some of these object counters to track the number of WINS queries your WINS server processes on your network.

EXERCISE 4.11

USING SYSTEM MONITOR TO MONITOR ACTIVE QUERIES PER SECOND

This exercise is designed to teach you how to use the Windows Server 2003 System Monitor to pinpoint and track WINS specific data.

1. Open the **Performance** MMC console (System Monitor) from your **Administrative Tools** menu (or type **perfmon** at the **Run** command).

2. At the bottom of the screen, click each of the predefined counters (for example Pages/sec) and press the **Delete** key. (This will clear all counters except the ones we are interested in seeing.)

3. Click the **Add** button (the *plus* icon) on the middle of the graphical menu bar, or select **Ctrl + I** on your keyboard, or right-click the graph and select **Add Counters**.

4. Drop-down the toggle box under **Performance objects** and select **WINS Server**.

5. From the **Select counters from list** window, select both **Queries/sec** and **Failed Queries /sec** and click **Add** as shown in Figure 4.77. Click **Close** to finish.

Figure 4.77 Selecting System Monitor Counters

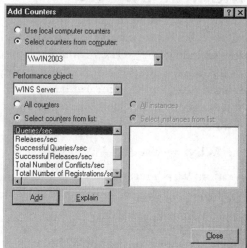

Your System Monitor will now display all of the WINS Query messages it is receiving in real time, as shown in Figure 4.78.

Figure 4.78 Viewing Live System Monitor Activity

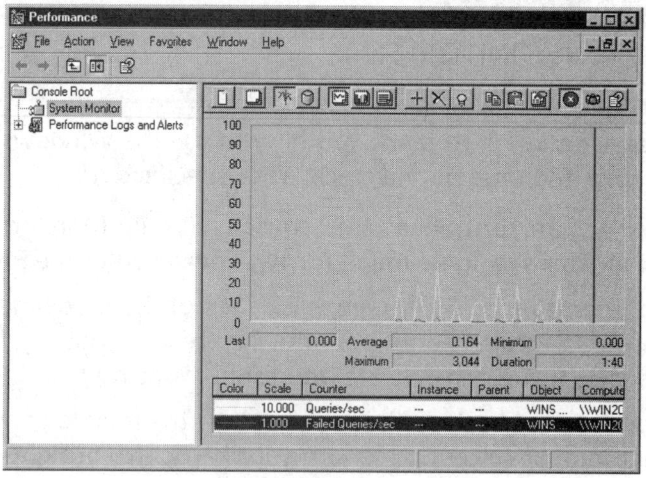

NOTE

Note that in addition to monitoring the local machine, you can also monitor another WINS server on the network remotely, by typing the UNC path for the remote server in the **Select counters from computer** box. If you have previously monitored other machines, their names will be in the drop-down box.

There are a number of other WINS-related counters that can be monitored. These are included with their descriptions in Table 4.8. If you forget the function of any particular counter, you can highlight it and click the **Explain** button for details about what the counter represents.

NOTE

System Monitor defaults to the **View Current Activity** mode, although there is also a **View Log Data** mode. On choosing the **View Log Data** mode, you are prompted to choose a previously recorded data log from a specific **Performance object** and all its counters.

NOTE

In order to simulate WINS related queries in an amount that may be equivalent to your production network, we used a batch file that did the following:

1. Mapped a drive to the WINS server (NetBIOS name query).

2. Deleted that mapping.
3. Flushed the local NetBIOS cache (so another query would result).
4. Repeated the preceding steps.

For those of you interested in using this code for your own testing purposes we have included it here:

```
@echo off

:loop

nbtstat -R

net use x: \\servername\c$

nbtstat -R

net use y: \\servername\admin$

nbtstat -R

net use x: /d

net use y: /d

goto loop
```

We changed the default scale for each of the object counters to 10, so it will show easily in the monitor window. We also increased the size of the display lines a bit to enhance visibility.

Windows Server 2003 provides the administrator with a number of very useful System Monitor counters that you can use to appropriately monitor, tune, or troubleshoot WINS related issues. Table 4.8 lists all of the specific WINS counters and gives a brief description as to what each of them can monitor when used with System Monitor.

Table 4.8 WINS Performance Counter Objects

Performance Counter	Description of Performance Counter
Failed Queries /sec	Total Number of Failed Queries/sec.
Failed Releases /sec	Total Number of Failed Releases/sec.
Group Conflicts /sec	The rate at which group registration received by the WINS server resulted in conflicts with records in the database.
Group Registrations /sec	The rate at which group registration are received by the WINS server.
Group Renewals /sec	The rate at which group renewals are received by the WINS server.
Queries /sec	The rate at which queries are received by the WINS server.
Releases /sec	The rate at which releases are received by the WINS server.
Successful Queries /sec	Total Number of Successful Queries/sec.
Successful Releases /sec	Total Number of Successful Releases/sec.
Total Number of Conflicts /sec	The sum of the Unique and Group conflicts per sec. This is the total rate at which conflicts were seen by the WINS server.
Total Number of Registrations /sec	The sum of the Unique and Group registrations per sec. This is the total rate at which registrations are received by the WINS server.
Total Number of Renewals /sec	The sum of the Unique and Group renewals per sec. This is the total rate at which renewals are received by the WINS server.
Unique Conflict /sec	The rate at which unique registrations/renewals received by the WINS server resulted in conflicts with records in the database.
Unique Registrations /sec	The rate at which unique registrations are received by the WINS server.
Unique Renewals /sec	The rate at which unique renewals are received by the WINS server.

Troubleshooting WINS Clients

There is nothing worse than getting a call from the help desk and hearing someone on the other end telling you they cannot connect to any of their network resources. If these are NetBIOS clients using a WINS server, troubleshooting whether it is a client or server issue is a relatively simple procedure, using a few command line utilities and following these steps (note that each one of the following commands requires you be inside a command shell window):

1. Click **Start | Run** and type **cmd**. Click **OK**.

2. Verify that your client is configured to use the correct WINS server using the ipconfig.exe utility with the **/all** switch as shown in Figure 4.79. Type ipconfig /all at your command prompt window. Make sure the **Node Type** is configured as it should be (usually **Hybrid**). Most importantly make sure the primary WINS server IP address is present and its IP address is correct. (If using a secondary WINS Server, check that as well.)

Figure 4.79 Determining Client Side WINS Settings

```
C:\WINDOWS\system32\cmd.exe                                    _ □ ×

C:\>ipconfig /all

Windows IP Configuration

        Host Name . . . . . . . . . . . . : Win2003
        Primary Dns Suffix  . . . . . . . : syngress.com
        Node Type . . . . . . . . . . . . : Hybrid
        IP Routing Enabled. . . . . . . . : Yes
        WINS Proxy Enabled. . . . . . . . : No
        DNS Suffix Search List. . . . . . : syngress.com
                                            vigil.ws
                                            columbia.vigil.ws
                                            domain.com

Ethernet adapter Local Area Connection:

        Connection-specific DNS Suffix  . : syngress.com
        Description . . . . . . . . . . . : AMD PCNET Family PCI Ethernet Adapter
        Physical Address. . . . . . . . . : 00-0C-29-F3-7C-80
        DHCP Enabled. . . . . . . . . . . : No
        IP Address. . . . . . . . . . . . : 192.168.0.192
        Subnet Mask . . . . . . . . . . . : 255.255.255.0
        Default Gateway . . . . . . . . . : 192.168.0.50
        DNS Servers . . . . . . . . . . . : 192.168.0.192
        Primary WINS Server . . . . . . . : 192.168.0.192

C:\>_
```

3. If those settings are correct, you can use the nbtstat.exe command line utility to see if your client is using WINS or if it is broadcasting most of its name resolution requests. Type nbtstat –r as shown in Figure 4.80.

NOTE

If you are using WINS for NetBIOS name resolution, there should be very few name requests resolved by means of a broadcast, as shown in **nbtstat**. If you see that **Resolved By Broadcast** is much higher than **Resolved By Name Server**, then you may have a WINS server issue.

Figure 4.80 Determining Client Side WINS Settings

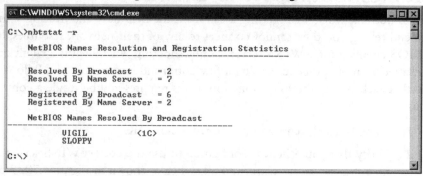

4. If it appears that you are using a WINS server for most of your name resolution requests, you can use the same utility again with the **–c** switch to see if you have an incorrectly cached NetBIOS name, possibly caused by an out of date LMHOSTS file using the #PRE tag prefixes. Type nbtstat –c as shown in Figure 4.81.

Figure 4.81 Determining Client Side WINS Settings

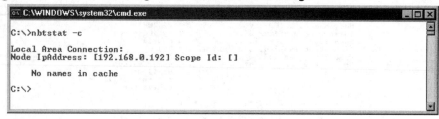

TEST DAY TIP

When troubleshooting a NetBIOS name resolution problem, don't rely on the more common **ping.exe** command line utility. Remember that **ping.exe** is a TCP/IP application layer program and does not use NetBIOS. This is a common mistake due to the fact that certain node types, like Microsoft's *Enhanced h-node*, use DNS and hosts files as a last means to resolve NetBIOS names. In situations where you want to be certain you have NetBIOS connectivity between two hosts, try mapping to the IPC$ share of a remote computer using the **net use** utility:

```
net use \\server\IPC$
```

If all of the outputs from these commands are correct, you may want to make sure that the problem exists for trying to resolve *all* NetBIOS and not just one. If the client cannot resolve *any* NetBIOS name, you may want to move on and examine your WINS server to see if the problem resides on it. If it is just a single NetBIOS name that is causing the problems, you should verify a few more things:

- Is that machine's NetBIOS name in conflict with another name?

- Is that NetBIOS name registered in WINS and if so is it *tombstoned*?

- Is that NetBIOS name registered in WINS with the correct IP address?

To verify that the NetBIOS name is not in a conflict state, you must be at a command prompt window on the machine in question. Type **nbtstat –n** to verify your NetBIOS names are in a Registered Status state, as shown in Figure 4.82. If the Status displays *Conflict*, then your problem resides with that NetBIOS name.

Figure 4.82 Determining Your NetBIOS Names Are in a Registered State

```
C:\WINDOWS\system32\cmd.exe

C:\>nbtstat -n

Local Area Connection:
Node IpAddress: [192.168.0.192] Scope Id: []

                NetBIOS Local Name Table

        Name              Type         Status
    ---------------------------------------------
    WIN2003       <00>  UNIQUE      Registered
    SYNGRESS      <00>  GROUP       Registered
    SYNGRESS      <1C>  GROUP       Registered
    WIN2003       <20>  UNIQUE      Registered
    SYNGRESS      <1B>  UNIQUE      Registered
    SYNGRESS      <1E>  GROUP       Registered
    SYNGRESS      <1D>  UNIQUE      Registered
    .._MSBROWSE__.<01>  GROUP       Registered

C:\>_
```

Next, open the WINS MMC snap-in and view the records in the WINS database. Refer to the section "Managing WINS Records and its Database" to search for the NetBIOS name in conflict. If you find the name in the database, verify that it is not tombstoned, has the correct IP address, and most importantly, that it exists. If the record does not exist, refer to steps 1 through 4 of the manual for this particular client. If you determine that this client is using the same WINS server to register its NetBIOS name and you verified that the WINS server is up, you can try manually reregistering the unreachable client with the WINS server by typing **nbtstat –RR** at the command line interface as shown in Figure 4.83.

Figure 4.83 Manually Reregistering a Client with WINS

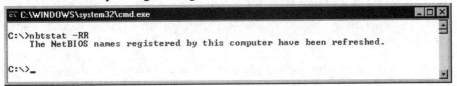

```
C:\WINDOWS\system32\cmd.exe

C:\>nbtstat -RR
    The NetBIOS names registered by this computer have been refreshed.

C:\>_
```

If the unreachable client is registering with a different WINS server than your client, and you verify that the record exists and is correct in its WINS server, you may have a WINS replication problem. You will need to refer to the next section on troubleshooting the WINS server.

TEST DAY TIP

A possible answer to a client's name still residing in the WINS database with a status of **active** when it is physically off the network could be one of four reasons:

- The client deliberately unplugged his or her PC from the network (possibly a laptop user).
- There was a power outage, causing the machine to shut down improperly and not successfully unregister its name from WINS.
- There was a loss of network connectivity between the client and server when the client shut down.
- The WINS server was down when the client shut down.

Head of the Class…

Network Monitor and Broadcast Storms

If you are running in a NetBIOS-heavy environment with a majority of your clients running downlevel Windows operating systems, you may want to periodically sniff your network segments for broadcast storm traffic. You can do this with an enhanced version of the Network Monitor utility. The standard version comes with Windows Server 2003, whereas the enhanced version ships with Microsoft's SMS Server suite, and lets you not only monitor traffic coming and going from a single machine, but lets you monitor, or sniff, *all* the traffic on a particular network segment. For this discussion, we will focus on the Windows Server 2003 version of Network Monitor and only sniff NetBIOS broadcast that a given machine can view.

If you want to examine all of the broadcast traffic that your client is listening to on its segment, follow these steps:

1. Install the tool from the **Add or Remove Programs** applet in **Control Panel**, since the Network Monitor is not installed by default. Choose **Add/Remove Windows Component | Management and Monitoring Tools | Network Monitor Tools**.

2. Click **OK** and point to your Windows Server 2003 source files.

3. After the installation completes, access the **Network Monitor** utility from the **Administrative Tools** menu.

4. In the Network Monitor interface, click **Capture | Start** from the **Tools** menu to begin capturing data, as shown in Figure 4.84.

When you believe that enough data traffic has been captured, simply click the **Capture | Stop and View** menu item and you will be looking at a low-level view of all your captured data packets as shown in Figure 4.85. Sorting through the data to find the packets you actually need is the time consuming part of using Network Monitor. In cases where there is just too much data to manage, you can use

Continued

Network Monitor's filtering ability to capture only specific network traffic, or to display only specified traffic from that which was previously captured.

Network Monitor is a very useful tool and is included with Windows Server 2003. You must understand how to configure and use this tool to effectively troubleshoot networking problems of all types, including those related to WINS and NetBIOS.

Figure 4.84 Capturing Data with Network Monitor

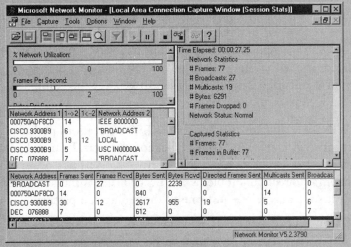

Figure 4.85 Viewing Captured Broadcast Data with Network Monitor

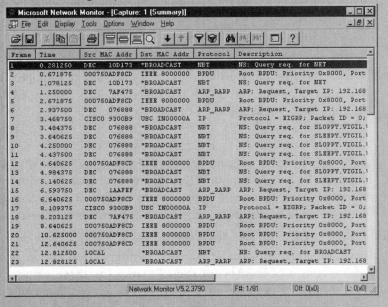

NOTE

If there are multiple network interfaces on the server, you will be asked to select a network on which you want to capture data. Select the appropriate interface (for example, the LAN interface).

Troubleshooting WINS Servers

Troubleshooting WINS server problems can be largely avoided by making sure you understand and correctly set up and configure your WINS database topology. Following are a few key clues that you may come across that point to a server-side WINS problem. All of these were discussed throughout the chapter, so we just reference them here as things to be aware of when troubleshooting your WINS server. To go over the configuration steps refer back to the related section of the chapter.

- **WINS replication problems** WINS replications problems can exist if you have incorrectly configured your replication partners. Remember that by default you must set up replication partners as two-way partners or replication will not work in either direction. Problems can occur if this is initially set up and then by accident someone deletes just one of the replication partners.

- **Static record issues** Remember, static records should be used only for non-WINS related client information. By default, they are configured to overwrite the same dynamic records in replication if they exist. This can appear to be a replication or server problem, when it really is a design and configuration issue. If you want to make static records appear to act as dynamic records you can do so by enabling the **Overwrite unique static mappings at this server (migrate on)** setting option.

- **WINS server load problems** When faced with an issue of WINS server load, you must reconsider the default burst handling mode discussed earlier in this chapter. Burst handling should be set to a value that is tuned for the number of WINS clients each WINS server will be handling. If you are seeing issues where clients are unable to successfully register with WINS because the server is too busy, consider lowering your burst handling value. On the same note if you are experiencing problems with WINS clients not being able to successfully resolve NetBIOS names because a majority of WINS clients are being deferred by the burst handling functionality, consider raising your burst handling value.

- **Rogue WINS servers** Be careful of rogue WINS servers on your network when using the **Automatic partner configuration** option. If using this option, take advantage of the **Accept records only for these owners** option to narrow your chances of running into a rogue WINS server. Once replication happens with a rogue WINS server, your next step may be to restore from backup.

- **WINS Database problems** Make sure you use one of the methods described in this chapter to back up your WINS database. You do not want to have 1500 WINS clients have to reregister with your new WINS server because you lost the database and had to create a new one from scratch. Be prepared and plan ahead. Backing up the database is not a tedious task and should be the second thing you set up after initial installation.

WINS Monitoring and Statistics

WINS keeps an ongoing history of statistical information within its database. These statistics can be viewed in the WINS MMC console by following these steps:

1. Click **Start | Administrative Tools | WINS** to open your WINS MMC snap-in console.

2. Right-click your **WINS** *server name* and select **Display Server Statistics** as shown in Figure 4.86.

Figure 4.86 Displaying WINS Server Statistics

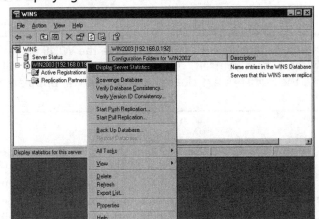

You can use the statistics shown in Figure 4.87 to determine any of the following bits of information:

- Last time the WINS service was started or the database was initialized

- Last periodic or manual replication time and date

- Total queries, releases, and unique and group registrations

- Last periodic or manual scavenging initiated

- A listing of configured replication partners as well as the number of replications and number of failed communications

Figure 4.87 Viewing WINS Server Statistics

Description	Details	
Server start time	6/23/2003 11:51:37 AM	
Database initialized		
Statistics last cleared		
Last periodic replication	6/23/2003 4:21:56 PM	
Last manual replication		
Last net update replication		
Last address change replication		
Total queries	42	
Records found	10	
Records not found	32	
Total releases	20	
Records found	20	
Records not found	0	
Unique registrations	5	
Conflicts	5	
Renewals	67	
Group registrations	3	
Conflicts	1	
Renewals	45	
Total registrations received	8	
Last periodic scavenging	6/23/2003 4:10:30 PM	
Last manual scavenging	6/23/2003 1:28:28 PM	
Last extinction scavenging		
Last verification scavenging		
WINS Partner	# of Replications	# of Comm Fails
66.150.161.133	0	10

NOTE

These database statistics are reset every time the WINS server is shut down. To manually reset them yourself, click the **Reset** button to set all counters to zero. You will notice the Statistics last cleared description will populate itself with the date and time.

If you are monitoring the server statistics in real time, you can configure the update interval to be refreshed on your screen periodically. To do this, click your **WINS** *server name* and select **Properties** from with the WINS MMC console. On the **General** tab, make sure **Automatically update statistics every** is checked. Type the *time interval* at which you wish to refresh your WINS server statistics as shown in Figure 4.88.

You also have the ability to turn on some advanced logging functionality on your WINS server. Turning this on enables you to fine tune your WINS troubleshooting by detailing very specific WINS related functions in the system event log, such as when WINS processes are stopped and started as seen in Figure 4.89, as well as more low-level database function messages shown in Figure 4.90.

To turn on advanced logging, click **Start | Administrative Tools | WINS** to open your WINS MMC snap-in console. Right-click your **WINS** *server name* and select **Properties**. Click the **Advanced** tab and click the option box **Log detailed events to Windows event log**.

Figure 4.88 Updating Server Statistics Interval

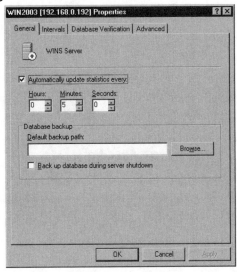

Figure 4.89 Logging of the Scavenging Process Being Started

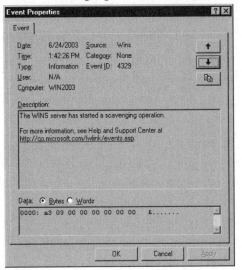

NOTE

Be careful when enabling WINS logging as it is very resource intensive. When it is enabled, be sure to increase the size of the system event logs or set them to overwrite as needed, or your newly generated WINS events will almost immediately fill your system event log if you are actively using WINS on your network. Microsoft recommends only enabling this logging during troubleshooting periods. When the problem is resolved, disable this functionality to enable your WINS server to operate at it best.

Figure 4.90 Logging of Lower Level Scavenging Information

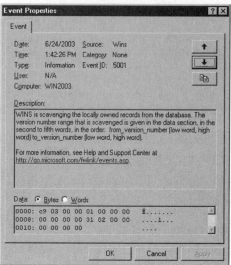

WINS Administration

Choose your WINS administrators wisely. WINS is an essential piece of your NetBIOS naming resolution infrastructure and should not be taken lightly. Take advantage of the built-in Active Directory WINS Users group when delegating users that need to view your database but not necessarily make changes. Be particular about who you add to the local administrators group on your WINS server.

Summary of Exam Objectives

With the release of Microsoft Windows 2000 and Windows Server 2003, Microsoft has changed its primary name resolution methods to use the Domain Naming Server over the Windows Internet Naming Server. This was a huge change for Microsoft as they have built NetBIOS and WINS into the heart of every operating system they built prior to Windows 2000. Though Microsoft states that NetBIOS is no longer needed for your Windows 2000 and Windows Server 2003 Active Directory domain environments, that does not mean that it is not needed for your downlevel clients as well as NetBIOS applications. What does all this mean? NetBIOS and WINS will be around for quite some time to come, so be prepared to learn about it and how to use it effectively on your network.

NetBIOS was first developed in 1983 by a company called Sytec, Inc. It was originally developed to be used as an application programming interface for programmers to tie into local area network aware applications. It later took on transport layer protocols like TCP/IP to use for network communication. Microsoft bought into this protocol and used it to develop its core line of Windows NT operating systems. NetBIOS stood at the heart of the Windows line of products and it was used to allow network communication, logon authentication, and browsing, just to name a few.

NetBIOS names must be unique on each network or communication will cease to function. For this reason, there resides a way to register NetBIOS names on your network. The NetBIOS name registration process consists of a three-phase process:

- Name Registration
- Name Discovery
- Name Release

Each of these steps is essential in making sure your NetBIOS name is authentic and can communicate on your NetBIOS network segment.

Client machines are configured to try and resolve NetBIOS names in a number of different ways. These are referred to as resolution methods and configured as node types. There are four node types that determine the order in which NetBIOS names get resolved from a NetBIOS enabled client machine. They are:

1. b-node
2. p-node
3. m-node
4. h-node

To these, Microsoft has added two more nodes types: Enhanced b-node and Enhanced h-node. Today's newer Windows 2000 and Windows XP operating systems are automatically configured as Enhanced h-node clients.

LAN Manager HOSTS files (LMHOSTS files) are one of the resolution methods used in the different Microsoft node types. They are single flat files that match names to IP addresses for client resolution. They can reside locally on each machine or can be configured to be used centrally on a file server. LMHOSTS files can come in handy when trying to establish trusts between firewalls or when you are having resolution issues between routers that do not allow broadcasts. It is good to know how to use them, but you should not rely on them in today's NetBIOS heavy network environments.

The Windows Internet Naming Service was created to replace the static LMHOSTS file. WINS is a central database that can be used to gather NetBIOS client information from thousands of clients and then later used as a query engine for NetBIOS name resolution. WINS is scaleable and its database can be replicated with WINS partners to unify the separate broadcast domains that are created by network routers. To be effective, your WINS server must use a static IP address and subnet mask when installed because clients must be set up with that static IP address to successfully register and query it in normal NetBIOS operation modes.

WINS clients can be configured in two ways. You can manually set each client IP stack up with the IP address of your WINS server, or you can configure your clients as DHCP clients and push those WINS IP addresses to them with DHCP configurable option 044. Microsoft recommends using DHCP for your clients and statically assigning WINS to your servers. With a simple registry key change, you can turn any Microsoft operating system into a listening beacon for non-WINS NetBIOS clients. This will enable your non-WINS clients to efficiently use your WINS server for their own name resolution queries. Computers configured this way are called WINS Proxy Agents and should reside on network segments that host non-WINS NetBIOS clients. It is not recommended to configure more than two of these proxy agents per network segment because it could cause extra broadcast traffic to occur.

The Microsoft WINS service can be integrated into your current DNS resolution backbone for use with DNS-only clients that are not set up as WINS clients by means of what Microsoft calls a WINS forwarder. Although your DNS clients now can use Windows 2003 DNS to authenticate and access service records, downlevel clients still require the use of NetBIOS and WINS to do those same functions. For this reason you must ensure that your Windows 2000 and Windows Server 2003 environment is set up to register with your WINS servers, so that needed logon information can be successfully located. These same downlevel clients also require WINS for network browsing. Active Directory allows you to publish resources in a directory, essentially eliminating the need for the chatty browsing protocol. In order to allow your downlevel clients to use this type of Active Directory searching you will need to install the Active Directory client on each of them.

WINS client troubleshooting can be accomplished using a few built-in command line tools called ipconfig.exe and nbtstat.exe. They are both accessible via the command line interface and are great for producing the client side troubleshooting information you need to solve NetBIOS naming issues.

Monitoring your WINS server can be done using the System Monitor and the built-in performance counters installed when you install WINS. You can also use Network Monitor to sniff your network for WINS related data. WINS has a server statistics page that you can periodically look at to see day-to-day server events. If the Windows event log does not give you enough detail of WINS-related issues, you can extend the limited logging that WINS initially has turned on. Although this is helpful it is very taxing to your system and should be used only when troubleshooting.

Be careful when assigning administrative rights to your WINS servers. WINS is an important component of your NetBIOS naming functionality and should be handled only by those who understand it. Consider using the built-in WINS Users group to give those users that just need to view your WINS database for troubleshooting purposes.

Exam Objectives Fast Track

Review of NetBIOS Name Resolution

☑ NetBIOS is a session layer protocol and needs to ride on something like TCP/IP as its transport in order for machines to communicate in a Windows environment.

☑ NetBIOS names use a flat namespace and thus can be used only once within similar networks.

☑ Though 16 bytes in length, NetBIOS names in Microsoft's implementation can be only 15 characters long as the sixteenth byte is used as a locator for service or application registration.

☑ NetBIOS is a broadcast-based protocol and thus creates a lot of network chatter. It is wise to use a name to IP mechanism like WINS to cut down on broadcast traffic in high volume NetBIOS domains.

The NetBIOS Node Types

☑ Windows 2000, Windows XP, and Windows Server 2003 operating systems ship with the default setting of Enhance h-node mode, if configured to use a WINS server. By default they are set to use DNS and HOSTS files in the name resolution process.

☑ You can manually change the node type of a machine by editing the local registry; however, Microsoft recommends using DHCP and pushing option 046 to your client base.

☑ If you want to completely eliminate the ability for clients to broadcast, set them up to use p-node mode. In this mode, clients are restricted to using either NetBIOS name cache or a configured WINS server.

☑ An easy way to remember the most commonly used NetBIOS naming resolution method is to use the sentence "**C**an **w**e **b**ark **l**ike **h**appy **d**ogs?". Use the first letter of each word to remember **Cache, WINS, Broadcast, LMHOSTS, HOSTS, DNS**.

The LMHOSTS File

☑ The LMHOSTS file is a static file located in the %systemroot%\system32\drivers\etc directory. Windows looks for this file every time it boots and loads whatever data exists in it into NetBIOS name cache for faster queries.

☑ To make LMHOSTS files use the NetBIOS name cache effectively, you can use the #PRE tag prefixes to make certain those entries remain in the cache permanently and are resolved instantly.

☑ The sample LMHOSTS file that ships with Windows Server 2003 has a default file extension of .SAM and will not be recognized until renamed to just LMHOSTS. It is recommended that you not use this file, but create your own as data is parsed and unnecessary data could result in performance loss.

The Windows Server 2003 Windows Internet Name Server

☑ WINS requires a static IP address and subnet mask to work effectively in any NetBIOS client environment.

☑ By default WINS is configured to issue six-day leases to every client. Clients will try to renew these leases at half the interval time (every three days).

☑ Be careful when importing LMHOSTS files into your WINS server, as all LMHOSTS file entries will become static WINS entries. Use only non-WINS client names in an LMHOSTS file when you use the import utility.

☑ By default the WINS server can replicate only with other servers set to replicate with it. You can turn this functionality off by disabling the **Only Replicate with Partners** option.

Configuring the WINS Client

☑ You can configure your WINS client by editing the TCP/IP stack and manually entering the IP address of both the primary and secondary WINS servers that are active on your network.

☑ It is a good idea to set up your WINS clients with both a primary and secondary WINS server, which happen to be replication partners.

☑ If you are using non-WINS clients, for example UNIX machines that are configured for SMB support, consider implementing a WINS proxy agent to give those clients the ability to use WINS for NetBIOS name resolution. Remember to limit the use to no more than two proxies per subnet.

Network Service Interoperability

☑ Using DHCP to distribute WINS servers is much more efficient and causes less administrative overhead. Use option 044 in your DHCP server options to distribute WINS server IP addresses to your clients.

☑ Integrating DNS to use WINS as a forward lookup would eliminate the need for you to set up your DNS-only clients, like Windows 2000 and Windows XP, as WINS clients. DNS will handle all the NetBIOS resolution by means of a WINS forward lookup.

☑ WINS is needed to supply downlevel NetBIOS clients, like Win9x and Windows NT machines, with needed authentication and logon information in your Windows Server 2003 active directory environment. This means that you need to set up your Windows Server 2003 domain controllers as WINS clients, so downlevel clients can retrieve the needed records.

Monitoring and Troubleshooting the Windows Server 2003 WINS Server

☑ If you are having an abnormal amount of WINS traffic, you can use System Monitor to actively monitor all queries to its server and alert you if it exceeds a certain threshold.

☑ You can use the ipconfig command line utility to run *ipconfig /all* and verify that your client is set up to use WINS and that the node type is correct.

☑ A sudden power outage may cause records in your WINS database to remain with an active status even though they are not on the network anymore. This may cause undesirable NetBIOS naming resolution failures.

Exam Objectives
Frequently Asked Questions

The following Frequently Asked Questions, answered by the authors of this book, are designed to both measure your understanding of the Exam Objectives presented in this chapter, and to assist you with real-life implementation of these concepts. You will also gain access to thousands of other FAQs at ITFAQnet.com.

Q: I have 100 Windows NT Servers and 25 Windows XP machines in a workgroup, functioning just fine on my single segment network. We plan on doubling these numbers by year end. Do I need a WINS server?

A: Yes. Working in a Windows NT workgroup, you are probably using NetBIOS over TCP/IP. NetBIOS is a broadcast-based protocol, and is not meant to scale to hundreds and thousands of machines without the help of some name to IP resolution solution like WINS.

Q: I have created a small Windows Server 2003 domain on my home network and called it Home.com. I am in the process of trying to build a Windows XP laptop machine named HOME and join it to the domain but cannot. Why?

A: When you create a Windows Server 2003 domain, it also creates a backward-compatible NetBIOS name for use with legacy Windows operating systems and products. It concatenates the first 15 letters of the domain name you choose by default as its NetBIOS name, in your case, HOME. Whether it is a single NetBIOS computer name or domain name, there can be only one instance of the same name on any network at a time.

Q: I have 20 computers on my single network segment and I want to split it up so there are two separate groups of 10, in which only those 10 computers can talk to other members of the group. My routers do not support IPSec and my switches do not support the use of VLANS. Is this still a possibility?

A: Yes, with the use of NetBIOS Scopes. A NetBIOS scope is an extension of the NetBIOS computer name and groups similar scoped members into a special class in which they can communicate only with NetBIOS machines names matching their scope. NetBIOS scopes are recommended only when other methods are unavailable.

Q: I have recently taken on the task of limiting my NetBIOS machines from broadcasting by pushing out the DHCP option to be configured as a p-node type client. Now none of my NetBIOS clients can access a handful of my Windows Server 2003 servers. Why?

A: Make sure those Windows Server 2003 servers are configured as WINS clients and have successfully registered their NetBIOS names in WINS. Be careful when implementing the p-node type to your clients because this does not just limit the use of broadcasting, it eliminates it permanently.

Q: I want to make sure my Windows XP clients use DNS and hosts files in the NetBIOS name resolution process. I have configured them as WINS clients. What else do I need to do?

A: Nothing. By default, these clients (like Windows 2000 and Windows Server 2003 clients) are set up as Enhanced h-node NetBIOS resolvers. The resolution order for enhanced h-node clients uses DNS and HOSTS files and is set up in the following order: *NetBIOS remote name cache, NetBIOS name server (WINS), Broadcast, LMHOSTS file, DNS named cache, HOSTS file, DNS.*

Q: We are having lots of problems with our network file share access being very slow. We run a Windows Server 2003 Active Directory with Windows 98 clients. We have set up these clients with the correct DNS servers, but it doesn't seem to help. What is the problem?

A: Windows 98 machines are considered downlevel clients that require the use of NetBIOS to access file share resources. Consider implementing a WINS server and setting up your clients as h-node type clients. This will enable them to first use the WINS server to resolve NetBIOS names, and let them broadcast if they are not successful with WINS. Your machines are now set up so that they are always broadcasting to resolve NetBIOS names, thus slowing up network performance.

Q: We have been experiencing some slower name resolution problems on a few of our older Windows NT workstation clients. To help speed up the name resolution process, we implemented LMHOSTS files using the #PRE tag prefix to load these entries in the local machine cache table. We have run the command **nbtstat –R** to purge and reload the name cache, but still have yet to see the #PRE switches show up in cache. Any ideas?

A: Make sure you have named the file LMHOSTS with no file extension and that you are not using the default sample file called LMHOSTS.SAM. You may need to enable the viewing of file extensions in your explorers **Folder options | View** configuration window. If you created the file with a text editor, it may have automatically saved it with the .TXT extension. If you moved the file to the appropriate directory rather than importing it, the .TXT extension would remain and prevent the file from being recognized by Windows as LMHOSTS.

Q: I am using an LMHOSTS file on two domain controllers that sit across a firewall boundary. One domain controller is part of a Windows Server 2003 Active Directory domain and acts as the PDC Emulator, and the other domain controller is in an NT 4.0 domain and acts as the PDC. I am trying to use the special hexadecimal service locator entries in my LMHOSTS file to help create a trust between these domains, but it does not seem to be working. I am using the following syntax:

```
192.168.0.50    "PDC  /0x1b"   #pre
```

A: When using hexadecimal locator numbers in an LMHOSTS file, you need to make sure you have specified the correct amount of blank spaces between the physical NetBIOS computer name and the actual hex number. The computer name plus the number of spaces between the hex number's beginning forward slash (/) can be no more or less than 15 characters. So, you would need to add 12 spaces if using the computer name PDC and to type it in the LMHOSTS file as follows:

```
192.168.0.50    "PDC            /0x1b"    #pre
```

Q: I want to use LMHOSTS files to try and speed up the logon process of my downlevel NT 4.0 workstation machines by adding all the domain controllers using the #PRE tag prefix and caching them on each machine. However, I have 200 machines. Is there a way I can use one LMHOSTS file and have everybody point to it?

A: Yes, by using the LMHOSTS file tag line entry **#INCLUDE** *<path to file>*. When using this entry, you can provide an alternate path to a shared file on a network resource. Remember, when using the tag, you must also include the NetBIOS name and IP address of the server that hosts the shared LMHOSTS file in another line entry.

Q: We are having a problem with certain static WINS mappings overwriting newly refreshed dynamic mappings. Why is this?

A: This is by design. Manually entered static records are set by default to not be overwritten, but to overwrite matching entries during replication. To turn this feature off, you can enable the option **Overwrite unique static mappings at this server (migrate on)** setting.

Q: Can I back up my WINS database in Windows Server 2003 without stopping the WINS service as I have to on my Windows NT 4.0 WINS servers?

A: Yes, you can. By using Windows Server 2003's new feature, Volume Shadow Copy, you can now back up your WINS server without taking the service offline.

Q: Do I have to manually choose each WINS server I want to replicate with?

A: No, you can choose to use the WINS option for automatic partner configuration. This feature will search for nearby WINS servers and create automatic replication partners at each end.

Q: Do I have to manually visit each machine I want to set up as a WINS client?

A: No, not if you are using DHCP. You can use DHCP and configure option 044 to push out and configure both primary and secondary WINS server IP addresses for your DHCP clients.

Q: Is there a way to allow my UNIX SMB clients to query my WINS server?

A: Yes, by installing a WINS proxy agent and pointing it to your WINS server. Just be certain that you do not install more than two proxy agents per network segment.

Q: How can I be sure my WINS client is configured with the right WINS server IP addresses?

A: An easy way is to run *ipconfig /all* at the command line of the client. Its output will tell you if your client is configured to use WINS and if the IP addresses of the WINS server are correct.

Q: How can I enable my DNS-only clients to use DNS to resolve names that reside only in my WINS database?

A: You can configure your DNS server to use WINS as a forwarder. When DNS queries are made to the DNS server for which it does not contain a record, it will forward the request over to the configured WINS server for resolution.

Q: Do I have to make my client services department local administrators of my WINS server in order for them to view the WINS database?

A: No, with Windows 2000 and Windows Server 2003 Active Directory comes a predelegated group called WINS Users. If you are a member of this group, you have view-only rights to all your WINS servers by default.

Q: Why is WINS required for me to browse my segmented network?

A: By design, segmented networks do not generally allow the transmission of broadcast packets outside their network interface boundaries because most routers do not forward broadcast messages by default. Without the use of WINS, browsing relies on broadcasts to gather browse list information. By using WINS on each network segment and implementing replication partners, you can eliminate the need to broadcast and use WINS to locate your browse lists.

Q: I am trying to troubleshoot a WINS server problem, but the System log does not seem to offer many events. What can I do?

A: You may want to turn on the advanced logging feature of WINS. This is turned off by default because it is very resource intensive, but can be used in cases like yours. You can enable this by clicking **Start | Administrative Tools | WINS** to open your WINS MMC snap-in console. Right-click your **WINS** *server name* and select **Properties**. Click the **Advanced** tab and click the option box **Log detailed events to Windows event**.

Self Test

A Quick Answer Key follows the Self Test questions. For complete questions, answers, and explanations to the Self Test questions in this chapter as well as the other chapters in this book, see the Self Test Appendix.

Review of NetBIOS Name Resolution

1. Tina, a network engineer for 123, Inc. corporation, is assigned the job of segmenting the company's internal network IP address scheme into five new networks from the current one network in place now. Four of the networks will be client broadcast domains and the fifth network will be the server network, consisting of all servers. The server network will continue to use their current IP addresses, whereas all other networks will have to change. The network consists of a native Windows Server 2003 domain with the Exchange 5.5 server being the only NT 4.0 server left in the environment because of some older applications build on top of this platform that are not ready for Exchange 2000. All clients run Windows XP on their desktops. Being very careful to prevent down time, Tina does her homework and gathers all the needed brainpower into a conference room to discuss possible problems and best practices for accomplishing the company's goals. She pulls together a member from each team, one from Systems Engineering, Desktop Support, Security, Application Support, and another from Network Engineering to put together an appropriate plan. She goes around the table and asks each group member what they will need to do in order to make this happen without causing unnecessary downtime. Here are their responses:

   - **Systems Engineering [Chad]** "We will need to create a new DHCP scope for each new network and assign it the appropriate IP address range and default gateway. Since the domain name suffix and DNS servers are common throughout, we can leave those as global scope options and be OK. I will also create an exclusion range for a handful of IP addresses for each network scope and give them to Gary to use when statically assigning certain needed workstations."

   - **Network Engineering [J.]** "We will need to subnet the class 10 network into five separate networks and break them out into ranges for Systems DHCP scopes. We will also let Chad know the appropriate default gateways to use for each new network. Lastly, we will enable the appropriate forwarding command on each router interface to allow DHCP broadcast to traverse the network."

- **Desktop Support [Gary]** "We will need to go through our list of statically assigned IP workstations in various departments and manually assign them a new IP address from the list Chad gives us and a new gateway IP address that J. gives us."

- **Security [Randy]** "There is really nothing we need to do."

- **Application Support [Doug]** "We will need to edit the access control lists for the accounting and human resource web applications with the static IP address assignments that Gary gives to the client workstations in these departments."

Tina feels comfortable that she has chosen the right group of people to get the job done and proceeds to schedule the work for the upcoming weekend. The project goes smoothly over the weekend. Chad confirms that each scope is handing out IP addresses correctly. J. confirms that the routers are allowing DHCP traffic across. Gary confirms that the DHCP clients can log on and authenticate with the domain controllers and browse the internet. He also confirms that the accounting and human resource users can access their Web applications. After these successful tests, Tina opens her Outlook Web Access client and sends an e-mail to upper management that everything was a success. On Monday morning, the Help Desk is flooded with calls. No one can log on to their outlook clients and get into mail. What did Chad forget to consider when evaluating the project plan?

A. Editing the access lists on the exchange database for the new static IP addresses

B. Creating new DNS entries for each new network scope

C. Adding a WINS server and distributing its IP address to each DHCP scope

D. Adding the ARP cache timeout option for each new DHCP scope

2. Computer Tech Inc. has recently been swamped with a lot of help desk calls from people complaining that computer connectivity is very intermittent throughout the day. Sometimes they can connect to a resource, but five minutes later they cannot. Based on the company's naming convention and frequent client turnaround, the support desk is also constantly typing computer names that no longer exist, or mistyping the computer name. The naming convention is based on a two–letter state identification ID plus a sequential number; for example, NJ1, NJ2, NJ3 or SC1, SC2, SC3. Computer Tech does not have a lot of network resources or the money to spend to get them. In order to afford equipment, they buy and deploy older, thus cheaper, technology. They are currently running their entire network on CAT3 cable with a 10BT network. They have only one router, segmenting the internal network from the Internet by way of a cable modem. All clients and servers currently connect daisy-chained network hubs and all use the same IP address scheme. Computer Tech hired a third-rate consulting company to come in and analyze their network to see if they

could help diagnose some of the problems. The consultants did some low-level sniffing tests and determined that based on the low grade wires deployed throughout the network, clients did not have enough time to successfully broadcast and hear a successful reply. They suggested that a script be written to slightly increase the amount of time clients were able to listen for broadcast query replies. Computer Tech asked their systems engineer Bart to write a system policy to increase this value on all clients. Bart got to work immediately and began writing a custom ADM file for the particular registry key. He made the following change over the weekend, pushing it out to the entire domain: HKLM\SYSTEM\CurrentControlSet\Services\NetBT\Parameters\BcastNameQueryCount=20. Throughout the next week, calls to the support desk did not get any better, and in fact increased. What did Bart do wrong?

A. Changed the key in the wrong registry hive

B. Did not make the registry value high enough

C. Did not make the registry value low enough

D. Changed the wrong key value

The NetBIOS Node Types

3. Mike owns a small advertising company in downtown Manhattan and commutes into work every day from New Jersey. With the economy picking up, his company has expanded over the last year, requiring him to hire a lot more people, buy more desktop machines, and more importantly, hire a group of people to manage his network. Mike originally set up his company network of five users, with a single NT 4.0 domain and static IP addresses for both the servers and clients. All network nodes share the same IP address scheme and reside on a single network segment. With the recent growth, his company now consists of over 100 employees and 20 servers. Mike's new network admin team is led by his most technical employee and long term neighbor, Scott. Scott has been working in the IT field for years and has seen small companies grow into large companies, knowing the barriers that need to be overcome. With his first week of employment, Scott opens up his network sniffer and begins gathering a baseline traffic report. After one week of sniffing the network, Scott reports back to Mike that there is an unusually large amount of network traffic on the network caused by client broadcasting. Realizing that all the clients are still running Windows 98 and require NetBIOS to resolve resource requests, Scott proposes a plan to greatly reduce the amount of broadcast traffic on the network. His plan consists of the following action items:

■   Convert all clients to DHCP

■   Install a WINS server

■   Set up a DHCP scope for the network address scheme

1. Exclude the server IP address

2. Add the WINS server as an option

3. Add the h-node type as an option

4. Add DNS as an option

5. Add the company's domain name suffix as an option

6. Add the default gateway as an option

Mike looks over his plan and is happy to have Scott on his team. He is eager to put the plan into action and schedules the work for the following evening. Between the two of them, they are able to install the networking components and touch all of the client machines to change their IP configuration to use DHCP. To test a successful implementation they log on to 15 different machines and test client to server connectivity. Everything seems to work great as they wrap up a late night and head back home to New Jersey. The next morning Scott receives no calls or complaints about network connectivity from his network administrators. Over the next week, Scott continues to sniff the network and monitor traffic flow. When he shows the report to Mike, he is surprised to see that network broadcast traffic has not been reduced by more than 1%. What did Scott forget to add to his plan?

A. P-node as an option as opposed to h-node

B. Configure servers to use DHCP

C. Configure servers with address of WINS server

D. M-node as an option as opposed to h-node

4. Keith was recently hired as a sales consultant for a software development company in Salt Lake City, Utah. Before attempting sales, Keith used to work in the computer industry as a contractor setting up small networks and configuring desktop machines. The late hours and technology overload pushed him into trying his luck in the sales arena. It has been almost a month and Keith is doing well. However, on Wednesday morning Keith is a bit frustrated about his network performance. His access to the sales application server is as slow as ever. Keith wishes he was back in IT and could fix the problem himself so he could get back to selling effectively. Because of his background, he decides to do a little digging before calling in a support desk ticket. He goes out to the command prompt window and types **ipconfig /all.** His results are shown in Figure 4.91.

Figure 4.91 Displaying IP Information Using IPCONFIG

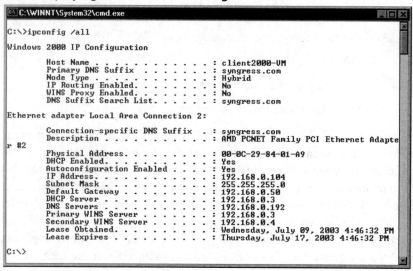

He verifies that he is using a WINS server. He then types **nbtstat –r** into his command window. The results show that half of his NetBIOS name resolutions are using broadcasts for name resolution. With this information, Keith calls the support desk and asks if the IP address of his WINS server is correct. They reply that it is. Keith thinks they are wrong because he knows that WINS servers should stop broadcasts. He continues to argue with support about his problem. What does support tell him next?

A. His node type supports broadcasting.

B. His node type does not support broadcasting.

C. They will reconfigure his node type for m-node.

D. They will reconfigure his node type for p-node.

5. Chris works as the systems manager for a bleeding edge computer company that is constantly trying to stay ahead of technology by implementing software days after it is released to the public. Until last weekend Chris and his network team supported a Windows 2000 native mode Active Directory domain using Exchange 2000. After the weekend, Chris was supporting a fully deployed Windows Server 2003 Active Directory environment. All of the clients at Chris's company are installed with either Windows 2000 Professional or Windows XP and are configured as DHCP clients. All servers are set up with static IP information. There is one group of NT 4.0 servers that run an ancient human resources payroll program. They do not yet currently support running on a Windows 2000 or Windows Server 2003 support platform. Because they are a somewhat smaller software company, all computer nodes are running on the same single network segment. Before the upgrade, Chris made sure to tell his systems

team that they need to leave the WINS server implementation in place as the payroll system still requires NetBIOS name resolution and everybody wants to make sure human resources can access and submit payroll checks! Eager to remove the old name resolution methods of Windows NT systems, Al conforms to the request yet suggests he has a way to at least eliminate the NetBIOS broadcast traffic. Chris agrees with him and says to make it so. Al changes the DHCP scope options and changes the node type from h-node to p-node. At the end of the month, the support desk starts receiving calls from the accounting department. They state that they are trying to access the payroll system to issue end of month checks but are unable to. They report a network error of "The network path was not found." Chris hears about the errors and is furious with Al because he had told him to leave the WINS server alone. In his defense, Al states that the WINS server is still up and that the Payroll applications server pool was able to communicate with each other just fine. Al runs nbtstat –r on one of the accounting machines and sees no broadcast activity, which is what he was trying to accomplish. What could be the problem?

A. The new node type has not taken effect yet.

B. The accounting client machines have not been rebooted yet.

C. The accounting servers were never configured to use WINS.

D. The accounting servers were not supposed to get the new node type.

The LMHOSTS file

6. You are a contractor working for a small Internet startup incubator, helping other companies get their companies on the right foot. One Friday afternoon, you find yourself at a local residence of someone trying to run a new business from his home. The owner, Joel, has run cat5e cable throughout his house and has two offices that are network and Internet-ready. You ask Joel a little bit about how his network is configured, and he tells you that he is running a Windows 2000 Active Directory mixed-mode backbone with one NT 4.0 BDC. All of his clients run Windows 98 or Windows ME. Because it is a small one-segment network, Joel tells you that he relies on broadcasts for name resolution and does not want to implement or manage a WINS server. However, he complains of slow network performance. You decide to work with him and recommend implementing LMHOSTS files on each of his Windows 98/ME workstations. Between the two of you, you create and test the LMHOSTS file on the owner's Windows 98 machine. It seems to greatly speed up his network performance. To save money, Joel sends you home and says he can add the same LMHOSTS file to each of the other machines. Twenty minutes later you get a call on your cell phone and Joel is complaining that the LMHOSTS file is not working on the other machines. What did you do, that Joel forgot to do?

A. Run **nbtstat -R**

B. Run **nbtstat -r**

C. Run **netstat -R**

D. Run **nbtstat -RR**

7. You work in the shipping and receiving warehouse for a small OEM computer supply company called The T-Group. It is your job as a desktop engineer to make sure that all clients are able to log on and authenticate to the corporate office from their NT 4.0 workstations. Currently, your client base of five workstations point to a WINS server at the corporate office to resolve logon and to authenticate to the correct domain controller. You get word that the systems engineering team is converting the functional level of the current Windows Server 2003 interim mode Active Directory domain over the weekend. They are raising the domain level to Windows Server 2003 native mode. You call the manager of this group and inquire about any changes you may need to make, so that your warehouse clients can still authenticate on Monday. Robert said that nothing would affect logon authentication, and in fact logon should be a lot quicker because he was removing some legacy protocols and services. Nervous about what he meant by this, as he is notorious for abrupt change without the correct research, you sit back and wait. Contrary to what was told to you, on Monday morning none of your NT 4.0 clients could log on. Knowing a little about network resolution, and more about Robert, you have a hunch and try to log on to using your Windows 2000 laptop machine that you built for emergencies. As you suspected, you are able to log on without a problem. You call Robert and ask him if he uninstalled the WINS server because he had heard that Windows Server 2003 no longer required NetBIOS. Robert replied, Yes. What can you do to quickly get your workstations logging onto the network again?

A. Distribute an LMHOSTS file using the #PRE and #DOM tags with the name and IP address of the new PDC Emulator and have everybody reboot.

B. Edit the default LMHOSTS file on everybody's workstation and use the #PRE and #DOM tags with the name and IP address of the new PDC Emulator.

C. Install WINS on one of the NT 4.0 workstations and have all your clients point to it.

D. Install a WINS proxy agent on one of your NT 4.0 workstations and have everybody point to it.

The Windows Server 2003
Windows Internet Name Server

8. You are working for the LAN Admin team at a local college in your home town of New Brunswick, NJ. It is your job to add and remove all user and computer names from the network as employees are hired and fired. The network you work on uses TCP/IP as its main network protocol, runs on a Windows 2003 Active Directory infrastructure with Windows NT 4.0 File Servers. All the clients are running Windows NT 4.0 workstation. As a LAN Admin team member, you have been added to the WINS Users active directory group in order to view WINS records and help troubleshoot workstation naming issues. Workstation names are based on cube number so that frequent turnaround does not require machine renaming. However, some employees use laptops and take their work home with them every night. On Monday morning, you received your weekly report detailing that last week's turnaround. On it were a few temps, some contractors, and some mobile users. You open Active Directory Users and Computers and delete all their usernames. On Tuesday, you receive a work order to add a new contractor to cube number 104. You venture over to cube 104 to begin the cleanup of the workstation for the new user. Based on the missing desktop, you realize that this must have been one of the mobile users that were recently fired. This means that you have to install a bare bone image on a new desktop. Based on the way names are created, the workstation name you would need to create would be NJ-104-NT40. You download your company's core OS image onto a new desktop PC and boot it up. Sysprep has been run on your image, so you go through all of the wizard's prompts in order to personalize this PC. When you get to the workstation name, you enter NJ-104-NT40. For some reason, you get the error message shown in Figure 4.92. You open up your WINS console and search for that name. To your surprise, you find it in an active state. You try to ping the name and IP address registered in your WINS database but get no response. What happened?

Figure 4.92 Workstation Naming Error

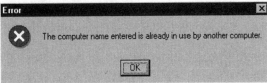

A. That is not a standard NetBIOS name.

B. That name is in use on your network.

C. That name is a hidden WINS record.

D. The computer holding that name was shut down incorrectly.

9. Jennifer, a long term employee, works as a systems engineer for a software development company you are planning to acquire. Before the two companies merge, you want to get a report from Jennifer, outlining her network design, server, and client node count, network protocols in use, and any needed application specific information. Your company employs the standard use of Windows XP on its client machines and has recently elevated the functional level of its domain to a Windows Server 2003 mode of active directory. The reason you are acquiring Jennifer's company is to take advantage of their very popular and world-renowned sales software product. You want to make sure the company merger does not interrupt the huge sales volumes level you currently demand when the switch to the new software is made. Jennifer is very aware of all your questions and gets the answers in a report back to you in a few days. In summary, it shows the following information:

- Windows 2003 interim functionality domain, with two Win2003 domain controllers and one NT 4.0 Backup Domain Controller

- Class A 10.0.0.0/24 network broken up into several broadcast domains

- 10 servers running a mix of Windows 2003 and Windows NT

- 50 client machines running a mix of Windows 98, Windows 2000, and Windows XP

- Network protocols in use: IP

- Network services in use: WINS, DHCP, DNS

- WINS and DHCP share a single server

- Sales software requires NetBIOS

You review the differences in the networks and devise a plan with Jennifer's help to merge the two companies. You decide to use Jennifer's domain as the source domain because it is already built with a generic *root.com* domain name and a simple OU design. You want to keep the internal domain structure generic and begin a new OU design from scratch rather than try to reorganize your own. Because of the scalability of Windows Server 2003, you decide that you do not need any more hardware to accommodate the additional 1000 workstations and 50 servers. The assumption was correct at first and the migration was scheduled and completed successfully over a long four-day weekend. Jennifer's company's NT 4.0 domain controller was removed and deleted from the domain, the functional level was raised to be equivalent to yours, and your company was migrated directly into their OU design. The current DHCP scopes were already configured with plenty of IP addresses to handle the new client load. On Monday morning, all the new clients come into work and boot up their machines. At first, everybody is able to log on and access the sales application just fine, but as more and more users come in and boot up, they are not even able to log on. After some investigation, Jennifer finds the following facts:

- Old users seem to be able to log on with cached credential but are using APIPA.

- New users are unable to log on to the domain at all, but can log on locally and also use APIPA.

- Users that are already logged on are up and working, but cannot access the sales application.

- The WINS server is hung.

What happened?

A. The DHCP scope ran out of addresses.

B. The WINS server's burst handling was set to *Low*.

C. The WINS server's burst handling was not installed.

D. The WINS server's burst handling was disabled.

Configuring the WINS Client

10. You are an ASP.NET Web developer working for an Application Solutions Provider in Seattle, Washington. Because of the kind of work you do, your company allows you the flexibility to work from home about 90 percent of the time. The other 10 percent of the time is spent in the office, at corporate meetings, or presenting new code to other development workers. Your manager Akin asks you to present your current code in a meeting on Wednesday afternoon, to show the other developers. You show up Wednesday morning prepared to wow your coworkers with your new code. About five minutes before the meeting you decide to print a copy of your code to hand out in the meeting. You gather your things and head into Conference Room A. You plug your Windows 2000 laptop into an available network jack and begin to set up a printer in accordance with the instruction card next to the conference room printer. The card states that the printer queue is named CONFA and the NT 4.0 print server is named PRINTSRV. As people start entering the room, you quickly realize that your IP information is set up for your home network. You make a quick call to one of your friends that works in the systems group and ask him for a valid IP address, subnet, and gateway for Conference Room A. You also get the IP address for the company DNS server and verify the NetBIOS name of the conference room print server. You set up your new information and test Internet connectivity successfully. Everyone is now seated and ready for your presentation. You say that you want to print a copy of your code and for everyone to grab it off the printer behind them. You quickly try to locate the printer to set it up by typing \\PRINTSRV\CONFA at the **Run** command window. You receive an error message that tells you the printer cannot be found. As you swallow your pride in front of your peers and call your friend back what does he tell you?

A. The correct IP address of the gateway

B. The IP address of the WINS server

C. The IP address of the CONFA printer

D. The IP address of the PRINTSRV server

11. Jamie has just opened her first consulting LLC in Nutley, NJ and is beginning to pull in some real business. She is starting off small with a few mom-and-pop shop administration jobs and a bit of integration work for some larger companies mixed in on the side. Jamie has been working in the IT business for quite some time and understands the importance of quick name resolution. She runs into a smaller, predominantly NetBIOS-based computer network company that seems to be having broadcast issues. They tell Jamie that they want to implement a solution with as little work as possible and that all the clients and servers must remain configured with static IP addresses. Jamie does a diagnosis of the computer network and finds that things rarely change, and the clients and servers have been running with the same names and IP addresses for 10 years. WINS is not in use on the network since broadcasts are now used for NetBIOS names resolution on the single segment network. Jamie decides to go with the following solution:

- Create a client side LMHOSTS file using the #INCLUDE tag to centrally point clients to a server side LMHOSTS file located on a common file server. Use the #BEGIN_ALTERNATE and #END_ALTERNATE tags to add another #INCLUDE statement for a pointer to a second copy of the server side LMHOST file for redundancy. The client side LMHOSTS file looks like this:

```
#BEGIN_ALTERNATE
#INCLUDE \\server1\public\lmhosts
#INCLUDE \\server2\public\lmhosts
#END_ALTERNATE
```

- Push the client side LMHOSTS file to each of the clients' %systemroot%\system32\drivers\etc directory by means of a logon script.

- Create a server side LMHOSTS file that includes all the NetBIOS server names using the #PRE tag to permanently cache the entries in each client's local name cache, for fast access and limited broadcasts.

Jamie puts this solution in place and is confident it will work because it is what she used to do at every administrator job she worked at previously. She drops by the office of Al, the owner, on the way out the door and tells him that clients will need to reboot their machines twice in order for the NetBIOS broadcast problem to go away. She explains that the first reboot will allow the LMHOSTS file to be copied locally, and the second reboot will read the local LMHOSTS file, telling it to load all the entries in name cache from the central server side LMHOSTS file. Jamie receives a call from Al about two hours later. He is complaining that it appears nothing has changed; client access is still slow. Jamie walks him through running the **nbtstat –r** command on five or six workstations. He reports that **Resolved by Broadcast** is 50 or higher on each of his client's workstations. She then has him search and look at the local LMHOSTS file to verify that it is correct. She has him manually reload it by typing **nbtstat –R**, but with no luck. As Al accesses resources that should be in the server side LMHOSTS file, the broadcast count gets higher. What did Jamie forget?

A. To include the #PRE and #DOM tags in the client side LMHOSTS file

B. To include the IP address and name of server1 and server2 in the client side LMHOSTS file

C. To include the IP address and name of server1 and server2 in the server side LMHOSTS file

D. To include the #REDIRECT tag instead of the older #INCLUDE tag

Network Service Interoperability

12. Kurt, the network administrator for Fantastic, Inc., a plastics manufacturing company, is a member of the DHCP Administrators group and is in charge of configuring all client DHCP scopes. Because it is a rather large client community, Kurt manages just over 20 DCHP scopes for the 20 or so different subnets on his company network. Though the network backend runs Windows Server 2003 Active Directory, most of the client community still runs Windows NT 4.0 on their desktops. Recently, the IP address of one of the secondary WINS servers had to change due to a revamp in its network subnet addressing scheme. In order to distribute this needed change to Kurt's clients, Kurt had to make the change 20 times, one for each subnet's scope. After the change was made and no users complained of any difficulties, Kurt looked into creating another solution for making a global change like this in the future. After some research, Kurt discovered DHCP Server Options. These are options that that be set once and applied globally on all scopes on a single server. Kurt put in a change control request to change all options that could be applied globally to the DHCP server. The options he chose were:

- Primary and secondary WINS Server IP Addresses

- Primary and secondary DNS Server IP addresses

- DNS Domain Name suffix

The request was approved and Kurt made the changes over the weekend. On Monday morning, the help desk starts receiving call tickets from people complaining of slow network logons and client server access times. The help desk confirmed, however, that although they are able to access network resources, including the Internet, some resources are very slow. You ask J, one of your network guys, to run a sniffer on the network and see if there are any abnormal broadcasts happening. He reports back to you that there is not a lot of broadcast traffic on the network. What has happened?

A. Kurt entered the wrong DNS server IP address in the scope.

B. Kurt forgot to switch the default gateway to a Global Scope option.

C. Kurt entered the wrong secondary WINS IP address.

D. Kurt entered the wrong primary WINS IP address.

13. As the network administrator, Kristy decides to implement the ability for clients to dial-in to the network to allow them the option to work from home if they want to, by installing and configuring an RRAS server. Kristy's internal network consists of a Windows 2000 domain, a single DNS and WINS server, multiple segmented broadcast domains, and a single DHCP server, configured to distribute the following information via four different IP address scopes:

- DNS Server (local option)

- Router (local option)

- WINS Server (local option)

- Node Type (global option)

- Domain Name (global option)

- ARP Timeout (local)

Kristy installs her RRAS server and configures the DHCP Relay Agent to point to the only internal DHCP server. She then configures a fifth DHCP scope to accommodate the DMZ network into which she has installed her RRAS server. Kristy hopes to be able to offer both internal Web mail and resource access to her NT 4.0 file server in the same way she is able to successfully offer it now to only internal users. Kristy composes an e-mail with detailed instructions on how to set up her Windows ME laptop users with the correct VPN settings to dial-in the company RRAS server. With the e-mail, Kristy asks for feedback as to ease of installation, setup, connectivity, speed, resource access, and so on. A few days later, Kristy receives e-mails from most of the users she sent the e-mail to. All of them said that they were able to access e-mail just fine and that the speeds were great. They also said they were able to browse the Internet without a problem, but none of them could access any of the file server resources that they needed to do their work. What is the easiest thing Kristy can do to facilitate this need?

A. Change the DNS server to a global option in DHCP

B. Change the WINS server to a global option in DHCP

C. Change the node type to a local option for each scope in DHCP

D. Add another WINS server to facilitate the dial-in users

Monitoring and Troubleshooting the Windows Server 2003 WINS Server

14. Jackie is the owner and administrator of network NetBIOS name resolution and replication. She has been the administrator for XYZ Corporation since it started using WINS back with Windows NT Server V3.51, so she is very familiar with the name resolution process. XYC Corporation is currently running Windows Server 2003 WINS servers and has set up two-way WINS Push/Pull replication between its hub in Boston, MA and all its satellite offices around the state. Gloucester is one of the satellite offices, and ever since the long weekend's scheduled database maintenance work, they are no longer receiving WINS replication records from the Boston hub. What could have possible happened over the weekend to prevent records in Boston from replicating to Gloucester? Boston is not having problems with any other site.

   A. Someone has added the Gloucester WINS server IP address in the Accept records for the owner's box on the Boston WINS server.

   B. Someone has added the Gloucester WINS server IP address in the Block records for the owner's box on the Boston WINS server.

   C. Someone has added the Boston WINS server IP address in the Accept records for the owner's box on the Gloucester WINS server.

   D. Someone has added the Boston WINS server IP address into the Block records for the owner's box on the Andover WINS server.

15. Chad is the network administrator for an online banking company located on the east coast of the United States. He has recently been involved with a team of engineers to help integrate their company with another online banking firm, and has been working closely with that company's lead engineer, Scott. Chad's company consists of a completely Windows NT 4.0 domain infrastructure, whereas Scott manages a fully native mode Windows 2000 Active Directory domain environment. The plan, as set forth by upper management, is to consolidate the NT 4.0 domain as an organizational unit in the Windows 2000 domain. To help facilitate this process, Chad and Scott set up a downlevel two-way trust between each of the domains. The trust is set up without a problem and now they are ready to start sharing resources. Scott tells Chad that before they are able to start accessing file share resources, they need to set up NetBIOS WINS replication. Chad informs Scott that he will need to get approval from his manager before going forth with that next step. Chad asks if there is any other way that some of his NT 4.0 clients can start accessing resources on some of the Windows 2000 servers. Scott tells him that there is a temporary solution and sends Chad a custom LMHOSTS file that has in it all the server names and downlevel domain controller information for the Windows 2000 domains PDC emulator and its

servers. Scott proceeds to tell Chad that he can place this file in the %systemroot%\ system32\drivers\etc directory of any server he wants to access resources in his domain. He will just need to reboot that server or run **nbtstat —R** to load the LMHOSTS file into name cache. Chad tries it on one of his servers and lets Scott know that it worked perfectly. Scott and Chad did not communicate for a few weeks after that because other projects seemed to pile up on each of their plates. The following Friday, Scott gave Chad a call and informed him he planned on changing one of the network segment's IP schemes, containing all the domain controllers. Although the WINS servers would not be affected, he discussed the fact that all the IP addresses of the DC's and some of the application servers had to change and that the LMHOSTS file would cease to work without changing it. Chad recommended they go forth with WINS replication instead as he had finally gotten approval from his manager. They scheduled the change for the Tuesday after the network change. Late Tuesday evening, both domains' WINS servers were set up as Push/Pull replication partners with each other, along with the help of a newly created LMHOSTS file to get initial name resolution working. Chad said that he noticed records flowing into his database, as did Scott. Both were satisfied with the results, and because it was late they were both ready to call it a day. Early Wednesday morning, Todd, Scott's boss, calls him complaining that none of his Windows 98 users can log on to the domain. He mentioned that his team was able to log on to the domain but they were not able to access the Exchange 5.5 server. You think to yourself about the differences and realize that Todd and his team members are using Windows XP. What happened?

A. Chad imported the original LMHOSTS file into his WINS server.

B. Chad forgot to remove the original LMHOSTS file from his WINS server.

C. Scott forgot to restart his WINS service after replication had taken place.

D. Scott forgot to change his DHCP server to hand out new WINS server IP addresses.

Self Test Quick Answer Key

For complete questions, answers, and explanations to the Self Test questions in this chapter as well as the other chapters in this book, see the Self Test Appendix.

1. **C**
2. **D**
3. **C**
4. **A**
5. **C**
6. **A**
7. **A**
8. **D**

9. **D**
10. **B**
11. **B**
12. **D**
13. **B**
14. **B**
15. **A**

Chapter 5

MCSA/MCSE 70-291

Domain Naming System Concepts

Exam Objectives in this Chapter:

2.2.3   Manage DNS server options.

☑   Summary of Exam Objectives

☑   Exam Objectives Fast Track

☑   Exam Objectives Frequently Asked Questions

☑   Self Test

☑   Self Test Quick Answer Key

Introduction

When internetworking was first conceived and implemented in the 1960s and 1970s, the Internet Protocol (IP) addressing scheme was also devised. It uses four sets of 8 bits (octets) to identify a unique address, which is composed of a network address and a unique host address. This provided enormous flexibility because this scheme allowed for millions of addresses. The original inventors of this system probably didn't envision the networking world as it is today—with millions of computers spanning the globe, many connected to one worldwide network, the Internet.

IP addressing works quite well, but most people have trouble remembering up to 12 digits at a time. If a friend says, "Yeah, just e-mail me, my e-mail address is me@247.84.132.167," you'll probably forget it, or transpose one or more numbers. If your friend says "Yeah, just e-mail me, my e-mail address is me@myname.com," you'll likely remember it. Similarly, it's easier to send a print job to a printer named HRLaserPrt1 rather than 154.39.187.241. Human brains can work well with numbers, but in terms of memory, we're more likely to remember a name than a long number. Computers, on the other hand, can only process binary information—numbers. As a result, computers connected to networks have both IP addresses and computer names. These names are sometimes referred to as *computer names* or *host names*.

In this chapter, we explore the *Domain Name System* (DNS). This is a method of creating hierarchical names that can be resolved to IP addresses (which, in turn, are resolved to MAC addresses). We explain the basis of DNS and compare it to alternative naming systems. We also explain how the DNS namespace is created and resolved to an IP address throughout the Internet or within a single organization. Once you have a solid foundation of understanding of DNS, you will learn about Windows Server 2003 DNS server, including the different roles DNS servers can play, the ways DNS Servers resolve names and replicate data, and how Windows Server 2003 Active Directory integrates with DNS. By the end of this chapter, you'll have a detailed understanding of DNS on the Internet as well as how DNS works within a Windows Server 2003 network.

NOTE

As with many of the networking constructs created years ago, the DNS framework is coming under increasing pressure as more and more servers are added around the world. For an interesting discussion of some of the new challenges facing the DNS framework, refer to RFC3467 (February 2003) at www.ietf.org/rfc/rfc3467.txt?number=3467 on the Internet Engineering Task Force (IETF) Web site. The International Engineering Task Force is an international organization that is concerned with the evolution of Internet architecture and the smooth operation and expansion of the Internet. It is open to any interested individual and work is done via working groups dedicated to specific tasks or areas of interest. RFCs are documents that outline methods to accomplish various Internet-related tasks.

Review of DNS

DNS initially was implemented on large networks in the late 1960s and early 1970s. It was widely used as computers were networked across dissimilar systems. The first network, ARPANET (discussed in Chapter 1), was a small network of large, mainframe computers. Each computer had a unique name, a *host name*, and an IP address, which were recorded in a file kept on each computer called the HOSTS file. It was a flat text file and was used by the computer to resolve host names to IP addresses. For example, the listing might look something like this:

```
66.154.14.9    UAserver1     # University A Server 1
66.154.14.10   UAserver2     # University A Server 2
62.99.74.8     Sciserver9    # Scientific Company A Server 9
62.99.74.19    Tecserver11   # Technical Company B Server 11
```

When there were five, ten, or even twenty computers, it wasn't difficult to keep the file current, nor was it difficult to choose a unique computer name. However, as the network expanded, it became increasingly difficult to do both. As organizations (universities, government agencies, and large corporations, at first) expanded their internal networks, the difficulty of ensuring unique computer names increased. It also became increasingly difficult to maintain an up-to-date version of the HOSTS file on each computer and the bandwidth required to transmit this file was expanding beyond the bandwidth capabilities of the time. Another system needed to be implemented.

What emerged from this were two RFCs, 882 and 883, that described the design of a domain name system based on a distributed database containing general resource information rather than relying on a distributed flat text file. Additional refinement to this concept was set out in RFCs 1034 and 1035. Further refinements have been made, but the schema for DNS was described in these four RFCs.

NOTE

For more information on RFCs 882, 883, 1034, and 1035, see www.ietf.org/rfc.html and search on the specific RFC number.

When the Windows operating system was developed, it began to incorporate networking capabilities, beginning with Windows 3.11. Microsoft chose to use the NetBIOS interface, which started as a high-level programming language developed by the Sytek Corporation for IBM, specifically for IBM-based PCs running the PC-DOS operating system. NetBIOS is a session layer interface that applications can use to communicate via transportation protocols that are NetBIOS compatible. One way to accomplish this is by using NetBIOS over TCP, or NetBT.

NetBIOS defines a software interface, not a protocol. The interface is designed to work over TCP and UDP, the two primary transport protocols in the TCP/IP suite. RFC1001 and 1002 define how NetBIOS works with TCP (RFC1001) and UDP (RFC1002) to provide a common framework for implementation. Prior to RFCs 1001 and 1002, NetBIOS was implemented over a variety of protocols and hardware systems, which meant that different implementations might not interoperate because they did not use the same protocols. Although adherence to RFCs 1001 and 1002 is voluntary, it is highly desirable because different implementations that adhere to these recommendations can interoperate.

RFC 1001 defines a NetBIOS name as a computer name that can contain 16 alphanumeric characters. The name is not permitted to not start with an asterisk (*) and each name must be unique. When RFCs 1001 and 1002 were developed, it was thought that most name resolution would occur over a local network, not across routers (gateways). Thus, there are limitations to NetBIOS with regard to wide area networks (WANs), including the fact that NetBIOS name resolution uses broadcasts to resolve names. Although this is fine for smaller networks, it becomes unmanageable over larger networks or across WANs. To address some of the constraints of NetBIOS name resolution, Microsoft implemented a unique system called Windows Internet Naming System (WINS). WINS is implemented only on Windows-based computers and is therefore proprietary to Windows, even though it is based on the wider NetBIOS RFCs that provide more generically for NetBIOS Name Servers (NBNSs). Although WINS is still supported in Windows Server 2003, the preferred (and default) method of name resolution became DNS beginning with Windows 2000. WINS is supported in order to provide backward compatibility for applications written to the NetBIOS interface.

Let's look at the similarities and differences of NetBIOS and DNS to better understand the evolution of naming, both on the Internet and in Windows operating systems.

Comparing NetBIOS and DNS Naming Conventions

As mentioned previously, the NetBIOS naming system originally was defined by the Sytek Corporation for IBM, for use on personal computers. It is a flat naming system with names that cannot exceed 16 characters. Although RFC1001 defines 16 characters for a NetBIOS name, Microsoft uses the sixteenth character as a NetBIOS suffix to define various functions, as you'll see in a moment.

By contrast, DNS is a more flexible system because names are not constrained by the 16 character limit. It is a hierarchical system, which allows for both longer names (up to 255 characters) and a more orderly method of naming. In addition, DNS has the ability to distribute and update a name resolution database across a WAN to provide more efficient name resolution services.

Test Day Tip

Remember that Microsoft NetBIOS names are limited to 15 characters even though RFC 1001 allows for 16. In Microsoft implementations of NetBIOS, the sixteenth character is a NetBIOS suffix. Keeping this in mind will help you identify illegal NetBIOS names on the exam.

Flat versus Hierarchical

The NetBIOS construction is a flat naming system. This means that only one computer can have a particular name, which must be unique on that network (or on any network to which that network is attached). Examples of a flat naming structure are SERVER1, SERVER2, and SERVER3. Under such a flat system, if Company A, connected to the Internet, had a server called SERVER1, then no other company connected to the Internet could have a server called SERVER1 or data packets would not be properly delivered to either computer. Clearly, this becomes a constraint very quickly, especially because all companies cannot possibly check with one another before naming a computer and bringing it online.

The hierarchical system, used by DNS, is a more flexible system that still guarantees a unique name. In this framework, the naming system is called the *domain namespace* and is structured similarly to a directory tree on a disk drive. In this system, the domain namespace begins at the root, which is unnamed and is identified by ".". As it expands, there are more and more branches to the tree and each node creates a unique name. An organization can choose to create a private domain namespace and it does not have to be unique as long as it does not interact with public networks such as the Internet.

Naming Conventions

If you're like most people, the first time you encounter some of the naming conventions in the computer world you can become quite confused. It seems there are names for everything but none of the names are quite the same. Let's take a moment to go through some of these to help answer any questions you might have.

- **Computer name** A computer name is just that, the name you give your computer. In many companies this name is assigned, although in some companies users can choose their computers' names. On a Windows XP/2000/Server 2003 computer, you can find your computer's name by right-clicking on **My Computer** and selecting **Properties**. (Alternately, you can select **System** from **Control Panel** to access the **System Properties** dialog box.) Then click the **Computer Name** tab to display (or change) your computer name. If you're on a network, this name must be unique. If you're not on a network, this name can be just about anything you choose. You can configure alternate names on the **Computer Name** tab by clicking **More** and entering your particular data. However, changing this information on a computer already connected to the network can cause the computer to lose connectivity due to naming conflicts. Most companies use a naming scheme to ensure all computer names are unique.

- **NetBIOS name** In a Windows-based computer, the name you see listed on the Computer Name tab of the My Computer properties *is* the NetBIOS name. This name can be up to 15 characters long (in Microsoft operating systems) and is used to identify the computer on the network. When NetBIOS name resolution occurs, the computer name (NetBIOS name) is mapped to an IP address.

- **Host name** This term originates in the mainframe and UNIX world. It was originally used in the same way a computer name is used in Windows. Technically, a host is any device with an IP address that is not a router and that is attached to the network. Host names are used in DNS and are resolved to IP addresses. Although host names are resolved to IP addresses as are NetBIOS names, the resolution process is different—do not confuse these two types of names. NetBIOS names must be resolved via an LMHOSTS file or via a NetBIOS name server, which in Windows is implemented as *Windows Internet Naming System* or WINS. Host names must be resolved via host name resolution, which is accomplished via a HOSTS file or via DNS servers, requesters, and resolvers (you'll learn more about this later in this chapter).

   A host name can be up to 255 characters long and can contain alphanumeric characters and the hyphen symbol (-). A period is used as the delimiter between segments in a DNS name, so it cannot be part of the name. Blank and space characters are not permitted. The first character, until recently, had to be an alpha character. That limitation has been removed and names can now begin with an alpha or numeric character. The last character cannot be a hyphen (-) or period (.). Case is not relevant, thus there is no difference between the names SERVER, SERver, and server.

NOTE

Some Microsoft documentation incorrectly states that the dot (.) character can be used in host names. This is incorrect and will result in errors. The dot character is interpreted as a delimiter and can be used in Fully Qualified Domain Names (FQDN). For more information, see Microsoft Knowledge Base article 122900.

By default, a computer's *host name* is set to the computer name (also known as the NetBIOS name), but a different host name can be assigned to the computer. To see the computer's host name, you can use the command line by choosing **Start | Run** and typing **cmd**. In the command prompt window, type **hostname**, then press **Enter**. The computer's host name is displayed. To compare it to the computer's NetBIOS name, use the command line again and type **net name** and press **Enter**. The computer's NetBIOS name is displayed (along with the logged on user's account name). To close the command prompt window, type **exit** and press **Enter**. Type the word **exit** to close the command prompt session.

- **DNS name** A DNS name can be a series of labels, each separated by a dot (.) to distinguish branches or nodes of the name within a hierarchy. An example of a DNS name is rosie.security.az.somecompany.com. When displayed in this manner, the name is called a *Fully Qualified Domain Name* (FQDN) because the entire path is shown. The left-most segment of a DNS name is the specific host name of the device; the remaining segments are the domain name (left to right from lowest to highest level domain).

- **Nickname** A *nickname* is an alternate name given a host name. It is often a shorter version of the FQDN. For instance, the computer named rosie.security.az.somecompany.com might also be called rosie1. As long as this nickname is unique on that node, the nickname can be used to map to the FQDN, which is then used to map to the IP address. In this case, rosie is the actual host name and rosie1 is the nickname. However, if another host is named rosie, it cannot also be called rosie1. Another host can be named rosie if it is on a different node, however. For instance, rosie.security.fl.somecompany.com is not the same name because it follows a different path. However, it cannot use the nickname rosie1. But it *can* use the nickname rosie2. You'll learn more on this topic throughout this chapter.

- **Alias** An alias is a any name used in place of another name. In DNS, an *alias* is called the *Canonical Name* (CNAME). A server named server1.somecompany.com might have an *alias* of dc1.somecompany.net, for example. You'll learn more about this later in this chapter, and we'll discuss how and why aliases are used.

NetBIOS Name Resolution Review

It is important to understand how NetBIOS names are resolved to IP addresses in order to understand the similarities and differences between NetBIOS and DNS naming conventions. We'll review NetBIOS name resolution briefly here.

A NetBIOS name can be 16 characters long, but in Windows, the sixteenth character is reserved for various NetBIOS functions. If a name is not 15 characters long, it is padded with spaces (in binary format, with 0s) so that all names are always 15 characters plus the sixteenth function character. The sixteenth character is used by Microsoft networking to define functions installed on the named device, such as Workstation Service, File Server Service, Master Browser Service, and so on. Several of the more common NetBIOS suffixes are shown here. The name type is shown with the hexadecimal (hex or h) suffix. They're shown in hex format because some of the characters are not printable.

\<computername\>	00	Workstation Service
\<computername\>	01	Messenger Service
\<computername\>	20	File Server Service
\<computername\>	21	Remote Access Server Client Service
\<domain\>	00	Domain Name
\<domain\>	1B	Domain Master Browser
\<domain\>	1C	Domain Controller
\<domain\>	1D	Master Browser

NOTE

For more information on how Microsoft uses the sixteenth character of the NetBIOS name to define various functions, see Microsoft Knowledge Base article 163409. Additional related articles are 119495 and 154608.

A NetBIOS name is either a unique name (belongs exclusively to one device) or a group name (belongs to a group and is nonexclusive). When a NetBIOS process needs to communicate across the network, it does so by specifying a unique name. When it needs to communicate with multiple processes on multiple computers, it does so using the group name.

A NetBIOS name must be resolved to an IP address on a network using TCP/IP in order for communications to occur. Thus, there must be a mechanism that translates or resolves the NetBIOS name to a specific IP address. This can be accomplished in several ways, but one that is commonly used in Windows is the NetBIOS over TCP (NetBT) interface at the session layer. NetBT either will send a broadcast containing a NetBIOS name query across the network or it will send a NetBIOS name query to a specific NetBIOS Name Server. In Windows, this function is provided (with a few proprietary modifications) by WINS. The process of resolving a NetBIOS name specified by an application using the NetBIOS API, then, is to broadcast or query for name-to-IP resolution. Prior to the implementation of WINS, NetBIOS name resolution was also accomplished using a file called the LMHOSTS file. Like the HOSTS file for host names, the LMHOSTS file is a flat text file that contains the mappings of specific NetBIOS names to IP addresses. LM stands for LAN Manager, which was the name used by IBM for networking functions in early PCs. LMHOSTS files can still be used for NetBIOS name resolution, though that function is most often handled by the WINS service on the Microsoft platform.

NetBIOS and Winsock Interface Name Resolution

The two most common ways applications running on a Windows-based platform can access the TCP/IP stack and communicate across a network are using the NetBIOS programming interface and the Windows Sockets programming interface. Both are *application programming interfaces* (APIs), providing a set of functions and commands that can be used by software developers when writing programs that need to perform network functions. The NetBIOS API provides applications written to the NetBIOS interface access to other computers across a network via the *computer name* (also called the NetBIOS name). It requires a session layer interface to access the TCP/IP protocol stack. This is accomplished via *NetBIOS over TCP*, also known as NetBT. NetBIOS provides name management, name resolution, delivery of datagrams (via UDP), and delivery of NetBIOS messages (via TCP).

By contrast, the Windows Sockets interface (Winsock) is another way Windows-based applications can communicate across the network. It allows applications written to the Winsock API to connect to remote computers via the *IP address* (in this case, it's called a *destination socket*, which contains the IP address), not the computer name. Thus, the Winsock API is independent from any specific *naming* convention since it relies solely on the IP address.

TEST DAY TIP

An application will be designed to run using either the NetBIOS interface via NetBIOS over TCP or the Windows Sockets interface, which runs directly over TCP.

The DNS Namespace

The DNS namespace is a hierarchical space. A *hierarchy* is defined as a structure in which an entity is subordinate to the entity above it. Many of us are familiar with hierarchies such as the military, where a private is subordinate to a corporal, who is subordinate to a sergeant, and so forth. In the DNS hierarchy, the DNS name is divided into separate levels, each denoted by a dot or period (.). The top of the hierarchy is the right-most part of the name and the lowest level of the hierarchy is the left-most part of the name.

Every node in the hierarchy has a name, referred to as a *label*, which can be zero to 63 octets in length. This is more commonly referred to as "up to 63 characters" because alphanumeric characters each are denoted within an octet. The 63 character limit is also referred to as 63 bytes, since a byte is 8 bits, or an octet. Nodes on the same branch cannot have the same name, but nodes on separate branches can.

The *domain name* for a specific node is the list of *labels* along the path from the root to the specific node. The full list of labels for a particular node is referred to as a FQDN. It is considered fully qualified because the entire list of labels is shown, leaving no doubt as to the entire path through the hierarchy to the specific node. Since we read domain names from left to right, we start with the most specific name and move up the hierarchy toward the more generic *top level domain* (TLD). This tree-like structure is shown in Figure 5.1, which shows only a few of the total number of TLDs now available.

Figure 5.1 DNS Name Structure

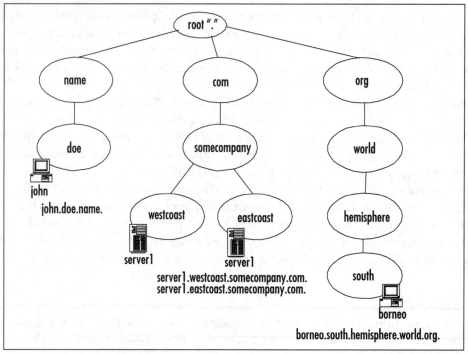

The root domain is denoted with the use of a dot (.) and has a length of zero characters. Technically, when written, all domain names end with the root character, though it is rarely denoted this way in common practice. Thus, a well-known domain name like *microsoft.com* should more correctly be denoted as *microsoft.com.*, with the final dot shown at the right end of the name. After the root, we move to the right, to the TLD. There are three types of TLDs: *ARPA*, *Generic*, and *Country Codes*.

The *ARPA* TLD is reserved for reverse name lookups and is discussed later in this chapter.

There were originally seven *generic* TLDs, as defined in RFC 1034: *com*, *net*, *org*, *edu*, *mil*, *gov*, and *int*. The seven TLDs were used by a variety of organizations, although the designations originally were intended for use by particular types of organizations. Table 5.1 shows the original intended use of the seven TLDs.

Table 5.1 Original Top Level Domain Designations

TLD	Original Use
com	Domains run by commercial businesses
net	Companies involved in Internet infrastructure activities
org	Nonprofit or not-for-profit organizations (though open to all)

Continued

Table 5.1 Original Top Level Domain Designations

TLD	Original Use
edu	Degree-granting accredited educational institutions
mil	United States military
gov	United States government
int	Registering organizations established by international treaties between governments
arpa	Reserved for reverse name lookup

As you can see, the seven original TLDs (excluding *arpa*, which is reserved) all were three letters long. This convention was used until November 2000 when the Internet Corporation for Assigned Names and Numbers (ICANN) authorized the use of new TLDs. There are now a total of 14 designated generic TLDs. The additions are shown in Table 5.2 along with their intended use.

Table 5.2 New Generic Top Level Domains

TLD	Intended Use
aero	Air-transportation industry (aviation)
coop	Cooperatives
biz	Businesses
museum	Museums
name	Individual names
info	Information
pro	Credentialed professions (such as accountants, attorneys)

The third category of TLDs are country code TLDs (ccTLD), which are two-letter country abbreviations, such as .uk for the United Kingdom, .jp for Japan, and so forth. The country codes are based on the country names used by the International Organization for Standardization (ISO). The one notable exception is that ISO uses .gb for Great Britain, as opposed to the ICANN designation .uk for United Kingdom. These country codes are regulated by the respective countries and are reserved for citizens of those countries.

TEST DAY TIP

Although there are new TLDs available, you're most likely to run into questions using the original TLDs such as .com, .org, or .net. The questions you'll encounter will most likely be focused on the structure of the domain rather than the details of the specific TLD. Being able to identify the commonly used TLDs and being aware of the new additions will be sufficient to successfully answer related questions on the exam.

Less specific than the TLDs are the second-level domain names. These identify specific organizations and must also be unique within their respective TLDs on the Internet. The uniqueness is regulated to ensure that the combination of second-level domain name plus TLD is always unique.

NOTE

For more information on top level domains, visit the Internet Assigned Numbers Authority (IANA) Web site, www.iana.org. IANA is responsible for the technical coordination of naming conventions on the Internet. Although IANA is responsible for TLDs and root name servers, it is also involved with additional Internet-related activities including defining and coordinating identifiers that include MIME media types, port numbers, private-enterprise numbers, and protocol numbers.

Domain and Host Names

A *host name* is a name assigned to a device to identify it as a TCP/IP host that has an IP address. This host name, unlike a NetBIOS computer name, can be up to 255 characters long and can contain alphanumeric and numeric characters as well as a hyphen (-). In Windows Server 2003 computers, the host name does not have to match the computer name. Host names can take a variety of forms, but the two most common are the nickname and the domain name. A *nickname* can be created by the user as an alias to the assigned IP address. The *domain name*, as you've just learned, is specified by the naming conventions used on the Internet. The name of the specific host in a DNS name is the left-most name in the hierarchy.

Applications using Windows Sockets, such as Internet Explorer and FTP in Windows, can use one of two values to connect to a destination—the host name or the IP address. If a host name is used, it must be resolved to an IP address before the data can be sent. NetBIOS applications, by contrast, use NetBIOS names to initiate communications. In Windows-based systems, NetBIOS names are resolved to IP addresses using either a NetBIOS broadcast or via the use of a WINS Server, which provides NetBIOS name-to-IP-address resolution.

EXAM WARNING

A Windows Server 2003 DNS server can be configured to enforce all, some, or none of the RFC naming restrictions related to allowable characters. FQDNs can use A through Z, a through z (there is no distinction between case when resolving names), 0 through 9, and the hyphen (-). The dot (.) is allowed only between domain name labels.

Naming Subdomains

Subdomains are below second-level domain names, and there can be multiple subdomains below the secondary level. The subdomains beginning at the third level are to the left of the organizationally specific second-level domain name. Subdomains are not regulated by any central authority, and each organization or company is free to use whatever subdomain naming structure it chooses, since the second-level and top-level domains are regulated to ensure uniqueness. Subdomain names can be duplicated at other organizations but cannot be duplicated within the same second-level domain. Organizations are responsible for maintaining their own internal naming structure, including subdomains. The relationship of TLDs, second-level domains, and subdomains is shown in Figure 5.2.

Figure 5.2 TLDs, Second-level Domains, and Subdomains

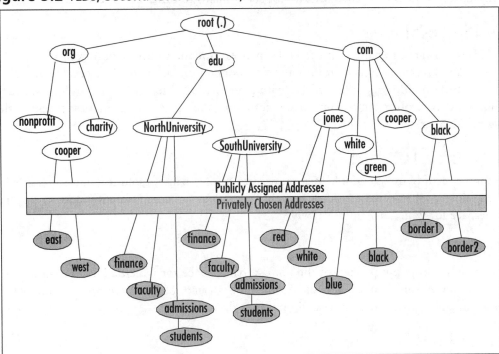

Basic DNS Concepts

Now that you've learned about DNS naming conventions, let's look at five basic concepts related to DNS. Each will be explored in more detail later in this chapter, but this introduction will give you an initial understanding of DNS concepts and terminology. There are five areas that we'll discuss: DNS servers, DNS resolvers, resource records, zones, and zone files.

DNS Servers

The DNS system relies on a distributed database for efficient name resolution. These databases reside on DNS servers that manage the database. Computers that act as DNS servers run a program that manages the database structure and the information in it. This information is used to provide responses to client requests for name resolution. A DNS server can either respond to the request directly or provide a pointer to another DNS server that can help resolve the query. It can also respond that it does not know or that the information does not exist. A Windows Server 2003-based computer can be configured to run DNS as a server service.

Each DNS server is assigned a portion of the namespace over which it presides. The DNS server responsible for a contiguous portion of the namespace is said to be *authoritative* for that contiguous portion. Authority for a zone can be delegated to another server. Administrators often delegate authority for subdomains to other DNS servers.

DNS Resolvers

DNS resolvers are programs that use DNS queries to request information from DNS servers. A resolver usually is built into a utility program or can be made accessible via library functions and can communicate with a remote DNS server or the DNS server running locally. A resolver can be run on any computer, including on a computer acting in the role of DNS server.

Resource Records

Resource records are sets of information used to resolve name resolution queries. A DNS server contains the resource records it needs to respond to name resolution queries for the namespace for which it is authoritative.

Zones

A zone is a contiguous portion of the domain name space for which a DNS server is authoritative. A zone is not a domain. A domain is a *branch* of the namespace; a zone is a *portion* of a namespace that can contain multiple domains.

Zone Files

Zone files are files that contain resource records for the zone for which the DNS server is authoritative. Typically, zone files are text files. In Windows Server 2003, they can also be stored in the Active Directory database. This implementation is discussed later in this chapter.

DNS Zones

A zone is a contiguous portion of a namespace. The term *contiguous* appears repeatedly and it's an important concept to understand. As you might know, things that are contiguous are in actual contact, adjacent or adjoining. Thus, the namespace that comprises a zone must be adjoining. Figure 5.3 shows a contiguous and noncontiguous namespace. The noncontiguous namespace cannot be a zone.

Figure 5.3 Contiguous and Noncontiguous Namespaces

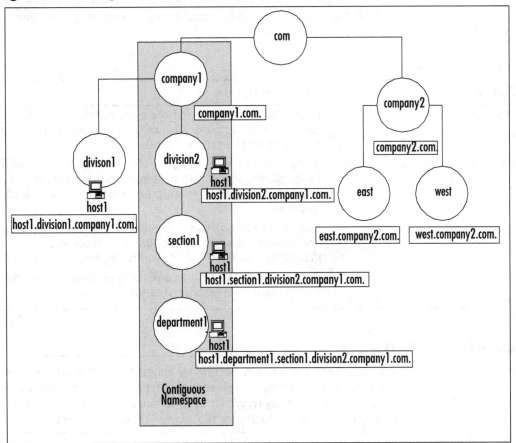

A DNS server is *authoritative* over one or more zones, meaning it maintains the database of resource records related to the nodes in the zone(s) for which is it responsible (or *authoritative*). Zones can be either primary or secondary. A *primary zone* is the copy of the zone to which updates are made. A DNS server that is authoritative for a particular zone will make updates to the primary zone. A *secondary zone* is a copy of the zone that is copied from the master server when replication of the zone occurs via *zone transfer*. A primary zone cannot be managed by two different DNS servers, except that multiple computers can be configured to manage zones that are integrated into Windows Active Directory. You'll learn more about Active Directory integration later in this chapter.

As mentioned earlier, a zone can be stored as a text file or within the Active Directory structure on a Windows 2000/Server 2003 DNS server. Some secondary DNS servers may store a zone in memory and perform a zone transfer whenever they are reinitialized. A *zone transfer* is when the zone resource records are replicated; we'll discuss this a little later in the chapter.

There are four types of zones supported in Windows Server 2003, shown in Table 5.3. The *primary*, *secondary*, and *Active Directory integrated* zones are discussed in detail later in this chapter. The *stub zone* is used to keep a parent zone up-to-date as to the authoritative DNS servers for a child zone. Stub zones are unique and contain a small subset of typical zone data. We'll look at stub zones a bit later in this chapter.

Table 5.3 Zone Types

Zone Name	Zone Description
Standard Primary	Holds the master copy of the zone database and is replicated to secondary zones. All changes to the zone are made to the primary zone.
Standard Secondary	A read-only copy of the zone database used to provide fault tolerance and faster name resolution across the network. The database is updated via the *zone transfer* process.
Active Directory Integrated	Zone information held in the Windows Active Directory and replicated using Active Directory replication, providing greater flexibility in the replication process.
Stub	Contains only the resource records needed to identify the authoritative DNS servers for the zone.

 EXAM WARNING

Make sure you're familiar with primary and secondary zones, as you'll most likely see this question on an exam either directly or indirectly as part of a scenario type question. The *primary* zone is the only copy to which updates are made. The *secondary* zone is a copy of the primary zone, which gets replicated via zone transfers.

DNS standards do not define the structure of the zone data to be stored, though it is generally stored in a text file format. One commonly used framework in non-Microsoft implementations is called the *Berkeley Internet Name Domain* (BIND) implementation, which defines the filenames in four ways, as shown in Table 5.4.

Table 5.4 Berkeley Internet Name Domain (BIND) Zone Names

BIND Zone Name	Description of Name
db.*addr*	Reverse lookup zone that contains the network ID. For instance, if your network ID is 66.24.0.0, the database filename would be db.66.24.0.0.
db.*cache*	This file maintains the names and IP addresses for the servers that maintain root DNS domain. All servers configured to use the Internet root DNS servers will have the same db.cache file. However, this can be modified for use on private networks (not connected to the Internet). This file is sometimes called the *root hints* file.
db.*domain*	Forward lookup zone that contains the domain name. For instance, if your domain is somecompany.com, the filename would be db.some-company.com.
db.127.0.0.1	This file is used to resolve queries to the loopback address and is the same on all name servers.

Microsoft uses a different naming convention, *zone_name*.dns, by default. However, if you are moving files from another DNS server to a Windows-based DNS server, you can configure Windows Server 2003 to use the BIND file names shown in Table 5.4. If you are integrating Microsoft and non-Microsoft DNS servers, you'll need to be familiar with the BIND naming convention.

TEST DAY TIP

BIND is used in non-Microsoft implementations of DNS such as DNS servers running on UNIX and Linux. Microsoft exams tend to cover Microsoft technologies exclusively, but you should be aware of BIND definitions. Also remember that Microsoft's naming convention is *zone_name.dns*. An example is *somecompany.dns* as the DNS zone name for somecompany.com.

A zone contains a set of resource records related to the domain namespace. *Resource records* (RRs) are records of information pertaining to the domain. These resource records can be retrieved and used by DNS clients but are stored in a database and are updated by the DNS server that is authoritative for that zone. There are a variety of types of resource records defined by RFCs 1034 and 1035 as well as in subsequent RFCs. Many types of RRs are no longer relevant in today's networking environment, but they are supported in Windows Server 2003. Table 5.5 shows some of the commonly used RRs in Windows Server 2003.

Table 5.5 Resource Records Types Used in Windows Server 2003

Resource Record Type	Description	Use
A	Host Address	Holds a specific host's IP address (IPv4 32-bit address). An IPv4 address is the standard four octet IP address with which you're familiar.
AAAA	IPv6 Host Record	Maps a DNS domain name to an IPv6 128-bit address. IPv6 is a later version of the Internet Protocol with additional functionality (described later in this chapter).
CNAME	Canonical Name (alias)	Creates an alias for a host.
KEY	Key	Key RRs are signed by the key from their parent zone. This record holds the public key for zones that are able to use DNS Security Extensions (DNSSEC). DNSSEC is discussed later in this chapter.
MX	Mail Exchanger	Routes messages to mail server and backup servers in the event the specified server is not available.
NS	Name Server	Provides list of authoritative servers for a domain or indicates the authoritative DNS server for delegated subdomains.
NXT	Next	Also part of DNSSEC, the NXT record indicated the next RR in a zone.
OPT	Option	This is a pseudo-RR that provides extended DNS functionality described by EDNS0.
PTR	Pointer	Resolves an IP address into a domain name (reverse lookup) using the *in-addr.arpa* domain.
SIG	Signature	Used by DNSSEC to store the digital signature for a RR or set of RRs.
SOA	Start of Authority	Stores zone property information and determines the primary server for a DNS zone.
SRV	Service Locator	Provides the ability to locate a particular service. Active Directory uses this record type to locate domain controllers, global catalog servers, and Lightweight Directory Access Protocol (LDAP) servers.

Each resource record contains a common set of information. Windows Server 2003's implementation of DNS is self-maintaining once properly configured, so you might not use this information on the job. However, understanding RRs is required when integrating with non-Windows DNS servers.

Commonly Used Resource Records

We've discussed the Start of Authority (SOA), which delineates important information about the zone and which is used during zone transfers. Other commonly used RRs include the NS, A, PTR, CNAME, MX, and SRV records.

The Name Server (NS) resource record indicates which DNS servers are authoritative for the zone. They specify both primary and secondary servers for the zone indicated in the SOA record. They also indicate servers for any delegated zones. Every zone must have at least one NS record at the zone root. If you want to delegate westcoast.somecompany.com to the domain controller WCDC1, the NS record might look like this:

```
westcoast.somecompany.com      IN      NS      wcdc1.westcoast.
     somecompany.com.
```

The IN indicates that it is an Internet Class record. As you'll recall, this is the Class designation and is almost always IN. No Time-to-Live interval is specified, so the default value will be derived from the SOA RR.

The Address (A) Resource Record associates an FQDN or host name to an IP address. This provides information for resolvers to request an IP address for a given FQDN. This is an example of an A RR:

```
wcdc1          IN          A          188.46.127.1
```

The Pointer (PTR) resource record is just the opposite of an A RR. It maps the IP address to the FQDN. An example of a PTR record is shown here. Recall that in-addr.arpa is a top level domain reserved for reverse lookups.

```
188.46.127.1.in-addr.arpa.      IN      PTR      wcdc1.westcoast.
     somecompany.com.
```

The Canonical Name (CNAME) resource record is used to create aliases that hide your network details from the clients that connect to it. For instance, suppose you want to create a server called FINANCE1 but you know that, because your finance department is growing quickly, you'll need to move those files to another server in six months. To keep these details hidden from the users, you can create an alias called FINANCE and point it to FINANCE1. When the new server, FINANCE2, is ready to be brought online, you can simply change the reference for FINANCE to point to FINANCE2. This way, all the applications and users will see is the FINANCE name, even though the destination of FINANCE may change from FINANCE1 to FINANCE2. An example of this type of record is shown here.

```
finance.somecompany.com      IN      CNAME      finance1.somecompany.com.
```

When a query for name resolution for *finance.somecompany.com* is received, the DNS server finds the CNAME record for *finance.somecompany.com* and is referred to *finance1.somecompany.com*. The DNS server then looks through the RRs for an **A** resource record for *finance1.somecompany.com* in order to resolve the FQDN to the IP address.

Exam Warning

According to RFC 2181, there can be only one CNAME per alias. Thus, if more than one CNAME is defined for an alias, an error is returned. Keep this limitation in mind if you get an exam question related to canonical names and resource records.

Another commonly used resource record type is the Mail Exchange (MX) resource record. This record specifies a mail exchange server that will process e-mail for the domain name. Only mail servers use the MX record type. Mail exchange servers can either send the mail directly or forward it to another mail server that is closer to the final destination. You can have more than one MX record in a DNS domain. If multiple MX records are present, a value is added to specify the priority or *preference value*, of the server, as indicated by the 0, 10, and 15 values in the records shown here.

```
*.westcoast.somecompany.com.    IN   MX    0     mailsvr1.somecompany.com.
*.westcoast.somecompany.com.    IN   MX    10    mailsvr2.somecompany.com.
*.westcoast.somecompany.com.    IN   MX    15    mailsvr3.somecompany.com.
```

Based on these MX RRs, the preferred mail server is mailsvr1.somecompany.com. By design, the lower preference value is used first. If the preferred mail server is down, the second two mail servers, mailsvr2 and mailsvr3, can be used. In this example, mailsvr2 will be used because it has a lower preference than mailsvr3.

Like the MX record, the Service (SRV) resource record is used to specify a preferred sever for a variety of other applications and protocols. For instance, if you have two FTP servers within your domain, you would use SRV resource records to identify those two servers as FTP servers. Thus, client resolvers can use the SRV records to locate the FTP servers within the domain.

SRV records have several fields, including the following:

- The name of the *service*
- The *protocol* used
- The *domain name* to which the SRV records refer
- The *TTL* and *class*

- The *priority* (similar to the preference value for the MX record)

- The *weight* (for load balancing, higher weight servers are tried more often)

- The *port* number for the service

- The *target* showing the FQDN for the host supporting the service

A sample SRV record is shown:

```
_ftp._tcp.somecompany.com.    IN    SRV   0  0   21    ftpsvr1.somecompany.com.
_ftp._tcp.somecompany.com.    IN    SRV   10 0   21    ftpsvr2.somecompany.com.
```

If a client resolver is attempting to locate an FTP server, it sends a query to the DNS server that looks like this: _ftp._tcp.somecompany.com. The DNS server replies with the SRV records shown. Because ftpsvr1.somecompany.com. has a lower priority than ftpsvr2.some-company.com. (0 vs. 10), the resolver will select ftpsvr1.somecompany.com. Next, it looks for an A resource record for ftpsvr1.somecompany.com. in order to resolve the FQDN to an IP address. Finally, the resolver will return the desired IP address to the client.

NOTE

For more information about SRV resource records, visit the Internet Engineering Task Force (IETF) Web site at ftp://ftp.rfc-editor.org/in-notes/rfc2782.txt. Both RFCs 2052 (obsolete) and 2782 (current) describe the SRV resource records in DNS.

There are many different types of resource records, but each must have data in several required fields. Additional information may be contained, but the required fields are shown in Table 5.6.

Table 5.6 Resource Record Common Fields

Resource Record Field Name	Use
Owner	Shows the DNS domain in which the RR is located.
TTL	Time to Live (TTL) is the length of time used by other DNS servers to determine how long information for the record should be cached before being discarded. For most RRs, this is an optional field. The value is shown in seconds, and a value of 0 indicates the RR should not be cached. SOA records have a default TTL value of 3600 (1 hour) to prevent these records from being cached any longer than one hour. When changes need to be propagated, this setting prevents delays.

Continued

Table 5.6 Resource Record Common Fields

Resource Record Field Name	Use
Class	This is another optional RR field. In earlier implementations of DNS, there were a variety of class types. Today, the only class type used (if at all) is IN, indicating the record belongs to the Internet class.
Type	This is a required field for a RR, indicating what type of information the RR holds. The commonly used type fields are described in Table 5.5.
Record-Specific Data	The format of this field varies depending on the type and class of the RR. It is a variable-length field and contains information that further describes the resource.

The **Start of Authority** (SOA) is a very important type of resource record. It is used in a number of situations but most importantly, it is the first and last record transferred during a traditional zone transfer. The SOA record contains the fields shown in Table 5.7.

Table 5.7 Fields in the Start of Authority Resource Record

Resource Record Field Name	Use
Owner, TTL, Class, Type	These fields are common to all resource records and are the same as discussed in Table 5.6.
Authoritative Server	This field shows the DNS server that is authoritative for this zone.
Responsible Person	This field contains the e-mail address of the administrator that is responsible for managing and maintaining this zone. This field uses a dot (.) rather than the @ symbol for the e-mail address.
Serial Number	Each time the zone information is updated, the zone's serial number is incremented. Serial numbers are used by other DNS servers to determine whether or not updates to their records are required. If the primary DNS server's serial number is higher than that of the secondary DNS server, the secondary DNS server knows it must initiate a *pull* transfer in order to update its records. Pull transfers are discussed later in this chapter.
Refresh	This field shows the interval at which the secondary DNS server will check for changes to the zone information.

Continued

Table 5.6 Resource Record Common Fields

Resource Record Field Name	Use
Retry	The secondary server will request zone changes from the primary server at a set interval. If the request goes unanswered, this field shows how long the secondary DNS server will wait for a response before it sends another query.
Expire	This field shows the expiration time of transferred zone data for the secondary DNS server. It shows how long after the previous zone transfer the secondary DNS server can use the zone data before it must be discarded. This prevents out-of-date DNS information from being used for name resolution.
Minimum TTL	This setting applies to all RRs that do not have a specific Time-to-Live (TTL) setting. Anytime a DNS server sends back a resource record in response to a name resolution request, it includes a minimum TTL value.

Delegation and Glue Records

Delegation and glue records are records added to the zone to delegate a subdomain into a separate zone. A stub zone, defined earlier, contains only the SOA, NS, and glue records for the zone. This helps the parent domain remain up-to-date with regard to the authority of delegated zones. The *delegation record* is a Name Space (NS) record in the parent zone that lists the parent zone as authoritative for the delegated zone. The glue record is an A type record (A RR) for the DNS server authoritative for the delegated zone. For example, in the zone to which authority is delegated, you would add these two records:

```
eastcoast.somecompany.com        IN     NS     ECNS1.eastcoast.somecompany.com
ECNS1.eastcoast.somecompany.com     IN     A     147.85.112.1
```

The first entry, the *delegation record*, delegates authority for eastcoast.somecompany.com to ECNS1.eastcoast.somecompany.com. The ECNS1 is the East Coast Name Server 1, which will maintain the zone records for eastcoast.somecompany.com. The second entry is the *glue record*, which is needed because ECNS1.eastcoast.somecompany.com is a member of the delegated domain, eastcoast.somecompany.com.

New & Noteworthy...

DNS Server Support for IPv6

Windows Server 2003 provides support for Internet Protocol version 6 (IPv6), the latest version of the IP protocol. The DNS Server service supports IPv6 by including several additional elements including:

- **AAAA Resource Record** Defined to store a host's IPv6 address. This "quad A" record is similar to an A RR but it uses a larger 128-bit IP address size. IPv6 is discussed in this book but is outside the scope of this chapter. The format of this record is:

```
6bone.somecompany.com.       IN   AAAA
   1243:123:456:789:1:2:3:456ab
```

- **AAAA Query** This query is for a specified domain name returns all associated AAAA RRs in the query response.

- **IP6.ARPA domain** This is the domain used for reverse lookup for IPv6. This is the equivalent of in-addr.arpa for the IPv4 protocol.

To support IPv6, all query types (NS, MX, etc.) must support both A and AAAA records. When processing a query, the DNS server adds all relevant IPv4 and IPv6 addresses to its responses.

EXERCISE 5.01

ADDING A RESOURCE RECORD TO A ZONE

In this exercise, you'll walk through the process of adding a new resource record to a zone.

1. Access the DNS Management Console by clicking **Start | Run | Administrative Tools | DNS**.

2. In the DNS Management Console, select the zone to which you want to add a record by clicking the zone name in the left pane.

3. On the menu, click **Action** and select the record type you want to create. The record type options listed on this menu are **New Host (A)**, **New Alias (CNAME)**, **New Mail Exchanger (MX)**, or **Other New Records**. Select **New Host (A)**.

4. The **New Host dialog** is displayed. Type the name of the new host. If you do not enter a FQDN, the parent domain name will be appended to the host name you enter. For example, if the parent domain is somecompany.com and you enter the name **salero**, the FQDN for the new host record will be salero.somecompany.com. Enter the desired name. As you

type the name, the resulting FQDN is displayed in the box entitled Fully qualified domain name (FQDN). You cannot directly edit this box.

5. Enter the IP address for the new host in the **IP address** box.

6. To create an associated pointer (PTR) record, click the checkbox to the left of that option.

7. To allow any authenticated user to update DNS records with the same owner name, click the checkbox to the left of that option.

8. When complete, click **Add Host** to add the host (A) resource record to the specified zone, or **Cancel** to exit without saving.

9. When you click **Add Host**, you should receive a DNS confirmation dialog box stating "The host record [*host's FQDN*] was successfully created." Click **OK** to close the dialog.

10. The New Host dialog box remains open to allow you to add additional new host (A) records. If you are finished adding new hosts, click **Done** to close the dialog.

Note that if you select the **Action | Other New Records** option, you can gain·access to a variety of RR types you may want to add manually, including CNAME, AAAA, MX, NXT, PTR, KEY, RP, SRV, SIG, and WKS, among others. Before exiting from the DNS Management Console, perform the following steps to review these choices.

1. Click **Action | Other New Records** from the menu within the DNS Management Console.

2. Scroll through the list of available resource records types. Click any resource type about which you'd like more information. The Description box below the resource record type provides a description about the selected resource record type. Take a moment to read these descriptions for the commonly used RR types.

3. Select any one of the RR types in this dialog and click **Create Record**. The options you'll be given depend on the RR type chosen. Explore these different types of RRs and options to become familiar with this function.

4. When finished, click **Cancel** to exit from the New Resource Record dialog for any given option you may have selected and click **Cancel** to exit from the Other New Records dialog.

5. Click **File** from the menu and click **Exit** to close the DNS Management Console.

Configuring a DNS Server

Windows Server 2003 provides extensive help files containing how-to information, including how to configure a DNS server, add zones, establishing forwarders, integrate DNS with Active Directory, and more. The first step is to access the DNS server installation checklist. This can be found by accessing the help files via **Start | Help and Support** and then searching using the phrase **DNS server installation checklist**. This same help file can be accessed via the **DNS Management Console.** Click **Action** and choose **Configure a DNS Server**. When the **Configure a DNS Server Wizard** is displayed, click the **DNS Checklists** button to access a variety of checklists. There are checklists for home-based networks, small to medium networks, and large networks. The DNS needs of each type of configuration are different and the DNS configuration changes based on that. For instance, a home or small business network might create only a forward lookup zone on the DNS server so that any names other than local names are forwarded to an ISP or designated external DNS servers. Larger enterprises will likely configure forward and reverse lookup zones as well as forwarders. The extensive help files contain very useful data on properly configuring and implementing DNS servers as well as how to integrate and manage Active Directory integrated DNS.

DNS Zone Transfer

A *DNS zone transfer* is the process by which the zone's resource records are copied, or replicated, to other DNS servers. The resource records in the zone are stored in a database that is copied at specified intervals to other DNS servers to ensure reliable host name resolution. Recall that the primary zone is the only copy of the DNS database that is updated. The secondary zone is the copy of the DNS database that is replicated to the other DNS servers. Let's take a closer look at this process.

In Windows Server 2003, there are three methods of transferring the zone information, which is composed of various types of resource records stored in a database. These three zone transfer methods are:

- **Traditional** As detailed in RFC1034, the traditional DNS zone transfer occurs when the secondary server requests a full copy of the zone from the primary server.

- **Incremental** An incremental zone transfer, defined in RFC1995, requires the primary DNS server (the one hosting the primary zone) to record incremental changes to the DNS database. These changes can be replicated to the secondary zone, updating only changed records.

- **Active Directory** Active Directory zone transfers occur when Active Directory zones are replicated to all domain controllers in the Windows Server 2003 domain. This replication is accomplished via the Active Directory replication function.

In a *traditional* (or *standard*) zone transfer, the secondary DNS server initiates a connection, via TCP, to the primary DNS server. After the connection is established, it requests a zone transfer. The transmission always begins and ends with the zone's SOA record. Once the SOA is transferred, the zone's resource records are transferred and the session is closed after the final record, the SOA, is received. This type of transfer is considered a *pull* transfer because the secondary DNS server "pulls" the data from the primary DNS server.

An *incremental* zone transfer is initiated by the secondary DNS server and again, it contacts the primary DNS server. In this case, however, the secondary DNS server queries the primary DNS server's SOA to determine if any changes have been made to the database that require an incremental zone transfer. The method by which this occurs is via a connectionless UDP datagram. If the reply is positive (changes do need to be replicated), a TCP connection is established and the incremental transfer occurs. This method of transferring, like the traditional transfer, is a *pull* transfer initiated by the receiving DNS server. The incremental zone transfer is supported in Windows 2000 and Windows Server 2003. Prior versions of Windows did not support incremental zone transfers.

Active Directory zone transfers can be done only within Windows 2000 or Window Server 2003. Active Directory is part of the Windows operating system and was introduced in Windows 2000. Active Directory integrated zone transfers, accomplished via Active Directory replication, is a *push* transfer, initiated by the domain controller hosting the primary DNS server function. When changes to the database occur, the domain controller sends updates to other domain controllers. This allows the changes to be updated more quickly and more efficiently. DNS servers do not need to check for updates constantly since updates will be received as changes are made on the primary DNS server. We'll discuss Active Directory integrated zones in greater detail later in this chapter.

NOTE

For an overview of Active Directory in Windows Server 2003, visit the Microsoft Web site at www.microsoft.com/windowsserver2003/techinfo/overview/activedirectory.mspx.

Host Name Resolution

DNS is the method used for resolving host names to IP addresses, which is required before packets can be delivered to their correct destinations in a TCP/IP environment. We've talked about how DNS records are stored and what types of DNS records are used. Now we'll look at the specific steps taken, through DNS, to resolve host names to IP addresses.

All name resolutions are done through queries, which are small messages sent back and forth between the DNS server(s) and the client. There are two types of queries—*recursive* and *iterative*. You'll learn how these two types of queries differ and how they're used. You'll also learn about *forward* and *reverse lookups* and when each is used. Let's begin by examining the order in which the processes of host name resolution occur.

Order of Host Name Resolution

Computers that require host name resolution use libraries called *resolvers*. These library files run on the local computer and perform the queries needed to resolve names. The resolver function resides on all computers that need to resolve DNS names, including DNS servers, which can act as a client in the name resolution procedure.

When a name needs to be resolved in a Windows Server 2003 environment, DNS resolution is the first option tried, even if the name turns out to be a NetBIOS name.

EXAM WARNING

In Windows NT Workstation or Windows NT Server 4.0, DNS name resolution was attempted only if the name contained a dot (as used in a FQDN) or was greater than 15 bytes (indicating that it could not be a NetBIOS name).

There are two primary ways host names are resolved to IP addresses. The first method involves using the copy of the HOSTS file on the local computer. This plain text file is parsed (read) by the DNS resolver on the client computer. If the desired host name is listed in the HOSTS file with a corresponding IP address, the IP address is used to send the packet to the IP address listed in the HOSTS file.

If the host name is not listed in the HOSTS file, a DNS server is queried. If the host name or IP address is misspelled in the HOSTS file, the host name will not be properly resolved to an IP address. Another error that can occur is if there are multiple entries for the host in the HOSTS file. You can use the command- line utilities nslookup or netdiag to help in diagnosing host name resolution problems.

If the host name is not found in the HOSTS file, the next step is to query the DNS server. The client computer requests name resolution from the DNS server using either a *recursive* or *iterative* query.

Recursive Queries

When a client issues a *recursive name query* to the DNS server, the DNS server must return either the requested resource record (typically the RR containing the IP address) for the specified host name or an error message. If the DNS server does not have the requested information, it will query other DNS servers for that information. If the name query fails (no other DNS servers are able to provide the requested information), an error is returned to the client stating that the host name or domain does not exist. A DNS server that is attempting to respond to a recursive name query from the client often uses an *iterative* process to resolve the name before responding to the client. Figure 5.4 shows the process by which a DNS client issues a recursive name query to resolve a host name to an IP address.

Figure 5.4 Recursive Name Query

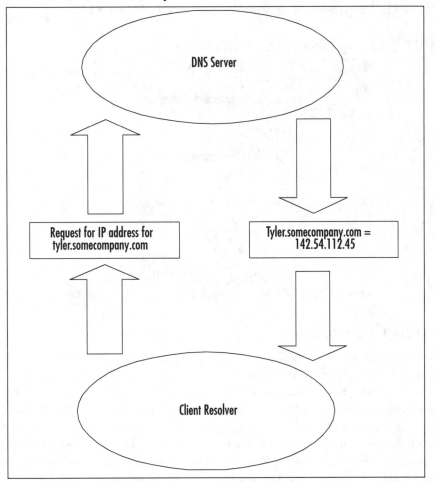

Recursive name queries are typically sent from a client to a DNS server requesting host name resolution. The DNS server, in turn, might issue a recursive or iterative query to another DNS server in order to resolve the name.

Recursive queries can be disabled on a DNS server. This is done in the **Advanced** tab of the **DNS Server Properties** accessed via the **DNS Management Console**. If this option is selected, it also disables forwarding. If the server is configured in this manner, it will be unable to resolve queries that are external to the domain (including the Internet) and it will be unable to work as a forwarder. Recursive queries by DNS servers typically are used to pass unresolved name queries to other DNS servers since the requirement of a recursive query is that it responds with either the requested information or an error. If a DNS server is configured not to use recursive queries, it will issue iterative queries only. You might use this configuration, for example, if the DNS server was configured to use a forwarder. Figure 5.5 shows the **DNS Server Properties** dialog with the **Advanced** tab selected.

Figure 5.5 Disabling Recursion on a DNS Server

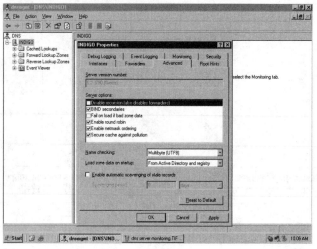

Iterative Queries

Iterative name queries are issued by the client computer and allow the DNS server to return the best answer it can based on its cached information or upon the information in the zone. If the DNS server does not have the information, it returns a referral, which is a pointer to another DNS server that is authoritative for a lower level of the domain name space. This is sometimes referred to as *walking the tree* because the name resolution starts at the top of the domain name space and works its way down, in an attempt to resolve the name. The most common use of the iterative name query is when a DNS server attempts to resolve a name so it can respond to a recursive name query from a client. Figure 5.6 shows the name resolution process using an iterative name query.

Figure 5.6 Iterative Name Query

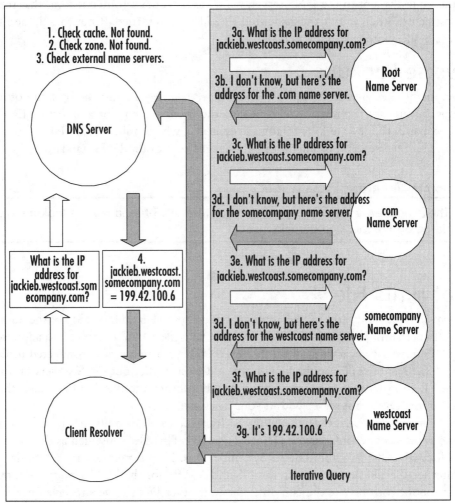

As you can see, the iterative process continues to walk down the tree until the name is resolved or until an error is returned. This process is commonly used by a DNS server attempting to resolve a host name via a recursive name query from a client. Remember, DNS servers can act as clients and use the client resolver function to query other DNS servers in an attempt to resolve host names for queries it receives.

Forward Lookups

Forward lookups (also called *forward queries*) contain information used to resolve host names to IP addresses within the DNS domain. They must include SOA and NS records and can include any type of resource record except for PTR, which map an IP address to an

FQDN. When a resolver requests the IP address for a particular host name, the forward lookup request is sent to the DNS server, which looks for A resource records that match the host name. When found, the associated IP address is returned. If not found, the DNS server can query other DNS servers.

Reverse Lookups

As you might guess, *reverse lookups* (also called *reverse queries*) are just the opposite of forward lookups. In this case, the resolver is requesting the domain name for a particular IP address. The query uses the reverse lookup zone, *in-addr.arpa*, which holds mostly PTR resource records. This reverse lookup function is an optional part of the DNS standard.

EXAM WARNING

The *in-addr.arpa* domain is used only for IPv4. IPv6-based reverse lookups are based on the *ip6.arpa* domain instead.

Root Hints File

The *root hints file* holds host information needed to resolve names outside of the authoritative DNS domains. This file, also called the *cache hints file*, contains names and addresses of root DNS servers, typically found on the Internet. If your network is connected to the Internet, the *root hints file* should contain the addresses of the root DNS servers on the Internet. If your network is not connected to the Internet, the file should contain the address of the DNS root server within your network.

When your network is connected to the Internet, the root hints file should contain the NS and A resource records for the DNS root servers. This file is installed as the *cache.dns* file and is located in the %SystemRoot%\System32\Dns. If your network is not connected to the Internet, the file should contain the NS and A RRs for the DNS server(s) authoritative for the root of your private domain. In this way, if other DNS servers receive queries they cannot resolve, they will query the internal root servers for the requested information.

Windows Server 2003's DNS Server wizard will make an effort to determine the correct configuration. If it cannot locate a DNS server on the Internet (because an Internet connection is not found or is not functioning), it will create its own cache file and will not point to Internet DNS servers.

EXAM
70-291
OBJECTIVE
2.2.3

Windows Server 2003 DNS Server Roles

In Windows Server 2003, DNS servers can be assigned one of several roles. The authoritative DNS server for a zone is the standard primary DNS server. Standard secondary DNS servers can be configured to provide three main benefits for the network:

- Fault tolerance

- Reduction of traffic on wide-area links

- Reduction of the load on the primary DNS server

A DNS server can also be configured as a caching-only server or a forwarder.

Standard Primary DNS Server

The *standard primary DNS server* contains the zone database for which it is authoritative. This zone has a SOA RR and a NS RR that specifies it as the primary zone. Any changes to the zone's RRs, including delegation of a portion of the zone to another DNS server, are made on the primary DNS server.

When a request for name resolution is received, the request is compared to the data in the primary DNS server's zone database. If there is a matching RR, the data is returned. If there is no matching data, the DNS server can carry out one or more methods of name resolution in an attempt to resolve the name. If those additional methods fail, the standard primary DNS server will return an error to the client requesting the resolution. You'll learn about additional resolution methods when we look at the other types of DNS servers.

Standard Secondary DNS Server

A *standard secondary DNS server* is one that contains a copy of the primary DNS server's zone database. It is replicated via a process called zone transfer, discussed earlier in this chapter. Many organizations configure secondary DNS servers to provide fault tolerance. If the primary DNS server is down, name resolution can be handled by the secondary DNS server(s) until the primary DNS server is restored. In addition to fault tolerance, configuring a secondary DNS server can be configured at a remote location with a large number of clients—a branch office, for instance. When those remote clients are configured to try the secondary DNS server first, name resolution traffic across the WAN is reduced. Name queries across a slower wide-area network can slow down local traffic and, obviously, increase WAN traffic as well. A third reason many organizations implement secondary DNS servers is to reduce the load on the primary DNS server. If a large number of clients are trying to simultaneously access name resolution services, the primary DNS server may get bogged down. Users may experience slow name resolution services through the perception that the network is slow. Configuring secondary DNS servers can help mitigate this effect.

Standard secondary DNS servers behave just like primary DNS servers except they cannot make updates to their zone information. Changes must be made on the primary zone and replicated out to secondary DNS servers. A server from which zone files are replicated can be either a primary or secondary server for the zone, and is often referred to as a master server. When a secondary DNS server starts up, it initiates a zone transfer from the master DNS server. It also checks periodically for updates on the master DNS server. If changes have been made, it initiates a zone transfer. As we discussed earlier, master servers in Active Directory integrated zones (discussed later in this chapter) can also *push* changes out to secondary servers when changes to the database have been made.

Caching-only DNS Server

As the name implies, *caching-only* DNS servers perform queries and store the results. They are not authoritative for any zones and they do not host any zones. The only data a caching-only DNS server stores is data it has collected via name resolution queries. The benefit of this type of server is that is does not add to network traffic by participating in zone transfers. The limitation of this server is that it does not store any zone information so when a caching-only DNS server is first initialized, it contains no data and must build up its cache of data slowly via queries and resolutions it performs.

All DNS servers cache name resolutions based on the RRs Time-to-Live (TTL) setting. This improves the speed of name resolution and can reduce name resolution traffic. Though this process is the same for all DNS servers, a caching-only DNS server has only this function and does not store a zone as do primary and secondary DNS servers.

DNS Forwarder and DNS Slave Servers

The first thing a DNS server does when it receives a query is to check its cache and then its local zone (for caching-only servers, it can check only cache). If the needed information cannot be found *and* the server is not authoritative for the requested data, it must check with other DNS servers to see if the query can be resolved.

There might be cases when you don't want your DNS server to communicate directly with DNS servers on the Internet, for example. In this case, you can configure DNS forwarders, which are servers configured to perform off-site name queries. One common use of this type of configuration is to use a *DNS forwarder* as the only DNS server that resolves Internet names. All queries from DNS servers within the organization to resolve names external to the organization can be sent through one (or more) forwarder for resolution. To accomplish this, the internal DNS servers must also be configured to forward queries for which they are not authoritative by providing the forwarding DNS server(s) IP address. No configuration is needed for the server designated as a forwarder. Figure 5.7 illustrates both the forwarder and slave configurations.

EXAM WARNING

You might be unable to configure a DNS server as a forwarder if the Active Directory Installation wizard did not detect any DNS servers during setup. In this case, it configures the DNS server as the root server, which cannot be configured as a forwarder. The root zone (".") must be deleted via the DNS Manager console or the command line *dnscmd /ZoneDelete . /DsDel*. The */DsDel* is used only for Active Directory integrated DNS. Question related to why a DNS server cannot reach the Internet may be related to this problem.

Figure 5.7 Forwarder and Slave DNS Servers

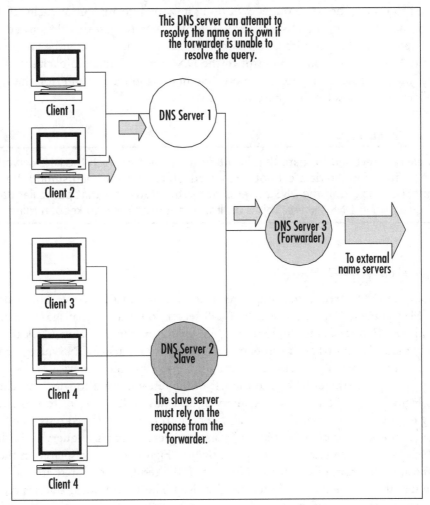

DNS servers configured with a forwarder's IP address will forward these queries in either exclusive or nonexclusive mode. In *exclusive* mode, a DNS server using a forwarder relies completely on the name resolution services of the forwarder. DNS servers configured in exclusive mode are known as *slaves*. A slave DNS server will first attempt to resolve the name query based on its own database and cache. If it cannot resolve the query, it forwards the request to the DNS forwarder, which carries out whatever name resolution activities are needed to resolve the name. If the name still cannot be resolved, the forwarder returns an error to the slave, which in turn returns an error to the requestor. The slave DNS server will not take any other actions to resolve the name.

Conversely, a DNS server using a forwarder can be configured in *nonexclusive mode*. In the nonexclusive mode, a DNS server receiving a query *is permitted* to resolve a query on its own if the forwarder fails to resolve a query. After receiving a query, the DNS server will first attempt to resolve the name on its own using its zone information or cache. If this does not resolve the query, the DNS server will forward the request to a designated forwarder for resolution. The forwarder carries out its name resolution activities and returns either the requested resolution or an error to the DNS server. Unlike in exclusive mode, however, if the forwarder is not able to resolve the query and returns an error, the DNS server will attempt to resolve the query on its own.

EXAM WARNING

If a query is received for data that is within the zone for which the DNS server is authoritative and the data cannot be located, an error is returned stating the address cannot be resolved. If the DNS server is not authoritative for that particular data, it will query other DNS servers. This is an important distinction to keep in mind.

Testing the DNS Server

You can test the DNS server using simple, recursive and automatic queries. This is done via the DNS Management Console. Select the DNS server you want to manage, click **Action**, and then choose **Properties** to display the DNS server's properties dialog. Click the **Monitoring** tab. On this tab, you can perform a simple or recursive DNS query or you can configure the server to perform automatic testing at a specified interval.

To run a test, click the checkbox to the left of the test you want to run. Your choices, as shown in Figure 5.8, are to run a simple query against this DNS server or to run a recursive query to other DNS servers. You can also choose to run the selected tests automatically at designated intervals. After you've selected a simple query, a recursive query or both, click the Test Now button. The results of the test, shown in Figure 5.8, are displayed in the Test results pane at the bottom of the dialog. Notice that the results of each test are shown separately, and that the time and date of each are displayed. The simple query queries the DNS files on the local computer. If this fails, there is a problem with DNS on this server. If the recursive query fails, there is most likely a problem finding or connecting to other DNS servers.

If you encounter an error, you can test your DNS server's connectivity via the command prompt. Open a command prompt via **Start | Run** and type **cmd**. Use the nslookup command in this format: **nslookup [dns_server_IP_address] 127.0.0.1**. For example, if your DNS server's IP address is 68.112.47.5, the command would be: **nslookup 68.112.47.5 127.0.0.1 [Enter]**. If the server is responding, it should return the name **localhost**. If it does not, you can begin troubleshooting the DNS connectivity problem.

Figure 5.8 DNS Server Testing Options

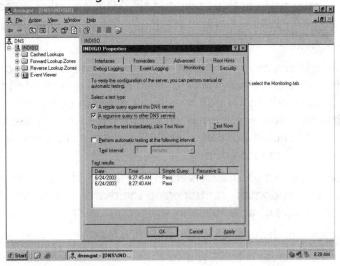

EXERCISE 5.02

ADDING A NEW ZONE TO A DNS SERVER

In this exercise, you'll learn how to add a zone to a DNS server by following the steps outlined. The options you'll encounter will depend on the configuration of your Windows Server 2003 computer, including whether or not it is a domain controller. The most common options are selected. Use the **Help** button on any of the dialog screens for more information.

1. Access the DNS Management Console by clicking **Start | Run | Administrative Tools**. Select **DNS**.

2. In the **DNS Management Console**, click the server on which you want to create a new zone by clicking the server name.

3. On the menu, click **Action** and select **New Zone**.

4. The New Zone Wizard is displayed. Click **Next** to continue.

5. Select **primary, secondary,** or **stub** zone type. If you want this zone to be integrated with Active Directory, make sure the check box to the left of **Store the zone in Active Directory (available only if DNS server is a domain controller)** is checked. This option will be available only if your server is a domain controller.

6. If you select **primary zone,** you will create a new zone on your computer. If you select **secondary zone,** you will create a copy of a primary

zone on your computer. If you select **stub zone**, you will create a copy of a zone that contains only the NS, SOA, and glue A records.

7. **Primary zone** is selected by default. Leave the default selection and click **Next**.

8. The next screen is the **Active Directory Zone Replication Scope**, which allows you to select how you want DNS data replicated throughout your network. By default, the **To all domain controllers in the Active Directory domain [domain name]** is selected. Choose this option if the zone should be loaded by DNS servers running on the domain controllers in the same domain.

9. You can select all DNS servers in the forest, all DNS servers in the domain, all domain controllers in the domain, or all domain controllers in the scope of an application directory partition.

10. Accept the default selection and click **Next**.

11. The next screen allows you to use forward or reverse lookup zones. Select **Forward lookup zone**, which should be selected by default, and click **Next**.

12. The next screen prompts you to select a zone name. The zone name selection is an option because you selected primary zone earlier. Type in the zone name, for example, north.somecompany.com. Caution: The zone name is not the name of the DNS server.

13. The next screen allows you to specify whether you want secure dynamic updates, nonsecure and secure dynamic updates, or no dynamic updates. If you are not using Active Directory integrated zones, the **Allow only secure dynamic updates (recommended for Active Directory)** option will not be available. Choosing **Allow both nonsecure and secure dynamic updates** can cause a severe security vulnerability because updates can be made by untrusted sources. Do not choose this option unless you understand how this will impact your network security. If you select **Do not allow dynamic updates**, you will have to make updates to your zone and resource records manually.

14. When you have selected the type of updates you want to allow, click **Next**.

15. The final screen of the **New Zone Wizard** confirms the information about the new zone you are adding. Review this information for accuracy and click **Finish** to complete adding the new zone or **Back** to go back through previous screens to modify any selections or inputs.

Dynamic DNS Servers

Starting with Windows 2000, DNS servers' resource records could be *dynamically* (or automatically) updated by the client. This ability to dynamically update records reduces administration time by eliminating the need to update zone resource records manually. Dynamic DNS (DDNS) updates can be done in conjunction with Dynamic Host Configuration Protocol (DHCP) to dynamically update resource records when a client's IP address is released or renewed via the DHCP functions. Computers running Windows 2000, Windows XP, or Windows Server 2003 can dynamically update their records.

NOTE

For more information on dynamic updates, review RFC 2136 at the Internet Engineering Task Force Web site, www.ietf.org/rfc/rfc2136.txt?number=2136.

With dynamic DNS updates, the client sends a DNS registration message to the DNS server indicating that the client's A resource record needs to be updated. If the client is also a DHCP client of a DHCP server, any time the client's DHCP configuration information changes, an update will be sent to the DNS server. The DHCP client sends a DHCP *Option 81* to the DHCP server with its FQDN. The Option 81 instruction tells the DHCP server to register a PTR RR with the DNS server on behalf of the client. If a Windows Server 2003 computer is statically configured (not a DHCP client), it will register both its A RR and PTR RR with the DNS server directly. Additionally, if the DHCP client is communicating with a down-level DHCP server that does not handle Option 81, the DHCP client will register its data directly with the DNS server. It's important that the DNS server be able to manage dynamic updates and beginning with Windows 2000, this ability was built into the DNS Server service.

EXERCISE 5.03

ENABLING DYNAMIC UPDATING ON DNS SERVERS

On a Windows Server 2003-based computer, dynamic updates can be managed through the Administrative Tools DNS console. To determine what types of dynamic updates are configured or to change the configuration:

1. Click **Start | Programs | Administrative Tools | DNS** to open the DNS Management Console.

2. In the DNS Management Console, click the + to the left of the DNS server to expand the DNS server that holds the authoritative zone that you want to check.

3. Locate and expand the Forward Lookup Zones folder.

4. Within the Forward Lookup Zones folder, locate the zone you want to check and right-click to display the shortcut menu.

5. On the shortcut menu, click **Properties** to display the zone properties. The **General** tab is selected by default.

6. On the **General** tab, locate the **Dynamic updates:** drop-down box as shown in Figure 5.9. The drop-down box allows three choices in this case: None, Nonsecure and secure, and Secure only.

Figure 5.9 Zone Properties Dialog

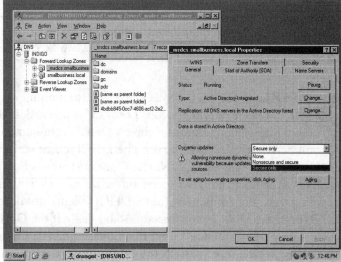

7. Select **Secure only** and click **OK** to accept changes or **Cancel** to exit without saving changes.

Allowing **Nonsecure and secure** updates poses a security risk to your network and should not be selected unless you understand the security implications and the appropriate environments in which this is an acceptable configuration. One such configuration is with DHCP servers, discussed later in this chapter.

If you create an Active Directory integrated zone, the zone is configured to allow only secure dynamic updates. If a zone was created on a standard DNS server (not integrated with Active Directory) and then converted to an Active Directory integrated zone, the zone will be configured for nonsecure or no dynamic updates, depending on how the original zone was configured. It's important to reconfigure this newly converted Active Directory integrated zone to allow only secure updates to maintain system-wide security.

Security is implemented via the *Access Control List* (ACL), which provides permission to create or modify the *dsnNode* objects within the zone within Active Directory. By default, the *Authenticated User* group is given *Create* permission, thus allowing any authenticated user or computer to create a new object in the zone. The creator of the object is also given full control of the object by default.

Head of the Class…

Secure Dynamic Updates in Windows Server 2003

Windows Server 2003 supports secure dynamic updates through the support of the specifications in RFC2078 (www.ietf.org/rfc/rfc2078.txt?number=2078) titled "Generic Security Service Application Programming Interface," or "GSS-API." Dynamic updates are also specified in RFC2535 ("Domain Name System Security Extensions") and RFC2137 ("Secure Domain Name System Dynamic Update"), but Windows Server 2003 supports RFC 2078. The GSS-API specification provides security services independent of the underlying security mechanism and secure dynamic updates in Windows Server 2003 are implemented in this manner.

The GSS-API specifies, among other things, a way to establish a secure context (or virtual connection) through the use of security tokens. In this framework, the client creates a token and passes it to the server. The server processes the token and returns a subsequent token to the client, if needed. This process, the *negotiation*, continues until it completes and a security context has been successfully established. After it is established, there is a finite time this context can be used to create and verify transaction signatures on messages between the client and server. When the specified time has expired, the negotiation must be re-established and new tokens must be created and used. This maintains a more secure environment through both the use of tokens and the use of finite connections.

The Windows implementation of GSS-API uses an algorithm specified in an IETF draft entitled "GSS Algorithm for TSID (GSS-TSIG)." This implementation uses the *Kerberos v5* authentication protocol as its security method. You should be familiar with Kerberos v5 authentication, which was introduced in Windows 2000 and used extensively throughout the Windows 2000/Server 2003 operating system. For more information about Kerberos v5, review RFC1510, www.ietf.org/rfc/rfc1510.txt, or review the Microsoft Knowledge Base article 266080.

Dynamic updates can be disabled on the host and for some environments, this might make sense. Dynamic updates can be disabled for the computer or for one or more interfaces on that computer. By changing this default value in the Windows Server 2003 registry, the DNS client is prevented from registering A and PTR RRs for whichever interfaces are specified. The registry key that you edit is one of the following (depending on the scope of the change—entire computer or specific interface):

```
HKEY_LOCAL_MACHINE\System\CurrentControlSet\Services\Tcpip\Parameters

HKEY_LOCAL_MACHINE\System\CurrentControlSet\Services\Tcpip\Parameters\
    Interface\<InterfaceGUID>
```

The **Valid range** is either 0 or 1 (false or true) and can be changed for either the entire computer (…*Parameters*) or for a particular interface (…*Parameters**Interface*…).

It typically makes sense to disable secure dynamic updates for any DHCP servers that will perform dynamic updates. The reason for this is that if the DHCP server performs a secure dynamic update on behalf of a client, it becomes the default owner of that name and then only that DHCP server can make updates. This can be a problem in a variety of ways, but the most common one is if a backup DHCP server attempts to make an update on that client's behalf. The update will fail because the primary DHCP server is the owner and the backup DHCP server will not have sufficient permissions to make the update in a secure update environment.

Exam Warning

Watch for questions that involve using DNS Servers in a mixed operating system environment. DNS Servers running Windows NT 4.0 or earlier do not support dynamic updates of resource records.

Exercise 5.04

Disabling Dynamic DNS Updates on a Host Computer

In this exercise, we'll go through the steps needed to disable dynamic updates on a host computer. It's critical to remember that improper editing of the registry can render a computer unusable, so use extreme care when editing the registry and always create a backup before making changes. You should back up your registry regularly (along with data backups on the system) and you should update your Automated System Recovery (ASR) disk after making any successful changes to the registry. For more information on recovering your system in the event the registry becomes corrupt, refer to the Microsoft Windows Server 2003 Resource Kit or Microsoft Knowledge Base article 322755 (which references Windows Server 2000 but is applicable to Windows Server 2003).

1. On your Windows Server 2003 computer, click **Start | Run** and type **regedt32** in the **Open** box. Click **OK**.

2. A quick way to back up the registry, for extra assurance, is to select **File | Export**. In the **Export Registry File** dialog, select a filename and a location to which you want to save the registry. Select whether you want to save the entire registry (which can be a large file) or just the selected branch. (For more on restoring your registry, see the Microsoft Knowledge Base article 322755.)

2. In the pane on the left, locate the **HKEY_LOCAL_MACHINE** key. Click the + to the left of that entry.

3. Locate **System** and click the + to the left of that entry to expand that tree.

4. Locate **CurrentControlSet** and click the + to expand that tree.

5. Locate **Services** and click the + to expand the tree.

6. Using the scroll bar for the left pane, scroll down until you locate **Tcpip**. Click the + to expand the tree.

7. Locate the **Parameters** node. If you want to disable the dynamic update function for the computer, click the **Parameters** node to list the names and values available under this node.

8. To disable dynamic update, locate the **DisableDynamicUpdate** name and value in the right pane. Double-click the entry to open the **Edit DWORD Value**. The value name is **DisableDynamicUpdate**. The default value data is 0. Change to 1 to set the disable function to true, meaning you want to disable the dynamic function. Click **OK** to accept the change or **Cancel** to exit without saving.

9. If you want to disable the dynamic update function for just one interface, expand the **Parameter** tree and locate the **Interface** node.

10. Expand the **Interface** node to expose the available interfaces. Click the desired interface in the left pane to view the available values in the right pane.

11. Locate the **DisableDynamicUpdate** name and value in the right pane. Double-click this entry to open the **Edit DWORD Value** dialog. Change the default value from 0 to 1 in the **Value data** box. Click **OK** to accept changes or **Cancel** to exit without saving changes.

If you are not in a domain using Active Directory, you will not have the dynamic update function available to you. You can verify this by noting the absence of the **DisableDynamicUpdate** value in either the **…\Parameters** node or the **…\Parameters\Interfaces** node in the registry.

Aging and Scavenging of Stale Records

With dynamic updating, records are added automatically to the zone information, but they are not always deleted when they are old or invalid. If a computer registers its own A RR and then that computer fails and disconnects from the network in an unusual (or improper) manner, the A RR record might not be purged from the zone data. This is particularly common with laptops that are added and removed from the network regularly.

Stale records obviously waste space and they can also unnecessarily use resources, such as when queries must sort through stale records before being resolved. Figure 5.10 shows the DNS Management Console interface that allows you to set variables related to aging and scavenging activities. You can manually enable or disable aging and scavenging on a per-server, per-zone, or per-record basis. By default, scavenging is disabled.

Care must be used when configuring scavenging because it is easy to inadvertently delete needed records. If you choose to enable scavenging, make sure you understand all the parameters before implementing this feature. One of the problems that can arise when scavenging is enabled is that a record is incorrectly removed, another computer uses a name that was in use by a server (for instance, a DHCP server), and it now owns the object. This can create a security risk and can also create serious network problems.

NOTE

For more information on the parameters used in aging and scavenging, refer to the appropriate Microsoft Windows Server 2003 product documentation (www.microsoft.com/windowsserver2003/proddoc/default.mspx) or Knowledge Base article number 816592, "How to Configure DNS Dynamic Update in Windows Server 2003."

Figure 5.10 Zone Aging/Scavenging Properties

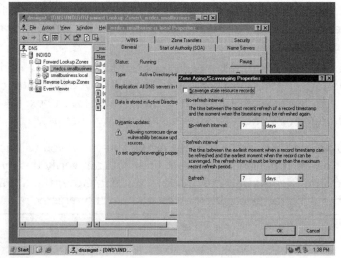

DNS Extensions

The DNS protocol defines and uses a number of fixed-length fields, each with a defined set of values. These fields, however, have been used for a variety of incremental improvements to the DNS protocol, and some method for further extending the DNS protocol's capabilities was needed. RFC2671 defines the first extension to the DNS protocol, EDNS0. It is assumed that subsequent extensions will be needed, thus the anticipated number scheme is EDNS0, EDNS1, EDNS2, and so forth.

NOTE

For more information on the extended DNS protocol, visit the Internet Engineering Task Force Web site, www.ietf.org/rfc/rfc2671.txt?number=2671 to read the RFC entitled "Extension Methods for DNS."

An example of how this is used in Windows Server 2003 is the extension of the DNS packet sent via the UDP, which was limited to 512 bytes under the original standards. This limitation became a problem because of the length and variety of information that needed to be sent by DNS via UDP. The extension defined in RFC2671 allows clients and servers to use larger DNS messages over UDP if both the client and server support the extension. This is implemented using a special OPT resource record, which is more accurately viewed as a pseudo-resource record. The OPT RR is not a RR that can be added to the database. Instead, it is generated if a host can handle DNS extensions. The OPT RR contains the client's maximum UDP size in the CLASS field as well as the number of octets in the largest UDP message the client can deliver within the client's network.

If a DNS server receives a DNS query that does not contain an OPT RR, it assumes the client does not support DNS extensions and all responses are limited to UDP's original maximum size of 512 bytes. If a DNS server receives a query that does contain an OPT RR, it caches this data for one week, by default. The default time-out value for the EDNS cache can be modified by changing the default value of 25200 in the registry key:

`HKEY_LOCAL_MACHINE\System\CurrentControlSet\Services\DNS\Parameters`

If the DNS server does not support the EDNS standard and it receives a query with the OPT RR included, it might return an error code. The three codes are:

- FORMERR(1)
- SERVFAIL(2)
- NOTIMPL(4)

FORMERR(1) indicates the server did not interpret the OPT resource record, SERV-FAIL(2) indicates the server did not process the query because of a problem with the name server, and NOTIMPL(4) indicates the name server does not support the type of query requested.

Test Day Tip

You will not be expected to name the error codes, but recognizing these three codes and what they indicate might help on questions related to the extensions of the DNS protocol. You will almost certainly run into a reference to extended DNS or, more specifically, the OPT RR.

Windows Server 2003 Active Directory Integrated DNS Servers

As with Windows 2000, DNS server services can be integrated into the Active Directory functions. This section assumes you are already familiar with Active Directory services in Windows 2000. As you know, Active Directory is the directory service included in Microsoft Windows beginning with Windows 2000. Active Directory stores information about network objects and also provides services that make this information available to users, applications, and computers. Using the DNS hierarchical naming system along with trust relationships, Active Directory provides a logical structure that helps organize and manage domains in a more consistent and efficient manner.

Exam Warning

Although DNS and Active Directory share the same domain name structure and use databases for name resolution, their roles should not be confused. DNS stores zones and resource records, whereas Active Directory stores domains and domain objects. Keep this distinction in mind when answering any questions that discuss both DNS and Active Directory.

The integration of DNS and Active Directory enables Active Directory to store and replicate DNS zone databases. The DNS Server service in Windows Server 2003 (and beginning with Windows 2000) supports storing zone data in the Active Directory as Active Directory objects. DNS files (zone resource records) are typically stored as text files on DNS servers. These files are synchronized and replicated via the zone transfer method discussed earlier. If you choose to use Active Directory-integrated DNS when you configure your DNS server in Windows Server 2003, the zone data is stored as an Active Directory object and is replicated during the normal Active Directory replication process. Note that the DNS server must be configured on a domain controller in order to implement Active Directory-integration since Active Directory is managed by the domain controllers.

EXAM WARNING

Only DNS servers running on domain controllers in Windows 2000/2003 can load Active Directory-integrated zones. If you run into a question about Active Directory-integrated zones on the exam, check to see whether or not the DNS server is running on a domain controller.

Secure Dynamic Updates

Windows Server 2003 supports the dynamic update protocol specified in RFC2136. The standard allows hosts to dynamically register their names in the DNS database, reducing the administrative overhead associated with manual updates. When DNS zone information is stored in Active Directory, DNS is automatically configured to accept dynamic updates. Secure dynamic updates are an additional feature provided by the integration of DNS and Active Directory. The DNS server accepts updates only from a client that has been authenticated in Active Directory and that has adequate permissions to use the dynamic update function.

NOTE

RFC2535 defines additional functionality called DNS Security (DNSSEC), which provides authentication and data integrity to resolvers when accessing DNS data. This security is based on encrypted digital signatures using private and public keys. Windows Server 2003 does not fully support DNSSEC but it does support the basic functionality designated in RFC2535. Windows Server 2003 does not provide a method for signing or verifying digital signatures and the Windows Server 2003 resolver does not verify any information returned by DNSSEC queries.

Active Directory Integrated Zones

An *Active Directory integrated zone* is a primary DNS zone held within Active Directory as an object and replicated to domain controllers through the Active Directory replication process. The DNS data is not replicated using the zone transfer process described earlier. Active Directory integrated zones can be a useful tool but it is important to remember that this configuration is proprietary to Microsoft Windows operating systems and is not available on non-Microsoft operating systems. This can lead to interoperability issues if mixed operating systems are used. However, the main benefits of the configuration are increased fault tolerance and more efficient replication.

When zone information is stored in Active Directory, it is stored on all domain controllers within the domain. This means that if one domain controller fails, the Active Directory information is present on other domain controllers in the domain, making the DNS zone data also available. Another benefit of Active Directory integrated zones is that because the zone data is an Active Directory object, it is replicated across slow WAN links more efficiently than via traditional zone transfers. When Active Directory replicates across slower WAN links, it compresses the data, reducing the time it takes to complete replication.

New & Noteworthy...

Active Directory Integrated Zone Locations

In Windows 2000, the DNS zone information was held in a single defined location, the *domain name context* of Active Directory. In Windows Server 2003, the AD integrated zones can be held in one of three locations:

1. All domain controllers in the domain
2. All domain controllers that are DNS servers
3. All domain controllers in the entire forest that are DNS servers

Windows Server 2003 stores Active Directory integrated zones in one of three places. The reason for this change is that under Windows 2000, the DNS zone data was replicated to all domain controllers in the domain regardless of whether or not they were DNS servers. This added unnecessary traffic and data to domain controllerss that were not also DNS servers. The ability, then, to replicate zone data only to domain controllerss that are also DNS servers either in the domain or in the entire forest provides a more efficient use of resources. This is particularly important in large enterprises where unnecessary replication can slow network traffic down significantly or increase replication time to an unacceptable level.

Active Directory Related DNS Entries

Resource records for Active Directory integrated zones are stored within Active Directory as Active Directory objects. The two primary objects used are the *dnsZone* and the *dnsNode* objects. The *dnsZone* object represents an Active Directory integrated zone that has dnsNode objects. This object is the equivalent of the standard zone stored in a text file on the DNS server for non–Active Directory integrated zones. The dnsZone object has a *dnsProperty* attribute, which defines details about the zone such as whether or not it supports dynamic updates. The *dnsNode* object corresponds to a standard DNS resource record. Each *dnsNode* object has a *dnsRecord* attribute, which contains information about the resource.

Summary of Exam Objectives

Windows Server 2003 fully supports the Domain Name System name resolution, in addition to supporting other name resolution methods such as Windows Internet Naming System (WINS) for NetBIOS name resolution. Names are used in addition to IP addresses because people can remember names more easily than they can recall a long string of numbers. Originally, all names were contained in a file called the HOSTS file. The file, a plain text file stored on each computer, held the names and associated IP addresses of all the computers on the small network back in the late 1960s and early 1970s. That solution quickly became untenable when the number of networked computers began to grow exponentially.

Fully Qualified Domain Names (FQDN) are host names that contain the full path to the host from the root, which is designated by a null character. An FQDN contains each branch of the network tree separated by the dot (.) character. The path is configured much like a tree structure for a directory on a computer hard drive. After the root is the top level domain (TLD) designation, which until recently was one of seven three-letter codes including *com*, *edu*, *org*, and *net*. The name to the left of the TLD is the second-level domain and both the TLD and the second-level domain are regulated by the Internet naming authority to ensure uniqueness on the Internet. Networks that do not connect to the Internet do not need to register their domain names and the names do not need to be unique (except within the organization). Each segment to the left of the second-level domain name is unregulated and companies can use any naming scheme that fits their requirements. Each of these subsequent sections is a branch on the network tree and the left-most segment of an FQDN is the specific host name. Names are resolved starting at the right side of the FQDN at the root domain and moving to the more specific data on the left.

The DNS system can resolve both a host name and the longer FQDN to the associated IP address using a DNS database. Although host names and FQDNs can still be resolved using a local HOSTS file, many companies do not want to deal with the administrative challenges of maintaining an up-to-date HOSTS file on every computer on the network. Although static HOSTS files can still be used and are still checked first, most name resolution in a Windows Server 2003-based network will occur through the use of the DNS name server. A host name can be the name of the computer or it can be an FQDN. In either case, the host name resolution is accomplished through the use of queries. A client requesting name resolution will send a query to the DNS server asking for the record associated with the name provided. The *forward lookup* or *forward query* requests the specific IP address for a host name. The DNS server responds with the specific *resource record* (RR), in this case the A RR, corresponding to the name given. This A RR includes the IP address of the requested host and is returned to the requesting client computer. If the client computer provides an IP address and requests the corresponding name, the request is a reverse lookup query and the corresponding host name for a given IP address is returned using a *Pointer* (PTR) RR. This is called a *reverse lookup* or *reverse query*.

Name resolution using DNS occurs through the use of queries. These queries can be *recursive* or *iterative*. A *recursive* query requires that either the requested information or an error be returned. Clients typically issue recursive queries to DNS servers. The DNS server, in turn, can issue a *recursive* or *iterative* query to other DNS servers if it does not have the requested information. An *iterative* query allows the DNS server to return its best answer, which might be the requested RR or a referral to another name server. This process, called "walking the tree," continues until the client receives either the requested information or an error stating the RR either does not exist or cannot be found. Iterative queries are most often used by DNS servers during their attempts to respond to a client's recursive query. It's important to note that DNS servers can act as clients to other DNS servers when they use resolvers to issue queries for name resolution in an attempt to provide name resolution to a client computer.

The data stored by DNS servers is stored in a database and is called a zone, which is simply a collection of database RRs associated with the namespace (typically a domain or subdomain). If the DNS server is responsible for maintaining those records it is said to be *authoritative* for that zone. If it is authoritative for the zone, it holds the *primary zone*. The primary zone is the only zone to which updates are made. The *secondary zone* is a copy of the primary zone and is copied to other DNS servers in the domain. The zone database is copied to secondary DNS servers via the *zone transfer* process, which occurs on a periodic basis to ensure accurate and timely name resolution.

A DNS server can assume one of several roles. It can be the *standard primary DNS server*, maintaining the primary zone database; a *standard secondary DNS server* receiving copies of the zone; or a *caching-only DNS server* that does not store zone information, does not participate in zone transfers, and does store resolutions received in response to queries in its memory, or cache. A DNS server can also be a forwarder or a slave. A DNS server can be configured as a forwarder so that all external name resolution requests are sent through the designated forwarder for resolution. This is often used when name resolution crosses the corporate network boundary (generally to the Internet). If a DNS server can only resolve a name using its cache, its zone information or the response from a forwarder, is it considered a *slave*. Otherwise, the DNS server will attempt to resolve the name on its own if it does not get a resolution via one of those three methods.

DNS servers can receive updates to their zone data via manual or dynamic entries. Dynamic updates are supported in Windows Server 2003 and these updates can be *secure* or *nonsecure*. With dynamic updating, the client provides information about its name, IP address, and other related information (contained in various types of resource records) to the DNS server, which updates its records.

DNS can be integrated with Active Directory, beginning with Windows 2000. The primary benefit of this ability to integrate DNS into the Active Directory structure is that replication can be done once (Active Directory replication containing DNS replication). Thus, separate zone transfers are not needed. When DNS is integrated into AD, the zone information is stored in Active Directory as Active Directory objects. The two primary objects are the *dnsZone* and the *dnsNode*. The *dnsZone* object is the entire zone and the *dnsNode* objects contain the individual resource records.

When integrated with Active Directory, DNS can use secure dynamic updating to update DNS RRs. The secure updating is managed via the Generic Security Service Application Program Interface (GSS-API) rather than via the methods outlined in RFCs 2535 or 2137. GSS-API provides security services that are independent of the underlying security mechanism. Secure dynamic updates are initiated by clients with appropriate permissions. Permissions are managed via the Access Control List (ACL) within the Active Directory security framework. Secure dynamic updates should not be enabled for DHCP servers who are performing dynamic updates on behalf of their DHCP clients because the DHCP server becomes the owner of the record and other DHCP servers will be unable to update the record due to inadequate ACL permissions. This is important if the primary DHCP server fails and the backup DHCP servers are called upon to perform primary functions.

DNS is a fundamental component of Windows Server 2003 networking. Thus, in this chapter, we provide you not only with information that is necessary to mastering the exam objectives in relation to DNS name resolution, but also with tips that will be invaluable to you in working with DNS in your daily duties as a network administrator.

Exam Objectives Fast Track

Review of DNS

- ☑ Domain Name System (DNS) uses host names and domain names to identify computers (hosts) on the Internet or on public networks.

- ☑ A Fully Qualified Domain Name (FQDN) contains the host name in the leftmost portion followed by the subdomain (if any), second level domain, and top level domain. Each is delimited by the use of the dot (.).

- ☑ DNS is a hierarchical naming system, as opposed to the flat NetBIOS naming structure.

- ☑ DNS is more scalable than NetBIOS naming, due to the ability to create a unique name based on the entire name (FQDN). Each name must be unique within its domain but can be repeated in separate domains because the FQDN created for each will be different.

- ☑ DNS names are resolved either using a HOSTS file or using name servers.

- ☑ DNS servers resolve name queries received from client resolvers.

- ☑ DNS servers resolve names using either recursive or iterative queries.

- ☑ A zone is a file located on the DNS server that provides name resolution data for the hosts within its zone.

☑ Zone files are composed of different types of resource records that provide information needed to resolve names and IP addresses for hosts.

☑ A DNS server that holds the primary zone is authoritative for that zone and changes can be made only to the primary zone.

☑ Zones can be primary, secondary, Active Directory integrated, or stub.

☑ Zones are copies to other DNS servers via the zone transfer process.

☑ Active Directory zones are replicated via the AD replication process.

Host Name Resolution

☑ Host names are resolved through the use of the HOSTS file or through a name server.

☑ The HOSTS file is located on each computer and can contain static information about hosts on the domain, including the location of servers.

☑ If the needed information is not located in the HOSTS file, a query is sent to the DNS name server.

☑ The DNS name server typically receives a recursive query from the host, meaning that it must either resolve the query or return an error.

☑ The DNS server checks its local cache then its zone database. If the name is present, the resolution is returned to the client resolver.

☑ If the name is not present, the DNS server will issue a query, either recursive or iterative, to other DNS servers.

☑ Other DNS servers (depending on the configuration of the DNS server issuing the query) will return either the resolved name, a pointer to another DNS server, or an error.

Windows Server 2003 DNS Server Roles

☑ A DNS server that is authoritative for a zone contains the primary zone and is considered to be a standard primary server.

☑ A DNS server that is not authoritative for a zone contains a secondary zone, which is a copy of the primary zone data.

☑ Changes are made only to the primary zone. Changes are replicated to other DNS servers via the secondary zone.

☑ DNS servers can be configured to be caching-only servers. In this case, no zone data is replicated to the server. All names are resolved via its cache or via queries. The cache data is built up as queries are resolved.

☑ DNS servers can be configured as forwarders and slaves. A forwarder is a DNS server that forwards external queries to appropriate DNS servers. It may perform iterative queries in an attempt to resolve the query.

☑ A slave server attempts to resolve the query using its cache and its zone data only. If it cannot be resolved, it forwards the query to a DNS forwarder. It does not perform iterative queries if the DNS forwarder is not able to resolve the query.

☑ DNS servers can accept dynamic updates, which automatically update RRs when information about the resource changes.

☑ Hosts that support dynamic updates can update their own records directly with a DNS server or they can allow the DHCP server, from which they obtain their IP configuration information, to register changes on their behalf.

☑ A client that permits the DHCP server to perform dynamic updates on its behalf will send DHCP Option 81 to the DHCP server.

Windows Server 2003 Active Directory Integrated DNS Servers

☑ Zones can be integrated into Active Directory either before or after they are created.

☑ Secure dynamic updates can be configured for any Active Directory integrated zones.

☑ Secure dynamic updates implement security via the ACL list using the Kerberos v5 protocol.

☑ Microsoft implements secure dynamic updates via GSS-API as outlined in RFC2078. It does not implement secure dynamic updates via methods outlined in either RFC 2535 or 2137.

☑ Active Directory integrated zones are stored within the Active Directory database as objects.

☑ The *dnsZone* object defines the zone, the *dnsProperty* object describes details about the *dnsZone* object, and the dnsNode object is the equivalent of a resource record in a standard zone file.

☑ Zone data is replicated when Active Directory replicates. This reduces administration and also reduces network traffic related to replication because Active Directory uses compression during replication.

Exam Objectives
Frequently Asked Questions

The following Frequently Asked Questions, answered by the authors of this book, are designed to both measure your understanding of the Exam Objectives presented in this chapter, and to assist you with real-life implementation of these concepts. You will also gain access to thousands of other FAQs at ITFAQnet.com.

Q: Aren't host names and NetBIOS names the same thing in Windows Server 2003?

A: By default, the host name assigned to the computer is used as the NetBIOS name in Windows Server 2003. However, an alternate NetBIOS name can be assigned to the computer, if desired. Even if the host name and NetBIOS name are the same, their functions and the methods by which they are resolved is different.

Q: On the exam, am I going to be expected to know all the different top level domains?

A: No. It's important that you understand what the top level domain designations are and how they're used on the Internet. However, questions on the exam will focus on applying your knowledge about top level domains to scenarios. In those cases, you'll need to understand that the root is unnamed and is designated with the dot (.). You'll also need to understand that the top level domains as well as the second level domains are managed so that each combination is guaranteed to be unique worldwide.

Q: What's the relationship between recursive and iterative queries and forward and reverse lookups?

A: Recursive and iterative queries specify what results are acceptable. A recursive query requires that either the information or an error be returned. An iterative query requires that either the information or a pointer be returned. When a DNS server is attempting to resolve a query, whether recursive or iterative, it will query its own cache and zone files first. There might be forward and reverse lookup zones defined. Forward lookup zones provide information needed to resolve names within the domain and reverse lookup zones provide information on reverse lookups, resolving an IP address to a name.

Q: What exactly is a stub zone?

A: A stub zone is a copy of a zone that contains only three resource records: SOA, NS, and glue A for the delegated zone. The stub zone typically is used to keep a parent zone aware of the authoritative DNS servers for child zones to maintain DNS name resolution efficiency. Just as a secondary zone is a copy of the primary zone, a stub zone is a copy as well, but it does not contain all the RRs, just those used to define authoritative DNS servers for child zones.

Q: Will I be expected to understand BIND for the exam?

A: Microsoft exams focus on Microsoft technologies and, in particular, what's new in the technology. In that regard, you would not expect to see questions about BIND. However, Microsoft technologies often are used in conjunction with non-Microsoft technologies. Where these two overlap or interact, you'll be expected to have a basic knowledge. What's important to understand about the BIND format is that although Microsoft does not use it, UNIX and Linux DNS servers do. If you are importing files, you'll need to understand how these interact and relate to the Microsoft convention.

Q: How much do I need to know about the types of resource records supported in Windows Server 2003?

A: It's important to understand the standard zone RRs such as A, PTR, CNAME, SOA, NS, MX, and SRV. Table 5.5 lists the more commonly used RRs. Understanding what each of these does and what information is contained in them will help you not only on the exam but on the job as well. You might be called upon to add manual RRs and you'll need to understand what effect they will have. The DNS Management Console provides the parameters for each RR type, so you won't need to memorize that data. You'll need to be able to recognize and understand the standard RRs used in Windows Server 2003.

Q: Do I need to know much about Internet Protocol version 6 for this exam?

A: Internet Protocol version 6 (IPv6) is the latest IP protocol version that provides support for 128-bit IP addresses, so you'll need to understand this protocol and how it's implemented in Windows Server 2003. That subject is outside the scope of this chapter. Within the scope, you'll need to know the RR types used to support IPv6 and also how IPv6 addresses are resolved (using either AAAA for name lookups or IP6.ARPA for reverse lookups). For more information about IPv6, you can visit the IETF Web site for information about the IPv6 standards or visit the Microsoft Windows Server 2003 Web site for information about IPv6 and how to install and route IPv6.

Self Test

A Quick Answer Key follows the Self Test questions. For complete questions, answers, and explanations to the Self Test questions in this chapter as well as the other chapters in this book, see the Self Test Appendix.

Review of DNS

1. Lisa Cooper works in the finance department, which has its own domain, finance.eastcoast.somecompany.com. Lisa Chandler works in the operations department in the same branch office as Lisa Cooper. While having lunch one day, Lisa Cooper mentions to Lisa Chandler that she'd renamed her computer to LISAC because it originally had come configured as HQV53X09 and she just didn't like that. Lisa Chandler becomes concerned when she hears this because *her* computer is named LISAC and she knows you can't have duplicate computer names on the network. If you overheard this conversation, what would you tell these two Lisa's?

    A. Since Lisa Chandler's computer was named LISAC first, it will be recognized as LISAC. Lisa Cooper's computer will lose connectivity to the network and will have to be renamed.

    B. Lisa Cooper's computer name will be seen as LISAC2 on the network since she chose the name after Lisa Chandler, whose computer name is LISAC.

    C. If Lisa Cooper changed the name without specifying the domain, there will be a conflict.

    D. Lisa Cooper's computer's FQDN is unique, so there is no conflict.

2. An application using NetBIOS needs a NetBIOS name resolved. To resolve the NetBIOS name, local cache is checked first. The needed resolution is not already cached, so the LMHOSTS file is checked next. The desired entry is not in the LMHOSTS file. Based on this, what is the next step taken in resolving the NetBIOS name?

    A. The DNS server issues a recursive query.

    B. The WINS server is queried.

    C. The DNS server is queried using an NS type record.

    D. NetBIOS over TCP resolves the name to an IP address.

3. The Cooper Company has just acquired a firm and they're trying to integrate their networks. The Cooper company has a domain name *somecompany.com*. As a temporary solution, the Cooper company uses the domain name newcompany.us as the domain name for the acquired company as a subdomain. However, another company on the Internet uses the domain name newcompany.us. Can the Cooper Company still use this domain name? Why or why not? Select the best response.

A. No. The Cooper Company must create a different domain name for the new company so it does not replicate a domain name already in use.

B. Yes. The Cooper Company can use this domain name because the FQDN of this new domain is newcompany.us.somecompany.com.

C. No. The Cooper Company cannot use this domain name because the .us indicates a TLD.

D. Yes, the Cooper Company can use this domain name because the new domain will not be connected to the Internet.

4. You've been asked to look at a DNS server that a junior member of the IT department worked on, which seems to be having problems. You browse to c:\windows03\system32\dns and locate the cache.dns file. You open this file using Notepad and see the following entry:

```
.                   360000   NS    somecompany.com.
somecompany.com     360000   A     184.22.63.1
```

You recognize the domain name as your company's domain name and the IP address as the root server for the domain. What do you conclude from this information?

A. The cache.dns file is corrupt and should be replaced by copying one from another DNS server.

B. You need an SOA record along with the NS and A type RRs in this file.

C. The DNS server was not connected to the Internet when DNS was initialized.

D. The server's root hints file is missing and should be copied from another DNS server that is working.

Host Name Resolution

5. You've been tasked with helping to set up some of the DNS servers for your company's expanded network. The domain name is somecompany.com and you're working on operations.somecompany.com. You have an older server, *bobcat*, that has been used for the operations department but is woefully inadequate. Due to serious budget constraints, you've been forced to delay purchases of hardware that you need to provide the services required by your users. The *bobcat* server is going to be temporarily replaced by another server with a slightly faster processor and more memory. This new server, *cheetah*, will be used only for a few months, until the new fiscal year. At that time, *bobcat* will be replaced with a significantly improved server that will provide more speed and processing power than either the old *bobcat* or the *cheetah*. Based on this information, what RR would you add to your DNS server when *cheetah* is operational?

A. cheetah   IN   SRV   bobcat.operations.somecompany.com

B. cheetah   IN   A   54.166.251.16

C. bobcat.operations.somecompany.com IN   PTR
    cheetah.operations.somecompany.com

D. bobcat.operations.somecompany.com IN   CNAME   cheetah.operations.some-company.com

6. A DNS server, NS1, receives a name resolution query via a client resolver. The name is not located in the DNS server's cache nor in its zone data. NS1 issues a query to NS2 in an attempt to resolve the name. NS2 checks its cache and its zone data and does not find an answer. It replies to NS1 with an A RR that has the name NS3 and the IP address for NS3. What will NS1 do next?

A. NS1 will forward the A record to the client resolver.

B. NS1 will issue a new query to the IP address listed in the A RR.

C. NS1 will forward the A record to NS2 requesting the NS and SOA records associated with the A RR.

D. NS1 will issue a new query to the NS2 server using the IP address listed in the A RR.

7. The IT department has seen a lot of traffic from a particular IP address outside of their corporate network. They'd like to know the name of this server. They know that a client resolver issues a request for the name associated with the IP address 118.54.78.9. Which is the correct RR they would expect to be returned?

A. 118.54.78.9 IN   PTR   njm.southwest.somecompany.com

B. njm.southwest.somecompany.com   IN-ADDR.ARPA   118.54.78.9

C. 118.54.78.9   in-addr-arpa IN   PTR   njm.southwest.somecompany.com

D. 118.54.78.9.in-addr.arpa   IN   PTR   njm.southwest.somecompany.com

8. Jackie is working with an associate, Bailey Scotland, on a market research project for a new product roll out. She's using a software application that will connect her to shared resources on Bailey's computer. Her computer on the somecompany.com domain issues a recursive query to a DNS server to resolve a host name, baileysc. What is the response you would expect to see in this case?

A. baileysc   IN   A   188.54.107.96

B. 188.54.107.96 IN   A   baileysc

C. baileysc   A   188.54.107.96

D. baileysc.somecompany.com   IN   CNAME   188.54.107.96

Windows Server 2003 DNS Server Roles

9. You're having trouble with name resolution for a particular host, jawbone. eastcoast.somecompany.com. You check the DNS server NS1.eastcoast. somecompany.com and see the following record:

Jawbone.eastcoast.somecompany.com   IN   AAAA   1.2.3.123.456.12.34.56ab

What can you conclude about jawbone.eastcoast.somecompany.com?

A. jawbone.eastcoast.somecompany.com should have an associated PTR record.

B. jawbone.eastcoast.somecompany.com's A RR is corrupt.

C. jawbone.eastcoast.somecompany.com is using IPv6.

D. jawbone.eastcoast.somecompany.com has an illegal IP address. Check the IP configuration for jawbone.

10. Your company's network runs Windows 2000 Server and Windows Server 2003 on all its servers. The server named reddog runs the DHCP server service. Two other servers, greenmonkey and bluefish, are backup DHCP servers. Thursday afternoon reddog goes down. A user contacts the help desk and states that her computer doesn't seem to connect to the Internet. She tried renewing her DHCP lease thinking that might fix the problem, but it hasn't. What is the most likely cause of this problem?

A. The DHCP servers greenmonkey and bluefish are not configured to perform dynamic updates so renewing the lease with either backup DHCP server will cause this problem.

B. The client should not have tried to renew her DHCP lease when reddog was down. She should wait until reddog is back online.

C. The DHCP scope information on greenmonkey or bluefish allowed the client to renew a lease using an already in-use IP address causing the connectivity problem.

D. The DHCP server, reddog, was using dynamic updating and registered with DNS on behalf of the user's computer making updates by greenmonkey or bluefish impossible.

11. Your network is running three DNS servers, NS1, NS2, and NS3. NS1 is running Windows Server 2003, whereas NS2 and NS3 are still running Windows NT 4.0. In reviewing the error log on NS1, you notice an error that lists NOTIMPL(4) being returned by NS3. What does this error indicate?

A. NS3 does not support extended DNS (EDNS0).

B. NS1 does not support extended DNS (EDNS0).

C. The OPT record received from NS3 contained an illegal Time-To-Live.

D. The OPT record needs to be added to all three name servers.

12. You've just created a new zone in DNS on a Windows Server 2003-based computer. You check the zone and notice that the only records in it are the SOA and NS RRs. You check the configuration and see that the zone is configured to accept dynamic updates. What should you do next?

    A. Manually add all RR for the zone including A, CNAME, PTR, and SRV records.

    B. Manually add A RR for all hosts that cannot use dynamic updating.

    C. Manually add A RR and PTR RR for all hosts that will be using dynamic updating.

    D. Manually initiate a zone transfer to replicate all the needed RR to the new zone.

13. A DNS server, Aspen, has been successfully resolving queries but with the wrong information. You use the Monitoring function in the DNS Management Console for Aspen and test the simple and recursive queries. Both work fine. What is the most likely cause of this problem?

    A. Aspen is not authoritative for the zone in which the wrong information is being returned.

    B. Aspen is not configured to perform iterative queries.

    C. Some clients do not support dynamic updates, or manually entered RR have errors.

    D. The clients that received the wrong information do not support the OPT record type.

Windows Server 2003 Active Directory Integrated DNS Servers

14. A DNS server, NS1Jones, on the domain us.somecompany.com, consistently fails to resolve names from the domain canada1company.com and mexicounocompany.com. It resolves names within the us.somecompany.com zone, for which it is authoritative, with no problems. What is the likely cause of this problem, assuming both external domains exist?

    A. NS1Jones is unable to perform recursive queries. Check the Advanced properties of the DNS server.

    B. NS1Jones is configured to be a forwarder. Disable forwarding in the NS1Jones properties.

    C. NS1Jones is unable to connect to the Internet's root DNS name servers.

    D. NS1Jones should be configured to be a secondary DNS server for both canada1.company.com and mexicuunocompany.com.

15. Your company has recently migrated from Windows NT 4.0 to Windows Server 2003 on all of its networked servers, including those running the DHCP and DNS server services. During the migration, you implemented Active Directory integrated zones. A colleague states that you cannot do this because the zones converted from non-AD aware operating systems will not allow secure updates, creating a significant security risk to the organization. What is your response?

A. When any zone is integrated into AD, it takes on the security features of AD.

B. If the zone is created outside of the AD, it will be configured for no secure updates and must be re-created to allow for secure updates.

C. If the zone is created outside of AD, it will not be configured for secure updates but can be modified via the DNS Management Console.

D. When any zone created before Windows 2000 is integrated into AD, it will use whatever update type other zones are configured to use.

Self Test Quick Answer Key

For complete questions, answers, and epxlanations to the Self Test questions in this chapter as well as the other chapters in this book, see the Self Test Appendix.

1. **D**	9. **C**
2. **B**	10. **D**
3. **B**	11. **A**
4. **C**	12. **B**
5. **D**	13. **C**
6. **B**	14. **A**
7. **D**	15. **C**
8. **A**	

Chapter 6

MCSA/MCSE 70-291

The Windows Server 2003 DNS Server

Exam Objectives in this Chapter:

2.1   Install and configure the DNS Server Service.

2.1.1   Configure DNS server options.

2.1.2   Configure DNS zone options.

2.1.3   Configure DNS forwarding.

2.2   Manage DNS.

2.2.1   Manage DNS zone settings.

2.2.2   Manage DNS record setting.

5.3   troubleshoot server services.

5.3.1   Diagnose and resolve issues related to service dependency.

5.3.2   Use service recovery options to diagnose and resolve service-related issues.

☑   Summary of Exam Objectives

☑   Exam Objectives Fast Track

☑   Exam Objectives Frequently Asked Questions

☑   Self Test

☑   Self Test Quick Answer Key

Introduction

With the release of Windows NT 4.0 in August of 1996, the Domain Name Service (DNS) Server entered the Microsoft Windows Server market, allowing for the first time an out-of-the-box solution for host name to IP address resolution in your Microsoft Windows TCP/IP network environment. Before this time, backend Microsoft shops were reliant upon third-party DNS solutions, like MetaIP or Berkley's BIND implementation. This created some configuration headaches and compatibility problems.

With the introduction of DNS into the Windows operating system, Microsoft started to tackle just one of the customer-dependant needs that have made them such a market leader in today's network operating systems shuffle. Since then, the Microsoft DNS Service has become the central brain for all communication within your native Active Directory Windows environment.

With this chapter, we will focus on installing, configuring, and integrating the Windows Server 2003 DNS service in your current environment. We will also discuss some basic monitoring and troubleshooting steps guided to help you solve some of the more common DNS problems facing most administrators today.

Installing and Configuring the Windows Server 2003 DNS Server

Installing the DNS server service into your Windows Server 2003 computer can be done in a number of different ways. For many, it will be installed via the first installation of a domain controller during the construction of a Windows Server 2003 Active Directory domain implementation. Others will find that a simple upgrade from their current Windows DNS will suffice as the best installation method. Lastly, Windows Server 2003 DNS can be installed and used without Active Directory on a stand-alone Windows Server 2003 server. For the purpose of learning how to install DNS onto a Windows Server 2003 machine, we will focus on the last method in the following exercise. Windows Server 2003 DNS is installed from the Networking Services option using the Add or Remove Program Files just as any other networking related Windows service. Exercise 6.01 will walk you through installing the DNS on a stand-alone Windows Server 2003 server.

EXERCISE 6.01

IINSTALLING THE WINDOWS SERVER 2003 DNS SERVICE

The following exercise will guide you through the Windows Server 2003 DNS wizards to successfully install the DNS server.

1. Click **Start | Control Panel | Add or Remove Programs**.

2. Click **Add/Remove Windows Components** in the Windows Components Wizard dialog window.

3. Scroll down and highlight **Network Services**. Click the **Details** button as shown in Figure 6.1.

Figure 6.1 Adding Windows Network Services

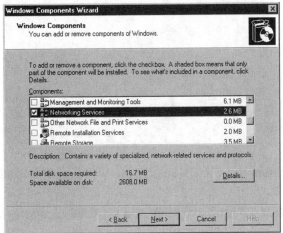

4. Select the **Domain Name System (DNS)** option checkbox and click **OK** as shown in Figure 6.2.

Figure 6.2 Adding the DNS Server Service

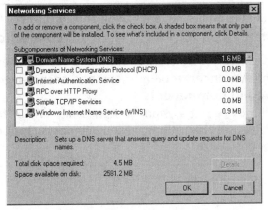

5. Make sure you have your Windows Server 2003 source CD in your CD-ROM (or you can type the path to a network share where the installation files are located when prompted). Click **Next**. Windows Server 2003 will start copying the needed source files and installing the DNS service as shown in Figure 6.3.

Figure 6.3 Copying DNS Source Files

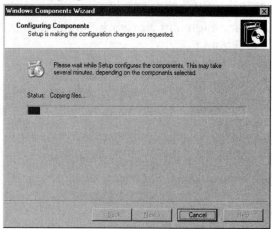

6. Click **Finish** and the DNS Server service will be installed and ready to be accessed.

7. Click **Start | Administrative Tools | DNS** to open your DNS MMC Console and to configure your DNS server.

NOTE

You can also install the DNS service via the **Network Connections** window.

1. Click **Start | Control Panel | Network Connections**.

2. Right-click **Network Connections** and select **Open**.

3. Click the **Advanced** toolbar menu and then select **Optional Networking Components**.

4. This will put you at a window somewhat similar to Figure 6.1, but with less available options, called Windows Optional Networking Components Wizard.

NOTE

Actually, the most efficient way to handle the DNS server's addressing is to make it a DHCP client and give it a *reserved* address in DHCP. That way, it will always have the same address—same effect as a static address—but the DHCP server will be able to update it with gateway changes and other TCP/IP configuration information.

Make a Habit of Using Static IP Addresses

Use static IP addresses for network critical services such as DNS, as discussed in Chapter 4. Use common sense and configure your Domain Naming System servers with a static IP address. If clients are to be hard-coded with the IP address of your DNS server, it is not wise to configure your DNS server with an IP address that uses Dynamic Host Configuration Protocol (DHCP), which could change over time. If you try to install DNS on a server that is configured to use DHCP, you will receive the errors displayed in Figures 6.4 and 6.5. Although the install will allow you to continue with the installation, Microsoft does not recommend that you do, and gives you the opportunity to set a static IP for your DNS installation, displayed after the first warning, as shown in Figure 6.5.

Figure 6.4 Installation Error Shown if Your Server Is Using DHCP

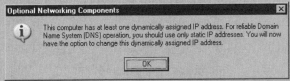

Figure 6.5 Installation Error Shown If You Continue Using DHCP

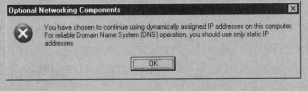

Along with configuring a static IP address before installing the DNS service, Microsoft also recommends preconfiguring the computer's *domain name*. This is to make certain the computer that is going to host DNS has a domain name that matches the zone it will be hosting for Active Directory purposes.

To configure a static domain name for your DNS server, follow these five steps:

1. Click **Start | Control Panel | Network Connections** and select **Local Area Connection**. Click the **Properties** button.

2. In the **Local Area Connections** dialog window, scroll down until you see **Internet Protocol (TCP/IP)** and highlight it. Click the **Properties** button.

3. In the **Internet Protocol (TCP/IP)** dialog window, click the **Advanced** button.

4. In the **Advanced TCP/IP Settings** dialog window, click the **DNS** tab as shown in Figure 6.6. Verify that the server's IP address that you are installing DNS onto is the first in the list in the **DNS server addresses, in order of use** window box.

5. In the **DNS suffix for this connection** field, type in your *primary* **domain name**, also shown in Figure 6.6. Click **OK**.

Figure 6.6 Pre-configuring Your Domain Name before Installing DNS

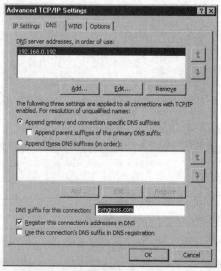

> ### New DNS Replication Options Using Windows Server 2003's Application Partition
>
> With the introduction of Windows Server 2003, you are now able to replicate Active Directory Integrated zone data to other domains, and even to the entire forest. If you install DNS on a domain controller, the **General** tab of your DNS server's **Properties** page has an option called **Replication: All DNS servers in the Active Directory domain** as shown in Figure 6.7. By default, Windows 2000 kept its Active Directory Integrated DNS database in the *domain partition*, which resided on every domain controller in only that domain. By default, Windows Server 2003 puts its DNS data into a mode that replicates only to all the Active Directory Integrated DNS servers in the domain. This is possible because of a new partition called the *Application Partition*.
>
> This new partition is replicated to all domain controllers in the forest, and it allows you as a DNS administrator to customize which domain controllers in the forest will contain this DNS zone database information. You can do this by clicking the **Change** button next to the **Replication: All DNS servers in the Active**

Continued

Directory domain option as shown in Figure 6.7. Figure 6.8 displays four different database replication options and explains which domain controllers will receive a copy of the replicated data.

Figure 6.7 Changing the DNS Replication Mode

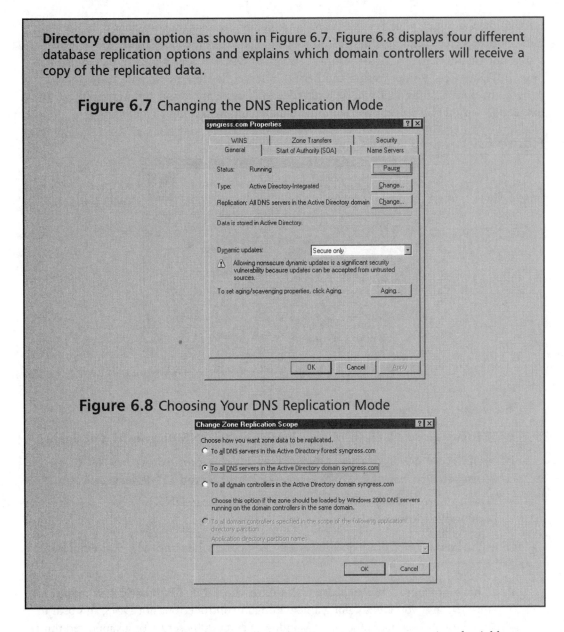

Figure 6.8 Choosing Your DNS Replication Mode

Previously, we discussed how to install the DNS service on a server using the Add or Remove Programs applet in the Control Panel. This typically is used to install DNS on a stand-alone or member server. You can also install DNS on a domain controller to take advantage of Windows Server 2003 Active Directory Integrated DNS. You can do this after the domain controller is already installed, or in instances where you are creating a new forest root domain, during the dcpromo process of your first domain controller (the dcpromo command invokes the Active Directory Installation Wizard. This wizard can also be invoked through the Configure your Server wizard, by selecting the domain controller role.) In the instance that you are creating a new forest root domain, dcpromo's execution will actively search out a DNS namespace based on its configured DNS IP addresses as displayed previously in Figure 6.6, in order to find another DNS server hosting the domain name for the domain the domain controller will be installed into. If none are found, the Active Directory Installation wizard will prompt you with the dialog window found in Figure 6.9.

Figure 6.9 Installing DNS via the Dcpromo Process

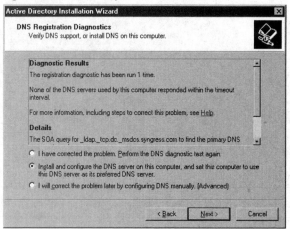

Three choices are available:

- **I have corrected the problem. Perform the DNS diagnostic test again.**

- **Install and configure the DNS server on this computer, and set this computer to use this DNS server as its preferred DNS server.**

- **I will correct the problem later by configuring DNS manually. (Advanced)**

We will discuss each of these options briefly, as well as when and why you would or would not want to use each of them.

- **I have corrected the problem. Perform the DNS diagnostic test again.** Use this option if you are installing a new domain controller but not DNS, and plan to use the DNS services of another Windows Server 2003 server or a supported third-party DNS application. When installing a DC, dcpromo needs to find a DNS server that supports both SRV records and Dynamic DNS in order for it to successfully promote and register itself as a domain controller in the domain. If, for any reason, your other DNS server was not available during the first attempt at promoting the computer to domain controller, select this option when you think the DNS server is contactable and try again.

EXAM WARNING

For a successful domain controller installation, you must configure the correct DNS IP address just discussed, and displayed in Figure 6.6. Unless you plan on installing DNS during the dcpromo process, it is best to have DNS properly configured prior to running a domain controller promotion.

- **Install and configure the DNS server on this computer, and set this computer to use this DNS server as its preferred DNS server.** Use this option if you want the **dcpromo** process to install and configure DNS for you based on your preconfigured DNS domain name. This is the Microsoft-recommended way if you do not already have DNS installed and configured.

- **I will correct the problem later by configuring DNS manually. (Advanced)** Use this option only if you are looking for a challenge later on. This option can be used if you are using a third-party DNS server that does not support Dynamic updates and thus cannot be updated with all of the needed DNS SRV records. You will have to use the **netlogon.dns** file located in %systemroot%\system32\config after the domain controller completes its installation, to populate the third-party DNS with the correct SRV record information. This is not recommended because it lends itself to human error and misconfiguration. Because Active Directory is completely dependant on a stable and working DNS, this method is frowned upon. See Figure 6.10 for an example of the netlogon.dns file.

Figure 6.10 Configuring Your DNS SRV Records Manually Using the netlogon.dns File

```
netlogon.dns - Notepad
File  Edit  Format  View  Help
syngress.com. 600 IN A 192.168.0.192
_ldap._tcp.syngress.com. 600 IN SRV 0 100 389 win2003.syngress.com.
_ldap._tcp.Default-First-Site-Name._sites.syngress.com. 600 IN SRV 0 100 389
win2003.syngress.com.
_ldap._tcp.pdc._msdcs.syngress.com. 600 IN SRV 0 100 389 win2003.syngress.com.
_ldap._tcp.gc._msdcs.syngress.com. 600 IN SRV 0 100 3268 win2003.syngress.com.
_ldap._tcp.Default-First-Site-Name._sites.gc._msdcs.syngress.com. 600 IN SRV 0 100 3268
win2003.syngress.com.
_ldap._tcp.e9a48969-e4ff-4453-ba6a-470c4959cc92.domains._msdcs.syngress.com. 600 IN SRV 0 100
389 win2003.syngress.com.
gc._msdcs.syngress.com. 600 IN A 192.168.0.192
6666df95-e9cd-49dc-ada8-e33d0fcfdc6b._msdcs.syngress.com. 600 IN CNAME win2003.syngress.com.
_kerberos._tcp.dc._msdcs.syngress.com. 600 IN SRV 0 100 88 win2003.syngress.com.
_kerberos._tcp.Default-First-Site-Name._sites.dc._msdcs.syngress.com. 600 IN SRV 0 100 88
win2003.syngress.com.
_ldap._tcp.dc._msdcs.syngress.com. 600 IN SRV 0 100 389 win2003.syngress.com.
_ldap._tcp.Default-First-Site-Name._sites.dc._msdcs.syngress.com. 600 IN SRV 0 100 389
win2003.syngress.com.
_kerberos._tcp.syngress.com. 600 IN SRV 0 100 88 win2003.syngress.com.
_kerberos._tcp.Default-First-Site-Name._sites.syngress.com. 600 IN SRV 0 100 88
win2003.syngress.com.
_gc._tcp.syngress.com. 600 IN SRV 0 100 3268 win2003.syngress.com.
_gc._tcp.Default-First-Site-Name._sites.syngress.com. 600 IN SRV 0 100 3268
win2003.syngress.com.
_kerberos._udp.syngress.com. 600 IN SRV 0 100 88 win2003.syngress.com.
_kpasswd._tcp.syngress.com. 600 IN SRV 0 100 464 win2003.syngress.com.
_kpasswd._udp.syngress.com. 600 IN SRV 0 100 464 win2003.syngress.com.
DomainDnsZones.syngress.com. 600 IN A 192.168.0.192
_ldap._tcp.DomainDnsZones.syngress.com. 600 IN SRV 0 100 389 win2003.syngress.com.
_ldap._tcp.Default-First-Site-Name._sites.DomainDnsZones.syngress.com. 600 IN SRV 0 100 389
win2003.syngress.com.
ForestDnsZones.syngress.com. 600 IN A 192.168.0.192
_ldap._tcp.ForestDnsZones.syngress.com. 600 IN SRV 0 100 389 win2003.syngress.com.
_ldap._tcp.Default-First-Site-Name._sites.ForestDnsZones.syngress.com. 600 IN SRV 0 100 389
win2003.syngress.com.
```

Configuring Your DNS Server

EXAM
70-291
OBJECTIVE
2.1.1

After you have successfully installed DNS, you must configure it to meet the needs of your organization. To open the DNS Management console, click **Start | Administrative Tools | DNS**. If you did not install DNS through the **Active Directory Installation** wizard, there are no zones configured by default. You are presented with a plain DNS console consisting of the following three folders or containers (as displayed in Figure 6.11):

- **Event Viewer** The Event Viewer folder is a shortcut to a new DNS Event Viewer log, installed when you installed DNS. Below it you will find the DNS Events folder. It contains DNS specific event information, alerts, warnings, and errors.

- **Forward Lookup Zones** The Forward Lookup Zones folder contains all of the forward lookup DNS domain zones that are hosted on the DNS server you are looking at.

- **Reverse Lookup Zones** The Reverse Lookup Zones folder contains all of the reverse lookup DNS domain zones that are hosted on the DNS server you are looking at.

Figure 6.11 Displaying the Stand-alone Install of the DNS Console

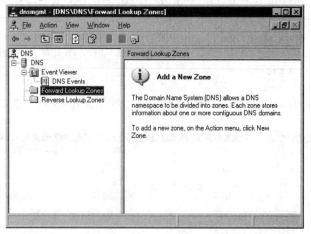

What you currently have set up is a DNS *caching-only* server. A DNS caching-only server is a DNS server set up to resolve the queries of DNS clients using its configured *root hints* or any *DNS forwarders*. Caching-only DNS servers build up a local cache of resolved queries while performing recursive DNS queries for its clients. DNS caching-only servers are not authoritative and thus do not host any local DNS zones.

NOTE

The ability to see the local server cache is not available by default. In order to see and manage your DNS cache, click **View** in the DNS console menu and select **Advanced**. You will then see the Cached Lookups folder as shown in Figure 6.12.

Figure 6.12 Displaying DNS Cached Lookups

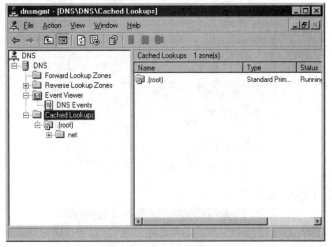

DNS root hints are defined as a listing of DNS servers that can be used to query against when a query for a domain name received is not authoritative on that DNS server. These are typically not altered, and are predefined when you install DNS. They can be viewed by right-clicking your **DNS** *server name* and clicking **Properties**. Click the **Root Hints** tab as shown in Figure 6.13. DNS forwarders are defined as a listing of DNS servers that are also used to query against, when a query for a domain name received is not authoritative on that DNS server. If DNS forwarders are set up, the DNS root hints are not used. Forwarders typically are used to lessen the load on the root hints DNS servers. You can configure DNS forwarders by right-clicking your **DNS** *server name* and clicking **Properties**. Click the **Forwarders** tab as shown in Figure 6.14.

Regardless of the caching-only server method used to gain domain name query resolution, after a domain name is successfully resolved and returned to your caching-only DNS server, that name is *cached* (saved locally). These cached query results later are used for future client queries to the same domain name, to help speed up resolution time. If you were to point clients to the IP address of this DNS server, it would first look in its cache to determine if it already has a resolution result. If so, it will send the answer directly back to the client, without having to use its root hints or configured forwarders.

Figure 6.13 Configuring DNS Root Hints

Figure 6.14 Configuring DNS Forwarders

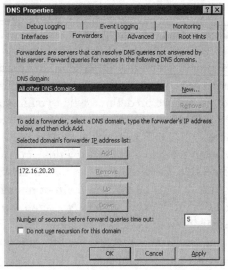

NOTE

Caching-only DNS servers are sometimes referred to as *forwarding-only* servers.

TEST DAY TIP

Caching-only DNS servers are best used at remote Wide Area Network (WAN) sites requiring domain name resolution, and are limited by the amount of bandwidth back to their main offices. Initially these servers will hold no cache, thus requiring more queries to be retrieved initially across the WAN. When these queries build up, less and less traffic will have to be sent across the WAN, and can be retrieved via the local server cache. Another benefit of caching-only DNS servers is that they are not subject to DNS zone transfer traffic as are DNS secondary zone servers.

EXAM WARNING

Caching-only DNS servers can limit the administrative overhead of primary or secondary servers, although it is necessary to occasionally delete stale domain names from the cache, or even to clear all contents of the local cache. To clear the DNS server cache, right-click on your **DNS server name** or the **Cached Lookups** folder as shown in Figure 6.12 and select **Clear Cache**.

Configuring Forward Lookup Zones

If your goal is to create an authoritative DNS zone for your or some other company's domain name, you must configure a *forward lookup zone*. Let's break that term up into two parts to define it more easily; *forward lookup* and *zone*:

- **Forward Lookup** Forward lookup refers to the manner in which a DNS server resolves a host name to an IP address. Forward means *name to IP*.

- **Zone** A zone is a portion of a contiguous name space in which a server has been given the authority to resolve DNS queries.

To configure a new DNS forward lookup zone, follow the steps outlined in Exercise 6.02.

EXERCISE 6.02

CREATING A NEW DNS FORWARD LOOKUP ZONE

This exercise will demonstrate how to create your first DNS domain forward lookup zone on your Windows Server 2003 server.

1. Click **Start | Administrative Tools | DNS**.
2. Highlight your **DNS server name**, right-click and select **New Zone** as shown in Figure 6.15.

Figure 6.15 Creating a New Forward Lookup Zone

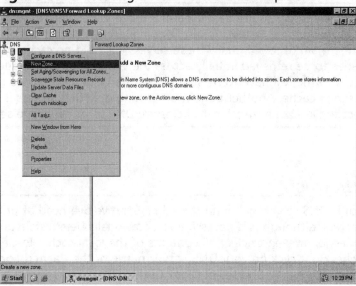

3. Click **Next** on the **Welcome to the New Zone Wizard** dialog window.

4. Select **Primary zone** for the configured zone type and click **Next** as shown in Figure 6.16.

Figure 6.16 Selecting a Primary Zone to Create

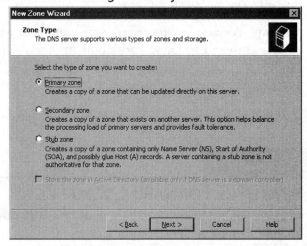

5. Select **Forward lookup zone** as shown in Figure 6.17 and click **Next**.

6. Type the **full domain name** of the domain for which you want to create a zone in the **Zone name** field as shown in Figure 6.18 and click **Next**.

Figure 6.17 Selecting a Forward Lookup Zone as the Zone Type

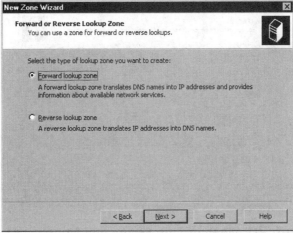

Figure 6.18 Creating the DNS Zone File

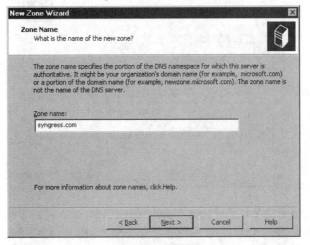

7. Unless you have a prepopulated zone configuration file, let the wizard create the default zone name file, appending **.dns** to your zone name as shown in Figure 6.19. Click **Next**.

8. Select **Allow both nonsecure and secure dynamic updates** as shown in Figure 6.20 and click **Next**.

9. Click **Finish** and your new zone will be created along with the Start of Authority (SOA), Name Server (NS), and Host (A) records of the DNS server, as shown in Figure 6.21.

Figure 6.19 Creating the DNS Zone Filename

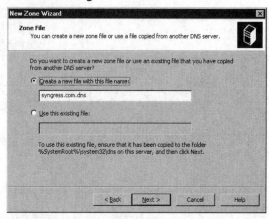

Figure 6.20 Allowing Both Secure and Nonsecure Dynamic Updates

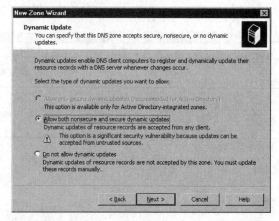

Figure 6.21 Viewing a Newly Created Zone and Default Records

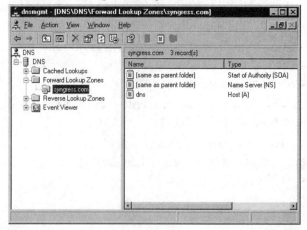

Adding DNS Database Records

Your Windows Server 2003 DNS database consists of many different types of records used by DNS clients to query and locate network resources. These records can be registered dynamically with your DNS server if it is configured to do so, or you can enter them manually as you had to do in the Windows NT 4.0 version of DNS. Table 6.1 lists the most common DNS record types you might find in your Windows Server 2003 DNS database.

Table 6.1 Common DNS Records

Record Name (Type)	Description
Host (A)	A record used to map machine or resource host names to IP addresses.
Alias (CNAME)	A record used to copy the name of an already existing host name. This record points to that existing host record and not to an IP address.
Mail Exchanger (MX)	A record identifying the location of your Internet mail server. This record points to the Host record of your mail server.
Pointer (PTR)	A record used for reverse lookup queries to resolve IP address to names.
Service Location (SRV)	A Windows 2000/Server 2003 record used to locate Active Directory infrastructure services.

To add DNS records to your database manually:

1. Click **Start | Administrative Tools | DNS** to open your DNS console.

2. Expand your **Forward Lookup Zones** folder and highlight the *DNS zone name* to which you want to add records.

3. Right-click your *DNS zone name* and select the record type you want to add as shown in Figure 6.22; for example **New Host (A)**.

4. In the **New Host** dialog window, type the name of your new host in the **Name (uses parent domain if blank)** field, and the hosts IP address in the **IP Address** field as shown in Figure 6.23.

5. Click **Add Host**, also shown in Figure 6.23.

NOTE

To add other types of DNS resource records manually, right-click on your **DNS zones name** and select **Other New Records**. A **Resource Record Type** dialog window will appear, giving you the ability to choose the type of resource record you want to enter. The most common are **A, CNAME (alias)**, and **MX** records, which is why they have a direct option to create them on the context drop-down menu.

Figure 6.22 Manually Adding DNS Records

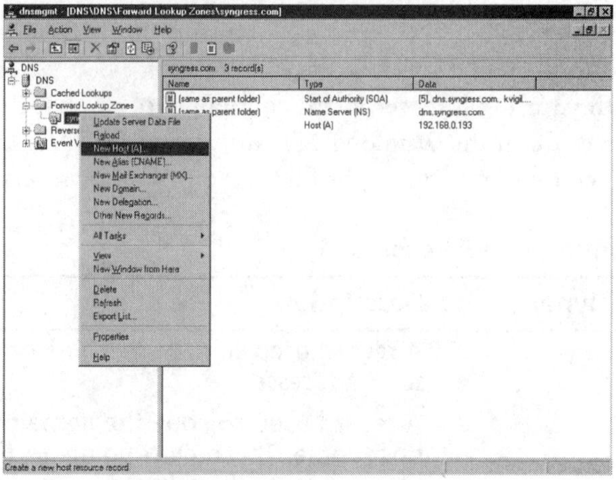

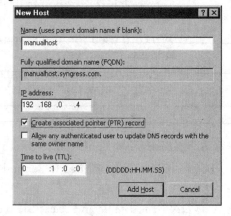

Figure 6.23 Adding a New Host (A) Record

You also have the option to create a Pointer (PTR) record if a reverse lookup zone for that network address space already exists. This record is used for queries looking to resolve an IP address to your host name. If you have already created a reverse lookup zone as discussed earlier in this section, click the option check box **Create associated pointer (PTR) record**.

In Exercise 6.02, we showed you how to configure a domain zone file for a Windows Server 2003 member server. If you were to create the same DNS zone for a Windows Server 2003 Active Directory, your zone database would look slightly different because it is used to house all of the domain controller's service, domain, and site locator records. For a look at the difference in appearance, refer to Figure 6.24 and compare the folder containers to that of Figure 6.21. For more of the different zone types and zones in general, refer to Chapter 5.

Figure 6.24 Viewing an Active Directory DNS Zone and Its Containers

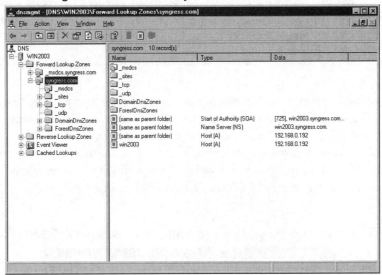

You can create two other types of forward lookup zones—*secondary* zones and *stub* zones. These zones were discussed in Chapter 5, but for a quick refresher, they are defined here:

- **Secondary zone** A secondary zone is a read-only copy of another delegated zone file. It continually updates its records from what is called a *master* server on a configured interval. It can be used as a client's primary DNS server because it maintains an exact copy of the original authoritative zone database. A secondary zone helps balance the load of primary DNS servers and can be used for fault tolerance

- **Stub zone** A stub zone is also a partial read-only copy of another zone file. It contains the start of authority (SOA) resource record, name server (NS) resource records, and the glue A resource records for the delegated subdomains. A glue record references a server that is authoritative for a subdomain. Glue records are used to enable DNS servers to send referrals directly to the DNS server authoritative for the child domain without having to forward the request up and down the DNS hierarchy. Stub zones are not authoritative for the zones they copy.

TEST DAY TIP

A secondary zone can be secondary to a primary zone or to another secondary zone. As long as the server to which it wants to transfer a file has given it the correct authority to do so, a secondary zone can transfer zone files.

TEST DAY TIP

Secondary and stub zone databases are read-only and cannot be edited. To create a record in a secondary zone file, it must be transferred from another zone in which the edit was made.

Creating secondary or stub zones is very similar to creating a primary zone as you did in Exercise 6.02. The only difference is you have to tell the secondary or stub zone which server to pull zone transfer data from. This is called the zone's *master* server. A master server is simply a server that allows zone data to be transferred from itself to another secondary server. When configuring a secondary or stub zone, you will be presented with another wizard prompting you to enter in the master server's IP address. This is displayed in Figure 6.25.

Figure 6.25 Configuring Secondary and Stub Zone Master DNS Servers

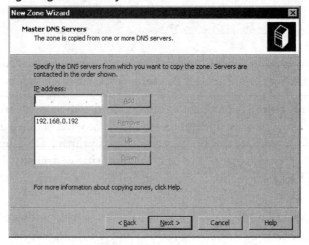

Configuring Reverse Lookup Zones

A second type of zone you can create on your DNS server is called a *reverse lookup* zone. A reverse lookup zone works in the exact opposite fashion from the forward lookup zone—its purpose is to resolve IP addresses to names. Reverse lookup zones are sometimes necessary for more secure applications to function properly. Reverse lookup zones are used to verify that the IP address the source host is using is actually coming from the location where that IP address name is authoritative. To create a reverse lookup zone, follow these steps:

1. Click **Start | Administrative Tools | DNS**.

2. Highlight your **DNS** *server name*, right-click and select **New Zone**.

3. Click **Next** on the **Welcome to the New Zone Wizard** dialog window.

4. Select **Primary zone** for the configured zone type and click **Next**.

5. Select **Reverse lookup zone** and click **Next**.

6. Type your *IP network* for the domain name for which you are creating this reverse lookup zone, in the **Network ID** field as shown in Figure 6.26. Click **Next**.

7. Click **Next** to accept the default zone filename.

8. Select **Allow both nonsecure and secure dynamic updates** and click **Next**.

9. Click **Finish** to create your new reverse lookup zone.

Figure 6.26 Creating a Reverse Lookup Zone Based on Your Network ID Number

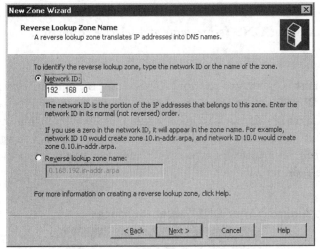

TEST DAY TIP

By default, there are three reverse lookup zones already created with each DNS server installation. These are necessary for DNS to function properly. They include:

- **0.in-addr.arpa** This represents a nonexistent network 0.0.0.0.
- **127.in-addr.arpa** This represents the local loopback network of the server on which DNS is installed.
- **255.in-addr.arpa** This represents the local broadcast network.

These are not visible by default. To see these zones, you must enable the Advanced view by clicking **View | Advanced** from the DNS console menu.

Configuring Your DNS Server

Configuring your DNS server consists of two separate configurable options:

- **DNS Server configuration settings** Affects all zones hosted on that DNS server.

- **DNS Zone configuration options** Affects only the zone for which you are configuring.

We will discuss each of these ways to configure your DNS server and its zones by going over each of the configurable dialog windows, accessible in the DNS Administrative console located in your Administrative Tools menu. Let's start with DNS server-specific options.

1. Click on **Start | Administrative Tools | DNS**.
2. Right-click your **DNS** *server name* and select **Properties**.

Interfaces

The first tab, **Interfaces**, is used to tell your DNS server on which Network Interface Cards (NIC), and IP addresses attached those cards, it will listen for DNS queries. The default is to pick up all IP addresses assigned to the DNS server during installation as shown in Figure 6.27. To limit the IP addresses on which your DNS server will listen, click **Only the following IP addresses**, type the IP addresses you want in the **IP Address** field, and click the **Add** button.

Figure 6.27 Configuring Your DNS Server Interfaces

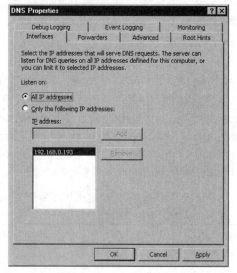

Forwarders

The second tab, **Forwarders**, is used to tell your DNS server to which DNS servers to forward requests when it is queried by a client for a name for which it is not authoritative. You can configure multiple DNS forwarders that will be queried from top to bottom in a recursive fashion. You can configure a time-out interval to tell your DNS server how long to wait between forwarders in the list before jumping to the next one. Use the **Number of seconds before forward queries time out** shown in Figure 6.28. The default is five seconds. If you select to check the **Do not use recursion for this domain** option check box, you are telling the server to not try any other means of name resolution if it cannot resolve a query using its list of forwarders. By default a DNS server will return to its root hints file if all the forwarders fail. For a graphical illustration of DNS forwarding, look at Figure 6.29.

Figure 6.28 Configuring Your DNS Forwarders

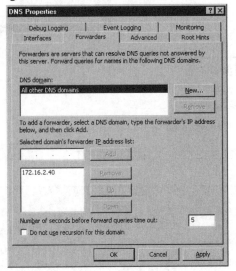

EXAM WARNING

Use the **Do not use recursion for this domain** option check box when you are sure that the forwarder to which you are pointing the domain for resolution requests will be able to resolve queries for that domain. Otherwise, you will be faced with a lot of failed queries because no other resolution methods will be attempted.

Figure 6.29 Using DNS Forwarding

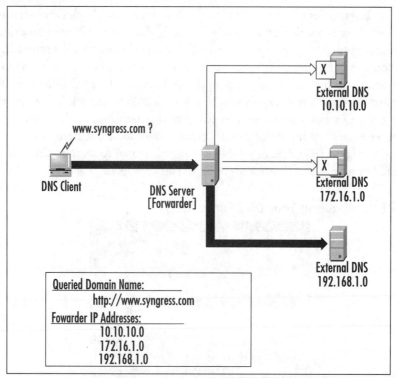

Designate Forwarders on a Per Domain Basis

With the introduction of Windows Server 2003, you are now able to selectively set up different forwarders for different domain names queried, sometimes referred to as *conditional forwarding*. At the same time, you are able to enable or disable recursion for each of those domains separately. Refer to Figure 6.28 and you will see that you can click the **New** button beside the **DNS domain** window to add different domain names to the window. In Figure 6.30 you can enter a domain name that you wish to use as a different forwarder than your default **All other DNS domains** forwarder. Click **OK** and notice that the settings for the default **All other DNS domains** are gone. You can type new DNS forwarders for each of your different domains. Check the **Do not use recursion for this domain** check box and you will effectively disable recursion for just that one domain. See Figure 6.31 for an illustration of conditional forwarding.

New & Noteworthy...

Figure 6.30 Forwarding Queries for a Domain to a Different Server

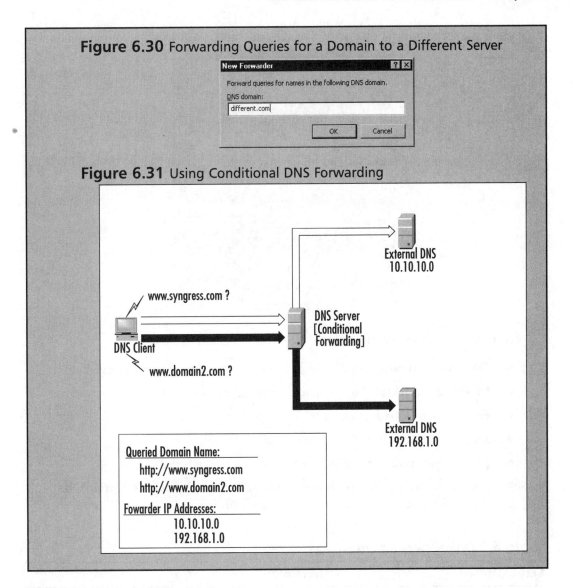

Figure 6.31 Using Conditional DNS Forwarding

Advanced

The third tab, **Advanced,** shown in Figure 6.32, is used to configure a variety of options on your DNS server. First, you will see the **Server version number**. This is a read-only display of your DNS server's software version number and can be used when diagnosing problems with service packs and hot fixes.

Figure 6.32 Configuring Your DNS Servers Advanced Features

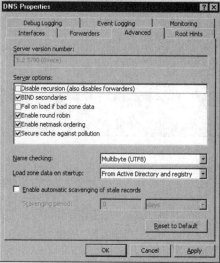

Next, you see **Server Options**, listed here and described in Table 6.2.

- **Disable recursion** (also disables forwarders) This option is *off* by default.

- **BIND secondaries** This option is *on* by default.

- **Fail to load if bad zone data** This option is *off* by default.

- **Enable round robin** This option is *on* by default.

- **Enable netmask ordering** This option is *on* by default.

- **Secure cache against pollution** This option is *on* by default (this was the default for Windows 2000 post Service Pack 3).

Table 6.2 DNS Server Options

Server Option	Description
Disable recursion (also disables forwarders)	Checking this option disables the use of recursive lookups on the entire server regardless of conditional settings on the **Forwarders** tab. It disables the use of forwarders.
BIND secondaries	This option is used to enable DNS to transfer a zone using the slower uncompressed transfer format. This enables successful zone transfers to be made with DNS servers that do not support the faster transfer method, such as BIND servers prior to version 4.9.4.

Continued

Table 6.2 DNS Server Options

Server Option	Description
Fail to load if bad zone data	By default, Windows Server 2003 DNS servers load their zones regardless of any errors in zone files. This option can be used to alter that behavior so that the DNS server service logs errors, but fails to load a zone file containing records data that is determined to have errors.
Enable round robin	Round robining enables DNS entries that have multiple IP addresses sharing the same host name to be alternately sequenced through when clients query that host name for name resolution. This means that clients querying the same host name will be directed to different IP addresses in a load balancing fashion.
Enable netmask ordering	Determines whether the DNS server reorders a list of multiple A resource records based on local subnet priority if the queried host name is for a multihomed computer.
Secure cache against pollution	This option disables the ability to spoof DNS queries and pollute DNS cache with wrong information. Spoofing describes the sending of nonsecure data in response to a DNS query and can be used to redirect queries to a rogue DNS server and can be malicious in nature.

 EXAM WARNING

DNS Round robining is enabled by default when you install Windows Server 2003 DNS. Though it is used for load balancing purposes, for example to balance the load on a Web server farm, note that it is not a fault tolerant solution. If one IP address in the pool of sequenced round robin IPs becomes unavailable, DNS will not know any better and will continue to hand it out as a successful name resolution. This causes clients to fail in their attempt to access the Web server. Failed IP addresses must be removed from the DNS round robining pool to continue to use round robining successfully.

Name checking is used by your DNS server service to find a compatible means to check names it receives and processes during normal operations. See Table 6.3 for the different name checking formats you can select from the drop-down box. Multibyte (UTF8) is the default and Microsoft recommends that it not be changed.

Table 6.3 Name Checking Format

Name Checking Format	Description
Strict RFC (ANSI)	This method strictly enforces RFC-compliant naming rules for all DNS names that the server processes. Names that are not RFC-compliant are treated as erred data by the server.
Non RFC (ANSI)	This method allows names that are not RFC-compliant to be used with the DNS server, such as names that use ASCII characters but are not compliant with RFC host naming requirements.
Multibyte (UTF8)	This method allows names that use the Unicode 8-bit translation encoding scheme, which is a proposed RFC draft, to be used with the DNS server. This is the default name checking method.
All names	Allows non-RFC (ANSI), strict RFC (ANSI), and multibyte (UTF8) naming conventions.

Load zone data on startup is an option that tells your DNS server service from where its zone data is to be physically loaded. Your three options are:

- **From Active Directory and registry (default setting)** Loads zone data from Active Directory if loaded on a domain controller and the Windows registry.
- **From registry** Loads data from the registry only.
- **From File** Loads data from a flat file.

Enable automatic scavenging of stale records is disabled by default. Enabling this option tells the DNS server to automatically purge stale record data from its database after a configurable time period set under the **Scavenging period** previously shown in Figure 6.32. By default, when you enable this option, stale records are purged from the database every seven days. You can configure this interval in either days or hours. You can also manually initiate the scavenging of stale resource records by right-clicking your **DNS** *server name* and selecting **Scavenge Stale Resource Records** as shown in Figure 6.33.

EXAM WARNING

Setting the **Enable scavenging of stale records** option affects both automatic and manual scavenging. Without enabling this check box option, you will not be able to manually initiate scavenging, although it appears as if you are able to in Figure 6.33. Although it appears available to run, and is not grayed out, the **Enable scavenging of stale records** check box needs to be selected for the **Scavenge Stale Resource Records** manual scavenging option to succeed.

Figure 6.33 Selecting to Manually Initiate Scavenging

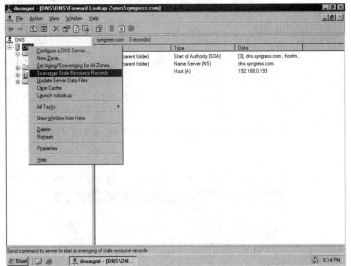

Stale records are determined by their individual **Record Time Stamp** as shown in Figure 6.34. Resource records that are dynamically registered with your DNS servers will receive a record time stamp and thus are subject to resource record *aging*. Aging is the process by which your DNS server decides that a resource record is available to be purged during the next scavenging interval.

Figure 6.34 Reviewing the Record Time Stamp of Your Resource Records

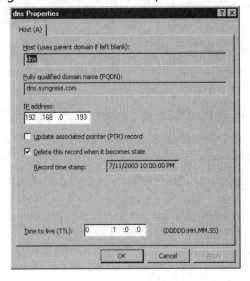

Clients will continually refresh their resource records with your DNS server to update their time stamps and not be subject to the aging process. Both DHCP and statically configured TCP/IP clients that have the ability to register themselves with DNS, or those downlevel clients that use the services of DHCP to register with DNS, (discussed in greater detail in Chapter 3 as well as in the section "Integrating the Windows Server 2003 DNS server with DHCP" later in this chapter), will try and refresh their time stamps every 24 hours by default. To globally set all of your DNS zone's aging and scavenging intervals at once, right-click your **DNS** *server name* and select **Set Aging/Scavenging for All Zones**, and you will see the **Server Aging/Scavenging Properties** dialog window as shown in Figure 6.35.

Figure 6.35 Globally Setting the Aging/Scavenging Settings for Your Zones

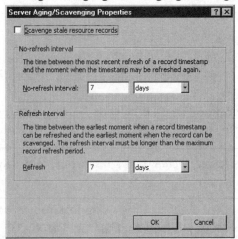

To enable your DNS server to age resource records, you must configure the no-refresh and refresh intervals shown in Figure 6.35. Both of these intervals can be configured in days or hours and are discussed in greater detail here:

- **No-refresh interval** An interval of time bounded by the following two events:

  1. The date and time when a resource record was last refreshed and its time stamp initially set.

  2. The date and time when a resource record next becomes eligible to be refreshed and have its time stamp updated.

     This value is needed to help decrease the number of write operations to the DNS database. This interval is set to 7 days by default. It should not be increased to an unreasonably high number, or stale record data may remain in the DNS database for longer periods of time, reducing the benefits of the aging and scavenging feature. *Unreasonably high* can be defined as not longer than a week between how often your resource records may change.

- **Refresh interval** An interval of time bounded by the following two distinct events:

    1. The earliest date and time when the record becomes eligible to be refreshed and have its time stamp updated.

    2. The earliest date and time when the record becomes eligible to be scavenged and purged from the zone database.
    This value should be large enough to allow all clients to refresh their records. This interval is set to seven days by default. This interval should not be smaller than the maximum refresh for any of your resource records that are typically based on DHCP lease intervals. The default DHCP lease interval is eight days and clients are set to renew their leases at 50 percent of the lease duration, causing the refresh to happen at four days.

Exam Warning

Be careful when enabling DNS scavenging and understand that it is disabled by default for a reason. You should not enable this feature until you fully understand each and every parameter and all possible outcomes of each setting. If it is set up incorrectly, vital DNS resource records could be deleted accidentally, causing more headaches than an abundance of stale records.

Note

Only dynamically registered records are considered available for scavenging and thus adhere to the rules of aging. Statically entered resource records are not subject to aging by default and thus are not purged via the scavenging interval. You can, however, edit a static record and manually set an expiration TTL on it, so that it follows the same rule of thumb as its dynamic partners. You can do this by checking the **Delete this record when it becomes stale** option box and manually entering a TTL value on the **Properties** window of any static resource record.

Root Hints

The forth tab, **Root Hints**, shown in Figure 6.36, is used by your DNS server to locate other DNS name servers on the network. By default, the Root Hints tab contains a listing of all the root or top level DNS servers that comprise the top level domains of the Internet namespace. It is typically not necessary to edit or add to these, but the option is available if you want to create your own custom root hints.

Figure 6.36 Configuring Your DNS Server Root Hints

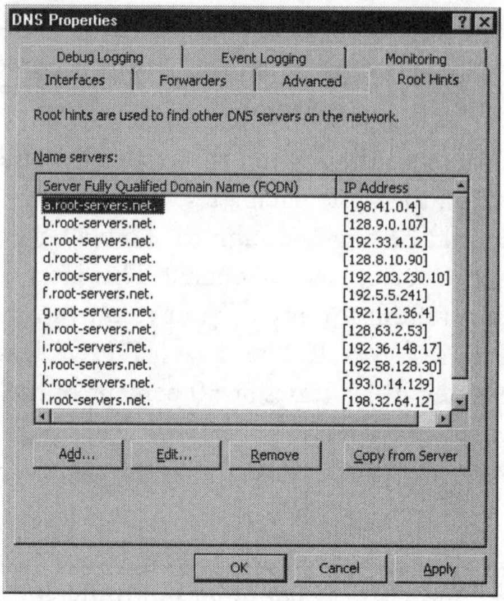

The last three DNS server property tabs, **Debug Logging**, **Event Logging**, and **Monitoring** all deal with monitoring and troubleshooting your DNS server and will be discussed later in this chapter.

EXAM 70-291

OBJECTIVE 2.1.2

Configuring Your DNS Zones

We finished discussing general server-specific configuration options that apply themselves globally to your server and all of its DNS zones. Now we'll discuss zone-specific configuration options, which apply only to the zone that you are configuring. You can access zone-specific properties by right-clicking on the *zone name* you want to administer and selecting **Properties** from the menu tab.

General

A zone's **General** tab gives you the ability to see the status of your DNS server service and pause it temporarily if you want, by clicking the **Pause** button shown in Figure 6.37. You might want to pause your primary DNS server to test and see if your secondary DNS server starts servicing client requests. After you click **Pause**, your DNS server will stop responding to requests and the status will display as paused. To start it up again, simply click the same button that now shows as **Start**. You can also change the type of DNS zone you have configured, whether you want to change it from Primary to Active-Directory integrated (only if installed on a domain controller), or if you want to change it from secondary to primary. Use the **Change** button to do so; you will see the options in Figure 6.38.

Figure 6.37 Configuring General Zone-Specific Options

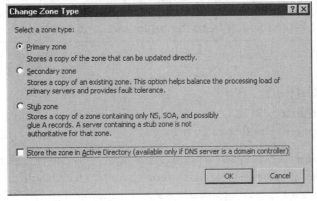

Figure 6.38 Changing the DNS Zone Type

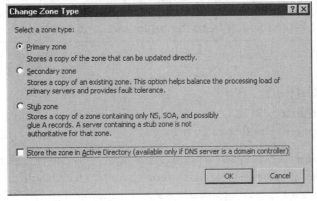

NOTE

The **Store the zone in Active Directory** option (available only if the DNS server is a domain controller) is grayed out if you are viewing this tab on a non-domain controller.

The **Zone file name** field displays the physical file name of your DNS zone, located under %systemroot%\system32\dns. Allowing the ability for clients to update their own records in DNS is referred to as *dynamic updates*. There are three configurable options for dynamic updates if you are viewing them from a domain controller; otherwise, only two exist. All three are outlined in Table 6.4.

Table 6.4 Dynamic Update Configuration Type

Dynamic Update Configuration	Description
None	Do not allow dynamic updates to take place on this zone.
Nonsecure and secure	Allow secure or nonsecure dynamic updates to take place.
Secure only (only on domain controllers)	Allow only secure dynamic updates to take place.

Discussed earlier in the section, "DNS Server Options," was the ability to set aging and scavenging properties on a global level, affecting all DNS zones on that server. The **General** tab of a zone's properties is where you enable zone-specific aging and scavenging properties. The settings are the same as if configured at the server level, and are set by clicking the **Aging** tab.

Exam Warning

When trying to enable resource record aging and the scavenging of those aged or stale records, either manually or at an automatic interval, remember that scavenging must be enabled at both the server level and the zone level.

Start of Authority (SOA)

The **Start of Authority (SOA)** tab, as shown in Figure 6.39, is used to configure and define a host of options. The first three fields are:

- **Serial number** Displays a number that is used to determine if a zone transfer is needed to update the zone. Each time a zone is changed, this number is incremented by a value of 1 to indicate a new zone version. This tells secondary zone transfer servers that a change has occurred and a zone transfer is needed.

- **Primary server** Defines the Fully Qualified Domain Name (FQDN) of the server that is designated as the primary master for that zone.

- **Responsible person** Lists the mail address of the person who is responsible for maintaining this domain zone. This name can be seen when using the popular Internet *whois* command to locate information about a domain name.

EXAM WARNING

The responsible person's mail address must be typed in FQDN format or it will not be accepted. Windows will ask if you want it to change it for you if you accidentally use an '@' symbol instead of the "." format between the user's name and the domain name. Example: joejones.syngress.com.

Figure 6.39 Configuring the DNS Zone Transfer Intervals

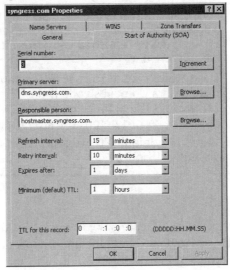

TEST DAY TIP

You can manually initiate a zone transfer by incrementing the **Serial number** field, which is done by clicking the **Increment** button to the right of its field.

EXAM WARNING

The **Start of Authority (SOA)** tab is configurable only on Primary and Active Directory Integrated zones because other zone types are read-only by default.

DNS zone data is kept up-to-date during zone transfers by using a number of configurable time intervals. These intervals are described in detail in Table 6.5.

Table 6.5 Zone Data Configuration Intervals

Interval Setting	Description
Refresh interval	This setting is used to determine how often the DNS server verifies the accuracy of the data in its secondary zone. The default is every 15 minutes.
Retry interval	This setting is used to determine how often a DNS server will attempt another zone transfer if the refresh interval time has expired without a successful transfer. The default is 10 minutes and is usually less than the refresh interval.
Expires after	This time interval is used to specify the amount of time before a secondary server discards a zone record if it has not received an updated or refreshed copy from its master server. The default is 1 day.
Minimum (default) TTL	This setting is used to specify a default TTL for all resource records in a domain's zone if the TTL is not already set. The TTL value is the amount of time a DNS server or resolver will cache the record before discarding it. The default is 1 hour.
TTL for this record	This is the default TTL value for the SOA record itself. The default is 1 hour.

Name Servers

The **Name Servers** tab, as shown in Figure 6.40, is used to list the all of the DNS servers that are authoritative for that zone. This should include any primary zones as well as any of its secondaries. By default, your DNS server will add itself to the list. If you want to add another server, acting as a secondary, click **Add**, enter the **IP address** of the DNS server, and click **OK**.

Figure 6.40 Configuring DNS Integration with WINS

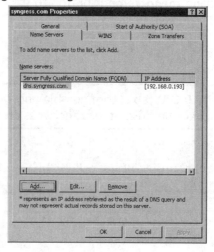

WINS

The **WINS** tab, as shown in Figure 6.41, is used to integrate the Windows Internet Naming service (WINS) into DNS. It is used to allow DNS-only clients the ability to query NetBIOS names registered to a WINS server. For more specific information about this integration, refer to Chapter 4.

Figure 6.41 Configuring DNS Integration with WINS

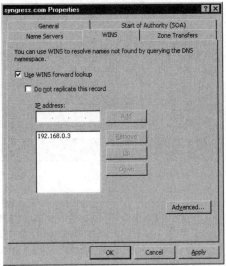

Zone Transfers

The **Zone Transfers** tab, as shown in Figure 6.42, is used to configure which DNS servers the master zone will allow to transfer its zone database. The default is to not allow zone transfers because the **Allow zone transfers** option checkbox is disabled. You have the ability to select one of three options:

- **To any server** This allows zone transfers to any server that points to it as its master.

- **Only to servers listed on the Name Servers tab** This allows zone transfers only to zones listed on the **Name Servers** tab on the zone's **Properties** page. This option tries to limit the number of servers that are authoritative for that zone by allowing zone transfers only to name servers your server has been configured to know about.

- **Only to the following servers** This allows you as an administrator to choose a specific number of DNS servers you wish to allow the transfer of zone data, using other DNS server's IP addresses.

Figure 6.42 Configuring Zone Transfer Security

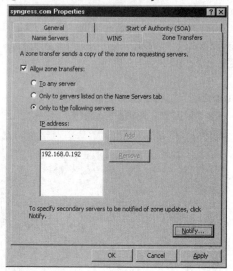

 EXAM WARNING

If using zone transfers in your environment, it is wise to limit the ability to transfer zone data and configure only those servers that you deem appropriate, because DNS zone data can be used by computer hackers as a means to attack your network both physically and socially. If at all possible, use Active Directory (AD) integrated zones and take advantage of the existing AD replication topology, avoiding zone transfers all together.

EXAM
70-291

OBJECTIVE

2.2

Configuring DNS Clients

In this section, we will discuss the different options that are available to configure your clients with the IP addresses of your DNS servers. You can choose to statically configure your DNS client as you do for all of your server DNS clients, or you can choose to assign DNS addresses via DHCP. Exercise 6.03 will walk you through the process of statically assigning DNS addresses to a DNS client, although this is uncommon for any but smaller environments.

EXERCISE 6.03

STATICALLY CONFIGURING YOUR DNS CLIENT

This exercise shows you how to statically set up your Windows Server 2003 server DNS client in a multidomain name environment.

1. Click **Start | Control Panel | Network Connections** and select **Local Area Connection**. Click the **Properties** button.

2. In the **Local Area Connections** dialog window, scroll down until you see **Internet Protocol (TCP/IP)** and highlight it. Click the **Properties** button.

3. In the **Internet Protocol (TCP/IP)** dialog window shown in Figure 6.43, click the **Use the following DNS server addresses** button and enter a **Preferred DNS server** IP address. Although not mandatory, you can also enter a backup DNS server by entering another IP address in the **Alternate DNS server** field.

Figure 6.43 Configuring Your DNS Client with DNS Server IP Addresses

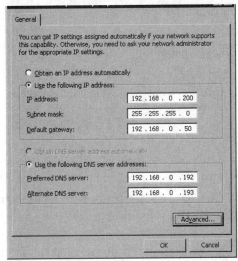

4. Click the **Advanced** button. In the **Advanced TCP/IP Settings** dialog window, click the **DNS** tab as shown in Figure 6.44.

5. If by chance you have a third DNS server you want to configure, sometimes called a *tertiary server*, you can click the **Add** button under the **DNS server addresses, in order of use** and type the IP address of the DNS server. Click **Add**.

6. If your DNS clients need to resolve hosts from multiple domains hosted on your DNS server, you will need to click **Append these DNS suffixes (in order)**. Click **Add** under this window and type the first domain name you wish to append to client queries as shown in Figure 6.45. Click **Add**. Repeat this step for each domain name you want to add.

7. In the **DNS suffix for this connection field**, type your primary **domain name** as shown in Figure 6.44.

Figure 6.44 Configuring Your DNS Client with DNS Server IP Addresses

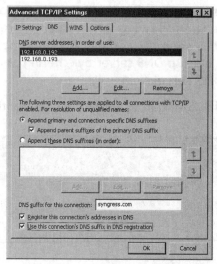

8. Leave the default option **Register this connection's addresses in DNS** enabled.

9. Check the option **Use this connection's DNS suffix in DNS registration** and click **OK**.

Figure 6.45 Entering Alternate DNS Suffix Domain Names

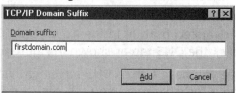

Using DHCP to Configure DNS Clients

DHCP is a powerful way to configure client side IP addresses and other options such as DNS server IP addresses. If you have configured your clients to use DHCP, you must make sure that you issue the DNS servers IP addresses to each of your DHCP server scopes. To do this, follow these steps:

1. Click on **Start | Program | Administrative Tools | DHCP**.

2. Click on the **+** button next to your **DHCP** *server name* and then again next to your **DHCP** *scope name*.

3. Highlight the **Scope Options** folder. Right-click and select **Configure Options**.

4. On the **General** tab of the **Scope Options** dialog window, scroll down until you see option **006 DNS Servers** as shown in Figure 6.46. Check this option, and enter each *DNS server IP address* in your environment into the **IP address** field and click **Add**.

5. Scroll down a bit further until you see option **015 DNS Domain Name**. Select it and enter your primary *DNS domain name suffix* in the **String Value** field for the data entry window as shown in Figure 6.47.

Figure 6.46 Configuring DNS as a DHCP Option

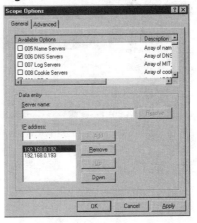

Figure 6.47 Configuring the DNS Domain Name as a DHCP Option

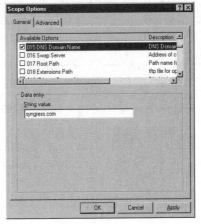

Configuring DNS Settings Using Group Policy

More and more client configuration options are being made available in the Group Policy console, and DNS client side settings is one of them. In Windows Server 2003, you can now configure almost all of your DNS client side settings via a Group Policy Object (GPO). One of these is the **DNS Suffix Search List** shown in Figure 6.48. Prior to Windows Server 2003, you had to configure this option manually on all your clients, or write some sort of startup or logon script to edit the clients' registries. It appears that many clients in today's heavily merging company marketplace have to use multiple domain name suffixes for proper name resolution. Now with Windows Server 2003 it is as simple as creating a Group Policy.

Figure 6.48 Configuring DNS Settings via Group Policy

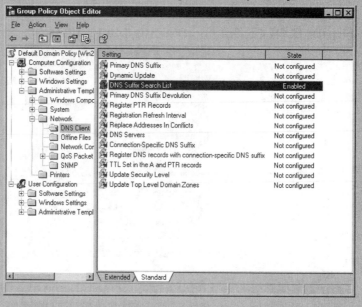

EXAM WARNING

By statically assigning DNS-specific information on the client, you override any setting that was delivered via a DHCP server option.

Configuring your clients for DNS is essential in a Windows 2000/2003 Active Directory environment. DNS is used as the resolution backbone for all host names and service locator records. After you have configured your DNS client, it will be ready to resolve host names to IP addresses and locate needed infrastructure services. Windows Server 2003 clients, sometimes called resolvers, try and resolve host names in a particular order, as shown here:

- DNS resolver cache

- HOSTS file

- DNS server (Preferred)

    1. Secondary DNS server

    2. Tertiary DNS server

- Cache (NetBIOS)

- WINS server

- Broadcast (NetBIOS)

- LMHOSTS file

TEST DAY TIP

To try and remember the DNS query order, remember this phase, and use the first letter of each word to identify the order: *Cindy Harris didn't cram well before leaving*.

- **[C]**indy – DNS *resolver* [C]ache
- **[H]**arris – [H]osts file
- **[D]**idn't – [D]NS
- **[C]**ram – NetBIOS [C]ache
- **[W]**ell – [W]INS
- **[B]**efore – NetBIOS [B]roadcast
- **[L]**eaving – [L]MHOSTS file

A client side DNS query is generated when a client tries to connect to a resource by way of using a friendly host name that is easy to remember. That name must then be turned into an IP address and ultimately translated into the Media Access Control (MAC) number of the Network Interface Card (NIC) residing on the destination host. Depending on the format of the host name entered at the client, DNS name resolution happens a bit differently. There are three separate name formats that can be submitted by a client as shown :

- **Fully Qualified Domain Name (FQDN)** Example: *host.domain.com.* (notice the trailing period)

- **Single-label unqualified domain name** Example: *host*

- **Multiple-label unqualified domain name** Example: *host.domain*

NOTE

DNS host names entered as host.domain.com may look like FQDN format, but without the trailing period, they are considered to be multiple-label unqualified domain names. Windows DNS clients will append a trailing period to qualify them correctly.

When a client enters a FQDN, that client immediately is sent to its configured DNS server for query resolution. Similarly, when a client enters what appears to be a FQDN, but without the trailing period ("."), the Windows DNS client will append the period and send the request to the configured DNS server. The differences in query resolution occur when clients enter incomplete names, defined as *single* or *multilabel unqualified* domain names. In these scenarios, any configured DNS suffixes in the search order list are then appended to the name submitted, along with a trailing period, and resent to the DNS server for resolution. As shown in Figure 6.49, resolution occurs in the following order for the query of the host name **computer**:

1. *computer.attempt1.com.*

2. *computer.attempt2.com.*

3. *computer.attempt3.com.*

4. *computer.attempt4.com.*

Figure 6.49 Querying DNS Using DNS Suffix Search Order List

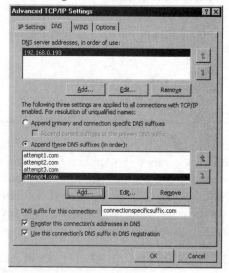

EXAM WARNING

If you choose **Append the DNS suffixes** (in order), only domain names listed in that window will be tried for resolution purposes. Both the connection-specific and primary DNS suffix are ignored.

If clients are not configured with multiple DNS suffixes as in Figure 6.50, their **Primary DNS suffix** is appended to the name and resent to DNS. The **Primary DNS suffix** can be found by going to **Start | Control Panel | System | Computer Name | Change | More** as shown in Figure 6.51. If resolution is still unsuccessful, each connection-specific DNS suffix is then tried and resubmitted to DNS. If resolution is again not successful, the client will attempt to append the parent suffix of the primary DNS name, the parent of its suffix, and so on until only two labels are left. This is the default and can be changed by clearing the option check box named **Append parent suffixes of the primary DNS suffix** shown in Figure 6.50.

Figure 6.50 Querying DNS Using Primary and Connection-Specific DNS Suffixes

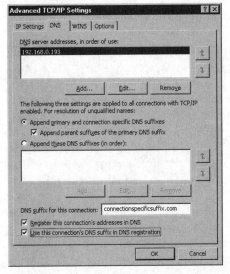

Figure 6.51 Accessing the Primary DNS Suffix of Your Computer

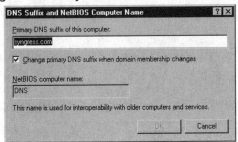

When a client's DNS query is resolved, it stores the results in its DNS cache to speed up future DNS queries to the same host. By default, Windows Server 2003 and XP clients store successful DNS resolution results for 24 hours, and they store negative DNS requests for 15 minutes. These values are referred to as Time to Live (TTL) intervals. If for some reason this cache gets stale before the TTL values expire, you can clear it manually using the ipconfig utility and typing **ipconfig /flushdns** as shown in Figure 6.52. To view what is present in your current DNS cache, type **ipconfig /displaydns**.

Figure 6.52 Entering Alternate DNS Suffix Domain Names

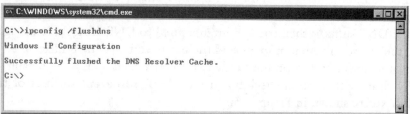

Disabling Client Side DNS Caching

Windows clients prior to Windows 2000 did not cache DNS queries locally and thus were able to test certain DNS server side features such as Round robining in real time. Windows 2000/XP and Windows Server 2003 clients do contain a client side cache and can give a user a false impression that DNS round robining is not working. This is because the first successful resolution was cached and all subsequent resolution queries use that cache and do not reference the DNS server again, although the round robining would actually occur. If you need to be able to resolve real time queries every time you query a new host, for load balancing purposes or for testing query resolution time, you might want to disable the ability to cache DNS host names. Alternatively, you might want to edit the TTL variables that are set when caching of DNS host names is enabled. To temporarily disable DNS caching on Windows Server 2003 and XP client machines, open a command prompt window by typing **Start | Run | cmd** and use either of the following two commands, depending on whether you are trying to disable your local machines DNS cache or a remote machines DNS cache:

1. **net stop dnscache** (local only)
2. **sc servername stop dnscache** (local or remote)

To permanently disable DNS client caching, set the DNS cache service to disabled by clicking **Start | Administrative Tools | Services**. Double-click on the **DNS Client** service, drop down the **Startup type** window, and select **Disabled**. Now when you reboot, that service will no longer start up. You can then click the **Stop** button and click **OK**.

Continued

To manually change the default TTL values for positive and negative DNS cached queries, open the registry editor by typing Start | Run | regedit.exe.

Traverse the registry to the following key: HKEY_LOCAL_MACHINE\SYSTEM\CurrentControlSet\Services\DNSCache\Parameters

The default TTL for positive responses is 86,400 seconds (1 day). To change this value, go to the **Edit** menu, point to **New**, click **DWORD Value**, and type **MaxCacheTtl** as the **Value Name**.

Double-click **MaxCacheTtl** and enter a number in the **Value Data** field, representing the number of seconds you want to cache positive DNS host name responses. If you lower the Maximum TTL value in the client's DNS cache to one second, this gives the appearance that the client-side DNS cache has been disabled.

The default TTL for negative responses is 900 seconds (15 minutes). To change this value, go to the **Edit** menu, point to **New**, click **DWORD Value**, and type **MaxNegativeCacheTtl** as the **Value Name**.

Double-click **MaxNegativeCacheTtl** and enter a number in the **Value Data** field, representing the number of seconds you want to cache negative DNS host name responses. Set the value to **0** if you do not want negative responses to be cached.

Integrating the Windows Server 2003 DNS Server with DHCP

With the abundance of clients in today's business marketplace, the Dynamic Host Configuration Protocol (DHCP) has become commonplace, and it is almost essential that it be used to configure client specific IP information. With the introduction of Windows 2000 and Windows Server 2003, DHCP-enabled clients lend themselves to some additional functionality when they are integrated into a DNS centric Windows Server 2003 environment. Because Windows Server 2003 Active Directory relies on DNS as its backbone communication resolution engine, it is imperative that other server host names and services are updated correctly in the DNS database. This is accomplished using Windows Server 2003's ability to dynamically accept and refresh DNS client information in its DNS database. As more and more clients are configured to use only DNS as a means to resolve names to IP addresses, they need to have their host names updated in the DNS database.

Windows 2000 and Windows XP clients are able to dynamically update their own records in the Windows Server 2003 DNS database. However, downlevel Windows clients, such as Windows NT 4.0 and Windows 9*x* clients, do not have the functionality built in to dynamically update DNS. Fortunately, if they are set up as DHCP-enabled clients, they can use DHCP to register and unregister their DNS hosts names on behalf of them. Although Windows 2000, Windows Server 2003, and Windows XP clients can register themselves,

they also use DHCP when set up as DHCP-enabled clients. You can set up this functionality by choosing one or many options configured on the **DNS** tab of each of your **DHCP
scopes Properties** pages. Click **Start | Administrative Tools | DHCP** to open your
DHCP console. Expand your **DHCP *server name*** and highlight your **DHCP scope**. Right-
click your **DHCP scope** and click **Properties**. Click the **DNS** tab as shown in Figure 6.53.

Figure 6.53 Configuring DNS Integration with Your DHCP Scopes

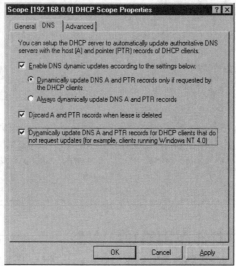

The configuration options displayed in Figure 6.53 are discussed in the next section, as
a recap of what was already outlined in Chapter 3.

DNS Updating Options

The DHCP updating DNS configuration options, shown in Figure 6.53, determine exactly
how various DHCP client leases are integrated into the DNS database. It is a huge benefit
to your network if you take advantage of these options for the most effective integration of
DNS and DHCP. Windows Server 2003 Active Directory is based on DNS, and Windows
2000, Windows Server 2003, and Windows XP clients use DNS first to try and resolve host
names to IP addresses. If you can maintain a list of your entire client and server base in your
DNS database, whether or not it consists of older downlevel clients, you can guarantee that
name resolution for Windows 2000, Windows Server 2003, and Windows XP machines will
be performed more quickly. This is because each name resolution request will not have to
be referred to a Windows Internet Naming Service (WINS) server to resolve names for
Windows NT 4.0 clients. In the following section, we will define each of the available
options in detail and discuss how they best can be used in your environment.

Enabling DNS Dynamic Updates

Checking this option turns **off** and **on** the function of allowing your DHCP server to dynamically update *any* of its clients. By default this option is turned **on**. This option has two additional settings:

- **Dynamically update DNS A and PTR records only if requested by DHCP clients** If this check box is selected, and the client is a Windows 2000, Windows XP, or Windows Server 2003 machine, the DHCP server updates only the PTR record. These clients will automatically update their own A records (if configured to do so on the client side). This option is turned on by default. However, if the clients are downlevel clients, the **Dynamically update DNS A and PTR records for DHCP clients that do not request updates** (for example, clients running Windows NT 4.0) check box must also be selected before DHCP will update the A and PTR records for these clients automatically. This check box is *not* checked by default.

- **Always dynamically update A and PTR records** If this check box is selected, and the client is a Windows 2000, Windows Server 2003, or Windows XP machine, the DHCP server will always update both the A and PTR records in DNS, regardless of what the client requests or how the client is configured. This option is turned off by default.

If the **Discard A and PTR records when lease is deleted** check box is selected, the server will automatically delete the A record associated with a client's PTR record when the client sends a *release message* to the DHCP server. By default, if the **Enable DNS Dynamic updates according to the settings below** check box also is enabled, the DHCP server automatically will delete the client's PTR record in DNS. This option allows the DHCP server to automatically delete the A record as well. This option is turned on by default.

When the **Dynamically update DNS A and PTR records for DHCP clients that do not request updates (for example clients running Windows NT 4.0)** check box is selected, it enables downlevel clients to participate in DHCP dynamic updates in a way that is similar to the behavior of Windows 2000, Windows XP, and Windows Server 2003 clients. One difference is that *all* DNS updates are funneled through the issuing DHCP server. We have included the illustrations shown in Figures 6.54 and 6.55 to illustrate the difference between dynamic DNS requests from downlevel Windows clients and clients post-Windows 2000.

TEST DAY TIP

The ability for Windows 2000, Windows Server 2003, and Windows XP clients to use dynamic updates relies on the addition of a new client side DHCP option (option 81). This option allows these types of clients to send their FQDNs to the DHCP server, along with informational data on how they should be updated in DNS. To emulate this ability for downlevel Windows clients, you must enable the **Dynamically update DNS A and PTR records for DHCP clients that do not request updates (for example clients running Windows NT 4.0)** option.

Figure 6.54 Displaying Dynamic DNS Requests for Windows 2000/XP/2003 Clients

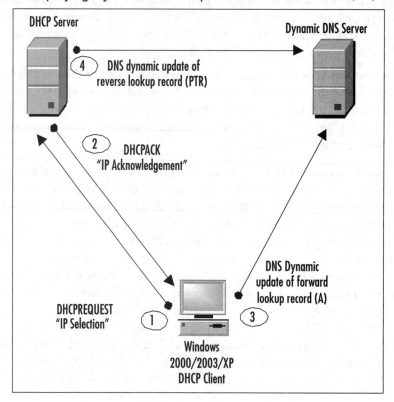

DNSUpdateProxy Group

Dynamic DNS provides a way to make sure all your clients, including downlevel clients, get updated in your DNS database. However, when your DHCP server updates its clients in DNS, the ownership of all the A and PTR records points directly back to the DHCP server itself (depending on the configuration discussed earlier in the section "DNS Updating Options"). This causes a problem when one of the following situations occurs:

Figure 6.55 Displaying Dynamic DNS Requests for Downlevel DHCP Clients

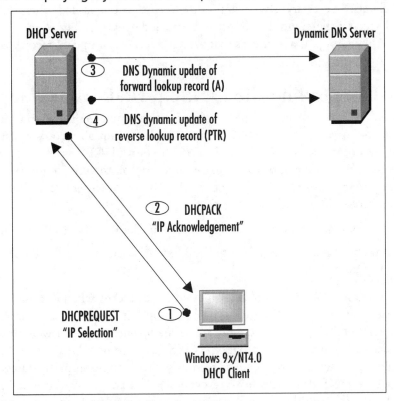

- You have to switch to using another DHCP Server.
- You change the configuration on your DHCP server to allow clients to update their own records.

If the original DHCP server that registered a client's record becomes unavailable and another DHCP server has to be brought online, the new DHCP server will not have any rights to update any of the older, already registered client records. Additionally, if you change the configuration on your DNS server from **Always dynamically update A and PTR records** to **Dynamically update DNA A and PTR records only if requested by DHCP clients** (or if you completely disable dynamic updating), clients will not have the rights to update their own records in DNS. Both of these situations arise because the registering DHCP server is the only one that has the proper security permissions to update these records. To prevent this from happening, Microsoft created the DNSUpdateProxy Active Directory Group.

The DNSUpdateProxy Group consists of computers that can update records on behalf of other DHCP clients. By putting all of your DHCP servers into this group, you can allow them to update records for your clients, but not take ownership of and stamp their own security credentials on these records. This means that the records can later be updated by the original clients if necessary. Ownership of the records is established when the first security principal accesses these entries. This does not include any member of the DNSUpdateProxy Group. It also means that DHCP servers can update records on behalf of other servers that fail.

Security Concerning the DNSUpdateProxy Group

There are some security concerns to be aware of when putting the DNSUpdateProxy Group into action. If you put your DHCP servers in this group, all records updated by those servers are not secure in your DNS database. If your DHCP server is a domain controller (as those in many branch office configurations are), all the service location (SRV) and forward lookup (A) records registered when starting the *Netlogon* service will not be secure. What can you do to address these concerns?

1. Do not put any of your domain controllers in the DNSUpdateProxy group.

2. If you choose to use the DNSUpdateProxy group, don't install DHCP on a domain controller.

Previous versions of Windows posed some serious concerns when dealing with DHCP's dynamic updating of DNS records. For example, if you were using an Active Directory integrated DNS zone configured for *secure updates only*, you were unable to use the DNSUpdateProxy group, because DHCP servers that are members of the DNSUpdateProxy group register all client records without ownership. To address some of these issues, a new **DNS dynamic update credentials** manager was created. Exercise 6.04 will walk you through the process of creating a separate Windows user account to register DNS records and retain ownership on behalf of clients, rather than letting the DHCP server retain ownership.

EXERCISE 6.04

USING DNS DYNAMIC UPDATE CREDENTIALS

This exercise will guide you through the process of creating a secure user account to be used by your DHCP server when registering host names on behalf of DNS-enabled clients.

You need to first create a dedicated user account in Active Directory whose credentials will be used by DHCP servers to perform dynamic updates. Next, configure each DHCP server to use that account by performing the following steps:

1. Click **Start | Administrative Tools | DHCP** to open your DHCP console.

2. Right-click your **DHCP server name** and select **Properties**.

3. Click the **Advanced** tab.

4. Under **DNS dynamic updates registration credentials,** click the **Credentials** button.

5. Enter the user name, domain, and password for the account you created for this purpose, and click **OK** as displayed in Figure 6.56.

Figure 6.56 Configuring Credentials for Use with Dynamic Updating

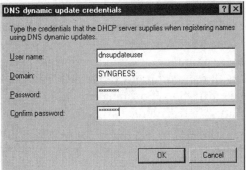

Follow Exercise 6.04 for all DHCP servers that will use these credentials. The credentials supplied in the **DNS dynamic update credentials** dialog box are used by DHCP servers that are members of the DNSUpdateProxy group to register client records in DNS. This prevents the registration of nonsecure records in DNS. The same account can be used on all your DHCP servers, thus eliminating one of the earlier issues described in the section, "Security Concerning the DNSUpdateProxy Group," in reference to switching to a new DHCP server after the original one has already registered client records under its ownership. By using the new credentials option, you create a configuration that allows the use of both the DNSUpdateProxy group and Active Directory integrated DNS with secure updates only.

To configure the dynamic DNS update credentials, you can use the graphical user interface (GUI) shown in Figure 6.56 or you can use the netsh command-line utility within the *servers context* using the *set dnscredentials* parameter.

NOTE

The user account whose credentials will be used by the DHCP servers for dynamic updates should be dedicated to this one task and should not be used for any other purpose.

Integrating the Windows Server 2003 DNS Server with WINS

WINS is used in the Windows NetBIOS world as DNS is used in the Windows host world. Whereas WINS resolves NetBIOS names to IP addresses, DNS resolves host names to IP addresses. Windows Server 2003 DNS allows the ability to integrate your existing WINS database into your DNS database to allow DNS-only clients name resolution of NetBIOS names. By default, downlevel Windows clients that do not use DNS for name resolution must rely on your WINS server. Thus your Windows 2000, Windows Server 2003, and Windows XP clients must use WINS to communicate with your downlevel clients due to their reliance on NetBIOS naming and its IP transport protocol. By default, DNS handles only host to IP name resolution and leaves NetBIOS to IP naming resolution to the WINS service. With Windows Server 2003's ability to integrate the two network services, you can effectively use only DNS for your higher level Windows clients. The majority of this section is a recap of what was covered earlier in Chapter 4, discussing WINS and Windows Server 2003.

WINS and DNS

Next we walk you through the process of integrating your WINS services into your Windows Server 2003 DNS backbone. To integrate your WINS installation with your Active Directory DNS zones, follow the steps outlined in Exercise 6.05.

EXERCISE 6.05

SETTING UP WINS TO INTEROPERATE WITH DNS

In this exercise, we will show you how you can set up your DNS zones to query your WINS database on behalf of your DNS clients for requests not found in DNS. This is useful if the majority of your server names are NetBIOS names stored in WINS, but you wish to use DNS to resolve these names.

1. Click **Start | Administrative Tools | DNS** to open your DNS console.
2. Expand your **Forward Lookup Zones** container.
3. **Highlight** the zone you want to configure, right-click it, and select **Properties**.
4. In your **DNS zone names Properties** dialog window, select the **WINS** tab as shown in Figure 6.57.
5. Click the option check box **Use WINS forward lookup**.
6. Type the **IP address** of your WINS server and click the **Add** button as displayed in Figure 6.57. Repeat this step for each server to which you want to forward lookups for name resolution.

Figure 6.57 Configuring WINS as a Forward Lookup for
Your DNS Zones

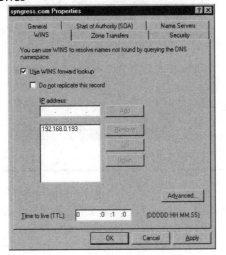

 NOTE

Check the option check box, **Do not replicate this record**, if you do not want
WINS-related entries replicated, or *transferred*, to your other DNS servers during
normal zone transfer operations. This option is useful when you want to avoid
zone update failures and loading errors in a mixed DNS environment consisting of
Microsoft and non-Microsoft DNS servers that might not understand your WINS
data records. By default this is not checked when enabling WINS lookup and thus
all WINS related records are slated to be replicated via zone transfers.

7. Click the **Advanced** button to configure both **Cache Time-outs** and
Lookup Time-outs as shown in Figure 6.58. The two advanced configuration options include the following:

- **Cache time-out** A time to live (TTL) value that determines how
long other DNS servers are allowed to cache WINS related entries
returned through the use of WINS lookup integration. The default
value is 15 minutes.

- **Lookup time-out** An interval that determines the amount of time
a DNS server will wait to get a successful response from its configured WINS forward lookup server before returning a *name not
found* error. The default value is 2 seconds.

Figure 6.58 Configuring Cache and Lookup Time-out Intervals

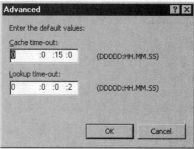

Configuring WINS forward lookup for your DNS implementation is *zone independent*. This means that if you have multiple zones, you will need to run through Exercise 6.05 for each zone you host. This is also true for any reverse lookups zones you host. However, reverse lookup zones ask you to specify a *domain name* that you want to append to the NetBIOS name record. Reverse WINS lookup also gives you the opportunity to return the DNS domain name as the *NetBIOS scope*. The latter should be used only if *NetBIOS scopes* are used in production already. Reverse WINS lookup is configured on the WINS-R tab of your zones properties. See Figure 6.59 for an illustration.

Figure 6.59 Configuring Reverse DNS to WINS Lookup

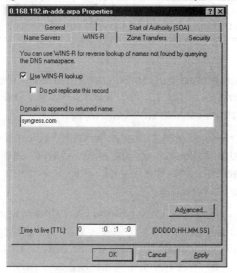

To better understand the way non–WINS, or DNS-only, clients use the WINS lookup feature of Windows Server 2003's DNS, take a look at the numbered steps while viewing the diagram depicted in Figure 6.60.

1. The DNS client queries its preferred DNS server.

2. The preferred DNS sever contacts the DNS server that is authoritative for that zone.

3. The authoritative server for that zone forwards that request to its configured WINS lookup server for resolution.

4. The WINS server resolves the name lookup and forwards the IP address back to the authoritative zone server.

5. The authoritative zone server returns the IP address back to the preferred DNS server.

6. The preferred DNS server returns the IP address back to the DNS client.

Figure 6.60 Tracing the Flow of the DNS to WINS Forward Lookup Process

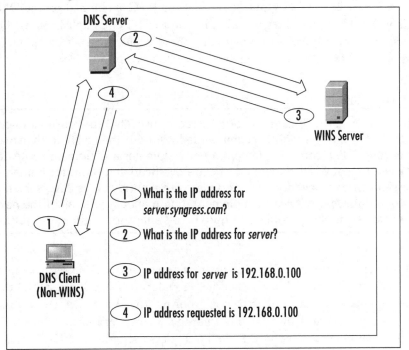

If you want your downlevel Windows clients to use DNS for name resolution, make sure they are set up as *Enhanced h-node* clients; if set up to use WINS, Windows 2000, Windows Server 2003, and Windows XP clients are enabled for *enhanced h-node* resolution by default. For more on this, refer to the *NetBIOS Node Types* section earlier in this chapter.

It depicts the different name resolution methods you can set up in order for DNS to be used as a means to resolving NetBIOS names.

Integrating the Windows Server 2003 DNS Server with BIND

Although Microsoft recommends using Windows Server 2003 DNS for your Active Directory implementations, they do not make it impossible to use other third-party versions of DNS. However, they do insist that you implement a DNS solution that adheres to two standard specifications that are crucial elements to successfully operating in a Windows Active Directory environment:

- Your DNS server must be able to support Service Locator (SRV) records.
- Your DNS server must be able to support Dynamic Updating or Dynamic DNS (DDNS).

Windows Server 2003 DNS supports most of the RFCs published on the DNS protocol and thus should support integration with a host of RFC-compliant non-Microsoft DNS servers. This section focuses on integrating the Berkeley Internet Name Domain or BIND version of DNS with your Windows Server 2003 version of DNS.

TEST DAY TIP

Support for Dynamic Updates is not required to use BIND for your main Active Directory DNS, but it is highly recommended. Without the ability to dynamically update your DNS records, implementing new domains and domain controllers into your environment will include a lot of extra overhead and room for human error. To successfully build a new domain controller with a nondynamic BIND server, you will have to update your BIND DNS implementation manually with all of the new DC's SRV records as displayed earlier in Figure 6.10's snapshot of the **netlogon.dns** file.

BIND is a very prominent DNS implementation and many DNS servers on the Internet, including many large Internet Service Providers (ISPs), still use BIND to service client name requests. In order to use BIND in your internal Active Directory domain environment, you must make sure that you are using the correct version to maintain Windows Server 2003 Active Directory support. Table 6.6 displays the different BIND versions and their support for the following items:

- Fast zone transfers
- SRV records
- Dynamic updating

Table 6.6 BIND Version Support

BIND Version	Supports Fast Zone Transfers	Supports SRV Records	Supports Dynamic Updating
4.9.3 and older			
4.9.4	X		
4.9.7	X	X	
8.1.2	X	X (used wrong format for Windows DNS)	X
8.1.3	X	X	X
8.2.2	X	X	X

NOTE

BIND version 8.2.2 requires patch 7 in order to properly function with Windows Server 2003 DNS. Microsoft highly recommends the use of BIND 8.2.2 over its 4.9.7 partner, which supports only SRV records.

TEST DAY TIP

Although BIND version 8.1.2 does not actually work with Windows Server 2003 SRV record support, it is what Microsoft expects you to know as the first version to support SRV records, for the exam.

NOTE

The following BIND DNS server versions were tested with Windows Server 2003 DNS Server and Client services by The Windows Server 2003 DNS development team:

- BIND 4.9.7
- BIND 8.1.2
- BIND 8.2
- BIND 9.1.0

Some versions of BIND that adhere to stricter RFC regulations might require that you change the name checking format of your Windows Server 2003 DNS server for zone transfer compatibility. Name checking is used by your DNS server service to find a compatible means to check names it receives and processes during normal operations. There might be a need to change the name checking format of your DNS server in order to be compatible with the version of BIND you implement in your environment. Some versions of BIND strictly adhere to RFC 1123, which supports only the standard DNS characters outlined in Table 6.7. See Table 6.8 for the different name checking formats available in Windows Server 2003. *Multibyte (UTF8)* is the default Windows Server 2003 name checking format, and Microsoft recommends that it not be changed. However, Exercise 6.06 will show you how to change this format on your Windows Server 2003 DNS server.

Table 6.7 Character Restrictions

Restrictions	Standard DNS	Windows Server 2003 DNS
Characters Supported	A-Z, a-z, 0-9, – (hyphen)	See Table 6.8.
FQDN Supported	63 bytes per label and 255 bytes per FQDN	63 bytes per label and 255 bytes per FQDN. DCs have a 155 byte limitation.

Table 6.8 Name Checking Format

Name Checking Format	Description
Strict RFC (ANSI)	This method strictly enforces RFC-compliant naming rules for all DNS names that the server processes. Names that are not RFC-compliant are treated as erred data by the server.
Non-RFC (ANSI)	This method allows names that are not RFC-compliant to be used with the DNS server, such as names that use ASCII characters but are not compliant with RFC host naming requirements.
Multibyte (UTF8)	This method allows names that use the Unicode 8-bit translation encoding scheme, which is a proposed RFC draft, to be used with the DNS server. This is the default name checking method.
All names	Allows Non-RFC (ANSI), Strict RFC (ANSI), and Multibyte (UTF8) naming conventions.

EXERCISE 6.06

CHANGING THE DNS NAME FORMAT

This exercise will this show you how to change the DNS naming format in order to co-exist with some other stricter versions of non-Microsoft DNS.

1. Click **Start | Administrative Tools | DNS** to open your DNS console.

2. Right-click your **DNS server name** and click **Properties**.

3. Click the **Advanced** tab as shown in Figure 6.61.

4. Click the drop-down box next to **Name checking** and select **Strict RFC (ANSI)**.

5. Click **OK**.

Figure 6.61 Configuring Strict RFC Name Checking Standards

If you are having problems with zone transfers and zones loading properly, check to see if you are replicating WINS records to your BIND DNS servers. Some versions of BIND might not support some of the Microsoft WINS record characters and this might be causing your failures. Integrating WINS into your DNS database could potentially cause problems when trying to replicate with other BIND-related versions of DNS. To disable WINS records form being included in DNS zone transfers, follow these steps:

1. Click **Start | Administrative Tools | DNS** to open your DNS console.

2. Expand your **Forward Lookup Zones** container.

3. **Highlight** the *DNS zone* you want to configure, then right-click and select **Properties**.

4. In your *zone names* **Properties** dialog window, select the **WINS** tab as shown in Figure 6.62.

Figure 6.62 Configuring WINS Records Not to Replicate During Zone Transfers

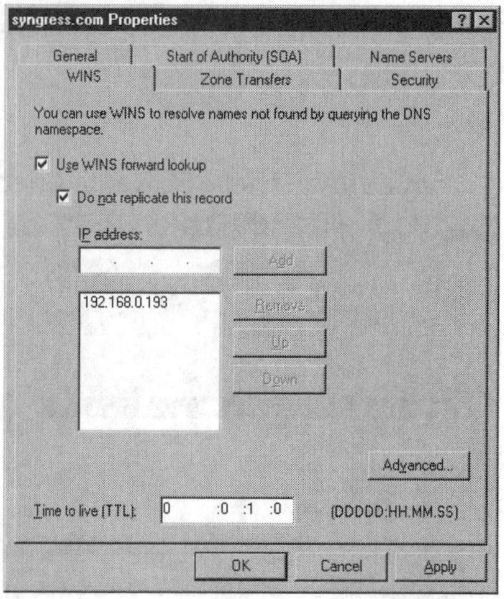

If you choose to use BIND DNS as a secondary DNS server, it is not as important to maintain the same version compatibility as needed with a primary DNS server. Secondary DNS zones maintain a read-only copy of the DNS database and thus are not subject to dynamic updates. For this reason, it is possible to use BIND versions such as 4.9.7, 8.1.2, and 8.1.3, which support only SRV records.

How to Maintain Older Versions of BIND and Windows Server 2003 DNS

Does your company want to take advantage of Windows Server 2003 Active Directory but thinks it is limited in this regard by your version of BIND? If you work in an environment that is currently using a BIND implementation not compatible with dynamic updates and you do not have the ability to upgrade it, you still have an option to upgrade to a Windows Server 2003 Active Directory domain that your clients can take advantage of without taking on the extra headache of manually updating your BIND server with needed Active Directory information.

You can build your Windows Server 2003 Active Directory with a Windows Server 2003 DNS server, making sure all domain controllers and infrastructure servers point to it for DNS resolution. This will ensure that all of your needed Active Directory information is kept up-to-date in its dynamic database. All you need to do next is configure your BIND DNS server as a secondary zone of your Windows Server 2003 DNS server. All of the needed Active Directory records will be populated in the BIND copy

Continued

> of the zone and your DNS-enabled clients will be able to search and locate all AD related services without having to physically point to the Windows Server 2003 DNS server. You can continue to use your BIND DNS server while you make all of your DNS edits on your Windows Server 2003 primary DNS server.

One thing to keep in mind when using BIND secondary servers that are set up to do zone transfers with Windows Server 2003 DNS servers is their ability to use fast zone transfers. By default, Windows Server 2003 DNS is configured to transfer its DNS database to all secondary servers in a compressed format that may include multiple records per TCP message. This is considered a fast zone transfer. BIND versions earlier than 4.9.4 do not support this functionality and will fail to pull a zone transfer from a Windows Server 2003 DNS server as shown in the BIND version support chart in Table 6.6. To turn off DNS fast zone transfers, you need to uncheck the **BIND secondaries** configuration check box displayed on the **Advanced** tab of your *DNS servers* **Properties** dialog window shown in Figure 6.61.

Monitoring the Windows Server 2003 DNS Server

Microsoft Windows Server 2003 ships with some out-of-the-box tools to help you monitor your DNS installation. It is important to monitor and test your DNS installation and its use on a scheduled basis to prevent or forecast unforeseen problems, taking a proactive approach. In this next section, we discuss three tools that help you monitor your DNS server. They are:

- DNS console
- System Monitor
- Network Monitor

DNS Console

You should already be somewhat familiar with the Windows Server 2003 DNS administrative console after reading this chapter. There is some monitoring functionality built right into this console. To access this functionality, open the **Monitoring** tab on the **Properties** of your **DNS** *server name*. To do this, right-click your **DNS** *server name* and select **Properties**. Click the **Monitoring** tab as shown in Figure 6.63.

Figure 6.63 Monitoring and Testing Your DNS Installation

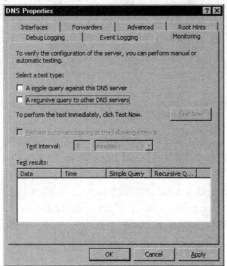

There are two types of monitoring tests you can run from your DNS consoles **Monitoring** tab window:

1.   A simple query against this DNS server *(iterative query)*

2.   A recursive query to other DNS servers *(recursive query)*

Both of these tests are designed to query your DNS server to see if it is still responsive to the same types of queries that DNS client resolvers would send to it on a normal day-to-day resolution request. Those DNS standard queries are called iterative and recursive, and are discussed in more detail in Chapter 5, but briefly here:

■   **Iterative query** A resolution request that asks the DNS server only what it knows. It does not ask that DNS server to ask another DNS server for any help resolving the request if it does not have a positive resolve. It simply sends the client resolver another DNS server to ask the same request.

■   **Recursive query** A resolution request that asks the DNS server to find out the most it can to resolve the name. The client resolver does not do any more work, but leaves the work in the hands of the server. The DNS server will go out in search of a resolution by querying another DNS server. These queries are also recursive in nature.

NOTE

To help you remember the differences between the query types, think of recursive queries as those that *pass the buck*, and iterative queries as the *worker bees*, doing all the work themselves.

To run either one of these tests, click one or both of the option check boxes, **A simple query against this DNS server** or **A recursive query to other DNS servers**, and click the **Test Now** button. See the results in Figure 6.64 if the queries were both successful.

Figure 6.64 Showing Successful DNS Queries

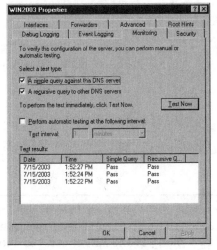

If, for some reason, one of the queries returned a failure, you would see a **Fail** event under the query type that failed, as shown in Figure 6.65. At this point, a yellow triangular warning icon will appear on top of your DNS icon in the console, alerting you that something has failed. This can be seen in Figure 6.66. If you want to continuously query your DNS server to see when a failure is occurring, click on the **Perform automatic testing at the following interval** option check box, and select an interval in hour, minute, or second increments.

Figure 6.65 Showing Failed DNS Queries

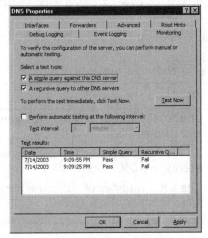

Figure 6.66 Alerting of DNS Query Failure

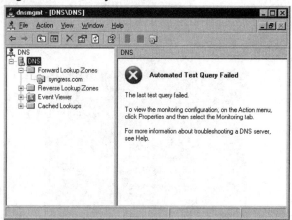

EXAM WARNING

If you are getting continual recursive query failures, you might want to make sure that another administrator has not disabled recursive queries on your DNS server. You can find this out by looking at the **Advanced** tab shown in Figure 6.61, and by making sure the **Disable recursion (also disables forwarders)** option check box is not checked.

System Monitor

Another very useful DNS monitoring tool is the Windows Server 2003 **System Monitor** found in your **Administrative Tools** folder. System Monitor can be used to actively monitor live performance statistics for your DNS server using over 60 different DNS-related performance counters. In Table 6.9, we have included each of these counters along with a description, to give you an easy location to look for and to help you decide which ones you want to use in combination to monitor your DNS a bit more specifically.

Table 6.9 Table of DNS Performance Counters

DNS Counter	Description
AXFR Request Received	The total number of full zone transfer requests received by the master DNS server
AXFR Request Sent	The total number of full zone transfer requests sent by the secondary DNS server
AXFR Response Received	The total number of full zone transfer responses received by the secondary DNS server

Continued

Table 6.9 Table of DNS Performance Counters

DNS Counter	Description
AXFR Success Received	The total number of successful full zone transfers received by the secondary DNS server
AXFR Success Sent	The total number of successful full zone transfers of the master DNS server
Caching Memory	The total caching memory used by DNS server
Database Node Memory	The total database node memory used by DNS server
Dynamic Update NoOperation	The total number of No-operation/Empty dynamic update requests received by the DNS server
Dynamic Update NoOperation/sec	The average number of No-operation/Empty dynamic update requests received by the DNS server in each second
Dynamic Update Queued	The total number of dynamic updates queued by the DNS server
Dynamic Update Received	The total number of dynamic update requests received by the DNS server
Dynamic Update Received/sec	The average number of dynamic update requests received by the DNS server in each second
Dynamic Update Rejected	The total number of dynamic updates rejected by the DNS server
Dynamic Update TimeOuts	The total number of dynamic update timeouts of the DNS server
Dynamic Update Written to Database/sec	The average number of dynamic updates written to the database by the DNS server in each second
IXFR Request Received	The total number of incremental zone transfer requests received by the master DNS server
IXFR Request Sent	The total number of incremental zone transfer requests sent by the secondary DNS server
IXFR Response Received	The total number of incremental zone transfer responses received by the secondary DNS server
IXFR Success Received	The total number of successful incremental zone transfers received by the secondary DNS server
IXFR Success Sent	The total number of successful incremental zone transfers of the master DNS server
IXFR TCP Success Received	The total number of successful TCP incremental zone transfers received by the secondary DNS server.
IXFR UDP Success Received	The total number of successful UDP incremental zone transfers received by the secondary DNS server
Nbstat Memory	The total Nbstat memory used by DNS server

Continued

Table 6.9 Table of DNS Performance Counters

DNS Counter	Description
Notify Received	The total number of notifies received by the secondary DNS server
Notify Sent	The total number of notifies sent by the master DNS server
Record Flow Memory	The total record flow memory used by DNS server
Recursive Queries	The total number of recursive queries received by DNS server
Recursive Queries/sec	The average number of recursive queries received by DNS server in each second
Recursive Query Failure	The total number of recursive query failures
Recursive Query Failure/sec	The average number of recursive query failures in each second
Recursive TimeOuts	The total number of recursive query sending timeouts
Recursive TimeOut/sec each second	The average number of recursive query sending timeouts in
Secure Update Failure	The total number of secure updates failed of the DNS server
Secure Update Received	The total number of secure update requests received by the DNS server
Secure Update Received/sec	The average number of secure update requests received by the DNS server in each second
TCP Message Memory	The total TCP message memory used by DNS server
TCP Query Received	The total number of TCP queries received by DNS server
TCP Query Received/sec	The average number of TCP queries received by DNS server in each second
TCP Response Sent	The total number of TCP responses sent by DNS server
TCP Response Sent/sec	The average number of TCP responses sent by DNS server in each second
Total Query Received	The total number of queries received by DNS server
Total Query Received/sec	The average number of queries received by DNS server in each second
Total Response Sent	The total number of responses sent by DNS server
Total Response Sent/sec	The average number of responses sent by DNS server in each second
UDP Message Memory	The total UDP message memory used by DNS server
UDP Query Received	The total number of UDP queries received by DNS server
UDP Query Received/sec	The average number of UDP queries received by DNS server in each second
UDP Response Sent	The total number of UDP responses sent by DNS server

Continued

Table 6.9 Table of DNS Performance Counters

DNS Counter	Description
UDP Response Sent/sec	The average number of UDP responses sent by DNS server in each second
WINS Lookup Received	The total number of WINS lookup requests received by the server
WINS Lookup Received/sec	The average number of WINS lookup requests received by the server in each second
WINS Response Sent	The total number of WINS lookup responses sent by the server
WINS Response Sent/sec	The average number of WINS lookup responses sent by the server in each second
WINS Reverse Lookup Received	The total number of WINS reverse lookup requests received by the server
WINS Reverse Lookup Received/sec	The average number of WINS reverse lookup requests received by the server in each second
WINS Reverse Response Sent	The total number of WINS Reverse lookup responses sent by the server
WINS Reverse Response Sent/sec	The average number of WINS Reverse lookup responses sent by the server in each second
Zone Transfer Request Received	The total number of failed zone transfers of the master DNS server
Zone Transfer Request Received	The total number of zone transfer requests received by the master DNS server
Zone Transfer SOA Request Sent	The total number of zone transfer SOA requests sent by the secondary DNS server
Zone Transfer Success	The total number of successful zone transfers of the master DNS server

Exercise 6.07 will step you through setting up System Monitor to monitor your DNS server's Total Queries Received/sec counter. In order to make a realistic DNS query count in our test environment, we used the following bit of code in a batch file called DNSQuery.bat along with a text file called addresses.txt. These were used to simulate many DNS resolvers querying the DNS server.

DNStest.bat

```
@echo off
net stop dnscache
:loop
for /f %%I in (c:\addresses.txt) do ping %%I
goto loop
```

Addresses.txt

```
test1
test2
test3
test4
test5
test6
test7
test8
test9
```

First, we disabled the local client from being able to cache DNS lookups, causing it always to look back to the DNS server. Next, we ran the command line **ping** utility against a list of machine names in a continuous loop.

EXERCISE 6.07

MONITORING DNS WITH SYSTEM MONITOR

This exercise is designed to help you set up an active performance monitor on your DNS server to monitor how many DNS queries it is receiving per second.

1. Click **Start | Administrative Tools | Performance** to open your System Monitor console.

2. Click **Ctrl+E** to clear the default counters.

3. Click **Ctrl+E** to open the **Add Counters** dialog window.

4. Click the drop-down box under **Performance object** and select **DNS** as shown in Figure 6.67.

Figure 6.67 Selecting the DNS Performance Object

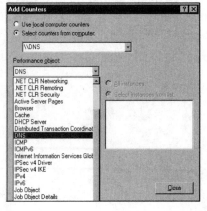

5. In the **Select counter from list** box, scroll down until you see **Total Queries Received/sec** and click **Add** as shown in Figure 6.68. Click **Close** to close the **Add Counter** dialog window.

Figure 6.68 Selecting the DNS Performance Object

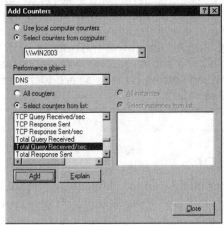

6. Right-click on the new **Total Queries Received/sec** counter at the bottom of your System Monitor console and select **Properties**.

7. On the **Scale** field, click the drop-down box and select **10.0**. Click **OK**.

8. Notice the performance meter line as it rises and falls with the DNS queries per second count as shown in Figure 6.69.

Figure 6.69 Showing Total DNS Queries per Second

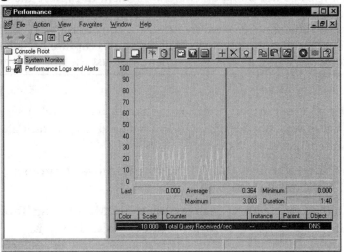

NOTE

You might think that with primary and secondary zones, or even with Active Directory Integrated zones, you have plenty of backup copies of your DNS zone records in case of a disaster. Well, we have found out differently, especially in smaller company environments. Setting up a server to do a zone transfer with your production DNS server is not all that much work, and well worth the effort in the face of a disaster. With the importance of DNS in today's Windows 2000 and Windows Server 2003 Active Directory infrastructure, you can never have too many copies of your domain zone and its records. We recommend installing the DNS service on a spare server and setting it up as a secondary server just for backup purposes. You'll be glad you did.

Network Monitor

Network Monitor is another useful tool to monitor and capture DNS-related data for analysis and reporting. Although this tool is useful, it is a bit more complex than System Monitor and it therefore should be used by the more experienced engineer. Network Monitor is a network sniffing software tool that is designed to look at and capture all of the network data frames that traverses the wire. The Network Monitor tool that ships with Windows Server 2003 is limited to sniffing only data sent to or from one machine at a time—the one on which it is running. To successfully monitor DNS traffic, you need to run Network Monitor from the DNS server.

NOTE

If you are interested in sniffing an entire IP segment to capture the DNS traffic of all resolvers on your network, you can obtain a copy of Microsoft's System Management Software (SMS), which includes a copy of Network Monitor that places your NIC in promiscuous mode, which allows you to capture packets sent to and from all computers on the network segment, not just the one on which it is installed.

To run Network Monitor, you first need to install it on your DNS server as it is not installed by default in Windows Server 2003. To install and start capturing data with Network Monitor:

1. Click **Start | Control Panel | Add or Remove Programs | Add/Remove Windows Components**.

2. Scroll down and highlight **Management and Monitoring Tools**. Click the **Details** button. Click **Network Monitor Tools**. Click **OK**.

3. Click **Next**, making sure your Windows Server 2003 source CD is in your CD-ROM (or you can type the path to a network share on which the installation files are located when prompted). Click **Finish** when it completes copying files.

4. After the installation completes, access the Network Monitor utility from the Administrative Tools menu by clicking **Start | Administrative Tools | Network Monitor**.

5. In the Network Monitor interface, click **Capture | Start** from the tools menu to begin capturing data, as shown in Figure 6.70.

NOTE

If there are multiple network interfaces on the server, you will be asked to select a network on which you want to capture data. Select the appropriate interface (for example, the LAN interface or Local Area Connection).

Figure 6.70 Capturing Data with Network Monitor

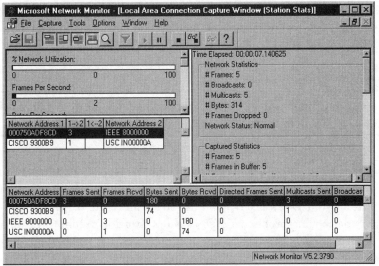

When you believe that enough data traffic has been captured, simply click the **Capture | Stop and View** menu item and you will see all of your network data frames that your DNS server was sending and receiving. Sorting through the data to find the packets you actually need is the time consuming part of using Network Monitor. In cases where there is just too much data to manage, you can use Network Monitor's filtering ability to capture only specific network traffic, or to display only specified traffic out of what was previously captured.

Network Monitor is a very useful tool that is included with Windows Server 2003. You must understand how to configure and use this tool to effectively troubleshoot networking problems of all types, including those related to DNS.

Troubleshooting the Windows Server 2003 DNS Server

With all the planning, configuring, and monitoring, you are bound to have to troubleshoot DNS server problems. In this section, we will show you a few of the tools and techniques used to effectively troubleshoot Windows Server 2003 DNS server. We will discuss two methods of troubleshooting:

- Logging
- Diagnostic Tools

Logging

Windows Server 2003 DNS server installs with all DNS events being logged to the DNS specific event log called **DNS Events** located either in your Event Viewer MMC console or the DNS console. Click **Start | Administrative Tools | Event Viewer** or **DNS**. In either console, you can click the DNS event log and search for detailed DNS warnings and alerts.

NOTE

If you are using the **Event Viewer** to access the DNS event log, it is called **DNS Server**; inside the DNS console it is referred to as **DNS Events**.

If you want to specifically log only errors, or just errors and warnings in the DNS event log, you can monitor the default behavior on the **Event Logging** tab on the **Properties** page of your **DNS** *server name* as shown in Figure 6.71.

If you are experiencing problematic DNS issues that don't seem to be able to be resolved via the maximum alerting features of the Windows Event Viewer, Windows Server 2003 DNS has the ability to enable debugging on your DNS server. The debugging feature of Windows Server 2003 DNS is disabled by default and should be enabled only as a last resort for solving DNS related problems. Debugging enables you as a DNS administrator to log every packet that is sent to your DNS server in a log file called **dns.log** located in %systemroot%\system32\dns by default. To successfully start logging data to this file, you must select at least the three following items from the **Debug Logging** tab on the **Properties** of your **DNS** *server name* as shown in Figure 6.72.

- Packet direction

- Transport protocol

- At least one other option (from the **Packet** contents or **Other Options** option check boxes)

Figure 6.71 Changing the Event Logging Defaults

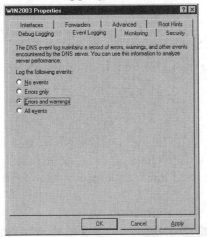

In order for debug logging to work correctly, it must be configured to look at data packets, either **inbound** or **outbound**. It must also be configured to look at a specific **transport protocol type**, either **UDP**, **TCP**, or both. For the "one other option," debug logging must be set to look at some sort of **packet content** or **packet type**. There are seven options to choose from. One of these must be selected, along with the previous two options, to have a full data set that can be used effectively by the debugging process.

Figure 6.72 Enabling DNS Debug Logging

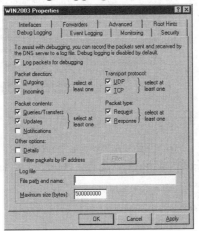

Diagnostic Tools

The following two tools are useful for troubleshooting DNS related server problems:

1. Nslookup.exe
2. Netdiag.exe

Nslookup is a standard TCP/IP utility that is commonly used as a DNS diagnostic troubleshooting tool. It has a wide range of functionality, allowing you to query your DNS server, as shown in the command line syntax snapshot in Figure 6.73.

Figure 6.73 Enabling DNS Debug Logging

```
C:\WINDOWS\system32\cmd.exe - nslookup

C:\>nslookup
Default Server:  win2003.syngress.com
Address:  192.168.0.192

> help
Commands:   (identifiers are shown in uppercase, [] means optional)
NAME            - print info about the host/domain NAME using default server
NAME1 NAME2     - as above, but use NAME2 as server
help or ?       - print info on common commands
set OPTION      - set an option
    all             - print options, current server and host
    [no]debug       - print debugging information
    [no]d2          - print exhaustive debugging information
    [no]defname     - append domain name to each query
    [no]recurse     - ask for recursive answer to query
    [no]search      - use domain search list
    [no]vc          - always use a virtual circuit
    domain=NAME     - set default domain name to NAME
    srchlist=N1[/N2/.../N6] - set domain to N1 and search list to N1,N2, etc.
    root=NAME       - set root server to NAME
    retry=X         - set number of retries to X
    timeout=X       - set initial time-out interval to X seconds
    type=X          - set query type (ex. A,ANY,CNAME,MX,NS,PTR,SOA,SRV)
    querytype=X     - same as type
    class=X         - set query class (ex. IN (Internet), ANY)
    [no]msxfr       - use MS fast zone transfer
    ixfrver=X       - current version to use in IXFR transfer request
server NAME     - set default server to NAME, using current default server
lserver NAME    - set default server to NAME, using initial server
finger [USER]   - finger the optional NAME at the current default host
root            - set current default server to the root
ls [opt] DOMAIN [> FILE] - list addresses in DOMAIN (optional: output to FILE)
    -a          -   list canonical names and aliases
    -d          -   list all records
    -t TYPE     -   list records of the given type (e.g. A,CNAME,MX,NS,PTR etc.)
view FILE       -   sort an 'ls' output file and view it with pg
exit            - exit the program

> _
```

To list the syntax displayed in Figure 6.73, you have to enter **nslookup** in a command prompt windows and type **Help** while in what is referred to as *interactive* mode. **Nslookup** will run in one of two modes:

- **Interactive**   Used to interact with **nslookup** when you require more than a single piece of information. It is accessed by typing **nslookup**.

- **Noninteractive**   Used when you need only a single piece of information or if you need to gather this information in a script or batch file. This is accessed by typing **nslookup** along with the syntax required for the information you are looking for. For example, if you wanted to find the name for the IP address 192.168.0.193, you would type **nslookup 192.168.0.193**.

EXAM WARNING

In order for **nslookup** to work properly, you must have a Reverse Lookup Zone set up for the domain you want to troubleshoot. When you launch **nslookup**, it does a reverse lookup against your configured DNS server, and reports an error if a reverse lookup zone is not configured. Any record you want to perform a lookup against must have an associated PTR record registered in the reverse lookup zone, or troubleshooting with **nslookup** will not work.

Windows Server 2003 has added the ability to run the handy command line **nslookup** utility right from within the DNS console window. Exercise 6.08 will guide you through the process of running **nslookup** to verify that specific SRV resource records within your DNS database are registered correctly.

EXERCISE 6.08

USING NSLOOKUP TO VERIFY SRV RECORDS

This exercise will teach you how to successfully use the **nslookup** utility to verify your DNS SRV resource record types.

1. Click **Start | Run** and type **cmd**. Click **OK**.

2. Type **nslookup** at the command prompt.

3. Type **ls –t SRV domainname.com** (where *domainname.com* is your forward lookup domain name; we used *syngress.com* in this example).

Notice the results in Figure 6.74. It shows a listing of all the SRV records of the domain you just specified.

Figure 6.74 Enabling DNS Debug Logging

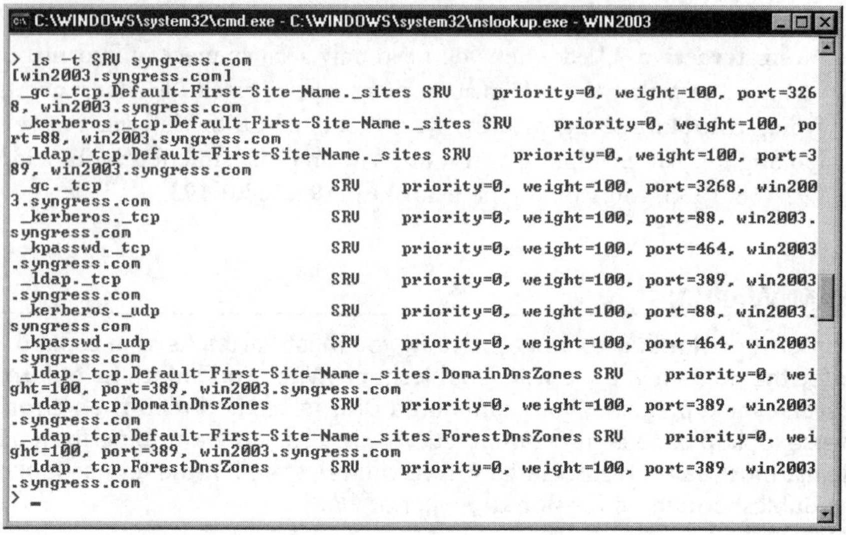

```
C:\WINDOWS\system32\cmd.exe - C:\WINDOWS\system32\nslookup.exe - WIN2003

> ls -t SRV syngress.com
[win2003.syngress.com]
 _gc._tcp.Default-First-Site-Name._sites SRV      priority=0, weight=100, port=326
8, win2003.syngress.com
 _kerberos._tcp.Default-First-Site-Name._sites SRV      priority=0, weight=100, po
rt=88, win2003.syngress.com
 _ldap._tcp.Default-First-Site-Name._sites SRV      priority=0, weight=100, port=3
89, win2003.syngress.com
 _gc._tcp                    SRV      priority=0, weight=100, port=3268, win200
3.syngress.com
 _kerberos._tcp              SRV      priority=0, weight=100, port=88, win2003.
syngress.com
 _kpasswd._tcp               SRV      priority=0, weight=100, port=464, win2003
.syngress.com
 _ldap._tcp                  SRV      priority=0, weight=100, port=389, win2003
.syngress.com
 _kerberos._udp              SRV      priority=0, weight=100, port=88, win2003.
syngress.com
 _kpasswd._udp               SRV      priority=0, weight=100, port=464, win2003
.syngress.com
 _ldap._tcp.Default-First-Site-Name._sites.DomainDnsZones SRV      priority=0, wei
ght=100, port=389, win2003.syngress.com
 _ldap._tcp.DomainDnsZones    SRV      priority=0, weight=100, port=389, win2003
.syngress.com
 _ldap._tcp.Default-First-Site-Name._sites.ForestDnsZones SRV      priority=0, wei
ght=100, port=389, win2003.syngress.com
 _ldap._tcp.ForestDnsZones    SRV      priority=0, weight=100, port=389, win2003
.syngress.com
> _
```

TEST DAY TIP

If you are already in the DNS console, you can launch the nslookup tool by right-clicking on your **DNS server name** and selecting **Launch nslookup** to put you in interactive mode. This is a new feature of Windows Server 2003.

netdiag.exe is a tool you can use on your DNS server to make sure everything is configured and working correctly. It is a more elaborate tool than nslookup and tests on a broad spectrum of server related configurations. To use netdiag to for DNS testing only, follow these steps:

1. Click **Start | Run | cmd**.
2. Type **netdiag /test:DNS**.

Notice the detailed results in Figure 6.75.

Figure 6.75 Testing Your DNS Server with netdiag

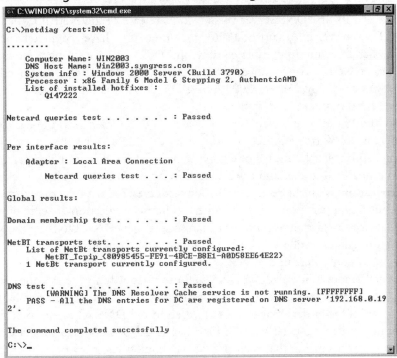

```
C:\WINDOWS\system32\cmd.exe

C:\>netdiag /test:DNS

.........
     Computer Name: WIN2003
     DNS Host Name: Win2003.syngress.com
     System info : Windows 2000 Server (Build 3790)
     Processor : x86 Family 6 Model 6 Stepping 2, AuthenticAMD
     List of installed hotfixes :
          Q147222

Netcard queries test . . . . . . . : Passed


Per interface results:

     Adapter : Local Area Connection

          Netcard queries test . . . : Passed


Global results:


Domain membership test . . . . . . : Passed


NetBT transports test. . . . . . . : Passed
     List of NetBt transports currently configured:
          NetBT_Tcpip_{80985455-FE91-4BCE-B8E1-A0D58EE64E22}
     1 NetBt transport currently configured.


DNS test . . . . . . . . . . . . : Passed
          [WARNING] The DNS Resolver Cache service is not running. [FFFFFFFF]
     PASS - All the DNS entries for DC are registered on DNS server '192.168.0.19
2'.


The command completed successfully

C:\>_
```

NOTE

In order to run the netdiag command-line utility successfully, you need to have the Remote Registry service started or you will receive an error.

NOTE

netdiag is part of the Windows Server 2003 Support Tools located on your source CD-ROM under SUPPORT\TOOLS. You can install it by installing the full tools MSI package file, **suptools.msi**, or by just extracting the netdiag.exe file from the **support.cab** file.

Summary of Exam Objectives

Microsoft released its first DNS server version in its release of the NetBIOS-dependant Windows NT 4.0 server in August of 1996. Since then, they have completely revamped their Windows architecture to completely rely on DNS, and have strongly moved away from their earlier NetBIOS-dependant protocol. Although NetBIOS is not needed to run Windows 2000 or Windows Server 2003 Active Directory, it is still needed to run down-level client operating systems and applications.

Windows DNS can be installed as a stand-alone DNS server or as the backbone on Windows Server 2003's Active Directory. It can host primary zones that can supplement secondary and stub zones by means of a zone transfer or it can be installed on a Windows Server 2003 domain controller and integrated into Active Directory, piggy-backing on its directory replication. With the release of Windows Server 2003, a new directory partition called the Application partition exists. It is used to house application-specific directory structures that need custom replication mechanisms, such as DNS. DNS can now be replicated among domain controllers in its own domain, domain controllers in other domains, or all the domain controllers in the forest.

By default, Windows Server 2003 DNS will use its root hints file as a means of locating other DNS servers for recursive query resolution. You can alter this behavior by setting up what are known as forwarders. Forwarders are used to tell DNS where to look for name resolution if not in its local database. Windows Server 2003 introduces the idea of conditional forwarding. This means that recursive query requests can now be subject to different DNS forwarder servers based on the domain name queried.

By default, reverse lookup zones are not created with the creation of forward lookup zones. In order to successfully use reverse lookups with say, the nslookup command line troubleshooting tool, it is necessary to configure reverse lookup zones.

Windows 2000 DNS introduced the idea of dynamic updating into the DNS database. This allows clients to dynamically update their own resource records in DNS. This may lend itself to an abundance of outdated or stale records as machines are added and removed from the network in today's quick changing and fast turnover environments. The use of DNS scavenging can be used to help purge these older records from the DNS database at prescheduled times or on a manual basis.

DNS allows the idea of secure or nonsecure dynamic updates. With secure updates configured, only members of the domain can successfully register their records. Microsoft recommends this way; however, it is available only if you install DNS on a domain controller and use Active Directory Integrated zones.

Client DNS configuration can be either automatic (with the use of DHCP) or static, by manually typing all the settings. Using DHCP is the recommended method for obvious overhead reasons, but for less obvious infrastructure reasons. DHCP can be integrated with DNS to greatly improve the way clients update DNS. DHCP can be used as a middle man to do the work for the clients. Better still, it can turn downlevel clients that are unable to dynamically register themselves with DNS into clients that can.

WINS can also be integrated into DNS for the purpose of servicing non-WINS, DNS-only clients. With the integration of WINS and DNS, DNS-only clients can now resolve NetBIOS names on behalf of their configured Windows Server 2003 DNS server.

Many organizations still use and want to continue to use a BIND implementation of DNS for their backbone name resolution methodology. However, they also want to take advantage of Microsoft's highly stable enterprise Network Operating System (NOS), Windows Server 2003. Microsoft has recognized this need and made Windows Server 2003 DNS able to integrate well with BIND. The only limitation is that the version of BIND in use must support Service Locator or RSV records. Microsoft also highly recommends that it support dynamic updates as well. BIND version 8.2.2 and later supports both of these features.

Microsoft has built some monitoring and troubleshooting functionality into its Windows Server 2003 version of DNS. Out of the box you can use the DNS console to run both iterative and recursive query tests against your DNS server. There is also the ability to enable debug mode logging, which will log every packet that is destined for your DNS server. Other tools such as System Monitor and Network Monitor can be used to run real time or base line tests against your DNS server. For you command line junkies, there are some handy tools included in Windows Server 2003 for you to use in monitoring and troubleshooting DNS. Both the nslookup and netdiag tools are an essential part of any DNS administrator's tool belt.

DNS is an integral component of your Windows Server 2003 Active Directory network, and this chapter covers information needed not only to master the exam objectives, but also to perform your everyday duties as a network administrator.

Exam Objectives Fast Track

Installing and Configuring the Windows Server 2003 DNS Server

☑ Forward lookup zones resolve names to IP addresses and Reverse lookup zones resolve IP addresses to names.

☑ Forwarders can be used on your DNS server to forward requests for which your DNS server does not have an authoritative answer. You can also set up your forwarders to conditionally forward requests to different forwarders based on domain names.

☑ Scavenging of stale records must be set up on both the server and the zone to work correctly.

☑ By default, zone transfers are not allowed. Microsoft recommends allowing zone transfers only to specific server IP addresses; best practice is to use Active Directory Integrated zones, which use Active Directory replication to copy zone data.

Configuring DNS Clients

☑ By default, only Windows Server 2003 and Windows XP DNS clients are set up to automatically register with their configured DNS server. Windows 2000 has this ability but is not configured to do so by default. Downlevel Windows clients must use the help of DHCP to register with DNS.

☑ Windows clients can contain more than two entries for a DNS server. In order to configure more DNS server for Windows 2000, Windows Server 2003, and Windows XP clients, you must use the **Advanced** properties page of your TCP/IP settings and configure it under the **DNS** tab.

☑ By default, DNS clients try and reregister their resource records with DNS every 24 hours.

☑ DNS clients can be configured with DNS suffixes if they are in need of resolving multiple hosts from multiple domains. These domains must be hosted on the DNS servers that the clients are configured to use.

Integrating the Windows Server 2003 DNS Server with DHCP

☑ When integrating DNS and DHCP, Windows 2000, Windows 2003, and Windows XP DHCP-enabled clients register only their A records with DNS by default. The DHCP server service registers their corresponding PTR records.

☑ Windows downlevel clients can automatically update the Windows Server 2003's dynamic DNS database with the assistance of a DHCP server.

☑ The DNSUpdateProxy group no longer has to pose the security threat of taking ownership of every record it registers in DNS on behalf of other clients with the introduction of the dynamic DNS credentials feature.

Integrating the Windows Server 2003 DNS Server with WINS

☑ You can pull all of your WINS addresses into your DNS database so that your DNS-only clients can resolve NetBIOS names without having to look at your WINS server.

☑ WINS resolves NetBIOS names to IP addresses and DNS resolves hosts names to IP addresses.

☑ When using WINS forward lookups, your non-WINS DNS clients communicate solely through your DNS server to resolve NetBIOS names.

Integrating the Windows Server 2003 DNS Server with BIND

- ☑ Windows Server 2003 SRV records were first supported in version 4.9.7 of the BIND implementation of DNS, and dynamic updating was first supported in version 8.1.2.

- ☑ Fast zone transfers are enabled by default in Windows Server 2003 DNS and need to be disabled if you set up zone transfers with BIND implementations prior to version 4.9.4.

- ☑ If you are integrating WINS with your Windows Server 2003 DNS it is good practice to disable replication of WINS records to other DNS servers that are acting as master DNS servers for secondary BIND implementations.

Monitoring the Windows Server 2003 DNS Server

- ☑ You can monitor your DNS server from within the DNS console by manually or automatically running iterative and recursive query tests against it.

- ☑ When DNS is installed on your Windows Server 2003 server, it also installs many performance counters that can be used to monitor such items as the amount of dynamic updates received or the amount of zone transfer requests received.

- ☑ Windows Server 2003 has a separate Event Log called the DNS Server log that makes searching for and weeding out DNS-related events much easier. You can turn up the logging event level when you want to monitor your server more closely and think there might be a problem.

Troubleshooting the Windows Server 2003 DNS Server

- ☑ Turning off recursion on your DNS servers can cause client queries to fail. Disable recursion on your DNS servers only if your clients are set up to be able to query other DNS servers iteratively.

- ☑ **Nslookup** is a powerful command line utility that can be used to query both forward and reverse lookup zones and to verify resource records in those zones.

- ☑ Logging is great for diagnosing DNS problems, but turn it on only when you have a problem because it tends to be a resource hog and can cause your DNS servers to perform poorly.

Exam Objectives
Frequently Asked Questions

The following Frequently Asked Questions, answered by the authors of this book, are designed to both measure your understanding of the Exam Objectives presented in this chapter, and to assist you with real-life implementation of these concepts. You will also gain access to thousands of other FAQs at ITFAQnet.com.

Q: I have been told that it is best to use an Active Directory integrated zone for my DNS zones; however, that option is grayed out on my server. What can I do?

A: You can either upgrade your DNS server to a domain controller, or move your DNS services to a domain controller. Active Directory integrated zones are supported only on domain controllers.

Q: My users are complaining that they can access any Internet site except one. They say they keep getting a response from the server that says the page cannot be found. Why are they unable to get to this one domain name?

A: Windows Server 2003 has the ability to use conditional forwarding. That domain name is probably set up to be forwarded to another server for resolution and that server is having problems or is down.

Q: We use a third-party help desk Web application from a company that just changed their Web page IP address. Now nobody can access the site. What can we do?

A: Clear the cache on your DNS server. Your DNS server has the old domain and IP address stored in cache.

Q: I have just changed my Windows XP network IP address on my laptop before I plugged it into the LAN. Now my coworkers cannot resolve my machine name. What can I do?

A: Type **ipconfig /registerdns** to reregister your IP address with DNS.

Q: When I try to ping a name I know is set up for round robining, why do I keep getting the same IP address?

A: You must be using a Windows 2000 or Windows XP machine, as they hold a local DNS cache. Type either ipconfig /flushdns to flush the DNS cache and query the DNS server again, or type net stop dnscache to temporarily disable DNS caching.

Q: My primary DNS server crashed this morning and now my DHCP clients are complaining that some Web pages are timing out while waiting for resolution from the secondary DNS server. What can I do?

A: Switch the DNS order in your DHCP scopes and have your clients renew their IP information by rebooting or typing ipconfig /renew at the command line.

Q: How can I use DHCP to register my client machines' A and PTR records without taking ownership of their records? We had a DHCP server that owned all my client records crash, and the new DHCP server could not update them.

A: Use the new Windows Server 2003 DNS Credential feature that allows you to specify an Active Directory user as the owner of all DHCP registered records.

Q: Does DHCP handle unregistering my laptop clients from DNS when they just unplug from my network?

A: No. DHCP only knows how to unregister addresses that are gracefully shutdown. DNS scavenging should be enabled to handle cleaning up records that linger in your DNS database from people unplugging from the network and not plugging back in for some time, such as mobile or laptop users.

Q: I have set up my DHCP server to dynamically update A and PTR records for my downlevel Windows clients; however, they do not seem to unregister themselves in DNS when these clients shut down. What is wrong?

A: It looks as if you do not have the **Discard A and PTR records when lease is deleted** option check box selected. This option ensures that DHCP will clean up those records when client leases expire or when their machines are shut down.

Q: I am having problems with my BIND zones loading ever since I integrated WINS into my Windows Server 2003 infrastructure. My BIND servers accept zone transfers from my Windows Server 2003 servers and they have worked prior to this. What is wrong?

A: You need to check the **Do not replicate this record** option on the WINS tab of your DNS zones properties. This tells DNS to not replicate WINS records with other DNS servers that might have problems understanding the NetBIOS name formats.

Q: Why do I need the ability to integrate WINS with DNS? I thought Windows Server 2003 didn't require WINS anymore?

A: You are correct in saying that Windows Server 2003 does not require WINS anymore; however, downlevel clients and applications that still rely on NetBIOS do. Integration with DNS is used to help non-WINS clients resolve WINS clients' NetBIOS names.

Q: I have integrated my WINS service with my DNS service and now all my non-WINS UNIX clients can talk to my NetBIOS machines. However, when they try to resolve their names using **nslookup**, they are not able to do so. Why not?

A: You also have to integrate your reverse lookup zones with WINS if you want to be able to use **nslookup**.

Q: We are currently using a BIND implementation version 4.9.7. Can we use this as our Active Directory DNS server?

A: Yes. You can, because BIND version 4.9.7 supports SRV records. However, it is recommended that you upgrade to version 8.2.2, which also supports dynamic updates. It will save lots of work and time and possible error.

Q: I am trying to do a zone transfer between my primary Windows Server 2003 DNS server and my older BIND server but keep getting zone transfer errors. What can I do?

A: Turn off BIND secondaries on your Windows Server 2003 DNS server or upgrade your version of BIND to a 4.9.4 or later. By default, Windows Server 2003 uses fast zone transfers which are not supported in versions of BIND before 4.9.4.

Q: If I decide to use my current version of BIND that supports only SRV records for my Active Directory DNS server, where can I get a list of the SRV records I need to manually enter into my BIND database?

A: After you install your Active Directory domain controller using the option to update DNS after the installation, you can use the **netlogon.dns** file found in %systemroot%\system32\config, because it contains all the necessary SRV records needed for AD functionality.

Q: When I try to run the query tests that are built into the DNS console, I keep getting recursive query failures. My clients are telling me that they cannot access many Internet sites. What is wrong?

A: Check and make sure another administrator did not turn off the ability for your server to do recursive query lookups.

Q: It seems that my DNS server is not working as well as it used to. Is it possible that my client load has overwhelmed my server's processing power and if so, how can I check?

A: Yes, that is possible. The tool you need to use is System Monitor. It will let you check both system load and specific DNS counter variables such as DNS queries per second to see if the server is getting an abundance of queries that it shouldn't.

Q: How can I actively monitor all the data packets that are going to my DNS server without buying a third-party sniffer program?

A: Windows Server 2003 comes with a utility called Network Monitor that will let you sniff the traffic coming to and going from only the server on which it is installed. This would work for your DNS request.

Q: When I type **nslookup**, I get an error saying that it cannot find the server. What's wrong and what can I do to make it work?

A: **Nslookup** requires that a reverse lookup zone be created. It uses PTR records to do a reverse lookup on queried names. Create a reverse lookup zone for the domain you want to query with **nslookup**.

Self Test

A Quick Answer Key follows the Self Test questions. For complete questions, answers, and explanations to the Self Test questions in this chapter as well as the other chapters in this book, see the Self Test Appendix.

Installing and Configuring the Windows Server 2003 DNS Server

1. Your company has been planning a migration from their Windows NT 4.0 domain to a new Windows Server 2003 domain for over a year. You have a corporate office in Charleston, SC and 15 satellite branches spread out over the east coast. In each branch, you are currently running a Windows NT 4.0 domain controller that is also functioning as a DNS, WINS, and DHCP server. In the corporate office you have three domain controllers and two member servers. The member servers in corporate are running WINS, DHCP, and DNS. The WINS servers at each branch are configured in a hub and spoke replication model with corporate. All branch DNS servers pull a secondary zone from a DNS server in corporate. Finally the time has come and you are ready to start your migration. You upgrade your primary DNS server to Windows 2000. You enable dynamic updates. You configure all of the domain controllers in corporate to point to the new Windows Server 2003 DNS server. Next you upgrade your PDC to Windows 2000. Everything seems to be working fine, but in a few hours you start getting calls from some of your branches that the DNS service is giving them Dr. Watson errors. What could be a cause of the problem?

A. The NT 4.0 servers are running service pack 5.

B. The NT 4.0 servers should not be running DNS since they are domain controllers.

C. The NT 4.0 servers are running service pack 3.

D. The NT 4.0 servers require full zone transfer, but Windows Server 2003 supports only incremental zone transfers.

2. Lisa works for a development company that has a native mode Windows Server 2003 Active Directory domain infrastructure in place. They are using Windows XP and Windows 2000 exclusively on all the client laptops and deploy all IP configuration options via DHCP. All DHCP servers are set up to automatically register A and PTR records on behalf of their clients. Lisa maintains an Active Directory integrated Windows Server 2003 DNS database. The corporate environment is heavily trafficked by mobile users moving from floor to floor, disconnecting their network cables and not properly shutting down or releasing old IP information. Developers are constantly adding machines to the domain via virtual software and then disconnecting them. Each of the four floors Lisa works on is set up as a subdomain of the first floor root domain. Each client is assigned a DNS suffix search order for each subdomain. After working there for quite some time, Lisa finds that her DNS database is filled with stagnant stale records. She thinks this is causing some performance problems and wants to initiate a manual scavenging of the database to see how many records it cleans up. Lisa has not changed any of the default DNS configuring setting since she installed it. Lisa goes into her DNS console, right-clicks her DNS server, and selects **Scavenge Stale Resource Records**. She answers **yes** to the question asking if she wants to scavenge all resource records in the database. She waits until the next day and checks the database only to find the records are still there. She then remembers that she read somewhere that the default refresh interval is 7 days, so she runs scavenging one more time to make sure and decides to check back in a week. Two weeks later, the stale database records are still around and do not seem to want to disappear. What is Lisa doing wrong?

A. Lisa forgot to enable scavenging on the server.

B. Lisa forgot to enable scavenging on the domain.

C. Lisa forgot to enable scavenging on the server and domain.

D. Lisa has not waited long enough.

Configuring DNS Clients

3. Joey is a desktop engineer for a computer software company in downtown New York City called Solutions. His company has just integrated themselves with two other smaller software development companies to try to build a stronger customer service application in their competitive market. The network groups have been combined and have successfully created a shared network backbone. They have also set up and confirmed that each company is now hosting secondary copies of the other's DNS domains. Cross-forest trusts have also been established and confirmed in a working order. Solutions is the only one of the three companies that has a Web presence, hosting a Web page at www.solutionsacme.com. It is Joey's responsibility to set up his 20 client users with the correct DNS suffixes to be able to resolve these new domains to access needed shared resources. He decides to test the adding of additional DNS suffixes on his Windows XP laptop first before scripting it out and applying it to the rest of his company workstations. He and most of the other users in his office use static IP addressing and are set up with a default connection-specific DNS suffix of solutionsacme.com. He leaves the default suffix in place on his laptop and adds the other companies' DNS suffixes in the DNS suffix search order window as shown in Figure 6.76. Joey starts his testing by trying to access the other company's shared network resources and is successful. Joey believes that he has set everything up correctly, until he tries to access his company Web site. He gets a Page cannot be displayed error. He invokes a command prompt and types **ping www** as he always had before. He gets a response of Ping request could not find host www. He calls support and asks if they can access the corporate Web site. They reply that they can. What is wrong with Joey's configuration?

Figure 6.76 Displaying DNS Suffix Configuration

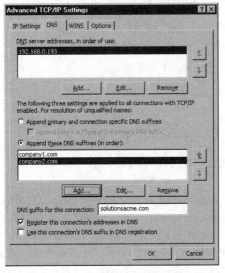

    A. Joey forgot to check **Use this connections DNS suffix in DNS registration** check box.

    B. Joey forgot to add the IP addresses of the other company's DNS servers in the DNS window.

    C. Joey forgot to add his domain name to the DNS suffix search order list.

    D. Nothing, there must be a problem with the Web site's host record.

4. John's network consists of a Windows Server 2003 Active Directory backbone using DHCP to distribute client IP addresses and network IP information. DHCP is set up to automatically update DNS with all Windows XP and Windows 2000 clients PTR records while they update their own A records. It is not set up to update downlevel clients because WINS is also in use on the network for some old Windows NT 4.0 applications servers running legacy human resource payroll and accounting applications. All clients are set up as default enhanced h-node clients. DNS is completely automated and does not contain any static entries. At the end of every month, human resources employees ftp all the payroll information to the accounting server, where an automatic process e-mails those files to a third-party processing firm to cut checks and mail them to employees. Due to an IP network overhaul, all of the servers' IP addresses had to be changed in order to accommodate a bigger IP address pool, for the accumulation of more servers and more employees. The change was scheduled for a weekend's worth of work. On the Monday following that weekend, there were just a handful of calls in the help desk queue. However, all of them were from human resource employees. The calls stated that they were no longer able to update end of month payroll files on the accounting server. John called one employee and asked her to send him a copy of the file in e-mail so he could try. When he tried, he was able to update the accounting server. What is the problem with accounting?

    A. A local LMHOSTS file needs updating.

    B. The DNS server was not updated correctly.

    C. A local HOSTS file needs updating.

    D. The WINS server needs updating.

Integrating the Windows Server 2003 DNS Server with DHCP

5. Your company has a Windows Server 2003 domain. All of your servers run Windows Server 2003 and all of your workstations run Windows XP Professional. Your DHCP server is configured with the default settings and all of your Windows XP machines are configured as DHCP clients with the default DHCP client settings. You want to use DNS dynamic updates to automatically register the host record and PTR record for all of your workstations. Which of the following must you do to accomplish your goal?

A. None. The default settings are sufficient.

B. Configure the DHCP server to always **Dynamically update DNS and PTR records**.

C. Configure the DHCP server to **Dynamically update DNS and PTR records only if requested by the DHCP clients**.

D. Configure the workstation to use dynamic updates.

6. Your network contains a mix of Windows 2000 and Windows Server 2003. You have three domain controllers running Windows Server 2003. Your file server, print server, and Exchange server are running Windows 2000 Server. Your DNS, DHCP, and WINS servers are running Windows Server 2003. All of your clients are running Windows XP Professional with service pack 1. All machines, other than the servers that require a static IP address, are configured as DHCP clients with the default settings. Your DNS server has been configured to allow dynamic updates. Which of the following records will be registered in DNS automatically? (Choose all that apply.)

A. MX

B. Host

C. SRV

D. PTR

Integrating the Windows Server 2003 DNS Server with WINS

7. You work as a systems administrator in a mixed UNIX/Windows environment. Until now, there has not been a real need for the two operating systems to communicate. The UNIX people operate in their own world and use their own file and print services, and the Windows people operate in their own Windows NT/2003 interim domain world. Your company is small enough that you are able to maintain both environments without too much overhead or doubling of work. Both environments do, however, share the same internal domain name and thus use the same Windows Server 2003 DNS servers for host name resolution. There are two DNS servers that perform zone transfers to stay in sync with one another. The systems team has handed out different preferred DNS servers to the client community as a whole in order to balance the load of network host resolution. On Wednesday afternoon, you are informed by your boss that network drive storage has become a real big issue. He says that based on recent reports he has seen, the duplication of static data is really increasing his backup window and he wants to put a stop to it. He tells you that by next week, he wants all file storage access stored on the Windows NT file server only, and to make sure that all static UNIX data is moved appropriately. You load up Samba on the UNIX file server so that you can access it from the Windows NT file server to copy the data. You also load the Services

for UNIX on the Windows NT server in order to create an NFS share for UNIX compatibility. By Friday of that week, you have copied all the data, and inform all of your UNIX folks that come Monday morning they will need to access the \\WINNTSRV\software share to get to any of their static software data. You set up your company's DNS domain to integrate with your WINS server in order for your DNS-only UNIX clients to be able to resolve WINNT as a host name in DNS. You test it out from one of your UNIX friend's laptops and you are able to successfully access the share. On Monday morning, all users start logging into the network. You don't hear any complaints until before lunch. A few of your UNIX cohorts approach you and tell you that they are unable to access the new Windows/UNIX share. They say they cannot get a successful ping of the name WINNTSRV. You call the friend with whom you originally tested access, and he states that he and three of his coworkers are able to access it, but his office mate is not. What is the problem?

A. You did not check WINS reverse lookup integration.

B. You checked **Do not replicate this record**.

C. You did not check WINS forward lookup integration.

D. You did not check **Do not replicate this record**.

8. You are using WINS Forward Lookup integration in your mixed UNIX/Windows environment to allow your DNS-only UNIX clients to use only their configured Windows Server 2003 DNS server to query and resolve resolution requests for down-level Windows NT 4.0 machines' NetBIOS names. This has been working well for your company for several months. You are informed that over the next several weeks, the Windows NT 4.0 servers are being moved to a different subnet in order to create a separate broadcast domain. They will still continue to register with the same WINS server, but their IP addresses will be changing, and they will no longer be able to be accessed via broadcasts. As these servers start their migration to the new subnet you begin to receive calls only from your UNIX community, complaining that they can no longer access servers that have moved until a day or so later. What can you do to fix the problem for all future migrated servers?

A. Type **nbtstat –RR** on the migrated NT servers.

B. Increase the TTL for WINS forward lookup records.

C. Type **ipconfig /registerdns** on the migrated NT servers.

D. Decrease the TTL for WINS forward lookups records.

Integrating the Windows Server 2003 DNS Server with Internet Publishing

9. Chris works for a ski enthusiast's online purchasing e-store hosting its external Web domain site at skimoreworkless.com. Chris has an internal group of Web designers that publish to this Web site via its www.skimoreworkless.com Internet address. Chris hired a group of network consultants to come in and build a new Windows Server 2003 Active Directory domain environment for their company's internal use. Chris sat down with the consultants to answer a few questions before they got started, one of which was, "What do you want me to call your internal DNS domain name?" That one was easy, Chris thought. He stated that he wanted to keep the internal name the same as the external name: skimoreworkless.com. The consultant asked if he was sure, and Chris said most definitely. Convinced, the consultants got to work that Friday morning, and by closing time, walked out the door leaving Chris with a fully implemented single forest, single domain Active Directory infrastructure using a powerful 4 processor Pentium IV server with 2G of memory. They had installed a second member server that served as a single scope DHCP server handing out the following information:

- Router: 192.1668.0.1
- DNS Server: 192.168.0.10
- Domain name: skimoreworkless.com

The consultants left Chris with the administrator password to the domain and told him that each of the users' logon names consisted of their first name with a blank password that would ask them to change it upon initial logon. The consultant also left instructions for Chris on how to change all his Windows XP laptop machines to use DHCP and how to join them to the domain. After a long weekend of skiing, Chris and crew came in to work early Monday morning to finish setting up their new Windows environment. By lunch time, Chris had successfully joined each of their PCs to the domain and made sure they were all able to log on and change their passwords before going to lunch. After lunch, everyone jumped back into a normal day of business, checking Web server hits, processing orders, and shipping them out. Chuck, a Web site developer, came up to Chris and said he was having trouble publishing to the Web site. At the same time, Chris noticed that he was unable to even get to the Web site. In a panic, they checked with everyone else, only to find the same results. Was the site down? Where they losing business? Chris scurried to find the consultant's number. When he called the consultant, what did he learn?

A. His Web site was actually down.

B. He hadn't published his Web site's A records internally.

C. He hadn't set up his internal DNS forwarders.

D. He hadn't set up a reverse lookup zone.

Integrating the Windows Server 2003 DNS Server with BIND

10. You have been hired as a consultant for CX2 Consulting. Your job is to assist in the migration from Windows NT 4.0 to Windows Server 2003. CX2 Consulting will be implementing Active Directory and Exchange 2003. The company is currently using a Linux DNS server running BIND 4.9.2. CX2 Consulting has given you a few requirements for DNS.

   ■ They want to take advantage of dynamic updates for their Windows 2000 Professional clients.

   ■ They want to continue using the BIND DNS server.

   Which of the following should you do to complete your migration while meeting the company's requirements?

   A. Upgrade the BIND DNS server to BIND version 4.9.3.

   B. Upgrade the BIND DNS server to BIND version 4.9.7.

   C. Upgrade the BIND DBS server to BIND version 8.1.3.

   D. Upgrade the BIND DBS server to BIND version 8.0.2.

11. Tina works for a software support company and has the responsibility for implementing and maintaining all of the DNS servers in her environment. Her network infrastructure is a very mixed hodge-podge of different operating systems, DNS implementations, messaging packages, and so on. Her company needs to keep such a large mix of products up and running at their office because they never know what the calling customers might have at their own company. They want to make sure they can replicate any environment or problem so they can be of better assistance to a wider variety of customers. Tina has just received a call from a customer in Columbia, SC that is trying to set up a DNS zone transfer between their Windows Server 2003 DNS server and a BIND UNIX DNS implementation. The Windows Server 2003 DNS server is set up as a master and the BIND is set up as a secondary. Tina already has this environment set up at work and is ready to tackle the customer's problem. The customer complains that when they try to initiate a zone transfer, it appears to connect and have the correct per-

missions, but then fails every time. Tina tries it on her test setup and everything works fine. Tina thinks about what might be different between the two environments and starts asking the following questions:

- Do you have any zone transfer permissions set up on your Windows Server 2003 server? No. Allow zone transfers to any servers is enabled.

- Have you made any other configuration changes or did you accept all the Windows Server 2003 DNS default? Yes, the defaults.

- Are both the DNS servers on the same network? Yes.

- Any firewalls, IDS systems, or egress filtering going on? No, nothing like that.

What is Tina's last question, and the one that solves the problem?

A. With what version of client are you initiating the zone transfer?

B. What version of BIND are you using?

C. Is your Windows Server 2003 DNS Active Directory Integrated?

D. Are you allowing secure-only dynamic updates?

Monitoring the Windows Server 2003 DNS Server

12. You are a new systems administrator for your company and have been asked to do some monitoring of several key servers in your environment. You use System Monitor to watch the performance of your DNS server and notice a lot of zone transfer traffic coming from your primary DNS server using the **AXFR Success Sent** performance counter. You alert your systems security team and ask them if this is normal. They tell you that you are running in an Active Directory domain with Active Directory DNS. Your company's zone is set to allow dynamic updates and your DHCP server is set to auto update PTR records for your Windows XP and Windows 2000 clients. They tell you that this generates a lot of zone transfers between the 20 domain controllers at the branches, as each branch office is set up locally as a DNS server. You ask if there are any DNS servers outside of the ones on the domain controllers (DC) and you are told that there are not. What should you do immediately?

A. Configure each of the DCs to be able to do zone transfers only with each other.

B. Configure each of the DCs to not allow zone transfers at all.

C. Change the Active Directory Integrated DNS DCs into primaries and configure them to allow only zone transfers from servers on the name server tab.

D. Nothing. Everything is as it should be.

13. You and four other members of your systems team work as DNS administrators for a small Internet Service Provider in Massachusetts. With more and more business coming into your company, you continually have to upgrade your DNS server as you host thousands of authoritative zones for Web sites locally and around the country. For the past week, you have noticed degradation in server performance and you asked one of your other DNS administrators to look into the problem and log what he finds, because you are going to be away for a week. Because you had not heard back, you assumed that everything was fine and that no news was good news. On Tuesday, you come back to work and notice that the DNS server was performing unbelievable sluggishly and you want to know why. You open up System Monitor on the DNS server and load the following counters with the following results:

- Total Query Received/sec: 88
- Total Response Sent/sec: 33
- Recursive Queries/sec: 60
- % Free Space: 2
- % Disk Time: 90
- Pages/sec: 1

What can you do to pick up performance?

A. Turn off debug logging.

B. Turn on debug logging.

C. Add more memory.

D. Add faster Disks.

Troubleshooting the Windows Server 2003 DNS Server

14. Your network consists of four Windows Server 2003 domain controllers, three Windows 2000 member servers, and 50 Windows XP Professional machines. Your users are reporting that they cannot log onto the network. You believe this problem is due to the client machines not being able to resolve names via the DNS server. You want to test and verify that the workstations can talk to the DNS server over the network. Which of the following tools could you use? (Choose all that apply.)

A. Ping

B. Nslookup

C. Nbtstat

D. Netstat

15. Your Web server is running Windows Server 2003 Web Edition. It hosts a Web application that is used by people over the Internet. You log all of your traffic to a log file so that you can see who has been connecting. You look through your log files and see that one IP address has connected and disconnected 3500 times in the last two hours. You are worried that this person might be trying to hack your Web server. You need to find the host computer name that goes along with this IP address. Which of the following tools could you use? (Choose all that apply.)

    A. Ping

    B. Nslookup

    C. Netdiag

    D. Netstat

Self Test Quick Answer Key

For complete questions, answers, and explanations to the Self Test questions in this chapter as well as the other chapters in this book, see the Self Test Appendix.

1.	**C**	9.	**B**
2.	**C**	10.	**C**
3.	**C**	11.	**B**
4.	**C**	12.	**B**
5.	**A**	13.	**A**
6.	**B, C, D**	14.	**A, B**
7.	**B**	15.	**A, B**
8.	**D**		

Chapter 7

MCSA/MCSE 70-291

Configuring the Windows Server 2003 Routing and Remote Access Service VPN Services

Exam Objectives in this Chapter:

4.1   Configure Routing and Remote Access user authentication.

4.1.1   Configure remote access authentication protocols.

4.5.1   Diagnose and resolve issues related to remote access VPNs.

4.6.2   Troubleshoot router-to-router VPNs.

     ☑   Summary of Exam Objectives

     ☑   Exam Objectives Fast Track

     ☑   Exam Objectives Frequently Asked Questions

     ☑   Self Test

     ☑   Self Test Quick Answer Key

569

Introduction

In the previous chapter, we discussed the Domain Naming System (DNS) for Windows Server 2003. The public incarnation of DNS relies on the interconnectivity of several different network infrastructures. These networks are brought together through various routing protocols to facilitate the vast global IP network that is known as the Internet.

Traditionally, WAN connections were provided via private data connections (such as a point-to-point dedicated leased line) or via dial-up connections using conventional modems. A private connection belonged only to the offices it connected and was not shared among various companies through the service provider's network. The conventional dial-up connection was provided via a modem on the user's computer and a modem bank or modem card at the access server.

In the last five years, many companies have expanded, from unconnected systems to LANs, and then to WANs utilizing the Internet for interoffice connectivity. As the low price and increasing availability of broadband services continues to bring high-speed Internet connectivity to more offices and homes at a blistering pace, the need for secure connectivity and interconnectivity has led to many different types of office, small office, and home routers. A technology has emerged that provides for the secure transfer of private data and a newer style of dial-up connections between these remote networks, utilizing the Internet as the transport mechanism. This technology provides for a private network in a virtual sense, hence the term Virtual Private Network (VPN).

In this chapter, we will examine how Windows Server 2003 provides a network infrastructure for interconnecting local and remote systems and networks through the Routing and Remote Access service (RRAS). The Windows Server 2003 Routing and Remote Access service provides interconnectivity for remote users and remote offices through two different configuration options. We will take a detailed look at the VPN options for Windows Server 2003 Routing and Remote Access service in this chapter, along with the numerous authentication protocols used by these VPN technologies.

Review of Windows Server 2003 Remote Access Concepts

A VPN is an extension of a private network that utilizes links through shared or public networks. VPN technology is built on extensions to the point-to-point (PPP) protocol. PPP encapsulates upper layer network traffic to carry it through media that typically could not carry this encapsulated traffic. Think of this is a method for packaging data before transporting it to another location. Data is packed, or encapsulated, on one end of the link and it is unpacked on the other end. This transport mechanism relies on special tunneling protocols to handle the data encapsulation. VPNs provide a relatively inexpensive, secure mechanism for transporting remote data.

One scenario where a VPN is useful involves a user in Tokyo requiring secure access to a shared folder on a server in Atlanta. VPN provides access to the folder using nothing more than an Internet connection at each end. Traditionally, a remote user would connect from Tokyo to Atlanta over a long-haul T-carrier line (a T-1 for example) or through a lower bandwidth option like an analog dial-up connection. The cost of a VPN in this case, compared to a long-haul T-1 or analog international long-distance connection, is minimal. The Tokyo portion of the VPN relies on inexpensive Internet access. The Atlanta portion of the connection is more costly, relying on a dedicated Internet connection. Let's look at a couple of scenarios where VPN technology would provide a nearly ideal solution.

The sales force to your corporation spends 80 percent of their time on the road. They travel all over the country, or all over the world meeting with customers. The sales employees need access to real-time production data to accurately inform customers of delivery schedules or product updates. Each salesperson needs secure access to corporate information. Each salesperson carries a laptop computer with a modem and a network card installed. Typically, your sales force stays in hotels that provide either an analog phone line to connect to the Internet, or in some cases, high-speed broadband access. In this scenario, a dedicated VPN server would provide your sales employees with secure access to your corporate data through the Internet connections that are readily available to them on the road. Again, compare this to the cost of long distance for each of the sales representatives that are on the road. The corporate office will incur the expense of a dedicated Internet connection, and the sales reps will utilize either dial-up connections to the Internet or broadband Internet connectivity provided by the hotels where they stay. This scenario provides secure connectivity while reducing long distance expenses.

Many corporations today are downsizing or, when possible, outsourcing certain staff members. With this downsizing and outsourcing, corporations are working hard to minimize the use of office space. Home-based employees are handling more and more of the corporate workload. Although home-based employees may not need office space to conduct their day-to-day duties, they typically need access to corporate information. The availability of broadband Internet access continues to increase while its cost continues to remain the same or, in many cases, to decrease. A dedicated corporate VPN server could provide relatively high-speed secure access to corporate data for the home-based broadband users at a fraction of the cost of dial-up connections or dedicated T-carrier private lines. Again, while providing this secure connection, you are typically saving money as well.

Another common scenario where VPN connectivity is useful involves remote office connectivity. Imagine a corporate office with several remote satellite offices requiring access to resources within the corporate office. Router-to-router VPNs could be configured for each remote office, connecting the remote offices to the corporate office. Again, the requirement for the corporate office is a dedicated Internet connection. The remote offices may connect to the Internet using a dedicated connection or through some form of dial-on-demand. In either case, connectivity through the VPN is typically less expensive than either a long-haul T-carrier line (T-1) or a persistent dial-up connection where long distance expenses and line costs will be incurred.

In our examples, compare the cost of a local Internet connection for each location with the cost of a persistent dial-up connection where long distance rates or international long distance rates would be assessed. Again, compare the cost of a local Internet connection on each end with a long-haul T-1 between the locations, where cost is assessed based on bandwidth and distance. VPNs are becoming prevalent because of their bang for the buck. You can achieve nearly equivalent performance to a long haul connection, while incurring only the cost of a local Internet connection on each end.

VPN connectivity works on a concept similar to the traditional analog dial-up connection. In an analog dial-up connection, upper layer traffic is wrapped or encapsulated by a special lower layer protocol. In the case of a VPN connection, we are talking about internal network traffic, usually Transport Control Protocol/Internet Protocol (TCP/IP), being encapsulated in external network packets. This encapsulation process is known as *tunneling*. Figure 7.1 illustrates the process of tunneling.

Figure 7.1 Tunneling TCP/IP Traffic through a TCP/IP Network

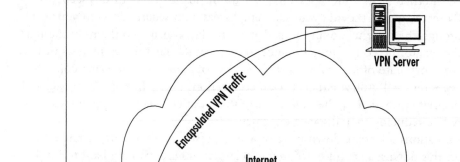

It is important to note here that the server in this model must always be available on the Internet. It is also important to understand each component in use in this model. To provide a VPN, traffic is tunneled between the two systems. This tunneling does not necessarily provide security or privacy. The encapsulation process merely provides a way to transport traffic through a connection that normally could not provide such a transport.

So we have provided for connectivity through the use of a tunnel, but how is this private? The encapsulation of data does not necessarily ensure privacy. To protect the data from eavesdroppers, it has to be encrypted. Encryption is the process of manipulating information through the use of mathematical formulas or algorithms to make the information unreadable or unusable to eavesdroppers. The scrambled information can be unscrambled only by using the proper mathematical formula to undo the encryption. There are several mechanisms available to provide encryption. We commonly use passwords to gain access to resources on computer networks. The password may be used as a component of the algorithm to encrypt the message. The recipient must have a way of unencrypting the information as well. One simple scheme for encryption using passwords involves preshared keys. Each end of the encryption channel needs to know the password to be used in order to encrypt and unencrypt the data in this scheme. The encrypted data, or hash, is considered symmetric, or two-way, in this scenario because the same process used to encrypt the data is used in reverse to unencrypt, in much the same way that Morse code is used to transmit telegraph information. The same algorithm is being used at each end.

Public Key Infrastructure (PKI) is an asymmetric encryption process where each endpoint uses its own key in conjunction with a publicly available key.

The Windows Server 2003 Routing and Remote Access service management console (the RRAS MMC) is the graphic interface for performing server-side network configurations. The RRAS MMC provides the following options:

- Remote access (dial-up or VPN)
- Network address translation (NAT)
- Virtual Private Network (VPN) access and NAT
- Secure connection between two private networks
- Custom configuration
- Routing protocol configuration
- DHCP Relay configuration
- Remote access policy configuration
- Remote access logging

Our primary focus throughout this chapter will be on the various aspects of Windows Server 2003 VPN configuration. We will examine the VPN authentication process, the two tunneling protocols used to carry VPN traffic in Windows Server 2003 (and their related encryption protocols), and the authentication and encryption processes. We will also discuss the function of the Point to Point Protocol (PPP) and its bearing on VPN authentication, encapsulation, and encryption techniques.

Keep in mind that the Remote Access Service for Windows Server 2003 is used to provide clients with remote access—not remote control of the server. This means that files, printers, and other resources are available to client computers. From the perspective of a remote access client, internal network resources appear to be available to the remote access user in the same fashion that they are available to any on-site system that is attached to the

LAN. Thus, for example, a remote user can open a document file that is stored on a server on the company LAN, if the user has an application on his or her own system that will open the document format.

Remote control, on the other hand, provides a desktop to the user remotely. In this scenario, a server is generating the desktop, providing the CPU clock cycles to run the applications, and controlling the user's interaction with the system resources. The user can use any applications that are installed on the server (as long as the user has the correct permissions to do so). Microsoft uses Windows Server 2003's Remote Desktop for Administration (RDA) feature and Terminal Services to provide remote control capabilities (for more information about using configuring and using Windows Server 2003's terminal services, see Chapter 6, "Managing and Troubleshooting Terminal Services" of the *MCSA/MCSE Exam 70-290 Study Guide: Managing and Maintaining a Microsoft Windows Server 2003 Environment* (Syngress Publishing, ISBN: 1-932266-60-7). Because remote control means running the application on the remote control server, remote control servers tend to be more resource-intensive than remote access servers, because the remote access server is providing a network connection or transport mechanism only for the remote users.

There are two different types of VPNs used today. The first type, as discussed in this chapter, is a software-based VPN. This system operates as a component to the operating system on a server. It is considered software-based because programs or programming modules handle all of the VPN functionality. In contrast, hardware-based VPNs provide the same functionality as a software-based VPN by utilizing specialized hardware designed strictly for the purpose of VPN traffic management. A VPN appliance, the typical reference to a hardware-based VPN, operates for the sole purpose of providing VPN connectivity. In this way, a hardware-based VPN oftentimes provides greater reliability and security because of its single-purpose nature. Because a software-based VPN is often expected to provide other network services like routing, file sharing, printer sharing, authentication, name resolution, and so on, the software-based VPN typically relies on more system resources per user than a hardware-based VPN. Although VPNs do not truly rely on physical links in the same way that a dedicated private-line does, the virtual nature of VPNs places a greater reliance on system resources. Each virtual link provided by a VPN relies on system memory, processor cycles, and network bandwidth in much the same way that multiple physical links rely on those very same resources.

Finally, note the difference between layer-two and layer-three VPN technologies. Cisco introduces Layer-2 Forwarding *L2F* as an Open Systems Interconnect *OSI* layer-two answer to VPN encapsulation requirements. L2F provides an OSI layer-two solution to VPN encapsulation in much the same way that PPP provides layer-two encapsulation for dial-up connections. Layer-two VPN technology does not rely on IP connectivity to provide a transport mechanism. This is beneficial where ATM, Frame-Relay, or other technologies may be implemented as a WAN transport medium. Microsoft Windows Server 2003 provides layer-two VPN connectivity through the Layer Two Tunneling Protocol *L2TP*. Other layer-two technologies include L2F as mentioned previously, and Multiprotocol Label Switching *MPLS*. While both PPTP and L2TP are layer-two Protocols, IPSEC is a layer-three protocol. We will compare and contrast PPTP and L2TP later in this chapter.

In the next section, we will explore the Windows Server 2003 Remote Access Service in greater detail. We will also walk through the steps required to enable the remote access service on a Windows Server 2003 Server.

TEST DAY TIP

Virtual private networking is a complex subject, and because the Microsoft 70-291 exam is skills-based, it is essential that you not only understand the concepts, but that you also get plenty of hands-on practice in deploying VPNs. The exams are focused on networking in the enterprise environment, so it is important that you be able to simulate that environment for your studies. We recommend that you reference the TechNet article *Step-by-Step Guide for Setting up VPN-based Remote Access in a Test Lab,* which describes how to use five computers in a test lab to simulate an Internet and private Internet (see http://www.microsoft.com/technet/treeview/default.asp?url=/technet/prodtechnol/windowsserver2003/deploy/confeat/RmoteVPN.asp). It is not always necessary to have multiple physical computers to emulate a multicomputer environment. You can use VMWare (www.vmware.com) or Connectix Virtual PC (www.connectix.com) to run multiple computers in virtual machines.

Enabling the Windows Server 2003 Remote Access Service

Like many of the features in Windows Server 2003, the Remote Access Service is enabled through a wizard. Normally, the purpose of a VPN connection is to allow secure access to a LAN from a remote location. Secure, remote access to a LAN implies two connections (network interfaces) on the server. This requirement exists because of the nature of a VPN server. A VPN server provides access to LAN-based resources from a remote location. One interface is required to make the connection to the medium shared for the remote users (usually a WAN interface), and another interface is required to connect to the LAN.

NOTE

Be aware that, if the system on which you want to enable RAS is a member of an Active Directory domain, the procedure requires that you log on with an account that is a member of either an administrator group (Enterprise Administrators or Domain Administrators) or the RAS and IAS security group. If the system uses local authentication or a RADIUS server, membership in the local administrator security group is sufficient.

The Routing and Remote Access Server Setup Wizard will allow you to configure the Custom configuration option only if your system has a single network interface. Configuring a single interface VPN server is not recommended for a production environment, as mentioned earlier. The only reasons for this type of configuration would be to provide remote access to resources hosted on the server itself (like a terminal server for example) or for lab testing purposes.

In the following exercise, we will walk through the initial configuration steps for the Windows Server 2003 Routing and Remote Access Service. The following configuration should work on any system that has a network connection. As noted previously, the majority of the configuration options covered in this chapter will require a minimum of two network connections. Two other methods exist for enabling the Routing and Remote Access service. One method utilizes the Manage Your Server wizard and the other method relies on the Configure Your Server wizard.

To enable Routing and Remote Access with the Manage Your Server wizard:

1. Click **Start | Manage Your Server** as shown in Figure 7.2.

Figure 7.2 Initiating the Manage Your Server Wizard

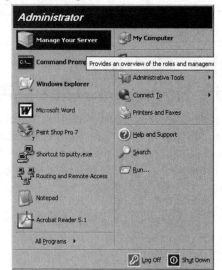

2. From the **Manage Your Server** main screen, select **Add or remove a role** as shown in Figure 7.3.

Figure 7.3 Adding a Role to Your Server

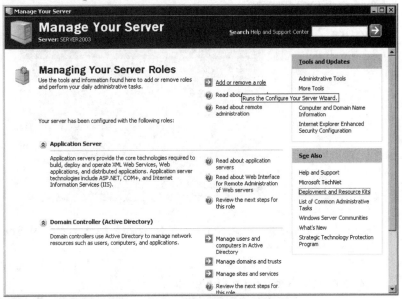

3. From the **Preliminary Steps** screen of the **Configure Your Server** wizard, select **Next** as shown in Figure 7.4.

Figure 7.4 The Preliminary Steps Screen

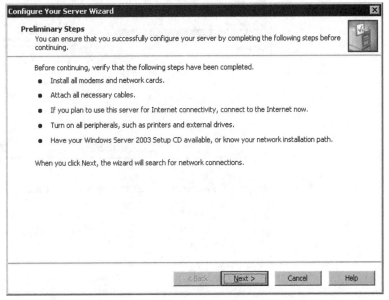

4. An animated pop-up will be displayed as information about your server is gathered, as shown in Figure 7.5.

Figure 7.5 Gathering Server Information

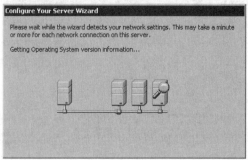

5. From the **Server Role** screen, select **Remote Access/VPN Server** as shown in Figure 7.6 then select **Next**.

Figure 7.6 Selecting a Server Role

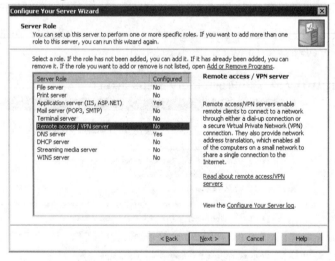

6. From the **Summary of Selections** screen as shown in Figure 7.7 select **Next**.

Figure 7.7 Summary of Selections Screen

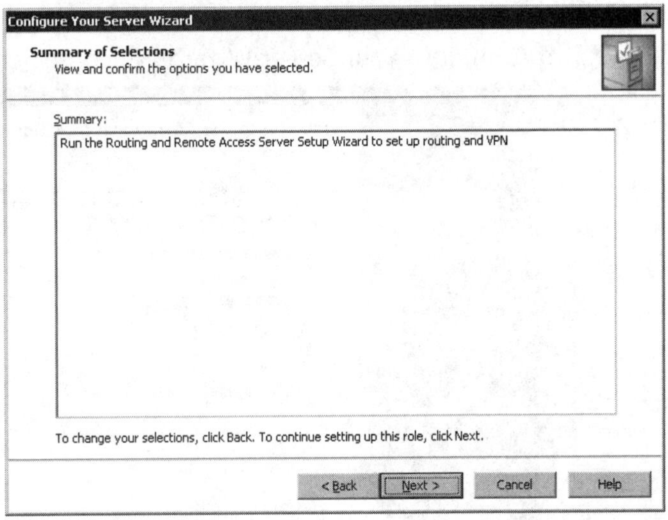

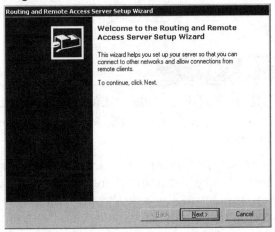

7. From the **Welcome to the Routing and Remote Access Server Setup Wizard** screen, select **Next** as shown in Figure 7.8.

Figure 7.8 Routing and Remote Access Welcome Screen

8. Continue the setup by following the steps listed in Exercise 7.01, beginning with step 5.

To use the **Configure Your Server** wizard to enable the Routing and Remote Access service:

1. Click **Start | Administrative Tools | Configure Your Server Wizard**.

2. From the **Welcome to the Configure Your Server Wizard** screen, select **Next** as shown in Figure 7.9.

Figure 7.9 Configure Your Server Wizard Welcome Screen

3. From the **Preliminary Steps** screen of the **Configure Your Server wizard**, select **Next** as shown previously in Figure 7.9.

4. Continue with step 4 in the previous section.

EXERCISE 7.01

ENABLING THE ROUTING AND REMOTE ACCESS SERVICE

This exercise will introduce you to the Routing and Remote Access Configuration Wizard.

1. Click **Start | Programs | Administrative Tools | Routing and Remote Access**. Initially, the Routing and Remote Access Service should be disabled, as indicated by a downward-pointing red arrow on the icon representing the local server. You'll see a "Welcome to Routing and Remote Access" message in the right console pane.

2. To start the Routing and Remote Access Server Setup Wizard, from the Routing and Remote Access management console, first select the icon for the local server name in the left pane, then select **Action | Configure and Enable Routing and Remote Access** as shown in Figure 7.10, or right-click the icon for the local server and select **Configure and Enable Routing and Remote Access** from the context menu.

Figure 7.10 Initiating the Routing and Remote Access Server
Setup Wizard

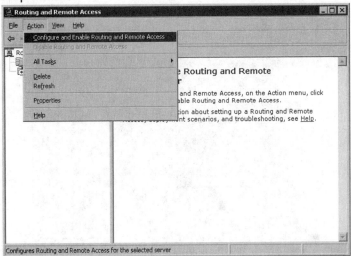

3. The Welcome page of the **Routing and Remote Access Server Setup Wizard** screen is displayed. Select **Next** to display the **Routing and Remote Access Server Setup Wizard Configuration** screen.

4. Select **Custom configuration** as shown in Figure 7.11 and click **Next**.

Figure 7.11 Routing and Remote Access Server Setup Wizard
Configuration Screen

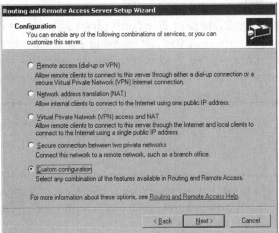

5. From the **Routing and Remote Access Server Setup Wizard Custom Configuration** screen, select **VPN Access** and then click **Next**, as shown in Figure 7.12.

Figure 7.12 Routing and Remote Access Server Setup Wizard Custom Configuration Screen

6. On the **Completing the Routing and Remote Access Server Setup Wizard** screen, review the summary of your selections, which should read **VPN access**. Click **Back** if you need to make changes. Click **Finish** to complete the initial configuration and enable the Routing and Remote Access Service.

7. A message box will be displayed to inform you that the Routing and Remote Access service has been installed, and asking if you want to start the service. Click **Yes**.

8. When the service is properly configured and started, the downward-pointing red arrow in the left console pane will change to an upward-pointing green arrow, and when you expand the server node, several new items will be listed below the server in the console tree.

NOTE

If you later want to disable remote access services on this server, right-click the server name in the left pane of the RRAS MMC, and on the **General** tab, uncheck the **Remote access server** checkbox.

Configuring & Implementing...

Tightening Security for Administrative Tasks

Many security exploits take advantage of elevated permissions, and any time an administrative account is logged on, a security vulnerability is created. If you are in the habit of logging on with an administrator account to do all of your day-to-day tasks, you should consider using the **Run As** command to elevate your user account permissions on an as-needed basis instead of always using your administrator account for nonadministrative tasks.

Run as, also called *secondary logon,* is a useful tool that was introduced with Windows 2000, and allows a user to run a specified program with permissions that are different from those belonging to the account with which the user is currently logged on.

To use the **Run as** command, in Windows Explorer or in the **Programs** menu or **Control Panel**, right-click the program that you want to run with your administrative permissions. From the **context** menu, select **Run As**. This will invoke the **Run as** dialog box. From the **Run as** dialog box, select **The following user** button and authenticate with your administrator account username and password. This method of administration will prevent inadvertent installation and deletion of applications and files due to unnecessarily escalated permissions.

The **Run as** selection will appear in the context menu only if the file you right-click is an executable (including .msc files, which are management consoles), or if you right-click an icon (in the **Start** menu, on the desktop, etc.) that is a shortcut to an executable. The **Printers** folder and desktop items such as **My Computer** and **My Network Places** cannot be started with the **Run as** function.

The **Run as** command can also be run from the command line, in which case there are a number of switches that can be used with it to specify whether to load the user's profile, whether to use the current network environment instead of the user's local environment, whether credentials are to be provided via a smart card, and the trust level at which the application is to be run.

The secondary logon service must be running in order for you to use **Run as.** If you are unable to use the command, check the status of the service by right-clicking **My Computer,** selecting **Manage| Services and Applications | Services** and ensuring that the status is **Started** and Startup Type is **Automatic.** If the service is stopped, you can right-click it and select **Start.**

TEST DAY TIP

You should run through the Configuration Wizard enough times to be sure that you know the details of the next screen before that screen is displayed.

Configuring the Windows Server 2003 VPN Server

Now that you have a grasp of the basics, it is time to look at the Windows Server 2003 configuration options in greater detail. In this section, we will focus on various aspects of VPN server configuration, including the following topics:

- The details of address management, and how VPN connectivity affects our address pool

- The world of PPP authentication, the myriad of PPP authentication protocols, and how they affect VPN configuration

- Choices of VPN protocols, detailing the advantages and disadvantages of each

When configuring a Windows Server 2003 VPN server, we need to consider the operating system in use by our client systems. In today's security-conscious business environment, you should generally use the strongest authentication method possible and provide the best encryption for tunneled traffic. Client operating systems usually dictate the type of authentication that can be used as well as the available encapsulation and encryption capabilities.

Server hardware places limitations on the number of clients that can connect simultaneously. For example, each VPN connection consumes about 40KB of RAM. As a rule of thumb, for 1,000 concurrent connections, 512 MB of RAM on the server is adequate. For every additional 1,000 connections, you should add 256 MB of RAM. Another factor affecting configuration is the existing network infrastructure and placement of VPN servers.

Supporting Network Infrastructure

There are several components that are required in order to establish a VPN connection and others that are desirable, or may be required in certain circumstances:

- VPN Services enabled on the server and VPN client software installed on the client

- Client and server must be connected to the same network (underlying network connection)

- Proper VPN server placement

- A certificate infrastructure or Public Key Infrastructure (PKI)

- A centralized accounting mechanism

- Common authentication and encryption methods on client and server

- Common tunneling protocols on client and server

VPN services must be enabled on the server to facilitate VPN connectivity. Also, VPN clients are required to have VPN software installed. Microsoft VPN software is prepackaged with the operating system. Network connectivity between the VPN client and VPN server also is required.

Depending on the VPN encapsulation protocol used, the VPN server may have to be placed on a publicly accessible network. If the VPN server is placed on a private network and clients will have to gain access from a public network, your NAT or firewall will have to be configured to accommodate the VPN clients' connection requests.
If you are using L2TP with IPSec, and you are not using preshared keys, a certificate infrastructure is required. In an effort to simplify administration, it is recommended that you implement a centralized accounting mechanism like RADIUS.

The VPN client and VPN server are required to use the same authentication protocol, the same encryption method and strength, as well as the same tunneling protocols.

We have already discussed how to enable VPN services on the server, and modern Microsoft client operating systems come with built-in VPN client software. In the following sections, we will discuss some of the other components.

Underlying Network Connection

The first, and fundamental requirement for a VPN connection is an underlying network connection (usually the Internet). Although VPNs are commonly associated with tunneling across the Internet, VPN connectivity is not limited to Internet connectivity for the base connection. A VPN connection may utilize a layer-two technology like Frame Relay or ATM for an underlying connection. There are scenarios where the security and privacy of a VPN connection may be beneficial on an internal network as well. Typically, a VPN would be used on an internal network to protect traffic as it traverses the network. Maybe a specialized financial application is used on your network or users in one office may need access to resources containing confidential information. A VPN in this scenario would ensure secure, private transmission of this data.

Again, the fundamental premise here is basic network connectivity between endpoints. Typically, the endpoints are either two VPN servers, or a VPN client and a VPN server. There are also router-to-router VPNs (also called gateway to gateway) that connect two LANs (for example, two branch offices). The endpoints of the VPN connection typically dictate which remote access protocols can be used.

VPN Server Placement

Another important consideration in VPN connectivity is server placement. It is often more beneficial to have a VPN server protected by a firewall, as opposed to placing the VPN server outside of the firewall with direct Internet connectivity available to the VPN server. Again, VPN client operating systems can affect this decision. Because VPN client operating systems will usually dictate the authentication protocols and encryption methods used, this in turn will affect the proper placement of the VPN servers.

If your network currently relies on a firewall for protected access, you would likely place the VPN server behind this firewall to minimize the vulnerability of your network due to the addition of the VPN server. If your firewall is not capable of handling the packet load or the firewall is not capable of passing the encrypted headers created by IPSec encrypted traffic, you may have to place the VPN server outside of the firewall or parallel to the firewall. Again, because of the nature of software-based firewalls, this introduces potential vulnerabilities to your network based on the security of the underlying operating system and system configuration.

A firewall or NAT system may not be able to pass IPSec traffic because of the process IPSec uses for securing network data. IPSec encrypts not only the data maintained in the body of the packet but also the packet header. NAT and firewall rules both typically operate based on information contained in the header. If the header is encrypted, NAT will not be able to translate the network traffic because it cannot determine source and destination ports and addresses. Likewise, firewall rules may not function with IPSec for the same reasons.

Certificate Infrastructure

Another factor to take into account when configuring a VPN server is the presence or absence of a certificate infrastructure. Certain protocols require the availability of a certificate infrastructure. We will look at VPN protocols later in this chapter, and discuss the influence of client operating systems and certificate infrastructure on selecting the right protocols for your situation.

A certificate is an electronic key used to encrypt or decrypt data. This certificate or key is a mix of upper- and lowercase alphanumeric characters. The combination of characters helps to provide uniqueness for the certificate. Generally, the longer the certificate (the greater the number of characters) the better the security provided. Currently, the more common certificate lengths are 40-bit, 56-bit, 128-bit, and 168-bit. There are five ways that a certificate would normally be used:

- Symmetric-key encryption: One key
- Public-key encryption: Two keys
- One-way hash algorithms
- Digital signature: Combine public key with hash
- Key exchange: Combine symmetric key with public key

Symmetric-key encryption involves the sharing of a single key. This key could be a password or a certificate. Public-key encryption uses two keys—a public key and a private key. The user's private key encrypts data and the public key decrypts the data. Likewise, data sent to the user uses the public key to encrypt the data and the private key to decrypt.

One-way hash algorithms use a mathematical function to generate a key that is not supposed to be decrypted. Typically, the algorithm is used to encrypt traffic that should be known by both parties, like a password used for authentication. The hashed value is created first by the user attempting to authenticate, then when the authentication machine receives the hash, a hash is also created using the stored password. If the hashes match, the password is correct. If the hashes do not match, the password is incorrect.

Digital signatures use a public key in conjunction with the data that is transmitted to create a special tag. This tag binds the user's identity to the data that was transmitted. This process ensures data integrity while providing identity verification for the sender.

Key exchange is the process of exchanging symmetric keys through a public key encryption mechanism. Public key encryption is a slow encryption mechanism; however, it provides relatively strong security. Using public key encryption as a mechanism for sharing the symmetric encryption key provides a method for securing the weakest part of symmetric keys—the key exchange.

A Public Key Infrastructure (PKI) is the subset of systems needed to provide public key encryption. This infrastructure provides a certificate enrollment, verification, and revocation system.

NOTE

Encryption strength and standards are greatly affected by the current capabilities of computer systems. The Data Encryption Standard (DES) was once believed to take thousands of years to decrypt using computers slightly better than modern computers of the time. Today, an array of computers has broken DES for an RSA challenge (www.rsa.com) in less than one day's time (22 hours). This reflects the effects of computing power on encryption.

Centralized Accounting

If we are deploying a fairly large remote access network, it may be beneficial to centralize the accounting functions. Windows Server 2003 provides for centralized account management of remote access users and devices through the Internet Authentication Service (IAS). IAS is Microsoft's implementation of Remote Authentication Dial-in User Service (RADIUS). RADIUS is an industry-standard centralized logon service for remote access networks. Microsoft IAS provides logon capabilities for Microsoft and (through RADIUS) non-Microsoft clients and devices.

IAS/RADIUS is not installed by default. From the control panel, IAS has to be installed as an additional Windows component. Do this by going to **Start | Control Panel | Add Remove Programs | Add Remove Windows Components | Networking Services | Internet Authentication Service**. Once installed, IAS is administered from the Administrative Tools menu.

TEST DAY TIP

The concept of client-server VPN versus server-server VPN is an important topic. Remember that a client dialing in to a VPN server is a voluntary tunnel. You should have a good understanding of what this means from a network infrastructure and IP address assignment perspective. The compulsory tunnel is created between two VPN gateways or servers. The compulsory tunnel should be transparent to the clients.

PPP Authentication Process and Protocols

Authentication is the process of verifying an identity. This verification could be for a user, a computer, or both. After a user has been authenticated, we can control access to resources and maintain information about logon and access rights used. Authentication is the first line of defense when securing a network. The Point-to-Point protocol (PPP) provides encapsulation capabilities for higher layer protocols like TCP/IP and IPX/SPX as well as multilink and authentication capabilities. In this section, we will look at the four phases of PPP negotiation with an emphasis on the PPP authentication protocols.

The PPP Authentication Process

The Point-to-Point Protocol (PPP) uses four phases of negotiation to establish a connection. The four phases of negotiation are:

1. PPP Link Establishment
2. User Authentication
3. PPP Callback Control
4. Invocation of Network Layer Protocol

During phase one, authentication protocols are negotiated. Also, the agreement between the client and server to use compression and encryption also occurs during phase one. Phase one does not involve the implementation of the authentication protocols that are selected, nor does it involve the selection of compression or encryption algorithms. The decision to use authentication and the type of authentication to use is negotiated, and the agreement to use compression and/or encryption completes the steps processed in phase one.

Phase two of the PPP negotiations involves authentication protocol implementation. The sole focus of phase two is the implementation of the authentication protocol selected in phase one. Windows Server 2003 Routing and Remote Access supports five different protocols for PPP authentication. We will discuss each of these protocols in more detail in the next section. Phase two of PPP negotiations involves collection of authentication data and comparison, either locally or remotely, of the data against stored authentication information.

Phase three handles PPP Callback Control. When used, this phase provides additional security by requiring the remote access server to call the client back at a specific number. This is a dial-up feature that is not used in VPN connections.

Phase four invokes the upper layer network control protocols. Typically, TCP/IP upper layer connectivity is provided through the Internet Protocol Control Protocol (IPCP). Also, Microsoft compression and encryption features are implemented during phase four of the PPP negotiations.

NOTE

IPCP is an Internet standard that is defined in RFCs 1332 and 3241. For more information about the function of this protocol, see http://rfc.sunsite.dk/rfc/rfc1332.html.

PPP Authentication Protocols

The five protocols supported by Windows Server 2003 for PPP authentication are:

- Password Authentication Protocol (PAP)

- Challenge Handshake Authentication Protocol (CHAP)

- Microsoft Challenge Handshake Authentication Protocol (MS-CHAP)

- MS-CHAP version 2 (MS-CHAP v2)

- Extensible Authentication Protocol (EAP)

In the following sections, we will take a closer look at each of the authentication protocols that can be implemented at phase two of the PPP negotiation stages.

Password Authentication Protocol (PAP)

PAP authentication is a basic, clear-text authentication scheme. During PAP authentication, the access server requests the username and password from the inbound connection. In response to the authentication request, the station sends the username and password in plain, unencrypted, clear-text.

This creates an obvious security issue. There are numerous programs that are readily available and can read TCP streams, allowing for extraction of clear-text information. Any savvy hacker can use a network sniffer to capture the user credentials and then use them for malevolent purposes. Consequently, PAP is not a preferred method of authentication because of the lack of password encryption or obfuscation. Additionally, you cannot use Microsoft Point-to-Point Encryption (MPPE), the standard protocol used for encryption in conjunction with the PPTP tunneling protocol, with PAP authentication.

However, in some cases, with client operating systems that don't support any other type of authentication, it may be necessary to use PAP for compatibility purposes. PAP should be used only as a last resort, especially for VPN connections.

Disabling PAP on the RAS Server

It is considered best practice to disable clear-text protocols like PAP. Although PAP is disabled by default, it is a good idea to verify this setting on your RRAS server. In this section, we will see how to verify which authentication protocols are supported by the server:

1. From the **Start** button, select **Administrative Tools | Routing and Remote Access**.

2. From the **Routing and Remote Access** management console, right-click the server name and select **Properties**.

3. From the **Properties** window, select the **Security** tab as shown in Figure 7.13.

Figure 7.13 Selecting Security from the RRAS Properties Window

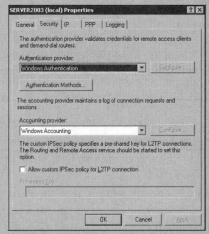

4. Select the **Authentication Methods...** button, as shown in Figure 7.13.

5. Ensure that PAP is not selected, as shown in Figure 7.14.

Figure 7.14 RRAS Authentication Methods

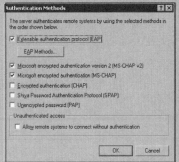

Shiva Password Authentication Protocol (SPAP)

SPAP authentication is a variation of PAP. It is slightly more secure than PAP but provides less security than CHAP authentication. It was developed for use by Shiva and is a proprietary authentication protocol, and is used for connecting to devices made by Shiva such as the LanRover. In Windows Server 2003, it would be used if you have Shiva clients that need to connect to the remote access server. It is also sometimes used when Windows 9x clients are connecting via a NetWare account.

SPAP authentication provides a reversible encrypted password, while offering an exchange of credentials and authorization similar to PAP authentication. When a user attempts to log on, the remote access server issues a challenge. In response to the challenge, the client provides the username and encrypted password. The server decrypts the password and checks it, along with the username, against its database. The server replies with either an acknowledgement (Authenticate-ACK) or a negative acknowledgement (Authenticate-NAK).

TEST DAY TIP

For the exam, ensure that you understand the ramifications of clear-text password usage. There are several packet capture programs or packet sniffers (also called protocol analyzers or network analyzers) available on the Internet. Download Ethereal or one of the other available packet capture programs, or use the Network Monitor built into Windows Server 2003, and capture your logon while using PAP authentication. This will give you a much greater appreciation and understanding of the problems with clear-text authentication.

Challenge Handshake Authentication Protocol (CHAP)

CHAP authentication is a more secure method of authentication than PAP or SPAP, because the password itself is not transmitted over the link. The remote access server passes a challenge to the client. This challenge consists of a challenge string and a session ID. The client uses a one-way Message Digest version 5 (MD5) hashing algorithm to send a hash of the password, along with the session identifier and username. As mentioned previously, the actual password is not sent during this authentication process. Instead, the password is used to create a hash value from the original challenge that was sent by the remote access server. The remote access server is also capable of creating this hash value because the remote access server knows the password and the challenge that were sent to the remote client. The remote access server will grant or deny access to the remote client based on a comparison of the hash values. The remote access server repeatedly sends challenges to the remote client during the connection. This process helps to prevent client impersonation. One disadvantage of CHAP is that the username is passed in clear-text format.

You would use CHAP instead of MS-CHAP for interoperability reasons. If your client or VPN server does not support MS-CHAP due to its proprietary nature, you may have to use the open-standard CHAP protocol. It is not uncommon today to find non-Microsoft VPN clients and servers that support MS-CHAP, however.

Understanding the Hashing Process

Hashing, or encrypting, is the process used to obfuscate or conceal data. Hashing exists as one-way hash values and two-way hash values. A one-way hash is encrypted using an algorithm or mathematical formula in such a way that it is considered impossible to decrypt. Two-way hash values are encrypted at one end of the transaction and decrypted at the other end of the transaction using either the same encryption key or through a special publicly available encryption key. The process involving public and private keys is known collectively as public key encryption. This is the process supported by PKI, as discussed earlier in this chapter.

Using one-way hashing, a user may be authenticated without actually passing the password across the network link. Since the user should know the correct password and the authentication server should also have the same password maintained in its security database, the user passes a one-way hash of the password to the authentication server. The authentication server will use the stored password to create a hash value using the same algorithm. The hashes are compared and the user is either granted access or denied access depending on the result from comparing the two hashed values.

Two-way hashing usually involves a public and a private key, although it is also possible to use a preshared key or symmetric hash as well. In the PKI example, the private key uses an algorithm that may be decrypted by the public key. Likewise, the public key transmits data that can be encrypted only by the private key that matches up to the public key.

Common hashing algorithms include the Digital Encryption Standard (DES), Advanced Encryption Standard (AES), and Message Digest 5 (MD5) to name a few.

Microsoft Challenge Handshake Authentication Protocol (MS-CHAP)

MS-CHAP authentication is another form of authentication that does not transmit the actual password over the link. MS-CHAP is Microsoft's implementation of CHAP, with a few improvements. For example, MS-CHAP has provisions built into the protocol to allow the remote access server to store passwords in a hashed format, instead of in the typical clear-text password store that is used by CHAP.

Initially, the remote access server sends a challenge to the client in the same fashion as CHAP. In return, the remote client must reply with the username, the challenge string in an encrypted form, an MD4 hash of the password, and the session identifier. In addition to the ability to store the password on the remote access server in a hashed format, MS-CHAP authentication provides a larger set of error codes than does CHAP, and provides capabilities for remote users to change their passwords during the authentication process. MS-CHAP also provides for Microsoft Point-to-Point Encryption (MPPE), an encryption technique based on the RSA/RC4 algorithm.

The original version of MS-CHAP is referred to as version 1. It has been largely replaced by MS-CHAPv2, discussed in the next section. If you are using pre-Windows 95 clients for remote access connectivity, if you are using Windows 95 for dial-up remote access; or if you are using certain non-Microsoft clients, you may have to use MS-CHAP version 1 for authentication.

Microsoft Challenge Handshake Authentication Protocol version 2 (MS-CHAP v2)

MS-CHAP v2 authentication is another improvement to the CHAP authentication protocol. As with the other versions of CHAP, the password is not transmitted during MS-CHAP v2 authentication. The process begins with a challenge, consisting of a session ID and a challenge string, sent from the remote access server (also called the authenticator) to the remote client. The remote client responds with the username, a peer challenge, the received challenge string, the session identifier, and the user's password. These last three are in encrypted format. The remote access server checks the client responses and replies with a success or failure indication and an authentication response based on the sent challenge, the peer challenge, the encrypted response of the client, and the user's password. The client then verifies the authentication response of the server and completes the connection if the response is correct. If the client receives an invalid response from the remote access server, the connection is dropped. This two-way, mutual authentication process ensures authenticity of the client and server.

Like MS-CHAPv1, v2 supports password change during the authentication process. Figure 7.15 illustrates the MS-CHAP v2 authentication process.

Figure 7.15 The MS-CHAP v2 Authentication Process

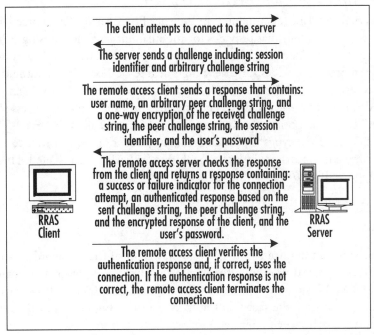

Table 7.1 compares MS–CHAP v1 and MS–CHAP v2.

Table 7.1 MS-CHAP v1 versus MS-CHAP v2

MS-CHAP version 1	MS-CHAP version 2
Uses LAN Manager encoding for backward compatibility with older Microsoft remote access clients.	MS-CHAP v2 does not allow LAN Manager encoded responses.
Only one-way authentication is possible. The remote access client is unable to verify the remote access server's identity. This opens the door for a masquerading remote access server to retrieve the one-way password hash.	MS-CHAP v2 provides mutual authentication, also known as two-way authentication. The client verifies the identity of the remote access server that it is dialing in to.
40-bit encryption is used and the cryptographic key is based on the user's password. If the user connects with the same password, the same cryptographic key is generated.	With MS-CHAP v2, the cryptographic key is always based on the user's password and an arbitrary challenge string. Each time the user connects with the same password, a different cryptographic key is used.
Transmitted and received data both use a single cryptographic key for the connection.	Cryptographic keys are generated for trans-mitted and received data.

Extensible Authentication Protocol (EAP)

EAP is an Internet standard (documented in Internet Engineering Task Force (IETF) Request For Comments (RFC) 2284) that provides for modular authentication using PPP. This protocol allows vendors to add new authentication modules to clients and servers using PPP. This open, modular approach provides for a very high degree of flexibility in authentication techniques. EAP is supported on Windows 2000 and Windows Server 2003 servers.

With EAP, the remote access client and the authenticator (remote access server or RADIUS/IAS server) negotiate the authentication scheme (called the *EAP type*) to use. Support for different EAP types is provided via plug-in modules. In order to use EAP, the client and server must both have at least one common EAP type installed. There are two EAP types supported by Windows Server 2003:

- MD5 Challenge
- EAP-TLS

MD5 Challenge authentication uses a one-way hash of the password to authenticate users. This challenge is also used to authenticate the client and server used for network communication. MD5 is considered to be relatively strong authentication because of the strength of the encryption, the fact that the hash is a one-way hash, and because of the mutual authentication between client and server.

EAP-TLS is also an IETF standard. It is documented in RFC 2716. This authentication protocol utilizes the extensibility of EAP to provide public-key-certificate-based authentication of users and remote access servers. A PIN number or username/password combination generally protects the user's key, which can be stored on the local PC or a smart card or security token.

EAP-TLS is the only authentication method supported when smart cards are used for remote authentication. A public key infrastructure (PKI) is required to implement EAP-TLS. A trusted certification authority verifies the user's identification based on the key the user provides. A trusted certificate authority also verifies the identity of the remote access server, to secure both ends of the communication channel. EAP is supported on Windows 2000, Windows XP, and Windows Server 2003. Standalone remote access servers or those that belong to a workgroup cannot use EAP-TLS; only remote access servers that belong to a domain can do so.

NOTE

Any discussions about wireless will inevitably turn to authentication protocols. Lightweight Extended Authentication Protocol (LEAP) and Protected Extensible Authentication Protocol (PEAP) are both password-based authentication schemes used for wireless client authentication. Microsoft does not provide support for Cisco's proprietary LEAP protocol due to its proprietary nature; however, the open-standard PEAP protocol is supported on Windows XP Service Pack 1, Windows Server 2003, Windows 2000 wireless clients and Windows 2000 Internet Authentication Service (IAS) with Microsoft's 802.1x Authentication Client.

EAP-RADIUS is not actually an EAP type in the way that EAP-TLS is, for example. EAP-RADIUS is actually a method for passing requests from the various EAP types available to a RADIUS or IAS server. EAP-RADIUS encapsulates EAP authentication traffic from remote access clients within RADIUS authentication packets and forwards them to the RADIUS server. The RADIUS server processes the EAP authentication request and forwards it to the originating EAP-RADIUS server within encapsulated RADIUS packets. The EAP-RADIUS server responds to the remote access client with the previously encapsulated EAP response.

NOTE

A very common cause of failed VPN connections involves authentication protocols and encryption mismatches. It is important to have your client and server or both servers (for compulsory tunnel mode in a gateway-to-gateway VPN) configured to use the same encryption strength and authentication protocol.

Be aware that the addition of service packs to systems sometimes changes the encryption strength available on the system. If your clients are not running the most recent service pack, they might not have the encryption strength available to meet your server's request.

EXAM WARNING

PPP negotiation, and PPP authentication in particular, is a prime concern in today's high security business environments. Ensure that you understand the progression of PPP authentication methods, from weakest to strongest. It is also important to note which methods use clear-text (unencrypted) exchanges of user names and or passwords.

The protocol selected determines the level of encryption supported. MPPE Standard supports 40-bit and 56-bit encryption, MPPE Strong supports 128-bit encryption, IPSec DES supports 56-bit encryption, and IPSec Triple DES supports 3DES (168-bit) encryption.

Selecting MS-CHAP, MS-CHAP v2, or EAP for dial-up or virtual private network (VPN) connections enables MPPE-based data encryption.

When configuring VPNs, if the VPN connection is configured to connect to a PPTP server, MPPE encryption is used. If the VPN will connect to an L2TP server, IPSec will be used. If the VPN is configured with the default selection (for an Automatic server type), which is L2TP, and its associated IPSec encryption, it will be attempted first, then PPTP and its associated MPPE encryption will be attempted.

In the next section, we will take a closer look at the VPN tunneling protocols that are supported by Windows Server 2003.

VPN Tunneling Protocols

Transport Control Protocol/Internet Protocol (TCP/IP) usually provides the underlying transport mechanism for VPN connectivity. Internal traffic, or that traffic being protected by the VPN encryption, is encapsulated within the underlying TCP/IP packets. The process of encapsulating VPN data traffic is called tunneling—one of the primary premises of VPN connectivity.

Understanding Tunneling

By *tunnel,* we are referring to a logical connection between two points. VPN tunnels allow authentication and encryption of the data that travels from one endpoint of the tunnel to the other. The data packets within the tunnel are *encapsulated*, or hidden inside a new packet. This new packet contains the address of the tunnel endpoint in its header, and the address of the final destination computer is on the original packet's header that is inside. The encapsulation header is removed when the packet gets to the endpoint, and the original packet is delivered to its destination.

Tunnels can be created at either Layer 2 or Layer 3 of the OSI networking model. Layer 2 (data link) tunneling protocols include PPTP and L2TP, both supported by Windows Server 2003. Another Layer 2 tunneling protocol (developed by Cisco and used as a basis for the creation of L2TP by Cisco and Microsoft) is called Layer 2 Forwarding (L2F). Windows Server 2003 does not support L2F, but it is used by Cisco routers and Shiva devices. Layer 3 tunnels can be created by IPSec. IPSec can function as a tunneling protocol itself (generally for gateway-to-gateway VPNs), or it can be used to provide encryption for L2TP tunnels. Windows Server 2003 uses IPSec in conjunction with L2TP.

VPN tunneling is generally accomplished in one of two ways: through voluntary tunnels or through compulsory tunnels. Let's look at the details of voluntary and compulsory tunneling.

Voluntary Tunneling

Voluntary tunneling is probably the more common method of VPN tunneling. Voluntary tunneling utilizes the client-server model of network communication. In this method, a VPN client initiates a connection with the VPN server. Earlier in this chapter, we discussed the basics of VPN connectivity, referring to some form of underlying connectivity (usually

IP connectivity) as a prerequisite for VPN encapsulation or tunneling. The voluntary tunnel requires an existing network connection between the client and the remote access server. The client uses this connection to establish a tunneled connection with the server; thereby gaining access to the protected LAN that lies behind the VPN server.

Compulsory Tunneling

Compulsory tunneling produces a connection between two VPN servers or two VPN access devices (such as VPN-enabled routers). This creates a gateway-to-gateway VPN. In a compulsory tunnel, a client dials-in to a remote access server, either through an Internet dial-up connection or via the local LAN connection. The server or device to which the client connects forms a tunnel with another remote access or VPN server to tunnel the data, allowing access between the client and a protected LAN or between two protected LANs. This method forces the client to use a VPN tunnel to connect to the remote resources, hence the name compulsory tunnel. In this scenario, a many-to-many relationship exists, in which several clients may be utilizing the same tunnel to access remote resources, compared to the one-to-many relationship of a typical voluntary tunnel, where one client may be accessing many systems behind the remote access server.

NOTE

If you've studied IPSec, you may recognize that the description of voluntary tunneling sounds similar to use of IPSec in Transport mode, and the description of compulsory tunneling sounds similar to that of IPSec in tunnel mode.

Tunneling Protocols Supported by Windows Server 2003

Windows Server 2003 includes two VPN tunneling protocols for remote access via VPN connections:

- PPTP, which uses MPPE for encryption.
- L2TP with IPSec to provide for higher layer encapsulation and encryption features necessary for VPN connectivity. This combination is known as L2TP/IPSec.

We will explore the features of both of these protocols in the following passages.

PPTP/MPPE

The PPTP Forum, a joint venture between Microsoft and several other companies with interests in remote access technology (3COM, U.S. Robotics, Ascend, and ECI Telematics), developed the PPTP. Microsoft first introduced PPTP with Windows NT 4.0 Beta Release 2. PPTP transmits data over a TCP/IP connection by encapsulating PPP frames in IP datagrams. PPTP works with remote access connections (remote client calling remote access server) or with router-to-router VPN connections. There are two components to a PPTP connection. First, a TCP connection handles tunnel management on TCP port number 1723. Next, a modified version of the Generic Route Encapsulation (GRE) protocol packages PPP frames for encapsulated tunnel data. The encapsulated tunnel data may either be encrypted, compressed, or both. PPTP can use any of the authentication schemes that are supported by PPP.

The version of PPTP that ships with Windows Server 2003 is PPTP version 2. After its release, several security vulnerabilities were discovered in Microsoft's original implementation of PPTP, which prompted a revamping of this protocol. The PPTPv2 protocol supports 40-bit and 128-bit encryption. PPTP is documented by the IETF in RFC 2637. This RFC specifies "a protocol which allows the Point to Point Protocol (PPP) to be tunneled through an IP network."

PPTP does not specify any changes to the PPP protocol, but rather describes a new vehicle for carrying PPP. The basic simplicity of PPTP is one of its biggest advantages because PPTP operation is not based on a certificate infrastructure. Also, a Network Address Translator (NAT) can translate PPTP traffic and consequently will allow PPTP traffic streams to be directed through routers or corporate firewalls. PPTP is also capable of carrying non-IP traffic, making it ideal for applications where legacy network transports such as IPX/SPX, NetBEUI, AppleTalk, or others may be required.

Microsoft's PPTP uses MPPE to encrypt the data in a PPTP VPN, providing the security for the data that travels between the VPN client and server. Although PPTP itself can use any PPP authentication mechanism, MPPE requires encryption keys generated by MS-CHAP v1 or v2, or EAP-TLS. The remote access server can be configured to require data encryption, or it can be configured to use optional encryption (in which case a connection will be made even if the client does not support encryption).

L2TP/IPSec

L2TP, first introduced with Windows 2000, combines the benefits of PPTP with Cisco System's Layer Two Forwarding (L2F) protocol. Generally, a layer-two connection is used to connect a remote client with a remote access server, and consequently the PPP connection also terminates at the same endpoints as the layer two connections.

L2TP extends PPP to allow the PPP and layer-two endpoints to reside on different devices. Whereas PPTP connects systems over an IP network only, L2TP allows for connectivity over IP, X.25, Frame Relay, or Asynchronous Transfer Mode (ATM). When IP is used as a transport mechanism, L2TP uses UDP packets and special L2TP messages to handle tunnel management. L2TP also carries the tunneled data in UDP encapsulated PPP frames. Remember that Microsoft's PPTP provides encryption via MPPE as well as compression via Microsoft Point-to-Point Compression (MPPC). L2TP has provisions for encrypted and compressed PPP encapsulated payloads; however, the Microsoft implementation of L2TP does not provide for these features directly. To encrypt the encapsulated PPP payload, Microsoft's implementation of L2TP must be used with IPSec's Encapsulating Security Payload (ESP) protocol.

NOTE

L2TP can be used only if both the VPN server and VPN client support it. Windows 2000 and Windows XP clients and Windows 2000 and Windows Server 2003 servers include built-in L2TP/IPSec support. Windows 9x and Windows NT clients do not include L2TP support, but you can download an L2TP/IPSec client for Windows 98, Windows ME, and Windows NT Workstation 4.0 from Microsoft's Web site at http://www.microsoft.com/windows2000/server/evaluation/news/bulletins/l2tpclient.asp.

L2TP is described in IETF RFC 2661. The combination of L2TP with IPSec is described in IETF RFC 3193.

Head of the Class…

NAT Traversal

Using IPSec encrypts not only the data payload, but also the UDP header. This presents a problem if the data needs to be tunneled behind a NAT server or router. The UDP header specifies the UDP port number for packet forwarding to a specific service. Encryption of the UDP header means encryption of the UDP port number information, and consequently no forwarding of L2TP/IPSec traffic.

The solution to this problem is a technology called *NAT traversal (NAT-T)*, which was developed by a consortium of technology companies, including Cisco Systems and Microsoft. NAT-T uses UDP encapsulation, placing the IPSec packet inside a UCP/IP header. This way, NAT devices can change the IP address or port number without changing the IPSec packet. NAT traversal communications are transmitted through UDP port 500 (which is normally open for IKE when IPSec is used).

If the VPN client and server both support NAT-T, the client and/or server may be placed behind a NAT server or router. Windows Server 2003, unlike Windows 2000 Server, provides special NAT-T capabilities. Microsoft offers a new VPN client that supports client-side NAT-T for Windows NT 4.0, Windows 98, and Windows ME clients, to be used when connecting to a Windows Server 2003 server.

Both L2TP/IPSec and PPTP/MPPE exhibit certain advantages and disadvantages. Table 7.2 compares L2TP/IPSec with PPTP/MPPE.

Table 7.2 Comparison of L2TP/IPSec and PPTP/MPPE

Factor	PPTP Advantages and Constraints	L2TP/IPSec Advantages and Constraints
Client operating systems supported	Supported on clients running Windows 2000, Windows XP, Windows Server 2003, Windows NT Workstation 4.0, Windows ME, or Windows 98.	Built-in support on clients running Windows 2000, Windows XP, or Windows Server 2003. Mls2tp.exe must be installed for support on clients running Windows 98, Windows Me, or Windows NT Workstation 4.0.
Certificate support	PPTP requires a certificate infrastructure for EAP-TLS authentication to issue computer certificates to the authenticating server and user certificates to all VPN clients or to issue smart cards to all users.	L2TP/IPSec requires a certificate infrastructure or a preshared key (PSK) to issue computer certificates to the VPN server and all VPN clients.
Security	Captured packets cannot be interpreted without the encryption key—confidentiality. Does not provide proof that the data was not modified in transit—data integrity. Does not provide proof that the data was sent by the authorized user—data origin authentication. Use MS-CHAP v2 as the authentication with strong passwords to increase security.	Provides data confidentiality, data integrity, data origin authentication, and replay protection. Offers the highest level of security.
Performance	A VPN server is capable of supporting more PPTP connections than L2TP/IPSec connections.	IPSec encryption is processing-intensive. A VPN server supports fewer L2TP connections than PPTP connections because of additional processing overhead. To support additional L2TP connections, increase CPU processing power or network adapters designed for encrypted traffic.
NAT support	PPTP-based VPN clients can be located behind a NAT if the NAT includes an editor that can translate PPTP.	If you locate L2TP/IPSec–based clients or servers behind a NAT, both client and server must support IPSec NAT traversal (NAT-T).

EXAM WARNING

L2TP is still the latest and greatest for VPN security. Ensure that you understand the similarities and differences between L2TP and PPTP. Although L2TP/IPSec tends to provide a more secure VPN solution, PPTP still has its advantages as well. Make sure you understand the advantages and disadvantages of each.

Now that you understand the basic concepts and terminology associated with Windows Server 2003 VPNs, we will move on to practice some hands-on configurations and you'll learn how to put the concepts to work. The following preconfiguration checklist will simplify the configuration settings outlined in the next section:

1. Review the basic VPN concepts. Determine the type of VPN you wish to configure: router-to-router or client-server.

2. Ensure hardware is compatible and install necessary hardware.

3. Install and enable the Routing and Remote Access service as outlined in Exercise 7.01.

Configuring the VPN Server

As mentioned earlier in this chapter, VPN configuration is initially accomplished through the Routing and Remote Access Server Setup Wizard. This wizard walks us through the step-by-step process of basic VPN configuration. It is only run once; after you have completed it, if you try to run it again, you will get a message that Routing and Remote Access is configured on the server, and changes to the current configuration should be made by selecting an item in the console tree and accessing its properties sheet. After we have completed the steps in the wizard, it is usually a matter of some fine-tuning to complete our VPN server configuration.

Planning Your VPN Server Deployment

The first and most important step should be the planning phase. There are a number of considerations for this phase:

- You need to determine the number of VPN client connections that you need to support.

- You need to determine the availability and logical location of a DHCP server. If you are not using a DHCP server on your network, or if it will exist on a different subnet from the VPN server, you will have to take this into account as you configure the VPN server.

- You need to determine where users will be authenticated and which users will have remote dial-in access available to them.

- You need to determine what operating systems will be used by VPN clients.

Our client operating systems will dictate many of your decisions about VPN tunneling protocols and authentication protocols. Older client operating systems may require the L2TP/IPSec client software that is available for download from Microsoft in order to support L2TP/IPSec, and some older operating systems (most notably, Windows 95) cannot use L2TP/IPSec. Also, the presence or absence of a certificate infrastructure will dictate the protocols used. Your basic network infrastructure and the type of connection that is available to the Internet will determine the type of VPN connection to implement. Persistent connections usually will be used over a more modern broadband network or one that is connected to the Internet via a dedicated leased line. Time-based and network traffic-based dial-up connections may be used in cases where connectivity costs are based on use.

After you have determined which authentication protocols and VPN protocols to use, along with the details of connection persistence, you must determine the restrictions you want to put in place for the users. There are a couple of options available when it comes to dial-in permissions. One option is to grant dial-in permission on a per user basis. This is done via the **Dial-in tab** on the **Properties** sheet for the user's account. Another, more common option, is to grant dial-in permission to groups through Remote Access Policies.

Remote Access Policies provide greater control of VPN user access by comparing inbound connection attempts to a set of predefined rules. If the connection attempt matches a particular rule, the connection is either accepted or rejected based on the Remote Access Policy's configuration settings. Remote Access Policies first compare the connection to different criteria such as remote access permission, group membership, type of connection, time of day, authentication methods, and several advanced conditions (access server identity, access client phone number or MAC address, whether user account dial-in properties are ignored, whether unauthenticated access is allowed) before authorizing the connection. After a connection has been authorized, connection restrictions can be specified to control various aspects of the session such as idle timeout time, maximum session time, encryption strength, IP packet filters, and advanced restrictions like IP address for PPP connections and static routes. Several other connection restriction settings also exist within the Remote Access Policy configuration options.

New & Noteworthy...

Network Access Quarantine Control

A new feature that comes with a new set of utilities for Windows Server 2003 is Network Access Quarantine Control. Using either the Connection Manager Administration Kit (CMAK) or the Windows Deployment and Resource Kits, administrators can configure special policies that restrict VPN client access using a quarantine mode until the client system is either brought into compliance with corporate VPN client specifications or determined to already be in accordance with specifications. This is a new feature for Windows Server 2003 that will help to increase network security.

Network Access Quarantine Control controls client access after initial authentication has been completed. The client uses an installed notification component (Rqc.exe) to communicate system compliance information to the Remote Access Server's listening component (Rqs.exe) after testing the client with a specially configured script known as the Connection Manager profile. Two attributes (MS-Quarantine-IPFilter and MS-Quarantine-Session-Timeout) filter IP traffic between the remote access client and the remote access server until the client system passes the configuration requirements or the timeout period is reached.

The process used to deploy Network Access Quarantine Control for your remote access network involves the following steps:

1. Either use the Rqc.exe notification component or create a notification component that provides verification to the remote access server that the remote access client computer complies with network policy requirements.

2. Create a validation script that authorizes the client configuration. The script runs the notification component with the appropriate parameters if the client configuration meets the requirements specified in the validation script.

3. Either use the Rqs.exe listener component or create a listener component that receives the network policy compliance notification from the notification component.

4. Using the Connection Manager Administration Kit CMAK) from the Windows Server 2003 Resource Kit create a Connection Manager (CM) profile. Configure a post-connect action to run the script with the required parameters and include the script and the notification component in the profile.

5. Distribute the CM profile for installation on remote access client computers.

6. After the CM profile has been installed on remote access client computers, configure a quarantine remote access policy on your IAS servers.

In the next section, we will discuss one of the most important keys to proper VPN configuration: client address assignment.

IP Addressing for VPN Clients

VPN data encapsulation is the process of taking LAN traffic or private network traffic and tunneling it through an insecure network (typically the Internet). From the perspective of a VPN server administrator, there are three methods for client address assignment:

- Automatic address assignment via a DHCP server

- Assignment of an address from a specified range

- Assignment of static addresses on a per-user basis

You will see two of the available options when you initially run the Routing and Remote Access Configuration Wizard. These are shown in Figure 7.16.

Figure 7.16 Routing and Remote Access Server Remote Client IP Address Assignment

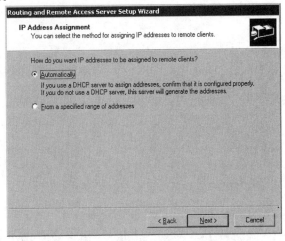

The two options presented within the wizard are **Automatically** and **From a specified range of addresses**. Using automatic address assignment, the VPN server will request addresses from the DHCP server in blocks of ten. Client messages to the DHCP server will be available to the DHCP server if it is on the same local subnet as the VPN server. If the DHCP server and the VPN server are on different subnets, the VPN server must be configured as a DHCP Relay Agent in order to direct client DHCP broadcast messages via unicast transport to the remote DHCP server.

Configuring the VPN server IP address assignment **From a specified range of addresses** allows for automatic address assignment when a DHCP server is not available, or when you would prefer to assign addresses from a range that is different than those provided by the DHCP server. If addresses in the static pool are depleted, clients will be assigned Automatic Private IP Addresses (APIPA) from the 169.254.y.z address range.

As a final option, you may provide addresses on a per user basis. In other words, you may assign static IP addresses to dial-in users, based on their user credentials. When a user authenticates through a VPN connection to the server, you can ensure that the user receives a specific address based on his or her account settings in Active Directory Users and Computers (for systems in an Active Directory domain) or through Local Users and Groups (for standalone servers).

TEST DAY TIP

If you are studying in a test lab or a home lab, viewing the IP configuration of your VPN client should help drive home the point of tunneling and encapsulation. While connected to the VPN server, run the **ipconfig /all** utility from a command prompt and note the **WAN (PPP/SLIP) Interface** IP address. You should see that your computer has an IP address consistent with the subnet of the remote LAN, giving you connectivity to systems on the remote LAN.

Adding Ports on the VPN Server

By default, there are 128 L2TP ports and 128 PPTP ports (called WAN miniports) available when you set up your Windows Server 2003 VPN server. If you need to allow more clients to connect simultaneously, you can increase the number of maximum ports up to 1000 for each protocol. However, Windows Server 2003 Standard Edition will support only 1000 total simultaneous VPN connections, and Web Edition will accept only one VPN connection at a time.

To add more L2TP or PPTP ports, in the RRAS console, expand the node for the remote access server in the left console pane and follow these steps:

1. Right-click the **Ports** node and click **Properties**.

2. On the **Ports Properties** sheet, highlight either **WAN Miniport (PPTP)** or **WAN Miniport (L2TP)** and click the **Configure** button.

3. In the **Maximum ports** box, click the up or down arrow to set the number of ports you want to allow. Click **OK** to apply the change, then click **OK** again to close the properties box.

To disable PPTP so that only L2TP connections can be made to the VPN server, in the **Configure Device** sheet for the WAN Miniport (PPTP), uncheck the **Remote access connections (inbound only)** and **Demand-dial routing connections (inbound and outbound)** check boxes.

EXERCISE 7.02

VPN SERVER CONFIGURATION FOR REMOTE ACCESS CLIENTS

In this exercise, you will configure the Routing and Remote Access service to support various numbers of remote clients first through DHCP server address allocation, and then using IP address allocation direct from the VPN server.

Before we begin, make sure you have two network interfaces available to you. For convenience, it helps to properly name your network connections through the Network Connections folder so that they will be easy to identify. For example, determine which network card is attached to the LAN and name it, aptly, "LAN." You might name the network connection that connects to the Internet "WAN" or "Internet" as shown in Figure 7.17.

Figure 7.17 Renaming Your Network Connections

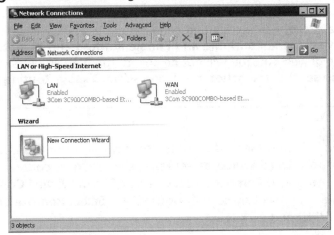

1. To rename a network connection, select the connection to rename, click on **File | Rename** and type the new, more descriptive name for the connection, to simplify identification. After you've done this for both connections, we'll move to the main focus of this exercise and configure your VPN server for remote client access.

NOTE

You might be unable to open the Network Connections folder as shown in Figure 7.17. Instead, when you click **Control Panel,** you see another menu displaying the Control Panel items, and when you click **Network Connections**, you get yet another menu instead of the folder view. To correct this, right-click an empty area of the taskbar, select **Properties,** and select the **Start Menu** tab. Select **Classic Start Menu,** and click the **Customize** button. Uncheck the **Expand Control Panel** and **Expand Network Connections** check boxes, then click **OK,** and then **OK** again.

2. Following the same basic procedure as in Exercise 7.01, begin by opening the Routing and Remote Access management console: **Start | Administrative Tools | Routing and Remote Access**.

3. From the Routing and Remote Access management console, select **Action | Configure and Enable Routing and Remote Access,** or right-click the name of the server on which you want to enable RRAS and make the same selection from the console menu.

NOTE

If you have already run the Routing and Remote Access Server Setup Wizard in the previous exercise, the **Configure and Enable Routing and Remote Access** selection will be grayed out. You will not be able to run it again unless you first disable RRAS. To do so, click the **Action** menu and select **Disable Routing and Remote Access**.

4. You will be presented with the **Routing and Remote Access Server Setup Wizard Welcome screen**. Select **Next** to continue to the **Routing and Remote Access Server Setup Wizard Configuration** page as previously seen in Figure 7.11. Select **Remote access (dial-up or VPN)** and click **Next**.

5. On the Remote Access page, select **VPN | Next**.

6. Now you will reap the rewards for naming your connections with names that identify them easily. From the VPN Connection page, select WAN to configure the VPN service to listen on the WAN interface. Notice that the IP address is also displayed, in case you decided not to name the connections. We will leave the default setting of Enable security on the selected interface by setting up static packet filters. Select **Next**.

7. This brings you to the address selection page. Your two options are to use DHCP or to select a range of addresses. First we will set up this server to use a DHCP server to allocate addresses. Select Automatically from the two options and click **Next**.

NOTE

You should not select the **Automatically** option unless you have a DHCP server set up on the internal network. Otherwise an error will be generated and VPN clients will not be able to connect.

8. Remote Access Dial-In User Service (RADIUS) is a method of authenticating remote users from a centralized database of accounts, similar to a domain logon compared to a workgroup logon. Without RADIUS, users' account information has to be available on the Remote Access Server. We will select **No, user Routing and Remote Access to authenticate connection requests**.

9. Click **Next** to display the **Completing the Routing and Remote Access Server Setup Wizard** and then click **Finish** to continue.

NOTE

You must have a RADIUS server on the network in order to use RADIUS for authentication. Otherwise, an error will be generated. VPN clients will fail to be authenticated and will not be able to connect.

10. You will be prompted with a message that tells you to configure the properties of the DHCP Relay Agent with the IP address of the DHCP server in order to support DHCP relay messages from remote clients. Select **OK** to complete the configuration and to allow the Routing and Remote Access service to be started.

When the Routing and Remote Access service is running on the server, you should see a management console similar to the one in Figure 7.18.

Now that the server is configured, you need to set up a client that has IP connectivity to your WAN interface.

You configure the client through the Network Connections folder on the client machine. In this example, we will use a Windows 2000 Professional system as the client.

Figure 7.18 Initial VPN Configurations

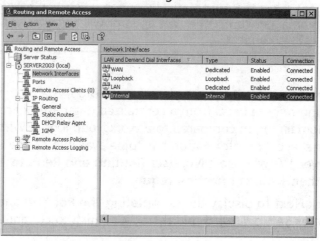

1. On the Windows 2000 Professional computer, select **Start | Settings | Control Panel**, right-click on **Network Connections**, and select **Open**.

2. From the **Network Connections** folder, select **New Connection Wizard**. From the **Welcome to the New Connection Wizard** page, select **Next**. From the **New Connection Wizard Network Connection Type** page, select **Connect to the network at my workplace** and select **Next**.

3. Select **Virtual Private Network Connection** from the next page and select **Next**.

4. In the **Connection Name** dialog box, type a name for this connection and select **Next**.

5. Enter either the external IP address or the FQDN of the VPN server computer. Select **Next**.

6. From the **Connection Availability** dialog box, select **Anyone's use (If you want the connection to be available to everyone who uses the computer)** and select **Next**.

7. Select **Finish** from the **Completing the New Connection Wizard** screen.

8. A logon screen will be displayed after you complete the **New Connection Wizard**, as shown in Figure 7.19.

Figure 7.19 Completing the New Connection Wizard—the VPN Logon Screen

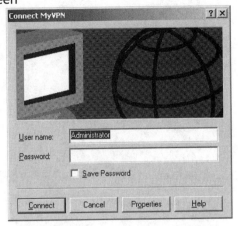

Now you have connectivity from the server and from the client, but you still need to grant access to the user for dial-in permission so you can test the connection. In our example, you are using local authentication so you need to grant dial-in permission to the user account through Local Users and Groups on the VPN server.

1. Select **Start | Administrative Tools | Computer Management**.

2. In the left pane of the Computer Management MMC, double-click **Local Users and Groups**.

3. Double-click **Users** in the right pane, and double-click the user account to which you want to grant dial-in access. You will grant dial-in access to the administrator account in this example. From the **Dial-in** tab of the **Administrator Properties** dialog box, select **Allow access** and click **OK** to grant dial-in permission to the administrator as shown in Figure 7.20.

NOTE

If the VPN server is a member of a Windows Server 2003 domain, dial-in permission is granted by accessing the user's account in the **Active Directory Users and Computers** administrative tool. Also be aware that the conditions in remote access policies set via Group Policy can override the settings in the user's Properties sheet.

Figure 7.20 Granting Dial-in Permission to the Administrator Account

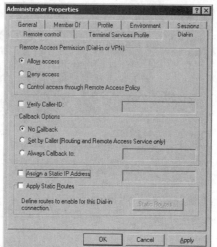

4. Notice that the third option for client IP address allocation is listed at the bottom of the **Dial-in** tab of the **Administrator Properties** dialog box. Selecting **Assign a Static IP Address** will provide a specific address to the administrator account immediately following account authentication. If the address entered here is invalid or another computer on the network is already using it, the remote access server will assign a dynamic IP address instead.

NOTE

The options to assign a static IP address or to apply static routes are not available (they will be grayed out) if the user is a member of a Windows 2000 mixed domain. Other options on the **Dial-in** tab that are not available in this circumstance include the **Control Access through Remote Access Policy** and **Verify Caller-ID** options. If you raise the domain functional level to Windows Server 2003, these options will become available. However, you should *not* raise the functional level unless *all* domain controllers in the domain are running Windows Server 2003. The domain functional level is raised by using the **Active Directory Domains and Trusts** administrative tool (right-click the domain name in the left pane and select **Raise domain functional level**). After it is raised, it cannot be lowered again.

5. From the **Network Connections** folder on the VPN client computer, double-click the VPN connection that you created earlier in this exercise.

6. An authentication challenge box will be displayed. Enter the credentials for the administrator account of the VPN server and select **Connect**. A message box will be displayed from the taskbar; you should see an icon with a message informing you that the connection has been made. To disconnect, in the **Network Connections** folder on the client computer, right-click on the icon for the VPN connection. Select **Disconnect**. The client will disconnect from the VPN server.

7. Change the address allocation settings to reflect local address allocation. On your VPN server, select **Start | Administrative Tools | Routing and Remote Access.**

8. Select the server name in the left pane and select **Action | Properties**.

9. On the **IP** tab, select **Static address pool**.

10. Select the **Add...** button from below the **Static address pool** selection.

11. A dialog box will be displayed, requesting a **Start IP address**, an **End IP address**, and a **Number of addresses**. Using this dialog box, a locally allocated store of IP addresses may be created to allow VPN client connectivity without utilizing a DHCP server to provide addresses.

NOTE

You can create multiple static addresses pools. Just repeat steps 28 through 30 for each range of addresses that you want to add. If any range of addresses in your pool are in a different subnet, you'll need to enable an IP routing protocol on the remote access server or configure static IP routes to the intranet routers.

EXAM
70-291

OBJECTIVE
4.4
4.5.1
4.6.2

Configuring the Windows Server 2003 VPN Gateway

A gateway is simply a connection point. In the case of protocol gateways, such as the old Gateway Services for NetWare in previous versions of Windows server, this connection is between dissimilar systems. In the case of the default gateway that you set in a computer's TCP/IP properties, the connection point is a router that joins two networks or subnets. In the case of a VPN gateway, the connection is between two LANs that are connected by the Internet or some other nonsecure network. A VPN gateway connects to another VPN gateway (or a series of other VPN gateways) to provide an extension to the existing LAN. VPN gateways are also called VPN routers.

Although this works differently in some respects from the VPN client/VPN server configuration we discussed in the previous sections, there is a designated client (the calling router) and server (the answering router). The client is authenticated to the server (and if two-way mutual authentication is supported by the authentication protocol, the server can also authenticate to the client).

From the perspective of the clients, a remote machine should appear as though it were on the same LAN segment as the local machines. Figure 7.21 illustrates the use of two VPN gateways to connect two geographically distant LANs via a broadband Internet connection. This VPN gateway provides a compulsory tunnel between the LANs that it will connect, in contrast to the voluntary tunnel that we created in the previous section.

Figure 7.21 VPN Gateway Connectivity

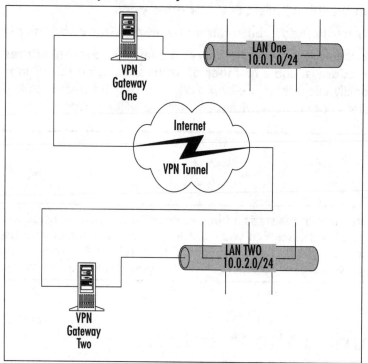

Unlike a client/server VPN configuration, within a compulsory tunnel the client operating systems do not play a part in the VPN configuration decision process. That's because the client computers are not tunnel endpoints. The tunnels are created and destroyed at the gateways and the clients connect via their normal network/transport protocols. In most cases, this is TCP/IP. Otherwise, the configuration process for compulsory tunnels is very similar to the VPN server configuration. There are, however, a couple of differences to consider:

- The use of routing protocols to provide adequate connectivity for all clients
- The use of inbound and outbound filters to secure the traffic types between the remote LANs

In an effort to keep nonsecure traffic off of the corporate LAN, inbound and outbound filters validate traffic by IP address, TCP port number, UDP port number, and protocol number.

As mentioned earlier, VPN gateways generally connect LANs that are geographically separated by large distances (several miles or more). The connecting medium between these LANs is typically the Internet. Thus, a VPN gateway will exhibit an IP address on the LAN to which it is attached, as well as a public IP address (assuming the VPN gateway is directly connected to the Internet and not hidden behind a NAT).

If you examine the client IP addresses, you will notice only single LAN addresses on each system. Again, the compulsory tunnel that is created through the VPN gateway is transparent to the clients. If you query the address of a remote client that is connected to the other end of your VPN gateway tunnel, you will receive a response as though the remote client were connected directly to our local LAN. VPN protocol usage and authentication protocol usage often dictate placement of the VPN server.

Supporting Network Infrastructure

Several design considerations need to be taken into account when designing a network infrastructure with VPN gateways. Address allocation, routing table maintenance, name resolution, auto-static routing update, and dynamic routing updates all affect the network infrastructure design. In this section, we will see how dynamic routing, name resolution, and auto-static updates are affected by VPN gateways in a network infrastructure.

DHCP clients, for example, may receive IP addresses from a DCHP server on their local LAN or through a DHCP Relay Agent that proxies local LAN client requests to a DHCP server on a remote LAN connected through the VPN. This design relies on the VPN connection to provide network connectivity on a persistent basis.

VPN gateway networks are usually designed in a hub and spoke configuration with the main corporate site in the middle or hub portion of the network. This allows the corporate network to control Internet access and to handle routing between satellite offices, if needed. The advantage to this configuration is the increased amount of control available through the corporate office network. This design also provides relatively simplified network routing configuration even when using static routes. Each remote office uses a default static route to the corporate office. The corporate office VPN gateway router will then require a route to each satellite office. The downside to this configuration is the bandwidth needed at the corporate site to handle the traffic from each satellite office and also to provide Internet access. Another downside is the increasing network complexity as more and more remote sites are added to the network.

Name resolution, which is provided through either WINS or DNS, relies on proper connectivity between clients and their respective name resolution servers. The WINS or

DNS servers may be located on the local LAN or clients may rely on the VPN connection to carry their requests to the remote servers. Also, DNS name resolution may be provided from Internet-based DNS servers as well as the intranet-based DNS servers. Clients need to properly determine where local and remote resources are located by querying the proper servers. It is generally preferable that clients are also able to find Internet-based resources through DNS name resolution. For VPN gateway networks, name resolution server addresses generally are provided from the DHCP server.

As networks increase in size and complexity, using a dynamic routing protocol to provide network routing updates provides simplified administration. Dynamic routing protocols like RIP and OSPF share routing update information between the routers on the network to maintain current routing tables for all network traffic. One problem, however, is that RIP advertises updates every 30 seconds. If your network design includes any demand-dial network connections, this RIP traffic could potentially keep your demand-dial link active even if there is no other network traffic running on your network at the time. This update traffic defeats the main purpose to demand-dial networking. The solution to this dilemma is auto-static updates. Auto-static updates maintain network routes by providing a mechanism to schedule route update advertisements. Auto-static updates may be configured for RIP routed networks only. Microsoft does not provide auto-static update for OSPF.

NOTE

Site-to-site VPN connections using L2TP with IPSec will not advertise routing updates through dynamic routing protocols because L2TP VPNs do not present the connection as a logical interface.

It is recommended to use the IP addresses of answering routers instead of the fully qualified domain names. If a name is resolved to a public IP address, traffic is sent in clear-text across the Internet. This will result in VPN traffic being passed in clear-text format instead of the encrypted, tunneled traffic that a VPN is meant to provide.

Also be aware that clients connecting to a VPN router directly will generally receive addresses and name resolution server information from the VPN server itself. Depending on the VPN server configuration, the client may receive either information that has been configured directly on the VPN server or proxied information from the VPN server acting as a DHCP Relay Agent.

In the next section, we will see how to implement a demand-dial connection, as discussed earlier in this section.

Creating the Demand-Dial Connection

Demand-dial routing provides a connection between networks on-demand. This scenario typically is used where a persistent network or Internet connection would be too costly. Connecting networks through a bonded set of analog lines, for example, might cause your company to incur long distance or international long distance charges for the time that the connection is established. Likewise, if your company is using ISDN to connect remote offices, you may be paying for the time the connection is established as well. Demand-dial routing provides the connection on an as-needed basis based on network traffic criteria specified in the demand-dial configuration. Demand-dial routing uses PPP to connect to remote networks on an as-needed basis. This is different from standard remote access in the fact that remote access connected individual systems to a remote network, whereas demand-dial routing connected entire networks to remote networks. Although demand-dial routing provides a different type of remote network access than standard remote access service, the configuration settings are very similar. Although the services can be configured and enabled independently of one another, they do share a common subset of configuration settings.

Persistent connections are full-time dedicated connections. Any type of always-on connection would be considered a persistent connection. T-1, cable, and DSL could all be classified as persistent connections. It is possible to configure analog and digital dial connections to operate in a persistent fashion.

In this section, we will look at the process used to create a demand-dial connection. This is necessary to connect our VPN gateways to create our compulsory VPN tunnel.

The first step in creating a demand dial VPN connection is the same as the first step in creating a standard VPN server configuration: the design phase. You must take into consideration several aspects of your VPN design requirements:

- Select your encapsulation protocol—PPTP or L2TP. The operating system used at each end of the tunnel is one major determining factor in this decision. If one system is running Windows NT 3.51 or Windows 95 or earlier, you will have to use PPTP. Windows NT 4.0 and Windows 98/ME clients require the new L2TP/IPSec client software to be installed in order to interoperate with Windows 2000 and Windows Server 2003 servers that use L2TP/IPSec.

- If you are not constrained by the operating system, and you want to use L2TP, we will have to use a Public Key Infrastructure (PKI). This means a certificate server or complete certificate server infrastructure needs to be available on the network.

- If you will be using a demand-dial circuit, determine whether you have a persistent Internet connection on each end of the tunnel. If one system dials to the Internet, you will have to configure a standard demand-dial connection as well as the demand-dial VPN. If both systems are connected to the Internet through a persistent connection, you need to determine whether or not you want both ends to be able to initiate the demand-dial connection.

Configuring & Implementing...

Installing Certificates on Calling and Answering Routers

When routers connect through L2TP/IPSec or authenticate using EAP-TLS, it is necessary to install certificates on the systems acting as VPN routers. A certificate authority is required in order to install certificates on computers within your organization. Once a certificate authority is in place, there are three options for installing certificates:

- Through automatic enrollment. Auto-enrollment of computer certificates is available to computers in a Windows Server 2003 domain.

- Through the local Certificates snap-in.

- Through your browser, connect to the CA Web enrollment pages. Install a certificate on the local computer or save it to removable media. Install the certificate on another computer.

We will outline the two most common methods for installing certificates: auto-enrollment and Web-based installation.

To auto-enroll computer certificates, create a group policy for auto-enrollment as follows:

1. Click **Start | Programs | Administrative Tools | Active Directory Users and Computers**.

2. In the left pane, double-click **Active Directory Users and Computers**, right-click the **domain name** that contains your CA, then click **Properties**.

3. From the **Group Policy** tab, click **Default Domain Policy**, and select **Edit**.

4. From the left pane, right-click **Automatic Certificate Request Settings | New**, and then click **Computer Configuration | Windows Settings | Security Settings | Public Key Policies | Automatic Certificate | Request Settings**. The **Automatic Certificate Request** wizard will appear.

5. Click **Next**.

6. From Certificate templates, click **Computer**, and then click **Next**. The enterprise root CA from your network will appear on the list.

7. Click **CA | Next | Finish**.

8. From a command prompt (**Start | Run** | type **cmd**) type gpupdate **/target:Computer**.

The steps for Web browser certificate installation are as follows:

1. Click **Start | Programs | Internet Explorer**.

Continued

2. In the Internet Explorer Address Box, type the **address** of the CA that issues the computer certificates followed by **/certsrv**. Example: **http://yourCA.com/certsrv**.

3. On the **Welcome page**, select **Request a certificate | Advanced certificate request | Create and submit a request to this CA**.

4. In **Certificate Template**, select **Router (Offline request)**, or the name of the template as directed by the CA administrator.

5. In **Name**, type the user account name that is used by the calling router.

6. From **Key Options**, click the **Mark keys as exportable** and **Store certificate in the local computer certificate store** check boxes.

7. Click **Submit**.

8. A confirmation message appears that asks you to confirm that you trust this Web site and that you want to request a certificate. Click **Yes**. From the **Certificate Issued page**, select **Install this certificate**.

After you make these decisions about the VPN protocols, the persistence of the connections, and who can initiate the calls, you will have to address IP addressing and routing.

IP Addressing Support for VPN Gateways

Unlike voluntary VPN tunnels, compulsory tunnels are configured only between intermediary machines (the VPN gateways). Consequently, we need to let each VPN gateway know which LAN addresses are available, and how to reach them. This can be accomplished by setting static routes or through the use of a routing protocol to advertise the routes available. For example, in Figure 7.21, we saw a LAN address in the 10.0.1.0/24 subnet for VPN Gateway One.

VPN Gateway Two is on the 10.0.2.0/24 subnet. In order for our clients on both LANs to be able to reach one another, each VPN server will require routes to its counterpart's LANs. This means that VPN Gateway One will have to know that requests from its LAN clients for any address in the 10.0.2.0/24 subnet should be directed to VPN Gateway Two via the VPN tunnel interface. Likewise, for traffic to come back from VPN Gateway Two's LAN, a route will have to be available on VPN Gateway Two for the 10.0.1.0/24 subnet via the VPN tunnel interface.

EXAM WARNING

Although the major focus of this chapter is not on IP addressing in particular, you must have a strong understanding of TCP/IP fundamentals to understand how VPNs work. All of our modern Internet-connected networks use TCP/IP as a transport mechanism. If you connect remote LANs through the Internet, IP addressing is the basis of the underlying infrastructure. The 70-291 exam will test your fundamental knowledge of TCP/IP. Understand the difference between public and private IP addresses and the implications of private addressing with regard to Internet connectivity (NAT).

Another option that we have available is to use dynamic routing instead of our static routes. We will fully address dynamic routing and the various routing protocols available on Windows Server 2003 in the next chapter, where we discuss the routing protocols that are supported, the configuration options for those protocols, and the factors to consider in selecting which protocol to use. We will address some of the basics of dynamic routing later in this chapter.

Calling routers receive IP addresses the same way that standard remote access clients receive their addresses. The answering router either can allocate an address from the DHCP server, an address may be allocated from a static address pool, or the calling router user account may have a specifically assigned address. If an address is not available for the calling router, a connection will still be established and the router will operate without an address. This process is known as an unnumbered connection. Be aware that the routing protocols provided by Windows Server 2003 RRAS do not support route advertisements over unnumbered connections, however. This means an unnumbered connection will need static routing configured for proper operation. When assigning addresses, each L2TP and PPTP port must have an IP address available for it, as well as an address for the calling router.

In the next section, we will look at the configuration options for our VPN gateways in greater detail.

Creating the Local and Remote Gateways

Once we have determined our network infrastructure considerations and we have determined a VPN protocol to carry our traffic, it's time to look at the configuration.

The configuration of local and remote VPN gateways is not so different than the configuration for a voluntary tunnel mode VPN server. We start from a basic VPN configuration for each of the servers. It is a good idea to test connectivity between your VPN gateways to ensure that the tunnel can be formed. A simple ping between servers should be sufficient to guarantee connectivity. Now, we need to add a couple of configuration settings to either server, or both servers depending on our design requirement here and the presence of persistent Internet connections at each end.

We can configure our demand-dial interface on the VPN Gateway that we intend to use to call the other gateway. If we are going to set up both VPN gateways as calling routers, we will have to configure both VPN gateways with demand-dial interfaces. We also have the option to create a persistent connection from the demand-dial interface, if our design calls for continuous connectivity between our remote LANs.

If we are using demand-dial interfaces to handle our tunnel connectivity, we can set our credentials and specify dial-out hours for the calling VPN gateway. We need to make sure we are using the same authentication protocols, encryption strength, and VPN protocols between our VPN gateways. As a rule of thumb, the majority of the settings configured on our local VPN gateway will be the same as the remote VPN gateway settings. We will need a route from each VPN gateway to its counterpart. This can be added as a static route or we can use a dynamic routing protocol here to advertise the routes. If we want to configure our routers to use a demand-dial circuit, we can add one last step here—demand-dial filters.

The demand-dial filter is the trigger used to initiate a demand-dial circuit. Here, we use rules to specify the type of traffic used to initiate a demand circuit. We can specify source address or network, destination address or network, TCP source and destination port number, UDP source and destination port number, ICMP, or protocol number to initiate the circuit.

For example, if we are using an ISDN connection to connect to the Internet we do not want to use a persistent connection. We could configure our demand-dial circuit to come up whenever traffic from our source network (LAN subnet) is headed to the destination network (remote LAN subnet). Maybe we only want certain traffic types to initiate the circuit. We might specify a packet filter based on the port number of the service being requested.

EXAM WARNING

Since the exam is liable to ask questions about filtering certain types of traffic, make sure you know the basic port numbers and protocols involved there. It is a good idea to know on which ports some of your more common services reside. Domain Name Service (DNS), Simple Mail Transport Protocol (SMTP), Post Office Protocol version 3 (POP3), World Wide Web (WWW), Terminal Services, L2TP, and PPTP are all fair game, just to name a few. If it is a fairly common service, it could be on the exam as part of one of your questions.

Creating the Static Packet Filter

In addition to demand-dial filters, we can also implement inbound and outbound packet filters to control inbound and outbound access to our resources through the VPN tunnel. VPN packet filters are very similar to demand-dial filters in the fact that they analyze packets based on a given criteria, and they make a decision to act on the analysis based on a given set of rules. The rule set that we put in place for the packet filter is based on source or destination IP address, source or destination TCP port, source or destination UDP port, protocol type, and ICMP.

The inbound and outbound packet filters are created within the Routing and Remote Access management console. To configure an inbound filter:

1. Select your server name from the Routing and Remote Access management console.

2. Select **General** beneath the **IP Routing** icon in the left pane of the management console.

3. Select your demand dial interface from the right pane. With the demand dial interface highlighted, select **Action | Properties** and select **Inbound Filters** from the **General Tab** of the demand-dial interface properties.

4. Select **New** from the **Inbound Filters** dialog box. From here, we can select almost any combination of IP addresses and either port or protocol numbers.

Figure 7.22 illustrates the **Add IP Filter** dialog box.

Figure 7.22 Add IP Filter Dialog Box

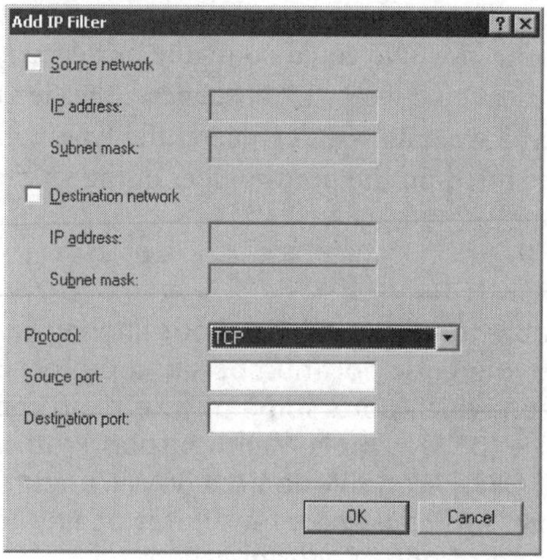

This is where a general understanding of your network infrastructure and of various application port numbers comes in handy. If you know what types of traffic you want to allow or disable and you know the port numbers associated with it, you'll find it a lot easier to implement the inbound and outbound filtering features.

Two types of filters are available for RRAS: demand-dial and IP packet filters. Demand-dial filters are applied before a connection is made and they are used to determine whether or not a connection is to be established. IP packet filters, on the other hand, are applied after the connection is made. To ensure proper interaction of demand-dial and IP packet filters, use the following rules for applying filters:

■   Configure the same set of filters as demand-dial filters with **Initiate connection** set to **For all traffic except** when your output IP packet filters are configured with the **Receive all packets except those that meet the criteria listed below** option.

■ Configure the same set of filters as demand-dial filters with **Initiate connection** set to **Only for the following traffic** when you have configured a set of output IP packet filters with the **Drop all packets except those that meet the criteria listed below** option.

Importance of Demand-Dial Filters

Broadband networking is becoming more and more popular and available every day. Before broadband, the best connection you could get for a home office or satellite office (short of a T1) was ISDN. One major difference between ISDN and a typical broadband (cable or DSL) connection today is the price structure. In some areas, ISDN is billed based on usage. This can mean a huge difference in your bill if you are using your ISDN unnecessarily.

Save your company a little (or a lot) of money by ensuring that your ISDN connection is being used only when necessary by properly configuring your demand-dial filters. Also, it is a good idea to set hour restrictions on your demand-dial connections to ensure the connections are being established only when needed. This can be considered added insurance and security when configuring demand-dial connections.

EXERCISE 7.03

VPN GATEWAY CONFIGURATION

In this exercise, you will configure a standard VPN gateway to provide connectivity between two geographically distant LANs, using the Internet as a transport mechanism for your compulsory VPN tunnel. You will configure a persistent connection and inbound and outbound packet filters to permit routing of all IP traffic that matches your LAN subnets.

Before we begin, make sure you have two network interfaces per server available to you. For convenience, it helps to properly name your network connections through the Network Connections folder. For example, determine which network card is attached to the LAN and name it "LAN." Name the network connection that connects to the Internet "WAN" or "Internet."

Your IP addresses should be configured to match the addresses in Figure 7.21 earlier in the chapter.

1. After properly configuring the IP addresses, initiate the **Routing and Remote Access Server Setup Wizard** by selecting your server name from the left pane in the Routing and Remote Access Microsoft management console and clicking **Action | Configure,** then clicking **Enable Routing and Remote Access** in the context menu. Select **Next** to begin the configuration process. Remember that if Routing and Remote Access has been previously enabled, you will have to disable it before you can perform this step to invoke the wizard.

2. From the **Routing and Remote Access Server Setup Wizard Configuration** dialog box, select **Remote access (dial-up or VPN)** and select **Next**.

3. From the **Remote Access** dialog box, select **VPN** and click **Next**.

4. Select your WAN or Internet interface on the next page while keeping the default setting to enable security, as shown in Figure 7.23. Select **Next** to bring up the IP Address Assignment dialog box.

Figure 7.23 Selecting the WAN Interface as the Listening Interface

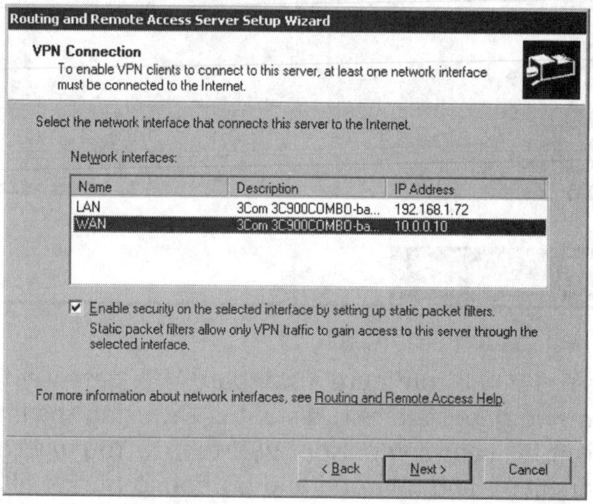

5. Select **From a specified range of addresses | Next**.

6. From the **Address Range Assignment** page, select **New...** and configure a range that consists of enough addresses to support each remote VPN Gateway. Ensure that the addresses in the range will not conflict with the existing DHCP server address pool. Click **Next**.

7. The **Managing Multiple Remote Access Servers** dialog box will be displayed. Select **Next**, keeping the default of **No, use Routing and Remote Access to authenticate connection requests**.

8. Select **Finish** from the **Completing the Routing and Remote Access Server Setup Wizard** page, then click **OK** in response to the DHCP Relay Message that is shown in Figure 7.24.

Figure 7.24 DHCP Relay Properties Message

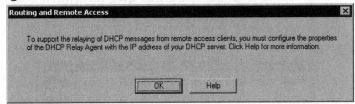

9. To configure a demand-dial interface, select **Network Interfaces** from the left pane of the Routing and Remote Access management console. Click **Action | New Demand-dial Interface...**, as shown in Figure 7.25.

Figure 7.25 Initiating Demand-Dial Interface Configuration

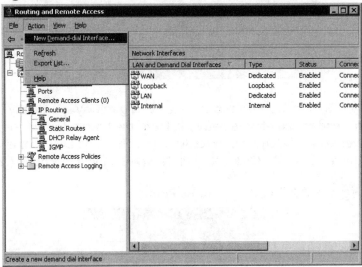

10. Select **Next**, then type in an **Interface name** in the next dialog box to describe this demand-dial VPN interface. Click **Next**.

11. From the **Connection Type** dialog box, select the second option, **Connect using virtual private networking (VPN),** then click **Next**.

12. Based on your decision regarding VPN protocols, select the VPN protocol you want to use from the **VPN Type** screen. In this example, we will go with the default of **Automatic selection** followed by **Next**.

13. Enter a name or IP address in the **Destination Address** dialog box, then click **Next**. This address should match the publicly available interface of the remote gateway.

14. In order to route packets between your gateways, select the default setting of **Route IP packets on this interface,** then click **Next** as shown in Figure 7.26.

Figure 7.26 Setting Routing Options

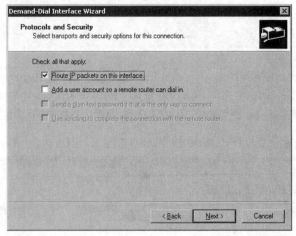

15. Add your static routes to tell your VPN gateway specifically which packets to send to the remote network. From the **Static Routes for Remote Networks** dialog box, select **Add** and enter the LAN subnet address for the remote LAN. Click **OK,** then **Next,** as shown in Figure 7.27.

Figure 7.27 Adding a Static Route

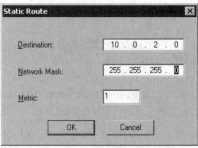

16. Configure authentication information for the **Username, Password, and Domain** and then click **Next**. Don't forget to grant dial-in permissions to the account that will be used to initiate the demand-dial connection. Select **Finish** to complete the basic demand-dial interface.

17. To configure the interface for a persistent connection, select the demand-dial interface name in the right pane of the **Routing and Remote Access management console**.

18. Select **Action | Options,** as shown in Figure 7.28.

Figure 7.28 Setting a Persistent Connection

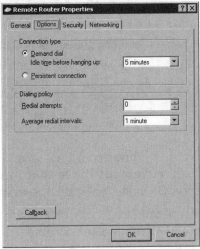

19. Select **Persistent Connection,** then click **OK** on the **Properties** dialog box.

20. Verify your static route to the remote LAN subnet and set the packet filtering capabilities. Under **IP Routing** on the left side of the management console, select **Static Routes**. There should be a static route listed in the right pane of the management console.

21. To set the **Inbound Filters** and **Outbound Filters,** select the demand-dial VPN interface from **IP Routing | General**.

22. Click **Action | Properties**, then the **General** tab of the **Properties** dialog box. Select **Inbound Filters | New**. Fill in the information about your LAN subnets here, as shown in Figure 7.29.

23. Select **OK**. Then select **Drop all packets except those that meet the criteria below**, and click **OK** again to return to the **General** tab to select the demand-dial VPN interface from **IP Routing | General**.

24. From **Action | Properties**, click the **General** tab of the **Properties** dialog box. Select **Outbound Filters | New**.

Figure 7.29 Enabling Inbound Filtering

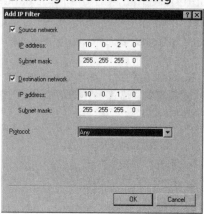

25. Fill in the information about your LAN subnets here. Select **OK**. Then click **Drop all packets except those that meet the criteria below**. Click **OK** and then **OK** again to apply the new settings.

26. Select the demand-dial circuit from **Network Interfaces** in the Routing and Remote Access management console.

27. Select **Action | Connect** to establish the persistent, compulsory tunnel. To verify the operation of your tunnel, look at the Status and Connection State columns, as shown in Figure 7.30.

Figure 7.30 Completed Connection Between Gateways

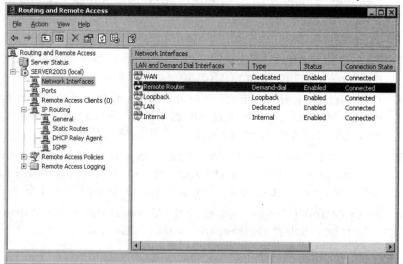

To test connectivity further, use the PING command. When the tunnel is connected, you should be able to ping a client on the remote LAN from one of your local systems. For example, if you are on the 10.0.1.0/24 network, try to ping one of the clients on the 10.0.2.0/24 network.

Troubleshooting Windows Server 2003 VPN Services

There are several possible problems that can prevent clients or other VPN routers from connecting to the VPN service. The best approach to troubleshoot connectivity problems is to follow the OSI reference model and approach the problem from the simplest possible connectivity problems first. Work your way up in complexity, climbing the OSI reference model as you go. Remote access connections in general have an added level of complexity because they first rely on an underlying connection before the actual remote access connection can be made. Remember that remote access connections rely on a PPP connection or some form of encapsulation (L2TP or PPTP).

First, test the underlying network connection. If you are connecting to a VPN server with a persistent Internet connection (this is the typical way of connecting), ensure the VPN server has Internet connectivity. Attempt to ping the VPN server from the calling machine. If the calling machine and the answering server are able to connect to resources on the Internet but pings fail, there may be a firewall between the machines that is blocking ICMP requests (ping). As long as you can verify Internet connectivity for the client and the server, you have removed one layer of complexity from the problem. Ensure that your connection attempts are to the correct IP address. If a firewall exists on either of your networks, make sure it is configured to allow the VPN connection. If you are attempting to connect to the right IP address and both systems have Internet connectivity, the problem may be a NAT configuration or NAT translation problem, or a firewall configuration problem. Remember that L2TP/IPSec connections require NAT-T on the client and server in order to provide proper NAT translation.

Once you have confirmed proper connectivity between the machines, move up in complexity to the authentication aspects of the connection. Make sure that client and server are using the same authentication protocols. Make sure that the encryption strength is the same on client and server. Also, make sure that client and server are both using the same VPN tunneling protocol (PPTP or L2TP). At this point, we have confirmed connectivity and we have ensured that once underlying connectivity exists, the systems will be able to authenticate the connection and establish the tunnel and encryption. Also, make sure that a supply of addresses exists for the calling router or client.

Verify that the calling account has proper permissions to establish a dial-in connection to the network. If you are using remote access policies, make sure that the policies are not preventing the connection. Also make sure, if you are using remote access policies, that the account is configured to use the policies. If you are not using remote access policies, make sure the account has dial-in permission from the **Dial-in** tab of the **Account Properties** dialog box. You may want to enable **Logon** auditing to begin logging access problems. This will provide **Event Viewer** log information in the **Security Log** of your **Event Viewer**.

Two other logging methods are available for remote access. L2TP/IPSec connections will maintain a text-based log in the **Isakmp.log** if the **Enable IPSec logging** check box in the **Microsoft IPSec VPN Configuration Utility** is selected. Another option for logging is to enable PPP logging. To enable PPP logging from the **PPP** tab on the **Properties** of the remote access server, select the **Enable Point-to-Point Protocol (PPP) logging** option.

If you are able to establish a VPN connection, but you are unable to access resources on the remote LAN, first check the IP address for the WAN/PPP Adaptor for the VPN client or VPN calling router. This address should be within the address range of the static IP address pool or it should be within the range of the DHCP scope. If the address is an APIPA address (169.254.y.z), check the static address pool or the DHCP server for available addresses. If the address is within the range of the DHCP scope or static address pool, test connectivity to remote resources using the respective remote LAN IP addresses. Lack of connectivity here would reflect a routing problem within the VPN connection itself. Make sure the VPN routers have correct route table entries for the respective remote networks. If IP connectivity exists but you are unable to connect to resources by name, either through UNC path (\\server\share) or FQDN (server.network.tld/share), check the name resolution for the connection. Your client should be configured to communicate with the proper WINS server for UNC connectivity and it should be configured to communicate with the proper DNS server for FQDN/host connectivity.

A troubleshooting utility is available for VPN and RRAS troubleshooting in the **netsh ras diagnostics** command. This command provides specific diagnostics for the RRAS connection. Another useful command-line utility is the **netdiag** command. Issuing a **netdiag /test:ipsec** from a command prompt will provide a quick test of network connectivity with verbose output to provide troubleshooting information.

The following resources and/or commands will aid in the troubleshooting process:

- **PING** to do basic connectivity testing.

- **IPCONFIG** to verify configuration settings for the local system. This will allow you to verify the correct WINS and DNS server settings, the correct PPP/WAN Adaptor settings, and other basic IP configuration settings.

- **NSLOOKUP** to troubleshoot DNS/Host problems in greater detail.

- **NBTSTAT** to provide basic troubleshooting information for WINS/NetBIOS problems.

- **Event Viewer** to provide basic logging information when **Logon** auditing is enabled.

- **Netsh ras diagnostics** to provide specific diagnostics capabilities for RRAS connections.

- **Netdiag /test:ipsec** to provide a basic network diagnostic exam with sufficient output to narrow down connectivity problems.

NOTE

When configuring logging for troubleshooting connections, understand the different logging options. Certain logs are maintained for security purposes, not for general troubleshooting. VPN server Remote Access Logging, for example, is not intended for general troubleshooting. The main purpose for Remote Access Logging is for security monitoring of Remote Access events.

Summary of Exam Objectives

VPNs have become a major part of the information technology landscape. As networking has evolved and the Internet has become a major part of corporate communication infrastructure, the need to connect remote users and offices has become increasingly more important. VPNs evolved as an extension of traditional dial-up networking, and the VPN technologies used today evolved from the dial-up networking PPP.

VPN authentication is built upon PPP. The various authentication protocols in use and supported by Windows Server 2003 vary in strength and features from PAP authentication with no encryption of password or user name to Microsoft Challenge Handshake Authentication Protocol version 2 (MS-CHAP v2), which provides encryption and user and system verification capabilities. The following list summarizes the authentication protocols used in Microsoft VPN technologies:

- **PAP** Clear-text username and password

- **SPAP** Clear-text username and reversible encrypted password

- **CHAP** Clear-text username and one-way hashed MD5 value in place of the password

- **MS-CHAP** Microsoft's improved implementation of CHAP with error codes and capabilities to change password at logon

- **MS-CHAP v2** Second, further improved version of MS-CHAP with server verification

- **EAP** Modular authentication capabilities that enable vendors to add new authentication methods

- **EAP-TLS** An EAP type that uses certificate-based modular authentication

Two VPN tunneling protocols exist in Microsoft's implementation of VPN. The original protocol available from Microsoft for VPNs, now available in version 2, is Point-to-Point Tunneling Protocol (PPTP). PPTP was introduced with Windows NT 4.0 Beta 2 and has been available in every Microsoft operating system released since then. After several vulnerabilities were discovered in Microsoft's original implementation of PPTP, they revamped it and released version 2 of the protocol. The current implementation of PPTP (used in Windows Server 2003) is PPTP v2. PPTP includes provisions for encryption and compression. The protocol is an extension of the Generic Route Encapsulation (GRE) protocol with a control mechanism that operates on TCP port 1723. Microsoft's PPTP uses the Microsoft Point to Point Encryption (MPPE) protocol for encryption.

Layer Two Tunneling Protocol with Internet Protocol Security (L2TP/IPSec) combines the benefits of PPTP with those of Cisco's Layer Two Forwarding (L2F). L2TP/IPSec provides increased encryption strength when compared to that provided by PPTP. The authentication process is protected by encryption through IPSec so that username and password information receives an extra level of security. L2TP offers these improvements at a cost, however. To implement L2TP, you need a certificate infrastructure in place. This adds complexity to the implementation and is generally perceived as a disadvantage, compared to the simplicity of PPTP, especially in small companies that would not normally implement a PKI. Additionally, the IPSec encryption used with L2TP encrypts the UDP header, the part of the IP packet that contains the destination UDP port number (usually UDP port 1701). This makes L2TP/IPSec difficult to translate when using Network Address Translation (NAT). However, one improvement in Windows Server 2003 over Windows 2000 is that the former offers NAT traversal (NAT-T) to circumvent the problem of using an L2TP/IPSec VPN behind a NAT. As long as both endpoints of the VPN have NAT-T capabilities, the use of NAT is not a problem.

VPN offers secure transfer of data by encapsulating the data packets through the VPN tunneling protocol that is used. Two methods of encapsulating or tunneling the traffic exist:

- **Compulsory Tunnels** Usually created between two VPN servers or gateways to connect remote LANs using the Internet as a transport mechanism
- **Voluntary Tunnels** The more typical use of VPNs, to connect remote users to the corporate LAN using the Internet as a transport mechanism

Configure Microsoft VPNs through the Routing and Remote Access Service management console. Voluntary tunneling and compulsory tunneling start out with basically the same configuration. Voluntary tunneling generally uses a single server. Multiple clients connect to the VPN server through a VPN dial-in. The clients' user accounts need to have dial-in permissions and the configuration of client and server must match with regard to authentication protocols, encryption strength, and VPN tunneling protocol. Compulsory tunnels are established between servers (VPN gateways or VPN routers). The servers usually will have nearly identical configurations. An option exists to initiate a compulsory VPN on-demand. This demand-dial circuit is initiated by interesting traffic, or traffic that is monitored for use as a trigger mechanism. The other option is to configure the VPN servers to use a persistent connection if constant connectivity is not cost prohibitive.

Designing and implementing VPN connectivity requires a good fundamental understanding of the Transport Control Protocol/Internet Protocol (TCP/IP). Because demand circuits are initiated by interesting traffic (TCP or UDP source and/or destination ports, IP source and/or destination addresses, and protocol types), you need to understand how the various port numbers play a part in providing IP connectivity. Also, because private addresses are often used on LANs, and private addresses are not routed on the Internet, you should understand how the private address space works to protect your internal LAN traffic. The inbound and outbound filtering features used in VPN gateways rely heavily upon protocol and port numbers, as well as IP addresses. Understanding how each of these fundamental network building blocks interact with one another and with services on the network will not only help you in your day-to-day networking design and support tasks, it might even help you pass the 70-291 exam.

In any networking implementation, there can and will be unexpected problems. Several methods and utilities exist for troubleshooting remote access VPN connections in Windows Server 2003. The typical utilities for troubleshooting a VPN connection in Windows Server 2003 are:

- **PING** to do basic connectivity testing.

- **IPCONFIG** to verify configuration settings for the local system. This will allow you to verify the correct WINS and DNS server settings, the correct PPP/WAN Adaptor settings, and other basic IP configuration settings.

- **NSLOOKUP** to allow you to troubleshoot DNS/Host problems in greater detail.

- **NBTSTAT** to provide basic troubleshooting information for WINS/NetBIOS problems.

- **Event Viewer** to provide basic logging information when **Logon** auditing is enabled.

- **Netsh ras diagnostics** to provide specific diagnostics capabilities for RRAS connections.

- **Netdiag /test:ipsec** to provide a basic network diagnostic exam with sufficient output to narrow down connectivity problems.

If the client or calling router is not establishing a VPN connection to the answering VPN router, test the underlying connectivity first. After you ensure proper connectivity, the next step is to verify the proper authentication protocols and VPN protocols as well as the proper encryption strengths are in use. At this point, you should have connectivity. If you are unable to reach resources beyond the VPN server, you should verify proper address allocation for the client or calling router. Test basic IP connectivity to resources on the remote LAN by issuing **PING** commands to the various IP addresses. If the **PING** commands fail, check the route table entries on the VPN server or servers. If connectivity exists, test connectivity through UNC or FQDN/Hosts naming. If connectivity by name is failing, the problem is in WINS for the UNC connectivity or in DNS for FQDN/Hosts connectivity.

Exam Objectives Fast Track

Review of Windows Server 2003 Remote Access Concepts

- ☑ Remote Access Service provides for remote access, not remote control.

- ☑ Remote Access Service generally makes remote resources appear as if they are on the local LAN.

☑ Remote Access Service provides for the following functions:

- Remote access (dial-up or VPN)
- Network address translation (NAT)
- Virtual Private Network (VPN) access and NAT
- Secure connection between two private networks
- Custom configuration
- Routing protocol configuration
- DHCP relay configuration
- Remote access policy configuration
- Remote access logging

Enabling the Windows Server 2003 Remote Access Service

☑ VPN configuration requires two network interfaces.

☑ VPN authentication may be provided through the Local System's security accounts database, Active Directory, or RADIUS/IAS.

☑ Several PPP authentication protocols are used for VPN and dial-up:

- PAP
- SPAP
- CHAP
- MS-CHAP
- MS-CHAP v2
- EAP
- EAP-TLS

Configuring the Windows Server 2003 VPN Server

☑ The VPN server is configured through the Routing and Remote Access Service Microsoft Management Console.

☑ Ensure the use of matching authentication protocols, VPN protocols, and matching encryption strength.

☑ Use the **Run As...** command to elevate your permissions to administrator-level on an as-needed basis instead of using the administrator account for normal day-to-day nonadministrative tasks.

Configuring the Windows Server 2003 VPN Gateway

☑ There are two tunneling modes:

- Compulsory (gateway to gateway)
- Voluntary (more common; multiple VPN clients to server)

☑ Options exist for either demand-dial or persistent connections.

☑ Demand-dial filters trigger tunnels when interesting traffic is detected.

☑ Inbound and outbound packet filters help to secure the VPN traffic at the gateway.

Troubleshooting Windows Server 2003 VPN Services

☑ Begin troubleshooting with the simplest variables first. Start at the low end of the OSI reference model.

☑ Ensure that the authentication and encapsulation protocols are the same on the client and server or the calling and answering routers. Make sure the same encryption strength is used on both ends of the connection.

☑ Various commands, utilities, and logging options exist including the following:

- PING
- IPCONFIG
- NSLOOKUP
- NBTSTAT
- Event Viewer
- Netsh ras diagnostics
- Netdiag /test:ipsec

Exam Objectives
Frequently Asked Questions

The following Frequently Asked Questions, answered by the authors of this book, are designed to both measure your understanding of the Exam Objectives presented in this chapter, and to assist you with real-life implementation of these concepts. You will also gain access to thousands of other FAQs at ITFAQnet.com.

Q: Can I mix authentication protocols between client and server?

A: Authentication protocols, VPN protocols, and encryption strength must match in order to establish a VPN tunnel. However, you can configure the client and/or server to support multiple protocols. As long as they have at least one in common, the connection can be made.

Q: I have configured everything as instructed but I am unable to connect. The server says the account does not have dial-in permission. What should I do?

A: Make sure the user account you are using has been configured with dial-in permission (either through remote access policy or individual user permissions in the Local users' properties or the Active Directory users' properties).

Q: How do VPNs and standard RAS requirements differ?

A: Since VPNs typically use a nonsecure public network as a transport medium, VPN authentication and data transfer are more prone to exploitation and consequently should utilize the best encryption and security practices available. A standard RAS connection is made over a private telephone line.

Q: What are strong passwords?

A: Strong passwords use a mix of upper- and lowercase characters in a random pattern, along with numbers and other symbols to provide greater complexity than simple dictionary or language-based passwords. According to IEEE documentation, a password of 10 characters using a dictionary-based password scheme is generally equivalent to a 13-bit key. Adding complexity and randomness to a 10-character password can result in the equivalent of a 40-bit key.

Q: What are smart cards and how are they used?

A: Smart cards are small credit-card-sized cards that usually store encryption keys, public-key certificates, and other types of account information. The card is inserted into a card reader attached to the computer, which reads the information stored on the card.

Typically, a password or Personal Identification Number (PIN) is required to release the account information for authentication within a network. This means that, in order to authenticate, a user must both have physical possession of the card and have knowledge of the PIN. This is commonly used with EAP-TLS authentication.

Q: How is a VPN different from Terminal Services?

A: Terminal Services provides remote control capabilities. VPNs provide remote access. A terminal server provides CPU, memory, and other resources to local applications that are used by remote clients. A VPN server provides a connection point and method for transporting local network traffic across a nonsecure network. The VPN server uses CPU, memory, and other resources to handle encryption capabilities and to transport packets from the LAN over the insecure network to the VPN client.

Q: What is a remote access policy?

A: Remote access policies are sets of rules used to determine access rights or permissions for remote users and hosts. A remote access policy compares connection criteria against a set of predefined rules in a predetermined order. If the connection criteria meet one of the rules in the order the rules are processed, the remote access server will stop comparing the connection criteria to the rule list and will act upon the connection using the method specified in the rule.

For example, your company wants to restrict inbound connections to the VPN server to a specific time. Apply a remote access policy to control logon hours for inbound connections. In this case, the rule is the scheduled hours. When comparing a logon request to the rule, the remote access policy will determine whether to grant access or deny access based in this case on the time of day.

Q: You mention 40-bit encryption, 56-bit encryption, and 128-bit encryption. What difference does it make if you use stronger encryption?

A: The bit number refers to the length of the encryption key. The more digits there are in a key, the longer will take to guess that key by randomly trying different combinations. Stronger encryption techniques make it more difficult to extract the clear-text password through brute-force attacks. In other words, the stronger the encryption, the longer it should take for an attacker to compromise the encrypted password if every possible combination of passwords is to be tried in a given scenario.

Q: Are PPTP and IPSec proprietary protocols? Do we have to use technologies supplied by one company if we put PPTP or IPSec in place in our network?

A: PPTP and IPSec are Internet standard protocols; however, Microsoft has implemented its own version of PPTP. Microsoft recommends using L2TP/IPSec if interoperability with non-Microsoft products is a concern.

Self Test

A Quick Answer Key follows the Self Test questions. For complete questions, answers, and explanations to the Self Test questions in this chapter as well as the other chapters in this book, see the Self Test Appendix.

Review of Windows Server 2003 Remote Access Concepts

1. The president of your company has asked you if VPN technology could benefit the company. What is the greatest benefit provided by VPN?

   A. VPN solutions provide secure connectivity at a significant price savings compared to long distance analog or dedicated circuit connections.

   B. VPN solutions utilize fewer resources than dedicated circuits or analog connections.

   C. VPN solutions provide better remote control capabilities than other third-party alternatives.

   D. VPN solutions provide higher speed connections than dedicated circuits or analog connections.

Enabling the Windows Server 2003 Remote Access Service

2. Your company's corporate security policy is very strict. No username or password information may be passed over the Internet without using the strongest encryption available. Your company does not yet have a certificate infrastructure in place. Which of these methods would be the best choice for VPN authentication to ensure that you are within your company's corporate security policy requirements?

   A. MS-CHAP v2

   B. PAP

   C. CHAP

   D. SPAP

3. You administer a network composed of your corporate office and four separate remote offices located throughout the state. In an effort to avoid long distance charges, you have acquired fractional T-1 Internet access for each office. Each office has a Windows Server 2003 server configured with Network Address Translation (NAT). You want to implement a VPN configuration that ensures that only users from the remote offices can access resources on your corporate network. You also want to ensure Internet connectivity for each office. How will you implement this solution?

A. Configure the corporate VPN gateway with routes for each of the remote LANs. Configure each remote LAN with a default route to the corporate LAN.

B. Configure the corporate VPN gateway with inbound and outbound filters that reflect the remote LANs' subnet addresses.

C. Configure compulsory tunnels between each of the remote offices and the corporate VPN gateway. Configure the corporate VPN gateway with routes for each of the remote LANs and inbound and outbound filters that reflect the remote LANs' subnet addresses. Configure each remote LAN with a default route to the corporate LAN.

D. Configure compulsory tunnels between each of the remote offices and the corporate VPN gateway. Configure the corporate VPN gateway with routes for each of the remote LANs and inbound and outbound filters that reflect the remote LANs' subnet addresses. Configure each remote LAN with a route to the corporate LAN and a default route to the Internet (split tunnel).

Configuring the Windows Server 2003 VPN Server

4. After the completion of your company's PKI project, the CIO of your company has asked you to design a secure solution to give users located at satellite offices access to a new Web-based intranet application. There are typically two or three users in each of the seventeen remote offices. Client computers are using a mix of Windows 98 and Windows XP Professional for their operating systems. Your corporate intranet server sits behind a NAT enabled router. What solution will provide the best security for client access to the intranet server?

A. Install the Microsoft L2TP/IPSec VPN Client on all Windows 98 systems. Configure all clients to connect to the server using EAP-TLS authentication with L2TP/IPSec.

B. Configure all clients to connect to the server using MS-CHAP v2 authentication with PPTP.

C. Configure all clients to connect to the server using EAP-TLS authentication with PPTP.

D. Install the Microsoft L2TP/IPSec VPN Client on all Windows 98 systems. Configure all clients to connect to the server using MS-CHAP v2 authentication with L2TP/IPSec.

5. Your network consists of Windows 98, Windows 2000 Professional, and Windows XP Professional clients. In a recent review of security logs for your network, you noticed several failed attempts to access your network through your VPN server. Examination of firewall logs indicates the attempted failed access came from the same IP address, and the account used was that of an ex-employee. What simple steps should be taken to prevent future unauthorized access attempts from this account and address?

A. Disable the user accounts for all ex-employees and enforce EAP-TLS authentication with IPSec.

B. Disable the user accounts for all ex-employees of the company. Configure a RAS policy to prevent authentication attempts from the IP address reported in the firewall logs. Make sure dial-in permissions are assigned based on RAS policy.

C. Disable the user accounts for all ex-employees and enforce MS-CHAP v2 authentication

D. Disable the user account for the ex-employee. Configure a RAS policy to prevent authentication attempts from the IP address reported in the firewall logs. Make sure dial-in permissions are assigned based on RAS policy.

Configuring the Windows Server 2003 VPN Gateway

6. You have been assigned the task of configuring a VPN server for several remote users to access your corporate network. You open the Routing and Remote Access Server Setup Wizard to begin this process. Using Figure 7.31 as a guide, which of the following options will provide you with a base VPN server for this task? (Choose all that apply.)

Figure 7.31 Routing and Remote Access Server Setup Wizard Configuration

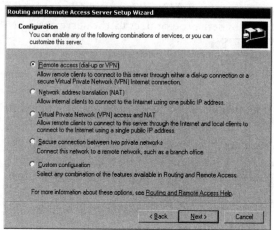

A. Remote access (dial-up or VPN)

B. Network address translation (NAT)

C. Virtual private network (VPN) access and NAT

D. Secure connection between two private networks

E. Custom configuration

7. Your company is designing a software package that will replace legacy applications that currently use IPX/SPX for connectivity with TCP/IP as a transport mechanism. Currently, the software engineers on your four remote office networks need access to a common test server located in your corporate office. The connectivity between the software engineers and server needs to be secure. Also, several sales engineers carrying Windows 98 laptops will need access to resources on the corporate LAN while they are on the road. What solution would best accommodate this scenario?

A. Configure VPN servers to provide remote access VPN and VPN gateway capabilities at each office utilizing L2TP/IPSec with MS-CHAP v2 authentication.

B. Configure the software engineers' systems to use L2TP/IPSec with EAP-TLS authentication.

C. Configure VPN servers to provide remote access VPN and VPN gateway capabilities at each office utilizing PPTP with MS-CHAP v2 authentication.

D. Configure the software engineers' systems to use PPTP with MS-CHAP v2 authentication.

8. You have installed an Exchange server on your corporate network to handle e-mail for all of the users within your organization. If you want to use compulsory VPN tunnels specifically to transport e-mail using SMTP and POP3 between clients and the Exchange server, which TCP ports will you configure in your VPN packet filters?

    A. TCP 25 and TCP 443

    B. TCP 80 and TCP 110

    C. TCP 110 and TCP 143

    D. TCP 25 and TCP 110

9. You are setting up two VPN gateways in a test lab to test configurations before implementing them in your production network. You are using two copies of Windows Server 2003 Server Web Edition to test the connectivity in your test scenario. You configure the two servers as VPN gateways. Five L2TP ports are visible in the management console as well as five PPTP ports. You connect the servers together with compulsory tunnel mode PPTP tunnels. Everything seems to be functioning correctly. When you try to connect a dial-in VPN client to one of the servers, the connection fails. Why is the client unable to connect?

    A. You do not have a sufficient public key infrastructure in place to provide PPTP connectivity.

    B. Windows Server 2003 Server–Web Edition does not support PPTP voluntary mode tunnels.

    C. Windows Server 2003 Server–Web Edition does not support more than one simultaneous tunnel, even though 1,000 tunnels may be installed.

    D. You do not have the same authentication modes on the client and server.

10. Several outside sales personnel need access to the corporate LAN. They are not direct-hire employees of your company but they will need access to certain resources. Because they are not direct-hire employees, it has been very difficult to control their system configurations to ensure security for the corporate LAN. How can you enforce corporate policies for this group of remote access clients?

    A. Configure a special Remote Access Policy to enforce your corporate security policy on their machines.

    B. Use the Network Access Quarantine Control utilities from the Connection Manager Administration Kit to ensure the VPN clients meet corporate standards for remote access.

    C. Use the **netsh** command to ensure users connect with proper client configurations.

    D. Configure the VPN server to use RADIUS for authentication. Use a RADIUS connection policy with Active Directory Group Policy to enforce corporate security.

11. You are planning to use IAS/RADIUS for authentication and account management of remote access users and devices. You go to the Administrative Tools menu but IAS is not listed. Where is IAS management conducted?

   A. IAS is an applet of the Administrative Tools menu but it must be installed as a Windows Component.

   B. IAS is managed through the Routing and Remote Access management console.

   C. IAS is administered under Active Directory Users and Computers.

   D. IAS is under the Option Pack submenu of the Administrative Tools menu.

Troubleshooting Windows Server 2003 VPN Services

12. You work for a small computer-consulting firm. One of your clients, who recently began working from home, calls to inform you that he cannot dial in to the company's Windows Server 2003 VPN from his Windows XP computer. He just completed the setup for his new DSL connection and, at the instruction of one of the other VPN users; he has configured his VPN client. He says that error 735 is being displayed. You use the Windows XP remote desktop to connect to his computer and see the error message displayed in Figure 7.32. How can you repair this connection to enable access to this user?

Figure 7.32 Connection Error 735

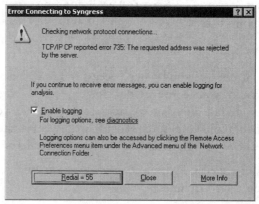

   A. Ensure the computer has a valid certificate on the network.

   B. Configure the **Host name or IP address of the destination** on the **General** tab of the VPN connection properties for the correct VPN server IP address.

C. Configure the VPN client to **Obtain an IP address automatically** and to **Obtain DNS server address automatically** from the **Internet Protocol Properties** of the **Networking** tab of the VPN connection.

D. From the **Internet Protocol Properties** of the **General** tab of the **Local Area Network** connection, configure the **Local Area Network** connection to **Obtain an IP address automatically** and to **Obtain DNS server address automatically**.

13. Your company is constantly growing and expanding to include more field personnel. There are currently approximately 60 employees accessing the VPN from various remote locations. You return to the office after a relaxing weekend to find that three users are unable to access the VPN server. You walk the users through the process of making a screen shot of the error generated. What is causing the error in Figure 7.33?

Figure 7.33 VPN User Logon Error

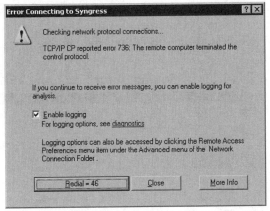

A. Ensure the computer has a valid certificate on the network.

B. Configure the **Host name or IP address of the destination** on the **General** tab of the VPN connection properties for the correct VPN server IP address.

C. Configure the VPN client to **Obtain an IP address automatically** and to **Obtain DNS server address automatically** from the **Internet Protocol Properties** of the **Networking** tab of the VPN connection.

D. Configure the DHCP server with a larger scope to accommodate IP addresses for all local and remote users.

14. One of your users calls about a problem accessing resources on the network. The client VPN connection shows a connection but none of the resources within your Active Directory domain are available. The user seems to have IP connectivity to the VPN LAN with his or her Windows 2000 Professional computer. Other remote users have not reported problems connecting to the network resources. What is causing this problem?

    A. The WINS server configuration settings for the VPN client are incorrect..

    B. The VPN server configuration for the DNS server is incorrect.

    C. The VPN server configuration for the WINS server is incorrect.

    D. The DNS server configuration settings for the VPN client are incorrect.

15. Your VPN server is configured to connect directly to the Internet, providing VPN connectivity and NAT for your office. Your broadband access provider recently went out of business and you have to reconfigure your server to connect to a new service. One of the junior administrators was in the process of reconfiguring the server but could not obtain connectivity to the Internet. You run ipconfig and see the IP address information shown in Figure 7.34. Why is the VPN server unable to connect to the Internet?

Figure 7.34 IP Configuration for Corporate VPN/NAT Server

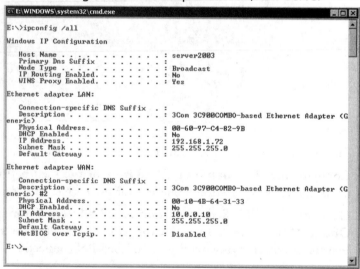

    A. This operation is by design.

    B. The VPN server does not have a correct route to the Internet.

    C. Both addresses are private addresses. This server cannot connect directly to the Internet.

    D. The DNS server addresses are incorrect.

Self Test Quick Answer Key

For complete questions, answers, and explanations to the Self Test questions in this chapter as well as the other chapters in this book, see the Self Test Appendix.

1.	**A**	9.	**C**
2.	**A**	10.	**B**
3.	**D**	11.	**A**
4.	**D**	12.	**C**
5.	**B**	13.	**D**
6.	**A, C, E**	14.	**D**
7.	**C**	15.	**C**
8.	**D**		

Chapter 8

MCSA/MCSE 70-291

Configuring the Windows 2003 Routing and Remote Access Service LAN Routing, Dial-up Services, and Routing Protocols

Exam Objectives in this Chapter:

4.3.3   Manage routing ports.

4.6   Troubleshoot Routing and Remote Access routing.

4.6.1   Troubleshoot demand-dial routing.

4.2   Manage Remote access.

4.2.1   Manage packet filters.

4.2.2   Manage Routing and Remote Access routing interfaces.

4.2.3   Manage devices and ports.

4.5.3   Diagnose and resolve user access to resources beyond the remote access server.

4.1.1   Configure remote access authentication protocols.

4.1.3   Configure Routing and Remote Access policies to permit or deny access.

4.2.5   Manage Routing and Remote Access clients.

4.2.4   Manage routing protocols.

4.3   Manage TCP/IP routing.

4.3.1   Manage routing protocols.

5.3   Troubleshoot server services.

5.3.1   Diagnose and resolve issues related to service dependency.

5.3.2   Use service recovery options to diagnose and resolve service-realted issues.

4.5   Troubleshoot user access to remote access services.

4.5.2   Diagnose and resolve issues realted to establishing a remote access connection.

4.1.2   Configure Internet Authentication Service (IAS) to provide authentication for Routing and Remote Access clients.

Introduction

In the previous chapter, we looked at the VPN capabilities of Windows Server 2003. We reviewed the importance of network infrastructure design and connectivity requirements when designing and implementing a VPN. Primary connectivity for Windows Server 2003 relies on Transmission Control Protocol/Internet Protocol (TCP/IP). The Internet relies on TCP/IP and consequently, the growth of the Internet has driven the use of this open protocol. Through this growth, other standards have developed to support TCP/IP network connectivity on a large scale. TCP/IP routing protocols are a fundamental necessity for Internet connectivity. The Internet would not support the scalability and redundancy that it now supports without the use of dynamic routing protocols like RIP and OSPF.

In this chapter, we will look at IP Routing Protocols in a local area network (LAN) environment. Since the outward growth of our LAN is being perpetuated by the abundance of Internet connectivity and the growing presence of corporate wide area networks (WANs), the growing need for corporate remote network access has grown proportionately. We will explore the Routing and Remote Access Service (RRAS) for Windows Server 2003 along with the protocols used to support remote access. One of the key protocols used in modern dial-up and VPN environments is Point-to-Point Protocol (PPP). We will look at PPP and special features available to PPP connections in Windows Server 2003.

Security is a major industry buzzword today. In this chapter, we will look at some of the features used to implement network security for Windows Server 2003. Connecting your corporate LAN, or even a small office, to the Internet can potentially compromise the security of your entire network. In the area of security, we will look at Windows Server 2003's basic firewall capabilities. Also, we will conduct an analysis of the Windows Server 2003 RRAS policy configuration and packet filter implementation. Because most internal systems today do not have a sufficient number of public IP addresses, we will discuss RRAS Network Address Translation (NAT) services. Finally, because even the best of intentions do not always go according to plan, we will look at troubleshooting remote access client and server configurations followed by a thorough review of Microsoft's implementation of Remote Access Dial-in User Service (RADIUS), also known as Internet Authentication Service (IAS) in the Microsoft world. Let's start with a look at something that has become very familiar to even the smallest of offices today, the LAN.

Configuring LAN Routing

Today, even the smallest of offices are starting to reap the rewards of the LAN. Sharing files, printers, and network services is commonplace today. As the availability of broadband services continues to increase, there is an increased need to share Internet connectivity for multiple users. Windows Server 2003 provides LAN routing through the Routing and Remote Access Service. Through this wizard-based configuration, we can implement the basic components needed to connect multiple LANs. In the previous chapter, we discussed VPN technologies provided by Windows Server 2003. In this section, we will look at the network infrastructure that can be built upon the VPN services in Windows Server 2003. Windows Server 2003 has support for static routing as well as a couple of open-standard dynamic routing protocols. We will look at the routing protocols in greater detail later in this chapter. First, however, we will review how Windows Server 2003 can provide LAN-to-LAN connectivity over various types of connections.

Several technologies exist today to provide connectivity between distant networks. There are various private line technologies utilizing non-Internet connectivity and the Internet can also provide LAN-to-LAN connectivity. To configure remote site connectivity or LAN routing, we have to take a methodical approach to design. First, based on bandwidth require-ments, distance between sites, and budget, we have to decide on a connection type.

Some of the most frequently implemented options for remote site connection type include:

- Frame Relay
- Dedicated leased line
- Dial-up
- VPN

Frame Relay and dedicated lines typically require other hardware components, such as Channel Service Unit/Data Service Unit (CSU/DSU) devices, to complete the connection between remote offices (these are sometimes referred to as Customer Premises Equipment, or CPE). Dial-up connections, depending on the technology used, will probably require extra hardware as well. In the case of dial-up connections, if your server does not already have one, you might need an analog modem or analog modem card depending on the number of lines used for the connection. Integrated Service Digital Network (ISDN) is another type of dial-up connection that will require either an external ISDN terminal adapter or an internal ISDN adapter card for your server. Some of the more common broadband Internet connections, including Digital Subscriber Line (DSL) and cable, often used as a base for a VPN network, provide Internet connectivity via Ethernet connection. Most new servers come with one, or sometimes two, Ethernet ports built in or preinstalled. If you are planning to use a VPN solution to connect remote offices, you will have to decide on the VPN technology to use. As discussed in the previous chapter, Microsoft Windows Server 2003 provides for L2TP/IPSec and PPTP VPN connectivity.

If you will be using a dial-up technology (either analog, ISDN, or VPN), you need to decide on persistent connectivity or demand-dial connectivity. If you will be using a demand-dial connection you need to determine which end of the dial-up connection will initiate the call. You can configure either end of your dial-up circuit to initiate the connec-tion or both ends can dial-up as needed. One-way connections are used for satellite offices to connect to a corporate office when the corporate office will not ever be required to ini-tiate a connection to the remote site. If there are ten or more remote offices in your net-work and offices need to have connectivity to one another, persistent one-way initiated connections are recommended. If there are less than ten offices requiring connectivity in both directions, two-way initiated connections are recommended. You also need to determine what traffic type will be considered interesting traffic. In other words, what type of network traffic should initiate your dial-up connection when it is down? As mentioned in the previous chapter, you can specify interesting traffic as well as dial-out hours to restrict the use of your demand-dial circuit.

Next, you need to determine security features to use for your network. VPN server placement, authentication provider, authentication method, VPN encryption type, router user accounts and groups, and remote access policy settings are all security features that should be decided at this point. If your network currently has perimeter devices in place, you will probably place your VPN server behind the perimeter. If you do not currently have a perimeter network, you should place the VPN server at the edge of the network to protect the inside systems. Also, the operating system in use on your servers will determine placement of VPN servers. As mentioned in the previous chapter, L2TP/IPSec will not work with all versions of NAT. This might force you to place your VPN servers outside of the perimeter of your network. Authentication providers include Windows authentication and RADIUS/IAS authentication. Preferred authentication methods include EAP-TLS and MS-CHAP v2 as discussed in the previous chapter. Preferred methods of VPN encryption include MPPE and IPSec, again as discussed in the previous chapter. Router user and group accounts will aid in the implementation of remote access policies. Remote access policies control user and group access to the network through the remote access connection.

After your security features have been planned out, you should move ahead to the issue of remote site integration with your existing network. In this stage, you will design your infrastructure, plan IP address allocation, and plan your Active Directory integration. You must decide whether to use static routing or one of the dynamic routing protocols available for Windows Server 2003. After determining which routing protocol will be used (if any), you must allocate the IP addresses to each site. The number of systems and network devices at each site, as well as the routing protocol in use, will determine the subnet mask to use and consequently the number of IP addresses available at each site. When your IP routing and allocation design is in place, you must decide how your remote site will interact with your Active Directory and other Active Directory servers on your network.

To complete the planning stages, you should inventory your existing routers, if you currently have any. It is advisable to migrate the Windows NT 4.0 or Windows 2000 based systems to Windows Server 2003. Although Windows 2000 has many of the features of Windows Server 2003, to gain the most from a Windows Server 2003 deployment, you should migrate all of the older systems to take advantage of the new improved features available in Windows Server 2003. This stage involves reviewing hardware requirements for Windows Server 2003 to ensure that your planned upgrade systems can support Windows Server 2003. Also, you will have to plan for the server capacities at each site. The number of connections the server will support, the expected data throughput, and the types of data encryption and compression that will be used all affect the capacity requirements for your remote access servers.

EXAM WARNING

This chapter focuses heavily on different forms of remote access. Because remote access usually involves systems that are beyond the scope of normal network administration, or systems that might not belong to the corporate network, and also because remote access potentially opens up network access to unwanted users, authentication plays a vital role. Understand the different types of authentication available in Windows Server 2003 and know what each protocol provides and requires.

It's finally time to deploy your solution. After navigating the myriad of design decisions, the final step is the actual deployment. It is a good idea to deploy this design in a test environment first, to work out any bugs in the configuration, and to determine the viability of the design. Deployment involves deploying the actual connection, the selected security features, and completing the integration of the remote site with the existing network. In the next section, we will look at the details of RRAS packet filters and how their selection and implementation can affect network performance and traffic patterns.

EXERCISE 8.01

ROUTING AND REMOTE ACCESS
BASIC LAN ROUTING CONFIGURATION

In this exercise, we will examine the basic setup procedure for Routing and Remote Access Service LAN Routing for Windows Server 2003. We will configure two Windows Server 2003 routers to advertise the RIP version 1 routing protocol. To configure RIP v1 for our network, we will walk through the configurations for one of the routers. The same basic configuration should be repeated on the second router. Begin by configuring the addresses as shown in Figure 8.1.

Figure 8.1 Configuration for a Two-Router Network

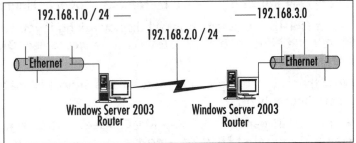

Now let's go to the Routing and Remote Access management console to enable routing and to configure RIP.

1. Click **Start | Programs | Administrative Tools | Routing and Remote Access**.

2. From the **Routing and Remote Access** management console, right-click on the server name in the left console pane and select **Configure and Enable Routing and Remote Access**. If this option is grayed out, select **Disable Routing and Remote Access** to start with a fresh configuration, and then you will be able to select the **Configure and Enable Routing and Remote Access** option.

3. On the first page of the Routing and Remote Access Server Setup Wizard, click **Next**.

4. Select **Custom Configuration** and click **Next** as shown in Figure 8.2.

Figure 8.2 Custom Routing and Remote Access Configuration

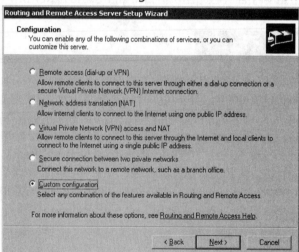

5. Select **LAN Routing** followed by **Next** as shown in Figure 8.3.

6. Select **Finish**. A message box will display asking if you would like to enable the Routing and Remote Access Service. Select **OK** to enable LAN routing.

7. Now that the Routing and Remote Access Service is enabled, we have to configure RIP v1.

8. From the left pane of the RRAS MMC, select **IP Routing**. Right-click **General** and select **New Routing Protocol** as shown in Figure 8.4.

Figure 8.3 LAN Routing Configuration

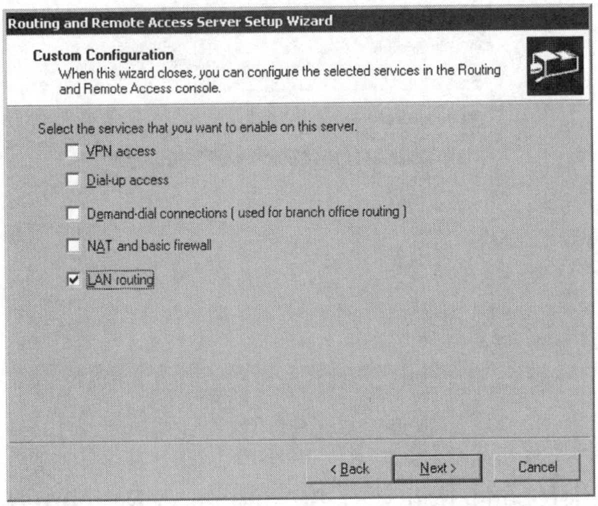

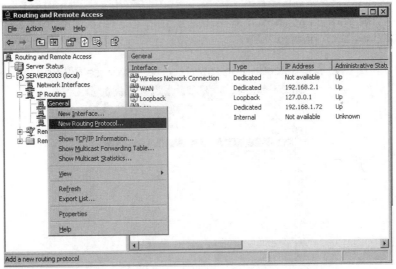

Figure 8.4 Adding a New Routing Protocol

9. From the next screen, select **RIP Version 2 for Internet Protocol** and click **OK** as shown in Figure 8.5.

10. Now an entry for **RIP** will be displayed in the left pane beneath the **IP Routing** icon. This means that RIP is enabled on the server, but at this point, RIP will not advertise any routes because we have to tell RIP which interfaces to use for route advertisement.

Figure 8.5 Adding RIP

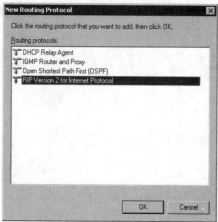

11. In the left pane, right-click **RIP** and select **New Interface….**

12. From the **New Interface for RIP Version 2 for Internet Protocol** dialog box, select the interface that provides the common link between the routers as shown in Figure 8.6. In this case, the common interface has been named **WAN**.

Figure 8.6 Selecting an Interface to Advertise RIP Routes Through

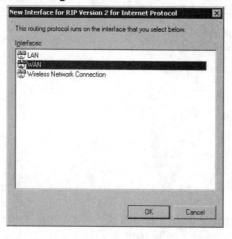

13. Because our initial configuration will support only RIP version 1, we have to configure the router to support only RIP version 1. Select **RIP version 1 broadcast** from the **Outgoing packet protocol:** drop-down box and **RIP version 1 only** from the **Incoming packet protocol:** drop-down box as shown in Figure 8.7 and click **OK.** You will notice a couple

of options in Figure 8.7. First, we can specify the cost of the route by modifying the **Added cost for routes:** option in the dialog box. Cost for RIP routes is the number of hops or the number of routers that traffic will traverse to reach the destination. If we want this route to be advertised as a less preferred route, we can increase the cost here. You will also see an option for tagged routes. By modifying the **Tag for announced routes:** option in the dialog box, we can mark specific routes with a special identifier. This is handy when mixing routing protocols. If you were to advertise RIP routes into another routing protocol, like OSPF or BGP, you might want to ensure that RIP routes advertised from this router are modified with a different weight value or a different cost value. Finally, you will also see an option for authentication. By selecting **Activate authentication** in this dialog box, we can specify a password for each RIP route exchange. This option adds a level of security to your network by protecting the RIP information exchanged between routers and consequently protecting information about your network.

Figure 8.7 Selecting RIP Version 1 for Inbound and Outbound Packets

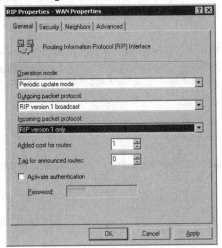

14. We have now completed the RIP configuration for this router. Repeat the previous steps on the other router to complete the end-to-end RIP advertisements for this network.

15. After you have completed the configuration for both routers, you should verify RIP operation between routers. There are three basic checks we can use to verify operation in this scenario. First, under the left pane of the **Routing and Remote Access Service** management

console, we can select **IP Routing**. Now, in the right pane of the management console, right-click **RIP** and select **Show Neighbors....**

16. You should see a message box with the address of the nearest RIP router as shown in Figure 8.8.

Figure 8.8 Viewing RIP Neighbors

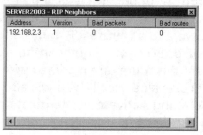

17. Since the routers see one another as neighbors, we should verify that they are properly advertising routes to one another. Select **General** beneath **IP Routing** in the left pane of the management console. Right-click any of the interfaces listed in the right pane and select **Show IP Routing Table...** to display the routing table as shown in Figure 8.9.

Figure 8.9 Displaying the Routing Table to Verify RIP Operation

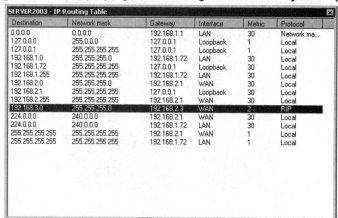

18. As a final verification step, we can ping any remote address on the network from a local system. If RIP v1 routing is working properly, a client on the 192.168.1.0/24 network should get a reply when pinging a client on the 192.168.3.0/24 network as shown in Figure 8.10.

Figure 8.10 Testing RIP with the PING Command

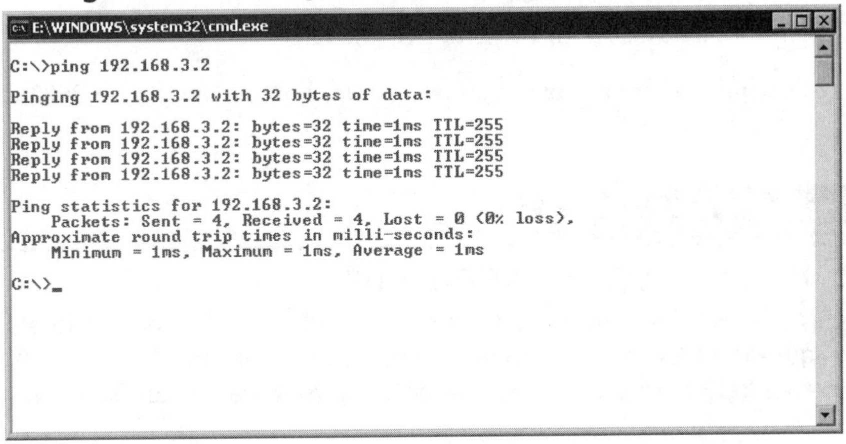

```
E:\WINDOWS\system32\cmd.exe                                    _ □ X

C:\>ping 192.168.3.2

Pinging 192.168.3.2 with 32 bytes of data:

Reply from 192.168.3.2: bytes=32 time=1ms TTL=255
Reply from 192.168.3.2: bytes=32 time=1ms TTL=255
Reply from 192.168.3.2: bytes=32 time=1ms TTL=255
Reply from 192.168.3.2: bytes=32 time=1ms TTL=255

Ping statistics for 192.168.3.2:
    Packets: Sent = 4, Received = 4, Lost = 0 (0% loss),
Approximate round trip times in milli-seconds:
    Minimum = 1ms, Maximum = 1ms, Average = 1ms

C:\>_
```

Configuring & Implementing...

Vendor Interoperability

There are many instances in which you will not have a uniform network. You don't always have the benefit of a clean slate when designing a network and often, when administering a network, you don't have the benefit of selecting the equipment to be used on your network. Maybe you are connecting a network from a new acquisition into your existing network. Maybe you are configuring a link between your network and a partner's network. In any case, you will likely have to connect your equipment to equipment from a different vendor or running a different operating system.

The nature of networking today is interoperability. The coverage of RIP and OSPF in this chapter will provide the capabilities to connect Cisco, Nortel, or any of several other vendors' equipment into your Microsoft network. This interoperability is a necessity today with the ever-changing network infrastructures that we are required to design and support. A basic understanding of the protocols covered here will help you to make your growing network communicate harmoniously with almost any equipment that may be thrown your way.

EXAM
70-291

OBJECTIVE
4.2
4.2.1
4.2.2
4.2.3

Configuring RRAS Packet Filters

Routing and Remote Access packet filters provide network security by controlling certain types of network traffic into or out of your LAN. RRAS packet filters are applied through the Routing and Remote Access Service MMC on a per-interface basis. RRAS packet filters work on an exception basis. This means that the filters can do either of the following:

- Allow all traffic except that specified in the filter
- Deny all traffic except that specified by the filter

Packet filtering rules are a vital part of security in the Windows Server 2003 remote access network environment.

EXERCISE 8.02

RRAS PACKET FILTER CONFIGURATION

In this exercise, we will configure inbound and outbound packet filters. We will configure the LAN interface to allow only traffic from the 192.168.0.0/16 series of networks. Figure 8.11 shows the network that we are configuring.

Figure 8.11 RRAS Network to Be Filtered

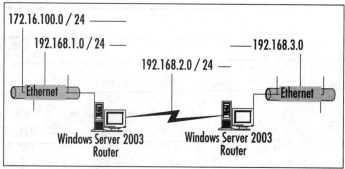

To start our configuration, we will configure a basic RIP version 2 network as seen in the previous exercise.

1. Start by opening **Routing and Remote Access** by selecting **Start | Programs | Administrative Tools | Routing and Remote Access**.

2. From the **Routing and Remote Access** management console, right-click the server name and select **Configure and Enable Routing and Remote Access**. If this option is grayed out, select **Disable Routing and Remote Access** to start with a fresh configuration.

3. On the first page of the Routing and Remote Access Server Setup Wizard, click **Next**.

4. Select **Custom Configuration** and click **Next**.

5. Select **LAN Routing** followed by **Next**, and then select **Finish**. A message box will display asking if you would like to enable the Routing and Remote Access Service. Select **OK** to enable LAN routing.

6. Now that the Routing and Remote Access Service is enabled, we have to configure RIP v2.

7. In the left pane, select **IP Routing**. Right-click **General** and select **New Routing Protocol**.

8. On the next screen, select **RIP Version 2 for Internet Protocol** and click **OK**.

9. Now an entry for **RIP** will be displayed in the left pane beneath the **IP Routing** icon. This means that RIP is enabled on the server but at this point, RIP will not advertise any routes because we have to tell RIP which interfaces to use for route advertisement.

10. In the left pane, right-click **RIP** and select **New Interface....**

11. From the **New Interface for RIP Version 2 for Internet Protocol** dialog box, select the interface that provides the common link between the routers as shown in Figure 8.11. In this case, the common interface has been named **WAN**.

12. The default setting for RIP in a Windows Server 2003 environment is **Rip version 2 broadcast** for the **Outgoing packet protocol:** drop-down list and **Rip version 1 and 2** for the **Incoming packet protocol:** drop-down box. If we are using only RIP version 2 throughout our network, and the transport medium will be Ethernet, it is preferred to use **RIP version 2 multicast** for the **Outbound packet protocol:** drop-down selection and to ensure only RIP version 2 operation, select **RIP version 2 only** from the **Incoming protocol packet:** drop-down list.

13. Repeat this process for the other Windows Server 2003 router that will be advertising RIP version 2 on your network.

In our example, we have configured another network at 172.16.100.0/24. This is the network we wish to block using the packet filters. The direct approach would be to specifically block this network. We intend to block all network traffic except for our current network addresses. We will begin with the **Routing and Remote Access** management console to configure the packet filters for inbound and outbound traffic.

1. Before we begin filtering, verify connectivity to the 172.16.100.0/24 network by pinging the 172.16.100.3 interface from your server as shown in Figure 8.12.

Figure 8.12 Verifying Connectivity to the 172.16.100.0 Network

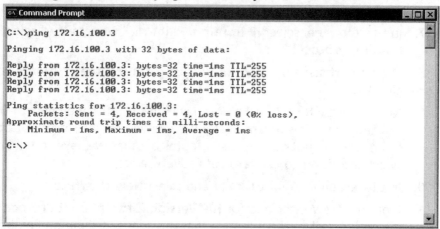

```
C:\>ping 172.16.100.3

Pinging 172.16.100.3 with 32 bytes of data:

Reply from 172.16.100.3: bytes=32 time=1ms TTL=255
Reply from 172.16.100.3: bytes=32 time=1ms TTL=255
Reply from 172.16.100.3: bytes=32 time=1ms TTL=255
Reply from 172.16.100.3: bytes=32 time=1ms TTL=255

Ping statistics for 172.16.100.3:
    Packets: Sent = 4, Received = 4, Lost = 0 (0% loss),
Approximate round trip times in milli-seconds:
    Minimum = 1ms, Maximum = 1ms, Average = 1ms

C:\>
```

2. We intend to block all traffic except traffic to and from the 192.168.1.0, 192.168.2.0, and 192.168.3.0 networks. To accomplish this, we will apply inbound and outbound packet filters on our WAN interface. Select **General** under the **IP Routing** icon in the left pane of the management console.

3. Right-click the **WAN** interface in the right pane of the management console and select **Properties**.

4. Under the **General** tab of the **WAN Properties** dialog box, select the **Inbound Filters...** button as shown in Figure 8.13.

Figure 8.13 Inbound and Outbound Filter Configuration

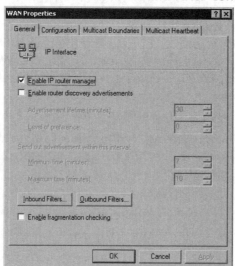

5. The inbound filters should allow traffic coming from the 192.168.2.0 and 192.168.3.0 networks only. We will add those networks as source networks for the inbound filter. Select **New** from the **Inbound Filters** dialog box. Then, select the **Source Network** check box and enter **192.168.2.0** for the **IP address:** and **255.255.255.0** for the **Subnet mask:** as shown in Figure 8.14.

Figure 8.14 Adding an Inbound Filter

6. Click **OK** to add the first filter to the inbound filter list.

7. Repeat this process for the 192.168.3.0 network. Select **New** from the **Inbound Filters** dialog box. Then, select the **Source Network** check box and enter **192.168.3.0** for the **IP address:** and **255.255.255.0** for the **Subnet mask:**.

8. Change the **Filter Action** to **Drop all packets except those that meet the criteria below** and click **OK** as shown in Figure 8.15.

Figure 8.15 Completed Inbound Filters

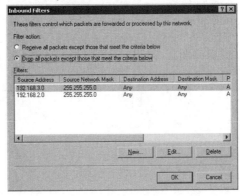

9. We will now configure **Outbound Filters** in the same fashion that we just configured the **Inbound Filters**. Select the **Outbound Filters...** button. The outbound filters should allow traffic going to the 192.168.2.0 and 192.168.3.0 networks only. We will add those networks as destination networks for the outbound filter. Select **New** from the **Outbound Filters** dialog box. Then, select the **Destination Network** check box and enter **192.168.2.0** for the **IP address:** and **255.255.255.0** for the **Subnet mask:**.

10. Repeat step number 9 for the 192.168.3.0 network. Select **New** from the **Outbound Filters** dialog box. Then, select the **Destination Network** check box and enter **192.168.3.0** for the **IP address:** and **255.255.255.0** for the **Subnet mask:**.

11. Change the **Filter Action** to **Drop all packets except those that meet the criteria below** and click **OK**.

12. From the **WAN Properties** dialog box, click **OK** to complete the configuration.

13. To verify your configuration, test connectivity to the 172.16.100.0/24 network by pinging the 172.16.100.3 interface from your server as shown in Figure 8.16.

Figure 8.16 Verifying the Packet Filter Is Working

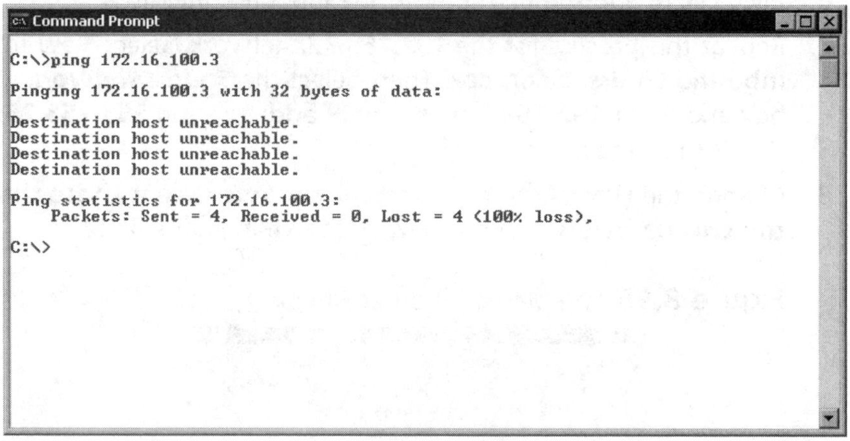

Configuring the Windows 2003 Dial-up RAS Server

When configured as a dial-up server, Windows Server 2003 Routing and Remote Access Service provides dial-up network connectivity to remote users via the public switched telephone network (PSTN) through either analog connections or digital ISDN connections. The RRAS server configured in this manner will provide remote access to users, not to be confused with remote control. Remote control features are provided through Windows Server 2003 Terminal Services.

NOTE

This chapter focuses on RRAS and the remote access capabilities of Windows Server 2003. Understand that remote access is not the same thing as remote control. Remote control provides a desktop and resources from the hosting server. Microsoft Terminal Server, AT&T's Virtual Network Computing VNC, and Symantec's PCAnywhere are a few examples of remote control software. Remote access provides network connectivity for remote clients. Remote access allows clients to connect to resources on a remote network as if the client were physically connected directly to that network.

Dial-up connectivity is generally provided through the Point-to-Point Protocol (PPP). PPP will be discussed later in this chapter. First, let's look at how an RRAS Dial-up server fits into a Windows Server 2003 network. Remote users dial in via the analog PSTN, in this example, to connect to the corporate LAN. This scenario would most typically be used where long distance charges will not be incurred. The remote user dials the server using a local modem. The corporate server would normally have a modem card or modem bank to provide multiple connections to remote users through the RRAS dial-up service. The RRAS dial-up server would authenticate the user and/or computer, verify logon privileges are allowed based on RRAS policies and account logon hours, and then grant or deny access. Figure 8.17 illustrates the network described in this scenario.

The dial-up scenario using analog phone lines is most typically for local phone calls to the corporate office. A similar configuration and scenario was discussed in the previous chapter in which the dial-up users were dialing the server through the Internet using a VPN connection instead of the PPP analog connection described here. A VPN connection is more appropriate if direct dialup calls would incur long distance charges.

Figure 8.17 RRAS Dial-up Server

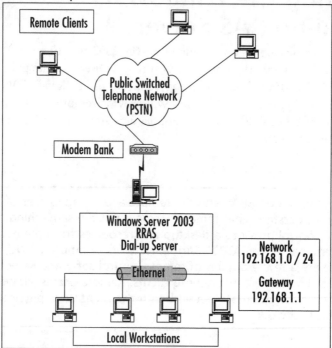

EXERCISE 8.03

RRAS DIAL-UP SERVER CONFIGURATION

In this exercise, we will configure a dial-up server to provide LAN access to remote users via the PSTN. RRAS remote dial-in support typically relies on a device known as a modem bank. This device provides multiple modem connections (with multiple phone lines) on one card. In this example, we will work with a standard modem configuration. Using a modem bank, we first configure the Routing and Remote Access service using the Custom configuration option.

1. Open **Routing and Remote Access**. **Start | Administrative Tools | Routing and Remote Access**.

2. From the **Routing and Remote Access** management console, right-click the server name and select **Configure and Enable Routing and Remote Access**. If this option is grayed out, select **Disable Routing and Remote Access** to start with a fresh configuration.

3. On the first page of the **Routing and Remote Access Server Setup Wizard**, click **Next**.

4. Select **Custom configuration** and click **Next** as shown in Figure 8.18. This configuration can also be accomplished by selecting **Remote Access (dial-up or VPN)** from the selection options. We will use the **Custom configuration** option instead, which provides the same basic result when using the wizard.

Figure 8.18 Custom Routing and Remote Access Configuration

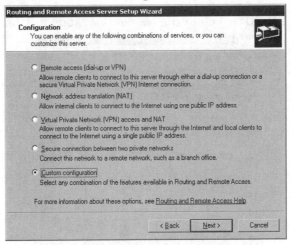

5. Next, select **Dial-up Access** as shown in Figure 8.19, then click **Next**.

Figure 8.19 Selecting Dial-up Access Configuration

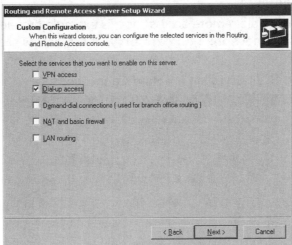

6. To complete the initial configuration, select **Finish** then click **Yes** to start the Routing and Remote Access service.

7. Now we will configure the modem bank ports to provide inbound connectivity. In the left pane, right-click **Ports**.

8. Select **Properties** to open the **Ports Properties** dialog box as shown in Figure 8.20.

Figure 8.20 Selecting the Modem or Modem Bank for Configuration

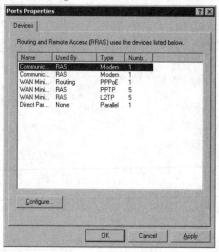

9. From the **Ports Properties** dialog box, select a device, and then select **Configure**.

10. We will enable remote access for this example by selecting the **Remote access connections (inbound only)** check box as seen in Figure 8.21.

Figure 8.21 Enabling Inbound Connections

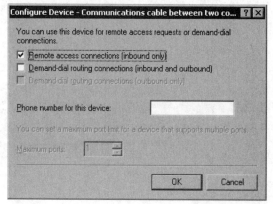

11. Now that the initial configuration is complete, we have to modify the Routing and Remote Access properties for the server. In the left pane, right-click on the server name and select **Properties**.

12. Click the **General** tab and make sure that the **Remote access server** check box is selected as shown in Figure 8.22.

Figure 8.22 Verifying Remote Access Server General Configuration

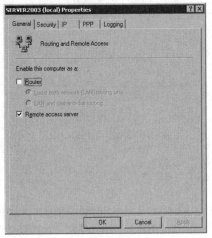

13. From the **Security** tab, select the **Authentication Provider** and make sure **Windows Authentication** is selected (this should be the default selection) as shown in Figure 8.23. We will look at RADIUS/IAS authentication later in this chapter.

Figure 8.23 Selecting the Authentication Provider

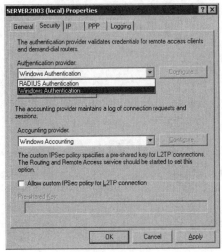

14. Now select **Authentication Methods** to select the authentication protocol that you want to make available to clients as seen in Figure 8.24. The default settings here should be sufficient for any Windows-based clients.

Figure 8.24 Selecting the Authentication Methods

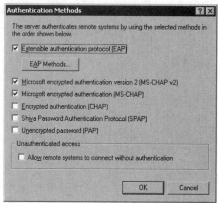

15. Next, select the **Accounting Provider** from the **Security** tab as shown in Figure 8.25. This option is used to record dial-up client activity for accounting or analysis. Again, we will use the default **Windows Accounting** option here, because we are not using a RADIUS server for accounting.

Figure 8.25 Selecting the Accounting Provider

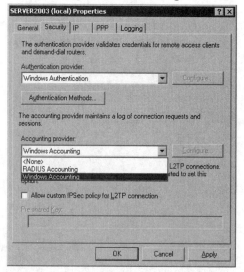

NOTE

The **Allow custom policy for L2TP connection** check box provides preshared key capabilities for L2TP. This setting uses a string of characters (up to 255) to be used in conjunction with the encryption algorithm in place of a Public Key Infrastructure.

16. The **IP** tab provides dial-in client IP address configuration options. For dial-in client connections to function properly, ensure the **Enable IP routing** and **Allow IP-based remote access and demand-dial connections** check boxes are selected as seen in Figure 8.26.

Figure 8.26 Setting the Basic Requirements to Enable Dial-in Support

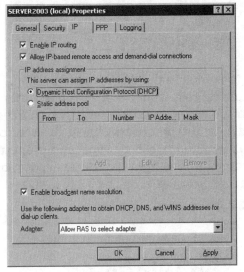

17. We are using a DHCP server to provide network address allocation in this scenario so clients will be provided IP addresses in this fashion. From the **IP** tab, make sure **Dynamic Host Configuration Protocol (DHCP)** is selected in the **IP address assignment** selection area.

18. From the **Adapter** drop-down list, select the **LAN** adapter to provide DHCP, DNS, and WINS services to dial-in clients as shown in Figure 8.27.

Figure 8.27 Selecting the Proper Adapter for IP Allocation and Name Resolution

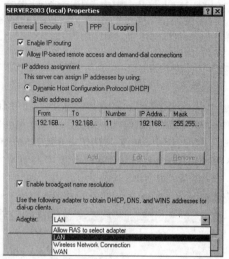

19. Select **OK** to complete the dial-in configuration. The server is ready to accept incoming calls from clients through a standard modem connection to provide access to corporate LAN resources in much the same way that dial-up Internet connections are used to provide access to the Internet. Make sure the client connection properties are configured with the correct phone number, address allocation method, and authentication protocol.

Configuring the Windows 2003 Dial-up RAS Gateway

A Windows Server 2003 Remote Access Server configured as a dial-up gateway provides dial-up connectivity for users located on the same LAN as the RRAS dial-up server. This RRAS gateway provides LAN-to-LAN connectivity for users of both the local and remote LAN or LANs. Figure 8.28 illustrates an example of an RRAS server configured to provide LAN-to-LAN connectivity for corporate LAN users.

Figure 8.28 RRAS Dial-up Gateway

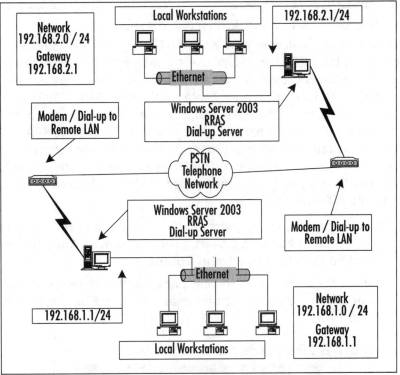

When configured to provide shared dial-up access via a common modem or modem pool, the RRAS dial-up server is providing remote access for all clients on the LAN connection. RRAS clients connecting to a remote LAN as seen in Figure 8.28 connect via a standard routed interface.

TEST DAY TIP

We have seen the routing and remote access service used in several different ways throughout this chapter and other chapters in this book. Make sure you understand the capabilities of RRAS. This Windows Server 2003 service provides so many capabilities that it is guaranteed to be an exam focal point. The service provides routing, VPN, dial-in, dial-out, NAT, and wireless capabilities. Make sure to do one last high-level overview of the capabilities one last time before the exam.

EXERCISE 8.04

RRAS DIAL-UP GATEWAY CONFIGURATION

In this exercise, we will configure an RRAS Dial-up Gateway for users connected to the local LAN. Local LAN users will be provided access to resources on a remote LAN as shown in Figure 8.28. This configuration is based on the demand dial interface options available in Windows Server 2003 Routing and Remote Access Service. There are basically three stages to this configuration. A user account must be created and configured for the dialing RRAS server to connect to the remote LAN and proper dial-in permissions should be granted to the account. Next, a demand dial interface to the remote network must be created. Finally, a default static route needs to be configured to direct non-LAN traffic to the dial-up connection.

1. Open Active Directory Users and Computers to create the accounts for the dialing RRAS servers: **Start | All Programs | Administrative Tools | Active Directory Users and Computers**.

2. Create the accounts. In the left pane, right-click **Users** and select **New | User**. Enter the user information as shown in Figure 8.29, then click **Next**.

Figure 8.29 Creating the Dial-in User

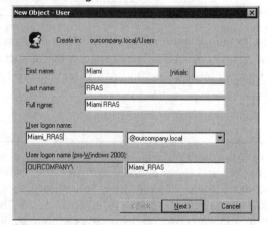

3. Enter a password for the account, confirm the password by retyping it in the second text box, remove the check from **User must change password at next logon,** and click **Next** as shown in Figure 8.30.

Figure 8.30 Setting the Password and Options for the Dial-in Account

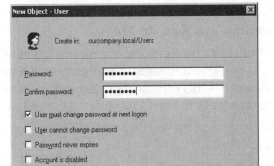

4. Click **Users** in the left pane. Right-click the user account that you just created in step 2 and select **Properties**.

5. From the **Dial-in** tab, select **Allow access** as shown in Figure 8.31 and click **OK**.

Figure 8.31 Setting Dial-in Permission for the RRAS Server Dial-in Account

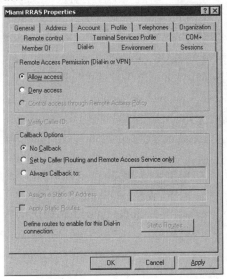

For the demand dial interface:

1. Open Routing and Remote Access: **Start | Programs | Administrative Tools | Routing and Remote Access**.

2. From the **Routing and Remote Access** management console, right-click the server name and select **Configure and Enable Routing and Remote Access**. If this option is grayed out, select **Disable Routing and Remote Access** to start with a fresh configuration.

3. On the first page of the **Routing and Remote Access Server Setup Wizard**, click **Next**.

4. Select **Custom configuration** and click **Next**.

5. From the **Custom configuration** screen, select **Demand-dial connections (used for branch office routing)** as shown in Figure 8.32 and click **Next**.

Figure 8.32 Enabling Demand-dial Connection

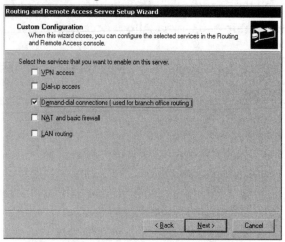

6. Click **Finish** to complete the basic demand-dial configuration and select **Yes** to start the Routing and Remote Access Service.

7. In the left pane, right-click **Network Interfaces** and select **New Demand-dial Interface...** as seen in Figure 8.33.

8. Select **Next**. Type a name for the connection, probably something refer-ring to the ISP you use, as shown in Figure 8.34.

Figure 8.33 Adding a Demand-dial Interface

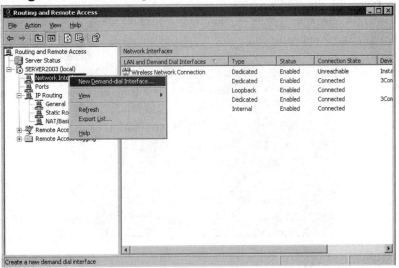

Figure 8.34 Naming the Demand-dial Connection

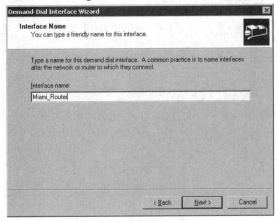

9. Click **Next** to move to the **Connection Type** screen and select **Connect using a modem, ISDN adapter, or other physical device** as shown in Figure 8.35.

10. Select **Next** to move to the **Select a Device** screen. Select the modem you will use for the dial-up connection to the ISP and click **Next**.

11. Make sure **Route IP packets on this interface** is selected (this should be the default selection) as shown in Figure 8.36.

Figure 8.35 Selecting the Connection Type for the Demand-dial Connection

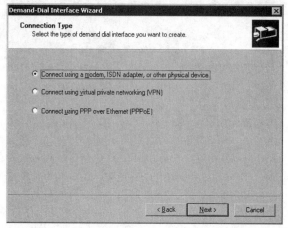

Figure 8.36 Selecting Protocol and Security Settings

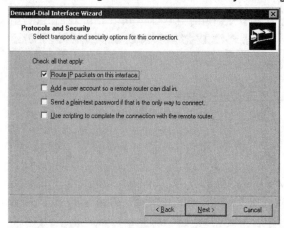

12. Click **Next**. From the **Static Routes for Remote Networks** screen, click **Add** as shown in Figure 8.37.

13. From the **Static Route** dialog box, select **OK** to configure a static route for the network, as shown in Figure 8.38.

Figure 8.37 Adding a Static Route to Invoke the Demand-dial Connection

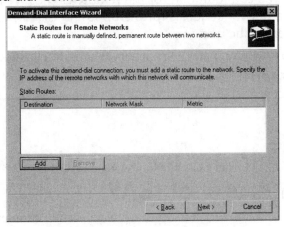

Figure 8.38 Configuring a Default Static Route

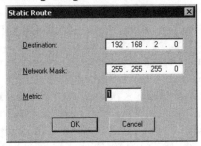

14. Click **Next**. From the **Dial Out Credentials** dialog box, enter the account information for your ISP account as shown in Figure 8.39 and click **Next**.

Figure 8.39 Entering Dial Out Credentials

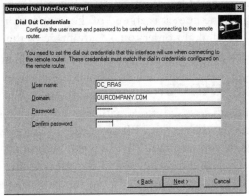

15. Select **Finish** to complete the demand-dial configuration.

16. Repeat the configuration for the remote LAN as we just outlined, providing a network address for the opposing LAN when configuring the necessary static route.

17. From a LAN attached client, attempt to connect to a resource on the remote LAN to verify operation of the gateway.

PPP Multilink and Bandwidth Allocation Protocol (BAP)

The Point-to-Point Protocol (PPP) provides encapsulation, authentication, and encryption functions for remote access connectivity. Most VPN and remote access technology today is built upon PPP or extensions of this protocol. One of the many features of PPP is Multilink. PPP is generally used for different types of dial-up connections. Sometimes, there is an advantage to providing a single virtual link that encompasses multiple physical links, like the B-channels on an ISDN connection. ISDN provides two bearer channels (2B) plus one control channel (D). This 2B+D connection can provide two separate physical links. Often, it is more beneficial to combine the two links. The combined links provide a virtual connection, in the case of ISDN, of 128kbps. This approach is not without drawbacks, however.

Since ISDN has traditionally been billed per usage, and analog long distance phone calls are also typically billed per usage, maintaining the virtual link when the bandwidth requirements are low could prove costly. Multilink itself does not include provisions to monitor the connection requirements. Enter Bandwidth Allocation Protocol (BAP). BAP adds features to PPP and Multilink to monitor the connection requirements and to adjust accordingly. If our ISDN link does not need the bandwidth provided through two B-channels, BAP will drop one of the two connections, based on our configuration settings. If the bandwidth requirements increase and the single B-channel in use cannot provide sufficient bandwidth, BAP will connect the second B-channel to double our bandwidth capabilities. This same configuration could include two analog phone lines at each end of the connection as opposed to the 2B+D ISDN configuration for Multilink. In order to take advantage of the capabilities of BAP, the remote access client and server must support BAP and have it enabled.

PPP Multilink Protocol

PPP has, by Internet standards, a long history with the Internet Engineering Task Force (IETF). The basic documented history of PPP dates back to 1989 when "A Proposal for Multi-Protocol Transmission of Datagrams Over Point-to-Point Links" was specified in Request For Comments (RFC) 1134. The official implementation, as used by Microsoft, comes from RFP 1990. Capabilities were added and subsequent modifications to the standard were made leading up to PPP as it exists today. In 1994, a documented standard was proposed for "The PPP Multilink Protocol" in RFC 1717. At the time, other proposals existed to combine streams of data at the bit level (basically a hardware solution). This proposal described a software-based solution for the need to combine multiple streams of data into one. This solution was well-suited to the twin bearer channels of ISDN (2B+D).

The PPP Multilink Protocol must be enabled on both the remote access client and the remote access server. PPP Multilink is enabled on the remote access server via remote access policy, using the Routing and Remote Access Service management console or the Internet Authentication Service (IAS). The nature of multilink requires dialing to multiple devices or endpoints. To enable Multilink on a remote access client, you must enable multiple device dialing on the client system through the **Network and Dial-up Connections** folder. Again, if unlimited connectivity is not available, the nature of Multilink presents cost prohibitive problems due to the lack of provisions to link and unlink extra physical connections on an as-needed basis.

NOTE

Be aware that if you use Multilink to dial a server that requires callback, only one of your devices is called back. Because you can store only one number in a user account, only one device connects and all other devices fail to complete the connection. Some ISDN service uses a single number for both B channels. If your ISDN uses only a single number for both B channels, then Multilink callback will work in this case. This attribute of callback means your connection loses Multilink functionality.

BAP Protocols

To facilitate dynamic allocation of links for Multilink, Microsoft provides dynamic BAP. Dynamic BAP is a series of interrelated protocols. Dynamic BAP consists of the following protocols:

- Bandwidth Allocation Protocol (BAP)
- Bandwidth Allocation Control Protocol (BACP)
- Extensions to the Link Control Protocol (LCP)

BAP, defined in RFC 2125, provisions additional links on an as-needed basis, in response to specific configuration settings. BAP is the control mechanism used in dynamic BAP. If, for example, your 56kbps dial-up connection is transmitting 35kbps of data for a predetermined amount of time, BAP will initiate a connection with your second modem to increase your available bandwidth to 112kbps (56kbps+56kbps). Once the bandwidth requirement drops below a predetermined setting for a predetermined amount of time, the second modem will disconnect.

BACP works in conjunction with BAP, utilizing the same mechanism as PPP's Link Control Protocol to provide connection control in a dynamic BAP environment. The sole purpose of BACP is to provide a negotiated, favored peer whose requests are implemented during a request to add or drop a connection.

PPP provides connections for upper layer protocols through the Link Control Protocol. Extensions to LCP are an integral part of dynamic BAP, just as they are with any other implementation or PPP. To transport TCP/IP traffic over an analog dial-up connection, Internet Protocol Connection Protocol (IPCP), an extension of LCP, carries the IP traffic through the PPP connection. Likewise, to carry IPX/SPX traffic over a PPP connection, Internetwork Packet Exchange Control Protocol (IPXCP) provides the connection between the PPP endpoints and the IPX/SPX client. This encapsulation of upper layer data is commonly known as *tunneling*.

Multilink with BAP support is implemented through the Routing and Remote Access management console and it is enabled by default. To configure your server to use Multilink with BAP, you must first enable BAP as follows:

1. Click **Start | Programs | Administrative Tools | Routing and Remote Access**.
2. Right-click the server name for which you want to enable BAP and BACP, and then click **Properties**.
3. On the **PPP** tab, select the **Dynamic bandwidth control using BAP and BACP** check box.

Now that we have enabled dynamic bandwidth control, we need to enable Multilink through a remote access policy as follows:

1. Click **Start | Programs | Administrative Tools | Routing and Remote Access**.
2. Double-click **Routing and Remote Access** and the server name, if necessary.
3. In the left pane, click **Remote Access Policies**.
4. In the right pane, double-click the remote access policy to modify.
5. Click **Edit Profile**.
6. On the **Multilink** tab, configure the specifics of the Multilink policy.

EXERCISE 8.05

CONFIGURING MULTILINK WITH BAP

In this exercise, we will see the basic configuration for Multilink with dynamic BAP capabilities for a Windows Server 2003 Routing and Remote Access server.

Later in this chapter we will revisit Multilink by configuring advanced settings through a Remote Access Policy for Multilink with BAP.

1. Because Multilink and BAP bind multiple physical connections together (usually dial-up) to increase available bandwidth, start with a basic gateway configuration as configured in Exercise 8.04.

2. From the Routing and Remote Access Microsoft management console of the configured gateway, right-click on the server name in the left pane of the management console and select **Properties** to display the **Server Properties** dialog box as shown in Figure 8.40.

Figure 8.40 The RRAS Properties Dialog Box

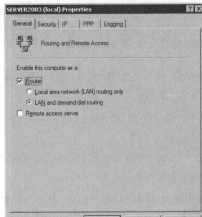

3. Select the **PPP** tab as shown in Figure 8.41. Verify that **Multilink connections** and **Dynamic bandwidth control using BAP or BACP** are selected. This is the default configuration option for a Routing and Remote Access using Windows Server 2003. Click **OK**.

BAP is not required for Multilink configuration. We will, however, look at advanced Multilink, BAP, and BACP options in the Remote Access Policy section of this chapter.

The nature of multilink requires dialing to multiple devices or endpoints. To enable Multilink on a remote access client, you must enable multiple device dialing on the client system through the **Network and Dial-up Connections** folder.

Figure 8.41 Verifying Multilink, BAP, and BACP Configuration

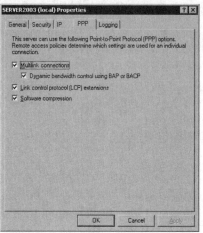

1. Click **Start | Settings | Control Panel | Network and Dial-up Connections**.

2. Right-click the connection to be used for multilink and select **Properties**.

3. Select **Options | Multiple devices**. Now, depending what you want to do, perform the following:

   ■ To dynamically dial and hang up devices, click **Dial devices only as needed | Configure**. From **Automatic dialing**, click and set **Activity at least** percentage and **Duration at least** time to your requirements. Once the connection activity level is reached for the amount of time specified, another line is dialed. From **Automatic hangup**, click and set **Activity no more than percentage** and **Duration at least** time to your requirements. Once the connection activity level is below the level specified for the amount of time specified, the line is disconnected.

   ■ To use all of your devices, click **Dial all devices**.

   ■ To dial only the first available device, click **Dial only first available device**.

Configuring Wireless Connections

EXAM
70-291
OBJECTIVE
4.1.1

If you have ever had to run wiring for a network, you will appreciate wireless networking. Microsoft Windows Server 2003 supports wireless networking utilizing either infrared communication (IR) or radio frequency (RF).

Categorizing Wireless Networks

Wireless networks can be categorized according to their scope, similarly to wired networking, as follows:

- Wireless personal area networks (WPANs)
- Wireless local area networks (WLANs)
- Wireless metropolitan area networks (WMANs)
- Wireless wide area networks (WWANs)

WPANs connect personal devices such as personal digital assistants (PDAs), cellular phones, laptop computers, and other devices together to share resources or data over a very limited area. WPANs can operate using either infrared or radio frequency. Bluetooth defines a radio frequency-based WPAN. Bluetooth is a technology that is moving toward IEEE standardization through the IEEE 802.15 working group. It provides wireless connectivity at distances up to 30 feet with capabilities to penetrate walls, briefcases, pockets, and so on. Infrared networking typically is limited to line of sight connectivity at a distance no greater than about three feet. Line of sight means that connectivity cannot be established between devices without an unobstructed path between them.

WLANs enable users to share resources throughout a local area (typically an office or a building). WLANs have evolved through the IEEE 802.11 standard. IEEE 802.11 WLANs started life at transfer speeds of 1 Mbps to 2 Mbps. Through evolution and improvement, 802.11b developed as a standard for 11 Mbps transfer rates and new implementations can operate at 22 Mbps, over areas of approximately 300 feet. Two new standards are evolving at 55 Mbps, 802.11a and 802.11g. IEEE 802.11a is an existing standard, and 802.11g is nearing completion as a standard. 802.11a provides better speed but shorter distances than 802.11b, whereas 802.11g combines the high speed of 802.11a with the greater distance span of 802.11b. 802.11 devices connect to existing wired LANs through wireless access points (WAPs) or to one another in peer-to-peer fashion. Wireless bridges can be used to connect devices to the wireless network or to connect two wireless networks together.

NOTE

The distances given for wireless networking are based on standard antennas. 802.11 network connectivity can be extended by using special high gain antennas, either omnidirectional (which can extend the range up to a kilometer or more) or directional antennas such as the Yagi (which can extend the range to over five kilometers).

WMANs connect buildings within a campus or city through infrared or radio frequency. Again, the disadvantage to infrared is the line of sight requirements. Clouds, aircraft, or anything else that can block line of sight transmission can disrupt infrared WMANs. Radio frequency WMAN technologies, such as multichannel multipoint distribution service (MMDS) and the local multipoint distribution services (LMDS), already exist but the IEEE 802.16 working group has not finalized on any standards at this point.

WWAN technology has been around for several years now. The current players in this field are Global System for Mobile Communications (GSM), Cellular Digital Packet Data (CDPD), and Code Division Multiple Access (CDMA). Current cellular phones use these second generation (2G) technologies. These antenna and satellite-based technologies exhibit compatibility problems with one another, hindering the ability to roam worldwide and utilize the same technology for connectivity worldwide. In an effort to provide standardization and worldwide roaming capabilities, the International Telecommunication Union is working currently working on the third generation of WWAN technology, known as 3G.

Wireless Security

Traditional wired networks tend to be easier to secure than their wireless counterparts because the access points to the network are generally well known to the network designers and administrators. Usually, wires are physically secured by the security of the office building itself; electronic security of the access points would be handled by a firewall. By their general nature, wireless networks cannot be secured as easily as traditional wired networks. Wireless networks provide access beyond the physical security of the office building and consequently, a WLAN generally has to be viewed in much the same way that a VPN is viewed. WLANs and VPNs require secure connectivity through an insecure transport medium. WLANs generally use methods similar to those used in VPNs (strong authentication methods, data encryption) to secure the open-air traffic. Let's look at the protocols in use for WLAN security.

The IEEE 802.1X standard provides for authenticated network access using either wired Ethernet networks or 802.11 WLANs. As discussed in the previous chapter, Extensible Authentication Protocol (EAP) is an extension to the PPP that provides for modular authentication mechanisms to be employed. EAP supports Kerberos, certificates, tokens, smart cards, and one-time passwords. The 802.1X standards use EAP to provide WLAN networking with a few security options:

- EAP-Transport Layer Security (EAP-TLS)
- EAP-Microsoft Challenge Handshake Authentication Protocol version 2 (EAP-MS-CHAP v2)
- Protected EAP (PEAP)

NOTE

It is important to understand that 802.1X is not itself an authentication method. It is the EAP type you specify that determines how authentication is performed.

EAP-TLS uses certificates to provide the strongest authentication available using Windows Server 2003. Certificate-based security relies on a special text file or certificate. The certificate is usually created by using user or company information in conjunction with a password to create a special hashed value. This hashed value is used in a similar fashion to a password to encrypt network traffic. Public key encryption, which utilizes certificates or keys for encryption, is a method of asymmetric encryption where a private key encrypts a user's outbound data only to be unencrypted by the public key, distributed by the user. Likewise, the public key encrypts traffic to be sent to the user, only to be unencrypted by the user's private key. When the private key is providing the encryption and the public key is decrypting, data confidentiality is not provided but authentication is provided. When the public key is providing the encryption and the private key is decrypting, data confidentiality is provided. EAP-TLS authenticates clients and servers through the certificate infrastructure while negotiating encryption method and encryption key.

EAP-MS-CHAP v2 supports password-based authentication of the user, the client computer, and the server. This method of authentication is not as strong as EAP-TLS due to the inherent weakness of password-based security. EAP-MS-CHAP v2 authentication requires proof of knowledge of the user's password to be demonstrated by the client and the server.

PEAP relies on TLS to provide several enhancements to EAP. PEAP authenticates servers to prevent the use of rogue access points. Also, PEAP has provisions for session caching, which allows fast reconnection while wireless users roam between access points. PEAP provides a special encryption conduit to protect other EAP processes running within PEAP.

EXAM WARNING

Wireless networks are all the rage. Since this is an up and coming technology and Windows Server 2003 provides significant support capabilities and simplified administration capabilities for wireless networking, make sure you understand the fundamentals covered through the exercises in this section.

Windows Server 2003 wireless networking relies on Active Directory-based wireless network policies. To configure the Active Directory-based wireless network policies, open the **Active Directory Users and Computers** management console and navigate to the **Wireless Network (IEEE 802.111) Policies** as follows:

1. Click **Start | Programs | Administrative Tools | Active Directory Users and Computers**.

2. In the left pane, right-click the domain or organizational unit for which you want to set Group Policy.

3. Select **Properties**, and then click the **Group Policy** tab.

4. Select **Edit** and open the Group Policy object that you want to edit. If you will be creating a new policy, click **New** to create a new Group Policy object, and then click **Edit**.

5. In the left pane, click **Computer Configuration | Windows Settings | Security Settings | Wireless Network (IEEE 802.11) Policies** as shown in Figure 8.42.

Figure 8.42 Wireless Policy Setup

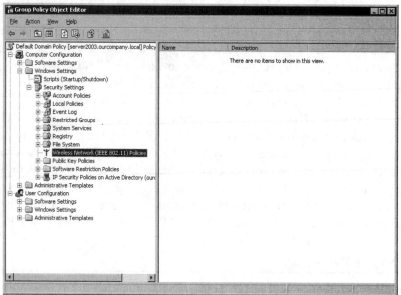

 EXAM WARNING

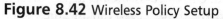

The Wireless Network Policy node in Group Policy and the Wireless Network Policy Wizard are new in Windows Server 2003; you will not find these in the Windows 2000 GPO.

Now we need to configure the actual policy settings. Here, Windows Server 2003 provides a convenient wizard to walk us through the configuration settings for the policy.

1. Right-click **Wireless Network (IEEE 802.11) Policies** and select **Create Wireless Network Policy**. Click **Next** on the Welcome page of the Wizard.

2. **The Wireless Network (IEEE 802.11) Policy** wizard requests a policy name and description. Name the policy by typing a unique name in the **Name** field. Provide a description of the wireless network policy by typing a description in the **Description** field. The description should contain something such as the groups or domains the policy affects. Figure 8.43 illustrates the **Wireless Network Policy Name** dialog box.

Figure 8.43 Setting a Name and Description for the Wireless Policy

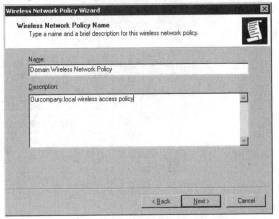

3. Click **Next** and leave the **Edit properties** check box checked as shown in Figure 8.44.

Figure 8.44 Completing the Wireless Network Policy Wizard

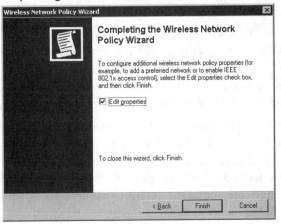

4. Click **Finish** to complete the initial wireless network policy configuration and to open the **Domain Wireless Network Policy Properties** dialog box as shown in Figure 8.45.

Figure 8.45 Setting the Wireless Networks Policy Properties

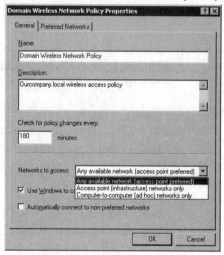

5. Specify how often Active Directory is to be polled for updates by typing a value in **Check for policy changes every number minutes**.

6. Specify the type of wireless network that clients can access by clicking a network type in the **Networks to access** list. Choices include any available network (access point preferred), access point (infrastructure) networks only, or computer to computer (ad hoc) networks only.

7. If you want to allow client systems to dictate wireless network settings, select the **Use Windows to configure wireless network settings for clients** check box. This is the default setting. If, instead, you wish to prevent clients from using Windows to configure their wireless network settings, clear the **Use Windows to configure wireless network settings for clients** check box.

8. If clients will be allowed to connect to available networks that do not appear on the Preferred Networks tab, select the **Automatically connect to non-preferred networks** check box. If, instead, you wish to ensure that clients connect only to networks that appear on the Preferred Networks tab, clear the **Automatically connect to non-preferred networks** check box (cleared by default).

9. Preferred Networks may be configured from the **Preferred Networks** tab as shown in Figure 8.46.

Figure 8.46 Selecting Preferred Networks

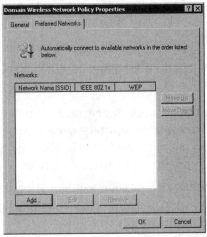

10.   Click **Add** to add a preferred network as shown in Figure 8.47.

Figure 8.47 Adding a Preferred Network

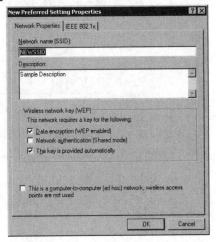

11.   In the **Network name (SSID)** box, enter a unique name.

12.   In the **Description** box, enter a description of the wireless network.

13.   From the **Wireless network key (WEP)** box, specify network encryption and authentication by configuring the following check boxes:

   ■   **Data encryption (WEP enabled)** setting will require a network key to be used for encryption.

- **Network authentication (Shared mode)** setting will require that a network key be used for authentication. Not selecting this option means that a network key is not required for authentication. In this configuration, the network will operate in open system mode.

- **The key is provided automatically** setting determines whether a network key is automatically provided for clients.

14. To configure the network to operate as a computer-to-computer (ad hoc) network, click **This is a computer-to-computer (ad hoc) network; wireless access points are not used check box**. The **Move Up** and **Move Down** buttons provide capabilities to change the preferred network search order.

15. The **IEEE 802.1x** tab provides configuration options for 802.1x—a port-based network access control discussed later in this chapter. Figure 8.48 displays the **IEEE 802.1x** configuration tab.

Figure 8.48 IEEE 802.1x Configuration Options

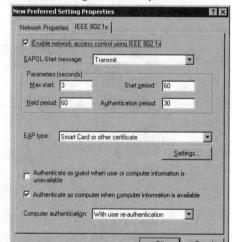

16. Click **OK | OK**. Close the Group Policy Editor by clicking on the **X** in the upper right corner of the **Group Policy Editor** management console. Click **OK** to close the domain properties dialog box. Close **Active Directory Users and Computers** by clicking the **X** in the upper-right corner of the **Active Directory Users and Computers** management console.

From a security perspective, we typically do not want clients to be part of the decision making process. It is more secure to configure network policies using a centralized policy like the policy settings provided in Active Directory Wireless Network (IEEE 802.11) Policies. It is possible to use Internet Authentication Service (IAS), Microsoft's implementation of Remote Authentication Dial-in User Service (RADIUS), with 802.1X to provide centralized policy implementation and administration as well. RADIUS works to isolate wireless connections from the wired LAN until the client provides a valid authentication key. We will look at IAS/RADIUS later in this chapter.

Head of the Class…

Network Overlap

Several of the topics in this chapter cover open standard protocols and Microsoft's implementation of them. Don't overlook a particular topic because it doesn't seem important. The OSI reference model, for example, is something that is discussed in almost every networking book that you will ever pick up. Some might think it's a trivial topic, but in fact it is the foundation of networking. The more time you spend in this industry, the more you will appreciate a well-structured guideline like the OSI reference model.

As you learn the various protocols available to provide networking communication, and as you learn how to use the myriad of networking troubleshooting tools at your disposal, the implications of the OSI reference model will prove to be an invaluable guide.

You will also see that as you work with other vendor's implementations of technologies studied here, your fundamental understanding of the materials will give you a solid base from which to work. Making Cisco equipment talk to Nortel equipment or making Linux equipment talk to Microsoft equipment becomes a lot less tasking when you understand the fundamentals.

EXERCISE 8.06

CONFIGURING WIRELESS NETWORKING

In this exercise, we will configure a client and server to use 802.11 wireless networking. The recommended best-practice for wireless networking in a Microsoft environment is to configure IAS/RADIUS to centralize authentication for the wireless access points used in the network. More detailed instructions for implementing IAS are listed in Exercise 8.13. The instructions for IAS installation and configuration listed here are just specific enough to meet the requirements for wireless networking. EAP-TLS is the recommended authentication protocol for wireless networking. EAP-TLS requires installation of a certificate on the IAS server. We will detail the process used to install the certificate here but the instructions for installing and configuring a certificate server are outside the scope of this exam (planning, implementing, and maintaining a public key infrastructure based on certificate services is covered in exam 70-293).

Begin by installing a certificate for the IAS server. It is recommended that you use the automatic certificate allocation feature available through Active Directory Group Policy.

1. Open **Active Directory Users and Computers**. Start | **Administrative Tools** | **Active Directory Users and Computers**.

2. In the left pane, double-click **Active Directory Users and Computers**, then right-click the domain name where your CA exists, and then click **Properties**.

3. On the **Group Policy** tab, click **Default Domain Policy**, and then click **Edit**.

4. In the left pane, click **Computer Configuration** | **Windows Settings** | **Security Settings** | **Public Key Policies** as seen in Figure 8.49.

Figure 8.49 Configuring Automatic Certificate Request

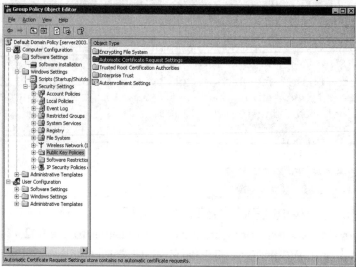

5. In the right pane, right-click **Automatic Certificate Request Settings**, point to **New**, and then click **Automatic Certificate Request**.

6. From the **Automatic Certificate Request** wizard, click **Next**.

7. In **Certificate templates**, click **Computer** as seen in Figure 8.50, and then click **Next**.

Figure 8.50 Specifying Computer Certificates

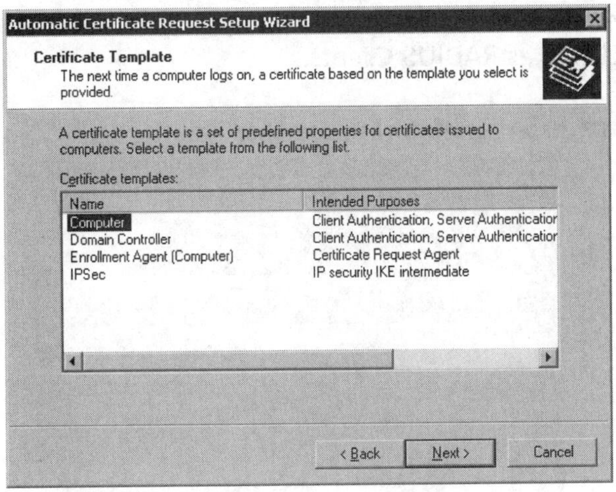

8. Your enterprise root CA appears on the list.

9. Click the CA, click **Next**, and then click **Finish**.

10. To create a computer certificate for the CA computer, type the following at the command prompt: **gpupdate /target:Computer**.

11. Install the IAS Windows component through **Add or Remove Programs. Start | Settings | Control Panel | Add or Remove Programs**. Click the **Windows Components** icon in the left side of the applet.

12. From the **Windows Components Wizard** dialog box, click **Networking Services**, then select **Details**.

13. From the **Networking Services** dialog box, click **Internet Authentication Service | OK | Next**.

14. You may be prompted to insert the Windows Server 2003 compact disc.

15. Once IAS is installed, click **Finish | Close**.

16. Open the **Internet Authentication Service** management console. **Start | Programs | Administrative Tools | Internet Authentication Service**.

17. The default port and event logging setting for IAS are sufficient for this exercise.

18. The default log file parameters for the IAS are sufficient for this exercise.

19. From the IAS management console, right-click **RADIUS Clients**, and select **New RADIUS Client**.

20. Using the **New RADIUS Client Wizard,** add basic client information for the wireless access point as shown in Figure 8.51. Also add your wireless clients as RADIUS Clients.

Figure 8.51 Configuring the IAS Client

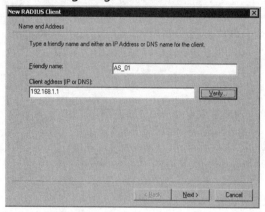

21. Click **Next**. Select **RADIUS Standard** from the **Client-Vendor** drop-down list on the **New RADIUS Client** screen and enter the shared secret password as shown in Figure 8.52; select **Finish**.

NOTE

If you have enabled the Message Authenticator attribute, then the entire RADIUS message is encrypted using the shared secret as the key. Be aware that shared secrets are case-sensitive. Also, be sure to verify that the client's shared secret and the shared secret that you type in the **Shared secret** field are identical.

Figure 8.52 New RADIUS Client Configuration

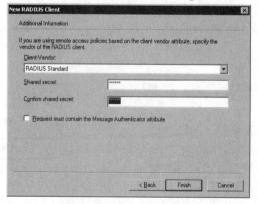

22. Configure a remote access policy for the IAS clients. From the IAS management console (**Start | Administrative Tools | Internet Authentication Service**) double-click **Internet Authentication Service** in the left pane.

23. In the left pane, click **Remote Access Policies**.

24. In the right pane, double-click the policy that you want to configure.

25. Click **Edit Profile**.

26. On the **Authentication** tab, click **EAP Methods**.

27. In **Select EAP providers**, click **Add**. Select the **Protected EAP (PEAP)** as shown in Figure 8.53 and then click **OK**.

Figure 8.53 Specifying PEAP Authentication

28. In **Select EAP providers**, click the **Protected EAP (PEAP)** and then click **Edit**.

29. From the **Protected EAP Properties** dialog box in **Certificate Issued**, select the certificate that the server uses to identify itself to client computers. Enable PEAP fast reconnect for 802.11 wireless client computers by selecting **Enable Fast Reconnect** as shown in Figure 8.54.

30. Select secure password authentication with EAP-MSCHAPv2 as the default EAP Type. The default settings for EAP-MSCHAPv2 are sufficient for this exercise.

Figure 8.54 Configuring PEAP Properties

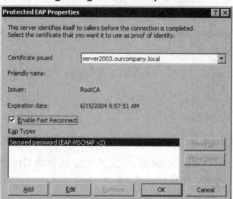

31. Select **OK**. Click **OK** again to complete the PEAP configuration. We will use PEAP as the only authentication protocol allowed for our wireless clients. Remove the other authentication check boxes as shown in Figure 8.55.

NOTE

PEAP uses Transport Layer Security (TLS) to provide an added layer of protection. PEAP also provides other benefits including an encryption channel that protects other EAP methods running within PEAP, fast reconnect—the capability to reconnect to a wireless access point using cached session keys facilitating quick roaming between wireless access points, TLS-generated dynamic keying material, and server authentication that prevents deployment of unauthorized wireless access points.

Figure 8.55 Using PEAP Exclusively for Authentication

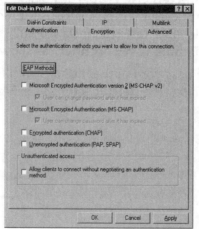

32. Select **OK** and select **OK** again to complete the configuration.

NOTE

Wireless networking has been developing in the background for several years now. It is finally on the forefront of networking technology. You will see PEAP and 802.1X listed as authentication protocols for wireless networking in Windows Server 2003. These capabilities have been added since the release of Windows 2000. This topic warrants a thorough review. As the price of wireless equipment gets lower and the bandwidth capabilities tend to keep increasing, wireless will likely increase in popularity. As any topic becomes more prevalent it also becomes more of a target. Expect Microsoft to put some emphasis on this hot topic.

EXAM 70-291
OBJECTIVE
4.1.3
4.2.5

Configuring Remote Access Policies

A traditional LAN is usually located within the physical confines of a building. The systems within the bounds of the LAN are administered by an individual or group of individuals and usually a policy is in place to guide the administration and configuration. When users connect from outside the confines of the LAN, often the system the client connects from is not administered by the corporate administrator or administrators. This can present configuration problems as well as security problems. Remote access policies help administrators apply a consistent policy to non-LAN machines, the machines that are often not directly administered within the confines of the corporate LAN. Through the use of remote access policies, administrators can limit the access rights and privileges of remote users and computers by validating connections and can specify connection restrictions. Connection settings that can be validated by standard remote access policy settings include the following:

- Authentication methods
- Group membership
- Remote access permission
- Time of day
- Type of connection

Advanced remote access policy validation settings include the following:

- Access server identity
- Access client phone number or MAC address

- Whether user account dial-in properties are ignored
- Whether unauthenticated access is allowed

Authentication methods include the following:

- PEAP
- EAP
- MS-CHAP
- MS-CHAP version 2
- CHAP
- PAP
- Unauthenticated access

NOTE

This is not an all inclusive list; there are many other condition attributes that can be set on a remote access policy, such as protocol type, service type, tunnel type (for VPN connections), client IP address, and vendor of the RADIUS proxy (IAS).

Authentication method refers to the authentication type being used by the client (EAP, CHAP, MS-CHAP, etc.).

Group membership is configured through Active Directory Users and Computers. Groups significantly reduce the necessary amount of administration by grouping users according to similar job functions, access rights and requirements, and other common similarities between users. Group membership policy restrictions can be used to allow corporate users to gain network access based on one set of criteria, whereas users from a specific vendor or partner might have a different set of remote access restrictions or rules.

Time of day restrictions ensure that users can log in only during certain times. This can be used to keep users disconnected during certain maintenance operations or to keep remote users out of the network after normal business hours.

Type of connection validation sets different remote access policies based on the method the user uses to connect. For example, VPN users can have one policy, whereas analog dial-up users are governed by a different policy.

Access server identity validation ensures that users connecting to a specific access server have a specific policy applied to them. This can be used to ensure that a user is connecting through proper channels. If someone were to attempt to break into the network through a nonauthorized connection, this restriction will prevent such access.

Access client phone number validation ensures the user is connecting from an authorized location or computer. Using the client's calling phone number (which is specified as the

Calling Station ID) as validation relies upon a certain amount of physical security as well as the password or certificate-based electronic security. Someone would theoretically have to break into the calling location and use that phone to connect based on this validation.

Once a remote access policy has authorized a connection, it can also set connection restrictions (called *constraints*) based on the following:

- Encryption strength
- Idle timeout
- IP packet filters
- Maximum session time

Also, remote access policies provide advanced connection restrictions based on the following:

- IP address for PPP connections
- Static routes

NOTE

Again, the dial-in constraints listed are not the only ones you can set. You can also specify that access is allowed only via specific media (FDDI, wireless, Token Ring, Ethernet, DSL, cable, etc.).

Encryption strength typically ranges from 40-bit to 168-bit. Encryption property settings for Windows Server 2003 include no encryption, Basic encryption (40-bit MPPE or 56-bit DES), Strong encryption (56-bit MPPE or 56-bit DES), and Strongest encryption (128-bit MPPE or 168-bit 3DES). Idle timeout is used to secure the network by disconnecting users after a specific amount of idle time has passed. IP packet filters restrict connections based on the services being requested. For example, Telnet access may be granted to a dial-in user by configuring an IP packet filter to allow traffic to TCP port 23 at a particular address. Maximum session time ensures security by disconnecting a user after a specified amount of time regardless of the current session status (idle or active). Specific IP addresses may be distributed through PPP connections to restrict access to portions of the network. This provides another method for securing network access through remote access policy. Static routes also set network access restrictions by routing or not routing specific traffic based on destination network address.

Finally, global remote access policies may be varied according to the following:

- Access client phone number or MAC address
- Authentication methods

- Group membership
- Identity of the access server
- Time of day
- Type of connection
- Whether unauthenticated access is allowed

Windows Server 2003 remote access servers provide remote access policy through the Routing and Remote Access Service on stand-alone machines. The RRAS policy applies to connections through that specific RRAS server in that case. If you are using IAS or RADIUS on your network, remote access policies are configured through the Internet Authentication Service or RADIUS server.

To configure a remote access policy for your RRAS server:

1. First, configure the user accounts to use remote access policy for dial-in access.

2. Click **Start | Programs | Administrative Tools | Active Directory Users and Computers**.

3. The user accounts should have the **Remote Access Permission (Dial-in or VPN)** option set to **Control access through Remote Access Policy**.

4. Now, open the Routing and Remote Access management console to configure the policy.

5. Click **Start | Programs | Administrative Tools | Routing and Remote Access**.

6. If necessary, double-click **Routing and Remote Access** and the server name.

7. In the left pane, right-click **Remote Access Policies**, and then click **New Remote Access Policy**.

8. Select the appropriate policy settings as discussed earlier.

9. Delete the default policies.

EXERCISE 8.07

CONFIGURING REMOTE ACCESS POLICIES

In this exercise, a group of users in our organization needs remote access through analog dial-in. Some users have the ability to dial in with multiple modems. We want to provide a remote access policy to grant access to this group of users and to provide them with multilink, if needed. To accomplish our goal, we will configure our remote access server to allow dial-up connections using group membership. The remote access policy will also provide for Multilink, BAP, and BACP client support.

1. Configure an RRAS dial-up gateway like that configured in Exercise 8.04.

2. Create a Group called Dial-Users. Click **Start | Administrative Tools | Active Directory Users and Computers.** Right-click the **Users** container or the container that the remote users belong to. Select **New | Group**. In the **Group Name** box, type **Dial-Users** in the **Group Name** text box as shown in Figure 8.56. Click **OK**.

Figure 8.56 Creating a Dial-Users Group

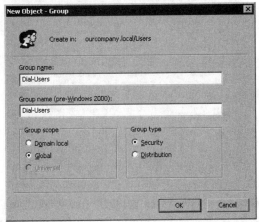

3. Create the policy condition and policy profile through the **New Remote Access Policy Wizard.** Click **Start | Administrative Tools | Routing and Remote Access**. Right-click **Remote Access Policies** in the left pane of the management console and select **New Remote Access Policy** to start the **New Remote Access Policy Wizard.** Click **Next**.

4. Select **Set up a custom policy** and enter **Dial-Users** in the **Policy Name** box as shown in Figure 8.57.

Figure 8.57 Creating the Dial-Users RRAS Policy

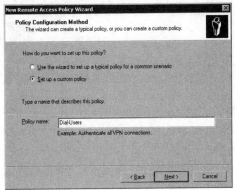

5. Click **Next** to move to the **Policy Conditions** screen. Click **Add** to specify **Windows-Group** for the condition portion of the RRAS Policy as shown in Figure 8.58.

Figure 8.58 Using a Windows-Group for the Condition

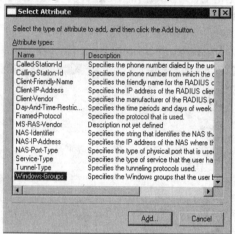

6. Click **Add** to open the **Groups** selection box. Click **Add** again. From the **Select Groups** dialog box, type **Dial** into the text box and click the **Check Names** button. The **Dial-Users** group should be displayed in the text box as shown in Figure 8.59.

Figure 8.59 Selecting the Dial-Users Group to Meet the Policy Conditions

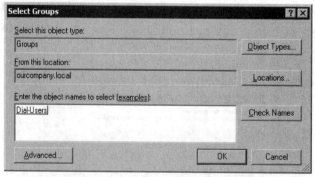

7. Click **OK**. Click **OK** again. Click **Next** to view the **Permissions** screen. Select **Grant remote access permission** as shown in Figure 8.60.

Figure 8.60 Granting Remote Access Permission to the Dial-Users Group

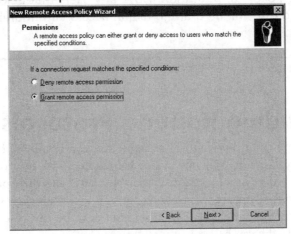

8. Click **Next** to proceed to the **Profile** screen. Click the **Edit Profile** button to invoke the **Edit Dial-in Profile** dialog box. Click the **Multilink** tab. We want to allow Multilink connections and we will drop the second line if the bandwidth requirement drops below 50 percent. Select **Allow Multilink connections**. Select **Require BAP for dynamic Multilink requests** and accept the defaults as shown in Figure 8.61.

Figure 8.61 Allowing Multilink Connections through the Policy Profile

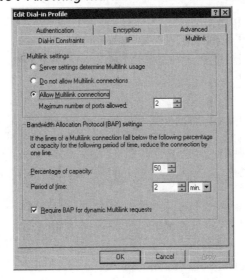

9. Click **OK**. Click **Next** and then click **Finish** to complete the Remote Access Policy configuration. Now, any users that belong to the Dial-Users group will be granted dial-in access with multilink capabilities available to them.

Understanding Routing Protocols

In this section, we will enter the world of dynamic routing. If you are familiar with TCP/IP and network addresses, you are probably somewhat familiar with the concept of routing. Routing protocols are designed to advertise available routes and their preference to other routers on the network. Compare this to static routing where every possible route must be entered into the router's routing table. The traffic routes to be advertised are typically unicast routes. TCP/IP traffic can be broken into three areas:

- Unicast

- Broadcast

- Multicast

Unicast traffic is point-to-point connectivity between TCP/IP systems. Each system communicates with one other system, with the systems using their respective IP addresses. For example, Figure 8.62 illustrates two clients communicating through TCP/IP unicast traffic.

Figure 8.62 Unicast IP Traffic

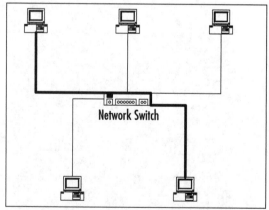

Broadcast traffic involves point-to-multipoint connectivity between TCP/IP systems. In this scenario, a system communicates with the broadcast address of its respective network, or through the global broadcast address. In either case, broadcast is represented in binary as all hosts or all bits in the host portion of the address turned on (for example, on a traditional class C network in which the fourth octet represents the host address, the broadcast address will notate that octet as 11111111, or 255 in decimal). All hosts will interact with a broadcast message to their respective network. Figure 8.63 represents a network experiencing broadcast traffic.

Figure 8.63 Broadcast IP Traffic

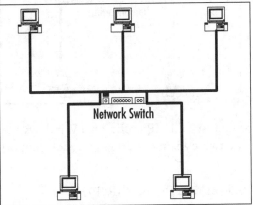

Multicast traffic involves point-to-multipoint traffic to specific participants. Where broadcast traffic is intended for every node on a given network segment or common IP network address, multicast is intended for a group of selected participants that have to join the multicast group. Traffic is sent to a special IP address that represents that multicast group. Multicast addresses are in the Class D range above the class C network range and below the experimental Class E IP range.

Some applications that utilize multicast traffic are:

- Norton Ghost multicast

- Windows Internet Naming Service (WINS) autodiscovery and replication

- OSPF routing protocol

- RIP v2 routing protocol

- Microsoft NetShow

Figure 8.64 illustrates typical multicast communication on a network segment.

Figure 8.64 Multicast IP Traffic

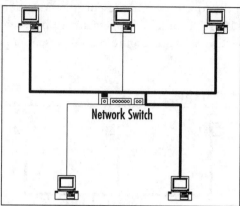

Dynamic routing for unicast TCP/IP traffic on a Windows Server 2003 system is achieved with either of the two dynamic routing protocols supported by the operating system:

- The Routing Information Protocol (RIP)
- The Open Shortest Path First (OSPF) protocol

Windows Server 2003 does not support multicast routing protocols but does come with provisions for multicast traffic through the Internet Group Management Protocol (IGMP). Before we get into the details of dynamic routing, let's review the basic concepts used in routing.

When two systems communicate through TCP/IP, the first thing that needs to be determined is the location of the recipient (destination computer). In other words, the sending system will determine whether the recipient is a local system or a remote system. A local system is one that is on the same network address as the sending system. A remote system is one that is on a separate network address so the sending system will send the traffic through a proxy server or a router. In our examples, we will use a router as the network gateway instead of a proxy server. A proxy server acts on behalf of the client to establish an IP connection with a remote machine. A router forwards the sending system's request to the next router in the preferred route to the destination.

Figure 8.65 illustrates our first example, where Computer A is attempting to communicate with Computer B.

Figure 8.65 Basic Local TCP/IP Communication

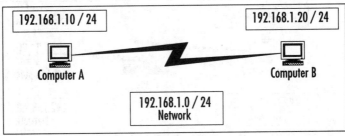

The basic process that Computer A will use to communicate with Computer B is as follows.

1. Computer A, in its effort to communicate with Computer B, will take Computer B's IP address and perform a binary AND of Computer B's address with its own subnet mask. This binary AND operation yields the network address of Computer B.

2. Computer A then compares this network address to its own network address.

3. If Computer B's network address is the same as Computer A's network address, Computer A will consider Computer B to be a local system. If Computer B's network address is different from Computer A's network address, Computer A will consider Computer B to be a remote system and will attempt to find an IP gateway to forward the traffic to.

4. In our case, Computer B is considered local so Computer A uses the local traffic approach to communicate with Computer B.

5. Computer A checks for the Media Access Control (MAC) address for Computer B in its own Address Resolution Protocol (ARP) cache. If Computer B's MAC address is in Computer A's ARP cache, Computer A will forward the traffic to Computer B's MAC address.

6. If Computer A does not have Computer B's MAC address in its ARP cache, Computer A will send out an ARP broadcast using Computer B's IP address to request the MAC address for Computer B.

7. Computer B will respond to Computer A with its MAC address and communication will begin.

Now, let's review the same example with Computer B configured as a remote host, as seen in Figure 8.66.

Figure 8.66 Basic Remote TCP/IP Communication

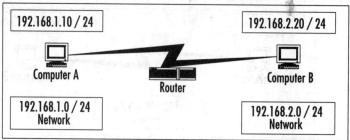

The basic process that Computer A will use to communicate with Computer B is as follows.

1. Computer A, in its effort to communicate with Computer B, will take Computer B's IP address and perform a binary AND of Computer B's address with its own subnet mask. This binary AND operation yields the network address of Computer B.

2. Computer A then compares this network address to its own network address.

3. If Computer B's network address is the same as Computer A's network address, Computer A will consider Computer B to be a local system. If Computer B's network address is different from Computer A's network address, Computer A will consider Computer B to be a remote system and will attempt to find an IP gateway to forward the traffic to.

4. In our case, Computer B is considered remote so Computer A uses the remote traffic approach to communicate with Computer B.

5. Computer A checks for the Media Access Control (MAC) address for an IP gateway (typically its default gateway address) in its own Address Resolution Protocol (ARP) cache. If the gateway's MAC address is in Computer A's ARP cache, Computer A will forward the traffic to the gateway's MAC address.

6. If Computer A does not have the gateway's MAC address in its ARP cache, Computer A will send out an ARP broadcast using the gateway's IP address to request the MAC address for the gateway.

7. The gateway will respond to Computer A with its MAC address and communication will begin between them.

8. The gateway (a router) will check its routing table to see if a route exists to Computer B's network address. If the route exists, the gateway will forward all traffic destined for Computer B to the next closest router along the route to Computer B's network. In our example, Computer B is on the gateway's second network interface. Consequently, local network communication begins between the gateway and Computer B in much the same fashion that local traffic was handled in the previous example.

Now that we have reviewed the basics, let's take a look at the dynamic routing protocols used for Windows Server 2003.

RIP

RIP is an open-standard dynamic routing protocol used to exchange routing information in small to mid-sized networks. Windows Server 2003 supports RIP versions 1 and 2. Although RIP is simple to configure, it suffers from a few drawbacks. RIP is limited to a hop count of 15. This means that an advertisement can pass through only 16 routers before the route is considered unreachable. Also, RIP is considered slow to recover when there is a change in the network topology. One other problem with RIP, along with the slow recovery times, is the possibility of routing loops. Routing loops are advertisements that send IP traffic through the same series of routers until the maximum hop count is reached. Basically, RIP does not scale well for use in large networks because of the reasons mentioned here.

RIP v1 operates through broadcast announcements. It follows classful routing characteristics. This means that route advertisements in RIP v1 do not carry subnet mask information. Consequently, only network addresses that use their default subnet mask, following their classful boundaries, will work properly in a RIP v1 configured environment.

NOTE

Classful boundaries are network boundaries that exist between networks that are configured with their default subnet masks. For example, a 192.168.1.0 network would have a subnet mask of 255.255.255.0 if it were configured to operate on its classful boundary and a 10.0.0.0 network would have a 255.0.0.0 subnet mask if it were configured to operate on its classful boundary.

RIP v2 uses multicast or broadcast advertisements and is considered a classless routing protocol. Therefore, unlike RIP v1, RIP v2 is not limited to classful boundaries. Routing advertisements that include subnet mask information are said to follow Classless InterDomain Routing (CIDR) rules.

NOTE

The acronym CIDR is pronounced "cider."

Some of the other features and characteristics of RIP as implemented in Windows Server 2003 are:

- Capability to disable subnet summarization—the process used to aggregate network addresses to a single address to reduce the size of routing tables and advertised route information

- Ability to configure announcement and route aging timers—route advertisements intervals and time to live values for existing routes

- Password authentication support

- Peer filters for choosing which router's announcements are accepted

- Route filters for choosing which networks to announce or accept

- Selection of which RIP version to run on each interface for incoming and outgoing packets

- Split-horizon, poison-reverse, and triggered-update algorithms that are used to avoid routing loops and speed recovery of the internetwork when topology changes occur

EXERCISE 8.08

CONFIGURING RIP ON A WINDOWS SERVER 2003 NETWORK

In this exercise, we will configure RIP v2.

1. Begin by configuring LAN Routing in **Routing and Remote Access**. Click **Start | Programs | Administrative Tools | Routing and Remote Access**.

2. In the left pane of the **Routing and Remote Access** management console, right-click the server name and select **Configure and Enable Routing and Remote Access**. If this option is grayed out, select **Disable Routing and Remote Access** to start with a fresh configuration.

3. On the first page of the **Routing and Remote Access Server Setup Wizard**, click **Next**.

4. Select **Custom Configuration** and click **Next** as shown in Figure 8.67.

Figure 8.67 Custom Routing and Remote Access Configuration

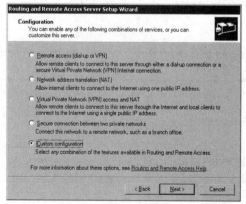

5. Select **LAN Routing** followed by **Next** as shown in Figure 8.68.

Figure 8.68 LAN Routing Configuration

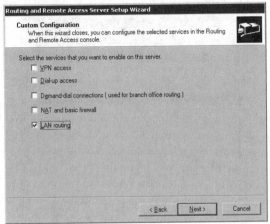

6. Select **Finish**. A message box will display asking if you would like to enable the Routing and Remote Access Service. Select **OK** to enable LAN routing.

7. Now that the Routing and Remote Access Service is enabled, we have to configure RIP v1.

8. In the left pane, select **IP Routing**. Right-click on **General** and select **New Routing Protocol** as shown in Figure 8.69.

Figure 8.69 Adding a New Routing Protocol

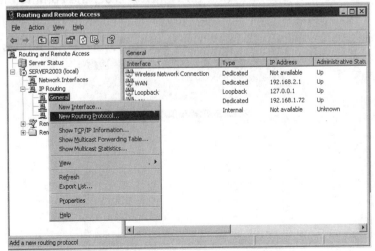

9. From the next screen, select **RIP Version 2 for Internet Protocol** and click **OK** as shown in Figure 8.70.

Figure 8.70 Adding RIP

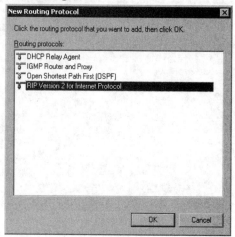

10. Now an entry for **RIP** will be displayed in the left pane beneath the **IP Routing** icon. This means that RIP is enabled on the server but at this point, RIP will not advertise any routes because we have to tell RIP which interfaces to use for route advertisement.

11. In the left pane, right-click **RIP** and select **New Interface....**

12. In the **New Interface for RIP Version 2 for Internet Protocol** dialog box, select the interface that provides the common link between your routers as shown in Figure 8.71. In this case, the common interface has been named **WAN**.

Figure 8.71 Selecting an Interface to Advertise RIP Routes Through

13. From the left pane, select **IP Routing | RIP**.

14. From the right pane, right-click **RIP** and select **Properties**.

15. The default setting for RIP in a Windows Server 2003 environment is **Rip version 2 broadcast** for the **Outgoing packet protocol:** drop-down list and **Rip version 1 and 2** for the **Incoming packet protocol:** drop-down box. If we are using only RIP version 2 throughout our network, and the transport medium will be Ethernet, it is best to use **RIP version 2 multicast** for the **Outbound packet protocol:** drop-down selection and to ensure only RIP version 2 operation, select **RIP version 2 only** from the **Incoming protocol packet:** drop-down list as shown in Figure 8.72.

Figure 8.72 Selecting RIP version 2 as the Only Routing Protocol

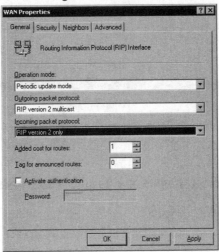

16. Repeat this process for the other Windows Server 2003 router that will be advertising RIP version 2 on your network.

Now that RIP is configured, verify the operation by using the **Show Neighbor...** command. From the left pane of the **Routing and Remote Access** management console, select **IP Routing**. From the right pane of the management console, right-click **RIP** and select **Show Neighbors....** You should see that RIP v2 is the protocol used for the advertisements as shown in Figure 8.73.

Figure 8.73 Verifying RIP version 2 for Neighboring Routers

SERVER2003 - RIP Neighbors

Address	Version	Bad packets	Bad routes
192.168.2.2	2	0	0

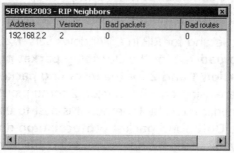

Verify the routing table entry for the RIP version 2 route by selecting **General** in the left pane of the management console under **IP Routing.** Next, in the right pane of the management console, right-click on any of the interfaces and select **Show IP Routing Table.** You should see the RIP table entry for the remote network as shown in Figure 8.74.

Figure 8.74 Verifying the RIP version 2 Routing Table Entry

SERVER2003 - IP Routing Table

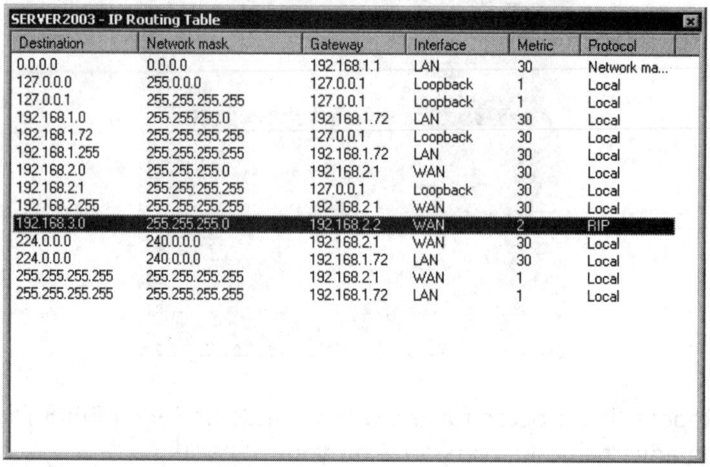

Destination	Network mask	Gateway	Interface	Metric	Protocol
0.0.0.0	0.0.0.0	192.168.1.1	LAN	30	Network ma...
127.0.0.0	255.0.0.0	127.0.0.1	Loopback	1	Local
127.0.0.1	255.255.255.255	127.0.0.1	Loopback	1	Local
192.168.1.0	255.255.255.0	192.168.1.72	LAN	30	Local
192.168.1.72	255.255.255.255	127.0.0.1	Loopback	30	Local
192.168.1.255	255.255.255.255	192.168.1.72	LAN	30	Local
192.168.2.0	255.255.255.0	192.168.2.1	WAN	30	Local
192.168.2.1	255.255.255.255	127.0.0.1	Loopback	30	Local
192.168.2.255	255.255.255.255	192.168.2.1	WAN	30	Local
192.168.3.0	255.255.255.0	192.168.2.2	WAN	2	RIP
224.0.0.0	240.0.0.0	192.168.2.1	WAN	30	Local
224.0.0.0	240.0.0.0	192.168.1.72	LAN	30	Local
255.255.255.255	255.255.255.255	192.168.2.1	WAN	1	Local
255.255.255.255	255.255.255.255	192.168.1.72	LAN	1	Local

Finally, we can ping any remote address on the network from a local system. If RIP v2 routing is working properly, a client on the 192.168.1.0/24 network should get a reply when pinging a client on the 192.168.3.0/24 network as shown in Figure 8.75.

Figure 8.75 Using the PING Command to Verify RIP version 2 Routing Operation

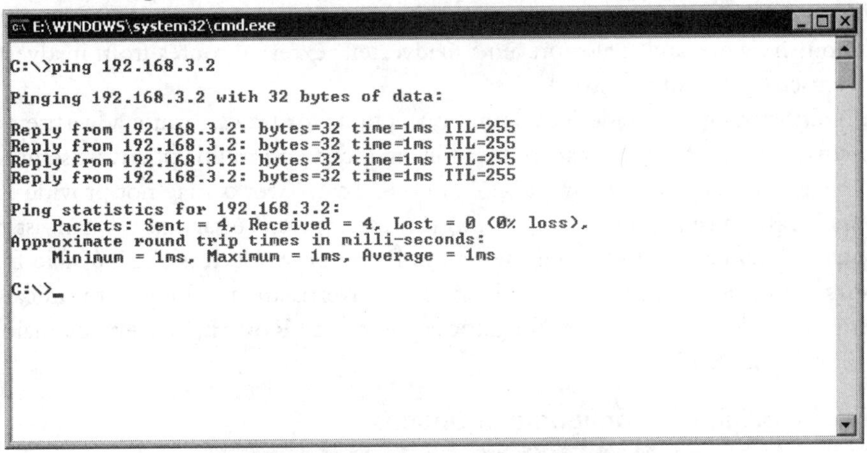

E:\WINDOWS\system32\cmd.exe
C:\>ping 192.168.3.2
Pinging 192.168.3.2 with 32 bytes of data:
Reply from 192.168.3.2: bytes=32 time=1ms TTL=255
Reply from 192.168.3.2: bytes=32 time=1ms TTL=255
Reply from 192.168.3.2: bytes=32 time=1ms TTL=255
Reply from 192.168.3.2: bytes=32 time=1ms TTL=255
Ping statistics for 192.168.3.2:
Packets: Sent = 4, Received = 4, Lost = 0 (0% loss),
Approximate round trip times in milli-seconds:
Minimum = 1ms, Maximum = 1ms, Average = 1ms
C:\>_

Let's look at a couple of the other configuration options for RIP before we begin our OSPF configuration. Open the RIP property settings by selecting **RIP** under **IP Routing** in the left pane of the **Routing and Remote Access** management console. In the right pane, right-click on the interface that is advertising RIP updates and select **Properties.** We have already reviewed the options in the **General** tab. Now, select the **Security** tab as shown in Figure 8.76.

Figure 8.76 RIP Security Configuration Options

WAN Properties
General
Security
Neighbors
Advanced
Action:
For incoming routes
Accept all routes
Accept all routes in the ranges listed
Ignore all routes in the ranges listed
From:
To:
Add
From
To
Edit
Remove
OK
Cancel
Apply

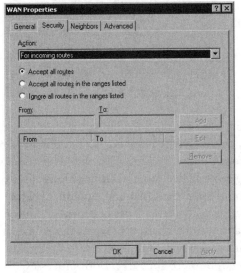

The **Security** tab provides route-filtering options for each interface that will advertise routing information. There are options to filter incoming and outgoing routes based on

addresses or address ranges. We can use this option to allow advertised routes only for network addresses in use. This prevents our internal routes from inadvertently being advertised outside of our network and it also prevents inadvertent external routes from inadvertently being advertised within our network.

The **Neighbors** tab provides configuration options for unicast route advertisements. Not all network media provides capabilities for broadcast and multicast advertisements. For example, depending on the configuration, Frame Relay networks may not provide broadcast and multicast transmission capabilities. In this case, it is necessary to use unicast route advertisements between routers using the Frame Relay network. It is also possible from the **Neighbors** tab to use broadcast or multicast route advertisements along with unicast route advertisements. The options for the **Neighbors** tab of the **Routing Interface** dialog box are shown in Figure 8.77.

Figure 8.77 Neighbors Configuration Options

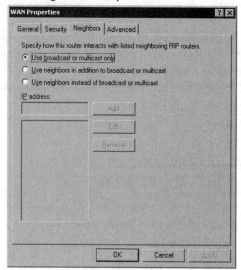

The **Advanced** tab provides options for routing timers, routing loop prevention options, and routing table tuning options. The **Advanced** tab options are shown in Figure 8.78.

The routing timers control how frequently advertisements are sent, how long routes are maintained in the routing table as live routes, and how long dead routes are kept in the routing table before removal. **Split horizon** and **poison reverse processing** are methods used to prevent resending route advertisements out through an interface where the route advertisement was just learned. Split horizon prevents the readvertisement of routes in the direction they were originally learned. Poison reverse is the process of advertising a route marked as infinite (a hop count of 16 for RIP). Both processes are implemented to alleviate the problem of counting to infinity, which delays route convergence and creates instability in routed a network.

Figure 8.78 Advanced Configuration Options

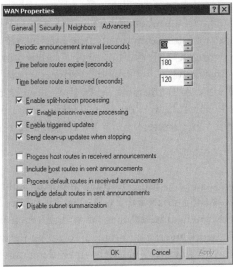

Routing loops occur when IP traffic is incorrectly routed between a series of routers, only to be routed back again within the series of routers. Routing loops trap IP traffic in a loop until the IP TTL is reached. *Route flapping* occurs when a route is advertised through one path, only to be advertised through a different route on the next, or subsequent route advertisements. The route is said to be flapping when its path is advertised alternately as available and unavailable, or as one route and then another.

Advanced Routing

Head of the Class...

In this chapter, we introduce RIP, RIP v2, and OSPF routing. There are entire books written about each one of these routing protocols. We have attempted to touch upon the major advantages and disadvantages of each protocol as well as the basic configurations of each. The entire Internet is held together by open standard protocols like RIP, OSPF, and BGP. If you are going to design networks on a global scale, it is worth having a better understanding of the dynamic routing protocols, especially RIP and OSPF.

Again, the strength of each one of these protocols lies in the fact that they are open standards. Almost every piece of networking equipment and nearly every networking operating system can handle RIP routing at a minimum. More and more vendors are building in OSPF capabilities as well. Microsoft has designed Active Directory to be a globally distributed, redundant database system for account administration, network management, and software deployment. The notion that this is a globally distributed system relies heavily on the fact that globally distributed systems can communicate with one another. This global communication relies on some type of dynamic routing protocol working behind the scenes.

RIP is a distance-vector protocol. Distance-vector protocols advertise full routes on a regular update interval. Preferred routes are determined based on a distance component (in the case of RIP this distance is the number of hops—the number of routers a packet will traverse on a given path) and a vector component (the interface the route will use to forward packets to a given network). OSPF, on the other hand, is a link state protocol. Link state protocols flood the network with link state advertisements to understand the network topology. Routers then advertise only the portion of the network to which they are physically attached. This process enables the routers to maintain separate tables describing the network topology, the neighboring routers, and a list of preferred routes.

OSPF

OSPF is an open-standard dynamic routing protocol used to exchange routing information in large to very large networks. Compared to RIP, OSPF is more difficult to configure and administer but it tends to be much more efficient than RIP even in very large networks. OSPF requires very little network overhead, even in complex networks.

OSPF uses the shortest path first (SPF) algorithm to determine routes that should be added to the routing table. OSPF routers maintain a map of the internetwork called the link state database. This database is synchronized by all OSPF routers and the information contained in the link state database is used to compute routing table entries. Each OSPF router forms an adjacency with its neighboring routers. Any time a change occurs in the internetwork, information about the change is flooded to the entire network.

Every time updated information about the link state database is received, the routes in the routing table are recalculated. This presents a problem in that the larger the network, the more system resources are required to maintain and calculate route information. OSPF allows for *routing areas* as a means to cut down on routing changes flooded to the network and also to reduce the resource requirements for OSPF routers. All routing areas must connect to the *backbone area* to facilitate proper route advertisements. An area is a group of contiguous networks and the hosts that are attached to them. OSPF uses Autonomous System (AS) numbers to label the areas. AS numbers are used to determine the authority for a network. In other words, an organization will be provided with a specific AS number or set of AS numbers to use for their network. This AS number provides accountability for routing information.

Each routing area maintains link state information only about itself, with the exception of the backbone. The backbone must maintain information about all other areas, including itself. This provides a hierarchical network infrastructure that, when designed correctly, promotes scalability.

Everywhere that a border exists between areas, there must be at least one area border router (ABR). This is a router with multiple interfaces that attach to multiple areas. The ABR maintains routing information for each area that it belongs to, with a separate database for each area. The backbone is made up of the ABRs and any networks that aren't completely within any of the areas (and their routers).

Also, OSPF has a special-case area in which only one entry and exit point exists for the network area. This area, known as a stub area, provides a default route for the area. A default route is a route listed with all zeros, providing a route for all external traffic where a specific route is not known. The stub area does not advertise external routes and, through the use of default route advertisement, significantly reduces the amount of link state advertisements and resource utilization within the stub area.

OSPF uses two different types of routes: inter-area and intra-area routes. Inter-area routes are advertisements passed between routing areas. Intra-area routes are routes advertised within a routing area. By design, all inter-area routes will eventually reach the backbone area in an OSPF network. The backbone area controls route advertisements to all surrounding areas. Figure 8.79 illustrates some of the OSPF terminology.

Figure 8.79 OSPF Terminology

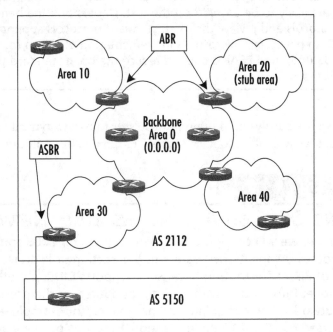

OSPF has the following advantages over RIP:

■ Network topology changes converge faster.

■ OSPF provides loop-free routes.

■ OSPF scales to large or very large internetworks.

The Microsoft Windows Server 2003 implementation of OSPF has the following features:

■ Coexistence with RIP

■ Dynamic addition and deletion of interfaces

- Dynamic reconfiguration of all OSPF settings
- Route filters for controlling interaction with other routing protocols

TEST DAY TIP

There is a trend in IT that seems to be a reflection of the popularity of the Internet itself. The Internet is based on the popular open standard TCP/IP. Companies have used proprietary methods for sharing information between their systems in the past. You will see in Window Server 2003 that most of the protocols reviewed here are open standard protocols. This ensures better interoperability between different vendor solutions and between partnering companies. These open standards are topics that are likely to be covered on the test. Understand the benefits of open standard protocols and review the open standard protocols supported in Windows Server 2003 (in particular, Microsoft's implementation of them) for this exam. RIP, OSPF, RADIUS (IAS), and PEAP are just a few of the open standard protocols that we have discussed.

So far, we have been analyzing routing protocols that provide dynamic routing for unicast IP traffic. Next we will take a look at Microsoft's support for multicast IP traffic.

EXERCISE 8.09

CONFIGURING OSPF ON A WINDOWS 2003 NETWORK

In this exercise, we will configure two Windows Server 2003 routers to advertise OSPF routes. As mentioned earlier in this section, it is preferable to use RIP v2 instead of RIP v1 for routing because it supports CIDR, a method capable of carrying subnet information within routing updates. In the previous example, if we used networks with nondefault subnet masks (for example, a 10.0.0.10/24 address instead of 10.0.0.10/8), RIP version 1 will not properly advertise the routes because it does not understand nonclassful addressing. We would use RIP v1 only for compatibility reasons. In other words, use RIP v1 only if you have equipment that does not support RIP v2 routing.

For the final portion of this exercise, we will change our routing protocol to OSPF, as shown in Figure 8.80. To demonstrate some of the features of OSPF, we will configure the common connection between the routers as the backbone area or Area 0. Each of the respective LAN connections on our routers will be configured as Area 10 for the 192.168.1.0/24 network and Area 30 for the 192.168.3.0/24 network. Because each of these networks has only a single source for external traffic, we will configure these areas as stub areas. Let's begin by disabling RIP and enabling OSPF for our router.

Figure 8.80 OSPF Router Configuration

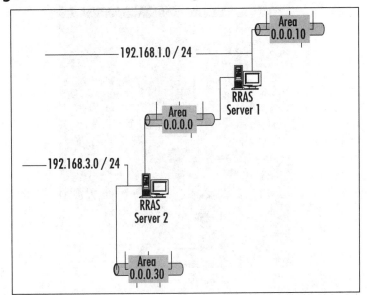

1. Open the Routing and Remote Access management console by selecting **Start | Programs | Administrative Tools | Routing and Remote Access**.

2. Disable RIP. Select **RIP** under **IP Routing** in the left pane of the management console. Right-click **RIP** and select **Delete**. Select **Yes** when the message box asks **Are you sure you want to remove RIP Version 2 for Internet Protocol?**

3. Right-click the **General** tab and select **Open Shortest Path First (OSPF)** and select **OK** to enable OSPF on the server.

4. Now that OSPF is enabled, we need to specify interfaces for OSPF participation. From the left pane of the **Routing and Remote Access** management console, below **IP Routing**, right-click **OSPF** and select **New Interface....** Select the common interface between the routers first (our WAN) interface. The **OSPF Properties** dialog box will be displayed as shown in Figure 8.81.

Figure 8.81 OSPF Properties Dialog Box

5. Router priority is used to determine which router will be the designated router on a broadcast network. We will go with the default settings here so select **OK**. Please note the other tabs on the **OSPF Properties** dialog box. The **NBMA Neighbors** tab provides configuration options for Non-Broadcast Multi-Access Neighbors as seen in multiaccess environments like ATM and Frame Relay. The **Advanced** tab provides configuration options for OSPF timers and packet limitations.

6. Now that we have created our backbone area, we have to configure it. Right-click **OSPF** in the left pane of the **Routing and Remote Access** management console and select **Properties**. Select the **Areas** tab, select the backbone area (0.0.0.0), and select **Edit** as shown in Figure 8.82.

Figure 8.82 Configuring the OSPF Backbone Area Options

7. We will not use OSPF authentication for this scenario so our first con-figuration change should be to remove the check box from **Enable plaintext password** under the **General** tab as shown in Figure 8.83.

Figure 8.83 Removing Authentication from OSPF

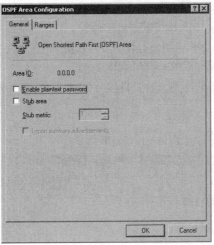

8. Under the **Ranges** tab, we will tell OSPF which interface range to advertise. Enter the network address for our backbone network (192.168.2.0) into the **Destination:** text box and the subnet mask (255.255.255.0) into the **Network mask:** text box and select **Add.** The **Ranges** tab should look like the one shown in Figure 8.84.

Figure 8.84 Configuring the OSPF Backbone Range

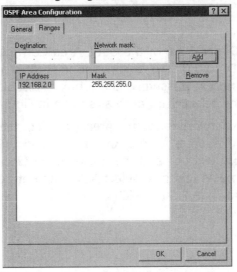

9. Select **OK** to commit the changes to the OSPF backbone.

10. Repeat the process outlined in steps 4 through 9 to configure Area 10.

11. Add the **LAN** interface to the OSPF process by right-clicking **OSPF** in the left pane of the management console and selecting **New Interface....** Select the **LAN** interface that will be used for Area 10 and then select **OK** to accept the default settings.

12. Right-click **OSPF** in the left pane below **IP Routing** and select **Properties**. Click the **Areas** tab.

13. From the **Areas** tab, add Area 10 by selecting **Add** as shown in Figure 8.85.

Figure 8.85 Adding an OSPF Area

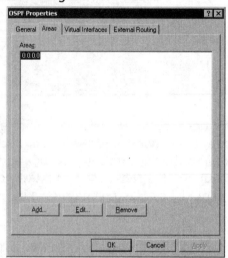

14. From the **General** tab of the **OSPF Area Configuration** dialog box, set the **Area ID:** to 0.0.0.10 to correspond to Area 10 and remove the **Enable plaintext password** check box to disable authentication for our scenario and select **Stub area** as shown in Figure 8.86.

15. To add the network range for Area 10, select the **Ranges** tab and enter the network address for the Area 10 network (192.168.1.0) into the **Destination:** text box and the subnet mask (255.255.255.0) into the **Network mask:** text box. Select **Add**. The **Ranges** tab should look like the one shown in Figure 8.87.

Figure 8.86 Configuring the New OSPF Area

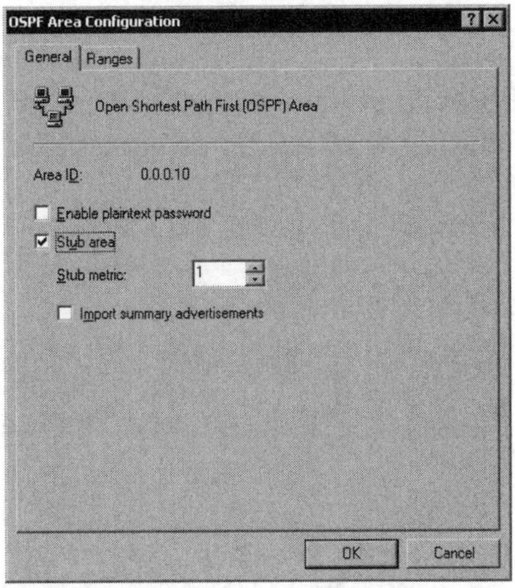

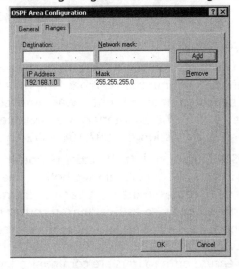

Figure 8.87 Configuring the Network Range for Area 10

16. Select **OK** to complete the configuration of the **OSPF Area Configuration** and select **OK** to complete this overall configuration for OSPF.

17. Click **OSPF** in the left pane under **IP Routing** and then from the right pane of the management console right-click on the **LAN** interface that will be in Area 10; select **Properties**.

18. In the **LAN Properties** dialog box, select **0.0.0.10** from the **Area ID:** drop-down box on the **General** tab as shown in Figure 8.88.

Figure 8.88 Assigning the Area ID to the LAN Interface

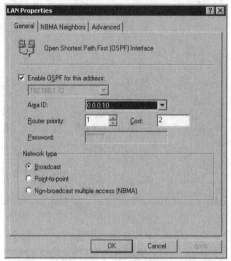

19. Select **OK** to complete the configuration.

20. The second Windows Server 2003 router will be configured using almost identical configuration options. The only difference is in Area 30. Since the first configured router was connected to Area 10 and Area 0, the 192.168.1.0/24 interface was assigned to Area 10. On the next router, we will assign the 192.168.3.0/24 network to Area 30.

21. To verify OSPF routing click **OSPF** under **IP Routing** in the left pane of the management console. You should see both of the interfaces that are advertising OSPF routes in the right pane of the management console. The **State** should be listed as **Designated-router** or **Backup designated-router**. If the state is **Waiting** and more than a few minutes have passed since you completed your configurations, check the OSPF configuration settings to ensure both routers are communicating properly.

22. Right-click **OSPF** in the left pane of the management console and select **Show Areas…** to verify Area advertisement for the router as shown in Figure 8.89.

Figure 8.89 Viewing Advertised OSPF Areas for the Server

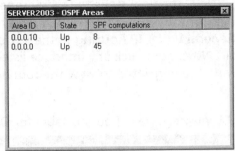

23. Verify neighbor adjacencies by right-clicking on **OSPF** in the left pane of the management console and selecting **Show Neighbors...** as shown in Figure 8.90.

Figure 8.90 Viewing OSPF Neighbors

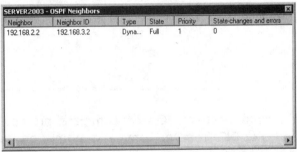

24. Again, right-click **OSPF** in the left pane of the management console and select **Show Link-state Database...** to view the Link-state Database information as shown in Figure 8.91.

Figure 8.91 Viewing the Link-state Database

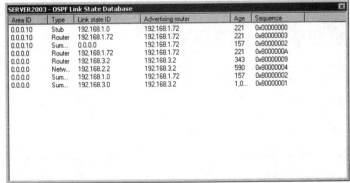

25. Each of the previous verification steps provided information about the operation of OSPF. The final steps to verify proper operation should include a check of the routing table and a ping to the remote network. First, click **General** under **IP Routing** in the left pane of the management console. Next, right-click any interface listed in the right pane and select **Show IP Routing Table** to view the routing table as shown in Figure 8.92.

Figure 8.92 Viewing the IP Routing Table for OSPF Routing

Destination	Network mask	Gateway	Interface	Metric	Protocol
255.255.255.255	255.255.255.255	192.168.2.1	WAN	1	Local
255.255.255.255	255.255.255.255	192.168.1.72	LAN	1	Local
224.0.0.0	240.0.0.0	192.168.2.1	WAN	30	Local
224.0.0.0	240.0.0.0	192.168.1.72	LAN	30	Local
192.168.2.255	255.255.255.255	192.168.2.1	WAN	30	Local
192.168.2.1	255.255.255.255	127.0.0.1	Loopback	30	Local
192.168.2.0	255.255.255.0	192.168.2.1	WAN	30	Local
192.168.1.255	255.255.255.255	192.168.1.72	LAN	30	Local
192.168.1.72	255.255.255.255	127.0.0.1	Loopback	30	Local
192.168.1.0	255.255.255.0	192.168.1.72	LAN	30	Local
127.0.0.1	255.255.255.255	127.0.0.1	Loopback	1	Local
127.0.0.0	255.0.0.0	127.0.0.1	Loopback	1	Local
0.0.0.0	0.0.0.0	192.168.1.1	LAN	30	Network ma...
192.168.3.0	255.255.255.0	192.168.2.2	WAN	3	OSPF
192.168.2.0	255.255.255.0	192.168.2.1	WAN	2	OSPF
192.168.1.0	255.255.255.0	192.168.1.72	LAN	2	OSPF

26. **Ping** the remote network. Open a command prompt **Start | Run |** type **cmd** and click **OK**. From the command prompt on the machine connected to Area 10 or any machine on the Area 10 LAN, type **ping 192.168.3.2** and press **Enter** to test connectivity between the networks as shown in Figure 8.93.

Figure 8.93 Testing Connectivity with the Ping Command

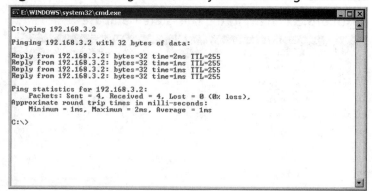

```
C:\>ping 192.168.3.2

Pinging 192.168.3.2 with 32 bytes of data:

Reply from 192.168.3.2: bytes=32 time=2ms TTL=255
Reply from 192.168.3.2: bytes=32 time=1ms TTL=255
Reply from 192.168.3.2: bytes=32 time=1ms TTL=255
Reply from 192.168.3.2: bytes=32 time=1ms TTL=255

Ping statistics for 192.168.3.2:
    Packets: Sent = 4, Received = 4, Lost = 0 (0% loss),
Approximate round trip times in milli-seconds:
    Minimum = 1ms, Maximum = 2ms, Average = 1ms

C:\>
```

IGMP

IGMP is an open-standard protocol used to communicate multicast membership information for an internetwork. IGMP version 1 is defined in RFC 1112 and IGMP version 2 is defined in RFC 2236. Both protocols provide a method for host to router communication about multicast membership. Hosts advertise joining and leaving multicast groups to multicast routers using IGMP. As with unicast, where route information is shared between routers using routing protocols like RIP and OSPF, multicast route information is also shared between routers using multicast routing protocols. Distance Vector Multicast Routing Protocol (DVMRP) is one of the more common multicast routing protocols. Microsoft Windows Server 2003 does not support multicast routing protocols directly. It does, however, support IGMP and IGMP proxy mode.

As mentioned, IGMP provides a transport mechanism for IP multicast group membership between participating hosts and multicast routers. Although Windows Server 2003 does not support multicast routing, it does provide forwarding of IGMP messages in single router environments. In other words, if one Windows Server 2003 router is attached to multiple networks, it can be configured to forward IGMP information from one interface to other attached interfaces. This process differs from routing in the fact that routing would provide directional information for multicast traffic whereas Windows Server 2003 only forwards multicast IGMP messages without truly directing the multicast traffic.

In IGMP proxy mode, a Windows Server 2003 router will forward all IGMP messages to Internet-based multicast routers on behalf of the IGMP hosts. Also, the Windows Server 2003 router will forward IGMP multicast information from Internet routers to the IGMP hosts attached to its local network.

To enable IGMP on a Windows Server 2003 router:

1. Open **Routing and Remote Access** from **Start | Programs | Administrative Tools | Routing and Remote Access**.

2. Right-click **General** and click **New Routing Protocol**.

3. From the **Select Routing Protocol** dialog box, click **IGMP Router and Proxy** and then click **OK**.

Configuring Basic Firewall Support

Now more than ever, security is a major concern in today's corporate environment. One way to improve basic security on an Internet-connected network is to install a firewall. Windows Server 2003 comes with basic firewall support built in. A firewall compares network traffic, as it passes through the firewall, to a set of preconfigured rules. Traffic streams are accepted or rejected based on the rules they match. To enable basic firewall support in Windows Server 2003, a public interface must be configured to utilize the basic firewall rules. Based on its configuration, the Windows Server 2003 basic firewall will have different rule sets applied.

If the public interface configured for basic firewall support is configured for private network traffic only, only computers on the private network will have their traffic routed. Private network computers will not be able to reach computers on the public network, and likewise, public computers will not be able to reach computers on the private network. VPN clients connecting to the network will be treated as private computers due to the nature of VPN.

If the public interface configured for basic firewall support is configured for private network traffic and also configured for NAT, source and destination addresses will be recorded in the NAT table. Using the NAT table, the basic firewall will determine which public computers can connect to private systems. If the private system initiated the connection, an entry will be in the NAT table for the private and public system and the basic firewall will allow the public computer to connect with the private system based on this NAT table entry. This means an external computer will be able to connect with a computer on the internal network only in response to communications initiated by the internal computer.

EXAM WARNING

Firewall support involves filtering traffic based on rules. The rules are either based on the addresses involved in the TCP/IP transmission or the port numbers associated with the TCP/IP transmission. Make sure you know the basic TCP and UDP port numbers for common Internet services such as FTP, DHCP, DNS, WWW, and e-mail (POP3, SMTP, and IMAP). These are called the *well-known ports,* and some of the most frequently used are as follows:

- **ftp-data** 20/tcp
- **ftp** 21/tcp
- **telnet** 23/tcp
- **smtp** 25/tcp
- **DNS** 53/tcp
- **DNS** 53/udp
- **tftp** 69/udp
- **http** 80/tcp
- **pop3** 110/tcp
- **imap** 143/tcp
- **https** 443/tcp
- **https** 443/udp
- **RDP/terminal server** 3389/tcp

A firewall functions in much the same way as do the packet filters discussed earlier in this chapter. There are a few things to consider when implementing a firewall. If you already have some other network firewall software installed, you do not need to use the basic firewall. Basic firewall configuration is applied only to public interfaces. The firewall might interfere with certain network applications such as e-mail or FTP. If this is the case, you will have to configure exceptions to the firewall rules. Also, it can be beneficial to configure packet filters to use in conjunction with the firewall. Packet filters can be applied to public or private interfaces.

EXERCISE 8.10

CONFIGURING BASIC FIREWALL SUPPORT

In this exercise, we will configure basic firewall support to allow LAN connections to connect only to intranet Web servers located on a different subnet than the client systems as shown in Figure 8.94.

Figure 8.94 Simple Intranet with Firewall

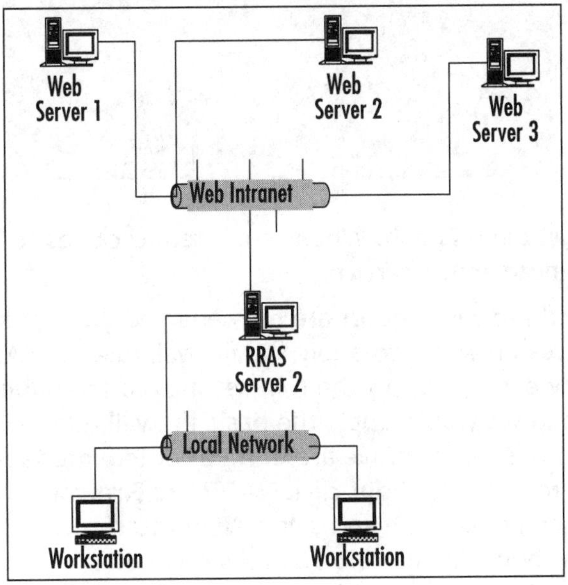

1. Open **Routing and Remote Access. Start | Administrative Tools | Routing and Remote Access.**

2. From the **Routing and Remote Access** management console, right-click the server name and select **Configure and Enable Routing and Remote Access.** If this option is grayed out, select **Disable Routing and Remote Access** to start with a fresh configuration.

3. From the **Routing and Remote Access Server Setup Wizard**, click **Next.**

4. Select **Custom configuration** and click **Next.**

5. From the **Custom Configuration** screen, select **NAT and basic firewall** as shown in Figure 8.95.

Figure 8.95 Selecting NAT and Basic Firewall for the Custom Configuration

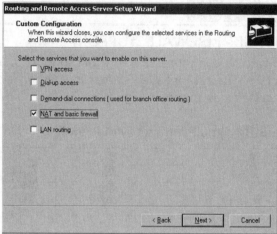

6. Click **Next** and **Finish**. When prompted, click **Yes** to start the routing and remote access service.

7. NAT and firewall support are now enabled, but we have to specify interfaces on which to apply the firewall rules. If NAT was in use on this server, we would apply the NAT settings to the public and private interfaces and we would apply the basic firewall rules to the public interface. In this scenario, we are using a routed interface and will apply the basic firewall only. Right-click **NAT/Basic Firewall** in the left pane of the management console and select **New Interface....** Select the **LAN** interface as shown in Figure 8.96 and select **OK**.

Figure 8.96 Adding the LAN Interface to the Basic Firewall

8. From the **Network Address Translation Properties** box, select **Basic firewall only** as shown in Figure 8.97.

Figure 8.97 Specifying Basic Firewall for the Interface

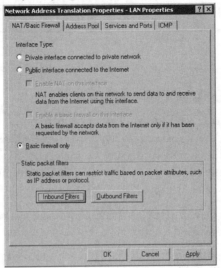

9. We will apply an inbound filter for all LAN traffic destined for the Web servers on the intranet subnet. Click the **Inbound Filters** button. Select **New** from the **Inbound Filters** screen. Select the **Source network** check box and enter **192.168.1.0** for the **IP address** and **255.255.255.0** for the **Subnet mask**. Select the **Destination network** check box and enter **10.0.0.0** for the **IP address** and **255.255.255.0** for the **Subnet mask**. In the **Protocol** drop-down box, select **TCP** and enter **80** for the **Destination port** as shown in Figure 8.98. This is our selection because by default, Web servers listen for traffic on TCP port 80.

Figure 8.98 Configuring the Addresses and Ports

10.   Click **OK**. Select **Drop all packets except those that meet the criteria below** from the **Inbound Filters** screen and click **OK**. Click **OK** one more time to complete the firewall configuration. Any LAN traffic destined for the Web servers on the 10.0.0.0/24 network will be passed. Any traffic not matching these criteria will be blocked.

RRAS NAT Services

Network Address Translation (NAT) was introduced in response to the concern that available public IP version 4 addresses were rapidly being depleted. NAT is defined in RFC 1631. NAT typically provides a translation service for private IP addresses to a public IP address or addresses. *IP masquerading* is another term frequently used (especially in the UNIX community) to describe this process. NAT works in the following manner:

1.   A system on the private network attempts to connect to a public address on the outside of the network.

2.   The NAT system (the client's default gateway) looks at the source and destination addresses and TCP and/or UDP port numbers.

3.   The NAT system enters this information into its NAT table, replaces the client address with the NAT system's public address, and possibly modifies the source port numbers.

4.   The remote system responds to the NAT system, sending any return information to the NAT system's public address and advertised port number or numbers.

5.   The NAT system checks its NAT table to determine whether or not to forward the request to the internal network.

6.   If a match is made in the NAT table, what is now the destination address for this traffic stream (the computer on the private network) replaces the NAT public address and again port numbers are modified if necessary.

7.   The client that originated the traffic receives the responses from the public computer.

NAT can provide address mappings for hundreds or even thousands of addresses. NAT also provides a level of security for private networks because NAT typically does not allow inbound TCP/IP traffic without initiation from the internal network. In other words, unless a client on the private network requests to connect to a system on the public network, the system on the public network will not be allowed to connect to the private network.

So, what happens when you want to host a public service that is connected to your private network? Figure 8.99 illustrates an example in which public systems need access to a Web server that is housed on the private network.

Figure 8.99 Private Network Web Server Available to the Public

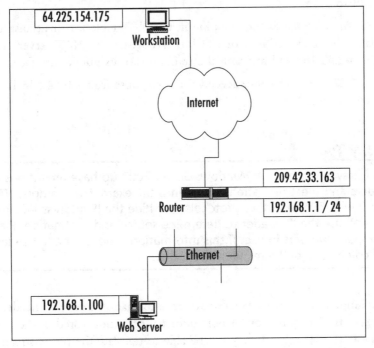

For a public system to reach a system on a private network hidden by NAT, the NAT system needs a static mapping for the service being requested. This static mapping will map the TCP or UDP port request to a private address on the inside of the NAT translated network. Let's look at an example to see how this works.

1. A user on the public network at address 64.225.154.175 attempts to connect to the Web server hidden behind a NAT translator at 209.42.33.163.

2. The public system sends a TCP Synchronize (SYN) segment from 64.225.154.175 on TCP port 2481 to the NAT translator at 209.42.33.163 on TCP port 80.

3. If the NAT translator did not have a static mapping, the connection would fail and the public system attempting to make the connection would display an error message. In our example, the NAT translator finds a mapping for 192.168.1.100, the private address for the Web server on the private LAN segment behind the NAT system.

4. The NAT translator removes the destination address of 209.42.33.163, replaces it with 192.168.1.100, and forwards the traffic out the NAT private interface to the private network Web server.

5. The Web server replies to the NAT system with traffic destined for 64.225.154.175.

6. The NAT system sees the mapping in the NAT table for this transaction and replaces the source address of 192.168.1.100 with the NAT server's public address of 209.42.33.163 and forwards the traffic out of its public interface.

7. The 64.225.154.175 system receives the response from 209.42.33.163 to complete the connection.

TEST DAY TIP

NAT and firewall features in Windows Server 2003 do have limitations. Make sure you understand these limitations going into the exam. For example, NAT does not work well with FTP and other protocols that hide the IP address information. NAT and firewall use the IP header to determine source and destination IP address and TCP/UDP port numbers in use. If this information is not in the IP header, NAT and firewall could have problems with the traffic.

There are limitations to NAT. NAT relies on information in the IP header and TCP header of packets. If IP information or port information is not stored in the header, the way it is in most TCP/IP traffic, NAT may not be able to translate the traffic stream. FTP, PPTP, and other forms of tunneled traffic can cause problems for NAT. A NAT editor is needed to translate FTP traffic through a NAT system, for example.

Typical NAT traffic is translated based on TCP port, UDP port, and IP addresses listed in the TCP header, UDP header, and IP header, respectively. NAT editors are special software components that translate traffic that contains TCP, UDP, or IP information in places other than their respective headers. Microsoft provides built-in NAT editor functions for some common protocols like FTP and PPTP within their recent operating system offerings.

EXERCISE 8.11

CONFIGURING NAT AND STATIC NAT MAPPING

In this exercise, we will configure NAT and a static NAT mapping for a Web server as shown in Figure 8.93.

1. Open **Routing and Remote Access. Start | Administrative Tools | Routing and Remote Access.**

2. From the **Routing and Remote Access** management console, right-click the server name and select **Configure and Enable Routing and Remote Access**. If this option is grayed out, select **Disable Routing and Remote Access** to start with a fresh configuration.

3. From the **Routing and Remote Access Server Setup Wizard**, click **Next**.

4. Select **Network address translation (NAT)** and click **Next**.

5. From the **NAT Internet Connection** dialog box, select the **WAN** interface and remove the **Enable security on the selected interface by setting up basic firewall** check box as shown in Figure 8.100; click **Next**.

Figure 8.100 Specifying the Public Interface and Removing Firewall Settings

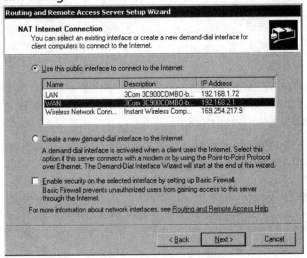

6. Select the **LAN** interface for the private NAT interface as shown in Figure 8.101 and select **Next**.

7. Click **Finish** to complete the basic NAT configuration. Now we will modify the configuration to provide public inbound requests for our private Web servers.

Figure 8.101 Specifying the LAN Interface as the Private NAT Interface

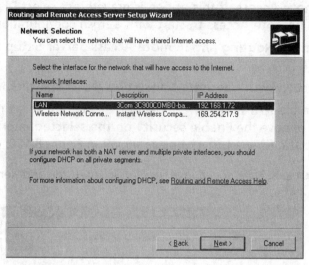

8. Click **NAT/Basic Firewall** in the left pane of the management console and right-click the **WAN** interface in the right pane of the management console. Select **Properties**.

9. From the **WAN Properties** dialog box, select the **Service and Ports** tab as shown in Figure 8.102.

Figure 8.102 Specifying Services Available through NAT

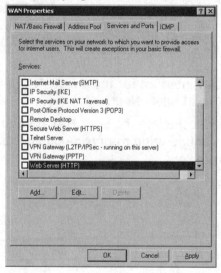

10. Select the **Web Server (HTTP)** check box. In the **Private address** box, enter **192.168.1.100** as shown in Figure 8.103 to direct inbound Web traffic to the Web server located at 192.168.1.100.

Figure 8.103 Specifying the Private Network Web Server Address

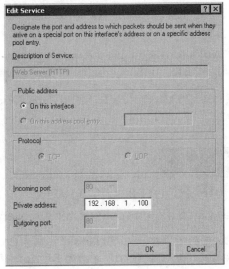

11. Click **OK**. Click **OK** again to complete the configuration.

NAT-Traversal

Using NAT with IPSec was not possible with previous implementations of Windows. Windows XP and Windows Server 2003 introduced a feature called NAT-Traversal, or NAT-T for short. NAT-T gets around the limitation imposed by the very nature of NAT. NAT looks at the IP header for address and port information for IP traffic streams. IPSec hides this information in the body of the packet and consequently did not work with previous versions of NAT. NAT-T is a new feature that allows Windows Server 2003 and Windows XP systems to overcome this previous limitation. NAT Traversal is not a proprietary Microsoft technology; the implementation used in Windows Server 2003 and Windows XP was developed by the UPnP Internet Gateway Device (IGD) Working Committee, made up of many member organizations, as a solution to the problems previously inherent in NAT.

New & Noteworthy...

ICMP Router Discovery

RFC 1256 describes a method for IP hosts to detect a router's availability by using Internet Control Message Protocol (ICMP). ICMP Router Discovery, the name for this process, works in two ways:

- Hosts send router solicitations using ICMP to discover available routers on the network.

- Routers send ICMP advertisements in response to the IP host solicitations as well as periodic ICMP updates to notify the hosts that the router is still available.

Although Windows Server 2003 supports ICMP Router Discovery, it is disabled by default.

EXERCISE 8.12

CONFIGURING ICMP ROUTER DISCOVERY

In this exercise, we will configure ICMP router discovery.

1. Open **Routing and Remote Access. Start | Programs | Administrative Tools | Routing and Remote Access**.

2. In the left pane of the RRAS console, click **General**.

3. In the right pane, right-click the interface on which you want to enable router discovery, and then click **Properties**.

4. On the **General** tab, select the **Enable router discovery advertisements** check box.

5. In **Advertisement lifetime (minutes)**, type or select the time after which a router is considered down after hearing its last router advertisement.

6. In **Minimum time (minutes)**, type or select the minimum rate at which the router periodically sends ICMP router advertisements.

7. **In Maximum time (minutes)**, type or select the maximum rate at which the router periodically sends ICMP router advertisements.

8. In **Level of preference**, type or select the level of preference for this router to be a default gateway for hosts.

TEST DAY TIP

It is important to know the limitations of RRAS, but it is also important to understand the features. Make sure you remember what multilink, BAP, NAT, ICS, and similar services do. Make sure you understand the basic differences between the routing protocols and how they are best applied. Microsoft has packed RRAS with lots of wonderful features. Exam 70-291 is sure to cover many of these.

EXAM
70-291
OBJECTIVE
4.2.5
4.5
4.5.2
4.5.3

Troubleshooting Remote Access Client Connections

Remote access client connections are often the most difficult connection problems to troubleshoot. In many cases, the system you are troubleshooting is not physically in front of you or even remotely accessible via remote control software, which makes it an added challenge. The best practice to follow when troubleshooting any type of connectivity problem is to start with the simpler areas and work your way up. The Open Systems Interconnect (OSI) reference model proves to be a handy guide for troubleshooting. Troubleshoot by starting at the lowest layers first, as seen in Table 8.1.

Table 8.1 The OSI Reference Model

Layer Number	Layer	Description
1	Physical Layer	Cabling, connectors
2	Data Link Layer	Network card, Hardware address (ARP, MAC, LLC)
3	Network Layer	Logical Addressing (IP address, IPX address)
4	Transport Layer	Segment and assemble upper layer information (TCP ports, UDP ports)
5	Session Layer	Connection control (RPC, SQL, NFS)
6	Presentation Layer	Data formatting (ASCII, MPEG, JPEG)
7	Application Layer	Applications (e-mail client, Web browser, word processor)

Most, if not all, networking problems will be solved within the first three or four layers. Begin the troubleshooting process with cabling. Work your way up the OSI reference model to test hardware settings and drivers next. At layer 3, the network layer, verify connectivity based on logical addressing like phone numbers or IP addresses. At the transport layer, verify available port numbers for your applications. Usually, transport layer problems will occur at a firewall or NAT system. This should be one of the first things to check if you have made it to layer 4 in the troubleshooting process. Session layer troubleshooting would entail verifying that services are started and running properly on your systems.

Presentation and application layer problems do not generally affect network and/or remote access connectivity. Let's take a closer look at the different types of remote access to see how our methodology applies.

If the client is connecting through a modem, check the phone cable connectors to make sure they are securely connected to the wall and the modem. Ensure the modem is getting power and displays proper diagnostic indicators if you are working with an external modem. You might try shutting off and restarting an external modem. Check the Windows Device Manager to verify operation and driver information. If necessary, update the drivers. Working our way toward the network layer, test full operation of the modem by dialing a phone number with the phone dialer. Test the modem itself to ensure it is dialing a different number using phone dialer. If possible, ensure that the routing and remote access service is operational on the remote access server. Make sure you are using the correct authentication algorithm.

If you are connecting through VPN using an Internet connection, first verify Internet connectivity. If you are using a dial-up Internet connection to provide a transport for the VPN, follow the steps in the previous paragraph to ensure dial-up connectivity to your ISP and the Internet. If you are able to reach Internet servers, verify connectivity to the VPN server by issuing a ping command to the VPN server's FQDN or IP address. Make sure that there are a sufficient number of L2TP or PPTP ports available on the VPN server. Make sure you are using the proper authentication algorithms and the proper encryption strength. Finally, verify remote access policy settings will allow connectivity. If any one of the remote access policy rules matches your client computer or your user account, rule processing ends at that step and the requested action is processed.

If you are able to connect to the remote access server but you are unable to connect to resources within the remote LAN, you have already ruled out the first two layers of the OSI reference model. Typical problems in this scenario include IP connectivity problems, name resolutions problems, and incorrect upper layer protocol selection. An approach here would be to check the IP address assigned to the PPP adaptor. Verify IP connectivity to the inside interface of the remote access server. This is the LAN interface on the RRAS server. Next, in a Windows 2000 or Windows Server 2003 Active Directory environment, issue an nslookup command to test DNS resolution for the client. If IP connectivity fails, name resolution will fail. When testing IP connectivity, verify that the address assigned to the PPP adaptor is a valid address for one of your LANs. If the address is in the range of 169.254.0.1 and 169.254.255.254, this is an Automatic Private IP Address assignment (APIPA). This signifies a problem in the address request process with the DHCP server. This problem could be between the client and the RRAS server or between the RRAS server and the DHCP server.

Some utilities for troubleshooting Windows Server 2003 connectivity include:

- Ipconfig

- Netsh

- Nslookup

- Ping

The **ipconfig** command, when used with the **all** switch (**ipconfig /all**), provides information about existing network interfaces, both real and virtual. Figure 8.104 shows the output from the **ipconfig** command when used with the **all** switch.

Figure 8.104 Ipconfig Command Display

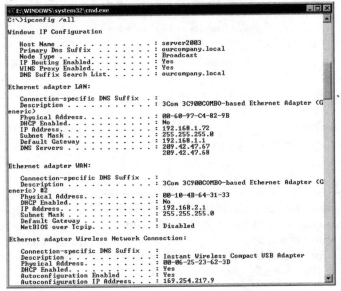

The **netsh** command utility was introduced with Windows 2000. It provides scripting, display, and modification capabilities for virtually every aspect of Windows Server 2003 networking. Figure 8.105 displays a list of available options from the **netsh** command line interface. The **netsh** command has been expanded with additional helper files and so has more functionality in its Windows Server 2003 version (for example, the IPSec context).

Figure 8.105 Netsh Command Line Options

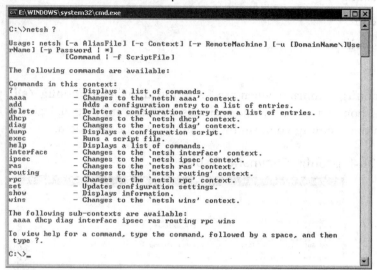

```
E:\WINDOWS\system32\cmd.exe

C:\>netsh ?

Usage: netsh [-a AliasFile] [-c Context] [-r RemoteMachine] [-u [DomainName\]Use
rName] [-p Password | *]
               [Command | -f ScriptFile]

The following commands are available:

Commands in this context:
?              - Displays a list of commands.
aaaa           - Changes to the 'netsh aaaa' context.
add            - Adds a configuration entry to a list of entries.
delete         - Deletes a configuration entry from a list of entries.
dhcp           - Changes to the 'netsh dhcp' context.
diag           - Changes to the 'netsh diag' context.
dump           - Displays a configuration script.
exec           - Runs a script file.
help           - Displays a list of commands.
interface      - Changes to the 'netsh interface' context.
ipsec          - Changes to the 'netsh ipsec' context.
ras            - Changes to the 'netsh ras' context.
routing        - Changes to the 'netsh routing' context.
rpc            - Changes to the 'netsh rpc' context.
set            - Updates configuration settings.
show           - Displays information.
wins           - Changes to the 'netsh wins' context.

The following sub-contexts are available:
 aaaa dhcp diag interface ipsec ras routing rpc wins

To view help for a command, type the command, followed by a space, and then
 type ?.

C:\>_
```

Several of the **netsh** commands typically are used more from the server but **netsh** provides functions for client side interaction as well.

TEST DAY TIP

Two very powerful commands in Windows Server 2003 are **pingpath** and **netsh**. Review this chapter and the Windows Help files to make sure you understand the power of these commands. Also, there is no substitute for basic experience. The more time you spend using the tools available to you, the better your understanding of their benefits and limitations.

The **nslookup** command is used to troubleshoot and test DNS information for client systems. When used with a computer name or FQDN within an Active Directory environment, **nslookup** can illustrate DNS name resolution mappings, as well as general DNS information. Figure 8.106 illustrates the output from a typical **nslookup** command.

Figure 8.106 Using the Nslookup Command

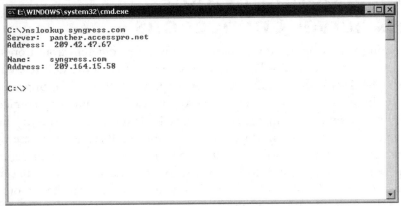

The **ping** command is used to test general network layer connectivity between hosts. Several switches are available for use with the **ping** command. **Ping** sends an ICMP echo request to the host that the **ping** command was issued to. The host, if available, will reply with an ICMP reply to the **ping** issued to the initiating system. From the initiating system, a successful **ping** will list the responses with TTL times displayed next to each request. Figure 8.107 displays one successful **ping** command and one failed **ping** command.

Figure 8.107 Using the Ping Command

```
E:\WINDOWS\system32\cmd.exe

C:\>ping 192.168.1.1

Pinging 192.168.1.1 with 32 bytes of data:

Reply from 192.168.1.1: bytes=32 time<1ms TTL=150
Reply from 192.168.1.1: bytes=32 time<1ms TTL=150
Reply from 192.168.1.1: bytes=32 time<1ms TTL=150
Reply from 192.168.1.1: bytes=32 time<1ms TTL=150

Ping statistics for 192.168.1.1:
    Packets: Sent = 4, Received = 4, Lost = 0 (0% loss),
Approximate round trip times in milli-seconds:
    Minimum = 0ms, Maximum = 0ms, Average = 0ms

C:\>ping 192.168.1.37

Pinging 192.168.1.37 with 32 bytes of data:

Request timed out.
Request timed out.
Request timed out.
Request timed out.

Ping statistics for 192.168.1.37:
    Packets: Sent = 4, Received = 0, Lost = 4 (100% loss),

C:\>
```

Troubleshooting Remote Access Server Connections

Troubleshooting remote access server connections is not so different from troubleshooting remote access client connections. The best approach is to follow the OSI reference model from the simple lower layers, working your way up through the various upper layers. Again, begin by checking physical layer attributes. Make sure cables are properly connected and secured. Ensure hardware is configured with the right drivers and, if necessary, hardware configurations. Verify the problem is truly a server problem. If some clients are able to connect and others are not, it is possible that the problem is with the client configurations.

It is quite common for clients to have access to a remote access server, but not to systems beyond the server. This could be a problem with IP routing on the remote access server. Verify IP connectivity beyond the remote access server by pinging either the inside network interface on the remote access server or ping another internal address on the remote LAN. If you are unable to reach internal addresses on the remote LAN, verify that IP Routing is enabled on the remote access server. For AppleTalk clients, verify that network access is allowed for AppleTalk clients on the **AppleTalk** tab on the server properties sheet. If the **AppleTalk** tab does not exist on the server, AppleTalk needs to be installed on the server. Another possible network layer problem involves static routing. If the remote LAN does not have a static route entry back to the client system, client traffic will enter the remote LAN only to die within the confines of the remote LAN.

Other network layer problems can occur with dynamic routing enabled (RIP or OSPF). One possible compatibility problem to consider: Windows XP 64-bit and Windows Server 2003 64-bit do not support OSPF routing. Also, as mentioned earlier in this chapter, RIP v1 is a classful routing protocol. This means that RIP v1 networks must be divided at standard default subnet mask boundaries. If two networks exist within your IP network that do not use standard network masks, this can present routing problems. RIP v1 cannot properly advertise a network that does not use default subnet masks. Also, when using DHCP to allocate addresses, it is possible to run out of addresses or to lose proper connectivity with the DHCP server. As mentioned in the previous section, this will result in APIPA assignment (unless APIPA has been disabled or there is an alternate configuration set). APIPA addresses fall within the range of 169.254.0.1 and 169.254.255.254, and having an APIPA assigned address could be the result of connectivity problems between the RRAS client and server or between the RRAS server and DHCP server. Check the RRAS server to ensure the server is using the proper network interface to communicate with the DHCP server. Look for an APIPA assigned address at the RRAS server. Also, try ping connectivity testing between the RRAS server and the DHCP server. Part of the address distribution troubleshooting process involves understanding where the addresses are coming from. If a DHCP server is supposed to provide clients with addresses, this server should be the next stop for troubleshooting address problems. Likewise, if the RRAS server is distributing addresses from a static address pool, this server will be the next stop for address troubleshooting.

In order to properly troubleshoot routing problems in a Windows Server 2003 environment, you have a few commands at your disposal. Along with the commands listed in the previous section, the following commands will be useful for troubleshooting network layer connectivity and routing problems:

- Pathping
- Tracert
- Route

The **pathping** command was introduced with Windows 2000. This command combines characteristics of the **ping** command, discussed in the previous section, with the **tracert** command. This command enumerates the routing path that IP traffic will take to a given destination, as well as listing statistical information about the path to each router along the route to the destination. This command is useful for testing packet loss along a path. If you suspect a router along the path is dropping packets, this is the command to use. From a command prompt, type **pathping w.x.y.z**, where **w.x.y.z** is the remote system address whose path you are testing. The results from a **pathping** are displayed in Figure 8.108.

Figure 8.108 Pathping Test Results

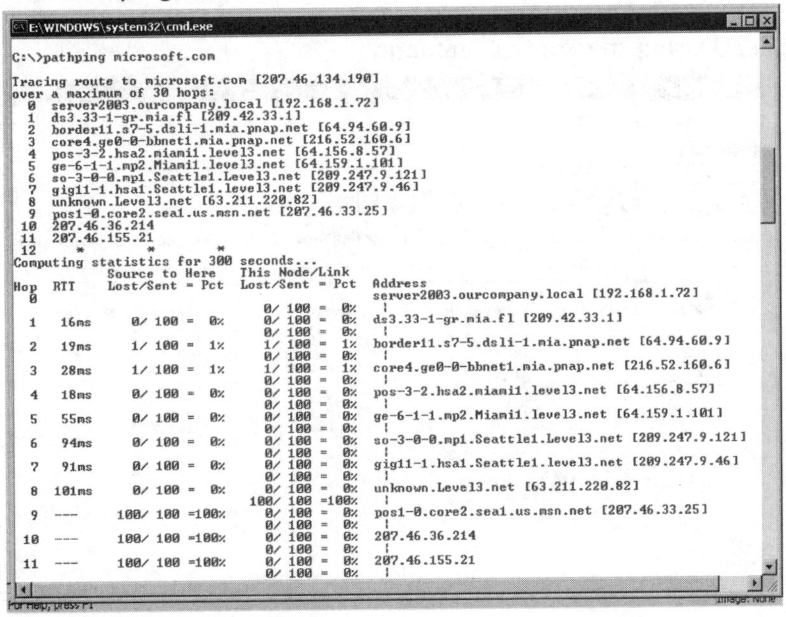

The **tracert** command enumerates the routing path that IP traffic will take to a given destination. Again, some basic statistical information is also listed with the trace. This command is a little less detailed than the **pathping** command. . From a command prompt, type **tracert w.x.y.z**, where **w.x.y.z** is the remote system address whose path you are testing. The results from a **tracert** are displayed in Figure 8.109.

Figure 8.109 Tracert Results

```
E:\WINDOWS\system32\cmd.exe                                          _ □ X

C:\>tracert microsoft.com

Tracing route to microsoft.com [207.46.134.222]
over a maximum of 30 hops:

  1    16 ms    17 ms    18 ms  ds3.33-1-gr.mia.fl [209.42.33.1]
  2    18 ms    19 ms    23 ms  border11.s7-5.dsli-1.mia.pnap.net [64.94.60.9]
  3    18 ms    19 ms    19 ms  core4.ge0-0-bbnet1.mia.pnap.net [216.52.160.6]
  4    21 ms    20 ms    24 ms  pos-3-2.hsa2.miami1.level3.net [64.156.8.57]
  5    20 ms    27 ms    20 ms  ge-6-2-1.mp2.Miami1.level3.net [64.159.1.177]
  6    91 ms    92 ms    91 ms  so-1-0-0.mp2.Seattle1.Level3.net [209.247.10.133
]
  7    91 ms    91 ms    92 ms  gig10-1.hsa1.Seattle1.level3.net [209.247.9.70]

  8    97 ms    97 ms    96 ms  unknown.Level3.net [63.211.220.82]
  9    96 ms    96 ms    97 ms  207.46.33.229
 10    95 ms    98 ms    97 ms  207.46.36.78
 11    98 ms    98 ms    98 ms  207.46.155.21
 12     *         *         *    Request timed out.
 13     *         *         *    Request timed out.
 14     *         *         *    Request timed out.
 15    ^C
C:\>_
```

The **route** command is used to add, modify, delete, and display routing information for a Windows Server 2003 router. This command is useful in determining existing routes available for IP traffic passing through the server. Figure 8.110 illustrates the **route** command with the **print** switch.

Figure 8.110 Using the Route Command

```
E:\WINDOWS\system32\cmd.exe                                          _ □ X

C:\>route print

IPv4 Route Table
===========================================================================
Interface List
0x1 ............................. MS TCP Loopback interface
0x2 ...00 60 97 c4 82 9b ...... 3Com 3C900COMBO-based Ethernet Adapter (Generic)

0x3 ...00 10 4b 64 31 33 ...... 3Com 3C900COMBO-based Ethernet Adapter (Generic)
#2
===========================================================================
===========================================================================
Active Routes:
Network Destination        Netmask          Gateway       Interface  Metric
        0.0.0.0          0.0.0.0      192.168.1.1    192.168.1.72     30
      127.0.0.0        255.0.0.0        127.0.0.1      127.0.0.1      1
    192.168.1.0    255.255.255.0    192.168.1.72    192.168.1.72     30
   192.168.1.72  255.255.255.255      127.0.0.1      127.0.0.1      30
  192.168.1.255  255.255.255.255    192.168.1.72    192.168.1.72     30
    192.168.2.0    255.255.255.0    192.168.2.1     192.168.2.1      30
    192.168.2.1  255.255.255.255      127.0.0.1      127.0.0.1      30
  192.168.2.255  255.255.255.255    192.168.2.1     192.168.2.1      30
      224.0.0.0        240.0.0.0    192.168.1.72    192.168.1.72     30
      224.0.0.0        240.0.0.0    192.168.2.1     192.168.2.1      30
255.255.255.255  255.255.255.255    192.168.1.72    192.168.1.72      1
255.255.255.255  255.255.255.255    192.168.2.1     192.168.2.1       1
Default Gateway:       192.168.1.1
===========================================================================
Persistent Routes:
  None

C:\>_
```

Finally, completing our network layer troubleshooting and working up to the transport layer, make sure the client traffic passes through any packet filters that might be in place. If the client's network settings match any single rule in the packet filter criteria for denied access, the client will be denied access. If this is the case, determine how the rule might be rewritten to allow client access. Another option would be to determine a way to modify the client configuration so the packet filter rule does not prevent client access to the network.

Exam Warning

Network troubleshooting involves a systematic approach. The OSI reference model provides an excellent framework to use when deciphering network connection problems. Understand where each of the tools available to you would be used. For example, if systems can connect based on address, you need to look at name resolution problems with a tool like NSLOOKUP. If connectivity is sporadic, you should check the routers between the endpoints with PINGPATH. Know which tool to use in a given scenario.

Configuring Internet Authentication Services

The Windows Server 2003 Internet Authentication Services (IAS) provide open standard centralized connection authentication, authorization, and accounting for several types of network access. This open standard is more commonly known as Remote Authentication Dial-In User Service (RADIUS). This Microsoft implementation of RADIUS provides authentication for the following network connection types:

- Authenticating switch
- Dial-up
- Router-to-router connections
- Virtual private network (VPN) remote access
- Wireless

The major advantage of IAS/RADIUS is that it provides an open standard solution. This means that equipment and software from various vendors can be tied together through the RADIUS authentication service, thereby simplifying account administration for remote access users and systems. Windows Server 2003 IAS supports the IETF RADIUS standards specified in RFC 2865 and 2866. One advantage to using the Microsoft implementation of RADIUS in conjunction with Active Directory is the capability for a single sign-on. The centralized authentication capabilities for IAS provide for authentication forwarding to Active Directory for authentication. In this fashion, all users are authenticated from the same source. If a user logs in to the local LAN, his or her username and password will be the same as the one used for remote access through VPN, wireless networking, or any other network connection whose authentication is provided by Microsoft IAS.

NOTE

RADIUS has developed as an open protocol since it was first proposed in the mid 1990s. RADIUS is not the only protocol providing centralized account management, authentication, and access control (AAA). Cisco's implementation of Terminal Access Controller Access Control System Plus (TACACS+) for example is a proprietary protocol providing AAA. Although the Cisco TACACS+ protocol offers certain advantages to RADIUS, the fact that it is a proprietary protocol provides a significant disadvantage to TACACS+ in a large enterprise environment where equipment is not all from the same vendor.

IAS must be installed as a separate Windows component. The first step in IAS configuration is installing the IAS component. Next, we must configure the properties for one of the IAS servers. After that, the remote access servers that will act as clients to this IAS server must be added. When IAS is implemented the IAS servers will carry out remote access policies. Remote access policies should be configured at this time on the IAS server. Logging methods must be configured for authentication and accounting. As the configuration of the first server is nearly complete, we can now copy the configuration from this IAS server to additional IAS servers on our network. The IAS servers must be registered in the correct Active Directory domains as a final configuration step. After completing the actual configuration, it is considered best practice to verify all configurations and operational settings. There are three ways to register the IAS servers in the appropriate Active Directory domains. You can use any one of these methods:

- Register the IAS server in the default domain using Active Directory Users and Computers.

- Register the IAS server in the default domain using Internet Authentication Service.

- Register the IAS server in the default domain using the **netsh** command.

EXAM WARNING

IAS is the Microsoft implementation of RADIUS. Generally, anything that simplifies network administration for larger networks, the way IAS does, is a target for the exam. IAS is no exception. You will probably see significant coverage of this topic on the exam. Read through this section and the exercises and make sure you understand the benefits of IAS and the tools and techniques used to implement and administer it.

We have completed the installation and configuration for the IAS server. Before placing the server into production, we should verify the configuration of RADIUS accounting and authentication on the access servers. Also, depending on the role of the server, we should verify that the access servers are properly configured for operation. For example, for dial-up and VPN connections we should establish a connection through standard dial-up as well as a VPN connection.

Configuring & Implementing…

IAS and Wireless

IAS provides centralized administration and support for your network. Accounts are administered using your familiar Active Directory Users and Computers management console. You might have users connecting through a Nortel VPN router, or a Cisco wireless access point, or any number of pieces of equipment. The beauty of IAS is that it provides a standard, simplified interface to administer the users when the equipment and software are in place.

As wireless technology continues to carve out its place in the networking landscape, you will learn to really appreciate IAS/RADIUS. Plugging in and setting up equipment from numerous vendors will not be the headache that it once was. Whether users are remote access clients or corporate LAN users, whether they log in from a laptop, workstation, or PDA, all administration will be handled with the same interface—Active Directory Users and Computers. This greatly simplifies our increasingly complex networks.

EXERCISE 8.13

CONFIGURING IAS

In this exercise, we will look at a basic IAS configuration.

1. Click **Start | Control Panel | Add Remove Programs**.

2. Click **Add/Remove Windows Components**.

3. From the dialog box in the Windows Components Wizard, select **Networking Services | Details**.

4. Select **Internet Authentication Service** followed by **OK | Next**.

Now that IAS is installed, it is time to configure the properties for the IAS server as follows:

1. Click **Start | Programs | Administrative Tools | Internet Authentication Service**.

2. Right-click **Internet Authentication Service** and select **Properties**.

3. Select the **Ports** tab, and configure the RADIUS authentication and accounting UDP ports if they differ from the defaults of 1812 and 1645 for authentication, and 1813 and 1646 for accounting, as shown in Figure 8.111.

Figure 8.111 Verifying the RADIUS UDP Port Numbers

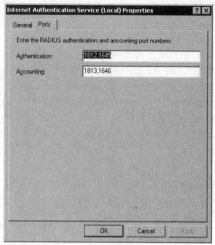

4. Continuing from Properties, on the **General** tab, select each required option for IAS event logging as shown in Figure 8.112, and then click **OK**.

Figure 8.112 Configuring IAS Event Logging

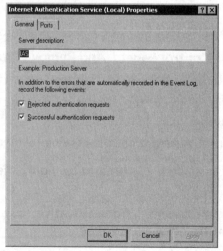

5. Right-click **RADIUS Clients** and select **New RADIUS Client**.

6. From the **New RADIUS Client Wizard** add basic client information as shown in Figure 8.113. Click **Next**.

Figure 8.113 Configuring the IAS Client

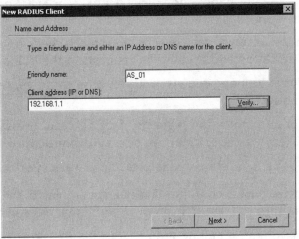

7. Select **RADIUS Standard** from the **Client-Vendor** drop-down list on the **New RADIUS Client** screen and enter the shared secret password as shown in Figure 8.114; then select **Finish**.

Figure 8.114 New RADIUS Client Configuration

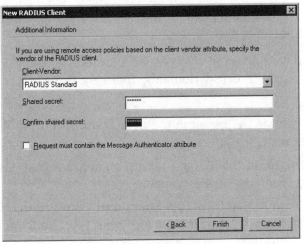

8. Configure the remote access policies as discussed earlier in this chapter. In our example, we will grant access to a Windows Global Group called

Radius-Clients. Configure the remote access policy to grant access to members of the Radius-Clients group as described in Exercise 8.07.

9. From the left pane of the Microsoft management console, select **Remote access logging**.

10. From the right pane, right-click **Local File** or **SQL Server**, and then select **Properties**.

11. From the **Settings** tab, select one or more check boxes for recording authentication and accounting requests in the IAS log files:

   ■ For accounting request and response captures, select **Accounting requests**.

   ■ For authentication requests, Access-Accept messages, and Access-Reject messages captures, select **Authentication requests**.

   ■ For periodic status update captures, select **Periodic status**.

Now that we have a configuration nearly completed, we can copy the IAS configuration from the first IAS server to additional IAS servers.

1. Begin from a Command Prompt. Click **Start | Run** and type **cmd**, then click **OK**.

2. From the command prompt, type **netsh aaaa show config > path\file.txt**. This stores all configuration settings in a text file. You can use a relative or absolute path, or a UNC path.

3. Copy this file to the destination computer or computers.

4. From a command prompt on the destination computer, type **netsh exec path\file.txt**.

As a final configuration step, we have to register the IAS servers in the appropriate Active Directory domains. There are three ways to accomplish this task:

■ Register the IAS server in the default domain using Active Directory Users and Computers:

   1. Log on to the IAS server with an account that has administrative credentials for the domain.

   2. Open **Active Directory Users and Computers**. Click **Start | Programs | Administrative Tools | Active Directory Users and Computers**.

   3. In the left pane of the ADUC console, click the **Users** folder for your domain.

4. In the right pane, right-click **RAS and IAS Servers**, and then click **Properties**.

5. In the **RAS and IAS Servers Properties** dialog box, on the **Members** tab, add each of the IAS servers.

■ To register the IAS server in the default domain using Internet Authentication Service:

1. Log on to the IAS server with an account that has administrative credentials for the domain.

2. Open **Internet Authentication Service**. Click **Start | Programs | Administrative Tools | Internet Authentication Service**.

3. Right-click **Internet Authentication Service**, and select **Register Server in Active Directory**.

4. Select **OK** when the **Register Internet Authentication Service in Active Directory** dialog box appears.

■ To register the IAS server in the default domain using the **netsh** command:

1. Log on to the IAS server with an account that has administrative credentials for the domain.

2. Open **Command Prompt**. Click **Start | Run** and type **cmd**, then click **OK**.

3. Type **netsh ras add registeredserver** at the command prompt.

Summary of Exam Objectives

This chapter detailed various options for Routing and Remote Access configuration in a corporate network. Windows Server 2003 supports static routing and two dynamic routing protocols for unicast IP routing. RIP is the dynamic routing protocol of choice for smaller to mid-sized networks. It is an easily configured open standard routing protocol available on most systems that support dynamic routing. RIP version 2 supports carrying subnet mask information in the routing updates. This means RIP version 2 supports Classless InterDomain Routing (CIDR). RIP version 2 is not limited to classful network boundaries. Windows Server 2003 supports RIP versions 1 and 2. RIP version 1 is available for backward compatibility to older systems. RIP does not scale well because it uses hop count as its routing metric (with a limit of 15 hops) and because of the general process used by RIP to determine routes. Larger RIP networks tend to exhibit stability problems because routing updates experience a noticeable delay due to the nature of RIP's routing algorithm.

OSPF is the dynamic routing protocol of choice in large to very large IP networks. It is more difficult to configure than RIP but it provides for many features to aid in its scalability. OSPF uses a link-state database and link-state advertisements to map the network topology. This topological map is used with the link-state algorithm to determine the best route available. OSPF does not burden a network with excess traffic when the link-state database has converged. This is an advantage to using OSPF in a larger network. Also, because the algorithm used by OSPF to determine best routes relies on the link-state database, OSPF tends to update its routes faster than RIP when a network change is encountered. OSPF uses areas to segment the network. This segmentation helps to decrease the general size of the link-state database and consequently speeds up network convergence when changes in the network are experienced.

Packet filters are configured through Routing and Remote Access on Windows Server 2003. Packet filters allow or prevent traffic that matches specific criteria or rules. Windows Server 2003 supports inbound and outbound packet filters with rules provided on an exception basis. This means that either all traffic will be allowed or all traffic will be denied *except* for those packets meeting the criteria listed.

Windows Server 2003 supports remote access services in various configurations and capacities. A typical RRAS dial-up server provides dial-in access to remote corporate LAN resources for remote users. Remote users dial in to the RRAS server through a standard analog modem. The RRAS server has a pool of modems (or a modem bank) and several physical phone lines. The remote user authenticates through the RRAS server and the RRAS server provides basic address, IP routing, and name resolution functions for the remote users.

Another typical scenario for a dial-up RRAS server is the RAS gateway. A RAS gateway provides Internet or remote network connectivity for local users. In this fashion, a RAS gateway is configured to share a particular network connection for LAN users. LAN users can connect through the RRAS gateway to access a shared dial-up Internet connection, or bonded dial-up Internet connections. This bonded connection is provided through a PPP extension known as PPP Multilink. PPP Multilink provides a virtual interface made up of a bundle of multiple real or physical interfaces. This allocation of multiple interfaces is controlled through the Bandwidth Allocation Protocol (BAP). BAP provides trigger points for adding or releasing extra lines to the Multilink connection.

Windows Server 2003 supports radio frequency wireless connectivity as well as infrared wireless connectivity. Wireless networking in Windows Server 2003 typically is provided through the IEEE 802.11 networking standards. Because wireless networks do not have the typical physical constraints that wired networks have, it is necessary to provide added security for wireless networks. Wireless security is provided through encryption and strong authentication. Strong authentication can be accomplished via a new extension of the Extensible Authentication Protocol (EAP) known as Protected EAP (PEAP). Also, a new IEEE standard for network authentication known as the IEEE 802.1x standard provides added security for wireless networking. Wireless network authentication typically is mainly provided through Microsoft's implementation of the Remote Authentication Dial-In Users Service (RADIUS) known as Internet Authentication Service (IAS).

Remote access policies are used to control remote user access to the network. Remote access policies are built around two distinct components. The first component is the condition. Incoming connections are compared to the conditions specified in the policy. If the incoming connection criteria match the condition statement, the rule for that policy will be applied. The second component of the policy is the policy profile. The policy profile is the actual rule that will be applied. For example, remote users dialing in to the network might be placed in a particular Global Group. The Global Group will be used for the condition statement. The condition statement will be set up to grant access to the Global Group. After access is granted, the policy profile will determine further details about the connection. If users will need multilink support available to them, for example, the policy profile can provide that. In short: The condition determines whether access will be granted at all, whereas the policy places restrictions and limitations on the extent of access that is granted.

Firewall support is provided through the routing and remote access service in Windows Server 2003. The basic firewall provides connection restrictions that are applied in a way similar to the remote access policies. Certain conditions are compared with incoming or outgoing traffic on an interface. When the traffic matches one of the conditions, the traffic is either allowed or denied based on the settings on the firewall.

Network Address Translation (NAT) provides port and address mappings typically used to extend a privately addressed LAN to the Internet. Users on the private LAN that try to connect to the Internet send their requests to the NAT server. The NAT server maps the internal IP address and port information to the public address or addresses available on the NAT server. The connection TCP or UDP connection is established between the NAT server and the public address. The public addressed connection is then remapped to the internal client, based on the existing requests from that client.

ICMP Router Discovery provides messaging capabilities to advertise the availability or lack of availability of particular routers to the network. Using ICMP Router Discovery, clients discover routers through ICMP requests and routers advertise their existence and continue to advertise their availability through ICMP messages.

As networks become more complicated, a systematic approach to troubleshooting is necessary to ensure fast resolution of network problems. The Open Systems Interconnection or OSI reference model provides a systematic approach to network troubleshooting. Begin with the simple, lower layers of the OSI reference model and work upwards to the more complex layers, after it has been determined that each lower layer is functioning properly. You have several troubleshooting tools available to troubleshoot remote access clients. Some common tools for remote access client troubleshooting include:

- Ipconfig
- Netsh
- Nslookup
- Ping

Troubleshooting remote access server connections typically is approached in the same fashion as client connections. The main difference with troubleshooting server connectivity is that the server usually has special services, logging capabilities, and extra commands available for troubleshooting. Some common commands used for troubleshooting remote access server problems include:

- Pathping
- Tracert
- Route

RADIUS/IAS is the centralized, open-standard authentication component of Windows Server 2003. IAS provides centralized, single sign-on authentication for remote access users. This single sign-on approach allows users to connect to the network through several different types of networking equipment supplied by many different vendors. As long as the equipment supports the RADIUS open-standard authentication system, the Windows Server 2003 Active Directory can provide authentication and account management.

Exam Objectives Fast Track

Configuring LAN Routing

☑ The first step in configuring LAN routing is to choose a remote site connection type. The connection type can be a private line connection, dial-up (analog or ISDN) or Internet-based private network (VPN).

☑ Choose the security features:

- Authentication provider
- Authentication method
- Encryption to be used
- Choose router users and groups
- Choose remote access policy settings

☑ Integrate the remote sites with the existing network or sites.

☑ Prepare the servers for configuration.

☑ Deploy a test deployment.

☑ Deploy the final deployment.

Configuring RRAS Packet Filters

☑ Packet filters regulate access for inbound and outbound connections.

☑ Packet filters work on an exception basis—all packets allowed except or all packets denied except.

☑ When a match is made to a packet filter rule, rule processing stops.

Configuring the Windows Server 2003 Dial-up RAS Server

☑ Windows Server 2003 provides LAN access for external users.

☑ Either PSTN, ISDN, or VPN supply the connection for Windows Server 2003 dial-up RAS connections.

☑ Windows Server 2003 provides client to server connections through dial-up RAS servers.

Configuring the Windows Server 2003 Dial-up RAS Gateway

☑ RRAS Gateway provides remote LAN access for local users.

☑ PSTN, ISDN, or VPN supply the connection for Windows Server 2003 RRAS Gateways.

☑ A server to server connection provides the transport between locations.

PPP Multilink and Bandwidth Allocation Protocol (BAP)

☑ Multiple connections are utilized as one virtual connection.

☑ Dynamic BAP consists of multiple protocols:

- **BAP** Control mechanism for dynamic BAP

- **BACP** Provides a negotiated, favored peer for link selection

☑ Multilink with dynamic BAP is enabled by default on Windows Server 2003 RRAS servers.

Configuring Wireless Connections

☑ Infrared and radio frequency are supported for the following connection types:

- WPAN

- WLAN

- WMAN

- WWAN

☑ 802.1x and 802.11 are the standards for authentication and data transmission.

☑ The following protocols are used in wireless networking:

- EAP-TLS

- EAP-MS-CHAP v2

- PEAP

Configuring Remote Access Policies

☑ Remote access policies are built using a condition and a policy profile.

☑ Remote access connections are compared against the conditions. If a match is made, the policy profile and permission are applied.

☑ Policy profiles provide settings to apply when the conditions are matched.

Understanding Router Protocols

☑ RIP version 1 supports small to mid-sized networks using broadcast advertisements. No subnet information is advertised (this is a classful routing protocol).

☑ RIP version 2 supports small to mid-sized networks using broadcast advertisements. Subnet information is advertised (classless routing protocol following CIDR—Classless InterDomain Routing).

☑ OSPF supports large to very large networks.

☑ IGMP is not really a routing protocol but a method for advertising multicast group membership information to multicast routers.

Configuring Basic Firewall Support

☑ The firewall private traffic only configuration is used with VPN to shield the private network from the public network. Only private and VPN client systems may communicate on the network. Private computers cannot reach public computers.

☑ The firewall private traffic with NAT configuration is used to protect internal systems from unauthorized public access. Private systems can reach public computers as well as other private systems within the network.

☑ When implementing basic firewall support, it is applied only to public interfaces.

☑ Security may be increased through the use of packet filters in conjunction with basic firewall.

RRAS NAT Services

☑ NAT is sometimes called IP masquerading because the private, nonroutable LAN addresses are mapped to a single or group of public addresses.

☑ Traffic originating on the LAN appears to come from one or one group of public addresses.

☑ Static mappings are necessary to connect from the public Internet to a system behind the NAT system.

ICMP Router Discovery

☑ Hosts automatically determine router availability using ICMP.

☑ Routers respond to hosts and periodically advertise availability using ICMP.

☑ This is disabled by default on Windows Server 2003.

Troubleshooting Remote Access Client Connections

☑ Follow the OSI reference model as a troubleshooting guide.

☑ The following troubleshooting commands will aid in the troubleshooting process:

- **Ipconfig** Displays IP information about the host, allows clients to release addresses back to the DHCP server and renew addresses from the DHCP server, allows clients to clear the DNS cache

- **Netsh** Provides various remote access troubleshooting options and configuration verification

- **Nslookup** Used to test DNS resolution

- **Ping** Tests basic connectivity between hosts

☑ Protocols must match for authentication, encryption, networking, and so on, for remote access to function properly.

Troubleshooting Remote Access Server Connections

☑ Use the OSI reference model as a troubleshooting guide.

☑ Check routing protocols, routing table entries, and verify routing operation.

☑ Use same commands as those used for client troubleshooting as well as the following:

- **Pathping** Tests availability and basic packet delivery information for all routers along a given path

- **Tracert** Used to test basic path information for a packet, less detail than pathping

- **Route** Used to display and manipulate routing table entries on a Windows-based router

Configuring Internet Authentication Services

☑ IAS provides centralized authentication for most types of remote access equipment.

☑ IAS is Microsoft's implementation of the open–standard RADIUS.

☑ IAS uses Active Directory for centralized authentication of users.

Exam Objectives
Frequently Asked Questions

The following Frequently Asked Questions, answered by the authors of this book, are designed to both measure your understanding of the Exam Objectives presented in this chapter, and to assist you with real-life implementation of these concepts. You will also gain access to thousands of other FAQs at ITFAQnet.com.

Q: Can I use Windows NT 4.0 and Windows 2000 remote access servers in my Windows Server 2003 network design?

A: Yes, Windows NT 4.0 remote access will interoperate with Windows 2000 and Windows Server 2003. Although interoperability exists, Microsoft recommends upgrading all remote access servers to Windows Server 2003 to take advantage of the new features available in Windows Server 2003 such as L2TP.

Q: Does configuring a dial-up connection for Windows Server 2003 imply analog dial connectivity or are there other connections supported?

A: Dial-up connectivity in Windows Server 2003 can mean analog dial-up, ISDN digital dial-up, or nonpersistent VPN connectivity.

Q: Are there any limitations to demand-dial routing in Windows Server 2003?

A: If you are trying to connect more than 10 remote sites, and each site is required to have access to the others, you should use persistent one-way initiated connections instead of demand-dial connections because of performance considerations.

Q: Why is my filter doing the opposite of what I expect it to do?

A: Packet filters work on an exception basis (allow all packets except the following, or deny all packets except the following). Ensure the settings are for allowing except… or denying except…

Q: Why does FTP traffic to our server constantly fail?

A: FTP connectivity behind a NAT requires a NAT editor to handle some of the unusual formatting of FTP packets.

Q: Which is better, ICS or NAT?

A: Internet Connection Sharing (ICS) is a preconfigured implementation of NAT. ICS provides specialized DHCP addressing direct from the ICS server, and ICS can use only one public address for translation. NAT is better if you need to customize your configuration or provide multiple public addresses for translation. ICS also provides name resolution and address allocation. If you have a DNS and/or DHCP server on the network, you need to use NAT rather than ICS.

Q: When clients dial in to the RRAS server, they have access to the server itself but LAN resources are unreachable. What is causing this problem?

A: When you configure a static address pool for RRAS dial-in clients, if the client address range is different from the LAN address range, there must be a static route or a routing protocol configured to provide a path for client traffic. Make sure a route exists on the RRAS server to connect the client address range with the LAN.

Q: When clients dial in to the RRAS server, they have access to the server itself but LAN resources are unreachable by name. A **ping** command to a LAN address is successful, however. What is causing this problem?

A: Make sure the LAN adapter is selected for DHCP, DNS, and WINS services. Selecting the incorrect adapter can result in IP connectivity but failed name resolution.

Q: Several RRAS dial-in clients have been connecting properly but this morning, several help desk calls were received from dial-in clients that cannot connect. In the past, the clients established connections with the current configuration. Nothing seems to have changed on the server or the client configurations. What could be the problem?

A: Check the address pool. If a static address pool is in use, make sure there are a sufficient number of available addresses for dial-in clients. If dial-in clients are receiving their addresses from a DHCP server, make sure the DHCP server is functioning properly and check to see that there are a sufficient number of available addresses for dial-in clients.

Q: Analog dial-up connections are used less and less all the time. Is there any other use for a Dial-up RAS Gateway?

A: Dial-up RAS gateways are not limited to analog connections. Digital dial-up connections (ISDN) can be made through a dial-up RAS gateway as well as other nonpersistent connections.

Q: Is it possible to increase the amount of bandwidth available to a Dial-up RAS Gateway?

A: Dial-up RAS Gateways provide connectivity through the Point-to-Point Protocol (PPP). The PPP protocol provides a mechanism called multilink that creates a virtual connection of multiple physical connections. So, if you are limited to an analog dial-up connection between sites, it is possible to add another, or multiple analog lines to increase the bandwidth between sites.

Q: Can a Microsoft Dial-up RAS Gateway connect to another vendor's equipment?

A: Because a Microsoft Dial-up RAS Gateway relies on PPP to establish a connection, any vendor's equipment with the capability to support PPP should provide connectivity to the Dial-up RAS Gateway.

Q: Is multilink only for analog dial-up connection aggregation?

A: No. Multilink provides aggregation of multiple links of many types. This could be analog dial-up, ISDN, or any other demand-dial type connection.

Q: Can our Microsoft Windows Server 2003 multilink work with our ISP's Cisco Access Server?

A: Multilink is based on the open standard PPP protocol and therefore provides connectivity to any PPP multilink supported equipment.

Q: We are using the callback capabilities of PPP. For some reason, multilink is not working. What can we do to enable multilink?

A: Generally, multilink used with callback results in only one of your multilinked devices being called back (unless you have the phone company assign the same phone number to both lines). This is because you can store only one number in a user account, so only one device connects and all other devices fail to connect. For this reason, multilink and callback are generally not used with one another when the phone lines have different numbers, as is the norm.

Q: We are reluctant to deploy wireless in our network because of the lack of proper security for wireless connectivity. Is there any way to ensure reasonable security using wireless?

A: Properly implemented wireless networking can be configured to use authentication and encryption methods similar to the ones used for VPN connectivity or VLAN segregation. If your company is using VPNs to secure office-to-office or remote client-to-office connections or VLANs to separate different portions of your organization on the network, you are probably using similar technologies to the ones you would use to secure wireless clients. Be aware that WLANs relying on 802.1x are generally considered to be superior to WEP networks because 802.1x can use a certificate authority to distribute certificates to access points. In this way, 802.1x provides a method for automatic key updates whereas WEP requires manually changing keys at each access point. Also, a properly configured certificate-based WLAN will help to ensure reasonably secure connectivity.

Q: We are using a mix of wireless access points from different vendors. Is there any way to use our current network and accounts to provide authentication at the access point?

A: Nearly every wireless access point on the market today provides RADIUS authentication support. If you configure your wireless network to use IAS authentication through your Active Directory implementation, you can maintain and administer wireless accounts using the same tools you would use to maintain and administer any of your other user accounts on the network.

Q: I read an article claiming that the biggest problem with wireless is the large administrative burden associated with maintaining certificates for all of the users and computers that access the network through a wireless connection. Is there any way to lessen this burden?

A: Active Directory Group Policy has provisions for automatic certificate request and allocation. This system helps to automate the certificate implementation and maintenance tasks associated with certificate-based wireless networking. Implementing Group Policy for this task will greatly reduce the administrative overhead incurred by wireless networking.

Q: One of the junior administrators modified our remote access policy and now no one can connect. What could be the problem?

A: If a condition in the remote access policy is set to deny access, any traffic matching that condition will be denied. Likewise, if none of the traffic matches the conditions set up in the remote access policy, the traffic is implicitly denied.

Q: We are trying to limit dial-in permissions to a specific time period during the day. After this policy was implemented, no one could connect to the network. What might cause this problem?

A: It is not uncommon to find the dial-in hours configured incorrectly. If a functioning policy has been modified to reflect different dial-in hours, or any other modification, it is likely a configuration problem. Check the times to make sure it is the time intended. For example, you might want to grant access between 1 P.M. and 4 P.M. Make sure it is not set to 1 A.M. and 4 A.M.

Q: Is it possible to limit connectivity or modify connection properties for a group of users through the use of remote access policies?

A: Yes, the Windows-Group can be configured as a condition. When a condition is set, it is a matter of setting the profile policy and determining whether to grant or deny access based on the condition.

Q: Can Windows Server 2003 routers running RIP or OSPF share route information with Cisco routers running RIP or OSPF?

A: RIP and OSPF are open-standard protocols, just like TCP/IP. Although not all features of RIP and OSPF completely interoperate, it is possible to integrate RIP advertising or OSPF advertising systems from different vendors.

Q: Documentation for RIP says that it works in networks up to approximately 40 routers but the maximum hop count is only 15 hops. How is this possible?

A: A RIP network configured in a hub and spoke configuration can have 40 routers while maintaining a diameter less than 15 hops. This means that the maximum distance an advertised route will travel in this type of network is still less than 15, even though there are more than 15 routers on the network.

Q: Does OSPF have to use multiple areas?

A: OSPF uses multiple areas to provide hierarchical network design and reduce resource requirements for routers by reducing link state advertisements and breaking down the network topology into smaller sections. All router areas must connect to the backbone if multiple areas are used but it is not a requirement to use multiple areas.

Q: I enabled basic firewall support on the Windows Server 2003 system on our network and none of the users can reach the Internet. What happened?

A: Basic firewall support for Windows Server 2003 provides for private traffic only or private traffic only plus NAT. In order to reach public systems on the Internet, you need to have NAT configured along with your firewall.

Q: Is the basic firewall enough security?

A: Depending on your network security requirements, you might want to implement packet filters along with the basic firewall or implement a full featured firewall package on the perimeter of your network, such as ISA Server.

Q: We are using firewall software on our server. Would the basic firewall add additional security to the network?

A: If you are currently using firewall software, there is no need to configure basic firewall support for your Windows Server 2003 system. The addition of basic firewall will not accomplish anything beyond the current firewall capabilities and presents the opportunity for conflicts between the settings on the two firewalls.

Q: I am setting up remote control software for a system on our private network and the connection is not working. Why isn't this working?

A: There are two different types of port numbers used by TCP/IP. TCP port numbers provide service mappings for connection-based communications whereas UDP provides service mappings for connectionless communications. Remote control software often relies on TCP and UDP port mappings. Make sure you have mapped the proper ports and services for both UDP and TCP.

Q: Modern Microsoft client operating systems have a feature called Internet Connection Sharing (ICS). Microsoft's modern server products have NAT and ICS. Is NAT different from ICS? If so, how?

A: ICS is a limited implementation of NAT. Basically ICS allows one public address to be translated for the internal private subnet systems. Also, ICS provides a form of dynamic address allocation to clients on the network in a way similar to DHCP. This dynamic address allocation does not provide any configuration options or features to control it when compared to standard DHCP. ICS also provides name resolution for the ICS clients. NAT provides more control over private address allocation and it also provides for multiple public addresses to be used when compared to the more limited implementation of NAT provided by ICS. NAT should be used instead of ICS when you want to use a DHCP server and/or DNS server on the network (which would include most business networks). However, ICS is easier to implement than NAT and can be useful in the SOHO environment or where a shared connection needs to be implemented quickly and simply.

Q: Are there any limitations to NAT?

A: NAT uses IP address information from the IP header. Any traffic that does not carry the IP address information in the IP header will not work with a basic NAT implementation. FTP is a classic example of this. Most implementations of NAT today provide capabilities to carry FTP traffic. Likewise L2TP tunneled traffic, for the same reason, does not work with all implementations of NAT. A traditional limitation of NAT, its inability to interoperate with IPSec has been addressed through the use of NAT traversal technology. Also called NAT-T, this technology makes it possible to use IPSec and NAT together, and is supported in Windows Server 2003.

Q: Windows Server 2003 supports ICMP router discovery. Why aren't my clients finding the routers?

A: Although Windows Server 2003 supports ICMP router discovery, it is disabled by default. You have to enable ICMP router discovery in **Routing and Remote Access**.

Q: I enabled Windows Server 2003 ICMP router discovery. Why is the address for a Cisco router on our network showing as one of the available routers?

A: Several Cisco routers come preconfigured with ICMP router discovery enabled. ICMP router discovery is an open standard provided on several modern pieces of networking equipment.

Self Test

A Quick Answer Key follows the Self Test questions. For complete questions, answers, and explanations to the Self Test questions in this chapter as well as the other chapters in this book, see the Self Test Appendix.

Configuring LAN Routing

1. You are designing the corporate global network for your company. You have to decide on an authentication method. What is the preferred authentication method for Windows Server 2003 in a high security environment?

    A. MS-CHAP

    B. EAP-TLS

    C. CHAP

    D. PAP

Configuring RRAS Packet Filters

2. The IT Manager has asked you to implement an intranet Web server on a separate subnet from the client systems in your network. How will you implement a packet filter for the scenario shown in Figure 8.115?

Figure 8.115 Intranet Web Server Packet Filtering

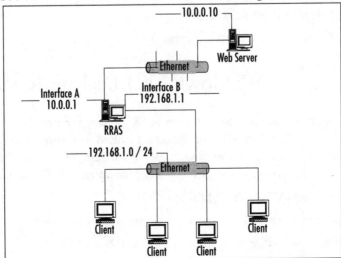

A. Filter inbound packets on Interface B with a source network of 192.168.1.0 and subnet mask of 255.255.255.0, a destination network of 10.0.0.0 and a destination subnet mask of 255.255.255.0, and destination TCP port 25. Select to drop all packets except those listed in your criteria.

B. Filter inbound packets on Interface B with a source network of 192.168.1.0 and subnet mask of 255.255.255.0, a destination network of 10.0.0.0 and a destination subnet mask of 255.255.255.0, and destination TCP port 25. Select to receive all packets except those listed in your criteria.

C. Filter inbound packets on Interface B with a source network of 192.168.1.0 and subnet mask of 255.255.255.0, a destination network of 10.0.0.0 and a destination subnet mask of 255.255.255.0, and destination TCP port 80. Select to drop all packets except those listed in your criteria.

D. Filter inbound packets on Interface B with a source network of 192.168.1.0 and subnet mask of 255.255.255.0, a destination network of 10.0.0.0 and a destination subnet mask of 255.255.255.0, and destination TCP port 80. Select to receive all packets except those listed in your criteria.

Configuring the Windows 2003 Dial-up RAS Server

3. You have been asked to set up a Windows 2003 dial-up RAS server for your company. Your clients use Windows XP and Windows 2000 Professional computers. Company policy requires the most secure authentication possible. How will you configure your dial-up RAS server to meet company policy?

A. Configure CHAP authentication.

B. Configure MS-CHAP v2 authentication.

C. Configure PAP authentication.

D. Configure EAP-TLS authentication.

Configuring the Windows 2003 Dial-up RAS Gateway

4. You configure a Windows 2003 dial-up RAS gateway for a remote office in your corporate network. A dial-up ISDN connection is used to connect the remote office to the corporate LAN. In order to provide access for the remote users to the corporate LAN, what two configuration settings do you need to complete? (Choose all that apply.)

A. Configure NAT on the ISDN interface.

B. Configure a demand-dial interface on the ISDN interface.

C. Configure a DHCP relay agent on the ISDN interface.

D. Configure a default static route on the ISDN interface.

5. You configure a Windows 2003 dial-up RAS Gateway providing Internet access for users on a remote LAN in your corporate network. The LAN is on the subnet 10.0.2.0/24. What RRAS mechanism will facilitate public Internet connectivity for users on this private network?

   A. The NAT component of Windows Server 2003 RRAS will provide connectivity in this case.

   B. RIP routing will provide connectivity in this case.

   C. OSPF routing will provide connectivity in this case.

   D. Dynamic DNS will provide connectivity in this case.

PPP Multilink and Bandwidth Allocation Protocol (BAP)

6. In Windows Server 2003 RRAS, PPP multilink is enabled by default. What controls the properties for the PPP multilink connection?

   A. Remote access policy controls the multilink connection properties.

   B. The dial-up networking properties for the client connection control the multilink connection properties.

   C. When a PPP multilink connection is established, the user is prompted with a dialog box to control the multilink connection properties.

   D. Active Directory controls multilink connection properties.

Configuring Wireless Connections

7. You are tasked with the design and implementation of a new wireless network for your corporate campus. Users will connect to various access points around campus using primarily laptops and PDAs. How will you design an authentication scheme to simplify the administration of the 1,000+ users of this system?

   A. Configure a single Windows Server 2003 system as the logon server. Create local accounts for all network users.

   B. Configure a pair of Windows Server 2003 systems as Active Directory domain controllers. Configure IAS to use the Active Directory user accounts for authentication.

   C. Configure a pair of Windows Server 2003 systems to share local account database information and use TACACS+ for user authentication.

   D. Configure a Windows Server 2003 system as a primary domain controller. Configure a second Windows Server 2003 system to replicate account database information using SQL.

Configuring Remote Access Policies

8. Your organization supports several users that work from home offices. Each home-based user connects to the network through a VPN. The DSL connections used by each home-based user are configured with static IP addresses. You want to use a remote access policy to ensure that the home-based users connect to the office only from their home office computers. What is the simplest way to accomplish this task?

   A. Configure smart-card authentication for each home-based user. Configure a remote access policy to deny access to all users except smart-card authenticated users.

   B. Configure biometric user authentication using EAP-TLS. Configure a remote access policy to deny access to all users except EAP-TLS authenticated users.

   C. Configure PEAP authentication. Configure a remote access policy to deny access to all users except PEAP authenticated users.

   D. Configure a remote access policy to deny access to all users except those verified with specific Client-IP-Address parameters.

Understanding Router Protocols

9. You are designing a small IP network with eight remote sites. You need to provide site-to-site connectivity through the corporate hub network. How can you provide a simple solution to routing this traffic and still accommodate the addition of new remote sites with the least amount of extra administration?

   A. Configure the network to use RIP v2 routing on all subnets.

   B. Configure the network to use OSPF on all subnets. Configure each remote site to be in area 0.0.0.0.

   C. Configure default static routes on each remote subnet.

   D. Configure IGMP on each subnet.

Configuring Basic Firewall Support

10. You are responsible for securing your corporate network using a Windows Server 2003 remote access server. Your network manager has asked you to install and configure the basic firewall features available in Windows Server 2003. Are there any concerns with using the basic firewall on your network?

A. Internet services that are provided from privately addressed systems will have to be provisioned in the firewall configuration.

B. Some public systems may experience problems connecting to systems on the LAN.

C. Some systems might not be able to connect to the Internet.

D. Some private systems might experience problems connecting to systems on the LAN.

RRAS NAT Services

11. You are talking with another network engineer about network address translation. She claims that ICS and Microsoft NAT are the same thing. What are two major differences between ICS and Microsoft's implementation of NAT as provided in Microsoft's server product line? (Choose all that apply.)

A. NAT supports multiple public addresses, ICS does not.

B. ICS works on Windows 2000 Server and Windows Server 2003, NAT does not.

C. ICS supports multiple public addresses, NAT does not.

D. NAT works with DHCP to accommodate different subnet addresses, ICS does not.

ICMP Router Discovery

12. To provide network redundancy, you have implemented ICMP Router Discovery on your company network. Clients are not detecting the routers on your network. What is preventing the clients from seeing the routers?

A. You have to enable ICMP Router Discovery on the network clients by implementing the proper group policy.

B. You have to enable ICMP Router Discovery on network clients by adding two entries to the registry.

C. You have to enable ICMP Router Discovery on the network clients through Active Directory Users and Computers.

D. You have to enable ICMP Router Discovery on the network clients through the Routing and Remote Access service Microsoft management console.

Troubleshooting Remote Access Client Connections

13. You move some of the servers on your network to a new subnet. You manually update the DNS server records for these servers. A client contacts you to complain that their computer cannot access resources on one of the moved servers. You successfully ping the server by IP address. When you ping the server by name, you notice that a different IP address is listed. How can you quickly rectify this problem?

    A. Run the **gpupdate** command to update the name resolution cache.

    B. Run the **ping -a** command with the server IP address to update the name resolution cache.

    C. Run the **ipconfig /flushdns** command to clear the DNS cache.

    D. Run the **nslookup** command. From the nslookup prompt, type **ls d** to repair the DNS cache.

Troubleshooting Remote Access Server Connections

14. Your remote access server provides a remote connection to your LAN-based terminal server. Several users are complaining that their connections to the server are frequently dropped. You suspect problems beyond the confines of your LAN. How can you determine the cause of this problem?

    A. Issue a **ping** command to several of the clients' addresses. Verify packet delivery.

    B. Issue a **pingpath** command to several of the clients' addresses. Look for high packet loss from routers along the path.

    C. Issue a **tracert** command to several of the clients' addresses. Look for high delivery times from routers along the path.

    D. Issue a **route** command to several of the clients' addresses. Look for high delivery times from routers along the path.

Configuring Internet Authentication Services

15. You configure IAS for centralized authentication of remote users. What are two major advantages of IAS for authentication?

    A. IAS provides open standard authentication, providing authentication for remote access devices from multiple vendors.

    B. IAS provides a proprietary authentication mechanism, providing authentication for remote access devices from multiple vendors.

    C. IAS provides single sign-on authentication for remote and local users through Active Directory.

    D. IAS provides single sign-on authentication for remote and local users through TACACS+.

Self Test Quick Answer Key

For complete questions, answers, and explanations to the Self Test questions in this chapter as well as the other chapters in this book, see the Self Test Appendix.

1.	**B**	9.	**A**
2.	**C**	10.	**A**
3.	**D**	11.	**A, D**
4.	**B, D**	12.	**B**
5.	**A**	13.	**C**
6.	**A**	14.	**B**
7.	**B**	15.	**A, C**
8.	**D**		

Chapter 9

MCSA/MCSE 70-291

Security Templates and Software Updates

Exam Objectives in this Chapter:

3.1 Implement secure network administration procedures.

3.1.3 Implement security baseline settings and audit security settings using security templates.

3.1.2 Implement the principle of least privelege.

☑ Summary of Exam Objectives

☑ Exam Objectives Fast Track

☑ Exam Objectives Frequently Asked Questions

☑ Self Test

☑ Self Test Quick Answer Key

Introduction

Security is becoming the snowball of information technology. In recent years, security has become a major concern for many companies. Security has become so much of a concern in fact, that several companies have created a position specifically for a security officer, someone responsible for a corporation's security policies and their implementation. In this chapter we will examine two of Microsoft's key security tools for Windows Server 2003, the Security Configuration and Analysis management console and the Software Update Service (SUS).

With each passing day, there are new security threats and system vulnerabilities discovered and, with their discovery, new security patches and hot fixes to apply. The Security Configuration and Analysis management console provides a utility for testing baseline security settings and a method for applying a consistent security configuration to machines throughout the enterprise. The SUS provides a mechanism to consistently apply hot fixes and updates to all Microsoft systems in your enterprise. When used together, the Security Configuration and Analysis management console and the SUS are intended to reduce administrative overhead while providing consistent application of current security settings to all Microsoft-based machines in your network.

With the release of Service Pack 4 (SP 4) for Windows NT 4.0, Microsoft introduced a new security configuration tool to ease administration of your Windows NT network. The release of the NT 4.0 Service Pack 4 CD introduced the Security Configuration Manager (SCM). The Security Configuration Manager is a product originally designed for Windows NT 5.0 (now known as Windows 2000). Now, with the release of Windows Server 2003, Microsoft continues to expand on the functionality of the SCM with the Security and Configuration Analysis management console. The Security Configuration and Analysis management console provides a tool for configuring, comparing, and applying security templates.

Security Templates

A security template is a Windows initialization (.INI) file that lists configuration parameters for various operating system settings for different server types. Using the Security Configuration and Analysis utility, you can analyze the current configuration of your server. This analysis creates a template for the existing system configuration while comparing the system configuration against a preconfigured template. The security template is divided into the following seven areas:

- Account Policies

- Local Policies

- Event Log

- Restricted Groups

- System Services
- Registry
- File System

EXAM WARNING

Know the difference between the various security templates and understand the basics of why each template may be used. The exam will test your knowledge of applying the templates.

Account Policies determine password policy, account lockout policy, and Kerberos policy. Through this portion of the security template you can configure password complexity, password history, and other password characteristics. Also, through the Account policy settings, you can configure account lockout threshold and duration.

Local Policies determine auditing policy, user rights assignment, and security options. Through Local Policy subcategories, you can configure system access settings, recovery options, system control permissions, account and system manipulation, and event auditing.

Event Log configurations modify application, system, and security Event Log settings. Through this category, you can configure event log storage capabilities and features.

The Restricted Groups category controls membership of security-sensitive groups. Through this category, group membership settings can be enforced and forced to override administrative changes to account settings that conflict with Restricted Groups membership settings.

The System Services category controls startup and permissions for system services. This configuration option helps to regulate system services available on the particular system. This carries an elevated level of importance for publicly connected servers, such as Web servers and VPN gateways. Publicly connected servers are exposed to malicious attacks from anywhere in the world. It is considered best practice to enable only services that are needed by the server. Maintaining unneeded services increases the potential vulnerabilities on the server. Different services are known to have certain vulnerabilities. For example, IIS has had a long list of buffer overflow vulnerabilities discovered and subsequently patched. If the machine is not being used as a Web server, there is no need to support IIS and maintain its series of patches and updates.

The Registry category offers configuration options for permissions for registry keys. This helps to control unwanted modification of registry values by users or programs operating under the context of particular users.

The File System category provides options to control permissions for folders and files. Figure 9.1 illustrates the Security Configuration and Analysis management console with a domain controller security template compared against the existing system configuration.

Figure 9.1 Security Configuration and Analysis Management Console

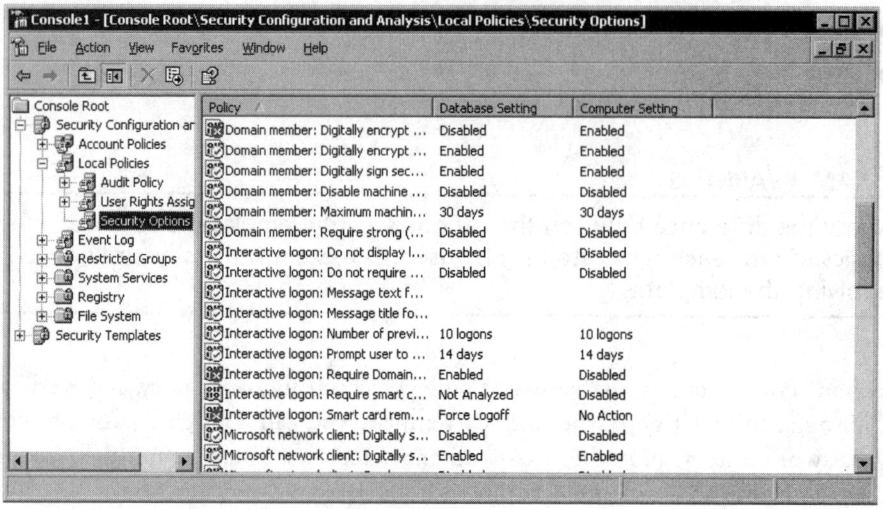

In the next section, we will look at the different types of security templates and explore the uses of and differences between each.

Types of Security Templates

Microsoft offers several preconfigured security templates through the Security Configuration and Analysis management console as well as online. You can apply a preconfigured security template to your system or use it to compare your existing configuration settings to predetermined settings provided by the security template. Templates are available for several configuration scenarios. Microsoft provides templates for the following:

- Default security (Setup security.inf)

- Compatible (Compatws.inf)

- Secure (Secure*.inf)

- Highly Secure (hisec*.inf)

- System root security (Rootsec.inf)

- No Terminal Server user SID (Notssid.inf)

The *Default* security template represents the default settings that are applied during installation of the operating system. This template also applies the default file permissions for the root of the system drive with the post-installation settings. This template was primarily designed for disaster recovery scenarios.

The *Compatible* security template modifies the permissions on files and registry settings to loosen the restrictive standard security settings for user accounts. This template provides limited capabilities for user accounts when compared to Power Users but provides greater freedom and capabilities than a standard user account.

The *Secure* security template increases security by modifying the password, lockout, and audit settings. This template increases security without adversely affecting application compatibility. Also, the Secure security template permits network authentication only through NT LAN Manager version 2 (NTLMv2). Microsoft network clients typically rely on LAN Manager and NTLM for network authentication. Windows for Workgroups, Windows 95, and Windows 98 clients that do not have the Directory Service client pack installed do not have NTLMv2 capabilities. Windows 95 and Windows 98 clients with the Directory Service client pack installed and Windows ME clients have provisions for NTLMv2 authentication.

The *Highly Secure* security template increases the security level provided by the Secure security template. The features modified by this template include the following:

- LAN Manager and NTLM authentication are refused

- Domain-to-member and domain-to-domain trust relationships require strong encryption and SMB packet signing

- All members of the Power Users group are removed

- Only Domain Admins and the local Administrator account remain members of the local Administrators group

The *System root security* template provides the same level of permissions as the default Windows XP file and folder permissions for the root system drive. This template can be used to reapply the default permissions to the root system drive if those permissions have been inadvertently modified or it can be used to apply the default permissions levels to other drives or volumes.

The *No Terminal Server user SID* security template removes the Terminal Server user SIDs that are used by Terminal Servers running in Application mode. Terminal Server user SIDs provide access control for users logged in to Terminal Servers running in Application mode. The Terminal Server user SIDs control access to the file system and default registry locations. Microsoft recommends running the Terminal Server in Full Security mode instead of removing the Terminal Server user SIDs to secure Terminal Servers. This template is generally used on a system that will not be used as a Terminal Server.

Network Security Settings

It was noted in the previous section that the use of *Secure* and *Highly Secure* security templates affects the authentication mechanisms used in network communication. Several of the security options under Local Policy affect network security for clients and servers. The Security Options listed under Local Policies provides several network security configuration options:

- Network security: Do not store LAN Manager hash value on next password change

- Network security: Force logoff when logon hours expire

- Network security: LAN Manager authentication level

- Network security: LDAP client signing requirements

- Network security: Minimum session security for NTLM SSP-based (including secure RPC) clients

- Network security: Minimum session security for NTLM SSP-based (including secure RPC) servers

The Network security: Do not store LAN Manager hash value on next password change security setting controls whether the weak LAN Manager (LM) hash value for the password will be stored in the local database next time the password is changed. The LM value is stored on the local computer in the security database. If the local computer's security database becomes compromised, the LM value might be used to extract the user's password. This setting is disabled by default.

NOTE

The LM authentication protocol is considered weak because of the method used to encrypt the password. If a password is less than seven characters in length, breaking down the LM protocol to extract the cleartext password is simplified because the last half of the LM hash follows the same predictable pattern. This weakness is known and exploited by hackers. Programs exist for extracting the LM hash and decrypting it. The best practice, if possible, is to not use LM authentication and to not store the LM hash.

The Network security: Force logoff when logon hours expire security setting affects users connected to the local computer through a network connection by manipulating the Server Message Block (SMB) communication between the systems. This setting, enabled by default, will disable network connectivity between the user's PC and the server configured with this security setting.

The Network security: LAN Manager authentication level security setting affects the authentication protocols used by clients and servers in a Microsoft network. Table 9.1 illustrates the relationship between security settings, client authentication protocol selection, and server authentication protocol selection.

NOTE

In a highly secure environment, you should implement the *principle of least privilege*, which states that any process or user should be allocated only the absolute minimum privileges that will allow the needed task(s) to be completed, and nothing more. In a Windows domain, this is accomplished through a combination of access permissions, user rights, and group policies. This term is derived from the government/security principle of *need to know*.

Table 9.1 Relationships between Client and Server Authentication Settings

Settings	Clients			Domain Controllers		
	LM	NTLM	NTLMv2	LM	NTLM	NTLMv2
Send LM & NTLM responses	Yes	Yes	No	Accepted	Accepted	Accepted
Send LM & NTLM— use NTLMv2 session security if negotiated	Yes	Yes	Yes*	Accepted	Accepted	Accepted
Send NTLM response only	No	Yes	Yes*	Accepted	Accepted	Accepted
Send NTLMv2 response only	No	No	Yes	Accepted	Accepted	Accepted
Send NTLMv2 response only\refuse LM	No	No	Yes	Refused	Accepted	Accepted
Send NTLMv2 response only\refuse LM & NTLM	No	No	Yes	Refused	Refused	Accepted

*If supported by the server

TEST DAY TIP

Review Table 9.1 before the exam. With the focus on security and the known weaknesses of LAN Manager authentication, this topic will probably warrant test coverage.

Normally, LAN Manager and NTLM authentication are used by Microsoft systems for network authentication. Implementing Secure and Highly Secure security templates affects network security by altering the typical LAN Manager and NTLM authentication request protocols.

A system configured with the Default security template or not configured with any security modifications will send LAN Manager and NTLM responses. Workstations do not have a defined configuration, meaning they will follow the server requests. Implementing security templates affects the use of LAN Manager and NTLM authentication used by the systems. Security settings determine which authentication protocol is used for network logons. The security settings determine the authentication protocol used by clients, the level of security negotiated, and the level of authentication accepted by servers. Figure 9.2 shows the options available through the Network security: LAN Manager authentication level security configuration setting.

Figure 9.2 Setting the Network Security: LAN Manager Authentication Level Options

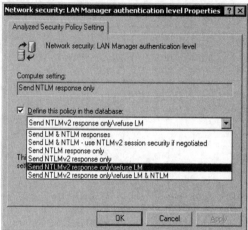

The Network security: LDAP client signing requirements security setting establishes the degree of data signing used in LDAP BIND requests. Digital signing is a method used to validate data integrity. This method uses keys to generate a hash of the actual data. This method of hashing, or encrypting the data, provides a mechanism to verify data integrity. If the data is modified in any way, the hash will not match. This ensures that data received by a client is the actual data sent by the server. The default setting is Negotiate signing. The three levels of LDAP client signing are:

- **None** Options are specified by the caller.

- **Negotiate signing** If Transport Layer Security/Secure Sockets Layer (TLS\SSL) is not being used, LDAP BIND requests occur with the LDAP data signing option set along with the options specified by the caller. If TLS\SSL is used, the LDAP BIND requests occur with the options that are specified by the caller. This is the default.

- **Require signature** If the client and server configurations do not match in this case, the client will receive an LDAP BIND request failed and the client will be unable to connect to the server.

The Network security: Minimum session security for NTLM SSP-based (including secure RPC) clients security setting provides message confidentiality, message integrity, 128-bit encryption, and NTLMv2 security connection requirements for client connections. In the default configuration, no options are set. The following options are available:

- **Require message integrity** Message integrity must be negotiated to continue the connection. Message integrity is verified through message signing. The signature ensures that the message has not been tampered with.

■ **Require message confidentiality** Encryption must be negotiated to continue the connection. Encryption converts data into an unreadable format until decrypted.

■ **Require NTLMv2 session security** NTLMv2 protocol must be negotiated or the connection will fail.

■ **Require 128-bit encryption** Without negotiating strong encryption (128-bit) the connection will fail.

Figure 9.3 demonstrates the available options for Network security: Minimum session security for NTLM SSP-based (including secure RPC) clients configuration.

Figure 9.3 Setting Minimum Session Security for NTLM SSP-based (Including Secure RPC) Clients

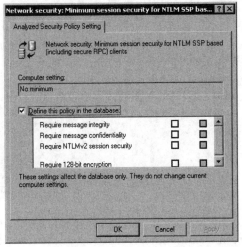

The Network security: Minimum session security for NTLM SSP-based (including secure RPC) servers security setting provides message confidentiality, message integrity, 128-bit encryption, and NTLMv2 security connection requirements for server connections. By default, no requirements are set. The following options (the same as those available for clients) are available:

■ **Require message integrity** Message integrity must be negotiated to continue the connection. Message integrity is verified through message signing. The signature ensures the message has not been tampered with.

■ **Require message confidentiality** Encryption must be negotiated to continue the connection. Encryption converts data into an unreadable format until decrypted.

- **Require NTLMv2 session security** NTLMv2 protocol must be negotiated or the connection will fail.

- **Require 128-bit encryption** Without negotiating strong encryption (128-bit) the connection will fail.

Figure 9.4 illustrates the available options for Network security: Minimum session security for NTLM SSP-based (including secure RPC) servers configuration.

Figure 9.4 Setting Minimum Session Security for NTLM SSP-based (Including Secure RPC) Servers

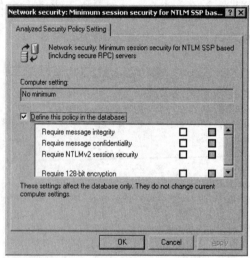

As mentioned previously, Microsoft provides several security templates to simplify basic security configurations to match common scenarios. In the next section, you will see how a predefined security template can be used to compare existing system security settings with the settings provided by the template.

Analyzing Baseline Security

In most types of analysis, the first step is to determine a baseline. If you want to measure network performance and determine how much difference certain modifications make, you have to start from a baseline or existing performance level. This approach also applies to security. If we want to tighten security on our network or on an individual system, we should first determine the baseline.

TEST DAY TIP

Try to run through several analysis scenarios during your test preparation. The Security Configuration and Analysis management console is an excellent tool for testing your existing security configurations. The exam will require that you understand what the analysis means, so be prepared.

Using the Microsoft Security Configuration and Analysis management console, you can compare existing security settings to one of the predefined templates or to a custom template. The baseline analysis is conducted through the following steps:

1. A baseline storage location is determined by creating a database file where the configuration information and comparison information will be saved.

2. A template is selected to compare the current configuration against.

3. To finish the analysis, you run an analysis between the selected template and the current configuration.

4. The analysis will display different icons depending on the comparison results.

Table 9.2 displays the possible results from a security analysis.

Table 9.2 Possible Security Analysis Results

Visual flag	Meaning
Red X	The entry is defined in the analysis database and on the system, but the security setting values do not match.
Green check	The entry is defined in the analysis database and on the system and the setting values match.
Question mark	The entry is not defined in the analysis database and, therefore, was not analyzed.
(No flag)	If an entry is not analyzed, it may be that it was not defined in the analysis database or that the user who is running the analysis may not have sufficient permission to perform analysis on a specific object or area.
Exclamation point	This item is defined in the analysis database, but does not exist on the actual system. For example, there may be a restricted group that is defined in the analysis database but does not actually exist on the analyzed system.

Exam Warning

Make sure you understand what each visual flag represents in the Security Configuration and Analysis management console. You will probably see sample scenarios in which templates have been compared and you will have to determine the preferred setting.

A comparison between the securedc.inf template file and a standard domain controller is displayed in Figure 9.5.

Figure 9.5 Comparing the securedc.inf Template to a Standard Domain Controller

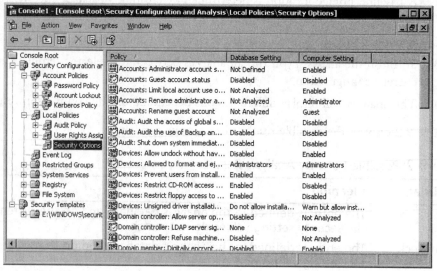

Exam Warning

A security analysis can be conducted through the GUI provided by the Security Configuration and Analysis management console or from a command-line using the secedit command.

EXERCISE 9.01

COMPARING SECURITY CONFIGURATIONS

In this exercise, we will import and compare the hisecdc.inf security template to a standard installation Windows Server 2003 domain controller.

1. We will customize a Microsoft Management Console (MMC) with the Security Configuration and Analysis Snap-in. Open the MMC click **Start | Run | MMC.exe** and click **OK**.

2. To add the Security Configuration and Analysis snap-in, click **File | Add Remove Snap-in** to open the **Add/Remove Snap-in** pop-up window as shown in Figure 9.6.

Figure 9.6 Adding Snap-ins to the MMC

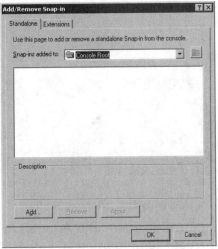

3. Click **Add** and scroll down and select the **Security Configuration and Analysis** snap-in as shown in Figure 9.7.

Figure 9.7 Adding the Security Configuration and Analysis Snap-in

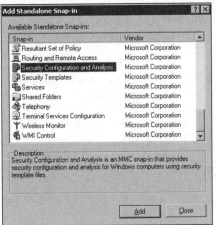

4. Click **Add** then click **Close** to return to the **Add/Remove Snap-in** dialog box as shown in Figure 9.8.

Figure 9.8 The Security Configuration and Analysis Snap-in Is Added

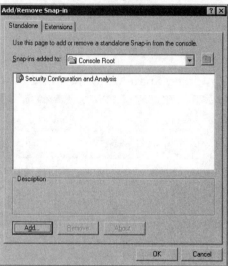

5. Click **OK** to move on to the analysis stage.

6. Click **Security Configuration and Analysis** in the left pane of the MMC to view instructions for importing and analyzing the templates as seen in Figure 9.9.

Figure 9.9 The MMC before Importing Templates

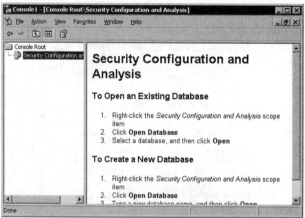

7. Right-click the **Security and Configuration Analysis** folder in the left pane of the MMC and select **Open database**.

8. Type **Exercise1** in the filename dialog box and click **OK**.

9. Select the hisecdc.inf security template as shown in Figure 9.10 and click **Open**.

Figure 9.10 Selecting the hisecdc.inf Template

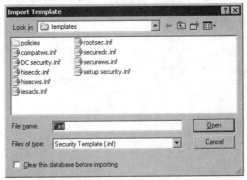

10. You will be returned to the blank Security Configuration and Analysis snap-in. Right-click the **Security Configuration and Analysis** folder in the left pane of the MMC and select **Analyze Computer Now.** A **Perform Analysis** dialog box will be displayed requesting the location for the **Error log file path:** as shown in Figure 9.11.

Figure 9.11 Specifying the Error Log File Path

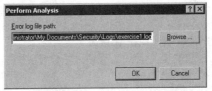

11. Click **OK** to begin the analysis. A progress screen like the one in Figure 9.12 will be displayed.

Figure 9.12 Analysis Progress Screen

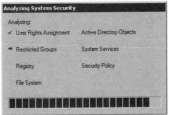

12. When the analysis is complete, you will see several new items listed below **Security Configuration and Analysis** in your MMC as shown in Figure 9.13.

Figure 9.13 Completed Analysis

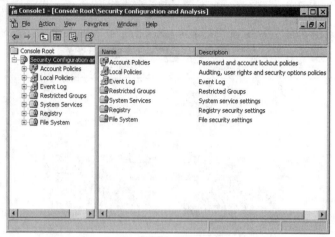

13. Browse through each category to see how the template will affect the configuration of your computer. Each item marked with a red X represents a discrepancy in the policy. Figure 9.14 illustrates an example of several discrepancies between the computer configuration and the template configuration. Each red X represents an increase in security, in this particular situation.

Figure 9.14 Discrepancies in the Analysis between the Current Configuration and the Template

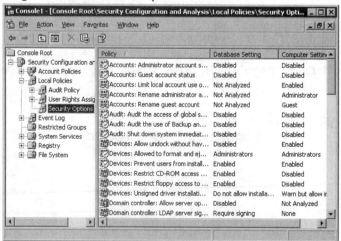

NOTE

Security templates provide a quick and easy checklist for your security configurations. It is a great idea to scan through the Security Configuration and Analysis utility after conducting an analysis on various systems. This utility will teach you a lot about basic network security and system security in a Microsoft environment. There are currently approximately 1,000 different configuration entries in this utility. Each entry provides a means to modify the registry without doing so directly with the regedit.exe utility.

Use this utility to see what you can do with Microsoft's latest and greatest operating systems. You will certainly learn about some new features that you were not aware of previously.

Applying Security Templates

There are multiple methods available for applying security templates in Windows Server 2003. The following tools provide mechanisms for applying security templates:

- secedit.exe
- Group Policy
- Security Configuration and Analysis management console

EXAM WARNING

Take some time to look at the different methods for applying the security templates. secedit is a less common way to apply templates but it has its benefits in some scenarios. Group Policy and Security Configuration and Analysis are basically the same interface. Again, there are reasons for using each. Typically, the secedit command would be used within a script to analyze and configure systems. The Security Configuration and Analysis utility is usually used for local security analysis and configuration on systems or in environments where Active Directory is not implemented. Group Policy provides the same interface as the Security Configuration and Analysis utility but the method for applying policies is centralized through Active Directory. Group Policy provides the simplest method for deploying new security policies because of its integration with Active Directory.

secedit.exe

The secedit.exe command-line tool provides a command line interface to analyze, modify, and apply security templates. The secedit.exe command works with the following switches:

- *secedit /analyze*
- *secedit /configure*
- *secedit /export*
- *secedit /validate*
- *secedit /import*
- *secedit /GenerateRollback*

The syntax used to apply a security template using the secedit.exe command is *secedit /configure /db FileName [/cfg FileName] [/overwrite][/areas area1 area2...] [/log FileName] [/quiet]*.

The *FileName* attribute used with the */db* switch specifies the filename of the database containing the security template to be applied. The *FileName* attribute used with the */cfg* switch is an optional parameter specifying the security template to be imported into the database. This option is valid only when used in conjunction with the */db* switch. The */overwrite* switch specifies to overwrite any information stored in the database instead of appending to the database. The */areas* switch specifies which areas of the template should be applied to the system. If no area is specified, all areas will be applied. The areas are the same categories discussed earlier in this chapter where we dissected the security template. Table 9.3 lists each area with a description of the configuration parameters provided.

Table 9.3 /areas Switch Options

Area Name	Description
SECURITYPOLICY	Local policy and domain policy for the system, including account policies, audit policies, and so on
GROUP_MGMT	Restricted group settings for any groups specified in the security template
USER_RIGHTS	User logon rights and granting of privileges
REGKEYS	Security on local registry keys
FILESTORE	Security on local file storage
SERVICES	Security for all defined services

The *FileName* parameter used with the */log* switch sets the filename and path for the log file. If this switch is not specified, the log file is stored in the default location. The */quiet* switch suppresses output to the screen.

Group Policy

Group Policy provides several configuration options for systems within your enterprise environment. You can install software packages, configure desktop options, configure Internet Explorer settings, and configure security settings just to name a few. Group Policy settings are applied through Active Directory Users and Computers for Domains and Organizational Units and through Active Directory Sites and Services for sites within your enterprise.

The security settings within Group Policy are identical to the configuration options in the Security Configuration and Analysis management console. When Group Policy is used, each area application of policy is applied in a cumulative fashion. The order of application is:

- local
- site
- domain
- organizational unit

First, locally configured security policies are applied to the system. Next, if a site-based security policy is configured, it will be applied on top of the local policy. This policy will overwrite the settings in the local policy. The domain policy is applied next, again over-writing previously applied policies. Finally, the organizational unit policy is applied. This policy also overwrites any previously written policies. If multiple (nested) organizational units hold the user or computer account, the nearest organizational unit to the user or computer account is applied last. This means that the nearest organizational unit-based policy will be the final policy applied and consequently, the settings from that policy will be the last ones written to the cumulative security settings.

NOTE

One of the newest features covered by previous Windows 2000 exams was Group Policy. Group Policy Objects (GPOs) are used to change system and security config-urations as well as to deploy software. To expedite group policy modifications in the past, we used the secedit command with the /refreshpolicy switch. Windows Server 2003 introduces a new command, specifically for expediting policy refresh settings. Instead of secedit /refreshpolicy, the gpupdate command is now used.

Security Configuration and Analysis

The Security Configuration and Analysis management console provides local security policy application to your system. As discussed in the previous section, the security settings applied by this type of policy are overwritten by site, domain, and organizational unit-based policies used in Group Policy application. The advantage of the Security Configuration and Analysis tool is that it provides analysis capabilities to determine cumulative affects from new policies. You can run the analysis portion of the Security Configuration and Analysis utility to determine what portion of your settings will change by applying a new template or to see where a template might not provide additional benefits to your configuration.

We used the Security Configuration and Analysis utility in Exercise 9.01 to compare the securedc.inf security template to our standard domain controller configuration.

Security Templates in the Real World

You might not find yourself using security templates in a production environment, but it is a good idea to be familiar with these. Are your corporate Web servers' access logs full of entries for http GET requests for /default.ida?. These requests generally come from IIS Web servers infected with the Nimda worm. Several other server vulnerabilities like Nimda are currently in existence and in the next few years, several more will be discovered. Security templates provide a way to test your systems beforehand, instead of waiting until after the fact to find that your configuration was insecure.

Take the time to analyze your servers, especially public servers, with appropriate security templates. The time it takes to do an analysis is very little in comparison to the time it takes to repair a compromised server.

Software Updates

Information technology is a dynamic industry. There is constant change and constant motion. Currently, security and cost of ownership are two of the hottest topics in IT. To maintain a secure, consistent environment requires keeping up-to-date on security patches and hot fixes. As new vulnerabilities are discovered, as new services are implemented, the onus is on the IT department to keep systems up-to-date and secure. Most people are now familiar with Windows Update. Using Windows Update, your computer polls Microsoft servers to determine whether your system is up-to-date with hot fixes and security patches. This process simplifies administration but creates a couple of other dilemmas.

Running Windows Update in a large network environment poses a number of questions:

- How do you provide consistency?

- How do you ensure that all systems are being updated?

- How do you make sure that the update will not cause problems with a software package installed on your client systems?

- What about the bandwidth consumed by all of your clients connecting over your expensive WAN links to retrieve the same information over and over again?

There must be a better way to keep clients consistently updated. Enter the Software Update Service. SUS provides a centralized, LAN-based solution for the Windows Update service. Using SUS, clients connect to a server within your network infrastructure to receive updates. This allows you to centrally control which updates are deployed and which updates are not deployed. In this manner, you are able to test updates before deploying them to clients. This process provides greater control over software updates for your clients while also cutting down on WAN traffic. Your SUS server connects to Microsoft's servers to keep up-to-date with current security patches and hot fixes. Now, instead of having multiple clients connecting through the WAN link to Microsoft's servers to each retrieve the same updates, your server connects once and the clients connect internally to your server. This system reduces WAN bandwidth requirements while also increasing security by minimizing the number of clients connecting outside of your network. Also, this centralized control allows you to test updates before deploying them.

There are basically two components to this system. SUS is the server component responsible for downloading the updates from Microsoft's servers. Also, the SUS component provides centralized control of updates. The second component to the system is the Automatic Updates client software. This software offers a mechanism for clients to connect to either Microsoft's update servers or to your centralized update server.

TEST DAY TIP

Know which clients work with SUS and know what it takes to make them work. NT 4.0 and Windows 98 are not supported as SUS clients. The supported client operating systems include Windows 2000 with Service Pack 2 (SP2) or later, Windows XP Professional, and Windows Server 2003 in order to run Automatic Updates. Windows ME, Windows 98, Windows 95, Windows for Workgroups, and other pre-Windows 2000 Microsoft operating systems are not supported as SUS clients.

Install and Configure Software Update Infrastructure

The SUS provides centralized administration and distribution of software updates within your organization's network. In this section, we will focus on the server components of the SUS infrastructure. The system is not a single piece of software but actually a combination of components that make up the infrastructure. To provide a centralized in-house SUS infrastructure, SUS uses the following three components:

- A new synchronization service called Windows Update Synchronization Service. This service downloads content to your SUS server.

- A server running an Internet Information Services (IIS) Web site. This server services the update requests from Automatic Updates clients.

- An SUS administration Web page.

SUS has the following software and minimum hardware requirements:

- Windows 2000 Server or Windows Server 2003

- Pentium III 700 MHz or higher processor

- A network card

- 512 megabytes of RAM

- 6 GB of free hard disk space on an NTFS partition for storage of update packages

- A minimum of 100MB of free space on an NTFS partition for installation of SUS

- Microsoft Internet Explorer v5.5 or above

Configuring & Implementing...

Implementing Software Update Service and Automatic Update for Your Production Environment

Automation and simplified management are important features in today's high-demand environments. We are expected to do more with less: Administer more systems with less administrative personnel, provide more services with less equipment, get more done in less time. Automating certain tasks and taking that responsibility out of the hands of the normal users is a good way to provide a more reliable, more consistent network.

Unfortunately, or maybe fortunately for people in the IT sector, none of the automation services are fool-proof and 100% reliable. Implementing an SUS server and automating your client configurations will simplify a huge portion of your day-to-day network administration tasks. If you are not testing and approving the updates as they are synchronized to your server, however, you are creating a consistent larger problem. A lot can be said for a standard routine, even in a highly automated environment.

According to Microsoft, this configuration should support up to 15,000 clients using one SUS server. To build the SUS server:

1. Download the sus10sp1.EXE file from the www.microsoft.com SUS page. The file is approximately 33 MB in size.

2. Copy the file to the server where you will install SUS.

3. Double-click the **sus10sp1.exe file**.

4. In the Welcome screen, click **Next**.

5. Accept the End User License Agreement, and click **Next**.

6. Select the **Typical** check box. At this point, a typical install has been completed for the SUS server. The next screen will display the URL used by client machines to connect to the SUS server being installed. Document the URL and click **Install**.

7. The IIS lockdown tool may run at this point, depending on current server configuration. The Finish page will be displayed next. Document the administration URL displayed on the Finish page.

8. Click **Finish** to launch the SUS administration Web site in your default Web browser.

EXAM WARNING

Make sure you understand the benefits of SUS. This is a fairly new service in Microsoft networking (introduced with Windows 2000) and it is likely to be a highlighted topic.

At this point, your SUS server has been installed with default configurations. In the next section, we will customize the server configuration. An SUS server provides two basic functions: synchronizing content and approving content. Before the SUS server can download content, it has to be configured.

1. Configuration settings are adjusted from the **Set Options** link, as shown in Figure 9.15.

Figure 9.15 Set Options Configuration Screen

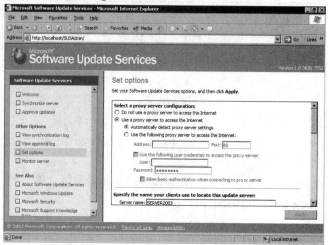

2. From the Set Options page, configure your network proxy settings if your network uses a proxy. The default setting is **Automatically detect proxy server settings**. This configuration will detect and automatically configure the proxy connection if your network supports this option. Otherwise, configure the proxy settings for your particular proxy.

3. Depending on whether your network uses DNS or NetBIOS for name resolution, you should configure the SUS server to support the proper name service for your network. This will determine the name used by clients to connect to the SUS server.

4. Configure the SUS server used to provide synchronized content. The options are to use Microsoft servers or to use a server on your internal network.

5. Specify how your server will handle new versions of previously approved updates.

6. Select a storage location for updates. The options are to maintain the updates on a Microsoft Windows Update server or to save the updates to a local folder. Also, locales may be selected from this portion of the configuration. Note that each locale that is selected will increase the amount of storage space necessary to maintain updates on your server.

There are two types of data associated with the SUS synchronization:

- The metadata stored in a file named aucatalog.cab. This file stores details about the packages and package availability.

- The actual package file that updates your systems.

No matter how the SUS server is configured, the aucatalog.cab file will always be downloaded. As previously mentioned, you have the option to store packages in a local folder or to use Maintain the updates on the Microsoft Windows Update servers. The benefit to the second option takes advantage of the global availability of the Microsoft Windows Update servers while still providing control over which updates your clients will receive. This does not provide bandwidth-saving advantages the way that keeping an internal SUS server does. It does, however, reduce the amount of free disk that you need on the SUS server.

NOTE

As mentioned earlier in this section, each locale that is selected on the Set Options page will increase the storage space required to maintain the update packages. Deselecting locales after synchronization has already occurred will not free up disk space because the packages that have already been downloaded will remain on the SUS server.

NOTE

If your network proxy server requires authentication, you must store the updates on your SUS server by selecting **Save the updates to a local Folder**. The Automatic Update client supports only proxy servers that do not require authentication.

Now that we have installed the Windows Update Synchronization Service to our SUS server and configured the update and storage settings, it is time to synchronize the server with the Microsoft Windows Update servers.

1. Click **Synchronize server** in the navigation panel on the left side of the Software Update Services administration page as shown in Figure 9.16.

Figure 9.16 Synchronize Server Page

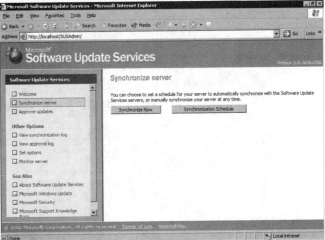

2. From this page, you should configure a synchronization schedule for your SUS server. The synchronization schedule setting allows for synchronization at a particular time of day on a weekly or daily basis. Determine a time when network traffic is low and your server is not in the process of being backed up or processing other service requests, if possible. Scheduling settings are shown in Figure 9.17.

Figure 9.17 Setting SUS Scheduling

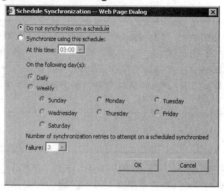

3. After specifying a schedule and completing the SUS server configuration, it is a good idea to manually synchronize the server the first time. Select **Synchronize Now** from the Synchronize Server page.

4. After synchronization is complete, depending on your server configuration, your server will either automatically approve the updates or you will have a list of updates to review for your approval. To review the updates, select **Approve updates** from the navigation menu as shown in Figure 9.18.

Figure 9.18 Update Review for Approval

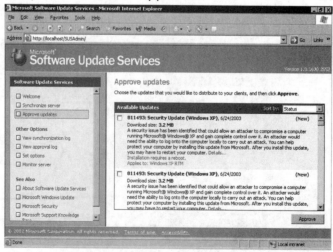

5. Review the updates available and select the updates that you want applied to your client systems, then click the **Approve** button to complete the SUS synchronization and update process. A pop-up message will appear to warn you that your update list will be modified as shown in Figure 9.19. Select **Yes** to continue.

Figure 9.19 Synchronization List Warning

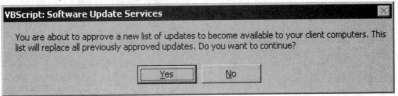

6. Depending on the update or updates selected, you may be prompted to accept an End User License Agreement (EULA) to continue as shown in Figure 9.20. Select **Accept** to continue.

Figure 9.20 EULA Prompt

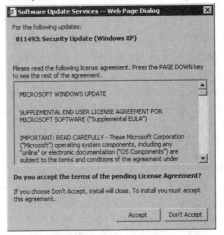

7. After the SUS server finishes downloading the selected updates, you are prompted with another pop-up window informing you that the updates have been successfully approved and are available for clients as shown in Figure 9.21.

Figure 9.21 Completed Approval Message

8.   The SUS server is now configured, and synchronization and approval have been completed.

9.   Your server may display one of the following messages next to each update in the approval list:

■   **New** This indicates that the update was recently downloaded. The update has not been approved and will not be offered to any client computers that query the server.

■   **Approved** This means that the update has been approved by an administrator and will be made available to client computers that query the server.

■   **Not Approved** This indicates that the update has not been approved and will not be made available to client computers that query the server.

■   **Updated** This indicates that the update has been changed during a recent synchronization.

■   **Temporarily Unavailable** This message is displayed only when updates are stored locally on the server. An update is in the Temporarily Unavailable state if one of the following is true: The associated update package file required to install the update is not available or a dependency required by the update is not available.

10.   Depending on your server configuration, the server may need periodic administration to approve new updates for your clients. It is best practice to test updates on non-production machines before approving them for your production environment. This ensures that the updates do not conflict with other software used by your client systems.

NOTE

Because SUS locks down the IIS service, turns off Internet printing, WebDAV, and indexing, and disables the session state, it is recommended that you dedicate an IIS server to the use of SUS and not use it for other Web services.

A Monitor server page is available for a high-level overview of updates available. Also, as synchronizations are performed, log entries are added to the Event Log to document the synchronization process and to provide information in the event of a synchronization failure.

In the next section, we will discuss the process used to install and configure SUS clients with the Automatic Client Update software on Windows Server 2003, Windows XP, and Windows 2000 client systems.

Install and Configure Automatic Client Update Settings

You now have a working SUS server on your corporate LAN so it is time to configure the clients. The updated Automatic Update client is available for Windows 2000 Professional, Windows 2000 Server, and Windows 2000 Advanced Server (all with Service Pack 2 or higher), Windows XP Professional, Windows XP Home Edition, and Windows Server 2003 family. Windows 2000 Data Center Server uses a special service for system update capabilities separate from the standard SUS service. Three options are available for client installation:

- Install Automatic Updates client using the MSI install package.
- Self-update from the STPP version Critical Update Notification (CUN).
- Install Windows 2000 Service Pack 3 (SP3).
- Install Windows XP SP1.
- Install Windows Server 2003.

Microsoft recommends using the MSI install package (filename WUAU22.msi) to update Windows 2000 and Windows XP client systems. The client software may be installed using the MSI package through Microsoft IntelliMirror, Microsoft Systems Management Server (SMS), or through a simple logon script.

Once the client software is installed, there are two basic configuration categories to complete:

- Automatic Updates functionality
- Automatic Updates server to use—from Microsoft Windows Updates servers or from a server running SUS on your local network

TEST DAY TIP

Installation of the Automatic Update client is best achieved through Group Policy. Review the concepts presented with Microsoft IntelliMirror for software deployment. You need a high-level understanding of Group Policy and IntelliMirror for this portion of the exam.

SUS clients use the Microsoft Windows Updates servers by default. Clients must be redirected to use the local SUS server or servers. The recommended approach for SUS client redirection to a local SUS server is through Group Policy settings.

NOTE

More and more services are taking advantage of the far-reaching networks in existence today. Several applications and services rely on the open http protocol to provide services to clients in a uniform manner. Microsoft has introduced Background Intelligent Transfer Service (BITS) to transfer files asynchronously between a client and an HTTP server. This service controls bandwidth utilization through http downloads while providing a connection history. If a client is downloading software that uses BITS technology, if the user is disconnected, shuts the system down, or logs off, the connection will be reestablished the next time the user is connected to the network. This ensures updates are received without overburdening the network with large amounts of traffic.

To configure Group Policy SUS server redirection in an Active Directory environment:

1. The WUAU.adm file that describes the new policy settings for the Automatic Updates client is automatically installed into the %windir%\inf folder when you install Automatic Updates. This file describes the new policy settings used for the Automatic Update configuration.

2. Load WUAU.adm as an administrative template in the **Group Policy Object Editor**.

3. From an Active Directory domain controller, click **Start | Programs | Administrative Tools | Active Directory Users and Computers**.

4. Right-click the Organizational Unit (OU) or domain where you want to create the policy, and then click **Properties**.

5. Click the **Group Policy** tab, and click **New**.

6. Type a name for the policy, and then click **Edit** to open the **Group Policy Object Editor**.

7. Under either Computer Settings or User Settings, right-click **Administrative Templates**.

8. Click **Add/Remove Templates** and **Add**.

9. Enter the name of the Automatic Updates ADM file: **%windir%\inf\WUAU.adm**.

10. Click **Open**.

11. From within the **Group Policy Object Editor, Computer Configuration | Administrative Templates | Windows Components | Windows Update** in the right pane of the management console, the two configuration options are listed as seen in Figure 9.22.

Figure 9.22 Configuring Windows Automatic Update Using Group Policy

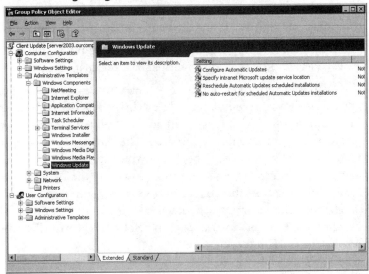

12. Configure the SUS server location information by double-clicking on **Specify intranet Microsoft update service location** and clicking **Enable** as shown in Figure 9.23.

Figure 9.23 Enabling SUS Client Redirection

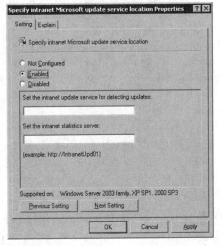

13. In the **Set the intranet update service for detecting updates** box, enter the URL for the SUS server.

14. In the **Set the intranet statistics server** box, enter the URL for the statistics server. Click **OK** to continue. This server can be the same server as the SUS server. The server has to have IIS installed and configured to be the statistics server.

15. Configure the **Automatic Update Properties** by double-clicking **Configure Automatic Updates** in the right pane of the management console.

16. Click **Enable** and select one of the three **Configure Automatic Updating** options as shown in Figure 9.24. The **Notify for download and notify for install** option notifies a logged-on administrative user prior to the download and prior to the installation of the updates. The **Auto download and notify for install** option automatically begins downloading updates and then notifies a logged-on administrative user prior to installing the updates. The **Auto download and schedule the install** option is configured to perform a scheduled installation. The recurring scheduled installation day and time must also be set using the **Scheduled install day** and **Scheduled install time** drop-down boxes. Click **OK** to continue.

Figure 9.24 Configuring Automatic Update Properties

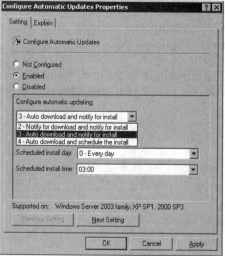

17. If the computer is not running when the scheduled install time arrives, the **Reschedule Automatic Updates scheduled installations** policy setting will provide a means to install the updates after the computer has been started. Double-click **Reschedule Automatic Updates scheduled installations**, click **Enable**, and specify a time in the **Wait after system startup(minutes)** box (a value between 1 and 60). Click **OK** to complete this configuration setting.

Twenty-four hours after the client first establishes a connection with the update service, a local administrator will be presented with a wizard-based configuration for the client update settings if no configuration settings have been specified through other methods. A local administrator can use the Automatic Updates applet in the Control Panel to configure Automatic Update or to modify the settings. If Group Policy has been configured for Automatic Updates, it will override the local settings. The order for policy application is the same as discussed earlier: Local, Site, Domain, Organizational Unit. Each policy overwrites the previous policy if conflicting parameters are encountered.

EXERCISE 9.02

AUTOMATIC UPDATE CLIENT CONFIGURATION

In this exercise, we will configure a domain Group Policy to install the client update software to Windows 2000 and Windows XP clients on our network. Then, we will configure clients to download and install updates at 3 A.M. without prompting users for any input whatsoever.

1. From a domain controller on your network, download the WUAU22.msi file from Microsoft's Web site. Open **Active Directory Users and Computers** to begin configuring the installation group policy. **Start | Programs | Administrative Tools | Active Directory Users and Computers**.

2. In the left pane of the MMC, right-click your domain name and select **Properties**.

3. From the domain properties dialog box, select the **Group Policy** tab as shown in Figure 9.25.

Figure 9.25 Opening the Group Policy Settings for the Domain

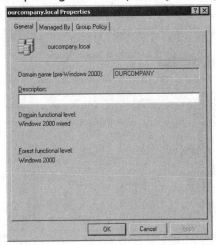

4. From the **Group Policy** tab, click **New** and type **Install AU**, and press **Enter** as shown in Figure 9.26.

Figure 9.26 Creating an Install GPO

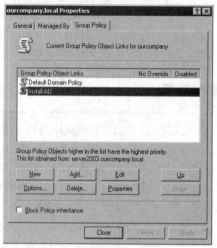

5. Click **Edit** to open the Group Policy Object Editor. Navigate to **Computer Configuration | Software Settings | Software Installation**.

6. In the right pane of the MMC, right-click in the white space and select **New | Package**.

7. Navigate to the WUAU22.msi file that you downloaded in the beginning of this exercise and select the file as shown in Figure 9.27.

Figure 9.27 Adding the WUAU22.msi file to the Group Policy

8. Click **Open** to continue. You will be prompted to **Assign** the package or for **Advanced** options as shown in Figure 9.28. Click **OK**.

Figure 9.28 Assigning the Package

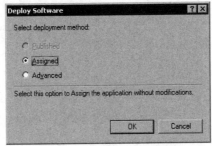

9. The package will be processed for distribution and the right pane of the MMC should update to reflect the addition of the new package as shown in Figure 9.29.

Figure 9.29 WUAU22.msi Package Ready for Assignment

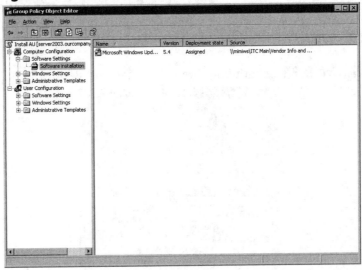

10. The software is configured for install. Now we will configure the Automatic Update client configuration using the same policy. Navigate to **Computer Configuration | Administrative Templates | Windows Components | Windows Update** as shown in Figure 9.30.

Figure 9.30 The Group Policy Windows Update Client Configuration

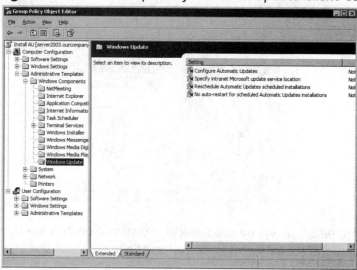

11. Double-click **Configure Automatic Updates** in the right pane of the MMC. Click **Enable**, and under **Configure automatic updating**, select **4 – Auto download and schedule the install** as shown in Figure 9.31. Click **OK**.

Figure 9.31 Scheduling Client Updates and Behavior

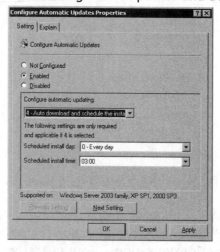

12. Double-click **Specify intranet Microsoft update service location** to configure the SUS server information for the clients. Click **Enable** and enter your SUS server URL and SUS statistics server URL as shown in Figure 9.32.

Figure 9.32 Specifying Service Locations

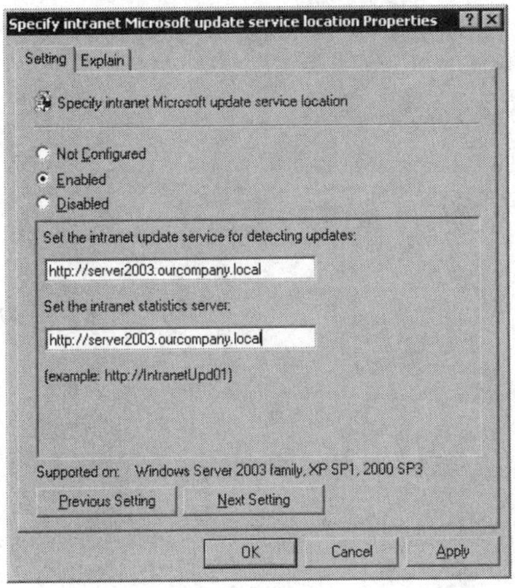

13. Click **OK** to continue with the configuration. In the right pane of the MMC, double-click **Reschedule Automatic Updates scheduled installations**. Click **Enable** and enter **15** for the **Wait after system startup(minutes)** as shown in Figure 9.33.

Figure 9.33 Entering the Rescheduled Automatic Update Setting

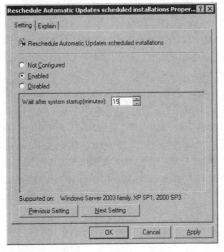

14. Click **OK** to continue. Double-click **No auto-restart for scheduled Automatic Updates installations** and click **Enabled** followed by **OK** as shown in Figure 9.34. If this is not configured, Automatic Update will inform any logged on user that the system will restart in five minutes. With this enabled, the user will be notified that the computer must be restarted, but the decision to restart is left up to the user.

Figure 9.34 Configuring No Auto-restart

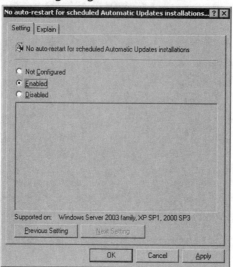

15. Click **OK** to return to the MMC, then close the MMC to return to the **Group Policy** tab for the domain. Click **Close** to close the **Group Policy** dialog box. From a command prompt, **Start | Run**, type **cmd**, and click **OK**. Type **gpupdate** and press **Enter** to update the group policy settings for the domain.

16. The policy is now configured. When client systems start up, they will download and install the Automatic Update client software from the domain controller. Clients will be configured to check for updates at 3 A.M. each morning. Updates will be installed at that time and the system rebooted, if the system is available at that time. If the system is off, 15 minutes after startup the system will check for updates. Next, updates will be downloaded and installed. If the update requires a reboot, and the user is logged on, the user will be prompted with a dialog box informing the user that the system must be rebooted. The **reboot now** option will have **No** grayed out but **Yes** will be available. When the user is ready, he or she can select **Yes** to reboot the system.

Supporting Legacy Clients

Legacy clients (running operating systems that predate Windows 2000) do not work with Group Policy. To take advantage of software update capabilities for Windows 98 and Windows 98SE systems, you will have to modify the registry. In a non–Active Directory environment (workgroup or NT 4.0 domain), there are several ways to configure registry keys for the SUS client settings. The most common ways to set the registry keys in a non-Active Directory environment are:

- Manually editing the registry using regedit.exe

- Centrally deploying these registry key changes using Windows NT 4.0 System Policy

TEST DAY TIP

Microsoft does not always focus on the latest and greatest features for their exams. Instead, they focus on real world situations. Many Windows Server 2003 administrators will also have to support older operating systems or domains. Windows NT 4.0 is not going to just disappear from the network landscape overnight, so you should make sure that you review the registry modification instructions from this portion of the chapter before the exam because this is the only real option for non-Active Directory domains.

First, update the Critical Update Notification (CUN) system to accommodate the new Automatic Update system. The option to update using self-update from the STPP version CUN involves editing the registry in the following manner:

1. Open the Registry Editor. Click **Start | Run** and type **regedit.exe**. Press **OK**.

2. Navigate to **HKEY_LOCAL_MACHINE\SOFTWARE\Microsoft\ Windows\CurrentVersion\WindowsUpdate\Critical Update**.

3. Create **SelfUpdServer** value under this key as **REG_SZ.."SelfUpdServer" ="http://<YourServer>/SelfUpdate/CUN5_4"**.

4. Navigate to **HKEY_LOCAL_MACHINE\SOFTWARE\Microsoft\ Windows\CurrentVersion\WindowsUpdate\Critical Update\Critical Update SelfUpdate**.

Create the **SelfUpdServer** value under this key as **REG_SZ. "SelfUpdServer"=** where *<YourServer>* is the name of the SUS server on your network.

After the Critical Update software has been upgraded, it is time to configure the software. Let's take a look at one of the methods used to update the registry on older client systems. To modify the Registry with regedit.exe, add the following settings to the Registry at this location: **HKEY_LOCAL_MACHINE\Software\Policies\ Microsoft\Windows\WindowsUpdate\AU**

- **RescheduleWaitTime**
  - Range: n; where n = time in minutes (1 through 60)
  - Registry Value Type: REG_DWORD

- **NoAutoRebootWithLoggedOnUsers**
  - Set this to 1 if you want the logged on users to choose whether or not to reboot their systems
  - Registry Value Type: REG_DWORD

- **NoAutoUpdate**
  - Range = 0 | 1. 0 = Automatic Updates is enabled (default), 1 = Automatic Updates is disabled
  - Registry Value Type: REG_DWORD

- **AUOptions**
  - Range = 2 | 3 | 4. 2 = notify of download and installation, 3 = automatically download and notify of installation, and 4 = automatic download and scheduled installation. All options notify the local administrator.
  - Registry Value Type: REG_DWORD

- **ScheduledInstallDay**
  - Range = 0 | 1 | 2 | 3 | 4 | 5 | 6 | 7. 0 = Every day; 1 through 7 = the days of the week from Sunday (1) to Saturday (7)
  - Registry Value Type: REG_DWORD

- **ScheduledInstallTime**
  - Range = n; where n = the time of day in 24-hour format (0 through 23)
  - Registry Value Type: REG_DWORD

- **UseWUServer**
  - Set this to 1 to enable Automatic Updates to use the server running Software Update Services as specified in WUServer
  - Registry Value Type: REG_DWORD

Now, in **HKEY_LOCAL_MACHINE\Software\Policies\Microsoft\Windows\ WindowsUpdate** add the following registry entries:

- **WUServer**
  - Sets the SUS server by HTTP name
  - Registry Value Type: REG_SZ

- **WUStatusServer**
  - Sets the SUS statistics server by HTTP name
  - Registry Value Type: REG_SZ

Testing Software Updates

Software updates were designed to fix security problems or to improve the performance or functionality of your network systems. With the enormous amount of software available for current Windows operating systems and with the massive amount of different types of hardware available, it is impossible from a practical standpoint to test every scenario in which a software update might be applied. Some software updates can have adverse affects on your client system performance or operating capabilities. It is considered best practice to try to simulate your network environment as accurately as possible in a test lab environment in an effort to pre-test software updates before deploying them to your production environment.

Testing should occur in a lab environment that models your production network. If possible, you should have at least two instances of each type of hardware used in your environment. This hardware should be configured with the same software and settings that typical clients with this type of system would have. You should have a server configured as a test SUS server for the network and you should have a sufficient number of servers set up in the lab to model the production network. As new updates become available, using the SUS test server, you should approve updates individually and test them against your lab systems to verify proper operation. Try to put the software through its paces, making sure that the update that was applied has not adversely affected the system. Maintain a list of tested updates, documenting any changes that you have observed as a result of the update. Now, once the client test systems seem to be functioning properly, you should approve the tested software updates on your production SUS server.

If, for some reason, an update does have adverse affects on certain systems in the test environment, do not deploy the update until a workaround has been determined. You should look on Microsoft's TechNet site to attempt to find solutions to the problems that the update is causing. Microsoft's TechNet site is located at www.microsoft.com/technet. This site maintains the Microsoft Knowledge Base, a database of known problems with Microsoft products and possible solutions. You might have to contact the hardware or software vendor to resolve the problem. It is possible that you may have to go through Microsoft's technical support to resolve the issues as well.

 EXAM WARNING

Not every environment will benefit from a full-fledged SUS test lab but it is a concept you should understand. Centralized deployment of software and configurations in a large environment can be a nightmare if applied incorrectly or in situations where the fix breaks something else. Review your basic networking topics to help prepare for this portion of the exam.

The Value of Testing

Nearly every company today is trying to save money in every way they can. Many companies are quick to throw out the idea of testing or keeping a lab to pretest software and configurations. There are many creative ways to provide your company with a test environment without buying several extra computers.

In an ideal world, you would test software on the same type of hardware used in your production environment. If that is not an option in your network, several utilities exist to provide you with virtual machines. In lieu of extra machines, invest in software-based solutions (or utilize freely available solutions) to test new updates with your software configurations. It will not provide you with the ideal solution, but it is still better than breaking production machines with the latest fix.

One way to set up elaborate testing scenarios without investing in hardware for dozens of machines is to use VMWare (www.vmware.com) to create virtual machines for your lab environment. This software allows you to run multiple machines, running different operating systems, on the same physical piece of hardware. The virtual machines can run simultaneously and interact with one another and with other physical and virtual machines on the network.

Head of the Class…

Summary of Exam Objectives

Security is a hot topic in IT today. With all of the concern about security, it is important to keep systems up-to-date with the latest security patches and hotfixes. It is also important that corporate security policies are consistently applied to all systems in your environment. This chapter focuses on the tools available to provide consistent security policy application and to keep systems up-to-date on a consistent basis as well.

The Security Configuration and Analysis management console provides a utility for security policy template creation, comparative analysis, and implementation. The utility provides several preconfigured templates to consistently apply security settings for various scenarios. You can import security templates to compare against current machine configurations and to apply new settings using the imported templates. Likewise, you can export current configuration settings to apply to other machines on your network.

Security templates are applied in the following ways: through local settings, to sites through the Active Directory Sites and Services management console, to Active Directory domains using Active Directory Users and Computers, and to Organizational Units (OUs) using Active Directory Users and Computers.

A command line utility is also available to handle security configuration and analysis duties. The secedit.exe command has several switches available that allow you to import, export, compare, and implement security policies via security template files.

After security configurations have been implemented, the dynamic nature of security requires frequent updates to the existing system. The Software Update Service provides centralized control over client software updates. You control when and if client updates are downloaded to the centralized SUS server. You also control which updates will be deployed to clients and also the client behavior for the download, installation, and (if necessary) reboot.

The SUS server uses Web-based administration and distribution of the updates. The administrator sets the synchronization schedule for the SUS server or selects to synchronize the server manually. After the server has been synchronized, the catalog is updated with the latest available software. The administrator selects which software to approve for distribution and, based on client configuration, the clients download the updates during their next scheduled update cycle. Updates typically are downloaded and installed transparently to the user. When updates have been downloaded and installed, the client can be configured to reboot if no users are logged on.

Exam Objectives Fast Track

Security Templates

- ☑ The use of security templates ensures consistent security settings throughout the enterprise.

- ☑ The Security Configuration and Analysis tool provides a mechanism for analyzing existing configurations and comparing them to a preconfigured template.

☑ Several preconfigured templates are available for Windows Server 2003. These include:

- Default security (Setup security.inf)

- Compatible (Compatws.inf)

- Secure (Secure★.inf)

- Highly Secure (hisec★.inf)

- System root security (Rootsec.inf)

- No Terminal Server user SID (Notssid.inf)

Software Updates

☑ SUS uses an IIS Web server to provide intranet-based, centralized control of client updates.

☑ There are two components to the SUS server configuration:

- The metadata stored in a file named aucatalog.cab. This file stores details about the packages and package availability.

- The actual package file that updates your systems.

☑ SUS client software is available through the following methods:

- Install Automatic Updates client using the MSI install package. (WUAU22.msi) This is the preferred method.

- Self-update from the STPP version Critical Update Notification (CUN).

- Install Windows 2000 Service Pack 3 (SP3).

- Install Windows XP SP1.

- Install Windows Server 2003.

☑ The following methods can be used for configuring SUS clients:

- Group Policy

- Windows NT 4.0 System Policy

- Edit Registry

Exam Objectives
Frequently Asked Questions

The following Frequently Asked Questions, answered by the authors of this book, are designed to both measure your understanding of the Exam Objectives presented in this chapter, and to assist you with real-life implementation of these concepts. You will also gain access to thousands of other FAQs at ITFAQnet.com.

Q: I am responsible for tightening security on our network. The network consists of Windows 98, Windows NT 4.0, Windows 2000, Windows XP, and Windows Server 2003 systems. Is it possible to apply security templates throughout this network to provide consistent security settings?

A: Security templates are available for Windows NT 4.0 systems with Service Pack 4 (SP4) or greater installed through the use of the Security Configuration Manager (SCM). Windows 2000, Windows XP, and Windows Server 2003 come with the Security Configuration and Analysis snap-in for the MMC preinstalled with the operating system. Windows 98 comes with capabilities to apply system policies through the system policy editor (poledit.exe); however, there are no provisions for security templates, like the ones used in this chapter, for Windows 98.

Q: Several security policy changes have been implemented on our domain controller. We are beginning to experience some adverse, unwanted affects from some of the settings. Is it possible to undo security settings to restore the machine to its original condition?

A: The DC security.inf template is available to undo security template policy settings and it is recommended that this template be applied before applying other templates to ensure consistent policy results.

Q: The corporate security officer sent a new template to me to apply to the servers in our office. How should I apply this template?

A: If security templates have been applied in the past or modifications to the standard security settings have been made in the past, it is a good idea to analyze the current configuration to compare it against the new template supplied by your corporate office. This allows you to see any discrepancies between the current configuration and the update to be applied. If no previous security configurations have been applied, apply the Setup secure*.inf security template first to configure the machine with a no-configuration configuration, and then apply the new security template.

Q: Is there a way to update Windows 98 systems with a LAN-based SUS server?

A: No. Windows 98 is not supported as a SUS client. Only Windows 2000 and newer clients will work with SUS.

Q: Not all of the clients in our Windows XP/Windows Server 2003 network are configured with the latest service packs and we do not currently have a consistent policy for Automatic Update. How can we apply a consistent policy to all of the clients on the network?

A: Use the Microsoft IntelliMirror capabilities of Windows Server 2003 to deploy the Automatic Update client software using the Automatic Update MSI package (WUAU22.msi). Configure Group Policy software installation (Computer Configuration) and apply it to the client systems through the domain or organizational unit (OU) containing the client systems.

Self Test

A Quick Answer Key follows the Self Test questions. For complete questions, answers, and explanations to the Self Test questions in this chapter as well as the other chapters in this book, see the Self Test Appendix.

Security Templates

1 . A junior administrator has modified the permissions on the c: drive of your file server. The operating system is installed on the C: drive and the data is stored on the D: drive. What is the simplest way to restore the default permissions for the file server?

A. Apply the securews.inf security template to the file server to apply the proper permissions.

B. Apply the Setup secure.inf security template to the file server to apply the proper permissions.

C. Apply the rootsec.inf security template to the file server to apply the proper permissions.

D. Apply the DC secure.inf security template to the file server to apply the proper permissions.

2. You upgrade three of the file servers on your network from Windows NT 4.0 Server to Windows Server 2003. Some applications originally used with Windows NT 4.0 are no longer functioning properly. When you are logged in with a local administrator account, the applications perform correctly. Corporate security policy does not allow standard users to have local administrator or power user membership on file servers. How can you provide sufficient privileges to the file servers while consistently providing the security required for the upgraded servers?

A. Apply the securews.inf security template to the file servers to adjust the security to the proper levels.

B. Apply the DC secure.inf security template to the file servers to adjust the security to the proper levels.

C. Apply the Setup secure.inf security template to the file servers to adjust the security to the proper levels.

D. Apply the compatws.inf security template to the file servers to adjust the security to the proper levels.

3. Your corporate network has several Windows 2000 file servers that will be upgraded to Windows Server 2003. You want to ensure that the upgraded servers' configurations are consistent with the new Windows Server 2003 servers that you are deploying. How can you ensure a consistent set of configurations for the Windows Server 2003 file servers?

A. Apply the setup security.inf security template to all upgraded servers to ensure consistency.

B. Apply the securews.inf security template to all upgraded servers to ensure consistency.

C. Apply the DC secure.inf security template to all upgraded servers to ensure consistency.

D. Apply the rootsec.inf security template to all upgraded servers to ensure consistency.

4. You administer systems in a satellite office for your multinational corporation. After analyzing one of your server's configurations against a new security template that you have received, you see that several question marks appear in the analysis. What is causing this?

A. The computer's configuration is different from the configurations specified in the new template file.

B. The computer's configuration has changed since the last configuration was applied.

C. The security template file has incorrect NTFS settings to perform the analysis.

D. You do not have sufficient permissions to compare the configurations in the areas indicated with question marks.

5. You want to increase security on your network. You analyze your new template against the current configuration as seen in Figure 9.35. Which configurations should you modify in the new template before applying the new template file?

Figure 9.35 Analysis Using New Security Template

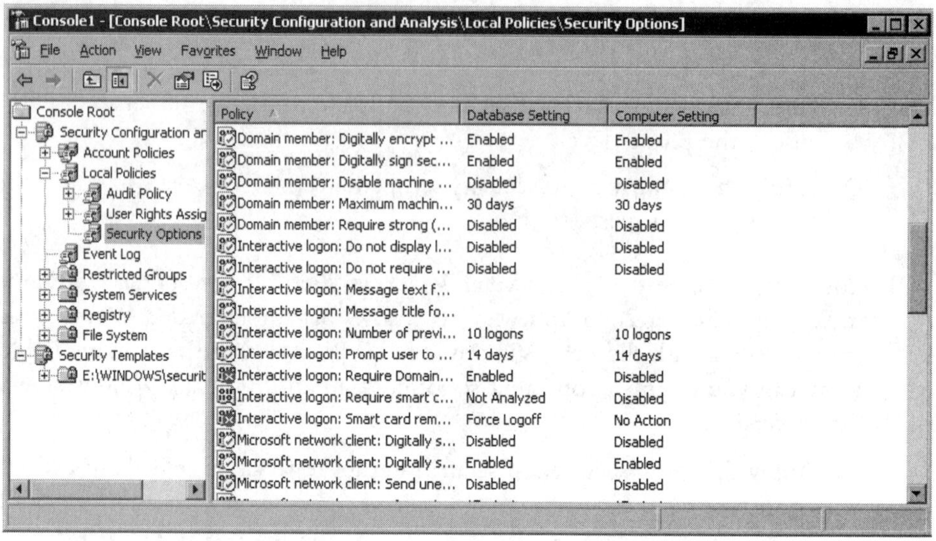

A. Change the **Interactive logon: Require Domain Controller authentication to unlock workstation** to **disabled**.

B. Based on the differences shown in Figure 9.35, you can apply the template as is, and it will not weaken the security in the areas shown.

C. Change the **Interactive logon: Smart card removal behavior** setting to **No Action**.

D. Change the **Interactive logon: Do not require CTRL + ALT + DEL** to **Enabled**.

6. You apply a new security setting to your domain using Group Policy. When you test the configuration, it has not been applied. What could be causing this?

A. A conflicting policy for the OU containing the machine you are testing has over-written the domain configuration that you created.

B. A conflicting policy for the site containing the machine you are testing has over-written the domain configuration that you created.

C. A conflicting local security policy for the machine you are testing has overwritten the domain configuration that you created.

D. A conflicting policy for the forest containing the machine you are testing has overwritten the domain configuration that you created.

7. You modify the domain security policy in the default domain group policy. There are no other policies configured for your network at this time. You implemented the policy about 15 minutes ago. The policy does not seem to be working. How can you make sure the policy is being applied with no service disruption?

    A. Reboot the domain controller that the policy was applied to.

    B. Use **secedit /refreshpolicy** to force a policy refresh instead of waiting for the policy interval to complete.

    C. Do nothing—you have to wait for the policy refresh interval to pass.

    D. Use the **gpupdate** command to force a policy refresh instead of waiting for the policy interval to complete.

8. A security audit has determined that one of your Active Directory sites should implement stronger security by increasing the minimum password length required. You implement the policy for the site through Active Directory Sites and Services but the policy does not seem to be taking affect. What is causing this policy to fail?

    A. Password and account related policies have to be applied to the domain, not to the site.

    B. You have to use the **gpupdate** command to force a policy refresh instead of waiting for the policy interval to complete.

    C. A local policy might be overwriting the new policy.

    D. Active Directory Sites and Services does not support security policies.

Software Updates

9. Your network consists of Windows XP, Windows 2000, and Windows Server 2003 systems. You implement a Group Policy to deploy and configure the Automatic Client Update software. Later in the day, some users report that the Windows Update information is no longer displayed on their task bars even though they did not go through the procedure of installing updates that were displayed there earlier in the day. What is causing this?

    A. The users reporting problems are not logging on to the domain.

    B. Check network connectivity. The users are not connecting to the SUS server.

    C. Restart the SUS service on the server—it is not responding to the client requests.

    D. This is the expected result from applying the Automatic Client Update configurations. Standard users do not have capabilities to modify the Automatic Update Client.

10. Your network consists of Windows XP, Windows 2000, and Windows Server 2003 systems. You implement a Group Policy to deploy and configure the Automatic Client Update software. The next day, some users report that a Windows Update information box is displayed on their systems, informing them that they must reboot now. The only option is to click **Yes**, because the **No** prompt is grayed out. What should the users do?

    A. Complete their current tasks and click **Yes** when it is convenient for them to reboot.

    B. Click **Yes** now, and all of their work will automatically be saved.

    C. Click **Yes** now, and all work will be lost.

    D. Click **Yes** now, and the system will not reboot until they have completed their current tasks.

11. Several users are logged on to one of the Terminal Servers on your network. A message is displayed that says the server has installed updates and must reboot. The **Yes** and **No** prompts are grayed out. What should the users do in this scenario?

    A. Open the task manager and end the rundll32.exe process.

    B. Close the Terminal Server window immediately.

    C. Complete their existing tasks on the Terminal Server and log off.

    D. From the **Start** button, select to shut down and restart the server.

12. Your network consists of Windows 98, Windows NT 4.0, and Windows Server 2003 computers. Depending on the technical level of the user, not all systems are kept up-to-date with security patches and hotfixes. With the least amount of administration and the lowest cost possible, what procedure should be used to ensure that timely, consistent updates are applied to all clients on your network?

    A. Upgrade all systems to Windows 2000 Professional or Windows XP Professional. Configure a Group Policy to keep systems up-to-date with an internal SUS server.

    B. Upgrade the NT 4.0 systems to Windows 2000 Professional or Windows XP Professional. Upgrade the critical update notification service on Windows 98 systems using the registry editor. Configure the Windows 98 clients using the Registry Editor. Configure a Group Policy to keep the Windows 2000, Windows XP, and Windows Server 2003 systems up-to-date with an internal SUS server.

    C. Upgrade the Windows 98 systems to Windows 2000 Professional or Windows XP Professional. Upgrade the critical update notification service on Windows NT 4.0 systems using the Registry Editor. Configure the Windows NT 4.0 clients using the Registry Editor. Configure a Group Policy to keep the Windows 2000, Windows XP, and Windows Server 2003 systems up-to-date with an internal SUS server.

    D. Install the Automatic Update Client MSI file to all systems through a logon script. Configure a Group Policy to keep systems up-to-date with an internal SUS server.

13. Your network consists of Windows Server 2003 server, Windows XP Professional, and Windows 98 clients. You have installed and configured an SUS server for your local network. You use a Group Policy to deploy the Automatic Update client software to the clients and you use Group Policy settings to configure the clients. Several days later, you notice that the Windows 98 systems are not being updated with the latest security patches and hot fixes. What is causing this problem?

A. Use the **gpupdate** command to force an update for the Group Policy refresh interval.

B. Use **secedit /refreshpolicy** to force an update for the Group Policy refresh interval.

C. Your Windows 98 clients use a different Group Policy setting from the other clients on the network. Create an OU for the Windows 98 clients and use a Group Policy to install and configure the Automatic Update client for these systems.

D. Your Windows 98 clients do not respond to Group Policy settings. You will have to upgrade the Windows 98 clients to Windows 2000 Professional or Windows XP Professional.

14. You approve several updates on your test environment SUS server. After testing, you decide to put the updates into production. How will you accomplish this?

A. Select **Production Update** under the set options page to update the production server with the changes.

B. Use the **Produpdate** script to update the production server with the changes.

C. Make sure the production server has synchronized. Manually approve the tested updates for the production SUS server.

D. Use the **gpupdate** command to force an update for the SUS server policies.

15. You are responsible for the SUS infrastructure deployment in your organization. Based on recommended best practice, you inform your manager that a test environment is necessary for software update testing. How many computers will be needed to accomplish this?

A. The environment should be a one-to-one correlation between the test lab and the production environment.

B. One or two systems for each type of client hardware used in your network as well as one or two systems representative of the software environment used in your network.

C. One SUS server and a terminal server to simulate the client environments.

D. One or two systems for each type of client hardware used in your network as well as one or two systems representative of the software environment used in your network. An SUS server and possibly servers to represent some of the other servers on your network.

Self Test Quick Answer Key

For complete questions, answers, and epxlanations to the Self Test questions in this chapter as well as the other chapters in this book, see the Self Test Appendix.

1.	**C**		9.	**D**
2.	**D**		10.	**A**
3.	**A**		11.	**C**
4.	**D**		12.	**A**
5.	**B**		13.	**D**
6.	**A**		14.	**C**
7.	**D**		15.	**D**
8.	**A**			

Chapter 10

MCSA/MCSE 70-254

Monitoring and Troubleshooting Network Activity

Exam Objectives in this Chapter:

3.3   Troubleshoot network protocol security. Tools might include the IP Security Monitor MMC snap-in, Event Viewer, and Network Monitor.

5.1   Monitor network traffic. Tools might include Network Monitor and System Monitor.

5.2   Troubleshoot connectivity to the Internet.

3.2   Monitor network protocol security. Tools might include the IP Security Monitor MMC snap-in and Kerberos support tools.

3.3   Troubleshoot network protocol security. Tools might include the IP Security Monitor MMC snap-in, Event Viewer, and Network Monitor.

☑   Summary of Exam Objectives

☑   Exam Objectives Fast Track

☑   Exam Objectives Frequently Asked Questions

☑   Self Test

☑   Self Test Quick Answer Key

Introduction

Managing a network involves a great deal of planning, design, and implementation. Even the most efficient networks require analysis and monitoring to validate your network design. Once your network is implemented, you will need to identify baselines for network activity, and be prepared to recognize abnormal behavior, and diagnose unexpected changes and troubleshoot problems with your network. Understanding your network will also provide you with the information necessary to plan for growth by examining trends and identifying the effects of adding hosts.

As challenging as it is to manage a regular local area network (LAN), we are expanding our scope of responsibility by allowing access to the Internet, and allowing our employees to access our networks from their homes, other businesses, and even hotels and coffee houses. With that perspective in mind, you spent all that time and effort to create a secure and reliable environment, and now you have clients transmitting company data from a network about which you know nothing. That fact alone makes it imperative that you implement strong security policies to protect loss of corporate data, and understand how to support and monitor the traffic in and out of your LAN from the Internet. It also places a burden on you to provide highly available and fast Internet access to support the telecommuters and any other remote clients that use the Internet to access the corporate LAN.

Due to the ever growing complexity with network design, and the large quantity of data flow on today's networks, we must understand the traffic and the tools that we use to capture and analyze that traffic. One of the most valuable tools we have at our disposal is Network Monitor. In this chapter, you will become familiar with network monitor and how to use Network Monitor to view your network traffic and identify information about the network traffic. Network Monitor is a great tool to help understand and troubleshoot connectivity problems.

We will discuss the identification and resolution for Internet connectivity problems. We will focus on Network Address Translation (NAT), name resolution, and IP addressing issues. In addition to troubleshooting and monitoring regular network traffic, we will also focus on monitoring network traffic that is encrypted. IP Security (IPSec) is based on open standards that are used to provide reliable transmission of encrypted data and authentication of data over IP. We will discuss how to use IPSec Security Monitor console to monitor and troubleshoot IPSec connections on your network.

Using Network Monitor

As a network administrator, you are tasked with understanding your network. One of the primary functions of the network is the reliable delivery of data. In addition to reliability, you must provide security and ensure that the data is accessible by those who are intended to receive it. Network Monitor provides network administrators with a window to the information being delivered over the network.

Network Monitor captures the frames of data as they are delivered over the wire, time stamps them, and provides statistical data about those frames. After you have captured the frames of data, Network Monitor will decode the headers and provide an easy-to-read summary of the type of packet, the source, the destination, and if the data is not encrypted, the data in the packet as well. In this section we will install Network Monitor. After we install Network Monitor, we explain the general layout of the main console, and then look at some captured frames. We teach you how to filter captured data by setting capture filters and capture triggers, and then view more concise data using display filters.

Installing Network Monitor

There are two versions of Network Monitor. The full featured version ships with both Microsoft Systems Management Server (SMS). The limited version is included with the operating system, but is not installed in Windows Server 2003 by default. Installing Network Monitor is actually a simple task—it is installed as a Windows Component via **Add/Remove Programs**.

In Exercise 10.01, we will install Network Monitor. During the installation, the driver for Network Monitor is automatically installed.

EXERCISE 10.01

INSTALLING NETWORK MONITOR

In this exercise, we will install the operating system component version of Network Monitor. You will need the Windows Server 2003 CD-ROM during the installation. It will be helpful to have other machines available to you after the exercise is complete to see network traffic and perform the captures.

1. Navigate to **Control Panel | Add/Remove Programs**. The Add or Remove programs dialog is displayed.

2. Select **Add/Remove Windows Components** from the shortcut bar.

3. The **Windows Components Wizard** is displayed (see Figure 10.1).

Figure 10.1 Windows Components Wizard

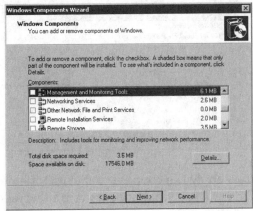

4. Select the item **Management and Monitoring Tools** as shown in Figure 10.1, and click the **Details** button.

5. The Management and Monitoring Tools dialog is shown as in Figure 10.2. Click the check box next to **Network Monitor Tools** and click **OK**.

Figure 10.2 Management and Monitoring Tools

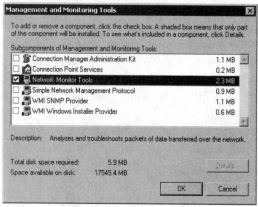

6. The **Windows Components Wizard** is displayed again (see Figure 10.3), this time with the check box next to **Management and Monitoring Tools selected** and **gray**.

Figure 10.3 Windows Components Wizard after Selecting the Network Monitoring Subcomponent

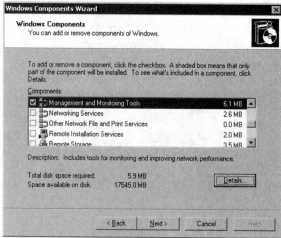

7. Click **Next** to apply the changes and install the necessary software components. You will see what appears to be several components that you

did not choose appear in the **Status** messages seen above the progress bar in Figure 10.4. This is part of a routine and there is no need for alarm. Only the necessary components for Network Monitor will be installed.

Figure 10.4 Configuring Components

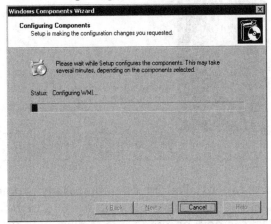

8. During the installation process, if the installation files for Windows Server 2003 are not accessible on the machine or existing network connections, then you will be prompted for the Windows Server 2003 setup disk as shown in Figure 10.5. If the installation files are located on the hard disk or a network share, you should still click **OK** and then you'll be able to enter the path on the next screen.

Figure 10.5 Insert Disk

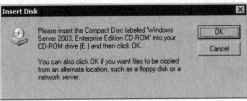

9. When the installation is complete, you will see the **Completing the Windows Components Wizard** message (see Figure 10.6). Click **Finish**.

Figure 10.6 Windows Components Wizard—Completing the Windows Components Wizard

In this exercise, we installed the operating system component version of Network Monitor. Now it is possible to capture and view frames of data from your network. We can now become more familiar with using Network Monitor and understand how to use it effectively.

Let's take a look at how to capture frames. Click **Start | Administrative Tools | Network Monitor**. The first time you launch Network Monitor, you will see a message informing you that you must select a network to monitor, or Network Monitor will select one for you, as shown in Figure 10.7.

Figure 10.7 Microsoft Network Monitor Console

Figures 10.8 and 10.9 show the dialog that you will use to select the network on which you will monitor traffic using this instance of Network Monitor. If you are capturing data from multiple LANS simultaneously, you must install and configure one adapter for each network and start a unique instance of Network Monitor for each adapter. You must select the network for each instance of Network Monitor by selecting **Capture | Networks** and selecting the appropriate network. The network for newly installed adapters will not be available until you restart Network Monitor.

Figure 10.8 Select a Network

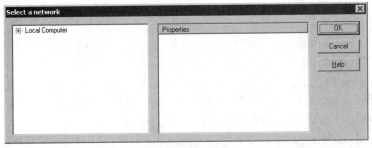

Figure 10.9 Select a Network with Multiple Adapters

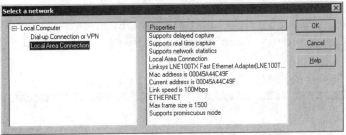

After you have selected a network, you will see the **Network Monitor Capture window** that is shown in Figure 10.10.

Figure 10.10 Network Monitor Console

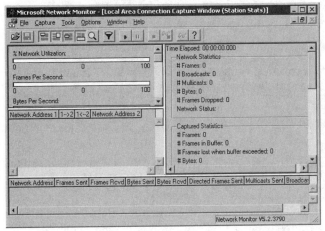

There are four panes in the Capture window:

- **Graph pane** is in the upper left corner and displays a graphical representation of the current total capture statistics from the collected capture data. See the Network Monitor help file for an explanation of each counter in this pane.

■ **Session Statistic pane** is located in the left center of the console and displays the current session statistics that constitute data sent to or from your computer. It displays the session's participants and the amount of data exchanged in either direction. See the Network Monitor help file for an explanation of each counter in this pane.

■ **Station Statistics pane** is the bottom-most pane that shows your computer's network activity. See the Network Monitor help file for an explanation of each counter in this pane.

■ **Total Statistics pane** is located in the upper right corner of the console. The Total Statistics pane shows the network traffic summaries for the inbound and outbound traffic on your computer.

Begin your first capture by selecting **Capture | Start** or clicking **Play** on the tool bar. You will begin to see data transmissions immediately, as shown in Figure 10.11.

Figure 10.11 Network Monitor Console Capturing Data

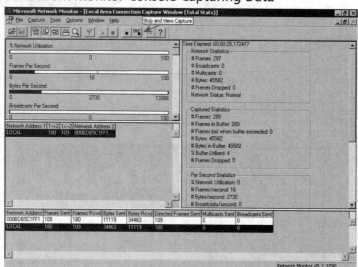

Click the **Stop and View Capture** icon (with the glasses and the square) shown in Figure 10.11, or **Capture | Stop** and **View** or **Shift+F11** to view the captured frames.

The window shown in Figure 10.12 is called the **Frame Viewer** window. Currently it is displaying a full window that contains the **Summary Pane**, which contains frames and their statistics to analyze. Three panes are part of the Frame Viewer window (see Figure 10.13):

Figure 10.12 Network Monitor Frame Viewer Window Summary Data

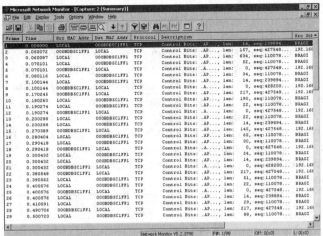

- **Summary Pane** shows the list of captured frames. You can filter this list to isolate the frames that you want to analyze. If you double-click an item in the list, the other two panes are visible.

- **Detail Pane** shows the detail of the frame that is currently selected in the Summary Pane, which now occupies only a third of the Frame Viewer window. This hierarchical representation is very informative, and can provide a valuable insight as to how you approach design and implementation for your network.

- **Hexadecimal Pane** is broken down into two views. The first view is the actual data in hexadecimal form that makes up the frame, and the second section is the alphanumeric ASCII representation of that frame.

Figure 10.13 Network Monitor Frame Viewer Window with All Panes Visible

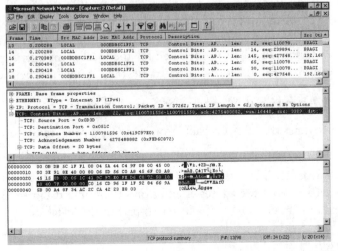

TEST DAY TIP

There are two different versions of Network Monitor. The one that ships with the Windows Server 2003 operating system allows you to analyze data destined for your machine and leaving your machine. The fully functional version of Network Monitor ships with Systems Management Server (SMS), and is licensed only with the SMS product. The SMS version can capture packets traveling on the network that are not sent from or to the machine on which it is installed (as long as the network adapter is capable of operating in "promiscuous" mode). Additional limitations of the operating system version are that it cannot use the features on the Tools Menu—Find Routers and Resolve Addresses From Name. In order for the SMS edition of Network Monitor to monitor traffic on a computer, you must install the Network Monitor driver.

Basic Configuration

As discussed in Exercise 10.01, there are certain settings that are required to monitor your network. For example, you must select a local network. If you don't set one, then Network Monitor will select your default adapter, which is the first in the network binding order. This may suit your current needs, but you might need to install additional adapters later to monitor multiple networks at the same time.

If you want to monitor more than one network, then you must have the additional adapter installed and configured prior to launching Network Monitor. If you install an adapter while Network Monitor is running, then you will need to restart Network Monitor after you install the adapter in order to select that network. Note, however, that if you want to monitor a specific protocol on the network, it is possible to capture that traffic without installing that protocol.

Network Monitor captures data by frames, which means that each packet contains the source and destination address, the header information, and the data itself. All the frames transmitted on the segment are processed by all the machines on that network. If the destination is not addressed to that adapter, then the frame is dropped. Broadcast frames are captured as well since technically they are destined for the local computer as part of the segment. If the adapter has initiated multicast traffic, then it will also be shown.

Network Monitor Default Settings

There are several settings that are accessible from the Capture menu. Two of the most important are:

- The **Capture | Addresses** menu item, which allows you to define addresses and the metadata about the addresses and stores them in a database. By default, the information about your local adapters is part of this database.

- The **Capture | Buffer settings** item, which allows you to set the Buffer Size in megabytes (MB), and Frame size in bytes. The buffer size determines how much data you can capture at one time before ceasing to gather data. The default setting for buffer size is 1MB. The maximum value for buffer size is 1024MB. Frame size is the setting that allows you to configure the number of bytes to capture from each frame. This is useful when on token ring networks that are particular about frame size. The default frame size is set to Full, which is the maximum size or 65,535 bytes. The list of frame sizes is a list of numbers that are incremented 64 bytes at a time, and the highest number listed is 65,472, even though 65,535 (Full) is the largest frame size. You have the option to type your own custom value in the range of 32 bytes to the maximum value, or you can select the values provided in the list.

The other menu items on the Capture menu are **Filter**, **Networks**, and **Trigger**. **Networks** has been discussed earlier in the chapter; **Filter** and **Trigger** will be discussed in later sections. By default there are no filters or triggers, and the network is the primary adapter on your machine.

 EXAM WARNING

Network Monitor uses parsers that are implemented in Dynamic Link Libraries (DLLs) with entries in the parser.ini file located in the WINDIR\System32\Netmon\ folder. The parser DLLs are in the WINDIR\System32\Netmon\parsers folder. Parsers are used to read and interpret the data in frames, and identify the different components that comprise the frame based on the protocol identified in the frame. You can add custom parsers for proprietary protocols by adding the entry in the parser.ini file with the name of the corresponding DLL, which you will place in the \parsers folder.

Configuring Monitoring Filters

Capture filters allow you to isolate different types of data transmitted to and from your machine on the specified network. You can use an address database to add addresses to your filter and restrict data to capture to those addresses. You can save the filter to a file so that you can use it again, and create standard address filters for your network. Using filters will reduce the buffer usage and save time fishing through an excessive number of frames captured. You can further restrict frames of data by designing a capture filter.

When you select **Capture | Filters** you will be presented with a **Capture Filter** dialog box (see Figure 10.14). You can use this dialog to create a logic base filter using a graphical representation of the Boolean logic you are using to define the filter.

You can filter on a specific protocol by clicking the **SAP/ETYPE=** line of the Capture Filter dialog and clicking **Edit**. For example, if you want to capture only IPv6

Figure 10.14 Capture Filter Dialog

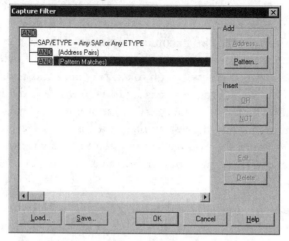

frames on your network, open the **Capture Filter** dialog and edit the **SAP/ETYPE** line, then select and disable all protocols except **IP ETYPE 0x86DD**.

You can add additional filters on addresses for up to four address pairs at the same time. This will capture packets only from that computer in Network Monitor, or you can define the filter to *exclude* that computer and its frames from the capture.

EXAM WARNING

Address pairs include the addresses that you want to capture data between (that is, the source and destination addresses of network communications). INCLUDE and EXCLUDE filters can be applied to multiple rules, but any EXCLUDE settings will always override INCLUDE filters, regardless of the order that the filters are defined in the Capture Filter dialog. Basically, if a frame meets the EXCLUDE criteria, it is discarded immediately, and therefore, no further processing can be done with it. The direction of the arrow indicates the direction of data flow as in Source—>Destination or Destination<—Source. When the arrow is both directions<——>, that indicates traffic in both directions.

The default filter is equivalent to INCLUDE MyComputer<——>ANY. The format is defined in the address expression dialog as **INCLUDE/EXCLUDE, Station1, Direction, Station2**. If you want to eliminate IP traffic originating from your machine outbound to another computer, you can define a filter to **EXCLUDE Machine1(IP)—> Machine2 (IP)**.

You can also specify a pattern to match in the frames you capture. It is possible to use pattern filters to limit the frames to only the ones that contain ASCII or hexadecimal data that you define in the pattern filter. If you have an idea where the data is located in the frame, you can improve the filter performance by defining bytes offsets from the **Start of the Frame**. The filter will ignore the offset number of hex bytes and then start searching for the filter criteria from that point in the frame. You can also specify **From End of Topology Header**. Topology Header is the definition of the network medium, such as Ethernet or Token Ring. If you are using Ethernet or Token Ring, you should specify the **From End of Topology Header** option, since Ethernet and Token Ring have variable size frames in the media access control (MAC) protocol. Pattern filters require the offset to be defined, and it defaults to 0 bytes from the start of the frame.

Configuring Display Filters

Once you have captured data, you can filter the data further by using a display filter. Display filters allow you to focus on the types of frames that you really care about. Display filters apply only to data that you have already captured and have no effect on the actual traffic. You can filter data that you want to analyze in the Frame Viewer window, or if you need only a subset of the information for later, you can apply a filter to restrict the data as you save it to a capture file.

Display filters can include criteria based on source or destination address, and protocol information in the frame. It is possible to use the properties of the protocol and the values the protocol contains in the header to filter data. Protocol properties are the definition of the protocol and its function. If you are inundated with unwanted traffic that is specific to a protocol or a machine address you can simply add a filter to exclude it by modifying the **Protocol==** line in the Display Filter dialog. By applying display filters, you reduce the data in the Capture window to a more manageable size. So if you want to limit the amount of frames that you want to allow Network Monitor to capture, use a capture filter to drop the frames you don't care about instead of adding the frames to the trace. After you have captured the data, use a display filter to hide the unwanted frames that are already captured.

Interpreting a Trace

Network Monitor can be used to capture frames of data transmitted to and from you machine. The captured frames are referred to a *network trace*. As previously discussed, you can identify capture filters that can be used to focus the trace on the types of frames that contain the information you need. For example, you can define capture filters that would enable you to trace IPSec traffic to your machine from a specific client, and view the data to ensure that it is encrypted. Exercise 10.02 will introduce you to performing network traces.

EXERCISE 10.02

PERFORMING A NETWORK TRACE

In this exercise, we are going to perform a network trace. We will begin a trace, identify a specific type of frame, and look at its contents. (Before you begin, you must complete Exercise 10.01.)

1. Open Network Monitor. Click **Start | Administrative Tools | Network Monitor**.

2. Click **Capture | Start Capture** or press **F10** to begin capturing frames.

3. From another computer, **ping** the interface that Network Monitor is capturing frames on for one series.

4. Once the ping is complete, click **Capture | Stop** or press **F11** to stop capturing frames.

5. Examine each of the panes in the Capture window and note the various values.

6. When you are satisfied that you did capture frames on that interface, click **Capture | Display Captured Data** or press **F12**. The **Capture Summary** (see Figure 10.15) appears.

Figure 10.15 Capture Summary

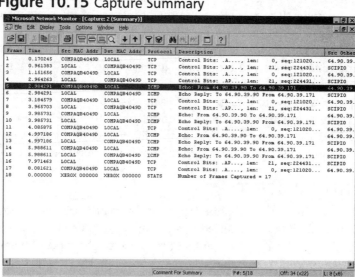

7. Use **Display | Filter** to open the filter dialog (see Figure 10.16).

8. Click **Protocol ==ANY** and then click **Edit Expression**.

9. The **Expression** dialog is displayed. Make sure you are on the **Protocol** tab, and click **Disable All**.

10. Locate **ICMP** in the **Disabled** protocols list and click **Enable** or double-click **ICMP**. The expression dialog should look like Figure 10.17.

Figure 10.16 Filter Dialog

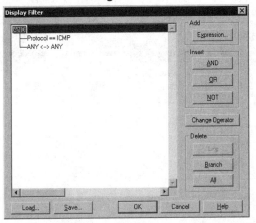

Figure 10.17 Expression Dialog with ICMP Enabled

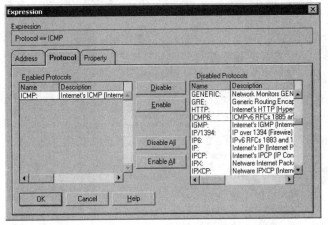

11. Click **OK**.

12. From the **Display filter** dialog, you will see that **Protocol==ANY** is now **Protocol==ICMP**. Click **OK**.

13. You should see only eight lines in the Capture Summary window as shown in Figure 10.18. Each of the lines represents either an inbound frame or an outbound frame for the ping we conducted. One ping cycle is four round trips.

14. Double-click one of the entries where the description begins **"Echo: From..."**. You should see the Capture Detail (middle) pane in Figure 10.19.

Figure 10.18 Capture Summary with ICMP Display Filter Enabled

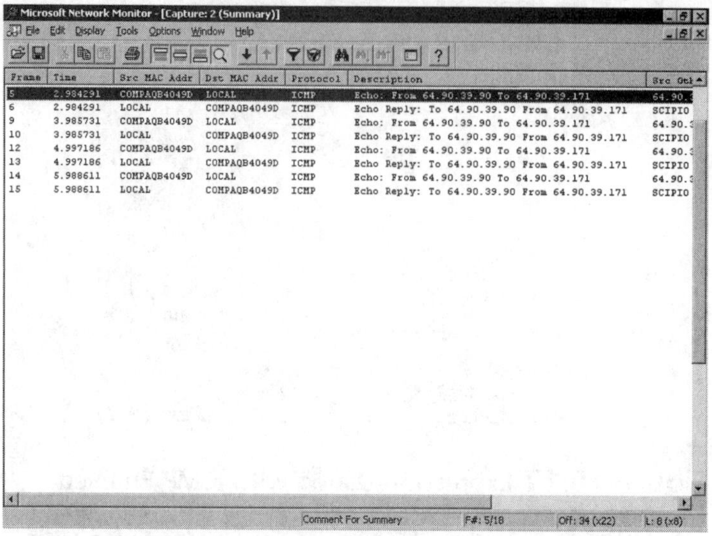

Figure 10.19 Capture Detail of ICMP Ping Traffic

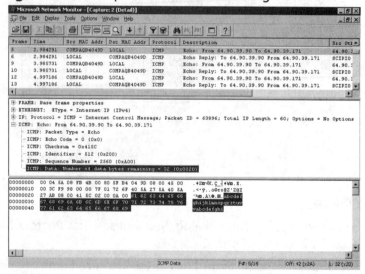

15. Expand the **ICMP** tree in the **Detail** pane and click the last item that begins **ICMP: Data:**.

16. Look in the Hexadecimal (bottom) pane at the highlighted text. Note the contents.

17. In the Capture Summary pane (top), click the next frame in the list. The Description should begin **"Echo Reply: To"**.

18. Expand the **ICMP** tree in the **Detail** pane and click the last item that begins **ICMP: Data: ....**

19. Look at the highlighted text in the bottom pane. Note the contents. They should be identical to the Data contents in the ICMP Echo. This is how ping is validated.

Now that you have analyzed a basic capture, locate a good TCP/IP reference and monitor traffic on your network for short periods of time and practice identifying details about the frames of data on your network. Don't forget to use capture and display filters to minimize the data gathered and then impact on network traffic.

Head of the Class...

Effective Use of Network Monitor

In order to make effective use of a very powerful tool, it is important to understand how to use it properly. It is very helpful to have protocol references for your hardware and operating system. There is no replacement for understanding the protocols and how they fit into your network topology. Here are some tips for how to use Network Monitor and make the best use of resources.

- **Spend some time creating and understanding detailed diagrams of your network topology.** It is critical that you understand the flow of data on your network. Identify points of failure and potential security points you should keep an eye on.

- **You should spend time getting to understand the expected traffic during different points on your network at different times of day.** This is typically what is referred to as a *baseline*. If you have not established a solid baseline, then you won't have anything to compare your current traces to, and it could be more difficult to analyze a problem.

- **Identify your objectives and capture only the amount of data you need.** Capturing more information can use up valuable resources, and makes it more challenging to find the information you need. This can be achieved by using capture filters to capture only the necessary data to help you identify the problem.

- **Use display filters to provide a more specific trace.** Even after providing a specific scope, it may still be necessary to pare down your capture results to help analyze the important data.

- **Special consideration must be made if you are capturing frames on a token ring network.** Because Token Ring networks are fussy about allowing packets that exceed your frame size setting of the network

Continued

interface card (NIC), you should configure the NIC to allow 17KB frame sizes, which is the biggest frame size expected on a Token Ring network.

■ **Capture data with Network Monitor at quiet times on your network to prevent any performance effects on your system.** On occasion, if you cannot wait until traffic dies down, be selective and capture data for only short intervals. Examine the date you have captured and plan the next capture using more specific filters to reduce the quantity of data.

Monitoring and Troubleshooting Internet Connectivity

Accessing the Internet has become commonplace over the last few years. The accessibility of information resources on the Internet alone makes it a necessity for day-to-day access. The ability to conduct business transactions using e-commerce applications has developed an online marketplace for business-to-business and business-to-consumer sales. It is also possible to provide remote technical support, connectivity between different company locations and voice communication over the Internet, and reduce the cost of travel and support.

With the onset of these new possibilities, you are now tasked with ensuring the high availability of Internet access. In addition to reliable access, you must ensure that the data transmitted over the Internet is protected from prying eyes, and that your network is not blatantly exposed to security threats from inside and outside your network. This section covers some of the various issues associated with Internet access and some of the tools used to monitor and troubleshoot Internet access.

NAT Logging

If you have a small, nonrouted network, you may have implemented the Network Address Translation protocol (NAT) to allow your private network users to access the Internet. There will be a need to monitor and possibly identify problems with applications that use the Internet over the interface that uses the NAT protocol. NAT requires Routing and Remote Access Services (RRAS) on a multihomed computer. One of the network interfaces must be configured with a public IP address or you may configure it to use demand dial routing, and obtain the public address from your Internet Service Provider (ISP). Take a look at this excellent overview at www.microsoft.com/WINDOWSXP/pro/techinfo/planning/networking/nattraversal.asp for more details on how NAT works.

EXAM WARNING

Internet Connection Sharing (ICS) and Network Address Translation (NAT) are very similar. They both provide private IP address translation to a public IP address, dynamic addressing to the private clients, and host name resolution. It is important to understand the differences between ICS and NAT. ICS is intended for a simple single check box configuration to allow a Small Office, Home Office (SOHO) network to access the Internet via a shared single public interface to the Internet. There is no other configuration beyond defining some basic services access. ICS is limited to a single public IP address, a single private interface to the SOHO network, and it uses a fixed address range in the pool of address it can assign to the SOHO clients.

NAT, on the other hand, requires the installation of Routing and Remote Access Services (RRAS), and manual configuration, although it is still quite simple to implement with the RRAS Server setup wizard. With NAT you can have multiple public IP addresses, which allows multiple private clients to use the same services through NAT simultaneously. The address range for the SOHO clients is configurable and allows multiple SOHO Interfaces. The NAT features are designed with the scope of providing Internet connectivity for small to medium businesses.

It is easy to confuse the two because ICS *is* a form of network address translation (NAT) in the generic sense, but Microsoft uses the term NAT to refer to its RRAS implementation of address translation.

The first step in troubleshooting NAT is to verify your configuration. There are a few basic settings to verify. Let's look at the RRAS server settings and identify some of the key details. Both the public interface to the Internet and the private LAN interfaces must be added to the NAT routing protocol and configured to use the correct settings. Figure 10.20 shows the **NAT/Basic Firewall** tab of the private interface. It must have the **Private interface connected to private network** option selected. Another common area for trouble is the **Static packet filters** options shown in the bottom of the dialog in Figure 10.21. The Static Packet Filters dialog is accessed by clicking the **Inbound Filters** button shown on the dialog in Figure 10.20. You can configure filters on the traffic Inbound (destined for the private network in this case) and Outbound (destined for the Internet in this case).

Filters are defined by two criteria. The first criterion is the action. The two actions are:

- Receive all packets except those that meet the criteria defined in the Filters list.

- Drop all except those that meet the criteria defined in the Filters list.

The second criterion is the filters that are listed in the Filters list. The filters contain settings for the following:

- The **Source network** IP address and subnet mask define where the packet is coming from.

Figure 10.20 NAT/Basic Firewall Tab of the Private Interface

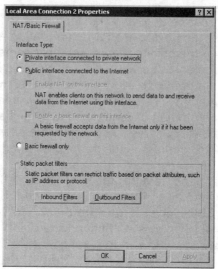

- The **Destination network** IP address and subnet mask define where the packet is going.

- **Protocol to filter** defines the protocol such as TCP, UDP, ICMP, and so on, and the source and destination ports used by the filter. You may also use **Any**, which includes all possible ports and protocols.

If you have defined filters that permit only specified traffic or deny all traffic except that which is defined in the filter list, you may use NAT logging to identify blocked traffic. We will discuss logging a little later in the chapter. Now you should examine the external interface.

Figure 10.21 Inbound Static Packet Filters Dialog

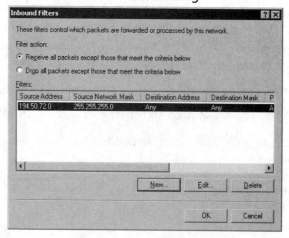

Shown in Figure 10.22 is the **NAT/Basic Firewall** tab of the public interface, which is configured as **Public interface connected to the Internet**. This properties dialog can be accessed from the **Routing and Remote Access Console** by expanding the **NAT/Basic Firewall** node, then right-clicking the LAN connection that is the external (public) interface adapter and selecting **Properties**. Also note that the check box for **Enable NAT on this interface** is checked. This turns the NAT protocol on, and is required for NAT protocol to map internal address and port requests to the public IP interface.

Figure 10.22 NAT/Basic Firewall Tab of the Public Interface

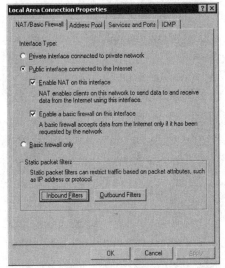

You can have the **Enable a basic firewall on this interface** option checked, which will block all public Internet access to the local private network. This is equivalent in concept to enabling filters on an interface. There are several methods you can use to define filters:

- **The TCP/IP filtering option**, which is located in the LAN properties, contains filter settings that are defined on the **Internet Protocol (TCP/IP) Properties**, **Advanced TCP/IP Settings**, **Options** tab.

- **In the RRAS snap-in, in the NAT/Basic Firewall node**, the Internal and each LAN Connection Interface properties there are the filters discussed previously.

- **In the RRAS snap-in, in the General node**, the Internal and each LAN Connection Interface properties there are the filters discussed previously.

You should check each location for filter settings to make sure that you are allowing or disallowing the appropriate traffic.

You can enable common services to access your network by simply checking the box next to the service name in the **Services and Ports** tab shown in Figure 10.23. You can also manage the behavior of ICMP by checking the boxes next to the functions you wish to allow on the ICMP tab seen in Figure 10.24. These settings are equivalent to setting filters and are disabled by default.

Figure 10.23 Services and Ports Tab

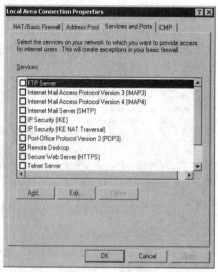

Figure 10.24 ICMP Tab

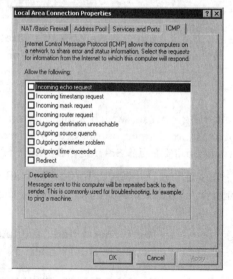

The client machines that use the NAT server will need their TCP/IP configuration set to obtain their IP addresses automatically. When the clients receive the IP configuration from the NAT server, they will be assigned:

- IP address from the defined pool (Defaults to 192.168.0.0/24)

- Subnet mask (Defaults to 255.255.255.0)

- Default gateway (NAT computer internal IP address)

- DNS server (NAT computer internal IP address)

Clients that obtain their address from the NAT server will use the NAT server to resolve DNS queries. The DNS server that is defined on the NAT server actually handles the request that is forwarded from the NAT server for the NAT client. This will limit your capabilities to resolve hostnames on your internal network if you have a DNS server providing the name resolution for internal hosts.

If the client machine is configured to use DHCP, or any of the TCP/IP settings were manually configured incorrectly, then it may not be able to access the Internet. If you are running DHCP service on another server on your network, and the client computer gets its IP address from the DHCP server, then it may not be able to access the Internet or resolve host names on the Internet. We will discuss name resolution in a later section. A nice feature of NAT is that you can disable NAT address assignment and allow your DHCP clients to use a DHCP server. This will simplify your network administration and provide you with the means to provide additional configuration information to DHCP clients in the scope options, such as WINS servers, which type of name resolution to use, and many others. With ICS you cannot disable address assignment.

To disable NAT addressing, using the RRAS Console, right-click on **NAT/Basic Firewall** and select **Properties**. You will be presented with the **Properties** dialog. Click the **Address Assignment** tab as shown in Figure 10.25. Simply uncheck the **Automatically assign IP addresses by using the DHCP allocator** check box, then click **OK**. Clients on your internal network will no longer obtain IP addresses from the NAT server.

Monitoring NAT Activity

Now that your LAN clients are using NAT, you will need to be able to monitor use, and to identify and resolve issues associated with NAT. There are several tools to provide you with the necessary information for identifying which clients are connected and to which address and port they are connected with what protocol. You may also need to identify causes of unreliable Internet access. All clients that use NAT to access the Internet will have their internal IP address mapped to an external IP address and the private address will need to map the appropriate port for the desired protocol to an external port for the same protocol.

You can view the mappings of NAT clients in the Network Address Translation Mappings Table shown in Figure 10.26, by right-clicking the interface listed in the

Figure 10.25 NAT/Basic Firewall Properties—Disable NAT Address Assignment

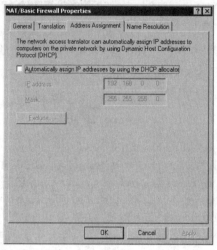

NAT/Basic Firewall pane of RRAS console. The route table (see Figure 10.27) and other TCP, UDP, and IP information is also accessible from RRAS by right-clicking the interface listed in the **General** pane.

Figure 10.26 Network Address Translation Mappings Table

SCIPIO - Network Address Translation Session Mapping Table

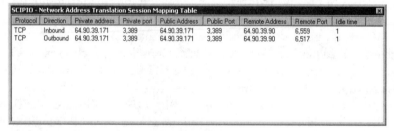

Protocol	Direction	Private address	Private port	Public Address	Public Port	Remote Address	Remote Port	Idle time
TCP	Inbound	64.90.39.171	3,389	64.90.39.171	3,389	64.90.39.90	6,559	1
TCP	Outbound	64.90.39.171	3,389	64.90.39.171	3,389	64.90.39.90	6,517	1

Figure 10.27 Routes Table

SCIPIO - IP Routing Table

Destination	Network mask	Gateway	Interface	Metric	Protocol
0.0.0.0	0.0.0.0	64.90.39.1	Local Area C...	20	Network management
64.90.39.0	255.255.255.0	64.90.39.171	Local Area C...	20	Local
64.90.39.171	255.255.255.255	127.0.0.1	Loopback	20	Local
64.255.255.255	255.255.255.255	64.90.39.171	Local Area C...	20	Local
127.0.0.0	255.0.0.0	127.0.0.1	Loopback	1	Local
127.0.0.1	255.255.255.255	127.0.0.1	Loopback	1	Local
224.0.0.0	240.0.0.0	64.90.39.171	Local Area C...	20	Local
255.255.255.255	255.255.255.255	64.90.39.171	Local Area C...	1	Local

There are other options to monitor the client Internet connections over NAT. In addition to providing an overview of mappings, the Netstat utility has a new option that allows you to find out what process is the owner of the connection. This is helpful when you have many connections through a routing server and need to identify what application is using which connection. The command is *netstat –o* and adds the Process column as you can see in Figure 10.28. The process can then be cross-referenced by id using Task Manager (see Figure 10.29). Another helpful utility to get details about a process is Process Explorer, a free utility from www.sysinternals.com. You can also enable logging.

Figure 10.28 Netstat Command with –o Option

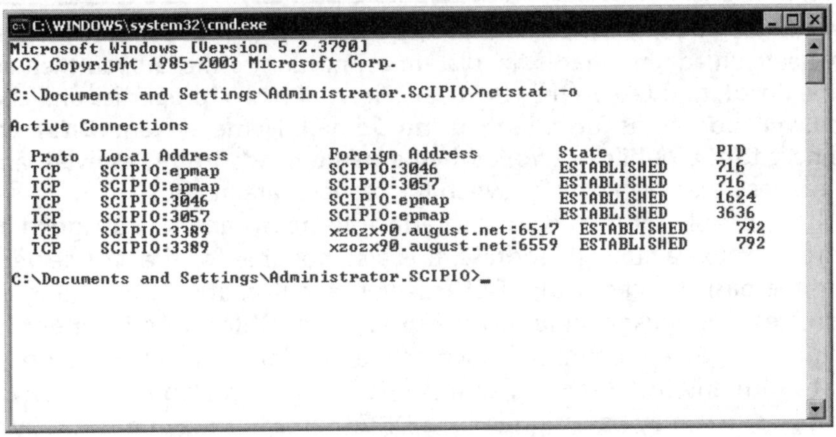

```
C:\WINDOWS\system32\cmd.exe
Microsoft Windows [Version 5.2.3790]
(C) Copyright 1985-2003 Microsoft Corp.

C:\Documents and Settings\Administrator.SCIPIO>netstat -o

Active Connections

  Proto  Local Address          Foreign Address        State           PID
  TCP    SCIPIO:epmap           SCIPIO:3046            ESTABLISHED      716
  TCP    SCIPIO:epmap           SCIPIO:3057            ESTABLISHED      716
  TCP    SCIPIO:3046            SCIPIO:epmap           ESTABLISHED     1624
  TCP    SCIPIO:3057            SCIPIO:epmap           ESTABLISHED     3636
  TCP    SCIPIO:3389            xzozx90.august.net:6517 ESTABLISHED      792
  TCP    SCIPIO:3389            xzozx90.august.net:6559 ESTABLISHED      792

C:\Documents and Settings\Administrator.SCIPIO>_
```

Figure 10.29 Task Manager Listing at the Same Time of the netstat –o Command

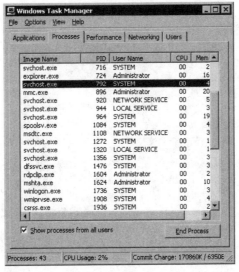

You can also log events associated with NAT. There are several different options for logging NAT events. One method you can use to configure NAT logging is by using *netsh:*

netsh routing ip nat set global LogLevel= none | info | warn | error, where LogLevel specifies the events you want to log. *none* turns off all NAT logging. The error parameter enables errors related to NAT to be logged, *warn* means that only warnings should be logged and info parameter logs all events related to NAT. Each of these options is configurable in the **General** tab of the **NAT/Basic Firewall Global** properties, as shown in Figure 10.30. The events that are logged are written to the Application Event log.

EXAM WARNING

Demand dial routing can be used on the external interface of your NAT server. You can create an adapter that is the dial-up connection to the ISP. You then access **Name Resolution** tab on the **NAT/Basic Firewall** global properties and check the **Resolve IP addresses for: Clients using Domain Name System (DNS)**, check the **Connect to the public network when a name needs to be resolved**, and define an interface that will be dialed when the requests are made.

It is possible for the external interface to be dynamically assigned an IP address, or use a static IP address. It is also possible for the NAT server to perform the basic functions of a DCHP server by automatically assigning IP addresses. You must enable this feature on the **Address Assignment** tab and ensure that you are defining a valid scope of addresses. NAT does not communicate with any DHCP servers, so it is necessary for you to exclude any addresses that may be assigned by a DHCP server, or may be statically assigned on your network.

Figure 10.30 NAT/Basic Firewall Global Properties

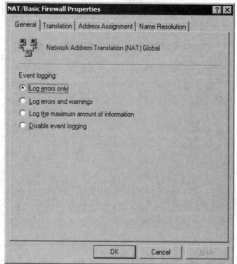

Name Resolution

The resources you provide on your LAN must be accessible by some means. Although you may be familiar with IP addresses, and may even know the IP address of every host on the network, it is not reasonable to assume that your clients will be able to use IP addresses to access those resources. The simple solution is to provide friendly names that can be used by your clients, such as www.syngress.com or \\BRAGI\PublicFiles, and so on. In order to facilitate friendly names, we must provide readily available services or mechanisms to resolve names to IP addresses. There are two basic types of name resolution, Host Name Resolution and NetBIOS Name Resolution.

Host Name Resolution

Host name resolution is defined as translating a host name to an IP address. A host name is a user-friendly reference, or alias, that is defined for an IP host. The name of the computer or device is called a label and is a maximum of 63 characters on the Windows platform. The entire host name can be no longer than 255 characters and must be alphanumeric, including hyphens and periods, but periods can be used only between labels and at the end of a fully qualified domain name (FQDN). You can also use an asterisk (*) or an underscore (_) as the first character in the label. You can assign an unlimited number of alias references to the same host.

There are two methods that Windows Sockets (WinSock) programs can use when configured to use host name resolution to connect to remote hosts:

- IP address
- Host name

If the IP address is specified, then you bypass the need to resolve any host names. If you use a host name, then it must be resolved to an IP address before you can connect to the destination host.

Aliases and FQDNs

There are two common forms of host names: aliases and fully qualified domain names (FQDNs). An *alias* is a nickname that is mapped to an IP address that is assigned to a host that can be used easily to connect to a host. The label or computer name would be an alias. A *fully qualified domain name* is structured so that it can be resolved hierarchically in a defined namespace, and includes the label for the host. The hierarchical namespace is implemented in DNS services. An example of a domain name is www.syngress.com. You can resolve aliases by defining the host to IP address pair in the Hosts file, located in the **WINDIR\System32\Drivers\etc** folder. The Hosts file contains examples that can be used to get you started. Hosts files are very effective in small environments with a limited number of hosts; however, the vast number of Internet resources led to the development of DNS.

The DNS Process

DNS answers name queries and responds with either the IP address of the DNS server that contains the information to resolve your host name mappings, or, if it is the mapping server, then it will resolve the name to an IP address and send the result back to the requestor. You must define an IP address for a DNS server to resolve domain names. If you are using Active Directory, then the Windows XP and Windows Server 2003 machines will need to be configured with a DNS server manually, or within the DHCP information defined in the scope properties.

Host Name Resolution Troubleshooting Tools

You can use nslookup to troubleshoot host name resolution. nslookup is an interactive command line utility that can be used to perform domain name queries against a specific DNS server, examine zone files, and validate the entries in the zone records in the DNS database. If the forward look up zone is not available, when you run nslookup to query that zone, it will timeout. netdiag, dnscmd, and dcdiag are all enhanced command line utilities that can also be used to resolve more Active Directory/DNS related issues. Netdiag is used to check distributed and network services such as IPSec, and to verify WINS and DNS name resolution and consistency. You can install the netdiag utility from the suptools.msi file located in the Support\Tools folder on the Windows Server 2003 product disc.

dnscmd is the command line version of the DNS configuration utility. This tool can be used to add, delete, or verify records in a DNS database, configure DNS servers, and manage zones. dcdiag can be used with netdiag and dnscmd to check the domain controllers in your enterprise and verify that the domain controllers are running properly.

NetBIOS Name Resolution

A NetBIOS name is a 16-byte address that maps to a network node that is defined as a NetBIOS resource on your network. NetBIOS name resolution entails resolving the NetBIOS name to the NetBIOS resource. NetBIOS names are unique names used by a host exclusively or a group name that can be resolved to more than one computer or process. If you request a single resource, then you use a unique name, otherwise you will use a group name to request resolution of more than one process on more than one computer.

Each 16-character NetBIOS name consists of a unique 15-character name based on the name of your host computer, followed by a special designator that defines the role of the NetBIOS host. If your hostname is shorter than 15 characters, then the appropriate number of spaces are added until it reaches 15 characters. Valid NetBIOS names can include Unicode characters, numbers, whitespace, and the symbols ~ ! @ # $ % ^ & ( ) . - _{ }. File and Printer Sharing for Microsoft Networks uses a sixteenth character of 0x20 to resolve NetBIOS requests for file shares and printer resources on your machine. Other values for the last byte include 0x1B (Domain Master Browser) and 0x1D (Master Browser) for browsing, 0x03 for the messenger service, and 0x00 for the workstation service. The workstation service for a machine named FRED would be **FRED** [00]. Notice the required padded spaces between the name and the final sixteenth byte.

If you wanted to retrieve files from a server named MAINFILESERVER1, then NetBIOS would attempt to resolve MAINFILESERVER1[20] and then connect. If you are using TCP/IP as your network protocol, then your machine will try to resolve the NetBIOS name to an IP address, then establish a TCP connection to the remote machine.

NetBIOS Node Types

There are different methods for resolving NetBIOS names to IP addresses. The order in which each of the methods is used to resolve NetBIOS names depends on the NetBIOS node type defined for the client host. You can configure DHCP scope to define the node type setting for each host that gets an address from that scope. See Table 10.1 for a description of each of the node types that can be defined.

Table 10.1 Definition of NetBIOS Node Types

Type of Node	Definition
b-node (broadcast)	B-node broadcasts NetBIOS name queries for resolution of NetBIOS names and registering NetBIOS resources. Since B-node is broadcast-based, it is confined to local segments and contributes a good deal to overall network traffic on a segment.
p-node (peer-peer)	P-node resolves NetBIOS names with a direct request to a NetBIOS name server (NBNS).
m-node (mixed)	M-node basically is made up of B-node and P-node resolution combined. M-Node hosts attempt to resolve hosts by using B-node broadcasts, and if that fails, then it will query a NetBIOS Name Server using a direct request using P-node.
h-node (hybrid)	H-node is a Hybrid made up of P-node and B-node resolution combined. H-Node requests are the opposite of M-node requests. The first attempt to resolve hosts is by a direct query to NetBIOS Name Server using P-node, and then it will use B-node broadcasts.

If a Windows Server 2003 machine is configured to use NetBIOS over TCP/IP, then it will use b-node broadcast to resolve NetBIOS names, unless a WINS server is defined, which will cause it to use h-Node resolution. You can also define the node type setting in DCHP for those hosts on your network that are set to dynamically configure the IP address.

LMHOSTS File

Much like the Hosts file in host name resolution, LMHosts files function similarly for NetBIOS name resolution. The LMHosts file is also located in the WINDIR\System32\Drivers\etc folder. There are differences in the file format of LMHosts. Instructions in the LMHosts.sam file located in the

WINDIR\System32\Drivers\etc folder can be used to create a file without the full name LMHosts (no .SAM extension). You can configure the clients with the option to use LMHosts files for resolution if you like. NBTStat can be used to purge the NetBIOS name cache and load the LMHosts file to the cache using **NBTStat –RR**, as well as troubleshooting NetBIOS name resolution. It is strongly recommended that if you are using a Windows operating systems other than Windows 2000/XP or Windows Server 2003, that you implement a WINS server to reduce broadcast traffic and aid in the resolution of the other Windows resources.

Using ipconfig to Troubleshoot Name Resolution

The front line in host name resolution problem solving is Ipconfig. You can use ipconfig to give you the details of your IP address settings for all your adapters. This allows you to verify the subnet mask, default gateway, and other settings for every adapter on the machine. The ipconfig utility with no command line options will provide the simple view as shown in Figure 10.31. For more detail you can use *ipconfig /all* for the results shown in Figure 10.32. In addition, you can now use ipconfig with the option */displaydns* to give you the list of host name resolutions cached on the client machine as shown in Figure 10.33.

Figure 10.31 Results of *ipconfig*

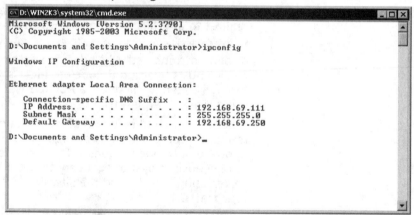

If you are having trouble resolving hosts, you can try clearing the resolver cache using *ipconfig /flushdns* as in Figure 10.34. On occasion, IP addresses change on the network. A common scenario is one in which a machine has a host name registered in DNS, you remove the computer account from Active Directory, and remove the entry from DNS. Then you add the machine with the same name as it had before, only now, it gets assigned a new IP address. When other machines attempt to resolve the machine by using the host name, if they have the old address for the same host name in cache, then the client machine will not be able to connect to the rebuilt machine. Simply use *ipconfig /flushdns* and the local resolver cache will be cleared, thus requiring the client to request resolution from DNS, where the current information can be obtained.

Figure 10.32 Results of *ipconfig /all*

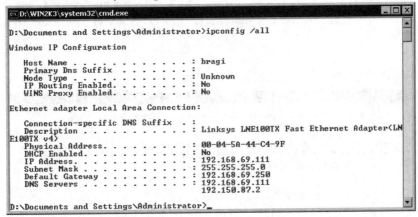

Figure 10.33 Results of *ipconfig /displaydns*

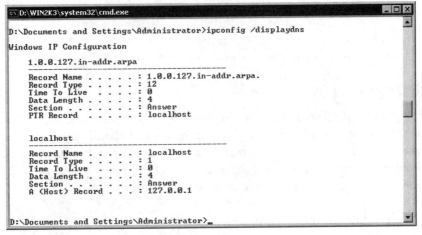

Figure 10.34 Results of *ipconfig /flushdns*

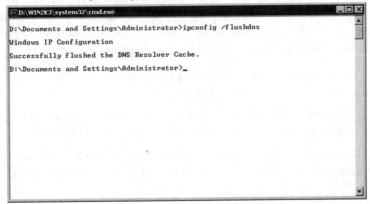

If required, you can use *ipconfig /registerdns* (see Figure 10.35) to add the client to the Dynamic DNS server if you are using dynamic DNS and your host name is not registered in DNS. Your machine name may not be registered in DNS if you have assigned a static IP address.

Figure 10.35 Results of ipconfig /registerdns

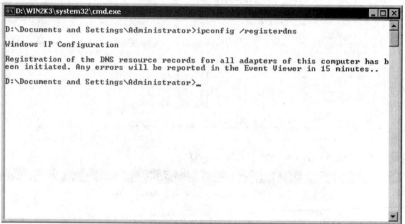

IP Addressing

The flexibility of TCP/IP contributes to the complexity of troubleshooting addresses and connections. There are several tools that can help isolate and identify issues with addressing, but it is also imperative that you understand IP addressing rules and subnetting. ipconfig, ping, and tracert are the most useful tools in identifying addressing problems with the client configurations and connections to other hosts on the Internet.

Client Configuration Issues

Some of the issues that occur with manual configuration of IP addresses include duplicate addresses, invalid subnet masks, invalid default gateways, and invalid or missing host name resolution settings (such as DNS and WINS). To help identify the problem, start by typing *ipconfig /all* at a command prompt. Verify the information that is output by the command is correct, and then continue by using ping to help isolate the problem.

1. Ping the loopback address (127.0.0.1) to verify that the TCP/IP protocol stack is configured correctly on the local computer.

2. Ping the external IP address of the local computer to ensure the host is on the network and using a valid IP address; that is, no address conflicts.

3. Ping the IP address of the default gateway to verify that the default gateway is accessible and your local network configuration contains the correct subnet mask.

4. Ping the IP address of a remote host to verify that you can transmit data over the default gateway.

If you are not able to get traffic through to a site, but you are making it through the default gateway, then you should use tracert to identify the break in the route to the destination. An example of using tracert is shown in Figure 10.36, using the command line tracert www.syngress.com. To prevent the resolution of the hostnames that are shown in the results of Figure 10.36, specify the command with the –*d* option: *tracert -d www.syngress.com.*

Figure 10.36 Results of tracert

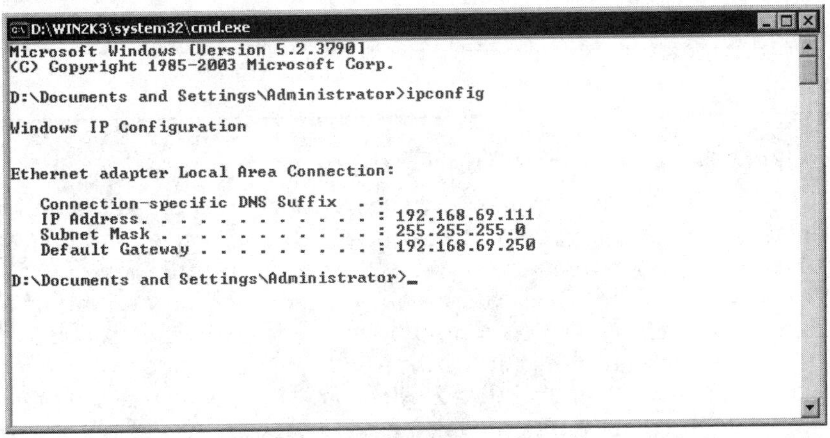

```
D:\WIN2K3\system32\cmd.exe

Microsoft Windows [Version 5.2.3790]
(C) Copyright 1985-2003 Microsoft Corp.

D:\Documents and Settings\Administrator>ipconfig

Windows IP Configuration

Ethernet adapter Local Area Connection:

        Connection-specific DNS Suffix  . :
        IP Address. . . . . . . . . . . . : 192.168.69.111
        Subnet Mask . . . . . . . . . . . : 255.255.255.0
        Default Gateway . . . . . . . . . : 192.168.69.250

D:\Documents and Settings\Administrator>_
```

Another utility that is more useful than tracert and ping combined is pathping. pathping is basically tracert and ping combined. The pathping command line utility provides an overview of latency and loss of data over a network at each hop from a source to a destination. The pathping utility will continue to ping over a specified period of time in seconds, but it will default to a value related to the total number of hops from the source to the destination. pathping computes the latency and packet loss from each router. This allows you to identify firewalls that block *icmp* but still provide information about latency on the hops past the firewall. You can also use *pathping* to zero in on problem routers, or slow connections on a route. An example of the command *pathping destination address* is shown in Figure 10.37. It is also possible to use pathping to trace the latency from a different source to the same destination. This provides a means for you to troubleshoot a connection on another machine, from a different client on the network. The command for specifying a different source address is *pathping –i<IP address of source> destination address*. It can also provide means for you to monitor a specific set of links in the route that may reduce the overall time to perform the trace. pathping command line options are case sensitive.

Figure 10.37 Results of pathping

```
D:\WIN2K3\system32\cmd.exe - pathping 64.90.39.1                          _ □ X

D:\Documents and Settings\Administrator>pathping 64.90.39.171

Tracing route to xzozx171.august.net [64.90.39.171]
over a maximum of 30 hops:
  0  bragi [192.168.69.111]
  1  192.168.69.250
  2  xzozx171.august.net [64.90.39.171]

Computing statistics for 50 seconds...
                Source to Here   This Node/Link
Hop  RTT      Lost/Sent = Pct  Lost/Sent = Pct  Address
  0                                              bragi [192.168.69.111]
                                0/ 100 =  0%   !
  1   9ms     0/ 100 =  0%      0/ 100 =  0%   192.168.69.250
                                0/ 100 =  0%   !
  2  11ms     0/ 100 =  0%      0/ 100 =  0%   xzozx171.august.net [64.90.39.171]

Trace complete.
```

New & Noteworthy...

Network Access Quarantine Control

There is a new feature incorporated in Windows Server 2003 called Network Access Quarantine Control. The purpose of Network Access Quarantine Control is to delay normal remote access to a private network pending the verification of the remote computer's configuration. The verification is implemented in the form of a script that executes on the quarantined computer when the connection is established.

Once the remote user has authenticated on the network and obtains an IP address, the connection is quarantined, which limits network access by the use of packet filters. The administrative script then executes on the remote access computer and examines the configuration. Once the remote client machine is validated the script notifies the remote access server providing the connection that it has run and the remote access computer satisfies the criteria defined by the network policies validated with the script. The remote access computer is subsequently granted normal access to the private network. Network Access Quarantine Control includes the ability to set a timer to limit the time a quarantined client connection can remain established before it is dropped. For more information visit www.microsoft.com/windowsserver2003/techinfo/overview/quarantine.mspx and read the whitepaper named Quarantine.doc available for download at this address.

Network Access Quarantine Control

Internet Authentication Service (IAS), combined with Remote Authentication Dial-In User Service (RADIUS) protocol and RRAS, provide a new function called Network Access Quarantine Control (NAQC). The primary function of NAQC is not to provide additional security, but to help protect your network from improperly configured clients that access your network using Virtual Private Networking (VPN). A perfect example of using NAQC would be ensuring that a client has the correct version of virus scan software, with the latest virus definitions, and also enable the software if it is currently disabled, all before allowing the client to access any other network resources.

The basic components involve all the services previously listed—RRAS, with MS Quarantine IPFilter and remote access policies such as MS Quarantine Session Timeout, and RADIUS with IAS. The client components to NAQC are a Connection Manager (CM) profile, which can be distributed with a CM policy from the RRAS servers, and a script using the client component RQC.exe. The remaining server components consist of the resources necessary to provide name resolution, script and file access, and the service component RQS.exe, which is installed on the RRAS server.

Generally, NAQC would function basically by a client using a CM profile that has the quarantine policy to connect to a RRAS server with quarantine capabilities and configured with the MS Quarantine IPFilter and MS Quarantine Session Timeout policies. The RRAS server forwards the RADIUS access request to the IAS server that will validate the user credentials and match the quarantine policy. The IAS server will provide a quarantine restricted access acceptance via RADIUS that will allow the client limited access to network resources such as obtaining an IP address, DNS access for name resolution, and the attributes that are part of the quarantine policies. Once the client has an IP address and policies, the client is restricted to accessing resources that match the quarantine filters, and only for the time allotted in the MS Quarantine Session Timeout policy.

The script is executed on the client by the CM profile, and is used to verify that the client configuration meets the requirements of the network policies. Once the verification is complete, the script executes rqc.exe with the necessary command line settings, which will send an unencrypted, unauthenticated notification to the RRAS server rqs.exe service. The rqs traffic is allowed to pass through the RRAS filters, since it is defined in the RRAS IPFilter settings with the MS Quarantine IPFilter attributes. Rqs then verifies the information and parameters passed from rqc, one of which is the script version passed in the rqc command line. If the client meets the requirements, then RRAS will get a notification from rqs that the client is valid, and subsequently RRAS will lift the MS Quarantine IPFilter and MS Quarantine Session Timeout policy restrictions and allow the client normal access to the LAN. Once this process is complete, the rqc component will write a message to the System event log.

Unfortunately, due to the fact that NAQC requires RRAS and the post connect script in the CM profile, it cannot be used on the LAN for regular clients. You can, however, implement similar functionality in logon scripts and domain policies since the LAN clients are very likely to be using domain accounts to access the network.

DHCP Issues

DHCP is an easy way to manage IP addressing schemes for larger networks. DHCP makes it possible to boot a machine and access the network without configuring any TCP/IP setting information. This eliminates many of the manual configuration issues such as using the wrong subnet mask, duplicate IP addresses, and limited or no host name resolution. Some of the items to consider when you implement and use DHCP include:

- Lease time

- Number of hosts in a scope

- Network traffic

- Scope options

- Topology

When a machine acquires an IP address from a DHCP server, it acquires a *lease*. The request for the lease is a message called a DHCPREQUEST, which is broadcast by the DHCP client looking for DHCPOFFERs of a lease from a DHCP server. The *lease duration* for a DCHP address is specified in the scope set on the server and defaults to eight days. At 50 percent of the lease duration, the DCHP client sends a directed request to the DHCP server that issued the lease and requests a renewal of the lease. If no DHCPACK (acknowledgement) is received from the server, the DHCP Client waits until 87.5 percent of the lease time and makes a final request to renew the IP address. If no DHCPACK is received at this point, then the client waits until the lease is expired and starts the process over. If a DHCP Client is unable to receive an IP address lease, then it will use an alternate configuration if one is specified. If there is no alternate configuration, the client will use APIPA to start the TCP/IP services and assign itself an address from the APIPA pool (169.254.0.0/16).

To determine the appropriate lease time for your network, consider the following:

- **Number of hosts** If the number of hosts is close to the number of total IP addresses in your DHCP server's scope, then the lease should be shorter—about three days. If there are a great deal more IP addresses than hosts, then a longer lease can be assigned.

- **Mobile Users** If you have a small number of mobile users and the client machines do not frequently move from one network to the other, then a longer lease duration is recommended; conversely, if you have more mobile users, then a shorter lease will be preferred so that the IP addresses will be released sooner and return to the available pool of addresses.

- **Unlimited** It is possible to set the lease duration to unlimited, but it presents a challenge if you wish to change the DHCP settings, since this setting requires the client to initiate the DHCPREQUEST.

Because they are broadcast, the DHCPREQUEST messages do not cross router boundaries, unless the router is capable of forwarding DHCP broadcast messages, in compliance with RFC2131. You can also configure a DHCP Relay Agent to forward the requests to a DHCP server.

Using DHCP can reduce IP address conflicts, by preventing the need for static IP addresses. It also can eliminate invalid subnet masks, since they are assigned by the DHCP server as well. Another advantage is the scope properties. By assigning scope properties, you can define default gateways, DNS servers, WINS servers, and the type of name resolution that is preferred. By managing name resolution settings, you can help eliminate broadcast traffic.

TEST DAY TIP

Wireless or authenticated clients on your LAN do not use the Routing and Remote Access service and therefore are not able to make use of Network Access Quarantine Control. It is possible to run a script on the client as long as the clients have a computer account for authentication on a domain on your network. You are then able to execute scripts that can enforce network policies as part of the computer's logon process to the domain.

EXAM
70-291
OBJECTIVE
3.2
3.3

Monitoring IPSec Connections

The connections established using the IPSec protocol are end-to-end connections, and are sometimes difficult to troubleshoot. Often the problems are related to connectivity of the networks over which the IPSec connection is established. There are also many different policies that we can apply that could have different effects depending on whether they are applied by the domain the machines are members of, or the ones that exist on the local computer. The network traffic is also a challenge, since it is responsible for delivering the data between the destinations. In this section, we are going to discuss the different methods to obtain useful information about IPSec connections and their settings.

IPSec Monitor Console

Information about IPSec traffic can be obtained using several different methods. One of the simplest methods is using the IPSec Monitor Console. IPSec monitor gives you information about domain and computer polices that are applied to the machine you are monitoring. In addition, it gives you information about main mode and quick mode statistics and filters. Most often, we may use IPSec monitor on the machine we are troubleshooting; however, it is possible to connect to a remote computer and view IPSec polices and settings using the IPSec Monitor snap-in.

IPSec Security Monitor allows us to watch for developing trends of security and authentication failures. This will help you to identify policy conflicts for specific IPSec tunnels. You can also determine the volume of traffic, the policies and associations, and how they are distributed. You can also evaluate the ESP packets with the total packets to identify potential holes in the security of the transmitted data and correct the security polices on the affected machines.

IPSec Management and Monitoring

Because of the complexity of IPSec policies and monitoring, you may find it helpful to create a special Microsoft Management Console File (.MSC file) with some of the useful tools associated with IPSec.

1. Click **Start | Run**, type **MMC**, and click **OK**.
2. From the MMC **File** menu, click **Add/Remove Snap-in**, and click **Add**.
3. Click **IP Security Monitor**, and then click **Add**.
4. Click **IP Security Polices**, click **Add**, and then choose to add the local computer, local computer's Active Directory domain, another Active Directory domain, or another computer. Click **Finish**.
5. Click **Resultant Set of Policy (RSoP)**, and then click **Add**.
6. Click **Link to Web Address**, and then click **Add**.
7. Click **Performance Logs and Alerts**, and then click **Add**.
8. Click **Close**, and then click **OK**.

Each of these snap-ins are valuable to you in different ways. To assist you with the standard monitoring of IPSec, you have the IPSec Security monitor. Another necessary tool is the IPSec Security Polices snap-in to allow you to manage the different IPSec policies on machines or domains on your network. The Resultant Set of Policy is a nice aid that provides a machine-specific overview of the Policy state for the defined machine. The link to the Web address is your portal to internal documentation, certificate authority Web pages where you obtain or issue certificates that can be used for IPSec. Finally, the Performance Logs and Alerts can be used to create and schedule monitoring of IPSec and IKE information, as well as alert us to conditions that may affect IPSec.

Enhancements to the IPSec Monitor in Windows Server 2003

IPSec monitor is now a Microsoft Management Console (MMC) snap-in. There is more information about security policies (SPs) and security associations (SAs). You can now monitor IPSec information for your local computer and using the same tool, connect to remote computers and view their IPSec information. There are now different filters and statistics for main mode (Internet Key Exchange (IKE)) and quick mode (IPSec). It is now possible for you to search for filters that match the source or destination host IP address. You can even specify the refresh rates. It is also possible to use DNS to resolve host names for filters and SAs.

Continued

Netsh now includes integration with IPSec to allow you to script SP and SA import and export, as well as use the command line utility to gather information and troubleshoot issues on your LAN. The netsh command replaces the IPSecpol.exe that was distributed with the Windows 2000 Server Resource Kit.

You can use either certificate authentication or Kerberos V5, and set restrictions to which computers can be allowed to access the network and log on to the domain. It is now possible to filter computers that are granted or denied access by the domain of which the workstation is a member: You can also filter on a single computer or a group of computers by name. If you have computers that have been issued a certificate, you can specify the list of issuing certification authorities that are valid and grant access to them.

Network Monitor

The Network Monitor software that is part of Windows Server 2003 includes all the necessary protocol parsers for Internet Key Exchange (IKE) Internet Security Association and Key Management Protocol (ISAKMP), IP Authentication Header (AH), and IP Encapsulating Security Payload (ESP) protocols. The ESP parsers only function if null-encryption is being used and the entire ESP packet is captured. Network Monitor cannot parse the encrypted portions of ESP traffic that is encapsulated by IPSec unless encryption is being performed by an IPSec hardware offload network adapter. This implies that the packets are decrypted by the hardware and as a result, the ESP packets are decrypted when Network Monitor captures them. This allows Network Monitor parsers to parse and interpret the data for the upper-layer protocols.

TEST DAY TIP

In order to monitor ESP-encrypted packets, you must use null ESP encryption on both machines using IPSec policy manager to disable the ESP encryption policy. Remember that the Windows component version of Network Monitor can view only traffic inbound and outbound from the machine on which it is installed; therefore, it can view only IPSec traffic that is part of an IPSec connection with that machine. To monitor other IPSec connections, you must have the full version of Network Monitor that ships with Systems Management Server.

netsh

IPSec packet event logging can be enabled using netsh command line utility. The command is *netsh ipsec dynamic set config ipsecdiagnostics Level*, where *level* is a whole value between 1 and 7. The option values are listed in Table 10.2. To see dropped packet events, you must set the logging level to 7. The change will be written to the registry and will not take effect until the next reboot, when the IPSec driver reads the registry on start up. The registry key that contains the logging level value is **HKEY_LOCAL_MACHINE\ System\CurrentControlSet\Services\IPSec\EnableDiagnostics**, and the value is a valid whole number in the DWORD registry setting between 1 and 7. All the events that are defined for the specified log level are written to the System event log once every hour or when the event buffer is full and must be written to the log.

Table 10.2 Log Level Options for IPSec Driver Using Netsh

Log level	Effective logging
1	Total number of incorrect Security Parameters Index (SPI) packets
2	Inbound only per-packet drop events
3	Combined effect of level 1 and 2 logging is enabled, as well as any unexpected plaintext packets (clear-text events) inbound or outbound
4	Outbound only per-packet drop events
5	Combined effect of level 1 and 4 logging is enabled
6	Combined effect of level 2 and 4 logging is enabled
7	All logging levels are enabled

The logging occurs at regular intervals based on the *LogInterval* setting in the registry, located in **HKEY_LOCAL_MACHINE\System\CurrentControlSet\ Services\IPSec**. You can set this value by using the registry, or by the preferred method of using *netsh ipsec dynamic set config ipsecloginterval Interval*, where *Interval* is the number of seconds between event log writes. The recommended value of the Interval parameter for troubleshooting is 60 seconds, which is also the minimum value. You can set the interval as high as 86400 seconds, which is equal to 1440 minutes or 24 hours. You can view information about IPSec policies using either the *netsh ipsec static show* command or the *netsh ipsec dynamic show* command.

EXAM WARNING

When you enable IPSec packet event logging, or change the logging interval, no changes to the logging will take effect until you reboot the computer. It is not necessary to reboot the machine to enable or disable IKE logging using the netsh command: *netsth ipse dynamic set config ikelogging 0 or 1*.

ipseccmd

The command line tool ipseccmd is used to script the creation of IPSec policy, and display active SAs and policy assignments. ipseccmd is no longer supported on Windows Server

2003 and its functionality is replaced by netsh. All IPSec-specific functionality is present in the netsh utility. You can view information about IPSec policies using either the *netsh ipsec static show* command or the *netsh ipsec dynamic show* command.

netdiag

Although **netdiag.exe** can still be used to obtain information about networking, Windows Server 2003 no longer uses the *netdiag /test:ipsec* option; it has been removed and replaced with the netsh commands for IPSec. All IPSec-specific functionality is present in the netsh utility. You can view information about IPSec policies using either the *netsh ipsec static show* command or the *netsh ipsec dynamic show* command.

TEST DAY TIP

Users without administrator rights cannot access current policy information. This prevents users from potentially gaining access to information without consent. The netsh utility will inform the user that the IPSec policy is in effect, or if they were unable to get the policy. You can view information about IPSec policies using either the *netsh ipsec static show* command or the *netsh ipsec dynamic show* command.

Event Viewer

To view Internet Key Exchange (IKE) events in the security log, you must enable success or failure auditing for the Audit logon events policy for your domain or workgroup, although these events are not exclusive to IPSec services. Enabling success or failure auditing will cause IPSec to record the success or failure of the negotiation, establishment, and termination of each main mode and quick mode connection as events.

You should be very cautious when enabling IKE events, especially if the server is exposed to the Internet, or provides IPSec services to lots of clients. Hack attempts on the IKE protocol could cause the security log to fill very quickly. IKE events can also fill the security log for servers that use IPSec to secure traffic to many clients. To avoid this, you can disable auditing for IKE events in the security log by modifying the registry.

To view IPSec policy change events in the Security log, enable success or failure auditing on the Audit policy node Audit Policy Change policy for your domain or local computer.

EXAM WARNING

To disable auditing of IKE events in the security log, create the **DisableIKEAudits** value. The value should be created in **HKEY_LOCAL_MACHINE\System\ CurrentControlSet\Control\Lsa\Audit**. Set the DWORD value of **DisableIKEAudits** to **1**. Remember this value does not exist by default so you must be created to disable IKE events. After you have created the key, you have to restart the **policyagent** service or reboot to make the changes take effect.

Summary of Exam Objectives

As a network administrator, you are responsible for managing and monitoring your network. It is important to understand how to use the tools to understand the behavior of traffic. Even the best design needs monitoring because things change. Network Monitor is one of the tools you can use to identify normal operations on your network.

Once you establish a baseline for your normal behavior, you are able to use Network Monitor to analyze frames of data in times of abnormal operation to troubleshoot and identify the problems. Other tools are used for quantity of data flow, but just looking at the quantity of data from node to node is not sufficient at times to solve problems. It is sometimes necessary to look at the frames themselves and verify the integrity of the frame or the validity of the data. There are two versions of Network Monitor—one is part of the operating system and the other is part of the SMS distribution. The version that ships with Windows is restricted to inbound and outbound traffic on the machine on which it is installed.

Filters can be defined to help analyze traffic. There are two types of filters, Capture and Display. Capture is used to drop frames that do not meet the criteria defined by the Capture filter, and Display is used to limit the frames that are visible in the captured frames. Exclusion filters will always exclude the specified criteria, so it is not possible to include portions of data that fall into a category that is excluded.

Today, most networks require access to the Internet. Due to the shortage of public IP addresses, Network Address Translation (NAT) is often implemented. NAT translates information in the headers to allow private addresses that are not routable over the Internet to be used internally and still gain access to the Internet by sharing a single address or multiple addresses that are public IP addresses.

NAT and ICS provide similar functionality, but ICS is simpler to implement and not configurable. NAT is more suited for small to medium-sized businesses, whereas ICS is good for the home or small office solution. NAT is part of Routing and Remote Services and is very configurable. However, because it is more configurable, there is more room for error. NAT Logging can be enabled in RRAS or using the netsh command, which will enable NAT to write specified levels of events to be written to the event log.

It is possible to define IP packet filters that can be used to restrict the type of traffic and where that traffic is coming from or going to. This can result in issues that prevent clients from accessing the Internet or specific resources that are not part of the network design. It is possible for NAT to function as a limited DHCP server and hand out IP addresses from its own pool of addresses to clients. This tends to eliminate the need for a DHCP server on a small network There is nothing that prevents NAT from handing out addresses that may be valid in a scope of IP addresses on a DHCP server or defined statically on one of the other machines on your network. Static NAT mappings can be used to define a route for inbound connections to be redirected to a specific host IP address and port.

Name resolution differs slightly depending on the type of name resolution you are using. There are certain types that you should be concerned with, including host name resolution, domain name resolution, and NetBIOS name resolution. Host name resolution is performed by searching entries in the Hosts file. Domain name resolution is performed by querying DNS servers. NetBIOS name resolution uses LMHosts, broadcasts, or a NetBIOS name server like WINS, depending on the node type setting for the computer.

Manual configuration of IP addresses could cause potential issues with network communication. The manual IP configuration is prone to mistakes, could result in assignment of a duplicate IP address, and potentially prevent access to other networks. DHCP provides a mechanism to overcome these challenges and prevent incorrect configuration.

The IPSec protocol allows us to transmit sensitive data over potentially less secure networks by creating a tunnel from one machine to the other. You can further encapsulate the data by encrypting the data using ESP protocol and adding an IP Authentication Header (AH). First, ESP encrypts the data then AH wraps it up and sends it to the destination. AH provides anti-replay security. There are several tools that can be used to monitor IPSec.

IPSec security monitor is useful in viewing quick and normal mode traffic, SAs and SPs, policy mismatches, and overall IPSec statistics. Network Monitor can help monitor IPSec data but it is limited to unencrypted data sent to or from the machine that is monitoring it. When troubleshooting, ESP can be defined with null encryption to allow us to validate ESP functionality without encrypting the data.

There are other command line tools that are helpful. netsh provides access to libraries that contain the information to view and configure certain aspect exchange newer resources. netdiag can be used to get information about IPSec as well. ipseccmd can do most everything that netsh and netdiag can do for IPSec, but is more enhanced and specialized to IPSec.

IKE and IPSec logging can be enabled, but must be watched carefully, since the quantity of messages that can be generated can fill up the event log very quickly. Enabling IPSec AND IKE logging can be done manually in the registry or using the netsh command. The IPSec driver reads the registry setting for IPSec on boot, so changing the logging settings will not take effect without rebooting.

Exam Objectives Fast Track

Using Network Monitor

- ☑ Network Monitor is a valuable tool in that it allows you to capture frames of data transmitted to or from your machine.

- ☑ Installation and configuration of Network Monitor is part of the operating system components, or the full version can be installed if you are using SMS.

- ☑ You can define Capture filters that apply to the data as it is captured and drop the frames that don't meet the criteria in the defined filters.

☑ After you have captured data, you can apply Display filters to the data in the Frame Viewer window, and use the filter to save specific data to a file for viewing later.

Monitoring and Troubleshooting Internet Connectivity

☑ NAT is used to provide small networks with a solution for accessing the Internet without obtaining multiple public IP addresses. NAT requires Routing and Remote Access Services and is more configurable than ICS, which can be implemented via one check box.

☑ NAT Logging can be enabled with **netsh** or the RRAS console.

☑ Domain name resolution is provided by DNS, and you can use nslookup, netdiag, and dnscmd to troubleshoot host name resolution.

☑ The Hosts file provides host name resolution on an IP-based network.

☑ LMHosts is used for NetBIOS name resolution. WINS servers should be installed on networks that support other Windows products besides Windows 2000/XP and Windows Server 2003.

☑ Configuration is an important part of troubleshooting Internet connectivity. Without the correct settings, clients will not be able to access Internet resources.

Monitoring IPSec Connections

☑ IPSec is end-to-end secure communication that has many facets. The primary monitoring tools are used to analyze and monitor IPSec security policies (SP) and security associations (SAs), IKE events, and network connectivity.

☑ Network Monitor enables you to parse the critical IPSec traffic, but it cannot view encrypted data.

☑ IPSec Security Monitor is now an MMC snap-in, and can give you information about IPSec SPs and SAs, as well as key exchanges and encryption of the data transmitted.

☑ ipseccmd, netdiag, and netsh are all command line utilities that will assist in scripting policy implementation, configuration, and troubleshooting IPSec connections.

Exam Objectives Frequently Asked Questions

The following Frequently Asked Questions, answered by the authors of this book, are designed to both measure your understanding of the Exam Objectives presented in this chapter, and to assist you with real-life implementation of these concepts. You will also gain access to thousands of other FAQs at ITFAQnet.com.

Q: Can I buy the full version of Network Monitor?

A: The full version of Network Monitor ships only as part of Systems Management Server. Although it has some valuable features, it should also be noted that the Network Monitor driver must be installed on all the machines you wish to monitor traffic on. The end result could be that the traffic you generate from all the Network Monitor clients sending information to the Network Monitoring console might cause more problems than the one you are trying to solve. There is no replacement for hardware-based network traffic sniffers when it comes to analyzing large and complex networks, but for the average LAN, the Network Monitor Windows component version should be more than sufficient.

Q: I am having trouble implementing IPSec on my network to allow remote users to connect to internal resources on my private IP network over NAT. Is this a configuration problem?

A: IPSec is not compatible for use over regular NAT since the data containing the IP address and port mappings of the destination host are encrypted. This architecture makes it impossible for standard NAT to translate the headers and redirect the traffic to an internal network. You can provide IPSec services using the new feature called NAT Traversal (NAT-T).

Q: Since most networks are using NAT to access the Internet because of the shortage of IP addresses, does that mean that IPSec is not really useful for those networks, since IPSec cannot be used over regular NAT?

A: Actually, no. Windows Server 2003 family includes a new feature called IPSec NAT Traversal (NAT-T). NAT-T uses ISAKMKP payloads encapsulated in UDP and slightly different methods of negotiation to allow IPSec/L2TP traffic to be translated by NAT, while ensuring the integrity of the data. This structure adds to security and integrity of your data when you require access to secure resources over the Internet. It should be noted that only clients that support negotiation of NAT traversal and UDP encapsulation of IPSec Packets can be used to establish these connections. Microsoft has released an update for Windows 2000 and XP clients. Search for the Knowledge base article KB818043 for more details on the update.

Q: I set up my IPSec connections to use tunneling, then apply the AH polices and then the ESP policies, but it does not seem to work. Can AH and ESP be used at the same time?

A: Yes—in fact it is good to use them both, since AH is used to protect the entire packet, and ESP applies only to the data field. It is possible that you have applied the policies in the wrong order. ESP policies should be applied first, resulting in the data being encrypted, and thus modified. If the AH policy was applied first, then the AH information would no longer be valid since it applies to the entire packet, and the packet changed. Next you apply the AH policy that will validate the encrypted data packet along with the rest of the packet to create another layer of protection for our data.

Q: Is it possible to use VPN to connect to an internal server using a private IP address over NAT?

A: Yes, but only because of the feature in RRAS that allows you to add static mappings to the NAT component. More broadly, you can provide access to many IP-based services inbound to your private network. Basically, you would identify the ports necessary to provide the connection, and the IP address of the server providing the service, in this case VPN. When the external clients connect to the public IP address using the address and port you defined, the request will be redirected to the internal address and port you specified in the NAT static mapping table.

Q: What do I need to do to use my existing Windows 2000 IPSec policies on Window Server 2003?

A: The default exemptions for traffic filtering, except for the IKE exemption, are removed on Windows Server 2003. You may need to change your existing IPSec policy designs in order to use the policies on Windows Server 2003 machines. You can prepare for the changes by setting **NoDefaultExempt=1** for all existing and new IPSec implementations on Windows 2000/XP-based machines, and the key will be preserved during upgrades to Windows Server 2003. By allowing Windows Server 2003 to support the **NoDefaultExempt=1** registry key, it enables administrators to use restored IPSec policies using the prior version behavior, which allows for backward compatibility with existing IPSec policies. It also provides some flexibility during the transition to Windows Server 2003. It should be noted that allowing the previous default exemption behavior may allow IPSec to be bypassed in some situations. See the Microsoft Knowledge Base article **KB811832—IPSec Default Exemptions Can Be Used to Bypass IPSec Protection in Some Scenarios** for more information.

Self Test

A Quick Answer Key follows the Self Test questions. For complete questions, answers, and explanations to the Self Test questions in this chapter as well as the other chapters in this book, see the Self Test Appendix.

Using Network Monitor

1. You have captured frames of traffic from your network. Unfortunately there is so much data you are having difficulty finding the data you need. Which methods can you use to quickly locate only the desired data from the packets you captured? (Choose all that apply.)

   A. Apply a Capture filter on the captured data that allows only the information you need in the Capture window.

   B. Apply a Display filter on the captured data that allows only the information you need in the Capture window.

   C. Search for the information using a property search and providing information about the data you are seeking.

   D. Use **Display | Colors** to change the appearance of the types of packets to display.

2. You are monitoring inbound requests using IP from a machine with named WKSTN01 to your server. You have installed and configured the Network Monitor Windows component. Select the proper filter representations of the Capture filter that you would configure to prevent any other traffic from being monitored. (Choose all that apply.)

   A. SAP/ETYPE = IP

   B. INCLUDE LOCAL <—> WKSTN01

   C. INCLUDE LOCAL <— WKSTN01

   D. EXCLUDE LOCAL <—>ANY

   E. EXCLUDE LOCAL —>ANY

3. You suspect that you are having problems with HyperText Transfer Protocol (HTTP) request traffic to and from your Windows Server 2003 intranet server, WEB1. You want to monitor HTTP requests on the network from another Windows Server 2003 machine in your office. You install the Windows component version of Network Monitor and begin a trace with the default filters specified. You notice frames are being captured, and then browse several Web pages on WEB1 using your Windows XP Professional workstation. Afterward, you stop and view the trace and notice that there are no HTTP Requests frames at all in the capture summary. Why?

A. The filters were not configured to allow HTTP requests to be captured.

B. You cannot monitor another server's traffic with the Windows component version of Network Monitor.

C. The subnet mask is invalid on the server WEB1.

D. IIS is not installed on WEB1.

Monitoring and Troubleshooting Internet Connectivity

4. A LAN client is unable to navigate to www.syngress.com using Internet Explorer. The user can access network resources, but cannot access any Web sites outside of the corporate domain. Which of the following tools will assist you in identifying the problem? (Choose all that apply.)

A. PING

B. NBTStat

C. Ipconfig

D. IPSec Monitor

5. Your company has added a new office and you are implementing a dial-on-demand interface one way to the new office over ISDN. You have configured all the information except the static route for the new connection. Where do you define that the static route? (Choose all that apply.)

A. In the RRAS configuration on the initiating computer

B. In the RRAS configuration on the destination computer at the new office

C. For the user account on the initiating computer

D. For the user account on the destination computer at the new office

6. You are responsible for the LAN at a branch office for a large corporation. You have a machine that is configured as a DNS server, and forwards FQDN resolution requests to the domain name server at the corporate office. You are testing the server's ability to perform the iterative, recursive, and simple queries. Which tools provide the necessary functionality? (Choose all that apply.)

A. nslookup

B. ipconfig

C. NBTStat

D. Monitoring tab of the DNS servers properties dialog

7. A client computer configured as a DCHP client was unable to obtain an address from the DCHP server. Upon investigation, you discovered that the DCHP scope was not activated, so you activated it. The client computer has an APIPA address of 169.254.0.1. What actions are required for the client to obtain an IP address from the DHCP server?

   A. Run **ipconfig /all** from a command prompt.

   B. Use **netsh** to assign an address to the network adapter.

   C. Log off of Windows XP and log on again.

   D. Take no action.

8. You are trying to ping a computer on the same subnet. When you ping the computer named WKSTN1 from WKSTN2, you get a valid ping response. When you ping WKSTN2 from WKSTN1, the ping request times out. You run **ipconfig** on the client machines. WKSTN1 has an IP address of 192.168.102.226 and a subnet mask of 255.255.255.0. WKSTN2 has an IP address of 192.168.102.5 and a subnet mask of 255.255.255.224. The router has an IP address of 192.168.102.1 and a subnet mask of 255.255.255.0. Your company deploys client machines configured to use the DCHP client. What can you do to correct the problem?

   A. Use the **IPConfig /registerdns** command.

   B. Use the **IPConfig /renew** command.

   C. Examine the properties of the WKSTN1 and correct the subnet mask.

   D. Examine the properties of the WKSTN2 and correct the subnet mask.

9. You have implemented a NAT/Basic Firewall configuration to allow your LAN clients to use private IP addresses and still access the Internet. You enabled the automatic assignment of IP addresses with the default scope. Things seem to be running well, but you get calls that the internal IIS server is occasionally unreachable. When you investigate, you see messages that indicate an IP address conflict. What is the best solution to prevent the IP address conflict from occurring?

   A. Manually assign and configure IP addresses for the internal clients and disable automatic assignment from NAT.

   B. Change the IP address of the IIS server.

   C. Implement a DHCP server and configure leases for each of the machines on your network. Set the lease duration to Unlimited.

   D. Exclude the IP address of the IIS server in the NAT automatic assignment configuration.

10. You want to configure your NAT server to allow users to access only Web pages on the Internet. Which solutions would provide the desired functionality?

    A. Configure an inbound filter on the internal adapter that includes the source network scope of the internal addresses and the TCP port 80. Select the option to **Receive all packets** except those listed in the Filters list.

    B. Configure an outbound filter on the internal adapter that includes the destination network scope of the internal addresses and the TCP port 80. Select the option to **Drop all packets** except those listed in the Filters list.

    C. Configure an outbound filter on the external adapter that includes the destination network scope of the internal addresses and the TCP port 80. Select the option to **Drop all packets** except those listed in the Filters list.

    D. Configure an inbound filter on the external adapter that includes the destination network scope of the internal addresses and the TCP port 80. Select the option to **Drop all packets** except those listed in the Filters list.

Monitoring IPSec Connections

11. Your HR department has spreadsheets with payroll information on a Windows Server 2003 file server to which only HR personnel have access. You have implemented IPSec policies on the server to ensure that data exchanged is more secure, by requiring IPSec for all connections to the server. All of your HR desktops are Windows XP Professional and Window NT 4.0 Workstation SP5 clients. The Windows XP clients can access the files without problems, but the Windows NT 4.0 clients cannot. What can you do to resolve this issue without changing the security on the file server?

    A. Install Windows NT 4.0 SP6a on the Windows NT clients.

    B. Upgrade the Windows NT 4.0 Workstation clients to Windows XP Professional.

    C. Install the IPSec client on the Windows NT 4.0 Workstations.

    D. Enable NetBIOS over TCP/IP on the Windows Server 2003 machine.

12. You are using Network Monitor to analyze IPSec packets that are using ESP. The data packet section is not viewable. What must you do to properly view the data packet section of the frames?

    A. Set ESP to use the same encryption policy as the Network Monitor machine.

    B. Disable AH policies.

    C. Install the ESP filter DLL and update the parser.ini file.

    D. Configure the ESP policy to use null encryption.

13. You are implementing Internet Protocol Security at your company and you wish to authenticate and encrypt connections. You must ensure that the tunnel header for every packet is authenticated. Which actions should you take? (Choose all that apply.)

    A. Use ESP for encryption.

    B. Use AH for encryption and authentication.

    C. Use AH for Authentication.

    D. Use ESP for encryption and RRAS for authentication.

14. You set a session key refresh limit of 1 for IPSec. What does this accomplish?

    A. Enables password lockout policy if the password entry fails only once

    B. Enables ESP

    C. Enables AH

    D. Enables master key PFS

15. What is the best solution to implement on your network computers to ensure that the appropriate packets of data transmitted from computers on your network are processed for signing and encryption with the IPSec protocol?

    A. Implement IPSec protocol

    B. Implement IPSec Group Policy

    C. Implement IPSec filters

    D. Implement IPSec profiles

Self Test Quick Answer Key

For complete questions, answers, and epxlanations to the Self Test questions in this chapter as well as the other chapters in this book, see the Self Test Appendix.

1.	**B, C, D**	9.	**D**
2.	**A, C**	10.	**B**
3.	**B**	11.	**B**
4.	**A, C**	12.	**D**
5.	**A, D**	13.	**A, C**
6.	**A, D**	14.	**D**
7.	**D**	15.	**C**
8.	**D**		

MCSA/MCSE 70-291

Self-Test Questions, Answers, and Explanations

This appendix provides complete Self Test Questions, Answers, and Explanations for each chapter.

Chapter 1 Reviewing TCP/IP Basics

Understanding the Purpose and Function of Networking Models

1. A beta version of an application you're testing to send and receive data on your network does not seem to be sending compressed data before sending packets across the network. You're looking at the architecture of the application to see if you can determine where the problem likely originates. Using the OSI model, from where is the problem probably originating?

    A. Transport layer

    B. Application layer

    C. Presentation layer

    D. Physical layer

    ☑   **C.** The Presentation layer in the OSI model is responsible for translating the data into a common format and for data compression to minimize the number of bits that must be transmitted, therefore Answer **C** is correct. If the data segments are too large, it is likely that there is a problem with the data compression at the Presentation layer.

    ☒   Answer **A** is incorrect, because the Transport layer is responsible for transporting the data from one node to another. It manages end-to-end flow control and error detection and recovery. This layer would not be involved if data segments were too large. Answer **B** is incorrect, because the Application layer is where the user connects with the communication process such as file or e-mail transfers. This layer is not responsible for the size of the data segment. Answer **D** is incorrect, because the Physical layer is responsible for taking the data and translating it onto the physical medium through electrical, optical, or other means. This layer simply takes the data given to it and sends it to the physical medium (or receives it from the medium).

2. Your firm is designing a new software driver that will employ a proprietary method of flow control for data being sent across a network medium. On which layer of the OSI model would be this flow control likely be implemented?

    A. Application

    B. Data Link

    C. Transport

    D. Media Access Control

    ☑   **B.** The Data Link layer of the OSI model has two components—the Logical Link Connection and the Media Access Control. Flow control is the responsibility of the Logical Link Connection, which is part of the Data Link layer; therefore Answer **B** is correct.

☒ Answer **A** is incorrect, because the Application layer is the top layer in the OSI model. This layer typically involves the user interface and would not be involved with flow control to the network medium. Answer **C** is incorrect, because in the OSI model, the Transport layer is responsible for connecting with the established session, adding headers to the packets, and sending them down through the rest of the OSI layers to the physical medium. This layer is not involved with flow control on the physical network medium. Answer **D** is incorrect, because the Media Access Control is a part of the Data Link layer and is not a discrete layer of the OSI model itself. The MAC provides *access* control, not *flow* control.

Understanding the TCP/IP Protocol Suite

3. You disabled TCP Port 80 on your Windows Server 2003, which is also running Web services via IIS, in hopes of increasing security on your network. However, users are now complaining that they can't reach your Web site. What is the most likely result of your actions?

   A. Disabling TCP Port 80 has no effect on your Web site, there must be another problem.

   B. FTP uses Port 80 and therefore the FTP function for your Web site was disabled.

   C. HTTP uses TCP Port 80 and therefore the HTTP protocol was disabled.

   D. The users need to enable HTTP on their local machines in order for them to browse to the Web site.

   ☑ **C.** The Hypertext Transport Protocol uses TCP Port 80. By disabling this port on your server, you shut down the HTTP function, causing your Web site to be unreachable. Therefore, Answer **C** is correct.

   ☒ Answer **A** is incorrect, because TCP Port 80 is used for HTTP, which is the protocol used to create and display Web pages on the Internet. This would impact your Web server. Answer **B** is incorrect, because FTP uses TCP Port 20 and 21 for data and control channels, respectively. The FTP function would not be impacted by disabling Port 80. Answer **D** is incorrect, because a browser such as Internet Explorer uses the HTTP protocol to display pages in the browser. However, users do not have to enable or disable anything on their local machines in order to browse Web sites using HTTP. It is enabled by default when a browser (or other application using HTTP) is installed.

4. A user notifies you that her computer is having trouble receiving e-mail via the corporate network. She has no trouble sending e-mail or connecting to files on public shares. She can also connect to the Internet. What would you check to begin troubleshooting this problem?

   A. Check to see if her computer is configured to use SMTP.

   B. Check to see if TCP/IP is installed on her computer.

   C. Check to see if she can ping localhost.

   D. Check to see if her computer is configured to use POP3.

☑ **D.** The user is able to connect to the corporate network but cannot receive e-mail. POP3 is the client side protocol typically used to retrieve e-mail from an e-mail server; therefore Answer **D** is correct.

☒ Answer **A** is incorrect, because Simple Mail Transport Protocol (SMTP) is used on the server side for e-mail and to send outgoing e-mail. It is not used by the client to *receive* e-mail at the client computer. Answer **B** is incorrect, because TCP/IP must be installed on her computer if she can connect to files on the network and to the Internet. Answer **C** is incorrect; since she can connect to the network, we can be confident that pinging the localhost will be successful. This will not provide any additional information to assist in resolving this problem.

Understanding IP Addressing

5. Your computer seems to have a problem with name resolution and you decide the problem may be in your hosts file. Your computer's IP address is 66.212.14.8. You open the hosts file and spot the likely problem. Which line from the hosts file is the most likely the cause of your name resolution problem?

   A. 66.214.41.1 router1

   B. 127.0.0.1 localhost

   C. 191.87.221.2 server.company.com pisces

   D. 66.212.14.8 localhost

☑ **D.** 66.212.14.8 is the IP address of your computer. However, the localhost is a loopback address that is a reserved network IP address of 127.0.0.0. This entry should not be in the hosts file; therefore Answer **D** is correct.

☒ Answer **A** is incorrect, because you may have selected this answer thinking that the router was not on your network. However, since we don't know the subnet mask, we are not exactly sure where this router is. Therefore, this is not the best answer. Answer **B** is incorrect, because this is the localhost loopback address. If you use the Ping utility and type **ping 127.0.0.1**, you will send a ping message to your own computer internally. This is useful to verify that your own computer's TCP/IP function is working properly. Answer **C** is incorrect, because this listing is a legitimate entry for a hosts.txt file. The IP address is followed by a Fully Qualified Domain Name (FQDN) and a host name "pisces."

6. You've just accepted a job at a small company as the IT Manager. The company network is not yet connected to the Internet and you've been asked to make this your top priority. You examine the IP addresses on several computers and find these addresses in use: 192.168.0.4, 192.168.0.19, 192.168.0.11. What is the next step you would have to take to connect your network to the Internet?

A. Purchase, configure, and install a server to act as a firewall for Internet connectivity.

B. Apply to the InterNIC for the appropriate IP address assignment.

C. Install and configure the common Internet protocols including SMTP, FTP, and HTTP.

D. Subnet the current network configuration using a custom Class C subnet mask.

☑ **B.** The 192.168.0.0/16 address range is a private Class C network configuration, therefore Answer **B** is correct. This can provide up to 256 Class C networks or the 16 bits can be used for host address spaces. In either case, this address range is reserved for private use and cannot connect to the Internet, nor can it be reached via the Internet. You would need to contact the InterNIC for a unique public address assignment.

☒ Answer **A** is incorrect, because when you have a public network address, you should certainly install and configure a firewall to prevent unauthorized network access via the Internet. However, that is not the first step involved. Answer **C** is incorrect, because when you have a legitimate public address, you can install and configure Internet-related services on a server. This is not the first step you would have to take for Internet connectivity. Answer **D** is incorrect, because the current network configuration may be subnetted but this has little to do with connecting the network to the Internet. As configured, it cannot be connected because the company elected to use a private network address, which must first be changed to a public network address.

7. A user contacts you to let you know his computer won't connect to the corporate network. You ask the user to go into his Network Connections properties and tell you both his IP address and subnet mask. He tells you his IP address is 180.10.254.36 and his subnet mask is 255.255.240.0. Based on this information, what is the correct binary representation of the network ID to which this user is connected?

A. 10110100.00001001.11110000.00000000

B. 10110100.00001010.11100000.00000000

C. 10110110.00001010.11110000.00000000

D. 10110100.00001010.11110000.00000000

☑ **D.** The user's IP address is 180.10.254.36 and the subnet mask is 255.255.240.0. To find the underlying network address, you need to use bitwise ANDing and compare the bits in the IP address to the bits in the subnet mask to find the underlying IP address. In this case, the bits look like this:

180.10.254.36 = 10110100.00001010.11111110.00100100

255.255.240.0 = 11111111.11111111.11110000.00000000

Network ID = 10110100.00001010.11110000.00000000 = 180.10.240.0

☒ Answer **A** is incorrect, because the dotted decimal representation of this number is 180.9.240.0. The ANDing comparison between the user's IP address and subnet mask yields 10 in the second octet, not 9. Answer **B** is incorrect, because the dotted decimal representation of this number is 180.10.224.0. The subnet mask sets the four-left most bits of the third octet to 1. The user's ID also has the four left-most bits of the third octet set to 1. ANDing these would result in 240, not 224. Answer **C** is incorrect, because the first octet in this answer equals 182 not 180. Bitwise ANDing the user's IP address and subnet mask results in the first octet being equal to 180, not 182.

8. Another IT staff person, Mike, tells you about a problem he's troubleshooting. He says that Jake's computer doesn't connect to the corporate network. The network uses DHCP to automatically assign IP addresses to computers, so he believes the IP address is correct and unique. He's tried pinging the localhost and that works fine but when he pings a server that is on the same subnet as Jake's computer, he gets an error message. What is the most likely cause of this problem?

   A. Mike's NIC card has a duplicate IP address.

   B. Mike's NIC card has a duplicate MAC address.

   C. Mike's NIC card has no IP address.

   D. Mike's Ethernet cable is loose.

   ☑ **D.** Although there could be a number of reasons that Mike's computer is having trouble connecting to the network, Answer **D** is the best answer. The success of the localhost ping indicates the computer's TCP/IP stack and NIC are functioning properly.

   ☒ Answer **A** is incorrect, because Mike would not be able to connect to the network with an invalid IP address. However, since the network is set to use DHCP, the IP address automatically assigned to Mike's computer is most likely correct and unique, unless Mike changed his computer's settings. However, this is not the best answer given the information provided. Answer **B** is incorrect, because unless there was a manufacturer's error or the NIC was purchased on the black market, each NIC has a unique MAC address and cannot be duplicated. This is not the likely cause of the problem. Answer **C** is incorrect, because the network employs DHCP to dynamically assign IP addresses, so Mike's computer probably has an IP address. If Mike inadvertently deleted the IP address, he may not have an IP address but he'd probably either tell you this or he'd reboot before calling you. Rebooting would cause his computer to request an IP address using the DHCP process. Therefore, this is not the most likely cause of the problem.

9. You're designing a network scheme from a Class A network address. You want to be able to have about 16,000 hosts on each subnet. Based on this, what is the maximum number of host address bits you can take to still allow up to 16,000 hosts per subnet?

   A. 8

   B. 16

   C. 24

   D. 17

☑ **B.** There are a number of ways to calculate this answer. One way is to start with your knowledge that bit 8 (left-most) of the first octet is equal to 128. As we move to the left, each bit is twice the one to its right. Thus, the string becomes (bit 9 =256), (bit 10 = 512)…(bit 16 = 16,384), (bit 17 = 32,768). Therefore, we need no fewer than 16 bits for our host address space to allow for up to 16,382 addresses per subnet.

☒ Answer **A** is incorrect, because eight bits would give us only 254 address spaces (128 + 64 + 32 + 16 + 8 + 4 + 2 + 1 = 256 − 2 − 254). Answer **C** is incorrect, because 24 bits would allow us far too many host address spaces. 2^{24} = 16,277,214 useable addresses. Answer **D** is incorrect, because 17 bits would give us just about double the number we need, 32,766. It's one more bit than we need. It's more common to take one more network bit than you think you need versus taking one more host bit, as it's typically better to have fewer hosts on more subnets for faster, more efficient networks.

Understanding Subnet Masking

10. As you review your firm's subnetting scheme, you notice that it was originally set up with a Class C network ID of 198.255.8.0 and was subdivided to yield four subnets, three of which are in use. Based on this information, what are the starting addresses of the available subnets?

    A. 198.255.8.0; 198.255.8.64;198.255.8.128

    B. 198.255.8.64; 198.255.8.128; 198.255.8.192; 198.255.8.224

    C. 198.255.8.0; 198.255.8.64; 198.255.8.128; 198.255.8.192

    D. 198.255.8.0; 198.255.8.1; 198.255.8.2; 198.255.8.3

    ☑ **C.** If you have three subnets, you would need to use two bits from the host address space. This yields four combinations (00, 01, 10, 11). The two-bit combinations equal, in order: 0, 64, 128, 192. Thus, the four subnet addresses are reflected in Answer **C**.

    ☒ Answer **A** is incorrect, because it includes only three of the four possible addresses. Setting both borrowed bits to 1 yield 128 + 64, or 192. This must be included as a possible network ID: 198.255.8.192. Answer **B** is incorrect, because the last IP address in this list cannot be included because it requires three bits from the host address space. Three bits could be used to create up to seven unique network IDs. This scenario states that only four were created. Answer **D** is incorrect, because these are host addresses on one network, not individual network IDs. They are all using the underlying 198.255.8.0 network ID, which is the first of the network IDs available.

11. You're working on a subnetting problem and you notice a host with the IP address of 146.64.195.36 and a subnet mask of 255.0.0.0. You compare this to another computer whose IP address is 146.64.195.38 and subnet mask is 255.0.0.0. Although you're not sure what's wrong, you do know that the maximum number of hosts your subnet supports is 65,534. What is the most likely cause of your subnetting problem?

A. The IP address is an illegal address.

B. The network portion of the IP address is incorrect.

C. The subnet mask is incorrect.

D. The host portion of the IP address is incorrect.

☑ **C.** The subnet mask used is a default subnet mask for a Class A network; therefore Answer **C** is correct. The IP address of this network is a Class B network (between 128.x.y.z and 191.255.y.z). Therefore, the subnet mask is incorrect. The correct default subnet mask for this network ID is 255.255.0.0.

☒ Answer **A** is incorrect, because the IP address is legal. Neither the network ID nor the host ID are all 0s or all 1s, which would be illegal in this classful system. Answer **B** is incorrect, because there is no indication that the network portion of the IP address is incorrect. If you can have 65.534 hosts, you are using a Class B network. The first octet, 146, falls within the Class B range. Therefore, we must work on the assumption that the network portion of the IP address is correct. The subnet mask used here is for a Class A network. Answer **D** is incorrect, because there is no indication that the host portion of the ID is incorrect. Again, we know that we have a Class B network and both IP addresses fall within those bounds.

12. The Class B network your firm was assigned needs to be subnetted. You have four divisions that are located in six cities around the U.S. You have approximately 5,000 employees, most of whom have computers on their desktops. In addition, you have approximately 47 servers and routers on your network. You want to create the most efficient network possible while providing for future growth, which is not yet quantified. Based on this information, what is the optimal number of bits to use for your subnetting task?

A. 20

B. 8

C. 24

D. 16

☑ **C.** A Class B network, by definition, uses the first two octets as the network ID, therefore Answer **C** is correct. In subnetting this network, we would take bits from the host address space. In this case, we need to balance network efficiency and expansion needs. The most common scenario for an efficient network is to have a maximum of 256 hosts per subnet. If we allow for 256 hosts, we must retain the right-most octet (z) for our host addressing. That leaves the third octet (y) available for network address expansion. The 16 default bits plus the 8 bits from the third octet yield 24 bits.

☒ Answer **A** is incorrect, because 20 bits would add four to the default configuration. This would allow for a maximum of 4,096 hosts per subnet, which is not optimal. This also unnecessarily limits the number of subnets you can create in the future by reducing the network bits from 24 (optimal) to 20 (suboptimal). This is not the best solution. Answer

B is incorrect, because you cannot use 8 bits for your network ID space because you have a Class B network ID that requires the use of at least 16 bits. Answer **D** is incorrect, because 16 bits is the default number of bits used for your network ID. This does not create any subnets and allows for 65,536 host addresses, far exceeding what would be practical on a network segment.

Understanding Basic IP Routing

13. A remote user reports that her computer doesn't seem to be able to connect to the corporate network. From your computer, you use the ping utilities to try to contact her computer, using its IP address. This returns the following message: "Packets: sent = 4, Received = 0, Lost = 4 (100% loss)." You also try pinging her computer by its name, *cooperjones*. Ping returns the following message: "Ping request could not find host cooperjones. Please check the name and try again." Based on these results, what would be your next logical step?

A. Verify her IP address.

B. Ask her to use the following command: **ping 127.0.0.1**

C. Ask her to use the following command: **ping 127.0.0.1 localhost**

D. Ask her to check her connection to the network cable.

☑ **B.** The next step would be to see if her computer can ping itself using the loopback address of 127.0.0.1. If it cannot, there is a problem within her computer—perhaps the NIC card is bad or the TCP/IP stack has a problem. If a computer cannot ping itself, there is no point in troubleshooting network connections, therefore Answer **B** is correct.

☒ Answer **A** is incorrect, because you may want to verify her IP address, which would depend on whether or not her computer uses DHCP or was manually set. However, you would likely do this after you run the loopback test so you can decide where the problem exists—internal or external to the computer itself. In troubleshooting, you always want to try to break the problem in half to narrow down the possible solutions faster. Answer **C** is incorrect, because the **ping** command uses either the IP address or the host name. The **ping** command interprets the word following the loopback address as a parameter, not as a name. This will return the error "Bad parameter localhost." Answer **D** is incorrect, because at some point, you may want the user to check her network cable connection. However, until you determine whether or not the computer can run an internal communication check (ping localhost), you should not ask the user to check the cable. Often cables are hard to reach and users can cause problems with other cables while trying to reach their own network connection. This may be part of the solution but should not be the next thing you try.

14. You work for a very small company that has computers in two physical locations, which are not currently connected. You're tasked with connecting the two locations. You purchase a server to act as both a server for the organization and as a dynamic router. You add a second NIC, and install Windows Server 2003. After you've enabled Routing and Remote Access on the server, what is the next step you must take to configure this computer as a dynamic router?

A. No additional steps. Once Routing and Remote Access is enabled, dynamic routing is enabled by default.

B. Bind your NIC to RIP and OSPF.

C. Add RIP and OSPF.

D. Set a default gateway for each NIC.

☑ **C.** RIP and OSPF are dynamic routing protocols required to implement dynamic routing in Windows Server 2003, therefore Answer **C** is correct. RIP has a 16-hop limitation and was designed for classful systems. OSPF was designed for classless systems and uses link state routing. RIP and OSPF are typically both implemented for dynamic routing in Windows Server 2003.

☒ Answer **A** is incorrect, because static routing is enabled when the Routing and Remote Access service is enabled via the registry key: *HKEY_LOCAL_MACHINE\System\ CurrentControlSet\Services\Tcpip\Parameters\IpEnableRouter = 1.* This does not, by default, enable dynamic routing. Dynamic routing protocols must be configured before dynamic routing can occur. Answer **B** is incorrect, because even though you do need to associate your NIC with both of these protocols, you first need to install or configure RIP and OSPF. This is the second step in this process, not the first. Answer **D** is incorrect, because in dynamic routing, default routes are seldom used. Therefore, it is not necessary to configure a default gateway on any of the NICs.

15. You notice that there are two servers on your network with the same name: salero215. You use the route utility to view your routing table and see the following entries:

196.6.14.5   salero215.building1.phoenix.somecompany.com salero215

196.6.17.5   salero215.building1.tubac.somecompany.com salero215

To solve this problem, you recommend the following change:

A. Change the first listing to salero215a.building1.phoenix.somecompany.com salero215.

B. Change the second listing to salero215.building2.tubac.somecompany.com.

C. Change the first listing to salero215.building1.phoenix.somecompany.com.

D. No change is needed. The FQDN for each server is unique.

☑ **C.** In the routing table, the IP address can be followed by the FQDN and the alias or nickname for the computer, therefore Answer **C** is correct. In this case, we have two aliases that are the same, which could cause a problem during name resolution. Each listing has a unique FQDN, so removing the alias (you could also change the alias) would resolve this problem.

☒ Answer **A** is incorrect, because there is no need to modify the FQDN for the server since both FQDNs are unique. The problem is the alias that follows the FQDN, which is not unique. This solution does not address the problem, which is the duplicate alias. Answer **B** is incorrect, because you cannot just randomly change the FQDN of the server to building2 since the full path indicates the server is in building1. Changing the FQDN in this way would make the server unreachable as it does not reside on the building2 network. Answer **D** is incorrect, because even though the FQDN is unique, the alias is not. Although the router will typically use the IP address or FQDN, if a request is received for "salero215," the router will not be able to resolve the address to an IP address.

Chapter 2 Variable Length Subnet Masking and Client Configuration

Classful Subnet Masking

1. What is the correct subnet mask for the IP address 120.66.10.5/10?

    A. 255.192.0.0

    B. 255.66.0.0

    C. 255.255.10.0

    D. 255.10.0.0

    ☑ **A.** The network ID given is a Class A network—the first (w) octet is between 1 and 126, the definition of a Class A network ID. Therefore, the default subnet mask would be 255.0.0.0. You can use this as your starting point and look at the /10 after the ID. This tells you how many network bits you're using. 10 indicates you have taken two address bits from the host space to extend the default network space by two bits. The value of the left-most two bits in the second (x) octet is 128 + 64 = 192. Therefore, the new subnet mask is 255.192.0.0, and Answer A is correct.

    ☒ Answer **B** is incorrect because the second octet has the left-most two bits as part of the network space and the right-most six bits as part of the address space. The value 66 is obtained using the following configuration for the second (x) octet: 01000010. This does not correspond to taking the two left-most bits as indicated by the /10 notation on the IP address and is therefore incorrect. Answer **C** is incorrect because this subnet mask might be used with a Class B network since the first two octets (w, x) are set to all 1s (255). In addition, if a Class A network were subdivided to yield 255 in the first two octets, the number of network bits would have to be 16, at a minimum. The notation would then be 120.66.10.5/16. This answer would actually require you to extend the network address space to 23 bits (original 8 + second octet 8 + the value of 10 in the third octet 7 bits =

/23). You are extending the network space by only two bits, not 16 bits. Answer **D** is incorrect because if you used this subnet mask, you would have to extend the network address space further than two bits. To generate the value 10 in the second octet, the configuration would be <u>00001010</u>. Thus, you would have to extend the network address space by seven bits (the bits underlined) and that would be indicated by 120.66.10.5/15.

2. Identify the underlying network ID for this IP address: 199.214.36.132/25.

    A. 199.214.36.0/24

    B. 199.214.36.0/25

    C. 199.214.36.128/25

    D. 199.214.36.128/24

    ☑ **C.** Begin by looking at the notation /25. This tells you that you're using 25 bits for the network ID portion of the IP address. Next, look at the beginning octet and see that it begins above 192, which indicates a Class C network. A Class C network uses the first three octets (*w, x, y*) as the network ID by default. In this case, you have a subnetted Class C network using the first three octets plus one additional bit from the fourth octet (8 + 8 + 8 + 1 = 25). Thus, you know that the underlying network ID uses the first three octets plus one bit. Recall that that one additional bit can be set to 0 or 1, yielding two possible addresses in the fourth octet: 0 or 128. The resulting subnets have starting addresses of 199.214.36.0/25 and 199.214.36.128/25. In this case, the given IP address has the fourth octet set to 132. The underlying network address is 199.214.36.128/25. Any IP address with the fourth octet value of 0 to 127 would be on the first subnet of 199.214.36.0/25. Therefore, Answer **C** is correct.

    ☒ Answer **A** is incorrect because the underlying network address would have to use as many network bits as the IP address given, which uses 25 bits, not 24 bits. Answer **B** is incorrect because the other subnet created by this subnetting scheme would have the underlying network ID of 199.214.36.0/25, but your IP address of 199.214.36.132/25 resides on the other subnet. If you were to use the subnet mask (using 25 bits) of 255.255.255.128 and perform bitwise ANDing on the IP address and subnet mask, you would see the following result: 11111111.11111111.11111111.10000000, and you could determine that the host address for this particular IP address is 5 (132 − 128). Answer **D** is incorrect; although the network address given in this answer is correct, the number of network bits used is incorrect, because it must match the IP address and use the same number of network bits. IP addresses using a different number of network address space bits are on different networks.

Variable Length or Nonclassful Subnet Masking

3. Your corporate network uses variable length subnetting to make more efficient use of IP addresses. One of the IP addresses for a host is 131.39.161.17 with a subnet mask of 255.255.248.0. What is the proper notation for the network to which this host is connected?

    A. 131.39.160.0/21

    B. 131.36.161.0/20

    C. 131.39.161.17/21

    D. 131.36.160.0/20

    ☑ **A.** Using the subnet mask to identify the number of network bits used, you can add bit values, starting from the left, until you reach 248. Thus, you add 128 + 64 + 32 + 16 + 8, or the left-most 5 bits, to generate 248 in the third octet. You know that you're using 21 bits for the network address space because the total number of bits set to 1 in the subnet mask is 21 (counting from left to right). Thus, the notation must end with /21. Next, you need to determine the underlying network address. Using bitwise ANDing to compare the IP address with the subnet mask yields this operation:

131.39.161.17	10000011.00100111.10100001.00010001
255.255.248.0	11111111.11111111.11111000.00000000
Result	10000011.00100111.10100000.00000000
Dotted decimal	131.39.160.0

Therefore, Answer **A** is correct: 131.36.160.0/21.

☒ In this example, the subnet mask's third octet determines the total number of network bits used. To equal 248, you must use the left-most five bits of the third octet. Therefore, the total number of bits set to 1 in the subnet mask is 21. The notation must end with /21, which eliminates Answer **B** as a possible answer. Performing bitwise ANDing would also help you determine that the underlying network address in the third octet is 160, not 161. To yield 161, the third octet of the subnet mask would have to be 249, not 248. Answer **C** provides the correct number of network bits (21) but uses the host's IP address. The question specified the underlying network address, not the host address; therefore Answer **C** is incorrect. Answer **D** is incorrect because the underlying network address is correct but the notation should be 21, not 20. If you selected this answer, it's possible you made an error in your math.

4. You need to create several subnets for your corporate network. Each subnet should have no more than two host addresses available per subnet. You have a subnet with the address of 136.42.255.0/24. What are the first two subnet addresses that would be created in this configuration?

A. 136.42.255.0/31, 136.42.255.4/31

B. 136.42.255.2/30, 136.42.255.4/30

C. 136.42.255.4/29, 136.42.255.8/29

D. 136.42.255.0/30, 136.42.255.4/30

☑ **D.** To end up with two host IP addresses per subnet, you need two bits for the host address space. Using one bit gives you two numbers (0 and 1) but a host address cannot be all 0s or all 1s. Thus, you need two bits so you can use two of the four possible configurations (01, and 10, discarding 00 and 11). Taking two bits for the host address space leaves 30 bits for the network address space. The notation must end with /30 to meet the requirements. Next, you need to determine the starting network addresses in this configuration. Begin with the given address of 136.42.255.0/24. This uses the first three octets for the network address space. You are extending this by six bits. Using the binary representation, you can see what happens in the fourth octet, showing the first three subnets created.

136.42.255.0/30   <u>10001000.00101010.11111111.000000</u>00
(network bits underlined)

136.42.255.4/30   <u>10001000.00101010.11111111.000001</u>00

136.42.255.8/30   10001000.00101010.11111111.00001000

The lowest bit value associated with the network address space is the bit with the weighted binary value of 4. You now know that your network address will increment by four each time, so each subnet will end with some multiple of 4 (4, 8, 12, 16, etc.). The first two addresses are 136.42.255.0/30 and 136.42.255.4/30. Therefore, Answer **D** is correct.

☒ The requirement is for two IP addresses per subnet. Using 31 bits would leave one bit for host addresses, but neither address (0, 1) is legal for a host address. Therefore, you need at least two bits to meet this requirement, reducing the number of network bits to 30, so Answer **A** is incorrect.. Answer **B** begins with the correct number of network bits used (as explained in the correct answer), but is incorrect. However, the network addresses increment by two, which is the 31st bit. For this answer to be correct, the network address would have to be 31 bits, making the notation 136.42.255.2/31, 136.42.255.4/31. In addition, these are the second and third addresses in this range (the first is 136.42.255.0/31), the question asked for the first two. Answer **C** is incorrect because if you used only 29 bits for your network space, you would have three bits left for the host address space. Three bits yields eight addresses, six of which can be used (000, 001, 010, 011, 100, 101, 110, 111). This does not meet the requirement of two IP addresses per subnet.

5. You've just accepted a position in the IT department at a small, growing company. You've been asked to devise a subnetting scheme for their network that will allow for a maximum of 30 hosts per subnet. The company's assigned network ID is 197.228.69.0. What is the subnet mask for the configuration you must develop?

   A. 255.255.255.248

   B. 255.255.255.240

   C. 255.255.255.224

   D. 255.225.248.0

   ☑ **C.** Your assigned network is a Class C network, which uses the subnet mask of 255.255.255.0 by default. To subnet this network to yield a maximum of 30 host addresses per subnet, you need to use five bits for the host address space and 27 (32 − 5) for the network address space. Three bits in the fourth octet equals 128 + 64 + 32 or 224. The correct subnet mask for a maximum of 30 hosts per subnet is 255.255.255.224; therefore Answer **C** is correct.

   ☒ Answer **A** is incorrect because it uses five bits from the fourth octet for the *network* address space. That leaves only three bits (8 − 5) for the host address space, which allows for only eight host addresses (six useable) per subnet. This does not meet the requirement. If you selected this answer, you may have gotten your network and host address bits mixed up. Answer **B** is incorrect because it uses four network bits and four host bits for the fourth octet. In this case, you have 16 host addresses (14 useable) per subnet, which does not meet the requirement. Answer **D** allows for 11 host address bits because the third octet is now set to 248, which uses the left-most five bits for the network address space. This configuration allows 2^{11} (2^{11}) host addresses per subnet, which equals 2,048. In addition, this violates the assigned Class C network configuration—you cannot use *fewer* network bits than your assigned public IP address allows; therefore Answer **D** is incorrect.

6. A Class A network is subnetted using the subnet mask 255.254.0.0. You are asked to further subnet this network to create a subnetting scheme that allows up to 65,534 hosts per subnet. The network address you've been given to work with is 65.254.0.0. What is the last network address in the new scheme you're to devise?

   A. 65.254.0.0/16

   B. 65.254.0.0/15

   C. 65.255.0.0/16

   D. 65.255.0.0/15

   ☑ **C.** Your current configuration is 65.254.0.0/15. The network bits are defined by the subnet mask. In this case, the second octet is set to 254. You can easily calculate that this uses the left-most seven bits because the entire octet set to 1s equals 255. This configuration, then, uses a total of 15 network bits. The number of host bits left to define host IP addresses is 32 − 15, or 17. Calculating 2^17 yields 131,072. The requirement is to create a subnetting scheme that has 65,534 host addresses per subnet. As you'll recall, each bit taken from the host space reduces the number of hosts by roughly half. Therefore, you can quickly determine that if you use 16 bits for the host address space, you'll end up with approximately 65,000 addresses. This adds only one bit to the network address space, yielding a total of two subnets. These subnets are 65.254.0.0/16 and 65.255.0.0/16. The question asked for the last network address, so the correct answer is Answer **C**, 65.255.0.0/16.

☒ The two subnets you created using 16 networks bits are 65.254.0.0/16 and 65.255.0.0/16. The required answer is the *last* network address, but Answer **A** is the first network address that meets the requirements, and is therefore incorrect. Answer **B** is incorrect because it is the current configuration. The given subnet mask uses a total of 15 network bits and the base network ID is 65.254.0.0, which could be notated as 65.254.0.0/15. This is your starting point but is not the correct answer to the question. Answer **D** is incorrect because 65.255.0.0/15 uses 15 network bits, which is your original configuration. This allows for 131,072 host addresses, exceeding the requirement of up to 65,534 hosts per subnet.

7. You're working on a subnet with this network address: 155.18.128.0/19. To make the most efficient use of your IP addresses and to improve the efficiency of the network, you are tasked with dividing this segment into subnets that have a maximum of 254 hosts per subnet. What are the last two network addresses you'll create and what is the correct subnet mask?

A. 155.18.128.0/24, 155.18.129.0/24, 255.255.255.0

B. 155.18.188.0/24, 155.18.190.0/24, 255.255.254.0

C. 155.18.254.0/24, 155.18.255.0/24, 255.255.255.0

D. 155.18.158.0/24, 155.18.159.0/24, 255.255.255.0

☑ **D.** To solve this problem, begin with the required number of hosts per subnet, 254. You know from your familiarity with Class C networks that this is the number of hosts on Class C networks, which immediately tells you that you must use eight bits for the host address space. That leaves 32 − 8, or 24 bits for the network address space. Thus, the starting network address is 155.18.128.0/24. Based on this, you know that the subnet mask must have the left-most 24 bits set to 1. This means that the left-most three octets (8 + 8 + 8) are set to 1, resulting in a subnet mask of 255.255.255.0. Finally, you must determine the resulting network addresses in order to determine the *last two* network addresses. The right-most network bit equates to the right-most bit of the third octet that has the binary weighted value of 1. Your network addresses will increment by 1. Since you are adding five bits to the network space, you have 2^5 (32) combinations. The third octet begins with 128 and increments by 1: (1) 128, (2) 129, (3) 130, ...(31) 158, (32) 159. The correct answer, then, is Answer **D**: 155.18.158.0/24, 155.18.159.0/24, 255.255.255.0.

☒ Answer **A** is incorrect; although the number of network bits needed, 24, is correct as is the subnet mask, the two addresses given represent the *first* two addresses, not the *last* two addresses as required. Answer **B** is incorrect. The subnet mask indicates that there are only 23 bits used for the network address space. 254 is derived by adding all but one of the bits from the third octet. Thus, the wrong subnet mask would eliminate this answer immediately. If you were using 23 bits for the network space, the network addresses would increment by two and the last two addresses would be 155.18.188.0 and 155.18.190.0, but the network would have to be denoted by /23, not /24. Answer **C** is incorrect. Using 24 bits for the network space, denoted by the use of the /24, is correct, as is the subnet mask. However, the last two network addresses created using this configuration are 158 and 159 because you started with the third octet value of 128, which is incremented by 1 for each subnet created.

The Windows XP/Windows 2000 Routing Table

8. Based on the partial routing table provided, what will happen to a packet with the IP address 133.94.228.52 and a default gateway of 133.94.128.1?

Network Destination	Netmask	Gateway	Interface	Metric
0.0.0.0	0.0.0.0	133.94.128.1	133.94.140.26	30
127.0.0.0	255.0.0.0	127.0.0.1	127.0.0.1	1
133.94.128.0	255.255.240.0	133.94.140.26	133.94.140.26	30
133.94.140.26	255.255.255.255	127.0.0.1	127.0.0.1	30

A. The packet will be sent directly to 133.94.228.52 for delivery.

B. The packet will be sent to 133.94.128.1 for delivery.

C. The packet will be sent to 133.94.140.26 for delivery.

D. The packet will be sent to 133.94.128.0 for delivery.

☑ **B.** Answer **B** is correct because the packet is not on the same subnet as the device. The network destination 133.94.128.0 shows the directly attached network route, which uses the computer's interface as the assigned gateway, meaning that the packet is sent directly to the IP address on the same subnet. However, by using this address's subnet mask, 255.255.240.0, we can determine that the IP address in question, 133.94.228.52, is not on the same subnet. Therefore, the packet will be sent to the default gateway for delivery. The default gateway's address is listed as 133.94.128.1.

☒ Answer **A** is incorrect because the packet cannot be sent directly because the IP address in question does not reside on the same subnet. It must go through a router and because no better route exists, the packet will be sent via the default gateway. Answer **C** is incorrect because based on the routing table information, the IP address for the computer from which the packet is to be sent has the IP address of 133.94.140.26. You know this because the netmask is all 1s and the gateway and interface are both the loopback address. Since the packet's IP address is located on a different subnet, the local computer's interface will not be used as the gateway. Answer **D** is incorrect because the network to which the sending computer is attached is defined as 133.94.128.0. The address for the gateway is 133.94.128.1.

9. Using the routing table provided, identify the destination of a packet with the IP address of 66.22.221.19 and a default gateway of 66.22.192.1.

Network Destination	Netmask	Gateway	Interface	Metric
0.0.0.0	0.0.0.0	66.22.192.1	66.22.200.13	30
127.0.0.0	255.0.0.0	127.0.0.1	127.0.0.1	1
66.22.192.0	255.255.224.0	66.22.200.13	66.22.200.13	30
66.22.200.13	255.255.255.255	127.0.0.1	127.0.0.1	30

A. 66.22.200.13

B. 66.22.192.0

C. 66.22.192.1

D. 66.22.221.19

☑ **D.** The local subnet address is 66.22.192.0; this is the address to which the computer (whose routing table we're viewing) is attached. The subnet mask is 255.255.224.0. This means that the network address space uses 8 + 8 + 3 bits, or 19 bits. You can use bitwise ANDing to compare the IP address to the subnet mask to determine whether the address is local or remote.

66.22.221.19	01000010.00010110.11011101.00010011
255.255.224.0	11111111.11111111.11100000.00000000
Result	01000010.00010110.11000000.00000000

Dotted decimal result   66.22.192.0

Based on the result of the bitwise ANDing, the IP address is attached to the same subnet as the sending computer so the packet is sent directly to the IP address indicated. Therefore Answer **D** is correct.

☒ **A.** Answer **A** is incorrect because this IP address is the address of the computer that is sending the data. This can be determined by the use of the loopback address for the gateway and interface IP addresses. The packet is not addressed to the loopback address or to the local computer. Answer **B** is incorrect because this is the address of the network to which the sending computer is attached. Although the packet will pass along this network, this is not the address to which the packet is sent because the packet is addressed to a host computer on the same network. Answer **C** is incorrect because a packet is sent to the default gateway only when the destination address is not on the local subnet and no other more suitable route exists. In this case, the destination of the packet is on the local subnet, so the packet is delivered directly to its destination without going through a router.

The Windows 2003 Routing Table

10. You've added several routes to a routing table on a heavily utilized server in the finance department, using the Routing and Remote Administration interface. However, you notice that this seems to be making things worse. You want to remove the routes you added, so you reboot the computer, knowing that the routing table will be recreated when TCP/IP is reinitialized, but the problem persists. What is the most likely cause of the problem?

A. When you add routes using the RRAS interface, they are not added to the routing table until you click Refresh. Therefore, the routes were never added.

B. The routes you added were not flagged with the −p to mark them as persistent. They should have been removed when you rebooted.

C. The routes you added will not be removed through rebooting because you added them through RRAS.

D. The routes you added can be removed only by using the command line interface.

☑ **C.** The routes added through the RRAS interface are persistent by default. Rebooting the computer will not remove the routes because they are persistent. Answer **C** is correct because to remove the routes added via the RRAS interface, you must return to the RRAS interface and select the route, then delete it.

☒ Answer **A** is incorrect because the routes you add via the RRAS interface are added immediately to the routing table. Refresh is used to refresh the screen, which is not dynamically updated when certain changes occur. It is not used to apply the changes. Answer **B** is incorrect because the −p parameter is used only with the command line **route add**. It is not available in RRAS. Answer **D** is incorrect because the routes that were added can be removed either via the command line interface or via the RRAS interface. However, this is not the problem.

11. You're examining the routing table on a Windows Server 2003. You see the following entries (partial routing table). What can you conclude about this computer?

Network Destination	Netmask	Gateway	Interface	Metric
0.0.0.0	0.0.0.0	66.22.192.1	66.22.200.13	30
10.84.112.0	255.255.255.0	10.84.112.8	10.84.112.8	30
10.84.112.8	255.255.255.255	127.0.0.1	127.0.0.1	1
66.22.192.0	255.255.224.0	66.22.200.13	66.22.200.13	30
66.22.200.13	255.255.255.255	127.0.0.1	127.0.0.1	30
127.0.0.0	255.0.0.0	127.0.0.1	127.0.0.1	1

A. There is a problem with the subnet mask associated with 10.84.112.0.

B. There is a problem with the TCP/IP protocol stack because two addresses are associated with the loopback address.

C. The computer is configured to use an alternate IP address.

D. The computer has two NICs installed.

☑ **D.** The computer has two network interface cards installed. This is shown in two ways. First, the directly attached network address is shown in two places, 10.84.112.0 and 66.22.192.0. Second, there are two addresses using the loopback address, indicating this computer has two network addresses, which occurs when you use two NICs to connect the computer to two different subnets. Therefore Answer **D** is correct.

☒ Answer **A** is incorrect because there is nothing to indicate the wrong subnet mask is being used. Remember, although 255.255.255.0 is used as the default subnet mask for a Class C network, it also can be used in variable length subnetting. So, while the address with which it is associated appears to be a Class A network address, it is subnetted using the variable length subnet mask. This means that the network could have been notated as 10.84.112.0/24. Answer **B** is incorrect because there is nothing to indicate a problem with the TCP/IP protocol stack. The loopback address is associated with two different IP addresses because there are two different IP addresses available to this computer via the two NICs installed. Answer **C** is incorrect; although the computer might be configured to use an alternate IP configuration, this is not the correct answer because there is no information in the routing table that would indicate the use of an alternate IP address.

Assigning Addressing Information to Network Clients

12. Your corporate network uses DHCP to dynamically assign IP addresses to clients. You're installing a new router and have been given the router's assigned static IP address. You configure the router and add it to the network. Immediately, you begin getting calls from users who cannot connect to the network. When you **ping** the router, you get errors. What is the most likely cause of this problem?

   A. The router is using an address within the scope of the DHCP addresses.

   B. The router is using a static IP address assigned to another router.

   C. The router is not configured to use a dynamic routing protocol.

   D. The router is on a different subnet from the DHCP server.

   ☑ **A.** The router is most likely using an address from within the scope assigned to the DHCP server, and that address also has been allocated by DHCP to a DHCP client. Answer **A** is correct because you cannot have duplicate IP addresses on a subnet, so either the router or the device using the duplicated IP address will not work on the network. The scope should be modified to exclude the static IP address used for the router.

   ☒ Answer **B** is incorrect. It is possible that the static IP address is assigned to another router. However, since you were given the IP address for the router, the more likely problem is that the DHCP scope includes the address, rather than the address being duplicated on another router. This is a possible answer but not the best answer, given the scenario. Answer **C** is incorrect. The router may or may not be configured to use dynamic routing protocols such as RIPv2, OSPF, or BGPv4. However, since the question does not specify that you are using variable length subnetting, there is no specific requirement to use a dynamic routing protocol. Answer **D** is incorrect because the router is very likely on a different subnet than the DHCP server but that makes no difference. The DHCP server can provide addresses for many different subnets via DHCP Relay Agents. The server can be configured with multiple scopes that define the addresses to be assigned to devices on a particular subnet along with the other required IP configuration information (subnet mask and default gateway).

13. Jack was away on vacation for three weeks and decided to come in Sunday afternoon to begin sorting through some of the work he knew would be waiting. Known to be a bit of a "button pusher," Jack started looking through some of his computer settings. He noticed that his IP address had changed to a completely new number. Before his vacation, his IP address was 62.128.47.55 but now it was 169.254.64.15. He wondered if something was wrong with his computer, but he noticed that he could still surf the Internet. When he mentions it to you over coffee Monday morning, what do you tell Jack about this?

A. Jack's computer is configured to automatically obtain IP configuration information from a backup DHCP server if the primary one is down.

B. The DHCP server was moved to a new subnet, causing client IP assignments to change.

C. The DHCP servers were offline for service on Sunday afternoon.

D. Someone must have changed the TCP/IP settings to a static IP address while Jack was on vacation.

☑ **C.** It appears the DHCP servers were offline on Sunday. Answer **C** is correct because if Jack's computer is configured to automatically obtain IP configuration information and the DHCP server is unavailable, the computer will use APIPA to provide a temporary IP address. It is randomly selected from a range starting with 169.254.0.0 and will be used until DHCP is available. Once available, the computer will request IP configuration information from the DHCP server.

☒ A computer configured to use DHCP will attempt to obtain its configuration information from any available DHCP server. Answer **A** is incorrect, however, because the assigned address will have to be on the same network and the address Jack reported was not at all the same. Answer **B** is incorrect because this is not the cause of the problem. Even if the server had been moved, the IP assignments would not change. DHCP servers can serve multiple subnets at once and have specific address ranges (scopes) defined for each of these subnets. The two addresses are clearly very different and are not related to one another, as are subnets of the same network. The original IP address is a Class A address and the one Jack discovered is a Class B network IP address. Answer **D** is incorrect because although it is possible that someone might have changed the IP settings on Jack's computer, because the address is a very specific APIPA address, this is almost certainly not the case.

14. A user has a laptop that she uses at home, at work to access both the corporate network and the Internet, and when she travels to client sites. She contacted you Monday morning to say that her laptop wouldn't connect to the network. She did mention something about having trouble on her home network over the weekend and working Sunday at home to fix the problem. You check the laptop's TCP/IP properties, and notice it is configured to "Use the following IP address." The address is 192.168.0.1 and the subnet mask is 255.255.255.0. What is the most likely cause of the user's connectivity problem at work?

A. The subnet mask does not match the network ID portion of the IP address.

B. Her laptop is configured to use a static IP address from the private address range.

C. Her laptop is configured to use an alternate IP address for her home connection.

D. Her laptop is configured to dynamically obtain an IP address, which caused a problem on her home network and is now causing a problem on the corporate network as well.

☑ **B.** The laptop is configured to use a static IP address from the private address range. How do you know this? First, the TCP/IP property specifies "Use the following IP address," which indicates the assignment of a static IP address. In addition, you know that 192.x.x.x is a private address range. This range can be used on networks of any type that do not connect to the Internet. Thus, the IP address she is using may not work on the corporate network. It was probably configured this way when she was working on the problem with her home network over the weekend. Therefore Answer **B** is correct.

☒ Answer **A** is incorrect because the subnet mask does match the IP address given. If you recall, a Class C network starts with the left-most three digits of the left-most octet (*w*) set to 110. This means that the address must start at 192 and it uses the first three octets for the network ID. The subnet mask has the first three octets set to all 1s (255) and therefore matches the Class C private network address of 192.168.0.1. Answer **C** is incorrect because her laptop could be configured to use an alternate IP address, but this option is available only if the general TCP/IP properties are set to "Obtain an IP address automatically" rather than "Use the following IP address." The alternate configuration is available only when using DHCP to automatically obtain an IP address for the primary connection. Answer **D** is incorrect because her laptop is not configured to dynamically obtain an IP address. If it were, the "Obtain an IP address automatically" would be selected rather than the "Use the following IP address" option.

15. You've configured a DHCP server to use the following range of IP addresses when assigning addresses to clients: 131.107.0.0/19 through 131.107.224.0/19. You set the subnet mask for this range of addresses to 255.255.240.0. Users are complaining that they cannot connect to the network. What is the most likely cause of this problem?

    A. The range of addresses is illegal. It should end at 131.107.192.0/19.

    B. The subnet mask is wrong. It should be 255.224.0.0.

    C. The range of addresses is illegal. The first address cannot be 131.107.0.0/19.

    D. The subnet mask is wrong. It should be 255.255.224.0.

    ☑ **D.** The address starting with 131 is a Class B network address. Therefore, the default subnet mask is 255.255.0.0. However, the notation /19 indicates that the network portion of the IP address occupies the left-most 19 bits, which is two octets (8 + 8) plus three additional bits from the third octet. Answer **D** is correct because the value of the three left-most bits is 128 + 64 + 32. This means that the dotted decimal value of the third octet must be 224, making the proper subnet mask 255.255.240.0.

    ☒ Answer **A** is incorrect. The address range is not illegal. The /19 indicates that the network portion of the IP address occupies 19 left-most bits. The base network ID is given: 131.107.0.0/19. If we set the left-most three bits from the third octet (bits 17, 18 and 19) to 1, the weighted binary value is 128 + 64 + 32 = 224. Thus, our network ID begins with 131.107.0.0/19 and ends with 131.107.224.0/19. This equates to the left-most three bits of the third octet beginning as 000 and incrementing through the various configurations to 111 (000, 001, 010, etc.). Answer **B** is incorrect. The subnet mask is incorrect. The network is a Class B network that uses the first two octets (*w, x*) as the network portion of the address. Thus, the subnet mask would have to *begin* with 255.255.x.x. The value of the third octet in the subnet mask is determined by the /19, which indicates three additional bits are needed for the subnet mask. Answer **C** is incorrect. The range of addresses is correct. A network ID *can* be 131.107.0.0/19. A network ID cannot be all 0s or all 1s, but it is not because we have 131.107.y.z as part of the network ID. We would not be able to use a *host* ID of 131.107.0.0 because the *host* portion cannot be all 0s or all 1s and the IP address of 131.107.0.0 would have a host address of 0. However, this is a legal address for a *network* ID.

Chapter 3 The Dynamic Host Configuration Protocol

Review of DHCP

1. About a week and a half ago, you hired Jamie, a new Systems Engineer, to help you fix some DHCP scope problems you had been having that resulted in a shortage of IP addresses. You configured a scope with a 24-bit mask and a network number of 192.168.0.0. You thought you had plenty of IP addresses because there are only 240 users in the company and this gives you 254 addresses. Your company employs a 50 percent sales force that is in and out of the office; sometimes sales personnel are gone for weeks at a time. With the recent addition of 10 new employees, your scope ran out of IP addresses and has been doing so intermittently for a few days. You put Jamie on the problem and she said she fixed it in a matter of minutes. She was right; you've had no more IP shortages. However, ever since the fix, your employees have been complaining to you about slow network performance. You asked one of your network engineers to run Network Monitor and he reported that hundreds and hundreds of DHCPREQUEST messages are traversing the wire. What did Jamie do to fix the problem?

A. Added more existing IP addresses to the scope range.

B. Turned off Dynamic DNS updating of downlevel Windows clients.

C. Reduced the default lease time.

D. Increased the default lease time.

☑ **C.** Answer **C** is correct, because it is the only thing that can account for an increase in DHCP client renewals. Jamie reduced the lease duration to 30 minutes, causing clients to begin the process of renewing their leases every fifteen minutes. This fixed the problem of mobile users docking into the network, getting an IP address lease of the default eight days, and then leaving with that IP for a week. However, even though it fixed the IP shortage problem, it caused a flood of DHCP broadcast traffic that slowed overall network performance.

☒ Answer **A** is incorrect because there were no more IP addresses to add. A network of 192.168.0.0/24 has only 254 existing IP addresses without subnetting it. Answer **B** is incorrect because turning off dynamic DNS would not cause increased DHCP traffic. Answer **D** is incorrect because increasing the default lease time would generate less DHCP broadcast traffic, not more.

2. Chris and Keith are two contractors you hired to help with your new data warehouse project for your Web site, the primary function of which is the online purchasing of ski apparel, equipment, and lift tickets for various ski resorts around the Untied States. Chris and Keith are very familiar with your entire product line and have been hired to customize an inventory database that is easily searchable from the Web site. To do this, they need the ability to gather information on site, sync it with the data on their portable Windows 2000 laptops, and bring this data into a prebuilt lab environment in their own office. Due to recent security policies, your company has mandated that consultant laptop machines using DHCP cannot leave the premises with any DHCP lease information from your network. Your manager asks you if this is possible. You reply yes. Was your reply correct?

A. Yes. There is no way to make sure leased IP addresses don't leave the building.

B. No. To do this, you need to make sure the lease duration is set to unlimited.

C. No. To do this, you need to set up a special User and Vendor class.

D. No. To do this, you need to make sure the lease duration is set to only a couple of days.

☑   **C.** Answer **C** is correct because it is possible to set specific options on specific machines with User and Vendor classes. In this situation, you should use the Vendor Class for Microsoft Windows 2000 and create a custom User class called Contractor Laptop Users, as shown in Figure 3.58. You can use the 002 option that specifies that all leases be released upon shutdown. Because Chris and Keith are using Windows 2000, their computers will match the Vendor Class. All that is left to do is use the **ipconfig** utility on Chris's and Keith's laptops to set the *classid* manually to Contractor Laptop Users in order for their machines to also match the User Class.

☒   Answer **A** is incorrect because there is a way to accomplish the task. Answer **B** is incorrect because, with an unlimited lease, contractors would be leaving the building and holding onto your IP addresses indefinitely. Answer **D** is incorrect, because even a lease of a few days would not stop the DHCP assigned IP addresses from leaving with the laptop.

Figure 3.58 Setting Up Vendor and User Specific Classes

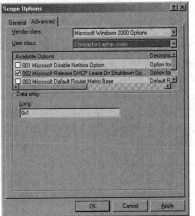

Configuring the Windows 2003 DHCP Server

3.   You are a contractor for a brand new mobile advertising company opening up in downtown Boston, MA, called Adstogo, Inc. You have been hired to configure DHCP for their new office of 200 employees. Fifty percent of their employees are mobile and usually out on the road, selling or driving advertising trucks. Every employee at Adstogo was offered a laptop with dial-in capabilities in order to stay in touch with corporate management because most of these road trips last one to two weeks at a time. You arrive onsite and begin configuring the Windows 2003 DHCP server as you have done many times before. You configure a scope with a 192.168.0.0/24 network address and exclude a range of 192.168.0.0 to 192.168.0.20 for network hardware and servers' static IP assignments. You configure the lease duration to three weeks and configure all the standard DHCP options. You authorize the server, activate the scope, and alert the 20 or so users in the office to hook up their already configured DHCP laptops. Presto! Everything works. You are congratulated, paid in full, and sent on your way. About two weeks later, you get a call from Mark, the owner of Adstogo. He says that he just hired 50 more employees to work in the office and only half of them can connect to network resources or get on the Internet. He rebooted the server and it appears to be working fine, other than the inability of some clients to obtain addresses. What is the problem?

A.   All users need to reboot to be assigned a new DHCP address.

B.   The DHCP server has crashed and is unable to hand out leases.

C.   Address conflicts are preventing clients from obtaining a lease.

D.   Your DHCP scope is out of addresses and able to renew only those that are already in use.

☑   **D.** You configured a scope that allowed only 234 addresses to be assigned. You also configured a lease duration that allowed your mobile users to leave the office with valid IP addresses for weeks at a time. With 234 addresses, 250 employees, and long lease durations, you are bound to come up short. Therefore, Answer **D** is correct.

☒   Answer **A** is incorrect because rebooting will not change anything that the DHCP client services weren't trying to do already. Clients are configured to search for a valid DHCP lease automatically every five minutes. Answer **B** is incorrect because if the DHCP server were down, no new users would be able to obtain an IP address and the question states that half of them can. Answer **C** is incorrect because you have not configured anything that might cause an address conflict to arise.

4.   For the past two years, you have been working as a systems engineer at a local bank in your hometown of Philadelphia. The bank has 17 branch offices that are participating in a Wide Area Network (WAN). Windows Server 2003 Active Directory has already been set up by the infrastructure team and they authorized all the DHCP servers currently in use today. Some of your responsibilities include the management of client and server IP addresses. This encompasses the setup and maintenance of all company DHCP servers. For this reason, your

user account has been made a member of the DHCP Administrators group. Your manager, Mike, alerts you that a new branch is opening and asks you to prepare the DHCP scope on the server that the infrastructure team installed. You gather the needed IP network information from your network team and start creating the new scope. About the same time, your manager calls you over with an urgent problem he needs fixed immediately. You select the option to configure the scope options at a later time and click Finish to build the new scope. After things have calmed down and the problems have subsided, you go back and finish configuring all the scope options as detailed in your IP information. You inform your manager that the server is ready to be deployed. However, clients at the new branch complain that they are unable to log on to the domain. You successfully ping the server from the Philadelphia branch to verify that it is up and responding. You also verify with the infrastructure team that they successfully authorized the DHCP server. Why are users unable to log onto the domain?

A. The local Domain Controller has not been activated.

B. The DHCP scope needs to be activated.

C. The users do not have any cached credentials on their local workstations.

D. The WAN link is down.

☑ **B.** Answer **B** is correct. The DHCP scope was created, but it was not activated, therefore it cannot hand out IP addresses. Because you did not configure the DHCP options when you initially ran the scope creation wizard, you were not prompted with a reminder to activate the scope.

☒ Answer **A** is incorrect because Domain Controllers do not have to be activated. Answer **C** is incorrect because users do not get cached credentials until they successfully log onto the domain at least once. Answer **D** is incorrect because you are able to ping the server from across the WAN, thus the WAN link can't be down.

5. Jennifer, the network administrator at a chain of bakery stores called The Cheesecake Factory, recently upgraded the corporate office of a single segmented network to one that supports four separate virtual networks, or Virtual Local Area Network segments (VLANS). Jennifer is very conscious of production change and thus contacted the systems group in order to make sure all the technical aspects of the project were met. Jennifer wanted to make sure that when all the client workstations were on the new network segments, they were still able to gain IP connectivity to the rest of the network as they had before. The Cheesecake Factory has been running a Windows 2003 Active Directory domain at the Windows 2000 mixed functional level for over two months. Jennifer created four network segments and labeled them VLAN1, VLAN2, VLAN3, and VLAN4. VLAN1 was the original network and hosts the original DHCP server, called SERVER1. Its network address did not change. The systems team decided to put DHCP Relay Agents on VLAN2 and VLAN3, configured to relay DHCP messages to the original DHCP server on VLAN1. Due to a reluctance to permit more DHCP broadcast traffic than the router could handle, Jennifer suggested to her systems team that VLAN4 should host its own DHCP server. The systems group installed

another DHCP server on VLAN4, set up the appropriate DHCP scopes on that server and set up the additional DHCP scopes for VLAN2 and VLAN3 on SERVER1. After the work was completed, all clients on all VLANs seemed to be working fine for about two weeks, until Jennifer got a call from the Help Desk stating that the users in the warehouse cannot boot up from their diskless workstations, where they run monthly accounting statistics, but can connect from all other workstations. Jennifer looks at her network diagram and determines that the warehouse is located on VLAN4. She also checks with users in the accounting department on VLAN1 to see if they can connect using their diskless workstations. They tell Jennifer that they can and have had no problems. What did the systems team most likely forget to do?

A. Install a DHCP Relay Agent on VLAN4.

B. Configure a BOOTP table on the new DHCP server on VLAN4.

C. Replace the router with an RFC 2131 compliant router.

D. Cold boot all the diskless workstations.

☑ **B.** Answer **B** is correct. Diskless workstations require a BOOTP table to be able to boot and communicate on the network. Clients on VLAN4 now get all their settings from a new DHCP server that has not been configured with a BOOTP table. The old DHCP server had a common BOOTP table that is still accessible by all other VLANS, because they are using a DHCP Relay Agent to forward requests to the original DHCP server.

☒ Answer **A** is incorrect because there is already a DHCP server on VLAN4 and a Relay Agent is not required. Answer **C** is incorrect for the same reason. There is no need to forward requests over the router due to the existence of a DHCP server on the local segment. Answer **D** is incorrect because simply cold booting the diskless workstation will not help them download a bootable image if one does not already exist on their network.

Configuring the DHCP Relay Agent

6. Ceste has been working for the client services department at a local bank in Richmond, Virginia for over a year. He is responsible for client connectivity to the corporate network backbone. Ceste is a member of the DHCP Users group and uses his privileges as a member of this group to gauge the status of DHCP leases and available IP addresses. Jamie is a systems engineer for the same bank, and is responsible for the back-end configuration of all DHCP servers and scope configuration. He is a member of both the Domain Users and DHCP Administrators groups. On Monday morning, SERVER2, the DHCP server servicing the first and second floor of the bank, crashes. SERVER2 sits on the same network segment as the first floor users' client machines. The second floor network segment has a Windows 2003 server with RRAS and a DHCP Relay Agent configured. Ceste is the first to be alerted that clients are unable to obtain an IP address, and further notices that he cannot connect to the DHCP Console on SERVER2. He notifies Jamie, telling him that he thinks SERVER2 has crashed. Jamie is already in the process of activating all the pre-existing backup scopes for all

the DHCP network segments at the bank. He tells Ceste to have all users on the first and second floor reboot their machines and everything should work. About 10 minutes later, Jamie receives a call from Ceste with the news that all first floor users' computers are now working, but nobody on the second floor can connect to any of their daily resources. What did Jamie forget to do in order to be fully prepared for this type of disaster?

A.   Add the IP address of the backup DHCP server to the DHCP Relay Agents.

B.   Configure a DHCP Relay Agent for the backup DHCP server.

C.   Authorize the backup DHCP server.

D.   Activate the DHCP scopes.

☑   **A.** Answer **A** is correct because users on the second floor used a DHCP Relay Agent to connect to their DHCP server. If a different DHCP server is now servicing IP leases, the DHCP Relay Agent needs to be configured with that server's IP address or client machines will attempt to negotiate only with a nonworking DHCP server.

☒   Answer **B** is incorrect because you can add multiple DHCP servers' IP addresses into a single installation of the DHCP Relay Agent. There is no need to configure another agent. Answer **C** is incorrect because users on the first floor are able to work and thus their machines have obtained valid IP addresses from an authorized server. Answer **D** is incorrect because the question states that all the scopes were activated and that users on the first floor are receiving IP addresses successfully.

Integrating the DHCP Server with Dynamic DNS

7.   You have been using Windows 2003 DHCP services to distribute IP addresses successfully to your mixed Windows XP/Windows NT DHCP enabled clients for over two months on your single segment LAN. Your Windows XP clients are configured with only the IP address of your DNS server for name resolution. NetBIOS broadcasts have been disabled on your network. Windows XP machines are able to successfully resolve all Windows NT workstations by means of DNS. Recently, you had a disaster with one of your domain controllers and had to promote your only DHCP server to a DC, due to corporate cutbacks and limited budgeting. You are concerned with security due to this situation and decide to update your password policy so that when an account is locked out, it stays locked out until an administrator unlocks it. You double-check and make sure that you are the only Enterprise and Domain Admin in your single domain forest. You have not made any changes to your network infrastructure since the crash. The problem: Your new DHCP Server/Domain Controller can no longer update any IP addresses for Windows NT clients in the Active Directory integrated DNS database. What is the most likely cause of this problem?

A. The original DHCP server was in the DNSUpdateProxy Group.

B. Coincidentally, someone recently turned on Secure only dynamic updates.

C. DNS and DHCP cannot coexist on the same Windows 2003 server.

D. The account credentials specified for Dynamic DNS updates has been locked out.

☑ **D**. More than likely, the account you configured to use for Dynamic DNS updates has been locked out because of your new password policy change. This could be due to an incorrect password being typed into the credentials password field used for dynamic DNS when the DHCP service was installed on your DC.

☒ Answer **A** is incorrect because even though the DHCP server is now a DC, being in the DNSUpdateProxy group would not have any effect on registering accounts, unless Secure only updates has been turned on in DNS. This cannot be and thus answer **B** incorrect, because you are the only one with the rights to turn on such a feature. Answer **C** is incorrect because it is simply not true that DNS and DHCP cannot coexist on a server.

8. Kim works for a consulting firm that services local Fortune 500 companies in the New York City tri-borough area, using Windows technology. She recently received a priority one call from a brokerage firm, stating that none of their Windows XP users who work collaboratively with each other's workstations can contact each other. Kim begins the troubleshooting process by gathering background data and recording recent changes. The systems administrator at the brokerage firm, Alan, said that the network team subnetted the network over the weekend and added five new virtual networks. He also told Kim that he installed and configured a new DHCP server to service these new networks. He said that the network team told him everything would be fine as long as he set up the correct DHCP server scopes ahead of time on the new DHCP server and had the clients reboot first thing Monday morning. The network team also noted that they were using DHCP forwarding on the routers and that there was no need to set up any DHCP Relay Agents. The DHCP forwarding address pointed to the new DHCP server. Kim asked how Dynamic updates were set up on the old and new DHCP servers and found that Alan always used the option Always dynamically update DNS A and PTR records. She asked what happens when a ping is attempted on one of the workstation names. Alan replied that he could ping the workstations by their new IP addresses, but not by name. When he pings the workstations by name, he receives the old DHCP IP addresses of the client machine. What should Kim suggest to fix the problem and make sure it does not happen again?

A. Enable secure dynamic updates on the DNS server.

B. Activate the new DHCP server scopes.

C. Add the new DHCP server to the DNSUpdateProxy Group and delete all the client records from DNS.

D. Add the new DHCP server to the DNSUpdateProxy Group.

☑ **C.** Answer **C** is correct. By default, a Windows 2003 DHCP server takes ownership of client records it records in DNS on behalf of those clients. This means that only that DHCP server can later update those records. Since *Always dynamically update DNS A and PTR records* was chosen, the DHCP server was updating and taking ownership of all A and PTR records. When the new DHCP server was installed and clients began receiving new network IP addresses, the new DHCP server couldn't update the records in DNS, and it is those records that are causing name resolution problems. To work around this, all the A and PTR records must be deleted so the new DHCP server can successfully register them. To prevent this from happening in the future, the DHCP servers should be added to the DNSUpdateProxy group, enabling the registration of A and PTR records to be nonsecure and updated by anyone.

☒ Answer **A** is incorrect because enabling secure dynamic updates does not help fix the problem with clients that are unable to communicate by name. When connectivity tests succeed using IP addresses but fail using names, this indicates a name resolution problem. Answer **B** is incorrect because the question states that clients are able to ping each other by IP address. This indicates that the scopes are working and thus are activated. Answer **D** is incorrect because just adding the new DHCP server to the DNSUpdateProxy group will not allow it to update the old client DNS records. They are still owned by the old DHCP server and must first be deleted to solve the problem.

Integrating the DHCP Server with Routing and Remote Access

9. You have been asked by upper management to implement a VPN solution in your newly built Windows 2003 Active Directory forest. All your users use Windows 2000 on portable laptops and their machines are successfully configured as DHCP clients. Management has asked that you not invest any more money in hardware or software but use the features that are packaged in the Windows 2003 product itself. You decide that this is feasible and begin by installing Routing and Remote Access (RRAS) on one of your dual-homed servers that is connected to both your internal network and your Internet Service Provider, and configuring it as a VPN server. You run the installation wizard and provide all the necessary answers. You have decided to use your RRAS server to assign client IP addresses by configuring it with a static pool of addresses that are routable on your internal network. Encouraged by the ease with which RRAS was set up, you send your CIO home for the day with the information needed to connect to your VPN server. You get a call from your CIO after he gets home. He says he is unable to connect to any resources on the internal network via the VPN. Which of the following is the most likely cause of the problem?

A. You forgot to exclude the static pool of IP addresses in your internal DHCP server's scope.

B. You forgot to configure your DHCP Relay Agent with the IP address of your internal DHCP server.

C. You gave your CIO the wrong IP address for the external network interface connected to your ISP.

D. You do not have a DNS server configured as an option on your RRAS server.

☑ **B.** Answer **B** is correct because, regardless of the DHCP mode in which you configure your DHCP server to hand out IP addresses, it must be configured with a DHCP Relay Agent that points to your internal DHCP server in order to receive DHCP options. In this configuration, the DHCP Relay Agent is responsible for sending client DHCPIN-FORM packets to the internal DHCP server in order to receive DHCP server options, such as a DNS server for name resolution.

☒ Answer **A** is incorrect because you would most likely receive DHCP conflict messages if you had overlapping DHCP scopes on your network. Even if you did not get a conflict message, this would not prevent you from connecting to internal resources. Answer **C** is incorrect because if your CIO had the wrong IP address, he would call complaining of not being able to connect at all, rather than not being able to connect to internal resources. Answer **D** is incorrect because the question states that DHCP is in use and working on your network. In order to work in an Active Directory forest, the remote DHCP clients must be using a DNS server configured by DHCP.

10. You are the systems administrator in charge of remote access at the corporate office for a multisite manufacturing company called BodyMetal, based in Chicago, Illinois. You have recently been tasked with the project of setting up a Routing and Remote Access Services (RRAS) server that will allow all of the company managers to work at home one day per week by dialing into the network, regardless of where they physically reside. Remote site managers live all over the United States and usually work from within their respective remote branch offices, using the high speed corporate WAN. You decide to install two RRAS servers to balance the user load, since you know all of your IT staff potentially will benefit from this project. All of your corporate DHCP servers reside on a single server, called SERVER1. You install the RRAS servers and configure them both with a locally hosted range of IP addresses. The two ranges you use do not overlap and have been excluded from the corporate DHCP server's scope. You also set up a DHCP Relay Agent on both RRAS servers and configure them with the internal IP address of your corporate DHCP server. You set up your external DNS to resolve to the names of your two RRAS servers, REMOTE1 and REMOTE2. You provide directions on setting up the VPN client software to all the users in the remote managers group and members of your IT staff, each randomly defined with a different RRAS server name. A week goes by and you start receiving a handful of calls from your remote VPN users, saying that they are unable to connect to any resources beyond the RRAS server itself. You ask some of your IT staff if they are also having prob-

lems. You receive mixed results, as some can connect to the rest of the network and some cannot. As you analyze the data about which users cannot connect, you come up with a common variable: they are all using the REMOTE1 RRAS server. What is the most likely cause of this problem?

A. The DHCP Relay Agent service on REMOTE1 is stopped and needs to be started via the Services MMC.

B. The RRAS server, REMOTE1, does not support BOOTP/DHCP forwarding.

C. The corporate DHCP server is down.

D. The DHCP Relay Agent on REMOTE1 is configured with the wrong IP address for the corporate DHCP server.

☑ **D**. Answer **D** is correct because the configuration described in the question was sufficient for REMOTE1 to allow RRAS connections. Since REMOTE2 is configured to allow the same access, and clients are able to connect to corporate resources through it, REMOTE1's DHCP Relay Agent must be configured with the wrong IP address.

☒ Answer **A** is incorrect because the Relay Agent is not a service that can be stopped and started through the Services MMC. The DHCP Relay Agent works as part of the RRAS service. Answer **B** is incorrect because the RRAS services use the DHCP service when configured with a Relay Agent. Answer **C** is incorrect because client machines using REMOTE2 are able to connect without a problem and they also use the corporate DHCP server.

Integrating the DHCP Server with Active Directory

11. You are the manager of the security division for an online banking startup company called BankNet.com. Security is of the utmost importance at your company, so you decided to implement Windows Server 2003 in an Active Directory infrastructure to take advantage of all the security features built into the new operating system and the AD environment. One of the features that most impresses you is the ability to control who can bring up DHCP servers on the network. At some of your other security jobs, you have seen a lot of client productivity lost due to the installation of a rogue DHCP server by one of the eager young IT guys. You decide that with Windows Server 2003's rogue detection feature, this will finally be a thing of the past. To assure yourself of this, you make sure that you are the only one who is a member of the Domain Admins, Enterprise Admins, and DHCP Administrators groups. One Tuesday afternoon, you get a call from the head of the Human Resources department, stating that he just rebooted his computer and now cannot connect to any network resources. You walk him through the process of running **ipconfig** with the **/all** switch at the command line, only to determine that this user has an IP address configuration that is not in the range of any scope configured on your DHCP servers. What has most likely happened?

A. One of the IT staff members has authorized a Windows 2003 server with the wrong scope information.

B. One of the IT staff members has reconfigured one of your existing scopes with the wrong IP range.

C. One of the IT staff members has installed a Windows NT 4.0 server running the DHCP service.

D. One of the IT staff members has changed the default gateway scope option for the segment on which the HR user's workstations sit.

☑ **C.** Answer **C** is correct because, although Windows Server 2003 Active Directory can prevent some rogue DHCP servers from causing havoc on your network, it can detect and shut down only unauthorized Windows 2000 or Windows 2003 DHCP servers. Any other operating system running the DHCP server service can be installed and go undetected by your Windows 2003 Active Directory defense mechanism of authorization.

☒ Answer **A** is incorrect, because no one other than you can authorize servers since no one else is a member of the Enterprise Administrators group. Answer **B** is incorrect because you are the only member of any of the groups that would have rights to reconfigure an existing DHCP scope. Answer **D** is incorrect for the same reason as answer **B**.

Understanding Automatic Private IP Addressing (APIPA)

12. You are the systems administrator for a small network of fewer than 10 users on a single network segment, which is configured for peer-to-peer network resource sharing. You are using Windows XP and Windows 2000 on all of your client desktops and you decide to avoid the hassle of installing DHCP or manually configuring static IP addresses by using APIPA. You are using two file servers, both running Windows Server 2003, which also have the ability to use APIPA. Everything is running smoothly and you applaud yourself for implementing such an easy alternative for IP distribution. As your small network grows, however, you start to see your single segment network begin to outgrow itself. You decide to add another segment to your network, and you do so, setting up a network router. You add five new employees and plug their computers into the switch that is attached to the new subnet. All these employees' computers are configured to use APIPA and are able to communicate with each other immediately. However, when the new users try to access anything on the network servers, they are unable to connect. They are also unable to connect to any existing shares on the original network. What have you overlooked in your use of APIPA as an IP alternative?

A. APIPA works only if you have fewer than 10 workstations.

B. APIPA has not been configured properly on the new workstations.

C. The router is not able to forward BOOTP/DHCP broadcasts.

D. APIPA cannot be routed.

☑ **D.** Answer **D** is correct because APIPA does not auto configure a default gateway and thus can't be routed. It can be used only on single-segment networks.

☒ Answer **A** is incorrect because, although APIPA should not be used for larger networks and is recommended for use with less than 20 workstations, it does not have a limit of 10. Answer **B** is incorrect because you do not have to configure APIPA on Windows XP workstations, as it is configured by default to be used if a DHCP server is not available. Answer **C** is incorrect because the router's ability to forward BOOTP/DHCP broadcasts is irrelevant in this situation. There are no BOOTP/DHCP servers to which the router could forward broadcasts.

Managing the Windows 2003 DHCP Server

13. You are working as a desktop engineer for a pharmaceutical company in Washington D.C., called SMB Inc. SMB Inc. has a fully functional Windows 2003 Active Directory domain in which they have implemented DHCP. You have been in the IT industry for nine years, working primarily with Windows NT 4.0, and consider yourself quite seasoned. When you hear your manager, Julie, asking one of the systems engineers why she is not able to obtain an IP address from the server, you go to your PC, open your DHCP MMC, and determine that the network scope for her subnet is not activated. You quickly activate it and tell her to try again. It now works. When the same thing happens two months later, you open the DHCP MMC and are pleased to find that is the same problem; you will be the first to fix it again. However, when you try to activate the scope this time, you find that you cannot. You report to Julie that there is a problem with the DHCP server, because it will not let you activate the scope, but it will let you open up the DHCP MMC and view everyone on the DHCP server. Most likely, what really has happened?

A. You have been removed from the Forest Admins Group.

B. You have been removed from the DHCP Administrators Group.

C. You have been placed in the DHCP Users Group.

D. You are correct that there is a DHCP server problem.

☑ **B.** Answer **B** is correct because the DHCP Administrators group gives you the ability to activate and deactivate scopes.

☒ Answer **A** is incorrect because there is no such group in Windows 2003 Active Directory. Answer **C** is incorrect because, although you now appear to be in the DHCP Users group since you have view-only DHCP server rights, it is not your membership in this group that prevented you from activating the DHCP scope. Answer **D** is incorrect, because the fact that you have insufficient rights to perform the task doesn't constitute a server problem.

Monitoring and Troubleshooting the Windows 2003 DHCP Server

14. Mike is the senior network analyst at a financial firm in downtown Manhattan. On a typical day, Mike monitors network traffic, compiles the traffic into a report, and submits any abnormalities to the appropriate technology team. The network is composed of a Windows 2003 Active Directory back end and a combination of Windows 2000 and Windows XP clients on the front end. On one particular Monday morning, Mike notices a large increase in the number of DHCPDECLINE messages coming from a majority of DHCP clients on subnet A. He checks the daily change control logs for any weekend work that might have caused this and comes across one entry of particular interest. The previous weekend, the systems team installed an additional DHCP server on subnet A to help balance the DHCP lease load on the existing DHCP server. With the data that Mike has already gathered, what conclusion can you come to as to the source of so many new DHCPDECLINE messages on Monday morning?

A. Conflict detection was not enabled on the new DHCP server.

B. The new DHCP server was configured with an overlapping scope of IP addresses.

C. The new DHCP server was not authorized, causing clients to decline its IP addresses.

D. The new DHCP server was not running Windows Server 2003.

☑ **B**. Answer **B** is correct, because DHCPDECLINE messages are generated by clients that determine an IP address is already in use on the network and decline its use, asking for another valid IP address. Windows 2000 and Windows XP clients have conflict detection built into their DHCP client software and thus generate these messages when DHCP servers with overlapping DHCP scopes hand out conflicting IP addresses.

☒ Answer **A** is incorrect because conflict detection on the server side would not generate DHCPDECLINE messages. Conflict detection on the server side is a means by which the server determines if the lease it is about to hand out is already is use; this reduces the incidence of clients issuing DHCPDECLINE messages. Answer **C** is incorrect because an unauthorized server does not cause clients to issue DHCPDECLINE messages, because it does not respond to client DHCP messages at all. Answer **D** is incorrect because running a DHCP server on a Windows 2003 server, as opposed to a Windows 2000 or Windows NT 4.0 server, has no bearing on the frequency of client DHCPDECLINE messages.

15. Gary has been the DHCP administrator for T&G Sporting Company for the past five years. When Gary retired last month, he gave the keys to the kingdom to Jeff, a newbie in the field of engineering but very eager to learn. Although new to a lot of Windows technology, Jeff was the only administrator at T&G and thus had full rights to manage anything and everything. Jeff immediately began poking around into all the systems and services to learn as much as he could, as quickly as he could, before something broke and he had to learn it on

the fly. Jeff was not quick enough. Jeff's manager, Jim, came up to him a few days after he took over, reporting that nobody on the second floor could access the Internet or anything else on the network. Jeff took a cursory look at the DHCP server service on the second floor and noticed that it was started. He then used the **netsh** utility to view the configuration of the DHCP scope, and noted that it appeared to be unchanged. He then looked at the System logs in the event viewer and noticed many specific errors with the source of DHCP server and Event ID of 1046. What did Jeff accidentally do to cause this problem while poking around in DHCP?

A. He deleted the DHCP database.

B. He unauthorized the DHCP server.

C. He turned off dynamic updates.

D. He created a multicast scope.

☑ **B.** Answer **B** is correct because event ID 1046 specifically states that your DHCP server is no longer authorized in Active Directory and therefore will not hand out IP leases. With Jeff's Enterprise Admins group rights, he had the ability to remove DHCP servers from the authorization list.

☒ Answer **A** is incorrect, because if Jeff had deleted the DHCP database, he would have had to stop the service first in order to free up the files in use. At this point, when the service started backup, a new database would have been created, which would have resulted in the output of the **netsh** command showing no scope data. Answers **C** and **D** are incorrect because these configurations have no effect on whether or not DHCP is handing out IP leases.

Chapter 4 NetBIOS Name Resolution and WINS

Review of NetBIOS Name Resolution

1. Tina, a network engineer for 123, Inc. corporation, is assigned the job of segmenting the company's internal network IP address scheme into five new networks from the current one network in place now. Four of the networks will be client broadcast domains and the fifth network will be the server network, consisting of all servers. The server network will continue to use their current IP addresses, whereas all other networks will have to change. The network consists of a native Windows Server 2003 domain with the Exchange 5.5 server being the only NT 4.0 server left in the environment because of some older applications build on top of this platform that are not ready for Exchange 2000. All clients run Windows XP on their desktops. Being very careful to prevent down time, Tina does her homework and gathers all the needed brainpower into a conference room to discuss possible problems and best practices for accomplishing the company's goals. She pulls together a member from each team, one from Systems Engineering, Desktop Support, Security, Application Support,

and another from Network Engineering to put together an appropriate plan. She goes around the table and asks each group member what they will need to do in order to make this happen without causing unnecessary downtime. Here are their responses:

- **Systems Engineering [Chad]** "We will need to create a new DHCP scope for each new network and assign it the appropriate IP address range and default gateway. Since the domain name suffix and DNS servers are common throughout, we can leave those as global scope options and be OK. I will also create an exclusion range for a handful of IP addresses for each network scope and give them to Gary to use when statically assigning certain needed workstations."

- **Network Engineering [J.]** "We will need to subnet the class 10 network into five separate networks and break them out into ranges for Systems DHCP scopes. We will also let Chad know the appropriate default gateways to use for each new network. Lastly, we will enable the appropriate forwarding command on each router interface to allow DHCP broadcast to traverse the network."

- **Desktop Support [Gary]** "We will need to go through our list of statically assigned IP workstations in various departments and manually assign them a new IP address from the list Chad gives us and a new gateway IP address that J. gives us."

- **Security [Randy]** "There is really nothing we need to do."

- **Application Support [Doug]** "We will need to edit the access control lists for the accounting and human resource web applications with the static IP address assignments that Gary gives to the client workstations in these departments."

Tina feels comfortable that she has chosen the right group of people to get the job done and proceeds to schedule the work for the upcoming weekend. The project goes smoothly over the weekend. Chad confirms that each scope is handing out IP addresses correctly. J. confirms that the routers are allowing DHCP traffic across. Gary confirms that the DHCP clients can log on and authenticate with the domain controllers and browse the internet. He also confirms that the accounting and human resource users can access their Web applications. After these successful tests, Tina opens her Outlook Web Access client and sends an e-mail to upper management that everything was a success. On Monday morning, the Help Desk is flooded with calls. No one can log on to their outlook clients and get into mail. What did Chad forget to consider when evaluating the project plan?

A. Editing the access lists on the exchange database for the new static IP addresses

B. Creating new DNS entries for each new network scope

C. Adding a WINS server and distributing its IP address to each DHCP scope

D. Adding the ARP cache timeout option for each new DHCP scope

☑ **C.** Answer **C** is correct because Chad forgot to consider the fact that based on the single network design prior to the network expansion project, users were all in the same broadcast domain. This enabled them to access NetBIOS-based applications via a broadcast since they were not configured as WINS clients. Tina was able to send an e-mail over the weekend because she used a Web application, which is based on DNS, to access her e-mail.

☒ Answer **A** is incorrect because there are no IP address access lists associated with exchange databases. Answer **B** is incorrect because the DNS servers have no changes and have been correctly set up in each of the DHCP scopes. Clients were able to access Web applications and browse the Internet. Answer **D** is incorrect because changing the ARP cache timeout would be effective only if the IP address of the Exchange server may have changes. If clients cached the MAC address and old IP address of the Exchange server for too long, they may not be able to connect. However, the IP address of the Exchange server did not change.

2. Computer Tech Inc. has recently been swamped with a lot of help desk calls from people complaining that computer connectivity is very intermittent throughout the day. Sometimes they can connect to a resource, but five minutes later they cannot. Based on the company's naming convention and frequent client turnaround, the support desk is also constantly typing computer names that no longer exist, or mistyping the computer name. The naming convention is based on a two-letter state identification ID plus a sequential number; for example, NJ1, NJ2, NJ3 or SC1, SC2, SC3. Computer Tech does not have a lot of network resources or the money to spend to get them. In order to afford equipment, they buy and deploy older, thus cheaper, technology. They are currently running their entire network on CAT3 cable with a 10BT network. They have only one router, segmenting the internal network from the Internet by way of a cable modem. All clients and servers currently connect daisy-chained network hubs and all use the same IP address scheme. Computer Tech hired a third-rate consulting company to come in and analyze their network to see if they could help diagnose some of the problems. The consultants did some low-level sniffing tests and determined that based on the low grade wires deployed throughout the network, clients did not have enough time to successfully broadcast and hear a successful reply. They suggested that a script be written to slightly increase the amount of time clients were able to listen for broadcast query replies. Computer Tech asked their systems engineer Bart to write a system policy to increase this value on all clients. Bart got to work immediately and began writing a custom ADM file for the particular registry key. He made the following change over the weekend, pushing it out to the entire domain: HKLM\SYSTEM\CurrentControlSet\Services\NetBT\Parameters\BcastNameQueryCount=20. Throughout the next week, calls to the support desk did not get any better, and in fact increased. What did Bart do wrong?

A. Changed the key in the wrong registry hive

B. Did not make the registry value high enough

C. Did not make the registry value low enough

D. Changed the wrong key value

☑ **D.** Answer **D** is correct because Bart choose the wrong key. In doing so, he effectively increased the amount of tries a client uses to resolve a query. Because of the computer naming convention and of the support desk constantly typing wrong computer names, broadcast tries were attempted 20 times before coming back with a negative response to the client. With the older less reliable CAT3 networking cable, and the use of hubs not switches, this would easily cause clients to be more unsuccessful when trying to connect to computer resources. The correct key should have been **BcastQueryTimeout** with a value of **200** milliseconds (ms). This setting would allow broadcasts to timeout after only 200ms instead of the default 750ms.

☒ Answer **A** is incorrect because HKLM is the correct registry hive. Answer **B** is incorrect because the registry key he changed was wrong. The correct key should have been **BcastQueryTimeout** with a value of **200** (ms). The value that was set on the incorrect key was also set much too high, causing a lot more broadcast traffic. Answer **C** is incorrect because again, the registry key was incorrect. If he set the key any lower than the default value of three, clients may not have had enough broadcast tries to reach a resolution.

The NetBIOS Node Types

3. Mike owns a small advertising company in downtown Manhattan and commutes into work every day from New Jersey. With the economy picking up, his company has expanded over the last year, requiring him to hire a lot more people, buy more desktop machines, and more importantly, hire a group of people to manage his network. Mike originally set up his company network of five users, with a single NT 4.0 domain and static IP addresses for both the servers and clients. All network nodes share the same IP address scheme and reside on a single network segment. With the recent growth, his company now consists of over 100 employees and 20 servers. Mike's new network admin team is led by his most technical employee and long term neighbor, Scott. Scott has been working in the IT field for years and has seen small companies grow into large companies, knowing the barriers that need to be overcome. With his first week of employment, Scott opens up his network sniffer and begins gathering a baseline traffic report. After one week of sniffing the network, Scott reports back to Mike that there is an unusually large amount of network traffic on the network caused by client broadcasting. Realizing that all the clients are still running Windows 98 and require NetBIOS to resolve resource requests, Scott proposes a plan to greatly reduce the amount of broadcast traffic on the network. His plan consists of the following action items:

- Convert all clients to DHCP
- Install a WINS server
- Set up a DHCP scope for the network address scheme

1. Exclude the server IP address

2. Add the WINS server as an option

3. Add the h-node type as an option

4. Add DNS as an option

5. Add the company's domain name suffix as an option

6. Add the default gateway as an option

Mike looks over his plan and is happy to have Scott on his team. He is eager to put the plan into action and schedules the work for the following evening. Between the two of them, they are able to install the networking components and touch all of the client machines to change their IP configuration to use DHCP. To test a successful implementation they log on to 15 different machines and test client to server connectivity. Everything seems to work great as they wrap up a late night and head back home to New Jersey. The next morning Scott receives no calls or complaints about network connectivity from his network administrators. Over the next week, Scott continues to sniff the network and monitor traffic flow. When he shows the report to Mike, he is surprised to see that network broadcast traffic has not been reduced by more than 1%. What did Scott forget to add to his plan?

A. P-node as an option as opposed to h-node

B. Configure servers to use DHCP

C. Configure servers with address of WINS server

D. M-node as an option as opposed to h-node

☑ **C.** Answer **C** is correct. If the servers are not set up to register themselves with the WINS servers, any client looking to resolve its NetBIOS name will still have to use a broadcast to locate them. Since all of the servers were statically assigned and their IP address stacks did not contain the address of the new WINS server, they will be able to be reached only via broadcast.

☒ Answer **A** is incorrect, because if p-node was configured as an option, the clients would not be able to use broadcasting at all to resolve NetBIOS names and thus would not be able to talk to any of the servers. P-node is set to use only a name server. Although Answer **B** may work, it is not the best available answer. Servers should not be set to use DHCP as it is best that most server IP addresses remain constant. Thus Answer **B** is incorrect. Answer **D** is incorrect because using m-node would set the clients to always broadcast first before trying to use a configured name server like WINS.

4. Keith was recently hired as a sales consultant for a software development company in Salt Lake City, Utah. Before attempting sales, Keith used to work in the computer industry as a contractor setting up small networks and configuring desktop machines. The late hours and technology overload pushed him into trying his luck in the sales arena. It has been almost a month and Keith is doing well. However, on Wednesday morning Keith is a bit frustrated

about his network performance. His access to the sales application server is as slow as ever. Keith wishes he was back in IT and could fix the problem himself so he could get back to selling effectively. Because of his background, he decides to do a little digging before calling in a support desk ticket. He goes out to the command prompt window and types ipconfig /all. His results are shown in Figure 4.91.

Figure 4.91 Displaying IP Information Using IPCONFIG

```
C:\WINNT\System32\cmd.exe                                    _ □ ✕

C:\>ipconfig /all

Windows 2000 IP Configuration

        Host Name . . . . . . . . . . . . : client2000-VM
        Primary DNS Suffix . . . . . . . : syngress.com
        Node Type . . . . . . . . . . . . : Hybrid
        IP Routing Enabled. . . . . . . . : No
        WINS Proxy Enabled. . . . . . . . : No
        DNS Suffix Search List. . . . . . : syngress.com

Ethernet adapter Local Area Connection 2:

        Connection-specific DNS Suffix  . : syngress.com
        Description . . . . . . . . . . . : AMD PCNET Family PCI Ethernet Adapte
r #2
        Physical Address. . . . . . . . . : 00-0C-29-84-01-A9
        DHCP Enabled. . . . . . . . . . . : Yes
        Autoconfiguration Enabled . . . . : Yes
        IP Address. . . . . . . . . . . . : 192.168.0.104
        Subnet Mask . . . . . . . . . . . : 255.255.255.0
        Default Gateway . . . . . . . . . : 192.168.0.50
        DHCP Server . . . . . . . . . . . : 192.168.0.3
        DNS Servers . . . . . . . . . . . : 192.168.0.192
        Primary WINS Server . . . . . . . : 192.168.0.3
        Secondary WINS Server . . . . . . : 192.168.0.4
        Lease Obtained. . . . . . . . . . : Wednesday, July 09, 2003 4:46:32 PM
        Lease Expires . . . . . . . . . . : Thursday, July 17, 2003 4:46:32 PM

C:\>
```

He verifies that he is using a WINS server. He then types **nbtstat −r** into his command window. The results show that half of his NetBIOS name resolutions are using broadcasts for name resolution. With this information, Keith calls the support desk and asks if the IP address of his WINS server is correct. They reply that it is. Keith thinks they are wrong because he knows that WINS servers should stop broadcasts. He continues to argue with support about his problem. What does support tell him next?

A. His node type supports broadcasting.

B. His node type does not support broadcasting.

C. They will reconfigure his node type for m-node.

D. They will reconfigure his node type for p-node.

☑ **A**. Answer **A** is correct. Hybrid or h-node configurations support the use of broadcasting. Just because a client is configured as a WINS client does not ensure that it will use WINS for name resolution. This is why there are a number of methods and node types to determine the method order. Only NetBIOS servers registered with WINS will be resolved using WINS.

☒ Answer **B** is incorrect because his node type of hybrid (h-node) does support broadcasting. Answer **C** is incorrect because an m-node type would make sure that all Keith's name resolutions would first try to broadcast before using his WINS server. Answer **D** is incorrect because a p-node configuration would make sure that Keith would be unable to resolve anything unless it was configured in WINS, which obviously is not the case due to his NetBIOS naming resolution stats.

5. Chris works as the systems manager for a bleeding edge computer company that is constantly trying to stay ahead of technology by implementing software days after it is released to the public. Until last weekend Chris and his network team supported a Windows 2000 native mode Active Directory domain using Exchange 2000. After the weekend, Chris was supporting a fully deployed Windows Server 2003 Active Directory environment. All of the clients at Chris's company are installed with either Windows 2000 Professional or Windows XP and are configured as DHCP clients. All servers are set up with static IP information. There is one group of NT 4.0 servers that run an ancient human resources payroll program. They do not yet currently support running on a Windows 2000 or Windows Server 2003 support platform. Because they are a somewhat smaller software company, all computer nodes are running on the same single network segment. Before the upgrade, Chris made sure to tell his systems team that they need to leave the WINS server implementation in place as the payroll system still requires NetBIOS name resolution and everybody wants to make sure human resources can access and submit payroll checks! Eager to remove the old name resolution methods of Windows NT systems, Al conforms to the request yet suggests he has a way to at least eliminate the NetBIOS broadcast traffic. Chris agrees with him and says to make it so. Al changes the DHCP scope options and changes the node type from h-node to p-node. At the end of the month, the support desk starts receiving calls from the accounting department. They state that they are trying to access the payroll system to issue end of month checks but are unable to. They report a network error of "The network path was not found." Chris hears about the errors and is furious with Al because he had told him to leave the WINS server alone. In his defense, Al states that the WINS server is still up and that the Payroll applications server pool was able to communicate with each other just fine. Al runs nbtstat –r on one of the accounting machines and sees no broadcast activity, which is what he was trying to accomplish. What could be the problem?

A. The new node type has not taken effect yet.

B. The accounting client machines have not been rebooted yet.

C. The accounting servers were never configured to use WINS.

D. The accounting servers were not supposed to get the new node type.

☑ **C.** Answer **C** is correct. Since broadcasting was disabled and no one in the accounting department can access the servers via their configured WINS servers, the accounting payroll servers must have never been configured to use a WINS server. The fact that the payroll servers can all still communicate with each other is due to their not being set up for DHCP and thus not being limited to WINS resolution with the p-node configuration parameter.

☒   Answer **A** is incorrect because it is apparent that the new node type has taken effect and restricted the ability for the accounting machines to broadcast and communicate with the payroll servers. Answer **B** is incorrect because regardless of whether the machines were rebooted, they still received the new DHCP option for p-node because they can no longer resolve NetBIOS names via broadcast. Answer **D** is incorrect because the accounting payroll servers would not have received the DHCP option as they are not DHCP clients and are configured statically.

The LMHOSTS file

6.   You are a contractor working for a small Internet startup incubator, helping other companies get their companies on the right foot. One Friday afternoon, you find yourself at a local residence of someone trying to run a new business from his home. The owner, Joel, has run cat5e cable throughout his house and has two offices that are network and Internet-ready. You ask Joel a little bit about how his network is configured, and he tells you that he is running a Windows 2000 Active Directory mixed-mode backbone with one NT 4.0 BDC. All of his clients run Windows 98 or Windows ME. Because it is a small one-segment network, Joel tells you that he relies on broadcasts for name resolution and does not want to implement or manage a WINS server. However, he complains of slow network performance. You decide to work with him and recommend implementing LMHOSTS files on each of his Windows 98/ME workstations. Between the two of you, you create and test the LMHOSTS file on the owner's Windows 98 machine. It seems to greatly speed up his network performance. To save money, Joel sends you home and says he can add the same LMHOSTS file to each of the other machines. Twenty minutes later you get a call on your cell phone and Joel is complaining that the LMHOSTS file is not working on the other machines. What did you do, that Joel forgot to do?

A.   Run **nbtstat -R**

B.   Run **nbtstat -r**

C.   Run **netstat -R**

D.   Run **nbtstat -RR**

☑   **A.** Answer **A** is correct because **nbtstat -R** is used to reload your LMHOSTS file located in %systemroot%\system32\drivers\etc. By default, this is loaded only upon initial boot of the computer. If you change or add an LMHOSTS file and do not reboot, you must reload the LMHOSTS file for your computer to the new name to IP settings.

☒   Answer **B** is incorrect because **nbtstat -r** will show you only which name resolutions have been answered via broadcasts, and which have been answered via a NetBIOS name server. Answer **C** is incorrect because **netstat** is not a utility to use when troubleshooting NetBIOS names, but is used to show what ports your computer is listening on. Answer **D** is incorrect because the **-RR** switch of the **nbtstat** command utility refreshes your NetBIOS name with a configured WINS server. Since you are not running a WINS server this would not work.

7. You work in the shipping and receiving warehouse for a small OEM computer supply com-
    pany called The T-Group. It is your job as a desktop engineer to make sure that all clients are
    able to log on and authenticate to the corporate office from their NT 4.0 workstations.
    Currently, your client base of five workstations point to a WINS server at the corporate
    office to resolve logon and to authenticate to the correct domain controller. You get word
    that the systems engineering team is converting the functional level of the current Windows
    Server 2003 interim mode Active Directory domain over the weekend. They are raising the
    domain level to Windows Server 2003 native mode. You call the manager of this group and
    inquire about any changes you may need to make, so that your warehouse clients can still
    authenticate on Monday. Robert said that nothing would affect logon authentication, and in
    fact logon should be a lot quicker because he was removing some legacy protocols and ser-
    vices. Nervous about what he meant by this, as he is notorious for abrupt change without
    the correct research, you sit back and wait. Contrary to what was told to you, on Monday
    morning none of your NT 4.0 clients could log on. Knowing a little about network resolu-
    tion, and more about Robert, you have a hunch and try to log on to using your Windows
    2000 laptop machine that you built for emergencies. As you suspected, you are able to log on
    without a problem. You call Robert and ask him if he uninstalled the WINS server because
    he had heard that Windows Server2003 no longer required NetBIOS. Robert replied, Yes.
    What can you do to quickly get your workstations logging onto the network again?

    A. Distribute an LMHOSTS file using the #PRE and #DOM tags with the name and IP
        address of the new PDC Emulator and have everybody reboot.

    B. Edit the default LMHOSTS file on everybody's workstation and use the #PRE and
        #DOM tags with the name and IP address of the new PDC Emulator.

    C. Install WINS on one of the NT 4.0 workstations and have all your clients point to it.

    D. Install a WINS proxy agent on one of your NT 4.0 workstations and have everybody
        point to it.

    ☑ **A.** Answer **A** is correct. Although Windows Server 2003 does not rely on NetBIOS
        itself, NT 4.0 machines require it to locate and authenticate with network domain con-
        trollers for successful logon. If you place the domain controller name in a file called
        LMHOSTS and use the domain controller identifier along with the preload tag prefixes,
        the NT 4.0 machines will cache the location of the domain controller's IP address upon
        next reboot and be able to authenticate for logon.

    ☒ Answer **B** is incorrect because the default LMHOSTS file is named LMHOSTS.SAM and
        is used only as a sample. If you were to rename that file and exclude the extension as well
        as run **nbtstat –R** to reload that fill, the solution would work. Answer **C** is incorrect
        because you cannot install WINS on an NT 4.0 workstation. WINS can be installed only
        on a server. Answer **D** is incorrect. Although you can configure an NT 4.0 workstation as a
        WINS proxy agent, a WINS proxy agent listens for only non-WINS client broadcasts.

The Windows 2003 Windows Internet Name Server

8. You are working for the LAN Admin team at a local college in your home town of New Brunswick, NJ. It is your job to add and remove all user and computer names from the network as employees are hired and fired. The network you work on uses TCP/IP as its main network protocol, runs on a Windows 2003 Active Directory infrastructure with Windows NT 4.0 File Servers. All the clients are running Windows NT 4.0 workstation. As a LAN Admin team member, you have been added to the WINS Users active directory group in order to view WINS records and help troubleshoot workstation naming issues. Workstation names are based on cube number so that frequent turnaround does not require machine renaming. However, some employees use laptops and take their work home with them every night. On Monday morning, you received your weekly report detailing that last week's turnaround. On it were a few temps, some contractors, and some mobile users. You open Active Directory users and computers and delete all their usernames. On Tuesday, you receive a work order to add a new contractor to cube number 104. You venture over to cube 104 to begin the cleanup of the workstation for the new user. Based on the missing desktop, you realize that this must have been one of the mobile users that were recently fired. This means that you have to install a bare bone image on a new desktop. Based on the way names are created, the workstation name you would need to create would be NJ-104-NT40. You download your company's core OS image onto a new desktop PC and boot it up. Sysprep has been run on your image, so you go through all of the wizard's prompts in order to personalize this PC. When you get to the workstation name, you enter NJ-104-NT40. For some reason, you get the error message shown in Figure 4.92. You open up your WINS console and search for that name. To your surprise, you find it in an active state. You try to ping the name and IP address registered in your WINS database but get no response. What happened?

Figure 4.92 Workstation Naming Error

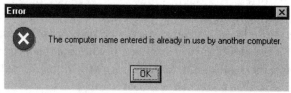

A. That is not a standard NetBIOS name.

B. That name is in use on your network.

C. That name is a hidden WINS record.

D. The computer holding that name was shut down incorrectly.

☑ **D.** Answer **D** is correct because computers that are not properly shut down will remain in the WINS database as active NetBIOS names until either that computer name comes back online and reregisters that name, or the TTL expires on that name and the name becomes tombstoned.

☒ Answer **A** is incorrect because all the characters used in that name are supported NetBIOS characters and the name does not exceed 15 characters in length. Answer **B** is incorrect because you try and ping it by name and IP address and are unable to communicate with it. Answer **C** is incorrect because there is no way to hide a WINS record. You can hide your NetBIOS name from the browse list but not the WINS database.

9. Jennifer, a long term employee, works as a systems engineer for a software development company you are planning to acquire. Before the two companies merge, you want to get a report from Jennifer, outlining her network design, server, and client node count, network protocols in use, and any needed application specific information. Your company employs the standard use of Windows XP on its client machines and has recently elevated the functional level of its domain to a Windows Server 2003 mode of active directory. The reason you are acquiring Jennifer's company is to take advantage of their very popular and world-renowned sales software product. You want to make sure the company merger does not interrupt the huge sales volumes level you currently demand when the switch to the new software is made. Jennifer is very aware of all your questions and gets the answers in a report back to you in a few days. In summary, it shows the following information:

- Windows 2003 interim functionality domain, with two Win2003 domain controllers and one NT 4.0 Backup Domain Controller

- Class A 10.0.0.0/24 network broken up into several broadcast domains

- 10 servers running a mix of Windows 2003 and Windows NT

- 50 client machines running a mix of Windows 98, Windows 2000, and Windows XP

- Network protocols in use: IP

- Network services in use: WINS, DHCP, DNS

- WINS and DHCP share a single server

- Sales software requires NetBIOS

You review the differences in the networks and devise a plan with Jennifer's help to merge the two companies. You decide to use Jennifer's domain as the source domain because it is already built with a generic *root.com* domain name and a simple OU design. You want to keep the internal domain structure generic and begin a new OU design from scratch rather than try to reorganize your own. Because of the scalability of Windows Server 2003, you decide that you do not need any more hardware to accommodate the additional 1000 workstations and 50 servers. The assumption was correct at first and the migration was scheduled and completed successfully over a long four-day weekend. Jennifer's company's NT 4.0 domain controller was removed and deleted from the domain, the functional level was raised to be equivalent to yours, and your company was migrated directly into their OU design. The current DHCP scopes were already configured with plenty of IP addresses to handle the new client load. On Monday morning, all the new clients come into work and boot up their machines. At first, everybody is able to log on and access the sales application just fine, but as more and more users come in and boot up, they are not even able to log on. After some investigation, Jennifer finds the following facts:

- Old users seem to be able to log on with cached credential but are using APIPA.

- New users are unable to log on to the domain at all, but can log on locally and also use APIPA.

- Users that are already logged on are up and working, but cannot access the sales application.

- The WINS server is hung.

What happened?

- A. The DHCP scope ran out of addresses.
- B. The WINS server's burst handling was set to *Low*.
- C. The WINS server's burst handling was not installed.
- D. The WINS server's burst handling was disabled.

☑ **D.** Answer **D** is correct because without burst handling enabled, the WINS server was unable to register and reply to the mass amount of new client requests and in an attempt to do so, hung. Because WINS was installed on the same server as DHCP, the DHCP service also hung, preventing new clients from obtaining an IP address and logging onto a domain in which they did not have the ability to use cached credentials. Clients were unable to access the NetBIOS sales application because they were trying to resolve its name from a hung WINS server. Broadcasting would not work because they were across router boundaries in which broadcasts do not pass.

☒ Answer **A** is incorrect because it was predetermined that there were plenty of IP addresses available for all networks. The DHCP server was running off the same server that WINS was and it was hung, unable to hand out any more addresses. Answer **B** is incorrect because if WINS burst handling was set to *Low*, then after 300 WINS registrations, bursting would have kicked in, and the server may not have hung. Answer **C** is incorrect because burst handling is not something you install, but a setting you can enable or disable.

Configuring the WINS Client

10. You are an ASP.NET Web developer working for an Application Solutions Provider in Seattle, Washington. Because of the kind of work you do, your company allows you the flexibility to work from home about 90 percent of the time. The other 10 percent of the time is spent in the office, at corporate meetings, or presenting new code to other development workers. Your manager Akin asks you to present your current code in a meeting on Wednesday afternoon, to show the other developers. You show up Wednesday morning prepared to wow your coworkers with your new code. About five minutes before the meeting you decide to print a copy of your code to hand out in the meeting. You gather your things and head into Conference Room A. You plug your Windows 2000 laptop into an available network jack and begin to set up a printer in accordance with the instruction card next to the conference room printer. The card states that the printer queue is named CONFA and the NT 4.0 print server is named PRINTSRV. As people start entering the room, you quickly realize that your IP information is set up for your home network. You make a quick call to one of your friends that works in the systems group and ask him for a valid IP address, subnet, and gateway for Conference Room A. You also get the IP address for the company DNS server and verify the NetBIOS name of the conference room print server. You set up your new information and test Internet connectivity successfully. Everyone is now seated and ready for your presentation. You say that you want to print a copy of your code and for everyone to grab it off the printer behind them. You quickly try to locate the printer to set it up by typing **\\PRINTSRV\CONFA** at the **Run** command window. You receive an error message that tells you the printer cannot be found. As you swallow your pride in front of your peers and call your friend back what does he tell you?

A. The correct IP address of the gateway

B. The IP address of the WINS server

C. The IP address of the CONFA printer

D. The IP address of the PRINTSRV server

☑ **B.** Answer **B** is correct because you are in need of NetBIOS name to IP address resolution for the NetBIOS-based NT 4.0 print server. Unless properly configured to integrate with DNS, WINS by default will not be passed requests from DNS queries for NetBIOS names.

☒ Answer **A** is incorrect because without the correct gateway IP address you would not have been able to access the Internet. Answer **C** is incorrect because you do not need to know the IP address of the physical printer if it is shared via a print server. Answer **D** is incorrect for the same reason. Although knowing the IP address of either the print server or the physical printer may help you set up the printer, it is not the correct solution in this manner. The uses of names on a network are there for a reason and are to be used instead of physical IP addresses for resource connectivity.

11. Jamie has just opened her first consulting LLC in Nutley, NJ and is beginning to pull in some real business. She is starting off small with a few mom-and-pop shop administration jobs and a bit of integration work for some larger companies mixed in on the side. Jamie has been working in the IT business for quite some time and understands the importance of quick name resolution. She runs into a smaller, predominantly NetBIOS-based computer network company that seems to be having broadcast issues. They tell Jamie that they want to implement a solution with as little work as possible and that all the clients and servers must remain configured with static IP addresses. Jamie does a diagnosis of the computer network and finds that things rarely change, and the clients and servers have been running with the same names and IP addresses for 10 years. WINS is not in use on the network since broadcasts are now used for NetBIOS names resolution on the single segment network. Jamie decides to go with the following solution:

■ Create a client side LMHOSTS file using the #INCLUDE tag to centrally point clients to a server side LMHOSTS file located on a common file server. Use the #BEGIN_ALTERNATE and #END_ALTERNATE tags to add another #INCLUDE statement for a pointer to a second copy of the server side LMHOST file for redundancy. The client side LMHOSTS file looks like this:

```
#BEGIN_ALTERNATE
#INCLUDE \\server1\public\lmhosts
#INCLUDE \\server2\public\lmhosts
#END_ALTERNATE
```

■ Push the client side LMHOSTS file to each of the clients' %systemroot%\system32\drivers\etc directory by means of a logon script.

■ Create a server side LMHOSTS file that includes all the NetBIOS server names using the #PRE tag to permanently cache the entries in each client's local name cache, for fast access and limited broadcasts.

Jamie puts this solution in place and is confident it will work because it is what she used to do at every administrator job she worked at previously. She drops by the office of Al, the owner, on the way out the door and tells him that clients will need to reboot their machines twice in order for the NetBIOS broadcast problem to go away. She explains that the first reboot will allow the LMHOSTS file to be copied locally, and the second reboot will read the local LMHOSTS file, telling it to load all the entries in name cache from the central server side LMHOSTS file. Jamie receives a call from Al about two hours later. He is complaining that it appears nothing has changed; client access is still slow. Jamie walks him through running the **nbtstat –r** command on five or six workstations. He reports that **Resolved by Broadcast** is 50 or higher on each of his client's workstations. She then has him search and look at the local LMHOSTS file to verify that it is correct. She has him manually reload it by typing **nbtstat –R**, but with no luck. As Al accesses resources that should be in the server side LMHOSTS file, the broadcast count gets higher. What did Jamie forget?

A. To include the #PRE and #DOM tags in the client side LMHOSTS file

B. To include the IP address and name of server1 and server2 in the client side LMHOSTS file

C. To include the IP address and name of server1 and server2 in the server side LMHOSTS file

D. To include the #REDIRECT tag instead of the older #INCLUDE tag

☑ **B.** Answer **B** is correct because in order for the client to use a centrally located LMHOSTS file, the physical server name and IP address where that file is located must be loaded into the local client's cache in order for it to use the central file.

☒ Answer **A** is incorrect because the #PRE and #DOM tags are not needed in the client side LMHOSTS file if using the #INCLUDE tag to look at another LMHOSTS file. You can use the #PRE and #DOM tags in the server side LMHOSTS file. Answer **C** is incorrect because the IP address and name are not necessary in the server side LMHOSTS file for the #INCLUDE redirect statement to work for the local client. Answer **D** is incorrect because there is no such #REDIRECT tag.

Network Service Interoperability

12. Kurt, the network administrator for Fantastic, Inc., a plastics manufacturing company, is a member of the DHCP Administrators group and is in charge of configuring all client DHCP scopes. Because it is a rather large client community, Kurt manages just over 20 DCHP scopes for the 20 or so different subnets on his company network. Though the network backend runs Windows Server 2003 Active Directory, most of the client community still runs Windows NT 4.0 on their desktops. Recently, the IP address of one of the secondary WINS servers had to change due to a revamp in its network subnet addressing scheme. In order to distribute this needed change to Kurt's clients, Kurt had to make the change 20 times, one for each subnet's scope. After the change was made and no users complained of any difficulties, Kurt looked into creating another solution for making a global change like this in the future. After some research, Kurt discovered DHCP Server Options. These are options that that be set once and applied globally on all scopes on a single server. Kurt put in a change control request to change all options that could be applied globally to the DHCP server. The options he chose were:

- Primary and secondary WINS Server IP Addresses

- Primary and secondary DNS Server IP addresses

- DNS Domain Name suffix

The request was approved and Kurt made the changes over the weekend. On Monday morning, the help desk starts receiving call tickets from people complaining of slow network logons and client server access times. The help desk confirmed, however, that although they are able to access network resources, including the Internet, some resources are very slow. You ask J, one of your network guys, to run a sniffer on the network and see if there are any abnormal broadcasts happening. He reports back to you that there is not a lot of broadcast traffic on the network. What has happened?

A. Kurt entered the wrong DNS server IP address in the scope.

B. Kurt forgot to switch the default gateway to a Global Scope option.

C. Kurt entered the wrong secondary WINS IP address.

D. Kurt entered the wrong primary WINS IP address.

☑ **D.** Answer **D** is correct. If a client's primary WINS server is misconfigured or physically offline, the client will attempt to contact it three times before defaulting to its secondary WINS server. This would definitely cause a noticeable degradation in log on performance and resource access in NetBIOS-dependant NT 4.0 workstations.

☒ Answer **A** is incorrect because NT 4.0 machines do not use DNS for logon or authentication. Reports also showed that clients could access the Internet, a DNS-dependent function. If the default gateway was used as a global scope option, only the subnets that were attached to that gateway interface would be able to log on at all. Default gateways are subnet independent and should be configured as regular scope options. Since everyone was able to log on and was complaining only of slow access, Answer **B** is incorrect. Although Answer **C** could be correct, it is not the best choice because clients would not use the secondary WINS server unless the primary WINS server was down. If just the secondary WINS server was down or misconfigured, clients would probably not notice any difference in network logon or resource access speed.

13. As the network administrator, Kristy decides to implement the ability for clients to dial-in to the network to allow them the option to work from home if they want to, by installing and configuring an RRAS server. Kristy's internal network consists of a Windows 2000 domain, a single DNS and WINS server, multiple segmented broadcast domains, and a single DHCP server, configured to distribute the following information via four different IP address scopes:

■ DNS Server (local option)

■ Router (local option)

■ WINS Server (local option)

■ Node Type (global option)

■ Domain Name (global option)

■ ARP Timeout (local)

Kristy installs her RRAS server and configures the DHCP Relay Agent to point to the only internal DHCP server. She then configures a fifth DHCP scope to accommodate the DMZ network into which she has installed her RRAS server. Kristy hopes to be able to offer both internal Web mail and resource access to her NT 4.0 file server in the same way she is able to successfully offer it now to only internal users. Kristy composes an e-mail with detailed instructions on how to set up her Windows ME laptop users with the correct VPN settings to dial-in the company RRAS server. With the e-mail, Kristy asks for feedback as to ease of installation, setup, connectivity, speed, resource access, and so on. A few days later, Kristy receives e-mails from most of the users she sent the e-mail to. All of them said that they were able to access e-mail just fine and that the speeds were great. They also said they were able to browse the Internet without a problem, but none of them could access any of the file server resources that they needed to do their work. What is the easiest thing Kristy can do to facilitate this need?

A. Change the DNS server to a global option in DHCP

B. Change the WINS server to a global option in DHCP

C. Change the node type to a local option for each scope in DHCP

D. Add another WINS server to facilitate the dial-in users

☑ **B.** Answer **B** is correct. Clients seem to be getting every setting DHCP is set up for except WINS. Since WINS is set locally, that means that it must be configured for each scope separately. The dial-in scope must have been missed. Since there is only one WINS server in use on the internal network, configuring this as a global option to apply to all scopes would be the best solution.

☒ Answer **A** is incorrect, because dial-in clients were able to access internal Web mail and the Internet meaning that they must be getting the correct DNS settings. Answer **C** is incorrect because the node type setting is globally set. This means that if there were a problem with its type, internal users would also have issues connecting to file share resources. Answer **D** is incorrect, because another WINS server would be more work than simply changing the WINS server option to global. It also does not state that you should change the DHCP option, which was the problem in the first place.

Monitoring and Troubleshooting the Windows 2003 WINS Server

14. Jackie is the owner and administrator of network NetBIOS name resolution and replication. She has been the administrator for XYZ Corporation since it started using WINS back with Windows NT Server V3.51, so she is very familiar with the name resolution process. XYC Corporation is currently running Windows Server 2003 WINS servers and has set up two-way WINS Push/Pull replication between its hub in Boston, MA and all its satellite offices around the state. Gloucester is one of the satellite offices, and ever since the long weekend's scheduled database maintenance work, they are no longer receiving WINS replication records from the Boston hub. What could have possible happened over the weekend to prevent records in Boston from replicating to Gloucester? Boston is not having problems with any other site.

A. Someone has added the Gloucester WINS server IP address in the Accept records for the owner's box on the Boston WINS server.

B. Someone has added the Gloucester WINS server IP address in the Block records for the owner's box on the Boston WINS server.

C. Someone has added the Boston WINS server IP address in the Accept records for the owner's box on the Gloucester WINS server.

D. Someone has added the Boston WINS server IP address into the Block records for the owner's box on the Andover WINS server.

☑ **B.** Answer **B** is correct. By adding Gloucester into the Block records for the owner's box on Boston's WINS server, you have effectively stopped replication traffic for Gloucester being able to pull data from Boston.

☒ Answer **A** in incorrect because accepting Gloucester as a valid WINS replication partner on the Boston WINS server would allow replication to happen, not prevent it. The problem also states that replication is not happening in the other direction; however, if the default configuration setting of Only replicate with partners is on, both replication partners must allow each other for successful replication to happen. Answer **C** is incorrect because accepting Boston as a valid replication partner on Gloucester's WINS server would not prevent Gloucester from receiving replication updates but again would allow replication updates. Answer **D** is incorrect because it states that Andover is not allowed to replicate with Boston, which has nothing to do with Gloucester.

15. Chad is the network administrator for an online banking company located on the east coast of the United States. He has recently been involved with a team of engineers to help integrate their company with another online banking firm, and has been working closely with that company's lead engineer, Scott. Chad's company consists of a completely Windows NT 4.0 domain infrastructure, whereas Scott manages a fully native mode Windows 2000 Active Directory domain environment. The plan, as set forth by upper management, is to consolidate the NT 4.0 domain as an organizational unit in the Windows 2000 domain. To help facilitate this process, Chad and Scott set up a downlevel two-way trust between each of the domains. The trust is set up without a problem and now they are ready to start sharing resources. Scott tells Chad that before they are able to start accessing file share resources, they need to set up NetBIOS WINS replication. Chad informs Scott that he will need to get approval from his manager before going forth with that next step. Chad asks if there is any other way that some of his NT 4.0 clients can start accessing resources on some of the Windows 2000 servers. Scott tells him that there is a temporary solution and sends Chad a custom LMHOSTS file that has in it all the server names and downlevel domain controller information for the Windows 2000 domains PDC emulator and its servers. Scott proceeds to tell Chad that he can place this file in the %systemroot%\system32\drivers\etc directory of any server he wants to access resources in his domain. He will just need to reboot that server or run **nbtstat −R** to load the LMHOSTS file into name cache. Chad tries it on one of his servers and lets Scott know that it worked perfectly. Scott and Chad did not communicate

for a few weeks after that because other projects seemed to pile up on each of their plates. The following Friday, Scott gave Chad a call and informed him he planned on changing one of the network segment's IP schemes, containing all the domain controllers. Although the WINS servers would not be affected, he discussed the fact that all the IP addresses of the DC's and some of the application servers had to change and that the LMHOSTS file would cease to work without changing it. Chad recommended they go forth with WINS replication instead as he had finally gotten approval from his manager. They scheduled the change for the Tuesday after the network change. Late Tuesday evening, both domains' WINS servers were set up as Push/Pull replication partners with each other, along with the help of a newly created LMHOSTS file to get initial name resolution working. Chad said that he noticed records flowing into his database, as did Scott. Both were satisfied with the results, and because it was late they were both ready to call it a day. Early Wednesday morning, Todd, Scott's boss, calls him complaining that none of his Windows 98 users can log on to the domain. He mentioned that his team was able to log on to the domain but they were not able to access the Exchange 5.5 server. You think to yourself about the differences and realize that Todd and his team members are using Windows XP. What happened?

A. Chad imported the original LMHOSTS file into his WINS server.

B. Chad forgot to remove the original LMHOSTS file from his WINS server.

C. Scott forgot to restart his WINS service after replication had taken place.

D. Scott forgot to change his DHCP server to hand out new WINS server IP addresses.

☑ **A. Answer A is correct.** If Chad had imported the original LMHOSTS file into his WINS server, it would have enabled all of his clients to access the resources he wanted them to access without the need to set up replication. However, in doing so, all records created within his WINS server were static records. Because static records overwrite dynamic records by default, when replication was set up between the two WINS servers, the older static IP entries overwrote the new IP addresses on the Windows 2000 domain controllers. This prevented the Windows 98 clients from successfully authenticating and logging on to the domain because they require NetBIOS domain controller records to log on. Windows XP machines, however, do not, because they use DNS, which was working. Exchange 5.5 is another NetBIOS application that requires WINS, and must have been in the original LMHOSTS file.

☒ Answer **B** is incorrect because an incorrect LMHOSTS file on Chad's domain WINS server would not affect Windows 98 logon on Scott's Windows 2000 domain. Answer **C** is incorrect because WINS does not need to be restarted after replication is set up. Answer **D** is incorrect because the question states that the WINS server IP address did not change.

Chapter 5 Domain Naming System Concepts

Review of DNS

1. Lisa Cooper works in the finance department, which has its own domain, finance.eastcoast.somecompany.com. Lisa Chandler works in the operations department in the same branch office as Lisa Cooper. While having lunch one day, Lisa Cooper mentions to Lisa Chandler that she'd renamed her computer to LISAC because it originally had come configured as HQV53X09 and she just didn't like that. Lisa Chandler becomes concerned when she hears this because her computer is named LISAC and she knows you can't have duplicate computer names on the network. If you overheard this conversation, what would you tell these two Lisa's?

   A. Since Lisa Chandler's computer was named LISAC first, it will be recognized as LISAC. Lisa Cooper's computer will lose connectivity to the network and will have to be renamed.

   B. Lisa Cooper's computer name will be seen as LISAC2 on the network since she chose the name after Lisa Chandler, whose computer name is LISAC.

   C. If Lisa Cooper changed the name without specifying the domain, there will be a conflict.

   D. Lisa Cooper's computer's FQDN is unique, so there is no conflict.

   ☑ **D.** The host name is appended to the domain name on a network resulting in a unique host name (FQDN). If Lisa Cooper and Lisa Chandler's computers were on the same subdomain, they could not both have the name LISAC because the FQDN would be identical. As it is, there is no problem. Lisa Cooper's computer's FQDN is lisac.finance.eastcoast.somecompany.com and Lisa Chandler's computer's FQDN is lisac.operations.eastcoast.somecompany.com; therefore, Answer **D** is correct.

   ☒ If the computers were in a small network or if they were on the same subdomain (or domain), they could not have the same name. In this case, the registration of a duplicate name would not be allowed. This is not the case since their computers are on different domains; therefore, Answer **A** is incorrect. Answer **B** is incorrect because the naming system does not automatically assign alternate names. A name is either accepted and registered or rejected. Answer **C** is incorrect because when the computer name is changed, the parent domain is appended unless another domain is specified. In this case, the parent domain is finance.eastcoast.somecompany.com, so there is no problem.

2. An application using NetBIOS needs a NetBIOS name resolved. To resolve the NetBIOS name, local cache is checked first. The needed resolution is not already cached, so the LMHOSTS file is checked next. The desired entry is not in the LMHOSTS file. Based on this, what is the next step taken in resolving the NetBIOS name?

A. The DNS server issues a recursive query.

B. The WINS server is queried.

C. The DNS server is queried using an NS type record.

D. NetBIOS over TCP resolves the name to an IP address.

☑ **B.** Answer **B** is correct because the next step taken is to resolve the name via WINS. In some cases, based on the NetBIOS node type (covered earlier in this book), a broadcast message may be sent. However, when WINS is implemented, it will be used to resolve NetBIOS name queries if the name is not found in either cache or an LMHOSTS file on the local computer.

☒ The DNS server can issue a recursive query to another DNS server in response to a host name query. In this case, the resolution involves a NetBIOS name, so WINS will be used to resolve the NetBIOS name to an IP address; therefore, Answer **A** is incorrect. Answer **C** is incorrect because DNS is not queried to resolve NetBIOS names. The NS record is for the name space, not for NetBIOS. NetBIOS over TCP is the interface used by NetBIOS applications across a TCP/IP network. It is not directly responsible for resolving NetBIOS names; therefore, Answer **D** is incorrect.

3. The Cooper Company has just acquired a firm and they're trying to integrate their networks. The Cooper company has a domain name somecompany.com. As a temporary solution, the Cooper company uses the domain name newcompany.us as the domain name for the acquired company as a subdomain. However, another company on the Internet uses the domain name newcompany.us. Can the Cooper Company still use this domain name? Why or why not? Select the best response.

A. No. The Cooper Company must create a different domain name for the new company so it does not replicate a domain name already in use.

B. Yes. The Cooper Company can use this domain name because the FQDN of this new domain is newcompany.us.somecompany.com.

C. No. The Cooper Company cannot use this domain name because the .us indicates a TLD.

D. Yes, the Cooper Company can use this domain name because the new domain will not be connected to the Internet.

☑ **B.** The Cooper Company can use this domain name because the subdomain name is appended to the second-level and TLD name. In this case, the FQDN becomes newcompany.us + somecompany.com or newcompany.us.somecompany.com. A computer connected to the new subdomain might have an FQDN of lisam.newcompany.us.somecompany.com. Therefore, Answer **B** is correct.

☒ The Cooper Company could not connect the subdomain directly to the Internet. This would be violating naming regulations that guarantee that domain names (second level plus TLD) are unique. Answer **A** is incorrect because as long as the subdomain newcompany.us is connected to the Internet via the second level domain, somecompany.com, there is no naming violation. The .us is a new TLD, but it can be used in other parts of a domain name. When used in other than the TLD location, it is interpreted as a node on the DNS name tree rather than as a TLD. Therefore, Answer **C** is incorrect. Answer **D** is incorrect because the Cooper Company can use any name it chooses as long as that domain does not connect to the Internet. However, in this case, there is no information as to whether or not the new domain will connect to the Internet. The relevant information here is that newcompany.us was labels as a subdomain, which indicates it is below the second level domain name. This means that it will use the second level domain name, somecompany.com, as part of its FQDN, thus creating (and guaranteeing) a unique name on the Internet.

4. You've been asked to look at a DNS server that a junior member of the IT department worked on, which seems to be having problems. You browse to c:\windows03\system32\dns and locate the cache.dns file. You open this file using Notepad and see the following entry:

```
.                    360000    NS      somecompany.com.
somecompany.com  360000    A        184.22.63.1
```

You recognize the domain name as your company's domain name and the IP address as the root server for the domain. What do you conclude from this information?

A. The cache.dns file is corrupt and should be replaced by copying one from another DNS server.

B. You need an SOA record along with the NS and A type RRs in this file.

C. The DNS server was not connected to the Internet when DNS was initialized.

D. The server's root hints file is missing and should be copied from another DNS server that is working.

☑ **C.** The DNS Wizard will attempt to locate the root servers on the Internet when it's initializing DNS. However, if it cannot locate Internet root servers, it will point to the internal root server instead. Answer **C** is correct because in this case, the system must not have been connected to the network when the junior IT staff member installed DNS on the server.

☒ Answer **A** is incorrect because there is no evidence the file is corrupt. This file, the
cache.dns file, is the correct file to check for root server information. However, the entries
are valid entries for the internal root server. Answer **B** is incorrect because you do not
need an SOA record in the cache.dns file. You do need an SOA and NS RR in the zone
to specify the DNS server is authoritative for the zone but that is not the problem in this
question. The root hints file is named cache.dns in Windows environments. If you are
viewing the contents of cache.dns, you are viewing the root hints file. Therefore, Answer **D**
is incorrect.

Host Name Resolution

5. You've been tasked with helping to set up some of the DNS servers for your company's
expanded network. The domain name is somecompany.com and you're working on opera-
tions.somecompany.com. You have an older server, bobcat, that has been used for the operations department but is woefully inadequate. Due to serious budget constraints, you've been
forced to delay purchases of hardware that you need to provide the services required by your
users. The bobcat server is going to be temporarily replaced by another server with a slightly
faster processor and more memory. This new server, cheetah, will be used only for a few
months, until the new fiscal year. At that time, bobcat will be replaced with a significantly
improved server that will provide more speed and processing power than either the old
bobcat or the cheetah. Based on this information, what RR would you add to your DNS
server when cheetah is operational?

A. cheetah IN   SRV   bobcat.operations.somecompany.com

B. cheetah IN   A   54.166.251.16

C. bobcat.operations.somecompany.com IN PTR   cheetah.operations.somecom-
pany.com

D. bobcat.operations.somecompany.com IN CNAME   cheetah.operations.somecom-
pany.com

☑ **D.** Answer **D** is correct because in this case, you want to create an alias, or CNAME, that
will allow you to point to another server. The *bobcat* server on
operations.somecompany.com will remain, in name, and the *cheetah* server will be used as
the actual server for a while. In this case, the CNAME record can be used to create an
alias so that when an application or user attempts to locate *bobcat*, it will find *cheetah*.
When you are ready to bring a new *bobcat* back online, you can remove the CNAME
record and users will return to using *bobcat* directly.

☒ Answer **A** is incorrect because the SRV record is a Service record, used to locate a particular service such as DNS or WINS. This would not be used to temporarily point to an
alternate resource. Answer **B** is incorrect because this is a type A record used to resolve
the name cheetah to an IP address. This would not help when setting up a temporary

server for which you do not want to change the infrastructure. Answer **C** is incorrect because the PTR record is just the opposite of a type A record. It resolves an IP address to a host name. However, this is not required for this scenario because we are not trying to resolve an IP address; we are trying to hide our infrastructure changes from our users to create less disruption to users. In addition, the PTR record format is incorrect. It must use the *in-addr.arpa* domain appended to the IP address, which this record does not. An example of a correct PTR record is 54.166.251.16.in-addr.arpa. IN PTR bob-cast.operations.somecompany.com.

6. A DNS server, NS1, receives a name resolution query via a client resolver. The name is not located in the DNS server's cache nor in its zone data. NS1 issues a query to NS2 in an attempt to resolve the name. NS2 checks its cache and its zone data and does not find an answer. It replies to NS1 with an A RR that has the name NS3 and the IP address for NS3. What will NS1 do next?

   A. NS1 will forward the A record to the client resolver.

   B. NS1 will issue a new query to the IP address listed in the A RR.

   C. NS1 will forward the A record to NS2 requesting the NS and SOA records associated with the A RR.

   D. NS1 will issue a new query to the NS2 server using the IP address listed in the A RR.

   ☑ **B**. NS2 responded with a pointer to another name server. This is the result of an iterative query issued by NS1, which requires either the requested IP address or a pointer be returned. Answer **B** is correct because in this case, NS2 could not resolve the name and it returned a pointer to another name server.

   ☒ Answer **A** is incorrect because the NS1 server will not forward the A RR to the client resolver. The information in the A RR is used by NS1 to locate another name server that may be able to help it resolve the requested name to an IP address. Client resolvers typically issue recursive queries meaning that it wants either the IP address (or name, in the case of a reverse lookup) or an error. Iterative queries result in the resolution or a pointer. Answer **C** is incorrect because NS2 has already indicated that it does not know the IP address. It has responded with a pointer to another name server. NS1 would have no need for the NS and SOA records of NS2. These RR types indicate zone authority and will not assist in resolving a name that NS2 cannot resolve based on its cache or zone file. Answer **D** is incorrect because NS1 will issue a new query but it will not send it back to NS2. NS2 responded with a pointer to another name server so NS1 will use that IP address and issue a new iterative query to the name server specified in the A RR.

7. The IT department has seen a lot of traffic from a particular IP address outside of their corporate network. They'd like to know the name of this server. They know that a client resolver issues a request for the name associated with the IP address 118.54.78.9. Which is the correct RR they would expect to be returned?

A. 118.54.78.9   IN   PTR   njm.southwest.somecompany.com

B. njm.southwest.somecompany.com   IN-ADDR.ARPA   118.54.78.9

C. 118.54.78.9   in-addr-arpa   IN   PTR   njm.southwest.somecompany.com

D. 118.54.78.9.in-addr.arpa   IN   PTR   njm.southwest.somecompany.com

☑ **D.** Answer **D** is correct because when a client requests a reverse name lookup (provide the IP address and requests the associated host name), the domain used is the top level domain of *.arpa*. The record will use the FQDN of the IP address appended with the in-addr.arpa domain. The RR type is the PTR followed by the name of the host.

☒ The only problem with this response is that the top level domain of *in-addr.arpa* is not specified. This TLD is reserved for reverse lookups and must be appended to the IP address for a reverse lookup. Therefore, Answer **A** is incorrect. Answer **B** is incorrect because there is no resource record type listed in this response, which makes it incorrect regardless of what other information is included. In addition, the reverse lookup response will begin with the listed IP address, not the host name. The correct format is the IP address's FQDN, which is composed of the IP address and the domain in-addr.arpa. This RR does not show that these two elements are in the same field and in-addr.arpa is not appended to the IP address, therefore, Answer **C** is incorrect.

8. Jackie is working with an associate, Bailey Scotland, on a market research project for a new product roll out. She's using a software application that will connect her to shared resources on Bailey's computer. Her computer on the somecompany.com domain issues a recursive query to a DNS server to resolve a host name, baileysc. What is the response you would expect to see in this case?

A. baileysc   IN   A   188.54.107.96

B. 188.54.107.96   IN   A   baileysc

C. baileysc   A   188.54.107.96

D. baileysc.somecompany.com   IN   CNAME   188.54.107.96

☑ **A.** The client computer needs to resolve the host name baileysc to an IP address. It issues a query to the DNS server. The DNS server either has that information available or it queries another DNS server. When resolved, it should return the IP address in the form of an A resource record type, which has the format of baileysc [host name]   IN [for Internet Class]   A [record type]   188.54.107.96 [IP address]. Therefore, Answer **A** is correct.

☒ Answer **B** is incorrect because the information contained in this response has all the right elements but in the wrong order. The A type record begins with the host name, not the IP address. Answer **C** is incorrect because this type A record is missing the Class type, which in almost all cases is IN for Internet but is required. Answer **D** is incorrect because this record shows the FQDN for the host name, which is not needed if the client and the requested host name are on the same domain. More importantly, however, is that the CNAME type record is the Canonical Name, which creates an alias for a host. This is not the correct format for the CNAME record type nor is it the correct response to the query.

Windows Server 2003 DNS Server Roles

9. You're having trouble with name resolution for a particular host, jawbone.eastcoast.some-company.com. You check the DNS server NS1.eastcoast.somecompany.com and see the following record:

Jawbone.eastcoast.somecompany.com   IN   AAAA   1.2.3.123.456.12.34.56ab

What can you conclude about jawbone.eastcoast.somecompany.com?

A. jawbone.eastcoast.somecompany.com should have an associated PTR record.

B. jawbone.eastcoast.somecompany.com's A RR is corrupt.

C. jawbone.eastcoast.somecompany.com is using IPv6.

D. jawbone.eastcoas.somecompany.com has an illegal IP address. Check the IP configuration for jawbone.

☑ **C.** Answer **C** is correct because this is the correct syntax for a computer using IPv6. The clue is that the record type is AAAA, the designation for IPv6 resource records, which use a 128-bit IP address instead of the standard 32-bit IP address used in IPv4.

☒ The PTR record is for reverse lookup. There may or may not be an associated PTR RR, but the question focuses on what you know about the host named jawbone; therefore, Answer **A** is incorrect. The host, jawbone, may have an associated IPv4 type A record, but this record is for IPv6. This is indicated by the type AAAA and the use of a 128-bit IP address. Therefore, Answer **B** is incorrect. Answer **D** is incorrect because there is nothing wrong with the resource record. If it were a type A RR, the IP address would be illegal. However, the IP address for a AAAA is a 128-bit IP address.

10. Your company's network runs Windows 2000 Server and Windows Server 2003 on all its servers. The server named reddog runs the DHCP server service. Two other servers, green-monkey and bluefish, are backup DHCP servers. Thursday afternoon reddog goes down. A user contacts the help desk and states that her computer doesn't seem to connect to the Internet. She tried renewing her DHCP lease thinking that might fix the problem, but it hasn't. What is the most likely cause of this problem?

A. The DHCP servers greenmonkey and bluefish are not configured to perform dynamic updates so renewing the lease with either backup DHCP server will cause this problem.

B. The client should not have tried to renew her DHCP lease when reddog was down. She should wait until reddog is back online.

C. The DHCP scope information on greenmonkey or bluefish allowed the client to renew a lease using an already in-use IP address causing the connectivity problem.

D. The DHCP server, reddog, was using dynamic updating and registered with DNS on behalf of the user's computer making updates by greenmonkey or bluefish impossible.

☑ **D.** Answer **D** is correct because if a DHCP server is using dynamic updates to update DNS information on behalf of a client, it owns those records. As a result, neither the client nor the backup DHCP servers have permission to modify the record created by the primary DHCP server. Thus, when reddog goes down, the client's record could not be modified.

☒ It might be wise to have the DHCP servers configured to not allow dynamic updates. Answer **A** is incorrect because the problem is just the reverse—the primary DHCP server was using dynamic updates. When it became unavailable, neither greenmonkey nor bluefish was able to make changes to the DNS server record to reflect the new lease information. If the client renews her lease when reddog is back up, this problem will be resolved. Answer **B** is incorrect because this is not the best answer. The reason an organization configures backup DHCP servers is for this very reason. The user should be able to renew her computer's DHCP lease at any time and greenmonkey or bluefish should have been able to do the job had reddog not used dynamic updates. A scope problem could, potentially, cause problems if there was a conflict with an existing statically configured host. However, the more likely cause of the problem is one of dynamic updates because the problem became apparent only when reddog went down. If there were scope problems, they would be seen on reddog as well and the problem would not likely surface when reddog went down. Therefore, Answer **C** is incorrect.

11. Your network is running three DNS servers, NS1, NS2, and NS3. NS1 is running Windows Server 2003, whereas NS2 and NS3 are still running Windows NT 4.0. In reviewing the error log on NS1, you notice an error that lists NOTIMPL(4) being returned by NS3. What does this error indicate?

A. NS3 does not support extended DNS (EDNS0).

B. NS1 does not support extended DNS (EDNS0).

C. The OPT record received from NS3 contained an illegal Time-To-Live.

D. The OPT record needs to be added to all three name servers.

☑ **A.** Answer **A** is correct because NS3 will return an error if it does not support extended DNS. This support was added in Windows 2000 and is not supported in Windows NT 4.0. Typically, a name server will respond with this type of error when it receives a query with an OPT record in it.

☒ Answer **B** is incorrect because the error is returned from NS3 to NS1 indicating the problem is on NS3. Answer **C** is incorrect because the OPT record is not a record that can be added. It is included in a query from a host that supports extended DNS. This record is sent to the name server as part of the query. If the server supports EDNS0, it will respond based on the information in the OPT record. Otherwise, it will respond with an error.

12. You've just created a new zone in DNS on a Windows Server 2003-based computer. You check the zone and notice that the only records in it are the SOA and NS RRs. You check the configuration and see that the zone is configured to accept dynamic updates. What should you do next?

    A. Manually add all RR for the zone including A, CNAME, PTR, and SRV records.

    B. Manually add A RR for all hosts that cannot use dynamic updating.

    C. Manually add A RR and PTR RR for all hosts that will be using dynamic updating.

    D. Manually initiate a zone transfer to replicate all the needed RR to the new zone.

    ☑ **B.** Answer **B** is correct because the zone will accept dynamic updates, so the zone data will be updated by clients that support dynamic updates. If you have clients that cannot support this feature (such as clients running earlier versions of Windows or non-Microsoft operating systems that do not support dynamic updates), you must manually enter A RR for these clients. Otherwise, the zone database will be updated as clients renew their leases through DHCP or directly with the DNS server.

    ☒ Answer **A** is incorrect because hosts that support dynamic updates will update their own A and PTR records. You do not need to manually enter CNAME and SRV records except in circumstances where these types of records are specifically called for, such as when you want to create an alias to hide infrastructure changes from users (CNAME). Answer **C** is incorrect because if hosts support dynamic updating, they will maintain their own records. Therefore, you would need to create these types of records for hosts that do *not* support dynamic updates. A zone transfer will replicate what is already in the primary zone. Since you are working on the primary zone, this would simply replicate the two existing records created by default, the SOA and NS for the zone. Therefore, Answer **D** is incorrect.

13. A DNS server, Aspen, has been successfully resolving queries but with the wrong information. You use the Monitoring function in the DNS Management Console for Aspen and test the simple and recursive queries. Both work fine. What is the most likely cause of this problem?

    A. Aspen is not authoritative for the zone in which the wrong information is being returned.

    B. Aspen is not configured to perform iterative queries.

    C. Some clients do not support dynamic updates, or manually entered RR have errors.

    D. The clients that received the wrong information do not support the OPT record type.

    ☑ **C.** Answer **C** is correct because if clients do not support dynamic updates and their DNS information changes, the information in the DNS server's zone database might be incorrect. Thus, the DNS server can successfully resolve a query with incorrect information. You need to check the RRs for any clients that do not perform dynamic updates or clients that do not use DHCP to perform dynamic updates on their behalf. Also check any RRs that were entered manually to ensure that the data within the RR is correct.

☒ If a DNS server is not authoritative for the zone, it will check its cache for the needed information and then query other DNS servers. If those other DNS servers cannot resolve the query, an error is returned. Answer **A** is incorrect because incorrect information will not be returned. Iterative queries return either the requested information or a pointer to another DNS server. If a recursive query was issued, the server would simply return either the needed data or an error. Again, incorrect information would not be returned as a result, so Answer **B** is incorrect. The OPT record type has to do with extending DNS over UDP from 512 byte to a larger size. The client will include an OPT record type in the query if it supports OPT, so this is not the issue. Incorrect information would not be returned if OPT was not supported. Instead, an error code would be returned. Therefore, Answer **D** is incorrect.

Windows Server 2003 Active Directory Integrated DNS Servers

14. A DNS server, NS1Jones, on the domain us.somecompany.com, consistently fails to resolve names from the domain canada1company.com and mexicounocompany.com. It resolves names within the us.somecompany.com zone, for which it is authoritative, with no problems. What is the likely cause of this problem, assuming both external domains exist?

   A. NS1Jones is unable to perform recursive queries. Check the Advanced properties of the DNS server.

   B. NS1Jones is configured to be a forwarder. Disable forwarding in the NS1Jones properties.

   C. NS1Jones is unable to connect to the Internet's root DNS name servers.

   D. NS1Jones should be configured to be a secondary DNS server for both canada1.company.com and mexicuunocompany.com.

   ☑ **A**. NS1Jones is most likely unable to perform recursive queries. Answer **A** is correct because recursive queries, which require either the resolution or an error be returned, can be disabled on a DNS server via the Advanced tab of the DNS server properties. This action also disables forwarders.

   ☒ If NS1Jones were configured to be a forwarder, it would send queries that it could not resolve to another DNS server for a response. Answer **B** is incorrect because the inability of NS1Jones to resolve an external query would suggest it was unable to forward or issue a recursive query. NS1Jones may be unable to connect to the Internet's root servers. However, if NS1Jones was configured to issue recursive queries, the problem would be resolved by other DNS servers query responses. If NS1Jones was configured as a forwarder, this could be a problem, but this is not the best answer for the given scenario;

therefore, Answer **C** is incorrect. Answer **D** is incorrect because the domain names for each of the external domains are different enough from the internal domain, us.some-company.com, that it cannot be assumed these domains are part of the same company. In fact, it is highly likely that they are not part of the same company given the differences in the naming conventions. However, that is not the issue in this case. The ability to resolve these names does not rely upon NS1Jones having a copy of the zone database for those two domains. This is exactly why DNS servers are configured as primary and secondary DNS servers and why root servers on the Internet exist—so that name resolution becomes a process of examining local data and then querying other name servers. If every name to be resolved had to be located on the local DNS server, name resolution across the Internet would virtually halt and DNS servers would grind to a halt. This distributed system obviates the need for DNS servers to hold all name resolution data.

15. Your company has recently migrated from Windows NT 4.0 to Windows Server 2003 on all of its networked servers, including those running the DHCP and DNS server services. During the migration, you implemented Active Directory integrated zones. A colleague states that you cannot do this because the zones converted from non-AD aware operating systems will not allow secure updates, creating a significant security risk to the organization. What is your response?

A. When any zone is integrated into AD, it takes on the security features of AD.

B. If the zone is created outside of the AD, it will be configured for no secure updates and must be re-created to allow for secure updates.

C. If the zone is created outside of AD, it will not be configured for secure updates but can be modified via the DNS Management Console.

D. When any zone created before Windows 2000 is integrated into AD, it will use whatever update type other zones are configured to use.

☑ **C.** If a zone is created outside of AD, is can be integrated into AD and its properties can be modified via the DNS Management Console. Answer **C** is correct because AD integration provides the ability to use the Access Control List (ACL) to manage security, including secure dynamic updates.

☒ Answer **A** is incorrect because when a zone is integrated into AD, it does not automatically take on the features of AD. The newly integrated zone must be modified by the administrator. Answer **B** is incorrect because when a zone is created outside of AD and integrated into AD, it will by default be configured for no secure updates. However, the zone does not need to be re-created in order to modify its properties. Once in AD, it can be modified via the DNS Management Console. Answer **D** is incorrect because a zone created outside of AD (whether in an earlier version of the Windows operating system that did not support AD or in a non-Microsoft implementation of DNS) typically will not use secure updates. When using the default DNS Server service, it is set to not allow secure updates. An AD integrated zone does not use whatever update types are used for other zones, but can be configured via the DNS Management Console.

Chapter 6 The Windows Server 2003 DNS Server

Installing and Configuring the Windows Server 2003 DNS Server

1. Your company has been planning a migration from their Windows NT 4.0 domain to a new Windows Server 2003 domain for over a year. You have a corporate office in Charleston, SC and 15 satellite branches spread out over the east coast. In each branch, you are currently running a Windows NT 4.0 domain controller that is also functioning as a DNS, WINS, and DHCP server. In the corporate office you have three domain controllers and two member servers. The member servers in corporate are running WINS, DHCP, and DNS. The WINS servers at each branch are configured in a hub and spoke replication model with corporate. All branch DNS servers pull a secondary zone from a DNS server in corporate. Finally the time has come and you are ready to start your migration. You upgrade your primary DNS server to Windows 2000. You enable dynamic updates. You configure all of the domain controllers in corporate to point to the new Windows Server 2003 DNS server. Next you upgrade your PDC to Windows 2000. Everything seems to be working fine, but in a few hours you start getting calls from some of your branches that the DNS service is giving them Dr. Watson errors. What could be a cause of the problem?

A. The NT 4.0 servers are running service pack 5.

B. The NT 4.0 servers should not be running DNS since they are domain controllers.

C. The NT 4.0 servers are running service pack 3.

D. The NT 4.0 servers require full zone transfer, but Windows Server 2003 supports only incremental zone transfers.

☑ **C.** Answer **C** is correct, because Windows NT 4.0 DNS servers can replicate with Windows Server 2003 DNS servers. However, if the 4.0 servers are not running at least service pack 4 they will not support SRV records. In this question, your primary DNS server has been upgraded to Windows 2000, which gives it built-in support for dynamic updates and service (SRV) records. It then replicates those records to all secondary Windows NT 4.0 DNS zones. Now when the zone file is loaded, Window performs a Dr. Watson (indicating that the system had a failure).

☒ Answer **A** is incorrect, because having service pack 5 is not required. Answer **B** is incorrect, because running DNS on a domain controller is completely acceptable. Answer **D** is there to try and throw you off. It is a true a statement, because Windows NT 4.0 supports only full zone transfers and Windows Server 2003 supports incremental zone transfers. However, this would not cause a problem because Windows Server 2003 also supports full zone transfers and would replicate with a Windows NT 4.0 DNS server with no problem.

2. Lisa works for a development company that has a native mode Windows Server 2003 Active Directory domain infrastructure in place. They are using Windows XP and Windows 2000 exclusively on all the client laptops and deploy all IP configuration options via DHCP. All DHCP servers are set up to automatically register A and PTR records on behalf of their clients. Lisa maintains an Active Directory integrated Windows Server 2003 DNS database. The corporate environment is heavily trafficked by mobile users moving from floor to floor, disconnecting their network cables and not properly shutting down or releasing old IP information. Developers are constantly adding machines to the domain via virtual software and then disconnecting them. Each of the four floors Lisa works on is set up as a subdomain of the first floor root domain. Each client is assigned a DNS suffix search order for each subdomain. After working there for quite some time, Lisa finds that her DNS database is filled with stagnant stale records. She thinks this is causing some performance problems and wants to initiate a manual scavenging of the database to see how many records it cleans up. Lisa has not changed any of the default DNS configuring setting since she installed it. Lisa goes into her DNS console, right-clicks her DNS server, and selects **Scavenge Stale Resource Records**. She answers **yes** to the question asking if she wants to scavenge all resource records in the database. She waits until the next day and checks the database only to find the records are still there. She then remembers that she read somewhere that the default refresh interval is 7 days, so she runs scavenging one more time to make sure and decides to check back in a week. Two weeks later, the stale database records are still around and do not seem to want to disappear. What is Lisa doing wrong?

A. Lisa forgot to enable scavenging on the server.

B. Lisa forgot to enable scavenging on the domain.

C. Lisa forgot to enable scavenging on the server and domain.

D. Lisa has not waited long enough.

☑ **C.** Answer **C** is correct, because in order for scavenging to work either manually or automatically, it must be enabled in both the server's properties and the domain's properties. If one of these is not enabled, manual scavenging will not work even though it does not give you an error message.

☒ Answer **A** is incorrect, because Lisa has not changed the default install. That means both the server and the domain have to be enabled, not just the server. Answer **B** is incorrect for the same reason. Answer **D** is incorrect, because the amount of time Lisa waits does not change the fact that scavenging is not working at all.

Configuring DNS Clients

3. Joey is a desktop engineer for a computer software company in downtown New York City called Solutions. His company has just integrated themselves with two other smaller software development companies to try to build a stronger customer service application in their com-

petitive market. The network groups have been combined and have successfully created a shared network backbone. They have also set up and confirmed that each company is now hosting secondary copies of the other's DNS domains. Cross-forest trusts have also been established and confirmed in a working order. Solutions is the only one of the three companies that has a Web presence, hosting a Web page at www.solutionsacme.com. It is Joey's responsibility to set up his 20 client users with the correct DNS suffixes to be able to resolve these new domains to access needed shared resources. He decides to test the adding of additional DNS suffixes on his Windows XP laptop first before scripting it out and applying it to the rest of his company workstations. He and most of the other users in his office use static IP addressing and are set up with a default connection-specific DNS suffix of solutionsacme.com. He leaves the default suffix in place on his laptop and adds the other companies' DNS suffixes in the DNS suffix search order window as shown in Figure 6.76. Joey starts his testing by trying to access the other company's shared network resources and is successful. Joey believes that he has set everything up correctly, until he tries to access his company Web site. He gets a Page cannot be displayed error. He invokes a command prompt and types **ping www** as he always had before. He gets a response of Ping request could not find host www. He calls support and asks if they can access the corporate Web site. They reply that they can. What is wrong with Joey's configuration?

Figure 6.76 Displaying DNS Suffix Configuration

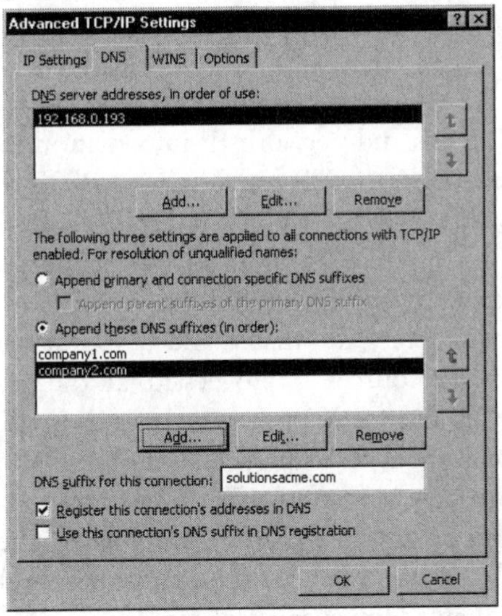

A. Joey forgot to check **Use this connections DNS suffix in DNS registration** check box.

B. Joey forgot to add the IP addresses of the other company's DNS servers in the DNS window.

C. Joey forgot to add his domain name to the DNS suffix search order list.

D. Nothing, there must be a problem with the Web site's host record.

☑ **C.** Answer **C** is correct, because as soon as you enter a single domain into the DNS suffix search order window, both your **DNS suffix for this connection** and your **Primary DNS suffix** are not used anymore to append to host names during the resolution process. Because the other companies do not maintain a Web presence, they have no need to host a record for their Web site; otherwise, Joey might have received a reply from one of those records. Joey needs to add his domain to the DNS suffix search order list to resolve the Web site's host record.

☒ Answer **A** is incorrect because registering his connection-specific DNS suffix in DNS would not alter the fact that it now is not part of the DNS search order list and thus is disregarded in DNS resolution. Answer **B** is incorrect, because there is no need to add the other companies' DNS IP addresses when you are maintaining a secondary zone on your DNS server. This also would not resolve the issue of not having a DNS suffix for solutionacme.com in his search window. Answer **D** is incorrect, because people other than Joey are able to access the company Web site using the www record without error.

4. John's network consists of a Windows Server 2003 Active Directory backbone using DHCP to distribute client IP addresses and network IP information. DHCP is set up to automatically update DNS with all Windows XP and Windows 2000 clients PTR records while they update their own A records. It is not set up to update downlevel clients because WINS is also in use on the network for some old Windows NT 4.0 applications servers running legacy human resource payroll and accounting applications. All clients are set up as default enhanced h-node clients. DNS is completely automated and does not contain any static entries. At the end of every month, human resources employees ftp all the payroll information to the accounting server, where an automatic process e-mails those files to a third-party processing firm to cut checks and mail them to employees. Due to an IP network overhaul, all of the servers' IP addresses had to be changed in order to accommodate a bigger IP address pool, for the accumulation of more servers and more employees. The change was scheduled for a weekend's worth of work. On the Monday following that weekend, there were just a handful of calls in the help desk queue. However, all of them were from human resource employees. The calls stated that they were no longer able to update end of month payroll files on the accounting server. John called one employee and asked her to send him a copy of the file in e-mail so he could try. When he tried, he was able to update the accounting server. What is the problem with accounting?

A. A local LMHOSTS file needs updating.

B. The DNS server was not updated correctly.

C. A local HOSTS file needs updating.

D. The WINS server needs updating.

☑ **C.** Answer **C** is correct, because it is the only variable that would cause accounting clients to get an incorrect resolution. DNS does not hold the accounting server's host name because Windows NT 4.0 servers cannot update DNS without the help of DHCP, which the question states is not set up for downlevel Windows NT 4.0 client updates. It also states that static records are not used. Thus, resolution must be coming from WINS via the host name resolution process below:

- [C]indy – DNS *resolver* [C]ache

- [H]arris – [H]osts file

- [D]idn't – [D]NS

- [C]ram – NetBIOS [C]ache

- [W]ell – [W]INS

- [B]efore – NetBIOS [B]roadcast

- [L]eaving – [L]MHOSTS file

☒ Answer **A** is incorrect. Although the LMHOSTS file might contain the old IP address of the accounting server, it comes after the HOSTS file in the host name resolution process for ftp application access. Answer **B** is incorrect, because the question states that no static entries are used in DNS, so the accounting clients must not have been getting ftp server resolution via DNS. Answer **D** is incorrect, because if WINS was incorrect John would not have been able to ftp the file either. If set up to use a WINS server, WINS will be tried in the host's name resolution process.

Integrating the Windows Server 2003 DNS Server with DHCP

5. Your company has a Windows Server 2003 domain. All of your servers run Windows Server 2003 and all of your workstations run Windows XP Professional. Your DHCP server is configured with the default settings and all of your Windows XP machines are configured as DHCP clients with the default DHCP client settings. You want to use DNS dynamic updates to automatically register the host record and PTR record for all of your workstations. Which of the following must you do to accomplish your goal?

A. None. The default settings are sufficient.

B. Configure the DHCP server to always **Dynamically update DNS and PTR records**.

C. Configure the DHCP server to **Dynamically update DNS and PTR records only if requested by the DHCP clients**.

D. Configure the workstation to use dynamic updates.

☑   **A**. Answer **A** is correct. By default Windows XP machines are configured to ask their DHCP server to update their PTR record and they will automatically update their host record with their DNS server. By default a Windows Server 2003 DHCP server is configured to **Dynamically update DNS and PTR records only if requested by the DHCP clients.** In other words, by using the default settings Windows XP machines will automatically have their host and PTR records updated in DNS.

☒   Answer **B** is incorrect, because you would need to use this option only if you wanted your DHCP to update host records and PTR records for machines that do not support dynamic updates. Answers **C** and **D** are incorrect, because they are enabled by default. Because this question says that we used the default client and server settings, there is nothing else to configure.

6. Your network contains a mix of Windows 2000 and Windows Server 2003. You have three domain controllers running Windows Server 2003. Your file server, print server, and Exchange server are running Windows 2000 Server. Your DNS, DHCP, and WINS servers are running Windows Server 2003. All of your clients are running Windows XP Professional with service pack 1. All machines, other than the servers that require a static IP address, are configured as DHCP clients with the default settings. Your DNS server has been configured to allow dynamic updates. Which of the following records will be registered in DNS automatically? (Choose all that apply.)

A. MX

B. Host

C. SRV

D. PT

☑   **B, C, D**. Answers **B** and **D** are correct, because Windows XP machines update their own host records in DNS and they request that their DHCP server update their PTR records in DNS by default. Also, by default a Windows Server 2003 DHCP server will update PTR records for any machine that requests it. Answer **C** is correct, because all Windows Server 2003 domain controllers register their SRV records in DNS by default.

☒   Answer **A** is incorrect because MX records must be created manually.

Integrating the Windows Server 2003 DNS Server with WINS

7. You work as a systems administrator in a mixed UNIX/Windows environment. Until now, there has not been a real need for the two operating systems to communicate. The UNIX people operate in their own world and use their own file and print services, and the Windows people operate in their own Windows NT/2003 interim domain world. Your company is small enough that you are able to maintain both environments without too much overhead or doubling of work. Both environments do, however, share the same internal domain name and thus use the same Windows Server 2003 DNS servers for host name resolution. There are two DNS servers that perform zone transfers to stay in sync with one another. The systems team has handed out different preferred DNS servers to the client community as a whole in order to balance the load of network host resolution. On Wednesday afternoon, you are informed by your boss that network drive storage has become a real big issue. He says that based on recent reports he has seen, the duplication of static data is really increasing his backup window and he wants to put a stop to it. He tells you that by next week, he wants all file storage access stored on the Windows NT file server only, and to make sure that all static UNIX data is moved appropriately. You load up Samba on the UNIX file server so that you can access it from the Windows NT file server to copy the data. You also load the Services for UNIX on the Windows NT server in order to create an NFS share for UNIX compatibility. By Friday of that week, you have copied all the data, and inform all of your UNIX folks that come Monday morning they will need to access the \\WINNTSRV\software share to get to any of their static software data. You set up your company's DNS domain to integrate with your WINS server in order for your DNS-only UNIX clients to be able to resolve WINNT as a host name in DNS. You test it out from one of your UNIX friend's laptops and you are able to successfully access the share. On Monday morning, all users start logging into the network. You don't hear any complaints until before lunch. A few of your UNIX cohorts approach you and tell you that they are unable to access the new Windows/UNIX share. They say they cannot get a successful ping of the name WINNTSRV. You call the friend with whom you originally tested access, and he states that he and three of his coworkers are able to access it, but his office mate is not. What is the problem?

A. You did not check WINS reverse lookup integration.

B. You checked **Do not replicate this record**.

C. You did not check WINS forward lookup integration.

D. You did not check **Do not replicate this record**.

☑ **B. Answer B** is correct. By checking **Do not replicate this record**, you effectively tell DNS not to replicate any WINS records it might have in its database to any of its DNS zone transfer partners. Because your company's clients are split, with some using the primary DNS and others using the secondary, only the users set to use the primary will be able to resolve the Windows NT 4.0 name WIINTSRV. Uncheck **Do not replicate this record** and the secondary zone will contain the replicated WINS records.

☒ Answer **A** is incorrect, because there is no need for reverse lookups in this scenario at all. Answer **C** is incorrect, because if you did not enable WINS forward lookups, no UNIX clients would be able to access the new share. Answer **D** is incorrect, because if you did not check **Do not replicate this record,** all WINS records would be replicated to the secondary DNS server and all UNIX clients would be able to access the share.

8. You are using WINS Forward Lookup integration in your mixed UNIX/Windows environment to allow your DNS-only UNIX clients to use only their configured Windows Server 2003 DNS server to query and resolve resolution requests for downlevel Windows NT 4.0 machines' NetBIOS names. This has been working well for your company for several months. You are informed that over the next several weeks, the Windows NT 4.0 servers are being moved to a different subnet in order to create a separate broadcast domain. They will still continue to register with the same WINS server, but their IP addresses will be changing, and they will no longer be able to be accessed via broadcasts. As these servers start their migration to the new subnet you begin to receive calls only from your UNIX community, complaining that they can no longer access servers that have moved until a day or so later. What can you do to fix the problem for all future migrated servers?

A. Type **nbtstat -RR** on the migrated NT servers.

B. Increase the TTL for WINS forward lookup records.

C. Type **ipconfig /registerdns** on the migrated NT servers.

D. Decrease the TTL for WINS forward lookups records.

☑ **D.** Answer **D** is correct. The default TTL on WINS forward lookups must have been changed from one minute to something greater than one day. When UNIX clients are accessing DNS to resolve the Windows NT server name, DNS has the old IP address cached because the TTL has yet to expire. After a day or so, the TTL expires and DNS forwards the request to WINS, which has the new IP information.

☒ Answer **A** is incorrect, because **nbtstat -RR** will refresh the NT server's NetBIOS name with its WINS server. This has already happened automatically, because other Windows clients can access them after the migration. Answer **B** is incorrect, because by increasing the TTL for WINS forward lookups, you ensure that the wrong IP address will stay in the DNS database for an even longer period of time, exacerbating the issue of UNIX clients not being able to access the migrated NT servers. Answer **C** is incorrect, because Window NT 4.0 clients cannot register their IP addresses with a DNS server, and require the help of a DHCP server to do so.

Integrating the Windows Server 2003 DNS Server with Internet Publishing

9. Chris works for a ski enthusiast's online purchasing e-store hosting its external Web domain site at skimoreworkless.com. Chris has an internal group of Web designers that publish to this Web site via its www.skimoreworkless.com Internet address. Chris hired a group of network consultants to come in and build a new Windows Server 2003 Active Directory domain environment for their company's internal use. Chris sat down with the consultants to answer a few questions before they got started, one of which was, "What do you want me to call your internal DNS domain name?" That one was easy, Chris thought. He stated that he wanted to keep the internal name the same as the external name: skimoreworkless.com. The consultant asked if he was sure, and Chris said most definitely. Convinced, the consultants got to work that Friday morning, and by closing time, walked out the door leaving Chris with a fully implemented single forest, single domain Active Directory infrastructure using a powerful 4 processor Pentium IV server with 2G of memory. They had installed a second member server that served as a single scope DHCP server handing out the following information:

- Router: 192.1668.0.1

- DNS Server: 192.168.0.10

- Domain name: skimoreworkless.com

The consultants left Chris with the administrator password to the domain and told him that each of the users' logon names consisted of their first name with a blank password that would ask them to change it upon initial logon. The consultant also left instructions for Chris on how to change all his Windows XP laptop machines to use DHCP and how to join them to the domain. After a long weekend of skiing, Chris and crew came in to work early Monday morning to finish setting up their new Windows environment. By lunch time, Chris had successfully joined each of their PCs to the domain and made sure they were all able to log on and change their passwords before going to lunch. After lunch, everyone jumped back into a normal day of business, checking Web server hits, processing orders, and shipping them out. Chuck, a Web site developer, came up to Chris and said he was having trouble publishing to the Web site. At the same time, Chris noticed that he was unable to even get to the Web site. In a panic, they checked with everyone else, only to find the same results. Was the site down? Where they losing business? Chris scurried to find the consultant's number. When he called the consultant, what did he learn?

A. His Web site was actually down.

B. He hadn't published his Web site's A records internally.

C. He hadn't set up his internal DNS forwarders.

D. He hadn't set up a reverse lookup zone.

☑ **B.** Answer **B** is correct. When you host an internal domain name that is identical to your external domain name, you add on the extra overhead of now having to host internal A records for each of your external host records' IP addresses. This is because when your client goes to find www.skimoreworkless.com, it first will first look at your internal domain's DNS for the record www. Because it is authoritative for that domain, it will not send that request anywhere else, but will return a negative response back to the client. The only way to change this behavior is by adding an A record for www and entering the external IP address that www uses, or better yet, when building your internal domain names, by using something different than your external domain names.

☒ Answer **A** is incorrect, because the results of what the consultant installed is the root cause of why the Web site is inaccessible internally. Externally, the Web site has not changed and is still resolving to the same host and IP address as before. Answer **C** is incorrect, because with the default install of Windows Server 2003 DNS uses the root hints file, and you do not need to set up forwarders to access the Internet. Although it is wise to set up forwarders to point to your external domain, you do not have to as the root hints will work fine. Answer **D** is incorrect, because a reverse lookup zone has nothing to do with why Chris can't resolve his www host record. Reverse lookup records are used to resolve IP address to host names.

Integrating the Windows Server 2003 DNS Server with BIND

10. You have been hired as a consultant for CX2 Consulting. Your job is to assist in the migration from Windows NT 4.0 to Windows Server 2003. CX2 Consulting will be implementing Active Directory and Exchange 2003. The company is currently using a Linux DNS server running BIND 4.9.2. CX2 Consulting has given you a few requirements for DNS.

- They want to take advantage of dynamic updates for their Windows 2000 Professional clients.

- They want to continue using the BIND DNS server.

Which of the following should you do to complete your migration while meeting the company's requirements?

A. Upgrade the BIND DNS server to BIND version 4.9.3.

B. Upgrade the BIND DNS server to BIND version 4.9.7.

C. Upgrade the BIND DBS server to BIND version 8.1.3.

D. Upgrade the BIND DBS server to BIND version 8.0.2.

☑ **C.** Answer **C** is correct, because the version of BIND that supports dynamic updates is version 8.1.3.

☒ Answers **A**, **B**, and **D** are incorrect, because these versions do not support dynamic updates.

11. Tina works for a software support company and has the responsibility for implementing and maintaining all of the DNS servers in her environment. Her network infrastructure is a very mixed hodge-podge of different operating systems, DNS implementations, messaging packages, and so on. Her company needs to keep such a large mix of products up and running at their office because they never know what the calling customers might have at their own company. They want to make sure they can replicate any environment or problem so they can be of better assistance to a wider variety of customers. Tina has just received a call from a customer in Columbia, SC that is trying to set up a DNS zone transfer between their Windows Server 2003 DNS server and a BIND UNIX DNS implementation. The Windows Server 2003 DNS server is set up as a master and the BIND is set up as a secondary. Tina already has this environment set up at work and is ready to tackle the customer's problem. The customer complains that when they try to initiate a zone transfer, it appears to connect and have the correct permissions, but then fails every time. Tina tries it on her test setup and everything works fine. Tina thinks about what might be different between the two environments and starts asking the following questions:

- Do you have any zone transfer permissions set up on your Windows Server 2003 server? No. Allow zone transfers to any servers is enabled.

- Have you made any other configuration changes or did you accept all the Windows Server 2003 DNS default? Yes, the defaults.

- Are both the DNS servers on the same network? Yes.

- Any firewalls, IDS systems, or egress filtering going on? No, nothing like that.

What is Tina's last question, and the one that solves the problem?

A. With what version of client are you initiating the zone transfer?

B. What version of BIND are you using?

C. Is your Windows Server 2003 DNS Active Directory Integrated?

D. Are you allowing secure-only dynamic updates?

☑ **B.** Answer **B** is correct. With the default install of Windows Server 2003, zone transfers to BIND servers are set to accept fast zone transfers. If the customer is running version 4.9.3 or earlier, then a zone transfer will never work, unless the BIND secondaries default option is disabled, or they upgrade their BIND implementation to version 4.9.4.

☒ Answer **A** is incorrect, because a client is not used to initiate a zone transfer, as the secondary zone pulls the data directory from its master at a scheduled transfer interval. Answer **C** is incorrect, because having an Active Directory integrated zone would not affect zone transfers. Answer **D** is incorrect for similar reasons. Accepting or not accepting dynamic updates does not allow or disallow zone transfers from occurring.

Monitoring the Windows Server 2003 DNS Server

12. You are a new systems administrator for your company and have been asked to do some monitoring of several key servers in your environment. You use System Monitor to watch the performance of your DNS server and notice a lot of zone transfer traffic coming from your primary DNS server using the **AXFR Success Sent** performance counter. You alert your systems security team and ask them if this is normal. They tell you that you are running in an Active Directory domain with Active Directory DNS. Your company's zone is set to allow dynamic updates and your DHCP server is set to auto update PTR records for your Windows XP and Windows 2000 clients. They tell you that this generates a lot of zone transfers between the 20 domain controllers at the branches, as each branch office is set up locally as a DNS server. You ask if there are any DNS servers outside of the ones on the domain controllers (DC) and you are told that there are not. What should you do immediately?

A. Configure each of the DCs to be able to do zone transfers only with each other.

B. Configure each of the DCs to not allow zone transfers at all.

C. Change the Active Directory Integrated DNS DCs into primaries and configure them to allow only zone transfers from servers on the name server tab.

D. Nothing. Everything is as it should be.

☑ **B.** Answer **B** is correct. Active Directory integrated zones do not require zone transfers as they use Active Directory replication in the new Windows Server 2003 application partition to synchronize zone data. Because security said that there should be no DNS servers other than those on the DCs, and those are Active Directory integrated, the zone transfer data you witnessed must be from an unknown insecure source. You should immediately disable the ability to transfer zones from your Active Directory DNS servers.

☒ Answer **A** is incorrect, because the DCs are not subject to zone transfers with each other if they are configured as Active Directory integrated DNS servers. Answer **C** is incorrect because changing all the Active Directory Integrated DC zones to primary would not allow you to set them up to transfer zones with each other. Only secondaries can transfer from their master primaries. Answer **D** is incorrect because there is an issue with a large number of suspicious zone transfers from the Active Directory Integrated DCs. Based on the information from the security team, there should not be any zone transfers going on in the environment because DNS should be replicated via Active Directory replication.

13. You and four other members of your systems team work as DNS administrators for a small Internet Service Provider in Massachusetts. With more and more business coming into your company, you continually have to upgrade your DNS server as you host thousands of authoritative zones for Web sites locally and around the country. For the past week, you have noticed degradation in server performance and you asked one of your other DNS administrators to look into the problem and log what he finds, because you are going to be away for a week. Because you had not heard back, you assumed that everything was fine and that no

news was good news. On Tuesday, you come back to work and notice that the DNS server was performing unbelievable sluggishly and you want to know why. You open up System Monitor on the DNS server and load the following counters with the following results:

- Total Query Received/sec: 88
- Total Response Sent/sec: 33
- Recursive Queries/sec: 60
- % Free Space: 2
- % Disk Time: 90
- Pages/sec: 1

What can you do to pick up performance?

A. Turn off debug logging.

B. Turn on debug logging.

C. Add more memory.

D. Add faster Disks.

☑ **A.** Answer **A** is correct. One of the other DNS administrators must have enabled debug logging to try and figure out why the DNS server was having issues. Debug logging is extremely taxing to a server and is very heavy on disk I/O, especially if you are an ISP getting a lot of resolution traffic. Because debug logging logs every packet in and out of the DNS server, it also consumes a lot of disk space and can quickly fill up a system's hard drive disk space. The %Disk Time shows the excessive amount of disk access. The % Free space shows that the logging has almost completely filled up the local system drive.

☒ Answer **B** is incorrect, because logging is already enabled and is, in fact, the problem. Answer **C** is incorrect, because memory is not a problem. Based on the very low pages/sec counter, there is almost no paging going on. Answer **D** is incorrect, because disk speed is not the issue, disk space is. When a system drive falls below 10% free space, system performance starts to decline at a faster rate.

Troubleshooting the Windows Server 2003 DNS Server

14. Your network consists of four Windows Server 2003 domain controllers, three Windows 2000 member servers, and 50 Windows XP Professional machines. Your users are reporting that they cannot log onto the network. You believe this problem is due to the client machines not being able to resolve names via the DNS server. You want to test and verify that the workstations can talk to the DNS server over the network. Which of the following tools could you use? (Choose all that apply.)

A. Ping

B. Nslookup

C. Nbtstat

D. Netstat

☑ **A, B**. Answer **A** is correct, because the **ping** command is used to test network connectivity between two machines. It uses the ICMP protocol to send echo request packets to a machine. When the target machine receives the request packets it will respond with a reply. The reply packets tell us that the machine is online and responding to network requests. Answer **B** is correct, because **nslookup** is used to query a DNS server for records over the network.

☒ Answer **C** is incorrect, because **nbtstat** is used to manage NetBIOS information. It has nothing to do with DNS. Answer **D** is incorrect because **Netstat** shows which ports are being used machines. It does not test network connectivity.

15. Your Web server is running Windows Server 2003 Web Edition. It hosts a Web application that is used by people over the Internet. You log all of your traffic to a log file so that you can see who has been connecting. You look through your log files and see that one IP address has connected and disconnected 3500 times in the last two hours. You are worried that this person might be trying to hack your Web server. You need to find the host computer name that goes along with this IP address. Which of the following tools could you use? (Choose all that apply.)

A. Ping

B. Nslookup

C. Netdiag

D. Netstat

☑ **A, B**. Answer **A** is correct. Normally when we think of **ping** we think of testing network connectivity only. However, **ping** has an option (**-a**) that allows it to do reverse lookup on the IP address it is sending ICMP packets to. The syntax is **ping –a** *ipaddress*, where *ipaddress* equals the IP address of the machine your are pinging. Answer **B** is correct, because **nslookup** is used to query a DNS server for records over the network. In this situation, you would use the **nslookup** command to query the DNS server for the PTR record of the machine whose name you need.

☒ Answer **C** is incorrect, because **netdiag** is used to run a diagnostics test against your server to see if anything is not working correctly. Answer **D** is incorrect, because netstat shows which ports are being used machines. It cannot be used to resolve PTR records.

Chapter 7 Configuring the Windows Server 2003 Routing and Remote Access Service VPN Services

Review of Windows Server 2003 Remote Access Concepts

1. The president of your company has asked you if VPN technology could benefit the company. What is the greatest benefit provided by VPN?

    A. VPN solutions provide secure connectivity at a significant price savings compared to long distance analog or dedicated circuit connections.

    B. VPN solutions utilize fewer resources than dedicated circuits or analog connections.

    C. VPN solutions provide better remote control capabilities than other third-party alternatives.

    D. VPN solutions provide higher speed connections than dedicated circuits or analog connections.

    ☑ **A.** Answer **A** is the correct answer. Relying on inexpensive, local phone-service Internet access to connect to remote servers, VPNs provide inexpensive alternatives to long distance analog connections. Also, providing an Internet-based solution to connectivity for higher bandwidth connections, VPNs provide an inexpensive alternative to long-haul T-carrier circuits.

    ☒ Answer **B** is incorrect, because oftentimes, VPN networks rely on more resources than a standard analog or dedicated circuit. Answer **C** is incorrect, because VPN services provide remote access capabilities, not remote control. Microsoft Terminal Server provides a remote control type of connection. Answer **D** is incorrect, because VPNs still rely on an underlying network connection of some type. The underlying network connection determines the bandwidth of the connection, not the VPN.

Enabling the Windows Server 2003 Remote Access Service

2. Your company's corporate security policy is very strict. No username or password information may be passed over the Internet without using the strongest encryption available. Your company does not yet have a certificate infrastructure in place. Which of these methods would be the best choice for VPN authentication to ensure that you are within your company's corporate security policy requirements?

    A. MS-CHAP v2

    B. PAP

    C. CHAP

    D. SPAP

☑ **A**. The strongest encryption available is EAP-TLS with certificates. The lack of a certificate infrastructure dictates the use of MS-CHAP v2. MS-CHAP v2 provides the strongest encryption for VPN authentication on Windows Server 2003 systems; therefore, Answer **A** is correct.

☒ Answer **B** is incorrect, because PAP sends passwords in clear-text. This completely violates the corporate security policy since no encryption is used on the password or username. Answer **C** is incorrect, because CHAP authentication is not the strongest available. Answer **D** is incorrect, because SPAP authentication uses reversible encryption on the password only. Reversible encryption generally is considered weaker than one-way hashed encryption or digest encryption.

3. You administer a network composed of your corporate office and four separate remote offices located throughout the state. In an effort to avoid long distance charges, you have acquired fractional T-1 Internet access for each office. Each office has a Windows Server 2003 server configured with Network Address Translation (NAT). You want to implement a VPN configuration that ensures that only users from the remote offices can access resources on your corporate network. You also want to ensure Internet connectivity for each office. How will you implement this solution?

A. Configure the corporate VPN gateway with routes for each of the remote LANs. Configure each remote LAN with a default route to the corporate LAN.

B. Configure the corporate VPN gateway with inbound and outbound filters that reflect the remote LANs' subnet addresses.

C. Configure compulsory tunnels between each of the remote offices and the corporate VPN gateway. Configure the corporate VPN gateway with routes for each of the remote LANs and inbound and outbound filters that reflect the remote LANs' subnet addresses. Configure each remote LAN with a default route to the corporate LAN.

D. Configure compulsory tunnels between each of the remote offices and the corporate VPN gateway. Configure the corporate VPN gateway with routes for each of the remote LANs and inbound and outbound filters that reflect the remote LANs' subnet addresses. Configure each remote LAN with a route to the corporate LAN and a default route to the Internet (split tunnel).

☑ **D**. Answer **D** is correct, because remote offices will need a route to the corporate LAN via the VPN gateway as well as a route to the Internet. The routes on the corporate VPN gateway and the inbound and outbound filters ensure only internal local and remote office network traffic will pass across the VPN tunnels.

☒ Answer **A** is incorrect, because the provisions for local and remote office secure traffic are not met by this solution, due to a lack of inbound and outbound filters. Also, the routing and tunneling are not completely configured in this scenario. Answer **B** is incorrect, because the routing and tunneling are not properly configured to meet all requirements. Answer **C** is incorrect, because the default routes should not point to the corporate network. A specific route should be specified for the corporate network and default routes should handle Internet traffic.

Configuring the Windows Server 2003 VPN Server

4. After the completion of your company's PKI project, the CIO of your company has asked you to design a secure solution to give users located at satellite offices access to a new Web-based intranet application. There are typically two or three users in each of the seventeen remote offices. Client computers are using a mix of Windows 98 and Windows XP Professional for their operating systems. Your corporate intranet server sits behind a NAT enabled router. What solution will provide the best security for client access to the intranet server?

A. Install the Microsoft L2TP/IPSec VPN Client on all Windows 98 systems. Configure all clients to connect to the server using EAP-TLS authentication with L2TP/IPSec.

B. Configure all clients to connect to the server using MS-CHAP v2 authentication with PPTP.

C. Configure all clients to connect to the server using EAP-TLS authentication with PPTP.

D. Install the Microsoft L2TP/IPSec VPN Client on all Windows 98 systems. Configure all clients to connect to the server using MS-CHAP v2 authentication with L2TP/IPSec.

☑ **D**. Answer **D** is the correct answer. Although EAP-TLS provides the best scenario for authentication, it is not available for Windows 98 clients. Since the Microsoft L2TP/IPSec VPN Client provides NAT-T for Windows 98 clients and Windows Server 2003, and the Windows XP Professional clients already have built-in support for L2TP/IPSec, L2TP/IPSec may be used for a transport. MS-CHAP v2 is the best authentication protocol available that is supported by the Windows 98 clients.

☒ Answer **A** is incorrect, because Windows 98 clients will not support EAP-TLS authentication. Answer **B** is incorrect, because L2TP/IPSec provides stronger encryption (168-bit) than PPTP (128-bit). Answer **C** is incorrect, because Windows 98 clients do not support EAP-TLS.

5. Your network consists of Windows 98, Windows 2000 Professional, and Windows XP Professional clients. In a recent review of security logs for your network, you noticed several failed attempts to access your network through your VPN server. Examination of firewall logs indicates the attempted failed access came from the same IP address, and the account used was that of an ex-employee. What simple steps should be taken to prevent future unauthorized access attempts from this account and address?

A. Disable the user accounts for all ex-employees and enforce EAP-TLS authentication with IPSec.

B. Disable the user accounts for all ex-employees of the company. Configure a RAS policy to prevent authentication attempts from the IP address reported in the firewall logs. Make sure dial-in permissions are assigned based on RAS policy.

C. Disable the user accounts for all ex-employees and enforce MS-CHAP v2 authentication

D. Disable the user account for the ex-employee. Configure a RAS policy to prevent authentication attempts from the IP address reported in the firewall logs. Make sure dial-in permissions are assigned based on RAS policy.

☑ **B**. Answer **B** is correct, because user accounts from all ex-employees present a possible vulnerability. A RAS policy can be put in place to prevent access from the IP address logged by the firewall. The remote access policy adds an extra level of security.

☒ Answer **A** is incorrect, because a solution utilizing EAP-TLS with IPSec will only work for Windows 98 clients. Also, this is not a simple solution to the problem. Answer **C** is incorrect, because no provisions have been made to prevent access from the IP address logged in the firewall. Answer **D** is incorrect, because it addresses the problem with only the current unauthorized user account. Answer **B** is a better solution because it takes an added step to prevent possible future unauthorized attempts at VPN network access.

Configuring the Windows Server 2003 VPN Gateway

6. You have been assigned the task of configuring a VPN server for several remote users to access your corporate network. You open the Routing and Remote Access Server Setup Wizard to begin this process. Using Figure 7.31 as a guide, which of the following options will provide you with a base VPN server for this task? (Choose all that apply.)

Figure 7.31 Routing and Remote Access Server Setup Wizard Configuration

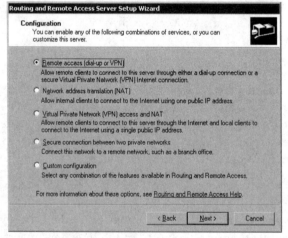

A. Remote access (dial-up or VPN)

B. Network address translation (NAT)

C. Virtual private network (VPN) access and NAT

D. Secure connection between two private networks

E. Custom configuration

☑ **A, C, E.** Answers **A, C,** and **E** are all correct answers because each one provides the basic VPN server configuration needed for remote access VPN clients.

☒ Answer **B** is incorrect, because NAT does not provide a basic VPN server of any type. Answer **D** is incorrect, because this option provides a VPN gateway, not a VPN server.

7. Your company is designing a software package that will replace legacy applications that currently use IPX/SPX for connectivity with TCP/IP as a transport mechanism. Currently, the software engineers on your four remote office networks need access to a common test server located in your corporate office. The connectivity between the software engineers and server needs to be secure. Also, several sales engineers carrying Windows 98 laptops will need access to resources on the corporate LAN while they are on the road. What solution would best accommodate this scenario?

A. Configure VPN servers to provide remote access VPN and VPN gateway capabilities at each office utilizing L2TP/IPSec with MS-CHAP v2 authentication.

B. Configure the software engineers' systems to use L2TP/IPSec with EAP-TLS authentication.

C. Configure VPN servers to provide remote access VPN and VPN gateway capabilities at each office utilizing PPTP with MS-CHAP v2 authentication.

D. Configure the software engineers' systems to use PPTP with MS-CHAP v2 authentication.

☑ **C.** Answer **C** is correct, because of the requirement to carry non-IP (IPX/SPX) traffic. Also, with the requirement to support Windows 98 clients, EAP-TLS is ruled out for authentication.

☒ Answer **A** is incorrect, because L2TP/IPSec does not provide a transport mechanism for non-IP traffic. Answer **B** is incorrect, because Windows 98 clients do not support EAP-TLS authentication. Answer **D** is incorrect, because the best solution involves connecting the offices through VPN gateways instead of relying on each client utilizing a VPN tunnel separately.

8. You have installed an Exchange server on your corporate network to handle e-mail for all of the users within your organization. If you want to use compulsory VPN tunnels specifically to transport e-mail using SMTP and POP3 between clients and the Exchange server, which TCP ports will you configure in your VPN packet filters?

A. TCP 25 and TCP 443

B. TCP 80 and TCP 110

C. TCP 110 and TCP 143

D. TCP 25 and TCP 110

☑ **D.** Answer **D** is correct because in this scenario, your Exchange clients connect via Simple Mail Transport Protocol (SMTP) and Post Office Protocol version 3 (POP3). SMTP uses TCP port 25 as a destination port while POP3 uses TCP port 110.

☒ Answer **A** is incorrect, because TCP port 25 would handle the SMTP correctly but TCP port 443 is for Secure Socket Layer connectivity (SSL). Although TCP port 110 is correct for POP3, Answer **B** is incorrect, because TCP port 80 handles World Wide Web (WWW) service. Although TCP port 110 is correct for POP3 service, Answer **C** is incorrect, because TCP port 143 handles Internet Message Access Protocol (IMAP).

9. You are setting up two VPN gateways in a test lab to test configurations before implementing them in your production network. You are using two copies of Windows Server 2003 Server Web Edition to test the connectivity in your test scenario. You configure the two servers as VPN gateways. Five L2TP ports are visible in the management console as well as five PPTP ports. You connect the servers together with compulsory tunnel mode PPTP tunnels. Everything seems to be functioning correctly. When you try to connect a dial-in VPN client to one of the servers, the connection fails. Why is the client unable to connect?

A. You do not have a sufficient public key infrastructure in place to provide PPTP connectivity.

B. Windows Server 2003 Server–Web Edition does not support PPTP voluntary mode tunnels.

C. Windows Server 2003 Server–Web Edition does not support more than one simultaneous tunnel, even though 1,000 tunnels may be installed.

D. You do not have the same authentication modes on the client and server.

☑ **C.** Answer **C** is the correct answer. In response to the prevalence of Linux installation with the Apache Web server, Microsoft released a special edition of Windows Server 2003 server to be more competitive in pricing, designed for Web hosting only. This was accomplished by limiting the features provided by Windows Server 2003 Server–Web Edition.

☒ Answer **A** is incorrect, because PPTP does not necessarily require a public key infrastructure. When EAP-TLS authentication is used with PPTP, then a certificate infrastructure needs to be in place. Answer **B** is incorrect, because Windows Server 2003 Server–Web Edition does support PPTP voluntary mode tunneling. It just limits the number of tunnels available. Answer **D** is incorrect, because the issue here is not a problem caused by mismatched VPN authentication protocols. This limitation is deliberate by design.

10. Several outside sales personnel need access to the corporate LAN. They are not direct-hire employees of your company but they will need access to certain resources. Because they are not direct-hire employees, it has been very difficult to control their system configurations to ensure security for the corporate LAN. How can you enforce corporate policies for this group of remote access clients?

A. Configure a special Remote Access Policy to enforce your corporate security policy on their machines.

B. Use the Network Access Quarantine Control utilities from the Connection Manager Administration Kit to ensure the VPN clients meet corporate standards for remote access.

C. Use the **netsh** command to ensure users connect with proper client configurations.

D. Configure the VPN server to use RADIUS for authentication. Use a RADIUS connection policy with Active Directory Group Policy to enforce corporate security.

☑ **B.** Answer **B** is the correct answer. The Network Access Quarantine Control feature of Windows Server 2003 is available through the Connection Manager Administration Kit (CMAK). It allows enforcement of corporate remote access policy configurations on client systems. This set of utilities quarantines remote access client systems until they are either brought into corporate compliance or determined to already be in compliance with corporate remote access policies.

☒ Answer **A** is incorrect, because remote access policies do not enforce or determine client configuration settings. Answer **C** is incorrect, because the **netsh** command is not used to apply network policies. Answer **D** is incorrect, because RADIUS is used only for centralized authentication of users and Group Policy does not enforce or determine client configuration settings.

11. You are planning to use IAS/RADIUS for authentication and account management of remote access users and devices. You go to the Administrative Tools menu but IAS is not listed. Where is IAS management conducted?

A. IAS is an applet of the Administrative Tools menu but it must be installed as a Windows Component.

B. IAS is managed through the Routing and Remote Access management console.

C. IAS is administered under Active Directory Users and Computers.

D. IAS is under the Option Pack submenu of the Administrative Tools menu.

☑ **A.** Answer **A** is correct. IAS is not installed on Windows Server 2003 by default. IAS must be added through the Add Remove Programs wizard as a Windows Component. After it is installed, Internet Authentication Service (IAS) is available as an applet of the Administrative Tools menu.

☒ Answer **B** is incorrect, because the Routing and Remote Access management console is used to administer remote access configuration for the local server. IAS/RADIUS is a centralized management interface for multiple RRAS servers, remote access users, and remote access devices. Answer **C** is incorrect, because Active Directory Users and Computers provides directory service administration for users and computers. The IAS management console is the utility for administering IAS/RADIUS on Windows Server 2003. Answer **D** is incorrect, because the Option Pack was a set of upgrades and utilities available on Windows NT 4.0 Server. IAS is a Windows Component that comes with Windows Server 2003. It is not installed by default, however, and must be installed through Add Remove Programs under the System Control Panel.

Troubleshooting Windows Server 2003 VPN Services

12. You work for a small computer-consulting firm. One of your clients, who recently began working from home, calls to inform you that he cannot dial in to the company's Windows Server 2003 VPN from his Windows XP computer. He just completed the setup for his new DSL connection and, at the instruction of one of the other VPN users; he has configured his VPN client. He says that error 735 is being displayed. You use the Windows XP remote desktop to connect to his computer and see the error message displayed in Figure 7.32. How can you repair this connection to enable access to this user?

Figure 7.32 Connection Error 735

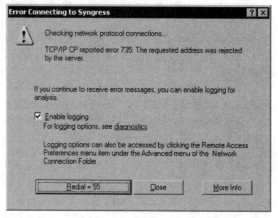

A. Ensure the computer has a valid certificate on the network.

B. Configure the **Host name or IP address of the destination** on the **General** tab of the VPN connection properties for the correct VPN server IP address.

C. Configure the VPN client to **Obtain an IP address automatically** and to **Obtain DNS server address automatically** from the **Internet Protocol Properties** of the **Networking** tab of the VPN connection.

D. From the **Internet Protocol Properties** of the **General** tab of the **Local Area Network** connection, configure the **Local Area Network** connection to **Obtain an IP address automatically** and to **Obtain DNS server address automatically**.

☑ **C.** Answer **C** is correct. The error that is being displayed results from an incorrectly configured static IP address on the VPN client connection for the internal network address. Typically, the VPN server provides addresses to clients via DHCP or through an address range configured within the VPN server. If the client sets an IP address for the client's internal connection, the system's IP address will be rejected without special settings on the server.

☒ Answer **A** is incorrect, because certificate errors typically are displayed under L2TP/IPSec client connections as a result of missing certificates or stalled services. This error reflects a TCP/IP CP problem—a problem with the IPCP binding. Answer **B** is incorrect, because an incorrect configuration for the **Host name or IP address of the destination** on the **General** tab of the VPN connection properties would result in an inability to connect to the VPN server. The error here reflects a connection, but an incorrect address setting for the client's address. IP connectivity through the Internet to the VPN server is a requirement for tunneling to take place. Answer **D** is incorrect, because reconfiguring the LAN connection for a home-based client using DSL would generally disrupt the Internet connection (DSL typically uses an Ethernet or LAN connection for non-PPPoE DSL). Again, the client needs IP connectivity through the Internet to the VPN server before a tunnel can be established. A loss of DSL connectivity would cause the computer to disconnect from the Internet. If the computer cannot reach the VPN server through the Internet, a tunnel cannot be established.

13. Your company is constantly growing and expanding to include more field personnel. There are currently approximately 60 employees accessing the VPN from various remote locations. You return to the office after a relaxing weekend to find that three users are unable to access the VPN server. You walk the users through the process of making a screen shot of the error generated. What is causing the error in Figure 7.33?

Figure 7.33 VPN User Logon Error

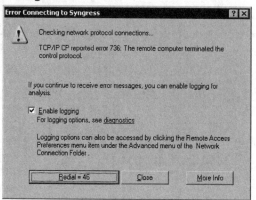

A. Ensure the computer has a valid certificate on the network.

B. Configure the **Host name or IP address of the destination** on the **General** tab of the VPN connection properties for the correct VPN server IP address.

C. Configure the VPN client to **Obtain an IP address automatically** and to **Obtain DNS server address automatically** from the **Internet Protocol Properties** of the **Networking** tab of the VPN connection.

D. Configure the DHCP server with a larger scope to accommodate IP addresses for all local and remote users.

☑ **D.** Answer **D** is correct, because the error that is being displayed comes from a lack of available IP addresses. A VPN server using DHCP for addressing requests IP addresses in blocks of 10. In all likelihood, there have never been more than 50 remote users connected at one time. On this particular Monday, more than 50 users have attempted to connect and the DHCP server did not have a sufficient block of addresses to provide to the VPN server.

☒ Answer **A** is incorrect, because certificate errors typically are displayed under L2TP/IPSec client connections as a result of missing certificates or stalled services. This error reflects a TCP/IP CP problem—a problem with the IPCP binding. Answer **B** is incorrect, because an incorrect configuration for the **Host name or IP address of the destination** on the **General** tab of the VPN connection properties would result in an inability to connect to the VPN server. The error here indicates that you have a connection, but an incorrect address setting for the client's address. IP connectivity through the Internet to the VPN server is a requirement for tunneling to take place. Answer **C** is incorrect, because this problem would not occur on systems that had been previously working. For three users to report the identical problem on systems that were working in the past indicates a server side or larger problem than individual systems might experience.

14. One of your users calls about a problem accessing resources on the network. The client VPN connection shows a connection but none of the resources within your Active Directory domain are available. The user seems to have IP connectivity to the VPN LAN with his or her Windows 2000 Professional computer. Other remote users have not reported problems connecting to the network resources. What is causing this problem?

    A. The WINS server configuration settings for the VPN client are incorrect..

    B. The VPN server configuration for the DNS server is incorrect.

    C. The VPN server configuration for the WINS server is incorrect.

    D. The DNS server configuration settings for the VPN client are incorrect.

    ☑ **D**. Answer **D** is the correct answer. The problem reported is a problem with a single user's connection. Windows Server 2003 Active Directory relies on DNS for connectivity. This scenario indicates a problem with the DNS VPN client configuration. Make sure the **Obtain DNS server address automatically** option is selected for the VPN client connection **TCP/IP Properties** dialog box.

    ☒ Answer **A** is incorrect, because this problem indicates a problem with name resolution. WINS is for Microsoft legacy systems and is only available for connectivity for older systems and non-Active Directory usage. Windows 2000 and Windows Server 2003 Active Directory utilizes DNS for name resolution. Answer **B** is incorrect, because this appears to be a client-side problem, not a server-side problem. Answer **C** is incorrect, because the problem appears to be a client-side problem, not a server-side problem. Also, WINS is used for legacy system connectivity. Active Directory relies on DNS for name resolution.

15. Your VPN server is configured to connect directly to the Internet, providing VPN connectivity and NAT for your office. Your broadband access provider recently went out of business and you have to reconfigure your server to connect to a new service. One of the junior administrators was in the process of reconfiguring the server but could not obtain connectivity to the Internet. You run ipconfig and see the IP address information shown in Figure 7.34. Why is the VPN server unable to connect to the Internet?

Figure 7.34 IP Configuration for Corporate VPN/NAT Server

```
E:\WINDOWS\system32\cmd.exe                                          _ □ ×

E:\>ipconfig /all

Windows IP Configuration

        Host Name . . . . . . . . . . . . : server2003
        Primary Dns Suffix  . . . . . . . :
        Node Type . . . . . . . . . . . . : Broadcast
        IP Routing Enabled. . . . . . . . : No
        WINS Proxy Enabled. . . . . . . . : Yes

Ethernet adapter LAN:

        Connection-specific DNS Suffix  . :
        Description . . . . . . . . . . . : 3Com 3C900COMBO-based Ethernet Adapter (G
eneric)
        Physical Address. . . . . . . . . : 00-60-97-C4-82-9B
        DHCP Enabled. . . . . . . . . . . : No
        IP Address. . . . . . . . . . . . : 192.168.1.72
        Subnet Mask . . . . . . . . . . . : 255.255.255.0
        Default Gateway . . . . . . . . . :

Ethernet adapter WAN:

        Connection-specific DNS Suffix  . :
        Description . . . . . . . . . . . : 3Com 3C900COMBO-based Ethernet Adapter (G
eneric) #2
        Physical Address. . . . . . . . . : 00-10-4B-64-31-33
        DHCP Enabled. . . . . . . . . . . : No
        IP Address. . . . . . . . . . . . : 10.0.0.10
        Subnet Mask . . . . . . . . . . . : 255.255.255.0
        Default Gateway . . . . . . . . . :
        NetBIOS over Tcpip. . . . . . . . : Disabled

E:\>_
```

A. This operation is by design.

B. The VPN server does not have a correct route to the Internet.

C. Both addresses are private addresses. This server cannot connect directly to the Internet.

D. The DNS server addresses are incorrect.

☑ **C.** Answer **C** is the correct answer. The more common private IP addresses are in the range of 10.0.0.0/8, 172.16.0.0/12, and 192.168.0.0/16.

☒ Answer **A** is incorrect, because VPN connectivity using the Internet as a transport medium requires proper Internet connectivity. There is nothing in the design of VPN that should prevent the VPN gateway from connecting to the Internet when a tunnel has not been initiated. Answer **B** is partially correct. Private IP addresses do not have routes defined on the Internet so this might be defined as a routing problem. The VPN server would need IP connectivity to its neighboring machine before we could truly say it had a routing problem, however. Answer **D** is incorrect, because the problem exists lower in the OSI reference model than the DNS naming service. This problem is a layer three IP addressing problem.

Chapter 8 Configuring the Windows 2003 Routing and Remote Access Service LAN Routing, Dial-up Services, and Routing Protocols

Configuring LAN Routing

1. You are designing the corporate global network for your company. You have to decide on an authentication method. What is the preferred authentication method for Windows Server 2003 in a high security environment?

   A. MS-CHAP

   B. EAP-TLS

   C. CHAP

   D. PAP

   ☑ **B**. Answer **B** is correct, because the Extensible Authentication Protocol with Transport Level Security (EAP-TLS) provides certificate-based authentication of users and computers in a Windows Server 2003 environment.

   ☒ Answer **A** is incorrect, because MS-CHAP does not provide authentication through certificates, so password selection can affect the security strength of the protocol. Answer **C** is incorrect, because CHAP does not provide authentication of computers, and like MS-CHAP, it uses passwords, which can compromise security based on the complexity of the passwords used. Answer **D** is incorrect, because PAP is a password-based protocol that uses clear-text transport of password information and it does not authenticate computers.

Configuring RRAS Packet Filters

2. The IT Manager has asked you to implement an intranet Web server on a separate subnet from the client systems in your network. How will you implement a packet filter for the scenario shown in Figure 8.115?

Figure 8.115 Intranet Web Server Packet Filtering

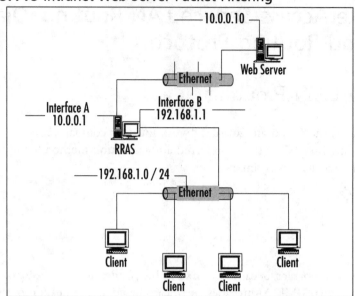

A. Filter inbound packets on Interface B with a source network of 192.168.1.0 and subnet mask of 255.255.255.0, a destination network of 10.0.0.0 and a destination subnet mask of 255.255.255.0, and destination TCP port 25. Select to drop all packets except those listed in your criteria.

B. Filter inbound packets on Interface B with a source network of 192.168.1.0 and subnet mask of 255.255.255.0, a destination network of 10.0.0.0 and a destination subnet mask of 255.255.255.0, and destination TCP port 25. Select to receive all packets except those listed in your criteria.

C. Filter inbound packets on Interface B with a source network of 192.168.1.0 and subnet mask of 255.255.255.0, a destination network of 10.0.0.0 and a destination subnet mask of 255.255.255.0, and destination TCP port 80. Select to drop all packets except those listed in your criteria.

D. Filter inbound packets on Interface B with a source network of 192.168.1.0 and subnet mask of 255.255.255.0, a destination network of 10.0.0.0 and a destination subnet mask of 255.255.255.0, and destination TCP port 80. Select to receive all packets except those listed in your criteria.

☑ **C**. Answer **C** is correct, because Web services are hosted on TCP port 80 and in this scenario on the destination network 10.0.0.0. We want to drop all packets except those coming from source 192.168.1.0 and destined for 10.0.0.0.

☒ Answer **A** is incorrect, because TCP port 25 is the port for basic e-mail transport through SMTP. We are trying to allow Web traffic, not e-mail. Answer **B** is incorrect, because the only traffic being restricted here is traffic through the SMTP e-mail transport protocol. Answer **D** is incorrect, because all traffic *except* Web traffic is being allowed in this configuration.

Configuring the Windows 2003 Dial-up RAS Server

3. You have been asked to set up a Windows 2003 dial-up RAS server for your company. Your clients use Windows XP and Windows 2000 Professional computers. Company policy requires the most secure authentication possible. How will you configure your dial-up RAS server to meet company policy?

   A. Configure CHAP authentication.

   B. Configure MS-CHAP v2 authentication.

   C. Configure PAP authentication.

   D. Configure EAP-TLS authentication.

   ☑ **D**. Answer **D** is correct, because the certificate-based EAP-TLS authentication provides the most secure authentication for Windows Server 2003.

   ☒ Answer **A** is incorrect, because CHAP is not the most secure authentication available. Answer **B** is incorrect; although MS-CHAP v2 provides mutual authentication of server and client systems as well as user authentication, it is still not consistently as strong of an authentication method as EAP-TLS. Answer **C** is incorrect, because PAP does not provide for encrypted usernames or passwords. Consequently, the clear-text PAP protocol is not nearly as secure as the encrypted, password-based EAP-TLS.

Configuring the Windows 2003 Dial-up RAS Gateway

4. You configure a Windows 2003 dial-up RAS gateway for a remote office in your corporate network. A dial-up ISDN connection is used to connect the remote office to the corporate LAN. In order to provide access for the remote users to the corporate LAN, what two configuration settings do you need to complete? (Choose all that apply.)

   A. Configure NAT on the ISDN interface.

   B. Configure a demand-dial interface on the ISDN interface.

   C. Configure a DHCP relay agent on the ISDN interface.

   D. Configure a default static route on the ISDN interface.

☑ **B, D.** To direct traffic from the remote LAN to the corporate LAN, a default static route needs to be configured on the ISDN interface to guide nonlocal LAN traffic off of the LAN, as described in Answer **D.** When traffic has been directed, a mechanism needs to be in place to carry the traffic from the remote LAN to the corporate LAN. The demand-dial interface on the ISDN interface initiates a connection between the remote ISDN interface and the ISDN interface on the corporate router as described in Answer **B.**

☒ Answer **A** is incorrect, because NAT is not usually needed for LAN-to-LAN connectivity. Answer **C** is incorrect, because a DHCP relay agent is not needed on the ISDN interface to provide connectivity. A DHCP relay agent listens for client broadcast requests for an IP address from a DHCP server. The DHCP relay agent sends the request through a unicast connection between the relay agent and the DHCP server, acting on behalf of the DHCP clients.

5. You configure a Windows 2003 dial-up RAS Gateway providing Internet access for users on a remote LAN in your corporate network. The LAN is on the subnet 10.0.2.0/24. What RRAS mechanism will facilitate public Internet connectivity for users on this private network?

A. The NAT component of Windows Server 2003 RRAS will provide connectivity in this case.

B. RIP routing will provide connectivity in this case.

C. OSPF routing will provide connectivity in this case.

D. Dynamic DNS will provide connectivity in this case.

☑ **A. A** is correct, because private network addresses rely on NAT to provide private network to public network mapping.

☒ Answer **B** is incorrect, because RIP is a dynamic routing protocol. Private IP addresses are not routed on the Internet. Answer **C** is incorrect, because OSPF is also a dynamic routing protocol. Answer **D** is incorrect, because dynamic DNS provides automatic mapping of changing IP addresses to DNS host name entries. The problem here involved IP address translations, not name resolution.

PPP Multilink and Bandwidth Allocation Protocol (BAP)

6. In Windows Server 2003 RRAS, PPP multilink is enabled by default. What controls the properties for the PPP multilink connection?

A. Remote access policy controls the multilink connection properties.

B. The dial-up networking properties for the client connection control the multilink connection properties.

C. When a PPP multilink connection is established, the user is prompted with a dialog box to control the multilink connection properties.

D. Active Directory controls multilink connection properties.

☑ **A. A** is correct, because remote access policy provides multilink property settings such as the number of ports available to the connection and BAP configuration options to control at what percentage of bandwidth extra ports will be dropped and how long extra connections will be carried while the bandwidth requirement is below the trigger percentage.

☒ Answer **B** is incorrect, because the client networking connection properties do not provide ultimate control over the multilink connection properties. Answer **C** is incorrect, because user prompts are not provided to control the multilink session properties. Answer **D** is incorrect, because Active Directory does not provide multilink connection properties, only authentication control and group policy implementation.

Configuring Wireless Connections

7. You are tasked with the design and implementation of a new wireless network for your corporate campus. Users will connect to various access points around campus using primarily laptops and PDAs. How will you design an authentication scheme to simplify the administration of the 1,000+ users of this system?

A. Configure a single Windows Server 2003 system as the logon server. Create local accounts for all network users.

B. Configure a pair of Windows Server 2003 systems as Active Directory domain controllers. Configure IAS to use the Active Directory user accounts for authentication.

C. Configure a pair of Windows Server 2003 systems to share local account database information and use TACACS+ for user authentication.

D. Configure a Windows Server 2003 system as a primary domain controller. Configure a second Windows Server 2003 system to replicate account database information using SQL.

☑ **B. B** is correct, because configuring IAS with Active Directory as the account management utility provides simplified administration, centralized accounting, redundancy, and single sign-on capabilities.

☒ Answer **A** is incorrect, because using a single system's local accounts is not possible with IAS. This would not provide a simplified method for account administration. Answer **C** is incorrect, because Terminal Access Controller Access Control System (TACACS+) is a family of security protocols used for Authentication, Authorization, and Accounting (AAA) that is not available in Windows Server 2003. TACACS is similar to IAS/RADIUS security protocol but is more flexible and powerful. Answer **D** is incorrect, because replicating SQL servers for authentication is not a wireless networking option for Windows Server 2003.

Configuring Remote Access Policies

8. Your organization supports several users that work from home offices. Each home-based user connects to the network through a VPN. The DSL connections used by each home-based user are configured with static IP addresses. You want to use a remote access policy to ensure that the home-based users connect to the office only from their home office computers. What is the simplest way to accomplish this task?

    A. Configure smart-card authentication for each home-based user. Configure a remote access policy to deny access to all users except smart-card authenticated users.

    B. Configure biometric user authentication using EAP-TLS. Configure a remote access policy to deny access to all users except EAP-TLS authenticated users.

    C. Configure PEAP authentication. Configure a remote access policy to deny access to all users except PEAP authenticated users.

    D. Configure a remote access policy to deny access to all users except those verified with specific Client-IP-Address parameters.

    ☑ **D.** Answer **D** is correct, because Client-IP-Address verification will ensure home-based users are connecting only from their static IP address assigned home offices.

    ☒ Answer **A** is incorrect, because smart-card authentication does not provide simplified administration and it does not necessarily ensure that users are connecting from their home offices. Answer **B** is incorrect, because biometric authentication with EAP-TLS does not provide simplified administration and again, it does not necessarily ensure that users are connecting from their home offices. Answer **C** is incorrect, because PEAP is an authentication protocol used in wireless networks.

Understanding Router Protocols

9. You are designing a small IP network with eight remote sites. You need to provide site-to-site connectivity through the corporate hub network. How can you provide a simple solution to routing this traffic and still accommodate the addition of new remote sites with the least amount of extra administration?

    A. Configure the network to use RIP v2 routing on all subnets.

    B. Configure the network to use OSPF on all subnets. Configure each remote site to be in area 0.0.0.0.

    C. Configure default static routes on each remote subnet.

    D. Configure IGMP on each subnet.

    ☑ **A.** Answer **A** is correct, because RIP v2 provides simple configuration and also accommodates the addition of new remote sites with a minimum of extra effort.

☒ Answer **B** is incorrect, because OSPF requires more planning and configuration than RIP. Answer **C** is incorrect, because default static routes will provide connectivity only to the corporate hub network. Traffic will not be carried through the hub to the other remote networks. Also, if more sites are added, default static routes would have to be configured for the new remote sites. Answer **D** is incorrect, because IGMP is a messaging protocol used to advertise multicast group membership information, not unicast IP routes.

Configuring Basic Firewall Support

10. You are responsible for securing your corporate network using a Windows Server 2003 remote access server. Your network manager has asked you to install and configure the basic firewall features available in Windows Server 2003. Are there any concerns with using the basic firewall on your network?

 A. Internet services that are provided from privately addressed systems will have to be provisioned in the firewall configuration.

 B. Some public systems may experience problems connecting to systems on the LAN.

 C. Some systems might not be able to connect to the Internet.

 D. Some private systems might experience problems connecting to systems on the LAN.

 ☑ **A.** Answer **A** is correct, because the filtering capabilities of the basic firewall will block Internet-based IP traffic to machines on the privately addressed LAN. The firewall has to be configured to support such machines and services.

 ☒ Answer **B** is incorrect, because the main purpose for using a firewall is to restrict inbound traffic from public systems to private LAN-based systems. Answer **C** is incorrect, because a properly functioning firewall should not restrict Internet access unintentionally. Answer **D** is incorrect, because the firewall should not affect internal network traffic on the LAN.

RRAS NAT Services

11. You are talking with another network engineer about network address translation. She claims that ICS and Microsoft NAT are the same thing. What are two major differences between ICS and Microsoft's implementation of NAT as provided in Microsoft's server product line? (Choose all that apply.)

 A. NAT supports multiple public addresses, ICS does not.

 B. ICS works on Windows 2000 Server and Windows Server 2003, NAT does not.

 C. ICS supports multiple public addresses, NAT does not.

 D. NAT works with DHCP to accommodate different subnet addresses, ICS does not.

☑ **A, D**. Answers **A** and **D** are correct. NAT supports multiple addresses on the public interface and provides address allocation through DHCP. ICS is a preconfigured implementation of NAT with several limitations due to its preconfigured nature.

☒ Answer **B** is incorrect, because ICS and NAT both work on Windows 2000 Server and Windows Server 2003. ICS is also available on Windows 98SE and newer Microsoft client operating systems. NAT is available only on Windows server operating systems, beginning with Windows 2000 server. Answer **C** is incorrect, because ICS does not support multiple public addresses on the public network interface.

ICMP Router Discovery

12. To provide network redundancy, you have implemented ICMP Router Discovery on your company network. Clients are not detecting the routers on your network. What is preventing the clients from seeing the routers?

A. You have to enable ICMP Router Discovery on the network clients by implementing the proper group policy.

B. You have to enable ICMP Router Discovery on network clients by adding two entries to the registry.

C. You have to enable ICMP Router Discovery on the network clients through Active Directory Users and Computers.

D. You have to enable ICMP Router Discovery on the network clients through the Routing and Remote Access service Microsoft management console.

☑ **B**. Answer **B** is correct. To enable ICMP Router Discovery on client computers, you have to add two registry entries. To implement ICMP on a client computer, add the following registry entries with a value of REG_DWORD 0x1:

1. PerformRouterDiscovery in the subkey HKEY_LOCAL_MACHINE\SYSTEM\CurrentControlSet\Services\Tcpip\Parameters

2. SolicitationAddressBcast in the subkey HKEY_LOCAL_MACHINE\SYSTEM\CurrentControlSet\Services\adaptername\Parameters\Tcpip.

☒ Answer **A** is incorrect, because group policy does not provide any client configuration options for ICMP Router Discovery. Answer **C** is incorrect, because Active Directory Users and Computers does not provide client configuration options for ICMP Router Discovery. Answer **D** is incorrect, because the Routing and Remote Access service Microsoft management console provides server configuration options for ICMP Router Discovery, not client configuration.

Troubleshooting Remote Access Client Connections

13. You move some of the servers on your network to a new subnet. You manually update the DNS server records for these servers. A client contacts you to complain that their computer cannot access resources on one of the moved servers. You successfully ping the server by IP address. When you ping the server by name, you notice that a different IP address is listed. How can you quickly rectify this problem?

    A. Run the **gpupdate** command to update the name resolution cache.

    B. Run the **ping -a** command with the server IP address to update the name resolution cache.

    C. Run the **ipconfig /flushdns** command to clear the DNS cache.

    D. Run the **nslookup** command. From the nslookup prompt, type **ls d** to repair the DNS cache.

    ☑ **C.** Answer **C** is correct because the **ipconfig /flushdns** command clears entries in the client's DNS cache. The problem described here is clearly a name resolution problem. In this case, it is a problem with cached name resolution information on the client system.

    ☒ Answer **A** is incorrect, because the **gpupdate** is used to update the group policy settings on a client computer. Answer **B** is incorrect, because the **ping -a** command is used to invoke an ICMP echo from the client at the IP address being pinged. The **-a** switch causes the command to request name information from the client. Answer **D** is incorrect, because the **nslookup** command is used to test DNS name resolution. When used with the **ls** command and the **d** switch, **nslookup** lists the naming information for the particular domain that the client uses for name resolution.

Troubleshooting Remote Access Server Connections

14. Your remote access server provides a remote connection to your LAN-based terminal server. Several users are complaining that their connections to the server are frequently dropped. You suspect problems beyond the confines of your LAN. How can you determine the cause of this problem?

    A. Issue a **ping** command to several of the clients' addresses. Verify packet delivery.

    B. Issue a **pingpath** command to several of the clients' addresses. Look for high packet loss from routers along the path.

    C. Issue a **tracert** command to several of the clients' addresses. Look for high delivery times from routers along the path.

    D. Issue a **route** command to several of the clients' addresses. Look for high delivery times from routers along the path.

☑ **B.** Answer **B** is correct because **pingpath** is the ideal command to test packet loss along a path. The problem described in this scenario is not an uncommon problem. The **pingpath** command works very well for testing networks outside of your LAN for connectivity problems.

☒ Answer **A** is incorrect, because the **ping** command only shows delivery information between two systems. This does not provide a capability to pinpoint the problems that may be occurring between the endpoints. Answer **C** is incorrect, because the **tracert** command does not provide sufficient detail about packet delivery along the traffic path. Answer **D** is incorrect, because the **route** command provides routing information only for your network, not external networks.

Configuring Internet Authentication Services

15. You configure IAS for centralized authentication of remote users. What are two major advantages of IAS for authentication?

A. IAS provides open standard authentication, providing authentication for remote access devices from multiple vendors.

B. IAS provides a proprietary authentication mechanism, providing authentication for remote access devices from multiple vendors.

C. IAS provides single sign-on authentication for remote and local users through Active Directory.

D. IAS provides single sign-on authentication for remote and local users through TACACS+.

☑ **A, C.** Answer **A** is correct, because IAS is Microsoft's implementation of the RADIUS open standard authentication protocol. This provides centralized authentication for equipment from various vendors. Answer **C** is correct, because IAS ties into Microsoft Active Directory for account administration. This provides multiple network access methods for a single account.

☒ Answer **B** is incorrect, because IAS is an implementation of RADIUS. The strength of IAS lies on the fact that RADIUS is an open standard, providing an authentication mechanism that is not vendor specific. A proprietary solution typically works with only one vendor's equipment. Answer **D** is incorrect, because IAS does not use Cisco's TACACS+ for authentication.

Chapter 9 Security Templates and Software Updates

Security Templates

1. A junior administrator has modified the permissions on the c: drive of your file server. The operating system is installed on the c: drive and the data is stored on the d: drive. What is the simplest way to restore the default permissions for the file server?

    A. Apply the securews.inf security template to the file server to apply the proper permissions.

    B. Apply the Setup secure.inf security template to the file server to apply the proper permissions.

    C. Apply the rootsec.inf security template to the file server to apply the proper permissions.

    D. Apply the DC secure.inf security template to the file server to apply the proper permissions.

    ☑ **C.** Answer **C** is correct because rootsec.inf applies the default set of permissions to the root drive.

    ☒ Answer **A** is incorrect because the securews.inf is used to increase security on workstations and servers, not to restore root file system permissions. Answer **B** is incorrect because the Setup secure.inf security template is used to reset the default settings on a workstation or server that has had local security settings modified with another security template or through direct modification with the Security Configuration and Analysis management console. Answer **D** is incorrect because the DC secure.inf security template is used to reset the default settings on a domain controller that has had local security settings modified with another security template or through direct modification with the Security Configuration and Analysis management console.

2. You upgrade three of the file servers on your network from Windows NT 4.0 Server to Windows Server 2003. Some applications originally used with Windows NT 4.0 are no longer functioning properly. When you are logged in with a local administrator account, the applications perform correctly. Corporate security policy does not allow standard users to have local administrator or power user membership on file servers. How can you provide sufficient privileges to the file servers while consistently providing the security required for the upgraded servers?

    A. Apply the securews.inf security template to the file servers to adjust the security to the proper levels.

    B. Apply the DC secure.inf security template to the file servers to adjust the security to the proper levels.

    C. Apply the Setup secure.inf security template to the file servers to adjust the security to the proper levels.

    D. Apply the compatws.inf security template to the file servers to adjust the security to the proper levels.

☑ **D.** Answer **D** is correct because the compatws.inf security template provides elevated user rights for standard users without utilizing the local administrator or power users groups.

☒ Answer **A** is incorrect because securews.inf provides increased security for workstations and servers. The problem here is a result of too much security. Increasing the security will not rectify the problem. Answer **B** is incorrect because the DC secure.inf security template is used to restore standard security configurations to a domain controller. Answer **C** is incorrect because the Setup secure.inf security template is used to restore standard security configurations to a workstation. The standard configuration of Windows Server 2003 is the problem here, so reconfiguring the Windows Server 2003 settings to their standard setting will not rectify the problem.

3. Your corporate network has several Windows 2000 file servers that will be upgraded to Windows Server 2003. You want to ensure that the upgraded servers' configurations are consistent with the new Windows Server 2003 servers that you are deploying. How can you ensure a consistent set of configurations for the Windows Server 2003 file servers?

A. Apply the setup security.inf security template to all upgraded servers to ensure consistency.

B. Apply the securews.inf security template to all upgraded servers to ensure consistency.

C. Apply the DC secure.inf security template to all upgraded servers to ensure consistency.

D. Apply the rootsec.inf security template to all upgraded servers to ensure consistency.

☑ **A.** Answer **A** is the correct answer because the setup security.inf security template provide configuration equivalent to a default installation.

☒ Answer **B** is incorrect because the securews.inf security template is used to supply increased security over a standard installation for workstations. Answer **C** is incorrect because the DC secure.inf security template provides a mechanism to restore standard security configuration for domain controllers. Answer **D** is incorrect because the rootsec.inf security template is used to restore permissions on the root file system, not to restore the overall system configuration settings.

4. You administer systems in a satellite office for your multinational corporation. After analyzing one of your server's configurations against a new security template that you have received, you see that several question marks appear in the analysis. What is causing this?

A. The computer's configuration is different from the configurations specified in the new template file.

B. The computer's configuration has changed since the last configuration was applied.

C. The security template file has incorrect NTFS settings to perform the analysis.

D. You do not have sufficient permissions to compare the configurations in the areas indicated with question marks.

☑ **D.** Answer **D** is correct. A question mark is an indication that the entry was not analyzed. This may be because it was not defined in the analysis database or because the user who is running the analysis does not have sufficient permission to perform analysis on a specific object or area.

☒ Answer **A** is incorrect because the question mark indicates that the particular entry could not be analyzed. Since the entry could not be analyzed, there is no way for the analysis to detect differences between the existing configuration and the new template configuration. Answer **B** is incorrect because the analysis does not track modifications to the existing system; it only compares imported templates to the existing system configuration. Answer **C** is incorrect because NTFS permissions are not causing a problem here.

5. You want to increase security on your network. You analyze your new template against the current configuration as seen in Figure 9.35. Which configurations should you modify in the new template before applying the new template file?

Figure 9.35 Analysis Using New Security Template

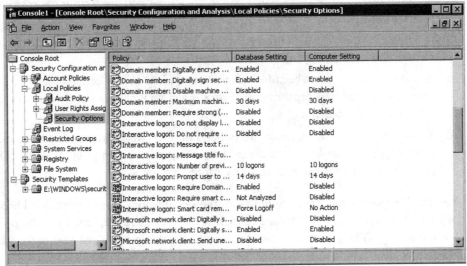

A. Change the **Interactive logon: Require Domain Controller authentication to unlock workstation** to **disabled**.

B. Based on the differences shown in Figure 9.35, you can apply the template as is, and it will not weaken the security in the areas shown.

C. Change the **Interactive logon: Smart card removal behavior** setting to **No Action**.

D. Change the **Interactive logon: Do not require CTRL+ALT+DEL** to **Enabled**.

☑ **B.** Answer **B** is correct because the settings listed will all improve security for the machine configuration displayed in Figure 9.35.

⊠ Answer **A** is incorrect because disabling the **Interactive logon: Require Domain Controller authentication to unlock workstation** will weaken the security configuration provided by the template. Answer **C** is incorrect because setting the **Interactive logon: Smart card removal behavior** setting to **No Action** will weaken the security configuration provided by the template. Answer **D** is incorrect because enabling the **Interactive logon: Do not require CTRL+ALT+DEL** setting will provide weaker security than the current system configuration and also will provide weaker security than that provided by the new template.

6. You apply a new security setting to your domain using Group Policy. When you test the configuration, it has not been applied. What could be causing this?

   A. A conflicting policy for the OU containing the machine you are testing has overwritten the domain configuration that you created.

   B. A conflicting policy for the site containing the machine you are testing has overwritten the domain configuration that you created.

   C. A conflicting local security policy for the machine you are testing has overwritten the domain configuration that you created.

   D. A conflicting policy for the forest containing the machine you are testing has overwritten the domain configuration that you created.

   ☑ **A.** Answer **A** is correct because policies are applied in this order: locally, to sites, to domains, and then to organizational units. Each consecutive policy overwrites conflicting settings for previous policies.

   ⊠ Answer **B** is incorrect because site policies do not overwrite domain policies. Answer **C** is incorrect because local policies do not overwrite domain policies. Answer **D** is incorrect because there is no such thing as a forest policy.

7. You modify the domain security policy in the default domain group policy. There are no other policies configured for your network at this time. You implemented the policy about 15 minutes ago. The policy does not seem to be working. How can you make sure the policy is being applied with no service disruption?

   A. Reboot the domain controller that the policy was applied to.

   B. Use **secedit /refreshpolicy** to force a policy refresh instead of waiting for the policy interval to complete.

   C. Do nothing—you have to wait for the policy refresh interval to pass.

   D. Use the **gpupdate** command to force a policy refresh instead of waiting for the policy interval to complete.

   ☑ **D.** Answer **D** is correct because for Windows Server 2003, security and group policy updates are expedited with the **gpupdate** command. The policy probably has not updated, so **gpupdate** will speed up the refresh process.

☒ Answer **A** is incorrect because although rebooting a server will update the policy, this is not a good approach because of the disruption to service that occurs due to server reboots. Answer **B** is incorrect because the **secedit /refreshpolicy** command and switch were used for Windows 2000. There is a new command, the **gpupdate** command, for Windows Server 2003. Answer **C** is incorrect because forcing a policy refresh will expedite the testing process to verify proper operation.

8. A security audit has determined that one of your Active Directory sites should implement stronger security by increasing the minimum password length required. You implement the policy for the site through Active Directory Sites and Services but the policy does not seem to be taking affect. What is causing this policy to fail?

A. Password and account related policies have to be applied to the domain, not to the site.

B. You have to use the **gpupdate** command to force a policy refresh instead of waiting for the policy interval to complete.

C. A local policy might be overwriting the new policy.

D. Active Directory Sites and Services does not support security policies.

☑ **A.** Answer **A** is correct because account and password related policies must be applied to the domain to take effect. You cannot apply these policies to sites.

☒ Answer **B** is incorrect because updating the policy will not make any difference in this case because the policy is not configured in the right place. Answer **C** is incorrect because local policies do not overwrite any policies. Answer **D** is incorrect because Active Directory Sites and Services does support security policies. It does not support account and password policies, however.

Software Updates

9. Your network consists of Windows XP, Windows 2000, and Windows Server 2003 systems. You implement a Group Policy to deploy and configure the Automatic Client Update software. Later in the day, some users report that the Windows Update information is no longer displayed on their task bars even though they did not go through the procedure of installing updates that were displayed there earlier in the day. What is causing this?

A. The users reporting problems are not logging on to the domain.

B. Check network connectivity. The users are not connecting to the SUS server.

C. Restart the SUS service on the server—it is not responding to the client requests.

D. This is the expected result from applying the Automatic Client Update configurations. Standard users do not have capabilities to modify the Automatic Update Client.

☑ **D.** Answer **D** is the correct answer. Once Automatic Client Update is installed and configured on the client systems, depending on configuration settings, users may see only minimal information about updates. The behavior being experienced here is expected.

☒ Answer **A** is incorrect because client update settings are configured on a per system basis, not on a per user basis. If Automatic Client Update is configured, updates will be deployed to systems regardless of whether users log on to their computers or the domain. Answer **B** is incorrect because network connectivity problems would result in other problems that would, in all likelihood, be visible to the user. Answer **C** is incorrect because the problem is not a problem with the server. This problem was reported by only some of the clients and the problem, in reality, is expected behavior.

10. Your network consists of Windows XP, Windows 2000, and Windows Server 2003 systems. You implement a Group Policy to deploy and configure the Automatic Client Update software. The next day, some users report that a Windows Update information box is displayed on their systems, informing them that they must reboot now. The only option is to click **Yes**, because the **No** prompt is grayed out. What should the users do?

A. Complete their current tasks and click **Yes** when it is convenient for them to reboot.

B. Click **Yes** now, and all of their work will automatically be saved.

C. Click **Yes** now, and all work will be lost.

D. Click **Yes** now, and the system will not reboot until they have completed their current tasks.

☑ **A.** Answer **A** is correct. This message box is being displayed because the users' systems were not running during the time that the client systems were configured to connect to the SUS server for updates. Consequently, when users logged on that morning, updates that were not downloaded and installed at the scheduled time were downloaded after startup. Now, the updates require a reboot and the user is being informed of the required reboot. The message does not have a timer associated with it so users may click **Yes** when it is convenient for them to reboot.

☒ Answer **B** is incorrect because work will not be saved automatically. Answer **C** is incorrect because it implies that the user has to click **Yes** right now, losing all of his or her work. The users should click **Yes** when it is convenient for them, after saving all of their work. Answer **D** is incorrect because the system will reboot as soon as **Yes** is clicked.

11. Several users are logged on to one of the terminal servers on your network. A message is displayed that says the server has installed updates and must reboot. The **Yes** and **No** prompts are grayed out. What should the users do in this scenario?

A. Open the task manager and end the Rundll32.exe process.

B. Close the terminal server window immediately.

C. Complete their existing tasks on the terminal server and log off.

D. From the **Start** button, select to shut down and restart the server.

☑ **C.** Answer **C** is correct. When nonadministrative users are logged on to a server and updates have been installed that require reboot, a message is displayed to all logged on users informing them that the server must reboot. Users should complete their tasks and log off. Once all users have logged off, the server will reboot.

☒ Answer **A** is incorrect because killing the **Rundll32.exe** process will usually close a message box. It is not necessary to close this box, even if the user had sufficient rights to do so, because this message is intended to be informational. Users should complete their tasks and log off as soon as possible when this prompt is displayed. Answer **B** is incorrect because closing the terminal window is unnecessary if the users have not completed their intended tasks. The message displayed is intended to inform users that the server is awaiting a reboot to complete updates that were just installed. The users should log off at the soonest convenient time. Answer **D** is incorrect because standard users should not have sufficient rights to reboot a terminal server. Furthermore, it is unnecessary for anyone to issue a reboot to the server. As soon as all users log off, the server will reboot automatically.

12. Your network consists of Windows 98, Windows NT 4.0, and Windows Server 2003 computers. Depending on the technical level of the user, not all systems are kept up-to-date with security patches and hot fixes. With the least amount of administration and the lowest cost possible, what procedure should be used to ensure that timely, consistent updates are applied to all clients on your network?

   A. Upgrade all systems to Windows 2000 Professional or Windows XP Professional. Configure a Group Policy to keep systems up-to-date with an internal SUS server.

   B. Upgrade the NT 4.0 systems to Windows 2000 Professional or Windows XP Professional. Upgrade the critical update notification service on Windows 98 systems using the registry editor. Configure the Windows 98 clients using the registry editor. Configure a Group Policy to keep the Windows 2000, Windows XP, and Windows Server 2003 systems up-to-date with an internal SUS server.

   C. Upgrade the Windows 98 systems to Windows 2000 Professional or Windows XP Professional. Upgrade the critical update notification service on Windows NT 4.0 systems using the registry editor. Configure the Windows NT 4.0 clients using the registry editor. Configure a Group Policy to keep the Windows 2000, Windows XP, and Windows Server 2003 systems up-to-date with an internal SUS server.

   D. Install the Automatic Update Client MSI file to all systems through a logon script. Configure a Group Policy to keep systems up-to-date with an internal SUS server.

   ☑ **A.** Answer **A** is the correct answer. Windows Critical Update Notification can be upgraded on Windows 2000 systems by modifying the registry in non-Active Directory environments or through Group Policy where an Active Directory domain is present. Windows 98 and Windows NT 4.0 will not work with an internal SUS server. All Windows 98 and Windows NT 4.0 systems will have to be upgraded to take advantage of the automated SUS service.

☒ Answer **B** is incorrect because the SUS service does not support Windows 98 or Windows NT 4.0. Answer **C** is incorrect because the SUS service does not support Windows 98 or Windows NT 4.0. Answer **D** is incorrect because the Automatic Update Client MSI is not intended for Windows 98 or Windows NT 4.0 systems. This solution will not work for the Windows 98 and Windows NT 4.0 clients on this network.

13. Your network consists of Windows Server 2003 server, Windows XP Professional, and Windows 98 clients. You have installed and configured an SUS server for your local network. You use a Group Policy to deploy the Automatic Update client software to the clients and you use Group Policy settings to configure the clients. Several days later, you notice that the Windows 98 systems are not being updated with the latest security patches and hot fixes. What is causing this problem?

A. Use the **gpupdate** command to force an update for the Group Policy refresh interval.

B. Use **secedit /refreshpolicy** to force an update for the Group Policy refresh interval.

C. Your Windows 98 clients use a different Group Policy setting from the other clients on the network. Create an OU for the Windows 98 clients and use a Group Policy to install and configure the Automatic Update client for these systems.

D. Your Windows 98 clients do not respond to Group Policy settings. You will have to upgrade the Windows 98 clients to Windows 2000 Professional or Windows XP Professional.

☑ **D.** Answer **D** is the correct answer because Windows 98 does not support Group Policy. It is necessary to upgrade Windows 98 systems to Windows 2000 or newer to take advantage of an internal SUS server.

☒ Answer **A** is incorrect because the **gpupdate** command is used to expedite a Group Policy refresh interval on Windows Server 2003 servers hosting the Group Policy. Since Group Policy does not support Windows 98 clients, this will not have any bearing on the problem stated here. Answer **B** is incorrect because the **secedit /refreshpolicy** command is used to expedite a Group Policy refresh interval on Windows 2000 Servers hosting the Group Policy. Since Group Policy does not support Windows 98 clients, this will not have any bearing on the problem stated here. Answer **C** is incorrect because Group Policy does not support Windows 98 clients at all.

14. You approve several updates on your test environment SUS server. After testing, you decide to put the updates into production. How will you accomplish this?

A. Select **Production Update** under the set options page to update the production server with the changes.

B. Use the **Produpdate** script to update the production server with the changes.

C. Make sure the production server has synchronized. Manually approve the tested updates for the production SUS server.

D. Use the **gpupdate** command to force an update for the SUS server policies.

☑ **C.** Answer **C** is the correct answer because Microsoft has not provided capabilities for SUS test servers to share information with SUS production servers at this point. The only option is to manually approve the tested updates on the production server.

☒ Answer **A** is incorrect because there are currently no provisions for sharing information between test SUS servers and production SUS servers. Answer **B** is incorrect because although it should be possible to write an administrative script to accomplish this, there are currently no provisions for sharing information between test SUS servers and production SUS servers. Answer **D** is incorrect because SUS servers are not configured or administered with Group Policy. The **gpupdate** command is used to update the policy for a server before the refresh interval is encountered.

15. You are responsible for the SUS infrastructure deployment in your organization. Based on recommended best practice, you inform your manager that a test environment is necessary for software update testing. How many computers will be needed to accomplish this?

A. The environment should be a one-to-one correlation between the test lab and the production environment.

B. One or two systems for each type of client hardware used in your network as well as one or two systems representative of the software environment used in your network.

C. One SUS server and a terminal server to simulate the client environments.

D. One or two systems for each type of client hardware used in your network as well as one or two systems representative of the software environment used in your network. An SUS server and possibly servers to represent some of the other servers on your network.

☑ **D.** Answer **D** is the correct answer. Ideally, you want a miniature representation of the production network. For each hardware/software combination, you typically will want one or two systems to test the configuration with. You will also need a test SUS server. It is possible for the test environment to consolidate some of the services on one or two servers, if necessary.

☒ Answer **A** is incorrect because a one-to-one representation is generally not economically feasible and it will require more configuration and testing than is really necessary. Answer **B** is incorrect because you have not specified any SUS server or other servers from the network. Answer **C** is incorrect because a terminal server solution will not represent hardware differences that could play a role in update functionality. Unless your environment is completely terminal server-based, this solution will not provide sufficient testing capabilities.

Chapter 10 Monitoring and Troubleshooting Network Activity

Using Network Monitor

1. You have captured frames of traffic from your network. Unfortunately there is so much data you are having difficulty finding the data you need. Which methods can you use to quickly locate only the desired data from the packets you captured? (Choose all that apply.)

   A. Apply a Capture filter on the captured data that allows only the information you need in the Capture window.

   B. Apply a Display filter on the captured data that allows only the information you need in the Capture window.

   C. Search for the information using a property search and providing information about the data you are seeking.

   D. Use **Display | Colors** to change the appearance of the types of packets to display.

   ☑ Answers **B**, **C**, and **D** are correct, because you can always use a display filter on captured data to limit the types of packets you wish to display. The property search is very useful if you know what you are looking for, and it will take you right to the data. Changing the colors of the display for different protocols can help you visually identify desired data instantly, and it provides it in the context of the other frames, which may be important.

   ☒ Answer **A** is incorrect, because capture filters can be applied only prior to capturing the data.

2. You are monitoring inbound requests using IP from a machine with named WKSTN01 to your server. You have installed and configured the Network Monitor Windows component. Select the proper filter representations of the Capture filter that you would configure to prevent any other traffic from being monitored. (Choose all that apply.)

   A. SAP/ETYPE = IP

   B. INCLUDE LOCAL <—> WKSTN01

   C. INCLUDE LOCAL <— WKSTN01

   D. EXCLUDE LOCAL <—>ANY

   E. EXCLUDE LOCAL —>ANY

   ☑ **A, C.** Answer **A** is correct, because setting SAP/ETYPE =IP will allow only IP traffic to be monitored. Answer **C** is correct, because INCLUDE LOCAL <— WKSTN01 will include only inbound traffic from WKSTN01. This is all that is required for the trace.

☒ Answer **B** is incorrect, because INCLUDE LOCAL <—> WKSTN01 additionally includes outbound traffic from the Local machine to the WKSTN01 machine. Answer **D** is incorrect, because EXCLUDE LOCAL<—>ANY effectively eliminates the capture of any network traffic on this machine. Answer **E** is incorrect, because EXCLUDE LOCAL—>ANY is not required since you are including only inbound IP traffic from WKSTN01. No other traffic will be captured because you did not configure it to do so.

3. You suspect that you are having problems with HyperText Transfer Protocol (HTTP) request traffic to and from your Windows Server 2003 intranet server, WEB1. You want to monitor HTTP requests on the network from another Windows Server 2003 machine in your office. You install the Windows component version of Network Monitor and begin a trace with the default filters specified. You notice frames are being captured, and then browse several Web pages on WEB1 using your Windows XP Professional workstation. Afterward, you stop and view the trace and notice that there are no HTTP Requests frames at all in the capture summary. Why?

   A. The filters were not configured to allow HTTP requests to be captured.

   B. You cannot monitor another server's traffic with the Windows component version of Network Monitor.

   C. The subnet mask is invalid on the server WEB1.

   D. IIS is not installed on WEB1.

   ☑ **B.** Answer **B** is correct, because you can monitor the local server's inbound and outbound traffic only with the windows component version of Network Monitor. The version of Network Monitor that ships with System Management Server (SMS) allows you to monitor any system with the Network Monitor Driver installed.

   ☒ Answer **A** is incorrect, because default capture filters include all IP traffic, including HTTP. Answer **C** is incorrect, because if the subnet mask was invalid you would not have been able to browse Web pages. Answer **D** is incorrect, because IIS is the service that hosts Web pages and responds to HTTP requests, and thus must have been installed in order to navigate the intranet Web pages.

Monitoring and Troubleshooting Internet Connectivity

4. A LAN client is unable to navigate to www.syngress.com using Internet Explorer. The user can access network resources, but cannot access any Web sites outside of the corporate domain. Which of the following tools will assist you in identifying the problem? (Choose all that apply.)

   A. PING

   B. NBTStat

   C. Ipconfig

   D. IPSec Monitor

☑ **A, C.** Answer **A** is correct, because PING can help you by starting with the local loop-back adapter, then the local adapters address, default gateway, and ultimately the destination, www.sysgress.com. Answer **C** is correct, because Ipconfig can tell you if the address configuration is valid, such as having a default gateway defined, the correct subnet mask, DNS server entries, and so on.

☒ Answer **B** is incorrect, because NBTStat is used for NetBIOS over TCP/IP name resolution information and does not apply to domain name resolution that is the case for this scenario. Answer **D** is incorrect, because IPSec Monitor is used for monitoring status messages, security policies (SP) and security assignments (SA), and other IPSec-related information, which is not in used in this scenario.

5. Your company has added a new office and you are implementing a dial-on-demand interface one way to the new office over ISDN. You have configured all the information except the static route for the new connection. Where do you define that the static route? (Choose all that apply.)

A. In the RRAS configuration on the initiating computer

B. In the RRAS configuration on the destination computer at the new office

C. For the user account on the initiating computer

D. For the user account on the destination computer at the new office

☑ **A, D.** Answer **A** is correct, because the static route must be defined on the initiating computer to cause the dial-on-demand to connect when packets are sent to that route. Answer **D** is correct; since it is dial-on-demand one way, the user account on the remote machine is used to establish the connection and there is no connection to establish a route back to the local network, so the user account used to connect must define the static routes back.

☒ Answer **B** is incorrect, because this is a one way connection and there is no indication that there is a RRAS server at the new office. If there was, then you could set up two-way dial-on-demand. Answer **C** is incorrect, because the client account on this machine is not used to make the remote connection; therefore it would serve no purpose to define static routes for the user, especially since RRAS is installed here.

6. You are responsible for the LAN at a branch office for a large corporation. You have a machine that is configured as a DNS server, and forwards FQDN resolution requests to the domain name server at the corporate office. You are testing the server's ability to perform the iterative, recursive, and simple queries. Which tools provide the necessary functionality? (Choose all that apply.)

A. nslookup

B. ipconfig

C. NBTStat

D. Monitoring tab of the DNS servers properties dialog

☑ **A, D.** Answer **A** is correct, because nslookup can be used from the command line to interactively perform name queries against a DNS server. Answer **D** is correct, because the Monitoring tab allows similar functionality as nslookup, where you are able to perform tests on the domain name resolution server such as iterative and simple tests.

☒ Answer **B** is incorrect, because ipconfig can definitely help with troubleshooting your IP connections, but does not specifically help with name resolution requests. Answer **C** is incorrect, because NBTStat is used for NetBIOS over TCP/IP name resolution information and does not apply to domain name resolution.

7. A client computer configured as a DCHP client was unable to obtain an address from the DCHP server. Upon investigation, you discovered that the DCHP scope was not activated, so you activated it. The client computer has an APIPA address of 169.254.0.1. What actions are required for the client to obtain an IP address from the DHCP server?

   A. Run **ipconfig /all** from a command prompt.
   B. Use **netsh** to assign an address to the network adapter.
   C. Log off of Windows XP and log on again.
   D. Take no action.

☑ **D.** Answer **D** is correct, because when a DCHP client fails to obtain an address, it will continue to request an address every five minutes until one is obtained.

☒ Answer **A** is incorrect, because **ipconfig /all** will display only the current configuration. If **ipconfig /renew** is run, then it would initiate the request immediately, although it is not required. Answer **B** is incorrect, because using **netsh** to assign an address would defeat the purpose of having a DHCP client. Answer **C** is incorrect, because logging off of Windows XP and logging on has no effect on obtaining a DHCP lease.

8. You are trying to ping a computer on the same subnet. When you ping the computer named WKSTN1 from WKSTN2, you get a valid ping response. When you ping WKSTN2 from WKSTN1, the ping request times out. You run **ipconfig** on the client machines. WKSTN1 has an IP address of 192.168.102.226 and a subnet mask of 255.255.255.0. WKSTN2 has an IP address of 192.168.102.5 and a subnet mask of 255.255.255.224. The router has an IP address of 192.168.102.1 and a subnet mask of 255.255.255.0. Your company deploys client machines configured to use the DCHP client. What can you do to correct the problem?

   A. Use the **IPConfig /registerdns** command.
   B. Use the **IPConfig /renew** command.
   C. Examine the properties of the WKSTN1 and correct the subnet mask.
   D. Examine the properties of the WKSTN2 and correct the subnet mask.

☑   **D.** Answer **D** is correct, because if the WKSTN2 machine has a different subnet mask from WKSTN1 and the router, the mask must have been entered manually, since DHCP supplies the subnet mask, and the mask of the router is the same as WKSTN1. Manual settings in the network configuration always override the settings provided by DHCP.

☒   Answer **A** is incorrect, because **ipconfig /registerdns** will only flush the resolution cache and update the clients records in DNS. Answer **B** is incorrect, because **ipconfig /renew** will not correct the issue unless the manually configured subnet mask is removed. Answer **C** is incorrect, because the subnet mask for WKSTN1 matches the subnet mask for the default gateway, so it is correct.

9. You have implemented a NAT/Basic Firewall configuration to allow your LAN clients to use private IP addresses and still access the Internet. You enabled the automatic assignment of IP addresses with the default scope. Things seem to be running well, but you get calls that the internal IIS server is occasionally unreachable. When you investigate, you see messages that indicate an IP address conflict. What is the best solution to prevent the IP address conflict from occurring?

A. Manually assign and configure IP addresses for the internal clients and disable automatic assignment from NAT.

B. Change the IP address of the IIS server.

C. Implement a DHCP server and configure leases for each of the machines on your network. Set the lease duration to Unlimited.

D. Exclude the IP address of the IIS server in the NAT automatic assignment configuration.

☑   **D.** NAT is very straightforward when assigning internal addresses, and does not coordinate with DHCP servers in attempts to use existing scopes when using automatic address assignment. It is necessary to exclude any addresses that you have assigned or may assign in the future to prevent address conflict from occurring; therefore, Answer **D** is correct.

☒   Answer **A** is incorrect; even though manual assignment of addresses would work, it makes it difficult for you to manage changes on your network, is prone to error, and involves more maintenance and it does not technically prevent address conflict. Answer **B** is incorrect, because even though changing the IP address of the IIS server may appear to solve the problem initially, it does not guarantee that the address won't be handed out eventually by NAT. Answer **C** is incorrect, because if you implement a DHCP server on your network, you should also disable NAT automatic assignment of addresses. DCHP is more robust, but may require more maintenance than is necessary for smaller networks.

10. You want to configure your NAT server to allow users to access only Web pages on the Internet. Which solutions would provide the desired functionality?

A. Configure an inbound filter on the internal adapter that includes the source network scope of the internal addresses and the TCP port 80. Select the option to **Receive all packets** except those listed in the Filters list.

B. Configure an outbound filter on the internal adapter that includes the destination network scope of the internal addresses and the TCP port 80. Select the option to **Drop all packets** except those listed in the Filters list.

C. Configure an outbound filter on the external adapter that includes the destination network scope of the internal addresses and the TCP port 80. Select the option to **Drop all packets** except those listed in the Filters list.

D. Configure an inbound filter on the external adapter that includes the destination network scope of the internal addresses and the TCP port 80. Select the option to **Drop all packets** except those listed in the Filters list.

☑ **B.** Answer **B** is correct, because Inbound means that it is on its way into the network and outbound means it is leaving the network.

- If the packets are leaving the internal network, then the internal network is the source.

- If the packets are entering the internal network, then the internal network is the destination.

- If the packets are leaving the external network, then the Internet is the destination.

- If the packets are entering the external network, then the Internet is the source.

By defining an outbound filter on the internal network and allowing only TCP port 80 by dropping all packets except those, you have effectively restricted traffic to the Internet to standard Web page requests.

☒ Answer **A** is incorrect, because inbound to the internal adapter is coming from the Internet, and **Receive all packets...** allows every thing but the listed filters, and so does not prevent outbound traffic at all. Answer **C** is incorrect, because the outbound filter of the external adapter is destined for the Internet, so restricting the destination hosts to internal addresses and setting **Dropping all packets...** will effectively block all Internet traffic. Answer **D** is incorrect, because the inbound filter on the external adapter serves to permit only Web traffic inbound, not outbound.

Monitoring IPSec Connections

11. Your HR department has spreadsheets with payroll information on a Windows Server 2003 file server to which only HR personnel have access. You have implemented IPSec policies on the server to ensure that data exchanged is more secure, by requiring IPSec for all connections to the server. All of your HR desktops are Windows XP Professional and Window NT 4.0 Workstation sp5 clients. The Windows XP clients can access the files without problems, but the Windows NT 4.0 clients cannot. What can you do to resolve this issue without changing the security on the file server?

A. Install Windows NT 4.0 sp 6a on the Windows NT clients.

B. Upgrade the Windows NT 4.0 Workstation clients to Windows XP Professional.

C. Install the IPSec client on the Windows NT 4.0 Workstations.

D. Enable NetBIOS over TCP/IP on the Windows Server 2003 machine.

☑ **B.** Answer **B** is correct, because Windows NT 4.0 does not support IPSec, therefore this is the only viable solution without disabling IPSec on the file server.

☒ Answer **A** is incorrect, because there is no service pack available for Windows NT 4.0 that enables IPSec. Answer **C** is incorrect, because there is not an IPSec client to install on Windows NT 4.0. Answer **D** is incorrect, because enabling NetBIOS over TCP/IP on the Windows Server 2003 machine does not enable Windows NT 4.0 to use IPSec.

12. You are using Network Monitor to analyze IPSec packets that are using ESP. The data packet section is not viewable. What must you do to properly view the data packet section of the frames?

A. Set ESP to use the same encryption policy as the Network Monitor machine.

B. Disable AH policies.

C. Install the ESP filter DLL and update the parser.ini file.

D. Configure the ESP policy to use null encryption.

☑ **D.** Answer **D** is correct, because ESP encrypts the data packet and encapsulates it in the ESP packet. If the data is encrypted then Network Monitor cannot parse the frame. You can test ESP by defining null encryption, which will still encapsulate the data packet with ESP, but it will not be encrypted.

☒ Answer **A** is incorrect, because both machines must be using the same policies to connect using IPSec. Answer **B** is incorrect, because AH policies provide authentication headers for static data in the entire packet, and do not encrypt data. Answer **C** is incorrect, because Network Monitor ships with the parser for ESP included in the WINDIR\System32\Netmon\parsers\tcpip.dll.

13. You are implementing Internet Protocol Security at your company and you wish to authenticate and encrypt connections. You must ensure that the tunnel header for every packet is authenticated. Which actions should you take? (Choose all that apply.)s

A. Use ESP for encryption.

B. Use AH for encryption and authentication.

C. Use AH for Authentication.

D. Use ESP for encryption and RRAS for authentication.

☑ **A, C.** Answer **A** is correct, because Encapsulating Security Payload (ESP) encryption will encrypt the data packet and encapsulate it in the ESP packet. Answer **C** is correct, because the Authentication Header (AH) protocol will verify the entire packet and encapsulate it so that the integrity can be ensured en route to the destination, and prevent data replay attacks.

☒ Answer **B** is incorrect, because AH is used for authentication and integrity, not data confidentiality, and doesn't encrypt the data that it encapsulates. Answer **D** is incorrect, because ESP is used for encryption of data, but RRAS does not implement header authentication on each packet.

14. You set a session key refresh limit of 1 for IPSec. What does this accomplish?
    A. Enables password lockout policy if the password entry fails only once
    B. Enables ESP
    C. Enables AH
    D. Enables master key PFS

    ☑ **D.** Answer **D** is correct, because setting the session key refresh limit of 1 implements master key Perfect Forward Security (PFS) by allowing the master key to be used only once for a single session. The refresh setting defines how many times a key can be used to generate keys for a session, and anything more than 1violates the definition of PFS.

    ☒ Answer **A** is incorrect, because the password lock out policy applies to domain access. Answer **B** is incorrect, because ESP is used for encapsulation of the data payload. Answer **C** is incorrect, because AH is used to provide packet authentication.

15. What is the best solution to implement on your network computers to ensure that the appropriate packets of data transmitted from computers on your network are processed for signing and encryption with the IPSec protocol?
    A. Implement IPSec protocol
    B. Implement IPSec Group Policy
    C. Implement IPSec filters
    D. Implement IPSec profiles

    ☑ **C.** Answer **C** is correct, because filtering will define which packets must be processed by IPSec and which do not.

    ☒ Answer **A** is incorrect, because the IPSec protocol would be required for IPSec to even function, but it does not ensure that the packets will be processed by IPSec. Answer **B** is incorrect, because Group IPSec policies define the behavior of IPSec and although it includes filtering, defining a Group policy does more than just define processing of IPSec packets. Answer **D** is incorrect, because profiles apply to users not protocols.

Index

* (wildcard), 137
. (dot) character, 414
! (exclamation point), 789
? (question mark), 789
0s
   network destination and, 131
   subnets using all, 106, 118
/0x1b tag, 297
10 Gigabit Ethernet Alliance, 26
100VG-AnyLAN architecture, 26
1s
   network destination and, 131
   subnets using all, 106, 118
3G (third generation) technology, 686
802.11
   standard, 5, 685
   wireless networking, 693–699
802.x standards, 5

A

AAA (account management, authentication, and access
   control), 752
ABR (area border router), 720
Accept records option, 321
access client phone number validation, 700–701
access server identity validation, 700
account management, authentication, and access control
   (AAA), 752
Account Policies, security template, 781
Accounting Provider, 670
Acknowledgement (ACK) message
   of connection-oriented protocol, 15
   Session layer and, 16
   in TCP connection process, 30, 32–33
Active Directory (AD)
   DHCP integration with, 226–228
   DHCP servers, authorizing in, 229–230
   DNS zone, 361–365, 524–528
   Group Policy SUS server redirection in, 808–811
   IAS/RADIUS and, 751
   integrated DNS servers, 454–456, 458–459, 461
   integrated zone, 424, 448–449
   need for WINS, 354
   rogue DHCP server detection, 230–231
   SUS can not be installed on, 801
   WINS and, 366–367
   zone transfer, 435
Active Directory-based wireless network policies, 687–693

Active Directory Installation Wizard, 477–478
Active Directory Sites and Services, 797
Active Directory Users and Computers
   for Automatic Update client configuration, 811–816
   for certificate installation, 618
   Group Policy settings applied through, 796–797
   for IAS administration, 753
   for RRAS dial-up gateway configuration, 674
active WINS record state, 330
AD. See Active Directory (AD)
adapters
   capturing frames and, 836–837
   Network Monitor configuration and, 840, 841
Add or Remove Programs applet, 472–474
Add/Remove Programs Control Panel, 307
Added cost for routes option, 657
Address (A) resource record, 427
address resolution
   IP to MAC address resolution, 76–77
   name resolution, 68–72
Address Resolution Protocol (ARP)
   in IP to MAC address resolution, 76–77
   responsibilities of, 29–30
Address Resolution Protocol (ARP) cache
   IP to MAC address resolution and, 76
   mappings stored in, 29
   in TCP/IP communication, 709, 710
addressing. See IP addressing
Administration Pack, Windows Server 2003, 179
administrator account, 583
advanced logging, 380
Advanced Research Projects Agency (DARPA), 4
Advanced Research Projects Agency Network
   (ARPANET)
   Domain Naming System, 410
   as foundation of Internet, 4
   FTP used on, 42
   host name-to-IP resolution in, 42–43
   Internet and, 89
   TCP/IP and, 85
Advanced tab
   in DNS server configuration, 495–501
   in OSPF configuration, 724
   in RIP configuration, 718
Advanced WINS options, 341–343
aging, 452, 499–501
Alias. See Canonical Name (CNAME)
All names name checking format, 530
All People Seem to Need Data Processing acronym, 9

Allow custom policy for L2TP connection check box, 671

Alternate Configuration tab, 145–146

alternate IP address configurations, 144–146, 153

AND function, 57–58

answering routers, 618–619, 620

antennas, 685

API. *See* Application Program Interface (API)

APIPA. *See* Automatic Private IP Addressing (APIPA)

AppleTalk, 748

Application layer
  DoD model, 8
  functions of, 17
  OSI model, 10
  protocols, 90
  TCP/IP, 35–44

Application partition, 476, 550

Application Program Interface (API)
  definition of, 21
  in Microsoft model, 20
  See also NetBIOS; Windows Sockets (WinSocks)

applications, 417

ARCnet (Attached Resource Computer Network), 26

area border router (ABR), 720

/ areas switch, 796

ARP. *See* Address Resolution Protocol (ARP)

ARP Reply, 76, 77

ARP Request, 76, 77

ARP responder, 76

ARPA TLDs, 418

ARPANET. *See* Advanced Research Projects Agency
    Network (ARPANET)

Attached Resource Computer Network (ARCnet), 26

Aucatalog.cab file, 802–803

audit log, 250

auditing, 871

authentication
  client operating systems and, 584
  PPP authentication process/protocols, 588–597
  for remote access, 653
  for remote access policy, 700
  in RRAS dial-up server configuration, 670
  in wireless networking configuration, 697–699
  for wireless security, 686–687

authentication protocol
  security settings determine, 785
  troubleshooting VPN services and, 629

Authentication Provider, 669

authoritative DNS forwarder server, 444

Authoritative Server, 430

auto-enrollment of certificates, 618

auto-static updates, 616

automatic backup, 344–345

automatic certificate allocation feature, 694

automatic metric calculation, disabling, 133–134

Automatic Partner Configuration feature
  for creating replication partners, 312–313
  replication to subset of WINS servers with, 320–321
  rogue WINS servers with, 378

Automatic Private IP Addressing (APIPA)
  description of, 68
  disabling, 232–233
  for IP address, 866
  IP address configuration, 143–144
  IP lease requests and, 168
  overview of, 231–232
  troubleshooting connectivity and, 748
  Windows Server 2003 and, 234–235

Automatic Update client software
  configuration exercise, 811–816
  function of, 799
  installing/configuring, 807–816
  supporting legacy clients, 816–819

Automatically detect proxy server settings, 802

B

B-channel, 680

b-node (broadcast)
  configuring, 293–294
  defined, 291, 859
  description of, 71

backbone area
  in OSPF configuration, 724–726
  routing areas connect to, 720

Background Intelligent Transfer Service (BITS), 808

backup
  of DNS zone records, 542
  of WINS database, 344–351

BACP (Bandwidth Allocation Control Protocol), 682

bandwidth, 680, 681–682, 683

Bandwidth Allocation Protocol (BAP)
  configuring PPP Multilink with, 682–684
  dynamic BAP protocols, 681–682
  function of, 680
  PPP Multilink and, 762

baseline, 847

baseline security, analyzing, 788–790

Berkeley Internet Name Domain (BIND)
  BIND secondaries, 496
  described, 425
  integrating DNS server with, 528–533, 551, 553

BGPv4 (Border Gateway Protocol version 4), 118, 122

BIA (Burned-In Address), 12

binary AND operation, 709, 710

binary numbering system
  conversion program question, 90

converting decimal numbering to, 45–50
as foundation of IP addressing, 2
for subnet mask creation, 66
for subnetted networks, 62, 63, 64
binary representation, 99–100
BIND. *See* Berkeley Internet Name Domain (BIND)
bits
  address classes and, 52–54
  in classful subnet masking, 99–100
  in decimal to binary conversion, 45, 46–47
  from host address for subnetting, 55–57
  of network/host IDs, 52
  subnet masking and, 57–68
  subnetting Class A network and, 107–109
  subnetting Class B network and, 110–113
  in variable length subnetting exercise, 115–118
BITS (Background Intelligent Transfer Service), 808
bitwise ANDing
  to find network ID, 100–101
  process of, 57–58
  for subnet mask creation, 64
block records, 320–321
Bluetooth, 685
BNC connector, 7
Boolean operators, 57–58
Bootstrap protocol (BOOTP)
  DHCP and, 163
  vs. DHCP relay, 210–211
  tables, 199–201
Border Gateway Protocol version 4 (BGPv4), 118, 122
boundary layers, 19–21
broadband, 571, 623
broadcast clients, 300
broadcast domains, 367–368
broadcast node. *See* b-node (broadcast)
broadcast query timeout, 286
broadcast storms, 376–378
broadcast traffic, 706–707
broadcasts, 171
Browse Lists, 283, 367
browsing, 283, 367–368
buffer size, 841
Burned-In Address (BIA), 12
burst handling
  for WINS, 342, 343
  WINS server load problems and, 378

C

CA (certificate authority), 618–619
cable, 6–7
cache hints file, 440
cache time-out, 363, 525

caching
  disabling client side DNS caching, 516–517
  option for WINS records, 324–325
caching-only DNS server, 442
calling routers, 618–619, 620
Canonical Name (CNAME), 415, 427–428, 487
Capture | Addresses menu item, 840
Capture | Buffer settings item, 841
Capture Filter dialog box, 841–842
capture filters
  display filters, 843
  monitoring filters, 841–843
  network trace, 843–847
Capture Summary, 844, 845–846
capturing frames, 836–840
Carrier Sense Multiple Access/Collision Avoidance
    (CSMA/CA), 25
Carrier Sense Multiple Access/Collision Detection
    (CSMA/CD), 24–25
cc TLD (country code TLD), 418, 419
CDMA (Code Division Multiple Access), 686
Cellular Digital Packet Data (CDPD), 686
centralized accounting, 587
certificate authority (CA), 618–619
certificate infrastructure
  for L2TP implementation, 633
  PPTP based on, 599
  support of PPTP/MPPE and L2TP/IPSec, 601
  for VPN server configuration, 585, 586–587
certificates
  of EAP-TLS, 687
  installing on routers, 618–619
Challenge Handshake Authentication Protocol (CHAP),
    591, 632
checksum, 28
CIDR (Classless Interdomain Routing), 121–124
CIFS (Common Internet File System), 37
Class A addresses
  default subnet mask for, 60
  explanation of, 52–53
  private IP address, 67
  summary of, 54–55
Class A network
  classful subnet masking and, 98–99
  subnetting, 55–56, 107–110
Class B addresses
  default subnet mask for, 60
  explanation of, 53
  private IP address, 67
  summary of, 54–55
Class B network
  classful subnet masking and, 98–99
  custom subnet mask with, 61–64

example of, 83–84
subnetting, 110–113
subnetting exercise for, 101–103
Class C addresses
default subnet mask for, 60
explanation of, 53–54
private IP address, 67
summary of, 54–55
Class C network
classful subnet masking and, 98–99
subnet masking, 57
subnetting, 113–115
supernetting, 120–123
supernetting/CIDR blocks exercise, 123–124
Class D addresses, 54, 131
Class D netmask, 148
Class E addresses, 54
classful boundaries, 711
classful IP addressing, 98
classful network, 83–84
Classless Interdomain Routing (CIDR), 121–124
classless subnet masking. *See* subnet masking, variable
length
classless system, 51–52
client address assignment, 605–606
client name registration, 302–303
client name renewal, 303–304
client name resolution query, 305–306
client-server VPN, 587
Client service, WINS, 37
client side DNS caching, 516–517
clients
IP lease requests and, 168
logon, 171
in VPN gateway, 614
CM (Connection Manager) profile, 604, 865
CMAK (Connection Manager Administration Kit), 604
CNAME (Canonical Name), 415, 427–428, 487
Code Division Multiple Access (CDMA), 686
collision detection, 25
collision domain, 25
combo cards, 7
command line
routing table access with, 125
routing utilities run from, 82
Telnet session at, 38–39
comment, 297
Common Internet File System (CIFS), 37
communication session, 16
compact, 340–341
Compatible security template, 782
component layers, Microsoft model, 21–22
compulsory tunneling

creation of, 587
described, 598
IP addressing for VPN gateway and, 619
summary of, 633
VPN gateway and, 614, 615
computer certificates, 694–695
computer name, 413–414
computer-to-computer (ad hoc) network, 692
conditional forwarding, 494–495
configuration intervals, 505–506
Configure Automatic Updating: options, 810
Configure Your Server wizard, 577–580
conflict detection options, 173
connection
BAP protocols and, 681–682
demand-dial connection for VPN gateway, 616–617
remote access client connections, troubleshooting,
743–747, 764
remote access server connections, troubleshooting,
748–751, 764
restrictions of remote access policy, 701
settings for remote access policy, 699
troubleshooting VPN services and, 629–630
Connection Manager Administration Kit (CMAK), 604
Connection Manager (CM) profile, 604, 865
connection-oriented protocol, 15
connection point, 613
connection types
for LAN routing, 651–652
for RRAS dial-up gateway, 677, 678
connectionless protocol, 15, 34
contiguous, 423
Count, 121
country code TLD (ccTLD), 418, 419
Critical Update Notification (CUN), 817
CSMA/CA (Carrier Sense Multiple Access/Collision
Avoidance), 25
CSMA/CD (Carrier Sense Multiple Access/Collision
Detection), 24–25
CUN (Critical Update Notification), 817
Custom Routing and Remote Access Configuration, 654

D

DARPA (Advanced Research Projects Agency), 4
data bits, 11
data compression, 17
Data Encryption Standard (DES), 587
data flow, 18, 19
Data Link layer, OSI model
function of, sublayers of, 11–13
Layer 2 switches in, 14
in OSI model diagram, 10

data packet routing
  description of, 72
  inverse ARP, 77
  IP routers, static/dynamic, 77–82
  IP routing tables, 73–75
  physical address resolution, 76–77
  proxy ARP, 77
  route processing, 75–76
  simple classful network example, 83–84
  utilities, 82–83
data packets
  in Data Link layer, 11–12
  header information attached to, 16
  routing in Network layer, 13
data traffic, 543
data translation, 17
data validity, 334–336
database
  consistency, 336–340
  management, 235–239
  path, 342, 343, 344–345
  size, 340–341
datagram service, NETBT, 36
/ db switch, 796
DC. See domain controller (DC)
dcdiag utility, 858
dcpromo command, 477–479
debugging, 544–545
dedicated lease line, 651
default backup path, 344–345
default gateway, 132
default route
  in classful network example, 84
  in routing table, 74, 125
  static routes in multihomed computers, 78
default routing tables, 147–148
default security template, 782, 785
default subnet mask, 59–60
default timing intervals, 331–333
delegation records, 431–434
demand-dial circuit, 621
demand-dial connection
  planning for, 651–652
  for VPN gateway, 616–617
demand-dial filters
  rules for applying, 622–623
  for VPN gateway, 621
demand-dial interface
  in RRAS dial-up gateway configuration, 676–678
  static packet filter and, 622
  for VPN gateway, 620–621, 625–627
demand-dial routing, 856
demand-priority access control method, 26

Department of Defense (DOD) networking model
  Application layer, 8
  development of, 3–4
  Host-to-Host Transport layer, 7–8
  Internet layer, 7
  media access control, 6
  network interface hardware/software, 6–7
  Network Interface layer, 4–5
  TCP/IP developed by DARPA, 85
  TCP/IP protocol suite and, 23, 24
DES (Data Encryption Standard), 587
destination IP address, 27
destination socket, 417
Destination Unreachable message, 28
Detail Pane, 839
DHCP. See Dynamic Host Configuration Protocol
    (DHCP)
DHCPACK, 166–167, 172–173
DHCPDECLINE, 167
DHCPDISCOVER
  described, 166, 167
  DHCPNACK and, 174
  overview of, 168–170
DHCPINFORM, 167
DHCPNACK, 167, 172–173
DHCPOFFER, 166–167, 170–171
DHCPRELEASE, 167
DHCPREQUEST, 166–167, 171–172, 866
diagnostic tools, 546–549
dial-in permission
  for RRAS dial-up gateway, 675
  troubleshooting VPN services and, 630
  in VPN gateway configuration, 626
  for VPN server, 603, 611–612
Dial Out Credentials, 679
dial-up connectivity, 672–680
dial-up server, RRAS, 665–672
dial-up technology
  for LAN routing, 651–652
  remote access policy for, 702–706
Dial-Users group, 703–706
digital signatures
  described, 587
  network security settings for, 786
direct delivery, 72
direct hosting, 44
Directly Attached Network ID Routes field, 125
directly attached network IDs, 74
disable recursion, 496
DisableIKEAudits value, 871
Discard A and PTR records when lease is deleted option,
    519
discover. See DHCPDISCOVER

Discover, Offer, Request, Acknowledgement (DORA)
  APIPA and, 144
  described, 166
  DHCPDISCOVER and, 170
display filters
  configuring, 843
  in network trace, 845–846
  for specific trace, 847
Distance Vector Multicast Routing Protocol (DVMRP), 731
distance-vector protocol, 720, 731
distributed systems architecture (DSA), 8
DNS. *See* Domain Name Server (DNS) Service; Domain Name System (DNS)
DNS A records, 519–521
DNS administrative console, 533–536
DNS caching, 516–517
DNS caching-only server, 480–483
DNS dynamic update credentials manager, 522–523
DNS event log, 544–546
DNS Events, 544
DNS forwarder/slave server, 442–444
DNS forwarders
  configuring, 481, 482, 493–495
  function of, 550
DNS Management console, 480
DNS name, 415
DNS name format, 530–531
DNS resolver, 70
DNS root hints
  configuring, 482
  defined, 481
  Root Hints tab in DNS configuration, 501–502
DNS Security (DNSSEC), 455
DNS suffix, 514–516
DNS Suffix Search List, 512
DNS tab, 518
DNS zone
  BIND, 425
  DNS server options for, 496–497
  forward lookup zones, configuring, 483–486
  in general, 423
  integration with WINS, 524–528
  resource records, 425–431
  reverse lookup zones, configuring, 490–491
  types, 424
  WINS installation integrated with, 361–365
DNS zone name, 487
DNS zones, configuring, 502–508
  General tab, 502–504
  Name Servers tab, 506
  Start of Authority (SOA) tab, 504–506
  WINS tab, 507
  Zone transfers tab, 507–508

dnscmd utility, 858
dns.log, 544, 546
dnsNode, 456
DNSSEC (DNS Security), 455
DNSUpdateProxy Group
  Dynamic DNS and, 218–222
  ownership issues, 520–522
  security concerning, 522
dnsZone, 456
Do not replicate this record option, 525
Do not use recursion for this domain option, 493, 494
DOD. *See* Department of Defense (DOD) networking model
domain, 494–495
domain controller (DC)
  AD integrated zones and, 455–456
  DNSUpdateProxy Group and, 522
  installing DNS on, 477–479
  record, WINS and Active Directory, 366
Domain Name Server (DNS) Service
  configuring, 480–483, 492–502
  configuring forward lookup zones, 483–486
  DNS clients, configuring, 508–517
  DNS database records, adding, 487–490
  DNS zones, configuring, 502–508
  installing, 472–479
  integrating with BIND, 528–533
  integrating with DHCP, 517–523
  integrating with WINS, 524–528
  monitoring, 533–544
  reverse lookup zones, configuring, 490–491
  summary of, 550–553
  troubleshooting, 544–549
Domain Name Server (DNS) Service, monitoring, 533–544
  DNS console, 533–536
  with Network Monitor, 542–544
  with System Monitor, 536–542
Domain Name System (DNS)
  AD integrated DNS servers, 454–456
  concepts, 421–423
  database records, adding to DNS Server, 487–490
  delegation/glue records, 431–434
  direct hosting and, 44
  DNS namespace, 417–421
  DNS zones, 423–431
  Enhanced h-node and, 292
  entries, AD related, 456
  extensions, 453–454
  function of/development of, 42–43
  host name resolution, 69, 435–440, 457–458
  integration with WINS, 361–365
  name characters, 282
  name resolution, 70, 615–616

NetBIOS/DNS, compared, 412–417

NetBIOS name resolution and, 290

nslookup to troubleshoot, 746–747

overview of, 410–412, 459–460

performance counters, 536–539

performance object, 540, 541

primary IP to name resolution method, 280

routing protocols for, 570

server roles, 440–454, 460–461

WINS and, 384

WINS replication and, 312

zone transfer, 434–435

Domain Name System (DNS) clients, configuring, 508–517

disabling client side DNS caching, 516–517

DNS query, 513–516

DNS settings using Group Policy, 512

resolving host names, 512–513

statically, 508–510

summary of, 550, 552

using DHCP for, 510–512

Domain Name System (DNS) query

count with System Monitor, 539–541

DNS client configuration and, 513–516

from DNS console, 534–536

Domain Name System (DNS) server

in DNS zone configuration, 506–507

host name resolution and, 858

name resolution and, 70

NAT configuration and, 853

needs static IP address, 140

domain name type, 326

domain names

hierarchical structure of, 417–419

host name resolution, 68–69

host names and, 420

second level, 420

domain namespace, 413

Domain Wireless Network Policy Properties dialog box, 690

DORA. *See* Discover, Offer, Request, Acknowledgement (DORA)

dot (.) character, 414

dotted decimal notation

conversion program question, 90

converting to binary, 45–50

explanation of, 45

for subnetted networks, 62, 64

dotted decimal values, 99–100

downlevel Windows clients, 368

Droms, Ralph, 163

DSA (distributed systems architecture), 8

DVMRP (Distance Vector Multicast Routing Protocol), 731

dynamic BAP

configuring Multilink with, 682–684

protocols of, 681–682

Dynamic DNS

DHCP server integration with, 214–216

DNSUpdateProxy Group, 218–222

servers, 447–451

updating options, 216–217

Windows NT 4.0/Win*9x*

clients and, 216

Dynamic Host Configuration Protocol (DHCP)

Active Directory integration with, 226–231

allocator, 146

APIPA, overview of, 231–235

client leases, 518

to configure DNS clients, 510–512

DNS server and, 474, 475

DNS server integration with, 517–523, 552

Dynamic DNS integration with, 214–222

function of, 39–40

implementation considerations, 865–867

leases, 164–175

overview of, 162–163

record time stamps and, 500

relay, 210–211

relay agent, 365

Relay Agent, configuring, 209–214

reservations, 141, 197–198

scope, troubleshooting VPN services and, 630

summary of, 256–258

WINS and, 359–361

WINS client configuration as, 384

Dynamic Host Configuration Protocol (DHCP) management console, 179

Dynamic Host Configuration Protocol (DHCP) server

address assignment via, 605–606

alternate IP configuration and, 144–145, 146

APIPA and, 143–144

audit log, using, 250

BOOTP tables, configuring, 199–201

configuring, 176–209

database, managing, 235–239

DHCP administration, delegating, 241–242

DHCP options, overview of, 186–188

DHCP Reservations, configuring, 197–198

DHCP service, installing, 176–179

DNS dynamic update credentials and, 522–523

DNSUpdateProxy Group and, 520–522

dynamic IP addressing and, 141–143

Event Viewer, using, 243–245

integrating with Dynamic DNS, 214–222

integrating with RRAS, 222–226

IP configuration with, 148

log files, using, 251–254

managing, 235–242
monitoring/troubleshooting, 243–255
multicast scopes, configuring, 203–206
NAT server performing functions of, 857
needs static IP address, 140–141
Network Monitor, using, 248–250
overview of, 235
routing problems and, 748
RRAS, integrating with, 222–226
scope allocation of IP addresses, configuring, 206–209
scopes, configuring, 179–186
server options, 189
statistics, viewing/recording, 239–241
superscopes, configuring, 201–203
System Monitor, using, 245–248
troubleshooting, client-side, 254–255
user/vendor class options, 189–197
VPN gateway and, 615
in VPN server configuration, 608–609
Dynamic Host Configuration Protocol (DHCP) service
installation of, 176–179
NAT and, 853
Windows 2003 installation, 176–179
dynamic IP addressing, 141–143
dynamic routing
configuring Windows 2003 Server for, 81
routing protocols for, 80–81
TCP/IP traffic categories and, 706–708
for VPN gateway, 620
dynamic routing protocols
support CIDR blocks, 122
for VPN gateway, 616
dynamic updates
BIND version support of, 529
disabling on host computer, 450–451
in DNS database, 550
DNS options for, 519–522
DNS server integration with BIND and, 528
on DNS servers, 447–450
in DNS zone configuration, 503–504
secure, 455
summarized, 459

E

e-mail, 40
EAP. *See* Extensible Authentication Protocol (EAP)
EAP-Microsoft Challenge Handshake Authentication
    Protocol version 2 (EAP-MS-CHAP v2), 687, 697
EAP-RADIUS, 595
EAP-Transport Layer Security (EAP-TLS)
    certificates for authentication, 687
    defined, 632

described, 595
for wireless networking, 693
enable burst handling option, 342
Enable LMHOSTS lookup, 293, 298, 360
Enable netmask ordering, 496, 497
Enable result caching option, 324–325
Enable round robin, 496, 497
enable scavenging of stale records option, 498–499
Encapsulating Payload (ESP) protocol, 599–600
Encapsulating Security Payload (ESP) parsers, 869
encapsulation, 588, 597
encryption
    certificate infrastructure, 586–587
    level, PPP protocols and, 596
    restrictions of remote access policy, 701
    for tunneling privacy, 572–573
End User License Agreement (EULA), 805
Enhanced b-node, 291
Enhanced h-node
    DNS in, 290
    for DNS name resolution, 527–528
    name resolution order for, 292–293
errors, 178–179
    See also troubleshooting
ESP (Encapsulating Payload) protocol, 599–600
ESP (Encapsulating Security Payload) parsers, 869
ESP packet, 869
Ethernet
    From End of Topology Header option for, 843
    media access control protocols for, 24–25
Ethernet NIC (network interface card)
    cable type for, 6–7
    MAC address on, 12
EULA (End User License Agreement), 805
Event Log configurations, 781
Event Viewer, 243–245, 630
Event Viewer folder, 480
exclamation point (!), 789
EXCLUDE filters, 842
Executive level, 21
expiration field, 330, 331–333
Expire, 431
expires after interval, 506
Expression dialog, 844, 845
Extensible Authentication Protocol (EAP)
    authentication process of, 594–595
    summary of, 632
    for wireless security, 686–687
extensions, DNS, 453–454
Extensions to the Link Control Protocol (LCP), 682
extinction interval
    of name release, 304
    of WINS records, 331

extinction timeout, 332

F

f switch, 136
Fail event, 535–536
Fail to load if bad zone data, 496, 497
fast zone transfers, 529, 533
FDDI network, 26
File System category, 781–782
file system drivers, 22
File Transfer Protocol (FTP), 42, 738
FileName attribute, 796
filter dialog, 844, 845
filter option, 324
filters
    demand-dial filters, 621
    display filters, 843
    monitoring filters, 841–843
    in NAT configuration, 849–851
    in network trace, 843–847
    static packet filter, 621–623
firewall
    configuring, 731–736, 763
    in NAT configuration, 851
    summary of, 759
    troubleshooting VPN services and, 629
    VPN server placement and, 585–586
flat naming system, 413
Flexible Single Master Operational (FSMO) roles, 366
flow control, 11
forward lookup
    configuring WINS as, 524–526, 527
    defined, 483
    host name resolution and, 439–440
forward lookup zones
    configuring, 483–486
    secondary zone/stub zone, 489–490
Forward Lookup Zones folder, 480
Forwarders tab, 493–495
FQDN. *See* Fully Qualified Domain Name (FQDN)
frame format, 31
Frame Relay, 651
Frame Viewer window, 838–839
frames
    capturing with Network Monitor, 836–839
    data organized in, 11
    size in Network Monitor configuration, 841
frames, capturing
    display filter configuration and, 843
    monitoring filters configuration and, 841–843
    Network Monitor configuration and, 840
    network trace, 843–847
From End of Topology Header option, 843

FSMO (Flexible Single Master Operational) roles, 366
FTP. *See* File Transfer Protocol (FTP)
full duplex information, 16
Fully Qualified Domain Name (FQDN)
    defined, 857
    described, 417
    DNS name resolution and, 513–514
    host name resolution and, 69, 70
    summarized, 457

G

gateway
    defined, 613
    RRAS dial-up gateway, configuring, 672–680
    See also routers; Virtual Private Network (VPN) gateway,
        configuring
Gateway field, 125, 130–132
gateway services, 17
gateway-to-gateway VPN, 598
General tab, 476, 502–504
Generic Route Encapsulation (GRE) protocol, 599, 632
Generic Security Service Application Programming
        Interface (GSS-API), 449
generic TLDs, 418–419
global communication, 719
global remote access policies, 701–702
Global System for Mobile Communications (GSM), 686
GlobalMaxTcpWindowSize setting, 31
glue records, 431–434
GPOs (Group Policy Objects), 797
gpupdate command, 797
Graph pane, 837
GRE (Generic Route Encapsulation) protocol, 599, 632
green check, 789
group membership, 700, 702–703
Group Policy
    applying security templates with, 795, 796–797
    Automatic Update client configuration with, 811–816
    configuring DNS settings with, 512
    SUS server redirection through, 807–811
    for wireless networking configuration, 694
    in wireless policy setup, 688–692
Group Policy Objects (GPOs), 797
group type, 326
GSM (Global System for Mobile Communications), 686
GSS-API (Generic Security Service Application
        Programming Interface), 449

H

h-node (hybrid)
    configuring, 293–294
    defined, 859

description of, 71
for name query resolution, 305–306
name resolution order for, 292
for WINS and DHCP, 360
half duplex communication, 16
hardware
requirements for SUS, 800
testing software updates and, 819, 820
hardware-based VPN, 574
hashing
of CHAP, 591
digital signing for data integrity, 786
one-way/two-way hashing, 592
header
information attached to data packets, 16
of TCP segment, 31
of UDP, 34
hexadecimal numbers
in WINS database, 322
of WINS records, 334, 336
Hexadecimal Pane, 839
hexadecimal switches, 297
hierarchical naming system, 413
hierarchy, 417
High Speed Token Ring (HSTR), 26
Highly Secure security template, 783
Honeywell, 8
hop count, 711
hops, 125
Host (A) DNS record, 487, 488
host address
address classes and, 52–55
definition of, 50
organization of, 51
rules for, 52
subnet masking and, 57–68, 98–103
subnets using host ID bits, 55–57
subnetting Class A network and, 107–110
subnetting Class B network and, 110–113
subnetting Class C network, 113–114
in supernetting/CIDR blocks exercise, 123–124
supernetting Class C network and, 120–123
in variable length subnetting exercise, 115–118
host name
defined, 420
described, 414–415
summarized, 457
host name resolution
aliases and FQDNs, 857
defined, 857
description of/methods for, 68–70
of DNS client, 513–516
DNS process, 858

forward lookups, 439–440
iterative queries, 438–439
overview of, 435–436, 460
recursive queries, 436–438
resolvers and, 436
reverse lookups, 440
root hints file, 440
troubleshooting tools, 858
host name-to-IP resolution
with DNS, 42–43
hosts file and, 69–70
host route, 74, 125
Host-to-Host Transport layer, DoD model, 7–8
Host-to-Host Transport layer, TCP/IP, 30–35
hosts, 866
hosts file
host name resolution and, 436
host name-to-IP resolution with, 42–43
LMHOSTS file *vs.*, 295
name resolution and, 69–70
hot fixes. *See* software updates
HSTR (High Speed Token Ring), 26
HTTP (Hypertext Transport Protocol), 41
hub and spoke configuration, 615
hybrid node. *See* h-node (hybrid)
Hypertext Transport Protocol (HTTP), 41

I

IANA. *See* Internet Assigned Numbers Authority (IANA)
IAS. *See* Internet Authentication Services (IAS)
IBM
NetBIOS designed for, 280
Server Message Block developed by, 37
See also Token Ring
ICMP (Internet Control Message Protocol), 28
ICS (Internet Connection Sharing), 146, 849
identification, 28
idle timeout, 701
IEEE 802.11 standard, 5, 685, 693–699
IEEE 802.1X configuration tab, 692
IEEE 802.1X standard, 686–693
IEEE (Institute of Electrical and Electronics Engineers), 4–5
IETF (International Engineering Task Force), 410
IGMP (Internet Group Management Protocol), 28–29, 731
IIS server, 806
IKE (Internet Key Exchange) events, 871
illegal addresses, 67
IMAP (Internet Message Access Protocol), 40
Import LMHOSTS feature, 298–299, 302
in-addr.arpa domain, 440
InARP (Inverse ARP), 77

inbound filter
    configuring, 621–622
    in firewall configuration, 735–736
    in VPN gateway configuration, 627–628
inbound packet filter, 662–663
INCLUDE filters, 842
incremental zone transfer, 434, 435
indirect delivery, 72
infrared, 686
Institute of Electrical and Electronics Engineers (IEEE),
    4–5
Integrated Service Digital Network (ISDN)
    broadband vs., 623
    channels, 680
    ISDN adapter card for, 651
    PPP Multilink and, 681
IntelliMirror, 807
inter-area routes, 721
interactive mode, 547
Interface field, 125, 130–132
interface, routing table, 74
interfaces
    to advertise RIP routes through, 656, 714
    boundary layers of Microsoft model, 19–21
    for OSPF router configuration, 723–724
Interfaces tab, 492
International Engineering Task Force (IETF), 410
International Standards Organization (ISO), 8, 281
Internet
    ARPANET and, 89
    demand dial VPN connection and, 617
    public/private addresses, 67–68
    supernetting and, 120–121
    for VPN connectivity, 570, 571, 585
    VPN gateway connectivity and, 615
Internet Assigned Numbers Authority (IANA)
    port numbers assigned by, 34
    supernetting and, 120
    Web site of, 420
Internet Authentication Services (IAS)
    centralized accounting through, 587
    configuring, 751–757, 764
    Network Access Quarantine Control and, 864–865
    for network policy, 692–693
    servers, 752–753
    summary of, 760
    in wireless networking configuration, 693–695
Internet Connection Sharing (ICS), 146, 849
Internet connectivity, 629
Internet connectivity, monitoring/troubleshooting
    IP addressing, 862–867
    name resolution, 857–862
    NAT logging, 848–856

summary of, 872–873, 874
Internet Control Message Protocol (ICMP), 28
Internet Control Message Protocol (ICMP) Router
        Discovery
    configuring, 742
    summary of, 759, 763
Internet Engineering Task Force (IETF), 680
Internet Group Management Protocol (IGMP), 28–29, 731
Internet group type, 326
Internet Key Exchange (IKE) events, 871
Internet layer, DOD model, 7
Internet layer, TCP/IP, 23, 27–30
Internet Message Access Protocol (IMAP), 40
Internet Network Information Center (InterNIC)
    DNS created by, 69
    primary network IDs managed by, 51
    public addresses assigned by, 67
Internet Printing Protocol (IPP), 37–38
Internet Protocol. See IP (Internet Protocol)
Internet Protocol version 6 (IPv6), 132, 432
interoperability, vendor, 659
intervals
    extinction, 304, 331
    for WINS/DNS server integration, 525–526
    zone data configuration intervals, 505–506
intra-area routes, 721
intranet, 733–736
Inverse ARP (InARP), 77
Invocation of Network Layer Protocol phase, 588
IP address
    in classful network, 84
    classful subnet masking and, 98–103
    DHCP and, 39–40
    in DNS client configuration, 510–512
    DNS server configuration and, 492
    IGMP and, 28–29
    IP routing tables and, 73, 74–75
    MAC address mapping with ARP, 29–30
    in manual WINS replication, 311–312
    mappings of NAT clients, 853–854
    name resolution, 68–72, 857–862
    NAT addressing, 853
    with NAT and ICS, 849
    NAT configuration and, 853
    NAT server and, 856
    NAT services and, 736–738
    in NetBIOS name resolution, 285–288
    packet routing and, 72
    physical address resolution, 76–77
    public/private, 67–68
    resolving NetBIOS names to, 289
    reverse lookup zones for, 490–491
    route processing and, 72, 75–76

routing table and, 124–125, 130–131
static, for DNS service, 475
subnet masking and, 57–66
supernetting Class C network and, 120–123
troubleshooting VPN services and, 630
VPN gateway and, 615, 623–624
WINS client configuration and, 355–356
in WINS client name registration, 302–303
of WINS server, 309
IP address class, 164
IP address configuration options, 671
IP address field, 330
IP addressing
    address class summary, 54–55
    Class A address, 52–53
    Class B address, 53
    Class C address, 53–54
    Class D/Class E addresses, 54
    decimal to binary conversion, 45–50
    fundamentals of, 87
    network ID/host ID, 50–52
    summary of, 85
    support for VPN gateways, 619–620
    troubleshooting, 862–867
    for VPN clients, 605–606
IP addressing, client configuration
    alternate configurations, 144–146
    with APIPA, 143–144
    dynamic IP addressing, 141–143
    review of, 151
    static IP addressing, 138–141
IP connectivity
    testing, 744
    troubleshooting connectivity, 748
IP gateway, 709, 710
IP header, 738
IP (Internet Protocol)
    addressing scheme, 410
    definition of, data in IP packets, 27–28
    routing as primary function of, 124
IP lease acknowledgement. See DHCPACK
IP lease request. See DHCPDISCOVER
IP masquerading, 736
IP multicast groups, 28–29
IP multicasting, 54
IP offer response. See DHCPOFFER
IP packet filters
    creating, 621–623
    in remote access policy, 701
    in VPN gateway configuration, 627–628
IP routers, 77–82
IP routing, 68–84
    fundamentals of, 88

name and address resolution, 68–72
process of, 72–83
simple classful network example, 83–84
IP routing table
    creation of, 72
    displaying to verify RIP operation, 716
    entries, 73–74
    route determination process, 74–75
    static/dynamic, 77–78
    viewing for OSPF routing, 730
IP Security (IPSec)
    L2TP/IPSec, 599–602
    NAT and firewall rules and, 586
    voluntary/compulsory tunneling and, 598
IP Security (IPSec) connections, monitoring, 867–871
    Event Viewer, using, 871
    IPSec enhancements, 868–869
    IPSec Monitor Console, 867
    ipseccmd, 870–871
    .MSC file for, 868
    netdiag.exe, 871
    netsh, 869–870
    Network Monitor, 869
    questions about, 875–876
    summary of, 873, 874
IP selection request. See DHCPREQUEST
IP tab, 671
ipconfig
    manual lease renewal and, 175
    for troubleshooting connectivity, 745
    for troubleshooting IP addressing, 862
    for troubleshooting name resolution, 860–862
    for troubleshooting VPN services, 630
ipconfig /all
    for name resolution, 860, 861
    for troubleshooting IP addressing, 862
    for troubleshooting WINS clients, 373
    for WINS client configuration, 306
ipconfig /displaydns, 860, 861
ipconfig /flushdns, 860, 861
ipconfig /registerdns, 862
IPCP standard, 589
IPP (Internet Printing Protocol), 37–38
IPSec. See IP Security (IPSec)
IPSec DES, 596
IPSec Monitor Console, 867, 868–869
IPSec NAT Traversal (NAT-T), 875
IPSec Security Monitor, 867, 868
IPSec Security Policies, 867
IPSec Triple DES, 596
ipseccmd command line utility, 870–871
IPv6 (Internet Protocol version 6), 132, 432
ISDN. See Integrated Service Digital Network (ISDN)

ISO (International Standards Organization), 8, 281
iterative query
    from DNS console, 534–535
    host name resolution and, 438–439

J

jetpack.exe tool, 340–341

K

Kernel area, 21
key exchange, 587

L

L2F (Layer 2 Forwarding), 574, 597
L2TP. *See* Layer Two Tunneling Protocol (L2TP)
L2TP/IPSec. *See* Layer Two Tunneling Protocol with
        Internet Protocol Security (L2TP/IPSec)
labels, 417
LAN. *See* Local Area Network (LAN)
LAN adapter, 671–672
LAN Manager (LM), 784–786
latency, 863
Layer 2 Forwarding (L2F), 574, 597
Layer 2 switches, 11, 14
Layer 2 tunneling protocols, 597
Layer 3 switches, 14
Layer 3 tunneling protocols, 597
Layer 4 switches, 14
Layer Two Tunneling Protocol (L2TP)
    described, 599–600
    ports, adding on VPN server, 606
    PPTP/MPPE *vs.*, 601–602
    for VPN connectivity, 574
Layer Two Tunneling Protocol with Internet Protocol
        Security (L2TP/IPSec)
    for demand dial VPN connection, 617
    described, 599–602
    logging, enabling, 630
    summary of, 632–633
    VPN server deployment and, 603
LDAP client signing requirements, 786
LEAP (Lightweight Extended Authentication Protocol),
        595
lease
    DHCP lease process, 166–173
    from DHCP server, 866
    duration, 174, 866
    duration rules, 165–166
    overview of, 164–165
    renewal, 173–175

of WINS record, 330–333
legacy clients, 816–819
Lightweight Extended Authentication Protocol (LEAP),
        595
line of sight connectivity, 685
link state advertisements (LSAs), 81
link state database, 720, 729
link state protocols, 720
LLC (Logical Link Control) sublayer, 11–12
LM (LAN Manager), 784–786
LMHOSTS file
    browsing broadcast domains with, 368
    described, 416
    NetBIOS and, 414
    for NetBIOS name resolution, 859–860
    reasons to use, 299–300
    with RRAS, 365
    static WINS records and, 328
    summary of, 384, 386
    tag options for, 294–297
    using an import to create, 298–299
    in WINS client configuration, 360
    WINS client name resolution query and, 305
    WINS records and, 325
LMHOSTS.SAM file, 297
Load zone on startup option, 498
Local Area Network (LAN)
    remote access policies, configuring, 699
    RRAS dial-up gateway for, 672–680
    VPN gateway configuration and, 623–629
    VPN gateway connectivity and, 613–615
Local Area Network (LAN) routing, 650–659
    connection types for, 651–652
    deployment process, 653
    planning stages for, 652
    for RIP configuration, 712–713
    RRAS LAN routing configuration, 653–659
    summary of, 760–761
local broadcast, 285–286
local LAN, 674–680
Local Policies, 781, 783–788
Local TCP/IP communication, 708, 709
Local Users and Groups, 611
local VPN gateway, 620–621
Log detailed events to Windows event log option, 341–342
log files, 251–254
logging
    NAT, 847–856
    for troubleshooting connections, 631
    for troubleshooting DNS server, 544–546
logical addressing, 13
Logical Link Control (LLC) sublayer, 11–12
Logon auditing, 630

lookup time-out, 363, 525
loopback address, 130–131
LSAs (link state advertisements), 81

M

m-node (mixed)
  configuring, 293–294
  defined, 859
  description of, 71
  name resolution order for, 291
MAC. *See* media access control (MAC)
Mail Exchange resource record, 428
Mail Exchanger (MX), 487
mainframe computers, 3
Manage Your Server wizard, 576–577
manual backup, 346–347
manual configuration of WINS replication partners,
    310–312
manual replication, 318–320
manual WINS database restore, 351–353
MAPI (Messaging API), 22
Master Browsers, 283
maximum session time, 701
MBONE (Multicast Backbone on the Internet), 54
mbstat -c, 374
MD5 (Message Digest version 5), 591
MD5 (Message Digest version 5) Challenge authentication,
    594
MDIS wrapper, 21
media access control (MAC)
  exam warning about, 27
  function of, 6
  handled at MAC sublayer, 12–13
media access control (MAC) address
  IGMP and, 28
  IP address mapping with ARP, 29–30
  of NIC, 12
  physical address resolution, 76–77
  in TCP/IP communication, 709, 710
media access control (MAC) protocols
  CSMA/CA, 25
  CSMA/CD, 24–25
  Token Passing, 25–26
media access control (MAC) sublayer, 12–13
Media Sense, 169
Message Digest version 5 (MD5), 591
Message Digest version 5 (MD5) Challenge authentication,
    594
Messaging API (MAPI), 22
metric, 74, 75
Metric field, 125, 130–132
Microsoft

b-nodes of, 291
BIND naming conventions and, 425
DNS in operating system, 280, 472
in NetBIOS history, 280–281, 383
PPTP/MPPE, 598–599
security templates by, 782–783
TechNet site, 819
Microsoft Challenge Handshake Authentication Protocol
    (MS-CHAP)
  CHAP instead of, 591
  described, 592–593
  MS-CHAP v2 *vs.*, 594
  summary of, 632
Microsoft Challenge Handshake Authentication Protocol
    version 2 (MS-CHAP v2)
  authentication process of, 593
  MS-CHAP v1 *vs.*, 594
  summary of, 632
Microsoft DNS Service. *See* Domain Name Server (DNS)
    Service
Microsoft Knowledgebase, 819
Microsoft Management Console File (.MSC file), 868
Microsoft model, 18–22
  benefits of, 3
  boundary layers, 19–21
  component layers, 21–22
  development of, 18
Microsoft Point-to-Point Encryption (MPPE) Protocol
  PPTP and, 599
  types of, 596
Microsoft Windows Server 2003 Network Infrastructure
    exam (Exam 70-291), 2
Microsoft Windows Update servers, 803–806
migrate on feature, 328–329
minimum (default) TTL, 506
Minimum TTL, 431
mobile users, 866
modem bank, 666, 668
modem, testing, 744
Modified b-node, 291
Monitor server page, 806
monitoring
  DHCP server, 243
  DNS Server, 533–544, 551, 553
  WINS monitoring statistics, 379–382
monitoring filters, 841–843
Monitoring tab, 533–534
monitoring/troubleshooting network activity, 832–882
  IP addressing, 862–867
  IPSec connections, 867–871
  name resolution, 857–862
  NAT logging, 848–856
  Network Monitor, capturing frames, 836–839

Network Monitor, configuration of, 840
Network Monitor, default settings, 840–841
Network Monitor, display filters, 843
Network Monitor, function of, 832–833
Network Monitor, installing, 833–836
Network Monitor, monitoring filters, 841–843
Network Monitor, network traces, 843–848
summary of, 872–873
monitoring/troubleshooting WINS server, 368–382
summary of, 384–385, 387
troubleshooting WINS clients, 373–378
troubleshooting WINS servers, 378–382
WINS System Monitor for, 369–372
MPPE. *See* Microsoft Point-to-Point Encryption (MPPE)
    Protocol
MPPE Standard, 596
MPPE Strong, 596
MS-CHAP. *See* Microsoft Challenge Handshake
    Authentication Protocol (MS-CHAP)
MS-CHAP v2. *See* Microsoft Challenge Handshake
    Authentication Protocol version 2 (MS-CHAP v2)
MS Quarantine IPFilter, 865
MS Quarantine Session Timeout, 865
.MSC (Microsoft Management Console File), 868
MSI install package, 807
Multibyte (UTF8) name checking format, 530
Multicast Backbone on the Internet (MBONE), 54
multicast routing, 731
multicast routing protocols, 731
multicast scopes, 203–206
multicast time to live (TTL), 312
multicast traffic, 707–708
multicasting
    IGMP and, 28–29
    WINS replication partners and, 312–313
multihomed type, 326
multihomed Windows Server 2003-based computers,
    78–80
Multilink connections, 705
multiple-label unqualified domain name, 513, 514
MX (Mail Exchanger), 487
My Network Places icon, 367

N

Nagle Algorithm, 32
Nagle, John, 32
name checking
    BIND/DNS server integration and, 529–531
    formats for DNS server configuration, 497–498
name release, 304–305
Name Release request, 304
name resolution

demand dial routing, 856
host name resolution, 68–70, 435–440, 513–516,
    857–858
ipconfig to troubleshoot, 860–862
services in TCP/IP, 44
at Transport layer, 15
VPN gateway and, 615–616
with WINS, 36–37
See also NetBIOS (Network Basic Input/Output System)
    name resolution
Name Server (NS) resource record, 427
Name Servers tab, 506
name service, NETBT, 36
namespace, DNS
    domain/host names, 420
    hierarchical naming system and, 413
    overview of, 417–420
    subdomains, naming, 421
naming conventions
    flat *vs.* hierarchical, 413
    Microsoft DNS zone, 425
    NetBIOS, 415–417
    overview of, 413–415
NAQC. *See* Network Access Quarantine Control (NAQC)
NAT. *See* Network Address Translation (NAT)
NAT/Basic Firewall tab
    to disable NAT addressing, 853, 854
    in NAT configuration, 849, 850, 851
    for netsh option, 856
NAT-Traversal (NAT-T)
    IPSec and, 600, 741
    L2TP/IPSec and, 633
NBMA Neighbors tab, 724
NBMA (non-broadcast-based multiple access) networks, 77
NBNS (NetBIOS name server), 288–289
nbstat -n, 375
nbstat -r
    for local broadcast, 285–286
    for NetBIOS name cache, 287–288
    for troubleshooting WINS clients, 373
nbstat -RR, 285, 304
nbtstat, 630
NDIS (Network Device Interface Specification), 20, 21
Negative Name Registration Response, 284
Neighbors tab, 718
net use utility, 374
NetBIOS name
    described, 414, 415–416
    registration process, 383
    for static WINS records, 325–327
NetBIOS name cache
    client name resolution query and, 306
    NetBIOS node types and, 290

viewing, 287–288
NetBIOS name discovery, 284
NetBIOS name query, 284
NetBIOS name registration
  for non-WINS clients, 357
  steps of, 283–285
NetBIOS name release
  described, 284
  WINS client name release, 304–305
NetBIOS name server (NBNS), 288–289
NetBIOS (Network Basic Input/Output System)
  applications, 420
  DNS *vs.*, 412–417
  NetBIOS API, 22, 417
  overview of, 411–412
  scope, 282, 283
  settings in WINS client configuration, 361
  WINS and, 36–37
NetBIOS (Network Basic Input/Output System) name
    resolution
  described, 281–283, 858–859
  DNS server integration with WINS, 524–528
  history of NetBIOS, 280–281
  LMHOSTS file, 294–300
  LMHOSTS file for, 294–300, 859–860
  methods for, 70–72, 289
  NetBIOS name discovery, 284
  NetBIOS name registration, 283–284
  NetBIOS name release, 284–285
  NetBIOS node types, 290–294, 849
  NetBIOS over TCP/IP, 289
  NetBT, 289
  network browsing, 283
  for non-WINS clients, 357–358
  standard, 285–289
  summary of, 383–384, 385
  troubleshooting WINS clients, 373–376
  with WINS and RRAS, 365
  See also Windows Internet Name Service (WINS)
NetBIOS node types
  adding via DHCP, 360
  b-node, 291
  enhanced h-node, 292–294
  in general, 290
  h-node, 292
  m-node, 291
  name resolution of, 70–71
  p-node, 291
  summary of, 383, 385–386
NetBIOS over TCP (NETBT)
  definition of, services of, 35–36
  described, 289
  Windows and, 416

netdiag /test:ipsec command, 630, 631
netdiag.exe
  for DNS server problems, 548–549
  for host name resolution, 858
  IPSec monitoring and, 871
netmask, 74, 132
Netmask field, 125, 130–132
netsh command line utility
  to backup WINS, 350
  to configure NAT logging, 855–856
  for IPSec monitoring, 869–870, 871
  for IPv6 routes, 132
  for troubleshooting connectivity, 745–746
  for WINS restore, 353–354
netsh ras diagnostics command, 630, 631
netstat utility, 855
Network Access Quarantine Control (NAQC)
  deployment process, 604
  function of, 864–865
  wireless clients and, 867
network address
  address classes, 52–55, 85
  definition of, 50
  IP routing tables and, 73–74
  organization of, 51–52
  route processing and, 75–76
  rules for, 52
  subnet masking and, 57–68, 98–103
  subnetting Class A network and, 107–110
  subnetting Class B network and, 110–113
  subnetting Class C network, 113–114
  supernetting Class C network and, 120–123
  in TCP/IP communication, 709, 710
Network Address Translation Mappings Table, 853–854
Network Address Translation (NAT)
  basic firewall support and, 732, 734
  DHCP allocator and, 146
  ICS *vs.*, 849
  PPTP and, 599
  for private address translation, 68
  support of PPTP/MPPE and L2TP/IPSec, 601
  VPN server placement and, 586
Network Address Translation (NAT) logging
  monitoring NAT activity, 853–856
  NAT configuration, 847–853
Network Address Translation (NAT) services, 736–741
  configuring NAT and static NAT mapping, 738–741
  process of/example of, 736–738
  summary of, 759, 763
Network and Dial-up Connections folder, 681
Network Basic Input/Output System. *See* NetBIOS
    (Network Basic Input/Output System)
network browsing, 283

network clients, configuring IP addressing
  alternate configurations, 145–146
  APIPA, 143–145
  dynamic IP addressing, 141–143
  review of, 151
  static IP addressing, 138–141
network connections
  naming for VPN gateway configuration, 623
  renaming, 607–608
  testing, 629
  for VPN server, 585
Network Connections folder, 177
Network Connections window, 309, 474
network destination, 74
Network Destination field, 125, 130–132
Network Device Interface Specification (NDIS), 20, 21
network infrastructure
  for VPN gateway, 615–616
  for VPN server, 584–587
network interface card (NIC)
  dynamic routing and, 81
  Ethernet, 24–25, 843
  hardware/software used by, 6–7
  IP address and, 50
  MAC address of, 12
  multiple, 169
  of Network Interface layer of DoD model, 4
  static routes and, 78
Network Interface layer, DOD model, 4–7, 89
Network Interface layer, TCP/IP
  function of, 24
  media access control protocols for, 24–26
  OSI model layers and, 23
network layer connectivity, 747, 748–751
Network layer, OSI model, 10, 13
Network Monitor
  capturing frames, 836–839
  configuration of, 840
  configuring display filters, 843
  configuring monitoring filters, 841–843
  default settings, 840–841
  effective use of, 847–848
  full version of, 875
  function of, 832–833
  installing, 833–836
  for IPSec monitoring, 869
  to monitor broadcast storms, 376–378
  monitoring DNS server with, 542–544
  network traces, 843–847
  summary of, 872, 873–874
  for troubleshooting DHCP traffic, 248–250
Network Monitor Capture window, 837–838
network security settings, 783–788

network service interoperability, 359–368
  summary of, 387
  WINS and Active Directory, 366–367
  WINS and browser service, 367–368
  WINS and DHCP, 359–361
  WINS and DNS, 361–365
  WINS and RRAS, 365
  WINS and Win9x/NT clients, 368
network trace, 843–847
network transport protocols, 2, 22
networking models
  DOD networking model, 3–8
  function of, 2–3
  Microsoft model, 18–22
  OSI model, 8–18
  purpose/function of, 86–87
New Connection Wizard, 610–611
New RADIUS Client Wizard, 696
New Remote Access Policy Wizard, 703
New Scope Wizard, 165
New Static Mapping dialog, 326–327
newsgroups, 41
next hop, 74
NIC. See network interface card (NIC)
nicknames
  described, 415, 420
  host name resolution, 68
Nimda worm, 798
NNTP (Network News Transfer Protocol), 41
No Auto-restart for scheduled Automatic Updates
    installations, 815–816
(no flag), 789
no-refresh interval, 500
No Terminal Server user SID security template, 783
non-Active Directory domains, 816–819
non-broadcast-based multiple access (NBMA) networks, 77
Non-RFC (ANSI) name checking format, 530
non-WINS clients
  static records for, 325–329
  WINS proxy agent for, 357–358
nonclassful subnetting. See subnet masking, variable length
noncontention access method, 25
noninteractive mode, 547
NS (Name Server) resource record, 427
nslookup
  host name resolution and, 436
  to troubleshoot connectivity, 746–747
  to troubleshoot DNS server problems, 546–548
  to troubleshoot host name resolution, 858
  to troubleshoot VPN services, 630
  troubleshooting with, 444
NT LAN Manager version 2 (NTLMv2), 783, 785–787
ntbackup.exe utility, 348, 349

NTLM authentication, 785–786

O

octets
  address classes and, 52–55
  in binary to decimal conversion, 49
  in classful subnet masking, 99–100
  explanation of, 45
  subnet masking and, 60, 61–62, 66
  subnetting and, 55
  for subnetting Class B network, 112
one-way hash algorithms, 586
one-way hashing, 592
Open Shortest Path First (OSPF)
  advantages/features of, 721–722
  configuring, 722–730
  for dynamic routing, 80, 81, 708
  frame relay questions about, 82
  in general, 720
  routing table view and, 129–130
  summary of, 758
  supports CIDR blocks, 122
  supports RFC 1812, 118
  terminology, 720–721
  for VPN gateway, 616
open standard protocols
  IAS/RADIUS solution, 751–752
  IGMP, 731
  trend in use of, 722
Open Systems Interconnection committee, 8
Open Systems Interconnection (OSI) model
  Application layer, 17
  data flow through, 18, 19
  Data Link layer, 11–13
  development of, 85
  development of, layers of, 8–9
  importance of, 693
  NetBIOS at session layer of, 281
  Network layer, 13
  for network troubleshooting, 751, 760
  Physical layer, 9–11
  Presentation layer, 17
  Session layer, 16
  TCP/IP protocol suite and, 22–24
  Transport layer, 14–15
  for troubleshooting connectivity, 748
  as troubleshooting guide, 743
  for troubleshooting VPN services, 629
operating systems
  compatible with Automatic Updates, 799
  configured as WINS clients, 356

support of PPTP/MPPE and L2TP/IPSec, 601
  VPN server and, 584, 603
OPT resource record, 453–454
option 044 WINS/NBSN Servers, 359
Option 046 WINS/NBT Node Type, 359, 360
OSI model. See Open Systems Interconnection (OSI)
    model
OSPF. See Open Shortest Path First (OSPF)
OSPF neighbors, 729
outbound filter, 621–622, 627–628
outbound packet filter, 664
Overwrite unique static mappings at this server (migrate
    on) option, 328–329, 378
Owner, 429
Owner field, 330

P

p-node (peer-to-peer)
  configuring, 293–294
  defined, 859
  description of, 71
  name resolution order for, 291
-p parameter
  for persistent route, 137
  for persistent route entry, 132, 135
  removing routing table entries and, 136
packet filters
  RRAS packet filter configuration, 660–664, 758
  used with firewall, 733
PAP. See Password Authentication Protocol (PAP)
parsers, 841
password
  of CHAP, 591
  encryption using, 573
  LM authentication protocol for, 784
  of MS-CHAP, 592
  of MS-CHAP v2, 593
  for RIP route exchange, 657
  of security templates, 781
  of SPAP, 591
  for user account, 674–675
Password Authentication Protocol (PAP)
  disabling on RRAS server, 590
  security risk of, 589
  summary of, 632
pathping utility
  function of, 82
  for troubleshooting connectivity, 749
  for troubleshooting IP addressing, 863–864
pattern filters, 842–843
PDC Emulator Role, 366

PEAP. *See* Protected Extensible Authentication Protocol (PEAP)
performance, 601
Performance Logs and Alerts, 867
permission. *See* dial-in permission
persistent connections
    planning for, 651–652
    for push/pull relationships, 316
    types of, 617
    for VPN gateway, 627
persistent route
    creating, 134–135
    -p parameter for, 137
    removing, 136
    routing table and, 132
physical addresses, 13
Physical layer, OSI model, 9–11
ping
    to check connectivity, 83
    function of, 82
    ICMP and, 28
    NetBIOS name resolution problems and, 374
    in network trace, 844, 845, 846
    to test OSPF router, 730
    to test VPN gateway connectivity, 629
    testing RIP with, 658–659
    to troubleshoot connectivity, 747–748
    to troubleshoot IP addressing, 862–863
    to troubleshoot VPN services, 630
    to verify RIP v2 operation, 716–717
pingpath, 746
PKI. *See* Public Key Infrastructure (PKI)
Point-to-Point Protocol (PPP)
    authentication process, 588–589
    authentication protocols, 589–602
    BAP protocols and, 682, 683
    demand-dial routing uses, 617
    dial-up connectivity via, 665
    functions for remote access connectivity, 680
    L2TP and, 599
    logging, enabling, 630
    PPTP and, 598–599
    VPN technology built on, 570
Point-to-Point Protocol (PPP) authentication protocols
    Challenge Handshake Authentication Protocol, 591
    exam warning about, 596–597
    Extensible Authentication Protocol, 594–595
    hashing process, 592
    Microsoft Challenge Handshake Authentication Protocol, 592–593
    Microsoft Challenge Handshake Authentication Protocol version 2, 593–594
    Password Authentication Protocol, 589–590

    in PPP authentication process, 588
    Shiva Password Authentication Protocol, 591
    summary of, 632
Point-to-Point Protocol (PPP) Multilink Protocol
    BAP and, 759, 762
    configuring with BAP, 682–684
    enabling, 681
    history of, 680–681
Point-to-Point Tunneling Protocol (PPTP)
    for demand dial VPN connection, 617
    described, 598–599
    L2TP/IPSec *vs.*, 601–602
    ports, 606
    summary of, 632
Pointer (PTR)
    creating, 488
    described, 487
    DNS update options for, 519–521
    resource record, 427
poison reverse processing, 718
POP (Post Office Protocol), 40
port numbers
    used by TCP and UDP, 34–35
    for well-known ports, 732
ports
    adding on VPN server, 606
    exam warning about, 621
    FTP ports, 42
    static packet filter and, 622
    Transport layer and, 15
Post Office Protocol (POP), 40
PPP. *See* Point-to-Point Protocol (PPP)
PPP Callback Control, 588
PPP Link Establishment phase, 588
PPP Multilink. *See* Point-to-Point Protocol (PPP) Multilink Protocol
PPTP. *See* Point-to-Point Tunneling Protocol (PPTP)
PPTPv2, 599
#PRE tag, 295
Preferred Networks, 690–691
Presentation layer, OSI model, 10, 17
Primary DNS suffix, 515
primary server, DNS zones, 504
primary WINS server
    client name registration and, 302
    client name renewal with, 303
    client name resolution query with, 305
primary zone, 424
private IP addresses, 67–68
private network, 736–738
process, 16
Process Explorer, 855
Protected Extensible Authentication Protocol (PEAP)

authentication method of, 687
  for wireless authentication, 595
  in wireless networking configuration, 697, 698–699
Protocol field, 129
protocol properties, 843
protocol stack, 2
protocol translation, 17
protocols, 844–845
Proxy ARP, 77
PSTN (public switched telephone network), 665, 666
PTR. *See* Pointer (PTR)
public interface, 731–732
public IP addresses, 67
public key encryption
  of EAP-TLS certificates, 687
  hashing process, 592
  pros/cons of, 587
Public Key Infrastructure (PKI)
  defined, 573, 587
  for demand dial VPN connection, 617
  for EAP-TLS, 595
public network, 736–738
public switched telephone network (PSTN), 665, 666
pull replication partners
  configuring, 314–315
  manually forcing replication, 318–320
Push/Pull partner relationships
  configuring, 313–318
  manually forcing replication, 318–320
push replication partners
  configuring, 316–318
  manually forcing replication, 318–320

Q

queries
  from DNS console, 534–536
  DNS query, 513–516, 539–541
  summarized, 458
  System Monitor to monitor, 369–372
  types of, 436
question mark (?), 789

R

radio frequency, 686
RADIUS. *See* Remote Authentication Dial-in User Service
  (RADIUS)
Ranges tab, 725, 726
RARP (Reverse Address Resolution protocol), 29–30
RDA (Remote Desktop for Administration), 574
Record Name field, 330
Record-Specific Data, 430

Record Time Stamp, 499–500
records
  adding DNS database records, 487–490
  delegation/glue, 431–434
  stale, aging/scavenging, 452
recursive queries
  from DNS console, 534–536
  host name resolution and, 436–438
  summarized, 458
recursive subnetting, 104
red X, 789, 794
Redirector, 22
Refresh, 430
refresh interval, 501, 506
regedit.exe, 817
registry, 79, 816–819
Registry category, 781
Relay Agent
  BOOTP *vs.* DHCP relay, 210–211
  configuration of, 211–214
  overview of, 209–210
  scopes and, 179
released WINS record state, 330, 331
remote access
  basics, 570–575
  clients, VPN server configuration for, 607–613
  concepts, 634–635
  connections, troubleshooting, 629, 743–747, 764
  defined, 665
  PPP Multilink and BAP, 680–684
  RRAS dial-up gateway configuration, 672–680
  RRAS dial-up server configuration, 665–672
remote access policies
  configuring, 699–706, 762
  for IAS clients, 697
  summary of, 759
  troubleshooting VPN services and, 629–630
  VPN server configuration and, 603
remote access server
  connections, troubleshooting, 748–751, 764
  PPP Multilink enabled on, 681
Remote Access Service (RAS). *See* Routing and Remote
    Access service (RRAS)
Remote Authentication Dial-in User Service (RADIUS)
  IAS/RADIUS, 587, 751–757
  for network policy, 693
  VPN server configuration and, 609
  in wireless networking configuration, 695–696
remote cache table, 287
remote control, 574, 665
Remote Desktop for Administration (RDA), 574
Remote Network ID Routes, 125
remote network IDs, 74

Remote Registry service, 549

remote TCP/IP communication, 708, 710

remote VPN gateway, 620–621

Renew interval setting, 303

renewal interval, 331

renewal, lease, 173–175

Replicate Only with Partners option, 329

replication

    manually stopping WINS records from, 329

    option with Application Partition, 476

    troubleshooting WINS servers and, 378

    WINS server replication, configuring, 310–321

Request for Comment (RFC) 1134, 680

Request for Comment (RFC) 1812, 106, 118

Request for Comment (RFC) 2125, 681

Request for Comment (RFC) 2131, 163

Request for Comment (RFC) 2535, 455

Request for Comment (RFC) 3467, 410

Request for Comment (RFC) 882/883, 411

Request for Comments (RFCs) 1001/1002, 412

Reschedule Automatic Updates scheduled installations

    policy setting, 810, 815

reserved address, 474

resolvers, 422, 436

resource records (RR)

    commonly used, 427–431

    enabling DNS server to age, 500–501

    overview of, 422

    scavenging of stale, 498–500

    Server 2003, types used in, 426–427

    zones, adding to, 432–433

    zones and, 425

Responsible Person, 430

responsible person field, 504–505

restore, 351–354

Restricted Groups category, 781

Resultant Set of Policy, 867

Retry, 431

retry interval, 506

Reverse Address Resolution protocol (RARP), 29–30

reverse lookup zones

    configuring, 490–491, 550

    host name resolution and, 440

    nslookup and, 547

    reverse DNS to WINS lookup, 526

Reverse Lookup Zones folder, 480

RFC. *See* specific Request for Comment (RFC) names

RFC 1001, 281

RIP. *See* Routing Information Protocol (RIP)

RIP Version 2 for Internet Protocol, 660–661

rogue DHCP server, 230–231

rogue WINS servers, 378

root domain, 418

root hints file, 440

Root Hints tab, 501–502

round robining, 497, 516

route add command, 127–128, 132

route change command, 127, 137

route command, 750

route command help, 127

route command line utility, 136

route delete command

    for removing routing table entries, 128, 136, 137

    for routing table, 127

route flapping, 719

route print command

    example of, 137

    for removing routing table entries, 136

    to view changes, 127

    in Windows Server 2003, 132

route utility, 82

routers

    CIDR blocks and, 122

    configuring static IP address for, 138

    definition of, 72

    installing certificates on, 618–619

    network/host addresses and, 51

    RRAS LAN routing configuration, 653–659

    subnet masking and, 61

    support of RFC 1812, 118

    in VPN gateway creation, 621

routing

    definition of, 72

    description of, 72

    inverse ARP, 77

    IP routers, static/dynamic, 77–82

    IP routing tables, 73–75

    in Network layer, 13

    physical address resolution, 76–77

    proxy ARP, 77

    route processing, 75–76

    simple classful network example, 83–84

    summary of, 86

    utilities, 82–83

    of VPN gateway, 615, 616

    See also IP routing

Routing and Remote Access Configuration Wizard,

    605–606

Routing and Remote Access management console

    configuring basic firewall support in, 733–736

    configuring NAT and static NAT mapping with,

    738–741

    OSPF router configuration in, 723–724

    for static packet filters, 621–622

Routing and Remote Access Server Setup Wizard
  configuring VPN server with, 602
  enabling RRAS with, 580–582
  for RRAS configuration, 575, 576
  for VPN gateway configuration, 623–629
  for VPN server configuration, 607–608
Routing and Remote Access Service (RRAS)
  DHCP server integration, 222–224
  dial-up gateway, configuring, 672–680
  dial-up server, configuring, 665–672
  for dynamic routing, 81
  enabling, 635
  enabling for static route, 78
  firewall support, configuring, 731–736
  IAS, configuring, 751–757
  LAN routing, configuring, 650–659
  for NAT, 848, 849
  NAT services, 736–741
  necessity of, 82
  Network Access Quarantine Control and, 864–865
  packet filters, 659–664, 761
  PPP Multilink and BAP, 680–684
  remote access policies, configuring, 699–706
  RIP configuration and, 712–719
  routing protocols, 706–731
  for routing table, 128
  for routing table modifications, 135–138
  for routing table view customization, 129
  server, 748
  summary of, 758–760
  troubleshooting remote access client connections,
    743–747
  troubleshooting remote access server connections,
    748–751
  user object IP addresses, assigning, 225–226
  WINS and, 365
  wireless connections, configuring, 685–699
Routing and Remote Access Service (RRAS) dial-up
    gateway
  configuring, 672–680, 761
  summary of, 758–759
Routing and Remote Access Service (RRAS) dial-up
    server
  configuring, 665–672, 761
  summary of, 758
Routing and Remote Access Service (RRAS) VPN
  configuring, 602–613
  enabling, 575–583
  network infrastructure for, 584–587
  PPP authentication process/protocols, 588–597
  remote access concepts, 570–575
  troubleshooting, 629–631
  VPN gateway, configuring, 613–629

VPN tunneling protocols, 597–602
routing areas, 720
Routing Information Protocol (RIP)
  configuring, 712–720
  for dynamic routing, 80, 81, 708
  features/characteristics of, 711–712
  function of, 43
  in LAN routing configuration, 653, 654–657
  neighbors, 658
  not for large network, 82
  summary of, 758
  for VPN gateway, 616
Routing Information Protocol (RIP) v1
  limited to classful boundaries, 711
  routing problems with, 748
  summary of, 758
  when to use, 722
Routing Information Protocol version 2 (RIPv2)
  configuring, 712–715
  described, 711
  preferable to use, 722
  summary of, 758
  supports CIDR blocks, 122
  supports RFC 1812, 118
routing loops, 711, 719
routing metric, 132, 133–134
routing options, 626
routing protocols, 706–731
  for dynamic/static routing, 80–82
  IGMP, 731
  for LAN routing, 652
  local TCP/IP communication example, 708, 709
  OSPF, 720–730
  remote TCP/IP communication example, 708, 710
  RIP, 711–720
  summary of, 758, 762–763
  TCP/IP traffic categories, 706–708
routing table
  automatic metric calculation, disabling, 133–134
  in classful network example, 83–84
  creating entries, 134–136
  displaying to verify RIP operation, 658
  entries, meaning of, 130–132
  fundamentals of, 147–148
  question about, 152
  removing entries, 136–138
  review of, 150–151
  for supernetting, 121
  viewing, 128–129
  in Windows XP/2000, 124–128
routing table entries
  adding, 127–128
  creating in Windows 2003, 134–136

removing, 128, 136–138
routing table, Window XP/2000, 150
routing table, Windows 2003
    automatic metric calculation, disabling, 133–134
    creating entries, 134–136
    entries, 130–132
    fundamentals of, 147–148
    removing entries, 136–138
    review of, 150–151
    viewing, 128–129
routing table, Windows XP, 147–148
routing timers, 718
rqc.exe, 865
Rqc.exe notification component, 604
rqs.exe, 865
Rqs.exe listener, 604
RR. See resource records (RR)
RRAS. See Routing and Remote Access Service (RRAS)
RRAS snap-in, 851
rules, lease duration, 164–166
Run As command, 583

S

SAP/ETYPE= line, 841–842
SBS (Small Business Server), 801
scavenging
    enabled at server/zone level, 504
    of stale records, 452, 498–500
    warning about, 501
SCM (Security Configuration Manager), 780
scope allocation of IP addresses, 206–209
scope properties, 876–877
scopes
    DHCP server, configuring with, 179–186
    dynamic IP addressing and, 142–143
    multicast, 203–206
search for WINS records, 322–325
secedit.exe, 790, 795–796
second generation (2G) technology, 686
secondary logon, 583
secondary WINS server
    client name registration and, 302
    client name renewal with, 303
    client name resolution query with, 305
secondary zone
    creating, 490
    defined, 424, 489
secure cache against pollution option, 496, 497
Secure security template, 783
security
    configurations, comparing, 790–795
    of DNSUpdateProxy Group, 522

features for LAN routing, 652
of PPTP/MPPE and L2TP/IPSec, 601
risks of PAP, 589
wireless security, 686–693
Security Configuration and Analysis management console
    for analyzing baseline security, 789–790
    for comparing security configurations, 790–795
    function of, 780
    for security templates, 780–782
    summary of, 821
Security Configuration and Analysis utility
    applying security templates with, 795, 797–798
    security template types from, 782–783
Security Configuration Manager (SCM), 780
security patches. See software updates
Security tab, 717–718
security templates, 780–798
    applying, 795–798
    baseline security, analyzing, 788–790
    categories of, 780–782
    network security settings, 783–788
    security configurations, comparing, 790–794
    summary of, 821–822
    types of, 782–783
SelfUpdServer value, 817
serial number, 430, 504
Server Message Block (SMB), 37, 784
Server options, 496–497
server-server VPN, 587
Server service, 22, 36–37
Service Locator (SRV) records
    BIND version support of, 529
    described, 428–429, 487
    nslookup to verify, 547–548
service packs, 596
Services and Ports tab, 852
Session layer, OSI model, 10, 16
session service, NETBT, 36
Session Statistic pane, 838
Set Options page, 802, 803
shared secret, 696
Shiva Password Authentication Protocol (SPAP), 591, 632
Show Neighbor command, 715–716
shut down, 305
Silly Window Syndrome (SWS), 32
Simple Mail Transport Protocol (SMTP), 40
Simple Network Management Protocol (SNMP), 43
simplex communication, 16
single-label unqualified domain name, 513
sixteenth character, NetBIOS name, 415, 416
Small Business Server (SBS), 801
Small Office Home Office (SOHO), 849
smart cards, 595

SMB (Server Message Block), 37, 784
SMS (System Management Software), 542
SMS (Systems Management Server), 823, 840
SMTP (Simple Mail Transport Protocol), 40
sniffing, 542–544
SNMP (Simple Network Management Protocol), 43
SOA (Start of Authority) resource record, 430
SOA (Start of Authority) tab, 504–506
software-based VPN, 574
software requirements, SUS, 800
Software Update Service (SUS)
  Automatic Update client, installing/configuring,
    807–816
  function of, 780, 799
  installing/configuring, 799–806
  summary of, 821, 822
  supporting legacy clients, 816–819
  testing software updates, 819–820
Software Update Service (SUS) server
  Automatic Update client directed to, 807
  building, 801
  components of, 799–800
  configuration of, 801–803
  redirection through Group Policy, 808–811
  requirements for, 800
  synchronizing, 803–806
  for testing software updates, 819
software updates
  automatic client update configuration, 811–816
  automatic client update settings, 807–811
  infrastructure, installing/configuring, 799–806
  legacy clients, supporting, 816–819
  Software Update Service, 799
  summary of, 821, 822
  testing, 819–820
  Windows Update, 798
SOHO (Small Office Home Office), 849
source IP address, 27
SPAP (Shiva Password Authentication Protocol), 591, 632
split horizon, 718
spoofing, 497
SRV. *See* Service Locator (SRV) records
stale records, 498–500
standard primary DNS Server, 441
standard secondary DNS Server, 441
standard switches. *See* Layer 2 switches
standard zone transfer. *See* traditional zone transfer
Start of Authority (SOA) resource record, 430
Start of Authority (SOA) tab, 504–506
Starting Network ID, 121, 122
state
  bitwise ANDing and, 57–58
  of OSPF routing, 728

of WINS records, 330–331
static address pool, 613
static domain name, 475–476
static entries
  adding to routing table, 135–136
  push replication partners and, 318
  in WINS database, 302
Static field, 330
static IP address
  alternate IP address and, 153
  configuring, 138–141
  DHCP server scope and, 142
  for DNS, 475
  in VPN server configuration, 612
static mapping, 737–738
static NAT mapping, 738–741
static packet filter, 621–623, 849
static records
  not subject to aging, 501
  troubleshooting WINS servers and, 378
  WINS, creating, 325–329
static route
  applications for, 77–78
  in multihomed Windows Server 2003 computers, 78–80
  removing, 137
  for RRAS dial-up gateway, 678–679
  for VPN gateway, 619–620
  in VPN gateway configuration, 626, 627
Station Statistics pane, 838
statistics, 239–241
*Step-by-Step Guide for Setting up VPN-based Remote Access in
  a Test Lab* (TechNet article), 575
Strict RFC (ANSI) name checking format, 530
stub area
  in OSPF configuration, 726
  of OSPF routers, 720–721
stub zone
  creating, 490
  defined, 489
  described, 424
  glue records and, 431
subdomains, 421
subnet mask
  route determination process and, 74–75
  in supernetting/CIDR blocks exercise, 123–124
  for supernetting Class C network, 121, 122
subnet mask, custom
  creating, 64, 66
  defining, 64–65
  determining number of host bits to use, 61–62
  function of, 60
  IP address, determining, 63–64
  subnetted network IDs, 62–63

subnet masking, 57–68
  bitwise ANDing, 57–59
  custom subnet mask, 60–66
  default subnet mask, 59–60
  function of, 57
  fundamentals of, 88
  public/private IP addresses, 67–68
subnet masking, classful
  limitations of, 104
  review of, 98–104, 148–149
  summary of, 147
subnet masking, variable length
  definition of, 98
  exercise for, 115–119
  networks divided into variable length subnets, 106
  process of, 104–105
  review of, 149
  subnetting Class A network, 107–110
  subnetting Class B network, 110–113
  subnetting Class C network, 113–115
  summary of, 119–120
subnets
  in classful network example, 83–84
  dotted decimal notation, 45
  static routing in, 78
  Windows 2003 routing table and, 131
subnetting
  function of, 2
  with host ID bits, 55–57
  summary of, 85–86
  variable length, 104–120, 147
Summary Pane, 838–839
supernetting
  CIDR blocks and, exercise for, 123–124
  Class C networks, 120–123
  definition of, 60, 98
superscopes, 201–203
SUS. See Software Update Service (SUS)
Sus10sp1.EXE, 801
switches, 14
SWS (Silly Window Syndrome), 32
symbol, 295
symmetric-key encryption, 586
synchronization, 802–806
Systek Corporation, 36
System Management Software (SMS), 542
System Monitor
  monitoring DNS server with, 536–542
  monitoring WINS with, 369–372
  using, 245–248
System root security template, 783
System Services category, 781
Systems Management Server (SMS), 833, 840

Sytec, Inc., 280, 383, 411

T

T-1 connection, 571, 572
TACACS+ (Terminal Access Controller Access Control System Plus), 752
Tag for announced routes option, 657
tag line options, 294–297
TAPI (Telephony API), 22
TCP. See Transmission Control Protocol (TCP)
TCP handshake, 32–33
TCP/IP. See Transmission Control Protocol/Internet Protocol (TCP/IP)
TCP Window Scale, 32
TcpWindowSize setting, 31–32
TDI (Transport Driver Interface) boundary layer, 21
telephony, 22
Telephony API (TAPI), 22
Telnet session, 38–39
templates. See security templates
Terminal Access Controller Access Control System Plus (TACACS+), 752
Terminal Server, 783
Terminal Services, 574
third generation (3G) technology, 686
three-part handshake, 32–33
time of day restrictions, 700
Time-to-Live (TTL)
  defined, 28
  of DNS resolution results, 516
  resource record field described, 429
  of WINS client names, 302, 303–305
TLD. See top level domain (TLD)
TLS (Transport Layer Security), 698
token passing and, 25–26
Token Ring
  development of, 25–26
  From End of Topology Header option for, 843
  network trace on, 847–848
  NIC, 12
tombstoned WINS record state
  described, 330
  manually deleting, 332, 333
  NetBIOS name resolution and, 375
top level domain (TLD), 417–420
  See also ARPA TLDs; generic TLDs
Total Queries Received/sec counter, 539, 541
Total Statistics pane, 838
tracert utility
  function of, 82
  for troubleshooting connectivity, 749–750
  for troubleshooting IP addressing, 863

traditional zone transfer, 434, 435

traffic, 661–664

transfer, zone, 424, 434–435

Transmission Control Protocol/Internet Protocol
(TCP/IP)
DHCP and, 162
DOD networking model, 3–8
filtering option in NAT configuration, 851
fundamentals of, 87
Internet's reliance on, 650
IP addressing, 45–55
IP lease requests and, 168
IP routing, 68–84
IP routing tables and, 73
Microsoft model, 18–22
NAT configuration and, 853
networking models, reason for, 2–3
OSI model, 8–18
overview, 2
stack, 178
subnet masking, 57–68
subnetting, 55–57
summary of, 85–86
TCP/IP protocol suite, 22–44
traffic categories, 706–708

Transmission Control Protocol/Internet Protocol
(TCP/IP) protocol suite, 22–44
Application layer, 35–44
DOD model/OSI model and, 22–24
Host-to-Host Transport layer, 30–35
Internet layer, 27–30
Network Interface layer, 24–27

Transmission Control Protocol (TCP)
connection process of, 30–33
port numbers, 34
ports, security of, 42
Transport layer and, 14, 15
UDP vs., 35
used at Host-to-Host Transport layer, 7–8

Transport Driver Interface (TDI) boundary layer, 21

Transport layer
OSI model, 10, 14–15
TCP/IP, 23
troubleshooting connectivity, 750–751

Transport Layer Security (TLS), 698

troubleshooting
client-side, 254–255
DHCP server, 243
DNS Server, 544–549, 553
remote access client connections, 743–747, 764
remote access server connections, 748–751, 764
summary of, 760
VPN services, 629–631, 634, 636

WINS server, 368–382
See also monitoring/troubleshooting network activity

TTL. See Time-to-Live (TTL)

TTL for this record interval, 506

tunnel, 597

tunneling
process of, 572
voluntary/compulsory, 587
VPN gateway and, 614–615, 620–621
VPN methods of, 633
VPN tunneling protocols, 597–602

two-way hashing, 592

type byte, 282

Type field, 330, 430

type of connection validation, 700

U

UDP. See User Datagram Protocol (UDP)

UDP Checksum, 34

UDP datagrams, 71

UDP header, 600

underlying network connection, 585, 629

unicast route advertisements, 718

unicast traffic, 706

Uniform Resource Locator (URL), 41

UNIX, 69

unnumbered connection, 620

updates
of DNS, 518–522
secure dynamic, 455
See also software updates

URL (Uniform Resource Locator), 41

U.S. Department of Defense, 4
See also Department of Defense (DOD) networking
model

Use computer names that are compatible with LAN
Manager option, 358

Usenet newsgroups, 41

user account, 674

User Authentication phase, 588

user class, 189–197

User Datagram Protocol (UDP)
description of, port numbers used by, 34–35
DNS extensions and, 453–454
NetBIOS announcement with, 281
routers and, 171
Transport layer and, 14
used at Host-to-Host Transport layer, 7, 8

User level, 21

user object IP addresses, 225–226

V

Variable Length Subnet Mask (VLSM), 98
  See also subnet mask, custom
vendor class, 189–197
vendor interoperability, 659
verification interval, 332
version consistency, 338–339
Version field, 330
version ID
  verifying, 338–339
  of WINS database, 336
  WINS starting version ID, 342
View Log Data mode, 371
virtual circuit, 13, 77
virtual link, 680
Virtual Private Network (VPN)
  connection type for, 651
  emergence of, 570
  IP addressing for clients, 605–606
  remote access client connections, troubleshooting, 744
  RRAS dial-up server and, 665
  types of, 574
  WLANs security and, 686
  See also Routing and Remote Access Service (RRAS)
    VPN
Virtual Private Network (VPN) gateway, configuring,
    613–629
  configuration exercise, 623–629
  connectivity, 613–615
  demand-dial connection, creating, 616–617
  installing certificates on routers, 618–619
  IP addressing support for, 619–620
  local/remote gateways, creating, 620–621
  static packet filter, creating, 621–623
  summary of, 636
  supporting network infrastructure for, 615–616
Virtual Private Network (VPN) server
  placement, 585–586
  security features for, 652
Virtual Private Network (VPN) server, configuring,
    602–613
  adding ports on VPN server, 606
  IP addressing for VPN clients, 605–606
  Network Access Quarantine Control process, 604
  planning VPN server deployment, 602–603
  PPP authentication process/protocols, 588–597
  for remote access clients, 607–613
  summary of, 635–636
  supporting network infrastructure for, 584–587
  VPN tunneling protocols, 597–602
Virtual Private Network (VPN) tunneling protocols,
    597–602
  compulsory tunneling, 598

L2TP/IPSec, 599–600
L2TP/IPSec *vs.* PPTP/MPPE, 601–602
PPTP/MPPE, 598–599
summary of, 632–633
troubleshooting VPN services and, 629
tunneling, 597
voluntary tunneling, 597–598
in VPN gateway configuration, 625
VPN server deployment and, 603
visual flags, 789–790
VLSM (Variable Length Subnet Mask), 98
VMWare, 820
Volume Shadow Copy, 348–349
voluntary tunneling
  client-server VPN model, 587
  described, 597–598
  summary of, 633
VPN. *See* Virtual Private Network (VPN)

W

"walking the tree", 438, 458
WAN. *See* Wide Area Network (WAN)
Web browser certificate installation, 618–619
Web sites
  for Active Directory, 435
  on aging/scavenging records, 452
  for ARP and RARP, 30
  on DNS extensions, 453
  DNS framework, 410
  on dynamic updates, 447, 449
  for FAQs, 152
  for IANA, 121
  for ICMP, 28
  IEEE standards, 5
  for IGMP, 29
  for Internet Printing Protocol, 38
  for list of commonly hacked ports, 35
  Microsoft's TechNet site, 819
  for NAQC information, 864
  for NAT, 848
  for Process Explorer, 855
  for RFCs 882, 883, 1034, 1035, 411
  for SMB, 37
  on SRV resource records, 429
  for TechNet article, 575
  on TLDs, 420
  Usenet newsgroups, 41
  VMWare, 820
well-known ports, 732
Wide Area Network (WAN)
  bandwidth, 799
  caching-only DNS servers for, 483

miniports, 606
  VPN and, 570
wildcard (*), 137
window size, TCP, 31–32
Windows 2000, 124–128, 150
Windows 9x clients, 216, 368
Windows Clustering Services, 169
Windows Components Wizard, 177, 833–836
Windows Internet Name Service (WINS)
  Active Directory and, 366–367
  administrators, 382
  advanced options for, 341–343
  back up /restore WINS database, 344–354
  broadcast storms, 376–377
  browser service and, 367–368
  clients, configuring, 354–358
  database consistency, 336–340
  database size, 340–341
  definition of, function of, 36–37
  DHCP and, 359–361
  disabling records from DNS zone transfers, 531–532
  DNS and, 361–365
  DNS integration with, 507
  forward lookup, 361–365, 384
  function of, 280
  installing WINS server, 307–309
  integrating DNS server with, 524–528, 551, 552
  for name resolution, 44
  NetBIOS and, 412
  overview of, 300–306
  performance counter objects, 372
  proxy agent, 357–358, 384
  record expiration, 331–333
  record reconciliation/integrity, 334–336
  record states, 330–331
  records, adding/removing, 325
  records, searching for, 322–325
  replication, configuring, 310–321
  Routing and Remote Access Server and, 365
  static records, creating, 325–330
  summary of, 384–385, 386
  troubleshooting clients, 373–376
  troubleshooting WINS server, 378–382
  troubleshooting with System Monitor, 369–372
  Win 9x/NT clients and, 368
Windows Internet Name Service (WINS) clients
  client name registration, 302–303
  client name release, 304–305
  client name renewal, 303–304
  configuring, 354–358, 384, 387
  configuring via DHCP, 359–361
  defined, 300
  name resolution query, 305–306
  troubleshooting, 373–378

Windows Internet Name Service (WINS) database,
    321–343
  adding/removing WINS records, 325
  advanced options for, 341–343
  database consistency, 336–340
  database size, 340–341
  key tasks, 321–322
  searching for WINS records, 322–325
  static records, adding, 326–327
  static records, creating, 325–326, 328–330
  troubleshooting WINS servers and, 379
  WINS record expiration field, 331–333
  WINS record state, 330–331
  WINS records, reconciling, 334–336
Windows Internet Name Service (WINS) records
  adding/removing, 325
  creating static, 325–329
  entry descriptions, 329–330
  expiration, 331–333
  reconciling, 334–336
  searching for, 322–325
  state, 330–331
Windows Internet Name Service (WINS) replication
  automatically creating replication partners, 312–313
  manual replication partners, 310–312
  push/pull partner relationships, configuring, 313–320
  to a subset of WINS servers, 320–321
Windows Internet Name Service (WINS) server
  client name registration and, 302–303
  client name release, 304–305
  client name renewal with, 303–304
  client name resolution query, 305–306
  installing, 307–309
  needs static IP address, 140
  NetBIOS name release, 285
  troubleshooting, 378–382
Windows NT 3.1, 18
Windows NT 4.0, 817
Windows NT 4.0 clients, 216
Windows NT 4.0 domains, 300
Windows NT 4.0 Service Pack, 780
Windows NT clients, 368
Windows operating systems, 411
  See also operating system
Windows Server 2003
  AD integrated DNS servers, 454–456, 461
  Administration Pak, 179
  alternate IP configuration in, 144–146
  basic firewall support, 731–736
  caching-only DNS server, 442
  configuring as dynamic router, 81
  configuring OSPF on, 722–730
  configuring RIP on, 712–715
  DNS extensions and, 453–454

DNS Forwarder/Slave server, 442–444
DNS name resolution and, 457
DNS server, configuring, 434
DNS server, RFC naming conventions and, 420
DNS server testing, 444
DNS stale records, aging/scavenging, 452
DNS zones, adding, 445–446
dynamic DNS and, 447–451
dynamic IP addressing in, 141–142
enabling as WINS client, 355–356
enabling IGMP on router, 731
host name resolution and, 436
installing DNS Service, 472–479
IP routing process on, 75–76
lease duration and, 165–166
LMHOSTS file, disabling in, 300
migrating older systems to, 652
name resolution in, 44
route commands in, 128
RRAS dial-up server configuration in, 665–672
RRAS LAN routing configuration for, 653–659
standard primary DNS Server, 441
standard secondary DNS Server, 441
static IP address, configuring, 138–140
static routes in multihomed computers, 78–80
statically configuring DNS client in, 508–510
troubleshooting utilities for, 744–747
tunneling protocols supported by, 598–602
viewing routing table, 126
WINS service in, 37
Windows Server 2003 DHCP Server. See Dynamic Host
    Configuration Protocol (DHCP) server
Windows Server 2003 DNS Server. See Domain Name
    Server (DNS) Service
Windows Server 2003 product disc, 833, 835
Windows Server 2003 routing table. See routing table
Windows Sockets (WinSocks)
    definition of, 22
    host name resolution and, 68–69
    NetBIOS and, 417
    uses for, 38
Windows Update Synchronization Service
    for hot fixes/security patches, 798–799
    installed to SUS server, 803
Windows XP
    alternate IP configuration in, 144–146
    routing table, 124–128, 150
    routing table self test, 155–156
WINS. See Windows Internet Name Service (WINS)
WINS MMC console
    backup of WINS database via, 344–347
    manually restoring WINS database with, 351–353
    monitoring statistics in, 379–380
    searching for WINS records in, 322–325

WINS tab, 507
WINS Users group, 366–367, 382
winscl.exe, 350–351
WinSocks. See Windows Sockets (WinSocks)
wireless authentication protocols, 595
wireless connections
    configuring, 762
    wireless networking, configuring, 693–699
    wireless networks categories, 685–686
    wireless security configuration, 686–693
wireless local area networks (WLANs), 685, 686
wireless metropolitan area networks (WMANs), 686
Wireless Network (IEEE 802.111) Policies, 687–693
Wireless network key (WEP) box, 691–692
Wireless Network Policy node, 688
Wireless Network Policy Wizard, 688–689
wireless networks
    categories of, 685–686
    configuring, 693–699
    IAS and, 753
    security, 686–693, 759
wireless personal area networks (WPANs), 685
wireless security protocols, 759
wireless wide are networks (WWANs), 686
WLANs (wireless local area networks), 685, 686
WMANs (wireless metropolitan area networks), 686
WPANs (wireless personal area networks), 685
WUAU22.msi file, 811, 812, 813
WUAU.adm file, 808
WWANs (wireless wide are networks), 686

Z

zone, defined, 483
zone files, 422
zone independent, 526
zone transfers
    BIND/DNS server integration and, 531–532
    configuring security, 507–508
Zone Transfers tab, 507–508
zones
    AD integrated, 455–456
    forward lookup zones, 483–486, 489–490
    overview of, 422
    resource records, adding to, 432–433
    summarized, 458
    transfer of, 424, 434–435
    See also DNS zone; reverse lookup zones